Conrad Black is a graduate of Carleton, Laval, and McGill universities in history and law and is the author of two other works of nonfiction, including an authoritative biography of one of French Canada's most successful political leaders. His articles and reviews on various subjects have appeared in the *Wall Street Journal*, *National Interest*, and *American Spectator*, as well as many British and Canadian publications. Conrad Black was the chairman of the *London Daily* and *Sunday Telegraph* from 1987 to 2004, the founding publisher of the *National Post* of Canada, and, with associates, is the controlling shareholder of Hollinger International, which owns the *Chicago Sun-Times* and many other newspapers. He has been a member of the British House of Lords as Lord Black of Crossharbour since 2001. Conrad Black is married to the writer Barbara Amiel Black, has three children from his previous marriage, and divides his time between London, New York, and Toronto.

Praise for
Franklin Delano Roosevelt: Champion of Freedom

"However unexpected, this enormous book is also one of the best one-volume biographies of Roosevelt yet. . . . It tells the remarkable story of Roosevelt's life with an engaging eloquence and with largely personal and mostly interesting opinions about the people and events he is describing. . . . [A] powerful and often moving picture of the life as a whole. It is a worthy and important addition to the vast literature on the most important modern American leader."
—Alan Brinkley, *The New York Times*

"*Franklin Delano Roosevelt* has received mostly glowing reviews from across the political spectrum—and with good reason. It is the best biography of Roosevelt by far, notwithstanding the fact that Conrad Black relies almost exclusively on secondary material. He tells Roosevelt's story engrossingly, combining historical rigor with a novelist's eye for detail and character. A marvelous book about a great president who richly earned the title Conrad Black bestows on him."
—*The Weekly Standard*

"Conrad Black's life of Franklin Roosevelt is a great achievement, and all the more welcome for being more than a little surprising. The book is well-researched, readable and judicious. It deserves to become the standard one-volume life of FDR." —*The Economist*

"*Franklin Delano Roosevelt* is in fact a rather superb book, eminently fair and very well researched . . . it deserves a wide audience. . . . Conrad Black's study presents in a fair and judicious way this controversial figure. His judgments are positive, not just toward FDR but also toward the American people, who became generous allies and idealistic warriors in the last great crusade for worldwide freedom." —*The Washington Times*

"A monumental and admirable biography . . . this book is not simply splendid and thorough, marvelously readable and valuable, it is also a sustained and challenging argument. A powerful and impassioned case is being made, in a strong and sinewy language, by a biographer who reveres his subject, relishes the thrust of debate and repeatedly engages his putative critics on the page. . . . Black has a fine eye for the telling anecdote, however it reflects on his subject. . . . Black's book is not just the best Roosevelt biography so far, but also by far the most enjoyable . . ." —*The National Interest*

"Conrad Black is strongest in his portrayal of FDR as war leader [and] excellent in describing the wrangling, misunderstandings, and often genuine hostility that characterized the relationship between Roosevelt and De Gaulle. He shows that FDR was profoundly wrong in searching for a French leader other than De Gaulle to lead the provisional government of France."
—James Chace, *The New York Review of Books*

"A deft writer who applies to one of the most influential men of the 20th century what he has learned from a career of sizing up people and their ambitions. The result is a sweeping, occasionally sprawling biography. At 1,280 pages, it's a companion for the long haul—and an engrossing one, thanks to the storytelling and pungency of its judgments."   —Daniel Yergin, *The Wall Street Journal*

"Black has an uncanny grasp of the intricacies of American politics. . . . His account of how Roosevelt swung the Democratic Convention of 1932, to win the nomination for the presidency, is one of the funniest and cleverest essays in the analysis of American politics ever written, worthy to rank beside the work of Theodore H. White or A.J. Liebling."
          —Historian John Keegan, *London Daily Telegraph*

"[An] unrivaled biography. . . . A major social history of the time. . . . [C]elebrates its long-elusive protagonist . . . while capturing Roosevelt in all his rich, baffling, and fascinating variety. [Black's] mastery of surrounding moment and personalities, of a vanished America, is often rendered in such a graceful sweep . . . that we hardly notice how thoroughly the author commands the material."
          —*Toronto Globe & Mail*

Franklin Delano Roosevelt

Champion of Freedom

CONRAD BLACK

PublicAffairs
New York

Book Design by Anne DeLozier

Library of Congress Cataloging-in-Publication Data
Black, Conrad.
Franklin Delano Roosevelt : champion of freedom / Conrad Black.—1st ed.
p.   cm.
Includes bibliographical references and index.
ISBN-13 978-1-58648-282-4   ISBN-10 1-58648-282-3
1. Roosevelt, Franklin D. (Franklin Delano), 1882–1945.   2. Presidents—
United States—Biography.   I. Title.
E807.B58 2003
973.917'092—dc21
[B]
2003047054

10 9 8 7 6 5 4 3 2

For
G. Montegu Black, 1940–2002
and
G. Emmett Cardinal Carter, 1912–2003

A noble brother and a dear friend,
who had both looked forward to this book.

Contents

Acknowledgments

I wish to thank first George (Lord) Weidenfeld, for inspiring me to write a biography of Franklin D. Roosevelt at all, and my wife, Barbara, for enduring unimaginable inconvenience and boredom throughout the life of this project.

For reading all or important parts of the manuscript, I wish to thank, apart from Barbara Black: Corelli Barnett, Christopher Breiseth, Anthony Beevor, William F. Buckley Jr., Henry A. Grunwald, Simon Heffer, Roger Hertog, Paul Johnson, George Jonas, Sir John Keegan, Henry A. Kissinger, John Lukacs, Robert Morgenthau, Frank Pearl, Andrew Roberts, Arthur Ross, Arthur M. Schlesinger Jr., Simon Sebag-Montefiore, Brian Stewart, William Vanden Heuvel, George Will, Tom Wolfe, David Woolner, and Ezra Zilkha. I tried to follow virtually every suggestion they made and am deeply indebted to all of them.

Christopher Breiseth, William Vanden Heuvel, and David Woolner were also very helpful in facilitating access to the Franklin D. Roosevelt Library, as were the personnel of that library and of the Franklin and Eleanor Roosevelt Institute.

For research and assistance in organizing the material, I am grateful to Janice Akerhielm, Adam Daifallah, Joan Maida, Rosemary Millar, and Kennan Moody.

My agent, Morton L. Janklow, was an early and constant source of wise counsel and support, and I wish also to thank for their encouragement and helpfulness in various ways Robert Hopkins, Mary (Lady) Soames, Ion Trewin, and Ed Victor.

My editor, William Whitworth, has been kind, patient, and thorough beyond all praise or duty. His unfailing good humor has made this often abrasive process a delight, at least for me. I hope our intense e-mail relationship graduates eventually to our actual meeting. Whatever this book's shortcomings now, they are a fraction of what they would have been without Bill Whitworth's attentions.

The publisher, Peter Osnos, and his colleagues at PublicAffairs, Robert Kimzey, Paul Golob, Clive Priddle, Gene Taft, David Patterson, Melanie Johnstone, and Vicky Dawes, have been a joy to work with even in the most difficult circumstances produced by crucial publishing deadlines. Ginny Carroll's work with the endnotes is all that has avoided chaos in that area; she is a heroine.

I am very grateful to all of the above.

PART I

The Predestined Squire

1882–1932

"I Like You and Trust You and Believe in You . . . and Golden Years Open before You"

*(President Theodore Roosevelt to his sixth cousin, Franklin Delano
Roosevelt, when Franklin became engaged to the President's niece,
Eleanor Roosevelt, 1904)*

I

T HE ASTONISHING LIFE of Franklin Delano Roosevelt began with great difficulty following a labor of over twenty-four hours on January 30, 1882. He finally emerged after the use of chloroform, blue and still and weighing an imposing ten pounds. The family doctor successfully applied mouth-to-mouth resuscitation to the infant. He proved at once and always to be tenacious of life. His father recorded the arrival of "a splendid, large, baby boy."[1]

Mrs. Roosevelt was confined to her bed for a month, and was advised that she should not have another child. Most of Sara Delano Roosevelt's ample energies and ambitions would for nearly sixty years be focused on her son.

Though young Roosevelt's passage into it was difficult, the world of his afflu-ent and affectionate parents was genteel. He was born at Springwood, the family home overlooking the Hudson River at Hyde Park, New York. James and Sara Roosevelt were among the fifty or so families that had commodious estates along (mainly) the eastern bank of the majestic Hudson, where it flowed slowly by Westchester and Dutchess counties, especially from Rhinebeck to Tarrytown — from seventy-five down to fifteen miles north of New York City. Washington Irv-ing had made Sleepy Hollow, near Tarrytown, famous with the legends of Rip Van Winkle and Ichabod Crane.

The Roosevelts were not the senior residents, an honor that went to earlier Dutch families such as the Schuylers and Van Rensselaers. And they were far from the wealthiest, distantly trailing the Astors, the Belmonts, the Vanderbilts, and eventually the Rockefellers and others in much grander homes. But they were comfortable, distinguished, and gentle people. In New York City, where they also had a home, they formed part of the Knickerbocker society described in the novels of Henry James and Edith Wharton.

All his life Roosevelt would be profoundly dedicated to the area around his home, compiling and studying obscurely detailed local histories and endlessly fascinated with the minutiae of local life. "I miss our river . . . Why is it that our River and our countryside seem so to be a part of us?" he wrote in the nineteen-thirties to his intimate cousin, Margaret Suckley. He convinced himself that a stand of timber near the driveway on his property was a primeval forest that ante-dated Henry Hudson and so described it eventually to the illustrious visitors he attracted to his house in the thirties and forties.[2] Franklin Roosevelt would early learn and never forget the distinction between new and old money.

The first Roosevelt in the new world was Claes Van Roosevelt, who emigrated to Nieuw Amsterdam in 1650, and the first Delano was Philippe de la Noye, a Huguenot arrival at Plymouth in 1621. It was among Claes Van Roosevelt's grandsons that the branches that gave twentieth century America two of its greatest leaders emerged; Franklin Roosevelt was descended from Jacobus (James) Roosevelt, and Theodore Roosevelt was descended from his brother Johannes.

There was a widespread theory, circulated largely in anti-Semitic circles in the thirties, that the Roosevelts were originally Jewish. In a famous letter in 1935, Franklin D. Roosevelt responded to a written question on this point from a Jewish scholar (Philip Slomovitz) that it was of no interest to him what the religion of his Dutch ancestors might have been, he only hoped that they were people "of good character and believers in God."[3]

The Roosevelts prospered in Manhattan real estate, dry goods, and the importation of sugar from the West Indies. They intermarried with good and wealthy families (a practice that continued even unto some of FDR's erratic children, though not with their ancestors' stubborn attachment to the indissolubility of marriage).

The most noteworthy of the eighteenth-century Roosevelts was "Isaac the Patriot," a well-to-do sugar importer who voted for independence at the provincial assembly in 1776 because of unreasonable taxation and had to flee New York when the British occupied the city. He moved to Dutchess County, where his family remained. He was one of the authors of the constitution of New York, a Federalist ally of Alexander Hamilton, and one of the founders, with Hamilton and others, and for a time the president, of the Bank of New York.

Philippe de la Noye came to the New World unsuccessfully pursuing Priscilla Mullens, a woman who would also be the subject of the attentions of the famous parliamentarians Myles Standish and John Alden. His enthusiasm unrequited, he found another wife, and one of their sons, Jonathan Delano (as the name had become), fought with such distinction in King Philip's War (with the Indians, 1675–6, which killed one-sixth of the male colonists in New England) that he was rewarded with an 800-acre grant of land. Included in the grant was the coastal village of Fairhaven, near New Bedford, Massachusetts. His grandson, Warren Delano, started a sailing career in the early nineteenth century, shipping agricultural products to Britain, the Canary Islands, and the Gulf of Mexico, and became a successful ship owner. Warren's son, Warren Delano II, Franklin D. Roosevelt's maternal grandfather, was born at Fairhaven in 1809.

At the end of the War of 1812 Warren Delano was detained on the high seas for two weeks by the British. This may have been the beginning of a durable family resentment of the British Empire. This prickly Yankee competitiveness was sometimes present even in the thoughts of Franklin Delano Roosevelt. (During the South African War, his sympathies would be entirely with the Boers.) As a scion of New York squires he was always an Anglophile. Yet as the descendant of New England seafarers, he felt a tinge of civilized rivalry.

Warren Delano II, inspired by his father's swashbuckling, launched himself on a career as an oriental trader when he shipped out to China in 1833. He made a substantial fortune with the principal American company in the China trade — Russell, Sturgis of Boston. He was inconvenienced by the Opium Wars of 1838–1842, which led to the cession of Hong Kong to Britain. His sympathies were with the Chinese over the British, provided Americans could continue to do what had angered the decrepit Chinese authorities in the first place: export opium and sell it in large quantities in China.

The latter-day Roosevelts, including Franklin, were not happy that much of their inherited millions came from the derring-do of the Delanos in the opium trade. When this was referred to by Westbrook Pegler, one of the premier muckrakers of the American media in the 1940s, FDR left it to a distant admiring relative, Daniel Delano, to offer a lame exculpation. Delano made the spurious claim that Warren Delano had been (and only during his second sojourn in China) the "special representative in China" of President Lincoln. Pegler's allegations were held to "dishonor the memory . . . and integrity" of Lincoln.[4]

Not even FDR, who in his prime had few peers as an imaginatively self-serving rewriter of history, would have tried anything so implausible. When dogged with such allegations, he would judge it wiser to emphasize the romance of the clipper ships and maintain a decorous silence about the Delanos' buccaneering past. There is no evidence that Abraham Lincoln was even aware of Warren Delano.

Warren Delano II happily returned to the United States in 1846 from his first stint in China. He had never liked China and was glad to be quit of it and to reinvest the proceeds of his work there in New York real estate, railroads, and various mining ventures. Warren's younger brother, Franklin (after whom Franklin D. Roosevelt was eventually named), had married the granddaughter of America's wealthiest man, John Jacob Astor, the beginning of a long association between the two families. Warren Delano built a splendid house, Algonac, twenty miles south of Hyde Park and on the western side of the Hudson, in 1852. "Algonac" was an Algonquin word for river and hill. In the Delano family it was long used as a synonym for good news. It was here on September 21, 1854, that Sara Delano, FDR's mother, was born.

The progress of the Roosevelts in the first half of the nineteenth century had been rather more prosaic. James, the son of Isaac the Patriot, built a comfortable house at Mount Hope, on the Hudson not far from Hyde Park, in 1820. He led a tranquil life there and on South Street in New York City. His eldest son, the inevitable Isaac, was an eccentric who qualified as a medical doctor but declined to practice his profession because he was repelled by the sight of blood. He moved to Mount Hope when it was completed and lived a solitary and scholarly life there, gloomily pious, hypochondriacal, and reclusive. Samuel F. B. Morse, a neighbor, was among his few friends. His family (his father had ten other children from three wives) was startled when, in 1827, with negligible previous contact with the opposite sex, he married Mary Rebecca Aspinwall, the daughter of a wealthy shipping family, who was nineteen, barely half Isaac's age. The next James Roosevelt, who would be Franklin D. Roosevelt's father, was born of this improbable couple at Mount Hope, on July 16, 1828.

He would be a very different person from his academic and timid father. James Roosevelt was a natural gentleman, discreet, civilized, mannerly—never boastful, idle, garish, or overtly snobbish, but tasteful and discriminating. He had a restrained but active sense of humor and was worldly but profoundly attached to his community, where he filled a number of worthy little offices, such as town manager of Hyde Park, Episcopal church warden, and hospital governor. Through most of his adult life, other than during the Civil War, he was one of the 30,000 Americans who travelled in Europe each year, where he was everywhere received by prominent people. He was also easy, courteous, and generous with the humblest people.

Emboldened by parenthood, Dr. Isaac built himself a fine home, Rosedale, across the Albany Post Road from Mount Hope. Mr. James, as Franklin D. Roosevelt's father was kindly known almost all his life, had a happy if lonely childhood. His parents doted on him. He was tutored at home until he was nine, was a day student at the progressive and gentle Poughkeepsie Collegiate School until he was thirteen, and then, shortly after the birth of a brother, John Aspinwall Roosevelt, was sent to Hyde's School in Lee, Massachusetts. This was a more pious and regimented place than Poughkeepsie, where James had been able to see the reassuring rooftops of Rosedale three miles away, but James did well and enrolled in the University of New York in 1843.

His father had grave reservations about the corrupting influence of New York City, requiring that James live with his paternal grandparents on Bleecker Street. As Dr. Isaac had feared, Sodom and Gomorrah worked their influence on the impressionable young man: James and three friends were admonished for causing "disorder," and failed to complete the year. Dr. Isaac, reasserting the virtues of less metropolitan places of study, sent him to Union College in Schenectady. This was a sort of cram school for turbulent freshmen, where the future president Chester Alan Arthur and Frederick Seward, son of New York's governor, who was later secretary of state under Presidents Abraham Lincoln, Andrew Johnson, and Ulysses S. Grant, were also enrolled.[5]

James was one of the few students who lived off campus. He scandalized his father by joining a secret society that met in a tavern, but he did quite well and graduated in good standing in 1847. To the intense consternation of his father, he left almost at once for Europe on the conventional grand tour for the young offspring of the wealthy. James travelled in England, France, Spain, Germany, Italy, and even in the Middle East, causing great anxiety to the ever-fretful Dr. Isaac.

In a robust gesture, James Roosevelt, aged twenty, enlisted in the reunificationist army of the Italian patriot and military leader Giuseppe Garibaldi. Mr. James's revolutionary career lasted for one rather boring and disorganized month. According to his son Franklin in 1941, Mr. James, with Garibaldi's permission, retired from the Red Shirt forces, which had attracted volunteers from the idealistic youth of all Europe, a little like the international brigades in the Spanish Civil War nearly a century later.[6]

Mr. James then resumed a walking tour of southern Italy with an impecunious priest with whom he had been travelling. He returned to the United States in the spring of 1849 and enrolled in Harvard Law School in the autumn of that year. An intelligent and popular student, he passed easily through to graduation in 1851 as an LL.B. He was elected an honorary member of the most sought-after campus society, the Porcellian Club, two years after graduation.

From 1851 to 1853 James Roosevelt was a junior in the distinguished New York law firm of Benjamin Silliman, and used it as a springboard to business. In 1852, he became a director of the newly incorporated Consolidated Coal Company, of which his uncle, William Aspinwall, was a co-founder. Railroads were America's most financially tumultuous and greatest growth industry. In his mid-twenties, Mr. James became general manager of the Cumberland and Pennsylvania Railway.

On April 27, 1853, Mr. James married his first cousin, Rebecca Brien Howland. After a honeymoon in Niagara Falls, they moved into Mount Hope, and in the autumn they went on the first of many extended visits they would take to Europe.

In London, James and Rebecca called upon the American minister, James Buchanan, who invited James to serve as his secretary at the embassy until the arrival of new personnel. James did so, beginning a tradition of Hyde Park Roosevelts working with Democratic presidents (as Buchanan became three years later) that would last over a century.[7]

When James's first son was born in March 1854, James and Rebecca emphasized familiar insularity (and ended the practice of alternating the names James and Isaac each generation) by giving him the singular name James Roosevelt Roosevelt. (This was a more distinguished alternative to adding "Junior" to the boy's name.) He was a jovial boy and man and was known from earliest days and all his life as Rosy. James and Rebecca took Rosy everywhere with them, including to Europe in 1865, after the Civil War. On this trip they travelled across the ocean with August Belmont. During a two-month stay at Le Havre, they met Count Alexandre Walewski, cousin of the French emperor, natural son of Napoleon I, and president of the French Legislative Assembly.[8] In these times, even a moderately social and itinerant gentleman like James Roosevelt could meet virtually everyone in the Western world of any importance.

At Interlaken in September, James learned from a letter from his brother John of the destruction by fire of the family home at Mount Hope. James always believed that it was an act of arson by a tenant's servant trying to disguise his own thefts of the Roosevelts' property, but no charge was ever laid. Although a tea service was the only family heirloom saved, James and Rebecca determined to remain in Europe and proceeded to Dresden for the winter.

One of their neighbors there, with whom James struck up a warm friendship, was General George B. McClellan. Abraham Lincoln had dismissed McClellan as Union Army commander in 1862 and defeated him in the presidential election of 1864.

Despite Franklin Roosevelt's later claim that his father had "rendered distinguished patriotic service" as a member of the Sanitary Commission succoring the wounded during the Civil War, there is no evidence that he did anything useful for the war effort. He may have done such work, or given logistical advice on the use of the railways and paid someone else to answer his draft call (as was perfectly legal), or by official oversight never have been called, but there is no evidence of any of it. Nor is there any evidence that his relative inactivity discountenanced him or his son. Passivity during the nation's greatest national and martial crisis did trouble his friend and cousin, the senior Theodore Roosevelt and his son, the future president, who would never be accused of passivity.[9]

It is not clear when James became a Democrat. He was an old Whig in the tradition of the Roosevelts, and he remembered the tempestuous populism of Andrew Jackson, which outraged the Roosevelt elders as much as his infant cousin Teddy and his own unborn son Franklin would horrify many of their peers forty and seventy years later. When the Whigs ceased to present respectable candidates after General Winfield Scott in 1852 (defeated by Franklin Pierce), James opted for the Democrats, perhaps because of his friendship with Buchanan. They were at this point the more genteel party.

At about the same time James abandoned the derelict Whigs, he departed the implacably gloomy Dutch Reform Church of his father. For Dr. Isaac the end was always nigh, and for him it finally came in 1863, when he was seventy-three. James, who was a regular churchgoer but not an overly pious or fervent man, joined his wife in the more urbane Episcopal Church. Mr. James was for decades a vestryman and intermittent senior warden of St. James Episcopal Church at Hyde Park, a tasteful little neo-Gothic chapel where the pews were allotted more or less on the basis of social standing. The brass plaque "J. Roosevelt" adorned his places on the aisle in the third row. Franklin and the illustrious guests whom he would conscientiously conduct to St. James, including the Supreme Governor of the affiliated Church of England, King George VI, would make the little church world famous.

Dr. Isaac's death had considerably enriched James and made him the head of his branch of the family. He had already been occupying Mount Hope. His brother John took Rosedale, and after the fire James was left to find a new country house. His first attempt was to buy John Jacob Astor III's opulent Ferncliffe, but his bid was insufficient, so he purchased the modest but well-situated estate that he renamed Springwood, at Hyde Park.[10] Here would be born America's greatest leader since Lincoln. And here he was raised and always returned.

Mr. James was elected town supervisor of Hyde Park as a Democrat in 1871. Thereafter he was frequently asked to stand for the New York state assembly or senate and for Congress. He was interested in politics and gratified to be approached, but he always declined, to the great relief of Rebecca.

Although Mr. James had cast his lot altogether with the sedate builders and conservators of traditional fortunes and did not envy the new rich, he was tempted by the tremendous explosion of wealth in the harum-scarum financial and industrial growth of post-Civil War America. He was often an imaginative though not reckless investor, hoping to raise his fortune without altering the gracious tenor of his life as a Hudson River gentleman. His devotion to that life and his penchant for trans-Atlantic travel ruled out a full-time political career and prevented him from giving finance and industry the undivided attention required for conspicuous success in the cut-throat age of the robber barons.

He may have been a slightly inconstant financier, but he was a formidable master of Springwood. Athletic and stylish, despite the claim of one acquaintance that his mutton-chop whiskers made him look more like Lord Lansdowne's coachman than like Lord Lansdowne, he was adept at all the appropriate sports. Mr. James was an accomplished skater, ice-boater, sailor, and fisherman, a fine horseman, a master of fox hounds, and commodore of the local yacht club. He was keenly interested in agriculture and forestry and was proud of operating

Springwood's farm (mainly trees, apples, horses, and hay) at a profit, though the accounting methods used to generate the profit may not have been rigorous.

Of all these interests, Mr. James was most interested in horses. He was a successful breeder of trotting horses and had an impressive array of horse-drawn vehicles. (Franklin had the four-foot tail of his father's best trotter mounted on a bedroom wall in the New York governor's mansion and in the White House.) Mr. James was a relentless improver of his property. He built Springwood up over decades from a little more than a hundred acres that he bought in 1866 to over a thousand, while expanding the house from Victorian farmhouse to a not especially well-proportioned thirty-room semi-Georgian residence. It eventually became a pleasant house, but was never grand or sumptuous. Save for the renown of the eventual occupants, the entire contents, from the stuffed birds in the entrance hall to the last overstuffed sofa and straight-backed chair, would not be worth one of their more prosperous neighbors' tapestries or dinner services.

The Roosevelts, whether at Hyde Park or Oyster Bay, were rugged and hardy, *mens sana in corpore sano*, practitioners of the strenuous life, refined and adequately learned but, except possibly for Teddy, not intellectual. They were gentlemen farmers and sportsmen. For the pharaonic opulence of the Gilded Age they lacked the means and probably the inclination. Such access to it as they ever enjoyed would be through marriage, neighborliness, and, finally, high political office. They disparaged the ostentation of the Vanderbilts, in particular.

Mr. James endured serious commercial disappointments in the 1870s. He invested in Thomas Scott's Southern Railway Securities Company, which controlled the lines between Richmond, Atlanta, New Orleans, and Memphis. Scott was one of the principals of the Pennsylvania Railway and a precursor of E.H. Harriman, James J. Hill, and other great railway financiers. He made James Roosevelt president of the S.R.S.C. in 1872.

In September 1871, the prominent Philadelphia bank Jay Cooke & Company abruptly collapsed, generating a panic in financial markets. Thomas Scott's grand scheme, reliant on inflated stock values, imploded a few weeks later. James Roosevelt resigned amid the debacle on October 3, 1871. There was no suggestion of the slightest impropriety on his part.

Even though Scott's Southern Railways Securities Company failed, the whole episode was a costly but affordable success for the Pennsylvania Railroad, which Thomas Scott represented, because it enabled further consolidation of rail-lines and a tighter cartel. For James Roosevelt and other outside investors, however, it was a severe setback.[11]

In the spring of 1875, Consolidation Coal, after being severely shaken by the repercussions of the Cooke fiasco, was the subject of a shareholders' revolt that swept out James, his uncle, William H. Aspinwall, and his subsequent in-law, Warren Delano II. The Baltimore and Ohio Railroad exploited the unfavorable conditions to take control of Consolidation, which it profitably retained for many years.[12] Mr. James had not invested—and never did invest—more than he could afford to lose, and he retreated to Springwood, sobered but not chastened.

His last great scheme to catapult himself into the ranks of America's wealthiest industrialists was an isthmian canal project in Nicaragua, in competition with the Ferdinand de Lesseps initiative in Panama, which failed financially in the late 1880s. Mr. James worked on this for fifteen years and relied heavily on his friendship with President Grover Cleveland, but the Nicaraguan project finally collapsed in 1899. Mr. James was a perceptive investor but lacked the intense concentration and killer instinct to make a huge fortune. (His investment decisions were, however, almost Midas-like compared with some of the ideas in which Franklin would invest in the twenties.)

From 1869 on, Rebecca Roosevelt's condition steadily declined. Overweight, constantly fatigued, racked by coughing, chest pains, and backaches, she bore up bravely, but neither the medical profession nor traditional travel cures availed. When James took her and Rosy to Europe in the summer of 1869, London, Paris, Rome, and the spa of Merau did nothing for her. In one of his countless remedial efforts, James took Rebecca out on his sailing yacht on Long Island Sound in August 1876. Rebecca suffered a heart attack shortly after embarking. She was conveyed back to their city home on Washington Square, where she died after a few days, on August 21, 1876. She was buried behind St. James's chapel in Hyde Park. James and Rosy sailed to England in October.

The Delanos were even more rugged individualists than the Roosevelts, or at least the Hyde Park Roosevelts. The third quarter of the nineteenth century had been very challenging for them. Warren Delano would harangue his children when they remained indoors on a rainy day: "All weather is good weather!"[13]

Reduced to straitened circumstances by investment reversals in the 1850s, Delano even thought of selling Algonac. He finally resolved that the only way to replenish his fortunes was to return to China, which he did from 1860 to 1866. He reentered the tea and opium trades in Hong Kong, and as the senior American merchant there became the American consul, as he had been in Canton in the 1840s. This was the post that gave birth to the canard about representing President Lincoln.

In 1862 Delano sent for his wife and seven children, including the eight-year-old Sara. The voyage from New York and around the Cape took 128 days on a clipper. They endured temperature variances of over 90 degrees Fahrenheit and sighted one vessel that was at first feared to be a Confederate warship. This was the subject of much eventual embellishment by FDR.[14] Sara and two of her brothers returned to the United States after three memorable years in Rose Hill, the family's large home overlooking the harbor of Hong Kong.

Warren Delano reinvigorated his fortunes in China and, with even greater satisfaction than in his original departure from that country in 1846, collected his family and moved to a fine apartment in Paris beside the Bois de Boulogne. Sara spent four years in Europe, suffered the only serious illness of her life, rheumatic fever, and convalesced watching the comings and goings around the Paris Universal Exhibition, glimpsing most of Europe's leading statesmen, including Bismarck, from her father's balcony.[15] The Delanos moved on to Dresden in 1867. Sara went to finishing school in Celle, Germany, from 1868 to 1870, summering on an island in the North Sea and in the Harz Mountains. Sara returned to New York in June 1870 on the last ship to leave Germany before the Franco-Prussian War.

In the mid-seventies Sara was ardently courted by the brilliant but bumptious young architect Stanford White, whom Sara's father detested and described as "the red-headed trial."[16] He was compulsively noisy and contrarian, always underfoot, loud in clothes as well as voice, and seemed to the redoubtable Warren Delano almost preternaturally precocious and abrasive. Delano sent his daughter away for nine months, the time-honored tactic of wealthy Victorian fathers hardpressed by the apprehended romantic misadventures of their children. Sara visited England, where she observed Disraeli and Gladstone from the parliamentary visitors' gallery, watching closely enough to be impressed by the accuracy of George Arliss' film portrayal of Disraeli more than fifty years later. She went on to Hong Kong to stay with her brother-in-law Will Forbes at Rose Hill, where Forbes was carrying on the lucrative Delano family participation in the opium and tea trades.[17]

Sara finally chose to retain her father's goodwill. She resisted her undoubted infatuation with Stanford White and returned to Algonac in 1877. White married seven years later, by which time he had already become one of the most successful and admired architects in the history of the United States. Delano may have underestimated White's professional genius, but in the more important matter of White's aptitudes as a husband, Delano's paternal instinct was exact. White was a compulsive womanizer, both a bounder and a cad. He was murdered in 1906 by the mad husband of his then current paramour. Even Sara, so majestic of will and personality in later years, would have found White a handful, or, as her father had said, a "trial."

At the time that the entanglement between Sara Delano and Stanford White was extinguished by the master of Algonac, the nearby squire of Springwood, Mr. James, threw himself into unrequited passion for his cousin, Bamie Roosevelt, the future president Theodore Roosevelt's elder sister. Mr. James was old enough to be her father, but that was not necessarily inhibiting; and there were precedents for Roosevelts marrying cousins, as James already had. Mr. James proposed in 1880 after another contemplative holiday in England and France. But the widow of the elder Theodore Roosevelt (who had died in 1878) gently intervened, and Bamie politely declined.

It was under these circumstances that Mr. James met Sara, in April 1880. It was virtually love at first sight (though it has been alleged that White was the only man Sara Delano ever romantically loved).[18] A woman undeterred by the vagaries of White's personality would not be overly bothered by the twenty-six-year disparity in age between Mr. James and herself. Warren Delano and his wife were inexpressibly relieved to see the back of Stanford White and gratefully grappled Mr. James, whom they knew and esteemed, to the bosom of their family.

James Roosevelt and Sara Delano were married in a Unitarian service at Algonac on October 7, 1880. The wedding was held to 125 guests because of family bereavements, most recently a cousin and an aunt after whom Sara had been named. According to the *New York World*, villagers in their "pretty country cottages" stood at the roadside "to do honor" like vassals emerging from under thatched roofs as the wedding party and guests passed in a long row of fine carriages.[19]

The newlyweds left for Europe a month later, just after the election of James's old school friend Chester A. Arthur as vice president with James A. Garfield. Arthur would succeed to the presidency on the assassination of Garfield the following summer. The Roosevelts returned in September after ten months abroad, with Sara almost five months pregnant.

At Springwood an informal understanding obtained: They would live exactly as Mr. James had with Rebecca, including the playing of bezique every night, but all holidays and family occasions would be spent with the Delanos. Mr. James would then be dragooned into the serried ranks of the in-laws.

The Delanos were further thinned in the autumn of 1881 by the death of a popular uncle and of Sara's younger brother Philippe, named after the first American Delano. Though scarcely twenty, Philippe succumbed to a series of seizures and strokes. (In 1884, Sara's beautiful nineteen-year-old sister Laura would die when an alcohol lamp fell over on her as she was heating curling irons and she was almost incinerated before the eyes of family members at Algonac. She was the fifth of Warren Delano's children to die; even his indomitable spirit was heavily taxed.)

Six weeks after Philippe's death, Franklin Delano Roosevelt was born. Thirteen days later, Warren Delano IV, aged four, died of typhoid fever. Sara had rejected James's proposal to revive the tradition of alternating James and Isaac each generation, because she disliked the name Isaac. Her intention was to name her son after her own father, but the parents of little Warren Delano IV asked her to desist.[20] Franklin therefore took his name from his wealthy and childless uncle and Astor in-law. One of his godfathers was Elliott Roosevelt, brother of the future president Theodore Roosevelt. Had he lived, Elliott would also have been Franklin's father-in-law.

II

S ARA WAS A departure from the usual young mother of her social station. She insisted on being involved in every aspect of her son's upbringing and becoming completely qualified to feed, change, and wash him. Franklin was never overly dependent on nannies. But he was quite affected when his mother called on Miss McRorie in an old-age home in Hamilton, Ontario, in 1934 and told him that his old nurse, then eighty-nine, always listened to his addresses on the radio and remembered everything about him. "You were such 'a good boy' and only sometimes full of mischief. I told her that I thought her fine sterling qualities had helped you always and given you a wonderful start," the President's mother wrote.[21]

Miss McRorie's successor, the Swiss Mlle. Sandoz, helped to fire Franklin's social conscience, and continued to write to him up to and into his presidency. She inspired her charge's essay on ancient Egypt in 1891: "The kings made them [the people] work so hard and gave them so little that by wingo! They nearly starved and by jinks! They had hardly any clothes so they died in quadrillions." [22] Mlle. Sandoz, "more than anyone else . . . laid the foundations of my education," he wrote to her forty years later.[23]

"Certainly, everything about his infancy seemed calculated to make him feel loved. His mother constantly carried and held him. She fed him at her breast for almost a year."[24] She did not let him bathe without her until he was eight.[25] Even his exacting grandfather, who found fault with practically everyone, judged the infant Franklin "a beautiful little fellow—well and strong and well-behaved . . . always bright and happy" and, turning to phrenology, "with a good-shaped head of the Delano type."[26] He even allowed Franklin, when his parents brought him to Algonac, alone among his seventeen grandchildren, to sleep in the cradle he had himself slept in nearly seventy-five years before.

Theodore Roosevelt's mother, no under-qualified judge of children, described Franklin as "such a fair, sweet, cunning little bright five-months old darling baby."[27] With suitable adjustments for maturation, this was essentially what an indefectible majority of the American people thought of him fifty years later: handsome, kind, cunning, and intelligent; only his eloquence and physical courage were indiscernible in these early days.

Sara Delano Roosevelt not only rejoiced in dressing Franklin, but insisted for an inordinate time that he have shoulder-length curls and wear skirts. When his mother finally liberated him from skirts in the fashion made popular in the contemporary romantic novel *Little Lord Fauntleroy*, it was to put him in kilts.[28] This was a preposterous affectation, since the Roosevelts and the Delanos had only a tenuous claim on Caledonian ancestry.[29] At the same time, she cut his hair but missed "his little blond curls bobbing" as he was "trotting along and chatting over his small affairs."[30]

Separations from his parents were rare and painful, but endured in dignified silence. In 1886 Mr. James (again a director of several railroads) took Sara to Mexico on his private railway car, the *Monon*, and left the four-year-old Franklin behind because of public health problems in Mexico. Franklin was undemonstrative, as he would be throughout his life, but spent hours rocking on a hobby horse at Algonac that he called "Mexico." When his parents returned, he held on to his mother in the carriage from the Newburgh ferry to Algonac without uttering a sound, "like a little soldier."[31]

Mr. James and Sara had agreed to travel very extensively and were away from Springwood for most of most years. In 1884 the two-year-old Franklin and his parents were two months in New York City and over six months in England. In 1885 they were back in Europe and had a harrowing experience on their return when it was feared that their ship, the *Germania*, might founder. Sara held on to Franklin in the cabin with water sloshing around on the floor and an almost hysterical commotion audible in the ship. She retrieved a toy Franklin asked for that was being borne about the room on the rolling tide of bilgewater. All the Roosevelts, as always, were calm through the crisis. The captain had been temporarily incapacitated when struck by an object sprung loose in the storm. He came to and commanded a limping return to Liverpool.[32] Franklin always remembered the experience as illustrative of the virtues of calm under pressure, of unflappable seamanship, and of family solidarity.

In 1885 Mr. James built a rambling, comfortable cottage on Campobello Island, New Brunswick. He was attracted by the sailing on Passamaquoddy Bay, which was made interesting by the unusually changeable tides, winds, and currents. Franklin spent most summers there for thirty-six years. Sara, unshakeable by world wars, depression, or family illness, would be a pillar of summer life on Campobello for nearly sixty years.

Mr. James taught Franklin to ride at four and to sail by six, and went tobogganing with him into his sixties. Their relations were close and affectionate; Franklin called his father, who was fifty-four when the boy was born, "Popsy," implying a good deal less formality than might have been expected from the Roosevelts.[33] In early years Franklin almost always accompanied his father, including one visit to the Hudson River State Hospital, a mental institution of which Mr. James was the manager, built on the grounds of the former family home at Mount Hope. A hallucinating woman patient who believed herself to be Queen Victoria chased Mr. James through the hospital, exclaiming that he was Prince Albert, come to take her back to Windsor.[34]

While his father taught and accompanied him in sports, his mother was a benign but unswerving figure of authority in almost all other things. Franklin knew only the tyranny of his mother's regimental routine. There was no spontaneity, variety, privacy, or unpredictability. He rose every day at seven, went to bed at eight, took his meals at eight, one, and six, did his lessons from nine to noon and one-thirty to four, and had supervised recreation from noon to one and four to six. His mother read to him every night and required him to pay attention. Literacy and knowledge of literature and history were encouraged. Like many small boys, he was an unenthusiastic piano student, and often claimed that headaches made churchgoing burdensome.[35]

Franklin Roosevelt was a reasonably learned young man. He had no allowance except when the family was travelling, and money was never an acceptable subject of conversation. Sometimes two young sons of one of the Roosevelt farmers were allowed to bobsled with Franklin and his father, but in informal exchange for this privilege, they took the sled back to the top of the run and the Roosevelts, father and son, followed unburdened.[36] Franklin had little other contact with young people outside his social stratum.

Mr. James believed that "There is not so much to luck as some people profess to believe. Indeed, most people fail because they do not deserve to succeed." But he did have a compassionate view of the underprivileged, devoid of condescension, which he certainly communicated to Franklin. He was horrified at the conditions in which the poor lived in the great cities of Europe and America. He considered it the duty of everyone to help the underprivileged of society, not only financially but with personal care and attention. "We must furnish work to do away with pauperism," he once famously said.[37]

Warren Delano was inspired by an even more advanced view of society. He was comprehensively generous to the poor and particularly concerned with the status of African-Americans. He supported the black educator Booker T. Washington financially and welcomed him to his house, where Sara met him. Franklin would be influenced by this view also, both directly and through his mother. His and his antecedents' concepts of public policy and private duty vastly transcended mere paternalism and were amplified by Mlle. Sandoz's advocacy of social Christianity. The roots of the New Deal were not in the factories or mines or union halls or universities or farmers' associations of America, but in Springwood and Algonac.

For such an intelligent child, faced with such a loving but strict mother, the choice between rebellion, submission, and the application of guile was constantly to be made. Franklin was too astute not to realize the impossibility of successful revolt and too conscious of his own value (a knowledge that his parents constantly reinforced) to carry submission to extremes. He gradually developed the skill of placatory acceptance of his mother's authority, tempered by as much leeway as he could carve out for himself. Many of the mundane political arts he would perfect, including obfuscation, prevarication, flattery, sophistical evasion, and various forms of pandering, were developed and tested on an involuntary focus group of one, whose acuity was far above the mean.

In 1885 the Democrats finally regained the White House, twenty-four years having been required to shed completely the stigma of being infested with southern secessionists and other unpatriotic elements. Grover Cleveland, governor of New York, was the new president, a friend of Mr. James, as had been President James Buchanan and General George McClellan. In 1887 Franklin went with his father to meet the new president, who was already so weary of the office that he patted Franklin, five, on the head and said: "My little man, I am making a strange wish for you. It is that you may never be president of the United States."[38]

That certainly conformed to the preferences of his parents. Mr. James was interested in politics but not as an office-holder, elected or appointed; he declined Cleveland's offer of embassies. The Hyde Park Roosevelts prior to Franklin had a concept of public life that was a patrician version of citizen-statesmanship. Sometimes the duty of public service could not be honorably escaped, but most of the family thought it was rarely a distinguished, or even comprehensible, ambition.

An exception to this family aversion to public office occurred in the case of Rosy, Franklin's half-brother, James Roosevelt Roosevelt. Pleasant and debonair, Rosy had style and was always kind to Franklin, but his principal interest was the purchase, maintenance, and driving of four-horse coaches. At this pastime Rosy was undoubtedly a formidable talent, but it was not a real vocation. He was twenty-eight years old when Franklin was born in 1882, a Columbia alumnus and a devotee of New York's most extravagant cotillions. More important, he was, from 1877, the husband of Helen Astor, the daughter of the Mrs. (William) Astor, grande doyenne of New York society for forty years. Beneath his elegant façade, he always remained the frightened child who slept in his parents' bedroom until he was ten and substituted society and the diversions of the rich for exposure to the competition of life. "He provided his far younger half brother with a vivid and instructive example of what wealth without ambition could make of a man."[39]

Rosy ostensibly worked in the real estate management section of the vast Astor interests and was a trustee of J. P. Morgan's Cathedral of St. John the Divine, but mainly he drove his coaches, hunted to hounds, and accompanied his immensely rich wife to sumptuous social outings. To give him some prospect of doing something useful, his father asked President Cleveland to make Rosy first secretary in the American embassy in Vienna, and the President obliged. Rosy took up his post and busied himself interviewing visa applicants. When Cleveland lost the 1888 election to Benjamin Harrison, Rosy insisted on withdrawing, to retain credibility with the Democrats, he claimed, though the new secretary of state, James G. Blaine, to whom Mr. James had written on Rosy's behalf, was agreeable to his continuation. His father tried without success to find an appropriate position for him when he returned to the United States.

In 1892 Grover Cleveland had his revenge on Benjamin Harrison and became the only man in American history to be elected to non-consecutive terms as president, despite the weariness of office he expressed to young Franklin in 1887. Rosy had made a $10,000 campaign donation and pressed his claim to become ambassador to Belgium. Cleveland gave him instead the first secretaryship of the embassy in London, where Rosy already had many friends, and where he chiefly sifted among the applications for the places allotted by Buckingham Palace for Queen Victoria's springtime receptions.

Rosy's wife, Helen Astor, fell sick and died in the last months of 1889, and Mr. James was offended when Rosy declined his initial offer to sail to England and be with his son while Helen was alive but in decline. Rosy showed unexpected grit and avarice over the Astors' money, though he had to endure the humiliation of the court's reducing the inheritance of his children, Helen and Taddy, instead of granting the increase he had sought.

Rosy asked his cousin Anna "Bamie" Roosevelt to help him take care of his children. She was the delightful person to whom Mr. James had initially proposed after the death of his first wife and just before he met Sara. Now thirty-eight and still unmarried, she conceived a fancy for the son of the man she had declined. In London she delighted everybody and became the very successful hostess for the entire embassy. Ironically, her designs on Rosy were as unsuccessful as Mr. James's desire for her had been. Rosy had had a paramour for some time—Elizabeth Riley, a beautiful younger woman whom he would finally marry in 1914. Bamie was philosophical and remained friendly. She conducted Rosy's negotiations with the Astors over financial affairs with great skill, showing herself fully equal in these matters to the legendary Mrs. Astor.* Rosy made a modest success of his London posting.

In 1889 the Roosevelts returned to England. Franklin had contracted typhoid fever, which was only diagnosed when they were shipboard on the White Star liner *Adriatic*. The captain gave his cabin to Franklin and arranged for his cousin, who was a doctor at Queenstown, to meet the family at the pier and take Franklin to his own home for a convalescence of several weeks. It was another demonstration of Mr. James's influence that his friend Sir Thomas Ismay, founder of the White Star Line, provided a special launch to evacuate Franklin from the *Adriatic* and sent flowers to him at the doctor's home every day of his stay there. Franklin again proved resilient, and continued on with his parents to a riding holiday at Pau in the Pyrenees (where there was a large English colony).[40]

Franklin would be physically indomitable and astoundingly resistant to pain and to danger all his life. When he was a small boy a curtain rod fell on him in his father's railway car, gashing his forehead. Rather than alarm his father, he wore a

---

*Bamie eventually married the amiable, portly, fiftyish Navy Commander William Sheffield Cowles.

cap to disguise the wound.[41] When he was fourteen and a friend accidentally flung an improvised bat in Franklin's face, splitting his lip and shattering a tooth, Franklin tried to hide the injury from his mother. She finally discovered a fully exposed and angry dental nerve. Neither then nor during his resulting visit to the dentist did he show any particular sensitivity to the pain.[42]

The life of the Roosevelt family was permanently altered when Mr. James suffered a mild but painful heart attack in 1890, at the age of only sixty-two. Thereafter the family's ambition was to spare him any alarm or discomfort. He ceased to be a sporting companion of Franklin and was increasingly an invalid. Henceforth, travel would be less the broadening and relaxing recreation it had been than a pursuit of air and waters and therapies to prolong James Roosevelt's life. The family went to Bad Nauheim six times, starting in 1891, so that Mr. James could take the supposedly curative waters. (Sara wished to avoid the Germans, whom she never liked; there were people of other nationalities there.) The theory that bathing up to the neck in warm bubbling water would expand blood vessels and relieve the heart was essentially nonsense. However, the Roosevelts attached some credence to it, and when Franklin was eventually faced with a mighty recuperative challenge to limbs and muscles, he acted on his conditioned instinct and sought out warm spring waters.

In 1892 at Bad Nauheim the Roosevelts met Mark Twain, and the ten-year-old Franklin learned to swim and went to a local German school for six weeks. This was his first experience of school and he took to it not badly, though he wasn't impressed by his German schoolmates. Forty years later when he became the president of the United States, he was much praised by the school's director, the effusive Herr Bommerscheim.[43]

By then, Roosevelt would claim that the school at Bad Nauheim had been his introduction to German discipline and militarism. He would claim conversationally, even to Churchill and Stalin, that at that time the recently elevated Emperor Wilhelm II required all German schoolboys to study maps and topography, and began gradually putting virtually the entire male population into uniform—a process, he seemed to believe, that transformed the Germans into militaristic soldier ants. As was often the case in his version of his own experiences, he claimed to have been an eyewitness to an earth-shaking event, which he described as the genesis of a hideous mutation in the culture of Beethoven and Goethe—the dawn of German militarism. (This did not prevent him, when claiming to be quite neutral in his views of the contending nationalities if not of their political regimes, at the outset of World War II, from asserting that as a youth he had known and liked Germany better than he liked France or Britain.)[44]

It became the practice to engage tutors and nannies for Franklin in Europe and to determine in the course of the summer whether it was appropriate to invite them back to Springwood. Franklin was a precocious judge of character and competences and of the foibles of human nature, quickly noting the sensitivities and absurd quirks of his governesses. Sara generally agreed with him. He executed one of his more imaginative revenges on a dour German governess with whom he especially lacked rapport, putting some effervescent powder in her chamber pot. When she used it in the dead of night the consequent foaming and fizzing so alarmed her with the thought that she might have a ghastly illness that she awakened Mrs. Roosevelt. For once even Sara was fooled. Mr. James was not but could scarcely contain his amusement when he wrung a confession from his son the next day.[45]

As Franklin grew older, he became a very ambitious collector. His best-known such pastime as president was stamp collecting. Once again, his mother played a key role. She had started a stamp collection when she was five and later handed it over to her brother Fred, who gave it to Franklin on his tenth birthday, in January 1892. Franklin worked steadily at this collection all his life, building it up into one of the most valuable assets he possessed, with over one million stamps in 150 albums.

He astonished his mother by repeating back to her verbatim tracts of books she read to him while he was apparently completely absorbed in inserting stamps in albums. He was proud of his ability to concentrate effectively on two very different things at once. His doctor, Admiral Ross McIntire, reckoned that he spent well over 2,000 hours on his stamp collection during his twelve years in the White House.[46] In these times, postage stamps evoked exotic places and were symbols of both the spirit of exploration and the genius of science that continually shrunk the world. The young Roosevelt's love of sailing and the sea and his curiosity about foreign lands and geography were well served by this pastime. He was, in any case, a natural collector. By the time he became president, he also had accumulated 15,000 books and an extensive collection of British political caricatures.

Another great preoccupation from his earliest years was birds. He started out collecting their eggs and then nests, but soon insisted on getting a shotgun. Since Mr. James no longer had the energy to accompany Franklin outdoors as he had done, he agreed to the request and Franklin became an avid shot. He had astonishing numbers of birds stuffed. They still festoon the walls of the entry hall of Springwood, where Sara proudly placed them.[47] In England in 1893, he persuaded his parents to allow him to go alone on the train to Nottinghamshire to see Lord Hawkesbury's internationally renowned mounted bird collection. The eleven-year-old made a very favorable impression on the venerable peer and ornithologist.

Franklin D. Roosevelt's greatest pastime was probably the sea. At the end of his life his library contained 2,000 books about U.S. naval history, 1,200 naval prints, 200 fully rigged ship models, and 37 albums of photographs of naval vessels, carefully assembled and annotated by himself.[48]

His interest in the sea began with seafaring tales from his grandfather Delano and from his mother, who got most of them from the same source but could add a few of her own. His father owned a yacht, the fifty-one-foot *Half Moon*, which

Franklin sailed when he was a teenager, sometimes with his mother reading aloud to him as he steered. When Franklin was sixteen, his father bought him a sloop of his own, the *New Moon*, which he sailed enthusiastically every day at Campobello. After 1900 he was responsible for his father's yacht, including engaging the captain and overseeing maintenance. In secondary school he avidly read Captain Alfred Thayer Mahan's seminal books on the influence of sea power on history (given him by an uncle at Christmas 1897 and for his sixteenth birthday a month later).[19] He eventually corresponded with (then) Admiral Mahan up to his death, by which time Roosevelt was assistant secretary of the navy.

Though he never had any experience before the mast or in a subordinate position at sea, he crossed the Atlantic constantly from his earliest days, cruised in all manner of sail and power yachts, and when in public office commandeered everything from patrol boats to battleships, ostensibly to inspect naval installations but more often to fish and play poker with cronies. He was never seasick (though on one crossing he greatly sympathized with the conscripts below decks, where the stench was "worse than a street in Haiti"). He was an extremely skillful sailor, a talent that was not diminished by the illness that eventually afflicted him. He never studied instrument navigation but was a remarkable sailor, with an instinctive ability to judge currents, tides, and winds; he loved maps, knew a great deal about geography, and knew at all times how to rig and adjust sail on any boat in any conditions.

It is likely and has been claimed[50] that his skill at dead reckoning navigation was of great help to him as a politician. In economic and foreign policy especially he was prone to tack fairly steadily. He famously would describe himself as a "juggler." This was not an inaccurate self-description, but he could just as well have called himself a sailor, who alone knew his destination and had an uncanny talent for reaching it. Winston Churchill would aptly praise "his power of gauging the tides and currents of [America's] mobile public opinion."

Franklin wanted to go to the Naval Academy at Annapolis instead of Harvard, but his father insisted it would be too painful to him and his wife to be separated as much from their son as a naval career would require. He claimed to have missed enrolling at Annapolis by only a week as a result of his parents' entreaties.[51] He thought of resigning from the Wilson administration in 1917 to become a uniformed naval officer but was dissuaded by the President.

No American president, not even his cousin, who wrote the definitive history *The Naval War of 1812* (when he was twenty-one years old) and part of the official history of the Royal Navy, came to office with as much knowledge of ships, the sea, and sea power and strategy as did FDR. In his first two terms as president, he spent an average of forty-five days per year at sea, his preferred escape from the political hothouse of Washington.

In September 1895, Mr. James engaged a young, robust clergyman and master of Latin and mathematics as a companion for Franklin. He rejoiced in the name of Arthur Dumper and went on to become Episcopal bishop of Newark. Apart from supplementing his lessons, Arthur played tennis and golf and bicycled and walked and explored and hunted birds and squirrels with Franklin at Springwood and Bad Nauheim.

On their way home from Bad Nauheim in the summer of 1896, Sara and Franklin stopped at Bayreuth and attended an entire *Ring* cycle in Richard Wagner's *Festspielhaus*, sitting not far from the box that the then seven-year-old Adolf Hitler would occupy faithfully every year from 1933 to 1940. To Winifried Wagner, the composer's daughter-in-law, Hitler said "Wagner is where it began."[52] This visit of the fourteen-year-old Roosevelt, as well as his reading of German myths and heroic legends in this period, may have strengthened his intuition about the nature of the German leader when they came to the highest offices in their countries in early 1933.

Franklin liked the *Ring*, which was a considerable achievement, because it requires fourteen hours of concentrated attention, a greater commitment to complicated Wagnerian Teutonic myth than most American teenage boys would enjoy. But he might have found the forest legends interesting in themselves; his wife, Eleanor, claimed later that the Black Forest, carefully tended, inspired much of his life-long love of forestry. Sara wrote that her son "was most attentive and rapt during the long acts and always sorry to leave, never tired or bored."[53]

In September—two years later than had originally been planned because his parents were so upset at the thought of being separated from him—it was time for Franklin, aged fourteen, to go off to Groton School. The school had been founded by Endicott Peabody, the closest American equivalent to Dr. Thomas Arnold, who was immortalized in *Tom Brown's School Days* and Lytton Strachey's *Eminent Victorians*. Dr. Peabody avoided the corporal punishment and stratification of British public schools but, like them, focused on character-building, rugged Christianity, and rounded boys rather than on academic excellence alone. After taking holy orders he had set up the first Episcopal church in Arizona Territory—in Tombstone, in 1882, under the guns of Wyatt Earp and his brothers. A year later, he secured the backing of some of his father's wealthy friends for an upper-class boys' boarding school, and the result was Groton, forty-five miles north of Boston. It opened its doors in 1885.

Franklin's parents took him to Groton on Mr. James's railway car on September 15, 1896. Except for his six weeks at summer school in Bad Nauheim in 1892, he had not been in a school before and didn't know many people his own age. Groton would change him.

III

I F LIFE AT Groton was not greatly more regimented than at Springwood, it was a great deal more spartan and impersonal and afforded no privacy; Franklin must have found it quite a shock. Because he was two years late beginning, he arrived after his peers had already formed their friendships. It was not helpful to him that Rosy's erratic and timid son Taddy was also at the school and not much admired by the boys. Days began with cold showers (there were no hot water taps). Franklin never had much problem with his studies and was always in the upper reaches of his class. The classics, Greek and Latin, were emphasized, as well as French and German, in which Roosevelt was already proficient. Dr. Peabody judged him "of more than ordinary intelligence . . . but not brilliant."[54] He came fourth of seventeen in his class in academic average in his first year.[55] This was ideal for the doctor, who was suspicious of excessively intelligent boys as not rounded and prone to intellectual vanity and indiscipline.

Franklin did have political problems. He never quite figured out the balance between gaining the esteem of his peers and pleasing his elders, the faculty, by such prosaic achievements as winning the annual prize (three times) for punctuality. He was too astute to fall altogether afoul of either, but he was always looked upon unenthusiastically by many of the boys his age. He seemed to them too European or English in accent and mannerisms (as in his habit, of which Dr. Peabody cured him, of bowing from the waist when saying goodnight to Mrs. Peabody). And the harder he tried to be liked, as he always had been before in his life, the more suspiciously he was regarded. He was always steering between being a swat to the faculty and a toady to the students. He wrote his parents that he was relieved to receive his first black mark, for talking in class: "I was very glad I got it, as I was thought to have no school spirit."[56]

It was here that Roosevelt seems to have settled his eventually famous accent, a combination of upper-class New York and Ivy League, with a broad "a" and almost indiscernible "r" other than at the start of words.

He was too slight to be a first-class athlete, the surest passage to popularity. At Mr. James's insistence he tried boxing, but this was not a great success, though in later years he claimed to have had some pugilistic skill. This was one of the many minor liberties he took with the facts of his early years. He made claims of boxing prowess in a letter from school to his mother, regretting that he wasn't present to avenge her against a bicyclist who had run her down. When president he frequently suffered severe sinus attacks and blamed them on having broken his nose twice while playing football at Groton, a complete fiction.

He was more successful as a debater. His first semi-public speech was a two-minute improvisation on his father's last great financial initiative, the Nicaraguan inter-ocean canal, which was well-received. He also sang in the choir, starting as a soprano and ending as a tenor.[57] All in all, he got on, and was never seriously disciplined by the faculty or hazed or picked on by the schoolboys.

It was a dour, exacting, and worthy regime Dr. Peabody had created, and Franklin Roosevelt's talents and tastes ran to intrigue, mischief, and political maneuver, and more than suited the doctor. He came through Groton adequately but cannot be said to have flourished there. It is a mystery why Roosevelt always in subsequent years had such veneration for Peabody. In 1934 he declared: "As long as I live, the influence of Dr. Peabody means and will mean more to me than that of any other people next to my father and mother."[58]

The distinguished public servant Averell Harriman was one of the few Groton alumni who dissented from the customary elegiacs about the doctor: "Peabody would be an awful bully if he weren't such a terrible Christian," Harriman wrote to his father at the age of thirteen. Another famous alumnus was future secretary of state Dean Acheson, who was rather loyal to Peabody. But after a visit from the rector in 1939, when Acheson had suggested Britain needed Churchill and Peabody said that his British friends didn't think Churchill enough of a gentleman, Acheson remarked: "Chamberlain doesn't understand what he's up against but he would be a great success as a student at Groton. Churchill does understand it. He would be kicked out of Groton in a week."[59] Peabody was obviously a formidable and memorable figure in the formation of generations of upper-class schoolboys, but he was priggish, pious, and, in some respects, almost a philistine.

Yet Roosevelt delighted in any opportunity to get close to him. He was happy to be appointed one of two mail sorters (known as "mail niggers," referring to menial work, not pigmentation), because it would enable him to have breakfast twice a year with the rector. He also attended the rector's confirmation class, which involved a good deal of direct contact in his last year, and he seems to have imbibed some of Peabody's rigorously uncomplicated ecclesiastical views. Life was an opportunity and obligation to do good works.

Franklin joined the Groton Missionary Society, in which capacity, with another boy, he assisted an eighty-four-year-old black woman, the widow of a Civil War Union Army drummer, plowing snow out of her driveway, feeding the chickens she kept, and bringing her coal on cold days. He was also the organist in an itinerant church group that sallied out from the school each week to bring divine worship to remote areas. He learned at least four hymns he could pound out on the organ. It is not clear whether this surge of religious practice was unthinking convention, one of his strategies for ingratiating himself with the pious rector, or a manifestation of his religious faith, which certainly became an important pillar of his adult worldview.

Franklin also served two two-week terms in the Missionary Society's summer camp in New Hampshire. This was a benefit for poor and slum children. Apart from showing the campers a healthier life than most of them had glimpsed before, it was supposed to combat complacency and elitism and encourage good works among the Groton participants. This was Franklin's first contact with poor people and with social work of any kind, and seems to have had some such effect on him. No one could have foreseen where it would lead, but he is one of the few U.S. presidents ever to have done such work.

He wrote twice a week to his parents for four years. Even a day's delay in receiving his letter caused them to telegraph the school to ascertain whether Franklin was unwell. His letters were in the chatty style of much of his correspondence and conversation as a mature man: fluent and superficially informative but entirely devoid of anything personal or profound. There was never a trace of disappointment or anguish. Everything was always excellent. Sara Roosevelt visited her son at Groton often and thought about him constantly. Sara and Mr. James sent Franklin the British magazines *Punch* and *The Spectator* throughout his time at Groton.[60]

One of the many doubtful stories that Franklin propagated about his youth was that on the outbreak of the Spanish-American War in 1898, he and two friends determined to enlist in the U.S. Navy at Boston and bribed a pie-truck driver to take them out of the school grounds in his truck. According to the story, they were prevented from executing their plan by the onset of scarlet fever.[61] This claim, at least, was real. Franklin's parents had just arrived at Bad Nauheim for another attempted cure for Mr. James, who had suffered a second heart attack in 1897. They came immediately back to New York on receiving a worrisome telegram. Sara wept with relief on being informed at dockside by waiting relatives that Franklin was out of danger. They went directly on to Groton, where Franklin was still in the school infirmary. After coming all the way from Germany they could only wave at him through a glass for fear of contracting scarlet fever themselves.

As a senior at Groton in 1899–1900, Franklin was more successful than in the preceding years. He became a dormitory prefect and was very generous and helpful to younger boys, who revered and admired him all their lives.[62] His academic performance was rewarded with one of the best single rooms at the school, a signal recognition from the austere rector, and he was a great hit as Uncle Boppady in the school play, W.S. Gilbert's *The Wedding March An Eccentricity in Three Acts.*[63] Mr. James and Sara came to see him perform twice. The reviews in the school paper were laudatory. He made the second football team but rode the bench most of the season because of his physical slightness.

There began to emerge in Franklin certain traits that would become notorious at the height of his public career. His devious tendencies were more evident than ever before in his letters home; his own achievements were exaggerated, shortcomings were never his fault, and reflections on rivals, no matter how narrow the field of competition, become acidulous.

He was worldlier than most of his schoolmates, but that did not help him fit in with them. "He may have known more than most boys about the bigger world beyond Groton, but they knew far more than he about being boys."[64] His apparently glib charm, which worked so well with his mother and most adults, seemed affected and obsequious to schoolboys. Similarly, his mastery of American public opinion as president would seem to many who had known him, at Groton and elsewhere, as vulgar pandering and ungentlemanly demagogy. When he was passed over as a senior prefect in his last year in favor of several others, including the rector's nephew, Franklin's reaction was not just disappointed but nasty. Too ambitious not to care, he attributed setbacks to malice or unfairness. This was possibly accurate but was not the spirit of disinterested service the rector was trying to inculcate in those entrusted to him.

Franklin claimed to his parents in a letter that he had come fourth in the all-school six-mile paper chase. He hadn't, but he knew that the *Grotonian* would publish only the names of the three first finishers. He told them an article he had written for the school paper about the Dreyfus case had been rejected by the paper because it had already published one on this subject. It hadn't; the editors were just not impressed with Franklin's piece.

Misinforming his doting parents on such trivial matters was unseemly, and potentially risky. The adulatory goodwill of his parents was a great asset, and Franklin Roosevelt, the eventual political sans pareil, should have recognized that he was putting too much at risk for too little possible reward. He already had tremendous confidence in his talents as a political manipulator. When those talents were under-rewarded, he became churlish, as when he represented to his parents that failing to be chosen a senior prefect didn't matter to him because Peabody had reduced the honor to insignificance by his nepotism.[65]

When he graduated in the spring of 1900, Franklin claimed to be sad to leave and to be nostalgic about his early years at Groton. Peabody graciously wrote that he had been a "thoroughly faithful scholar and most satisfactory member of this school . . . I part with Franklin with reluctance." Roosevelt spoke admiringly of Dr. Peabody and had him perform private religious services for him before his first three presidential inaugurations and at family occasions.

At the party Groton alumni held for Dr. Peabody on his eightieth birthday, the rector concluded his remarks: "I believe Franklin Roosevelt to be a gallant and courageous gentleman. I am happy to count him as my friend."[66] Satisfied as Roosevelt surely was with this commendation, he was probably not very displeased when not one of the 400 alumni applauded. He had won in the end. That his schoolmates continued to withhold their approval no longer disturbed him; he had run the gauntlet of their little world. Who were they compared with the tens of millions of his loyal voters?

He would send all four of his sons to Groton at twelve, not holding them back until they were fourteen, which he felt had been a mistake in his case. Franklin D. Roosevelt Jr. was senior prefect at Groton in November 1932 and was awakened at 6 A.M. by the rector in his night shirt, who informed him that his father had been elected president of the United States—"the first Groton student to be so honored and very much in the tradition of Groton School," he said to the sleepy young man.[67] It is not obvious what tradition the rector, who had voted for Hoover, had in mind. In their very different ways, Roosevelt and Peabody served each other's ends. Peabody's public admiration conferred official victory over the indifference of the President's erstwhile peers. Roosevelt's power and fame amplified the prestige of Groton and its founder.

———————

Franklin Roosevelt went to Harvard in September 1900. He lived in the Westmorly university residence on Mount Auburn Street with his Groton friend Lathrap Brown, and settled into a relaxed freshman year. Franklin became captain of the freshman football team and a staff member at the university newspaper, the *Crimson.* Harvard had an extremely distinguished faculty, including William James, Josiah Royce, George Santayana, A. Lawrence Lowell, and, as a visitor, Frederick Jackson Turner. Franklin's attendance was spotty and he was never overly interested in academics. He sailed through Harvard with Cs; his development was more of the personality than of the intellect. He took a class in public speaking and had to present speech texts every two weeks. The only one that survives urges Southerners to resolve the "Negro problem" through education, and declares that it is the ambition of North and South "to make a man out of a semibeast."

He joined the Republican Club of Harvard, though he was too young to vote, in order to agitate for the election of cousin Teddy as McKinley's vice president. (When he had been obliged to get eyeglasses at Groton, he bought a pince-nez modeled on Teddy's now famous one.) Teddy was always gracious and charming to Franklin and invited him to Oyster Bay for the Fourth of July celebrations in successive years.

In the autumn of 1900, Mr. James was in gradual decline. He had been very saddened by the mysterious explosion and sinking of his yacht, the *Half Moon,* while it was being towed up the Hudson to Hyde Park in 1898. He was touched by Franklin's selfless offer to sell the *New Moon* to help pay for a replacement. This was not necessary, and Mr. James had taken delivery of *Half Moon II* at Campobello in July 1899. Though the cause of the fire was apparently spontaneous combustion of naptha, Franklin was outraged that there was no crew member aboard the *Half Moon.* Mr. James, characteristically, was more forgiving.[68]

The greatest shock to Mr. James in these last months was the erratic behavior of his grandson Taddy, Rosy's son, who had preceded Franklin through Groton and Harvard. In June 1900 Taddy dropped out of Harvard and disappeared. This afforded Franklin, for whom kinship with Taddy had been a heavy burden in school and university, the opportunity for some self-righteous letters to his mother, accusing Taddy of "asininity" and adding, just before the scandal broke: "He may be off on a bat now for ought I know. I think the very strictest measures should be taken."[69] In June Taddy married a Hungarian-born prostitute, Sadie Mesinger, whom he had met at a notorious dance hall in the Tenderloin district of Manhattan, on the Lower West Side. This produced an immense controversy and a good deal of mockery in the press, all an unbearable indignity for Mr. James. Taddy's grandmother, the unshakably majestic Mrs. Astor, was not too pleased either. (Taddy remained married to Sadie until she died forty years later.) He eventually gave up drink, worked on automobiles as an occupation, and never touched his extensive inheritance, which he left to the Salvation Army when he died, in 1958. Rosy disowned him, which was financially irrelevant since Taddy's money came from the Astors.[70] As far as is known, Franklin never saw or spoke or corresponded with Taddy again after 1900.

Buffeted by Taddy's peccadillo, Mr. James suffered another coronary four days after that story broke and convalesced over the summer. Rosy bought a car, a Locomobile, which through the fall gave considerable enjoyment to his father, who also still rode occasionally. Mr. James conscientiously carried out from home his duties as chairman of the Delaware and Hudson Railway. But Mr. James was laid low by another heart attack in late November 1900 and was moved to the family's apartment on West 40th Street in New York. He did not respond to treatment and died at 2:20 in the morning of December 8, with Sara, Franklin, and Rosy at his bedside. He had lived to see his friend and cousin Teddy elected vice president the previous month. His last recorded words about Franklin were very optimistic and appreciative: "I know he is good and will be good," he had said to Sara.[71]

There was a simple service at St. James, Hyde Park, and eventual burial in the churchyard beside his first wife. The obituarists were respectful and condolences were numerous and profuse. One fellow Groton parent, grateful for the attention Mr. James had shown her son when he visited Franklin after Franklin's attack of scarlet fever in 1898, wrote to Sara of her husband: "He was so wonderfully sympathetic with a boy, full of interest and the warmth of affection . . . I think it never entered his mind that he was better than other people."[72] This was the essence of Mr. James's undoubted distinction: courteous, honest, dignified, modest, intelligent, dutiful, and gently humorous.

Mr. James had neither the preternatural cunning nor the insatiable ambition of his younger son. But Franklin learned from his father the ability to masquerade as an unambitious draftee to public life serving the country that had been so generous to his forefathers and himself. He was certainly a patriotic American and during his presidency genuinely did wish to go back to Hyde Park, but not as much as he wished to remain president. At every stage he represented sacrifice and the implacable national interest as his only considerations, and he did so plausibly in the judgment of an adequate number of his countrymen. This was Mr. James speaking through his son. There was enough truth to it for Franklin Delano Roosevelt to appear as the generous, stylish, Christian, noblesse oblige gentleman that, like his father, he was, up to a point. He managed to seem more disinterested than he really was, and, at his histrionic best, almost as selfless as Mr. James. This was a great legacy, which helped FDR to outwit his opponents again and again (to use one of his eventually famous oratorical flourishes).

If Mr. James taught FDR how to appear the patrician squire, Dr. Peabody had shown him how to sound overwhelmingly righteous. Even as a child and schoolboy, Franklin Roosevelt was frequently duplicitous. As a political leader he was almost compulsively devious. While he found some of the exigencies of political life distasteful, gentleman as he was, he resorted to them naturally and was proud of his manipulative virtuosity and skill as a dissembler. So well had he learned from these two early mentors how to seem upright, even perceptive historians have tended to believe that Roosevelt was a largely guileless man and that he became distressed when his puckish love of mischief led him to tactical excess.

Thus: "He was not really Machiavellian, Endicott Peabody had done his work too well. The rather simple-hearted idealism which lay so near the core of Roosevelt's personality could not indefinitely support the experiments in smart-aleckness and trickiness."[73] Franklin Roosevelt's talent at deception extended to appearing as a kindly sentimentalist who couldn't stand to fire people, who was straightforward by nature but enjoyed the occasional ruse. Ironically, Roosevelt's academic admirers, by presenting this picture of him, have made him a better man but lesser statesman than he was.

Their version of Roosevelt made him more vulnerable than he should have been to the charges levelled by his enemies that he was naïve and gullible when dealing with Stalin. His most fervent admirers have made him seem an amiable and capable man carried along to four terms in the White House on a tide of events over which he had little influence. This narrative will demonstrate otherwise. He was a less admirable character, perhaps, than his admirers have traditionally believed. But in applying his ruthless and often amoral political genius to almost wholly desirable ends, he was a greater statesman than even his most vocal supporters have generally appreciated.

IV

SARA'S FAMILY RALLIED round and various of them stayed with her in Springwood in relays. Franklin, whose own grief was profound, though, as always, borne with discretion, was certainly a great comfort. Sara began to manage the estate as Mr. James had done, and took to riding around it on his horse Bobby. Between her husband and her father (who had died in 1898, aged eighty-eight), she had been left several million dollars (the current equivalent is probably fifty times as much). Franklin and Rosy received trust funds of $120,000 each.

In the summer of 1901, Sara and Franklin; Franklin's cousin (Theodore Robinson, a nephew of Theodore Roosevelt); their neighbor from Campobello, Mrs. Pell, whose husband had also died, and her daughter Frances, travelled in Europe for ten weeks. They took a cruising yacht, the *Prinzessin Victoria Luisa* up the Norwegian coast and into many fjords. They were surprised to encounter the German Imperial yacht *Hohenzollern*, flying the emperor's standard, at Molde. The kaiser, Wilhelm II, came aboard the Roosevelts' yacht for tea and invited the young members of the party back aboard the *Hohenzollern*. They found him extremely forceful but rather grim. Franklin stole a pencil bearing (presumably) Wilhelm's teeth-marks from the emperor's desk as a souvenir.[74] They carried on to Dresden, Zurich, Geneva, and Paris, visiting relatives and old haunts. On their arrival in New York, they learned that President McKinley had been assassinated and Cousin Theodore was now the president.

In his capacity as a *Crimson* reporter at Harvard, Roosevelt broke the scoop that President Roosevelt was coming to the campus. The President, who was always kind to Franklin, greeted him warmly in front of hundreds of other students. At the social debut of the President's daughter Alice at Christmastime, Theodore had two private conversations with Franklin and his mother, "something always to be remembered,"[75] Franklin wrote of the second one. The TR story helped get Franklin elected one of the five *Crimson* editors in the coming year.

True to his penchant for self-serving history, Franklin would claim credit for having wrung from the president of Harvard, Charles W. Eliot, that he intended to vote Republican in 1900. In fact the story was broken by someone else, and Franklin subsequently claimed he had no knowledge of how the version featuring himself was launched.[76]

Less successful than his advance at the *Crimson*, and one of the most disagreeable experiences of his entire career, was Franklin's candidacy for the prestigious Porcellian Club, of which his father had been elected an honorary member and of which Theodore Roosevelt was the most prominent current member. First, 100 of the class of 500 were elected to the Institute of 1770. Then some of them would be elected to a fraternity known as the Dickey, from its Greek letters. From this group the best clubs chose their members. Franklin made it over the first two hurdles all right, but was blackballed for the Porcellian.

It was a severe humiliation. Porcellian members were selected by sixteen juniors and seniors, and one negative vote would kill any aspirant. It was an absolutely secret process; not even the electors would know who cast the opposing vote or votes. Franklin felt let down by the five Groton alumni in the group of sixteen. Eleanor would eventually claim that his peers found Franklin too bookish, an improbable explanation. She claimed he suffered "an inferiority complex" from this rebuff, but that it made him more sensitive to underprivileged people. Franklin himself acknowledged it as "the greatest disappointment of my life" nearly twenty years later, though he also called such interpretations "a damned canard" more than a decade after that in conversation with his son James.[77]

He had his electoral successes. As a member of the Dickey he automatically became a member of the Hasty Pudding Society and was elected to the "Fly" (another short form from the Greek letters), serving as the librarian for both, and he was elected to the Signet Literary Society and the Memorial Society (concerned with the history of the university). His election as managing editor of the *Crimson* was a considerable achievement, and it brought automatic elevation to the editorship the following year.

Roosevelt ran for election as one of five class marshals at the end of 1903, trying to use his position at the newspaper to buck the slates run by the clubs. He knew he would not succeed and didn't, but put on a fairly strong showing in an open election in which the three candidates first past the post won and there were no blackballs. He represented his campaign as a struggle for reform against what he would describe a decade later as the autocracy of the bosses. A few days later he won his first ever electoral victory by a comfortable margin, as chairman of the 1904 class committee.

He chose to remain at Harvard through 1904, ostensibly pursuing a master's degree but really to exercise the power that being editor of the *Crimson* gave him. His editorials were fairly pedestrian: advocacy of better pathways and fire escapes and general boosterism, especially in honor of the football team. Roosevelt became so strident in his editorial exhortations and excoriations of the football team that Henry James II, a law student, wrote criticizing his practice of "dealing out editorial sarcasms . . . to amateur athletes."[78] He was undoubtedly a successful manager and was credited by his successor with having "liked people and having made them instinctively like him . . . In his geniality there was a kind of frictionless command."[79] The *Harvard Alumni Bulletin* considered his time as editor "at least mildly distinguished for the animation of his many editorials and for certain college reforms which he engineered."[80]

His Harvard experiences were formative. The Groton problem of not being altogether accepted by his peers persisted, but he did better with larger electorates and had graduated to a democratic pursuit of popular approval. He was already developing political techniques for attracting the support of people he didn't actually know and for projecting himself through strategic positions, such as that of a campus newspaper editor, into a position of increasing influence. Not least, he was an almost constant campaigner, seeking out offices to run for and considering the electoral process a pleasing activity in itself, not, as his father had felt and counselled, an irritation sometimes necessary to the performance of one's civic duty.

Thirty years later it would be alleged that Roosevelt was paying back the wealthy and well-born elements that had rejected him at Groton and Harvard. He always denied this. Still, there must have been some special gratification in running as a champion of the common man against caricatured groups of complacent and greedy inheritors. As always with him, his motives became a subtle blend of expediency and principle, both lofty and vindictive. He was rather frugal in his own tastes and despised the gaudy and vulgar parvenus of the Gilded Age as he would those of the Roaring Twenties. He would not have been his mother's son if he were not, in some measure, a snob. Yet he was a meritocrat who was profoundly contemptuous of frivolous and foppish inheritors.

He wanted to make the world safe for the style of living he enjoyed, but he didn't want to confer excessive deference on either genteel, underworked squirearchies or economic plunderers, nor on any special interests. His informal and largely intuitive understanding of the nature of political power in America, which began at Springwood and developed at Groton, reached a much higher level of sophistication at Harvard.

Sara moved to Boston for Franklin's last two winters there. She was a New Englander originally and had many friends and relatives in the Boston area. Winter was a bit barren at Springwood, where with neither James nor Franklin, she was very much alone. Franklin professed to welcome her presence in Boston but also found his mother's close attentions oppressive at times.

In the summer of 1903 Franklin went to Europe with a friend, Charles Bradley. It was his first trip to Europe unaccompanied by an older person. Franklin stayed at Claridge's, bought suits on Savile Row, and visited friends of his parents in their country houses. He wrote home virtually every day. On returning in August, Franklin had his tonsils out with "his usual stoicism and cheerfulness" (Sara's account),[81] and cast his first vote, in an off-year municipal election. He voted Democratic.

Around this time Franklin seems to have begun to take the pursuit of girls more seriously. In correspondence with his mother he tended to refer to girls that he thought ill-favored as "ice-carts" or as "pills," or as being "elephantine."[82] He was a fine-looking young man, but some considered him exaggeratedly chirpy and affectedly courteous. A prolonged schism between Hyde Park and Oyster Bay was already opening up, though TR would never be a party to it himself. His niece Corinne Alsop said that she and her friends called Franklin "the feather duster" and "the handkerchief-box young man," because he looked like the smarmily solicitous young men on ladies' handkerchief-presentation boxes. As would often be the case, Alice Roosevelt, the President's daughter, would be the most sarcastic commentator on this subject. Alice called Franklin "a good little mother's boy" and associated him with "dull friends," "minor clubs," and indifferent parties.

Franklin seems to have been reasonably active socially at Harvard. A number of attractive women have been mentioned as early interests, including Dorothy Quincy and Frances Dana, who was the granddaughter of the newspaper publisher Charles Henry Dana and of Henry Wadsworth Longfellow, but was a Roman Catholic, which according to FDR's sons Elliott and James disconcerted Franklin's mother. But Alice Sohier was undoubtedly the main subject of Franklin's ardent attentions, which she seems not to have requited. They at least discussed marriage, though he was only twenty and she seventeen. He had ambitious plans to have a large family while young enough to enjoy the children himself, having felt keenly the loneliness of Springwood with an aged father. This was not what Alice had in mind, and she demurred, saying many years later that she "did not wish to be a cow."[83]

As with other setbacks in other fields of endeavor, Franklin could never acknowledge defeat, though this must have been another bruising rebuff. He developed a little yarn about how he had been beguiled by the sleepy and insular life of the Boston Brahmins into musing about taking a wife there and settling down in Back Bay, but had gone on a reflective trip "meeting numbers of real Americans—i.e., those from the west and south. I was saved but it was an awfully narrow escape." In fact, Alice had taken the trip and Alice said no.[84]

Franklin D. Roosevelt never mastered the art of self-deprecation or even detached comment about himself, much less the virtues of confession and repentance. This was partly because he emerged from his early years a bonhomous but unusually self-contained young man. He never had any real intimates. But it is also because his considerable vanity could never allow that he had been defeated or outsmarted.

After the onset of his illness with polio, this would oddly cease to be a problem. He could not be considered vain anymore. No one could ask anyone who bore such a burden with such light-hearted courage to make a practice of self-deprecation. As will be seen, cruel though it was, Roosevelt's polio not only made him more admirable by highlighting his courage and unconquerable spirit. In some ways it masked egoistic traits that otherwise might have made him more vulnerable politically.

As for the girl who got away, Alice Sohier married an insurance executive in 1910, had two children, was divorced in 1925, and never remarried. She was highly critical of Roosevelt throughout his presidency and proclaimed to her dying breath in 1972, aged eighty-six, her pleasure at not having married him. All in all, it was probably a good thing for both of them that she didn't. Eleanor, stiff-necked though she often was, seems emollient by comparison.[85]

V

A ND IT WAS to the somewhat improbable figure of Eleanor that young Franklin's attentions now turned in all their vigor. At the boisterous annual Thanksgiving Weekend at Fairhaven in November 1903, Franklin took his mother aside and told her that he intended to marry Eleanor Roosevelt.[86] Sara was startled, uttered precautionary words about Franklin's youth compared with his father and grandfathers when they married, and wrung from him a promise to keep the engagement a secret for a year to give him and Eleanor time to think it through. (She was referring to Mr. James's marriage to her, of course, not to his first wife, happy though that marriage was.)

Eleanor was the daughter of Elliott Roosevelt, Theodore's younger brother, and his wife, Anna Hall. Elliott Roosevelt met Mr. James and Sara when they were starting out on their honeymoon trip to Europe, on which Franklin was conceived, in 1881, and when Elliott was setting out on a round-the-world pleasure trip. The Hyde Park Roosevelts found him such an engaging shipboard companion that they asked him to be one of Franklin's godparents. Elliott returned to New York in 1882, took a job in the real estate business, fell in love with Anna, and became engaged to her at a house party at the Delanos' home, Algonac, in June. Theodore Roosevelt was best man at their wedding, in New York in December 1883. Anna was startlingly beautiful; Robert Browning would be among those dazzled by her grace and pulchritude.

In February 1884, Theodore and Elliott Roosevelt's mother and Theodore's wife Alice died on the same day, as Alice was giving birth to their only child, the Alice Roosevelt who would be entwined, generally disagreeably so, in the affairs of Franklin and Eleanor Roosevelt for almost all their lives.

Anna Eleanor Roosevelt was born on October 11, 1884. From the earliest days she was a disappointment to her mother, Anna. Plain, serious, and diffident, she lacked the beauty and effervescence that the Hall women possessed and required.

Her father, Elliott, shortly revealed himself as an unstable and in many ways weak character. Terribly overshadowed by his older brother, he was an alcoholic incapable of steady work or consistent behavior. He oscillated unpredictably between irrational jubilation and blank depression. His marriage to Anna had started breaking down almost as soon as it began. But Elliott doted on his daughter, who passionately adored him, rebuffed as she was by her mother.

In 1887 Elliott threw over his real estate job (with his brother-in-law Douglas Robinson, who was married to Elliot's sister Corinne) and set out for Europe with Anna, Eleanor, and Anna's sister. They were scarcely out of New York harbor when their ship, the *Britannic*, was rammed by another liner, the *Celtic* (on which the James Roosevelts sometimes travelled). In a rather disorderly scene the women and children took to the boats and Elliott was the only adult male cabin-class passenger who did so with them, as the railway magnate Collis P. Huntington ungraciously pointed out to the *New York World*. Elliott's conduct had not been cowardly: he followed the request of one of the ship's officers in an undermanned lifeboat. Still, he did not publicly defend himself from Huntington's slur and the effect of it lingered.

This was a most inauspicious beginning for Eleanor's seafaring career, and she became hysterical at the thought of reembarking. She was so demonstrative that she was left with her great aunt and uncle, Mr. and Mrs. James King Gracie, at Oyster Bay while her parents went to Europe for six months. This was the first of many abandonments that "Little Nell," as her father called her, after the character in Dickens's *Old Curiosity Shop*, would have to endure. When they returned, Elliott went back to selling real estate (for Mr. Gracie) but also to reckless and dangerous sporting endeavors such as night fox-hunting. He broke a succession of limbs and other bones, most seriously his ankle, was kicked in the head by his horse, and became dependent again on alcohol as an antidote to pain and depressive thoughts. His mood was sometimes explicitly suicidal.

Elliott and Anna had a son, Elliott Jr., in the autumn of 1889. Elliott unsuccessfully sought a cure in the southern states, and in the summer of 1890 the whole family was propelled by Anna to Europe in the hope of finding help for Elliott in the spas of Germany and Switzerland. Further searing unpleasantnesses awaited Eleanor here. She remembered all her life her father's calling her a coward when she was reluctant to descend a steep slope above Sorrento on a donkey. Anna monitored her husband closely, sometimes pursuing him in the dead of night in her nightclothes through houses where they were staying, to redeem him from the temptation of drink. When it became clear that he was not making it, he went to a sanitarium in Austria.

Anna was again pregnant. After three months the family moved to the west Paris suburb of Neuilly, where Eleanor was sent to a convent. She was discriminated against as a Protestant and eventually expelled for seeking attention by confecting a fairly innocuous tale about swallowing a coin. Her mother excoriated her fiercely, a terrible punishment for the seven-year-old girl, who was very vulnerable at the best of times. (This may have been the beginning of her lifelong distaste for the Roman Catholic Church.)

Paris proved an irresistible trap for Elliott, who was terribly depressed when sober. He gave way to debauchery on a prodigious scale, and took up with an expatriate American woman, Florence Bagley Sherman, of Detroit. Mrs. Sherman infuriated the Roosevelts by blaming all Elliott's problems on Anna's supposedly miserable and domineering personality. In the midst of this domestic turmoil, Elliott was accused in absentia in New York by the Roosevelts' maid, Katy Mann, of siring her illegitimate child. He could not promise Anna that the claim was not true.

Brother Theodore, now a federal public service commissioner, his righteousness magnified by his political ambition, denounced his brother as "a flagrant man-swine . . . and maniac" and urged Anna to leave him. The Roosevelts paid off Katy Mann, and that story didn't emerge for decades. But Theodore threatened to have Elliott committed. Elliott countered with a threat of divorce and disinheritance of his three young children. There were frightful scenes, seizures for Anna, almost constant delirium tremens for Elliott, in between stupors and catatonic depressions. This was the household to which Eleanor returned on her expulsion from the convent. She must at times have yearned even for the cold severity of the nuns.

Elliott's sister Bamie, the helpful family firefighter in times of crisis for both main branches of the Roosevelt family, was in Paris to assist Anna. She accompanied her and her children back to New York when the marriage finally collapsed altogether in August 1891. Elliott was confined for a time to the Chateau Suresne, a Paris asylum, where Theodore went to visit after launching a court action in New York that led to a spate of newspaper stories alleging Elliott's insanity. Elliott claimed in a letter written from the Chateau Suresne in response to the New York committal action that he was neither insane nor an alcoholic as his wife and brother had alleged but only recuperating from riding accidents. But once in the physical presence of his overpowering brother, he collapsed. The pathetic arrangement the brothers made was that Elliott would stay six months at the Chateau Suresne, return to the United States, take a five-week alcoholic cure at an institution in Illinois, and then spend two years on a sort of probation, completely separated from his wife and children. Anna would then desist from divorcing him for the duration of this hoped-for rehabilitative period. (Years later, Mrs.

Sherman gave to Elliott's most supportive sibling, his sister Corinne Robinson, some diary notes written after Elliott's departure from France expressing her contempt for Anna and Theodore and her sympathy for Elliott. Mrs. Robinson later gave the notes to Eleanor, who cherished them all her life, and kept them in a little album started by Anna's mother.)

Elliott tried to renegotiate the terms of his probation after Illinois, and when that failed accused Anna of infidelity and claimed that Hall was not his son. His banishment proceeded despite his wails and threats, and he settled over a store in Abingdon, Virginia, in 1891, where he kept dogs and horses and became a popular village personality. He was ostensibly overseeing (brother-in-law) Douglas Robinson's extensive properties. He did not cease his quasi-suicidal daredevil antics, such as galloping along the railway trestle just ahead of the train for the amusement of the townsfolk.

Eleanor knew almost nothing of the rights and wrongs of the fierce disputes between her parents, only that her harassed and distracted mother had sent her beloved father away. Her resentment of her mother, whose physical condition was crumbling under the strain of her shattered marriage, grew steadily. They moved into a house on 61st Street, where Eleanor and some young friends were tutored in an improvised classroom by a specially engaged teacher. Anna required exploratory surgery in October 1892. She contracted diphtheria, hovered in serious condition for six weeks—during which Elliott pitifully petitioned his mother-in-law for the right to visit his stricken wife, without success—and died on December 7, 1892, aged twenty-nine and still a great beauty. The second wife of Theodore Roosevelt, Edith, said sadly of Eleanor: "I do not feel she has much chance, poor little soul." Not even Franklin was subjected to such benign but colossal underestimation by another Roosevelt.

Elliott returned to New York, broke down at the sight of his wife in her open coffin, and then plunged into merriment before being packed off back to Virginia. Eleanor and her little brothers went to live with their grandmother, Mrs. Hall, on West 37th Street, where the boys too were attacked by diphtheria in the spring of 1893. Elliott Jr. died, aged three. Many years later Eleanor wrote: "My little brother Ellie was simply too good for this world." For the Oyster Bay Roosevelts, even more than for their Hyde Park cousins or the Delanos, wealth was no protection against tragedy.

Elliott lapsed back into dissolution and visited his daughter only occasionally. Once he left her holding his three leashed dogs for six hours in front of the Knickerbocker Club while he drank himself into unconsciousness within, and was finally carried out past the ever-patient Eleanor and her canine charges. He moved to New York in 1893, living under an assumed name, "Maxwell Elliott," with a new mistress, but rarely contacted his daughter. She continued to adore him and all her life kept his letters, which became steadily less frequent and coherent. As with the ravished housemaid Katy Mann, Elliott's last paramour received a stipend from the Roosevelts when her cuckolded husband turned up in the family office brandishing a revolver.

Elliott declined steeply, blundering into drunken mishaps every few days, subject to seizures and frenzies. On August 13, 1894, he ran up and down the stairs of his home on 102nd Street until he stiffened and fell backwards down the stairs; he died the next day. He was thirty-two and probably the most tragic of all the Roosevelts. Eleanor never ceased to love him and burnish his memory. In 1933 she published a volume of his letters that revealed him as a discerning and witty writer. And in 1952, aged sixty-seven, she visited the Taj Mahal, about which Elliott had written eloquently in 1881, during the trip on the first leg of which he had met Mr. James and Sara. Eleanor kept at her bedside all her life a little Bible from which her father had once read to Anna.

Eleanor plodded grimly through adolescence, living with her desiccated and unremitting grandmother. She was plain, shy, tall, and dowdy looking, condescended to by her more stylish and gregarious cousins, such as Alice. But in 1899 her luck turned for the better, when she was sent to the French-language Allenswood School in the London district of Putney, presided over by the famous Mlle. Marie Souvestre. Eleanor's French was already exemplary. Mlle. Souvestre, though a lesbian and an atheist (only the second preference was visited upon the girls), gave Eleanor confidence, encouraged her intellectual curiosity, spruced up her wardrobe, and made possible her levitation from the almost unrelieved emotional misery of her whole previous life. Eleanor continued to be worthy and earnest, as the nation would discover thirty years later. But she also emerged from Allenswood determined, poised, and much less intimidated by the clannish and often catty Roosevelt women.

Eleanor studied avidly and at Easter 1900 travelled with Mlle. Souvestre to Florence, where she plunged appreciatively into churches and galleries. Mme. Souvestre was a much more enlightened teacher than Endicott Peabody, and Eleanor made a much greater success of Allenswood than Franklin did of Groton. She was the favored student of the headmistress, yet was universally liked and admired by the students. She was kind to the younger students and forthright and thoughtful to everyone. She did not then or ever have any of her future husband's vanity, flippancy, or cynical tendency to political maneuver. Where Franklin had arrived at Groton having known nothing but affection and admiration, Eleanor arrived at Allenswood having known nothing but their almost complete absence.

Franklin the master politician in the making had been unable to straddle altogether the requirements of impressing the school authorities while gaining the affection of his peers. Dr. Peabody suspected the presence of a political operator and so did many of the students. Eleanor arrived at Allenswood a fugitive from a terrible past, grateful to be there, guileless, and full of good intentions. Her kindliness, sincerity, and intelligence delighted everyone.

The rector had promoted athletics, Christian devotion, abstinence, modesty, and the avoidance of excessive intellectualism. Mademoiselle fired the intelligence, treated Anglo-Saxon pieties with delightful French cynicism and a dose of Cartesian scorn, and emphasized reasonable sensual pleasures—especially the arts, female glamour, and good food and wine. Dour Protestantism inconvenienced the irrepressible and prematurely worldly Franklin. French savoir faire liberated the withdrawn Eleanor.

When Eleanor finally departed Allenswood in 1902, Mlle. Souvestre wrote: "I miss you every day of my life." The sentiment was undoubtedly reciprocated, because life with grandmother Hall was even more lugubrious than ever, but Eleanor was now better equipped to deal with it. The Hall family rivalled even the more neurotically sociopathic of the Roosevelts. When Eleanor returned, they were all gathered around their reclusive mother (Eleanor's grandmother) on the family's estate at Tivoli, about twenty-five miles north of Hyde Park.

Eleanor's aunt Edith "Pussie" Hall careened through a series of catastrophic romances. She had accompanied Eleanor on the way home from England and constantly threatened to commit suicide by jumping overboard in mid-Atlantic. Eleanor's uncle Valentine "Vallie" Hall was almost as helpless an alcoholic as Elliott had been, without Elliott's (admittedly rare) bright moments. He was frequently violent and fired rifles out of his bedroom window, obliging the household to dodge between trees at all times when strolling on the property so as not to be picked off by Vallie in one of his drunken rages. (He would continue this practice right up to his death in 1934, blazing away at the neighbors' children, who taunted him by creeping about in the undergrowth like Burnham Wood coming to Dunsinane and calling out to him.)

He could have caused serious embarrassment to his nephew by marriage, who was then the president, and did turn up, drunk and noisy, at the residence of the governor of New York in 1930 when Franklin and Eleanor lived there. He was subdued by the dashing officer in charge of Eleanor's security, Earl Miller. Vallie's brother Eddie was incompetent and another heavy and boorish drinker. Eleanor moved to the family's house on 37th Street with Pussie, who needed her regular attention. She had to put heavy locks on her bedroom door to keep out her drunken uncles when they visited, and she often retrieved them from sodden binges. Her brother Hall combined many of the worst features of Elliott and Vallie.[87]

Franklin and Eleanor had naturally known each other as children. Once when she was very little, Eleanor had spent much of one afternoon being carried around on Franklin's back.[88] Franklin and Eleanor Roosevelt met for the first time in more than a general family group in the autumn of 1902, at the New York

Horse Show, and went to dinner afterwards as Rosy's guests. They met a few more times and then again at Theodore's levee at the White House at New Year's, 1903. They went to the theater together in the President's entourage. When Franklin returned to Harvard, they continued to meet. Sara invited Eleanor to Spring-wood several times, and when the summer came, Franklin took Eleanor sailing and joined her in other recreations in a wholesome family setting.

In the autumn, Eleanor, with several relatives, visited Franklin in Boston and had the edifying experience of watching him perform as male cheerleader at the Harvard-Yale game, which the home team lost despite Franklin's energetic encouragements. Franklin engaged in this activity to follow his own counsel in the *Crimson*, that the Harvard fans had to show more enthusiasm. (He wrote that he "felt like a Damn Fool waving my arms and legs before several thousand amused spectators.")[89] After the game, he took Eleanor on to Groton and a church service presided over by the inevitable Dr. Peabody.

There was some similarity in their religious views. There is no evidence that Franklin ever bought into Dr. Peabody's rather hair-shirted view of Christianity. He did agree with the rector's more optimistic reflections, as when he quoted him in his fourth inaugural address on the subject of secular progress. Franklin believed in a just and generous God. The United States was His preferred country. Gradually, between his fifteenth and twenty-fifth years, during the rise and ascendancy of Theodore Roosevelt, Franklin began to persuade himself that he would become God's chosen, and the American people's constitutionally elected, instrument for the stewardship of the country.

In his great career, Franklin Delano Roosevelt acted as if, and so presumably believed that, his role was to be the bridge between the divine ideal of what his mighty nation could be and the reality of what its talented and generous but very human population could be led to achieve. His role was more instrumental than messianic in the implementation of what he thought to be right.

Many have speculated on what his source of calm, confidence, and detached judgment was. He almost never had trouble sleeping in middle age and rarely betrayed any nervosity. His 1930s advisor Rexford Tugwell wrote: "The secret of his unassailable serenity and his easy gaiety lay in this sense of oneness with the ongoing processes of the universe and his feeling of being, as Emerson said, in tune with the infinite."[90]

He knew God would test him, especially after the onset of his illness, and that great achievements would not come easily. But he believed that perseverance in desirable causes would be rewarded and, apparently, that a certain amount of mundane and even squalid methodology was permitted in pursuit of an admirable purpose. Franklin D. Roosevelt's God was indulgent but exacting, fair and condign and ultimately forgiving. Beyond this, his exact ecclesiastical views, like most of his inner thoughts, are indiscernible. As he told Eleanor, he didn't question his own beliefs: "It is just as well not to think about things like that too much."[91]

Eleanor's religion was less convenient for her. She sometimes verged on reproach of Providence for the tragedies and sadnesses that so afflicted her life, especially her early years. Franklin did so only once, during the monumental crisis of his illness. But generally Eleanor endured life stoically, armed with stubborn and fearless convictions of what was right and an unswerving sense of duty, unencumbered by tactics, practicality, or any indulgence of human foibles. She didn't feel she was in touch with God as Franklin may have, but believed that God would make all things and all people, particularly her poor tragic father, well in the end. They were not incompatible views.

Theirs was a pretty staid and chaste romance. The question has often been posed about what it was in the much-improved but still rather sober Eleanor that so attracted the dashing Franklin. Eleanor was tall and had a good figure and lovely hair, easily forgotten if we remember her only in her matronly middle age. She wasn't Anna or Sara or even Alice but was pleasant in appearance and more so in manner. She was also the niece and goddaughter of an immensely popular president to whose goodwill Franklin attached great importance. She was very intelligent, a refreshing departure from the usual vacuous social flibbertigibits who abounded in debutante circles in and near New York, Boston, and Washington. Franklin had had plenty of exposure to but not unlimited rapport with such people.

Eleanor was obviously a splendid and admirable character, and if rather serious, was also marriageable, reliable, and interesting. In fact, she seemed to many to be more of a catch than he. Handsome though he was, he was still widely regarded as a "feather duster" and a cheerleader, and not just on football days. He was six feet one inch tall and weighed barely 160 pounds, and his other Oyster Bay cousins called him "Miss Nancy" because of what they considered the affected way that he played tennis. Both Franklin and Eleanor smarted under the disparagements of their relatives and both were underestimated in what passed for society. Franklin had recently been rejected by the haughty Alice Sohier, and he didn't enjoy or wish to run the risk of replicating that fiasco. He was, as we have already seen, conspicuously averse to failure.

Finally, Eleanor was a Roosevelt. There was precedent for marrying within the family, an act of ultimate self-confidence by a man whose half-brother unselfconsciously bore the name James Roosevelt Roosevelt. Mr. James had proposed to Bamie, who had pursued Rosy, and there had been lesser overtures between the Hyde Park and Oyster Bay Roosevelts. Franklin was determined to succeed in bridging the two. As Theodore Roosevelt would tell him on the wedding day, "There's nothing like keeping the name in the family."[92]

Franklin had before him the example of waiting too long to build a family, as his father had with him, and as had Isaac or even Mr. Delano. He also had had Sara in Boston for two winters. The constraints of marriage, even to Eleanor at her most overbearing, would be a comparative liberation from the shackles his mother maintained. And this was the only liberation that Sara could not oppose, with one of the very few girls of whom Sara could not possibly disapprove. As always with Franklin, there was an element of tactics. But he also loved Eleanor and she loved him. This is hardly to be wondered at; they were exceptional people, and their reciprocated esteem was not misplaced and rarely wavered, even though their mutual affection did. Franklin was only getting away from the benign despotism of Sara; Eleanor was escaping the gruesome and psychotic menagerie of what was left of her family.

What would unite them would be courage, high intelligence, burning though differing ambitions, and an unusual concern for the disadvantaged. Franklin the precocious secondary school and university politician already showed some of the form of the giant of national and world politics that he was to become. Eleanor, when she graduated from school in 1902, was aware at last of her potential to do good and do well. Already faintly discernible was the woman who would achieve the remarkable feat of adding even more luster to the great name that would soon be hers by right of marriage as well as birth. They almost certainly saw in each other the qualities that would carry them to heights that even Franklin, great though his ambition was, could not have imagined. And though their marriage would have many difficulties, from a distance at least it would be a huge and historic success.

In the interregnum between Franklin's revelation of his marital plans to his mother and the public disclosure of the engagement, the relations between Sara and Eleanor and Franklin often shifted. Eleanor whiled away the time in the Junior League, which she did not treat as a luncheon club or thrift-store operation but rather as challenging social work. She taught callisthenics and "fancy dancing" to Jewish and Italian immigrant children on the Lower East Side, south of Houston Street, the fashionable SoHo of a century later. At first she was defensive about this with Franklin, but she wanted him to realize the conditions of the urban poor and often arranged for him to accompany her home from there. After one such occasion, when Franklin carried a sick girl from Eleanor's class home to an upper floor tenement, he said: "I didn't know anyone lived like that." In 1961, aged seventy-seven, Eleanor said to a friend, of her effort to educate Franklin: "It worked. He saw how people lived and he never forgot."[93] Thanks to Eleanor, Roosevelt was probably the only president in American history who had any direct familiarity with urban poverty.

During the Christmas holidays of 1903, Sara did her best to urge Franklin out into society to meet as many people—i.e., nubile young ladies—as possible. To placate her, Franklin proposed that she take a Caribbean winter cruise with him and Lathrop Brown. Sara accepted happily, and the two seniors skipped a full month of courses and, in Franklin's case, of the editorship of the *Crimson*. The trip was quite a success and was the backdrop for another of FDR's famous fictionalized stories. He told the president of Venezuela, who was on a state visit to Washington in 1944, that he had heard Caruso sing at the Caracas opera house in 1904, that Caruso was then an obscure itinerant tenor unheard of in New York, and that he and Lathrop had "discovered" Caruso. It was a harmless fiction, but Caruso was not then in Caracas, he had appeared often in New York, and he had been the most illustrious tenor and one of the most famous people in the world for some years by then.[94]

The cruise ended at Miami. The Roosevelt party went to Palm Beach, where Sara was appalled by the "crowds of overdressed vulgar people," an opinion of Palm Beach that Franklin would renew at long intervals throughout his life. Once back in Washington, Sara unsuccessfully sought for Franklin the post of secretary to the U.S. ambassador in London, Joseph Choate. This was an ambitious but somewhat desperate diversionary tactic. The ambassador had already filled the post, and Franklin's qualifications, apart from being related to the President, were not clear.[95]

Franklin began his law studies at Columbia in October 1904, but they didn't much interest him and his academic performance was mediocre. He failed two courses in his first year, something that he characteristically blamed on administrative pettifogging. He had planned to announce his engagement at the Delano Thanksgiving dinner at Fairhaven on the exact anniversary of his advice of it to his mother, but jaundice prevented him from attending, so he sent a letter of announcement that was read at the family dinner to great celebration. Franklin recovered at home in New York fairly quickly, with Sara reading to him from the memoirs of General Robert E. Lee and Rosy playing piquet with him.

Announcements were made in the press on December 1. Almost all the attention was focused on Eleanor, who was portrayed as the beautiful and gracious niece of the President. Franklin was tersely described as the former editor of the Crimson and a member of the New York Yacht Club. It was to be an almost all-Roosevelt wedding party, with Rosy as best man and the rather injudicious choice of Alice Roosevelt as maid of honor, who declared the news "simply too nice to be true." The ubiquitous President, who had just been reelected by a huge majority, including Franklin's first presidential ballot, would give the bride away.

Franklin was undoubtedly gratified by the President's letter to him: "I am as fond of Eleanor as if she were my daughter, and I like you, and trust you, and believe in you . . . You and Eleanor are true and brave, and I believe you love each other unselfishly; and golden years open before you. May all good fortune attend you both, ever . . . Your affectionate cousin."[96]

Theodore Roosevelt was by then was the most admired man in America. He continued to be unfailingly generous to Franklin and Eleanor right to the premature end of his life. He soon signed himself off in correspondence to Franklin as "your affectionate uncle," a slight but felicitous liberty with the facts. The President invited the engaged couple to his reinauguration March 4, 1905, and seated them just behind his own family on the steps of the Capitol. Franklin listened carefully as TR promised every American "a square deal."[97]

Endicott Peabody went to some inconvenience to accept Franklin's request that he officiate at the wedding, which took place on St. Patrick's Day, March 17, 1905, at the 76th Street home of Eleanor's grandmother, Mary Livingston Ludlow Hall. By opening up the interconnecting drawing room of the neighboring house, owned by a cousin, 200 guests could be accommodated. As she was dressing before the wedding, Eleanor received a very welcome cable from England: "Bonheur. Souvestre." It was the last contact between Eleanor and the woman to whom she owed much of the happiness she now enjoyed. Mme. Souvestre died of cancer just two days later.

There were great ovations as the President arrived and bounded up the stairs. The rector had to make himself heard over the noisy revelry of the St. Patrick's Day celebrants thronging the streets beyond the windows. Rosy was unwell and Lathrop Brown took his place as best man. The ushers were all relatives or classmates.[98]

The newlyweds entrained for Hyde Park. Sara remained in New York as the couple that would become the most famous in American history spent their first night together. Franklin and Eleanor were alone for a week at Hyde Park; Sara thought that Eleanor should have the same launch of her marriage that she had had. Then they went to a modest apartment Sara had chosen for them on West 45th Street. Eleanor was concerned about her lack of domestic skills, such as cooking, but Franklin was his usual cheerful and undemanding self. Eleanor went to great lengths to ingratiate herself with Sara, writing frequent variations of: "You are just the sweetest, dearest Mama to your children," including herself as one.[99] Eleanor's desire to belong to a family was understandable, and Sara certainly welcomed it, but the triangular Roosevelt relationship would require endless fine-tuning over the next thirty-five years.

This was presumably the beginning of their sexual lives, an area in which Eleanor was uneducated and that she seems never to have been able to enjoy. Franklin may have been somewhat experienced, but this is conjecture. The source of Eleanor's exposure to the subject appears to have been her cousin Alice, over Eleanor's protests against what she regarded as blasphemy, noisily reading the "begat" sections of the Old Testament.[100] Eleanor's view may have been similar to Sara's statement of purposeful resignation on the same subject (in response to a question from a grandson): "I knew my obligations as a wife and did my duty." Eleanor, according to her own daughter, Anna (who was a sexually well-adjusted and attractive woman), considered the subject "an ordeal to be borne."[101]

Franklin was always affable and equable and even affectionate, but almost never intimate, other than physically. Eleanor, starved for affection, sought intimacy but was always fearful of rejection and never optimistic that she would retain the love of Franklin or the friendship of anyone for very long. Franklin, who had basked in the love of his parents, did not share Eleanor's desire for a very close relationship. He was courteous, always and sometimes maddeningly chipper, but unrevealing about himself, accustomed to doing whatever he wanted, and disinclined to change.

⚜

CHAPTER 2

"The Hardest Trader I've Ever Run Against"

(Joseph P. Kennedy's description of Franklin D. Roosevelt as assistant secretary of the navy, 1917)

I

T HE NEWLYWEDS DEPARTED on their honeymoon trip to Europe on the British liner *Oceanic* on June 7, 1905. To Franklin, the most interesting passengers they encountered were six Japanese naval officers on their way to Britain to take over two new warships built for Japan by British shipbuilders. Franklin grilled them quite intensively. (At this time, Japan relied on the British for sophisticated warship construction, which the Japanese then copied and refined.)[1]

Despite his outward serenity, Franklin was clearly afflicted by some anxieties. He regularly had inexplicable attacks of hives and also had terrible nightmares and intermittent bouts of sleepwalking. Eleanor several times had to rouse him from upsetting dreams and deter him from somnambulating out of his hotel room.[2] There were also strains arising from Eleanor's penchant for jealousy. She resented Franklin's going mountain climbing at Cortina with another woman who was staying in their hotel, even though he had invited his wife and she had declined and nothing unseemly occurred on the three-hour outing. There was a hotel dance that Franklin attended after Eleanor declined. This all sent Eleanor into one of her "Griselda" moods, as she would always call the grim, mute funks that periodically overcame her.[3]

Another problem in Switzerland arose when the Palace Hotel in St. Moritz refused them entry to the main dining room in the evening because their dress was too casual. Eleanor never forgot this. When she finally returned to St. Moritz nearly fifty years later as the proverbial "First Lady of the World," she declined to stay in the Palace Hotel.[4]

In Britain, France, and Italy, they spent a good deal of time browsing in secondhand bookstores, and Eleanor, who spoke passable Italian, negotiated with the Italian booksellers for Franklin until he fired her for siding with the vendors (she found any haggling extremely distasteful).[5] In 1906 Sara found that Franklin hadn't paid all his bills in two Paris bookstores she visited. She settled the accounts herself and scolded Franklin as a delinquent.[6]

In Paris Eleanor was somewhat scandalized by a bawdy farce to which Franklin and some touring Harvard friends took her and Dora Forbes, Sara's sister.[7] Franklin and Eleanor also had their fortunes read by a famous seer and palmist in Paris, Mme. Noel, who predicted a large inheritance for Eleanor and the presidency of the United States for Franklin (perhaps not such a feat of clairvoyance given the name of the incumbent at the time). When they arrived in Paris on August 11, Franklin learned of his failure in two first-year law courses, Contracts and Pleading and Practice. He wrote to his mother asking that the relevant texts be sent to him, without explaining why. When the books arrived from New York, Franklin began swotting up the courses in the mornings and toured and honeymooned in the afternoons. Franklin easily passed supplemental examinations at Columbia and began his second year of law school in October 1905.

Another minor incident that Franklin later magnified as a raconteur occurred on the railroad from St. Moritz to Augsburg. Four large Germans entered the Roosevelts' compartment and a squabble developed over the blinds and the window, which Franklin succeeded in reopening. Franklin worked this up to a claim of successful fisticuffs with the (predictable) Prussian officer and his comrades.[8]

Eleanor returned to Allenswood School, but Franklin was unable to accompany her on this sentimental visit, the venue of her happiest memories, because he was visiting his bank. Given the importance of the place to his wife, this was rather insensitive. She found it not at all the same without Mme. Souvestre. They visited the homes of some of Franklin's parents' friends, including the great collector of stuffed birds, Lord Hawkesbury. They also visited the Scottish home of Eleanor's best friend, Isabella Selmes, and her husband, Robert Ferguson, a taciturn Scottish adventurer who had been a Rough Rider with Theodore Roosevelt in Cuba in the Spanish-American War.[9] The Fergusons had Sidney and Beatrice Webb to lunch one day, the supreme ideological inspirers of the British Labour Party and, with George Bernard Shaw, stars of the socialist Fabian Society. Franklin discussed teaching techniques at Harvard with Sidney, while Eleanor discussed what she described in a letter to Sara as "the servant problem" with Beatrice, an unlikely preoccupation for one of the world's most famous socialists.[10]

While at the Fergusons' Franklin gave his first known adult public speech, other than an explanation as an eighteen-year-old to an audience at Campobello of the rationale for a new golf course with which he was associated, and not counting his remarks in Harvard speech-making classes. On those occasions in 1900, he already knew most of the audience and was at ease. He had been congratulated on the lucidity of his explanation at Campobello by a visiting justice of the U.S. Supreme Court, Horace Gray. On the Fergusons' estate he addressed a small group of Scottish crofters at the opening of a flower show. It was a rather banal and loquacious effort, digressing into the standard methods of preparation of vegetables in Great Britain and the United States. Eleanor was generous in her description of it. He was, for once, excessively self-critical, writing to his mother that "the foolishness" of his smile was equalled only by the "extreme idiocy" of his remarks.[11]

Like Sara, Eleanor returned home from her honeymoon trip in Europe pregnant. She shouldered the difficulties of child-bearing uncomplainingly, earning the praise of her mother-in-law. Sara tried to encourage her with recollections of Chinese peasant women she had learned about when in the Orient in her youth, who took an hour off from their menial labor and gave birth on a bench, then returned to their toils. Eleanor did not find this uplifting, however.

Franklin was not pleased when, at the wedding reception of his cousin Alice and Congressman Nicholas Longworth in February 1906, the Porcellian Club members, led by the bridegroom and the President, withdrew to a side room for toasts and club songs, attended upon by the club's elderly black steward.

Franklin and Eleanor's first child, Anna Eleanor, was born, big and healthy, on May 3, 1906. Franklin was delighted, but Eleanor, intense and introspective, seems to have seen the event as another joyless burden. Unfortunately, she fell under the influence of an opinionated pediatrician, L. Emmett Holt, an advocate of stern discipline and absolute fixity of schedule for newborns. Thumb-sucking should be discouraged by tying the baby's arms to its sides; kissing should be avoided for fear of diphtheria, tuberculosis, and venereal disease, and children should be "aired" for up to five hours a day. Eleanor fulfilled the latter requirement by putting her daughter in a wooden basket with a chicken wire top and suspending it out of her bedroom window, until a neighbor threatened to report her to the Society for the Prevention of Cruelty to Children.[12] Another flourish of Eleanor's was to tie three-year-old Anna's hands to the top of her crib at night as "the prescribed cure" to prevent masturbation.[13]

In later years Eleanor would strongly regret that she had been too regimental and unbending with her children when they were little. The problem was compounded by an unimaginably authoritarian nanny, hired, like the rest of the young Roosevelts' servants, by Sara, whose retreat from control of their lives would be conducted with the skill and tenacity of Robert E. Lee at Richmond.

When one of the Roosevelts' sons would be accused of falsely claiming to have brushed his teeth, Nanny forced him to don one of his sister's dresses and march back and forth wearing a sandwich board proclaiming "I am a liar" on the sidewalk of 65th Street, an area unaccustomed to such spectacles. She locked others of them in a cupboard for hours, with, they believed, lasting resulting claustrophobia and dread of darkness. Jimmy, the eldest son, believed her forcing him to eat a pot of hot mustard caused him to be susceptible to ulcers as an adult. Her reign was a great and malign change from that of Franklin's Miss McCrorie and Mlle. Sandoz. Franklin and Eleanor were aware of these incidents, but the nanny was dismissed only when Eleanor discovered a cache of her empty liquor bottles. Cruelty to children was less serious a transgression than dipsomania.[14] Henceforth, Eleanor hired her own staff.

Sara retained power of the purse, since Franklin's inheritance did not produce the income necessary to live as he did. Instead of settling something on him or advancing money regularly with no strings attached, Sara ensured that she was constantly being asked for financial and other favors. As soon as her grandchildren were old enough to be pawns in the game, she began making direct gifts to them, which complicated Franklin and Eleanor's parenting efforts, erratic at the best of times.[15]

Franklin let his mother and his wife keep each other busy while he reverted more or less to the life of a bachelor. This was a net gain for Sara, who was able to assert herself in matronly manner over Eleanor, while it was not at all what the new Mrs. Roosevelt had imagined her married life would be. She became disillusioned with her lot.

Although their religious views were reasonably compatible, Eleanor's grim nature required slavish church attendance, while Franklin breezily excused himself on Sunday mornings to golf, sail, or sleep in.[16] Eleanor dutifully attended history classes at Hyde Park organized by her mother-in-law, and even sewing lessons provided for the local girls, that they might qualify as maids in the homes of the rich. Franklin, ever the spontaneous dilettante, briefly started two novels, the second about Egbert Valentine, a love-struck bibliophile. He abandoned this project after four pages.

Franklin was skilled at all the manly arts—including almost all sports and carving meat—as well as dancing and all aspects of socializing. On occasion, he stayed out to 4 A.M., which seriously irritated Eleanor, who was beginning to think that there might be some merit in the allegations of relatives and some classmates that Franklin was frivolous. Eleanor's attempt to learn to play golf was a failure, and her husband advised her to abandon it. She did not overcome her fear of the water sufficiently to learn to swim properly until middle age. She did fish and sail a little but never really took to either activity. When she tried riding Mr. James's horse, unaware—because Franklin and Sara had neglected to tell her—that the horse burst into a spontaneous gallop on parts of the trails she followed, as Mr. James had taught it to do, she had a nerve-racking and dangerous ride and did not take to a horse again for many years.[17]

The following summer the whole family went to Seabright on the Atlantic shore of New Jersey. Franklin commuted and was somewhat discountenanced when Eleanor, as part of her intermittent campaign to be a more serviceable wife by learning to drive, smashed up Franklin's Ford while toppling a gatepost and shearing off part of the landlord's porch.[18] Driving automobiles became yet another activity she did not try again for some time. The Seabright experiment was not a great success, and the summer apostasy from Campobello was not repeated.

Franklin desultorily pursued his law studies at Columbia, but never took the law seriously as a possible occupation. Many of his classmates were Jews, a fact that even Eleanor commented on, though reasonably neutrally. Enlightened people regarded Jews as aliens, very different though not necessarily bad. Less enlightened people, but none of the Roosevelts so far as is known, regarded Jews as considerably more sinister. This was Franklin's first serious exposure to the complicated sociology of his country. There is no evidence that he found the experience disagreeable or even noteworthy. (He did on one occasion refer to "blessed little men of the 'chosen race' " in a note to Eleanor accompanying a check for a children's hospital in a Jewish and Italian district, but it was a poor attempt at humor, not a slur.)

———————

Franklin took and passed the bar examinations for the state of New York June 19, 1906, and his formal education ended. (His achievement in passing an eight-hour examination was considerable, because he was suffering a severe attack of sinusitis, an ailment that would bedevil him throughout his life.) The university degree of bachelor of laws would have meant another year's study, and Franklin, who had gone happily back to Harvard for a superfluous year to be editor of the *Crimson*, saw no need for a second degree once he was able to practice law, which he had no intention of doing for long.

He landed a position in the well-known Wall Street law firm Carter, Ledyard & Milburn, through interventions with a fellow member of the New York Yacht Club who was a partner. According to Columbia law professor Jackson Reynolds, Sara requested the position of the senior partner, Lewis C. Ledyard, who was the commodore of the Yacht Club.[19]

Franklin's legal practice was not a very impassioned affair; he defended a few Harvard friends on a drunk and disorderly charge, and seems to have had only one criminal case, in 1910, involving a second-degree assault charge, in which Franklin won an acquittal. He graduated to admiralty law—"those ferryboat cases," he later called them—which was somewhat more interesting.

Ledyard eventually claimed that he told Sara that Franklin had to leave the firm, because he had no aptitude for the law. Franklin seems to have convinced his mother, who put it in her hagiographical book about him, that he had had a very successful time as a downtown lawyer and only threw it over to enter public service, out of duty. He always maintained that the law was a world and an occupation that he had easily mastered but gave up as unfulfilling. The truth seems to be that Franklin, as he had at Groton, Harvard, and Columbia, merely got by in his law practice, though he sometimes took overlong and even slightly liquified lunches.[20] He didn't have to work and, far from being a martyr to the work ethic, was biding his time until he could launch his political career. As he languidly explained to his fellow juniors at Carter, Ledyard & Milburn one day in 1907, he intended soon to get himself elected to the New York State Assembly, then gain appointment to the post of assistant secretary of the navy, and then be elected governor of New York. This was exactly the route that Theodore Roosevelt had followed. Franklin's young legal friends, who were well accustomed to his breezy dissertations on a vast range of subjects, were in this case very impressed with his candor.

Even at this early date there was the division of opinion about Franklin Roosevelt that persisted much of his life. To serious young legal careerists, he was "a harmless bust. He had a sanguine temperament almost adolescent in its buoyancy."[21] His more prescient peers, undeterred by his breezy confidence, had not "deprecated his ambition or even smiled at it as we might perhaps have done. It seemed proper and sincere; and moreover, as he put it, entirely reasonable."[22]

Those who liked, or at least were not put off by, his manner, saw him from the beginning as a great developing talent and possibly the author of a remarkable career. Those who were irked by his flippant, collegiate self-assurance, tinged with superficiality and cynicism, discounted him. Roosevelt early divided acquaintances into the two groups, and never forgot who had belonged in which in the decades before the fulfilment of his ambitions resolved the issue. His admirers were always more numerous, but not necessarily more vocal.

In these days, very few people became president who had cherished virtually no other ambition all their conscient lives. The custom was for men to build a distinguished career in some respectable occupation such as law or the military, gravitate to public life, and be elevated more or less by merit or accident to a great public office and ultimately to the presidency, which they had come to seek only lately. (From General Jackson in 1824 to General Winfield Scott Hancock in 1880, someone who had been principally known as a distinguished military officer had been a candidate for president in every election except 1844 and 1860. It was part of the American tradition, begun by George Washington, of the citizen-soldier-leader. Voluntarism, heroism, and service to the nation in dangerous times were considered desirable in a president. Franklin D. Roosevelt was able to maintain some of this tradition by glamorizing his performance in World War I, but he was really the greatest of the nation's professional politicians.

Franklin lived somewhat like a bachelor, though faithful to his wife and procreating with her. The Roosevelts' second child, James, was born on December 23, 1907.

In June 1908, Franklin went with his uncle, Warren Delano III, on a weeklong inspection of the family's coal lands in the Cumberland Mountains in Kentucky, largely on horseback. It did not fire in him any enthusiasm for the coal business.[23] Franklin had retained his skill as an equestrian (and had ridden and driven his father's favorite trotter, Bobby, to two blue-ribbon victories, one trotting, the other saddled, at the Dutchess County fair, September 27, 1905).

———————

The Roosevelts' third child, Franklin Jr., was born March 18, 1909, a whopping baby of eleven pounds. In October he developed endocarditis, an inflammation of the wall of the heart, and he died on November 2. Eleanor had not been with her son when he initially took ill, having entrusted him to Sara and staff. She almost had to be coerced to leave the infant's graveside, and remembered: "How cruel it seemed to leave him out there alone in the cold."[24] Franklin, though evidently upset by the occurrence of every parent's nightmare, recovered his equilibrium with what Eleanor considered to be unseemly haste. She was already rather resentful of her husband, who often stopped off after work and came in very late, sometimes with alcohol on his breath, which the temperate Eleanor found repulsive.

She had expected and felt she had been promised a good deal more companionship than she was getting in this marriage. "I was horribly disappointed yesterday, with your hasty little scrap of a letter after not getting anything for two days," she wrote in August 1909 as she soldiered on in Campobello without him.[25]

Franklin was moved by family tragedy to join the board of the New York Milk Committee, to fight infant mortality, which from various causes claimed the lives of more than a thousand other babies in Manhattan less than a year old in the summer of 1909 alone. He became reacquainted with the miserable annals of the poor for the first time since he used to pick Eleanor up from her slum callisthenics and dancing classes five years before. The Roosevelts continued to seek a larger family, and their fourth child, Elliott, was born September 23, 1910. This time no unusual medical problems arose.

Franklin became a Democrat because his father had been one, and because he became disenchanted with the fat-cat complacency of New York Republicans. All this and Franklin's other political sensibilities were altered by the rise of Theodore Roosevelt, whom Franklin always referred to as the greatest man he had ever met. Franklin was a militant booster of Teddy, even more so when, nearly four years after the end of his presidential term, Teddy became thoroughly estranged from his party, thus legitimizing in Franklin's eyes his own continuing adherence to the Democrats.

By his energy, reforming zeal, youth, and iconoclastic contempt for the party bosses, Theodore inspired Franklin with a burning vision of what could be done by a determined politician. He could come from a prominent family, be educated by tutors, attend Harvard and Columbia, but still attract the people and harvest their votes. Franklin also felt that being a Democrat spared him from invidious family comparisons with Teddy. Tactically he always envisioned an alliance between progressive Republican and reform Democrats. Theodore Roosevelt's disappointment with his selected successor, William Howard Taft, a giant walrus of a man, was already beginning to divide the Republicans between conservative and reform (progressive) factions. This was a very dangerous schism within the party. Theodore Roosevelt was the leader of the progressives and was capable of anything; he was likely to put the Democratic presidential candidate and many lesser candidates across if he split the Republican vote.

The Dutchess County district attorney, Judge John E. Mack, called on Franklin at his law office at 54 Wall Street in early 1910. He had come to deliver some papers for signing but ended by offering Franklin the Democratic nomination for the state assembly seat for Poughkeepsie.[26] This place was apparently about to be vacated by the former lieutenant governor (who had won in 1906 on the ticket headed unsuccessfully by publisher William Randolph Hearst) and Democratic candidate for governor in 1908 (defeated by the Republican nominee, Charles Evans Hughes), Lewis Stuyvesant Chandler, an Astor and a distant cousin of Franklin's.

Franklin sought the advice of his most illustrious kinsman. TR encouraged him to run.[27] There would be a good deal of to-ing and fro-ing, including the announcement by Chandler that he had changed his mind and wished to retain his place in the state assembly. Franklin became so incensed that he threatened to run as an independent, throwing the race to the Republicans. Because of his surname, his general aura of serene confidence, and his considerable means, this threat was taken seriously. In response, Judge Mack suggested that Franklin might try for the state senate instead, in which case he could be nominated unopposed but would face real difficulty getting elected in a habitually Republican district.

Franklin was nominated by the chairman of the Fishkill Democratic Committee, Morgan Hoyt (who would perform the same task for him again seven times—four times for president). Franklin campaigned with the other local Democratic nominees, including the Poughkeepsie congressional candidate, the editor of the *Poughkeepsie News-Press*, Richard E. Connell. From this picturesque character FDR learned the technique of addressing large crowds of uncertain political persuasion as "My friends."

The most gripping drama in the campaign was when Franklin's campaign car ran over a dog. There weren't witnesses, but Franklin insisted on stopping, meeting the bereaved owner, and paying him five dollars.[28] The incident was thus transformed into a vote-winner. Franklin campaigned with tremendous energy. What he lacked in gravitas was made up in exuberance and gregariousness. On one long campaign day, Franklin's road show finished up at a little town where the candidate stood all the occupants of the town bar to drinks before asking the town's name and learning that he had strayed all the way into Connecticut.[29] This was the sort of story Franklin was happy in later years to tell about himself. Like many people who are incapable of admitting error, he engaged in occasional innocuous self-mockery instead.

Franklin so impressed one young elector, Tom Lynch, the son of an Irish-American Poughkeepsie florist whom Franklin referred to thereafter as "my wild

Irish Rose," that Lynch set aside two bottles of champagne for Franklin's nomination as president of the United States. The bottles were uncorked twenty-two years later.[30]

Franklin evoked his famous cousin at every opportunity. Like him, he was often "deelighted" with anything that was "bully." He rebutted the charge of being a carpetbagger by accusing his opponent, Senator John Schlosser, of being a stooge of the Republican Party bosses, an argument that accorded exactly with what Theodore Roosevelt was saying about the Taft Republicans at the time. Franklin Roosevelt was an underdog given little chance of winning. The Republicans were complacent almost until election day. As the campaign wound up in early November, Franklin spoke in Poughkeepsie and Tivoli (the home of Eleanor's Hall relatives), and his wife, mother, and a bevy of aunts and cousins attended. But these performances were underwhelming. Eleanor wrote that he appeared "thin . . . high-strung, and at times, nervous."[31] These seem to have been unrepresentative addresses, his nervousness perhaps provoked by the presence of too much family.

The results came in quickly on election day. Franklin Roosevelt prevailed, running in his district ahead of the entire Democratic ticket, including the successful Democratic candidate for governor, John Alden Dix, wresting the senate seat from the Republicans, who had held it for many years, and piling up an impressive victory, 15,708 to 14,568.[32] Aged twenty-eight, Franklin D. Roosevelt had finally launched his career; there would be no more dilettantism, no mere going through the motions just to get along, as at Groton, Harvard, and Wall Street. This apparently trivial election was a seminal event in modern American history.

II

ROOSEVELT WAS ALMOST an instant celebrity in Albany. He had been visiting the state capital since he went with his father to see veterans of Governor Cleveland's administration.

The Roosevelts moved into a comfortable house on Upper State Street in a genteel residential area, and were well taken care of by servants. The most interesting decorative motif was a fist holding a club carved above the library fireplace, which Franklin pointed out to visitors as a heraldic representation of his famous cousin's legendary "big stick." For this first winter, little James Roosevelt, having a slight heart murmur, had to be carried up and down the stairs of the house, an additional trial for the always rather beleaguered Eleanor.

The then-leading member of the assembly (and soon to be its speaker) was Alfred E. Smith, a four-term assemblyman from a poor but respectable Irish family in the Bowery, who was to develop a very complex relationship with Roosevelt that would continue almost to the end of their lives. Roosevelt's daughter, Anna, once said that the greatest motive in her father's political career, at least well into his presidency, was not to be outdistanced by Al Smith. Their relations were sometimes affectionate, sometimes very abrasive, but never altogether hostile and never wholly trusting.

Another young and promising figure in New York Democratic politics, whose career would also be entwined with Smith's and Roosevelt's for many years, was state senator Robert Wagner. These men were members of the Tammany Hall political machine, but of a reform variety, financially honest and passionately dedicated to the interests of New York's immigrant communities. Tammany's history and current status were more complicated than its folkloric notoriety would indicate. Tammany drew its name from a benign Delaware Indian chief, Tammanend, and was founded in 1789 in middle-class opposition to the more comfortable Federalists. It was incorporated as a benevolent society in 1805 and thereafter had the same leadership as the New York Democratic Party. It became the advocate of according the franchise to successive waves of propertyless immigrants, starting with the Irish. Paternalistic and authoritarian, and generally based on the sale of votes for patronage, Tammany quickly became, by traditional standards, a retrograde organization. But it was also the principal agency of charity and a start in life in the New World for New York's immigrants.

Tammany's crooked bosses were colorful scoundrels of astonishing shamelessness, most notably William Marcy Tweed (1823–1878), who stole scores of millions of dollars of public money and died in prison after being extradited from Spain. But Tammany's progressive leaders, and Al Smith would be the most famous and popular of all, were outstanding pioneers of reform.

Franklin Roosevelt had never had any contact with such people, and his effortless Ivy League and Upper Hudson squirely charm was unlikely to be too serviceable with this political breed. But Roosevelt never doubted that he could bridge the patrician world of his origins and upbringing and the ward-heeling, log-rolling rough and tumble of New York politics he now encountered. His cousin Teddy, especially as New York City police commissioner, had met these same elements, but as a reform Republican, an emissary from the gentlemen's party of Lincoln to the rougher districts of New York. There had been distinguished New York reform Democrats like Grover Cleveland of Buffalo and Samuel Tilden (1814–1886), who reorganized the New York Democrats after the Civil War, sent Tweed to prison, and was cheated out of the presidency in favor of Rutherford B. Hayes by the House of Representatives in the election of 1876. But these men were not so wealthy or socially exalted in origin as Franklin D. Roosevelt, and did not master the byzantine intricacies of New York machine politics as he would.

Franklin was always more genteel than Teddy, the cowboy and Rough Rider, and taller and more aristocratic in bearing. Slender, clean-shaven, mellifluous, and prone to make his points with a debonair wave of his cigarette-holder, he was a less plausible occupant of a proverbial smoke-filled room than the mustachioed, barrel-chested, bellowing, cigar-chomping TR. Franklin had always known how to be subtle and devious, and was never over-scrupulous in approaching his objectives. He was as jejune as TR was guileless and direct, as euphonious as Teddy was stentorian. His effete quality would largely disappear with a few more years in the great world beyond Springwood, Groton, Harvard, and Wall Street, and was never more than the manner of a privately schooled only son accustomed to pleasing his elders. He would never aspire to Theodore's rugged individualism or bellicosity but developed a style of the natural, relaxed, supremely confident gentleman, patrician without snobbery, ambitious without exhausting those about him.

This would all come in stages, but at the outset of his political career he already knew his vocation and his own and human nature well enough to develop quite quickly. The party bosses were always wary of FDR, in New York as elsewhere, until his dominance of his party became so overwhelming that they acclaimed him as their natural leader.

In these first days, the bosses knew that unlike them, young Roosevelt did not embark on a political career because he was incapable of doing as well in other fields. And unlike most other blue-bloods, he wasn't a Republican; but, being a Roosevelt, he could attract all the press attention he wanted, was largely impervious to the threats and blandishments of the machine, and would probably prove energetic and unpredictable, if not as terrifying to them as Teddy had been. He was an exotic arrival in Albany in 1910 and was watched with great curiosity from the start. Whatever the suspicion with which the Democratic bosses regarded him, Franklin was ever a Roosevelt and was, with Eleanor, and with Sara when she visited Albany, a frequent invitee to the executive mansion.

Franklin D. Roosevelt's first test was not long in coming. In these times United States senators were chosen by both houses of the legislatures of their states. The New York incumbent, the prosperous Republican Chauncey Depew, could count on the support of eighty-six Republican legislators. The 114 Democrats were divided between Edward Shepard, a respected Cleveland-era railway lawyer, and William F. Sheehan, a smooth but corrupt political roué (who had been associated with Judge Alton B. Parker, the hugely unsuccessful Democratic candidate for president against Theodore Roosevelt in 1904). The Democratic legislators were in principle bound to support the choice of their majority in order that they would prevail as a party over Depew. In charge of the maintenance of party unity, incumbency, and preferments was the Tammany Hall boss, Charles F. Murphy, a very formidable but considerably more refined boss than Tammany had had before. Murphy was confident he had the votes for Sheehan.

The reformers won an early victory when the machine senator Thomas A. Grady was dumped as leader pro tempore of the senate in favor of Smith and Robert Wagner. A group of younger, mainly upstate reform Democrats, to whom Franklin Roosevelt naturally adhered, caucused separately on the morning of January 16, 1911, to send Murphy the message that they would rather have the

Republican Depew than Sheehan. Young Roosevelt had plunged into the thickets of rebellion within two weeks of taking up his position. There were twenty-one insurgents, and they regularly met in the Roosevelt house throughout the ten-week insurrection. Franklin was known as "the shepherd."[33] A veteran Albany political reporter, Louis McHenry Howe, a gnomish cynic plying around in a miasma of whiskey and cigar smoke on behalf of the *New York Herald,* wrote that "Never in the history of Albany have 21 men threatened such ruin of machine plans. It is the most humanly interesting political fight of many years." He quickly recognized the newsworthiness and the potentialities of Franklin Roosevelt. These were the first glimmerings of a much more improbable relationship even than that between Roosevelt and Smith.

The unfolding drama attracted Eleanor to politics for the first time. Sheehan warned Roosevelt early on in the controversy that he would use not only the party apparatus but his own resources to besmirch his opponents in their own districts. There were various trivial acts of machine oppression, including the firing of FDR's long-time nominator for successively higher offices, Morgan Hoyt, as clerk of the assembly's Forest, Fish, and Game Committee, of which Roosevelt was the chairman. (In his most resolute activities as a new legislator, Roosevelt transformed this docile committee into a ceaseless breeding ground of conservationist ideas, and pushed through a modest reforestation bill.)[34]

Roosevelt gallantly announced that he would use his family's means to help some of the more financially vulnerable renegades.[35] This was widely acclaimed as selfless altruism, but there is no evidence that it was actually translated into check-writing by him or Sara. Several of the insurgents were threatened with mortgage foreclosures, and one small newspaper-owner lost state government advertising and eventually folded the paper.

One of Sheehan's most predictable tactics was to accuse his opponents, and Roosevelt in particular, of anti-Catholic bias.[36] Roosevelt was rather naively nonplussed by this gambit and self-righteously denied it. In fact, Roosevelt and his family had generally looked with some suspicion on the Roman Catholic Church as a vast, secretive, autocratic, alien, and somewhat primitive institution and on many of its adherents as loyalty risks. Mr. James had preferred to avoid hiring Irish Catholic domestics.

Once FDR introduced basic political arithmetic into sectarian notions, he became an ostentatious champion of some prominent Roman Catholic public figures. Many of his closest collaborators, his principal law partner, his personal assistants (who revered their boss like secular nuns), and his party chairmen would be Roman Catholics. There was doubtless a large element of sincerity in this metamorphosis, as Roosevelt seemed to outgrow his anti-papist prejudices, especially when he began to correspond with the popes. However, Catholicism always rankled with Eleanor as authoritarian, if not saturnine.

Boss Murphy invited Roosevelt for a talk on his twenty-ninth birthday, January 30, 1911, and acknowledged that Sheehan could not make it. He asked Roosevelt to help him persuade Sheehan to withdraw, and Franklin and Eleanor had the Sheehans to lunch three days later. It was a civilized but strained encounter of several hours, and nothing directly resulted from it. Roosevelt started casting about for a fusion candidate between reform Democrats and Republicans. He abandoned his original candidate, Edward Shepard, and followed the advice that he now needed to bury the anti-Catholic charge by finding a Catholic candidate. There was a good deal of farcical shuttling back and forth as Murphy proposed candidates, the renegades mistakenly boycotted a deserving nominee, and the renegades supported another candidate of Murphy's, who then declined. Finally a sachem of Tammany who had some reputation for independence, Justice James A. O'Gorman, was put forward; the insurrection started to melt away; and, on Smith's and Wagner's assurance that there would be no reprisals against the renegades, Roosevelt pledged support to Murphy's candidate.

As usual with Roosevelt, a prodigious effort was deployed from the outset to represent the O'Gorman election as a tremendous and precocious victory. He had already mastered the technique he would eventually make famous of teasing and manipulating reporters: smilingly refusing to answer, putting partially truthful answers off the record, and answering questions with other questions.

All these skills were hurled into the fray on this occasion, with mixed results. To skeptics, the Sheehan affair was a fiasco. "Virtually every knowledgeable observer at the time . . . was convinced that the insurgency, so bravely sustained for so long, had in the end suffered ignominious defeat at the hands of the wily Murphy."[37] "Progressives within both parties soon became hazy about the outcome . . . They did remember that Sheehan had not been elected. Roosevelt began to say that he would have favored O'Gorman from the start, and Murphy was in no position to deny this."[38] Roosevelt even claimed credit for getting an Irish Catholic elected, and "the general impression grew that the insurgents had won. Eventually the smile passed completely from the [Tammany] tiger's face to Roosevelt." [39]

On balance, the fact that O'Gorman wasn't a huge qualitative leap forward from Sheehan wasn't as important as the fact that Franklin D. Roosevelt established in his first weeks that he was someone to be reckoned with. He cast his vote (in the Albany city hall, because fire had gutted the capitol) amid tumultuous heckling and the loud singing of the Tammany Hall anthem, but in the state and in the country he had established himself as a coming reformer worthy of his surname. He and his public relations machine would overwhelm the doubters and propagate the myth of "the Murphy surrender."[40] "The flag of truce was brought to me by Al Smith . . . and Bob Wagner. What a change has taken place!"[41] In one of these debates, Wagner said in the state senate, "Senator Roosevelt has made his point. What he wants is a headline in the newspapers. Let us proceed to our business."[42]

Roosevelt probably does deserve credit for a cameo role in securing the direct election of U.S. senators, the subject of the Seventeenth Amendment to the Constitution, which was adopted two years later and for which he was one of the local floor managers in the New York State Senate. This reform avoided repetitions of the Sheehan affair.

Franklin Roosevelt was often a rather bumptious freshman senator, regularly raising absurd objections to footling points and on one occasion managing to get himself physically ejected from the caucus, muttering chirpily about his talents as a pugilist at Groton (which was not true, as we have seen). According to Frances Perkins, a suffragette and labor lobbyist, he had an unfortunate manner of tossing his head and appearing to look down his nose at people through his pince-nez. He was, she thought, a somewhat unserious figure at this time: "his small mouth pursed up and slightly open, his nostrils distended, his head in the air, and his cool, remote voice saying: 'No, no, I won't hear of it!' "[43]

He was easy to underestimate, and only after he moved on to a greater office was it possible to realize how skillfully he had performed in his former role. Roosevelt loped about the state capitol, ignored by many, certainly not overly companionable, but, as it turned out, fixed constantly on all that might raise him up from this mundane place to the heights where he was sure he belonged. He wasn't as sure-footed as he later became at judging the mood of the times and of his colleagues. He waffled for some time about the right of women to vote; even though his wife and mother were opposed to it, he decided by 1912 that women should vote.

He alienated all sections of opinion on the issue of a new charter for New York City in 1911. The reform-minded mayor, William Gaynor, and Tammany Hall agreed on a new charter and promised Franklin Roosevelt a free ride in a safe congressional district if he would support them. He wobbled back and forth unbecomingly all summer before finally voting against. He outraged his opponents, who thought they had a commitment from him, and his reformist friends, who saw that he was somewhat resistless against temptation, though he had, ultimately, rejected the offer of a safe seat in the Congress.

On March 25, 1911, the infamous Triangle Shirtwaist Company fire, near Washington Square in New York City, killed 146 people, largely because there were no fire escapes and no fireproofing precautions. No one was prosecuted, and the owners of the building collected insurance payments of $65,000 while the families of the dead were rewarded with seventy-five dollars per corpse. It was one of the defining moments in the American urban reform movement. The state legislature created the New York Factory Commission, with Robert Wagner as chairman, Alfred E. Smith as vice chairman, and Frances Perkins as chief investigator. This commission poured forth reform bills over the next several years governing wages and hours, safety provisions in workplaces, improved building codes, the banning of child labor, and categories of workmens' compensation. One of the pivotal measures was a bill limiting women's and children's working hours to fifty-four per week. Tammany split as Murphy was induced by his rich friends to oppose it while Wagner and Smith led the charge in favor. Once again, Franklin Roosevelt's vote was important, and both sides laid siege to him.

Frances Perkins lobbied Roosevelt personally, but he refused her an interview in his most imperious and insolent manner, tossing his head back and claiming "Much more important things" (than to talk to her about this bill).[44] The bill passed on the vote and support of Big Tim Sullivan, one of the most corrupt of the Tammany politicians, but a warm-hearted man of the people in the better Tammany tradition. Roosevelt did not attend the session where the decisive vote was taken, but had his vote recorded for the bill in absentia and then set about his customary life-long task of rewriting history.

He ran for successively higher offices representing himself falsely as one of the fathers of this vital measure. He even claimed in the *Saturday Evening Post* in 1932 to have forced Sullivan to support the measure, and to have conducted a filibuster until the necessary votes were assembled—unmitigated falsehoods. He must have known how untruthful this posturing was, and ultimately rewarded Frances Perkins handsomely, both personally and in policy terms, but his initial response to this soul-wrenching issue had been, to say the least, pusillanimous.[45] Those who in later years would represent him as a radical champion of the left ignored how conservative, cautious, and at times ruthlessly opportunistic he was.

He now did grasp that he couldn't allow Tammany to get to the left of him and he did support all of the bills that emerged from the Wagner-Smith-Perkins commission. He learned that his natural allies would be an ever-shifting group of greatly varied social and cultural origins, constantly assembled and reassembled on the basis of current policy questions. The last vestiges of the gentleman-politician and dabbler were giving way to the emerging profound tactician who sought not just high office but the ability to implement a program that would make his incumbency memorable and benignly significant to posterity.

Yet he was not about to become a conviction politician either. He personally thought that banning sporting matches on Sunday was humbug, but voted to maintain a ban on Sunday baseball when an avalanche of constituents' mail came in against this desecration of the sabbath. As with some important issues that arose during his presidency, he didn't care either to defy or redirect the currents of public opinion. The one area where he put himself out at all in his first eighteen months was reforestation, which he managed slightly to promote, with a further tepid gesture toward public ownership of electricity—issues to which he would return in higher offices and on a grand scale.

On March 3, 1912, in a speech to the People's Forum at Troy, New York, Roosevelt attempted the most ambitious formulation to date of his social and political views. At that it was a rather muddled Hegelian perception that technological and demographic changes had created a requirement for the greater liberty of groups rather than exclusively of individuals. "Competition has been shown to be useful up to a certain point and no further." Beyond that point, "cooperation" would be necessary. Clearly the state would be required to encourage, if not impose, that degree of cooperation "for the liberty of the community," a concept that Roosevelt left fairly fuzzy. He seems not to have inspired much curiosity in the people of Troy, New York, but a glimmer of some of his future interventionist policies can be found in this address.[46]

At the recess of the New York State Senate in April 1912, Franklin and his brother-in-law, Hall Roosevelt, set out on a trip to the Panama Canal, where, at the request of Theodore Roosevelt, they were received like dignitaries by the chief constructor of the canal, George Washington Goethals. Franklin was awestruck by this great project, then nearly completed. It appealed to his naval interest, fired by reading the works of Admiral Mahan. And he loved the idea of remaking nature in grandiose and useful ways. He wrote home excitedly and returned on a number of occasions to the canal, which was always an inspiration as well as a reminder of his illustrious cousin and of his father's championship of the isthmian canal through Nicaragua.[47]

While this tour was under way and Eleanor was closing the Albany house and moving their family back to New York, R.M.S. *Titanic* struck an iceberg in the North Atlantic on her maiden voyage and foundered, with the loss of over fifteen hundred souls. Among these were many friends of the Roosevelts, such as John Jacob Astor IV, Rosy's brother-in-law, who left an estate of nearly $90 million to Franklin's young neighbor and life-long admirer, Vincent Astor. The Roosevelts had often travelled on the White Star Line, the ship's owner, and well knew the Ismays, who ran the line and had taken such good care of Franklin when he contracted typhoid fever aboard the *Adriatic* in 1889.

Returning to the United States at New Orleans, Franklin was greeted by Eleanor and the two set off on a motor trip to New Mexico to see Eleanor's best friend, Isabella Ferguson, and her husband, Bob, the Scottish former comrade-in-arms of Theodore Roosevelt, who was a severe tubercular case in search of dry air in New Mexico. Isabella's cheerfulness in coping with a practically hopeless medical crisis while raising young children was an inspiration to Eleanor, and would be much in her thoughts when severe medical misfortune came upon the Roosevelts nearly a decade later.

————————

This was a presidential election year, and Franklin Roosevelt was already a partisan of the governor of New Jersey and former president of Princeton University, Thomas Woodrow Wilson. A prodigious intellect and author, generally reckoned one of the country's most distinguished educators, Wilson had amassed an impressive reform record in a normally boss-ridden and corruptly governed state. Roosevelt strongly regretted that the Democratic Party had fallen under what he considered the Mephistophelian influence of William Jennings Bryan, who had run unsuccessfully as the party's candidate for president in 1896, 1900, and 1908.

Roosevelt thought Bryan a cranky, unworldly, demagogic western malcontent, more or less a one-issue candidate on the subject of silver coinage, and a Bible-thumping fundamentalist quack besides.

The Democrats had lost the last four elections and eleven of the last thirteen. Such a pattern didn't bode well for the fulfilment of Franklin's ambitions. Yet the Democrats' prospects were particularly enhanced by the gaping split in Republican ranks. Theodore Roosevelt was so disgusted at what he regarded as the plutocratic flabbiness of his chosen successor, William Howard Taft, that he was threatening to run as an independent candidate if he did not succeed in wresting the party nomination from Taft. He won the primaries and only the Republican bosses could stop him, by strangling the will of the party rank and file at the convention.

Franklin Roosevelt had already pledged his support to Wilson in the autumn of 1911, after being impressed with his progressive views in a lengthy interview and train trip to Trenton (New Jersey's capital) with Wilson and his secretary, Joseph Tumulty.[48] Wilson was originally put forward as governor of New Jersey by J.P. Morgan's partner, Colonel George Harvey, to take the Democratic Party away from Bryan and his followers. This tactic succeeded, but Wilson was neither as conservative nor as malleable as Harvey had hoped.[49]

Roosevelt had been working hard ever since on cracking open the New York delegation for Wilson. This was another uphill battle against the party bosses, because New York had a unit rule requiring that all the delegation's votes be cast as the majority decided. And Tammany Boss Charles Murphy, as Roosevelt had often had occasion to notice, controlled a permanent majority. Murphy had ensured that Roosevelt was not a delegate or alternate delegate at the Democratic National Convention in Baltimore in June 1912. But Roosevelt, undeterred by such inconveniences, had cobbled together, and set himself at the head of, a group of 150 agitators that he portentously called the New York State Wilson Conference.

At the Republican convention in Chicago, June 22, 1912, the party bosses, who had never liked Theodore Roosevelt and had accepted him as President McKinley's vice president in 1900 only to ward off the prairie wildfire of William Jennings Bryan, ignored TR's primary victories and renominated Taft. This was a stupefying error, since they must have known that Roosevelt would split the party and take most of the rank and file with him. This is exactly what happened. Never a man to understate matters, Theodore Roosevelt stalked out of the party saying, "We stand at Armageddon and we battle for the Lord." President Taft, less grandiloquently, had said: "I don't want to fight, but even a rat in a corner will fight."[50] If Roosevelt had encouraged the Wisconsin progressive Robert La Follette and stayed out of it himself, La Follette might have won and led a united Republican Party into the 1912 election.

The Democratic nomination, so often a doubtful prize since the Civil War, was now an almost certain ticket to victory, unless the inept Republican wheelhorses around Taft could find some way to placate Theodore Roosevelt, which they were little disposed to do, and which would have been a challenging task in any case.

Eleanor accompanied Franklin to the convention, the first for both of them, but was dismayed by the "lumpy" beds in their scruffy hotel beside a dark alley from which "the most unearthly sounds emanated."[51] Franklin and Eleanor had fairly good seats in the visitors' gallery but Franklin was constantly shaking hands, lobbying delegates, and leading pro-Wilson demonstrations with all the enthusiasm he had formerly reserved for the Harvard football team. Although she found the proceedings interesting, as she had found some of the policy issues in Albany interesting, Eleanor eventually concluded that she wouldn't be missed, left Baltimore, and gathered the children up for the summer at Campobello.

The convention became a battle between Wilson and the Speaker of the House of Representatives, Beauchamp "Champ" Clark of Missouri. A two-thirds majority was required for nomination. After the tenth ballot, Charles Murphy threw New York behind Clark, but this put him only barely in front of Wilson. Bryan, on the fourteenth ballot, finally abandoning hope of an unheard of (until the elevation of the young man from Hyde Park a generation later) fourth nomination as president, threw his support to Wilson. He held the convention spellbound as he so often had before, starting with his famous "Cross of Gold" speech, which had stampeded the 1896 convention toward him. Bryan declaimed that he could not support anyone who would accept the support of Tammany Hall or the Wall Street fat cats such as (the Roosevelts' friend and quasi in-law) August Belmont. That Tammany and Wall Street were generally mortal enemies and that Belmont despised Murphy as much as Bryan did was a subtlety too profound for the rabble-rousing Nebraskan. (Mrs. Belmont steamed majestically out of the convention in protest, which may have emboldened Eleanor, who was sitting near her, to make her exit.)[52]

The battle continued for thirty-two more ballots, but with Wilson steadily inching closer to the required majority. William Jennings Bryan, the thrice-chosen standard-bearer of his party always frustrated in his supreme ambition, was the decisive force in the elevation of Wilson. Incapable of election himself, he at least had the privilege of virtually naming the next president of the United States. (Theodore Roosevelt's son Kermit had bumped into Franklin on his way to Baltimore and told him that TR "was praying for Clark," to have the reform field of the electorate to himself.) By his unceasing efforts on Wilson's behalf, Franklin Roosevelt had significantly enhanced his political career.

While Eleanor was at Campobello, Franklin campaigned with great energy for renomination against the antagonism of the Murphy machine, which could make itself felt even in Poughkeepsie. He did prevail and was selected unanimously on August 24.

The Roosevelts were divided on the presidential election. Sara preferred Theodore to Wilson. Alice Longworth's husband was a congressman from Taft's home city of Cincinnati, Ohio, and owed Taft as much politically as he owed TR.

And though Theodore was philosophical about Franklin's candidacy as a Democrat and his support for Wilson, it opened a rift with other members of his family that would not heal until many elections and two world wars later.

Franklin's career suffered another severe jolt when he again contracted typhoid fever on the steamer that brought him and his family back from his short stay at Campobello. The ailment laid him low all through September. He despaired of holding his state senate seat if unable to campaign. Then one of the most improbable figures in modern American political history came to the rescue.

———

Louis McHenry Howe was the journeyman reporter for the *New York Herald* whose comments on the Sheehan affair have been mentioned. A native of Indianapolis who was brought up in the horse-racing community of Saratoga Springs, where his parents fled in the 1870s after a spectacular business failure, Howe was forty-two in 1912. Asthmatic, simian, small and stooped, with large ears and eyes, a bulbous nose, and poor complexion (aggravated by a bicycling accident that ground gravel into facial lesions), he had a permanently startled expression.

Howe was, to put it flatteringly, unprepossessing. A more complete physical and sociological contrast to Franklin D. Roosevelt could scarcely be found among white Americans. An exceedingly sickly youth, young Howe had to wear a supportive belt to prevent internal ruptures from his compulsive coughing. He left a girls' school near his parents' house (where he had been one of only two boys) to work at the *Saratoga Sun*, an uneconomic weekly newspaper his father had taken over in a tentative relaunch of his career. Howe joined his father in his little newspaper while still in his teens and supplemented his income by becoming a stringer for the *Herald*.

He took over the *Saratoga Sun* after his father had a nervous breakdown, but the paper was seized by its creditors in 1899. (The elder Howe died in 1908.) Howe worked for the new owner until fired by him and even then worked for him as a freelancer. He had married a girl from a good family in Fall River secretly in 1898, and then publicly the following year. They had three sons (one of whom died in infancy) and a daughter, but the marriage was a shambles as the couple quarrelled and separated for months at a time over decades.

Howe had an overbearing mother and an even more domineering mother-in-law. He was in fact a good reporter, wrote famously of Theodore Roosevelt's presidential inauguration in rural New York after the death of William McKinley, and became the Albany reporter for the *Herald* in 1906. He was an amusing and unforgettable figure whose high intelligence became clear only when people who met him rose above his absurd and ill-favored appearance. Because of his appearance and his ragged career he knew he could never fulfil his ambitions in a conventional progress through life, and sought instead to attach himself as a person of influence to someone whose political career could lift him as well.

For Howe Roosevelt was political love at first sight. Roosevelt, unaware that he needed anyone of Howe's talents, did not instantly requite his interest. Howe was the first Albany journalist to give Franklin Roosevelt serious favorable publicity, informally gave him tactical advice in the Sheehan affair, and did most of the work for Roosevelt and his allies in the so-called New York State Wilson Conference in 1912. He took to referring to FDR as a future president of the United States even before they got to Baltimore. Lurking beneath Howe's rumpled clothes and clouds of tobacco smoke was a tactical political genius. It was a "Damon and Pythias relationship."[53]

Effectively taking over Roosevelt's re-election campaign, Howe devised a series of initiatives to ingratiate the candidate with sections of his electorate. He and Roosevelt both assumed Wilson would win the White House and Roosevelt would leave the state senate and parachute himself into the administration, so delivering on all Howe's thoughtful munificences to Roosevelt's constituents was not a huge preoccupation.[54]

Howe spent a good deal of money on newspaper advertising and campaigned in person all around Roosevelt's district. When the Republican opponent, Jacob Southard, hauled out the old bugbear that Roosevelt was anti-Catholic, Howe arranged for some patronage for local Catholics, while Roosevelt wrote out a pompous letter, lauding himself, that he proposed to prevail upon someone to sign and send to one of the local newspapers. (Roosevelt thought better of this; he learned a lot, quickly, about the real world of politics from Howe.)[55]

On election day, Woodrow Wilson won easily against Theodore Roosevelt and President Taft, albeit with only about 42 percent of the vote. Franklin Roosevelt increased his majority, though he was in a three-party race, and ran ahead of Woodrow Wilson in the district. Howe transferred his allegiance formally to Roosevelt, and they would remain inseparable until Howe's death in 1936. Still unsteady in the aftermath of his illness, Roosevelt returned to Albany in January 1913 and was made chairman of the agriculture committee of the state senate, a position of some importance, but immediately began dickering for a position in the new federal administration.

Woodrow Wilson invited him to the New Jersey capital, Trenton, and the new Treasury secretary, William Gibbs McAdoo, offered him deputy secretary of the Treasury, and when that was declined, customs collector of the Port of New York, a position that some previous occupants had turned into a lucrative license to milk the huge traffic under its authority. It would certainly have enabled Roosevelt to build a base of influence that would provide an alternative to Tammany in New York, but he was already focused on national affairs and especially his life-long love of the navy.

It is not known whether he asked Wilson for a navy appointment, but the offer of the post of assistant secretary of the navy, which his cousin had held, was finally made by the secretary, Josephus Daniels, whom Franklin had met and impressed (especially by his dashing and patrician appearance) at the convention in Baltimore. (It was when they met that Daniels had introduced Roosevelt to McAdoo, then the party vice chairman but not yet Wilson's son-in-law, and to Tennessee congressman Cordell Hull, with whom Roosevelt would serve intimately in historic circumstances a generation later.)[56]

Daniels formally offered the appointment on inauguration day morning, March 4, in the lobby of the Willard Hotel in Washington. Roosevelt accepted with instant enthusiasm. (Senator Elihu Root, formerly TR's secretary of state, warned Daniels when consulted by him, "Whenever a Roosevelt rides, he wishes to be in front.") The Albany establishment and its Tammany supporters were happy to see Roosevelt go, as Robert Wagner made clear when they parted.

More perceptive people, including Theodore Roosevelt himself and Endicott Peabody (both of whom sent cordial letters of good wishes), saw the possibilities for the thirty-one-year-old Roosevelt in serving as deputy to a good-natured, paunchy, puritanical, languid North Carolina newspaper publisher with no maritime background but pacifist and isolationist leanings. Daniels, publisher of the *Raleigh News and Observer*, which he built into one of the most influential newspapers in the South, may have sought out Roosevelt precisely because he knew nothing of naval affairs and strategy and felt he could use some help from the bearer of the name of the greatest booster of the modern U.S. Navy. His term as assistant secretary of the navy would be the only time in his life that Roosevelt actually worked in a subordinate position to anybody. His Springwood, Groton, and Harvard talents at doing what he wanted while ingratiating himself with his elders would be reasserted. This time, he was no new boy or freshman. Josephus Daniels was nobody's fool either, but he was far from being an authority figure like Mr. James or Dr. Peabody to his assistant secretary.

Roosevelt's Groton roommate and best man at his wedding, Lathrop Brown, had been elected a Democratic congressman from Long Island, and Dr. Peabody wrote Roosevelt that with them "among our rulers, we are feeling very influential."[57]

III

FRANKLIN D. ROOSEVELT assumed his new position on St. Patrick's Day, 1913, his eighth wedding anniversary, and promptly wrote to his wife and then his mother on his impressive new official stationery.[58] His position required him to deal with procurement, supply, and civilian and land-bound personnel, while the secretary was responsible for the fleet, which at that time was the third in the world but a good deal smaller than the British Royal or even the Imperial German Navy. (Britain had 84 battleships and battlecruisers, including 35 modern battleships; compared, respectively, with Germany's 48 and 20 and the United States's 41 and 18. France, Japan, Italy, Russia, and Austria-Hungary trailed.) Yet the Great White Fleet that President Theodore Roosevelt had largely created and sent round the world in 1907, and strengthened by building the Panama Canal, was formidable. It counted in the geopolitical equations of all important countries, as the strategic mentor of both Roosevelts, Admiral Mahan, had written that it must.

Early in his appointment, Franklin was unable to resist the temptation, when Daniels was away, to quip that a Roosevelt was in charge and to remind people of the last time a Roosevelt was in charge of the Navy Department. (Teddy had positioned Admiral Dewey to attack the Spanish at Manila.) Eleanor, in one of her earlier known severe criticisms of Franklin, stirred perhaps by the comparison with her uncle and godfather, denounced this reflection as "horrid."[59]

In August 1913 the Mexican Civil War threatened to involve the United States directly, as Wilson mused publicly about "an orderly and righteous" government of Mexico while the factions there pillaged the entire country.[60] Franklin Roosevelt noisily announced that any major U.S. intervention would cause him to resign his post, organize a regiment of Rough Riders of his own, and proceed into combat as his cousin had done in the Spanish-American War (and was considering doing again).

Roosevelt seemed to think that his cousin had devised some magic formula for swift ascent of the political ladder to the presidency, and that all he needed to do was proclaim his surname and scramble through his cousin's career manual.

Wilson didn't intervene militarily in Mexico at this time, contenting himself with a posture of "watchful waiting," which irritated the Roosevelts as pious humbug but satisfied a national and official reticence about committing significant numbers of ground forces to an open-ended involvement in the unpromising cauldron of Mexico. The following year, in April 1914, while Franklin Roosevelt was on an inspection tour on the West Coast, three American sailors were briefly detained and the local U.S. commander—"not," as Howe wrote to Roosevelt, "a good watchful waiter"—demanded a grovelling apology and a ceremony of respect for the U.S. flag.[61] Wilson supported this, and after nineteen Americans were killed seizing the customs house at Vera Cruz on Daniels's orders, to prevent the importation of a boatload of arms and munitions from Germany, Franklin became a screeching war hawk charging around the Pacific Coast spewing out blood-curdling utterances. Wilson referred the controversy for arbitration by Argentina, Brazil, and Chile, and Daniels telegraphed his request that Roosevelt return to Washington. Even from his train on the way east, Franklin publicly predicted in Minneapolis that war was unavoidable, and in Chicago flirted with outright annexation of all of Mexico. The crisis swiftly subsided, and Roosevelt's eve of Agincourt purposefulness evaporated with it.[62]

———

Franklin settled into Washington officialdom and, with Eleanor, into Washington society. Eleanor dutifully delivered her calling card to the home of every significant official in the city. She received unannounced visitors in great variety on Wednesdays. Franklin designed a naval standard and a uniform (a dashing blue cape over a blue suit or a blue jacket and white trousers, depending on the season). He arranged for the battleship *North Dakota* to come to Campobello for the Fourth of July, and for the seventeen-gun salute to which he was entitled when he boarded.[63]

Roosevelt made many useful contacts. Among the young navy captains he encountered, who were quickly impressed with his knowledge of sailing and navigation, were future admirals William F. Halsey, William D. Leahy, Harold R. Stark, and Husband E. Kimmel. Roosevelt successfully wrote a letter of recommendation to Secretary of State Bryan on behalf of Sumner Welles, a fellow Grotonian (and a page at his wedding).[64]

Apart from Roosevelt, the Wilson administration was a pretty dour operation. The President and his wife were not at all gregarious. There were no inaugural balls and no social dinners at the White House, and Mrs. Wilson was commendably preoccupied with the poor of Washington, D.C., particularly the black poor. Even Eleanor found that the Wilsons' daughter, also named Eleanor, lacked "breeding"—not a lacuna she would often lament at any stage in her career.

The Roosevelts were more often than not with the residue of the TR era in Washington or with their own circle of ambitious contemporaries. Of Teddy's friends, the premier were the British ambassador, Sir Cecil Spring-Rice (composer of the hymn "I Pledge To Thee My Country"), the French ambassador, Jules Jusserand, and Senator Henry Cabot Lodge.[65] In their own group were the secretary of the interior, Franklin K. Lane; the third assistant secretary of state, William Phillips; Federal Reserve Board member Adolph Miller; and Assistant Secretary of the Treasury Charles Hamlin, whose wife was a childhood friend of Franklin's from Albany.[66]

Alice Roosevelt Longworth was still one of the capital's leading hostesses. Her husband, Nicholas Longworth, had been narrowly defeated in his congressional district in the debacle of the 1912 election. They returned to Cincinnati for a time, but when in Washington, though they both had numerous affairs and liaisons with other people, their marriage was a linchpin of Washington society in the earnest and sober Wilson years. Their parties were rollicking and well-lubricated, unlike Franklin and Eleanor's, which Alice considered rather staid, though she said that Franklin came visibly to life when Eleanor wasn't present. Franklin was a lively man at a party, and his reputation as a convivial lightweight was not alleviated by this stint in Washington, where his social life largely consisted of almost collegiate activity. There is no indication that anyone except Louis Howe (now FDR's secretary and special assistant, at the highest income he had ever earned) thought Franklin Roosevelt was likely to have a particularly brilliant future.

Josephus Daniels was not such a preposterous choice as secretary of the navy as he had first appeared, even though he regarded military ceremony as "flummery" and his wife had responded to his initial nomination with "hilarity."[67] The tremendous initial impression Roosevelt made on Daniels was not reciprocated, as Roosevelt thought his chief "the funniest looking hillbilly I had ever seen."[68] Daniels's father had been a naval carpenter and his brother-in-law had been the very first American fatality in the Spanish-American War. Daniels was a pacifist, a prohibitionist, and a white supremacist and arch-segregationist. But he was also a progressive opponent of the trusts and a man of unquestionable integrity.

He turned the U.S. Navy into a dry navy and altered nautical language and customs to be more democratic, accessible, and unceremonious. In strictly administrative terms, he was efficient. (FDR eventually concluded that the navy was better off not serving spirits while at sea. In his usual breezy disregard for the facts, he claimed the "credit" for this decree by Daniels, even though Louis Howe congratulated him at the time for being on a West Coast inspection trip when the decree was issued. Roosevelt himself generally ignored the "dry" decree when he was aboard a U.S. Navy ship, in his present and higher offices.)

While Daniels tickled some of Roosevelt's snobbish instincts, generally the younger man practiced what he had learned of successful subordinacy at Groton, and appreciated Daniels's better qualities. At Christmas 1913, Roosevelt gave his chief a framed photograph of a watercolor of a nineteenth-century American battleship, for which Daniels was deeply appreciative. "My most prized Christmas present," he wrote in his diary.[69] Roosevelt put on a strenuous pretense of enthused accord when Daniels lent a navy band to the renowned evangelist Billy Sunday during a prayer crusade in Washington.[70] Franklin and Eleanor even attended one of the revival sessions. Though they must have been culturally and theologically horrified, they were discreet.

In some of the most important aspects of his job, Daniels early won Roosevelt's thorough admiration. He lobbied Congress with unfailing assiduity and success, resisted the ant-like movements of the admirals to take away his authority and usurp his ability to decide departmental policy, and secured significant concessions from avaricious contractors. These were all areas that required high natural intelligence and considerable experience and Daniels was unfailingly capable in them.

When admirals, especially the secretary's aide for operations, Admiral Bradley Fiske, attempted to appeal to the White House over Daniels, Wilson forbade the relevant committee to meet again without his approval. (After a particularly difficult session with the admiral, Daniels and Roosevelt were on their way back to Washington by train from Annapolis, and Daniels commended to Roosevelt as uniquely true a well-known automotive rubber company's message on a billboard they passed. It read: "Fisk Tires.")[71] Roosevelt learned from Daniels a good deal about how the federal government worked and about the interaction between the president, department heads, service chiefs, and congressional leaders.

He himself became a mercilessly hard bargainer on behalf of the federal government, as the young financier Joseph Kennedy would discover at their first substantive encounter, in 1917. Kennedy refused, on behalf of Charles Schwab, chairman of Bethlehem Steel Corporation, to release ships built for Argentina until Bethlehem was paid. Roosevelt amiably said that in that case the Navy Department would have to take them and leave Bethlehem to collect its receivable from Argentina itself. Kennedy assured Schwab this was a bluff. A few days later, navy tugs arrived carrying marines, who shooed the Bethlehem personnel from the ships, which they removed and delivered to the waiting Argentinians. Roosevelt was unfailingly polite throughout, and Kennedy revised his opinion of him from another overindulged Harvard rich man's son to "the hardest trader I've ever run against." Kennedy, always as combative as a bantam rooster, later admitted: "I broke down and cried."[72] President Wilson himself had dinner on the Argentinian battleship *Moreno* before she sailed.[73]

With the guidance of Louis Howe, Roosevelt also acquainted himself with the concerns of organized labor regarding dealings with the Navy Department, and was popular with the union representatives who were constantly visiting. His visits to ships, which were astonishingly frequent and conducted with great and unfeigned enthusiasm, were always morale-raisers. Roosevelt's love of the navy was evident to and always appreciated by the officers and men he met.

Howe tended to the political aspects of the job in the assistant secretary's home state of New York. His manipulative aptitudes flourished with each augmentation of his status. He virtually mesmerized the assistant postmaster general, Daniel Roper (whose credulity would not go unrewarded), and took over the awarding of postal jobs in New York. He even intruded on the competitive examination process for job candidates in a manner that would have scandalized Wilson had he been aware of it.

Roosevelt and Howe set about building an organization of their own, thinking of a return to New York electoral politics in 1914, with Franklin running either for governor or U.S. senator. Their attempt to have Roosevelt loyalist Mayor John Sague of Poughkeepsie named customs collector of New York, the supreme spigot of patronage that Roosevelt had declined when Wilson offered it to him just a year before, was spiked by Wilson's Svengalian confidant, Colonel Edward Mandel House. House was spooked when Tammany shrieked like a wounded animal at Roosevelt's skulduggery.[74]

Roosevelt and Howe had never stopped conniving from Washington to take over and strengthen the anti-Tammany forces in New York. Roosevelt appealed to President Wilson to appoint him as the President's agent to cleanse the New York Democrats, but Wilson responded with his usual recipe of "watchful waiting."

Tammany had impeached and removed Governor William Sulzer, who had taken his claims of independence from the machine too seriously, and selected the docile Martin Glynn as its candidate for the gubernatorial nomination in 1914. Howe floated a story that the President had asked Roosevelt to run for the nomination against Glynn, which FDR then denied with great unctuousness.

(To Glynn himself, who didn't believe a word Roosevelt wrote about it, he referred to the source of the rumor as an "inspiring idiot" and to the suggestion that he would "under any circumstances" be a candidate for governor as "absolutely mistaken.")[75] In March 1914, Roosevelt asked if the President would see him for an article the *New York World* had asked him to write about the unfolding New York political scene. Wilson could not spare the time but advised him in a note to resist the electoral temptation.[76]

Roosevelt's star was rising, more through Howe's feverish efforts than from any general recognition of his surging merit. But to his political elders in the Wilson inner circles in New York and Washington, the thirty-two-year-old Franklin Roosevelt was like an over-energetic child or family dog. The state party chairman, William Osborn, a former patron of Roosevelt's, undoubtedly had him in mind when he referred to "self-appointed little busybodies" in Washington.[77] Wilson was moved to make a tepidly pro-Tammany statement. Roosevelt's antics were traditional for ambitious young politicians, unsubtle and slightly irksome, but were not unpardonable and possessed a vital force that could not simply be ignored.

Franklin Roosevelt now made perhaps the most inexplicable error of his political career, in deciding at the last moment to run in the Democratic primary for U.S. senator from New York. He was encouraged to make the race by Secretary of the Treasury William Gibbs McAdoo, who was generally favorable to Roosevelt and whose sponsorship Roosevelt mistakenly took as indicative of the views of McAdoo's father-in-law, as Wilson became in May 1914. Though McAdoo never implied any such thing, Roosevelt inferred that the President would endorse him and that Tammany was incapable of putting up a reputable candidate. Howe hoped for William Randolph Hearst, the flamboyant newspaper publisher, who he thought would be easy to defeat as an irresponsible fat cat. Roosevelt also hoped for support from TR's aggrieved Progressives.

Roosevelt was at Campobello in July 1914, about to leave for the ceremonies opening the Cape Cod Canal, when he learned that Austria-Hungary had declared war on Serbia, which was guaranteed by Russia, which would likely bring France and Germany into the hostilities. He proceeded through the night from Cape Cod to Washington "like Paul Revere," as he said.[78] He was astounded by the lethargic atmosphere in the U.S. government, punctuated only by hand-wringing from Josephus Daniels and Secretary of State William Jennings Bryan. These men, wrote Roosevelt, were motivated by the collapse of their pacifistic "idealistic nonsense."[79] Roosevelt was particularly amused that Bryan didn't know the difference between a battleship and a gunboat. ("Roosevelt," he said, "after this, when I talk about battleships don't think I mean anything technical."[80] In fact, there wasn't much for the U.S. government to do.

Affairs were further immobilized by the impending death of the President's wife from cancer. She died on August 6, and FDR feared that Wilson might suffer "a breakdown."[81] Wilson absorbed the heavy news (they had been married twenty-nine years) with his customary dignity.

Hearst didn't run, and the Tammany candidate was the distinguished former U.S. ambassador to Germany, James W. Gerard. Roosevelt was "not yet willing to believe that [Murphy] can drag Gerard away from important duties to make him a respectable figurehead for a bad ticket."[82] Gerard sought guidance from Bryan and Wilson. Bryan, with McAdoo and Colonel House, favored Roosevelt, but Tumulty and the attorney general, James McReynolds, were for Gerard. Wilson declined to intervene, and Gerard left Berlin early in the war and made the race. The Roosevelt campaign started late, was not run with Howe's usual efficiency, and failed to ignite any enthusiasm from the Progressives or anyone else. Gerard won by a popular margin of three to one, with Roosevelt carrying only one-third of New York's sixty-six counties. Roosevelt, as always following unpleasant developments that reflected on his own performance, professed total unconcern and personal blamelessness.

The lesson that emerged from the primary election and from the easy Republican victory of James Wadsworth over Gerard in the general election in November was that an upstate reformer couldn't wrest a state-wide nomination from Tammany and that Tammany couldn't win against the Republicans, even with a respectable candidate, without the support of the upstate Democratic reformers. In the general election campaign, roles were reversed, as Roosevelt ignored the urgings of Colonel House, relayed by McAdoo and Daniels, to endorse Gerard.

Roosevelt was a federal commissioner of the Panama-Pacific Exposition in San Francisco in March 1915. Daniels had initially invited naval participation from many countries (including the Swiss, not being very familiar with European geography), but the war required that the proposed international armada be cancelled.

Wilson's representative at San Francisco was his diminutive vice president, Thomas R. Marshall, immortalized in American history for his comment "What this country needs is a good five-cent cigar." Marshall was dwarfed by his overbearing wife and was a droll master of self-deprecation and understatement. The Roosevelts traveled to San Francisco with the Marshalls. At one point, as the train approached the Rocky Mountains, Marshall was prevailed upon to observe the looming mountain peaks from the observation car. He gazed at them momentarily, drew on his cigar, and declared: "I never did like scenery," and returned to the parlor car.[83]

Roosevelt's illustrious cousin continued to attract immense public attention. In October 1913, TR had gone on a challenging trip up the Amazon, "my last chance to be a boy," he called it. He infected a leg, lost thirty-five pounds, and was dogged thereafter by tropical diseases. The trip almost certainly shortened TR's life, which foiled his ultimate plan for a return as president. He campaigned for Progressive candidates in the 1914 congressional election, unsuccessfully. Not wishing to complicate Franklin's life, he thoughtfully declined Sara's offer to stay in Springwood while barnstorming the area.

In the spring of 1915 Franklin Roosevelt was delighted to be able to repay some of the great kindness Theodore Roosevelt had always shown to Eleanor and to him. TR was accused of defamation in Syracuse for likening the Republican boss in Albany and party state chairman, William J. Barnes, to Tammany boss Charles Murphy. The respondent had great difficulty getting credible witnesses to testify against the two parties' respective machine bosses by giving evidence of the collusion between them, but Franklin was able to give testimony about Barnes's apparent arrangements with Murphy in the Sheehan affair. He gave his evidence well, and Barnes's counsel totally failed to shake him. TR, undoubtedly helped by Franklin's testimony, won the case. The former and future presidents exchanged warm letters of congratulation. "I shall never forget [your] capital . . . testimony and the impression upon the jury," the elder man wrote.[84]

The court case was complicated by the sinking by a German submarine, on May 7, 1915, in the middle of the trial, of the Cunard liner *Lusitania*, with the loss of 1,200 lives, including 128 Americans. Theodore Roosevelt immediately demanded a U.S. declaration of war against Germany, despite the presence of two German-born jurors in his case.

———————

Franklin Roosevelt, who had periodically agitated for war with Mexico as a consolation for absence from the main event, had believed from the start of the world war that the United States must take the side of the Allies or face the prospect of being dangerously threatened by a militant and rampaging Germany. Despite the naval and merchant rivalry of his Yankee relatives and ancestors with the British, all his sympathies were with the British and the French. The Roosevelts' nanny had three brothers in the British army, and the whole Roosevelt family heard of their perils and exploits at the front.[85]

(The nanny's charges now included a third son, FDR Jr., born in the summer of 1914 and replacing the child of the same name who had died in infancy in 1909. Their last child, John Aspinwall Roosevelt, would be born in March 1916. Franklin would then have sired as many children as Theodore and fulfilled the desire he expressed to Alice Sohier during their unsuccessful courtship in 1902, which she described as requiring her to become "a cow.")

There was by 1916 an ambiance of war hysteria, at least in the eastern part of the country. When a fire flared up at Springwood from the materials of some artisans doing the remodelling work that separated the Roosevelts' bedrooms and caused $200 damage, the *New York Times* solemnly announced, without any evidence, that this was the work of German saboteurs seeking revenge on the pro-British assistant secretary of the navy.[86]

Roosevelt was terribly disappointed with President Wilson's statement on May

10, 1915, three days after the sinking of the *Lusitania,* that a man could be "too proud to fight." Wilson personally favored the British and French and considered the Germans dangerous militarists, but thought even intellectual neutrality to be his moral duty.

In 1915, 1916, and 1917, Roosevelt would remain within the administration, though profoundly opposed to the Wilson-Bryan-Daniels pacifist views; would work secretly with his cousin, the government's most formidable domestic adversary; and would do all he could while retaining his official post to further the participationist cause. TR, no mean source of partisan invective, called William Jennings Bryan a "yodeler . . . a human trombone" and Wilson a "logothete . . . a real sophist," the worst president since Buchanan, a "silly doctrinaire . . . neither a gentleman nor a real man." Wilson, though a cold and inaccessible intellectual, was a formidable polemicist himself, and accused his opponents of being "nervous and excited" and of seeking to turn the United States into an "armed camp."

Privately Franklin Roosevelt was even exasperated at the reluctance of the German Navy to give battle to the Royal Navy, which blockaded it. The Germans encountered the British in a full fleet action only once, at Jutland in 1916, an immense but indecisive engagement, following which the German High Seas Fleet returned to port for the duration of the war.

Roosevelt secretly fed information to TR and his principal allies, Senator Henry Cabot Lodge and the latter's son-in-law, Congressman Augustus Gardner, chairman of the House Military Affairs Committee after 1916. When he testified before Gardner's committee Roosevelt did an artful job of seeming to support the administration of which he was a member. But subtly, he also reinforced, over five hours of testimony, his previously expressed concerns about the shortfall of manpower, which Daniels had already asked him to clarify publicly. He dazzled the committee with his grasp of massive detail and ability to bury questioners in a cascade of statistics and precise information.[87]

The increased attention the Great War focused on the navy assisted Roosevelt in his objective to become a noteworthy national political personality. And his physical appearance had lost the delicacy that Alice Longworth and others had mocked. He had filled out and had become an impressive-looking man in his mid-thirties.

Franklin D. Roosevelt had already developed many of the unique political skills he would display at the most critical moments of his career. Yet it says something for the liberality of Wilson and Daniels that they never turned on him throughout these very tense years, when the administration was regularly the victim of indiscretions to the press from insiders and when FDR must have been, with good reason, a prime suspect. They were well aware of his social friendship with Gardner and Lodge, and they could scarcely be unaware of his relations with his famous cousin.

As the hatred deepened between Theodore Roosevelt and Woodrow Wilson, the nation's two leading politicians and both generally reckoned to be outstanding presidents, Franklin Roosevelt found himself under increasing pressure from both. His loyalties and sympathies were entirely with his cousin, but his career required that he not burn his bridges with the president he served.

William Jennings Bryan abruptly resigned as secretary of state a month after the sinking of the *Lusitania*, in June 1915, because he thought Wilson's policy was not really neutral in that it did not condemn the British naval blockade of Germany as vehemently as the German use of submarine warfare around the British Isles. (This was a silly view, not only because of the legitimate American preference for an Allied victory, but because the British blockade did not lead to the sinking of any significant number of ships nor to the death of more than a very few civilians, and was therefore hardly comparable to German submarine warfare.)

Franklin Roosevelt was delighted to see the back of Bryan, whom he considered an absurd figure and a menace in foreign policy. Neither Roosevelt nor anyone else was much impressed with Bryan's successor, Robert Lansing, though Roosevelt was personally friendly with him, and his conduct at official functions was less buffoonish than Bryan's. (The venerable Nebraskan had never taken the trouble to acquaint himself with any of the requirements of protocol.) Roosevelt was also pretty scathing about Daniels's jeremiads, though even Daniels conceded that the United States couldn't continue indefinitely "negotiating by notes and more notes [of protest delivered to the combatants]."[88]

Roosevelt suffered a burst appendix at the beginning of July 1915 and Daniels generously sent him on the secretary of the navy's yacht to Campobello, where he convalesced for five weeks. Once back at his desk, Roosevelt took it upon himself, without consulting his chief, to set up a naval reserve of 50,000 and squadrons of power boats, many of them provided by FDR's yachting friends. Daniels expressed no irritation at not having been consulted. He approved of the reserve. With any less indulgent a boss, Roosevelt would have had a very difficult tenure.

In February 1916, six months after Bryan's resignation, the secretary of war, Lindley Garrison, and the assistant secretary, Henry Breckinridge, resigned for the opposite reason to Bryan's. They did not think the President adequately determined in the matter of military preparedness, and dissented from this refusal to seek universal conscription. This too was a lesson that Franklin Roosevelt, who advocated conscription but not publicly, would remember. (His own equally strong disagreement with the President didn't seem to cause him for a moment to consider resigning; he would remain and advance the cause surreptitiously.)

Roosevelt undoubtedly hoped to succeed Garrison and was happy when it was suggested in the press that Wilson might ask him. But the post went instead to the mayor of Cleveland, Newton D. Baker, and there is no reason to believe that FDR was seriously considered.

He did enjoy a success when Wilson proposed and the Congress established the Council of National Defense in August 1916, which Roosevelt had proposed a year before. This proved a very effective agency, which recruited some of America's outstanding experts from various walks of life to assist in preparedness and in every aspect of national defense and related fields. Among the early star recruits was Herbert Hoover, who in April 1917 became chairman of a committee on food supply and prices. From there he graduated to supervision of food distribution in war-torn Europe.

———

The separation of the Roosevelts in the summer of 1916 was longer than usual, almost four months, because there was an epidemic of infantile paralysis that afflicted 27,000 people in the Northeast and made it necessary to keep the children away from any possible exposure to the disease. It was an election year, and Franklin Roosevelt was much in demand. However inconstant his true devotion to his president, he was a preparedness advocate and a Roosevelt and highly valued by the Democratic Party strategists.

He campaigned extensively for Wilson around the country, not returning to Campobello to collect his family until almost the end of September, again in the secretary's official yacht, the *Dolphin*. The commander of the vessel, William D. Leahy, remembered the homeward journey to New York as a nightmare because of the undisciplined antics of the Roosevelt children—"brats," he would call them thirty-two years later.[89]

Wilson ran as a preparedness advocate, but a man of peace. "He kept us out of war" was the party's effective slogan, although Wilson privately acknowledged that any "little German lieutenant can put us into war at any time by some calculated outrage." Wilson ran an intelligent campaign based on the promise of peace through strength.

The Republican candidate, Charles Evans Hughes, a distinguished jurist and former governor of New York (who had defeated William Randolph Hearst for that office in 1906), proved not to be a particularly strong campaigner. Hirsute but impeccable, Hughes had been described by Theodore Roosevelt, who was annoyed that Hughes didn't testify for him in the Barnes trial, as "the bearded lady."[90] Hughes started out surpassing Wilson in evasiveness about neutrality, but under pressure from Theodore Roosevelt, Lodge, and others, began to tilt toward the Allies, while still pledging to stay out of war. He was trying to suck and blow at the same time, and Wilson was too clever to let him off lightly. Mindful of the fact that he had had only 42 percent of the vote in the three-party fight of 1912, Wilson tried to outflank the Progressives and cast a wide net in a more artful manner than Hughes, but it was a close election all through the autumn.

Despite Hughes's shortcomings as a candidate, Wilson was an underdog, because of the long Republican advantage that had prevailed since the Civil War. Franklin Roosevelt was hurled into the breach constantly, and on one occasion his partisan enthusiasm caused him to attack his cousin's record on naval preparedness. This was an inexplicable and ungracious blunder. TR wrote gently to Franklin about it when he returned from a Caribbean holiday, where he had been when the ill-considered volley was launched. Franklin apologized abjectly in writing, but not in public. Franklin had more success exchanging fire with Hughes on navy matters. The lack of rapport between these two was not new and did not stop here.

On election night, Hughes, Wilson, and Franklin Roosevelt all concluded that the Republicans had won. Roosevelt left his party's New York headquarters at midnight to catch the last train to Washington, assuming that he would shortly be returning to the private sector. Hughes had carried most of the eastern states, but Wilson gained fairly steadily as the results moved westwards. It was widely believed that Hughes made a catastrophic error when he was campaigning in California by conspicuously ignoring the state's leading politician, U.S. Senator Hiram W. Johnson. Hughes was cool toward Johnson because he had been Theodore Roosevelt's Progressive candidate for vice president in 1912. The California Progressives did not migrate back to the Republicans in adequate numbers, and Wilson narrowly won the state and the election, the first presidential election decided in California.

A very early caller to Hughes's home on the morning after the election, when informed by the candidate's son that the President-elect was asleep, responded that when he woke up it would be appropriate to tell the President-elect that he had lost the election.[91] Wilson won the popular vote 9.13 million to 8.54 million for Hughes, who only conceded November 22, two weeks after the election. Hughes's congratulations, Wilson recounted, arrived "a little moth-eaten, but quite legible."[92]

Franklin D. Roosevelt, by working hard and effectively for the party's victory, had earned Wilson's gratitude. Memorable chapters remained to be written in Roosevelt's relations with many people he had encountered in this first term in official Washington, including William McAdoo, Cordell Hull, Joseph Kennedy, William D. Leahy, Newton D. Baker, James McReynolds, and Charles Evans Hughes.

IV

ROOSEVELT SENT WILSON a memorandum written by James Monroe when he was secretary of state in 1814, warning that excessive endurance of provocations from European powers merely makes their ultimate redress more difficult. Shortly before Christmas, and following a German offer to negotiate peace, Wilson had proposed a negotiated peace and expressed readiness to consider the formation of a "league of nations to insure peace and justice throughout the world." He offered his services as a mediator between the warring powers. Germany declined, preferring direct talks with its enemies.

After great public enthusiasm in the United States for the President's position, William Borah, beginning a twenty-five year struggle in the Senate against any "foreign entanglements" of the kind he believed the Founding Fathers had abjured, attacked the proposal. Theodore Roosevelt and Henry Cabot Lodge, having initially supported the President's initiative, changed course, presumably motivated in part by their personal animosity for Wilson, and warned against surrender of any sovereignty in TR's case and against activity outside the American hemisphere in Lodge's.

On the day of Lodge's address to the Senate deserting Wilson, January 3, 1916, Colonel House found Wilson emboldened by the hostility of Lodge and Borah to spell out the peace terms he thought appropriate. Wilson prepared a speech, which he delivered January 22, calling for "a peace without victory," because "only a peace between equals can last." He called for a community rather than a balance of power, and the extension of the Monroe Doctrine throughout the world as a guarantee of non-intervention by countries in the affairs of other countries. He was apparently inspired by the success of the War of 1812, not as combat, but as a stalemate that had led to over a century of peace between the United States and Great Britain. His idealistic notions inspired many, were greeted with cynicism by some, and were seen as vainglorious, cowardly, and politically suicidal by his domestic opponents, scarcely recovered from their narrow electoral defeat in 1916.

Wilson's great electoral peace-and-preparedness straddle barely stretched through the election period. It was not "a little German lieutenant" but the German emperor himself who posed the act of "calculated outrage" Wilson had feared, by the adoption on February 1, 1917, of a policy of unrestricted submarine warfare. The kaiser, Wilhelm II, thus committed one of the most colossal military and strategic blunders in the history of the world.

While the Hohenzollern emperor was contemplating the decision that would cost him the war and his throne and the future of his dynasty, the U.S. assistant secretary of the navy was assembling an inspection trip to Haiti and the Dominican Republic, both of which were under occupation by the U.S. Marines, as well as to Cuba. In 1915, the gruesome murder of the president of Haiti following his massacre of 167 political opponents had motivated Wilson to send in marines for fear the Europeans might otherwise construe it as their business to do so. The Dominican Republic was seized, in circumstances only slightly less disorderly, in 1916. Daniels was very uneasy with this unsought imperialism, unlike his assistant secretary, who, whatever his reservations then and subsequently about the British Empire, was an enthusiastic advocate of having American protectorates wherever there was the slightest justification for them.

Roosevelt's preferred winter holiday was finally approved by Daniels, and he set out on a destroyer for Havana with a few cronies. Unfortunately, the mayor of New York, John P. Mitchell, whom FDR invited and in whom he doubtless saw political possibilities, was unable to spare the time. Havana was more or less of a club crawl in elaborate tropical formal wear, leading to tenacious hangovers. The spirit of the trip was of Harvard alumni reliving their peppier undergraduate days.

Franklin's adoring Harvard friend Livingston Davis, now an underworked Boston stockbroker living off the avails of a rich marriage and his college tie, set a challenging bacchanalian pace.

The party attended upon the president of Cuba, about whom Franklin wrote encouraging things to his superiors, though he had waded through blood to his position. The challenges to him in the next few weeks were so severe that Wilson, who unlike the Roosevelts was genuinely reluctant to do so, felt compelled to send in the marines there, too, to restore and maintain order. The Roosevelt party went by train to Santiago in the private car of the Cuban railways chairman, Benny Van Horne, son of the legendary founder of the Canadian Pacific Railway, Sir William Cornelius Van Horne, who had been a friend of Roosevelt's father.

Roosevelt and his friends moved on by destroyer to Haiti, where in Port-au-Prince harbor the entire U.S. Atlantic Fleet of seventy-two ships, in festive rigging, was present in two rows, ready for the assistant secretary's review. As his destroyer proceeded down the channel between the two lines, each ship fired a seventeen-gun salute in Roosevelt's honor. It was a bracing moment for the thirty-four-year-old FDR. He went with his entourage to the president of Haiti's palace and repeated the little address, in French, that he had rehearsed and already rendered to the welcoming party and then to the mayor.[93]

The American marine commander, General Smedley D. Butler, was a vintage proconsul, winner of the Congressional Medal of Honor and a fierce veteran of many campaigns in primitive Latin American places, whose name for generations afterwards was bandied about by native mothers to frighten their children. He regarded the locals, including the president of the country, as "niggers, coons, and gooks." When Butler seized the president by the collar to permit Roosevelt to enter the official car first, Roosevelt raised his top hat and urged President Dartiguenave to enter the car first, addressing him as "Excellence" in his confident "Roosevelt French," to Butler's disconcertion.[94]

The inspection tour continued on for a four-day horseback ride into the interior, with Roosevelt in a marine uniform and tall in his finest Hyde Park saddle leading a single file that included Butler and 50 of his marines and 150 of his trained Haitian militia. According to Roosevelt there was frequent gunfire in the distance and occasionally overhead in the bandit-infested jungles, but no one else on the trip remembered any gunfire, and this is probably Roosevelt's usual embellishment.[95]

The party was happy to be observed swimming in the altogether by a large group of voyeurs and exhibitionists and admiring native women, all performing their roles with exquisite composure and deliberateness.[96] Roosevelt's thirty-fifth birthday, January 30, 1917, was celebrated on this leg of the trip. Roosevelt was so impressed by the tour Butler gave him of the fortress where he had suppressed the local brigands (armed by the Germans) who had reduced the country to chaos that he unsuccessfully nominated the general for a second Medal of Honor. (When he ultimately failed to become commandant of the Marine Corps, Butler would claim that he had spent his life in Mexico, Cuba, Nicaragua, Haiti, the Dominican Republic, and ultimately China as the unwitting dupe of avaricious American bankers and traders, a line happily quoted for the rest of the twentieth century by America's leftist enemies.)

This visit to Haiti had a profound impact on Roosevelt. In 1943 he even would compare his attitude toward the forlorn Caribbean country to Queen Mary I's attachment to Calais: "When I die I think that 'Haiti' is going to be written on my heart, because for all these years I have had the most intense interest in the Republic of Haiti."[97]

When the group moved on by ship to the Dominican Republic, Franklin was recalled to Washington (by a message in a code he had devised and shared with Daniels and Howe) because of a political crisis that he surmised meant the imminence of war with Germany.

But there was still a last, excruciating suspensive period. Two days after the Germans announced that they would sink any ship of any nationality en route to any Allied port, they sank the American ship *Housatonic*. This was the day Roosevelt was recalled from the Dominican Republic (February 3, 1917). On that day Wilson informed the Congress that he had severed diplomatic relations with Germany. Gerard was recalled from Germany, and the German ambassador was expelled. The final extremity before war had been reached.

With Daniels out of Washington, Roosevelt asked to see the President and requested that Wilson authorize him to recall the Atlantic Fleet from Guantanamo Bay and prepare it for a war emergency. Wilson declined even to do that, saying to Roosevelt that the United States must "come into the court of history with clean hands."[98]

Both principal Roosevelts were now disgusted. Wilson told Daniels, whose dismissal was widely demanded by the hawkish press, that "The Junkerthurm . . . [is] trying to creep in under cover of the patriotic feeling of the moment." Franklin Roosevelt, through Louis Howe, encouraged a press campaign calling for the sacking of Daniels and his replacement by the "virileminded, hard-fisted" assistant secretary (the *Chicago Post*), while piously pledging public and private allegiance to his chief. Roosevelt even wrote to fellow Grotonian "Bert" McCormick, the proprietor of the *Chicago Tribune*, implying impatience at the administration's shilly-shallying and urging a naval rearmament editorial line.[99]

In his inaugural address on March 5, Wilson spoke of "armed neutrality" and then further disappointed his assistant secretary of the navy by reviewing the inaugural parade from "a glass cage" that protected him from the wind. Roosevelt, sitting in the elements behind his leader, considered this conduct unbecoming a commander in chief. He advised his tenant in his New York house, Thomas Lamont, that he might be returning to New York, which is plausibly

cited as evidence that he was finally considering retiring in protest from the government.[100] On inauguration evening Roosevelt called on Colonel House, the
President's closest advisor and an advocate of participation in the war. Then (in
the White House) and five days later when they met in New York, Roosevelt told
House unflattering things about the lack of preparedness of the navy and the general lassitude of Josephus Daniels.[101] House had been urging Wilson to dump
Daniels, and Roosevelt was happy to provide more ammunition.

On inauguration day, a bill of Wilson's authorizing the arming of merchant
ships had been filibustered to death by midwestern isolationists led by Robert M.
La Follette and including, to Roosevelt's particular irritation, New York's O'Gorman, whom Roosevelt had helped to elect over Tammany's William Sheehan.
The President (who less than a month before had refused to recall the fleet from
Cuba at FDR's urging) called them "a little group of wilful men" and then
awarded himself the power to order the arming of merchantmen.

Wilson had resented Britain's naval blockade much more than he made public. He felt it had narrowed his options and, combined with German bellicosity,
had placed the United States on a conveyer belt that would dump it into the war
he sought to avoid. He knew Bryan's equivocation between the unequal provocations of the Germans and the British was nonsense, but came to consider the
naval buildup Roosevelt had been clamoring for as desirable. He thought such a
buildup would be almost a second Declaration of Independence. Wilson even
exasperatedly said to his grey eminence, Colonel House, on September 24, 1916:
"Let us build a navy bigger than Britain's and do what we please." By March of
1917, this was both a churlish and an impractical sentiment. In fact, the British
would not have prevented American shipping from going to German ports if Wilson had made it an issue of war and peace as Madison had a century earlier. In
the intervening century, the power of the United States had increased from
insignificance to decisive control of the balance of power between the Allied and
Central powers.

On the same day as his meeting in New York with House (March 11, 1917),
Franklin Roosevelt had dinner at the Metropolitan Club with his leader's most
mortal enemies: Theodore Roosevelt, General Leonard Wood, former secretary
of state Elihu Root, J.P. Morgan Jr., and the mayor of New York, John P. Mitchell,
among others.[102] This was a tour de force of conspiracy by a young and relatively
junior, if well-connected, government official whom many persisted in considering a lightweight for another fifteen years. The two Roosevelts were the most pugnacious warmongers in this group, which determined to increase pressure on the
administration in various ways.

Franklin Roosevelt returned to Washington and found Josephus Daniels as
mournfully dilatory as ever. There were gloomy meetings about implementing
the arming of merchant vessels. And Roosevelt was exasperated by Daniels's
refusal to order American captains to fire on German submarines on sight, given
that German orders were now to sink any shipping that appeared to be destined

for Allied ports. In practice this would be all shipping, since the British blockade of Germany was impenetrable. Another American ship was torpedoed and sunk on the twelfth.

On the ides of March, Czar Nicholas II abdicated in favor of Prince Georgy Lvov's provisional government. Wilson was relieved, because now if the United States entered the war he would not be making common cause with a notorious despotism. Russia's war-making abilities were clearly almost exhausted, but Wilson greeted the news from there with almost pathetic euphoria.

The German emperor would have been on the verge of victory, or at least of a satisfactory peace, if he hadn't provoked the United States to enter the war against him. On March 18, 1917, three more American ships were sunk. On the twentieth Wilson consulted his cabinet. Daniels was asked last, after all nine of his colleagues had told the President there was now no alternative to asking Congress for a declaration of war. On the verge of tears, feeling himself, as he subsequently wrote, "at a Gethsemane," Daniels concurred that there was now no choice but war.[103]

President Wilson finally gave the Congress his war address on the evening of April 2, 1917. It was one of American history's dramatic moments, full of portents and ironies. Daniels and Roosevelt sat immediately in front of Wilson in the places traditionally reserved at presidential addresses to the Congress for the cabinet, the Supreme Court, and the chiefs of staff of the armed forces. The Speaker of the House, Champ Clark, who introduced Wilson, would have been the president himself if he had not been deserted at the convention in Baltimore by William Jennings Bryan, who had deserted Wilson too, because Bryan thought him insufficiently peace-loving.

The President was dressed in black and appeared even more gaunt than usual. The power of his intellect, idealism, and articulation silenced his critics among both the war hawks and the pacifists, and stirred the nation. He recounted all he had done to keep the country out of war. Then: "We will not choose the path of submission and suffer the most sacred rights of our Nation and our people to be ignored or violated." He spoke of "the solemn and even tragical character of the step I am taking," and accepted that Germany had, in fact, already gone to war against the United States.

Wilson was encouraged by "the wonderful and heartening" events in Russia, which had "been always in fact democratic at heart . . . The great generous Russian people have been added in all their native majesty and might to the forces of freedom. We are now about to accept the gauge of battle with [Germany], this natural foe to liberty and shall, if necessary, spend the whole force of the Nation . . . to fight for the ultimate peace of the world and for the liberalism of its peoples, the German people included."

The President was frequently interrupted by fervent applause, some of it led by the chief justice, Confederate Army veteran Edward D. White, who was several times reduced to tears by Wilson's eloquence.[104] As he reached his peroration the President looked above his rapt audience, and his learned and glacial voice achieved an almost mystical and hypnotic clarity: "The world must be made safe for democracy . . . It is a fearful thing to lead this most peaceful people into the most terrible and disastrous of all wars . . . [Yet] The right is more precious than peace and . . . to such a task we can dedicate our lives and our fortunes, everything that we are and everything that we have, with the pride of those who know the day has come when America is privileged to spend her blood and her might for the principles that gave her birth and happiness and the peace which she has treasured. God helping her, she can do no other."

The President grimly ignored the thunder of applause that followed from the members of the Congress, who waved small American flags given them for the occasion. Even Senator Lodge approached Wilson with outstretched hand and congratulated him on a brilliant address. Only La Follette, arms folded and chewing gum, remained seated and silent.[105] The rest of the Congress and the galleries, including Franklin and Eleanor Roosevelt, were in uplifted tumult.[106]

By the narrowest of margins and with one more desperate effort by the terribly embattled French and almost equally beleaguered British, a tenuous victory for liberal democracy would be snatched almost from the stomach of defeat by the improbable coalition now led by this brilliant but unlikely war leader.

Even Theodore Roosevelt, visiting Wilson a few days later, called the speech "a great state paper," in the same category as those of Washington and Lincoln (with whom, Roosevelt had claimed a few weeks before, Wilson, because of his moral enfeeblement, had no right to the same citizenship). TR came to ask to be allowed to assemble and lead a division of volunteers to Europe, a request that Franklin Roosevelt did his best to assist by intervening with Daniels and Baker. Wilson remarked to his predecessor that modern war was no longer "the Charge of the Light Brigade." He told his secretary, Joseph Tumulty, that TR was "a great big boy . . . There is a sweetness about him that is very compelling. You can't resist the man."[107]

Wilson, however, declined the request. Theodore Roosevelt was fifty-eight, in poor health, half-blind, and an ex-president of great prestige, whose life should not be risked. The War Department was not much interested in volunteers, and General John J. Pershing, who was about to lead the American Expeditionary Force, having just conducted a rather unsuccessful punitive mission against Pancho Villa in Mexico, wasn't interested in being upstaged by TR. (He did say that he would be proud to have TR's sons, and all four of them volunteered and served with distinction. The youngest, Quentin, became an aviator and was shot down and killed in France. The Germans respectfully buried him with full honors.)

Wilson would only have been human if he was reticent about assisting Colonel Roosevelt's well-intentioned grandstanding. TR had reviled him as a fishy, cowardly shilly-shallier. His attempt at this point to relive San Juan Hill would not do much for the war effort, Wilson must have thought, despite French leader Georges Clemenceau's request for Roosevelt as a hero who would inspirit France and her brave but decimated army. (Clemenceau would be called to the premiership and vested with virtually unlimited emergency powers seven months later.)

Franklin Roosevelt always believed that the ex-president could have helped end the war earlier and might have kept Russia in the war longer. This was a doubtful bit of Roosevelt self-importance, given that Lenin and Trotsky took Russia out of the war and were unlikely to be moved to fight on by the Roosevelts. However, rejecting the former president's request inflamed the progressive Republicans. Their animosity would weigh heavily against Wilson when he set out to organize the peace.

FDR would put to good use Wilson's example in waiting until the country was united behind him before leading it to war. Wilson's righteousness, though grating at times, was not misplaced, and created an atmosphere of mighty, crusading zeal that he expressed with great eloquence. His combination of ascetic Protestantism, intense intellectuality, and high culture caught the moment better than Theodore Roosevelt's brave and benign jingoism.

This really was Armageddon; the United States thought it might be about to sustain hundreds of thousands or even millions of casualties, as the other major combatants had already done. The Roosevelts would have been no less courageous and determined had such losses been incurred. But there were limits in the transportability of *Boys' Own Annual* enthusiasm from the toy-soldiers wars against helpless adversaries, where Colonel Roosevelt's reputation had been built, to the bloodbath of the Western Front.

Theodore Roosevelt beseeched Franklin to resign and "get into uniform at once."[108] Franklin, who undoubtedly saw that he had greater possibilities for propelling the navy into maximum effectiveness by supplementing the efforts of the somewhat languid Daniels and continuing his promising career as a political intriguer, saw the attractions of military service sincerely as well as tactically. He did in fact resign, but Daniels and Wilson himself rejected his resignation and demanded that he remain at his post. Apart from valuing him where he was, they weren't interested in creating another Roosevelt war hero-politician. "I always thought he had this in mind," wrote Daniels later. "Theodore Roosevelt had gone up that way."[109] Wilson said that he and Daniels and Franklin Roosevelt did not have the right to choose the manner of their service and must do their duty where they were.

Roosevelt was surely sincere in offering his resignation, and his judgment was undoubtedly correct when he withdrew it (even, as may have been the case, with relief) after the Commander in Chief asked him to do so. He leapt into the war he had agitated to join with tremendous vigor, even for a Roosevelt.

Franklin Roosevelt inherited from his forbears his fighting instinct and contempt for the appeasement of evil, supplemented by his cousin's hortatory example. And from Wilson he learned to marshal patiently the moral force of the nation. The fecundity of his own personality eventually furnished a gift for political dexterity and cunning maneuver that would not have been seen in a major chancellery since Bismarck and Disraeli and Salisbury, if not Palmerston, Metternich, and Talleyrand. A generation later, this unique combination of aptitudes, convincingly masked by Franklin D. Roosevelt's vast joviality and idealism, would be indispensable to the salvation of the civilization America earnestly thought it was helping to rescue for all time in 1917.

CHAPTER 3

❧

"That Battle Can Still Be Won"

*(President Woodrow Wilson, speaking of the League of Nations
and the Treaty of Versailles to James M. Cox and Franklin D.
Roosevelt, Democratic candidates for president and vice president,
July 18, 1920)*

I

FRANKLIN ROOSEVELT WAS an advocate of a program to keep government leaders fit through regular exercise under the supervision of Yale athletics coach Walter Camp. That he was a splendid young man is clear from Camp's assertion that "Mr. Roosevelt is a beautifully built man, with the long muscles of the athlete."[1] "Government girls used to watch with admiration as he strode past on his way to work."[2] The *New York Tribune* similarly reported: "His face is long, firmly shaped and set with marks of confidence. There are faint wrinkles on a high straight forehead. Intensely blue eyes rest in light shadow. A firm thin mouth breaks quickly to laugh, openly and freely. His voice is pitched well."[3]

As throughout his life, neither Roosevelt's fine appearance nor his great energy assured him good health. He was plagued by sinus infections and vulnerable to bacterial infections and severe illnesses, including typhus, pneumonia, and ultimately polio. His sinusitis was enervating and his frequent bouts of congestion and heavy coughing were ultimately thought to have aggravated his cardiological problems. His chief, Daniels, who was obese and dumpy and never exercised in his adult life, did not have a day's sick leave during the war, and was almost never ill in his nearly eighty-six years, surviving his assistant by several years despite being twenty years his senior.

Roosevelt was always popular with those who worked for him—courteous, even-tempered, efficient, and solicitous. A teacher of shorthand whom Roosevelt engaged to help him deal with his extensive correspondence was impressed with the rapidity and clarity of his dictation, but even more by his congeniality and sense of humor. When an underling forged Roosevelt's name on his stationery in a note to his wife stating that the addressee's husband was to be awarded the Congressional Medal of Honor for exposing an espionage ring, the joker's wife believed it and told the local newspaper, which wired the assistant secretary for more information. Roosevelt had the man in, extracted a confession, and gravely advised him of the many crimes he had committed: forgery, impersonation, insubordination, desecration. When the enlisted man was convinced he would be court martialed and imprisoned, Roosevelt roared with laughter and made clear that he had appreciated the joke.[4]

At the suggestion of the American ambassador in London, Walter Hines Page, Admiral William S. Sims, president of the Naval War College, had already been sent to London to coordinate the anticipated joint naval war effort. Sims was a very intelligent and dynamic careerist who regularly went around his superiors and appealed directly to the civilian leadership, a practice that served him well under Theodore Roosevelt but didn't endear him to his fellow officers. Daniels chose him for this vital position despite his closeness to Theodore Roosevelt and his frequent criticism of the secretary of the navy and the President, because in a national emergency Daniels put the national interest before any personal consideration. Franklin Roosevelt, crowding onto the bandwagon of the admiral's popularity at the end of the war, as politicians frequently do with war heroes, would falsely claim to have been responsible for Sims's appointment. This was the overeager, superficial young FDR at his worst. "Not a word of it was true."[5]

Sims, in England, quickly learned that the naval situation was extremely stretched. The toll of German submarines on allied shipping had been 900,000 tons in March 1917 alone, and the British could not spare destroyers to protect convoys because they were afraid to leave the British Grand Fleet without them. This meant that the destroyers were virtually as inactive as the Royal Navy's heavy units, which were waiting for the harbor-bound German High Seas Fleet to come out—not a likely prospect.

Britain was now down to a three-week supply of grain, and famine was stalking the home islands. A British delegation led by former prime minister Arthur James Balfour and a French mission headed officially by former premier Rene Viviani but in fact by Marshal Joseph Joffre, victor of the Battle of the Marne, arrived in April and May. Franklin Roosevelt met both groups and urged them to ask all they needed. He promised, on his own and not Daniels's or Wilson's authority, thirty destroyers. This bold and intelligent step was ratified by his superiors and immediately improved Allied ability to protect convoys.

At a Navy League dinner in May in honor of the British delegation, FDR spoke after several others and made an impassioned plea for a pledge of definite numbers of ships and men to be delivered on a definite date. It made a strong impression on the visitors. So much so in Joffre's case that he accepted Sara's request that she be allowed to present Anna, James, and Elliott to the marshal, who was staying in the Frick mansion on Fifth Avenue. The children all had whooping cough, but Sara shepherded them over and the marshal kissed them and presented their grandmother with an autographed photograph of himself, which resided thereafter in a place of honor in her sitting room ("the snuggery," it was called) at Hyde Park.[6]

Sara was greatly impressed by Joffre, and she was equally impressed by Balfour when he spoke at Carnegie Hall and came to a special service at St. John the Divine, where Rosy was a trustee and made sure that Sara met the distinguished visitor. The British—and, to a lesser degree, the French—had already developed a talent for charming the Americans, in which they were never rivalled by the Germans, despite a residual Anglophobic sentiment in some Irish and German-American circles and among some senior ranks of the U.S. Navy. It would prove a vital strategic asset.

Franklin Roosevelt would subsequently claim, and is probably credible in this case, that Wilson himself asked him not to requisition supplies with such efficiency that there was nothing left for the army. He secured a commission for his contractor at Springwood and put him in charge of building new naval installations for the housing of draftees and for the collection of supplies. The speed of construction drastically increased as the unit costs plummeted. Roosevelt promised to "sign the requisitions with my eyes closed."[7]

Roosevelt would eventually claim that he had been second on a list of German elimination targets seized in the German consulate in New York, in consequence of which he had briefly carried a revolver in a shoulder holster. Louis Howe's flacking operation had become more successful now that his client was actually doing something more useful than just scheming against his superiors. As a result, there were a lot of positive stories in the press, such as the *Wall Street Journal* demand that Daniels be swept out in favor of his dynamic assistant.[8] But it is unlikely that the Germans were taken in.

In his unceasing campaign for a greater sense of urgency in the Navy Department, Roosevelt not only supported Howe's endless series of leaks to the press derogatory of Daniels and contrasting the energetic assistant secretary, he employed the well-known novelist Winston Churchill (an American Naval Academy graduate and no relation to the British statesman), an acquaintance of Wilson's, as a conduit to the President. Churchill researched navy affairs, at Roosevelt's instigation and under his tutelage, starting from a secret memorandum that was highly critical of Daniels. Churchill had known the President for many years and had rented a cottage in New Hampshire to him some years before. He submitted his report directly to Wilson in July 1917. Churchill's recommendations did quicken the pace of the department when endorsed by the President, but were not overtly critical of Daniels.[9]

Roosevelt did play a vital part in two important initiatives, the use of 110-foot wooden submarine chasers and the deployment of an anti-submarine mine barrage designed, in Wilson's phrase, to "shut up the hornets in their nests."[10] The idea was to extend the barrage of mines across the English Channel and the North Sea between Norway and Scotland, where all German submarines had to make their way into the sea lanes. This scheme was regarded skeptically by Daniels, Sims, and most of the other admirals and by the British, who treated every American suggestion with the condescension of seasoned veterans hearing the effusions of rank amateurs.

Wilson wearied of British negativism. "Nothing was ever done so systematically as nothing is being done now," he said in an address to officers aboard the battleship *Pennsylvania* on August 11, 1917.[11] Wilson wrote to Sims that the British Admiralty seemed "helpless to the point of panic."[12] To the British, the Americans were naïve interlopers insufficiently respectful of the vast and tragic war experience of the senior allies. To the Americans, the British and French were in extremis beseeching American assistance. If they were such consummate strategic warriors how did they get to the edge of such a precipice? There was doubtless merit in both positions, and the interplay of them was another experience that would be useful to Franklin D. Roosevelt (and at least one already prominent British statesman) a generation later.

Wilson supported Roosevelt on the mine barrage, and it was a contact of Roosevelt's that produced the device that was adapted to become "the Browne submerged gun." In February 1918, a convoy of Great Lakes transports carried 50,000 feet of wire cable and 100,000 mines to Britain to begin the deployment of the barrage. It was not completed when the war ended but accounted for at least three German submarines. Roosevelt always claimed that the prospect of it demoralized the Germans and that it would have worked. He eventually engaged in his usual hyperbole, claiming that "it may not be too far-fetched . . . to say that the North Sea mine barrage . . . had something definite to do with the German naval mutiny, the subsequent army mutiny, and the ending of the World War."[13]

In fact it would be too far-fetched, but it was still constructive new thinking and was a relatively inexpensive means to try to turn the tide of battle in the Atlantic. Daniels and the British and American admirals were unjustifiably negative, but Sims eventually called it "one of the wonders of the war."[14]

The submarine-chasers made a contribution too. Here Daniels had supported Roosevelt, but he relentlessly and successfully opposed one of FDR's other hobby horses, a fifty-foot anti-submarine vessel that Daniels felt would be too small to function usefully on any but freakishly calm days. Roosevelt wanted the vessels for American coastal waters. They might have accomplished something, but the German threat on the American coast never assumed the proportions that caused FDR to warn his wife to "grab the children and beat it into the woods" if a German submarine arrived at Campobello. The navy didn't miss these little boats.[15]

There was a perception that Roosevelt was headstrong and impressionable, a sucker for gadgeteers and cranks, and particularly so if they were old university or school chums or just clubbable Hooray Henrys who fitted into his socioeconomic group. As throughout his life after he left Springwood for Groton in 1896, it was hard for people to see where the substantive gave way to the tactical in his incandescent charm.

Near the end of 1917, Roosevelt gave new depth and meaning to his penchant for favoring old school and university chums by hiring Livingston (Livy) Davis as his special assistant. Roosevelt continued for a while longer to be most comfortable with these breezy, unchallenging relationships, which must have assisted him in feeling young and unattached as he aged and his family grew. Livy's chief contribution to the war effort was a program in which several thousand yachtsmen, bird-watchers, and opera-goers lent their binoculars and telescopes to the navy until peace came.

———————

A return to electoral politics was for a time as much a preoccupation for Roosevelt and Howe as was the flickering temptation to throw over the assistant secretary's office for the status of a uniformed officer. On July 4, 1917, Roosevelt effectively buried the hatchet with Tammany Hall by speaking at their Independence Day festivities and appearing in newspaper photographs side-by-side with Boss Charles F. Murphy. The rapport between the two men was no greater than it had been, but both had learned a lesson from the debacle of the U.S. Senate race in 1914—that they had to cooperate if they were to win a state-wide election.

Howe had been promoting Roosevelt for the nomination for governor of New York in 1918, and in May of that year Roosevelt raised the subject with Wilson. Al Smith was the leading candidate for the Democratic nomination. The President was a good deal warmer to this suggestion than he had been to Roosevelt's ill-starred candidacy for the U.S. Senate. When Roosevelt raised the matter of Smith's Catholicism as a possible obstacle to success, Wilson refused to hear of it, saying that no one asked the religion of the young men who were dying every day in combat and whose names were printed in growing numbers in the newspapers.[16] Roosevelt thereafter took the same line as Wilson in sectarian matters, on which FDR had never had any history of illiberal views anyway.

In response to his undoubtedly effective performance at the Navy Department, Wilson was probably more appreciative of Roosevelt generally than he had been. He subsequently told Daniels, who transmitted it to FDR, that he should take the nomination if it were offered. But Roosevelt and Howe soon decided that they didn't want the nomination in 1918.[17] Deserting the Navy Department for electoral politics in the midst of the war would be unseemly, as well as un-Rooseveltian—and might incite suspicions that his contribution to the war effort was less important than Howe's tireless propagation of a personality cult in Roosevelt's favor had led the public to believe. It was bound to be a difficult year for the Democrats, as off-year elections often are for the party in the White House, and Roosevelt and Howe might have been consolable if Smith had lost.

Roosevelt wrote his old patron, John E. Mack, shutting down his candidacy on June 22, 1918, and confirmed that he had done so in a letter to President Wilson July 8.[18] He endorsed Smith heartily when he was nominated, though he had endorsed his opponent (William C. Osborn) in the primary while telling Tammany's Boss Murphy that Smith should be the candidate. It was a tortuous performance even for FDR. And he has been suspected of having "privately knifed" Osborn. Howe urged him to remain on the trip he was about to take overseas until the primary had occurred.[19] Alfred E. Smith was easily nominated and was elected governor of New York for the first of four terms in 1918, escalating the rivalry that already existed between him and Roosevelt.

II

ROOSEVELT HAD SUCCESSFULLY SET his sights on a visit to the Western Front. Doubtless he was sincere about the benefits of such a visit for the navy's efficiency, but it is inconceivable that he didn't think it would be politically beneficial as well as interesting to see the greatest war in history at close quarters. Daniels responded coolly at first, thinking it another of his assistant's publicity stunts that would contribute more confusion than progress, but he relented eventually (after even Admiral Sims, who tended to have little use for his civilian chiefs, urged such a visit). Daniels concluded that members of the administration, tied down in Washington, ran a risk of being "chess players moving their pieces in the dark," and authorized his assistant secretary to go.[20] Roosevelt sailed on the destroyer U.S.S. *Dyer*, on July 9, 1918. She encountered heavy seas, but Roosevelt did not lose his appetite and, unlike some officers, was not at all sick.[21] He landed at Portsmouth July 21.

The Great War was approaching its supreme climax. With the help of steadily increasing numbers of Americans, a mighty German onslaught toward Paris was clearly running out of momentum. Marshal Foch, commander in chief of the Allied armies, had won the Second Battle of the Marne, as dramatic and much larger than the First, four years before. July 18, 1918, he would launch his great counter-offensive on the north-central section of the front. In succeeding weeks Foch wound unleash, in stages, his entire command, nearly six million men, then the greatest human host in history, against the Germans along the whole Western Front from the English Channel to the Swiss border.

The visiting assistant secretary of the navy had a broad mandate from his chief, and the British displayed their usual talent at receiving foreigners who could be vitally important to them. In London Roosevelt stayed in a fine suite in the Ritz and received the full treatment for distinguished visitors, including a forty-minute audience with King George V on July 29, 1918. His Imperial Britannic Majesty thoroughly charmed his young visitor, and there is no reason to doubt that the reverse also occurred. Roosevelt considered the king "open, quick and cordial . . . and a delightfully easy person to talk to, and we got on so well that part of the time we were both talking at the same time." Roosevelt gave the king his standard refrain of "having been to school in Germany and having seen their preparation for the first stages of the war machine." In Teutonic studies, the visitor was somewhat out of his depth; the king said he had also gone to school in Germany, for a year (compared with Roosevelt's six weeks), and added, "with a twinkle in his eye, 'You know I have a number of relations in Germany, but I can tell you frankly that in all my life I have never seen a German gentleman.' "[22]

That evening Roosevelt went to a dinner for Allied war ministers at Gray's Inn and was called upon to speak, impromptu, after Lord Curzon, General Smuts (then organizing the Royal Air Force, though a South African), and others. It may not have been his greatest oratorical performance, judging from the reaction of Winston (Spencer) Churchill, then minister of munitions, who "acted like a stinker" to him, and was "one of the few men in public life who was rude to me," as Roosevelt would explain to Joseph Kennedy in 1939. Churchill had no recollection of their meeting, as became clear when they met in Newfoundland in August 1941. In his memoirs, Churchill purported vividly to remember the 1918 encounter after all, including Roosevelt's "magnificent presence in all his youth and strength." Theodore Roosevelt, who met Churchill in 1899, when he was governor of New York, had not liked Churchill either, because he did not stand up when ladies or older men entered the room and was "generally obnoxious."[23]

The following day, July 30, Roosevelt had a wide-ranging conversation with Prime Minister Lloyd George and was most impressed by "his tremendous vitality." Lloyd George asserted that Britain had made a disastrous error in not imposing universal conscription at the start of the war. There had been some in the United States who opposed conscription after the country entered the war, but Roosevelt was one of their fiercest opponents, and the British prime minister's comments fortified him in his views, which would strongly influence the world a generation later.

That evening Roosevelt attended a dinner at the House of Commons and had a long talk with the foreign secretary, former prime minister Arthur Balfour, whom he had met the previous year in Washington. Their conversation took place as they strode in the dark on the terrace of Westminster Palace (Parliament). Balfour inspired Roosevelt to write: "What has pleased me more than anything else is the . . . determination of the British Cabinet to go through with the war to a definitely successful end."[24]

The inevitable Livy Davis was along on the trip, and when Roosevelt wasn't with the great and the good, he had time to shop, visit the country houses of old friends, and dine sumptuously with his entourage. They went to the Astors' home at Cliveden, and FDR found Nancy Astor "the same, enthusiastic, amusing, and talkative soul as always."[25]

On July 31, the Roosevelt party set out for France, from Dover to Dunkirk, in a

British destroyer flying the assistant secretary's standard, the first time a foreign naval standard had flown on a British ship, Roosevelt was told. (This is unlikely, but this time Roosevelt could be the recipient rather than the author of a tall tale[26].) The Americans were conveyed from Dunkirk to Paris in limousines along roads that had been heavily cratered by artillery fire. Roosevelt had a splendid room in the Hotel de Crillon overlooking Place de la Concorde, and began his day by taking Sara's sister, Dora Forbes, to visit Versailles, as he and Eleanor had on their honeymoon thirteen years before.

He visited Theodore Roosevelt Jr. and his brother Archie, who were convalescing in Paris from wounds and had been decorated for valor. Their brother Quentin had been killed while Franklin was on the high seas on the U.S.S. *Dyer*. Franklin wrote in the diary he kept of the trip with unalloyed admiration of the bravery and character of his relatives.

He was received by the French Navy minister Georges Leygues; the "liaison" (with America) minister, Andre Tardieu; Marshal Joffre; the president of the republic, the formidable Raymond Poincaré; and the even more formidable premier, the seventy-seven-year-old Georges Clemenceau. "I knew at once that I was in the presence of the greatest civilian in France," Roosevelt wrote in his diary. Clemenceau told Roosevelt about a dead poilu and a dead German soldier he had seen in a shell hole where they had been killed simultaneously by an artillery round while trying to bite each other to death. "He grabbed me by both shoulders and shook me with a grip of steel to illustrate his words, thrusting his teeth toward my neck."[27]

Clemenceau was a captivating figure who had been a schoolteacher in the United States as a young man. He was mayor of Montmartre during the Franco-Prussian War and the Paris Commune, one of Emile Zola's foremost allies in the battle to acquit Captain Dreyfus (he published Zola's famous letter *J'Accuse*), and a great cultural figure—an intimate of the artist Claude Monet and of many other icons of French art and literature.

Roosevelt also found the visit with Marshal Joffre agreeable. In his usual suspect manner where his own role in historic events was involved, Roosevelt claimed that Joffre credited him with the success of Joffre's military mission to Washington in May 1917. "He kept insisting that the friendly advice I had given him from the very first day when I met him . . . at Hampton Roads had in the end enabled him to obtain the answers for which he had come to America . . . I think he felt, and rightly so, that only a small part of the million and a quarter Americans now in France would be here had it not been for his mission."[28]

Franklin D. Roosevelt was in most respects an attractive as well as a capable young man. But he apparently considered himself largely responsible for the mutiny of the German Navy (with the prospect of the North Sea mine barrage), the American presence in France (with his advice to Joffre), and the consequent collapse of the German war effort and the salvation of France. This indicates an imbalance of judgment and an immaturity that, with his naked opportunism at times and alongside his undoubted qualities, help explain the frustration with him felt by some intelligent older men who worked with him, like Wilson and Daniels.

———————

Franklin and Livy had a tour of five-star restaurants and risqué nightclubs for a few days and then left for the front August 4, 1918. Roosevelt quickly fired his security aide, who was trying to keep him thirty miles behind the front looking at areas that had been cleared weeks before. Even at this distance, the evidence of battle was fearful—huge numbers of wounded, utter devastation of the country-side, and the pathetic spectacle of refugees returning to rebuild their homes and lives. The tour he devised for the next few days seems to have been the basis of his histrionic claims in the thirties to have seen an immense amount of the horrors and ravages of war.

He visited Verdun, the site of the greatest battle in the history of the world up to that time, where 975,000 casualties were taken by the French and the Germans combined in 1915 and 1916. He went to the Douaumont Fort, the largest in the world, where a then-unknown captain and prisoner of war with whom Roosevelt would eventually be quite well acquainted, Charles de Gaulle, was wounded and captured in March 1915. He saw what was claimed to be the original sign, "Ils ne passeront pas," that was the French pledge throughout the epic battle. ("They will not prevail.")[29]

The first prominent person Roosevelt met on the trip, Sir Eric Geddes, first lord of the Admiralty, had intrigued him with the thought of going to Italy to work out the sort of joint command that the British, French, and American navies and armies had.[30] His would be a fresh perspective, and Geddes persuaded him that the Italians, who insisted on control in the Adriatic but refused to leave their ports, might take robust advice better from the Americans than from the British or French. The British wanted command of the whole Mediterranean and a much more aggressive approach to the naval war there, where German and Austrian submarines from Trieste were now sinking more Allied shipping than was being lost in the Atlantic.

The addition of American destroyers and more intelligent antisubmarine tactics generally had greatly improved delivery of grain and the materiel of war to Britain and France, making the German decision to provoke the United States to war by unrestricted submarine warfare seem even more insane than it had in 1917.

Roosevelt was naturally happy to embark on the diplomatic mission to Italy, which if successful would serve the Allies as well as his own political cause. With Daniels's approval,[31] he entrained for Rome on August 8, the day of the beginning of the British part of Foch's grand offensive, and met with the Italian foreign minister, Baron Sidney Sonnino, with the navy minister and many naval officers, and finally with the prime minister, Vittorio Orlando.

However, the most durably important meeting he had on this excursion was probably with the young American Army Air Service captain Fiorello La Guardia of New York. Roosevelt assisted him in increasing supplies crossing the Italian-French border by intervening with the head of the American Red Cross in Italy.[32]

Roosevelt found the young Italian officers eager for a more active role, but the navy minister was "insistent on no risks being taken by the battleships." When Roosevelt suggested that it might have been unwise to leave the entire Italian battle fleet in Taranto in the heel of Italy without even coming out for target practice for a whole year, he was disconcerted to be told by the navy chief of staff, Admiral Thaon de Revel, "You must not forget that the Austrian fleet have not had any either."[33] He wrote in his diary of the trip: "This is a naval classic which is hard to beat."[34]

Roosevelt had great difficulty taking Italy seriously as a military power after this experience. (The future regent of Hungary, Admiral Miklos Horthy, would claim in his memoirs that his aggressive handling of his Adriatic fleet intimidated the Italians and disconcerted the young Roosevelt.[35] But the Austro-Hungarians don't seem to have been much more energetic than the Italians, and Roosevelt had little regard for Horthy, then or subsequently.)

Roosevelt thought when he finished with Orlando that his mission had been a success; he reported to Daniels that the Italians had agreed to a unified command. Orlando claimed that he had agreed only to a chairman of a joint naval staff and retention of Italian control over the Adriatic. Roosevelt irritated the Italians and the French by suggesting a British Mediterranean commander. He did propose Italian command in the Adriatic and French command in the Mediterranean outside the Adriatic, with the grandiloquent title Commander of the Mediterranean Grand Fleet. The British theater commander would chair a Mediterranean command council that would also include American and Japanese members. (Neither power had any naval presence in the Mediterranean.) Roosevelt had written Daniels August 13, 1918, that he surmised from cables that Daniels and the State Department supported the British ambition to a Mediterranean command, though he must have had some idea that he was considerably exceeding his authority, which was confined to permission from Daniels for exploratory talks.

When Roosevelt's friend the French ambassador in Washington, Jean Jusserand, on instruction from his aroused government, asked Roosevelt's friend the secretary of state, Robert Lansing, on September 3, 1918, what authority Roosevelt had to propose to the government of Italy a British Mediterranean naval commander, Lansing replied, after consulting Daniels, that he had no authority to do so. Wilson wrote Daniels that he was annoyed at unofficial missions (i.e., Roosevelt's) exaggerating their standing to speak for the U.S. government.[36]

Daniels wrote in his diary that he had told Lansing to tell Jusserand that the United States favored a unified command but not necessarily under British leadership. It would have been out of character for the generous and indulgent

Daniels to betray his own assistant. The likeliest explanation for what happened to Roosevelt's Italian mission is that there was a legitimate misunderstanding between Roosevelt and Daniels. This was probably compounded by Roosevelt's eagerness to play as great a role as possible, egged on by the duplicitous British first lord, Geddes. Daniels seems to have distanced himself from his assistant when Wilson, prodded by Clemenceau and Orlando, via their ambassadors and Lansing, expressed displeasure.[37]

Roosevelt performed competently but impetuously in a theater where the United States had little influence. He acknowledged in a letter to Geddes at the end of August that "I have not reached the milk in the coconut." He was, however, accurate in his quick assessment of the political fragility of Italy and in his judgment of Italy's limited maritime war-making capacities.[38]

Not at all fazed, as always, by this fiasco, including what amounted to a (not entirely just) rebuke from his own president, Roosevelt returned to France and inspected Atlantic coast antisubmarine bases and then a ninety-ton, fourteen-inch bore, rail-mounted artillery battery that had been intended for a battle cruiser but that he had been instrumental in sending to France. This part of the visit seems to have determined him finally to resign his position and return to the front as a U.S. Marine on such a battery. (He had had a particular affinity for the marines since he had donned a quasi-marine outfit in Haiti the year before.)

The American admiral commanding the battery offered to take him on as a lieutenant commander. He wrote to Eleanor that he might not be in Washington much longer, having a few days before told 3,000 American enlisted men at Pauillac, "It is hard for me to go back to a dull office job at Washington after having visited the lines where our boys are making history." It seems these batteries appealed to him because they united his love of the navy and marines with his desire to serve at the front. This is the only possible explanation for why he was more attracted to a battle cruiser gun on rails than to a sea command such as one of his beloved destroyers. He wrote out, but did not send, a letter to Daniels resigning as assistant secretary to pursue his "proper duty" at the front, and asking for a navy or marines commission to do so.[39]

At about this time, Eleanor was set upon by her Uncle Theodore at a family funeral. The former president demanded that Eleanor require her husband to enlist in the armed forces at once. Eleanor defended Franklin strenuously and became annoyed with TR for meddling, aware that her husband was thinking along the same lines as those her uncle was recommending.[40]

Roosevelt went on to a courtesy visit with the British commander in France, Field Marshal Douglas Haig, and then with King Albert I of the Belgians. He came under steady enemy artillery fire and two air raids, earning a legitimate claim to having been in combat. This claim was strengthened a few days later when the destroyer on which he recrossed the Channel was bombed twice by the German Air Force.

Roosevelt was once again coming down with a heavy flu, an ailment to which he was always vulnerable, but drove 240 miles through the night to Paris with a temperature of 102 and met with General Pershing and Marshal Foch. He was impressed with Foch's unpretentious manner and simple headquarters, and spoke with him for almost an hour, largely about coordinating the American Marine railroad artillery batteries with the French high command.[41]

Oblivious of his fever, Roosevelt even managed a bit of book shopping in Paris and then went to Scotland to inspect progress on the antisubmarine barrage and the U.S. battleship squadron at the Firth of Forth. The night before he left for home he was up with Livy Davis and others until 4:30 A.M. He arose at 7 A.M., and when he got on the ship for the return trip, the *Leviathan*, he collapsed with double pneumonia. When the ship docked at New York, September 19, he had to be taken off on a stretcher and carried into his mother's house on 65th Street by four orderlies.

Four weeks of convalescence was required, during which Roosevelt dictated a perceptive memo to Daniels about his trip, which the secretary praised to Wilson as the "clear, concise, and illuminating report [of the] clear-headed and able" FDR.[42] He received a large volume of good wishes, including affectionate notes from his children and: "Dear Franklin, We are deeply concerned about your sickness, and trust you will soon be well. We are very proud of you. With love, Aff. Yours, Theodore Roosevelt."[43]

III

AS THE WORLD war finally approached its end, Franklin D. Roosevelt blundered into what quickly became, next to his long struggle with polio, the greatest crisis of his personal life. He had fallen in love with an unmarried woman, and unless Cupid had deprived him of all his judgment, he could not possibly have imagined that this new relationship could end happily.

The woman was Lucy Page Mercer, who had been Eleanor's social secretary. While unpacking some of her still-sick husband's things in Sara's New York house, Eleanor came upon a batch of love letters from Lucy to Franklin.* All her ancient premonitions and insecurities naturally surged forward in her thoughts, and her sense of betrayal was overwhelming. She had been let down and humiliated by her husband and betrayed by an employee whom she had welcomed into her house.

Lucy Mercer was seven years younger than Eleanor, only twenty-seven when the liaison was discovered. She was by all accounts an extremely attractive, cultivated, and charming woman. Her ancestors, an eminent Roman Catholic family that had helped settle Maryland, had come to the New World in 1630. Her par-

---

* Columnist Drew Pearson mistakenly wrote that Eleanor discovered her husband's infidelity when she drove past Franklin and Lucy in a parked car, on the vacant area where the Pentagon was subsequently built.[44]

ents had gone through a substantial inheritance before their marriage collapsed when Lucy was twelve. She had attended a convent in Austria for a year and lived with her mother in modest accommodation in Washington.

It seems that Eleanor's aunt suggested Lucy to help Eleanor with all the social details that had befallen her since arriving in Washington, and Lucy started working for the Roosevelts in 1914. She and Franklin began an intense physical relationship shortly after the departure of Eleanor and the children for Campobello that summer. While she started out with the Roosevelts very much as an employee, she rapidly became virtually a member of the family, and was often a spare dinner guest.

Eleanor's suspicions were aroused despite the great lengths Franklin and Lucy went to to preserve discretion. Whenever they both attended a party, even when Eleanor was away, there was always another man ostensibly accompanying Lucy—usually Nigel Law, third secretary of the British Embassy and almost as worshipful an admirer of Franklin Roosevelt as Livy Davis was. Eleanor let Lucy go in the summer of 1917, explaining that the war would prevent her from carrying on the social life she had conducted for the first four years in Washington.

This didn't end Lucy's proximity to Franklin, because Lucy enlisted as a yeoman third class in the U.S. Navy and became a secretary in the Navy Department, working in an office near FDR's. Eleanor was also understandably suspicious of this arrangement. Her suspicion, and the whooping cough of the Roosevelt children, delayed the family's departure to Campobello until mid-July of 1917.

Eleanor had just finally departed when the *New York Times* produced an article (July 17, 1917) entitled "How to Save in Big Homes." She was quoted extensively praising "the servants" for assisting in using scraps and leftovers and filling out pledge cards promising to economize on food and clothes. Franklin wrote her, with a sarcasm he normally reserved for political opponents: "I am proud to be the husband of the Originator, Discoverer and Inventor of the New Household Economy for Millionaires." He asked for a photograph of the "cooperating servants" and said "all Washington is talking of the Roosevelt Plan." Eleanor was sheepish and blamed the journalist for quoting her. The tenor of the exchange between the spouses makes it clear that after twelve years the marriage was under great strain.[45]

Rumors were audible, particularly when Alice Roosevelt Longworth began to comment on the subject, saying that Franklin deserved some fun because he had Eleanor as a wife. Alice saw Franklin and Lucy together in Roosevelt's open car and called her cousin to tease him.[46] It is a testament to Lucy's allure that even the acidulous Alice always spoke well of her.

In October 1917, Josephus Daniels, an extreme conservative in marital matters, and unwaveringly fond of his assistant secretary despite his provocative behavior at times, relieved Lucy of her duties at the Navy Department. She had been promoted to yeoman second class, and was too competent and equable to have been removed for cause.

Given the level of Eleanor's suspicions and the indiscretions of Alice and her circle, Franklin's ineptitude in leaving Lucy's letters in the house, in his luggage, accessible to his wife, is incomprehensible without recourse to posthumous psychiatry. When Eleanor discovered the evidence in September 1918, she told Franklin he could have a divorce if he wanted one. Sara told Franklin that if he broke up his marriage in this way he would be disinherited and could forget about owning or even living at Springwood again. For good measure, Louis Howe told him that such a divorce would be the end of his political career. According to Drew Pearson, who, though well informed was always far from an impeccable source but is plausible in this case, Eleanor "was not one to give up easily. And she knew that her dashing young husband had more than his wife and children to sacrifice—his political ambition. 'If you want to be President, Franklin,' she told her husband very sweetly, 'you'll have to take me with you.'" (If she said any such thing, it was unlikely to have been sweetly.) Given the stance of his mother and Louis Howe, it is unlikely that Franklin Roosevelt needed much of a political tutorial from Eleanor on where his career was going if he didn't end his extramarital liaison.

Lucy Mercer was an observant Roman Catholic and could not break up a marriage or marry a divorced man unless Franklin could obtain an annulment, which in these times and circumstances would be practically impossible. Eleanor held all the cards and told Franklin that if he ever saw Lucy again, she would divorce him.

The impulses of all the principals are understandable. Lucy Mercer was considerably better looking than Eleanor, had an unfailingly pleasing manner, a gentle voice, and a subtle way of advancing her views. Eleanor was a remarkable woman, but as a wife was argumentative and hectoring. Lucy indulged Franklin's foibles and vanities; Eleanor challenged them. Even at the end of Franklin D. Roosevelt's life Lucy would speak affectionately of "his beloved presence . . . ringing laugh . . . his extraordinarily beautiful head." Eleanor rarely spoke of her husband in quite such superlatives, even before she became aware of his peccadillo. While Eleanor was a difficult personality at times, it is hard not to sympathize with her moral indignation. The attraction of Franklin to Lucy was obvious enough. All these impulses are comprehensible. But only Eleanor's reasonableness and the interventions of Sara and Louis Howe prevented this from becoming the terminal debacle of Roosevelt's public career.

Even allowing for Lucy Mercer's undoubted attractions and fine character, Roosevelt, who had so astutely managed his political career, who played a creditable second-echelon role in the victorious outcome of the greatest war in history and was nothing if not a cunning careerist, had behaved with unfathomable stupidity. He had advanced steadily into a cul-de-sac, knowing the stakes he was playing for, with no exit strategy and without even removing documentary evidence of his infidelity from the house he shared with his wife and mother and often his five children.

Franklin's leavetaking of Lucy must have been poignant and was obviously handled with exquisite discretion. There seems a possibility that he claimed to Lucy that they had to part because Eleanor would not give him a divorce. This was not the case but would be the most elegant grounds for ending their relationship he could have invoked. This was the version of events that survived among Lucy's relatives many years later.[47]

After Daniels's removal of Lucy from the Navy Department, she became the governess for Winthrop Rutherfurd, a distinguished and well-to-do widower in his early fifties. He was well known to and well liked by the Roosevelts. Lucy helped him through the horrible crisis of the slow death of his teenage son in the winter of 1919, and they were married in February 1920. It was apparently a happy marriage.

The talented journalist Murray Kempton wrote a brief fantasy of Franklin's leaving Eleanor and having a civil marriage with Lucy. It was almost a Gray's Elegiacal version of the Duke and Duchess of Windsor. Franklin would be a journeyman lawyer and Lucy, barred from the sacraments, would occasionally enter a Catholic church to pray and light a candle. It's an amusing parody, but to read it is to realize how little choice Franklin really had. Instead of keeping an option open, he had almost destroyed himself. He was an ambitious man, not an incurable romantic.[48]

It was a thoroughly bedraggled and distracted couple that returned to Washington when Franklin was well enough, on October 18, 1918. Franklin was scarcely back at his desk in the Navy Department when he succumbed to the influenza that laid low all his children and three of Eleanor's still-famous "cooperative servants." When clear of this, and after Howe had leaked the usual preparatory stories to the press (as predictable in Roosevelt's affairs at this time as an artillery barrage preceding an infantry charge), he made his final appeal to President Wilson that he be allowed to join the marines. This was on the evening of October 31, 1918, and Wilson told him that peace was about to break out. This was one option that he had kept open so long it expired of old age.*

German Field Marshal Ludendorff had broken down in his headquarters September 28, screaming wild accusations at his staff, and he and the supreme commander, Field Marshal von Hindenburg, agreed that it was no longer possible to be assured of a stalemate. Germany was at the end of endurance and could crack—militarily, under Foch's relentless offensive, or in civil disorder and revolution—at any moment. A liberal-socialist government under Prince Max of

---

* In 1921, when Groton School was raising a memorial to its sons who had served in the armed forces in the Great War, Roosevelt wrote that he deserved to be listed with those who were in uniform, because "I saw service on the other side, was missed by torpedoes and shell and had actual command."[49]

Baden was installed and asked President Wilson for an immediate armistice, a stand-still ceasefire in place pending comprehensive negotiations.

It was a foretaste of Wilson's lack of tactical judgment in the peace-making process that he corresponded with the German chancellor without informing his allies, congressional leaders, or his own military commanders. Wilson's position was that Britain, France, Italy, and the others were "associated states," rather than allies, because the United States was not bound by treaty to them as they were to each other. He was trying to preserve his status as a righteous champion of a new world brotherhood rather than a traditionally victorious coalition power. His motives were exemplary but, as the assistant navy secretary noted, his methods were impractical and his goals were not entirely attainable.

Wilson demanded immediate Central Powers withdrawal from all invaded territory, the abdication of the kaiser, and transformation of Germany into a constitutional democracy. These were not inappropriate demands, but it was dangerously reckless to conceal the existence of the exchanges for several weeks from his British, French, and Italian "associates," who had sustained over six million casualties fighting the common enemies, and from the leaders of the Senate, which would have to ratify any peace agreement. The German government informed Wilson on October 20 that it had ceased its policy of unrestricted submarine warfare, and Wilson then, finally, advised his allies of developments.

Wilson had revealed his program, called the Fourteen Points, for ending the war and securing peace in the world, on January 8, 1918, and had Colonel House represent him in a preliminary discussion of it in the Supreme Allied War Council in Paris, on October 29, 1918. It was a difficult meeting that should have given the American president all the notice he needed that he could not simply bring down the canons of his new world order like a demiurge. Clemenceau and Lloyd George as well as the foreign ministers, Balfour, Pichon, and Sonnino, represented their countries along with the military chiefs. Clemenceau and Lloyd George agreed at the outset that they had never been asked to approve the Fourteen Points. House affirmed that acceptance of an armistice would be deemed by the United States to be acceptance of the President's peace plan. This was a preposterous state of affairs. Clemenceau, an atheist, remarked that God had only had ten commandments. A point-by-point discussion ensued.

Point 1, "Open covenants openly arrived at," was objected to as making diplomacy impossible, but House got over this hurdle by saying that all that was intended was that agreements be published after they were agreed. This was not what Wilson had meant but was the best that could be done, and was accepted.

Point 2, "absolute freedom of navigation upon the seas in peace and war," was violently objected to by Lloyd George as ending Britain's power of blockade. House effectively threatened a separate peace between the United States and Germany and Austria-Hungary.

Balfour intervened and proposed agreement on the uncontentious points—Point 3, freedom of trade, and Points 4 to 8—arms reduction; equitable adjustment of colonial claims, with attention to local concerns; evacuation of Russia, which had been invaded by the Western powers after the Bolshevik coup d' état; restoration of Belgium; and restoration of France, including Alsace-Lorraine—were all fairly unexceptionable.

Italy objected to the Point 9, calling for adjustment of its boundaries along national lines. Points 10 to 14, at least theoretically, could be managed. These were autonomy for the constituent national units of the Austro-Hungarian Empire; restoration and expansion of Serbia, Rumania, and Montenegro, and unspecific pacification of the Balkans; "absolutely unmolested opportunity of autonomous development" of the non-Turkish parts of the Ottoman Empire and opening of the Dardanelles; an independent Polish state; and a "general association of nations."

Overnight, House devised the idea of sending back to the U.S. Congress the question of whether the United States should agree to an armistice on the basis of the Fourteen Points or advise Germany that it would require fulfillment of the demands of Britain, France, and Italy as well, when these were made known. This was a clever ploy, and Lloyd George proposed that the Fourteen Points be accepted as the basis of an armistice with a declared reservation about the power of maritime blockade in war and a clarification about the restoration of conquered territories. He and Clemenceau wanted chunks of the German and Turkish empires and reparations for damage to occupied areas, which in the case of France was immense. House realized that the discussion was leading to unsustainable reparations, which Wilson had promised to avoid, but accepted the compromise and the meeting adjourned. House had played his hand with great skill, but there were, as he advised Wilson, clear storm signals. Wilson chose to ignore them.

Wilson's demand for the abdication of the German emperor delayed agreement through October. But the ceasefire, leading to the armistice—a German surrender, in fact—was signed in Marshal Foch's railway carriage, the famous Wagon-Lit, in the Compiègne Forest, at 11 A.M., November 11, 1918.

IV

FRANKLIN AND ELEANOR, having gone to the brink, now made an effort to reinforce their relationship. She went out more socially and even danced occasionally. He went to church with her, involved her more in his work, and spent more time with all his children. He convinced Daniels that he should return to Europe and got an authorization for Eleanor to accompany him. (Sara may have played a role in this; she called upon Josephus Daniels just before he issued the travel orders.) The younger Roosevelts had twenty-four convalescent sailors to Christmas dinner in 1918. On Boxing Day they reviewed the returning fleet in a snowstorm in New York harbor.

The Roosevelts sailed for France on New Year's Day, 1919, on the liner *George Washington*, with the inseparable Livy Davis and a few others in the party. Also on board were Walter Camp, the financiers Charles Schwab and Bernard Baruch, and the Mexican and Chinese delegations to the Paris Peace Conference, which was to open on January 18.[50]

Theodore Roosevelt, who had spent six weeks in hospital with severe rheumatism, and was generally debilitated and overweight despite his legendarily strenuous life, died in his sleep in the early morning of January 6, 1919. (The entertaining and cynical vice president, Thomas R. Marshall, graciously said, "Death had to take him sleeping—if he had been awake there would have been a fight."[51]) He was only sixty. If he had not made the trip up the Amazon in 1909, he would probably have had the energy to run again for president in 1920, almost certainly successfully, and with important and positive consequences for America and the world. The contrast between his reforming and internationalist activism and personal integrity and the incompetence, corruption, and philistinism of the Harding administration could hardly be more vivid. The twenties would have been very different with TR ushering them in. Franklin and Eleanor were at sea and both were deeply shaken by the news.

Wilson, who was on his train in Italy, was observed to show shock and pity as well as relief when he received the telegram informing him of Roosevelt's death. He wrote to Edith Roosevelt, the late president's widow, but before dispatching his message, changed the claim that he was "grieved" to the more believable assertion that he was "shocked."[52] Obituarists were generous, in the United States and throughout the world, and the nation grieved, even if the President did not. The funeral was at Oyster Bay on January 8. Wilson and Roosevelt had been the greatest American statesmen since Abraham Lincoln, and the President was now unrivalled in American public esteem.

His position was far from invulnerable, however, as the midterm elections, a few days before the armistice, had demonstrated. Wilson, in the midst of what he had until a few days before been pleased to consider his private correspondence with the German government about the peace and the constitutional future of Germany, called upon his people for a vote of confidence. On October 25 he released to the press a statement he had typed himself on his own portable typewriter, without any consultation. He stated that the "Congressional elections . . . occur in the most critical period our country has ever faced. If you have approved of my leadership and wish me to continue to be your unembarrassed spokesman at home and abroad, I earnestly beg" your vote. "A Republican Congress would divide the leadership," and would, in the event of a Republican majority in either house, "certainly be interpreted on the other side of the water as a repudiation of my leadership."

Thus phrased, this was a mad initiative. The public ignored this imperious counsel and, to the audible amusement of the "associated powers," who for the most part had no idea how unsympathetic they would find the Republicans, elected 237 Republican congressmen to 190 of Wilson's Democrats and gave the

Republicans a Senate majority of two, enough to organize the foreign relations and other committees.

In what proved to be the last important public utterance of his career, Theodore Roosevelt jubilantly declared from New York's Roosevelt Hospital: "Our Allies and our enemies and Mr. Wilson himself should all understand that Mr. Wilson has no authority to speak for the American people . . . His leadership has just been emphatically repudiated by them . . . Mr. Wilson and his Fourteen Points and his four supplementary points and his five complementary points and all his utterances every which way have ceased to have any shadow of right to be accepted as expressive of the will of the American people." Roosevelt had still as great a place in the country's affections and esteem as Wilson, so when TR died ten weeks later, these, almost his last words to his countrymen, naturally resonated even more strongly. There is no evidence that Wilson reflected for an instant that if he had given TR the commission he sought, TR could not, as a serving officer, have spoken against the Commander in Chief, even if enemy fire and his own ailments had not felled him before the end of hostilities. America's next war leader was being given a gripping lesson by his two political mentors on how not to win a peace.

Heedless of the practical implications of what he himself had declared in advance to be a repudiation, Wilson took in his entourage to Europe no members of the Senate, which would have to ratify whatever he brought back, and where the Foreign Relations Committee would soon be chaired by Henry Cabot Lodge. Wilson also took no interest at all, when he got to Europe, in visiting the front, reviewing or encouraging his troops, visiting hospitals, or showing any human side to his hosts. He was a desiccated academic, brilliant and virtuous and, at his best, arrestingly eloquent, but the least gregarious successful politician anyone in Europe had ever seen.

———————

The Roosevelts had a fine suite in the Ritz, and Paris was an unforgettable sight, crowded with prizes of war along the great boulevards, as elegant as ever, but with a great number of war widows and wounded men, and colorful peace conference delegations from virtually every ethnic group in Europe, Asia, and the Middle East, all pressing their claims as Wilson, Clemenceau, Lloyd George, and Orlando set out to redraw the map of much of the world.

The President's Fourteen Points were received with great skepticism in official circles. But Wilson was now a mighty prophet, the first man to inspire the masses of the world with a vision of enduring peace. His path was strewn with flowers when he arrived at London's Charing Cross station. Paris was festooned with banners hailing him as "Wilson the Just," an almost biblical lawgiver to the world. There were votive candles before his photograph in simple homes throughout Europe.

The highlight of Roosevelt's activities in France was his negotiation with Andre Tardieu, the sometime French premier who was now in charge of inter-allied relations, over the fate of a naval radio station at Bordeaux. The French were hoping the Americans would leave it behind, but when Roosevelt threat-ened to pack it up and transport it, Tardieu finally agreed to pay a fair price for it.*[53]

The Roosevelts went from Paris to London on January 18. Eleanor was suffer-ing from pleurisy and was put into the care of doctors in London, where they also stayed in the Ritz.

Admiral Sims quickly made it clear that there was nothing more for Roosevelt to do in England. He could review some men and ships if he wanted, but the naval officers had everything under control and could do without interference from him. It was pretty galling from someone he had always treated with consid-erable deference. He returned to Ostend on January 31, 1919 (the day after his thirty-seventh birthday), to inspect marine installations in Germany. He took with him Livy Davis, whom Eleanor had already identified as a bad influence, frivolous and immature and a heavy drinker, and whom she must also have sus-pected of having a role in the Lucy Mercer affair. Eleanor soon made clear her view that it was high time that Franklin outgrew Livy and stopped wasting in col-legiate nostalgia time that could be better spent with his wife and family and seri-ous people. She succeeded, because Livy did not return with them but stayed on working in the food-distribution operations of Herbert Hoover. Famine was a des-perate problem in much of Europe, and Hoover had declared: "The wolf is at the door of the world."[54]

Roosevelt and Davis went by destroyer to lunch with the king of the Belgians. Seeing that the German flag was still flying over the great German fortress of Ehrenbreitstein out of respect for German sensibilities, Roosevelt later prevailed upon General Pershing to raise the Stars and Stripes in its place.

––––––––––

Roosevelt knew almost nothing about the peace negotiations. The discussions had been impossibly condensed and complicated. Lloyd George told Parlia-ment: "I am doubtful whether any body of men with a difficult task have worked under greater difficulties—stones crackling on the roof and crashing through the windows, and sometimes wild men screaming through the keyholes."[55]

Lloyd George had been overwhelmingly reelected on December 19, 1918, at the head of a coalition government after a grand jingoistic campaign that prom-ised to "Hang the Kaiser" and "Squeeze the Huns until the pips squeak." On December 21, Clemenceau was granted a huge mandate by the National Assem-bly to extract a Carthaginian peace from the Germans. This was not only at vari-

---

* Roosevelt's hard bargaining with Tardieu did not alienate the French statesman, who in 1932 expressed great pleasure at the success of his "very dear friend."[56]

ance with Wilson's pacifistic fantasies, and in contrast to his own recent electoral misfortune. It also gave the lie to the American president's theory that he, and not the other government leaders, represented the people of the world, including the other "associated countries." He purported to represent the future, while they represented the past, and the United States was the only country the world trusted.[57]

The agreement that emerged from the tumultuous proceedings in Paris bore little resemblance to Wilson's original pristine vision. He put Point 14 first and obtained his League of Nations, with an executive council of five: the United States, the British Empire, France, Italy, and Japan; but it had rather vague powers. The Covenant of the League, which Franklin and Eleanor were apprised of by a *New York Times* journalist as they boarded their train for Brest just ahead of Wilson, had twenty-three clauses. There was a good deal of sonorous Wilsonian assurance of peace and consultation, but the rest of his plan would have to await the peace treaty.

Wilson put all his faith and hopes in the League of Nations; that once it was launched, with American support and participation in world affairs for the first time, all other problems would be gradually resolved and the forces of history would be positive and inexorable. The League was a novelty and Woodrow Wilson was now at a supreme pinnacle of public esteem and expectations. Such hopes were invested in him as could not possibly be satisfied.

The French turned out in large and enthusiastic numbers to greet the President's boat train, but after such a horrible inferno of a war, no peace was going to redeem the indescribable sacrifices that had been borne in France, Germany, Britain, the Balkans, Italy, and Russia, now in the unsteady and blood-stained hands of the Bolsheviks.

———————

The Roosevelts left Europe with President Wilson on the *George Washington* from Brest, on February 15, 1919,* as the President came home to begin selling his version of the League of Nations and the peace based on it. Wilson was less sociable even than usual on the homeward trip and had no small talk, no common touch. He declined to attend the Washington Day boxing matches put on for his entertainment, and only sourly attended an evening amusement that included a number of sailors dressed as women, one of whom, begirt in pink tulle and rouged face as a chorus girl, ran up to the grim Commander in Chief and "chucked him under the chin."[58] Wilson recoiled, but he did sign the program of the cross-dressing evening for the Roosevelts. The Wilsons did invite the Roosevelts to lunch with them at sea one day. The President startled both Roosevelts by telling them that he never read the press, but left it to Tumulty to summarize it for him, which struck both of them as unwise. Wilson also said and apparently

---

* Roosevelt's old friend from Haiti, General Smedley Butler, was in command of a vast camp for returning American soldiers nearby, and they had a brief reunion.

believed that the United States was "the only nation that all feel is disinterested and that all trust."[59]

Wilson changed the port of destination to Boston from New York, on Tumulty's advice that he receive the greetings of the population in Lodge's home city.[60] Franklin Roosevelt naturally claimed that he had saved the captain from grounding in fog and piloted the ship through New England waters that he well knew from his many years of sailing on the New England coast. There appears to have been no truth whatever to this claim. Some habits of Franklin Roosevelt's youth would die hard, if at all. It was on this trip that Roosevelt told his cousin by marriage, Sheffield Cowles, that rejection at the Porcellian had been the greatest disappointment of his life.[61]

Huge crowds greeted President Wilson in Boston. More startling than the crowds was the exuberance of the Republican governor, Calvin Coolidge, who compared the welcome favorably to Boston's welcomes of George Washington and Abraham Lincoln and hailed Wilson as "a great statesman . . . to whom we have entrusted our destinies."[62]

Franklin Roosevelt was now again a very secondary player. There was nothing for the navy to do except transport American servicemen home and prepare for partial demobilization. The Covenant of the League of Nations and the text of the peace treaty were the issues that absorbed and commanded the attention of the whole world, and Wilson shared his confidences only with Colonel House and a few others. He seemed at this point to like Roosevelt adequately, but he was too intelligent not to realize what a careerist FDR was, and considered him an unserious and tiringly energetic young man. The world was on Woodrow Wilson's shoulders now, and there wasn't much Roosevelt could do for him.

A belated meeting at the White House on February 26, 1919, with members of the Senate and House Foreign Affairs Committees, which Borah refused to attend, went pleasantly enough but clearly did not change the minds of Lodge and the hard core of his Republican colleagues. Wilson returned in March to Versailles to work on the peace treaty, taking no notice of Senator Lodge's organization of thirty-six allies in the Senate, enough to prevent ratification, who signed a statement that they couldn't accept Wilson's Covenant in its present form. Wilson would not hear of compromise when Colonel House and others suggested it; he was confident he could sustain public enthusiasm and overwhelm doubters in the Congress. He seemed to think that with the death of Theodore Roosevelt, he no longer had any dangerous opponents.

Franklin D. Roosevelt was at this point a loyal supporter of the party line, as he revealed in an effective and widely remarked speech to the Democratic National Committee in Chicago in May. Roosevelt declared that there had been a war between progressive and reactionary forces in both major parties and that both struggles had been resolved. The Republicans now gave themselves "over to the principles of little Americanism and jingo bluff, to the old hypocrisy of Mark Hanna and Blaine" (McKinley's chief backer and Cleveland's unsuccessful first opponent for the presidency). The Republicans were concerned for "those unfortunate individuals who have incomes of $1,000,000 a year or more . . . and pet groups of manufacturers." Their foreign policy, devised by Lodge, was the "diametrical opposite" of whatever Wilson proposed. As for the Democrats, "Mr. Bryan [may have] gone too far in one direction," but the attempt to placate the reactionaries in 1904 had been a disaster and had been abandoned once and for all. He prepared the address in a couple of hours, delivered it with great flair, and invigorated his partisans. One of his eminent biographers has called it "a fighting speech—the first of Roosevelt's great political addresses."[63] As the Democratic Party began to think of candidates for 1920, he began to be mentioned as a senator or even, occasionally, for national office.

His marriage slowly mended, but Eleanor felt keenly, as she despairingly said to Franklin one night shortly after their return from Europe, that social Washington thought she was "dull and unattractive."[64] Franklin still stayed out late partying, though he was now absolutely circumspect about the other sex. The marriage must have been very taxing for both of them. Franklin found aspects of it a prison, and Eleanor was a specialist in putting on the airs of martyrdom, one night sitting for four hours on her doorstep waiting for Franklin and relatives to come home from a party she had left early. She explained to her incredulous husband that she hadn't wanted to ring the doorbell or go back to the party for a key.[65] For a time Eleanor couldn't take communion in her church because she was so bitter and unhappy.[66] In Washington she used to go to Rock Creek Park to commune instead with the statue of Mrs. Henry Adams, who had committed suicide in 1885. She became a Red Cross visitor in hospitals and began her remarkable career as an agent for social change.

In the evening of June 2, 1919, eight anarchist bombs in eight different cities in the United States went off, causing little damage. One of them, intended for the Washington home of the attorney general of the United States, Mitchell Palmer, was across the street from the Roosevelts. The anarchist himself was the only fatality, but it was a nerve-racking experience for the Roosevelts and ushered in a Red scare of unwholesome proportions. The following month there was a four-day race riot in Washington, in which fifteen people were killed. Unrelated to the communist and anarchist agitation, there were more than twenty other such riots in the United States that summer—the worst outbreak of racial violence in the United States since the notorious East St. Louis riots of 1917, in which artillery pieces were fired down the principal streets to quell the disturbances, with many hundreds of casualties and many blocks levelled by artillery or arson. (This particular disturbance drove the noted dancer Josephine Baker out of the United States and to Paris.)

V

ROOSEVELT'S PRINCIPAL PREOCCUPATION for much of 1919 and 1920 was purging homosexuals from the naval installations at Newport, Rhode Island, and, on the heels of this ostensible success, employing naval intelligence to entrap sexual wrongdoers among the town's civilian population. These initiatives ramified in ways unforeseen by the assistant secretary and caused him considerable embarrassment. Daniels had ordered that a court of inquiry clean up the alleged problem of a homosexual ring among naval personnel in Newport. The station commander set up a zealous navy doctor to send out a group of men pretending to be homosexuals to entice and ensnare potential naval deviants (by contemporary moral and legal standards). Fourteen men were eventually court martialed as a result of this sting operation.

Not content to leave the matter at this level, Roosevelt wrote to Attorney General Palmer, March 22, 1919, alleging "such conditions of vice and depravity" that they required action by the Justice Department.[67] Neither the attorney general nor the admiral in charge of naval intelligence thought it was appropriate for them to get involved in a general vice dragnet for "moral perversion and drugs" (Roosevelt's phrase) among the civil population of Newport. Both thought any such problems rightly belonged with the local civilian law enforcement authorities.

Franklin D. Roosevelt on the trail of moral turpitude was not to be put off. He armed his investigators with a letter from himself and attached them as "Section A" to his own office. As with the initial operation within navy ranks, controversial, in fact outrageous, acts were committed in pursuit of inculpatory evidence. Sixteen civilians were arrested, including the Episcopalian chaplain of the Newport naval hospital, who was charged with being "lewd and wanton." The clergyman was acquitted, and his trial brought to light the questionable entrapment methods employed by Section A, with the result that in September Roosevelt received a delegation of prominent Newport residents objecting to the operation. In vintage fashion, he claimed that the chaplain had been guilty and that the judge was incompetent or corrupt, and expressed qualified disbelief that any entrapment techniques had been employed.[68]

The acting director of the Bureau of Navigation, to whom Roosevelt referred his visitors, discontinued the operation. But Secretary Daniels handed the case back to the director of naval intelligence, who determined that the chaplain probably was guilty. The chaplain was hunted down in a sanitorium in Michigan where he had gone to reconstruct his life after suffering a nervous breakdown, and prosecuted again.

The chaplain's ordeal continued to January 1920, when he was acquitted at his second trial. The presiding judge excoriated the process that had led to the charge. The bishop of Rhode Island and a group of prominent clergymen petitioned the President for a serious investigation into the antics of Section A. The rabbits were about to chase the hunters. Roosevelt completed his customary majestic shift from self-righteously aggressive to sanctimoniously defensive, to unaware of bad things done by others, to severity in his condemnation of the over-righteous wrongdoers whom he had himself unleashed.

His opening gambit was to tell the *Boston Herald* that if allegations of objectionable methods in the collection of evidence were true, he "would take great pleasure in resigning my present office."[69] Daniels felt compelled to set up a court of inquiry on January 17, under Roosevelt's friend Admiral Herbert O. Dunn. Roosevelt and Howe now had to consume a little of their own medicine, when the editor of the *Providence Journal,* John Rathom, who had always been suspicious of Roosevelt's role in this affair, suggested he had been the real culprit. When the assistant secretary, as was his habit at such times, fulminated about "morally dishonest" journalism and so forth, Rathom circulated the most damning summary of the story to date to newspapers around the country. He demanded to know who had made enlisted men "perverts by official order."

Roosevelt then unsuccessfully asked the chairman of the Senate Naval Affairs Committee to suppress further coverage of the matter as potentially damaging to naval recruitment. He testified before the Dunn committee May 20, 1920, and stonewalled from start to finish; he had known nothing of the methods or activities of Section A. The committee deliberated harmlessly on through the 1920 election and reported its findings to Daniels early in 1921.

Its criticism of the assistant secretary was confined to suggestions that he had been "unfortunate and ill-advised."[70] He was dissatisfied even with this mild reproof and would remonstrate fiercely with a Senate subcommittee that had also taken up the Newport matter. The attorney general did choose not to prosecute. The legal aspect was thus wound down just before the administration went out of office, but Roosevelt's Republican opponents hadn't finished with it.

The chairman of the subcommittee, Senator L. Heisler Ball of Delaware, promised Roosevelt that he would allow him to testify before closing out its report and then reneged and proposed to bring out his report without notifying Roosevelt, when he knew him to be out of the country (in Campobello) on his summer holiday. Daniels warned Roosevelt by telegram of what was afoot and Roosevelt raced back to Washington on the promise that he would be heard. Ball gave him from 10 A.M. to 8 P.M., July 18, 1921, to give his reply to the fifteen-volume report he was seeing for the first time.

His press secretary, Stephen T. Early, and his personal secretary, Missy LeHand, assisted him. The subcommittee report called Roosevelt's testimony to the Dunn committee "incredible" and all but accused him of lying under oath. It made the point, not easily refuted, that since he had founded Section A, either he had a better idea than he admitted to of its proceedings or he was negligent in the administration of his office. Since the subcommittee regarded the assistant secretary as "a man of unusual intelligence and attainments," it did not doubt that he knew more than he admitted and that he and Daniels "showed an utter lack of moral perspective."[71]

As he toiled to assimilate the 6,000 pages of testimony, focusing because of the acute time shortage on the damaging conclusions, he learned that Senator Ball had double-crossed him again and released his report, which Daniels considered to be "libellous," to the press.[72] Roosevelt, sweltering through the July Washington heat, did his best at a disdainful polemical reply. Before asserting that the report did not "worry" him and that being attacked "so maliciously and savagely . . . rather amuses me," Roosevelt accused the authors of the report of "deliberate falsification of evidence, of perversion of facts, of misstatements of the record, and of a deliberate attempt to deceive."[73]

The newspapers didn't pay much attention to the controversy, and it didn't do Roosevelt any lasting damage. His performance had been absurdly impetuous in unleashing a navy undercover operation on the state of public morals in Newport. His unconcern with a likely terrible injustice to a well-regarded clergyman was unbecoming in someone so swift to represent himself as the victim of defamation.*

Unfortunately, this was not the only controversy that bedevilled the last months of the Daniels-Roosevelt era at the Navy Department. Daniels and Roosevelt sought to rehabilitate the men who had been disciplinary cases in the navy and confined to correctional centers, and enlisted Roosevelt and Howe's old New York reform ally, Thomas M. Osborne, who had been chairman of the New York State Commission on prison reform and warden of Sing Sing.

Osborne regularly changed into complicated disguises late in the night and drifted around seamy areas acquainting himself with the demimonde at the intersection of civil and criminal society. He had written a book on the experience of pretending for several weeks to be a prisoner in Auburn Prison. All of this was controversial and he had his enemies, including some who accused him of homosexual activity. He defended himself on these charges successfully, and Roosevelt supported him unreservedly as just the man to turn the detention facility at Portsmouth from, as Osborne put it, "a scrap-heap" into a "repair shop."[74]

In his period as commandant of the Portsmouth Prison, 4,000 of the 6,000 prisoners who came through were recycled into the navy. The whole program rankled the senior officers, including the much-decorated Admiral William S. Sims, now back as head of the Naval War College in Newport. He had always disliked Daniels and not taken much notice of Roosevelt, and the secretary delegated to his assistant the task of reminding the admiral of the naval regulation forbidding serving officers from engaging in public criticism of the Navy Department. Sims, whose disrespect for authority and official channels was well known,

---

* The head of Section A, Dr. E.M. Hudson, went on to be a dogmatic but confused and unconvincing witness in the trial of Bruno Richard Hauptmann, the accused killer of the kidnapped baby son of Colonel and Mrs. Charles A. Lindbergh, in 1933.

was particularly incensed by Daniels's overruling of many of his recommendations for awards and honors for those who had served under him. Sims highlighted his irritation by refusing the Distinguished Service Medal that was offered to him.

Sims had an even more serious grievance against Daniels. In January 1920, Sims had sent Daniels a paper summarizing what the admiral believed to be a catalogue of extravagances and blunders for which Daniels was responsible. In summary, Sims claimed that Daniels's dithering, inefficiency, and hostility to the British had cost half a million lives, 2.5 million tons of shipping, and $15 billion. He titled his bristling indictment "Certain Lessons of the Great War" and leaked it to the press. In the ensuing public controversy, a subcommittee of the Senate Naval Affairs Committee scheduled hearings on Sims's charges.

Roosevelt, despite Sims's condescending treatment of him in France in 1919, began to attach himself to the admiral, falsely claimed the credit (as described above) for sending him to Britain, and accompanied him from New York to Washington when he returned from Britain in the spring. He also successfully put Sims up for an honorary degree from Harvard. Sims sensed that he might be able to detach Roosevelt from Daniels and use him in the assault upon the secretary he had been preparing. He prevailed upon his wife to write to Eleanor that she had heard from a "high-ranking officer" that the sexual explorations with enlisted men "as decoys" in Newport had been Roosevelt's doing and that Daniels had had nothing to do with it. As a favor, she thought the Roosevelts should know this.

Franklin Roosevelt replied, denying any responsibility for the now infamous sex dragnet, but only mentioning Daniels as having ordered that that investigation proceed, on the recommendation of the admiral directing naval intelligence. He ended his letter somewhat fatuously, "Give my love to the Admiral [Sims] . . . Strictly between ourselves, I should like to shake the admiral warmly by the hand."[75]

Roosevelt, who had navigated the approaching end of the Wilson regime skillfully so far, now deserted his chief and jumped, prematurely as it turned out, to Sims. He gave a speech in Brooklyn on February 1, 1920, in which he claimed not only to have selected Sims for the British position (which as we have seen, was untrue), but against the wishes of Wilson and Daniels to have ordered guns with which to arm merchantmen, to remedy the state of unpreparedness for which his superiors were responsible.[76] It was one of the most discreditable episodes in Roosevelt's entire career, which ultimately contained a full catalogue of shabby moments.

When Roosevelt arrived at his office the next day as if nothing had happened, the long-suffering Daniels exploded with indignation. As always, Roosevelt claimed he had been misquoted and then prepared a clarification for the press that Daniels would not allow to go out because of its terminal blandness. In fact, Daniels had armed the merchant vessels on an executive order from Wilson, and the navy was not in an unprepared state at the outbreak of the war. The navy was a well-managed service, and most of the credit for that fact resided with the secretary, as Franklin Roosevelt well knew.

Having made his spurious case publicly, Roosevelt worked assiduously to capitalize on the Job-like forbearance of his chief, and even had Daniels and his wife to dinner on February 17, 1920, barely two weeks after Roosevelt's outrageous speech in Brooklyn. Daniels was still considering sacking Roosevelt, and visited the President to discuss it on February 21. By then the condition of the administration and of Wilson's health had become so parlous that Daniels thought better of it.

Wilson was already in an almost stuporous rage against Roosevelt, because he had had the effrontery to entertain to dinner Lord Grey, the former British foreign secretary, a birdwatching chum of Theodore Roosevelt's, who had come to tell Wilson that Britain could accept most of the amendments being proposed to the League of Nations Covenant in the Senate.

The reason for Wilson's anger against Grey and therefore Roosevelt was that Grey had in his entourage a Major Crauford-Stuart, who was known to have made an insulting joke about Mrs. Wilson and whom Wilson had the year before declared persona non grata and expelled from the country in consequence.* (The major was then a second-rank official in the British embassy.) It was undiplomatic of Grey, one of Britain's greatest foreign secretaries, but Wilson was by this time irrational. In the circumstances, and with Sims testifying at the Senate about his allegations of incompetence against the secretary of the navy, Daniels decided to accept Roosevelt's olive branch.

Roosevelt had said he would testify in the hearings if called, but truthfully and not as a partisan, which was enough to deter either side calling him; he further proclaimed that the Republicans shouldn't expect to derive any pleasure from an appearance of his. He gave written answers to written questions only. Sims cast no aspersions on Roosevelt, and Daniels proved a brilliant witness and floor manager for the administration.

As a newspaper publisher and former editor, Daniels knew how to orchestrate the press. He frogmarched in a long sequence of friendly admirals who were more than happy to puncture the balloon of Sims's vanity. Sims wasn't able to substantiate his charges of naval unpreparedness, and he proved a vainglorious megalomaniac, intelligent, but with only a tenuous hold on reality. (He was almost a miniaturized prototype of the last professional version of Douglas MacArthur.) Roosevelt wrote Daniels in 1922 that he objected to the movement to make Sims a full admiral. Sims, he wrote, had seen less sea service in the war than he, Roosevelt, had.[77]

Sims, who left the hearings a significantly diminished man, bitterly referred to

---

* The joke of Crauford-Stewart's that caused Wilson to expel him from the United States was: "What did Mrs. Galt do when the President proposed to her? She fell out of bed." Not very raunchy by subsequent standards, but too much for the severe Wilson.

Roosevelt, not altogether inaccurately at this stage, as "a simon-pure politician." Roosevelt evinced no further desire to "shake the Admiral warmly by the hand." (The throat perhaps, and the ambition was reciprocated.) Roosevelt had been as lucky as cunning, and even more than usually unscrupulous, to come through this affair unscathed.

Roosevelt did have some legitimate navy business to attend to, and fought successfully against a move to take naval aviation away from the navy and military aviation from the army and concentrate it in a new air department, as some other countries had done.

Less positively, he badgered Daniels into the construction of an oil refinery in Fall River, Massachusetts, for processing Mexican crude oil and saving the navy money. Roosevelt effusively assured audiences that he and Daniels had saved the taxpayers millions and cracked an oil cartel. In fact, by the time the refinery opened, the world's oil price had descended and the facility was a minor white elephant. It was a cheap and valuable lesson in the hazards of state-run enterprises.[78]

There was yet another controversy that Roosevelt had to deal with that was virtually entirely his own creation. In January 1920 he published an unsigned article in the *Army and Navy Journal* praising Osborne's efforts at rehabilitating convicted navy legal and moral offenders. A Captain J.K. Taussig wrote a sharply worded rebuttal, claiming that the number of sodomites sent back to sea was not the two Roosevelt claimed, but almost a hundred. Daniels appointed yet another board to look into this controversy but packed it by putting Roosevelt himself and his friend Admiral Dunn on the board of three (which makes all the more unpardonable Roosevelt's ungrateful, self-laudatory panegyric in Brooklyn, February 1, 1920). Daniels, in a further act of paternal forgiveness, declined Taussig's request for a full court of inquiry, saving his undeserving assistant from a potentially serious embarrassment in an election year.

Daniels must have recognized Roosevelt's finer qualities despite his many acts of ingratitude and occasional lapses into outright treachery, or he would have dispensed with him. Roosevelt was essentially vindicated in his apprehensions of impending war, and there was not one recorded instance where he was guilty of incompetence. Roosevelt may have learned from Daniels the virtues of loyalty to subordinates. He may also have taught himself the dangers of insubordinacy, because when his turn came he fired many people, including some distinguished men, for much less serious offenses than those that he regularly visited on Daniels.

Daniels was a good secretary and Roosevelt was a good assistant secretary, and although the navy functioned largely in a logistical role in the war, it performed well. Ship construction was intelligent, and despite Roosevelt's unsuccessful advocacy of fifty-foot patrol boats, the United States never became distracted with designs that didn't really work, like the battle cruiser. The surrender and ultimate scuttling of the German fleet at Scapa Flow in 1919 instantly elevated the United

States Navy to second place, behind only the British as the world's greatest navy, an incidental achievement for the Daniels-Roosevelt regime.

VI

I F THE RETURN to America of Woodrow Wilson in February 1919 after the establishment of the League of Nations was the pinnacle of his life, what then unfolded was a tragedy at every level. Wilson was back in France in March to hammer out a peace treaty. He returned to America once again on July 8 with the Treaty of Versailles and presented it to the Senate two days later. He claimed, indicating perhaps that the epochal struggle and unprecedented mass adulation had affected his judgment, that the treaty was the work of "the hand of God . . . It was of this time that we dreamed at our birth. America in truth shall show the way. The light streams upon the path ahead, and nowhere else." This uplifting vision was not universally shared. When he learned the terms of the treaty, Marshal Foch exclaimed: "This is not a peace, it is a twenty-year armistice!" He was accurate within two months, though events could have unfolded differently had the United States ratified the treaty and played a full part in world affairs.

Points 5 and 12 of Wilson's original program were gutted. The four other senior Allies helped themselves to the German colonies and the non-Turkish parts of the Ottoman Empire, and Italy nibbled at the former Habsburg Empire with little regard to matters of nationality. So much for the "absolutely unmolested opportunity for autonomy" of Turkey's Arab subjects. This was translated in fact into suzerainty of the British and French over the Asian Arabs—arguably more enlightened hands, but less durable ones, than Turkey's. Britain took the poisoned chalice of Arab-Jewish problems in Palestine and would drink the bitter cup to the lees.

Wilson had thought he had won the battle when he secured approval of the League of Nations and its charter from the conference first. When he returned to negotiate the peace treaty, the associated countries made it clear that the confirmation of and adherence to the League was mortgaged to almost every detail of the treaty. Since the League had no supranational authority, France's taking the Saar, Italy's seizing the Tyrol, Japan's exploiting Shantung, and many other traditional abuses by the victors of the defeated powers were effectively irreversible, except through restoration by force when Germany would have the strength to rise again.

To launch the League, Wilson made endless concessions of this kind. If his health had not been declining, he would have been better able to act on House's threat of October 1918, and make a separate peace with Germany. Instead, he gave way, and recriminations, reparations, and ostracism were piled on Germany, almost assuring the oppression of Europe's strongest country by its neighbors, and the likely incitement of an unquenchable spirit of German revanchism.

Some of the more idealistic members of the United States Peace Commission were outraged, and three, Adolf Berle, Samuel Eliot Morrison, and William C. Bullitt, resigned—Bullitt in an open and vitriolic letter to the President, which was cited by the President's enemies in the ratification debate.[79] (All these men would ultimately serve and work closely with Roosevelt many years later.) Roosevelt himself acknowledged that he had had the grace of conversion in favor of the League when he had gone to Europe in 1918.*

Wilson was prepared to compromise at the Paris conference, but not with Lodge. Roosevelt sensed how shallow and vulnerable was the support for the League, and from July of 1919 through the summer and autumn he spoke little about it publicly.[81] Wilson, ineptly leading domestic pro-League sentiment, failed to notice it melt away behind him.

The welcoming crowds were much thinner on Wilson's return in July 1919 than they had been only five months before and included, as he returned to the White House, the inimitable Alice Roosevelt Longworth attempting to put a hex on the returning President. ("A murrain on him!")[82] Lodge's motivations, as between statesmanly reservations and personal detestation of Wilson, have never been precisely unraveled. He ordered a word-by-word reading of the Versailles treaty into the record, which was preposterous, and six weeks of hearings in which every ethnic group in America was encouraged to express its disappointment at what the treaty did or failed to do to its ancestral homeland.

The anti-League movement arose and was well, though surreptitiously, financed. A campaign of demagogy and irresponsible editorial comment, claiming a sell-out to the British, the pope, and others spread across the country. Wilson, in the full transports of messianism, was unaware of the forces snapping and gnawing at his popular support. He had no rapport with the leaders of the Congress and took his time appealing directly to the public in terrestrial terms that the people would find comprehensible. While there is some mystery about Lodge's motives, there is no doubt that Wilson, in rejecting any compromise, was moved in large part by his unbecoming hatred of Lodge.

Lodge and his hard-line opponents to ratification of the treaty in the Senate early became known as "irreconcilables." In July 1919 when Wilson presented the treaty to the Senate, there were only fourteen of them. By August it was clear to the President's strategists that he would have to accept some modifications to assure passage. Wilson had maneuvered skillfully in his first term as president, getting a comprehensive reform program through a Congress where subtle coalition-building was often required. But now he recoiled at the thought of compromise and resolved instead to appeal to the country, despite deteriorating health, which seemed to decline in tandem with his tactical judgment.

The greatest and most civilized states of Europe having massacred the cream

* "This is a time when more ideals are properly demanded of us, and over there on the other side, every man, woman, and child looks to us to make good the high purpose with which we came into this war."[80]

of their youth and impoverished themselves, much of the world was eager to believe that Thomas Woodrow Wilson was not only the personification of the New World coming to the rescue of the Old. He was almost a redeemer of man, bringing forth a post-national order and, by making the Great War a victorious struggle against war itself, justifying the unimaginable slaughter that Europe had endured. It must be said that by his high intellect, soaring eloquence, and incorruptible attachment to principle, Woodrow Wilson had the great stature this unique role required. It was the objective that was unattainable. As euphoria gave way to disillusionment, Wilson refused to descend the mountain he had scaled, and was gradually transformed from a prophet to a tragic idealist whose benign ambitions were not of this world.

He failed, but he never lost his dignity or distinction as man and statesman, even under the battering of political defeat and withered health. With all the severity of his uncompromising personality he remains a formidable historic figure and one of the great, though not one of the very greatest, presidents of the United States. And he was right. His passion for openness and his attempt to rise above the criterion of the national interest were naïve and probably harmful. But the peace of the world required a more comprehensive approach to international relations and American engagement in the world.

Wilson had suffered a minor stroke in Paris in April 1919, and thereafter twitched and trembled, often compulsively. He ignored the advice of his wife, cabinet, doctor, and intimates like House and Tumulty, that he not undertake a transcontinental speaking tour. He had become a crusader. He was not playing a role on the world's stage; he had become convinced that he was a providential instrument in the reformation of the world from its violent past.

In his war upon war he had become intolerant even of tolerance if he thought it was misapplied. For the future of the world he would risk his life; he declared that he didn't care if he died if the treaty were adopted. He evidently considered that if it were not adopted, the only value his life retained was to be sacrificed to the cause. He was to be accused of almost everything, but not ambiguity of purpose.

Wilson left Washington on his speaking campaign on behalf of the League and the treaty on September 3, 1919 (twenty years to the day before the outbreak of the next world war, which it was his holy purpose to prevent). The President's train travelled over 8,000 miles in twenty-two days, and he gave forty formal speeches and a great many improvised ones. He repeated at each opportunity that the country owed it to all those who had died in the Great War to adopt a treaty that would end war. Referring to "mothers who have lost their sons in France [who] have said 'God bless you Mr. President,' " he declared that "they believe that their sons died for something that vastly transcends the immediate and palpable objects of the war."

At Pueblo, Colorado, on September 25 his emotion almost surpassed his great powers of expression as he evoked "the serried ranks . . . of those dear ghosts who still deploy upon the fields of France," and promised to lead the nation and the world "into pastures of quietness and peace such as the world never dreamed of before." That night, in his railway car, painted blue and called the Mayflower, the President suffered a severe stroke. The rest of the tour was cancelled. The crusade was over.

At his and his wife's insistence, the only announcement was that he was suffering from "nervous exhaustion" as the train conveyed him back to Washington. Other than on very brief automobile drives, he did not leave the White House again for seventeen months. The left side of his face was frozen. On October 2, 1919, Wilson suffered a further stroke and the complete paralysis of his left side.

On October 17, Wilson was almost killed by a prostatic obstruction. He survived but was confined to bed for two weeks, and was terribly frail, purblind, immobile, and almost incomprehensible after that. Medical bulletins dissembled. The new Mrs. Wilson fiercely protected her husband and masterminded a conspiracy to withhold from the cabinet and Congress the fact that he was incapacitated. In doing so she destroyed the only hope that remained of the substantial adoption of the treaty he sent to the Senate.

If the extent of his indisposition had been made known, it would have attracted considerable public and congressional sympathy. This was the course counselled in vain by Josephus Daniels. If the President had been declared incapacitated, as he should have been, Marshall and Lansing, who had none of Wilson's intellectual power, moral authority, or capacity to lead, but were realistic men of reasonable intelligence, could have secured adoption of a treaty that Lodge would have lightly modified but not completely emasculated.

Mrs. Wilson arranged for her husband to see visitors only very briefly after he was well-rested, when he would seem mentally competent, and he remained in office stubbornly refusing any compromise with his opponents but unable to lead the pro-League forces. These would have responded to his leadership or to knowledge of his personal sacrifice for the cause, but not to sullen silence behind the locked gates and drawn shades of the White House, with ghoulish rumors in constant circulation. The distinguished Kansas editor William Allen White, a reform Republican, said: "With calumny rampant about him he tasted the ingratitude of his republic, the statesman's ancient cup of hemlock."

On October 18, Franklin Roosevelt, Livy Davis, and the celebrated aviator Richard Byrd departed Washington for a three-week moose hunt in New Brunswick and Nova Scotia. Roosevelt would thus avoid the embarrassment of being in Washington but not seeing King Albert. (He had been planning to show the king all the letters he had received addressed to him as King Roosevelt or other royal salutations, always eager to emphasize any connection, however attenuated, to those whose positions were of majestic or even supposedly divine origin, but Wilson and his staff had excluded Roosevelt from the invitation to meet the king.)

The king and queen of the Belgians arrived on October 30 and visited the

White House briefly. The President, too ill to get out of bed, received his royal visitors propped up on pillows, wearing a dressing gown, and with a full white beard, because his doctors were afraid that shaving him might be too much of a strain.

In early November the Democratic leader in the Senate, Gilbert Hitchcock of Nebraska, visited the President and told him he no longer had a bare majority, much less the two-thirds required for ratification. Hitchcock urged a compromise offer to Lodge, but Wilson demanded that Lodge take the initiative. When the senator returned on November 18 even Mrs. Wilson asked her husband to compromise, but he wouldn't hear of it and begged her not to desert him. "It is not I who will not accept it; it is the nation's honor that is at stake. Better a thousand times to go down fighting than to dip your colors to dishonorable compromise."[83] He dictated a brief note asking his supporters to vote against the Lodge amendments. It was French and British Remembrance Day, the first anniversary of Foch's armistice. The next day the Senate rejected both the Lodge and the Wilson version of the treaty.

The sublime and the ridiculous were even closer together than Napoleon had originally observed. Everything that could go wrong did. Wilson's hour of glory had lasted only a few months. The dream of useful American participation in the world died, though not in the mind of the assistant secretary of the navy. But twenty-five years and scores of millions more victims would be wasted.

VII

O N JANUARY 10, 1920, an old friend of Roosevelt's from Harvard, Louis Wehle, a member of the War Industries Board and a nephew of Supreme Court justice Louis Brandeis, visited him to discuss politics. Wehle suggested that Roosevelt start a campaign within the Democratic Party to nominate Herbert C. Hoover, now the head of the Commission for Relief in Belgium and U.S. Food Administrator in Europe, a widely admired non-partisan figure, for president and Roosevelt for vice president. Roosevelt was cagey but urged Wehle to launch such a campaign if he wished, and Wehle started with Colonel House, who was strongly in favor. Hoover met with House, and with Roosevelt and their mutual friend Interior Secretary Franklin K. Lane. Roosevelt described Hoover as "a wonder," and added, "I wish we could make him President of the United States. There could not be a better one." (The ultimate ironies of this assertion need hardly be emphasized.) "Like Winston Churchill in London in 1918, [Hoover] made much more of an impression upon Roosevelt than Roosevelt did upon him."[84]

Hoover was pledged to support the League of Nations but had no affiliation with any party. He was tempted by high public office. Franklin and Eleanor Roosevelt dined with him on March 6, and were very impressed, but with American participation in the League of Nations dead, and the Democrats a discredited party waiting for the executioner on election day, Hoover publicly declared himself a progressive Republican on March 30. Not even Roosevelt could change parties easily, so if he wanted to run for vice president it would have to be with a candidate less likely to be elected than Hoover would have been. Given Hoover's espousal of the League, it is hard not to attribute his adherence to the Republicans to rank political opportunism.

The Eighteenth Amendment to the Constitution of the United States, banning the sale and consumption of alcoholic beverages, the fruit of a mighty campaign by the primordial forces of American Puritanism, went into effect at midnight, January 14–15, 1920. Representatives of the non-conformist Protestantism that produced the Prohibitionist movement, such as Josephus Daniels and William Jennings Bryan, celebrated. Those two were at the First Congregational Church of Washington as the clock struck midnight, with the author of the congressional enforcement act, Congressman Andrew Volstead. In such matters of personal and cultural habits of consumption, as in international affairs, there was a strong body of American opinion that the country was so different from the Old World that inconvenient aspects of human nature could simply be repealed by legislative fiat at home and made the subject of a grand abstention abroad.[85]

The American public was always repelled by Communism, particularly its anti-democratic and redistributive tenets, its collectivism, and its atheism. But many Americans shared a notion of the perfectibility of man that was almost as madly unrealistic as that of the Marxists. Franklin D. Roosevelt was not one of them. He was a worldly man and he liked a drink. He paid no attention to Prohibition in his personal habits and never believed for an instant that it would be a successful initiative. He never doubted that it would prove as great a failure as isolationism, and that the deformed idealism that gave rise to both would have to be redirected to more practical goals. He also had an idea of who might be the best person to lead America out of its current susceptibility to such mistaken public policy.

The Wilson administration began to disintegrate. McAdoo's successor as secretary of the Treasury resigned on February 2, frustrated at his inability to communicate with the President. On February 5 the secretary of the interior took the same step for the same reason. On February 7 the President demanded to know from Secretary of State Lansing if he had been convening the cabinet in his absence. Lansing replied that since the members of the cabinet were unable to get any direction from the President, they informally met among themselves from time to time. Wilson immediately demanded and received Lansing's resignation.

It was widely felt that Wilson was now mad. He had failed in his great project, failed even in his apparent effort to die in pursuit of the project if it were unsuccessful. His supreme wish and alternate death wish were both unfulfilled. In the spring he went for a brief automobile drive around Washington. On returning to the White House he was applauded by a small group of onlookers as his car went back through the gates of the executive mansion. The President lifted his right hand and gratefully said to his wife, "They still love me," unaware that it was a group of White House staff and their families organized by the head of Wilson's security detail. Edith Wilson wept.[86]

Wilson even attempted to float the idea of an unprecedented third term, dismissing the leading Democratic candidates: his son-in-law, William Gibbs McAdoo; the attorney general and chief author of the overworked Red Scare, A. Mitchell Palmer; and the governor of Ohio, James M. Cox. (He called Cox's candidacy "a joke.") Only those personally or professionally interested in the President's clinical condition still listened to him.

The U.S. government was now derelict and hopeless. There was little to be done until a new administration would be installed a year hence. In learning the lesson of not clinging to the presidency in declining health, Franklin D. Roosevelt was not as observant as he was of TR's mistake in leaving it prematurely, or of other aspects of this tragedy.

VIII

THE REPUBLICAN PARTY convened in Chicago in June under the chairmanship of Henry Cabot Lodge, who treated the delegates to an unbecomingly violent personal attack on Wilson. Governor Frank Lowden of Illinois and Theodore Roosevelt's friend and fellow Rough Rider General Leonard Wood were the leading candidates, and stalemated the convention. In the late evening of June 12 the party elders met in the original and famous smoke-filled room in the Blackstone Hotel and decided to give the nomination to the handsome, amiable lightweight Senator Warren Gamaliel Harding of Ohio. The most vocal dissenter against the customary motion to make Harding's nomination unanimous came from "stocky, clamp-jawed Chicago delegate" Harold Ickes, now thoroughly disillusioned with the Republicans, but Lodge, as convention chairman, gavelled the motion through.[87] The taciturn Calvin Coolidge, who had impressed the country by his suppression of a strike of Boston policemen in his capacity as governor of Massachusetts, was chosen as the candidate for vice president.

The Democratic convention opened in San Francisco on July 28. Roosevelt, claiming to have difficulty getting a hotel room (which was unlikely given his position and his status as a New York delegate), asked the commander of the Pacific Fleet, Admiral Hugh Rodman, to put him up in the flagship, the battleship *New Mexico*, which would be in San Francisco with the rest of the Pacific battle fleet at that time. Rodman considered Roosevelt a brash and precocious upstart but felt he had to comply. He didn't much care for Daniels, either, and when the secretary made the same request replied that there was only one suitable stateroom on the *New Mexico* and Roosevelt had reserved it. Daniels, who must have had quite enough of Roosevelt's impertinences by now, cabled back that he would stay on the *New Mexico* and Rodman could make other arrangements for his assistant secretary. Roosevelt took a cabin on the slightly older battleship *New York* and entertained the entire New York delegation on board.

Roosevelt's first noteworthy appearance at the convention came when a great demonstration occurred at the unveiling of a large floodlit portrait of President Wilson. The hall erupted in spontaneous demonstrations in Wilson's honor, but Tammany Boss Charles Murphy ordered New York delegates not to join in in any way, including carrying about the New York State standard demarcating the seats assigned to the New York delegates. With the mayor of Schenectady, Franklin Roosevelt wrested the standard from the local judge designated by Murphy to hold it and, followed by many of the New York delegates, carried it into the aisle and around the auditorium, in direct contravention of Murphy's orders.

As always with Roosevelt, only a few days were necessary for him to transform his feat of cheerleading, a bizarre interest he developed at Groton and honed at Harvard, to victorious fisticuffs with half a dozen Tammany goons, unassisted by the mayor of Schenectady or anyone else. Exaggerated though it was in the retelling, it was a peppy performance. No one else in the hall who was thirty-eight years old, deputy head of a large executive department, and hoping to be nominated for vice president, was likely to scuffle physically over such a sophomoric issue.

Roosevelt was at his charming squirely best when he entertained the New York delegates aboard the U.S.S. *New York,* in what would have been considered in any subsequent time to be a questionable use of his office and of government property. Here as elsewhere at this convention, the fact that the country had for six months (and the navy for seven years) been under Prohibition and was officially free of liquor was ignored. Liquor was not offered by the host, but was brought in quantities by some of the guests, and flowed in torrents at other places in the convention.

Governor Alfred E. Smith came aboard with his wife and family and took Roosevelt aside to ask if he would second Smith's nomination for president as the favorite son candidate of New York. Roosevelt accepted instantly and with pleasure. The candidacy had no chance of success. Smith was not well known outside New York, and the convention and the country were certainly not ready for a Roman Catholic candidate. The purpose of the candidacy was to hold the New York delegates together and give Murphy and Smith maximum influence in the choice between Secretary McAdoo, Attorney General Palmer, and Governor Cox.

Smith's motive in asking Roosevelt was to associate himself with upper-class Protestantism, anti-Tammany reform sentiment, and the great Roosevelt name. Roosevelt's motive was to give himself a platform from which to impress the delegates with his presence and oratorical talents and to indebt Tammany to him, whether he would be running for vice president or U.S. senator. Roosevelt had had tried to mend fences with Tammany and had worked hard with New York congressmen during the war on patronage issues and to help constituents in the navy.

Alfred Emmanuel Smith was a florid Irish New Yorker in loud suits and a brown derby hat, with gold-capped teeth, a heavy New York working-class accent, a large ruddy nose, a paunch, and, invariably, a big cigar. He was nine years older and four inches shorter than Franklin D. Roosevelt, a strenuously practicing but not at all intolerant Catholic. Born in 1873 in the old fourth ward near where the Brooklyn Bridge was later built, he had to leave school after the eighth grade when his father, a freight-handler, died. (Smith was younger when he left school than Roosevelt was when he was taken from his tutors and started school at Groton.)

Smith worked in the Fulton fish market but drifted to the local Democratic Party clubhouse, where he was popular because of his stentorian voice, love of histrionic entertainment, evident intelligence, and high ambition. His first white-collar job was as a court investigator rounding up jurors, a patronage position, and he personified the best aspects of the machine system. He personally was honest, diligent, and decent, a brilliant governor, and a credit to all he represented. He was an autodidact who with his friend Robert Wagner taught himself how to read and understand bills and statutes after he was elected to the New York State Assembly in 1903.

He had never seen a farm or a forest before he boarded the train to Albany to take his place in the state capitol in March 1904. The Triangle fire in 1911 and the New York State Factory Commission, which Wagner and Smith and Frances Perkins ran, took him all over the state for the first time. He became speaker of the assembly in 1913, and was a constant source of reform legislation governing working conditions, industrial safety, and minimum wages, with particular attention to women and children. Even Elihu Root and other exalted and learned men acknowledged Smith's pre-eminent role at the constitutional convention of New York State in 1915. He was sheriff of New York County (1915–1917) and president of the Board of Aldermen of Greater New York (1917) prior to his first election as governor of New York in 1918.

Smith and Roosevelt were not particularly friendly at the beginning of Roosevelt's career. Smith thought him another rich man's son, a snobbish, ineffectual dilettante masquerading as a public-spirited reformer who was grandstanding on his mother's money and his cousin's renown. It is unlikely that Roosevelt was greatly more appreciative of the rough-hewn assemblyman from the Bowery. The relationship they built was the bridge between the upstate, Protestant, reform Democrats and New York City, Catholic, machine Democrats.

They often celebrated their friendship, though their relations were only occasionally very cordial. But there were moments when the achievements of Smith in overcoming his socioeconomic disadvantages and of Roosevelt in overcoming the infirmity that struck him in the twenties, and of both in defeating political adversaries, stirred them to genuine mutual admiration.

Smith was nominated for president at San Francisco by his old friend and elocution teacher (from whom even Winston Churchill, who was an admirer of Smith and a fascinated devotee of U.S. politics, claimed to have learned), Bourke Cockran, the ne plus ultra of colorful Tammany orators. The band struck up and the convention dissolved into dancing and partying, including Roosevelt, who waltzed with female delegates to "The Sidewalks of New York" and other Irish Gotham ditties. When he saw the convention returning to order, Roosevelt vaulted over several rows of chairs to get to the podium, his first appearance there at a national convention.

Roosevelt was eloquent and generous in his praise of the favorite son of New York: "I love him as a friend; I look up to him as a man; I am with him as a Democrat, and we all know his record throughout the nation . . . The nominee of this convention will not be chosen at two A.M. in a hotel room!" He made a tremendous impression: confident but not haughty, energetic without the gawky boisterousness he had had as a younger man. He had learned the personal political arts and turned his mighty charm on great numbers of delegates.

Smith withdrew after eight ballots and Murphy swung most of the state to Cox, although Roosevelt personally went to McAdoo. Cox gradually crept toward the nomination, inching up in each ballot. Roosevelt and Murphy reached an agreement that if Roosevelt didn't obstruct Murphy's efforts on behalf of Cox, Murphy would not oppose Roosevelt as vice president or as senator. Roosevelt's supporters fanned out around the convention touting their man as vice president even before the presidential nomination had been completed, and met no opposition from the Tammany forces. Cox—judged almost as innocuous as Harding, his fellow Ohioan—was chiefly known for banning the teaching of German in Ohio in 1917 so as not to subvert the loyalty of Ohio's children in wartime. Cox was nominated on the 46th ballot at dawn on July 6, 1920.

When his floor manger phoned him with the news of his nomination and asked his preference for vice president, Cox responded, "Young Roosevelt." He had heard that Roosevelt was capable, attractive, and anti-Tammany, and he presumably was mindful that insofar as the Democrats had any hope of winning, it rode on bringing in the Republican progressives, which no one could do as well as the bearer of the magic name. (In later years Roosevelt would become sensitive about the value of TR's name, though he was happy to bandy it about at this stage. He claimed to the friendly biographer Emil Ludwig that "my name had become known during the war," and that he was a bridge between the administration and Cox, who had not worked in Washington. There is no evidence that Cox would have accepted either explanation.)

In deference to Boss Murphy, without whom he would not have been nominated and without whom he could not win, Cox asked that Murphy be consulted. When asked, Murphy said, "This young Roosevelt is no good, but if you want him go ahead and we'll vote for him." Murphy thus adhered to his word to Roosevelt and demonstrated his gratitude at being treated seriously as a respectable political chieftain by a presidential nominee. He had been ostracized during the Wilson and Bryan years.

Judge Timothy T. Ansberry nominated Franklin Roosevelt, and he was seconded by several others, including Al Smith, who was less effusive than Roosevelt had been for him, calling him "a leader in local legislative reform . . . who has held a position of great power and importance." Just before he was acclaimed, Josephus Daniels came to the podium. "To five hundred thousand men in the United States Navy and to five million men in the Army," he said, "it is a matter of peculiar gratification that this convention unanimously has chosen as a candidate for vice president that clear-headed and able executive and patriotic citizen of New York and the assistant secretary of the navy, Franklin D. Roosevelt."[88]

Daniels emphasized that only his own intervention had prevented the nominee from seeking active service during the Great War. (In fact it was Wilson's intervention, but after all Roosevelt's liberties with the truth at Daniels's expense, the secretary had certainly earned the right to exaggerate.) Roosevelt was nominated without opposition.

The electoral prospects were poor, but the possibilities for Roosevelt to impress huge numbers of Democrats around the country and the public generally were very interesting to him. He was doubly gratified because of the success he had earned according to his two main competitive yardsticks: he had lapped Theodore Roosevelt and leap-frogged Al Smith. He had been nominated for vice president at an age three years younger than the age at which TR had been nominated to the same post twenty years before, and hadn't had to be governor of New York first. And he was running for national office while Smith would be seeking reelection as governor. The comparison with his cousin was somewhat forced, since Theodore Roosevelt had been taken on by an incumbent president almost certain of reelection, while FDR was likely to sink with Cox. But it was still an ambitious jump up the political ladder for someone who looked more and more like an irresistible force in Democratic politics. Walter Lippmann, the newspaper and magazine editor (*The New Republic*) who became one of the most influential political columnists in the world, generously telegraphed the candidate: "When parties can pick a man like Frank Roosevelt, there is a decent future in politics."[89]

Roosevelt returned to Hyde Park on July 13. Bunting had been hung in a few places, and Sara was eager to tell her son how proud his father would have been. President Wilson fell far short of the usual effusive congratulations, though that may have been because of his disability. He sent a telegram of "warm congratulations and good wishes" to Roosevelt. The greeting to Cox was only slightly less tepid. Herbert Hoover sent Roosevelt "my personal congratulations of an old friend . . . it will bring the merit of a great public servant to the front." Roosevelt wrote his wife on July 17 that he had met Cox's train and that there was "a huge, cheering crowd, more enthusiastic than any Washington crowd I have ever seen."[90]

Roosevelt wrote a formal letter of resignation to Wilson on July 13, in which he referred to the President in terms normally reserved for Dr. Peabody: "All my life I shall never fail to remember the splendid principles you have kept to the fore and the devotion to unselfish service which you have given us as an example." Wilson responded with "sincere regret" that Roosevelt was leaving and had Daniels draft a letter of acceptance of his resignation.[91]

Cox and Roosevelt called on Wilson five days later. An informant of Lodge's thought Roosevelt "a little silly in his exuberance," and Lodge himself now thought him "a well-meaning, nice young fellow, but light . . . His head is evidently turned and the effect upon a not very strong man is obvious."[92] While Cox wore a grey suit, Roosevelt wore white shoes, white trousers, and a double-breasted dark-blue jacket, as if on his way to a yacht club, accentuating his almost collegiate youthfulness.[93] Roosevelt issued a statement regretting that not every American could be "a silent witness to the meeting of these two great men."[94]

Roosevelt had not seen his president for ten months, and Mrs. Wilson said she would never forget the shock and sympathy in his face when he saw the gravity of her husband's physical deterioration.[95] Wilson sat in his wheelchair, half-paralyzed and with downcast eyes. Cox expressed his admiration and pledged his support for Wilson's fight for the League. Wilson, who had considered Cox an absurd candidate, was grateful and said, "That battle can still be won."[96] Cox stopped in Tumulty's office and drafted a statement proclaiming the League the principal issue of the election. Not long after, Wilson told Daniels that he was "deeply resentful" of Roosevelt, as a precocious careerist of questionable loyalty.

His endorsement of the Democratic candidates consisted of a brief statement he made in a reedy voice to a little knot of supporters a week before the election encouraging them to vote according to which candidate (regardless of party) would redeem the honor of the United States. Unsuccessful in his grand project and in his effort to die in pursuit of it, he was reduced to seeking its rejection and being grimly vindicated in years that he would not see. This was the lugubrious sunset of the man probably rivalled only by Thomas Jefferson as the foremost intellect ever to occupy the White House.

IX

R OOSEVELT COMMANDEERED a destroyer to take him to Campobello for a brief holiday, irritating the Hearst newspapers, which accused him of self-indulgent extravagance. Shortly before departing for Campobello he wrote Eleanor that "Reports are distinctly encouraging about the sentiment throughout the nation."[97] This indicates that Roosevelt may have initially entertained greater hopes for the prospects of the Democratic ticket than he subsequently admitted.

He returned from Campobello to retire from the Navy Department officially on August 6. He received a warm sendoff from 2,000 employees and told them, "My heart will always be with the navy."[98] He would be faithful to that promise. He gave Josephus Daniels a hand-written note: "You have taught me so wisely and kept my feet on the ground when I was about to sky-rocket—and in it all there has never been a real dispute or antagonism or distrust."[99] (This last, a nice thought, took slight liberty with the facts.)

The secretary replied with his own note: "My thought and feeling has been that of an older brother . . . I shall share in the happiness [of] your beautiful home life" (he was well aware there had been problems), "and we will indeed be brothers in all things that make for the good of our country."[100] He wrote in his diary that night that he was glad he had resisted the temptation to deal harshly with his young assistant over his more egregious actions.[101] Roosevelt had judged his chief astutely, and theirs was a successful relationship in the end. They continued to be cordial for the rest of Roosevelt's days; FDR was able and happy to befriend both Daniels and his son when he was in a position to do so a generation later.

In these times it was the quaint practice that presidential and vice presidential nominees received formal notification of their nomination in their hometowns. Franklin, Eleanor, Anna (now an attractive golden-haired fourteen-year-old), and James travelled on August 8 to Dayton, Ohio, where James M. Cox owned the newspaper. Roosevelt was full of purposeful comments about how he would transform the vice presidency into a serious office. But when he asked Cox to promise that he would be invited to cabinet meetings, Cox demurred, saying he didn't want the Senate, over which the vice president presides, to think Roosevelt a White House spy. Roosevelt promised a campaign that would "drag the enemy off the front porch."[102]

Roosevelt's own notification took place the next day at Springwood. Five thousand people were in attendance on the lawn in front of the house, including Josephus Daniels, William G. McAdoo, and Al Smith. Roosevelt personally invited tenant farmers and people of the same general social echelon into the library of Springwood for the ceremony itself, and introduced many of his economically humblest neighbors to many of the important office-holders who attended. His graciousness was long and gratefully remembered by his neighbors, some of whom knew him throughout all his life and almost all of whom always liked and admired him.

In his remarks, the vice presidential nominee said that it was "impossible to be in this world and not of it."[103] He condemned isolationism: "The League will not die. An idea does not die which meets the call of the hearts of our mothers. . . . War may be 'declared'; peace cannot. It must be established by mutual consent. . . . We cannot anchor our ship of state in this world tempest, nor can we return to the placid harbor of long years ago." Regarding domestic matters he said: "We oppose money in politics, we oppose the private control of national finances. We oppose the treatment of human beings as commodities, we oppose the saloon-bossed city, we oppose starvation wages, we oppose rule by groups or cliques. . . . We oppose a mere period of coma in our national life."[104] (This was a fairly accurate prognosis of what a Harding administration would produce.) It was a prescient speech, and parts of it were a foretaste of addresses he would give to much larger audiences, often to tens of millions over the radio, fifteen or so years later. A distinguished Harvard economist said that "in comparison to Harding's performance it was like Hyperion to a satyr."[105]

It was a fine occasion, though tragically marred for the Roosevelt family by the death later in the day of Sara's brother, Warren Delano III, who had attended the notification ceremony. Frightened by a train whistle, his horse panicked forward and pulled his carriage in front of an oncoming locomotive.[106]

The campaign began on August 10, when Roosevelt boarded a private car attached to a regular train going west from Chicago. He travelled over 8,000 miles and, as he said many years later, "got to know the country as only a candidate for office or a traveling salesman can get to know it."[107] He delivered a daily average of seven formal addresses and many improvised ones. His advance man was his press secretary, Steve Early, who had been a staffer of the *Stars and Stripes* armed forces newspaper in Europe during the war. Early was a blunt southern journalist who would remain with Roosevelt throughout his public career. He would later tell Harold Ickes that Roosevelt in 1920 had a "playboy" approach.[108] "He couldn't be made to prepare speeches in advance, preferring to play cards instead."[109] To him the campaign was just "a great lark."[110]

Another aide who would always be there was Marvin McIntyre, who had handled public relations at the navy for FDR and continued to do so during the campaign. Also aboard the campaign train were Roosevelt's rotund male navy stenographer, Renah Camalier, and his florist friend from Poughkeepsie, Tom Lynch, who wrote the checks and tried to shepherd the meager resources of the campaign. These were supplemented by personal transfers from the candidate ($5,000) and his mother ($3,000). The highlight of the campaign for Camalier was when he was challenged to fisticuffs by the emaciated, asthmatic Louis Howe, whom Camalier outweighed by over a hundred pounds. They gestured and shadowboxed until the candidate could be fetched to separate them.[111]

With Theodore dead, relations between Oyster Bay and Hyde Park started to deteriorate seriously. Theodore Roosevelt Jr. had been elected to the New York State Assembly from Nassau County in 1919, but was narrowly defeated in his bid for the Republican nomination for governor to run against Al Smith. He happily accepted a Republican National Committee invitation to shadow his cousin's tour and said in Sheridan, Wyoming, that FDR was "a maverick. He does not have the brand of our family."[112] This was a rabbit punch; Franklin Roosevelt had always been very respectful of President Roosevelt and solicitous of his sons. He responded that in 1912 when TR had been trying to wrest control of the Republican Party from "the same old gang that now has it by the throat . . . [Harding had called TR] . . . first a Benedict Arnold, then an Aaron Burr. This is one thing at least some members of the Roosevelt family will not forget."[113]

Roosevelt was a popular performer on the campaign trail and fulfilled the expectations Cox had when he chose him as his running mate. He was remarkably impressive in appearance, a confident and eloquent speaker already endowed with the melodious voice, rich inflection, and animated gestures that would eventually be world-famous. And he was a tireless campaigner, prepared to go anywhere, no matter how remote or politically hostile. He had not, however, completely cured himself of the habit of taking liberties with the truth that the press or his adversaries could expose.

On August 18, 1920, at Deer Lodge, Montana, he rebutted the Republican claim that Britain would control the League of Nations because her Dominions—Canada, Australia, etc.—would always vote with her. Roosevelt replied, accurately but injudiciously; "Does anyone suppose that the votes of Cuba, Haiti, Santo Domingo, Panama, Nicaragua and the other Central American states would be cast differently from the vote of the United States? We are . . . the big brother of these little states." This was passable, though it could have been better phrased; the relationships hadn't changed much when he substituted "Good Neighbor" for "big brother" twelve years later. He was pushing it when he said, "I have always thought President Wilson slipped one over on Lloyd George when he was in Paris." Unfortunately, the candidate became altogether intoxicated with his own forensic powers and went on to say, "You know I have had something to do with running a couple of little Republics. The facts are that I wrote Haiti's constitution myself and, if I do say so, I think it's a pretty good constitution." He repeated this claim in Butte and Helena later the same day.[114]

This was the usual Rooseveltian flight of self-serving invention. He had nothing to do with the Haitian constitution and nothing to do with governing any of the countries referred to; his only experience with them was dinner and elemental ceremonies with a couple of the Caribbean presidents during the boozy 1917 trip. Much of that was given over to his horseback ride through the interior of Hispaniola (dodging, as he claimed, bullets that other members of the expedition did not recall having been fired).

Yet he continued in this line for some time, saying in San Francisco August 23: "Why, I have been running Haiti or San Domingo for the past seven years."[115] This was another falsehood, though Roosevelt's predictions of voting patterns by the Latin American countries in the League would doubtless have been reasonably accurate had the U.S. joined the League.

Warren Harding leapt at this indiscretion. There was already controversy over the severity of the marines and their firebrand leader Smedley Butler's administration of Haiti (prior to Butler's shipping out to France). Harding jubilantly declared that he would not appoint an assistant secretary of the navy who would impose his own constitution on helpless neighbors "at the point of bayo-nets . . . Thousands of native Haitians have been killed by American Marines, and . . . many of our own gallant men have sacrificed their lives . . . in order to establish laws drafted by the Assistant Secretary of the Navy to secure a vote in the League." Harding called this "the first official admission of the rape of Haiti and Santo Domingo by the present Administration. To my mind, moreover, it is the most shocking assertion that ever emanated from a responsible member of the government of the United States."[116]

Roosevelt swiftly learned that his customary response to such imbroglios, to deny that he had ever said it, wasn't effective in a national campaign. After he accused the Associated Press reporter who filed the story of misquoting him, thirty-one people among his audience at Butte signed an attestation that his remarks had been reported fairly.

The Republican newspapers gave him a pretty thorough going-over. The *New York Telegram* called him "a spoiled child, to be spanked."[117] He did not mention Haiti again in the campaign, and it probably didn't have a material impact on the election result, but the notion of "The Roosevelt Constitution" of Haiti kept pop-ping up in reporters' stories and Republican speeches. Roosevelt continued to dismiss the whole basis of the story as journalistic fiction. He was, in his own account, as always, immaculately blameless.

Roosevelt trimmed his message to suit his surroundings with more than the usual candidate's dexterity. He spoke at Tacoma, Washington, against the Repub-licans' pandering to the special interests of the wealthy. The same day, at Cen-tralia, he honored the members of the American Legion who had died in a brawl a year before with members of the marxist-tinged International Workers of the World in "a pilgrimage to the very graves of the martyred members of the Ameri-can Legion who here gave their lives in the sacred cause of Americanism."[118]

The election in Maine was held September 19, because of traditional con-cerns that inclemency might reduce the turnout in November. Roosevelt cam-paigned there for a few days to try to keep the Republican majority down. He wasn't successful and the Republican landslide was such that Harding and Coolidge took up the state slogan of Maine: "As Maine Goes, So Goes the Nation!"*

When Roosevelt went to the Democratic headquarters in New York, where he had planted his assistant at the Navy Department, Charles McCarthy, he found that apathy and defeatism abounded. There was little money, and none at all for the vice presidential campaign. Neither candidate excited the voters, who were accustomed to the electoral leadership of William Jennings Bryan, Theodore Roosevelt, and Woodrow Wilson. Bryan was unworldly and much of his platform

---

* The shoe would be on the other foot four elections later, when only Vermont joined Maine in voting against Roosevelt and he remarked, on the most one-sided presidential election since James Monroe ran unopposed in 1820, "As Maine Goes So Goes Vermont!"

was unworkable, but he was a mighty orator and a god to the discontented and the underprivileged, especially in the farm states. Cox and Harding had none of the greatness or galvanizing presence and personality of Wilson or TR. Cox would prove an inspired businessman, live to a great age, and leave a great fortune that his heirs further multiplied, but governor of Ohio was the outer limit of his political capabilities. The New York headquarters was "alarmingly dead." McCarthy told FDR that "the real work around headquarters" was done by the revolving electric sign bearing pictures of Cox and Roosevelt.[119]

Harding was out of his depth in the U.S. Senate. As events would prove, elevating him to the White House was a hazardous enterprise. Cox campaigned hard but stridently. Harding spoke rarely, was carefully scripted, and didn't stray from the tutelage of his handlers, the party bosses who had chosen him largely for his docility in the original smoke-filled room in Chicago. Harding said he was opposed to the "Paris League" or "Wilson's League," but he did claim to favor an Association of Nations, which he never defined. This was enough for Republican internationalists like Hoover. There was great disillusionment with Wilson, who to much of the public, unaware of the extent of his illness, seemed a sullen recluse, if not a coward. And the country thought it time for a change.

Roosevelt was soon perfectly aware of all of this, but believed he could gain ground even in defeat. He was putting up a plucky fight and meeting party executives and the rank and file all around the country. He had never been in most of the states before, only New York, Illinois, the New England states, and those states with naval installations. Roosevelt set out in his railway car, the *Westboro*, again at the end of September.[120] He asked Eleanor to join him, claiming, presumably with some sincerity, to miss her, and also probably hopeful that in the first election where women were entitled to vote it would be an advantage for the candidate's wife to be visible. Eleanor did not find the campaign train agreeable. The politicking was repetitive and boring and the evenings were overwhelmingly masculine: whiskey-soaked, boisterous, raunchy, with a good deal of poker-playing.

The bright spot in this foray for Eleanor was the bond that developed between her and Louis Howe. Howe knew all there was to know about tumultuous marriages. He knew that if Roosevelt were to scale the heights he thought him capable of, Eleanor must be supportive, and he knew that Franklin Roosevelt was so cavalier at times that he might not think to do what was necessary to make Eleanor feel at home. Howe asked her views on subjects that would arise in speeches, gradually became an intimate, and introduced her to some members of the press, who started to make funny faces at her in the crowd to try to reduce her countenance from that of the earnest listener as she heard her husband go through his set speech for the thousandth time. She came to be involved in the campaign and, through Howe, made some useful contributions to it. She also asked the candidate and his entourage to be less boisterous because they were disturbing the sleep of the porter.[121]

It became a nasty campaign. There were allegations in a circular distributed to many thousands of homes by a Negro-baiting professor that Harding had a black ancestor. Harding produced a family tree that was invulnerable to such a charge and the Democrats accused the Republicans of being behind the allegation. (Both parties were in fact innocent.) The counter-attack came with a widely circulated and partially publicized assault on Roosevelt by his old nemesis from the Newport, Rhode Island, controversy, John R. Rathom, editor of the *Providence Journal.*

Rathom's latest effort accused Roosevelt of cowardice and dissembling throughout the Newport affair (unfortunately with some reason, as we have seen) and criticized him for preventing Captain Taussig from getting a full inquiry into that dispute (over how many convicted homosexuals had been readmitted to shipboard service in the navy—again, there was a kernel of truth in Rathom's charges against Roosevelt). But by far the most sensational of Rathom's reflections was the suggestion that Roosevelt himself was a homosexual.

This was an outrageous insinuation and an odd claim to press against a young father of five children. It was based entirely on the fact that Roosevelt had commuted a seven-year prison sentence of a navy electrician convicted of sodomy. Rathom also accused him of seizing and destroying files in the case.[122] Roosevelt immediately sued Rathom for the formidable sum (in 1920) of $500,000 for libel and issued a denial, which the young Arthur Krock, the future *New York Times* columnist, helped him write. There were just ten days before the election. It turned out that Admiral Sims, embittered by the failure of his attack on Daniels and at being outmaneuverd by Roosevelt, had sent Taussig to Rathom. Through Thomas Spellacy, a U.S. district attorney whom Roosevelt had befriended when he had been the assistant secretary's legal adviser in Europe in 1919, Roosevelt got access to Rathom's file in the Department of Justice.[123]

Rathom was a very vulnerable assailant. The autobiography he had written was revealed to be a tissue of lies and exaggerations; he was a convicted adulterer, and the district attorney for New York, Frank G. Caffey, issued a statement that Rathom had been obliged to confess the complete falsehood of claims he had made about his role in the apprehension of German agents in the United States during the war. Rathom was completely discredited.

There is some dispute about whether Roosevelt had any illusions about the election results by late in the campaign. Eleanor recollected that he did not expect to win, and she would know best. But he and Cox exchanged encouraging telegrams; "The fight is won," wired Roosevelt, who promised to carry New York State.[124] It's unlikely he believed it, but he could never stand defeatism.

No matter how realistic Roosevelt had been, he could scarcely have been prepared for the tidal wave that overwhelmed the Democrats on November 2. Harding and Coolidge took sixty-one percent of the vote and every state outside the old South, which was still loyal to the Democrats as the opponents of the Union Army and its infamous carpetbaggers. The Electoral College was 404 to 127, and in the popular vote it was the greatest plurality in history, seven million votes, and the greatest percentage for one party since James Monroe, who was acclaimed in 1820. Roosevelt made a gracious public statement and sent a prompt congratulatory message to Coolidge.[125]

Roosevelt's ability to represent it as a moral victory for himself was somewhat diminished by the fact that, contrary to his confident predictions to Cox, the Republicans carried every county and every state-wide office in New York, including the state house—Al Smith was defeated for the only time in his five elections for the governorship of New York. Roosevelt was doubtless not too upset at the setback to his rival, especially since, contrary to Boss Murphy's promise, Tammany and its allies had devoted all their energies to Smith and done nothing to help Cox and Roosevelt.

In a characteristic reaction, Roosevelt privately expressed relief at not having to serve in the ambiguous office of vice president. He jauntily called the campaign "a darned fine sail."[126] More seriously, he said it was his duty to make the race, that he had done his best, and that since the opposition were going to win with a program he was convinced would be proved mistaken, they might as well have a clear mandate to implement that program. "The whole responsibility will be theirs," he wrote.[127] This was a prescient perception and not just the usual glib Roosevelt ex post facto rationalization. His greatest concern was that the Republicans would prove so reactionary that they would transform Democratic moderates and liberals into radicals and extremists. This too, showed his remarkable insight into the American political process.[128]

Inevitably, he also had to devise an explanation for any debacle in which he was involved; he privately blamed this one on vengeance-taking by German-Americans, and on the canard about Harding's black ancestry.[129]

The old allies of Theodore Roosevelt were jubilant, unworthy heir to TR though they knew Harding was. "We have torn up Wilsonism by the roots," exulted Henry Cabot Lodge. The cadaverous Wilson was closer to the truth and more elevated in his perspective when he commented to one of his staff: "We had a chance to gain the leadership of the world. We have lost it and soon will be witnessing the tragedy of it all."*[130]

---

* The rejection of Wilson, though unique in its proportions, was not without parallels. Roosevelt had written from England in 1918 that Lloyd George's support was based "on the sole issue of winning the war. The Conservatives who used to despise him as a demagogue; the Liberals who used to fear him as a radical; and most of the Labor people who now look upon him as a reactionary, may hate him just as much as ever and be unwilling after the war to trust reconstruction to his hands, but they will stand by him just as long as his administration keeps the winning of the war as its only political aim."[131] This was accurate. Lloyd George's coalition would collapse in 1922, and the Liberal Party of Gladstone and Asquith and himself would be surpassed by Labour and would never lead a government, nor Lloyd George himself serve in one, again.

In addition to all other principal aspects of this tragic drama, Roosevelt would well remem-

X

A FTER THE ELECTION Roosevelt went to Louisiana with his brother-in-law, Hall Roosevelt, to shoot ducks and geese, and assisted in the rescue of a fourteen-year-old boy who became lost overnight in the marshes. Then as Christmas approached, he gave gold cufflinks with his initials on one side and the recipient's initials on the other to everyone who had worked closely with him on the campaign. This founded the Cuff Links Club, which met annually on his birthday (January 30) to celebrate and reminisce, a practice that continued to the end of his life, with members being added as his career fluctuated and flourished.

The club was the beginning of his durable political organization, a cell that would grow to exercise great power in the United States for a prolonged and historic time. Louis Howe had recorded the names of a large number of party officials all around the country on thousands of individual file cards, with whom he now began to correspond, as the agonizing task of reconstructing the party began.

Roosevelt clairvoyantly told James M. Cox that the Democrats would not be back until an economic collapse drove the Republicans out.[132] He intended to be the beneficiary of that ejection and both his analysis and his ambitions were fulfilled. He had made his own name for himself and had generally made a good impression. There was no anti-Roosevelt vote in the result, and minor fiascoes such as the Haitian constitutional rodomontade did no lasting damage.

To prepare for the long siege of Republican rule, Roosevelt quickly moved away from the positions he had been best known for holding in the Wilson administration — advocacy of American adherence to the League of Nations and a big navy. The former was a dead letter in any event, and Roosevelt now advocated a separate peace with Germany and bilateral arrangements with the other major powers. With the scuttling of the German Navy, there was no point in a naval construction race with Britain, a recent ally with which the United States had no significant disagreement. And calling for a moratorium on naval con-

ber the parlous condition of the European war coalition leaders when the emergency was over, and would even caution Winston Churchill about the condition of his political support, insightfully but unsuccessfully, in 1943.

Clemenceau fared even less well. He quickly ceased to be indispensable and ran to succeed Ramond Poincaré as president of France in January 1920, and was defeated by the much less prominent Paul Deschanel. Seven months later, Deschanel leapt from a train and was found flopping around in a pond, hallucinating, and was obliged to retire for reasons of mental instability. Clemenceau withdrew from public life, other than to exchange barbs with Foch in successive editions of their memoirs.

Orlando resigned in June 1919, and the entire parliamentary system of Italy collapsed into the hands of the Fascist leader, Benito Mussolini, in 1922. Lloyd George, Clemenceau, and Orlando at least absorbed their downfalls more philosophically than Wilson, having never been intoxicated by apostolic airs and hopes. They soldiered rather acerbically on to the ages of eighty-two, eighty-eight, and ninety-two, Orlando even running unsuccessfully for the position of president of post-Fascist Italy at the age of eighty-seven.

struction enabled Roosevelt, formerly a verbose naval expansionist, to look more contemporary in Warren Harding's America.

Roosevelt's first priority was to put himself in a position to earn some money so he would be less dependent on the rather capriciously distributed largesse of his mother. His salary at the navy had been only $5,000 per year. Since 1914, shortly after he left Carter, Ledyard & Milburn, he had been a silent partner in the law firm he set up with his friends Grenville Emmett and Langdon Marvin. If he wanted to take this role more seriously, he could doubtless bring in more business to this small firm, which had served him more as a New York office than a professional workplace while he was in government. He quickly arranged with his friend Van Lear Black, proprietor of the *Baltimore Sun*, whom he had met at the convention in Baltimore that nominated Woodrow Wilson for president in 1912, to become vice president of the Fidelity & Deposit Company of Maryland (F&D), for New York, New Jersey, and New England. He was to be paid $25,000 per year and work only half days. Black officially welcomed Roosevelt to this company, which he controlled, at a sumptuous dinner at Delmonico's restaurant on January 7, 1921. Among those present were Adolf S. Ochs, proprietor of the *New York Times*; Owen D. Young, of General Electric; and Edward R. Stettinius, of United States Steel Corporation (and father of a future secretary of state of Roosevelt's).[133]

FDR's hustling of business for the F&D was apparently quite successful. He and Louis Howe had handled the patronage aspects of the Navy Department with great aplomb throughout their time there, and Roosevelt was not shy about mining his contacts and cashing in on past favors. He did virtually no professional legal analysis or court pleadings.

It was here that he retained Marguerite LeHand (called "Missy," because one of the Roosevelt children had trouble pronouncing "Miss"), a talented and devoted secretary who would remain with him for more than twenty years, until her health broke down. She had handled Roosevelt's schedule during the 1920 campaign and became a fixture in the Roosevelt inner circle. Discreet, diligent, attractive, and cheerful, she was engaged at Eleanor Roosevelt's suggestion and became a confidante of FDR through all the phases of his career from this date.

Roosevelt became very active on the speaking circuit around New York, keeping his name constantly before the media and playing a part in many civic activities such as the Boy Scout Foundation, National Civic Foundation, Near East Relief Committee, the Cathedral of St. John the Divine (where Rosy remained a trustee), and at least one charity for the blind. He had sublet the 12th Street house to Thomas Lamont at the beginning of the Wilson administration, and until the sublease expired in the autumn of 1921, the Roosevelt family was divided between Springwood and Sara's house on 65th Street.

Eleanor became highly industrious, determined to emancipate herself from the tyranny of her mother-in-law and get out from the shadow of her husband. In her purposeful way, she became proficient at typing and shorthand, and studied and developed some aptitude for cooking. Sara, who assumed people were hired to perform such feats, was nonplussed. Eleanor joined the board of the League of Women Voters, and became a close friend of the able lawyer Elizabeth Read and of her colleague in women's issues and advocacy, Esther Lape. With them, in addition to becoming a keen student of legislation with implications for women, she resumed her interest in poetry and French, which had largely lapsed since she left Allenswood nearly twenty years before.

She began to develop political opinions at some variance with her husband's and was increasingly insouciant about whether he agreed with her or whether her identification with some issues, especially in the general enhancement of the status of women, was convenient to him. The disparity in their personalities was more evident than ever. Eleanor, as she became more confident and independent, became less interested in conforming to or even abiding her husband's compulsive and sometimes disingenuous joviality.

He quailed at her grim worthiness and grew impatient with her impracticality. She grew more disenchanted with what she considered his frivolity and insincere careerism. When his political career resumed, abrasions between them would be a problem that would arise often. They would manage it better than not, but it was never absent for long.

Another family matter that became a considerable vexation was the elevation of Theodore Roosevelt Jr. to the family seat of assistant secretary of the navy in the Harding administration. Franklin Roosevelt's exchanges with his cousin had been fairly acerbic during the campaign as young TR was deployed by the Republican strategists to deny FDR the political succession to President TR. There was bound to be a rivalry, and this was heightened by the Oyster Bay view that Franklin Roosevelt was a usurper of the family's political renown and a shirker for apparently ignoring his late distinguished cousin's advice to wear the country's uniform during the Great War. This skirmishing, with the inimitable Alice playing her predictable role, would run and run.

On July 28, 1921, Roosevelt and about fifty other prominent supporters of the Boy Scout Foundation in New York went from New York to Bear Mountain on his friend Baron Collier's commodious steam yacht to visit 2,100 boys at the summer camps there. Many of the patrons drank profusely on the brief voyage, in violation of the law and the canons of the scout movement as enunciated by its founder, Lord Baden-Powell. Roosevelt always enjoyed this sort of outing and encouraged many of the transplanted city boys as they displayed their newly acquired skills in the manly outdoors life. It seems that it was on this trip that he contracted a virus that would mortally threaten and irrevocably change his life.

Having had to forego Campobello for all or almost all of his Washington summers, Roosevelt was looking forward to a long holiday there with his family, possibly the more so because his mother had resumed her pre-war habit of summering in Europe. (Aged sixty-seven, she flew in an early passenger airplane from London to Paris.)

He became more tired each day after his foray to the Boy Scout camp, and left New York on Van Lear Black's 140-foot yacht, *Sabalo*, for Campobello on August 5. It wasn't the U.S. Navy destroyer he and his neighbors had been used to, but it was a comfortable boat and a generous gesture by his friend and employer. It was a difficult passage; he had to pilot the yacht through the fog in Canadian waters, arriving at Welshpool, near Campobello Island, on the evening of August 7. Roosevelt was greeted at dockside by all his family and Louis Howe's as well. He was very tired but very cheerful. What was about to happen was almost unimaginable.

CHAPTER 4

"Trial By Fire"

(Eleanor Roosevelt's description of her husband's battle with polio)

I

FRANKLIN D. ROOSEVELT was up early at Campobello on August 8, 1921. He took his employer, Van Lear Black, and his party fishing on the tender to Black's yacht and was his usual attentive and energetic self, baiting everyone's hook and assisting every aspect of the sport. At one point he lost his balance and fell into the waters of the Bay of Fundy, where he had been immersed countless times before. He remembered feeling that on this occasion the water was stabbingly cold. That evening, the tiredness he had felt since his day trip from New York to Bear Mountain July 28 persisted and was compounded by some aches in his legs, which he thought at first must be lumbago.

On the afternoon of August 9, Black sailed out of the Bay on his way back to New York. The following day Roosevelt took his wife and his two eldest sons, James and Elliott, for a sail, deftly guiding the little boat near shoals and through the tides and currents with which he had been intimately familiar since he was a young boy. They stopped to extinguish a spontaneous pine-needle fire on one of the smaller islands by thrashing out the embers underfoot with pine boughs. They were all grimy and hot after an hour of this strenuous work. When they returned from the expedition at about four o'clock, Roosevelt felt weak and determined on more exercise; he invited his family to run with him to his favorite swimming place, a pond about two miles from the house. The run took place, a simulation of some of cousin Theodore's high-spirited exercises at Oyster Bay, followed by a swim in the pond, a splash in the very cold Bay of Fundy, and then a run back to the main house, though a horse-drawn wagon was available for the return trip.

Roosevelt was too tired to get out of his bathing suit when he got home, and sat and read the mail that had been delivered. After an hour he started to shiver and went to bed, well-wrapped in blankets and with no appetite for dinner. The next morning, August 11, after an indifferent sleep, with the aches in his legs worse than ever and extended into his neck and throughout his back, he stumbled to the bathroom and shaved. He was too weak, unstable, and pain-wracked to get dressed, and returned with difficulty to bed. The three-day camping trip he had promised his children was laid off on Grace Howe, an employee's wife. Roosevelt's temperature was 102, and first his left and then his right leg failed to function at all. He tried to exercise the muscles as long as he could, until they failed to respond.

Eleanor sent for the local doctor, a family general practitioner who was competent enough at routine ailments but was so dismayed by what he discovered with this patient that he confusedly declared that Roosevelt had a heavy cold, which FDR knew to be false, and promised to return the next day. When he did return, his patient could not stand unassisted and was having trouble urinating. There was only one telephone in Welshpool, which was not reliable, so Louis Howe (who was now Roosevelt's secretary at the Fidelity & Deposit) went with the doctor to his home in Lubec and telephoned down the New England coast until he found a doctor, an eighty-four-year-old Philadelphia surgeon vacationing at Bar Harbor.*

This doctor arrived August 14 and diagnosed a blood clot in the spinal cord that, because Roosevelt was able to move his toes in one foot, was already starting to dissolve. Eleanor called for a masseuse from New York, and she and Howe took turns rubbing his feet. Yet Roosevelt's condition continued to deteriorate. His bowels and bladder ceased to function and he lost the control he had retained of some of his toes. The Welshpool general practitioner taught Eleanor how to apply an enema and a glass catheter which had to be inserted with extreme care in the urethra. Eleanor would apply suction to draw off urine, and she and Howe managed to move the patient on and off the bedpan. This was a terribly awkward and demeaning condition for so vigorous a man as Franklin Roosevelt.

Despite Eleanor's and Howe's selfless efforts, Roosevelt started to slide into delirium, so it was almost impossible to address his sanitary needs. As his fever climbed, his religious faith, which he had always lightly assumed and invoked, faltered, and he feared he had been forsaken by the God he had confidently, if somewhat mechanically, worshipped.

But on August 15, he started to turn the corner and regain control of himself. The fever subsided, a few toes could again be moved, and hope tentatively returned. The octogenarian Philadelphian doctor wrote back, having reconsidered his diagnosis of a blood clot. He now believed that the problem had been caused by a more intractable spinal lesion. This was a bizarre conclusion, since there was no evidence or recollection of any particular harm to Roosevelt's back.

---

* The doctor, W.W. Keen, was a famous surgeon, and was one of those who secretly and successfully operated on President Cleveland for throat cancer on a yacht in 1893. There had been some questions about his diagnostic capabilities even then.

(He eventually sent a bill for the preposterous amount of $8,000 which the Roosevelts paid with reluctance.)

Louis Howe, who had had his share of medical problems and of slipshod medical analysis, wrote to Roosevelt's uncle, Fred Delano, summarizing the symptoms and asking that serious doctors in New York and Boston be canvassed. When Delano did this, the consensus that began to emerge was that Franklin Roosevelt had been stricken by infantile paralysis. Delano was urged to put his nephew in the hands of the leading authority on infantile paralysis in the United States, Dr. Robert W. Lovett, a Harvard professor and chief surgeon at Children's Hospital and at the New England Home for Crippled Children, both in Boston.

Dr. Lovett, the venerable Philadelphian, and the Welshpool general practitioner arrived en masse on August 25 to visit the patient, who had now been flat on his back for two weeks. Lovett noted that Roosevelt's face was partially paralyzed, that his arms were weak, and that one of his thumbs couldn't be opposed. His bladder was still paralyzed, but Eleanor had performed her mundane but exacting tasks so well that there was no infection. The muscles in Roosevelt's hips and legs had already lost a great deal of force but had not entirely atrophied. Lovett conferred briefly with his colleagues and then, leaving no room for doubt, diagnosed poliomyelitis.

He was able to reassure Eleanor that the children were not in any danger and insisted that the massages of her husband end at once, because they only served to exacerbate pain. He recommended retention of a registered nurse to relieve Eleanor of most of her drudgery. He felt that as polio cases went, this one was not overly severe and that there was a legitimate possibility of restoring full use of Roosevelt's limbs. Roosevelt became icily composed yet somewhat relieved when he received the diagnosis, Eleanor noted later, adding that his reaction was similar twenty years later when the Japanese attacked Pearl Harbor. In later years she would describe the ordeal of his polio as a "trial by fire."[1]

This early composure fluctuated somewhat as the days passed with no moderation of pain and a steady erosion of the withering muscles. Sara returned from abroad September 1, to be greeted at dockside by her stepson Rosy and her brother Fred Delano. Rosy gave her a letter from Eleanor that explained that she and Franklin couldn't greet her themselves because "Franklin has been quite ill."[2] Sara embarked at once on the arduous trek to Campobello, changing trains at Boston and then boarding the one-car train drawn by a wood-burning engine at Ayers Junction for the last leg of the trip.

When she arrived, her son, although he had been rather discouraged with the lack of progress, was determined, as always—as when he had had a broken tooth or gashed forehead as a youth—not to alarm his mother, and put a brave face on recent events. Sara touchingly wrote that she "came up to a brave, smiling, and beautiful son, who said: 'Well, I'm glad you're back Mummy' " (addressing his mother in the upper-class British style then still prevalent in the higher echelons of American society).[3]

Missy LeHand spent the last week in August at Campobello helping with correspondence from concerned friends. Roosevelt developed an elaborate deception based on "a severe chill" that had followed his swim in the unusually difficult and cold waters of the Bay of Fundy. He could not sign the letters himself because both his thumbs were paralyzed. Louis Howe forged his signature and dissembled to the press, including an Associated Press stringer in the area, even more than usual. There was no thought of allowing the true gravity of the situation to be known. The first newspaper account of Roosevelt's illness, which also reported that he was recovering, was published August 27.[4]

Dr. Lovett continued to prescribe complete rest into September. Roosevelt and his family understandably thought that if they kept exercising and massaging, the erosion of the muscles would be slowed or reversed, but Lovett insisted that exactly the reverse was true. He did recommend a gentle daily transfer to a warm bath, where the patient could do a great deal more with his limbs than when entirely fighting the force of gravity. Even the bedclothes irritated Roosevelt's skin as he lay all day in bed, reading or being read to and hearing the sounds of the sea leavened by the cheerful noises of his children. It was an agony of suspense. It was not clear what sort of a life he would be left with. For someone so ambitious and confident, it was a heavy burden to contemplate that his political career might have ended.

As summer moved toward autumn, steps had to be taken to move Roosevelt out of his cottage to an all-weather center. A private railway car was arranged and brought to Eastport.[5] On September 13, Roosevelt was carefully bundled up and carried by six local men on an improvised stretcher made from pine trunks and sailcloth out of the bedroom where he had lain inert for a month, down the steep stairs, through his drawing room, out through the veranda, and down to the sea. Louis Howe had put his hat over FDR's almost dysfunctional left hand. Roosevelt wanly smiled and tried to wave at his shocked children, who hadn't really seen him since the onset of the illness. As he disappeared down the hill carried backwards on the stretcher, he called out to them the assurance that "I will be all right."[6]

He crossed the bay to Eastport in his little dory, every few yards of the choppy water being very painful to the ever-stoical stretcher-borne evacuee. Eleanor and the nurse specially engaged for the trip sat beside him. The boat went to a crude landing point at the end of town opposite where Howe had directed the small contingent of metropolitan reporters who had assembled to judge the former vice presidential candidate's real condition. As the tide began to ebb, the men who had received the stretcher from the boat were on wet moss-covered stone and had to move with extreme caution to prevent slipping or pitching the convalescent into the water, which might well have been fatal, since he now had no ability to stay afloat.

He was successfully laid on a flat luggage cart and, with his wife and others who had helped him across the bay walking beside to mask him from onlookers, was conveyed to the train. There was a delay while a window frame on the train was removed, because Roosevelt could not be transferred through the door. Howe lit a cigarette and put it in FDR's holder to enable him to convey a more casual look as the reporters who had been misdirected finally realized their error and rushed toward the railway car. All they saw was a smiling Roosevelt with a cigarette in its holder at a jaunty angle in his mouth. The party line of incapacitation that was not severe and was strictly temporary was upheld and reported in the press. The departing polio sufferer would not return to Campobello for twelve years, when the world and his place in it would be much changed.[7]

Roosevelt was grateful to the railway engineer, who drove slowly to make life easier for his famous passenger. (As president of the United States, he would insist that his special trains not exceed forty miles per hour, because any faster speed could pitchfork him out of chairs.)

He finally returned to New York City the following day, September 14, coming into Grand Central Station on a special siding well away from the curious members of the press. A group of friends awaited, including one of Dr. Lovett's understudies and FDR's Poughkeepsie florist and organizer—his "wild Irish rose," Tom Lynch. An ambulance took him to the New York Presbyterian Hospital on Fifth Avenue and 70th Street. On September 16 the *New York Times* carried on page one the story that he was a polio victim, that his legs had been affected, but that he was recovering. The story showed the Louis Howe spin of olden times.[8]

He stayed in the hospital until October 28 and did make substantial progress. At first only Eleanor, Sara, and Louis Howe were admitted, but a torrent of letters of solidarity and condolence came in, including from the Oyster Bay Roosevelts and Dr. Peabody. Dr. Lovett's understudy, Dr. George Draper, was concerned about what he considered Roosevelt's unjustified optimism, and about what he thought was an absence of progress in FDR's upper body muscles. On this last point, he quickly became more optimistic after Roosevelt started sitting up October 11.[9]

Roosevelt early developed and never lost the technique of impressing observers and acquaintances with his unflappable optimism concerning his illness. One of the first to be subjected to Roosevelt's sunny outlook as a polio patient was Josephus Daniels, who came to visit him in hospital. He remembered his former assistant as "young and debonair, striding and strong," and was visibly shaken to see him immobilized. Roosevelt beckoned him closer and then punched him in his ample stomach, joking that Daniels was not visiting an invalid, but someone who could "knock you out."[10]

Astute judge of human nature as he was, he soon mastered the techniques of attracting sympathy and admiration but not pity. It required great finesse first to enlist the solidarity of onlookers and then to astonish them with his aplomb—inciting solicitude, then reassurance, then admiration. It was not an affectation or a fraud. Roosevelt had always been brave and determined. He came to regard polio as his supreme test, ultimately elevating him from his fortunate youth and confirming his resilience in the face of adversity. Those who had dismissed him as a well-born lightweight would see how unconquerable was his determination. Those predisposed to resent him would be compelled to respect. His tendency to boastful revisionism would be overlooked and, in any case, moderated.

He finally returned to 65th Street on October 28, and was carried all the way through the house to a quiet room at the top. His hospital chart was marked: "Not Improving."[11] But his back and chest muscles and arms and hands were improving, and he had by then recovered control of his bowels, and his sexual potency had returned. He was slowly starting to adjust, though the intermittent spikes in temperature kept recurring and his morale fluctuated, but not as seriously as during the earlier days of intense pain and almost unbearable suspense about the ultimate extent of the illness. The most serious of the sudden inflammations that occurred in the first months after the onset of polio was in mid-November, when his temperature shot up and his eyesight deteriorated, but both conditions corrected themselves after a few days.[12]

From the start of December, treatment was in the hands of a capable professional physiotherapist, Mrs. Kathleen Lake, who administered daily exercises to every affected limb. Roosevelt had not varied from his confident assertion that he would be up and around within a few weeks, even though he knew this was unlikely. But he plunged into Mrs. Lake's painful and exhausting regimen with unquenchable determination.

It was an adjustment for Roosevelt's family. When young James came home from Groton for the Christmas holidays, he later recorded, he dreaded seeing what condition his father might be in, and found him in his bed under all the apparatus with which he strengthened his upper-body muscles. "His chin still stuck out and he was grinning and he stretched out his arms to me. 'Come here, old man,' he said. I rushed over and received his embrace . . . Then though I was a Roosevelt and a Grotonian, I cried a bit, but, with Pa squeezing me and slapping me on the back and carrying on enthusiastically about how 'grand' I looked, I soon was chattering along with him."[13] Roosevelt showed his withered limbs to his children, rewarded them for memorizing the names of damaged muscles, and conducted cheers as he had at Harvard for toe movement and other small examples of muscular progress. Their dread of his infirmity quickly eroded.[14]

"There would grow up about him a legend of mortal agony and transfiguration, of spiritual rebirth and purification through suffering."[15] The positive effects of his illness on his character may have been exaggerated by some. Frances Perkins claimed he had undergone a "spiritual transformation . . . [and] emerged completely warm-hearted, with humility of spirit and deeper philosophy." Eleanor went even further and called her husband's polio "a blessing in disguise; for it gave him a strength and courage he had not had before [and] . . . infinite patience and never-ending perseverance." Roosevelt himself would almost certainly have agreed with his son James, who could not "accept the theory that

Father would not have been a great man and a great public figure if he had not gone through his personal Gethsemane."[16]

With his family as with others, Roosevelt's charm became more irresistible than ever. It was no longer merely the good manners and attentiveness of a vain young man. It was now the valiant perseverance of a man even more impressive in appearance than before as he built up the muscles in his ever-more massive torso to do the work of both arms and legs. Now he would no longer be merely a fine-looking man, but a man of ruggedness and uncommon courage as well. Even the dreaded cousin Alice, who would retain a tongue that could clip a hedge until the end of her days more than fifty years later, would become for a time comparatively restrained.

It is a reasonable inference that part of his determination not to abandon hope of a political career was his dawning realization that if he could implicitly present his ailment as a severe challenge that had been mastered without leaving a residue of pitiful incapacity, a proof of strength without the appearance of vulnerability, it might not be an electoral liability, only a heavy but surmountable inconvenience. His effort to overcome polio would be approximately equalled by his prodigious effort to disguise its impact.

The fact that no one as severely handicapped as he had ever been elected to such high offices as he would contest did not deter him in the slightest. Once his physical condition stabilized, he focused increasingly on the presentational problem. Prior to the onslaught of polio, he had won two elections (for state senator) and lost two (for a U.S. Senate primary and vice president). Henceforth, though no one could have foreseen it, his electoral record was entirely and unprecedentedly successful.

II

ELEANOR WAS CONCERNED that she not lose the independent life she had painstakingly built up. Her alliance with Louis Howe was amplified to proportions that alarmed Sara and the children, who all looked upon Howe as a dodgy and repulsive little gnome of doubtful motivation. Eleanor and Louis wanted to resuscitate FDR's career, Eleanor to inspirit her husband and to liberate herself from being an invalid's wife. She considered her husband's political ambitions to be "hopeless" but encouraged them anyway, to give him purpose.[17] Howe's ambition to wield real power from the White House and his faith in Roosevelt's ability to get him there were undimmed. What Sara wanted was precisely the opposite—for her son to return to Springwood, where she would care for him as she had cared for his father, her first beloved invalid, after the onset of his heart disease in 1892.

Since FDR had the same ambition that Eleanor and Louis Howe did, Sara was bound to lose this contest. Howe moved into the Roosevelt house, where he was a very difficult guest, coughing in frightful spasms that awakened the house many nights, constantly smoking, and a messy, rumpled, enigmatic, and, to the children, disturbing presence. His popularity was not enhanced by the fact that he usurped Anna's bedroom, banishing her to a much smaller one at the back of the house. This winter of 1921–1922 was "the most trying . . . of my entire life," Eleanor wrote.[18] A resident nurse took up another bedroom, and Eleanor slept on a cot and dressed in her husband's bathroom. The resulting abrasions of over-crowded living conditions did not improve the ambiance of the convalescent's house.

Roosevelt's infirmity did restore his relationship with his former chief, Woodrow Wilson, himself still confined to a wheelchair and partly paralyzed. Shortly after Wilson left office in March 1921, Roosevelt had become chairman of a preliminary committee to raise $500,000 to endow an award for humanitarian services named after and commemorating Woodrow Wilson. Wilson declined at first to see him, but did see him in June 1921, when Roosevelt was in Washington to attend a service for his recently deceased friend, Wilson's interior secretary, Franklin K. Lane. Wilson considered "Memorial" inappropriate usage, "inasmuch as I hope in the near future to give frequent evidences that I am not dead."[19] They eventually settled on the words "Woodrow Wilson Foundation."

But Wilson remained sufficiently irritated with Roosevelt that he refused him an autograph on a copy of Washington's farewell address that Roosevelt had published in Wilson's honor. Wilson claimed, through his secretary, that this was consistent with a rule he had against autographing such things.[20] However, after learning of Roosevelt's illness, Wilson sent "My dear Roosevelt" a note of "heartfelt sympathy."[21]

When the former president learned a few months later that Roosevelt was starting to move upright with the help of braces and crutches, he wrote: "I am indeed delighted to hear you are getting well so fast and so confidently, and I shall try to be generous enough not to envy you." On November 9, 1921, he wrote to Eleanor that he was "greatly relieved to hear of your husband's improvement," and asked her to convey his congratulations. And in response to Roosevelt's birthday greetings, on December 28, wrote him of his "peculiar gratification [for Roosevelt's] friendship and unselfish devotion."[22] Considering the historic role of both men, it was a seemly reconciliation.*

Roosevelt's fortieth birthday on January 30, 1922, found him straining for progress. Matters shortly went awry and his hamstrings contracted, forcing his knees up and threatening to reduce him permanently into a fetal position. His legs were placed in casts from hip to ankle, and wedges were gradually ham-

---

* Wilson was now living in a comfortable house on S Street in Washington, bought for him by some of his wealthy friends, including Bernard Baruch. As Roosevelt's relations with his former chief warmed, his former friendship with Senator Henry Cabot Lodge withered. Roosevelt now regarded Lodge, with whom he had conspired against the policy of Wilson and Daniels, as a dangerously primitive and malicious figure who should be "forcibly enrolled" in Johns Hopkins University's School of International Relations.[23]

mered into openings behind the knees to straighten his legs. Though the process was extremely painful, the patient never acknowledged that there was even a problem and never uttered a hint of complaint.[24]

The trivial muscular recovery that had occurred under Mrs. Lake's tutelage evaporated in February during the phase in the casts, but was gradually restored. Through all of this there is no evidence that Roosevelt's determination flagged. He was worried by setbacks but confined these concerns to the doctors and the therapist. To his family and friends he claimed to be on an inexorable march to a virtually full recovery. His fortitude was, and remains, an inspiration.

Finally, in March 1922, after seven months off his feet, Roosevelt was fitted for a fourteen-pound set of braces, which extended from his heels to above his waist and had a leather pelvic band. When snapped straight, these braces at least enabled him to stand precariously, as if on stilts. His initial efforts at motion were with crutches, dragging his legs behind him, thrusting his neck forward to move ahead of his crutches, and pulling his neck and head back to afford the momentary opportunity to thrust the crutches forward. It was inelegant, hazardous, and exhausting, but it was progress and a great refreshment to Roosevelt's morale.[25] Reporting to Dr. Lovett in April, Dr. Draper saluted the patient's progress at mobility and said the hips and quadriceps were coming back but that there was no visible reason for hope below the knee. At about this time, one of the doctors, in a graphic and chilling description, referred to his limbs as "flail legs," attached to but uncontrolled by his torso.[26]

Louis Howe effectively did most of his boss's work at the Fidelity & Deposit, which was writing letters rounding up clients for the firm. The firm's New York strategy sessions took place in the Roosevelt library on 65th Street every Tuesday afternoon starting in January. Van Lear Black was not restless with his employee and did not feel short-changed, and was in any case eager to be helpful. But Roosevelt keenly insisted on plausibly earning his paycheck.

On the doctors' recommendation and to relieve the congestion on 65th Street, the family moved to Springwood for the summer of 1922. Roosevelt remained in bed each day until ten or eleven in the morning, breakfasting there and exercising on the overhead apparatus to build his back, chest, and arm muscles. Sara installed ramps and reconditioned the luggage elevator that had been adapted to Mr. James's use. Her son would come downstairs by these routes and remain on the veranda or in the library, reading, whittling wood, or working on his stamp collection. Lunch was at one, followed by a nap, tea with his mother, more reading, dinner at seven, reading until retirement at eleven.

He needed help dressing and undressing and for some ablutions. Sometimes he would be wheeled around the property or even to see Rosy, whose house was several hundred yards distant, and who was now white-haired and gouty. To brighten things up for her son and make the squire's life more interesting, Sara invited guests to Springwood, particularly two distant and attractive young cousins, Laura Delano and Margaret L. Suckley.

Eleanor was recruited for the women's division of the state Democratic Party by Nancy Cook, the executive secretary of the group. Her husband was happy to acquiesce, because this kept his name before the public also. A friendship quickly developed between Eleanor and Nancy Cook and her friend Marion Dickerman, a social worker. Their neighbors on 12th Street were Molly Dewson of the Red Cross and Polly Porter, an educator of workers. As with her relationship with Esther Lape and Elizabeth Read, Eleanor was inviting the ridicule of her waspish relatives, and some speculation about her own proclivities. The ineffable cousin Alice called all these women friends Eleanor's "female impersonators" and claimed they found "pillow fights as jolly a form of communication as any."

Even FDR referred to Eleanor's "she-males," but took the trouble to get on well with them.[27] When Marion Dickerman came to dinner in the spring of 1922 and spoke of visiting a particularly abominable coal mine, unaware that it was owned by the Delanos, Sara was not amused.[28]

The great struggle between Eleanor, who wanted Franklin to exercise and strive to mitigate his illness, and Sara, who wanted him to relax and accept the life of an invalid as his father had done (when twenty years older), enervated Roosevelt, and his doctors told him he had to be separated from his family for a time.

When he went to Boston in June for therapy to increase his mobility, his attractive nurse, Edna Rockey, whose constant presence was already a sore point with Eleanor, went with him. Dr. Lovett's assistant, Wilhemine Wright, was an authority on instructing polio victims on how to recover as much mobility as possible, and considered it a specialized skill that had to be taught, like skating or dancing. She taught Roosevelt how to get out of a chair on his own—moving to the edge of it, lifting one leg over the other, turning toward his legs, raising himself against the back of the chair, pushing himself up onto his legs, and reaching for his crutches one at a time. It was very laborious and not easy to master, but another important step on the road to recovery.[29] Roosevelt's natural indomitability seemed to be exemplified by his frequent references to his ailment as a "childish" disease.[30]

Climbing stairs was very difficult. If there was a rail, both crutches were put under one shoulder and the other arm was used to pull upwards on the rail as the crutches pushed downwards, producing an elevation. Coming down the stairs was very hazardous, requiring a jump on a crutch and dragging one leg behind, steadying the movement with one hand clutching the railing. If there was no railing, astonishing strength and agility were required, because the stairs had to be mounted backwards. This meant relying entirely on a balancing of head and hips as the crutches were placed behind on the next upper step and the lifting was done by the forearms; it was virtually a feat of acrobatics. Descending stairs without a railing and unassisted was so dangerous that it normally would have been attempted only to escape fires or in comparable emergencies.[31] (Roosevelt's lifelong fear of fires, derived perhaps from those at Algonac, was intensified by his new vulnerability. He refused to have the old elevator at Springwood operated by electricity, which he feared would not be as reliable in a fire as manual operation of the ropes.)

In practice, it was usually easier to mount or descend stairs sitting down, protracted and undignified though this process was. Even Franklin Roosevelt, with all his determination, could never manage more than a few stair steps with his crutches alone. But he was able to move around with increasing agility—including around his bathroom, for example—and was substantially recovered a year after being attacked by a disease that defeated many and drove some to suicide.

That summer Sara took James and Anna on a strenuous tour of France, Switzerland, and Britain, their first trip to Europe. Eleanor, who had finally learned to drive, took young Franklin and John, two young friends, and Marion Dickerman and Nancy Cook on a motorized camping trip through New England and New Brunswick to Campobello. She found Campobello "in spite of all our trials . . . still serene, beautiful, and enjoyable."[32]

And Franklin, who stayed at Springwood, on being recognized for his role in World War I by the town historian of Hyde Park, Benjamin Haviland, took up with him the writing of a history of the town, a pastime that would happily engage him for the rest of his life. He could get in and out of automobiles relatively easily and drove around with Haviland inspecting overgrown cemeteries and other obscure local sites. Haviland was one of the very few people who continued to call him Franklin even when he was president of the United States. On one occasion, when discussing the relations of their own ancestors, Haviland questioned whether a story was true and Roosevelt allegedly replied: "Never mind the truth. It's a good story and the truth will take care of itself." This was a method he would sometimes apply to worldlier matters than the genealogy of Dutchess County.[33]

III

IN THE SUMMER of 1922 preparations were under way for the New York and congressional elections. William Randolph Hearst, who intermittently rose up like a cobra's head in American public life for forty years, was angling for the Democratic nomination for governor, as he had in 1906. He was typically unconcerned by the fact that he had relentlessly attacked Wilson and supported Harding in 1920.

More of a problem was his attack on then-governor Al Smith in 1919, alleging that Smith had been responsible for the death of babies by permitting the sale of diseased milk in poor areas of New York City. This was a monstrous falsehood, and when Hearst declined Smith's invitation to a public debate at Carnegie Hall, Smith harangued the audience himself and denounced Hearst as a cowardly liar. "The pestilence that walks in the darkness," he called him. Smith's mother, who was convalescing from pneumonia, was so shaken by the lies about her son that she babbled deliriously that "My son didn't kill the babies."[34]

Smith was an amiable man who enjoyed a good political knockabout, but he was a man of probity. Hearst was everything he hated: a wealthy poseur-reformer, without loyalty to the party he wished to lead, a cad who affronted Smith's Catholic fidelities, a charlatan who had already transferred his interests and loyalties to California, and an evil mudslinger. His better qualities, such as his sense of humor, genius as a showman, status as a media pioneer, talents as a builder and collector, and general grandiosity were not accessible to Smith, though Roosevelt appreciated them. In a phrase of Theodore Roosevelt's from 1907, Smith thought Hearst "a malefactor of great wealth."

Smith had enjoyed a large income and a life of ease for the first time in his life as chairman of the United States Trucking Company, but his sights were still set on politics, and the opportunity to chase Hearst out of the New York Democratic Party was a powerful added incentive. Besieged by the orthodox Democrats, Tammany and reform, to deliver the party from the ravening predator trying to take it over, Smith asked Roosevelt, as the most prominent New York Democrat outside New York City, to write him a public letter urging him to run. Roosevelt was delighted to oblige and was flattered by the recognition after a desperate year on the sidelines. A rather cosy "Dear Al" and "Dear Frank" public exchange followed. Hearst withdrew as candidate for governor and expressed interest in the Senate, trying to paper over his ulcerous relationship with Smith, who rebuffed the overture and barred the way, but accepted the nomination of a Hearst protégé, the New York City health commissioner, Dr. Royal Copeland.

Franklin Roosevelt predictably claimed privately that he had played a key role in blocking Hearst, which was customary exaggeration. But he accepted the honorary chairmanship of the Copeland campaign and gave Copeland an inspiriting lecture on the evils of defeatism when he visited him at Hyde Park. He was careful to retain cordial relations with Hearst. Given his long compulsory absence from politics, this was an impressively deft and cunning reentry that would yield positive results with Hearst in dramatic circumstances ten years later.

Smith won easily in November, turning out Nathan Miller, the Republican who had narrowly defeated him in 1920. Roosevelt wrote a warm letter of congratulation to Smith, including greetings to Smith's mother, whom "I have never had the honor of meeting."[35]

Roosevelt now took to swimming, saying "the water put me where I am, the water will bring me back."[36] (This was the contemporary view. As recorded, it is now thought that he contracted the polio virus at Bear Mountain in July 1921, even if the dips in the Bay of Fundy August 8 and 10 exacerbated the problem.) He swam first in the old ice pond near Springwood where he had learned to swim as a boy, and then several times a week in Vincent Astor's heated swimming pool at nearby Rhinebeck. He could make his legs partially functional in the water, which was useful and encouraging therapy. He also set up parallel bars on one of Springwood's lawns and spent a good deal of each afternoon in the awkward motion of swinging each leg from the hip in a forward circular movement, that, though cumbersome, would eventually enable him to dispense with his crutches and walk with a cane and an arm on the upper arm of a sturdy man, or even with two canes, which was further progress from the crutches. This would prove to be his most sophisticated form of locomotion and the furthest point of his recovery.

He developed the technique of chatting constantly while he did this, distracting visitors from his cumbrous and ungainly progress. Despite his apparently unshakeable optimism, it was starting to dawn on Franklin Roosevelt that it would be a very long and largely unremitting slog, and that in relaunching his career as he was determined to do, the effort to downplay the effects of the disease would indeed be as important as the prodigies expended to surmount it.

Franklin Roosevelt made his return debut as a functioning office-goer surmounting his handicap on October 9, 1922. He arrived in his chauffeur-driven Buick at about 11 A.M. at the Fidelity & Deposit office, 120 Broadway. He moved himself to the jump seat, and the driver held his legs out straight and snapped his braces into the rigid position. When a car behind him honked impatiently, the chauffeur went to remonstrate with the driver, leaving his employer holding himself sitting upright by grasping the car's door-frame, with his legs protruding stiffly onto the sidewalk. The chauffeur returned and raised him upright so he could support himself by leaning back on the car, put his hat on his head, and handed him his crutches. Passersby assembled, including one who helpfully replaced his hat on his head when it blew off. As he moved determinedly into and through the lobby of the building, the extent of his perspiration quickly became evident even through his jacket, so great were the exertions and the pressure of performing this exercise before strangers for the first time. (He would always perspire heavily while walking on crutches, even when surrounded by helpful aides.)

Within the building lobby, moving toward the elevators, his left crutch slipped (his left leg was not as strong as the right), and he fell in a great clatter, despite the chauffeur's efforts to break his fall. Roosevelt, seemingly unflappable and good-humored, turned over, sat upright, reassured the embarrassed spectators, and asked two apparently strong men to help him to his feet. One of them was Basil O'Connor. This was their introduction. O'Connor became his law partner and friend for life. The rest of the day proceeded uneventfully. It was a satisfactory beginning, but he did not return for two months.[37]

Roosevelt did not appear often at the F&D throughout the twenties, and had a rather abrasive relationship with the New York manager, Vincent Cullen, who did the work but was a humorless, diligent Dickensian caricature of a functionary, lacking only a visor, quill pen, and roll-top desk. Cullen resented the glamorous and affable Roosevelt, and there was intermittent skirmishing between them for control of the company's affairs in New York, especially over the Albany and Brooklyn branches, which Roosevelt had proposed setting up but control of which was retained by Baltimore, acting on advice from Cullen.

Roosevelt rather petulantly complained of this and other jurisdictional slights. Cullen finally quit in 1928, taking to a competitor some personnel and one or two clients. The firm did not miss them, and Roosevelt's stay at F&D was successful.[38] Roosevelt was a persevering pursuer of business on behalf of F&D, even writing William G. McAdoo that the mastermind of what became the Teapot Dome scandal, Edward L. Doheny, "is a good friend of mine and I feel very sure he will be pleased to have you place the [sought-after] business our way."[39]

In 1923 he set up Roosevelt & O'Connor with the man who had helped him through the lobby of the F&D building in his first visit there as a disabled person, although the partnership was only announced on New Year's Day, 1925. O'Connor was a self-made dynamo and a Dartmouth alumnus from Taunton, Massachusetts, who worked so hard at Harvard Law School that he temporarily lost his sight. FDR drew $10,000 a year and was happy to be at the front of the letterhead and to have a partner who could make the most of the association with him rather than begrudge him his undemanding work schedule as his law school chums at Marvin, Hooker and Roosevelt had done. As one of his partners in that firm put it: "I feel sorry for him. But we can never make a lawyer out of him. . . . He comes to conclusions. He hasn't got the patience to work things out." An Irish American workaholic was a more congenial and appreciative partner than WASP bluebloods. The implications of this would not be lost on Roosevelt the politician. Roosevelt explained to Marvin that his only motive in establishing the new partnership was to go to an office that didn't have steps in front of it, as Marvin's had. It was also convenient that his law chambers be so proximate to Fidelity & Deposit.

Roosevelt plunged into the speculative spirit of the twenties. What he described to huge jubilating audiences a decade later as "Nine mocking years of the golden calf . . . nine mad years of mirage . . . nine crazy years of the ticker" were years in which he was a frequent, if often incompetent, speculator.[40] His enthusiasm for novelty led him astray. Like many politicians, he lacked commercial intuition and was far too receptive to far-fetched financial projects.

Among those he took seriously, and in which he was in many cases an investor, albeit modestly, like a man at the horse races never gambling more than he could afford to lose, were a coffee substitute, a lobster-hoarding and price-rigging plan, fleets of coastal vessels and blimps, oil drilling, resort hotels, premoistened postage stamp dispensers (with Henry Morgenthau Sr.), and talking vending machines. The vending machines, which graciously uttered "Thank you" after each purchase, were, to say the least, ahead of their time. They were easily tricked by false coins and also erratically stingy about yielding what had been honestly paid for. They aroused the vocal concern of organized labor, but there was nothing to worry about, since guards soon had to be employed to protect the machines from furious customers who had been politely cheated, which rather defeated the purpose of automatic dispensing. The scheme was a fiasco, and after a merger and reorganization, went into bankruptcy.

His blimp company unsuccessfuly operated helium dirigibles between New York and Chicago. Roosevelt and a number of other prominent investors, including Owen D. Young of General Electric, did not like airplanes and believed dirigibles had a greater future. His ideas ranged from purchase of virgin forests through the issuance of bonds on the assumption that the price of forest products would inevitably rise, to selling advertising in taxicabs, to tidal electric power in the Bay of Fundy. None of these ventures got off the ground except, briefly, the blimps.

Others, unfortunately, did. In 1927, he became one of the minor backers of the International Germanic Trust Company, which was to promote American-German commercial relations. He eventually retired when difficulties arose, invoking a policy of his law firm, and the enterprise descended slowly into receivership.

He was one of the incorporators of the Federal International Investment Trust, which was well supported but could not disentangle itself from legal problems sufficiently to be brought to market. It was at least a respectable, though not a successful, venture. Less presentable was the Compo Bond Corporation, which tried to sell thrift bonds through the retail banking system. Roosevelt was a director of this company and of the Associated Bankers Corporation, which marketed commercial paper for small banks. Roosevelt resigned as a director an uncomfortably short time before Compo went bankrupt. This did not inhibit him from writing a homily about the need to avoid excessive securities legislation and to give the public "a sound education on the worth of securities."[41] In any such process, he would more appropriately have been a student than a teacher.

As it happened, the general secretary of the Society for Promoting Financial Knowledge wrote him that he noted with "a great deal of concern the use of your name to further . . . new promotions that . . . are business risks of the more hazardous type [that] are being offered . . . as 'safe investments.' " The writer regretted that "such an honored name should be commercialized in such a manner, when there are so many opportunities for employing the prestige that it carries in activities designed to promote some public good." Roosevelt resorted to his customary reply that in the case objected to, the use of his name had not been authorized.[42]

In 1925, Roosevelt had been sufficiently concerned about his financial condition that he auctioned off some of his naval prints, though they fetched less than a thousand dollars. He also wore somewhat unstylish and frayed clothes for awhile.[43] But this did not deter him from an energetic practice of eccentric investing and idiosyncratic commercial associations. His business career was like his poker playing, zestful, full of bluff and impetuosity, and not at all like his political approach, which varied between caution and boldness but was informed by an almost infallible clarity of intuition, subtlety of method, and judgment of people. He even referred to some of the ventures as "games." While he was in the shipping "game" himself, in the pages of the *New York Times* and elsewhere, he excoriated the government for aid to U.S. flag carriers other than his.[44]

In 1934 the *Chicago Tribune* would quote from a Roosevelt Fireside Chat attacking the "mad chase [during the twenties] for unearned riches, and an unwillingness of leaders in almost every walk of life to look beyond their own schemes and speculations." Beside this quotation was printed a comment on the talking vending machine company: "Extravagant estimates of earnings were put forward." The stock had declined from eighteen dollars to twelve cents and the company was then in reorganization, and "in 1928 numbered among its directors Mr. Franklin D. Roosevelt."[45]

The patrician squire resented new money. The self-proclaimed farmer resented modern industrial capitalism. The inept speculator resented not only the successful investors but all those implicated in the culture of unrestricted and unregulated investment. And the political genius resented both his own lack of commercial genius and the people who did possess commercial genius and who he thought were fundamentally at odds with the interests of what would become the vast army of his political followers.

For six years Roosevelt took on the presidency of the American Construction Council. In theory, this organization coordinated self-regulation for the construction industry, and Roosevelt inveighed against the undesirability of government regulation (of precisely the kind he imposed in the New Deal): "Government regulation is not feasible. It is unwieldy. It is expensive," he told the *New York Times* in 1922.[46]

In fact, the members of the council ignored his guidelines and often didn't even pay their dues, which may have helped cause Roosevelt to reconsider the merits of government regulation. Roosevelt used the council as a pulpit to keep his name in front of a large number of people in advocacy of esoteric causes. He praised the value of manual labor and tried to enlist Henry Ford to assist him. He wrote: "If the Puritan fathers had sat down on the Plymouth shore and opened up real estate offices [and] city planning bureaus, instead of chopping wood and drawing water, I'm afraid our progress towards being a nation would have been considerably retarded."[47]

Roosevelt, from this platform, even championed a revival of what he called "the guild spirit." He felt that, as they had in the late Middle Ages and early modern era, the skilled craftsman should have the same social standing as the professional. He believed that construction, if people of high standards entered it in greater numbers, could become more of a science than a trade. He railed against construction "distinctly inferior in quality and unsound in financing." Inadequately secured building mortgages were a particular (and prophetically justi-fied) bugbear.[48]

Roosevelt did have some successes, especially United European Investors Limited, a Canadian incorporation that invested in cash-strapped German indus-try while the Deutschmark was severely undervalued. The business operated from 1922 to 1924, when it was wound up at a 200 percent profit.[49]*

In his business activities, as Eleanor Roosevelt wrote, Roosevelt "was not expe-rienced and not always wise."[50] They showed him some of the other side of the business-government relationship different from the one he had learned in the Navy Department. He saw some of the venality and recklessness of undiscrimi-nating and unregulated capitalism. He is not immune to charges of envy, snob-bery, and misplaced vindictiveness for his own limitations as an investor. As one of his most distinguished biographers has written: "Undoubtedly his disappoint-ments as a business leader had some bearing upon his triumphs as a political leader."[51]

IV

ROOSEVELT TOOK THE FIRST of many houseboat cruises in the Florida Keys in February 1923. There was a good deal of exacting calculation of the navigability of the stairs between the sixty-foot *Weona II*'s two decks, and there was concern about the integration of his indispensable black valet, LeRoy Jones (whom Roosevelt invariably addressed as "Roy").[†] Both Eleanor and Louis Howe came on the trip initially, but did not enjoy themselves. Eleanor didn't like fish-ing, found it "eerie and menacing" at night, and disliked the lubricated, idle, and enforced conviviality of it. Louis Howe was not the most companionable of peo-ple at the best of times and had no interest in the great outdoors on land, much less at sea.

When the boat called at Miami, Roosevelt's presidential running mate of 1920, James M. Cox, came aboard and was so shaken at Roosevelt's appearance that he wept, convinced that FDR had had a stroke and was on the verge of death. He could not disguise his concerns from Roosevelt, who referred to them thereafter detachedly, masked by a pretense of wry amusement, with defiant determination to prove Cox's fears unwarranted.[53] (FDR also let his sideburns grow on the voy-

---

* It was not the least irony of the antagonism that arose between Roosevelt and Hitler that when the German leader sarcastically referred in 1941 to the American president's undistin-guished record as a speculator, he was presumably unaware of Roosevelt's success in German finance (while Hitler was languishing in Landsberg prison, after the fiasco of the 1923 Munich Putsch, dictating *Mein Kampf* to Rudolf Hess).
† The renting agent thought this a manageable problem if Roy would behave like other "well brought-up darkies."[52]

age, but when he returned to Hyde Park, Sara was so upset at his resemblance to Mr. James that she made him shave them back to contemporary length.[54]) Roosevelt declared in a letter to Senator Carter Glass after this trip: "Except for the braces, I have never been in better health in my life."[55]

The inevitable Livy Davis and Lewis Ledyard had been among the passengers on the *Weona II*. When Ledyard caught a forty-two pound Jewfish, Roosevelt was so amused by Mrs. Ledyard's remark that she thought they had left New York to escape the Jews that he put it in the log of the trip.[56]

With Jews as with blacks, Roosevelt never initiated slurs against them nor behaved discourteously toward or about them. Nor was he amused by virulent disparagements of African-Americans, sometimes remonstrating with southern arch-segregationist staff members such as Steve Early that they should be less racist. His view of these matters seems to have been like that of classes of accommodation on a ship. All Americans must have a ticket for the passage: basic freedoms and the right to achieve their maximum potential.

If white Protestants were the first-class passengers and blacks were the fourth class, Roman Catholics occupied the second-class cabins and Jews the third. There is no evidence of his ever disparaging Catholics or Catholicism. He had considerable experience of and deep respect for the pinnacles of Catholic culture in all the arts and for the great Catholic civilizations, especially France and Italy. He did, however, consider that the Roman Catholic Church occupied too great a place in the lives of its adherents, and while he believed in an episcopal rather than a congregational church, he was opposed to the bishops of any church having any capacity to intrude unduly into the lives of communicants, much less contest with the secular leaders.

Like many Protestants, he thought of the Roman Catholic Church as secretive, powerful, and somewhat un-American. Eleanor, at least initially, was more skeptical about Jews and Roman Catholics (influenced perhaps by the anticlerical atheism of Mlle. Souvestre and by her unhappy time in the French convent). But she was always, from her earliest adulthood to the end of her days, a courageous champion of the rights of blacks. Sara, though courteous and correct to almost everyone, thought the Jews aliens and the Roman Catholics priest-ridden victims of the occult, apart from the worldliest of the Latin Europeans, Austrians, and southern and Rhineland Germans. Her son never paid any attention to her opinions on such subjects.

The women closest to Franklin Roosevelt as an adult (his secretaries, Missy LeHand and Grace Tully, and Lucy Mercer) and most of the leading New York Democrats, including his party chairmen and one of his attorneys general, were Roman Catholics. And he was widely identified with the effort to elect Alfred E. Smith the first Roman Catholic president. He was a close friend of several of the leading American Catholic clergymen, especially Archbishop Spellman of New York, Cardinal Mundelein of Chicago, and Cardinal Gibbons of Baltimore. (Gibbons, as Roosevelt liked to recount, when asked whether he believed in the infallibility of the pope replied that he did but that he had met the pope many times and the pope invariably called him "Jibbons."[57])

To Roosevelt bigotry was a good deal more un-American than any individuals or groups who were the victims of it. Beyond that, he was eventually offended by the failure of his natural peers to support him as he set out to make safe their sheltered world, which the Great Depression so mortally threatened.

This heightened his appreciation of the groups that they despised and that voted in overwhelming numbers for him. He enjoyed ethnic jokes, including those directed against WASPS, but not ethnic or sectarian slurs. He believed in himself and in the Anglo-Saxon, Protestant, Yankee sociological type of which he was such an exemplar. But he was more impressed with those who strove and achieved in American society with few initial advantages than he was with those who claimed for themselves from the existence of their well-placed forebears a license to condescend to the less fortunate.

Withal, it is not at all clear that he thought of the United States as basically a Protestant and white country. He certainly saw the potential for recruiting Catholic and Jewish voters. Henry Morgenthau, Roosevelt's Jewish treasury secretary (and a fervent admirer of his), wrote in his diary (January 27, 1942) that Roosevelt had said three days before to Leo Crowley, a Roman Catholic (chairman of the Federal Deposit Insurance Corporation, Alien Property custodian, head of the Office of Economic Warfare, and ultimately Lend-Lease administrator), that "this is a Protestant country and the Catholics and Jews are here under sufferance. It is up to you to go along with anything I want." This sounds improbably callous. There is no documentary support for it; Crowley's biographer (Professor Stuart Weiss) makes no reference to it. Crowley and Morgenthau disliked each other. Crowley is not a reliable source and Morgenthau was a rather credulous recipient of this sort of reflection. The United States was an overwhelmingly Protestant country then, and the Jews and Catholics would wait a long time for a president better disposed to them than Roosevelt. Unfortunately, like the allegation that Justice Holmes thought Roosevelt a "second class intellect" (chapter 7), and several remarks about war-time relations with Stalin attributed to Roosevelt, this alleged claim of Crowley's has been widely accepted, even by some serious historians. It is unlikely that Roosevelt ever said, and there is no evidence that he believed, anything of the kind.[58]

Most of the Jews Roosevelt knew well were from the scholarly tradition, especially jurists like Supreme Court justice Felix Frankfurter and New York state Supreme Court justice Samuel I. Rosenman. He preferred the somewhat pedantic but loyal Frankfurter to the opportunistic financier Bernard Baruch, but they were both useful and they were both rather obsequious to him. Roosevelt had first encountered Frankfurter when he was assistant secretary of the navy and Frankfurter came to his attention as a very astute labor lawyer. During World War I, after FDR had brought Frankfurter home for lunch, Eleanor, unprejudiced though she was, described Frankfurter to Sara as "an interesting little man, but very Jew." She was less generous after a dinner at about the same time with Bernard Baruch. "The Jew party was appalling. I never wish to hear money, jewels, or labels mentioned again."[59]

When he was president, though Jews represented only 3 percent of the population, they occupied 15 per cent of the government's senior appointments. This enabled domestic anti-Semites such as Joseph P. Kennedy, the radio priest Charles E. Coughlin, long-time Boston mayor and Massachusetts governor James Michael Curley, and United Mine Workers leader John L. Lewis as well as foreign enemies, Adolf Hitler in particular, to claim that Roosevelt was dominated and manipulated by Jews pursuing an international Jewish interest. He reviled such incitements to bigotry with memorable eloquence.

V

S OCIAL LIFE IN New York sapped the painstaking progress of Roosevelt's muscles, and his therapist, Mrs. Lake, thought he suffered from being bullied by his wife and his mother. Dr. Lovett, who regarded Eleanor's and Louis Howe's hortatory influence as useful, examined him a year after his first visit to Boston. He pronounced that the muscles on balance had not progressed, although the patient had made great progress at getting around. Lovett thought Roosevelt too independent and prone to listen to quack suggestions. Roosevelt thought Lovett a tedious and unimaginative autocrat. Lovett became another skeptic whom he would amaze with his relaunched life, and Roosevelt saw little of him after 1923. He continued to experiment with gadgets and therapies—an electrified belt, a giant tricycle, and his theory that sunlight and water were the keys to muscular resuscitation.

Roosevelt was briefly inspired by Emile Coué, the French proponent of the doctrine that "Every day in every way, I'm getting better and better." Coué acknowledged to a friend of Roosevelt's who had inquired about it that there was little he could do for a polio case.[60] When an English noblewoman of his acquaintance recommended a new elixir, Roosevelt wrote jokingly to Dr. Draper about the merits of a concoction made from "the dried eyes of the extinct three-toed rhinoceros . . . [or] the distilling of the remains of King Tut-Ankh-Amen. The serum might put new life into some of our mutual friends."[61]

Roosevelt took up some of his hobbies with greater fervor than ever, especially stamp, book, and print collecting, and carving wooden model boats, which he sailed on the Hudson. As with almost anything requiring hand-eye coordination, from carving the Thanksgiving turkey to sailing in tricky waters, to mixing complex cocktails, he became an expert wood ship-modeler, using tools given him by his parents before he went to Groton in 1896.[*62]

---

* He made his model sailboats out of balsa wood at a uniform length of thirty-eight inches. In the right winds and currents his fastest boats gradually achieved an average speed in crossing the Hudson at Springwood of almost five miles per hour.[63]

He tried his hand at writing, without much success. He did manage an unexceptional article about Japan for *Asia* magazine. Before the war Roosevelt had been an advocate of a hard line against the Japanese in trade and in regard to any territorial expansion but had become a champion of trans-Pacific cooperation. Americans, he wrote, should "appreciate a little more readily the . . . greater necessity to Japan of the markets and raw materials" of China. The Japanese should understand that Americans felt a need for immigration restrictions, he wrote, just as the Japanese would not wish to be flooded with American settlers in their home islands.[64] The article was well received in Japan. The correspondent of the Tokyo *Nichi-Nichi* commended Roosevelt for being "broad-minded and fair."[65]

Roosevelt also wrote a banal article about Alexander Hamilton, whom he credited with organizing the finances of the nascent American republic with such skill that he had "removed for all time the risk of disturbance of the state."

This commendation quickly succumbed to the grace of conversion when Roosevelt read and reviewed for the *New York World* future ambassador Claude G. Bowers's biographies of Jefferson and Hamilton. Roosevelt was persuaded that Hamilton was in fact the slave and protagonist of wealth and high finance, while Jefferson was a genuine democrat. Both opinions were rather simplistic, but the second at least facilitated his masquerade as a continuator of a Jeffersonian tradition against Republican indulgence of the abuses of capitalism when he returned to politics.[66]

But his proposed history of the United States, beginning in 1000 A.D., meandered unconvincingly through a small part of the European Dark Ages before he abandoned it. He did some preparatory work on a life of John Paul Jones and a few other projects, but nothing proceeded except his work on local histories of Dutchess County.[67] He was an actor rather than an author, a dramatist only if he was in the lead role, making up the script as he went along, and, as would become clear, not really a historian but a subject for historians.

In late 1923 Roosevelt bought a seventy-one-foot houseboat with his friend John Lawrence, which they called, after themselves, *Larooco*. (Lawrence, too, did not have full use of his legs.[68]) Roosevelt was undeterred, but wounded for once, by Eleanor's scolding about his financial insouciance. After she asked for his golf socks to give to their son James, since "you don't use them now," and questioned the affordability of the houseboat, Roosevelt bitterly pledged to try not to be "a useless burden to my family." Eleanor had a glimpse of what a struggle he had conducted beneath his jovial exterior and thought better of her home economics lecture. She never forgot this outburst.[69]

(Her real grievance, Frances Perkins thought, was that her husband never relied on her opinions or really listened to her. He eventually asked her to report on things for him or represent him but almost never attached any weight to what she thought.[70] It may be that much of her prodigious hectoring was a demand for attention and a complaint at not receiving it.)

Larooco cost $3,750 and was ready for its new owners when they went south to embark in February 1924. *Larooco* was not a lucky or very seaworthy craft; her engines frequently failed and she grounded constantly—six times in one day. Nor was the weather entirely obliging that first winter; they were several times engulfed in teeming tropical rainstorms while bumbling about in mangrove swamps in the Everglades. Roosevelt was as indefatigable as always.

He had been advised by Dr. Draper that no further muscular improvement could be expected, and there were many times on this cruise when he had a melancholy air. As far as the medical profession was concerned, no more could be done for him—Franklin Roosevelt was on his own, he was told. According to Missy LeHand, who made the cruise although Eleanor did not, he often stayed in his cabin until noon, presumably unable until then to fix the happy countenance behind which he hid all his fears and sorrows.[71]

Missy, twenty-five years old at the time of the first *Larooco* cruise, called him "EffDee" and served him with a selfless devotion that consumed the rest of her life. She was an attractive woman, with a slightly long face and square jaw but beautiful dark, blue-grey eyes. She served as an efficient and congenial hostess in addition to being her employer's private secretary. Eventually, rumors arose about whether there was anything romantic in the relationship. Certainly Missy loved Roosevelt. Her letters are of the kind that wives or close companions write, volunteering dental advice, giving him a flower she had found on a Norwegian glacier while on holiday, and telling him "you are sweet to write."[72]

She was candid but diplomatic and reminded many of his friends of Lucy Mercer, her co-religionist with a similar background—including a wayward father. She never publicly contradicted him as his wife did, and was so wholly admiring, like Lucy, that her comments, because always unquestionably well-intended, often carried more weight than Eleanor's. Other men would become infatuated with Missy, including the dashing former Paris peace delegate and future U.S. ambassador to Russia and France, William C. Bullitt, and the state policeman in the Roosevelts' security unit, Earl Miller. Miller would be the subject of extensive rumors connecting him to Eleanor. Bullitt was even briefly engaged to Missy, but she never ceased to be completely devoted to Franklin D. Roosevelt.

The extent of Roosevelt's affection for Missy is not clear. Examining doctors repeatedly confirmed in their reports that his illness had not rendered him impotent, though the psychological barriers to sexual activity might have been considerable even for him. From 1925 to 1928 Roosevelt spent 116 of 208 weeks away from home, trying to regain full use of his limbs. Eleanor was with him for four of those weeks, Sara for two, and Missy LeHand for 110.[73] She and Roosevelt spent many nights alone on the *Larooco*, except for Roy Jones and crew. She often stayed at Springwood, and had her own bedroom in the executive mansion in Albany and in the White House, when Roosevelt lived there.

They had plentiful opportunity for a very comprehensive relationship. His mischievous son Elliott claimed that Missy and his father were lovers, but he had no real evidence of it and his siblings disagreed. The ever-suspicious and obsessively watchful Eleanor was astonished by Missy's relatively uncritical admiration of her husband but was not resentful of the relationship. She always considered her an employee of indifferent social origins (and apparently therefore not much of a threat) as well as a pleasant and valuable collaborator. Missy, in any case, went to great lengths to placate Eleanor and Sara.

Eleanor was wildly jealous of some other women and their relations with her husband, including eventually her own daughter, and James's first wife, Betsy Cushing. Betsy Cushing Roosevelt Whitney told the distinguished author and columnist William Safire after Missy and her boss were dead that she had seen Missy and the President in acts of physical affection, including Missy sitting on Roosevelt's lap, and a range of embraces and kisses.[74]

Once he was president, Roosevelt's romantic life and particularly the question of his libido were the subject of widespread private speculation in the press corps and among other close observers. Roosevelt may have had some relatively restrained sexual release with Missy LeHand and one or two other women. But the energy and ambition that he might otherwise have devoted to that activity was much more likely diverted to his quest for and execution of his office, and the vast complexity of his political designs, which steadily projected his influence over the whole earth. The truth will never be known, and more than cursory speculation is unseemly. But it is unlikely that Franklin D. Roosevelt compounded all the other obstacles he surmounted in his ascent to historic heights by conducting a physically ambitious extramarital romantic life from a wheelchair under the sensitive and intrusive noses of his wife and mother, two of the most assertive and puritanical women in American history.[75]

On February 23, 1924, Woodrow Wilson died. He had lived long enough to attend Warren Harding's funeral the previous summer, but never made any real recovery from his stroke. Roosevelt wrote out a statement for the press saying that Wilson had given "mankind a new vision of pure democracy," and the *Larooco's* flag flew at half-mast for thirty days.[76] In Miami, Roosevelt and his party disembarked and called upon William Jennings Bryan, who had a winter home there. Roosevelt had always regarded him as a yokel and a demagogue, though a formidable populist leader. But they had "a nice chat."[77] Bryan now saw Roosevelt as a progressive ally against Democrats who wished to emulate big-business-dominated Republicans.

This was the last of the many trips Franklin Roosevelt and Livy Davis took together. The *Larooco* would sail again with its owners aboard, but without Livy. When he married again, in 1927, FDR was invited to be best man at the wedding but didn't feel able to accept; he entertained the newlyweds to lunch in New

York. Davis came to FDR's first inauguration as governor, but their correspondence tapered off somewhat and on January 11, 1932, Davis died of a self-inflicted gunshot wound. Roosevelt seated his widow prominently at his first presidential inaugural and wrote a generous remembrance of his old friend for their 1934 Harvard class publication.

Roosevelt, showing some of the skill that would become one of his hallmarks in the thirties, elaborately finessed the international and even the Prohibition issue. In 1923, he had responded to a noted magazine editor, Edward Bok, who had offered an award for the best plan he received for the preservation of world peace. The failings of the League were obvious to Roosevelt, and he proposed scrapping it and replacing it with a new international organization that would be acceptable to an adequate majority in the United States. He recognized that the surest guarantee of the avoidance of wars between the great powers was to have the United States engaged in the world. Once emancipated from the fool's paradise of isolation, Roosevelt reasoned with great insight, the United States would tilt the correlation of forces in the world in favor of the democracies and the relatively responsible countries.

He had also outgrown his enthusiasm for imperial adventure. He had wished in March 1918 to try to buy Curaçao from the Dutch, and against Josephus Daniels's direct orders commissioned Marley Hay, an authority on submarines, to inquire when visiting the Netherlands whether the Dutch could be interested. The Dutch foreign minister declined, citing fear that Germany would consider the sale a violation of neutrality by the Netherlands. Presumably, Roosevelt did not try again after the war ended in November because he knew Wilson would not approve any such initiative.[78]

He had defended General Leonard Wood, the Republican governor general of the Philippines, who in 1922 had declined to grant the Filipinos any more self-government. Ironically, given events nearly twenty years later, in responses to letters he had received about his article on Japan, he opposed "Britain's new fortifications at Singapore [and] Holland's new fleet for the Dutch East Indies . . . [as offensive] to the spirit of the day."[79] He advocated that critics of the marines' presence in Haiti be transported to Haiti [and] "turned loose up country for about thirty days—those who come back (alive) would be in favor of sending down the whole of that bloodthirsty organization known as the Marine Corps."[80] His views evolved through the twenties to support for bringing all the colonial and sub-autonomous countries and peoples of the world to independence as quickly as they could meet reasonable criteria for the responsible exercise of it.[81]

His public views on Prohibition evolved with public opinion. Personally, as we have seen, Roosevelt thought Prohibition to be nonsense and paid almost no attention to it in the continuity of his own drinking habits. In the mid-twenties, a majority of Americans still favored it (a great majority of rural and small-town dwellers), while the majority of the urban population were opposed. Roosevelt's initial public position, in September 1922, was to claim to a supporter in Dutchess County that 3–4 percent beer was non-intoxicating and should be permitted to be sold. He cautioned the same person to be wary of advocating the legal sale of light wine, which at 10–15 percent alcoholic content undoubtedly was intoxicating.

He settled upon the device of a national referendum, privately assuring supporters on both sides of the Prohibition debate that their side would win. This arose in his conversation with William Jennings Bryan in Miami in 1925, and Bryan was noncomittal.

Roosevelt had advised Al Smith over the prohibition act that had passed through the state legislature in 1923, effectively revoking Prohibition in the state. Vetoing it would offend the urban anti-Prohibition majority and most of Smith's own followers. Roosevelt, again showing some of the fancy footwork that would befuddle his opponents later in his career, suggested Smith should veto the bill because New York was morally obligated to support the federal government in carrying out the national Prohibition laws, and that Smith should, at the same time, summon the legislature to a special session to prepare a new state law that would ostensibly support the federal Prohibition law but provide no commitment to do so. In other words, he should appease the Prohibitionists by vetoing revocation of Prohibition, and appease the anti-Prohibitionists by replacing the existing law with one that would largely negate the federal law by providing minimum funding for its enforcement. This was too devious for Smith, who followed his own principles and virtually abandoned Prohibition in the country's largest state, while issuing a bland denial that he had undercut the Volstead (Prohibition) Act.[82] Smith did ostentatiously abstain from drinking beer, his preferred beverage, until after the Democratic convention, but it didn't much impress the delegates he was trying to woo.

In 1924, Roosevelt had prepared a statement for Smith describing Prohibition as a "red herring" and adding "a temperate people are a happy and contented people and to that all my acts and words will bend." Smith wouldn't hear of it. He bravely stuck with his demand for outright repeal.[83]

VI

THE ROOSEVELTS MADE a substantial political comeback in 1924. Eleanor turned the women's division of the New York Democratic Party into a powerhouse and, with Smith's assistance, secured the ability for the women to name their own delegates to the state convention. This was a clear defeat for Boss Charles F. Murphy, who had wanted to name the delegates himself. Murphy died suddenly of a heart attack a few days later, and Franklin Roosevelt managed a generous statement regretting the demise of New York's "most powerful and wisest leader."[84]

It was shortly after this remarkable feat of Roosevelt's of setting bygones to rest that Smith's close advisors, Belle Moskowitz and state supreme court justice Joseph Proskauer, called upon Roosevelt at 65th Street and asked him to become the chairman of Citizens for Smith, Al Smith's 1924 campaign for the Democratic nomination for president of the United States. Assured that his disability, which would prevent his getting around the country very much, was not a problem, Roosevelt accepted. He did not in fact believe Smith had a great chance of nomination, much less of election. But he did see it as an opportunity for himself to solidify his position as New York's second most prominent Democrat.

Roosevelt and Howe foresaw a deadlocked 1924 convention between the anti-Prohibitionist (wet) Smith and the conservative Republican-imitating Prohibitionists (dries), probably led by McAdoo. Roosevelt had urged Smith to speak out on national questions to enhance his salability throughout the country. Smith declined to follow Roosevelt's advice, other than over Prohibition, reducing his credibility as a candidate and aggravating his problems at the convention.

Roosevelt had initially welcomed the elevation to the presidency of his 1920 opponent, Calvin Coolidge, on the death of Harding—apparently of a coronary—in August 1923. Roosevelt thought Coolidge "not a world beater,"[85] but it became clear that Coolidge's taciturn conservatism reassured and satisfied the country. Roosevelt judged Harding and Coolidge quite accurately: "Poor old Harding was perfectly honest himself, but was not the kind of man who could ever tell the difference between a real friend and a crooked one, and he allowed himself to be surrounded by a pretty rotten crowd."[86] Roosevelt was impressed by Harding's magnanimity in pardoning jailed Socialist Party leader Eugene V. Debs, who had received 900,000 votes running for president in 1920, and by his persuading the steel industry to reduce the steel mill workday from twelve hours to ten.[87]

He regarded Coolidge as someone just coasting on the prosperity of the time, which Roosevelt saw was not carrying the whole country upward. The middle classes were doing well, the working class holding its own, but farm income was not gaining. Apart from his own biases, Roosevelt's analysis of the weaknesses of the great Republican boom proved exact.[88] "Coolidge," he wrote, "is inarticulate to the extent of being thought a mystery. To stick the knife into ghosts is always hard."[89]

The Republicans should have been vulnerable because of the Teapot Dome and Elk Hills oil scandals. The secretary of the interior, Albert B. Fall, had taken large bribes and had transferred naval reserve oil leases to Harry Sinclair's Mammoth Oil Company and (Roosevelt's purported and soon-forgotten "friend") Edward L. Doheny and his Pan-American Petroleum and Transport Company. Doheny had paid the front-runner for the 1924 Democratic presidential nomination, William G. McAdoo, $250,000 over several years for services that were unspecified except for Doheny's testimony about McAdoo and others: "I paid them for their influence."[90] The Smith camp thought the scandal might give them a chance.*

Franklin Roosevelt noted with satisfaction that his cousin Ted Roosevelt (TR Jr.), the assistant secretary of the navy, did not come through unscathed. The secretary, Edward Denby, had been forced to retire for turning over the oil interests to the Interior Department, though there was no suggestion of financial impropriety by Denby or his assistant secretary. Ted Roosevelt survived and ran for governor of New York, and McAdoo retained his status as leading candidate.

The Republicans met in Cleveland June 10 to 13, 1924, nominated Coolidge and Charles G. Dawes, promised tax cuts and farm relief, and adjourned. Henry Cabot Lodge had alienated even the Republicans by the ferocity of his assault on Wilson. Having been Republican convention chairman in 1920, he was only a delegate and largely ignored in 1924.[91]

Roosevelt, as Smith's campaign chairman, manfully tried to head off a La Follette Progressive candidacy, which was threatened. He wrote the Wisconsinite in June 1924, enclosing his advocacy of farm relief, emphasizing Smith's credentials as a reformer, and requesting a personal meeting with La Follette.[92] La Follette found such a meeting inconvenient, and it did not take place. Any rapprochement with the anti-Prohibitionist, Tammany-backed, Roman Catholic Smith was impossible by then, anyway. (La Follette, like Bryan, Wilson, and Hoover, was much more of a crusading zealot than the more pragmatic Smith and Roosevelt.) Smith should have recognized Roosevelt's tactical skill but did not.[93]

For strictly tactical reasons, Proskauer proposed Roosevelt to Smith as his nominator at the convention again in 1924 as he had been in 1920, and Smith accepted for the same reasons. So did Roosevelt. They thought of him as a Protestant with a famous name and a pleasant face and accent, untainted by Tammany and with no potential to be a rival. (Smith would later claim to the anti-Roosevelt writer John T. Flynn that Roosevelt asked to be allowed to nominate him, but this doesn't square with all other accounts.)

Smith still regarded the senator from Hyde Park as a priggish, pompous mother's boy—not "the kind of man you can take into the pissroom and talk intimately with," as he once put it, before the onset of Roosevelt's disability made such a conversation, or at least such a criterion, impractical.[94] Roosevelt and Howe wanted to collect some votes at the convention for Roosevelt, just as a sign of prestige and future credibility.

When Proskauer asked Roosevelt to give the speech, FDR asked Proskauer to write it, which he did. It was, in fact Joseph Proskauer, not Franklin D. Roosevelt,

---

* Doheny had also employed Wilson's former secretaries of war and the interior, Lindley Garrison and Franklin Lane, and Wilson's attorney general, Thomas Gregory. And Sinclair had taken on Archibald Roosevelt, Ted's brother, in a well-paid sinecure from which he abruptly resigned at the first sign of wrongdoing.

who plucked the phrase "the happy warrior" from Wordsworth and applied it to Smith. Roosevelt thought Proskauer's draft too poetic for a political convention and produced his own draft. (He dictated it to Missy LeHand while sitting on a blanket on the lawn at Hyde Park.[95]) Finally, Herbert Bayard Swope, managing editor of the *New York World*, became the agreed arbiter of the dispute that arose over the competing versions of the speech, and adjudicated in favor of Proskauer's text. After heated words, Roosevelt agreed to speak from that draft with minor modifications.

The irony of what occurred was heavy; Smith and his friends thoroughly underestimated the political potential for Roosevelt before his illness, and completely discounted him now. They produced for him a slogan that would be all anyone would remember of the vapid oratory of the 1924 convention, and they gave him a platform from which he would relaunch his career and, ultimately, vastly eclipse Smith himself.

The convention opened in New York's Madison Square Garden on June 24, 1924. Roosevelt felt as keenly as ever in his life the pressure to perform. He was now the state's second most powerful Democrat despite his nearly three-year hiatus, and he was glad, though apprehensive, of this opportunity to return to the forefront of his party's affairs. He was to speak at noon two days later. Sara, Eleanor, all the Roosevelt children (except for James, who was with his father), and Eleanor's friends Nancy Cook and Marion Dickerman were in the gallery. Eleanor was knitting assiduously to distract herself from the intense scrutiny of her husband's public post-illness debut. Franklin Roosevelt had rehearsed the walk up the aisle many times in his home. He had developed a technique with his sixteen-year-old son James, using only his right crutch and grasping James's right upper arm tenaciously with his left hand, hitching his legs forward from the hip while chatting animatedly with his son. As he did so he made eye contact with nearby observers to distract them from the laboriousness of his progress. They paused at the rear of the dais while Franklin D. Roosevelt was for the third time introduced to a Democratic national convention.

After getting one of the national committeemen (Senator Joseph Guffey) to ensure that the speaker's platform was sturdy, Roosevelt made his way alone, on two crutches, to the podium. It was a dramatic and an affecting moment. The distance he had to cover was only fifteen feet, but the vast auditorium was absolutely silent; the solidarity of moral support for Franklin Roosevelt in his personal struggle with infirmity was unanimous and profound. Perspiring heavily and concentrating fiercely, he made the passage without incident and then thrust his head and shoulders back and smiled broadly at the convention in the distinctive way that in a few years would become familiar to the whole world. Twenty thousand people rose as one and erupted in thunderous applause that lasted for several minutes. The sun broke through the clouds and streamed through the skylight of Madison Square Garden.

His rich and melodious voice and confident Dutchess County/Ivy League accent filled and uplifted the hall. Buoyed by the affection of his party, he rendered Proskauer's speech with tremendous verve. Having attracted the fervent attention and goodwill of the convention, he startled it with his imposing presence and ringing eloquence. He concluded: "He has a power to strike at error and wrongdoing that makes his adversaries quail before him. He has a personality that carries to every hearer not only the sincerity but the righteousness of what he says. The 'Happy Warrior' of the political battlefield, Alfred E. Smith."

The audience was again moved to a mighty ovation that gave way to Smith demonstrations and continued for over an hour. Roosevelt had been on his feet and exerting himself for over half an hour. He smiled and responded happily to his great triumph, but his hands were starting to shake and no provision had been made to cover his withdrawal. Frances Perkins and another female delegate nimbly rushed up to congratulate the speaker and masked his retirement from the podium, which, once out of sight of the wildly demonstrating delegates, was conducted by wheelchair.

The convention went downhill after that. It lasted for thirteen days and went through 103 ballots, because McAdoo could not open up enough of a lead against Smith to secure the two-thirds majority needed for nomination. Smith demanded a severe condemnation of the Ku Klux Klan, which was then almost as hostile to Roman Catholics as to blacks, while McAdoo, in a gesture to the bigotry of the old South, the Democrats' last bulwark, favored a rather tepid demurral from its objectives. Smith was for the outright abolition of Prohibition (the Volstead Act). McAdoo was prepared to retain Prohibition. Roosevelt squarely opposed the Klan and wanted to finesse Prohibition, as has been mentioned, by playing with acceptable levels of alcoholic content. Smith and his Tammany friends had packed the convention galleries to the rafters. Many of their supporters were coarse and obnoxious, and the bad feeling between the Catholics and Protestants and the wets and dries within the Democratic Party was very abrasive.

When a southern delegate attacked the Ku Klux Klan, the Tammany galleries went happily wild and the organ played the Civil War Union Army song "Marching Through Georgia." Roosevelt had intervened to great applause, asking for unity and quoting Lincoln on malice and charity. Bryan, in a final and discreditable appearance at a Democratic convention, asked that the Klan not be named in a resolution opposing it. Bryan was loudly heckled by the Tammany forces, but his soft anti-Klan position passed—by a hair's breadth, 543.15 to 542.35. (Some delegate votes split into fractions, because several or more people shared the right to cast a single vote.) The split down the center of the Democratic Party could hardly have been more dramatic.

Roosevelt moved adjournment on one occasion, at 2 A.M. "on the Sabbath."

This passed. He intervened again less successfully after the sixty-sixth ballot, when he won majority support but less than the required two-thirds for inviting Smith and McAdoo to address the convention, and after the ninety-third ballot, when he proposed that both leading candidates withdraw. McAdoo refused. On all occasions, Roosevelt was greeted with great applause. He received one or two votes on sixteen of the ballots, undoubtedly less than he and Howe had hoped for, but the convention was still, for him and for him alone, a great success.

Finally, John W. Davis, a former ambassador to Great Britain and a distinguished conservative Wall Street lawyer (from West Virginia originally), was nominated for president when McAdoo realized he could not prevail. Charles W. Bryan, William Jennings Bryan's brother, was chosen as the vice presidential candidate. But the real victor was Franklin D. Roosevelt. Had the convention been confident that he was ready for a national campaign, it could have been stampeded towards him. He wasn't, and would not have wished or accepted nomination in this unpromising year. But Boss Tom Pendergast of Kansas City (patron of the then forty-year-old county judge Harry S Truman) called him "the most magnetic personality of any individual I have ever met . . . I predict he will be the candidate . . . in 1928." Franklin D. Roosevelt was edging ineluctably toward the national stage.[96]

After the convention many New York Catholics, previously a group that had been stand-offish to Roosevelt, wrote to him in terms of great gratitude, including future legendary party chairman James A. Farley, then of the New York State Athletic Commission. Roosevelt buried forever the suspicion of him, raised by the Sheehan affair in 1911, as anti-Catholic. As one historian wrote, for a time a list of his correspondents "read like a sampling from the Dublin telephone directory."[97] Perhaps the most illustrious of Roosevelt's correspondents at this time was the greatest American sports hero of all time, George Herman "Babe" Ruth, the great home-run king of the New York Yankees, who inspired the construction of Yankee Stadium. Ruth identified with Smith more on sociological than sectarian grounds. He wrote of "the humble beginning of Governor Smith. Maybe you know I wasn't fed with a gold spoon when I was a kid. No poor boy can go any too high in this world to suit me."[98]

Future House Speaker Henry T. Rainey of Illinois wrote Roosevelt that the convention had been a "contest between Morgan's lawyer [Davis] and Doheny's lawyer [McAdoo]." He also thought the Democrats would not be back in the White House until Republican policies had laid the economy low.[99] Commentator Walter Lippmann wrote a "Dear Frank" letter to Roosevelt, calling his speech "moving and distinguished . . . and most eloquent," and ending "We are all proud of you."[100] A wealthy New York banker writing under the pseudonym of Jedediah Tingle wrote Roosevelt that his "very crutches have helped you to the stature of the Gods."[101]

Faced with the conservative Tweedledum and Tweedledee of Coolidge and Davis, the La Follette campaign was off and running, assured of extensive farm and labor support. It was clear to Roosevelt and Howe from the outset that Davis would fail to rival Coolidge for the conservative vote, and that La Follette would take the liberal Democrats and the disgruntled Republican farmers, in a proportion of about two to one, adding to the Republican landslide.[102] Yet Roosevelt saw better days for his party ahead: "The Republican leaders are not through with dishonesty nor will the present prosperity continue unabated," he wrote.[103] He predicted the Republicans would produce "depression and unemployment" in time for the 1932 election.[104]

Denied the presidential nomination, Al Smith ran for a third term as governor of New York. His Republican opponent was Ted Roosevelt. The campaign between them was an uneven one. Smith's campaign for the presidential nomination had raised his stature. One of the more piquant vignettes of the campaign was Eleanor Roosevelt traveling about the state accompanied by her mannish lady friends, all kitted out in brown-tweed riding breeches or plus-fours, in a car surmounted by a large papier-mache teapot that emitted simulated steam, to remind the voters of her first cousin's involvement in the oil scandals of the Harding administration. (Teapot Dome, Wyoming, was the site of many of the oil reserves transferred from Ted Roosevelt's Navy Department to the Interior Department and then improperly leased.) "You should have seen her [Eleanor] in those pants!" said one cousin. "A sight . . . no artist could paint," said another.[105] Eleanor eventually acknowledged that this had been "a rough stunt."

This was at least the symbolic nadir of the falling-out between the Oyster Bay Roosevelts and the Hyde Park Roosevelts, to whom Eleanor had now been acculturated.[106]

The election was an easy third-term victory for Smith. He won by an unprecedented majority of 387,000, although Coolidge carried New York by 700,000. The presidential election was a debacle. Robert M. La Follette, as Roosevelt and Howe had predicted, took most of his votes from the Democrats. It was another great sweep for the Republicans. Coolidge received 15,724,000 votes to 8,400,000 for Davis and 4,823,000 for La Follette. Coolidge won 382 electoral votes to 136 for Davis and 13 (Wisconsin) for La Follette, though La Follette came second in eleven western states. Alfred E. Smith was now the leading Democrat in the country, but Franklin D. Roosevelt was arguably the second contender, contingent upon continued medical progress.

Roosevelt and Howe sent a circular letter to every delegate asking for suggestions on how to avoid a third successive disaster in 1928, and suggesting an off-year conference. The effort was looked upon with suspicion by the anti-Smith forces and with no great enthusiasm by the governor himself, and was stillborn.

Roosevelt conducted scores of extended interviews and built whole relationships around the quest for greater information about the vagaries of the storied boom of the twenties. One such relationship was with a young Jewish tailor who stayed with Roosevelt for much of one summer, as he worked on restoration of his legs, telling him about the living and working conditions of the poor urban working class. He became very informed about the grievances and dreams of these disadvantaged people, of whose existence Coolidge and Hoover were only dimly aware.[107]

With his resolution of the lingering suspicion that he was anti-Catholic, and his exposure to the prairie progressives, Roosevelt was devising a strategy for Democratic electoral victory. He was now looking at a way of broadening his exposure to the Democratic South while accelerating his progress against his illness. Smith was the likely presidential nominee, and the likely loser, for 1928. But 1932, as Roosevelt had written to Willard Saulsbury,[108] was the year for the Democrats to lead the Catholics, Jews, southern whites, northern blacks, western farmers, and urban working class to victory. Roosevelt was working to make his physical and political rehabilitation timetable conform to that schedule.[109]

VII

E VEN BEFORE THE Democratic convention, Roosevelt had begun to think of a project that would become one of the great preoccupations of his life. In his quest for a full recovery he continued a regime of arduous exercise, ignoring the advice of his doctors, who told him that further improvement was virtually impossible. He also concentrated on getting more sunshine and warm water. An old friend and sometime campaign contributor, New York banker George Foster Peabody (unrelated to the rector of Groton School), told him in June of a resort hotel near thermal springs in Georgia in which Peabody had an interest. (He had a winter home in nearby Columbus, Georgia.) Peabody wanted to sell it and thought of Roosevelt as a possible buyer of it for its therapeutic potential.

Roosevelt didn't pay much attention until Peabody wrote back in the summer of 1924 that a polio victim, Louis Joseph, had vacated his wheelchair as a result of therapy in the warm thermal waters adjacent to his hotel. Peabody's partner, a brave newspaperman and opponent of the Ku Klux Klan (at considerable risk to his life), Tom Loyless, came to New York to describe the resort and the particular cure of Louis Joseph.

Franklin and Eleanor Roosevelt came to Bullochville, Georgia (population 450), on October 3, 1924. In the classic manner of a used-car salesman, Peabody repainted his Meriwether Inn, a large Victorian wooden hotel, when he learned that Roosevelt would be visiting it. It was still, wrote Roosevelt, "in awful condition."[110] It turned out that Louis Joseph had discarded his braces almost as soon as he arrived, but he did attribute his steady subsequent improvement to exercise in the warm water.

Roosevelt tried out the Meriwether swimming pool the day after his arrival. The slight sulphurous odor of the warm water was bracing, and swimming had a splendid effect. Any muscular activity in depleted limbs could achieve infinitely more in water than on land. Polio sufferers could endure two hours or more at ninety degrees (Fahrenheit) in this water, which would become excessive to unafflicted people after ten or fifteen minutes. For the first time since August 1921, Roosevelt felt life in his toes. He said: "I walk around in water 4 feet deep without braces or crutches almost as well as if I had nothing the matter with my legs."[111] A local doctor familiar with the Joseph case advised Roosevelt that if his condition was at all similar he could start to respond in three weeks.

Loyless gave the Roosevelts a drive around the area. Roosevelt liked the scent of pine, but Eleanor found the poverty-stricken and oppressed state of the blacks obnoxious, and wasn't much impressed with the rural white Georgians, either. Anything Franklin was apt to invest in set alarm bells ringing with Eleanor, who had become very mistrustful of his commercial intuition, with some justification. Everyone whom he consulted shared Eleanor's reservations about the Georgia project, including Basil O'Connor, who came to visit and thought Roosevelt's idea—he wanted to combine a resort with a polio spa—grossly impractical. He foresaw that the polio cases would be awkward for the able-bodied visitors and that the general public could inhibit the polio victims. Roosevelt no longer seemed to take notice of the difference between those who did and those who did not suffer from polio. This was commendable, but it would be a stumbling block to commercial success if the project depended on others having the same enlightened perspective.

The Roosevelts stayed two weeks, as FDR steadily became more enthusiastic about the idea of buying Peabody's white elephant of a hotel. Peabody possessed considerable talents as a salesman, and in the middle of the Roosevelts' visit he persuaded the mayor and council of Bullochville to change the name of the town to Warm Springs.

Roosevelt returned to Warm Springs in April 1925. The publicity about his interest in Warm Springs had motivated several people suffering from polio to arrive unannounced at the Meriwether seeking treatment. Finding himself at the head of about ten fellow polio cases, he had them examined by the local general practitioner to make sure they had no other serious medical problems and then started to apply the muscle tests and exercises that had been given to him by Dr. Lovett.

He devised an exercise and water-therapy regime for each person who checked into the program at Warm Springs and infected almost everyone with his own determination and optimism. He personally led the exercises in the pool. His was a selfless and pioneering role. He claimed and possessed no medical expertise, but he knew the subject well. The combination of water, sun, exercises, companionship, and the inspiring manner of the leader did help most of those who attended. And Roosevelt was not overly concerned about being paid for his services. Those who could afford to pay were expected to; those who couldn't were not.

He also organized a great many picnics, especially to Dowdell's Knob, a 1,400-foot elevation with a splendid view that never failed to raise the morale of visitors. He became so relaxed with his troop of fellow patients that he sometimes wore his braces outside his trousers so he could adjust them himself. He even started a newspaper column in the *Macon Daily Telegraph*, composed of rather humdrum random opinions (that there should be a reduction in immigration, for instance), which was not successfully syndicated. Roosevelt later bound the columns and circulated them to a few intimates as an "Exegesis of the New Deal." It is difficult to find anything very prophetic in them.[112]

As Basil O'Connor had predicted, when the Meriwether's regular clientele arrived in May, they were alarmed at the presence of so many disabled people. Loyless attempted to placate them by setting up a separate dining room and swimming pool for the guests taking treatment.

Roosevelt spent June and July 1925 in New York and went in August to Horseneck Beach on Buzzard's Bay, Massachusetts, where Louis Howe had a cottage. Despite Dr. Draper's assertion two years before that the medical profession could do no more for him, he started treatment at nearby Marion, Massachusetts, with the energetic Dr. William McDonald.

McDonald, who had been recommended by Roosevelt's uncle Fred Delano, focused heavily on exercise and believed in braces as merely a transitional phase. Matters progressed until, in October, Roosevelt stood with his left brace only and McDonald and the faithful valet Roy Jones supporting him under the shoulders. He stayed throughout the autumn, and in early December walked several hundred feet with crutches but only his left brace, exulting to McDonald and Roy, "I can walk! . . . I begin to see actual daylight ahead."[113]

This proved to be optimistic. Roosevelt passed now into the hands of a new therapist, Alice Plastridge, who helped him economize on muscular effort so that he didn't exhaust himself with minor exertions. (She was ultimately chief therapist at Warm Springs and continued as an active member of the American Physical Therapy Association until she was one hundred years old.) He concluded his treatment with Dr. McDonald, who had oversold his own talents and considered Roosevelt, unjustly, something of an ingrate.

Roosevelt was losing interest in the *Larooco*, on which he had had a nasty accident in 1925, slipping and bumping his knee. For a time he feared gangrene. Because of large numbers of sharks in deep water, Roosevelt chose to swim only in shallow water, which reduced the hydro-therapeutic virtues of cruising in the *Larooco*, especially when, as in 1926, the weather was indifferent. He had written of this to John Lawrence in 1925, to explain his desire to sell the boat and concentrate on Warm Springs.[114]

When the boat had not been sold by the end of 1925, Roosevelt embarked once more, in February 1926. Eleanor joined him for a few days of engine trouble, bad weather, and navigational problems. Roosevelt often had a variety of guests on board (including, in 1925, the head of the American Federation of Labor, William Green, and his AFL executive).[115] The most exotic guests on this cruise were Oswald and Cynthia Mosley, he a British socialist member of parliament and future interned leader of the British Fascists, she the daughter of the former foreign secretary and viceroy of India, Lord Curzon.

Mosley had stayed with the Roosevelts in New York and would later write of the extraordinary contrast between "this magnificent man with his fine head and massive torso, handsome as a classic Greek and radiating charm" and "the exceptionally ugly woman, all movement and vivacity with an aura of gentle kindness, but without even a reflection of his attraction."

Eleanor left the *Larooco* before the Mosleys arrived. Mosley was impressed at his host's ingenuity in entertaining his guests. Among the divertissements was putting out shark-bait in the evening and then shooting the sharks that appeared "with FDR's revolver" and observing the carnage the next day when other sharks had devoured those that had been blooded by gunfire. Another was moving at speed through shallow lagoons and harpooning stingrays with such accuracy that when their stinging tails lashed up, the speedboat was out of reach. A good deal of drinking went on, virtually all day. By his solicitousness and ingenuity and charm, Mosley wrote, "F.D.R. reminded me of one of the great hostesses of Europe."[116] Mosley thought Roosevelt "charming and remarkable," and had been told that he was "the next governor of New York . . . They say [he might] eventually be President." Evidently, even at this point, discerning people could see Roosevelt coming, politically. But Mosley thought he had "too much will and too little intellect," embodying the weakness of America as a whole—it was, thought the socialist and future fascist Mosley, a country that lurched about without thinking things through, while Europe deliberated endlessly but was afraid of action. Mosley was perceptive up to a point, but he thought in caricatures, which ultimately ruined his career.[117] Roosevelt considered the Mosleys at this point "a most delightful couple."[118] Roosevelt continued to correspond amiably with Mosley into his presidency. He could tolerate fascists up to a point, but not adherents of Hitler and not after about 1935.

Roosevelt went directly from the *Larooco** to Warm Springs in March 1926. Tom Loyless had died of cancer, so Roosevelt had to see to the preparations himself. He had determined to buy the old hotel, which he did for $195,000, almost two-thirds of his personal fortune. Eleanor accompanied him at the outset of this trip and was again appalled at the poverty and the white supremacist segregation of rural Georgia, and unimpressed by her husband's new assets.

---

*The doughty old houseboat was finally sold at a handsome profit and eventually perished in a hurricane when thrown inland from its anchorage, landing in a pine forest.

She disputed the investment with him, highlighting the irresponsibility of such a commitment when he had five children in school. She seems to have cast aspersions on his aptitudes as an investor yet again, and to have suggested that he was prone to move fecklessly from project to project without ever finishing what he started. Roosevelt convinced her that this time he was durably serious about what he was doing and that if everything failed, including the uncommitted part of his fortune, his mother would help with the children's tuition.

Roosevelt's attendance at Warm Springs now reached its highest point. He returned there on September 21, 1926, and spent almost exactly half of the next two years there. He developed plans for a sophisticated polio treatment center and a full winter resort. He commissioned the construction of a cottage for himself, all on one level, easily accessible. (This was not "The Little White House," which was built in 1932.) Both were similar to the "top cottage" that he built ten years later at Hyde Park, above and not far from Eleanor's house at Val Kill. He deployed his public relations talents in favor of his polio treatment project, assuring the *New York Times* that after building the necessary pools and a separate health resort, he would build a splendid "cottage colony around the magnificent country club," which would feature a quail-shooting preserve, riding trails and stables, a bass-fishing lake, a palatial clubhouse, and two eighteen-hole golf courses. (Little of this ever materialized; the golfing facilities never progressed beyond a scratch nine-hole course.)[119] His promotional offensive worked with the wealthy who had polio victims in their families. But Warm Springs was never even slightly fashionable as a resort, and was scarcely competitive as a resort with Palm Beach.

(In 1927 FDR wrote to his cousin Bamie, now very handicapped herself (with arthritis), inviting her to visit him in Warm Springs and saying that his only fear was that his resort "will appeal to some of our rich friends who are suffering from nervous prosperity.")[120]

Sara kindly bought a cottage at Warm Springs she had no intention of occupying, to show tangible support for her son. From the earliest days he attempted various forms of farming at Warm Springs. None of it was successful, but Roosevelt never stopped tinkering with different types of sawmill pine, apples, peaches, grapes, and cattle. He engaged a local blacksmith to modify a Model T Ford with hand controls for the accelerator and the brakes so he could drive himself around the rural roads of Georgia. The car was a great success; Roosevelt eventually had it replicated by the manufacturer in grander versions, and cut automobile trails around his properties in Hyde Park and in Georgia. As with powerboats and sailboats, he became an expert and daring driver, compensating—or over-compensating, as many of his passengers would feel—for his physical immobility.

Roosevelt had asked to address the American Orthopedic Association about his work at Warm Springs in April 1926, but had been rebuffed. He and Eleanor attended the association's convention anyway, though officially uninvited, and Roosevelt lobbied the hall in his wheelchair. The doctors were not ready for and had no ability to resist such a charm offensive. It was indicative of Roosevelt's imperishable self-confidence that he crashed a professional association meeting and achieved the purposes that the doctors who had declined to invite him suspected were his object. His possibilities as a vote-getter would have been obvious to anyone who observed this evangelization of learned skeptics. He emerged with a promise of professional evaluation of his therapeutic program. In January 1927 the association reported favorably on his work, acknowledging improvement in the condition of all twenty-three of the monitored polio patients. The association then recommended the "establishment of a permanent hydrotherapeutic center at Warm Springs."[121]

Also in 1927, the Georgia Warm Springs Foundation was set up, with Franklin D. Roosevelt as chief fundraiser and Louis Howe as principal strategist, urging his boss to use before-and-after photographs "in your conversations with malefactors of great wealth." Roosevelt set up a patients' aid fund to help the indigent, and when that was exhausted, he took care of the bills himself. He would have no one turned away. He would have no uniforms or other evidence of a hospital atmosphere. Warm Springs undoubtedly achieved a great deal for almost all the polio sufferers who went there, and Roosevelt was a daring creator and lifelong and posthumous inspiration. Establishing Warm Springs was a bold financial move for him, as his wife and advisors pointed out. It was also a valuable paramedical initiative that has probably been underestimated because of the immense importance of his public career.

There were skits and menus making fun of the impact of polio (at the "Palais Polio"), and all the patients found such farcical touches hilarious. Roosevelt gave hope to these people, but they encouraged him also. The founder's comings and goings at Warm Springs, especially when he was president, were always great and heartfelt occasions. The financial condition of the foundation would be lifted free from concern only when he became president and some of his wealthy friends launched the March of Dimes campaign, which funded polio research generally until Dr. Jonas Salk developed a vaccine. (This great breakthrough was announced by Basil O'Connor on behalf of the Warm Springs Foundation in 1955, on the tenth anniversary of Franklin D. Roosevelt's death. For a time after he died, the foundation's annual meeting took place with his chair left vacant as a symbolic act of respect.[122])

Roosevelt continued to make inching progress at becoming more mobile. He could now walk with one crutch under his left arm and a cane in his right hand. This was awkward, and he had made some headway with two canes, but this looked disconcertingly ungainly to onlookers. In 1927 and 1928 Roosevelt further improved his walk, holding a cane in his right hand and grasping someone's right upper arm with his left hand. It was slow, awkward, and strenuous, but it was motion and a tremendous comeback from the first year of his polio, when he had to be carried everywhere.

He did this under the tutelage of another pleasant Warm Springs physiotherapist, Mary Hudson. Only a few film clips survive of Roosevelt in motion in this way. Swinging his legs in a semi-circle from the hip emphasized the lifelessness of his legs, and the sway of his great torso was somewhat alarming. But the indomitable countenance and the presence of a strong man to his left created an air of great resolution. The image could not be described as majestic, but it was formidable in its way and achieved Roosevelt's necessary political objective of inciting respect and not pity. As Winston Churchill's daughter, Lady Soames, told the author many years later, "It was painful, but impressive, to see."[123] (12/7/02)

———————

Eleanor too, had embarked on a new undertaking. Franklin Roosevelt himself had suggested that a cottage be built for her and her friends Marion Dickerman and Nancy Cook at Val Kill, a beautiful greensward that he had bought himself beside a creek about two miles from Springwood. When the house was built, Eleanor effectively moved into it with her friends, to the dismay of her mother-in-law. It was the first home Eleanor thought was truly hers. The creek was interrupted with a dam that furnished a place where Roosevelt could swim without having to impose on his neighbor Vincent Astor. A small furniture and handicrafts workshop was set up nearby and operated successfully under Nancy Cook's supervision.

A great deal of speculation has occurred about the nature of Eleanor's relationship with these and other women. As with her husband's heterosexual life after the onset of his illness, it will never be known whether Eleanor had homosexual relationships, as the enemies of both of them loved to claim, and as lesbian advocates would posthumously allege. Certainly it was possible, though the atmosphere at Val Kill was always more like a cheerful nunnery than a center of sapphic (or any other) debauchery. Eleanor had passionate and changeable affections, but generally seemed to be uninterested in sex and repelled by heterosexual activity, rather than physically attracted to other women.

In a further act of liberation, Eleanor, Nancy, and Marion bought the Todhunter School in Manhattan, where, starting in 1927, Eleanor set out to emulate Mlle. Souvestre and be a stimulating teacher. Marion would be the principal. Just as her husband was unconcerned with the economic condition of the polio patients who came to Warm Springs and with their pigmentation and ethnicity, Eleanor was a perfect egalitarian and, from all accounts, an inspiring and devoted teacher. She taught three days a week and frequently took her students on interesting field trips of great practical value.

———————

Anna Roosevelt married a nondescript and rather pedestrian conservative stockbroker, Curtis Dall, in 1926, to "get out," as she later put it, of her dysfunctional family.[124] She had refused to go to Cornell as her parents had wished, but spent one summer at the agricultural college at Geneva because she liked dogs and horses and thought she might be able to help operate the farm at Springwood. It was not a success, other than the hot pursuit of her conducted by many undergraduates, including the successful suitor, all beguiled by her long blonde hair, blue eyes, shapely figure, and vivacious personality. This was the sum of Anna's try at higher education.

Dr. Peabody presided at the wedding at St. James, Hyde Park, and it was a jovial enough occasion, though marred by Eleanor's irritation at Sara for giving the newlyweds an apartment in New York without telling the bride's mother. A year later Anna and Curtis had a daughter, Anna Eleanor, an event that occasioned a revival in contact between Lucy Mercer Rutherfurd and Franklin D. Roosevelt. First there was an innocuous note of congratulations, on March 25, 1927. The correspondence became fairly regular from then on. Roosevelt arranged for Lucy to see all four of his presidential inaugurations from an official car that was specially allowed to approach the official platform. Missy and Grace Tully gave the White House switchboard standing instructions to put her calls through, and after Missy's incapacitating stroke in 1941, Lucy and FDR would see each other fairly often, to the very end of his life. (Missy had disapproved the relationship, apparently from a mixture of envy and Catholic scruple.)

On May 7, 1927, James Roosevelt Roosevelt, the popular if rather unserious Rosy, died at Hyde Park, aged 73. Franklin Roosevelt was more saddened than he had perhaps expected, because his half brother had always been a source of disinterested and friendly companionship and advice, not brilliant but trustworthy. His will left a substantial amount to Franklin, which greatly assisted in the financing of Warm Springs and relieved Eleanor's more extreme fears about going to Sara with a begging bowl to prevent the children's being put out of their schools for lack of tuition money.

Roosevelt was often mentioned as a potential candidate for U.S. senator from New York in 1926, but repeatedly refused to be considered, pleading a need for more time to complete his recovery and a lack of aptitude for a non-executive position. "I am temperamentally unfitted to be a member of the uninteresting body known as the United States Senate," he said.[125] He gave the keynote address at the state convention that nominated his old Albany colleague Robert F. Wagner for U.S. senator,* and again generously lauded Al Smith, the reigning New York (and national) Democrat, who was about to seek his fourth term as governor.

Roosevelt's old friend Louis Wehle, who had been the first to promote him for the vice presidential nomination in 1920, albeit on a ticket headed by Herbert

---

* The author who had inspired Roosevelt with the Jeffersonian legacy of the Democrats, Claude G. Bowers, had become editor of the *New York World* and a speechwriter for Wagner.

Hoover, enhanced his record for historical clairvoyance by being the very first person to urge that he seek the nomination for governor if Smith were reelected in 1926 and vacated the statehouse to run for president in 1928. Roosevelt elaborately demurred, as he would with unfeigned sincerity until the very last minute.[126]

Smith was reelected easily over the wealthy Republican conservative Ogden Mills (by 257,000 votes). Wagner was elected U.S. senator by 116,000 votes, but would have lost to the Republican incumbent, James Wadsworth (who had been elected in 1914 when Roosevelt unsuccessfully sought the Democratic nomination), if the Republicans had not split on the Prohibition issue.

Continuing his gradual move to a more Wilsonian view of the world, Roosevelt released, just after the 1926 elections, "A Parable on War Debts," advocating relative debt forgiveness and rhetorically concluding: "Shall we place alongside the old words 'With malice toward none, with charity for all,' the newer saying [from Coolidge], 'Well, you hired the money, didn't you?' "[127]

The political year 1928 began for the Democrats as a rerun of 1924. Roosevelt had had a minor skirmish with Al Smith over Louis Howe's position. When Smith rewarded Roosevelt for his brilliant nominating effort in 1924 by naming him chairman of the Taconic State Park Commission, Roosevelt tried to put Howe in as commission secretary at $5,000 per year. This was blocked by Robert Moses, the legendary builder of New York City and its environs for forty years, secretary of state of New York, and holder of many other important positions, including chairman of the state Council of Parks.

Moses said that if Roosevelt wanted a "secretary and a valet" he could pay for him himself. Roosevelt abruptly resigned from the Taconic commission, but Smith talked him out of it by insisting in a five-page letter that there was "no man I have met in my whole public career who I have stronger affection for than for yourself." (Their professions of mutual love and respect were becoming steadily more extravagant, but no more truthful.[128]) Smith assured Roosevelt that the problem was really the legislature. Roosevelt didn't believe it but was interested in the Taconic commission's objective of extending the Bronx River Parkway to Albany, making his beloved Hudson Valley more accessible to New York City. He remained as chairman, but his relations with Moses were always antagonistic.

Moses and Howe stirred a mutual repulsion. Moses considered Howe a "fierce, fanatical" secretary, "a strange, ailing, gnomish, little man . . . free from personal and political ambition," exercising "immense power from the sickroom and the shadows . . . like the NKVD men in the USSR. . . . He was a second story man."[129]

Improbably, Franklin D. Roosevelt was lying in wait for the end of the ascendancy of the parvenu, the "mocking years of the golden calf." As a patrician, as a Democrat, as a convalescent, perhaps even as an unsuccessful speculator, and as a politician of immense ambition made more remarkable for its apparent implausibility, he was urgently and impatiently awaiting his time. Supported only by Louis Howe, to an extent by his wife and a few old friends, he believed with mounting conviction that his turn would come, soon.

No one knew, or will ever know, what dark nights of fear and despair he had to endure in the twenties. For his career and his morale, these were Franklin D. Roosevelt's wilderness years. They were surely deeper and more forbidding, because of their medical character, than Winston Churchill's famous ten years as an involuntary backbencher (1929–1939) or Charles de Gaulle's twelve years (1946–1958) waiting for the call at Colombey-les-deux-Eglises while the Fourth Republic floundered to an end.

Roosevelt's perseverance through these years, to unheard-of triumphs of political success and statesmanship, is a lesson in human faith, courage, and intelligence.

—— ✻ ——

CHAPTER 5

"Devote That Intelligent Mind of Yours to the Problems of the State"

(Alfred E. Smith's advice to Franklin D. Roosevelt on handing over the governorship of New York to him, January 1, 1929)

I

ROOSEVELT set out for Houston, the Democratic convention site, by rail on June 17, 1928. He had again been asked to nominate Al Smith for president, and would be accompanied this year by his eighteen-year-old son Elliott, who was to provide a strong upper arm to grasp. He called on Fidelity & Deposit clients in the Midwest and gave a number of speeches for Al Smith, rehearsing his techniques with his son. His appearance at Houston, though not as dramatic as at Madison Square Garden four years before, since there was little fear that he had not now largely prevailed over his ailment, was more helpful politically. In New York he won everyone's admiration for his courage and impressed them by his demeanor, but no one imagined he was ready for a political campaign. In Houston there were no crutches, he moved more quickly and confidently, and his physical presence was more imposing than ever. Eleanor did not attend this year, though Marion and Nancy loyally did. Eleanor self-importantly announced that she didn't like the "hurly-burly" of a convention. She listened to her husband on the radio, along with 15 million other Americans.

The versatile Claude Bowers was convention keynote speaker. He delighted the delegates with his standard abstruse claim that the Republicans could not simultaneously follow Abraham Lincoln and Alexander Hamilton.[1]

The crowd of 15,000 cheered steadily and without anxiety as Franklin and Elliott Roosevelt made their way to the rostrum. Though FDR's pace was faster in the eyes of onlookers, this took nothing from the ordeal he had obviously endured and surmounted. Roosevelt scaled new heights in the exchange of laudations with Alfred E. Smith. He warmed up Proskauer's old text to have Smith "loved by little children, by dumb animals . . . Between him and the people is that subtle bond which makes him their champion and makes them enthusiastically trust him with their loyalty and their love." Smith, the Brown Derby from the Bowery, was "a pathfinder, a blazer of the trail to the high road that will avoid the bottomless morass of crass materialism." (Roosevelt was obviously both irritated by and ever more suspicious of the endless Republican boom of the Roaring Twenties; he both believed and hoped that the bubble would burst.) "I offer one who has the will to win, who not only deserves success but commands it. Victory is his habit—the happy warrior of the political battlefield—Alfred E. Smith."

It was an electrifying speech, delivered by a now very accomplished orator, able to gesticulate gracefully with one hand at a time, while steadying himself by holding the podium with the other. He was an awesome presence at the podium, leonine head tossing with emphasis, massive shoulders thrust back, rich tenor more versatile and persuasive than ever. The effect on the convention was very great. Smith was nominated easily, but the press and the party faithful were dazzled by the man who formally nominated him.

Even Colonel Robert McCormick, the famously reactionary editor and publisher, praised the speech in the *Chicago Tribune.* In an editorial entitled "The Last of the Silver Tongues," Roosevelt was praised as "the only Republican in the Democratic Party." Other comment was entirely laudatory. The historian Will Durant, writing for the *New York World,* was idolatrous: Roosevelt was "tall and proud . . . a face of classic profile, pale with years of struggle . . . nervous and yet self-controlled with that tense, taut unity of spirit which lifts the complex soul above those whose calmness is only a stolidity . . . a gentleman and a scholar . . . softened and cleansed and illumined with pain. What in the name of Croker and Tweed is he doing here?"[2]

Smith himself sent Roosevelt a cutting from the *New York Times* and added that the Smith family had cried when they listened to FDR. Yet Smith seems to have been virtually the only listener who didn't realize that Roosevelt's rolling thunder of eloquent superlatives was better applied to himself than to the dumpy, ruddy, bulbous Tammany sachem Smith.

Few expected Smith to win, although he stirred a good deal of urban sentiment and was emphatic again in his opposition to Prohibition, which increasing numbers of people were seeing as a failure that did more for organized crime than for temperance. Coolidge was retiring, and the Republican candidate would be Roosevelt's old friend Herbert C. Hoover, the secretary of commerce under Harding and Coolidge through this great economic boom and still very respected.

Roosevelt was outraged when Smith put in John J. Raskob, the DuPont executive who had made that company the principal shareholder of General Motors, as party chairman and campaign manager. Raskob, an original businessman (and a devout Catholic), had created General Motors Acceptance Company to facilitate credit purchases, and pioneered the view that customers should be encouraged to be shareholders and vice versa.

Smith was not running as a credible reform candidate, as he had done in New York. He was challenging Hoover, as Davis had challenged Coolidge, for the conservative vote. It couldn't possibly work. Both candidates accepted the permanence of prosperity, ignored those who had been left out of it, endlessly praised the country's business leaders, and allowed the campaign to focus on Prohibition and the fitness of Roman Catholics for high public office. Roosevelt believed that Smith, for whom it was a cultural shock going from the Lower East Side to Albany, was kidnapped by unnatural allies when he became a national candidate.

Eleanor spurred her women's division into action and had an active election, but FDR, who was supposed to be a fundraiser among his socioeconomic peers, had Howe write form letters and secretaries forge his signature while he returned to Springwood and lived as he liked, with his mother in Europe and Eleanor on the hustings.

What now happened was one of the great ironies of American political history. Smith, convinced that only Roosevelt could hold the statehouse for the Democrats and that without a victory there he would not be able to carry his home state and would have no chance against Hoover, begged Roosevelt to run in his place for governor of New York. Roosevelt and Howe thought Hoover was probably good for two terms, that the gubernatorial race would be an uphill fight in 1928, and that with four more years Roosevelt would make great progress toward walking only with a cane.

Smith never seems to have considered the consequences if Roosevelt ran for governor and won while he, Smith, lost his race for president. This was not an implausible scenario, but Smith convinced himself that Roosevelt had been transformed by his illness from a lightweight to a dyspeptic (if well-spoken) lightweight. Smith was an intelligent man, but he had so little exposure to the nuances of the upper classes that he couldn't tell an indolent mama's boy from a man with a casual exterior who was fanatically determined to become president of the United States.

He hadn't noticed that in pursuit of that objective Roosevelt had risen up from paralysis, rebuilt his body, virtually invented a new method of locomotion, and convinced the world that although almost half of him had atrophied, and he couldn't stand up for more than forty-five minutes, he was only "lame." Roosevelt had known that he and Smith had been on a collision course virtually since they met in Albany in 1910. The closer they came to the collision the more excessive became Roosevelt's public praise of his governor. Roosevelt certainly knew the game he was playing, but it is not clear whether he realized how completely Smith did not.

On August 27, 1928, Coolidge's secretary of state, Frank B. Kellogg, and French foreign minister Aristide Briand, and ultimately all other countries, signed the

Pact of Paris, by which, with great fanfare, war was renounced "as an instrument of national policy." Roosevelt, who was an inexhaustible storehouse of opinions on foreign as on domestic affairs, attacked the pact, because "It leads to a false belief in America that we have taken great step forward. It does not contribute in any way to settling matters of international controversy." He offered this (accurate) opinion in the July 1928 issue of *Foreign Affairs*, (v.VI, p.585). He had the article preprinted and distributed to all the delegates at Houston.[3]

———

As the presidential campaign began, Smith attempted a few times by telephone to persuade Roosevelt to run for governor. This became a more urgent requirement when the Republicans nominated Albert Ottinger, the able and respected (Jewish) attorney general of New York. Ottinger had an interesting record—he had campaigned effectively against loan sharks, marketers of impure food, and petty graft-takers but was a member of the far right, opposed to the income tax and virtually any regulation of business, and was an advocate of very high tariffs.

The Democrats would nominate their candidate on October 1. Roosevelt went to Warm Springs, where telephone contact was difficult. When he learned that Smith was phoning for him (to a booth in the lobby of the old Meriwether), he gave elaborate instructions to the bellboy that he had gone on a picnic and then hastily did so. Smith corralled Eleanor in Rochester on the evening of September 30 and told her that Herbert Lehman would run for lieutenant governor and do all the work, and Raskob's organization would take care of the debt at Warm Springs. Smith was now beseeching the wife of, and offering financial inducements to, the one man who could make his reign at the head of the Democratic Party an evanescent moment. And the subject of these blandishments was sincerely resisting them.

Eleanor refused to intervene with her husband but did agree to try to get him on the telephone. He was in the third-floor school auditorium at Manchester, Georgia, about to give a speech for Smith, when he heard that his wife was calling on a telephone that was in a drugstore four blocks away. He asked that she be told he was on his way to the telephone and to hang on. He hurriedly gave his address and shook hands with well-wishers. Then he was carried down the three flights of stairs, driven to the drugstore, and helped to the phone booth, the doors of which, because of his braces, could not be closed to give him any privacy. Eleanor was annoyed at such a long wait and had to catch a train to Manhattan, so she handed the telephone to Al Smith. Roosevelt then claimed it was a bad connection and shouted that it was hopeless and that he was hanging up. Smith called back with a message that he had to speak to Roosevelt and asking that he go to the Meriwether and await a call.

Roosevelt's entourage was divided. Eleanor was neutral, Louis Howe was still opposed, Missy was strongly opposed, and Anna sent a telegram urging acceptance. Her father cabled back: "You ought to be spanked." When the telephone call that would alter American and world history came, Raskob started by saying he would take care of the losses at Warm Springs. Then Smith, clinging to the idea that Roosevelt was really a helpless invalid and a cipher as well, said that he could spend nine months of the year at Warm Springs and Lehman would do the work.

Lehman took the phone and said that if Roosevelt ran for governor he would run with him as lieutenant governor and would do anything he was asked. (Lehman was heavily influenced by Smith's powerful assistant Belle Moskowitz. What Smith and Mrs. Moskowitz didn't realize was that he was also a strenuous admirer of Roosevelt's. The Smith idyll of Roosevelt in office but Smith, through Lehman, Moskowitz, and Proskauer, in power was a plan that Roosevelt saw through from the start, though there was no need to vaporize it unless Roosevelt chose to run and was successful.)

Smith then took the telephone back for his closing pitch and put things on a "personal basis" as a favor. Implicit was the threat that refusal would incur the hostility of Smith and the machine that had elected him governor an unprecedented four times. Smith asked whether Roosevelt would reject a genuine draft. Roosevelt said he didn't want the nomination and wouldn't consent to having his name placed in nomination, but that if the delegates acted on their own, he wasn't sure what he would do. That was all Smith needed.

Raskob sent Roosevelt a check for $250,000, which he returned, saying it was enough to know that he was being underwritten. It was later put about that Raskob had effectively bribed Roosevelt, who responded that Raskob had promised $50,000 but had welshed on the promise. This was pretty shabby, because Raskob in fact contributed over $100,000 personally. (It remains unclear why Raskob didn't rebut the allegations against him by producing the cancelled checks or demanding an audit of the Warm Springs Foundation's accounts.) Some interesting contributions were already flowing in; Edsel Ford had contributed a glass-enclosed swimming pool.

On the motion of the legendary New York mayor James J. Walker acting for Al Smith, the state Democratic convention delegates did stampede for Roosevelt the next day. Roosevelt engaged, on Howe's recommendation, Grace Tully, the woman who would share the duties of principal secretary with Missy LeHand. Roosevelt cabled her that they would have "a grand campaign."

So they did. The Republicans and their friends in the press were not long in questioning Roosevelt's ability to campaign and serve as governor. The *New York Post* described the "drafting" of Roosevelt by Smith as "pathetic and pitiless." Smith responded that 95 percent of the governor's job was conducted at his desk. He did not have to be an "acrobat," and Roosevelt's intellectual faculties were greater than ever. Roosevelt good-naturedly announced, in New York on October 7: "Most people who are nominated for the governorship have to run, but obviously I am not in condition to run, and therefore I am counting on my friends all over the state to make it possible for me to walk in." He campaigned vigorously and effectively. It was understood that the press would not take pictures of him getting out of his car or in other activities that could alarm the voters. This protocol was never violated.

There is no discernible truth at all in the arguments later presented by some that he didn't really want to win this election. Missy LeHand allegedly said, out of concern for his physical condition, that she hoped he would lose, and Louis Howe expressed a similar hope to his wife in a letter October 2, but this is almost certainly because of attachment to his own timetable of waiting another four years for his patron's bid for governor. There is no doubt that Roosevelt, persuaded with the utmost difficulty to make the race, thought that the circumstances just might be right. He thought he had a good underdog's chance, that Smith would lose badly to Hoover, and that this would enable him to judge the best moment to try to make the jump to the White House. The circumstances of Smith's importuning of Roosevelt and the apparent invincibility of the Republicans quickened Roosevelt's ever-active intuition that destiny might, at last, be knocking.

Roosevelt had a natural instinct for the momentum of events, and once Smith's entreatites became irresistible, he began to believe that he might be riding a tide. He began to assemble a campaign team around Howe that would serve him for a long time and in historic circumstances. Edward J. Flynn was the party boss of the Bronx, a protégé of Boss Charles Murphy but an urbane lawyer from Fordham and an abstainer from the back-slapping, garrulous approach for being an urban party organizer. While Howe became the campaign manager, Flynn, a considerable intellect, though also a man of moods prone to occasional attacks of melancholia, was in effect the deputy manager. He liked and worked well with Howe, whose foibles he found endearing and whose political acumen was obvious to him.

Raymond Moley, a forty-one-year-old Columbia political science professor from Cleveland, was recruited as an issues expert and speech-drafter, especially on crime questions. Howe had met Moley on the National Crime Commission, another sinecure Roosevelt had found for Howe in 1925 that yielded him, and thus spared Roosevelt, about $4,000 per year.

Another Roosevelt political organizer who would pass into American folklore was James A. Farley, who had moved from the New York Athletic Commission to be secretary of the Democratic State Committee and a determined rebuilder of the party organization in upstate New York. He was the ultimate American synthetic Irishman, writing in green ink and known to virtually every member of the Elks Lodge in the United States. Astonishingly gregarious and universally liked, he "never forgot a face," knew over 10,000 people by their first names, and was an encyclopedia of grass-roots American politics. He was an impressive-looking man who, unusually for a political organizer, neither smoked nor drank and was another in Roosevelt's entourage who was a strong but not narrow-minded Roman Catholic.

Agricultural advice would come from Roosevelt's Hyde Park neighbor Henry Morgenthau, a successful wealthy farmer and publisher of the *American Agriculturist*, fiercely loyal to Franklin and Eleanor Roosevelt, and a rather fussy, slightly Dickensian man, the most country-gentrified of Jews at the time. Morgenthau's father, Wilson's ambassador to Turkey, was an early Roosevelt financial backer.

A key fundraiser would be William Woodin, a shy but nimble and engaging railway rolling-stock manufacturing executive with a passion and talent for music, who had published several concertos.

Then there was Samuel Rosenman, recruited for Roosevelt by the Democratic leader in the New York assembly, Maurice Bloch, to advise on legislation. A thirty-one-year-old lawyer originally from Texas, he was overwhelmed by Roosevelt's splendid appearance—"broad jaw and upthrust chin, the piercing flashing eyes, the firm hands." He was almost as quickly impressed by Roosevelt's ability to grasp complicated points and rework unexciting speech drafts into galvanizing public addresses. He was one of those most rapidly converted from the notion of Roosevelt as a lightweight to the lasting recollection of Roosevelt the political leader of peerless agility.

Roosevelt conducted a vigorous and original campaign for governor, violently attacking bigotry in every form, which endeared him to the huge Catholic and Jewish (and perhaps even black) populations of New York. He promised to complete the reforms sought by Al Smith, especially the eight-hour day and forty-eight-hour work week for women and children industrial workers. He called for an old-age pension and, in moving terms, for the abrogation "forever and ever" of the Poor Law and the end of the County Poor House. Even more evocative was his call for better care for handicapped and crippled people. He referred straightforwardly to his own experience, asserting that only his and his family's resources had enabled him to make the recovery he had, and that the same care should be available to everyone (as it was in Warm Springs).

In early October, the betting had been two to one against Roosevelt. Because of his vigorous campaign, the skillful handling of the handicapped question, and his status as continuator of a popular governor, by the beginning of November the oddsmakers were calling the race a tossup with a possible slight edge to Roosevelt.

———————

Election day fell on November 6, and in the evening of that day Roosevelt and his campaign team met at the Biltmore Hotel in New York, which had been the headquarters throughout the campaign. It quickly became clear that Smith was going down to a thumping defeat and that he was even going to lose New York.

Even though La Follette and the Progressives weren't running and Smith had almost doubled Davis's vote from 1924 and had run strongly in the cities all across the country, it was a third consecutive Republican sweep. Smith got more votes than any previous Democrat, and more than Coolidge had in 1924. The Democratic percentage of the total vote had increased from 34 in 1920 and 29 in the three-way race of 1924, to 41. Despite the appearance of another Democratic debacle, Smith had won a net plurality of 38,000 (reversing a Republican lead of over 1.25 million in 1924) in the combination of the country's twelve largest cities—New York, Chicago, Philadelphia, Detroit, Boston, St. Louis, Pittsburgh, Cleveland, Baltimore, Milwaukee, San Francisco, and Los Angeles. The urban voters were stirring. Roosevelt knew the farmers were not very contented, either, but Smith had been inaccessible to them. The great Republican incumbency depended on Main Street, Middle America, and was not as unassailable as it seemed. Smith made a respectable showing, but it was not a close election.

The governor's race in New York was much closer, although Ottinger led all evening. Roosevelt telephoned several upstate sheriffs and said he was relying on them to ensure that the fact that returns from their districts were coming in late did not imply skulduggery. He claimed that he could easily prevail upon Governor Smith to take over the counting process with the state police.

Smith and his wife, whose birthday it was, gamely visited Roosevelt's headquarters. The outgoing governor said that it would be a while before anyone "said his beads [rosary] in the White House." Roosevelt was running ahead of him in New York but still apparently trailing Ottinger. The Smiths were understandably shaken by the depths of anti-Catholic prejudice that had been exhibited in many places as Smith toured the country.

Eleanor's performance was undistinguished. She had not campaigned with her husband but entirely for Smith, despite her support of Prohibition—influenced, no doubt, by the problems her family had had with drink. "Governor Smith's election means something, but whether Franklin spends two years in Albany or not matters comparatively little," she had said to a friend. She told a *New York Post* reporter when the result was in: "I am not excited about my husband's election. I don't care." Her husband must have found this interesting reading. Sara had not been enthused at first, but once her son was nominated, she was a fierce partisan and promised that if he were elected she would make good the diminution of his income.

After the newspapers were delivered to the Roosevelt headquarters at the Biltmore, all proclaiming Ottinger's victory in tandem with Hoover's, Roosevelt thanked his supporters and, without explicitly conceding the election, went home with Eleanor and Anna at about midnight. Louis Howe, Sara Delano Roosevelt, Frances Perkins, Ed Flynn, and Jim Farley were among those who remained behind in the headquarters. Howe, who thought there was still a chance, was terribly afraid that if his man lost there would arise a theory that a handicapped person was unelectable.

Flynn and Farley continued to telephone upstate and chase up votes. At about one o'clock in the morning, Flynn telephoned Roosevelt's home and had the butler awaken him so Flynn could tell him that he was now pulling well ahead of Smith in New York and had a chance to win. Roosevelt was incredulous and went back to sleep. Flynn issued belligerent statements to the press about having "a thousand lawyers" to comb the results upstate. Between 2 and 4 A.M., the balance slowly shifted as the results from remote areas came in more quickly.

Shortly after four, it was clear Roosevelt had won. Sara and Frances Perkins toasted him in milk and shared a taxi, dropping Sara first at 65th Street, so she could have the pleasure of informing her son he had been elected governor of New York, the choice of the second largest electorate in the country, exceeded only by the nation as a whole voting for president and vice president. In fact, it seems to have been Ed Flynn who informed the candidate. He stopped at 65th Street on his way home a little later and awakened Roosevelt to give him the good news, the candidate's mother not having wished to interrupt his sleep.

Roosevelt had won by a razor's edge of 25,564 votes out of 4,234,822 cast. He had benefited from the fact that there were 50,000 fewer votes cast for governor than for president in New York State. Despite that, he ran 40,000 ahead of Smith in the state, though 33,000 behind Smith in New York City. With Lehman as his candidate for lieutenant governor, he appears to have been well rewarded by Roman Catholic and Jewish voters for his well-known liberality toward those groups, while benefiting also from the fact that he was even better known as a practicing Episcopalian, running against a Jewish opponent, Ottinger, and on a ticket headed by the Catholic Smith. About 73,000 electors voted for both Hoover and Roosevelt, many of them apparently influenced by Roosevelt's highly successful speaking tour in upstate New York, representing himself as a Hudson Valley farmer, albeit a wealthy Protestant one with an esteemed surname.

The day after the election, Smith said he would not be running for elective office again. The man he had beseeched to run in his place for tactical reasons, who would thereafter be free to spend nine months a year in Warm Springs, had taken his place as the country's foremost Democrat. The *New York Times* and less influential elements of the press were soon commenting on Roosevelt's presidential possibilities.[4] It was not imaginative speculation. A governor of New York had been a major party candidate for president in nine of the sixteen elections since the Civil War (and would be for the next five consecutive presidential elections). Southerners, who had seen their party's stranglehold on the South put in doubt by Smith's Catholicism and opposition to Prohibition, flocked to the part-time Georgian, Roosevelt. Joel Chandler Harris's son Julian, a southern editor, wrote of "the fervor of the devotion of the Georgians to Governor-elect Roosevelt." (The senior Harris was the creator of Uncle Remus.)[5] Roosevelt himself moved early to discourage such talk other than among Democratic professionals.[6]

The organization of the governor's office would be the first test of the Smith scenario of a regency by the ex-governor. Smith wished Roosevelt to retain his chief strategist and speechwriter, Mrs. Belle Moskowitz, as the governor's principal secretary, and the talented but egocentric and irascible Robert Moses as sec-

retary of state of New York. The former would run the political office and the latter the administration. Herbert Lehman, the incoming lieutenant governor, was
a protégé of Belle Moskowitz and would be the cat's paw of the Smith regency
while the titular governor played water polo with handicapped people in Warm
Springs. Eleanor, who had worked closely with the Smith campaign, warned her
husband that Moskowitz, Moses, and Lehman intended to put him in a cocoon.
Frances Perkins was convinced thereafter that without Eleanor, the Smith design
might have had some chance of success, but it is unlikely the Roosevelt the world
would come to know would have been taken in by such an obvious scheme.
Smith had reserved a suite of rooms in the DeWitt Clinton Hotel in Albany from
which to launch the regency.

Roosevelt was having none of it. Far from being self-conscious about his infirmity, he was anxious to show everyone how lightly he wore it. On December 14,
he and Smith met for four hours at 65th Street. Roosevelt nodded noncommittally when Smith suggested Belle Moskowitz be retained. He acknowledged her
qualities but did not commit to retain her. Roosevelt held her and Raskob responsible for isolating him from the presidential campaign "as though I was one of
those pieces of window-dressing that had to be borne with because of a certain
political value in non-New York city areas." Howe had told him Mrs. Moskowitz
had vetoed use of FDR's Happy Warrior speech as campaign literature.[7]

He balked altogether at the idea of retaining Robert Moses. The incoming
governor said he was prepared to retain Moses as state parks commissioner and
commissioner of parks of Long Island, but not as secretary of state, adding that he
found Moses an irritating personality. "He rubs me the wrong way," said Roosevelt in a considerable understatement. (Moses had predicted: "Roosevelt will
be a good candidate but a lousy governor."[8])

The meeting ended cordially, without Roosevelt's having shattered Smith's
madly self-serving idea that the new governor was a malleable cipher. Smith
thought that Roosevelt owed him the governor's chair. Roosevelt thought he
owed Smith nothing, having more than repaid any past favors by his efforts to
nominate Smith for the presidency and assist him to reach it. He had also given
Smith a lot of advice about different issues that would have made him a much
more serviceable presidential candidate, but Smith had ignored all of it.

According to Roosevelt, Smith came back to see him on December 18, and
told him that Mrs. Moskowitz was working on his inaugural address and message
to the legislature. The governor-elect claimed that he had replied that he had
already written his own and didn't require any more help. Only gradually did
Smith realize that Belle Moskowitz was now virtually unemployed.

When Edward Flynn returned to New York from a European holiday in
December, Basil O'Connor met him at dockside and conducted him to 65th
Street. Roosevelt piled on "all the great charm and persuasiveness of that remark-
able man," as Flynn later wrote, in what proved a successful effort to persuade
Flynn to move into Moses's job as secretary of state of New York. Frances Perkins

made a final effort on behalf of Belle Moskowitz, despite Smith's expressed lack of enthusiasm for Perkins as Roosevelt's apointee as state industrial commissioner. Roosevelt declined, and Moskowitz was as jobless as Smith was about to be, while Moses had his wings severely clipped. Roosevelt kept sixteen of Smith's eighteen department heads. Perkins and Flynn were excellent appointees. Roosevelt also offered Smith the Port Authority, but he declined anything subordinate to the governor. As 1928 drew to an end, Smith must have had an uneasy feeling that he had created a political Frankenstein's monster and that it was all going to be a good deal more complicated than he had imagined. Inexplicably, he was almost the last person to have any inkling of what was to come.

In barely six weeks, Al Smith had been eclipsed by Franklin D. Roosevelt, who had wanted to remain a while longer in the shadows. But he was now the unofficial leader of the opposition. Should anything go awry with the endless prosperity of the time, he would be the president in waiting. At the decisive moments of their political lives, Al Smith's judgment was defective, Franklin D. Roosevelt's luck was good, and Herbert Hoover would prove to be both lacking in judgment and highly unlucky. Thus were the greatest political fortunes won and lost and the world changed.

II

THE ACTUAL HANDING over of the governorship went smoothly. The Roosevelts arrived at the executive mansion in Albany in the afternoon of the last day of 1928. As their car pulled up in front of the governor's house, Al Smith charged out the door and down the steps, right hand outstretched, and exclaimed for the press and the many assembled well-wishers to hear: "God bless and keep you, Frank. A thousand welcomes. We've got the home fires burning and you'll find this a fine place to live." They kissed or embraced each other's wives.

The Smiths drove off with their admirers singing "Auld Lang Syne" after them but were back at the mansion in the evening for a dinner with members of the Smith and Roosevelt families and a few intimates. An elevator had been installed for the new governor, and in place of Smith's private zoo and greenhouse, a swimming pool was being built. The Roosevelts went out of their way to be respectful and convivial to the departing governor and his family. The official end of the Smith era was at the stroke of midnight on New Year's Eve. Roosevelt was concerned for his predecessor. He was a beloved figure, a brilliant governor, a gallant man, and as Roosevelt once confided to an admiring future biographer, Ernest Lindley: "No man ever willingly gives up public life—no man who has ever tasted it."[9] He would prove to be a personification of the truthfulness of that aphorism.

The formal transition and swearing-in of the new governor was at noon on January 1, 1929. Roosevelt was overshadowed at his inauguration by Smith, as he had been by TR at his wedding.[10] He would not be upstaged again. It was arranged for the outgoing governor to give a valedictory. After a gracious preamble, Smith patronizingly expressed the hope that "Frank" would "be able to devote that intelligent mind of yours to the problems of this state." He spoke movingly of the undoubted pride of the new governor's mother. The redoubtable Sara had tears in her eyes when Al Smith reminisced that his own mother had attended two of his gubernatorial installations and said that he knew about a mother's pride on such occasions.[11] (Sara was probably touched by thoughts of what her son had achieved in overcoming illness; to be elected governor was not considered such an achievement by the Roosevelts as it was for someone who left school at the age of twelve to work in the Fulton Fish Market, as Smith had.)

In his remarks, Roosevelt again paid a warm tribute to his predecessor, promised to build on what he had done, and urged non-partisanship on the Republicans, who controlled the legislature. The programs of the two were similar, but the contrast in voice and style was described by one Republican legislator as "the voice of Jacob and the hands of Esau."[12] On January 13, 1929, Louis Howe, who remained in New York City to begin Roosevelt's efforts to become president of the United States, issued a statement on the governor's behalf excoriating the conduct and outcome of the 1928 presidential election campaign. Howe and Roosevelt had again corresponded with thousands of party officials all around the country and concluded that the election had been won by the Republicans by recourse to "bigotry, ignorance of democratic principles . . . unspeakable and un-American methods . . . the most atrocious falsehoods, and improper pressures." But Smith had lost by seven million votes, and no such margin could have been produced by fanning anti-Catholic prejudices alone.

The Roosevelts were very social, Eleanor holding a large tea every afternoon when she was in Albany. There were many dinners and a showing of a new movie on the third floor of the mansion at least once a week.

The governor settled into a vigorous routine. Dr. Leroy Hubbard of the Warm Springs Foundation had publicly guaranteed Roosevelt's fitness, as long as he got twelve hours sleep a day. Roosevelt ignored this recommendation. He was awakened at eight by his butler, breakfasted and read the newspapers in bed, washed and shaved himself, dressed with the butler's assistance, and descended in the elevator to greet guests at his residence for about an hour. He went by car to his office at about 10:30 and dealt with correspondence for an hour. He lunched at his desk. He normally left at 6:15 after a day crowded with engagements, but if he did not have other commitments, he often had his dinner at his desk also. He usually took some work home with him and retired around midnight. He almost never had trouble sleeping. It was not an invalid's schedule, and he flourished under it.

He was unfailingly cheerful, even when the governor's mail room discovered an apparent letter bomb addressed to him. He claimed to have been the subject of such a missive when at the navy (which no one else remembered and was presumably another of his tall tales). When it came to light that it was a civil servant wishing to masquerade as the governor's savior to gain a reward to help him support his family, Roosevelt sent him $100 and later asked Frances Perkins to get him a job.[13]

Roosevelt set up a Democratic publicity bureau to counter the fact that most small newspapers in New York were Republican. This cost $100,000 per year, provided by wealthy Democrats, and was an effective counter to the Republicans in areas where they were unaccustomed to being contradicted.

Roosevelt also pioneered the extensive use of the radio among U.S. political officeholders. He appeared on a state-wide radio network at least once a month and was very effective in speaking with apparent intimacy, as if he were in the home of every listener.

Assemblymen were elected every year at this time, and Roosevelt seemed sometimes to be cranking up to campaign for a Democratic legislature in 1929. He was an even less inhibited dispenser of patronage than he had been while at the Navy Department. He packed every agency and commission with Democrats and his appointments were relentlessly partisan.

Roosevelt emulated the Republicans in calling for a commission to look into the state's agricultural problems and was the first Democratic governor in the state's recent history to hold himself out as a serious defender of New York's farmers. He was planning to cut into the Republicans' traditional lead in upstate New York and delighted in claiming to be a farmer by occupation, an imposture that was belied by his accent, mannerisms, and general appearance. New York had 190,000 farms, 25,000 more than Kansas, but the rural population had been ignored by Smith and taken for granted by the Republicans. Eventually the farmers of New York did benefit from Roosevelt's proposals, and he harvested the political reward for it.

He was able to offer early tax relief to the state's farmers as well as a 20 percent reduction in the state income tax, compensating with a gasoline tax. A tremendous struggle ensued. Roosevelt was accused of "avarice, usurpation, and presumption," and responded by blaming the Republican legislators of "an unintelligent riot," in which his bills were returned to him as "merely changelings dressed up to look like meritocratic legislation."[14]

Roosevelt proposed a commission funded with $25 million to look into a comprehensive old-age security scheme and to alleviate the problem at once with grants to institutions that cared for the elderly indigent. The governor coordinated with the well-known liberal rabbi Stephen S. Wise the rabbi's appearance at a boisterous public hearing on the issue on March 5. Wise denounced interests that had expressed opposition to the idea of old-age security, especially real estate groups that complained that such a measure would raise land taxes. Though the Republican legislature did not give him exactly the commission he wanted, one was established and the public relations impact for Roosevelt was wholly positive. Working so closely with Wise didn't harm his relations with New York's large Jewish community, either, though he would eventually sometimes know the rabbi better than he would have liked.

The governor presented, with great pomp and ceremony, his suggestions about hydroelectricity in a personal appearance before the legislature on March 12. He lamented a series of court decisions that enabled power companies to charge for electricity on a basis of a percentage on the replacement cost of hydroelectric facilities rather than actual cash invested. He contended that this criterion could provide astronomical profits for the supplier and deprive the consumer of all protection. Roosevelt proposed the setting up of a five-member authority to finance, build, and operate power generating facilities on sites owned or subsequently purchased by the state. He preferred transmission by the private sector, but he specifically threatened that New York State would go into the power transmission business if the private sector tried to overcharge as a distributor of publicly owned and generated power. Roosevelt approved an 8 percent dividend for electricity shareholders, and regulation provided them protection against extreme competition but not much more.[15] In June, he dramatically told a meeting of Massachusetts Democrats that only two heartbeats, his and Lehman's, separated the power monopoly from control of the resources of New York State.[16]

His power initiative gained him considerable attention throughout the country. The chief national advocate on the issue, Senator George W. Norris of Nebraska, a progressive Republican, expressed his approval, while lamenting that Roosevelt hadn't committed to provide comprehensive public-sector competition with the power companies from the source all the way to the user. Both Roosevelt and Norris were impressed by the example of the Canadian province of Ontario, on the other side of Lake Ontario and the St. Lawrence River from New York, which had a state-owned power system that furnished power at half to a quarter the rates charged by the private-sector suppliers in New York. Roosevelt also demanded a new rate-setting apparatus on criteria friendlier to the users. The legislature ignored Roosevelt's proposals, confirming his view that Norris's dream of complete competition was a non-starter in New York as long as the legislature was in the hands of reactionary Republicans.

In order to try to deprive him of the full value of the electricity question, where Roosevelt was clearly gaining ground against his opponents, the Republican leaders in the legislature came to him shortly before Christmas 1929 with a proposal that a five-person commission be set up to look into all the possible arrangements for the St. Lawrence and to provide recommendations for the 1931 legislature. Roosevelt read it carefully, seemed to approve, and thanked them for their proposal. As yet unaccustomed to Roosevelt's vast repertoire of tactics of dissimulation, his opponents withdrew happily, thinking they had deprived the governor of this greatest reelectoral weapon.

What followed was "a masterpiece of Rooseveltian political jujitsu."[17] Roosevelt declared a triumph for public ownership of electricity and a Republican concession of defeat. With the hyperbole he would make famous in his subsequent office, he declared: "This is one of the happiest days of my life and one of the most important for the people of the State of New York."[18] He represented it as a Republican surrender rather than the attempted stall that it was. Instead of neutralizing the issue, the Republicans had enabled their opponent to claim the consummation of decades of work. He sent such a telegraph to Smith, and received voluminous congratulations; like a sports team claiming to celebrate a disputed goal, all the advocates of public ownership of electric power joined in.

The public didn't follow these questions too closely, though the general impression of a politically progressive and effective governor was fostered. But the political community, including the national media, took note of Roosevelt's dexterity. Even Walter Lippmann, who had been skeptical of Roosevelt and would be again, was gulled into calling this development a "complete triumph."

In the selection of members of the Public Service Investigations Committee, Roosevelt followed the advice of Harvard law professor Felix Frankfurter. Frankfurter had already adopted a policy of exaggerated truckling to Roosevelt, insinuating himself into the inner councils of the man he saw as the most promising politician of the future. He would prove as formidable a courtier as a legal mind.

Roosevelt wrote an article for *Forum* magazine in the late summer of 1929 for publication at the end of 1929 in which he farseeingly called for state and federal collaboration to develop the hydroelectric potential of the St. Lawrence, the Tennessee, and the Colorado. He declared that such initiatives would "remain forever as a yardstick with which to measure the cost of producing and transforming electricity." He would make this happen.

In February 1930, Roosevelt would succeed in deposing the chairman of the Public Service Commission, William Prendergast, and replace him with Milo Maltbie, who was anything but an apologist for utility excesses. (In May 1930, the Commission would roll back telephone rate increases, an almost unprecedented development in New York State.) In March 1930, Roosevelt would wring from the legislature the right to appoint the members of the St. Lawrence Power Development Commission. A combination of Roosevelt's tactical skill and the beginnings of economic deterioration would effect a shift in the balance of power in Albany from the legislature to the governor.

Roosevelt and his supporters in the legislature presented hundreds of reform bills that were ignored, killed in committee, or voted down by the Republican leadership. These included many social and labor measures, a proposed $50 million bond issue for hospital construction (although Roosevelt did gain approval for a marked increase in state hospital beds), and a proposed change to a four-year term for the governor. Roosevelt did succeed in setting up his commission on old-age security and another to study reform of judicial administration, but with such a restricted mandate that when the bill returned to him he vetoed it as a "waste of $60,000." A Saratoga Springs Commission was set up as Roosevelt had asked, but packed with philistine Republican legislators. Roosevelt had wanted a nonpartisan commission of experts chaired by Bernard Baruch. His idea was to develop plans to turn Saratoga Springs into a modern resort and spa such as existed in various European towns like Marienbad and Bad Nauheim.

In the budget that he submitted for the fiscal year beginning July 1, 1929, Roosevelt included $25 million in lump-sum payments under various titles but at his discretion, out of total forecast expenditures of $260 million. The legislature increased the lump-sum payments to $54 million but took the discretion for allocation back from the governor and made it conditional upon agreement of the relevant committees of the legislature. Roosevelt vetoed these provisions of the budget and scores of other measures that he considered mere "pork-barreling" by his partisan opponents.

He left Albany for a month at Warm Springs at the end of April 1929, with the budget imbroglio referred to the appellate division of the state supreme court for settlement of constitutional prerogatives. The case hinged on the validity of Roosevelt's contention that the legislative committee chairmen, in arrogating to themselves authority over the disposition of lump-sum budgetary dispositions, were usurping the powers of the executive. The initial judgment in June was against the governor, but he appealed and instructed his pedantic and elderly counsel, William Guthrie, to employ more compelling arguments than he had at first instance, and the Court of Appeals reversed the lower court and found for Roosevelt in October. These were arcane issues of no great concern to the public, but the political community was watching closely to see if Roosevelt had the aptitude to govern the country's most populous state and deal with a hostile legislature. This was a considerable victory for him and a chastening experience for his opponents, who had hoped for a more pliable successor to the tenacious and battle-hardened Al Smith.

In June 1929, Roosevelt was pleased to receive honorary degrees from Dartmouth, Fordham, and most satisfyingly, Harvard. Even more agreeable was his election as grand marshal of the alumni observances, in keeping with the tradition that this position be held by a member of the twenty-fifth reunion class. Roosevelt never entirely outgrew his reverence for Groton and Harvard. When advised of his election by James Jackson, a Groton classmate and president of the Harvard class of 1904, he wrote, apparently without hyperbole: "I am quite overcome . . . and realize to the full the very great honor that has been given to me by the class and the university." He and Eleanor spent five days in a freshman dormitory much less commodious than where he had lived as an undergraduate. He revelled in a great range of collegiate activity.[19]

On July 4, 1929, Roosevelt again addressed the Tammany Hall Independence Day celebrations, as he had when reconciling himself to Boss Murphy twelve years before. On this occasion, Tammany was dedicating its new clubhouse on Union Square. Roosevelt lamented the inability of shopkeepers and other small businessmen to operate independently. He ruefully warned of the dangers of "highly centralized industrial control" as requiring reconsideration of the "whole problem of liberty," and expressed fear of a new kind of "economic feudalism." Tammany was an unlikely place for Roosevelt to warn that American citizens might have to put on "the liberty caps of their revolutionary forefathers and fight anew for independence." He called for the supplementing of the ancient doctrine of separation of church and state with an absolute separation of government and business.

With his elevation to high office and the extension of the great economic boom, Roosevelt's political views took shape more clearly. He would later reminisce: "I in common with most liberals did not at the start visualize the effects of the period, or the drastic changes that were even then necessary for a lasting economy." He knew that monopolies and concentration of wealth had to be addressed in the TR-Wilson tradition. "But we did not understand the real depths of the problem."[20] Just before his installation as governor and while the boom was in full strength, he said: "I believe that in the future the state . . . will assume a much larger role in the lives of its citizens. Public health . . . is a responsibility of the state as was the duty to promote general welfare. The state educates its children. Why not also keep them well?" He described his views as "social" rather than "socialistic," and yet confirmed that beyond that "the best government is the least government."[21]

He elaborated on the same theme at Tammany on July 4, 1929. It is not clear what his hosts thought of it, including sachem John R. Voorhis, then on the eve of his one hundredth birthday. Roosevelt declined to distribute his text, claiming (inaccurately) that he had spoken extemporaneously. A year later, with the economy in decline, in correspondence arising from his address, he wrote: "There will be a gain throughout the country of communistic thought unless we can keep Democracy up to its old ideals and original purposes . . . We face . . . not only the danger of communism but the equal danger of the concentration of power, economic and political, in the hands of what the ancient Greeks would have called an Oligarchy."[22]

The widely popular humorist and columnist Will Rogers wrote that with his address to Tammany and his performance generally, Roosevelt had practically assured himself of the Democratic presidential nomination in 1932.[23]

After destructive riots in July 1929 at two New York prisons—Dannemora and Auburn—Roosevelt tried his hand at prison reform. He built five lesser-security camps to promote outdoors work and reduce overcrowding, each initially taking a hundred men. He set up a committee to propose parole reforms, chaired a conference, and made some purposeful noises. This was about all he could do in these economic times and with a balky legislature, but it was a start.

Roosevelt disrupted the governor's conference at New London, Connecticut, also in July, by speaking about law enforcement and then, without any clearance from the author, reading a hand-written letter he had received from George Wickersham, head of President Hoover's commission on crime and Prohibition. Wickersham had suggested that the states share the cost of enforcing Prohibition with the federal government, and the conference now degenerated into a wild argument between supporters and opponents of Prohibition (in which Roosevelt remained scrupulously neutral).

The remarks of several of the governors at the conference reflected that it was a mockery of the prosperity of the late twenties that many of America's greatest cities, including the two largest, were mired in corruption.

The reform movement was stirring in New York City also. Mayor James J. Walker, a dapper former Broadway songwriter and theatrical personality, had retained his popularity with the public, but was becoming a serious embarrassment to his political allies. (Twenty-five years before, Walker had had been a protégé of songwriter Paul Dresser, the older brother of Theodore Dreiser and the author of the lyrics of "On the Banks of the Wabash" and "My Gal Sal." Walker himself had written the lyrics of "Kiss all the Girls For Me," "There's Music in the Rustle of a Skirt," and his greatest hit, "Will You Love Me in December as You Do in May?")

Corruption was out of control in New York City, and Walker's endless womanizing, frequent and prolonged holidays, erratic attendance at important events even when he was in New York, and notorious frequenting of speakeasies caused Al Smith to urge him not to run for reelection as mayor in 1929. Aware of his own popularity, Walker ignored this advice and ran again, challenged by reform Republican Fiorello H. La Guardia and the courageous if somewhat plodding perennial Socialist candidate Norman Thomas. Walker won with the astonishing plurality of over 500,000 votes. But Thomas raised the Socialist vote from 39,000 in the 1925 mayoral election to 175,000 in 1929, which Roosevelt, Howe, and Flynn immediately recognized as a significant portent.

A committee of prominent and thoroughly respectable Chicagoans had called on President Hoover in April 1929 to "reveal" to him the condition of their city, the second largest in the country. As Hoover put it in his memoirs, "Chicago was in the hands of the gangsters . . . the police and magistrates were completely under their control . . . the governor of the state was futile." This was the catalyst for Hoover's order to use the federal power to enforce tax and Prohibition laws against the notorious and folkloric gangster Al Capone, who was convicted of tax evasion in 1931 and sentenced to eleven years in prison, which were served in Alcatraz, the new maximum-security prison in San Francisco Bay.

III

THERE WERE DARKER SIDES to the America of the Roaring Twenties that has been so rhapsodised about in popular culture and that fascinated F. Scott Fitzgerald, Ernest Hemingway, and their readers. America then was a place of witless isolationism, massive corruption (largely but not wholly based on the inane attempt to ban alcoholic beverages), segregated oppression of the rights and opportunities of the ten percent of the population that was black, and an economic system that was now about to be revealed as built upon an unstable foundation, operated by industrialists and financiers indifferently qualified and motivated to exercise the vast unregulated power that they possessed. Most believed America to be on a "permanently high plateau" (in the phrase of the Yale economist Irving Fisher, uttered October 16, 1929, a few days before the market crash).

Franklin D. Roosevelt, having had to spend much of the decade in absentia from the temptations of society, convalescent and contemplative, was aware of many of these shortcomings and not complicit in them. This was an unsuspected advantage provided by his illness.

In the world, Benito Mussolini was generally regarded as the most prestigious political figure then active. He had shaped up Italy and caused it to be taken seriously in the world, famously made the trains run on time, drained the Pontine Marshes, and concluded his Concordat with the Vatican. Such diverse people as Winston Churchill and Will Rogers referred to Italy's Duce as a great man. (Roosevelt was more reticent, regularly referring to Italy and Russia as countries that abused civil rights.)

The problems of war reparations and international payments had been addressed in 1924 by Charles Gates Dawes, who had been rewarded with the vice presidency of the United States under Coolidge. It had been addressed again in 1929 by Owen D. Young of General Electric, who arranged a payments system less onerous than that which Germany was already observing. When Germany accepted this plan, France and Belgium discontinued their occupation of the Rhineland, which they had conducted since 1923.

In March 1929, sharp fluctuations in interest rates gave a hint of potential problems underlying the great Wall Street bull market, which had been rarely and only briefly interrupted in the last seven years. When the banking system withdrew $25 million from margin loans to miscellaneous stockholders, the call loan rate jumped sharply, rising three percent from March 25 to March 26, to 12 percent, then to 15 percent, 17 percent, and finally 20 percent, all in a few days, causing an unprecedented inundation of sell orders. Astute observers realized from this astounding elasticity in loan rates how fragile the levitation of the stock market had become, but official and public monitoring of such key indices was very primitive by the standards of subsequent decades.

The powerful president of the National City Bank, Charles E. Mitchell, announced that his bank would advance $20 million in call margin loans, in $5 million tranches and in 1 percent increments, from 15 percent to 18 percent, with a potential top rate of 20 percent. Other banks followed, and the immediate crisis seemed to subside. The call rate on unsecured stock market portfolio loans went back to a wide range of 6 percent to 15 percent. Many of the great industrial corporations entered the moneylending business by advancing loans to brokers from undistributed profits or secured on the basis of their high-grade credit ratings as borrowers, and profited from the wide spread between their cost of money and the call margin rate. This was very irresponsible, but the world had never known a time like this. Only the cleverest and most irreverent financial analysts, such as Bernard Baruch and Joseph Kennedy, or the most conservative, such as Vincent Astor and Averell Harriman, knew to avoid or cease financial impetuosity.

Another straw in the wind that might have been detected by the discerning was the failure of the City Trust Company, a New York bank for Italian Americans of modest means, in February 1929, a few days after the death of its founder, Francesco Ferrari. Shortly after that the state superintendent of banks, Frank H. Warder, abruptly resigned and applied for a passport, as he planned a prolonged European holiday. He was later sentenced to five to ten years in prison for taking a bribe from Ferrari. Because Roosevelt was in Warm Springs, Herbert Lehman dealt with the crisis by empowering a special commissioner to inquire into the failure of the bank. Inexplicably he selected Robert Moses for this role, though he certainly knew of Roosevelt's detestation of Moses.

Lehman gave a rather labored defense of his choice in correspondence with the governor and Howe, and Roosevelt now put Lehman on a loyalty watch to detect whether he would be a waverer in any contest for control of the Democratic Party between Smith and Roosevelt, as was almost certain to occur at the latest in 1932. (Smith was just publishing his autobiography, "Up To Now," the title implying that he intended to reenter public life, as Roosevelt expected.) Moses' recommendations were prompt and sensible and well-received. Roosevelt made no comment on Moses' report but did enact those of his recommendations that the legislature passed (in diluted form).

In his maiden speech in the United States Senate on March 5, 1928, Robert F. Wagner revealed that he had inquired of the Department of Labor what the unemployment rate was in the country and had been informed that there was no official knowledge of that figure. Yet the golden optimism of permanent prosperity was cantilevered on borrowed money farther and farther out over a financial abyss.

Al Smith's great backer (still Democratic Party chairman) and Roosevelt's ostensible friend (although in fact there was a complete absence of rapport between them), John J. Raskob, wrote in the August 1929 issue of the *Ladies' Home Journal*—of all places—in an article entitled "Everybody Ought to Be Rich," that if people just saved half their income and invested it in common stocks, they would become rich within twenty years. There was, he implied, no excuse not to do so. He was not encouraging borrowing, but just as irresponsibly for a man in his position, he was urging the average wage and salary earners of America to scrimp and pour their savings into a market afloat in oceans of borrowed money secured by stocks that had been inflated in price by the investment of that same borrowed money.

Raskob, mainly by large personal contributions, had founded a permanent Democratic National Committee whose publicity director would be the colorful Hearst and Pulitzer journalist Charles Michelson. Raskob engaged as head of the National Committee his protégé Jouett Shouse of Kansas City, who was not amenable to Roosevelt's relatively liberal views. This did not inhibit Roosevelt from writing to Shouse as if they were ancient comrades-in-arms. These party structures, if not the personnel in charge of them, would serve future Democratic leaders well.

———————

The Roosevelts spent the last golden summer, before the twenties imploded and the world changed forever, touring. The governor commandeered New York State's inland waterway inspection boat, named the *Inspector*, which had a glass roof and a fine sundeck. The boat went from Albany to Buffalo by canal, to Lake Ontario, and then into the St. Lawrence to Montreal, then along the Champlain canal and down the Hudson. The governor's official car met *Inspector* at each stop. These tours, ostensibly non-partisan information inspections, gave a foretaste of elaborate supposedly non-political railway trips Roosevelt would take around the country when president.

Eleanor and the two younger Roosevelts, Franklin Jr. and John, went as far as Montreal and there were joined by Eleanor's two inseparable companions, Marion Dickerman and Nancy Cook, who had driven from Val Kill. The three women and two boys would embark at Montreal on a tour of Europe, taking one of the Val Kill automobiles with them in the hold of the passenger liner for a motor tour that would somewhat emulate the motor excursions they had made the six previous summers from Hyde Park to Campobello. The governor, supposedly on a goodwill tour to Montreal to look at the hydroelectric and canalization possibilities of the St. Lawrence, gave the five Europe-bound tourists a farewell dinner on July 26, 1929, at the roof-top restaurant in Montreal's Mount Royal Hotel.

One result of these excursions, apart from a good rest, was to educate Roosevelt about the deteriorating plight of New York's farmers. He took seriously his claim to be a farmer, even if few others did, and he discovered that while agricultural production had grown, demand had not, and farm incomes had fallen off markedly.

Eleanor did not have an agreeable summer in Europe, and resolved never to conduct young people around on a sightseeing tour again. To conform with

Sara's magniloquent notions of a grand tour for her grandchildren, Eleanor required them to dress formally, and they were conducted in a chauffeur-driven Daimler, while Nancy and Marion drove around spontaneously in their Buick roadster. Eleanor's description of the Verdun battlefield, which FDR had asked her to show their sons, was eloquent. But in general her letters home were even gloomier than usual.

When Eleanor returned from Europe, Roosevelt asked her to resume her activities in the Democratic State Committee and the League of Women voters as long as she didn't give speeches that would be quoted in the press. She began to tour state facilities as a surrogate for her husband—hospitals, prisons, and schools as well as work-sites in the private sector. He counselled her on what to look for and how to avoid being fooled about quality of food, the confines of the public building, and so forth. Eleanor Roosevelt shortly proved extremely adept in this role.[24]

Her personal life became more controversial than ever. In addition to the time she spent with mannish and unmarried women, she was almost as much with her rather dashing security policeman, Corporal (later Sergeant) Earl Miller. Miller was a powerful, athletic, fine-looking former acrobat, boxer, and judo instructor. He was pleasant and presentable, and Eleanor brought him to the dinner table at Springwood, which considerably irritated Sara.

Franklin Roosevelt never evinced the slightest interest in whom his wife saw or what she did with them. He was perfectly cordial to all her friends, relying on her prudish nature to avoid any serious outrages. There remains a complete absence of evidence that Eleanor had any sexual interests of any kind after about 1917. The marriage worked as a fusion of efforts, and Eleanor performed a number of useful services for her husband. In 1949 in her book *This I Remember*, she resignedly wrote of her relationship with Franklin Roosevelt: "I was one of those who served his purposes." There must have been more to it than that, but this is clearly how she often felt, even after he died. In any event, Eleanor Roosevelt and Earl Miller made an unlikely couple.

At the beginning of September 1929, the stock market reached new highs. Since the slight flutter in March 1928, General Electric shares had jumped from $129 to $396; its competitor Westinghouse from $92 to $313; RCA from $93 to $505, and Union Carbide from $145 to $414. These were all well-managed companies that would weather the coming difficulties, and they had outperformed the market, but there was no commercial rationale at all for such a rise as they and the market generally had enjoyed in the previous eighteen months.

The stock market was a good deal more ragged for the rest of September as Roosevelt relaxed in Warm Springs, refusing in telephone press interviews La Guardia's and Norman Thomas's calls for a formal investigation into the murder of the famous gambler and racketeer Arnold Rothstein. On September 24, 4.4

million shares, a very heavy volume for Wall Street, traded and prices were off about two percent. A few ambivalent days followed, and then on October 3 there was a repetition of September 24—substantial declines on a volume of 4.7 million shares.

There were almost two weeks of further sideways movement until another similar reversal occurred on October 16. On October 19, a Saturday (the New York Stock Exchange was still open Saturday mornings), an astonishing 3.5 million shares were traded on that normally sleepy half day. On Monday the 21st, 6.1 million shares were traded, and the averages slumped again. The market was now declining by 1 to 2 percent every day or two. The market revived somewhat on Tuesday the 22nd, partly on rumors of organized support and partly on an optimistic statement by Charles Mitchell of the National City Bank as he returned from Britain and disembarked in New York. The following day brought the beginnings of panic: 6.4 million shares traded, 2.6 million in the last hour. Prices slid almost 4 percent, a paper loss of $4 billion in the value of listed securities. The ticker ran almost two hours behind the trading as sell orders flooded the dealers, many of them compulsory margin calls (where the shares secured the loans used to finance their purchase and the stock was sold in partial reduction of the loans, leaving the investor with an outstanding loan and no asset against it).

The next day, October 24, Mitchell and the heads of Chase National, Guaranty Trust, Bankers Trust, and First National gathered at the J.P. Morgan office at 23 Wall Street. (The First National chairman, the legendary George Baker, was on the telephone.) Morgan's vice president and senior trader, Richard Whitney, marched majestically about the Exchange floor casually putting in buy orders for about twenty blue chip stocks. The market plunged before noon and rallied appreciatively to Whitney's histrionic stroll on behalf of the nation's leading bank chairmen, closing the day almost even on a record-setting trade of 12.9 million shares.

On Friday, October 25, Roosevelt's friend and war-time tenant, Thomas Lamont of Morgan, confirmed that there was a backstop consortium of big banks to stabilize the stock market. There also began a crescendo of assurances from prominent financiers and politicians that the economy and stock market were "fundamentally" sound. Charles Mitchell, Charles Schwab of Bethlehem Steel, and President Hoover himself were among those who confidently bandied about assurances of the country's "fundamental" economic resilience.

Roosevelt, speaking to a church group in Poughkeepsie, sounded a slightly discordant note that was little noticed at the time when he criticized the "theory of getting something for nothing" and took the stock market to task for "improper schemes and questionable methods in stock promotions." He did claim that market ethics were improving and certainly did not fan the flames of the recent worries. The market was solid on Friday and Saturday, and the prestige of the country's leading bankers briefly scaled a new height in the nation's grateful perceptions.

Monday, October 28, 9.9 million shares traded and the market fell throughout the session, having one of its worst days ever and losing about 5 per cent of its total value. A meeting of the big bankers, joined by Owen Young of General Electric and the president of Equitable Trust, lasted two hours, not the perfunctory council of the previous Thursday. Thomas Lamont finally issued a statement that there had never been the intention to stabilize prices but only to retain an orderly market. He predicted that the market would stabilize eventually.

This set the scene for what became known to history as Black Tuesday, October 29, 1929. The New York Stock Exchange opened down, and three million shares traded in the first half hour. No statement came from the bankers' group as volume reached the astounding figure of 16.4 million shares, which would not be equalled until 1968. The ticker ran several hours behind the trades, and though the plunge eventually slowed late in the day, the market lost almost one-fifth of its entire ostensible value on that day alone. The Dow Jones Industrial Average was off 48 points, the equivalent seventy years later, when that average was around 12,000, of a loss of over 2,000 points (following the previous day's loss of the equivalent of 600 points). In fact it was worse, since much of the stock that was sold had been bought with borrowed money. People were being financially wiped out in large numbers, and the implications backed quickly into every area of the economy.

That vital part of economics that is psychology had been mortally wounded. The confidence of the financial community had been shattered. "The Jazz Age," wrote F. Scott Fitzgerald, who gave it its name, "leaped to a spectacular death in October, 1929." Calvin Coolidge's "business civilization" and Herbert Hoover's "American system" were exposed, again in Fitzgerald's words, as a "flimsy structure."

Writers and intellectuals are rarely impressed with commercial systems, and many of America's greatest writers, including Fitzgerald and Hemingway, had fled to Paris, as a generation earlier Henry James and some others had fled to London. But it wasn't only writers who had been skeptical about the business culture of the twenties, and not just the expatriate writers, either. Sinclair Lewis, H.L. Mencken, and Eugene O'Neill were as caustic as any and were often amused at the reversals suffered by the speculators and the fat cats. Edmund Wilson, who found the crash "stimulating," wrote: "One couldn't help being exhilarated at the sudden collapse of that stupid gigantic fraud."

This was a timeless response. Much of the cultural and media communities greeted any economic reversals with ululations of joy throughout the rest of the twentieth century, so great was their dislike of the ethos of commercial success and accompanying political conservatism.

Roosevelt had been awaiting a sharp correction, not a collapse. On October 26, 1929, he had telegraphed a New York newspaper: "Do not know detailed conditions but firmly believe fundamental industrial trade conditions are sound."[25] But with all his feline talents as observer and courtier of the American public,

Roosevelt saw the vindication of his own ambivalent attitudes, partly disdainful and partly envious. He also saw the opening of the opportunity he had been awaiting all his adult life. For a time he did not see that he would be seeking the leadership of his country in the most calamitous circumstances since the Civil War.

———

By mid-November, as the market continued to slump, about $40 billion had been wiped off the apparent wealth of Americans—in the terms of the year 2000, about $25,000 for every man, woman and child in the entire country—and it had only begun. All economic indicators, imprecise as they were, were now negative. In November President Hoover met with leaders of one industry after another and asked them to redouble their job-creating activities. The "fundamental" mantra having been unavailing, some of the country's wealthiest men—Henry Ford, John D. Rockefeller Jr. and Charles M. Schwab—announced they were buying equities to take advantage of the bargains that stock market reversals had created. This was more successful, as the stock market rose slightly in the first three months of 1930.

Hoover realized that the shock waves from the stock market had ramified very damagingly in the country, and cut income taxes slightly to encourage demand and ordered the Federal Farm Bureau to buy agricultural products and make loans at generous rates to farmers to try to resuscitate farm income. Public works appropriations were increased and the President wrote all the state governors asking the "energetic yet prudent pursuit of public works." Roosevelt responded that he had already intended to do so, without raising taxes or incurring a deficit.[26] The Smoot-Hawley tariff was imposed to protect American farmers and manufacturers. It raised the average tariff on dutiable imports from 26 percent to 50 percent. The tax reductions were insignificant and were reversed the following year. Tariff increases, the Federal Reserve's shrinking of the money supply, and the tax increases, when they came, were catastrophic policies in the economic downturn, and even Hoover seems to have had reservations about Treasury Secretary Andrew Mellon's inflexible responses.

Roosevelt, with an eye on national politics, spoke in Chicago on December 10, 1929. He mocked those who might refer to the Midwest as backward and said the region was rather the "backbone of the nation." And he had a Biblical admonition for reactionary Republican senator George Moses, who had referred to the western progressives (Borah, Norris, Wheeler, the La Follettes) as "sons of the wild jackass." To the great delight of western listeners and readers, Roosevelt reminded Moses that "it was to Balaam's ass that God granted the miraculous gift of sudden speech to warn his master from proceeding further on a path that led to irretrievable destruction."[27] FDR declared himself "quite flabbergasted" when even the *Chicago Tribune* supported him.[28]

Roosevelt congratulated state industrial commissioner Frances Perkins at the end of January 1930 when she publicly disputed Hoover's claim that unemployment was declining. "Bully for you" said FDR, emulating his famous cousin.

For the first few months after Black Tuesday, Roosevelt was unaware of the proportions of the debacle that was unfolding, and contented himself with panegyrics on the evils of greedy and dishonest stock promotion activities and generally of business combinations. It wasn't too different from what Theodore Roosevelt and Woodrow Wilson had been saying twenty years before.

On March 29, he became the first state governor to warn that unemployment was becoming a serious problem. He identified seasonal, technological, and cyclical causes, set up one of his inevitable commissions, and proposed community emergency relief, job-creation, and public works activities. Tepid though it was, it was a first step. As always, Roosevelt went on his intuition. He had known the boom was unsustainable and he knew some possibly radical remedial work would be necessary now. Knowing nothing of economics, he had no real idea of what or how much.

John J. Raskob and the Smith faction's early reaction to the deteriorating economy was concern that Democrats not fall to attacking business. Instead Raskob blamed Hoover for insufficient fervor at laissez faire economics. This was the ideal tactic from Roosevelt's standpoint, because Smith and Raskob vacated the field of serious reform advocacy, leaving him in sole occupancy of it. Smith had been intellectually kidnapped by Raskob and his rich friends. They were in a time warp, fighting Prohibition, which even Hoover had largely abandoned. Raskob was the chief financier for the world's tallest building—the Empire State Building, at Fifth Avenue and 34th Street—and Alfred E. Smith was to be the chairman of it. Their brief time at the summit of the Democratic Party had already ended, though they would not go altogether quietly. There was almost no political agreement between Roosevelt and Raskob other than on the absurdity of Prohibition, and little disagreement between Raskob, Smith, and Hoover.

In a Jefferson Day address in New York on April 26, 1930, Roosevelt alleged that 80 percent of America's industrial economy was controlled by fifty or sixty corporations and that the financial markets were as tightly controlled. "If Thomas Jefferson were alive he would be the first to question this concentration of economic power," he said. He was followed to the podium on this occasion by Montana's progressive senator, Burton K. Wheeler, who became the first prominent elected official to endorse Roosevelt for president. Wheeler received the customary note of thanks and the implausible disclaimer of any such ambition.

As he moved inexorably toward reelection as governor, Roosevelt was concerned to position himself at the head of as large a number of votes as possible. He had a good record on electricity and public utilities generally, hospital and road construction, and social welfare. He had run a clean administration, more than held his own with a mulishly partisan legislature, and debunked the theory that he lacked the stamina for the position, and he was an impressive physical presence and formidable orator who was already using the radio to advantage.

At the Governors' Conference at Salt Lake City on June 30, 1930, Roosevelt became the first governor to propose unemployment insurance and old-age pensions, though he was clear in opposing a "mere dole." He had in mind insurance against unemployment, not a substitute income as an unconditional *ex gratia* payment to the idle. This was less comprehensive than Frances Perkins, who had prepared a paper on it for him, had hoped, though she acknowledged later that Roosevelt had caught exactly the Democratic Party's mood—help for the desperate but not a war against the work ethic. This was what the party and the country were seeking, not hair-shirt platitudes from millionaires like Raskob and the Republican oligarchs.

Roosevelt claimed that the Hoover administration had authored the "wholly new economic theory that high wages and high pressure selling could guarantee prosperity at all times regardless of supply and demand."

IV

THE GREATEST POLITICAL problem facing Roosevelt was the corruption in New York City. The likely Republican candidate for governor against Roosevelt, District Attorney Charles Tuttle, was running on the Tammany corruption issue. Roosevelt had the problem of keeping the Tammany votes, as evidenced by Walker's colossal majority in 1929, without being lumbered with the appearance of being overly influenced by the Tammany bosses. There were special problems with the lower courts in the New York boroughs; in particular, La Guardia had unearthed the "loan" of nearly $20,000 from the murdered gambler Arnold Rothstein to Magistrate Albert H. Vitale. The legislature authorized, and implicitly urged, Roosevelt to investigate the government of the nation's largest city.

Mayor Walker and Tammany boss John Curry responded quickly. They revealed that to their great horror Vitale had actually taken $30,000 from Rothstein, and had him removed from the bench and disbarred. District Attorney Tuttle had found a good deal of Tammany-related skulduggery involving the sale of pier leases, zoning variances, and fraudulent stock issues. Roosevelt was in danger of being mired in a Damon Runyan world of hoods and scoundrels if he got into this too far. He was still trying to straddle between his upstate reform bearings and the need for Tammany's organizational support in the big boroughs of New York City.

The Republicans and Norman Thomas's Socialists demanded a special session of the legislature to empower and require the governor to plumb the cesspool. Roosevelt skillfully replied in an open letter to the Democratic leadership July 20, 1930, that the state Supreme Court had all the power necessary to investigate the magistrates' courts and that he was further prepared to send the attorney general to New York to convene an extraordinary grand jury for an extended term if the evidence justified it.

Roosevelt was now reembarked on the *Inspector,* touring the lakes and rivers and canals of New York, but the tireless District Attorney Tuttle was back in early August with strong evidence that a magistracy had been bought. The Tammany district attorney for Manhattan, Thomas Crain, claimed he could not secure indictments from a grand jury. The public outcry was so great at this evident cover-up that Roosevelt shifted the issue from Crain to the Republican attorney general of the state, Hamilton Ward, but circumscribed him to the one suborned magistracy.

Roosevelt commissioned a general investigation, not by elected Republican officeholders but by the state supreme court and specifically by respected appeals court judge Samuel Seabury, who had been the Democratic candidate for governor in 1916. Seabury was on holiday in Britain, and when he returned on September 5 he announced that an exhaustive investigation would have to precede public hearings. Seabury was a man of unimpeachable integrity as well as methodical thoroughness. This largely defanged the issue for the purposes of Roosevelt's reelection campaign. (The atmosphere of corruption became more pungent when on August 6 a Tammany member of the state supreme court, Joseph Crater, got into a taxi on West 45th Street after lunch with a showgirl, and was never seen again.)

Ward secured criminal indictments in the case that had been referred to him, and the grand jury asked the governor on September 24 to order an extended investigation. Roosevelt declined to do so on constitutional grounds but bullied Walker into requiring that all subpoenaed Tammany officials who had invoked the Fifth Amendment against self-incrimination waive their immunity or resign their posts. They had twenty-four hours to make this choice. Roosevelt had gone as far as he could with his old enemies in the New York machine; he wasn't going to go down with them. He had a testy public correspondence with the Reverend Russell Bowie, a friend and Harvard classmate and now rector of Grace Church in New York. In it he defensively and somewhat piously announced that the issue was due process.

When public funds ran out, civic groups paid for an extension, and the grand jury continued to adduce controversial evidence, much of it concerning the vanished Judge Crater, all through October. Judge Amadeo Bertini, whom Roosevelt had named to the bench in 1929 at the request of Tammany boss John Curry, despite his having been declared professionally and ethically unqualified, took the Fifth Amendment at the grand jury. Bertini partially recovered his position by issuing a clever statement impugning the motives of the partisan Republican attorney general in the middle of the election campaign. Roosevelt ignored these proceedings, unctuously announcing that justice must take its course.

The Republican gubernatorial nominating convention had opened on September 25, 1930, in Albany. The U.S. secretary of state, Henry L. Stimson, a former Republican candidate for governor, gave a keynote address that did nothing for the local Republicans but extolled the performance of the Hoover administration. The Republican delegates voted three to one in favor of repealing Prohibition. Roosevelt wrote at once to Senator Robert Wagner, who would be the Democrats' keynote speaker, also calling for repeal and the sale of alcoholic beverages through state outlets.

Roosevelt was not about to be outflanked on this issue by the Republicans, whose incumbent president was still waffling about it. He had been very discreet about it as governor, unlike his predecessor, because he did not want to split the Democratic Party again on that issue. The New York Republicans still tried to straddle by nominating a repeal advocate, or "wet"—Charles Tuttle—for governor, and a continuing prohibitionist, or "dry," for lieutenant governor, enabling Roosevelt to refer sarcastically to his opponents as an "amphibian." He devised a Latin technical name for the Republican ticket: "amphibius ichthyosaurus."

Franklin D. Roosevelt was renominated as the Democratic candidate for governor of New York on September 30, at Syracuse. He used the convention to complete the packing of the state organization with his own loyalists, installing James A. Farley as state Democratic chairman, replacing Smith appointee William Bray. Farley, like Howe and Flynn, was about to ride Roosevelt's coattails, where they were all attached almost at the waistband, into American political folklore. One of Howe's innovations was the first political talking movie, *The Roosevelt Record.* It was booked into hundreds of theaters and shown at Democratic rallies throughout the campaign. (The first full-length talking movie, *The Jazz Singer,* with Al Jolson, had appeared in 1927.)

In his acceptance remarks, Roosevelt did not name Tuttle but scorned him for ignoring every issue except municipal corruption, and piled upon him all the reactionary obstructionism of the Republican leaders in the legislature. He also engaged in a tactic that he would often employ—purporting to distinguish his primitive opponent from the rank and file of reasonable Republicans. This was a nostalgic play for the remaining followers of his progressive cousin. Campaign funds were plentiful, with the fundraising effort headed by Henry Morgenthau Sr., Broadway producer and commissioner of the Port of New York Howard Cullman, railway magnate Arthur James, and Roosevelt's 1914 opponent, Ambassador James Gerard.* Eleanor's friend Molly Dewson, in charge of the women's campaign, had prepared a handbill comparing the cost of operation of different household appliances in New York with the cost in neighboring Ontario. All registered Democratic women voters were sent a wad of these handbills and invited to pass them on to their friends. Many New York women always remembered this as the "waffle iron campaign."

Roosevelt released medical reports October 18 showing that he was in excel-

---

* Among the contributors were the Lehmans and Morgenthaus; members of the Dodge, Whitney, Pulitzer, and Warburg families; and Vincent Astor, Raskob, Al Smith, William Woodin, Samuel Seabury, and Theodore Roosevelt's son Archibald. [29]

lent health and had fully recovered from polio other than in his legs. He took out $560,000 of medical insurance, of which the beneficiary was the Warm Springs Foundation. There were twenty-two insurers, the rates were the normal ones, and he was offered up to a million dollars coverage if he wished. His physique, apart from his legs, was splendid; he had a greater chest expansion than Jack Dempsey and weighed 182 pounds, ideal for a man six feet, one and one-half inches tall, except that given his withered legs, his torso was very heavy, mainly with muscle acquired in his endless exercises. If his legs had had their normal weight but he had built his upper body strength anyway, he would have weighed about 225 pounds, very solid for his height.

His own campaign hammered the Hoover economic depression. He quoted sarcastically from some of Hoover's speeches in the 1928 campaign. Hoover sent senior officials into the state to answer Roosevelt. There was Secretary of War Patrick Hurley (whom Roosevelt was happy to portray as an Oklahoman), along with Undersecretary of the Treasury Ogden Mills (Smith's opponent in 1926) and, by radio, Henry Stimson, both of whom Roosevelt was happy to dismiss as former unsuccessful candidates for governor. Stimson harped, as Tuttle did, on Tammany corruption issues and represented them as evidence of Roosevelt's "unfitness to deal with" the problem. The resulting newspaper headlines screaming "Roosevelt Unfit" angered Roosevelt more than anything in the campaign, because he thought Stimson was referring to his medical condition. Roosevelt was eventually satisfied that this was a consequence unintended by Stimson.

This had been a radically different campaign from that of two years before. Instead of being rushed in at the last moment, Roosevelt and his advisors had prepared and conducted it very carefully. He had a creditable record and didn't have to stand on that of Al Smith (whose name was scarcely mentioned in this campaign). And he did not have to swim against the tide of permanent Republican prosperity.

Roosevelt received the election results at his campaign headquarters in the Biltmore Hotel on the evening of November 4. Only Roosevelts and intimates such as Henry Morgenthau Jr., who had accompanied him from Hyde Park, and Al Smith were admitted to the governor's own suite. By nine o'clock he had a gracious telegram of concession from Charles Tuttle. When he went home to 65th Street at ten it was clear that he was carrying New York City with a majority bigger than Jimmie Walker's half million plurality the year before and was even piling up a lead in the state outside of New York City, which no Democrat had done for decades. He almost doubled Smith's record-breaking 1924 majority of 387,000, racking up an astonishing lead of 725,000 over Tuttle. This was the first real sign of Franklin D. Roosevelt's mighty powers as a campaign strategist and vote-getter, and was a portent of historic election nights to come. Eleanor was in much more effusive spirits this night than she had been two years before. She retired early because she had to teach her class at Todhunter the next morning, but left her husband a note: "Much love and a world of congratulations. It is a triumph in so many ways, dear and so well earned. Bless you and good luck these next two years."[30]

Tammany, fighting for its life, had delivered for the governor as rarely before: the voter turnout in New York City was over 91 percent, against 71 percent upstate. Incredibly, Roosevelt had also carried upstate New York by 167,000 votes, but he was assisted by the Prohibitionist candidate, who had polled 181,000 votes upstate, most of them presumably taken from the Republicans.

The Democrats ran strongly cross the country, taking control of the House of Representatives for the first time since 1916 and reducing the Republican lead in the Senate to two, which was no lead at all when progressives like Robert La Follette and George Norris, who were only nominal Republicans, were deducted from the Republican total. Will Rogers said, "The Democrats nominated their president yesterday, Franklin D. Roosevelt."[31]

V

THE ROAD TO the presidential nomination would not be as effortless as Roosevelt hoped. He concentrated on building up such an overwhelming lead that he would become the inevitable candidate well in advance of the 1932 Democratic National Convention. A two-thirds vote continued to be necessary for nomination, and as a veteran of the terribly protracted conventions of 1912 (Baltimore and Wilson), 1920 (San Francisco and Cox), and 1924 (New York and Davis), he well knew the dangers of not coming to the convention with an insurmountable lead. In order to flatten any incipient stop-Roosevelt movement he allowed himself to be talked into impetuosity in his selection of primaries to enter. And although he had stick-handled through the Tammany-corruption problems in his 1930 gubernatorial race, this issue would be much more complicated in the run-up to a federal election. This was doubly so because as the election approached, the issue became not so much one of dispensable, low-level machine graft-takers but of the hugely popular mayor, Jimmy Walker himself.

A consummate dissembler, Roosevelt relentlessly denied that he had any presidential ambitions, writing at the end of November 1930 to one of Eleanor's friends very active in the League of Women Voters that having "seen so much of the White House ever since 1892 . . . I have no hankering . . . to be a candidate," as if visiting it as a young man reduced a practicing politician's ambition to be president. He had already asked Bronx boss Edward J. Flynn to take over his national delegate roundup effort. When Flynn declined, on the grounds that he was too reticent personally and too attached to his wife and home to travel all over the country as would be required, Roosevelt asked James A. Farley, who happily accepted in December 1930. Howe set up an informal Roosevelt-for-President headquarters at Madison Avenue and 43rd Street, across from Roosevelt's traditional election-night headquarters in the Biltmore Hotel.

Immediately following the 1930 election, Raskob and Shouse composed a conciliatory open letter to Hoover signed by the last three Democratic presidential nominees, Smith, Davis, and Cox, and the party's congressional leaders, John Nance Garner, who was about to become Speaker of the House of Representatives, and Senator Joseph T. Robinson. It promised bipartisan support for measures that would promote business recovery, and purported to abandon the party's longstanding opposition to high tariffs. Raskob was still trying to make the Democrats into a neo-Republican pro-business party. This was what Walter Lippmann would describe as Raskob's effort to turn large contributors into preferred shareholders of political parties.

In the shambles of his misjudgment of Roosevelt, Smith allowed himself to be coopted by this movement, which was contrary to the entire meaning of his long and distinguished career as a champion of the disadvantaged.

Raskob's next gambit was a call on February 10, 1931, for a special meeting of the Democratic National Committee for March 5, to commit the Democratic Party, almost two years in advance of the presidential election, to outright repeal of Prohibition and to a high tariff—support of the Smoot-Hawley measure that had been passed a year before over Democratic opposition. Roosevelt and Howe recognized this as the preemptive conservative strike against their campaign that it was, and Farley raced around the country rounding up opposition while Roosevelt bombarded Democratic Party officials with letters, telegrams, and telephone calls remonstrating against this attempted usurpation of the role of the party convention by means of a Hooverite Trojan Horse.

Farley summoned the New York Democratic committee on March 2 and had it adopt a resolution drafted by Roosevelt, Howe, Flynn, and himself condemning Raskob's initiative. When the national committee met three days later, Senator Robinson, an anti-Catholic prohibitionist, though he had run for vice president with Smith in 1928, gave a magisterial address condemning Raskob's attempted coup. Al Smith took the floor and gave a conciliatory speech, and Raskob ignominiously withdrew his motion. The first test of the stop-Roosevelt campaign was a fiasco.

One of those who emerged from the past to become a Roosevelt advisor and financial backer was Woodrow Wilson's shadowy grey eminence, Colonel Edward Mandell House. He was one of the original group of fifteen that bankrolled the start of the first Roosevelt presidential campaign.* House was a useful bridge to the old Wilson Democrats, who, unlike the bedraggled factions identified with Cox, Davis, and Smith, had actually frequented the White House and conceived of the Democrats as a reform party.

Just before Roosevelt left New York for his annual April holiday at Warm Springs in 1931, he learned that his mother had contracted pneumonia in France.

---

* They included Flynn himself, James Gerard, Joseph P. Kennedy, Herbert Lehman, Henry Morgenthau Sr., Sara Roosevelt, Harry Warner, William Woodin, Jesse Straus, Robert Bingham, Frank Walker, and Basil O'Connor.

In the grand Roosevelt tradition of dropping everything to cross the Atlantic in family medical emergencies, he embarked on the *Aquitania* with Elliott. He was returning his parents' flight from Bad Nauheim to his school infirmary when he had scarlet fever at Groton in 1898. His mother had already largely recovered when Roosevelt arrived in France. He remained about five weeks, toured the battlefields of the Great War with Elliott, and was pleased to find that the shattered farms and towns of northeastern France had been largely rebuilt. He had a reunion with Andre Tardieu, with whom he had jousted over the American radio station at Bordeaux in 1919. One of his returning shipmates on the new German blue riband superliner *Bremen*, whom he had to dinner in his stateroom twice, was the former vice president and now U.S. ambassador to Great Britain, Charles G. Dawes. The dinners were a huge success. Dawes wrote in his diary of Roosevelt that "if he is the next President of the United States, he will serve with honor to his country and credit to himself. He seems to have strength and equipoise, clarity of mind with soundness of judgment, and . . . common sense."[32]

On June 12, Roosevelt delivered the commencement address at Groton and was resonantly praised by Rector Peabody. The tide had finally turned in this relationship, and Franklin Roosevelt, whose obeisances to Peabody had never been entirely sufficient when he was in his charge, savored the compliments of his former headmaster. All four of the Roosevelt sons were present and young Franklin and John were still students at the school. James had married the beautiful, vivacious, and rich Betsy Cushing. He was about to quit Harvard Law School, which he was not enjoying, to set up in the insurance business, where he would trade heavily on his father's name and his wealthy in-laws' money and connections.

The day after Groton, Colonel House held a large and well-publicized luncheon for Roosevelt at his farm at Beverly, Massachusetts, which was attended by most of the Democratic establishment of the state. Among those present was Al Smith's only rival as the quintessential Irish urban politician, Boston's mayor James Michael Curley. Curley eventually persuaded Roosevelt to run in the Massachusetts primary, with the promise that he could deliver the state. Believing in Curley's promise was one of the few significant tactical political errors committed by Roosevelt in his prime. The crafty and worldly Colonel House went even further, and unsuccessfully proposed Curley as ambassador to Italy in 1933. It would have been a very strange appointment.[33]

Jim Farley set out on a national tour of delegate collection and a general preemptive strike against rival candidates on June 29, 1931. Roosevelt, Howe, and Farley together devised the itinerary, and Howe's years of corresponding with huge numbers of the party organization now bore fruit. Farley, one of the country's most prominent and enthusiastic Elks, professed to be travelling on Elks' business as well as neutrally canvassing preferences between New York's three possible candidates, Roosevelt, Smith, and businessman Owen Young. It is unlikely that either disguise fooled many he met.

He reported back that he found only occasional support for Alfred E. Smith, from militant Roman Catholics or anti-prohibitionists. Newton D. Baker, Wilson's wartime war secretary, was mentioned a few times. Roosevelt support was somewhat less extensive in California, which Farley ascribed to the favorite-son candidacy of William G. McAdoo who—illustrating the politician's timeless propensity to self-indulgent dreams—fancied that he had a chance to be the compromise candidate between Smith and Roosevelt, as Davis had been in 1924 between Smith and himself.

The only problem Farley encountered was concern about Roosevelt's physical condition and general stamina. By the time of his return Roosevelt had laid this issue largely to rest with an article in *Liberty* magazine published July 25, 1931, in which a team of doctors examined Roosevelt, and the author of the article, the respected journalist Earle Looker, followed the governor around for some days. Looker concluded that Roosevelt was "able to take more punishment than many men ten years younger."

On March 7, 1932, Roosevelt would write to Russell Hungerford of Washington, D.C., objecting to journalistic references to his disability as "yellow journalism. The losing my balance and toppling is not true. As you know, I wear a leg brace to lock the knee and on one occasion when I was speaking, the brace broke with the result that I went half way down. Frankly I cannot see the importance of all this nonsense when I am in perfect health and get through three times as much work in the average day as three ordinary men do." It is a testament to his relations with the press that Roosevelt thought he could pretend to wear only one leg brace instead of two. This contrasts with his letter of seven years before, when he had been upbraided for not standing at a ceremony honoring President Coolidge at Madison Square Garden. He wrote that he needed the "help of two people . . . as I wear steel braces on both legs and use crutches . . . It is not exactly pleasant for me."[34] The change in the descriptions was progress not so much in FDR's recovery as in his effort to minimize the importance of his affliction.

By the autumn of 1931, the Great Depression was evidently deepening. The three most ubiquitous urban symbols of the time were the bread line, the apple peddler, and the shantytowns of boxes and scrap metal that sprang up on the edges or in vacant parts of every large city in America. These were commonly called Hoovervilles, and it was illustrative of Hoover's incomprehension of the disaster that was overwhelming the country that in his memoirs he wrote that the apple peddler was an ingenious marketing device of the apple growers' associations. He wrote that they had induced many people to leave their jobs "for the more profitable one of selling apples." That the explanation for this phenomenon might be the utter destitution of the unemployed seems not to have occurred to the ex-president, writing long after the proportions of the Great Depression had been well documented and had caused his involuntary career change.

Unemployment had climbed to four million, or about 9 percent of the work force, by the end of the summer of 1930. It had approximately doubled in the following year, and continued to rise at the same alarming rate into and through 1932. Roosevelt had convened a conference of governors of neighboring states in Albany in January 1931 to discuss unemployment. It was at this point that he abandoned his Jeffersonian states' rights view of how to deal with the problem. This view had been amplified by his own resentment of Washington's presumptions upon New York State. But he now realized that only a national solution was possible, and began to describe the economic condition of the country as an emergency as serious as war.

The business index declined half a point a week from August 1929 into 1931 and, with minor interruptions, continued on this course through 1932. One year after the 1929 crash, steel production was down 30 percent and automobile production 55 percent.[35] The first major bank failure in New York after the City Trust Company (which had been the victim of an embezzlement problem rather than a Depression casualty) was the Bank of the United States, which closed its doors on December 10, 1930, after a run aggravated by agitators from the nearby 13th Street headquarters of the American Communist Party. Where City Trust had been an institution frequented by the Italian American working class and directed by Italian Americans, the Bank of the United States was a Jewish institution and was locally known as "the pants-pressers' bank." There had been a large element of simple mismanagement in this episode, but Tammany connections were also eventually revealed.

Robert Moses, when commissioned by Lieutenant Governor Lehman to look into the City Trust debacle, had warned that the Bank of the United States could be insolvent. This had not prevented Roosevelt, in the full fugue of his detestation of Moses, from appointing an executive of the Bank of the United States, Henry Pollack, to the special commission he set up to consider Moses' recommendations. (While most of those recommendations were ignored or diluted by the Republican legislators, it is not clear that Roosevelt pressed very hard for their adoption, either.)

In banking matters, Roosevelt tended at this point to follow the advice of Lehman, who, with his family, was steeped in the Wall Street merchant banking tradition. This advice proved too trusting of the competence and the honesty of many of those managing New York's financial institutions in these desperate times. In October 1930, while campaigning for reelection, Roosevelt had representatives of the Bank of the United States and several of the country's greatest banks meet at his home on 65th Street to try to arrange a takeover that would protect the depositors. The talks seemed to be productive but were ultimately unsuccessful. With a proper monitoring and regulatory system, the depositors, at least, of the Bank of the United States would have been rescued.[36]

This was the beginning of the rockslide of the banking system in New York, as the Chelsea Bank and the State Bank of Binghamton folded a few weeks later. Roosevelt evinced no embarrassment about having appointed Pollack to the banking commission and now opened, belatedly in the opinion of some observers, an agitation in favor of the protection of depositors. There was no depositor protection in the United States at this time, other than for those cautious souls who insured their deposits privately. If the bank and thrift equity holders went to the wall, the depositors largely followed them.

In such circumstances, panic was not difficult to generate and was not always unfounded; and as the Communists demonstrated in the Bank of the United States debacle, capitalism's enemies were happy to pitch in. Despite the omens, the New York Republican legislators, faithful to the end to their reactionary death wish, rejected the governor's eloquent and well-publicized advocacy of depositor protection, handing him yet another deadly weapon for his electoral arsenal.

VI

THE NEW YORK CITY municipal scandals were stirred by the slowly grinding wheels of Judge Samuel Seabury's investigation. Seabury was determined to rouse public opinion to force reforms and, incidentally, it was alleged, to confer renown upon himself. The judge had been laborious enough to get Roosevelt through his reelection as governor without further public relations emergencies, but throughout 1931 the public consciousness was shaken by revelations that put Roosevelt's relations with Tammany Hall under great pressure. In a bizarre twist, Seabury's chief counsel, Isidor Kresel, was implicated in the Bank of the United States skulduggery and was forced to resign from the judge's commission, where he had performed very effectively. In the dissolute Byzantine labyrinth of Jimmy Walker's New York, the more sophisticated and cynical players turned up everywhere, like the medieval Italian inspirers of Machiavelli.

Blasé New York public opinion was much more profoundly scandalized when Seabury brought to light that a number of New York women who failed to pay protection money to police officers to avoid arrest had been unjustly convicted of, or at least charged with, prostitution. Mayor Walker "confessed" to be "more or less shocked" and then departed on vacation to Palm Springs. Roosevelt's disquietude was more robust, and on Seabury's recommendation he issued six full pardons to women on parole and handed this investigation entirely to Seabury as well. Tammany started to put it about that Roosevelt's banking superintendent, Joseph Broderick, was up to his eyeballs in improprieties and that the governor was trying to protect him by falling in with Seabury's selection of Tammany as a scapegoat.

One of the women who had been falsely arrested on a vice charge was interviewed by Seabury's investigators, then found strangled in a park in the Bronx the next day. The unfortunate woman's teenage daughter, shocked by the revelations as well as bereaved, committed suicide a week later. New York City asserted its famous penchant for instant transformation from world-weary complacency to big-hearted righteousness. Public opinion exploded. The City Affairs Committee, led by the now, to Roosevelt, tiresomely familiar figure of Rabbi Stephen Wise and other faith and civic leaders, including the even more inevitable socialist leader Norman Thomas and the philosopher John Dewey, issued a public statement virtually putting America's largest city in the company of Sodom and Gomorrah. (They might have found it informative to make a well-organized field trip to Al Capone's Chicago.)

On St. Patrick's Day night, March 17, 1931, Roosevelt returned to his home on 65th Street from an Irish celebratory dinner at the Astor Hotel to find Rabbi Wise and the Reverend John H. Holmes of the Community Church waiting for him in his drawing room. They had come to present him with a 4,000-word petition charging ten counts of gross negligence against Mayor Walker and demanding his dismissal. Roosevelt was trying to run for president, not immerse himself in the civic quagmire of New York City. He rather testily saw his visitors out and a week later gave the charges to Walker to deal with.

Walker composed, without benefit of counsel, a disorganized, emotional, and apparently heartfelt statement of his good intentions, which Roosevelt accepted as an adequate defense. He rejected the petition for removal of Walker on April 27, 1931, but while he was ostensibly considering it, the legislature constituted a committee for the investigation of the government of New York City. With the governor's agreement, Seabury was placed in charge of this investigation too.

Roosevelt looked somewhat indulgently upon Walker as a mischievous but charming scoundrel and a considerable political figure. He was beginning to regard Wise and his apostles as dangerously naïve zealots. (Roosevelt had conferred much prominence on Wise by bringing him into his campaign for old-age security in 1929.) Wise had a well-publicized opinion on everything, and declared that he would oppose assistance to persecuted European Jews, as he would military assistance to a Jewish state in Palestine. People as outspoken as Rabbi Wise usually find themselves on the wrong side of many issues eventually, as he did.

Roosevelt clung as long as he could to a spurious theory of sanctity of local government, departure from which would be "moral cowardice" depriving the country of a much-needed antidote to the "type of new government now in effect in Russia and Italy," as he wrote to the editor of *Forum* magazine, Henry G. Leach, on December 11, 1930. He continued for a time to inflict platitudes on the public about the equal rights to municipal self-rule of Hyde Park and New York City. He steered close to the wind for some months before tacking artfully ahead of it in full sail. Several times he seemed unnecessarily on the verge of losing public support.

Seabury declined to urge removal of Tammany district attorney Thomas Crain, whose prosecution of most crimes, and any to do with his civic masters, was notoriously sluggish. Walker and Tammany boss John Curry had let it be known that they were going to renominate and reelect Crain whatever Seabury did, and the judge did not wish to appear ineffectual.

Acting on the judicial opinion of state court of appeals justice Benjamin Cardozo, Seabury asked Roosevelt for a special session of the legislature to grant statutory immunity to certain witnesses before him, to expedite his proceedings. Roosevelt, on his return in late August 1931, from what must have been a serene respite on the *Inspector* on the waterways of the state, granted this request, though not with any enthusiasm.

At the end of 1931 Seabury officially asked the governor to remove the sheriff of New York County, Thomas M. Farley (not related to James Farley of Rockland). Sheriff Farley had regaled the Seabury Commission with stories of how he had parlayed his $8,500 annual salary into a personal fortune of $400,000 in six years.

When asked where all this money had come from, he replied that it had come from "a tin box" he kept in his safe. Seabury asked if it was a "magic box." Farley acknowledged that it was "a wonderful box."[37] He hilariously described the antics of the Thomas M. Farley Association, which he represented as a harmless social and sporting club that planned picnics and peewee baseball matches. It emerged fairly clearly that the association was an illicit gambling club that had been frequented by Arnold Rothstein and his ilk. Roosevelt removed Farley as sheriff in February 1932.

———————

At the annual governor's conference at French Lick, Indiana, in June 1931, Roosevelt again took the opportunity to outline a program for dealing with the ever-worsening economic crisis. He explicitly called for reduction of tariffs, reduction of most taxes with a more progressive tax system (i.e., more tax from those who could afford it), unemployment and health insurance, and what he called a better balance between rural and urban life.

This last was partly a sop to the ignored farmers and partly an imprecise plan to encourage rural youth to remain on the land. Roosevelt knew better than to try to induce or coerce large numbers of urban dwellers back on the land, but he had a romantic Jeffersonian notion, supplemented by TR's Country Life movement and his own days as a patron of the Boy Scouts, that some might opt for such a course, given the chance. There was a back-to-the-land movement in many depression-racked places, but it was not much of a success, and the whole concept of thinning out the cities in favor of the country was chimerical. Roosevelt was again the star of the governors' conference.

Frances Perkins reckoned that by the autumn of 1931 there were one million unemployed in New York State, a staggering and completely unprecedented figure. It was about 24 percent of the work force, and this number would rise over the next year to about one-third of the work force in New York State and in the country as a whole. The economic crisis was assuming Old Testament proportions. It was not to endure such calamities that the forbears of the American people had embarked on the dangerous enterprise of emigration to the New World (not that the world their ancestors departed was faring any better).

Roosevelt delegated to Samuel Rosenman, as a matter of great urgency, the drafting of an emergency relief bill providing the unemployed with food and clothing and shelter and as much "useful work" as possible, but respecting Roosevelt's aversion to "the dole"—straight cash payments to the idle unemployed. Throughout the Depression, Roosevelt's preference was for workfare rather than cash payments unconnected to any activity. Roosevelt delivered his message in person to the legislature on August 28, 1931, and the Temporary Emergency Relief Administration (TERA) resulted, fairly promptly and in time for the winter of 1931–1932. The governor financed it through modest supplementary taxes on those with relatively high incomes, but it was not overly onerous: $26 more of tax on an income of over $10,000, $402 more of tax on an income of over $50,000, and $1,128 more tax on an income of over $100,000.

In his message and subsequent comments, Roosevelt made it clear that he considered Hoover responsible for the steady deterioration of the country's economic conditions. He condemned what he considered the President's dogmatic refusal to distribute aid directly to those in need, rather than through his well-paid and -fed cronies in big business. He was referring to the Reconstruction Finance Corporation, which could invest only in businesses and could make no direct payments to individuals.

TERA was up and running by early October, and was an initiative that put Franklin D. Roosevelt ahead of any other politician or government executive in the nation in the struggle with the Depression and the scourge of unemployment. Because nothing in Washington or all the other states was as prompt or direct a response to the crisis, it attracted and deserved great national attention and widespread praise. The director was Roosevelt's friend and financial supporter Jesse Straus, president of Macy's department store. In 1931, Straus had commissioned and paid for a very valuable poll of delegates at the 1928 Democratic convention. (The results clearly showed the success of Roosevelt's strategy in befriending the western progressives, the rural population, and the ethnic minorities, even though these elements were underrepresented in the poll. When the poll was published in April 1931, it helped solidify Roosevelt's status as the front-running candidate.)

If Straus was the chairman of the relief effort, the operational head of TERA was a forty-two-year old Iowa-born social worker, Harry Hopkins, who would become Roosevelt's most intimate and versatile collaborator through all the tumultuous and world-shaking events to come. Hopkins was slender, gangling, intense, a chain-smoker and sometimes heavy drinker, but extremely intelligent, tirelessly energetic, and a personality and administrator of very rare capability. By February 1932, TERA was distributing relief to 160,000 New Yorkers, but the state's unemployed had jumped by 50 percent in six months to 1,500,000. Roosevelt proposed in March 1932 that TERA's "life and work" be extended, and allocated $5 million and urged a referendum for a $30-million special bond issue to continue the program to 1934 and broaden it among the proliferating ranks of the helpless victims of the economic crisis. The crisis had finally imposed some discipline of responsibility even on the Republican legislators, who with uncharacteristic docility did what the governor asked. (The New York voters would overwhelmingly approve the bond issue in November 1932.) Faithful to his romantic notions of rural life, Roosevelt had TERA subsidize the resettlement of as many unemployed as possible on marginal farmland, with tools and instruction on how to cultivate it. In six years TERA assisted five million people, 40 percent of the population of New York State, at a cost of $1,555,000. At the end of the period, 70 percent of these were no longer reliant on government assistance.[38]

In his frustration at the meteoric rise of the successor he had beseeched to take his place and be his marionette, Al Smith lashed out almost mindlessly at Roosevelt without choosing his ground with any care. On October 15, 1931, he attacked one of Roosevelt's treasured but uncontroversial hobby horses, a $19 million bond issue to purchase sub-marginal land over eleven years and plant trees on it, strengthening the soil and providing both timber limits and state parkland. Smith claimed the measure was socialistic, because it would (eventually, when the seedlings grew up) put the state in the lumber business in competition with private enterprise. This was an odd complaint for a former brave advocate of public ownership of hydroelectricity.

Edward J. Flynn and Herbert Lehman had called on Al Smith separately in his splendid office on the 32nd floor of Raskob's Empire State Building in September and asked him if he stood by his resolve to refrain from electoral politics. Both had had loyalties to both Smith and Roosevelt and wanted to resolve them honorably. (The Empire State Building, like the equally grandiose and even more magnificent Rockefeller Center fifteen blocks north on Fifth Avenue, would be largely unoccupied for most of the thirties, though immensely successful thereafter.)

Smith emphasized that he did mean what he had said about staying out of politics, because two of his sons and a nephew had been ruined in the early months after the 1929 crash and he felt it his responsibility to pay off their debts. He spread out a sheaf of commercial IOUs on his desk and said he thought it would take him the rest of his life to clear up the mess. He had taken on the chairmanship of the County Trust Company, where his relatives had borrowed. He took the place of the former chairman of the company, James J. Riordan, a family friend and big financial supporter, who had committed suicide in November 1929 when he lost his personal fortune and County Trust became unstable. Smith's presence was intended to reassure depositors and did have that effect. In the circumstances, Smith was obviously very susceptible to the blandishments of Raskob, whose fortune seems not to have been overly affected by the crash.

Roosevelt took Smith's opposition to the bond issue, and the opportunity to crush it, seriously. He drafted a letter that Farley sent to every Democratic worker in the state. Amazingly, the Republicans supported Roosevelt on this question, and Tammany, where Smith was still a grand sachem and a beloved figure, refused to oppose the incumbent governor, recognizing that he was probably all that stood between several of their number and a jail cell. Roosevelt took to the airwaves and the amendment enabling the $19 million bond issue was adopted by referendum by a wide margin, November 3, 1931.

Roosevelt attempted a reconciliation with his predecessor, having proved his point, and invited Smith to lunch with him. This occurred at 65th Street on November 17, 1931, but was not a success. Roosevelt and Smith talked about practically everything under the sun except politics, and Smith left offended that he had merely been exposed to another demonstration of his host's facile manners without coming to grips with the evident rivalry between them. One of their mutual friends, Clark Howell, publisher of the *Atlanta Constitution*, told Roosevelt in early December 1931 that Smith had raged at him that while Roosevelt had always been personally considerate, he had never once asked Smith's advice "on a damned thing" since becoming governor, and had had him to lunch and never mentioned his candidacy for president.

Smith's disillusionment was inevitable, given his total misjudgment of Roosevelt's motives and capacities, but it was aggravated by his successor's breezy and almost sadistic refusal to refer explicitly to the real issues between them. It is hard and useless to apportion blame for the deterioration of their relationship. It was a hazard of their occupation. Al Smith was an outstanding politician, but he was no match for Roosevelt as a national politician.

Chicago mayor Anton Cermak had conferred with Smith and Raskob on November 5, 1931, and declared he wanted a strong anti-Prohibition nominee for president, an evident crack at Roosevelt. Though Cermak did not have the power within the Democratic Party of some of his successors, he was still an important king-maker. Then as subsequently, the mayor of Chicago, in disposing a majority of Illinois' votes, could enforce a unit rule on the state delegation, then the third largest in the country, and deliver Illinois at the national convention. Cermak's position became more important when Chicago was chosen by the Democratic National Committee, under Raskob's urging, to be the site of the 1932 convention. Roosevelt had hoped for Kansas City, where Boss Tom Pendergast could fill the galleries with Roosevelt supporters. The Roosevelt camp was concerned at the consequences if Cermak set out to pack the convention hall against him. The Roosevelt forces did get Robert H. Jackson of New Hampshire installed as secretary of the national committee. His assistance at the convention would be invaluable.

At this point, the governor of Maryland, Albert Ritchie, a staunch opponent of Prohibition, was thought to be a possible stop-Roosevelt candidate, if Smith did not really want to play this role himself. Waiting in the wings in case of a deadlock was Newton Baker and, at least in his imagination, the well-travelled wheel horse William G. McAdoo.

Bernard Baruch, a clever political and financial hustler, objected to a newspaper report by Roosevelt's acolyte Ernest Lindley that Baruch was in league with Raskob, Smith, and Ritchie in the incipient stop-Roosevelt movement. Baruch wrote Roosevelt[39] that FDR would know better than to imagine that there was any truth to such a suggestion. It gave Roosevelt evident pleasure to reply in rather patronizing terms, having been told of Baruch's references to him as "the boy scout governor." (He had said this to Morris L. Cooke.[40]) Roosevelt wrote: "I can not, of course, help knowing of the conversations of some people who profess friendship but nevertheless emit innuendos and false statements behind my back with the blissful assumption that they will never be repeated to me." Baruch was henceforth a good deal more guarded, and even more obsequious to Roosevelt than he had been.

A further wild card from a familiar source was thrown into the game on January 2, 1932. William Randolph Hearst, "his shadow long over the land," as the recently launched and phenomenally successful *Time* magazine put it, took to the radio to lambaste Roosevelt, Smith, Baker, Young, and others he perceived to be dangerous Wilsonian internationalists. Hearst recommended the Speaker of the House, John Nance Garner of Texas, as the Democratic presidential nominee, and followed this up with a front-page editorial to the same effect in all the Hearst newspapers the next day. Garner had not been consulted by Hearst and did not take his own candidacy seriously. He declined to campaign or even speak publicly about it. But he could deprive Roosevelt of a good many southwestern and possibly far-western convention delegates. Hearst could not possibly cooperate with Smith after the venomous disputes they had had, but if the Smith-Raskob elements fell in behind Garner, Roosevelt's nightmare of a deadlocked convention was conceivable.

This was the last time that Hearst would have any serious influence on an American presidential election. As a last hurrah, it was a discreditable intrusion from someone whose sympathies in decisive moments tended to be more with America's enemies than with her allies, though he was always a muscular patriot once the United States herself was directly engaged in hostilities. For a man as familiar with Europe as Hearst was and as discerning as he was in many ways, it was astonishing that he failed to see both the opportunities for America in, and the necessity for Western civilization of, greater U.S. engagement in the world's affairs. The same could be said of the formidable Colonel Robert Rutherford McCormick, proprietor of the *Chicago Tribune*, next to the *New York Times* the country's most influential newspaper.

Hearst's intervention had a substantial impact on the stance of the candidates. Newton Baker, embarking on a Mexican vacation on January 26, told journalists that while he continued to favor League of Nations membership for the United States, he did not want the Democratic platform to take a stand on the issue. This was a straddle that displeased everyone, but it confirmed that Baker too was interested in the nomination. The stop-Roosevelt bandwagon was becoming crowded with discordant office seekers.

Franklin D. Roosevelt announced his candidacy for the office he had been loudly proclaiming he had no wish to occupy by sending a letter on January 22, 1932, to the state Democratic Committee of North Dakota allowing his name to stand in the state's presidential primary. In the letter he pompously declared that it was a great honor to be nominated but that he couldn't campaign in North Dakota, since that would be cavalier toward the thirteen million New Yorkers he was serving by remaining in his state while the legislature was in session. Roosevelt never thereafter cured himself of the habit of aerated pieties about his implacable duty to seek or retain the nation's greatest office, as if his almost insatiable ambition for power had nothing to do with it.

Roosevelt and Howe sent Jim Farley to call on the editor of Hearst's *New York American* a few days later. Colonel House, Joseph Kennedy, and James Michael Curley all tried to persuade Hearst of Roosevelt's virtues. Farley told him that Hearst's outburst against Roosevelt on January 2 was based on the obsolete information that Roosevelt was still a League enthusiast, but that his views had evolved. Hearst was having none of this, and publicly revealed the Farley visit. He demanded that Roosevelt stop playing political "shell games" and added: "If Mr. Roosevelt has any statement to make about his not being an internationalist he should make it to the public publicly, and not to me privately." For once, Hearst had a point; Roosevelt should have known better than to imagine that he could placate so willful, powerful, and experienced a man as Hearst with an embassy of underlings conveying a message of evident flim-flam.

Roosevelt now confirmed the worst fears of those who saw him as Walter Lippmann did, as a slippery, unprincipled, amiable lightweight, "carrying water on both shoulders . . . [and] too eager to please . . . to be a danger to anyone." Lippmann had been scandalized by Roosevelt's shilly-shallying over the Tammany corruption issue, and had favored Charles Tuttle in the 1930 New York gubernatorial election. He was a frequent and acerbic critic, according the governor of New York praise only rarely, as on electric power and emergency relief issues. Roosevelt maneuvered constantly, giving little hint of what he really intended to do, and Lippmann, like so many other professional politicians and political observers, and as he would subsequently acknowledge, seriously underestimated him. Lippmann described Roosevelt in 1932 as a "pleasant man who without any important qualifications for the office, would very much like to be President."*

Lippmann and many people who had been Roosevelt partisans were disgusted by Roosevelt's appeasement of William Randolph Hearst in his address to the New York State Grange in Albany on February 2. Roosevelt tried to distinguish between economic and political internationalism, upheld the traditional Democratic opposition to high tariffs, which Raskob had abandoned, and demanded

---

* Lippmann's critics, as his biographer has pointed out, would never let him forget that assessment.

repayment of war debts owed to the United States. Then Roosevelt recanted on the League of Nations. He declared that he had no apology to make for having supported the League of Nations when he was in the Wilson administration and when he had been a candidate for vice president. But he declared that the League as it had evolved was not the League that Wilson had envisioned and founded. He blamed the failure of the United States to join at the beginning for the degeneration of the League into "a mere meeting place for the political discussion of strictly European political national difficulties." He decried the failure of the leading members of the League to deal with urgent problems such as armaments, declared that American participation would not further the avoidance of war for which the League was conceived, and concluded: "I do not favor American participation."

He was also prepared, as his intimates were aware, to oppose joining the World Court, which even Harding and Coolidge had supported, but Hearst, satisfied at this deference from the leading candidate of his party, was satiated and asked nothing more. Hearst ceased to attack Roosevelt in the same breath with the other internationalists.

Eleanor, in a representative liberal view, was so disappointed with her husband that she didn't speak to him for some time, despite Louis Howe's vigorous attempt to bring her around with a reminder of political realities. One of Eleanor's friends even declined to have lunch with Roosevelt because she did not wish to be asked to mediate with his wife, so "shabby" did she consider the candidate's speech to be.[41]

Shabby it was, but effective and, in its way, intelligent. The League of Nations had become a mere talking shop, and American membership would not in itself have markedly changed the tragic flow of events in the next decade. Only American military alliance with the other democracies would have done that. There was no chance of American public opinion subscribing to any such policy, and no serious American was advocating such a policy on this issue. Eleanor and her enlightened world federalist friends didn't represent anyone except a few feminists and socialists around Washington Square.

What made Roosevelt's performance so disappointing to many commentators was that he appeared to be grovelling to William Randolph Hearst, a celebrated and baroque but politically disreputable figure. But tactically, Roosevelt was adept. He was on the verge of the presidency, Hearst of oblivion. Hearst might have a sensation, one of the last of a political career that had been generally and deservedly unsuccessful, of his own power, but it would be evanescent, if not illusory. If Hearst's comparative goodwill would put Roosevelt over the top as Democratic nominee in a Democratic year, Roosevelt would be able to change the world. The only other candidate who could raise the delegates in sufficient numbers to challenge Roosevelt's two-thirds majority was Smith, unless unimaginable prodigies could be performed for Governor Albert Ritchie. Roosevelt had become ostensibly less internationalist than Newton Baker. Since Hearst could not support Smith because of the extreme animosity between them, Roosevelt had taken another step toward the White House.

In a strange way he had shown an aptitude for leadership. Since the principle of adherence to the League was now a lifeless heirloom of a bygone era with no chance of enactment, this was less of a principle than a tactical and nostalgic detail. In valuing his expedient interest above the approval of the chattering classes and the most energetic moralists (including his own wife), in doffing his cap to the ogre in the castle at San Simeon, he had shown the particular ruthless attachment to a strategic objective that gives rise to unholy alliances of convenience.

When courage was required and principles were important, Franklin D. Roosevelt would usually not be found wanting. When tactical skill was necessary to achieve a potential strategic advantage, Franklin D. Roosevelt would not be found wanting then, either. Whatever columnists, academics, or feminists might think about it, he was the pre-eminent Democrat and the Republican era was about to expire. His standing as a man who had mastered illness, as the successful governor of the country's most populous state, as a political leader of great dexterity, and as an inspiring figure in depressing times was very considerable. The office sought the man, which was convenient, because the man was ardently seeking the office.

PART II

The Great Depression and the New Deal

1932–1938

CHAPTER 6

"Stay Alive 'til November"

*(Vice presidential nominee John Nance Garner's advice
to Franklin D. Roosevelt on how to win the 1932 election)*

I

ALFRED E. SMITH, reversing what he had said to Edward J. Flynn and Herbert H. Lehman just a few months before, announced on February 8, 1932, that he was "available" (i.e., running) for the Democratic nomination for president. This came less than three weeks after Roosevelt had launched his candidacy. (Raskob had presumably alleviated the Smith family's financial discomfort.) Ten days after that, William G. McAdoo announced his support for John Nance Garner. Smith's move would open up a serious challenge for control of the New York delegation and McAdoo's would attach some, possibly all, of California's votes to Garner's and Hearst's diversion. The general effect was to chip away at the big block of convention votes that had already been assembled on behalf of Roosevelt.

The continuing crisis of Tammany ethics and scandals became ever more dangerous in light of the contest of Smith and Roosevelt for Tammany, for New York, and for both the reform and the machine vote in big-city states outside New York. Roosevelt tried to follow a middle path, giving the steady procession of Tammany accused plentiful opportunity to clear themselves and when they could not, removing them. To Tammany he claimed to be the most benign regime they had any chance of seeing in Albany; to the reformers in New York and outside, he was the most effective sweeper-out of machine corruption New York had had in many decades. And he was uprooting it with a deliberateness and respect for due process that would make it practically impossible for the weeds to return. Even Roosevelt couldn't walk this tightrope for long, because the machine demanded vengeance for the heat that was put on it. And Rabbi Wise and the Reverend Holmes kept producing demands for the removal of junior officials, supported by herniating wads of incontrovertible evidence of their skulduggery.

On March 30, Roosevelt issued a public letter accusing Wise and Holmes of being publicity hounds less concerned with clean government than with the augmentation of their own celebrity status. This was an unjust as well as an inexpedient charge. Wise and Holmes were tiresome in the manner of strident, godly, righteous men, but there was nothing wrong with their motives, and their charges were never unsubstantiated. Roosevelt's irritation at their endless immersion in secular politics was understandable, but the answer to it was to clean up government by conventional means, liberating the clergy to go back to pastoral and theological matters.

By contrast, his conduct in response to the indictment of his banking superintendent, Joseph A. Broderick, showed the most admirable side of Roosevelt. Tammany had complained that the Bank of the United States debacle had been not so much a failure due to machine infiltration as a botch by the governor's own appointee. When Seabury's commission had wrung an indictment against Broderick from the grand jury in October 1931, Roosevelt stuck with his superintendent publicly and privately when many men launching their campaigns for president would have cut him loose. Roosevelt constantly sent him letters of encouragement over the New Year's holiday and then, at great inconvenience to himself, testified voluntarily at his trial. There he declared that much of the oversight of the state's two hundred licensed banks properly resided with the governor and not the superintendent. Seabury's prosecutor declined to cross-examine the governor, who had effectively cowed him in his own court. Broderick was acquitted. When he was able to, Roosevelt named Broderick to the Federal Reserve Board.

Walter Lippmann, Eleanor Roosevelt, and others should have paid more attention to this episode than to the gesture to Hearst over the League of Nations. Roosevelt had shown unshakable loyalty to his own (almost certainly innocent) protégé. He had served notice on Tammany that they could not drag the governor into the dock with them. He had shown the reformers that if they wanted to prosecute the machine, they had better make clearer distinctions between the guilty and the innocent. He had shown that disregard for him and the power of the position he now occupied in U.S. public affairs could be detrimental to anyone's political career.

In mid-March 1932, Samuel Rosenman, whom Roosevelt was nominating to fill an unexpired term on the New York Supreme Court, advised him to assemble from the universities the beginnings of a team that could provide him with adequate background on the whole range of issues they would shortly be getting into and to provide the volume of speeches that would be necessary. This was the origin of the famous "Brain Trust" that gave Roosevelt a great advantage over his rivals in the quality of his policy positions and potential for rapid reaction to requirements for stances on new issues. (Roosevelt first called it the "privy council" but soon saw the dangers of that name.) Up to this point it had just been Howe executing tactical moves, Flynn and Farley pressed into service on special projects and delegate collection, and Rosenman cracking off the odd speech.

None of them had much to do with policy, other than frequent outbursts of opportunistic pandering by Howe, who considered all policy an adjunct to electioneering, and a few legal concepts of Rosenman's.

Raymond Moley, a Columbia political science professor whom Rosenman had recruited from time to time to provide the governor with some specialized advice, was invited to round up a few other faculty members who could give the Roosevelt campaign some intellectual energy and ensure that it was more than competitive with anyone else in policy areas. Party platforms were not so much policy manifestoes as a few talking points on a couple of perennial questions. Roosevelt would change that, too.

Rosenman, Moley, and Basil O'Connor (Roosevelt's law partner) met and agreed upon two new recruits, who accepted the draft: Rexford G. Tugwell as an agricultural expert and Adolf A. Berle as an authority on public finance and credit. Tugwell was in some respects an odd choice, because he had become such a strident advocate of economic planning that he was effectively an authoritarian opponent of many manifestations of the free market. Roosevelt recognized fairly early on that he would have to treat Tugwell's views with caution. Moley brought Tugwell to see Roosevelt in the third week of March 1932. They stayed for dinner in the mansion in Albany. Meeting Roosevelt, Tugwell wrote twenty-five years later, "was somewhat like coming into contact with destiny itself."[1]

On April 7 Roosevelt gave a nationwide radio address that borrowed a good deal from Tugwell, advocating comprehensive planning to restore purchasing power to the agricultural sector, mortgage relief through aid to local agencies, public-works projects to relieve unemployment, and reduced tariffs. Roosevelt attacked Hoover's Reconstruction Finance Corporation as a feedbag for the president's friends in big business. He coined the phrase "the forgotten man at the bottom of the economic pyramid" and purported to be speaking for him. The address caused considerable controversy, and Moley worried that Roosevelt might be displeased. The reverse was true, because the candidate was more concerned with appearing radical enough to enlist the forces of discontent than he was with upsetting his socioeconomic peers, whose slights he had not forgotten and for whose political acumen he would never have the slightest respect.

Al Smith responded in a Jefferson Day dinner on April 13 that he would "fight to the end against any candidate who persists in any demagogic appeal to the masses of the working people of this country to destroy themselves by setting class against class or rich against poor." It was clearly meant as an attack on Roosevelt. The battle for the nomination was shaping up as an effort by Smith to deny Roosevelt the two-thirds majority, with the Hearst-Garner-McAdoo group poised to cast the decisive vote or even benefit from a deadlock. Roosevelt responded to Smith in St. Paul, Minnesota, on April 18. He spoke of his well-known views of hydroelectric utilities and called for a "concert of interests" in the country. Though his remarks were more hortatory than specific, apart from utility questions, Walter Lippmann pronounced them worthy of "ungrudging praise." On his way west, Roosevelt learned that the great Insull utilities group had collapsed. This was another hard shock to public confidence.

Where Tugwell was a rurally originated pure academic from the Wharton School, the University of Washington, and Columbia, Adolf Berle had a varied background. He graduated from Harvard aged eighteen, having entered at only fourteen. He had been a Russian expert in Wilson's entourage at Versailles at the age of twenty-four.* With Gardiner C. Means he wrote *The Modern Corporation and Private Property*, a very influential book for many years, the basic point of which was concern at the concentration of American economic power in relatively few hands. It was published in 1932, but its contents were fairly well known for at least a year prior to that. Berle and Means and Berle and Louis Faulkner (a young economist with whom he produced a lengthy policy paper in 1932) predicted that without drastic planning measures, the United States would shortly be at the brink of violent revolution. Their principal practical proposals were for regulating security issues, recognizing the Soviet Union, tying debt cancellation to tariff reduction, restructuring the banking system along retail-branch lines, amending monopolies legislation to allow for monopolies and for their regulation, and establishing a comprehensive system of old age, sickness, and unemployment insurance. It was an imaginative though uneven series of proposals.

Roosevelt arranged for Moley to preside over a group—including Tugwell, Berle, and Rosenman—that would prepare a series of positions for him on this range of issues by the time he returned from Warm Springs at the end of May 1932. Primaries and state delegate selections had been rolling in favorably:† Boss Tom Pendergast, the only one of the big city bosses to support FDR and an admirer since the 1924 convention, arranged for Missouri to cast some votes for its own senator but gradually to deliver itself wholly to Roosevelt over several ballots to create a sense of momentum if it was needed.

Senators Joe Robinson of Arkansas and Alben Barkley of Kentucky withdrew as favorite son candidates, and Barkley endorsed Roosevelt. Former national committee chairman Homer Cummings of Connecticut had visited Barkley on Roosevelt's behalf with an offer of convention temporary chairman and keynote speaker in place of Shouse. Since such appointments were by majority vote of the convention, Roosevelt could deliver. Barkley accepted and brought Kentucky in behind him for Roosevelt.

Roosevelt had already craftily outmaneuvered Shouse and Raskob at a

---

* In company with Walter Lippmann, William Bullitt, future secretary of state Christian Herter, and future admiral Samuel E. Morrison. And with Bullitt and Morrison, Moley resigned in protest over the agreement that emerged (Chapter 3).

† New Hampshire, Minnesota, North Dakota, Georgia, Iowa, Maine, Wisconsin, South Dakota, Kansas, Wyoming, Arizona, New Mexico, Montana, Oregon, Nevada, Colorado, Utah, Alabama, West Virginia, Florida, and Mississippi, where Senator Pat Harrison narrowly retained control for Roosevelt, had all come in favorably. (Warm Springs, Georgia, voted 218 to one for Roosevelt.)

preparatory meeting on April 4, 1932. Several of his committee members had committed themselves to Shouse as temporary convention chairman, thinking the position merely honorific. Roosevelt, in order not to seem completely duplicitous, dictated to Farley a declaration "commending" rather than "recommending" Shouse. This was approved, and the Roosevelt forces then were able to dump Shouse in favor of Barkley. It required a subtle grasp of casuistry to produce this sophistical formula. This was vintage Roosevelt, and a foretaste of techniques of his that would become increasingly familiar.

Michigan, under the lead of Detroit mayor Frank Murphy, came in solidly for Roosevelt. Murphy was assisted by the city controller, Eleanor Roosevelt's brother, Hall. The radio priest Charles E. Coughlin, from Royal Oak, Michigan (later notorious for his controversial views), came with Murphy to see Roosevelt in New York and offered to speak in his favor on his radio program, which enjoyed a steadily growing audience.

Huey Long, persuaded by Burton Wheeler and George Norris (who was officially a Republican), threw Louisiana in for Roosevelt. A contesting delegation was formed and Huey Long turned the battle into a complete farce by recruiting a further contesting delegation. His loyalty to Roosevelt was assured because delegations, too, when contested, were seated by a majority vote of the whole convention, and the Roosevelt forces clearly already had that.

Tammany stuck with Al Smith. Flynn brought in the Bronx for Roosevelt and the governor held most of the upstate delegates, but the other four boroughs of New York City were solid for Smith under Tammany's influence.

On April 26, Massachusetts in its primary, which Boston's Mayor Curley had talked Roosevelt into entering, voted three to one for Smith over Roosevelt. The same day Roosevelt narrowly carried the Pennsylvania primary. Rhode Island, Connecticut, and New Jersey went to Smith, and California voted for Garner, with 214,000 votes to Roosevelt's 169,000 and Smith's 137,000. Smith and McAdoo arranged a reconciliation over the telephone, a remarkable alliance for the two men who had so radically divided the Democratic Party in 1924. These were not welcome developments for Roosevelt; the factions opposed to him had now locked arms and were clearly not going to be blown away by the first volley from the front-runner.

Ohio supported its native son, Governor George White, but these votes would move to fellow Ohioan Newton Baker if White didn't gain momentum. Chicago's Mayor Anton Cermak held Illinois for native son candidate Senator Hamilton Lewis. The Indiana vote was fragmented. McAdoo, the leading California politician and a champion of the Prohibitionists, came out for Garner, who for the last twelve years had exclaimed as he reached for his bourbon: "Let's strike a blow for liberty!" Smith, McAdoo, Garner, Ritchie, and Baker had created enough doubt about the strength of the Roosevelt bandwagon that local candidates tied up a sufficient number of votes to deny Roosevelt the two-thirds required for nomination.

The unit rule, binding all delegates from a state to the candidate who won a majority, created some anomalies. In Connecticut, Homer Cummings, a key Roosevelt organizer, was bound to vote for Smith. And in Kansas, Jouett Shouse was compelled by the governor, Harry Woodring, who held the state for Roosevelt, to vote with the other Kansas delegates for the New York governor.

The problem of dealing with New York City's scandals also flared up again, as Seabury unearthed the fact that Mayor Walker had deposited more than one million dollars in his own bank accounts in the last five years. There was a series of transactions linking Walker to official favors conferred on his contributors, including the Equitable Coach and Checker Cab companies. Seabury subpoenaed Walker, who testified all one day in May 1932. He didn't deal with the court's serious questions, and many of his answers were tossed off with the mayor's well-known wit and felicity.

The pressure on Roosevelt to face up to the Walker problem was now overwhelming. Walter Lippmann was far from the only critic of Roosevelt's handling of this issue. Lippmann described it as a "squalid mess" that had arisen because of the "weakness and timidity" of the governor of New York. The major newspapers were now calling for Roosevelt to sack Walker. Roosevelt sent Seabury's transcript of the mayor's appearance before him, and his fifteen unanswered accusations of corruption and abuse of office, to Walker for reply, having previously said that he had no evidence to justify removing Walker. The mayor said that he would reply after the convention. So, as one historian put it, "Roosevelt was forced to go through the convention with the putrefying Walker albatross around his neck."[2] Hoover had been dejectedly renominated on June 16. The Democrats began to gather in Chicago ten days later.

The Roosevelt effort was planned down to the last detail by Louis Howe from the "Friends of Roosevelt" headquarters on Madison Avenue. He had a large map of the United States on which all those states that had committed wholly or largely to Roosevelt were colored pink. It was such a formidable array of states that he had a duplicate map made and displayed on James A. Farley's convention headquarters wall in Chicago. Howe composed a ninety-second message of greeting that Roosevelt read into a microphone in his most honeyed tones. Howe sent a record of this message, a personal letter from the candidate, and an individually autographed photograph of him to every delegate.

Howe mobilized the vast network of the party faithful with which he had been keeping in touch since Roosevelt's campaign for vice president twelve years before. (Usually Howe's correspondents thought they were communicating with the governor, because Howe used his stationery and had a secretary who was expert at forging Roosevelt's confident signature.) Howe arranged for Farley to have a three-room suite at the convention site, the Chicago Stadium (then the largest indoor sports arena in the world) where Farley would buttonhole or harangue delegates or conspire with Roosevelt operatives in the middle room.

The adjoining rooms would serve as sonic insulation and would be occupied by Roosevelt agents who would ensure the absence of listening devices.

Howe imported his own switchboard operator to take over the Roosevelt head-quarters switchboard in the Congress Hotel. He arranged a direct line to the executive mansion in Albany and attached a loudspeaker to the telephone in the sitting room of his own suite on the seventeenth floor, so that Roosevelt could directly address delegates convened by Howe. He frequently did so in the next few days, his disembodied voice ringing out: "My friends of Virginia!" or what-ever. Access to Howe's suite was only upon approval of his son Hartley and his secretary, Margaret "Rabbit" Durand. Farley and Flynn, prepared for a massive recruitment and proselytization effort, had suites on different floors of the same hotel.

Howe left New York for Chicago on the luxury train the Twentieth Century Limited with Nancy Cook and Marion Dickerman on June 23. After an agreeable dinner they retired, having agreed to reconvene for breakfast in the dining car the next morning. When Howe did not appear for breakfast, his companions became alarmed and prevailed upon the conductor to open his room, where they found Howe in the midst of one of his asthmatic seizures, grey, gasping, prostrate in his bed, and apparently on the verge of death. But Howe soon revived, suppressed his cough, regained color, sat up, and began to function, growling at those who had tried to help him and demanding the newspapers (He had done the same thing years before, when he had been pronounced dead and then opened his eyes and gone about his business as if nothing unusual had occurred.)

On the eve of Howe's arrival in Chicago, Farley had convened about sixty-five key supporters to concert strategy. Louisiana's colorful and crafty leader Huey P. Long called for the abolition of the requirement for a two-thirds majority for nomination. Howe and Farley doubted this measure could pass, because of the desire of many states, especially in the South, to conserve greater leverage over the convention as a whole. Farley's effort to shut the measure down failed and Long spoke for his own motion, supported by Burton Wheeler, Senator Cordell Hull of Tennessee, Roosevelt's old boss Josephus Daniels, and Homer Cum-mings. Long's measure passed and had the effect that Howe and Farley had pre-dicted. Outrage was expressed by all the living former presidential candidates (Smith, Davis, and Cox), by McAdoo and Newton Baker (both of whom were angling for a deadlock), by Virginia's influential Senator Carter Glass, and by Sam Rayburn, Garner's floor manager and the House of Representatives whip.

John Raskob gaveled the convention to order on the morning of Monday, June 27. At the same time Roosevelt sent a statement from Albany opposing the move to eliminate the two-thirds majority rule. He declared that the rule was indeed undemocratic but that inadequate notice of a motion to eliminate the rule was unfair, and that he was therefore asking his supporters, an undoubted majority at the convention, to desist. He did ask the rules committee to take some steps to ensure that there not be a hopelessly deadlocked convention. His supporters on the committee, led by Huey Long, picked up this request and moved for adoption of a majority rule after six ballots. Amid screams of trickery from the stop-Roosevelt forces, Farley barely prevailed upon the rules committee to drop the whole initiative.

Chicago was suffering through the Depression in a desperate condition. The city had 700,000 unemployed, more than 40 percent of its workforce. The collapse of Samuel Insull's utilities pyramid had thoroughly deflated the Chicago financial community. Even former vice president Charles G. Dawes's Central Republic Bank, one of Chicago's greatest financial institutions, was teetering on the brink of insolvency, unknown for some months to the public, and was salvaged only at the last minute by an emergency loan of $90 million from the Reconstruction Finance Corporation (from the presidency of which Dawes had just abruptly resigned), on the orders of President Hoover himself. (The loan was only $5 million less than the total deposits of the bank and three times what the federal government would lend to the states for direct relief in 1932. Even then it would be insufficient—Dawes's bank shortly closed.) The city owed $20 million in back pay to schoolteachers. Chicago, like the whole nation, was in utter despair.

After the bewigged and mustachioed Senator Hamilton Lewis, at Farley's incessant urgings, released the Illinois delegates, Chicago's mayor, Anton Cermak, prevailed upon Melvin Traylor, chief executive of Chicago's First National Bank, to become the favorite son candidate from Illinois, and held the state's fifty-eight delegates en bloc and free of the serious candidates. On the evening of June 26, William G. McAdoo, Alfred E. Smith, and Herbert Bayard Swope met in Bernard Baruch's hotel suite. The fervor of the anti-Roosevelt forces had reached a point where the two men who had so severely split the 1924 convention would parley and even so cunning a man as Baruch would take them seriously. The issue of this meeting was that Smith and McAdoo both believed that if they could keep Roosevelt under two-thirds for four ballots, they could stampede delegates wary of a hung convention away from him. At that point, they and a few others would sit down and choose the candidate. It was understood that it would not be Smith, but the probable choice was not agreed, though participants subsequently expressed the consensus that Newton Baker was the most likely.

Smith, Raskob, Tammany boss John Curry, New Jersey boss Frank Hague, and such disparate figures as Walter Lippmann, Clare Booth Brokaw (later Mrs. Henry Luce), *New York Times* columnist Arthur Krock, and Judge Samuel Seabury were all milling about Chicago trying to stop Roosevelt. But they weren't very enthusiastic about each other. (The future Mrs. Luce promised to start a women's party if Roosevelt was nominated.) Smith described the optimism of the Roosevelt camp as "Farley's Fairy Stories."[3]

Senator Alben W. Barkley gave a stemwinding two-hour keynote address, heaping obloquy on the Hoover administration. The platform committee, chaired by Cordell Hull and former attorney general Mitchell Palmer, signed off on a "covenant with the people," a brief, largely economic document calling for a reduced tariff, balanced budget, reduced federal expenditures but increased public works for combating unemployment, and insurance schemes for the elderly and the unemployed operated by the states.

The platform was partly dictated by Roosevelt and was much to his liking, but it was obviously impossible. None of the people associated with it, including the candidates ultimately elected on it, could have imagined it was remotely possible to provide such relief in a country suffering from an unemployment rate of approximately 30 percent while reducing expenditures. (This did not prevent Lippmann from claiming that the platform was the best of either major party in twenty years.)

The convention, driven by Roosevelt's majority of the delegates, seated the pro-Roosevelt delegations from Louisiana and Minnesota, where there had also been a contest, while Huey Long clowned and joked. The convention also elevated Roosevelt loyalist Senator Thomas Walsh of Montana as permanent chairman of the convention over Shouse.

The only serious debate was over Prohibition, and Al Smith easily carried a strongly worded demand for full repeal. There were huge demonstrations while the great pipe organ mockingly thundered out "How Dry I Am."[4] Roosevelt wisely avoided the controversy, making it clear that he was for repeal and would live happily with any version of repeal. He lost no support by his stance, while Smith further antagonized the bedraggled "drys" like Josephus Daniels. Drys preferred Roosevelt's line, which he had used in his 1930 reelection campaign in New York, "Bread not Booze." His own feelings were not less emphatic than Smith's on this issue, but Roosevelt knew how not to grate on the sensibilities of a large bloc of his fellow Democrats.

As the many candidates were placed in nomination, the atmosphere of intense political gossip and horse-trading became febrile. Farley met with the leaders of the Texas delegation, Silliman Evans and Sam Rayburn, and informally explored the possibility of Garner retiring in favor of Roosevelt and becoming his vice presidential running mate. The Texans spoke well of Roosevelt and swore not to drag the convention out as in 1924. McAdoo was happy to cooperate with his old enemy Smith, but had not made his peace with another old enemy, Baker, the likely beneficiary of a successful resistance to Roosevelt. Howe was doubtful that much could be done with the Texans and was preoccupied with Virginia, at that point pledged to favorite son candidate Harry Flood Byrd. Roosevelt was called upon to adjudicate between the Howe and Farley strategies by telephone and urged both to continue what they were doing, Farley courting Texas and Howe Virginia.

Franklin D. Roosevelt was nominated by his old patron, Judge John E. Mack

of Poughkeepsie, who had first attracted him into public life in 1910. Claude
Bowers had regretfully declined this honor because he didn't want to offend his
employer, W.R. Hearst.[5] Mack's was an uninspiring speech that aroused little
enthusiasm and was followed by Roosevelt's chosen song, "Anchors Aweigh."
Howe and Flynn, agitated by the mounting tension of the convention and by
Mack's ineptitude as an orator, demanded a new anthem. Both later claimed the
credit for choosing "Happy Days Are Here Again." Whoever caused that tune to
be substituted, it became identified with Franklin D. Roosevelt ever after.

The nominating procedures dragged interminably on into the early morning
of Friday, July 1. The Roosevelt camp decided to hold the convention in session
all night to start the voting, hoping that tiredness would militate in favor of an
early result. The roll was called for the first ballot starting at 4:25 A.M. The almost
empty galleries, which Cermak had largely packed with Smith supporters,
refilled promptly and loudly cheered Curry's and Mayor Jimmy Walker's votes
for Smith. The result gave Roosevelt 664¼ votes to 201¼ for Smith and 90¼ for
Garner, with the gaggle of favorite sons taking the rest except for 8½ Indiana votes
for Baker. Roosevelt cleared a majority by 89 votes but fell 104 short of two-thirds.

The second ballot was called at once and produced a similar result. Roosevelt
inched up to 677¾, Smith eased to 195¼ and Garner and Baker and most of the
favorite sons were practically unchanged. Roosevelt's modest gain was due to the
prearranged, phased-in support of Boss Tom Pendergast of Kansas City.[6] The
stop-Roosevelt advocates were insistent on proceeding at once with a third ballot.
It produced another slight gain for Roosevelt, again largely thanks to Pendergast,
to 682.79 votes. Smith retained 194½ and Garner moved up to 101¼.

There had been great strains on the Mississippi delegation in particular, but
Huey Long and Pat Harrison held the Deep South in place for Roosevelt. It was
9:15 A.M. when the results of the third ballot were announced, and there was no
opposition when McAdoo, seconded by Roosevelt's floor manager, Arthur
Mullen, moved to adjourn until 8:30 that evening. Many felt the Roosevelt bandwagon had stalled.

Howe's physical condition deteriorated under the strain of the convention,
although he did not leave his suite in the first five days he was in Chicago. By Friday morning, he was prostrate on the floor on his back, scarcely audible, and with
two electric fans focused on his face. Farley, Flynn, and a few of the other senior
strategists came to meet with him at 11 A.M. Farley, to speak confidentially, had to
lie down on the floor beside Howe and whisper into his ear. It was agreed that
now was the time to concentrate all effort on Texas.

There has been much controversy in subsequent years to the effect that Roosevelt was within one ballot of losing the convention in a stampede to Baker.
Whether that is true will never be known, but much of Roosevelt's support was
quite solid. While Smith could support Baker, McAdoo would not, and Garner,
given his dependence on Hearst, would not either. This convention was more

likely to be like that of 1912, where Wilson's vote grew gradually. Roosevelt could certainly have slipped, and Baker, using Smith as a building block, could have challenged strongly. But Roosevelt was unlikely to implode like a fallen soufflé; he could expect to pick up his share of each departing candidate's support. Baker was sixty years old, had had a heart attack four years before, and, while a respected former war secretary, was not an especially galvanizing figure.

Smith, beloved and courageous figure though he had been in the past, was in Chicago obviously only as a spoiler. He had no chance of winning; his support was now down to Tammany, the Jersey City machine, delegates from the most heavily Catholic parts of New England, and little else. H.L. Mencken was right when he wrote that Smith now "was animated only by his fierce hatred of Roosevelt, the cuckoo who had seized his nest. He has ceased to be the wonder and glory of the East Side and becomes simply a minor figure of Park Avenue." (Mencken, obsessed by Prohibition, was less accurate when he prophesied that in endorsing repeal, the Democrats had lost the election.)[7]

Garner's candidacy was a favorite son operation that never got beyond the Lone Star state and California, despite William Randolph Hearst's attempt to breathe wind into its sails. McAdoo's availability was even flimsier. Unlike Garner, McAdoo had some autonomy from Hearst and some ambition for national office. If he had moved effectively now, he might have been able to write a brilliant final chapter of his career. He didn't.

C.H. Cramer, a reputable historian, later wrote that in interviews with Newton Baker, Baker claimed that on the afternoon of July 1, Franklin D. Roosevelt called him and offered to withdraw in his favor if that was his wish. No one else has ever referred to such a conversation, and no one else among the many who have written their own intimate recollections of all these events has ever suggested anything remotely resembling it. It is possible that Roosevelt called Baker with a provisional offer conditional on a dwindling of his own support. A master of obfuscation, Roosevelt was capable of intimating almost anything, but a direct offer to withdraw unconditionally is inconceivable. While Baker may have been confused, Roosevelt was not.[8]

The end came suddenly on the first of July. Joseph Kennedy telephoned William Randolph Hearst at his magnificent palace at San Simeon, California, at 5 A.M. Pacific Time. It was not the least of the many feats of ingenuity in Kennedy's extraordinary career that he managed to get through at that inconvenient hour when many others had failed. Kennedy emphasized that if Hearst and Garner did not throw their support to Roosevelt, Smith or Baker would win and everything Hearst detested in internationalism, demagogy (in Smith's case), or enfeebled upper-class altruism in Baker's, would prevail. Hearst agreed and said he would urge Garner to withdraw. Hearst wrote to his wife that Garner had responded "nobly."[9]

Hearst's wishes were conveyed to Garner by Hearst's Washington bureau chief. When Farley spoke to Sam Rayburn shortly before noon that day and conveyed the same message, Rayburn replied, "We'll see what can be done." Garner telephoned Rayburn at 3 P.M. and said it was time to nominate Roosevelt as the clear choice of the convention. He had no interest in the vice presidency, which he dismissed as "not worth a bucket of warm piss." He would prefer to remain as Speaker of the House of Representatives.

Rayburn prevailed in the Texas delegation caucus at 6:30 P.M., but with great difficulty and by only two votes, preserving the unit rule and delivering the entire delegation to Roosevelt. On his way to this meeting Rayburn had talked with McAdoo, who addressed a stormy meeting of the California delegation in a neighboring room starting at 7 P.M. The decision of when to move away from Garner was entrusted to a committee of four, on which McAdoo was the dominant personality. When the fourth ballot of the reassembled convention began, California, as the fourth state alphabetically, came up after only a couple of minutes, and McAdoo sought and received unanimous consent to explain his state's position.

He began by saying that California's delegation had come to Chicago to nominate a president of the United States, not deadlock a convention. The hall erupted in noise and disorder for half an hour, until the convention chairman, Thomas Walsh, summoned Mayor Cermak to the podium and demanded that he quiet his partisans, which the mayor, with difficulty, accomplished. McAdoo then concluded, thanking the convention for its "compliment" and urging delegates to fight the Republicans and not each other. He then cast all his state's votes for Franklin D. Roosevelt and the rockslide of delegates began. McAdoo had waited too long and did not receive the payoff he sought. He had finished Smith's career, returning Smith's damage to him in the 1924 convention. Garner, who desired only to remain as Speaker of the House, received the vice presidential nomination, a reward he would have preferred to avoid.

Mayor Cermak and the Illinois delegation, the third largest in the convention, and the packed galleries with it, fell in behind California and in lockstep with Texas. Only Smith's 190½ resisted. He held 63 of New York's 94 votes, 14½ of Pennsylvania's 76, plus Connecticut, Massachusetts, New Jersey, Rhode Island, and a scattered few others.

The fact that Smith held on to most of the New York delegation shows the importance of Roosevelt's narrow gubernatorial victory in 1928. Roosevelt was the only Democrat apart from Smith who could have won the New York governorship in 1928. If he had not run, or had lost, Smith almost certainly could have gained renomination and a fifth term as governor of New York in 1930. Smith then probably could have been renominated for president in 1932. He probably would have won, but, as the economic nostrums he sponsored during the thirties demonstrated, he could not have been as effective in dealing with the Depression as Roosevelt was, and he knew nothing of international affairs.

In these scenarios, Roosevelt could have become governor in 1932, and could have had a crack at the presidency in 1936 or 1940, depending on Smith's performance. But Smith's conscription of Roosevelt as the candidate for governor in 1928 and Roosevelt's hair's-breadth victory in that election were decisive events in American and world history, ultimately more important than Roosevelt's subsequent elections, which were virtually inevitable in the prevailing circumstances, with the partial exception of 1940.

Lost in contemporary (and most historic) analysis was the fact that if Roosevelt had not placated Hearst as he did in his "shabby" address to the New York Grange in April, and even in his support of Hearst's candidate for U.S. senator from New York in 1922, Royal Copeland, he could have lost the 1932 nomination. Apart from the minor indignity incurred in any deference to the overbearing and slightly mad publisher, Roosevelt had lost virtually nothing, but had won the right to rebuild America and, ultimately, the world. If he had not made these gestures, Hearst would not have responded as he did to the importunings of Kennedy and others. And the results would have been unpredictable.*

A disgusted Smith left the hall in Chicago before the vote was officially announced, without releasing his delegates, preventing the customary move to unanimous acclamation. Roosevelt's old adversary and now ardent recent supporter James Gerard, the party treasurer, sent Mrs. Charles Dana Gibson, a close friend of Smith's, to the gallery to ask Smith to move a unanimous nomination. She returned after a few minutes with Smith's reply: "I won't do it," repeated mindlessly and fixedly as in a mantra. The proportions of his underestimation of Roosevelt and of the madness of insisting that Roosevelt take his place as governor of New York must finally have become evident to him. It was an unsportsmanlike and therefore uncharacteristic and unseemly end to Smith's great career as the official Democratic Party leader. Even now he could have salvaged a significant role for himself, albeit in a subordinate position to someone formerly junior to him, had he behaved sensibly. Instead he opted for a bitter exile and was marginalized as an ever-popular figure of a receding past (whom Mencken had once described as "the greatest rabble-rouser since Peter the Hermit").

---

* Given his ambitions, Hearst should have cleaned up his own behavior, rationalized his opinions for the several preceding years, when he could see a Democratic victory coming, and taken the vice presidential nomination for himself, which probably could have been negotiated with Roosevelt. At his best Hearst would have been a stylish vice president and would have had something to show for the political exertions of his long life. He would probably even have avoided the financial embarrassment that befell him in 1937, the consequence of decades of extravagance as a collector and builder. Instead, he said: "I have had my day in politics. It was not a very long day, nor a very brilliant one. But it is over."[10]

Walsh declared Roosevelt the Democratic nominee for president, with 945 votes, at 10:32 P.M. July 1, 1932. He then read a message from the nominee stating that he would, for the first time in American conventions, come in person the next day to accept his party's nomination.

II

FRANKLIN D. ROOSEVELT emplaned from Albany at 7:30 A.M. on July 2, 1932, for Chicago in a Ford tri-motor, accompanied by his wife and all their children (except Franklin Jr.), both his secretaries, and his principal security men. The flight took almost ten hours, with stops at Buffalo and Cleveland, strong headwinds, and considerable turbulence. The candidate dozed off for parts of the trip, as oblivious of the vagaries of air travel as he always was of rough seas when sailing, and showing the serenity at key moments of his career that never deserted him.

Louis Howe finally left his hotel suite to greet the nominee at the Chicago airport and sat with him in the open car downtown, through streets packed with huge and enthusiastic crowds. After having given over his life to Roosevelt these twenty years Howe was entitled to this one public moment at least. Howe had taxed his exhausted constitution by sitting up most of the night writing a speech for Roosevelt's acceptance that he purported to believe Roosevelt should deliver on faith, discarding the address that Roosevelt himself and Moley and Rosenman had prepared.

Roosevelt, who had always had the remarkable gift of being able to do at least two things at once ever since he worked on his stamp collection while listening to his mother read the classics to him when a small boy, glanced at it while waving his hat to scores of thousands of people from the back of his open car on his way downtown. He adapted Howe's first page to the address that had already been prepared; the rest of Howe's draft was not at all appropriate, but this enabled Roosevelt to call Howe a coauthor of what would be a historic speech.

Roosevelt began his remarks at the convention shortly after 7 P.M. with Howe's assertion that his appearance personally at the convention was "unprecedented and unusual" (in his exhaustion, Howe did not notice that the first implied the second) but that so were the times. He proposed various employment schemes, including one of reforestation that he said was a great success in New York. (Hoover's researchers shortly revealed that his program employed only 72 people full-time and 272 part-time. Roosevelt was sheepish with Rosenman and Moley for having improvised this reference but assured them that Hoover wouldn't stoop to making an issue out of it and the embarrassment would be fleeting. His analysis was correct.)

Though the candidate, like his party's platform committee, couldn't square the circle between providing the massive relief the economic emergency required and a balanced budget to which everyone paid lip service, the acceptance speech soared in many places, and FDR gave hope to his beleaguered listeners throughout a nation thirsting for better times and intelligent change.

Roosevelt concluded by evoking those who look "for a more equitable opportunity to share in the distribution of national wealth. Those millions cannot and shall not hope in vain. I pledge you, I pledge myself to a New Deal for the American people. . . . This is more than a political campaign; it is a call to arms. Give me your help, not to win votes alone, but to win this crusade to restore America to its own people." As always, Roosevelt's delivery was brilliant, in what Al Smith's daughter demurely described as "his cultured and pleasantly modulated voice." Garner accepted his theoretical elevation, in fact a final payoff to Hearst, with his usual droll asperity. The effect of Roosevelt's sudden aerial appearance and of his dramatic and eloquent message was galvanizing. He was already the president-elect. The hapless Hoover was going through the motions. He was like a conscientious convict, not exactly penitent but resigned to his execution as inevitable, if excessive.

Despite the outraged howls of those who claimed a year later to be disillusioned with Roosevelt, and the general perception that his campaign remarks were vague, Roosevelt, on this as on many other pre-electoral occasions, gave a fair insight into his policy preferences. He spoke of reduction of conventional government spending, job creation through emergency public works, the end of Prohibition, securities regulation, the elevation of farm prices through voluntary production controls, mortgage relief, and lower tariffs. This was a relatively accurate summary of his program in his first two years, and no informed person had any right to claim ignorance of it as Walter Lippmann and many others would.

In this hour of triumph, Roosevelt did not neglect the practicalities of politics. He greeted many hundreds of party stalwarts, spoke glowingly of "My old friend Al" Smith, and arranged for Rosenman's wife, whom Smith liked, to prevent an open breach. Mrs. Rosenman asked one of Smith's closest friends, Judge Bernard Shientag, later a justice of the New York Supreme Court, to get on Smith's train at Harmon, New York, and ride with him into Grand Central Station and persuade him not to say anything hot-headed. It worked; Smith said nothing at all until the next day, when he condemned the Republican record and endorsed the Democratic nominees without naming them. (Belle Moskowitz sent Roosevelt a generous congratulatory wire.[11]) Roosevelt spoke of "my very good and old friend John Raskob" even as he had the Democratic National Committee, which he had convened in special session, remove Raskob as party chairman and replace him with James A. Farley. He wasted no time taking absolute control of the party machinery, a control he would only relinquish posthumously.

The process of popularizing the words "New Deal" was begun in a cartoon the next day that showed a frail farmer looking skyward at an airplane with those words written on the underside of its wings. They entered, and have remained in, American political language.

Eleanor was privately seized with fear that she could become virtually a prisoner in the White House. She shared her despair only with her most intimate women friends, Nancy Cook and Marion Dickerman, who shared them with Louis Howe, who vitally helped assuage Eleanor's concerns.

———————

Roosevelt returned to New York and announced that he and his sons, James, Franklin, and John, were going on a cruise in New England waters in a forty-foot yawl, *Myth II.* He histrionically offered to cancel this holiday and come to the White House to discuss with the president New York State's interest in the St. Lawrence Seaway project now under intensive discussion with Canada. He knew Hoover would archly decline the offer, which he did, and the talks subsequently aborted. The project would not be revived for more than twenty years.

The Roosevelts on their cruise were shadowed by one boat hired by the press and by Jesse Straus's commodious steam yacht *Ambassadress*, which had aboard Joseph Kennedy (who would for a time stick to Roosevelt like flypaper), William Woodin, Farley, Flynn, and others.

Roosevelt skilfully captained the *Myth II* past Fairhaven, the ancient concession of the Delanos where he had happily vacationed as a child; past Marion, where he had exercised so strenuously with Dr. William McDonald to overcome the immobility of polio; through the Cape Cod Canal, which he had opened officially as assistant secretary of the navy on the day the First World War broke out; and on to Portsmouth, where Colonel House and Robert Jackson entertained him. He addressed a crowd of 50,000 at Hampton Beach on July 17, but respectfully avoided politics, because it was a New England Sunday. Roosevelt received the leading officials of the New England Democratic parties at each port of call on his trip. Roosevelt turned the full power of his charm and his position on all these people and had little difficulty seducing the detritus of the Smith faction to his cause. Most useful were the photographs, newsreels, and news stories about the expedition, which highlighted the candidate's health and fitness.

———————

As if not enough had gone awry for the ill-starred Hoover regime, it had now to cope with the arrival in Washington of thousands of war veterans demanding immediate payment of supplementary benefit to rescue them from indigence. They called themselves the Bonus Expeditionary Force, in emulation of Pershing's army in France, and wore parts of their uniforms to demonstrate that they were veterans of the Great War. They formed up in companies and platoons, and descended on Washington mainly by railway boxcar and flatcar, starting in late May. Their specific purpose was to demand payment of bonuses Congress had voted payable in 1945. Congressman Wright Patman of Texas had introduced and Congress had passed a bill for the payment of $2.4 billion of non-gold-backed money as bonus to the veterans.

Both Hoover and Roosevelt opposed paying the bonus, because they favored a balanced budget and objected to such a large special payment to a single interest group. The first group of 300 so-called Bonus Marchers (they were also called the Bonus Army) had set out by rail from Portland, Oregon. The railways had not objected to their unpaid passage until in East St. Louis there was a fracas with the security detail of the Baltimore and Ohio Railroad. Local groups bought the bonus marchers some food and paid for their transportation eastward as far as Indiana. They now attracted considerable publicity, and veterans set out for Washington from all parts of the country. The first group arrived May 29; within a couple of months there were over 20,000 Bonus Marchers, staying in the wretched improvised Hooverville in Anacostia Flats, within sight of the Capitol.

The marchers were at first sympathetically treated by the District of Columbia police. Roosevelt offered to pay the return rail fare for the New York Bonus Marchers, but only a few accepted. Hoover made the same offer to all of them, and about half accepted.

The ostensible leader of the Bonus Marchers was Sergeant Walter W. Waters, who by late June was starting to lose control of his improvised army, partly to meticulously-instructed Communist agitators. He was also getting a little carried away with his own position and was audibly making comparisons with Mussolini's 1922 march on Rome. On July 28 Waters ordered the assembly of all the marchers. They had occupied four government buildings on Pennsylvania Avenue. The chief of the D.C. police, Brigadier General Pelham Glassford, arrived with a hundred men and ordered an immediate withdrawal. A considerable melee ensued, which Glassford broke off. Glassford proposed a cooling-off period, but the D.C. Board of Commissioners instead advised Hoover that a dangerous situation existed and asked for the army.

Hoover, who had ignored all requests for a meeting with Waters and his people, agreed to the request for soldiers, but ordered only that the marchers be conducted back to their camp. Not for the last time, the chief of staff of the U.S. Army, General Douglas MacArthur, exceeded his orders. He insisted on leading the repulse of the ragged Bonus Army himself, despite the advice of his aide, the forty-two-year-old Major Dwight D. Eisenhower, who told his chief that this would make the army and MacArthur himself unpopular with the Congress and the public. The views of the fierce forty-seven-year-old Major George S. Patton, though he was not consulted, were more to MacArthur's liking. (Patton even refused to see the Bonus Army veteran who had saved his life after Patton was severely wounded in action in France in 1918, so strongly did he disapprove of the marchers.)

MacArthur claimed that there was "incipient revolution in the air," and marched up Pennsylvania Avenue in full parade regalia (including his father's Congressional Medal of Honor) at the head of 1,000 men equipped with gas masks, tear-gas grenades, and fixed bayonets, accompanied by six tanks and a cavalry squadron. By 7 P.M. the Bonus Army had been routed by MacArthur's forces, and their shantytown was put to the torch behind them. Hoover issued a rather insensitive statement congratulating himself for repulsing the challenge of "those who would destroy all government." MacArthur followed with a press conference in which he declared that 90 percent of the Anacostia campers were not veterans at all and uttered self-serving comments about having emancipated the country from the specter of "insurrection."

Roosevelt, back in Albany, was disgusted by Hoover's handling of the Bonus Marchers. He believed that the President should have received Waters and that the army should never have become involved. He privately recanted his former high opinion of Hoover and said to Tugwell: "There was nothing left inside the man but jelly; maybe there never had been anything."

Roosevelt's personal relations with Hoover had soured after Hoover had kept him standing for half an hour at a reception for the country's governors at the White House in the spring of 1932.[12] (Roosevelt had been offered a chair while waiting for the President, but declined. The great inconvenience he endured was surely not deliberately inflicted, but Roosevelt was not convinced.)

———————

Roosevelt had received a visit from the ineffable Bernard Baruch, who brought with him one of his senior collaborators, General Hugh Johnson. Johnson joined the Brain Trust and was a source of much colorful speechwriting. Baruch, unabashed by his promiscuous flirtation with Roosevelt's recent rivals, began offering advice himself. Another wealthy collaborator who joined the Roosevelt team at this time was Averell Harriman, co-inheritor and chairman of the Union Pacific Railway. His government service would be long and varied.

Roosevelt advised Tugwell that in these difficult times when many questioned the efficacy of democracy, the two most dangerous men in America were Douglas MacArthur and Huey Long. Roosevelt had known MacArthur since he was an aide to his cousin President Theodore Roosevelt. He thought him a brave and capable military commander but also an American Bonapartist, a vainglorious man on horseback prone to confuse legitimate democratic popular opinion with mob rule. Long, whom the Roosevelt entourage had originally underestimated, he saw as a populist demagogue who could stir and mislead large sections of the population if he weren't handled with caution. Long asked to be allowed to campaign around the country for Roosevelt, but Farley, one of those who underestimated him, sent him only into safe or hopeless states and later regretted it.[13]

Roosevelt was always wary of those susceptible of becoming, in Richelieu's phrase, "a state within a state." In addition to his almost unfailing grasp of the possibilities and limits of American public opinion, he had a professional's cunning, almost feminine, insight into the potential of other public figures. From William Randolph Hearst and Colonel McCormick to the labor leader John L. Lewis, through MacArthur, Long, the misguided hero Charles A. Lindbergh, the rabidly ambitious Joseph Kennedy, and lesser figures, Roosevelt was always sensitive to potential disloyalty and danger to the democratic system. He knew the type of personality that could easily consider itself above such constraints, and he almost never exaggerated or underestimated the political aptitudes of a rival.

One long-time rival that had badly misplayed its hand was Tammany. Mayor Walker and Boss John Curry had ostentatiously voted for Smith at Chicago, although Walker's fate now lay in Roosevelt's hands. The nominee had also had to endure the antics of Judge Seabury, who had padded around the hotel suites and corridors of the Chicago convention promoting the stop-Roosevelt movement. Given that he owed the revival of his prominence to Roosevelt, this was rather ungrateful. It was also nakedly partisan for the holder of a judicial office.

The mayor's response to the Seabury charges was completely inadequate. Now was the time, in high summer and with the Democratic Party completely in his control but before the final electoral march to the White House began in earnest, to deal with Walker. Basil O'Connor, one of the few whom Roosevelt was generally disposed to listen to, urged that Walker not be removed. He had less credibility in this case than usual because he was Walker's lawyer, though obviously not, as Roosevelt's law partner, in these proceedings.

Roosevelt retained the distinguished (Roman Catholic) lawyer Martin Conboy, briefed himself profoundly on all the facts and issues, and summoned Mayor Walker and his counsel to appear before him in public hearings in Albany starting August 11. Roosevelt began somewhat quaveringly but quickly asserted himself and became, and remained, master of the proceedings. His brilliant performance demonstrated the accuracy of his long-held contention that had he wished to make his way as a lawyer he could certainly have been an outstanding one. He parried and effortlessly outmaneuvered all Walker's counsel's efforts to transform the proceedings into a Walker-Roosevelt duel. He was judicious, procedurally alert, authoritative, quick, and eloquent. Walker was stripped bare and revealed not in his Irish charm but in his cynical, graft-ridden Tammany licentiousness. Roosevelt was sitting in the library of the executive mansion on the evening of September 1, 1932, with Moley, O'Connor, Rosenman, Farley, and several others, and had just declared that on the evidence Walker would have to be removed, though most of his guests disagreed.[14] The telephone rang and one of the governor's staff informed him that James J. Walker had resigned as mayor of New York.*

This had been another masterpiece of Roosevelt's tactical political skill. He

---

* After a sojourn in Britain until his tax status was cleared, Jimmy Walker returned to New York and lived quietly with his second wife and adopted child. Unlike Smith, he remained loyal to Roosevelt, and Farley arranged for him to visit the White House in 1938. Roosevelt had always liked him personally, since 1911, when they met in the state senate.[15] Walker was briefly succeeded as mayor by John P. O'Brien, a Tammany hack best remembered for having referred to Albert Einstein as "Dr. Weinstein." Then, in 1934, with Roosevelt's support, the irrepressible Fiorello H. La Guardia defeated Tammany and ushered in a new and more salubrious era in New York. La Guardia named Walker impartial arbitrator of the garment industry, where he was generally reckoned to do a good job. Walker returned to the practice of Catholicism and spent his last years quite soberly, supporting good causes and counselling

had finessed his way through his reelection as governor by setting up Seabury's inquiry. He had got through his own presidential nomination by an elaborate exercise of due process in favor of Tammany and the mayor. Tammany had defanged itself by supporting Smith over Roosevelt at the convention. Roosevelt had secured the nomination anyway. He had returned as anointed candidate and inevitable president and set himself up as a Solomonic magistrate in a season of little publicity. He had conducted the hearings fairly and knowledgeably and in such a way as to confound Walker's effort to turn them into a circus, and had compelled the mayor to resign and avoided being forced to sack him.

The sequence had been a matter of perfect orchestration of naturally uncooperative elements. Roosevelt surgically removed rebarbative factions without leaving his fingerprints on the scalpel.

Boss Curry attempted revenge by denying Rosenman renomination as a judge. Roosevelt wrote Rosenman: "I have a long memory and a long arm for my friends."[17] Curry overplayed his hand, and Smith and Roosevelt had a grand public reconciliation at the Armory in Albany before thousands of relieved Democrats when Roosevelt returned from his western tour. Rosenman was back as a judge within a year, Curry was out as Tammany leader, Smith campaigned effectively for Roosevelt, Lehman was elected, and Tammany would never rise again.

Roosevelt even for a time maintained good relations with Colonel McCormick. Roosevelt received him at home, they exchanged cordial letters, and McCormick assigned an admiring young reporter, John Boettiger, to cover his activities. (Boettiger would become, some years later, Anna Roosevelt's second husband.)[18] Roosevelt also enjoyed the strong support of W.R. Hearst and his media, and they had an agreeable meeting in Los Angeles when Roosevelt was campaigning in California in September. The candidate sensibly declined to spend the night at Hearst's fantastic castle, San Simeon, near San Luis Obispo.[19]

On August 27, 1932, Roosevelt had received the profession of fealty of Smith's floor manager in Chicago, Boss Frank Hague of Jersey City. Hague was best-known for his statement at the height of the Prohibition Era that "I set the price of beer in this town," and Roosevelt used the occasion of an address at Sea Girt, New Jersey, where Hague had turned out an audience of 100,000 people, to attack Prohibition.

———————

Roosevelt embarked on a speaking tour through the western states to the Pacific coast with an address at Topeka, Kansas, on September 14, 1932. In setting out on

———————

moderation in all things. He died in 1946, aged 65, surpassed only by La Guardia in popularity among all New York's mayors, and was given a splendid funeral in St. Patrick's Cathedral. Prominent restaurateur Toots Shor reminisced that Walker "livened up the joint," and the famous barrister Louis Nizer reflected: "James J. Walker met success like a gentleman and failure like a man."[16]

such a strenuous tour, Roosevelt was ignoring the advice of many, including Hearst and his running mate, Garner, who told him: "All you have to do is stay alive 'til November."[20]

Roosevelt loved to campaign. He was an eloquent and versatile public speaker and campaign presence, and had great affection for and interest in all parts of the country. He knew the dangers of getting out of touch with the electors, and he wanted to take over the Democratic Party root and branch and not be dependent on local barons and bosses. He also wanted to encourage the frightened masses of America, to give them hope and show them that their new leader was as vigorous as the incumbent administration was flaccid and demoralized.

In Roosevelt's entourage now there was a Babel of contrary advice on how to deal with the Depression. The candidate gave no hint of his real views. He had laid out an economic smorgasbord but declined to indicate the weighting he would give the conflicting elements.

He suggested that the Hoover administration's policy prescription—increased taxes and tariffs, reduced spending, and a shrinking money supply—were the worst that could have been devised.

The immediate challenge for Roosevelt was to appear to have an idea of what to do about the crisis without putting out precise notions that would be easily ridiculed. The difficulty of the policy-making group in the Brain Trust around Roosevelt was illustrated by the tariff question, which was a good deal more tractable than most. Half the Democratic Party was for high tariffs and half for reduced tariffs. It was agreed that Moley would compose a speech for the candidate on this subject, but when he sought FDR's guidance, Moley was appalled to be told to "weave the two together."

The expedient settled upon was two speeches for the delectation of different audiences but not sufficiently contradictory to attract the stark incredulity of the press. In Seattle on September 20, Roosevelt used the draft composed by Moley and by Baruch's subaltern General Hugh Johnson, calling for a gradual ratchet down of some tariffs. In Sioux City, Iowa, nine days later he called for negotiated reciprocal reductions of tariffs.

The only reason Roosevelt wasn't successfully roasted over these woolly proposals was that Hoover's position was absurd: high tariffs and loans to foreign countries designed to facilitate purchases of American "surpluses," even though many of these countries were now in default. Roosevelt finessed it with attacks on the "outrageously high" existing tariffs under Smoot-Hawley, adopted by the previous Republican Congress. But he objected to the "stigmatization" of the Democrats as a free-trade party.

Hoover predicted that tariff reduction would cause the grass to "grow in the streets of a hundred cities, a thousand towns; the weeds will overrun millions of farms . . . their churches and schoolhouses will decay." This was graphic bunk, of course, but it did cause Roosevelt to emphasize to farm audiences that he was opposed to reduction of agricultural tariffs. Hoover was close to the mark when he declared that Roosevelt's tariff policy was "the dreadful position of the chameleon on the Scotch plaid."[21]

More successful was the Democratic candidate's effort to deal with agricultural prices and surpluses. In his acceptance speech in Chicago, Roosevelt called for voluntary subsidized production restraint by farmers, and implied opposition to the policy of trying to dump surplus production abroad.

Roosevelt took up this idea blissfully unconcerned that he had endorsed the Hoover agricultural dumping policy several times in the past year, including in a little book portentously entitled "Government Not Politics" which was ghostwritten for him by the journalist Earle Looker. So lethargic and unobservant was the Republican campaign that it didn't pick up on this contradiction, even though "Roosevelt's" book, which the putative author hadn't bothered to read himself and whose agricultural proposals he was mildly surprised to learn of from Tugwell, was on general sale.

Roosevelt's breezy disdain for convention that would inhibit most people was sometimes maddening, sometimes infectiously entertaining. It is possible to see from an episode like this how some found him excessively glib and superficial and others found him such a compelling and amusing companion and leader. Napoleon said the greatest attribute of a general was luck. Roosevelt often demonstrated that the same could be said for a political leader.

Hoover was doubly vulnerable to farm discontent after he accepted renomination for president with a convention speech that rejected and condemned the concept of direct loans to farmers.[22]

The address Roosevelt gave to 20,000 Kansans in Topeka on September 14, 1932, outlining his farm policy had been worked on by twenty-five different authors. It was a remarkable hybrid, and Tugwell was impressed by Roosevelt's ability to approach conflicting positions sufficiently to give comfort to those who held them without embracing them to the exclusion of contrasting views. He went through his usual oratorical masquerade for the benefit of rural audiences of pretending to be a farmer himself, and his delivery was very effective. Apart from an elaboration on domestic allotment, which to the audience meant subsidized underproduction and increased farm prices, he was unspecific but full of well-formulated empathy. It was none too soon, since the Farm Holiday Association was already spreading, at pitchfork point across Iowa, the doctrine of "organized refusal" to allow farm products to be marketed below their cost of production. This would obviously be self-defeating before long, but desperate—even starving—farmers, led by the locally well-known Iowa populist Milo Reno, were beginning by the summer of 1932 to cause havoc in several states. Dangerous though such an omen was for the country, it was a fortuitous atmosphere for Roosevelt in which to launch his garbled agricultural program.

In San Francisco on September 23 Roosevelt gave the most philosophically revealing address of his campaign. It had been written with great care by Berle and edited with equal attention by Berle's wife, and effectively exalted personal rights over property rights. The developing theme was that property rights had been corrupted into corporate rights and unjustly endowed with a status they did not deserve, of equality with the rights of the individual. Berle wrote, and Roosevelt claimed, that Jefferson had been the champion of personal rights and Hamilton of property rights, and that these were the original foundations of and distinction between the Democratic and Republican parties. This was, of course, a very simplistic economic and historical view, but a convenient one for the case Roosevelt was making. It was the bowdlerized Claude Bowers view of Hamilton and Jefferson warmed over again. Roosevelt explained, with allusions adapted to a Californian audience, that the transcontinental railways had been built at great cost to the country with the help of Republican administrations, but that the benefit outweighed the cost. But now that there was no frontier left, immigration could not be accepted, and America was "providing a drab living for our own people."

He mourned the passage of an age where there had been almost "no paupers" and "few who could live without labor." He was praising an era when the gap between the richest and poorest was relatively slight, but he was also nostalgically evoking an age when people like him, who had no aptitude for modern capitalism but were substantial landowners, were the wealthiest people in the society and did not have to endure the garish pre-eminence of post-Industrial Revolution pure capitalists. It was a warning that individual rights included the right to a degree of comparative distributive equality and that the implementation of such rights was the prerogative and duty of the federal government. High finance could not solve the present problems, and Roosevelt spoke of "enlightened administration" in the people's interest. He was clearly hinting at some degree of wealth redistribution. He spoke only of restricting "the speculator, the manipulator, even the financier," and then "not to hamper individualism but to protect it."

Roosevelt reaffirmed in San Francisco that he construed the right to life to mean the right "to make a comfortable living." A person "may by sloth or crime decline to exercise that right but it may not be denied him." He also affirmed every man's "right to his own property," including his savings. Beyond cracking down on the infamous but unspecified manipulators and speculators (most of whom, whoever they were, were bankrupt by 1933), he gave little hint of his position on taxing rightfully earned savings and incomes to transfer the resources for a comfortable life to those who could not achieve it without government assistance.

The implication was that the problem could be solved by discouraging irresponsible financial behavior. Discerning observers knew this to be moonshine. If the poor were to be refinanced, the virtuously well-to-do, and not just a few scoundrels, were going to have to pay for it, as Roosevelt himself perfectly well knew. He had not faced up to the magnitude of expenditure that his program would involve. He had estimated in a letter in June to Colonel McCormick that government expenses could be reduced by 20 percent, but he knew from his experiences in New York that this would not pay for job-creating public works on the scale he had in mind.[23] He would either have to tax the wealth of the country or run big deficits.

The speech resonated well in intellectual circles but presaged some worrisome and economically erroneous thinking in the administration to come. Reticence about unrestrained speculation was reasonable, but declaring it the state's duty and purpose to dismantle the consequences of economic competition evinced a desire to impose statism over the natural interplay of the free, but not unregulated, market.

The vigilant could see Roosevelt invoking the Depression as an excuse for revising American history, claiming a right to repeal one hundred years of economic history, and establishing government by a single member of the landed gentry in the paternalistically interpreted interests of the suffering people. The infallible system of checks and balances in the American Constitution would prevent the enactment of any such design. But the very fact that the likely next president thought in such terms was disquieting. The Industrial Revolution had not failed, and even if it had, it could not be rolled back. Government clearly had to do more to prevent and to remedy bad times, but property rights were an aspect of individual rights and not in competition with them, and there had been no practical dispute between Jefferson and Hamilton on that point. Monticello had not been a commune, other than for Jefferson's slaves. The great intellectual tour de force of Roosevelt's campaign was in fact largely an unsettling melange of socialism, atavism, humbug, and snobbery.

He gave his conservative address, for which Howe, Baruch, and others had been agitating, at Pittsburgh on October 19, and denounced Hoover for "unprecedented deficits in spite of increased taxation." He said the federal government then cost the country $125 per capita per year and thought this unsustainable. Hoover's record was "the most reckless and extravagant . . . that I have been able to discover in the peacetime record of any government anywhere, anytime."[24] He implied he would deal with the costs of his unemployment relief program with cuts in other categories of government spending, and did allow that even he would accept a deficit rather than have unrelieved destitution among the American people. In later years he would claim, when accused of broken campaign pledges, that he not had sufficient time to consider this address before delivering it. In fact, it had been composed early and discussed often, and conformed to the candidate's rather traditional notions of national (and household) economy.*

There were a great many whistle stops on the speaking tour. Roosevelt would emerge, beaming, say he was "glad to be back" (whether he had ever been there

---

* Colonel House, James M. Cox, and Felix Frankfurter were among those who thought the Pittsburgh address a great speech. [25]

before or not), announce he was there to listen and learn, and introduce his daughter and daughter-in-law and his son Jimmy, who, FDR would inevitably add, "has less hair than I do." (Jimmy got pretty tired of this routine.) Then the train would start to move and the candidate would depart, having listened to no one and learned nothing. But it was an effective performance. As Clinton Mosher of the *Brooklyn Eagle* put it: "It doesn't get tiresome. . . . Roosevelt can smile more than any man in American politics without being insipid."[26] Roosevelt travelled thirteen thousand miles and gave sixteen major addresses, sixty-seven stump speeches, and hundreds of greetings from the back of his train.

In Baltimore, on October 25, Roosevelt sounded an apocalyptic note in invoking the Republican "Four Horsemen of Destruction, Delay, Deceit, Despair." In Boston on October 31 he called for and promised direct relief for the unemployed. In a campaign windup at Madison Square Garden on November 5, he reiterated all the more coherent themes he had sounded throughout the campaign.

Walter Lippmann finally endorsed Roosevelt, though he had "the deepest reservations" about him. Senator William Borah attacked Hoover without endorsing Roosevelt.[27] Other Republican senators—George Norris, Hiram Johnson, and Bronson Cutting—and Progressive senator Robert LaFollette Jr. all endorsed Roosevelt. Writers from H.L. Mencken on the right to Edmund Wilson on the left were skeptical of the Democratic candidate but detested the Republicans. The people clearly wanted a change. All polls showed Roosevelt leading by a sizeable margin at the end of the campaign.

On election eve Roosevelt delivered a nationwide broadcast in Poughkeepsie. He was statesmanlike and concluded: "With your help and your patience and your generous good will we can mend the torn fabric of our common life."

Hoover had written his own speeches and campaigned doggedly. His words were intelligent but defensive and unimaginative, and contained no spark of hope. This was the man who in accepting the presidential nomination in 1928 had predicted the imminent end of poverty in the United States. All was inevitable, nothing was his fault, and there was nothing to do but plod on. His secretary of state, Henry Stimson, said it was "like sitting in a bath of ink to sit in his room," and the sculptor of Mount Rushmore, Gutzon Borglum, said that a rose placed in Hoover's hand "would wilt."[28]

Victory for the Democrats came early on election night, though Louis Howe for a long time refused to believe it and left the campaign headquarters in the Biltmore Hotel and went across the street to his Friends of Roosevelt headquarters. Eleanor and Jim Farley came to fetch him at eleven o'clock, just before Roosevelt spoke to his supporters across the street at the hotel. Louis Howe and Jim Farley stood beside Roosevelt as he described them as "the two people in the United States more than anybody else who are responsible for this great victory." A great victory it was. He had won 22,815,539 votes to Hoover's 15,759,930 and the Socialist Norman Thomas's 900,000—almost 57 percent of the total vote to 40 percent for Hoover. Roosevelt had more than fully reversed the proportions of Smith's loss to Hoover four years before, and Thomas had quadrupled the Socialist vote. The Communists received only 70,000 votes, despite the temporary support of influential writers Theodore Dreiser, John Dos Passos, Sherwood Anderson, and, intermittently, Edmund Wilson. Roosevelt won 42 states—all but Pennsylvania, Delaware, Connecticut, New Hampshire, Vermont, and Maine. He had 472 electoral votes to Hoover's 59. The Democrats had an almost two-to-one lead in the Senate and nearly a three-to-one command of the House of Representatives (310 Democrats to 117 Republicans).

It was the most varied bloc of electors that Roosevelt would have in his presidential elections; he took particularly big majorities among Roman Catholics, Jews, anti-Prohibitionists, and the foreign-born, as well as the discontented urban and rural masses and bourgeoisie of all descriptions. Franklin D. Roosevelt "was unique among American politicians of his day in his instinctive understanding of the variety of the nation he sought to lead—and his hunger to learn more about every facet of it. He could believe that all of this was his country."[29]

Roosevelt carried 88 percent of the vote in the Old South, 64 percent in the border states (Maryland, West Virginia, Kentucky, Tennessee, Oklahoma) and 61 percent in Wisconsin, Minnesota, and the Dakotas, where no Democratic presidential candidate had ever won a majority. In the Northeast, east of the western border of Illinois and north of the Ohio River, the Republican candidate retained a majority, 50 percent to 47 percent if New York City is excluded. Roosevelt took New York City 66 percent to 27 percent, carrying the whole Northeast as a result, 50 percent to 46 percent. This area cast 38 percent of the total vote, including New York City. In the entire remainder of the electorate, 62 percent of the total, Roosevelt had a 62 percent to 36 percent majority over Hoover. Roosevelt had carried about 61 percent of the Midwest and 58 percent of Pacific and mountain state voters but led Hoover in New England by only 49 to 48 percent. Roosevelt had painstakingly cast a wide net over ethnic and rural votes, aiming to unite the southern Democrats, Catholic urban machine voters, and midwestern progressives. The strategy he had been developing since shortly after his and Cox's defeat in 1920 was an overwhelming success.

Roosevelt ran 3 percent ahead of the congressional Democrats, and the Democrats swept every congressional district in the South, all but one in the Rockies and in the Pacific Northwest, almost all of the districts in Illinois and Ohio, and all but two in the border states. The Republicans held the Lincolnian seat of the Unionist majority: most of New England and upstate New York, almost all of Philadelphia and most of the rest of Pennsylvania, and prosperous areas of most of the other great cities of the East and the Midwest. Roosevelt was determined to assault and seize these electoral bastions next.

A desperate nation had given Franklin Delano Roosevelt almost all that it had to give. They were the worst of times, but he would be president at last. On election eve he had sat with Moley beside the fireplace in the drawing room at Springwood, serene and enigmatic. On election night, when his son Jimmy helped him to bed, he said that he wasn't sure if he was strong enough to do the job; he said he would pray for that strength and asked his son to pray for him too. In the circumstances this note of solemnity, though unprecedented for the Roosevelts, was certainly understandable. Despite it, when he had returned to 65th Street at 1:40 A.M. on election night and his mother embraced him, the press heard him say to Sara: "This is the greatest night of my life." After the unprecedented obstacles he had overcome, it could scarcely have been otherwise.[30]

III

THE PROPORTIONS of the economic crisis now justified fears for the viability of the country's institutions and the stability of international relations. There was no sign whatever that the traditional oscillation of the business cycle was reasserting itself; all indicators had continued in free fall almost uninterruptedly for over two years. Though unemployment figures were not—incredibly—compiled by the Department of Commerce, believable estimates ranged from 24 percent to 36 percent, with the likeliest number 30 percent or slightly above. There was minimal direct government relief for the unemployed. Their condition was alleviated mainly by the efforts of the private sector, supplemented by whatever self-help the indigent could achieve from theft and mendicancy.

The volume of check transactions and of stock market transactions in the United States had declined by 60 percent since 1929. The amount of new capital financing had declined by over 95 percent since 1929. The volume of new building contracts had declined by 75 percent in the same period. By inauguration day in March 1933, the Dow Jones Industrial Average would be down by 90 percent from its high in September 1929. There had been 5,000 bank failures in three years, wiping out nine million individual bank accounts. Steel production was under 20 percent of capacity, and United States Steel Corporation, which had had 225,000 full-time employees in 1929, now had no full-time employees, apart from the executive officers, and only a corporal's guard of part-time blue-collar employees. Total non-agricultural production was less than half of its 1929 level. The urban population had shrunk by 400,000 as some people sought refuge in the country, but agricultural production, while approximately equal in physical volume to that of 1929, had shrunk in farm income from $12 billion to slightly above $5 billion. Many local and state governments, including Chicago and Georgia, could not pay their teachers. Georgia closed over a thousand schools attended by 170,000 students. Most rural Alabama white schools were closed through the early months of 1933.[31] Forty-five percent of homes had been or were in danger of being foreclosed by mortgage holders. Through the first six months of 1933, 250,000 homes would be foreclosed, well over a thousand per day, the families pitched out into the street.[32] The money supply, deflation-adjusted, had declined by 25 percent in four years; taxes had risen; national production and income had declined by approximately half, farm income by 70 percent, manufacturing income by 65 percent (nonpostponable purchases such as shoes were down by only 3 percent but automobiles by over 65 percent), and stock market values by about 85 percent.

When the Soviet Union advertised for 6,000 skilled workers to go to Russia in 1932 for a period of several years, its New York office was swamped with 100,000 applications. The natives of West Africa sent New York $3.77 to help with relief for the poor.[33] When the city of Birmingham, Alabama, advertised for 750 ditch-diggers to work ten-hour days for two dollars per day, 12,000 applications immediately arrived. Hoover had long maintained that only the private sector should provide direct relief, then that it was a state and local matter. Finally the Reconstruction Finance Corporation was authorized to lend hard-pressed local and state authorities $300 million for emergency relief, but only one-tenth of this had actually been used by the end of 1932.

In the coal mining regions of West Virginia and Kentucky, and some other poor areas, over 90 percent of children were suffering from malnutrition. Two-thirds of the whole population was still adequately prosperous, though deeply worried, but millions of Americans faced the distinct possibility of death from starvation or exposure to the elements. Stories were legion, and generally true, of large numbers of people living from the scraps and leftovers thrown out in the garbage by restaurants and hotels. American literature achieved a virtual golden age with writers such as John Steinbeck, Erskine Caldwell, Edmund Wilson, and John Dos Passos describing the condition of, in Emma Lazarus's famous phrase applied to those seeking to come to the New World, "the wretched refuse" of America.

The decline of industrial production in the United States from 1929 to 1932 was, along with Germany's, the worst among the advanced countries. With 1929 as 100, the United States and Germany at the end of 1932 stood at 53, Italy at 67, France at 72. The United Kingdom—which, having been brought back onto the gold standard by Winston Churchill when he was chancellor of the exchequer, had struggled through the late twenties and was not enjoying a boom in 1929— was at 84. Japan, which had already commenced massive and inflationary military expenditures and aggressive actions in China, was at 98.[34]

The Soviet Union claimed an aberrant 198 as a result of Stalin's five-year plans. In fact, the figures were false and much of the increased production in the Communist command economy was useless and wasted. The U.S.S.R.'s performance in the thirties was further complicated by the distinctive Stalinist initiatives of quintupling the money supply and physically exterminating approximately 12 percent of the entire population, making comparisons with other countries inapplicable. Unfortunately, this did not prevent a large number of credulous western intellectuals and other notables from being completely gulled by Stalin's propaganda apparatus. Many, such as George Bernard Shaw, returned from trips to

Russia as, in Lenin's famous phrase, "useful idiots," urging Soviet practices on the West.

The whole world was profoundly depressed, economically and psychologically.

In America all hopes were now invested in Franklin Roosevelt, who as we have seen had only the most general notions of what to do and would have to sort out a very divided entourage. However, he had faith in himself. His basic concepts envisioned in the election campaign were sensible: direct relief, institutional reforms, an inspirational effort to reinvigorate the country's morale, conservation, public ownership of some electricity generation, programs to raise farm prices by reducing production, and progress toward a balanced budget when the crisis had started to subside.

———————

Roosevelt and Hoover had a gracious exchange of telegrams on election night and the following day, but there shortly began what Roosevelt came to regard as an effort to ensnare the president-elect in the outgoing president's failed and rejected policymaking. Hoover professed to believe he was merely showing normal courtesy to his successor, in the interests of continuity. Hoover blamed the economic crisis on foreign developments, and the Europeans generally blamed it on the American Depression. Roosevelt had dismissed Hoover's attribution of blame to foreign causes during the campaign as "the boldest alibi in history." He suggested that Hoover was unsure where "abroad" was, and mockingly wondered if he ascribed the causes of the depression to "Abyssinia." He was concerned about being drawn into a legitimization of this view now.

Hoover also wished to involve him in a discussion of the upcoming World Monetary and Economic Conference, which would be prepared under Hoover but take place in Roosevelt's term. Roosevelt had one of his frequent sinus cold attacks right after the election and had been confined to bed for five days, delaying his planned annual trip to Warm Springs leading up to Thanksgiving, always an elaborate occasion on which he carved the turkey for handicapped children.

Roosevelt stopped at Washington on his way south and met with the President at the White House on November 22. He was greeted at Washington's Union Station by the chief of protocol, his cousin Warren Delano Robbins. The meeting with Hoover, also attended by Raymond Moley and the secretary of the Treasury, Ogden Mills, was a rather frosty affair despite Roosevelt's usual effort at conviviality. (The long-serving Treasury secretary Andrew Mellon had gone to the embassy in London.) Other than a couple of glances, Hoover never looked at or even addressed Roosevelt directly. He gave a learned monologue of almost an hour on the many aspects of the international debt problem. He concluded that default on large amounts of debt owed the United States was now imminent, and either default or cancellation would be very destabilizing. What Hoover proposed was a debt commission, like that which had produced international debt agreements in the twenties, with equal representation from each house of the Congress and the administration. The Congress had already rejected this. The outgoing president's objective was to negotiate new arrangements with the debtor nations before they defaulted and international financial conditions deteriorated further.

In a formula with which many people would become disagreeably familiar, Roosevelt smiled, nodded, and said yes at least once. As far as Hoover was concerned, he had agreed to the idea of the commission. Roosevelt was just being polite and taking note of the President's proposal, and asked Moley to respond. Moley adhered scrupulously to what he knew to be the sacrosanct Roosevelt policy of giving no hint of his policy intentions in advance of taking office. He endorsed the principles Hoover had enunciated, that debts were business and not political obligations to the United States from other countries; that each was discrete and would not be considered on a debtor-bloc basis; that the debts were unrelated, as far as the United States was concerned, to German reparations; and that the United States was prepared to consider any country's claim of inability to pay.

Moley suggested that there was no need for such a commission as the President proposed, involving an act of Congress—that normal negotiations through the State Department should be sufficient. Roosevelt and Moley agreed with Hoover's view that the December 15 payments due to the United States would have to be paid. As was something of a tradition, Hoover underestimated his guest, telling Stimson that he and Mills had been "educating a very ignorant, though well-meaning young man."[35] The thought that Hoover might have made an unspeakable mess of this and related problems, and that Roosevelt might be a good deal cleverer than Hoover, seems not to have entered his mind.

Roosevelt met the Democratic congressional leaders that evening and described the meeting as a cordial exchange of opinion. The Democratic plan was for a very unambitious closing session of the old Congress, calling for the partial repeal of Prohibition (legalizing the sale of beer), some farm relief, and some modest budget-balancing measures. The session achieved virtually nothing, as Huey Long, abetted by some conservative Republicans, filibustered a bill to assist distressed banks because he was outraged at the rise of the branch banking system, which he represented as a threat to the neighborhood bank.

On the day of Roosevelt's meeting with Hoover, Britain made her payment to the United States but France did not. Hoover sent Roosevelt a long telegram December 17 urging that "machinery" be "erected" to deal with the problem thus created. He suggested that the delegation chosen for the World Monetary and Economic Conference should include some delegates to the previous disarmament conferences and should be empowered to enter into negotiations over the debt and related problems. Hoover added that he would be advising Congress that this was his opinion and inquired whether Roosevelt agreed with it. Roosevelt responded on December 19, after Hoover's message had gone to the Congress. In that message, Hoover blamed the departure from the gold standard for the erosion of prices in almost every area and called for the swiftest possible resumption of the gold standard. (This was orthodox conservative opinion at the time but was completely impractical. The reinflation of prices and incomes could not possibly be achieved by forcing the principal currencies into the hair-shirted straitjacket of deflation that would be required for them to resubscribe to the gold standard.) Hoover also referred to his intention to set up a special commission to deal with the connected problems of the world economy, international debts, and disarmament.

In his reply to Hoover, FDR, almost certainly accurately, questioned the wisdom of tying the three questions together as closely as he had. He approved Hoover's stance on disarmament, urged him to deal with the debt question as he saw fit but not to purport to bind the new administration, and opposed having the World Monetary and Economic Conference delegates be the same people who would be negotiating debt and disarmament questions. He further declined to join in naming the delegates to that conference and explicitly stated that he could not enter into any form of joint representation with Hoover, because he was "wholly lacking in attendant authority" until inauguration day—after which date, of course, Hoover would have no authority and Roosevelt wouldn't have to bother with him.

Hoover was back the next day with a telegram claiming that the scale of the international problems required cooperation between them, that he couldn't believe that it wasn't possible to avoid wasting valuable time, and even asking that Owen Young, Colonel House, "or any other men of your party" be named as representatives to coordinate a policy.

Roosevelt fundamentally thought that the focusing on foreign causes for the Depression was a scam and an evasion. He believed that the Depression in the United States was caused in the United States and would be solved there. He believed that efforts to lay great stress on the potential of international conferences to achieve much that would be useful were just attempts to shirk responsibility for the monstrous failure for which Herbert Hoover as president, and for eight years before that as secretary of commerce, was more personally responsible than anyone else. He responded on December 21, again declining to go further than exploratory talks to see where cooperation might be possible.

Hoover testily released all the correspondence and expressed regret that Roosevelt did not wish to cooperate with him. Roosevelt replied the same day, December 22, that he was happy to cooperate as much as was practical and to have exploratory discussions. He subtly implied that he did not highly appreciate an attempt to mousetrap him into agreement with the policies of a discredited and defeated administration that he had been elected to replace. Roosevelt's interviews with the Democratic congressional leaders from Huey Long to arch-conservative Carter Glass, cofounder of the Federal Reserve, were masterful—all charm, reassurance, and unspecific purpose.

Roosevelt did, toward the end of the year, float the idea of a "parallel budget," separating normal expenditures from emergency expenditures, which he would categorize as investments. The implication was that these investments would bear a return that would distinguish them from normal government expenses. The distinction was spurious and was greeted unenthusiastically. But it did reveal that the president-elect was finally starting to square the circle between emergency relief and budget balancing.[36]

Roosevelt had not commented on Hoover's proposals to raise taxes yet again to reduce the deficit, and the President's congressional supporters, even Garner, claimed that Roosevelt supported Hoover's measure. Finally, in late December, Roosevelt declared his emphatic opposition to an income tax increase and Hoover's tax increase died.

On January 9, 1933, Roosevelt had a protracted luncheon meeting at Hyde Park with Secretary of State Henry L. Stimson to talk about the new administration's attitudes to the World Monetary and Economic Conference and related matters. Hoover had initially forbidden this meeting, because he thought Roosevelt "a very dangerous and contrary man" after their disagreement in November. Stimson insisted and prevailed. The secretary of state recorded in his diary that he was highly impressed by Roosevelt in every way, especially his great courtesy and his easy unselfconsciousness about his polio.

Stimson had thought that Hoover was a distinctly more impressive man than Roosevelt, but now revised his opinion of the incoming president upwards.[37] Roosevelt was much closer to Stimson in his view of Far Eastern affairs than Stimson was to Hoover. The Stimson Doctrine, formulated the previous year over Japanese aggressions in Manchuria, had decreed that the United States would not recognize territorial or jurisdictional changes achieved in contravention of the Kellogg-Briand Pact of 1928, which had grandiloquently outlawed war as an instrument of national policy.

This was the limit to which Hoover would go. Stimson, like Roosevelt, was not averse to the imposition of sanctions or even, in some cases, military force to deter or respond to military aggression. Stimson had written in his diary (March 9, 1932[38]) that it was "almost impossible that there should not be an armed clash between two such different civilizations" (the United States and Japan). He would play a central role in enacting his own prophesy. After their meeting, Roosevelt endorsed the Stimson Doctrine and issued a bland statement in New York that "American foreign policy must uphold the sanctity of international relations."[39]

Roosevelt held steadfastly to his support of the Stimson Doctrine even when Tugwell and Moley called on him in New York on January 18 and Tugwell apocalyptically warned that Stimson's policy could lead to war with Japan. Roosevelt acknowledged that it could and that, given Japan's aggressive imperialism, if war was inevitable it might be best to have it sooner than later. He spoke at length and with some emotion of his family's history in and sympathy for China. Tugwell offered the outrageous view that Japanese imperialism might not be greatly more offensive than Britain's.* Roosevelt had lost his kindly disposition to Japan expressed in his article of 1922, and had returned to his pre-World War I view of likely potential conflict between Japan and the United States. This Roosevelt-Stimson meeting prepared the way for the remarkable relationship the two men would enjoy a decade later.

Other elements of Roosevelt's foreign policy began to emerge in the interregnum between the election and inauguration. He had wished to travel to Europe and meet with some of the principal European statesmen, and Hoover, who had travelled to South America at the corresponding moment in his career, offered the president-elect a warship for such a trip. Roosevelt reluctantly concluded that worsening economic conditions in the United States made such a voyage impractical. He was tempted to encourage prominent European leaders to visit him, but on the advice of Louis Brandeis and Felix Frankfurter did not do so.[40]

Roosevelt had extensive and successful interviews with the British and French ambassadors, Sir Ronald Lindsay and Paul Claudel. Lindsay visited him at Warm Springs on January 29. Lindsay noted that Roosevelt had a comprehensive idea of what he wished to achieve in foreign policy matters, and did not think the Senate would approve many piecemeal steps. He found the president-elect prone to take up certain issues lightly and then let them go when challenged, and found him "rather weak" on economic issues. He was impressed with Roosevelt's grasp of the nature of relations between the principal countries; he reported that FDR sought increased international trade and disarmament based on the prohibition of military aircraft and aircraft carriers and restriction of the size of submarines and battleships. Roosevelt favored containment of Japan by the retention of "strain" on that country, economically and morally.[41]

Roosevelt had already received Paul Claudel, a leading figure in French literature, at his New York home on January 10. Claudel described it as a very stimulating meeting with "A man of the world full of simplicity and humanity . . . a real friend of France." On the subject of debt repayments, Roosevelt gave Claudel "a little history lesson," recalling that in 1777 France had lent America fifteen million livres. The principal was not repaid until about 1815, and France had not agitated with the United States about payment. "This should never be forgotten. We do not consider that France defaulted. A great people never default. This word should not be allowed to be uttered. We simply consider that France for reasons she considered very important has postponed one of her payments."

---

* Tugwell was an academic agrarian economist; that he would feel free to compare Britain's empire-building activities to Japan's putting of ever-larger areas of China to fire and sword was an unfavorable augury about the practical judgment of the Brain Trust.

The president-elect also showed great solicitude for France's security concerns. He quoted Clemenceau, who had told him in 1918 that the meaning of security was that a newborn French child should never have to fear that there would be war on French soil in his lifetime. Roosevelt thought greater quantities of perfume could be imported from France and that repeal of Prohibition would require two or three years; he was touched that a wine-loading wharf in Paris was already called Quai Roosevelt.[42]*

Roosevelt and Hoover and their aides had another thoroughly unproductive meeting at the White House on January 20. Hoover, Stimson, Mills, and Norman Davis, who had been preparing the World Monetary and Economic Conference and who invited himself to the meeting on the Roosevelt side, argued with Moley. Finally, Roosevelt, who had said almost nothing, declared that debt, disarmament, and the world economy could not be approached together and that he would not agree to the selection of any delegates to the economic conference nor of its agenda until after his inauguration March 4.

He left the next day with Senator George Norris of Nebraska, the country's leading advocate of publicly owned electric power, and toured the Muscle Shoals area of the Tennessee River in Alabama. He promised a tremendous effort in rural electrification, nitrate production, irrigation, flood control, conservation, and job creation. Norris declared that he saw his "dreams come true." Roosevelt went on to Montgomery, Alabama, and gave an impromptu address on the possibilities for the Tennessee River to a large crowd on the lawn of the state capitol from what he called the "sacred spot" where Jefferson Davis had taken the oath as president of the Confederate States.

Roosevelt went on to Warm Springs, Georgia, and while he was relaxing there at his thermal resort on his fifty-first birthday, January 30, the eighty-six-year-old president of Germany, Field Marshal Paul von Hindenburg, called upon Adolf Hitler to become chancellor of Germany. New German elections were called for March 5, the day after Roosevelt's inauguration. The brutal intimidation of opponents by Hitler's Nazis, which was intensified at once and much reported in the Western press, left little doubt of the outcome of the election or the nature of the regime that would emerge in Berlin.

The relationship between Adolf Hitler and Franklin D. Roosevelt, coming to office within a few weeks of each other, would be almost openly hostile from the first. They would die less than three weeks apart, still holding those offices, but in circumstances as different as it was possible to conceive. They represented two

---

* Roosevelt had already given an interview to the London *News Chronicle* expressing the hope that the U.S., Canada, and Britain would act "with a complete identity of political and economic interests and will in that way acquire the leadership of the world."[43] To the Paris daily *Le Matin* he emphasized his great friendship and admiration for France.[44]

diametrically different views of how to govern and of what human society and international relations should be.

The competition between them, for the esteem of the world and finally in mortal combat, would be a Manichean epic. Apart from policy matters, Roosevelt detested Hitler's racism, militarism, totalitarianism, and espousal, both ludicrous and horrifying, of the mythic amoral superman of German legend and philosophy. Hitler resented America's wealth and despised its polyglotism. He was viscerally repelled by Roosevelt's infirmity and by the number of Jews in his entourage and blacks in his household. He affected to regard the United States as an "excrescence" of Europe, inhabited by an oafish lumpenproletariat in a culture that had no aptitude for music and that was "half judaized and half negrified."[45]

Almost Hitler's only appreciation of America was through Karl May's Western novels about cowboys and the frontier, which he had read avidly. (These were a considerable feat of fiction writing by May, since he had not been in America himself.) Roosevelt knew Germany well and had never much liked it, and saw Hitler at once as a hideous mutation of the worst Teutonic tendencies.[*]

In the public relations contest between Roosevelt and Hoover over cooperation before the change of administration, Hoover had somewhat got the better of it. But Roosevelt wasn't concerned. He wanted no association with the dead hand of the outgoing government. He departed Warm Springs on February 3 for Jacksonville, where he boarded the yacht of his admiring neighbor Vincent Astor, the luxurious 264-foot *Nourmahal*, for a fishing cruise down the Florida coast and through the Bahama Islands. This was in part a substitute for an official visit to Europe.[46]

Ed Flynn wished that the president-elect in this grimmest of winters in living memory might have chosen a more populist form of recreation. Vincent Astor's other guests stood at the rail in garish sporting attire as the yacht cast off, and Flynn sarcastically remarked, in reference to one of FDR's Harvard clubs: "The Hasty Pudding Society puts out to sea."[47]

The country's banking system continued to crumble. Huey Long had had to declare a bank holiday (through his governor, Oscar Allen) in Louisiana on the day one of the state's largest banks reached the edge of the abyss.[†] Ten days later the governor of Michigan, William Comstock, was forced to shut all of Michigan's banks for eight days after Henry Ford, who hated bankers, refused to guarantee retention of $7.5 million in one troubled bank, which was one of the conditions precedent to a loan to that bank from Hoover's Reconstruction Finance Corporation.

---

[*] Being taken by his mother to see Wagner's *Ring* cycle at Bayreuth in 1896 had probably not raised his appreciation of Hitler's world-view.
[†] He technically declared a holiday to observe the anniversary of breaking relations with Germany.

Roosevelt's cabinet selection process was rather idiosyncratic. He would not have anyone who actively opposed his nomination as president, and he was very leery of big industrialists, financiers, and corporate lawyers. This militated against Newton Baker, Bernard Baruch, and William G. McAdoo. Hearst, McAdoo, and Senator Carter Glass urged the merits of Baruch—who had contributed the extraordinary sum of $53,000 to his campaign—as secretary of state. Roosevelt put off Baruch's many sponsors by saying he could be better used elsewhere, but never offered him anything. Baruch always claimed he would not have accepted a cabinet position.[48]

Jim Farley was a sure thing from election night on as postmaster general, the traditional patronage-dispensing position of the party chairman. Senator Thomas Walsh of Montana, helpful chairman of the Chicago convention, was Roosevelt's first choice for attorney general, and Frances Perkins was his choice for labor secretary and first female cabinet member.

Burton Wheeler, the first prominent politician to get on the Roosevelt bandwagon, came to see Roosevelt to ask for the appointment of a protégé, Edward Keating, a former congressman and editor of the railway union newspaper, as secretary of labor. Roosevelt revealed that he proposed to nominate Wheeler's Montana colleague, Senator Walsh, for attorney general, which, with Farley as postmaster general, would give the cabinet two Roman Catholics. He also insisted on a woman cabinet member, and would choose either Frances Perkins or William Jennings Bryan's daughter Ruth Bryan Owen. If he chose Miss Perkins, which was likely, she would be labor secretary. On both counts, Keating was struck out: he was a Catholic and not a woman, and was only fit for the position being warmed up for Frances Perkins. Roosevelt prevailed on Wheeler to help him with the persuasion of Walsh to accept the position of attorney general. Wheeler had come sponsoring a protégé and left trying to enlist someone he (mistakenly) thought would not accept what was on offer.[49]

Roosevelt was considering Owen Young of General Electric as secretary of state, but once this became known the outcry from anti-utility western senators (even though his company was largely an appliance manufacturer) was such that Roosevelt was relieved when Young withdrew, citing his wife's illness. Apart from Young, Baker, and Baruch, a principal contender for secretary of state was Norman Davis, an elegant and bipartisan figure with a good deal of foreign policy experience. Frankfurter violently objected to Davis, alleging business skulduggery in Cuba decades before. (Frankfurter would become, in the opinion of some observers, the Iago of this administration.)

This narrowed the field to Senators Carter Glass and Cordell Hull, and Roosevelt offered Hull state and Glass Treasury. Hull had been a great loyalist of Roosevelt's for many years, and had cooperated with Roosevelt in an informal caucus of internationalist Democrats at the start of the Harding years. Hull's chief foreign policy preoccupation was an obsession with reducing tariffs, which he considered a panacea. Hull kept Roosevelt waiting almost a month after his invitation January 19. He doubted that his wife would be up to the required socializing, so Roosevelt engaged his prosperous and affable friend William Phillips as undersecretary of state and Hull accepted.

A number of Hull's Senate colleagues, hearing of this possibility, advised Roosevelt through Moley that Hull was not up to the post. Roosevelt was well aware of Hull's shortcomings but intended to conduct foreign policy himself and had no interest in having a particularly brilliant person as secretary of state. Hull, who was well-liked by the Senate and was a man of unquestioned integrity, would be useful in selling policies to the Senate.

Raymond Moley would become assistant secretary of state with special responsibility for foreign debt, the World Economic Conference, directing the office of the economic advisor (the capable Herbert Feis), and whatever else Roosevelt might wish to give him.

The president-elect pressed Carter Glass, cofounder of the Federal Reserve and a former secretary of the Treasury, to return to the post. Glass was suspicious of Roosevelt's propensity to reduce or depart the gold standard and inflate the currency, and he ultimately declined. One of his motives for accepting would have been to get Harry F. Byrd into the Senate. When Roosevelt offered the other Virginia senator, Claude Swanson, the navy, that opened up a place for Byrd and also freed up the position of chairman of the Senate Foreign Relations Committee for Roosevelt loyalist Senator Key Pittman of Nevada. (Byrd would rule Virginia for thirty-five years.)

The Treasury was then offered to William Woodin of Philadelphia, the diminutive head of American Car and Foundry and a strenuous admirer of Roosevelt's since he had been on the board of the Warm Springs Foundation several years before. Woodin had deserted the Republicans to support Roosevelt in 1928 and had been a sizeable financial contributor. He was a musician (piano, violin, guitar) and a composer (*Covered Wagon Suite*, the *Oriental Suite*, and, for the upcoming inauguration, the *Franklin Delano Roosevelt March*). His appointment was suggested in a coded message Howe sent Roosevelt on the *Nourmahal*: "Prefer a wooden roof to a glass roof." Woodin was not seeking a position, and needed a ninety-minute taxi ride around Central Park with Basil O'Connor before he accepted.[50] He was a good deal more flexible than Glass would have been.

Roosevelt was going to ask his friend Jesse Straus, chairman of retailer R.H. Macy, to be secretary of commerce. But when McAdoo agitated fiercely for Daniel Roper, who had been McAdoo's floor manager in 1924 and who, McAdoo said, had been instrumental in bringing California over at Chicago, Roosevelt offered him the Commerce Department and persuaded Straus to accept the embassy in Paris instead.*

Henry Wallace, the editor of a well-known farm magazine and the son of Harding's agriculture secretary, became secretary of agriculture, strongly recommended by the farm organizations, and Rexford Tugwell became the assistant secretary. George Dern of Utah had carried a lot of heavy water for the president-elect. He was owed something and was offered and accepted secretary of war, not a very exacting position at this time of a shrunken army. Dern was best remembered for his slogan when running for governor against Charles Mabey: "We need a Dern good governor and we don't mean Mabey."[51]

Senator Walsh of Montana eventually accepted the offer to become attorney general, but dropped dead just before inauguration day and a week after marrying a woman more than thirty years younger than he. Roosevelt then took the leader of the Democrats in Connecticut, Homer S. Cummings, and moved him up from governor of the Philippines, where he was about to send him, to attorney general.[†]

Interior was offered first to the indestructible Senator Hiram W. Johnson of California, who had played such important roles in the 1912 and 1916 presidential elections (as Theodore Roosevelt's Progressive Party vice presidential candidate and then in denying victory to Charles Evans Hughes in California). Johnson declined, however, and interior was offered to Senator Bronson Cutting of New Mexico. Cutting, a Grotonian and a tuberculosis victim, declined also, citing health reasons, but was in fact unconvinced of Roosevelt's liberalism and of his stature generally.

Johnson and Cutting had recommended the abrasive, but intelligent and courageous, progressive Chicago lawyer Harold L. Ickes. (His name rhymed with "Mikey's.") When Roosevelt was wheeled into the anteroom of his New York house, where Ickes had been invited and was sitting with about ten other people, as in a dentist's waiting room, Roosevelt asked: "Which one of you gentlemen is Ikes?" (Rhyming with "bikes.") After barely three minutes conversation, the president-elect said: "I like the cut of his jib." Ickes accepted the post, and this was the beginning of a long, complex, and generally satisfactory association (and Ickes was a much better choice than Hiram Johnson or Cutting would have been).

Fiscal conservatives were appeased with the appointment of Lewis Douglas of Arizona, a budget-balancing gold standardist, as director of the budget.

---

* Roper had been very cooperative with patronage when he was assistant postmaster general and Roosevelt was at the navy, and Straus had paid for some key polls for Roosevelt in 1931 and had headed the Roosevelt Business and Professional Men's League.
† Cummings had been on the Democratic National Committee for thirty years and was a former chairman of that committee. He had been an effective Roosevelt operator and had negotiated the adherence of Alben Barkley and the Kentucky delegation in Chicago.

The White House staff was not a difficult selection: Louis Howe, Missy LeHand, Grace Tully, Stephen Early (press relations), and Marvin McIntyre (scheduling) continued what they were already doing.

The *Nourmahal* docked at Miami on the evening of February 15, 1933. After a brief press conference Roosevelt and his party went to a welcoming celebration at Miami's Bay Front Park. About 20,000 people were assembled, including many dignitaries. Among these was the mayor of Chicago, Anton Cermak, come to make amends after his convention-packing efforts on behalf of Al Smith. He was particularly interested in federal aid to help him with back pay to the city's 20,000 schoolteachers whose salaries were still in arrears. Roosevelt's car pulled into the park; his security detail, led by Gus Gennerich, helped him nimbly to sit on the back of the open car with his feet on the back seat. The mayor of Miami introduced him in the correct brief style, and he spoke a few words into the microphone handed him. He recalled his many visits to Florida on the *Larooco* and otherwise, said he had had a splendid time fishing, promised the crowd that he wouldn't tell any fish stories and would try to come back next year. It was an innocuous address of the kind he had given thousands of times before.

When Mayor Cermak approached, Roosevelt shook hands cordially with him and agreed that they would meet on his railway car about an hour later. Another man appeared with a long telegram for FDR, and just then five shots rang out in quick succession. The car lurched forward as the driver sought to remove his passenger from danger. Roosevelt, imperturbable, noticed that Cermak had been wounded, shouted for the car to stop, and directed that Cermak to be helped into the car beside him. They sped off to Jackson Memorial Hospital. Roosevelt held Cermak with his left arm, felt for his pulse with his right hand, and when the mayor revived, encouraged him and urged him to conserve his strength and say nothing. The trailing car, in which Moley and Astor were seated, conveyed an injured policeman, but also the apprehended gunman, forced onto the luggage rack with two policemen sitting on him and another on the running board.

This car deposited the lightly wounded policeman at the hospital, and Moley and Astor joined Roosevelt to await a report on the mayor's prospects. Roosevelt briefly telephoned his wife, who was in New York. Eleanor nonchalantly told the press: "These things are to be expected."[52] In addition to Cermak, a New York policeman assigned to Roosevelt was in critical condition with a head wound, as was the wife of the president of the Florida Light and Power Company, with an abdominal wound. With five shots, the gunman, Guiseppe Zangara, had critically wounded three people and lightly wounded two.

Roosevelt professed to believe that with a name like Zangara he might well have been a Chicago gangster aiming at Cermak. Otherwise, he asked, why didn't he shoot at Roosevelt when he was speaking and a much easier target? Roosevelt's complete calm and concern for those who had been injured impressed all observers and the American public.*

Zangara was an anarchist and considered assassination a desirable response to government in general. Roosevelt had been saved by the quick thinking of a Miami housewife, Lillian Cross, who had been jostled by Zangara as he jumped up on a bench and took aim. She shoved his arm upward, and he had to jump down and forward to get away from her.

Roosevelt stayed overnight in Miami and visited the victims the next morning, February 16. His secret security detail attested that he slept soundly.[54] Cermak bravely said to Roosevelt: "I'm glad it was me instead of you." After they briefly discussed what Cermak had hoped to talk to the president-elect about, Roosevelt departed Miami on his train at 10:15 A.M. He sent a telegram of thanks when he learned of Mrs. Cross's role and never mentioned the episode again, as far as anyone can recall. This unaffected aplomb in the face of real danger is a vivid contrast to Roosevelt's penchant for inflating his own role in events, though he generally outgrew that habit once he occupied a position of such importance that exaggerations were hardly necessary. Cermak, further battered by colitis, pneumonia, and gangrene, listened to Roosevelt's inaugural address on the radio March 4 and died two days later. The other victims all survived. Zangara was convicted of first-degree murder and, defiant and unrepentant to the end, complaining only at the absence of photographers to record his execution, went fearlessly to the electric chair on March 20.

On the return trip to New York, Bronson Cutting and Carter Glass came on board from Washington to Baltimore and confirmed that they would not serve in the cabinet. Glass failed, once again, to get a promise from Roosevelt that he would not "tamper" with the currency.

The New York police absurdly overreacted to the events in Miami. Roosevelt was met by over 1,000 security people at Jersey City, and proceeded to 65th Street with several security people in his own car, preceded and followed by a total of fourteen carloads of police officers and security people. Roosevelt prohibited such excesses in the future.

Hoover had one last try at smoking out Roosevelt: he sent the president-elect a ten-page handwritten letter February 18 declaring that there was now a state of alarm in the country that threatened the recovery Hoover professed to believe was in progress. Hoover wrote that what was necessary was a clear statement from Roosevelt that there would be a balanced budget whatever the cost in taxation,

---

* Zangara confessed garrulously and proudly to the Miami police. Roosevelt certainly was his target. Moley, a criminologist, took part in the interrogation. Zangara had in his pocket a newspaper cutting about the assassination of William McKinley. Moley, as a young person, had been not far from McKinley when he was shot in Buffalo in 1901.[53]

and that the gold standard would be defended and inflation completely resisted. Roosevelt regarded this as "cheeky" (particularly so, as Hoover's secretary had committed the astonishing error of misspelling the president-elect's name). Roosevelt didn't bother to respond for eleven days and when he did it was in response to another urgent letter that Hoover sent on March 1. Roosevelt professed to have written a reply to the earlier message, claiming that his secretary had apparently thought it was only a draft and had not sent it. This, of course, was untrue; Roosevelt would not have sent a letter to the President unsigned and would not have signed a draft, so Hoover knew that he was being ignored.

The outgoing president is not greatly to be pitied, however. In a memorandum to Senator David Reed of Pennsylvania on February 20, Hoover wrote that the problem was national uncertainty due to concern that Roosevelt might inflate, fail to raise taxes, have recourse to deficit financing—in short, all that was in fact required to alleviate the horrible crisis that Hoover had presided over. Hoover's stated belief that a recovery had been in progress prior to the 1932 election was supported by a few transitory statistics of economic activity only and was not discernible to any identifiable segment of the American public.

For the rest of his life, Hoover claimed the recovery was under way but that Roosevelt had sabotaged it by leaving the country uncertain whether he would continue Hoover's program (which he had been elected to discontinue). Between the conventions and election day, Hoover was convinced the Democrats were conducting "bear raids" on the stock market, to break the momentum of returning prosperity. Roosevelt and his team were convinced the Republican newspaper owners were hyping the story of an economic revival to help Hoover. There isn't much evidence that either conspiracy actually occurred.

In Pennsylvania, where under Governor Gifford Pinchot relatively exact statistics were kept, unemployment increased by 28 percent from July 1932 to March 1933, and stood at 1,500,000 in that state on inauguration day, and at 13 to 18 million in the country as a whole.[55] Most states had reached the legal limit of debt, and many states and municipalities could not have sold bonds had they chosen, and been legally entitled, to issue them. Only the federal government possessed the potential to redeem the nation from economic collapse and social disorder. Hoover had proclaimed in the summer of 1930 that "the depression is over." National income had declined by over 50 percent since then. The banks were collapsing in droves. Frances Perkins wrote: "Relief stations were closing down for lack of funds. Hunger marchers were on parade. Food riots were becoming more common. Crime, born of the need for food, clothing, and other necessities of life, was on the upsurge. There were insecurity and terror in the agricultural regions. The increase in petty larceny was alarming."[56] Investment had declined by 90 percent since 1929, automobile production by 75 percent and half of all rural families lived at or below half of the accepted definition of poverty.[57]

In these terrible circumstances, Hoover wrote to Senator Reed that stability could be reasserted only by an unqualified endorsement of Hoover's policies by

Roosevelt and that this meant "the abandonment of 90 percent of the so-called 'new deal.' But unless this is done, they run the grave danger of precipitating a complete financial debacle."[58] Given the circumstances in which the country was then gasping, it is difficult to discern what ingredients Hoover thought were still missing from such a debacle.

While Hoover was completely demoralized politically, he retained his arrogant self-assurance about the virtues of his own policy right to the end of his life more than thirty years later. He had been, as Roosevelt had regarded him when he sought to be his running mate in 1920, a great public servant and continued to be so as an ex-president, but he had been completely defeated by the Great Depression. He seems to have believed that the public had suddenly become frightened at the prospect of the inauguration of the regime it had just elected by a heavy majority. Most astonishingly, he seems to have thought he could trick Roosevelt into abandoning his entire program and the majority of those who had elevated him.

As the banking crisis deepened through February, Roosevelt was besieged with letters about it, including one from his old friend Tom Lamont, who wrote in late February that "it could not be worse," and likened what was afoot to "pestilence and famine." Agnes Meyer, wife of Federal Reserve Governor Eugene Meyer and mother of the future newspaper and magazine publisher Katherine Graham, wrote in her diary: "World literally rocking beneath our feet." Hoover was going out "to the sound of crashing banks."[59] Hoover had reached such a state of alarm by mid-February that he was prepared to ask the Federal Reserve for a temporary guarantee of bank deposits until the crisis subsided.

Confidence had indeed declined even from the depths it had plumbed by election day, not because of Roosevelt, but because of the worsening crisis and the revelations of the Senate Banking and Currency and Finance committees. In the first, Charles G. Dawes acknowledged grossly imprudent and in fact illegal loans to the failed Insull utility empire. Before the same committee, the able counsel Ferdinand Pecora elicited from Charles Mitchell, the once all-powerful chairman of the National City Bank, that he had been wash-trading his own bank's shares, using the depositors' money as backing for questionable underwritings, and violating bank rules by stock-market promotions from which lending banks were supposed to abstain.

The Senate Finance Committee received a long procession of witnesses from the country's leading industrialists and financiers, lawyers, university presidents, and publishers, and it received almost no sensible views about what caused the Depression or what to do about it. Even relatively intelligent financiers like Bernard Baruch just gave Hooverish advice about soldiering on, as if through bad weather. Probably the American public has never been so disgusted and contemptuous toward its private-sector business leadership as at the beginning of 1933. There was an almost total dearth of imagination, inspiration, or even candor in the testimony before the committee.

By March 2, more than half the states had closed their banks. The New York Stock Exchange, the Chicago Board of Trade (for the first time since 1848), and most lesser places of exchange across the country had shut down. "In the once busy grain pits of Chicago, in the canyons of Wall Street, all was silent."[60]

The chief justice, Charles Evans Hughes, wrote on February 28 of his "earnest wish that you will have a most successful administration . . . and I especially prize the opportunity of being associated with you in our great American enterprise."[61] No doubt, but the entire financial system of the country was on the verge of collapse. The most prosperous nation in the history of the world, which had enticed millions of persecuted and penniless people from all over Europe to its shores, was on the verge of the failure of the brave experiment in democracy and individualism that had inspired, or at least aroused the curiosity of, the whole world for 150 years.

The redemption of the past and the salvation of the future all now depended on Franklin Delano Roosevelt. He and Moley had prepared the inaugural address, which would be delivered at 1 P.M. on March 4. It would signal a decisive change, not the assurance of continuity that Hoover had been pathetically beseeching Roosevelt to make. Roosevelt was almost transfigured in his serene outward composure on the train to Washington as he shared some of his ecclesiastical thoughts with Jim Farley, the most spiritual though far from the most intellectual of his entourage. "He told me of his own religious training [and said] the faith of the people was far more important than any other single element and . . . would be a great factor in seeing the nation through."[62] Roosevelt would appeal to that faith soon and often.

After surmounting the terrible personal ordeal of his illness, Roosevelt had resurrected his youthful conviction that he was the person to lead the American people back to the confidence and benignity of their forefathers. If he failed, the consequences would be as grave for the country as if Washington or Lincoln had failed in the same great office he was about to assume, and graver for the world. Franklin Delano Roosevelt believed in God, in the American people and their political institutions, in himself, and in the timely and intimate connection between them about to be solemnized. These were his thoughts as his train sped through the night and early hours of March 3, 1933, to Washington.

᷎

CHAPTER 7

"His Essence Was Force . . . the Relish of Power, and Command"

(Future Secretary of State Dean Acheson remembering Franklin D. Roosevelt in his early days as president)

ROOSEVELT WAS GREETED by tens of thousands of enthusiastic Washingtonians when his train arrived at Union Station at 9:25 on the cold and gloomy Friday morning of March 3, 1933. Flags were at half-mast in respect for Thomas Walsh, Roosevelt's attorney general-designate. Guards manning machine guns around public buildings added to an atmosphere of foreboding.[1] Roosevelt went to the presidential suite in the Mayflower Hotel and conferred until early afternoon with the Democratic leaders of the Congress. Eleanor took a friend in a taxi to visit St. Gaudens's allegorical statue *Grief* at the grave of Mrs. Henry Adams in Rock Creek Park, where she had often gone after her discovery of the Lucy Mercer affair fifteen years before.[2]

The usual dinner with the outgoing president had been condensed to a courtesy call and cup of tea at four o'clock on this afternoon, to the relief of both the Hoovers and the Roosevelts.

But Hoover made one final and unmannerly effort to ensnare Roosevelt in complicity with his own economic policy. Shortly after the arrival at the White House of the president-elect, his wife, his son James, and James's wife Betsy Cushing Roosevelt, Hoover announced that the secretary of the Treasury, Ogden Mills, and Federal Reserve governor Eugene Meyer were waiting to have a discussion about the banking crisis. Roosevelt prevailed upon his cousin, protocol chief Warren Delano Robbins, to call Moley, who arose from an afternoon nap and arrived just as the discussion got under way.

It continued for an hour, in which Roosevelt made it clear that it was Hoover's problem to deal with until the middle of the following day and that all he wished was to be advised of the President's decisions. He added that he understood that normally the outgoing president would now reciprocate his successor's visit but that he, Roosevelt, would perfectly understand if Hoover, in the circumstances, would wish to forgo that tradition. Hoover coldly responded that when Roosevelt had been in Washington as long as he had he would have learned that "the President of the United States calls upon no one." Roosevelt resolved to make a habit of calling frequently on appropriate people after he was installed in the White House. He and his party abruptly departed, asking to be advised of any important decisions.

Hoover telephoned Roosevelt twice on inauguration eve, still trying to secure Roosevelt's approval of an order restricting bank withdrawals and gold exports. Roosevelt declined yet again to be mousetrapped and retired shortly after one o'clock. Woodin and Moley then went over to the Treasury to familiarize themselves with the crisis that was about to fall into their laps and to help in the planning process that would have to be implemented by the end of the weekend that had just begun.

At the end of Friday, March 3, thirty-two states had closed all their banks *sine die*. Six other states had closed almost all their banks. In the other ten states and in the District of Columbia withdrawals were limited to 5 percent of deposits and in Texas to ten dollars per day. The U.S. financial system had reached the last extremity before it would collapse completely, taking the life's savings of tens of millions of people and what was left of the international economic system with it.

At ten o'clock on inauguration day morning, March 4, the Roosevelts went to a special service at St. John's Episcopal Church, across Lafayette Square from the White House. The timeless Endicott Peabody presided. The rector had voted for Hoover as the "more capable man" before rejoicing in the elevation of his former student, whose courtship of his favor had not wavered these nearly forty years.

When politics and religion intersected with Roosevelt, there was often a mixture of faith and tactics in his motives. There is no question of his sincere religiosity, but he also believed that he could achieve greater adherence to his leadership when seeming to lead the country toward a divinely inspired goal rather than merely invoking God's blessing on his own chosen course of action. He was also reluctant to be seen in the act of worship, though he was insistent on being known as a religious believer and churchgoer. Ecclesiastical modesty was doubtless compounded by the awkwardness of his physical condition and was addressed on this occasion by making it an invitation-only attendance. He "remained on his knees for some time, his face cupped in his hands."[3]

On his return to the Mayflower Hotel, Woodin and Moley briefed him on their night at the Treasury. They recommended that an obscure clause in the Trading with the Enemy Act be invoked to declare a bank holiday and that an emergency session of Congress be called to legislate a bank reorganization plan, both of which steps Roosevelt had already discussed and resolved to take, and that senior bankers from the eastern states as far west as Chicago be summoned to Washington to discuss the legislation starting the following day, Sunday, March 5. Roosevelt concurred and asked for the enabling documentation to be ready when he returned from his induction into the presidency. The Hoover administration did most of the preparatory work.

———————

The ride from the White House to the Capitol in an open car with Hoover for the inauguration was extremely frosty. Roosevelt made his usual effort at conviviality but was reduced as a conversational gambit to commenting on the "lovely steel" in the construction site of the new Department of Commerce building they passed (to be named after Hoover). Since nothing elicited any response from Hoover, the president-elect turned to wave his top hat at the large crowds on Pennsylvania Avenue. He went to the Senate chamber for the swearing in of John Nance Garner as vice president, and then at one o'clock, with his left hand grasping his son James's right upper arm and surrounded by aides so that he appeared to be walking stiffly and slowly but otherwise normally in the middle of the group, Franklin D. Roosevelt advanced to the rostrum on the steps of the Capitol. Here "the bearded iceberg," as Theodore Roosevelt had described the present Chief Justice (when he wasn't so irritated as to call him "the bearded lady"), Charles Evans Hughes, administered the brief constitutional oath to the new president.

The 400,000 spectators, more than half the population of greater Washington, covered forty acres of greensward beside the Capitol. They were much less festive than usual on such occasions, and now fell silent. In prior American history only Abraham Lincoln's second inaugural address is as well-known an opening presidential speech as the one Franklin D. Roosevelt now delivered. And in subsequent history, only John F. Kennedy's in 1961 is remotely as famous. The speaker described the occasion as a day "of national consecration" and promised "a candor and a decision which the present situation of our Nation impels. This great Nation will endure as it has endured, will revive and will prosper. So first of all let me assert my firm belief that the only thing we have to fear is fear itself—nameless unreasoning, unjustified terror which paralyzes needed efforts to convert retreat into advance." It is not clear whether this resonant phrase came from Louis Howe, as Howe claimed, or from Roosevelt's reading of Thoreau ("Nothing is so much to be feared as fear"), as Eleanor suggested to Samuel Rosenman. The thought was not original, but the application of it was dramatically effective.[4]

The country's difficulties, the new president said, "concern, thank God, only material things. Values have shrunken to fantastic levels; taxes have risen; our ability to pay has fallen; government of all kinds is faced by serious curtailment of income; the means of exchange are frozen in the currents of trade; the withered leaves of industrial enterprise lie on every side; farmers find no market for their produce; the savings of many years in thousands of families have gone.

"More important, a host of unemployed citizens face the grim problem of existence. Yet our distress comes from no failure of substance. We are stricken by no plague of locusts. Compared with the perils which our forefathers conquered because they believed and were not afraid, we have still much to be thankful for.

Nature still offers her bounty and human efforts have multiplied it. Plenty is at our doorstep but a generous use of it languishes in the very sight of the supply. Practices of the unscrupulous money changers stand indicted in the court of public opinion, rejected by the hearts and minds of men. . . . Faced by the failure of credit they have proposed only the lending of more money. Stripped of the lure of profit by which to induce our people to follow their false leadership, they have resorted to exhortations, pleading tearfully for restored confidence. They know only the rules of a generation of self-seekers. They have no vision and when there is no vision, the people perish.

"The money changers have fled from their high seats in the temple of our civilization. We may now restore that temple to the ancient truths." The vast audience before him and the tens of millions listening on the radio loved it, though Herbert Hoover, sitting six feet away, must have found it disconcerting. Nor would he have enjoyed the hereditary squire of Hyde Park's assertion that "Happiness lies not in the mere possession of money; it lies in the joy of achievement, in the thrill of creative effort." It would also have been galling to some to hear the person who would become the most avid political office-seeker in American history demand "the abandonment of the false belief that public office and high political position are to be valued only by the standards of pride of place."

This was the beginning of Roosevelt's consistent and inspired policy as president of channeling all the anger and frustration of these terrible times against unnamed forces, described only in broad moralistic caricatures. In this way he dispersed the country's rage harmlessly and conserved the moral integrality of America for eventual mobilization against real (external) enemies. As the decade progressed, he would arraign others in the dock beside the money changers: war profiteers, monopolists, malefactors of great wealth, economic royalists, and so forth. Audiences were delighted, an atmosphere of purgative reform prevailed, but there were no specified culprits.

Many businessmen and people from similar backgrounds to the President's would shriek with outrage at his demagogy and what they saw as his dishonorable desertion of his own peers. They were unaware, as businessmen often are, especially in America, of the subtleties of politics—that Roosevelt had spared them the status of scapegoats hated and reviled by 80 percent of the population; that Roosevelt had made the country safe again for the wealthy. He never ceased to be the man who had said with the debonair cynicism that caused those who knew him well to relish his company, that "It is hard for a man with five children and ten servants to make both ends meet."[5]

Franklin D. Roosevelt was assuredly well to the left of most businessmen, who tended to be orthodox reactionaries politically. But he was conservative socially. He was more concerned to prevent the extremes of American society from crowding the center and stampeding the masses into unacceptable attitudes than he was with the candor he pledged to employ in his first minute as president of the United States. Like Bismarck and Disraeli and his cousin Theodore, he wished to reform the system sufficiently to immunize it against extremes and ensure that everyone shared in the general prosperity, but meritocratically, not through imposed redistributive equality. He and they did not wish it reformed at the expense of their own ability to enjoy the lordly standards of living they had inherited and earned.

In all circumstances Roosevelt would remember where the majority of the voters were and how to produce as little division as possible in the nation as a whole. It was a providential talent in these tumultuous times, and would distinguish the United States from all the other major powers, which either embraced dictatorship or were riven by severe fissures between left and right.

Beyond his impassioned plea for more elevated ethics, Roosevelt recognized in his first moments as president that "This Nation asks for action and action now. Our greatest primary task is to put people to work." He promised direct job-creating relief "accomplishing greatly needed projects to stimulate and reorganize the use of our natural resources." He also promised government intervention to raise agricultural prices, aid to urban and rural home owners, comprehensive regulation of utilities and of the financial securities industries, and, in a gesture to the fiscal conservatives, "an adequate but sound currency . . . and making income balance outgo." He called for a revival of the "American spirit of the pioneer," and pledged the United States to the international policy of "the good neighbor."

He asked his countrymen to "move as a trained and loyal army willing to sacrifice for the good of a common discipline. The larger purposes will bind upon us all as a sacred obligation with a unity of duty hitherto evoked only in time of armed strife." This was reasonable enough, but it aroused Roosevelt's critics, then and subsequently, with the specter of dictatorial aspirations that they would have ample opportunity to impute as his presidency unfolded. The President promised to recommend the "measures that a stricken Nation in the midst of a stricken world may require." But if Congress failed to act, he would ask "for the one remaining instrument to meet the crisis—broad Executive power to wage a war against the emergency, as great as the power that would be given to me if we were in fact invaded by a foreign foe.

"For the trust reposed in me I will return the courage and the devotion that befit the time. I can do no less.

"We face the arduous days that lie ahead in the warm courage of national unity. . . . We do not distrust the future of essential democracy. The people of the United States have not failed. In their need, they have registered a mandate that they want direct, vigorous action. They have asked for discipline and direction under leadership. They have made me the present instrument of their wishes. In the spirit of the gift I take it."

The effect of the speech was electrifying. The long dreary years of Hoover's pettifogging and sermonizing and evasions passed noiselessly into a despised oblivion. When Roosevelt finished his fifteen-minute address, no one doubted that a drastically new era had begun, based on the pursuit of ambitious goals and not Dickensian humbug and claptrap about imminent spontaneous recovery. It was heard around the world—the first American political address to be so widely broadcast. Among the listeners were King George V and Queen Mary, British prime minister Ramsey MacDonald, and former prime minister Lloyd George, with his houseguests Oswald Mosley and the Soviet ambassador. Lady Cynthia Mosley wrote to Roosevelt that Lloyd George had been "terrifically excited" and thought the speech "most remarkable."[6]

(Benito Mussolini warmly thanked Roosevelt in July, in a handwritten letter in perfect English,[7] for the copy of the inaugural address delivered by the incoming U.S. ambassador, Breckinridge Long, and quoted Roosevelt admiringly and at length in an article in *Il Popolo d'Italia*, also in July. "This courage of youth," wrote the Italian leader of the New Deal, "facing the conflict with decision and with manly pessimism, belong to . . . 'that way of life' to which Fascism has educated . . . the Italian people.")[8]

Roosevelt came to regard his first inaugural address as "sacred ground," thought Frances Perkins. "It was something not of his own making. I'm sure he thought of it as direct divine guidance."[9]

President Hoover shook hands with his successor and departed for New York. The two men never met again, though they were often in the same city. Hoover observed a polite silence for some months of the new administration before taking up a prolonged opposition to most of Roosevelt's domestic program and much of his pre-war foreign policy.

Roosevelt had suggested a reduction in the scale of the inaugural celebrations. But the Democrats wanted to celebrate their return to office, and the customary festivities were not curtailed.[10] After a brief buffet lunch the President and other dignitaries, including many survivors of the Wilson administration, Mrs. Edith Wilson among them, watched the parade from the reviewing stand, which was a replica of the façade of Andrew Jackson's Tennessee house, the Hermitage.[11] Mindful of what he had considered Wilson's somewhat unmanly performance in 1917 of standing in a glass enclosure, Roosevelt watched bare-headed and subjected to the elements as the forty bands and hundreds of other formations went by. (Several of the bands played *The Franklin Delano Roosevelt March*, the latest musical creation of the new Treasury secretary, William Woodin.) General MacArthur was beside the President while the numerous army units came past. The civilian highlight and recipient of the greatest applause was Al Smith in a brown derby and the regalia of a sachem of Tammany Hall, walking briskly along at the head of the New York delegation, one of thirty-three state parade groups. The two former New York governors waved warmly to each other. It is unlikely that Smith's inner feelings were of unalloyed happiness as he contemplated, from his own position as a Raskob employee, his former stand-in as the repository of the hopes of the nation and the powers of its government.

As the light faded, Roosevelt returned to the White House, though the parade continued, and presided over the mass swearing-in of his cabinet. There was then a huge reception. He paid particular attention to a group of thirteen children on crutches from Warm Springs whom he had personally invited. There was a buffet dinner for family, including a substantial delegation from the Oyster Bay Roosevelts. After dinner Roosevelt sent his wife, daughter, and sons off to the inaugural balls and sat for a long time in Lincoln's study alone with Louis Howe, who had been planning this residential and career move for more than twenty years. The White House would be their official address for the rest of their lives.

———————

On Sunday, March 5, 1933, Roosevelt went unobtrusively to St. Thomas's Church, held a brief cabinet meeting, and gave a short radio address directed to the American Legion. He also issued proclamations closing all the banks in the country until March 10, prohibiting gold and silver exports and foreign-exchange transactions, and summoning Congress into emergency session for March 9.

On Monday, Roosevelt's first official workday in his new position, he was wheeled by his valet, Irwin McDuffie, to his new office, which still had bare walls and an uncluttered and empty desk. He was left there, behind closed doors and windows with nothing to read or to write upon. Roosevelt (according to Tugwell) found this unnerving, and after half a minute or so called out for someone to join him. Missy LeHand, who had arranged this contemplative moment at the start of this supreme stage of his career, hastily entered and a normal workday began.[12]

Roosevelt held his first of 998 presidential press conferences on the morning of Wednesday, March 8. Warren Harding had badly bobbled a question about naval disarmament in 1921, and after that Roosevelt's three Republican predecessors had required questions to be written out in advance. Roosevelt dispensed with this and started out with two press conferences per week. The journalists would come into his office and stand around his desk with notepads and pencils in hand. The President remained seated at his desk, his legs invisible to the press, and he unselfconsciously employed such phrases as "I have to run," "as funny as a crutch," etc. He established three categories of comments — attributable to a White House source; background, which could be used by reporters on their own authority and not attributed to the White House; and totally off the record.

He completely charmed the 125 journalists, was a master of the duplicitous answer and of the partial, evasive, or half-true answer, and always knew how to give most of the journalists something useful. He exuded a comprehension of the requirements of their job and manipulated them with such surpassing finesse that few of them realized the extent to which they were being used, or were flattered to play the role. He secured their support in the first days of his administration and never yielded it. In this first press conference his sons Franklin and John came in to say goodbye to their father as they were returning to school (Groton). It was a well-appreciated familial touch. At the end of the press briefing the reporters broke into spontaneous applause.

The deliberations with the bankers over the banking legislation were tense and acrimonious. Melvin Traylor, chief executive of Chicago's First National Bank, who had been put up by the late Mayor Anton Cermak as the favorite son candidate of Illinois at the Democratic convention nine months before, was an excitable participant in the talks, bursting several times into rages and tears. He never recovered from the strain of this week, and died less than a year later. The tensions even erupted among the White House representatives, as Berle and Moley squabbled fiercely at times.

The basis of what went to the Congress March 9 had been prepared by Hoover's Treasury secretary, Ogden Mills. Roosevelt was strongly urged by the urban left and the western progressive and populist members of the Congress to nationalize the banking business. He knew that any such initiative would be insane—would completely distract the administration and the Congress from the underlying task of resolving the Depression, would bitterly divide the politicians and the public, and if successful would catapult the government into the operation of a huge business for which it had no aptitude and in which it would attract infinite ill will for any loan declined or called, or any rise in interest rates. He maneuvered deftly to appear a savior of the industry to the conservatives and a reformer of a flawed banking system to the nationalization advocates.

As the final touches were being put on the banking legislation on Wednesday, March 8, Roosevelt unsuccessfully tried to persuade Felix Frankfurter to become solicitor general of the United States. Then, in violation of Hoover's practice that the president didn't call on anyone, he visited retired Supreme Court Justice Oliver Wendell Holmes, who was celebrating his ninety-second birthday with two of his former secretaries, Thomas G. Corcoran and Donald Hiss (brother of Holmes's former law clerk Alger Hiss), and with Frankfurter. Corcoran would go on to a prominent and controversial role in the New Deal. He was a strenuous and intelligent Irishman of the synthetic New England variety, who took his accordion with him to dinner parties to regale the guests with Irish songs (until Frankfurter told him in 1940 that he would not have anti-British songs in his house while Britain was defending Western civilization).

Three stories have emerged from this half-hour visit. One was that Holmes was in his library reading Plato when Roosevelt arrived and when Roosevelt asked why Holmes was reading *The Republic*, the justice replied: "To improve my mind, Mr. President." A second story is that Roosevelt asked if Holmes had any advice for him in the current economic crisis. The nonagenarian hero of the Civil War responded: "You are in a war, Mr. President, and in a war there is only one rule, form your battalions and fight!" Holmes and Roosevelt chatted about prize-fighting and John L. Sullivan. Finally, it is alleged that after the President left, Holmes remarked that his distinguished visitor's cousin had appointed him to the Supreme Court, and then said: "A second-class intellect but a first-class temperament."[13]

Corcoran is the chief source for this last quote, which was corroborated by Donald Hiss, but it is not clear which President Roosevelt Holmes was talking about.[14] This may even have been the first meeting between Holmes and Franklin Roosevelt, and Holmes had often referred to Theodore Roosevelt in similar terms in his correspondence.[15] Whether Holmes said it or not, Franklin Roosevelt has been arraigned on this patronizing charge by historians for some time. Just which presidents Holmes might have considered first-class intellects, apart from possibly Jefferson, Wilson, and Madison, is not clear.

If Holmes said this about FDR, it was an uncharacteristically ungentlemanly reward for the President's great courtesy in visiting him. And it does not square with the note Holmes sent a few days later thanking the President for his "kind thoughtfulness," praising "a most fortunate beginning of the term," and adding a "brief expression of confident prophecies for the future."[16]*

The House of Representatives passed the President's banking bill when it was presented on March 9, on a voice vote and without debate. The Senate passed it seventy-three to seven after a debate of a few hours. Roosevelt determined to hold Congress in special session and try to put through substantial parts of the New Deal at once if his draftsmen could prepare the legislation quickly enough.

On March 10, Roosevelt sent the Congress his economy bill, drafted by Director of the Budget Lewis Douglas and entitled "A Bill to Maintain the Credit of the United States Government." It authorized the President to reduce veterans' pensions and cut all government salaries by up to 15 percent. This was not as draconian as it sounds, because the cost of living had declined by more than 15 percent. But it was deflationary.

Roosevelt went on the radio at 10 P.M. Eastern Time on Sunday, March 12, to explain the banking crisis and the government's response to it. A large majority of the 17 million families that owned radio receivers are thought to have listened to Roosevelt's talk. Broadcaster Robert Trout, with the approval of the White House, introduced the President to an estimated 60 million listeners with the information that "The President wants to come into your home and sit beside your fireside for a little fireside chat." This description caught on, and was used, as Roosevelt said in 1938, "even when the radio talk is delivered on a very hot midsummer evening." A pharmacist's assistant swabbed Roosevelt's nasal passages

---

* If allowance is made for the supernatural acuity of his intuition and his almost infallible memory, which Holmes would have had little opportunity to appreciate, Roosevelt's intellect was first-class. His cultural attainments could be regarded as second-class by a man of Holmes's erudition, but they were considerable, if haphazard and esoteric. Roosevelt was not a polymath, but he was a learned man, a competent lawyer, a widely read expert on several historical areas, a passable naturalist, and the only president in the country's history who was reasonably fluent in French and German.[17]

before every important speech or broadcast to improve the quality of the sound of his rich tenor. Corcoran said that where "the sound of his voice was concerned, Roosevelt looked upon a speech with the same care that a prima donna would take care of her voice before a singing appearance."[18]

On this occasion, Roosevelt, in his best country doctor bedside manner, with solicitude but without a hint of condescension, explained how the banks functioned. He explained that the current problem had arisen because confidence had fled and demands for withdrawals had outstripped the ability of even the strongest banks to convert sound investments of depositors' money back into cash. He commended the Republicans as well as the members of his own party for putting his bill through the Congress "promptly and patriotically." His legislative measure authorized the issuance of special currency backed by bank assets, which was being distributed around the banking system to deal with further heavy withdrawals if these continued, without forcing uneconomic liquidations of bank assets.

The President gave the timetable of bank reopenings. The following day, March 13, banks certified by the Treasury to be sound would reopen in the twelve Federal Reserve cities. The day after, banks certified sound in 250 other cities would be reopened, and the day after that large numbers of banks throughout the country in smaller centers would reopen. More and more banks would continue to open in the larger cities too, as they were deemed by the Treasury to be fit to do so, by improvement in their condition, by recapitalization, or by merger. The government would encourage existing shareholders of banks to make supplementary investments in them where this was desirable, and the Reconstruction Finance Corporation would also do so, but on a more prudent basis than Hoover's squandered investment of $90 million in Charles G. Dawes's Central Republic Bank, which sank without a ripple. "Let me make it clear to you that if your bank does not open the first day you are by no means justified in believing that it will not open. A bank that opens on one of the subsequent days is in exactly the same status as the bank that opens tomorrow. It is my belief that hoarding during the past week has become a very unfashionable pastime. I can assure you that it is safer to keep your money in a reopened bank than under the mattress."

Roosevelt was careful not to play the anti-banking card. He expressed confidence in the system and in the great majority of bankers, and declared that problems arose from the incompetence or dishonesty of only an unspecified and unrepresentative few.

At Senator Glass's insistence, the state banks were excluded from the legislation; only Federal Reserve members were included. However, the RFC was specifically authorized to invest in both categories of banks, and under its aggressive chairman, Jesse Jones, it did so, becoming a huge corporation and a very successful one. The Federal Reserve also aided state banks, and brought a great many of them under federal control, with assistance as an enticement. Many banks were initially standoffish about having the U.S. government as a shareholder, fearing de facto nationalization, despite Jones's efforts at persuasion. Finally, on September 5, 1933, speaking off the record to the American Bankers' Association, Jones told them: "Half the banks represented in this room are insolvent; and those of you representing these banks know it better than anyone else." This appeal was successful. The cooperative effort that followed led to RFC investments in several thousand banks and greatly strengthened the banking system.[19]

It was clear within two days that the President's banking bill and his explanation of it had been an overwhelming success. By the end of March $1.25 billion had returned to the banks in deposits, and another billion dollars returned in April. By the third day of the reopening program, March 15, 76 percent of the Federal Reserve member banks had already reopened and this number rose steadily over succeeding months. Depositors' losses were a very small percentage of the total of deposits.

A particular case was Amadeo Peter Giannini's Bank of America in San Francisco, which had a very large number of small accounts, many with the Italian-American community, and was resented by the San Francisco banking establishment, which dominated the local Federal Reserve. It was also the pioneering bank of the California film industry. The head of the San Francisco Federal Reserve, John U. Calkins, wished to withhold the reopening of Giannini's bank, and Woodin asked Roosevelt's advice. The President stated that either the Bank of America should reopen on the first day, March 13, or Calkins should publicly take personal responsibility for the decision not to do so. This caused Calkins to retreat. The Bank of America opened on the first day, grew steadily larger and stronger, and became the largest bank in the country. Giannini was an unshakeable Roosevelt loyalist ever after.

An $800 million U.S. Treasury issue was oversubscribed by 100 percent in the first week of the bank reopenings. And the New York Stock Exchange, which had been unprecedentedly closed from March 3 to March 15, on reopening surged to its greatest one-day rise in history, over 15 percent on the heaviest volume in six months. It had been an astounding change of atmosphere and prospects in ten days. No administration in history had had such a brilliant launch. The handling of the banking crisis, the inaugural address itself, the new ground rules for dealing with the press, and the master stroke of the Fireside Chat were all brilliant advances for the new president.

The novelist John Dos Passos described years later the sensation of listening to a Fireside Chat: "People edge their chairs up to the radio. There is a man leaning across his desk, speaking clearly and cordially so that you and me will completely understand that he has his fingers on all the switchboards of the federal government, operating the intricate machinery of the departments, drafting codes and regulations and bills for the benefit of you and me worried about things, sitting close to the radio in small houses on rainy nights, for the benefit of us wagearners,

us homeowners, us farmers, us mechanics, us miners, us mortgagees, us proces-
sors, us mortgageholders, us bank depositors, us consumers, retail merchants,
bankers, brokers, stockholders, bondholders, creditors, debtors, jobless and job-
holders. 'Not a sparrow falleth but . . .' "[20]

British ambassador Sir Ronald Lindsay reported to the foreign secretary, Sir
John Simon, on March 15: "There is little doubt that [Roosevelt's] vigorous and
determined assault on the national problems has already induced a revival of
confidence across the country."[21]

II

ROOSEVELT NEXT THREW out the mad experiment of Prohibition. It had
achieved nothing for temperance proponents, nor for anyone else except a
few gangsters and lesser bootleggers. Prohibition was lamented only by the
underworld and by some whose families were afflicted with drunkenness and by
some fundamentalist Christian advocates of the earnest and joyless life, like, in
some respects, Josephus Daniels (and Eleanor Roosevelt). To sophisticated
Americans and especially to foreigners, Prohibition had been an inexplicable
crusade against one of life's noteworthy pleasures. It was just two months since
Roosevelt had told French ambassador Claudel that repeal would require two to
three years. Le Quai Roosevelt became very active shipping French wine to
America, including to the White House.

On April 7, 1933, the first day since 1920 that beer was legally sold in America,
a richly liveried horse-drawn Anheuser-Busch beer wagon delivered a ceremonial
case to Alfred E. Smith at his Empire State Building office, out of gratitude for
his long fight against Prohibition.[22]

The President moved to two more priorities, his domestic-allotment plan for
raising agricultural prices and direct employment in conservation projects. The
core of the new Agricultural Adjustment Act was to obtain voluntary reductions
of acreage and hog production on a decentralized basis, with benefit payments,
as they were called, going in compensation to farmers who observed agreed quotas. Producers of each crop governed by these arrangements would be invited to
ratify the quotas and benefit-payment levels by referendum before they could
take effect. It was declared that the ambition of the government was to establish a
parity of farm and industrial prices and to confer on the rural population a benefit comparable to that which manufacturers enjoyed from tariffs. That it was subject to the approval of those affected was a noteworthy exercise in popular
democracy. For a great many African-American farmers, it was the first time they
had ever been allowed to cast a ballot about anything.

Because Roosevelt refused to countenance further deficit spending, the program was to be paid for by an agricultural processing tax. The affected groups—
millers, packers, and canners—swarmed the Congress with opposition to the

measure. A raft of amendments, some of them special-interest moves, some simply dilatory, were filed. Roosevelt, well-skilled in this form of logrolling from his days in Albany, was ready with a counter strategy. On March 27, he united by executive order nine federal agencies dispensing different categories of farm relief in a single agency to be called the Farm Credit Administration. It was understood from an accompanying presidential message that the FCA would soon be charged with a comprehensive refinancing of farm mortgages, a desperately serious problem affecting the agricultural population, half of whom were threatened with dispossession of their farms. Henry Morgenthau, Roosevelt's Hudson valley neighbor, was bruited as the FCA governor. (Parallel legislation, refinancing urban mortgages through the Home Owners Loan Corporation, was successfully proposed a few weeks later.)

On April 3, Roosevelt sent the Congress the request for farm-mortgage relief legislation and had the resulting bill attached to the Agricultural Adjustment Act as Title II of that bill. The following day he summoned the entire Agriculture Committee to the White House and told them that the bottling up of his legislation in committee was intolerable. He said that in these desperate circumstances—and with planting about to begin, requiring immediate action if production was to be curtailed—his bill had to be reported out at once. If it were not, he warned, the committee would be publicly held responsible by him for continued collapsed farm prices and any further farm mortgage foreclosures.

The congressmen were resistless against such a threat, and the bill was reported out the next day and was promptly enacted.

With great difficulty Roosevelt recruited George Peek, formerly of the Moline Plow Company, which had failed financially, an agrarian capitalist and dirt farmer (and business associate of General Hugh Johnson and of Bernard Baruch), who opposed production constraints, as head of the Agricultural Adjustment Administration. To Peek's argument that he couldn't accept the appointment because he disapproved of domestic allotment, Roosevelt responded that since Peek opposed it because he feared that it would be administered in a bureaucratic and unjust manner, he must take the post and ensure that what he feared would not come to pass. Peek's acceptance helped carry the final vote on the AAA, because he enjoyed considerable credibility with the traditional agrarian comunity.

Roosevelt was still smarting from the fiasco of extemporizing a reference to job creation through reforestation in his acceptance speech in Chicago, when the number of jobs created was soon shown to be minimal. He determined to proceed with a Civilian Conservation Corps to employ 250,000 unemployed workers in many types of conservation projects. He presented the Congress with the appropriate bill on March 21. William Green, head of the American Federation of Labor, opposed the measure at first, because he feared that the modest wage scale would undercut his workers. He also expressed reservations about having the U.S. Army play any role in billeting, transporting, and supervising the workers, because it smacked to him of Fascism. Roosevelt, pointing out that there were approximately 14 million unemployed people in the country, dismissed these concerns as "utter rubbish," and appeased Green by appointing as director the Machinists' Union vice president, Robert Fechner. The bill passed easily.

The CCC normally employed only unmarried men between the ages of 18 and 25 from families on relief. The Forest and National Park Services planned work for them under the supervision of the army. Colonel George C. Marshall organized seventeen camps in the southeastern states with the efficiency he would later display in much greater and less bucolic operations. The corpsmen shortly numbered over 300,000 in about 1,500 camps, and numbered over 500,000 in 1935. Their duties included flood control, reforestation, suppression of tree diseases, clearing forest firebreaks and building fire observation towers, the creation or improvement of parks, beaches, and historic battlefields, and the preservation of endangered species such as the whooping crane. Four million acres of trees were thinned, one billion fish were stocked, and 30,000 wildlife shelters were built.[23] It was a hugely imaginative and successful program.

The CCC also helped to resolve the return of the Bonus Marchers. Several thousand of them had returned to Washington by mid-May. Where Hoover had ignored them while their ranks swelled and festered in cardboard and corrugated shantytowns, and ultimately unleashed upon them the disturbing figure of MacArthur, snorting of "insurrection" and in full dress uniform at the head of tanks, cavalry, and infantry with fixed bayonets, Roosevelt had the marchers put up in an underused army fort. He saw to it that they were given three meals a day and medical attention, and he received their leaders in the White House. He sent Eleanor out to visit them and lead them in singing the wartime ditty "It's a Long, Long, Trail A'Winding." They were offered membership in the CCC, which 90 percent accepted. They voted to disperse, and those that wished to return home rather than join the CCC were given free rail passage.

————————

Harry Hopkins, director of New York's Temporary Emergency Relief Administration, came to Washington with William Hodson of the New York Welfare Council in mid-March. They sought an interview with the President to present him with their plan for direct unemployment-relief grants to the states. This was at some variance with the Democratic platform, which called for credits to the states. Roosevelt was apprised of the idea by Frances Perkins, who met with Hopkins and Hodson when an appointment with the President was not easily available.

Miss Perkins was so enthusiastic about their idea that she insisted that Roosevelt meet them. He too agreed with the idea, and proclaimed that it fulfilled the platform commitment, despite the well-known difference between a credit and a grant. Roosevelt asked the Congress, which quickly complied, to set up the

Federal Emergency Relief Administration. Hopkins was named to the position of federal relief administrator. He would prove enormously effective and would quickly establish himself as the President's closest, most trusted, and most versatile collaborator. (Hopkins took a 40 percent cut in pay in moving from New York to Washington, but he was set at the head of what soon became a vast emergency relief apparatus dealing efficiently with millions of people.)

While the Senate hesitated over the farm-relief bill in late March and the House was relatively unoccupied, the administration sent in a minor measure of securities regulation to keep the congressmen occupied. Unfortunately, Roosevelt, in a gesture that typified his methods of assigning the same work to parallel and competing groups within his government, had requested a legislative draft from both Raymond Moley and Commerce Secretary Daniel Roper. He then forgot the duplication until both reported back to him, and then he asked Moley to deal with commodity and stock exchanges and Roper with securities marketing.

Roosevelt handed the drafting to Felix Frankfurter, who involved three of the stars in the early firmament of the New Deal. James M. Landis, Princeton and Harvard Law alumnus, former clerk to Justice Brandeis, and son of a Presbyterian missionary in Japan; Benjamin V. Cohen (University of Chicago and Harvard Law), counsel for the American Zionists at Versailles; and Thomas G. Corcoran (Brown and Harvard Law), protégé of both Frankfurter and Oliver Wendell Holmes. In their academic attainments, idealism, and ambition, as in their sectarian diversity, they quickly rose from this impromptu launch to legendary prominence in the new administration.

Roosevelt returned to the main lines of his reform program on April 10, when he asked Congress to establish the Tennessee Valley Authority, "a corporation clothed with the power of Government but possessed of the flexibility and initiative of a private enterprise." Along with matters concerning the U.S. Navy, to which he would never cease to be devoted, and the Civilian Conservation Corps, this was the measure closest to the President's heart. This was far more grandiose a project than any envisioned in eight previous Muscle Shoals bills introduced by George Norris, and would be one of the world's mighty feats of engineering. A 650-mile navigable channel was to be opened up from Knoxville, Tennesse, to Paducah, Kentucky and huge ancillary enterprises were to be created in fertilizer production and in electricity generation and distribution.

The bill sent to the Congress called for the TVA to be able to produce electricity and to distribute it over its own transmission lines to the public. This would be direct competition with the private sector. Following the collapse of the Insull empire, the Georgia and Alabama Light and Power Companies and the Tennessee Electric Power Company came under the control of Commonwealth and Southern, whose president was the energetic and capable transplanted (to Wall

Street) Indianan, Wendell L. Willkie. Willkie and others immediately began lob-bying the Congress and questioning the fairness and practicality of aspects of the bill, while lauding its scale and professed motivations.*

Roosevelt was unmoved by such arguments, and power utilities had few friends in the Congress. The President strong-armed the measure through and signed it on May 18, 1933. He appointed a three-man board of the TVA, with Arthur Morgan as chairman. Morgan had been in charge of flood control and dam construction in the Miami Conservancy District in Ohio. The other mem-bers were the president of the University of Tennessee, Harcourt Morgan (a fertil-izer specialist), and the young Harvard lawyer and Frankfurter protégé David E. Lilienthal. Despite being only thirty-four, Lilienthal had already served two years as Governor Robert La Follette's chairman of the Wisconsin Public Service Commission and was an authority on electric power policy.

Roosevelt came under considerable pressure in the Congress in April and May to take his reforms radically further. Senator Hugo Black of Alabama urged a thirty-hour work week, claiming this would spread employment around. Senators Bronson Cutting, Edward Costigan, and Robert La Follette Jr. proposed a $6 bil-lion public works employment program. Roosevelt did not approve of either of these measures but didn't want a direct dispute with his reform friends, and didn't want to be boxed in with the reactionary right.

A measure presented by Oklahoma's Senator Elmer Thomas, who had long claimed the country would have to inflate its way out of the crisis, presaged departure from the gold standard. Roosevelt's emergency banking legislation had suspended export sales of gold and silver. Thomas proposed that the President be required to print more money, monetize silver, or reduce the gold content of the dollar. The President's congressional floor managers had told him that they did not have the votes to prevent passage of the Thomas Amendment, so Roosevelt said he would accept it if the inflationary powers created were altered to be dis-cretionary to him rather than mandatory. In this form the bill passed. Conferring discretionary inflationary powers on the President was a momentous step but the advisability of it was supported by Britain's experience. Britain had made consid-erable progress and reduced domestic unrest when it abandoned the gold stan-dard. Germany had delivered itself into the hands of the Nazis in part by resisting this step. Gold standardist Budget Director Lewis Douglas gloomily announced to Moley and James Warburg: "This is the end of Western civilization."[24] The Treasury secretary, the musically and otherwise talented William Woodin, wrote a cheery little composition called "Lullaby to Silver."[25]

---

* Willkie was at this stage a Democrat who had attended the Chicago convention and had been one of the 8½ Indianans who voted for Newton D. Baker, undeterred by the fact that Baker had not been placed in nomination.

Roosevelt's workday in the White House was much like it had been in Albany. He awakened at 8:30, had a breakfast in bed of orange juice, scrambled eggs, toast, and coffee, and read the *New York Times* and *Herald Tribune, Washington Post* and *Herald,* the *Baltimore Sun,* and Louis Howe's digest of cuttings from other papers, called the *Daily Bugle.* With his breakfast, Roosevelt had the first cigarette of about two daily packs of Camels. These were smoked through a long-stemmed ivory cigarette holder designed not to aggravate his sensitive and receding gums. While still reading, and while he shaved (sitting), wearing mended pajamas, and even when he had started to dress, with the help of his valet, he received visitors. At the start of his administration, apart from family members, these were Raymond Moley and Lewis Douglas. With them, and their successors, and later McIntyre and Early, he would start to organize the workday.

At 10:30, on his simple, wheeled kitchen chair with an attached ashtray but no arms, he went by elevator to his office, where he remained until about 6 P.M. He received visitors, supposedly at fifteen-minute intervals, but he often went overtime and had in his office together sequential visitors who didn't even know each other. His conviviality almost never flagged. He had his simple lunch at his desk; for the first few months, the White House could not even give him a hot meal there until a rolling warming oven was bought. From two to three he dictated correspondence. He received between four and seven thousand letters and telegrams per day, and his staff sifted out the items he would like to see himself. They became highly proficient at dealing with most of the mail in as apparently personalized a way as possible. He was a lively and sometimes elegant correspondent, but rarely wrote letters of particular academic or stylistic distinction and almost never revealed anything about himself.

After three were the biweekly press conferences and the weekly cabinet meetings. He steadily built and maintained his relations with the working press. The convivial press conferences generated immense publicity for him. In early 1934, the managing editor of the *New York Times* reckoned that that newspaper had published one million words in articles generated by the press conferences. At five FDR would hold his "Children's Hour," when he would go over some of the day's events, usually in an amusing way, for half an hour. Then he might go for a swim in the indoor pool, paid for by subscriptions promoted by the *New York Daily News* before it and its owners deserted Roosevelt. The necessary funds, $10,000, were largely raised from schoolchildren. Most days he would have a massage and some swabbing and inhalations for his sinuses. Then he would mix his pre-dinner cocktails, usually a very wet martini or an old fashioned verging on punch. He often worked or strategized about work after dinner, retired shortly after midnight, and was asleep within five minutes.

The core of the New Deal, the National Industrial Recovery Act, had been sent to the Congress on May 17. It was a ramshackle measure combining the hobby horses of most of the prominent factions in the administration and the Congress, and had been thrown quickly together to counteract Hugo Black's thirty-hour workweek bill, which Roosevelt thought unconstitutional (as a restraint on the freedom of employers and employees), inflexible, and altogether bad.

Title I of the NIRA provided for suspension of antitrust constraints against price-fixing and urged industries to adopt and submit to the government codes for price levels in each industry. In the interests of raising prices and generating profits, taxes, and investments, the government was prepared to tolerate temporary recourse to state-approved cartelism. Proportionately, industries were required to engage in collective bargaining, thus placating the government's powerful constituency in organized labor by the greatest legal encouragement it had yet received from Washington.

Title II was a $3.3 billion allocation for an emergency Public Works Administration, which would build and repair federal buildings, roads, bridges, dams, and other assets and facilities, employing as many as two million of the unemployed.

Title III was presented in vague form, to be filled out by the Congress to provide some offsetting revenue for the billions to be spent in Title II. Since this was a radical departure from Roosevelt's balanced-budget pledges, especially the speech at Pittsburgh on September 19, 1932, the President went public with the distinction he had been trying for several months to sell privately, and referred to these expenses as "investments."

The bill incorporated most of everyone's wish list, from the inflationists through the Keynesians to the advocates of a balanced budget and a hard currency, though the last group was not going to be easily mollified. It reflected Roosevelt's own uncertainty about the cause of the Depression and his suspicion of those who claimed to have sure remedies for resolving it. All of the main solutions that had been proposed would be tried simultaneously.

Roosevelt knew that unemployment had to be reduced drastically, and the Civilian Conservation Corps, the Tennessee Valley Authority, and the Public Works Administration might absorb as much as one-third of the unemployed. He hoped that the stand-by authorities that had been voted for him to increase the money supply, reflate the currency, stimulate the economy, and put more demand into the system would be a jump-start to recovery.

The partial abandonment of the gold standard through prohibition of the exportation of gold and silver and the gold revaluation powers given the President had already produced a 12 percent reduction in the gold value of the dollar in June, and had produced some rise in commodity prices and industrial production. Industrial production was already up by 60 percent, and it would be up 80 percent by July. These facts and the President's inspirational talents had also excited stock market expectations of better times and inflationary pressures. Stock market prices, coming off a very depressed floor, had risen 65 percent in April and May.

By sending the Congress a measure that had in it something for (as well as something to offend) almost all schools of thought, but containing the fundamental steps aimed at raising incomes and prices and moving millions of people into workfare projects, he intended to reinvigorate the morale of the country. As the NIRA was presented, it was informally revealed that it would be administered by Baruch's colorful, forceful, and hard-drinking protégé, General Hugh Johnson, a well-regarded practical rather than theoretical man, and a florid speaker and writer.

Franklin D. Roosevelt, the former football cheerleader and current hero of the film and arts communities (a status he would retain throughout his presidency), intended to apply all his aptitudes for showmanship and elegant boosterism, including the recruitment of celebrities to help him sell the proposition that the economy was in full recovery. He gambled that the mass fervent desire for economic revival, the complexity of the recovery program, and the razzmatazz with which it was presented would compel a general adherence to its goals durable enough to enable the country to bootstrap itself out of the morass.

The National Industrial Recovery bill was assured of, and had, a stormy reception in the Congress. Organized labor, led by William Green of the American Federation of Labor and John L. Lewis of the United Mine Workers of America, generally favored it because of the collective-bargaining requirements. They had considered that industry was generally operating informal cartels anyway, and were relatively undisturbed by these provisions. Business was much more divided. Populists and Progressives were not at all sympathetic to cartels and weren't particularly impressed with the big unions, either. Fiscal conservatives were scandalized by the cost of the public works programs of Title II and unsatisfied by the revenue increases envisioned in Title III. There was little enthusiasm anywhere except among a few fiscal purists for the idea of raising taxes in the middle of the worst depression in the country's history.

One of the arguments that arose against the bill, raised by Senator Huey Long in particular, was that the appointment of Hugh Johnson as director would confer too much power on the shadowy figure of Bernard Baruch. This was ironic, because Baruch was already lobbying against Johnson as one who becomes "dangerous and unstable . . . [and] gets nervous and sometimes goes away for days without notice" (on drunken benders).

Huey Long found in the bill "every fault of socialism . . . every crime of monarchy . . . worse than anything proposed under the Soviets." These rhetorical flourishes did not deter him from ultimately voting for it. There were fierce battles over amendments, but on June 13, with Roosevelt pouring on the pressure, the National Industrial Recovery Act received congressional assent.

Roosevelt's winning tactic had been to keep the titles together so that the job creation under Title II, which had broad support, could not be voted without the corporatist and collective-bargaining features of Title I. Roosevelt allowed most of the revenue-generating potential of Title III to be scrapped, putting his conservative colleagues, led by Budget Director Lewis Douglas, over the side. With even more than his usual hyperbole Roosevelt announced: "History will probably record the National Industrial Recovery Act as the most important and far-reaching legislation ever enacted by the American Congress. It represents a supreme effort to stabilize for all time the many factors which make for the prosperity of the nation, and the preservation of American standards."[26]

Having got the bill through by attaching the first two titles so inseparably to each other, he now gave way to his reservations about Hugh Johnson by giving the administration of the huge public-works program to Interior Secretary Harold Ickes, leaving Johnson with only administration of the pricing and industrial-relations codes. Roosevelt invited Johnson in for the signing ceremony, and even heard a gracious speech of thanks from the general before gently informing him that he was, in effect, forced from most of his position before he assumed it. At the end of the meeting Roosevelt asked Frances Perkins to stay close to Johnson. "Don't let him explode," he said. Miss Perkins was efficient, as always, and effectively hosed down the crestfallen general.[27]

The NIRA became the model for vast amorphous programs to achieve universally desired ends in the future, such as wartime price and production controls and Richard Nixon's anti-inflation measures in 1971, replete with a "pay board" and "price commission." Nixon was no more optimistic about the real efficacy of these creations than Roosevelt probably was about elements of Title I of the NIRA, but they both hoped that the process and the cause would distract or enlist the population while concrete action, market forces, and White House–led inspirational psychology caused the crisis to subside. (Mr. Nixon confirmed to the author in 1991 that he had been influenced by the NIRA in presenting his anti-inflation measures in 1971.)

———

As if to accentuate the dangers of a speculative revival, the ingenious Ferdinand Pecora, in his examination of witnesses before the Senate Banking Committee, unearthed the fact that J.P. Morgan & Company had made an outright gift in 1929 to a number of prominent people of stock in the Allegheny Corporation at almost a 50 percent reduction to its market price. Among the fortunate recipients of this windfall, usually worth between fifteen and twenty thousand dollars per recipient, were Newton Baker, Bernard Baruch, John W. Davis, Norman Davis, William G. McAdoo, John J. Raskob, Calvin Coolidge, General John J. Pershing, Colonel Charles A. Lindbergh, and, more important, Roosevelt's secretary of the treasury, William Woodin.

Woodin offered his resignation, which some, including Garner, suggested be accepted, but Roosevelt declined it, explaining that Woodin had no expectation in 1929 of being associated with government and was a Republican at the time.

Nor did he ask for Norman Davis's resignation. Roosevelt made no public comment on the controversy, which quickly passed.

Pecora had roughly handled the Morgan witnesses, including J. P. Morgan II, son of the titan. Morgan was subjected to the crowning indignity of having a Ringling Brothers Circus publicity agent drop a woman midget in Morgan's lap, so "the world's smallest woman could meet the world's richest man" (which Morgan was not). It was, reminisced veteran members of the Congress, quite a change from the "massive dignity" with which J. P. Morgan, father, had testified twenty years before.[28]

The last measures of the congressional session did not reveal Roosevelt at his most distinguished. There was a serious dispute with important sections of the Congress over pay and an almost inexplicable disagreement over guarantees of bank deposits.

As a sop to Lewis Douglas and the bedraggled forces of fiscal conservatism in the administration, Roosevelt had agreed to cut veterans' benefits in line with deflation generally, as part of his administrative economy measures. Bronson Cutting attacked the President savagely for short-changing the veterans. Cutting had wanted to nationalize the banks and had become a western radical in his time in the Southwest, far to the left of the President and somewhat dismissive of him as a poseur. Groton, Harvard, and infirmity (tuberculosis in Cutting's case) had made their relations abrasive, and Roosevelt and Cutting never enjoyed a cordial relationship thereafter. Even the relatively philosophical Roosevelt found some of Cutting's reflections unforgivable. Quickly recognizing that he had misjudged the issue, Roosevelt saved minor cuts for Douglas but allowed the veterans' pension measure to go through in much more generous form than originally planned—cuts were held to 25 percent.

Roosevelt initially clung to the astonishing view that bank deposits should not be guaranteed, privately opposing even his own vice president and most of his party, and departing from the course he had advocated as governor. He now felt that the collapse of some banks would be so severe that, if guaranteed, they would endanger the entire system. Fortunately, Roosevelt the political genius came swiftly to the rescue of Roosevelt the commercial and economic novice. Under the Glass-Steagall Act, as it was called, all deposits were guaranteed up to $2,500—95 percent of them in number, and almost as high in total amount, as most people with more cash put it in short-term instruments or spread it over a number of accounts.

The act passed easily, with the President having swiftly changed his colors and advanced to the head of the bill's supporters. It was one of the most successful measures of his entire administration. Bank failures became extremely rare. Public confidence was heavily reinforced, especially since Huey Long managed to get the state banks included in the scheme. And it was one of the greatest advances in the monetary history of the United States, as bank deposits effectively joined most definitions of the money supply.

The superlatives the President lavished implausibly on his Rube Goldberg monstrosity of the NIRA would have been better applied to the Glass-Steagall Act. As with the Wagner-Smith-Perkins reforms following the 1911 Triangle Shirtwaist fire, the lateness of the President's conversion to the virtues of Glass-Steagall did not inhibit Roosevelt from claiming for the rest of his life to be the guardian of the nation's savings and protector of its bank deposits.

It had been the most diversely productive session in the 144-year history of the United States Congress, and it had been rich in good legislation. The banking measures, ratifying closures, scheduling reopenings, and guaranteeing deposits; the Tennessee Valley Authority; the Civilian Conservation Corps; the substantial abandonment of the gold standard; the system of voluntary subsidized reduction in agricultural production; the discretionary reflationary powers accorded the President; the public-works elements of NIRA; and the abandonment of the folly of Prohibition were all brilliant initiatives. Roosevelt's direction of part of the public-works budget toward naval reconstruction, starting with two heavy cruisers, was another innovation that would later be amplified to the great good fortune of the country and its eventual allies. Despite his quest for disarmament, the President moved early to bring the United States Navy up to treaty strength within the framework of his job-creation program. Roosevelt's handling of the press and his use of Fireside Chats were also brilliant. His inaugural address would occupy a permanent and distinguished place in the nation's history.

There was no coherent macroeconomic budgetary or monetary strategy for recovery but rather a laboratory in which Roosevelt had released a bunch of competing measures to observe which performed most usefully. He had also produced with them some durable reforms. These First Hundred Days are generally regarded as the First New Deal, and despite the many improvisations, the New Deal encouraged the nation and was off to an excellent start.

III

THE STRIDENCY OF the new German government caused British Prime Minister Ramsay MacDonald to produce a disarmament plan based on doubling the size of the German Army allowable under the Versailles Treaty while bringing the French Army down to the same size. The plan did not include a British guarantee of France, nor any boundary revisions in favor of Germany, and so was unacceptable to both.

At Roosevelt's invitation, MacDonald came to Washington in late April, arriving in New York on the *Berengaria*. While he was aboard ship in mid-ocean, he learned that Roosevelt had effectively departed the gold standard with the Thomas Amendment. His advisors suggested that when they arrived in New York they reembark on the *Mauretania* and return to Britain, since the American move had made agreement on monetary questions very unlikely. This would have been farcical, and MacDonald, an optimistic, pacifistic man almost at the end of his career, propped up by the king at the head of a coalition government dominated by the opposition Conservatives, was determined to pursue agreement with the American president.

Roosevelt and his wife and daughter received MacDonald and his daughter and advisors with great charm and informality at the White House. Little was accomplished by the visit, but Roosevelt greatly impressed MacDonald. MacDonald was still staying in the Lincoln bedroom when the just-resigned French premier, Edouard Herriot, still chairman of the National Assembly foreign affairs committee, arrived. At one point in the afternoon of April 24, the British and French delegations and the Canadian prime minister, Richard B. Bennett, were all milling about in the corridors of the White House.

The anti-Semitic oppressions of the German government began early in Hitler's term and escalated fairly steadily. Roosevelt and the State Department regarded these pogroms, disgusting as they were, as internal German matters. Hitler, in April, in response to massive unofficial criticism of his actions, publicly accused the United States of bigotry and hypocrisy. "Through its immigration laws [America] has prevented the entry of those races which seemed unwelcome. . . . And America today is by no means ready to open its doors to so-called refugee Jews from Germany."[29] Hitler always regarded the American Jews with particular suspicion, and would often try to divide Jewish from non-Jewish American opinion.

Brandeis and Frankfurter tried very gently to persuade Roosevelt to permit greater numbers of persecuted German Jews to enter the United States. The State Department opposed this on the implausible grounds that it would be an interference in German internal affairs. This was Secretary of State Hull's view, though he deplored the German hostility to Jews and his own wife was Jewish.

Roosevelt told French ambassador Paul Claudel in early April 1933, just two months after Hitler's installation as German chancellor, that "Hitler is a madman and his counselors, some of whom I personally know, are even madder than he is." (He knew the vice chancellor, Franz von Papen, from World War I. Von Papen and Hjalmar Schacht, president of the Reichsbank, were two of the sanest and most respectable members of the German government, and were among the few who were acquitted in the Nuremberg trials at the end of World War II.)

Hitler sent Schacht to Washington in May 1933, to negotiate Germany out of its debt obligations.* Schacht claimed that when he told Roosevelt that Germany was about to default on its debt interest payments, Roosevelt slapped his thigh amusedly and remarked that this would "serve the Wall Street bankers right."[30] Schacht's recollection is unverifiable.

---

* Schacht's father had been working in the United States during the 1872 election when Horace Greeley ran against Ulysses S. Grant for the presidency. The future central banker was born five years later and was named Horace Greeley Hjalmar Schacht.

If Schacht's account was true, Roosevelt later thought better of whatever he had said to Schacht, because the next day he commissioned a sternly worded memo in which he professed himself to be "shocked" by the German's information. This adjective survived despite Warburg's attempt to have it removed (as an inadvertent pun on Schacht's name). Roosevelt's version of his meetings with Schacht was that he had knocked Schacht about quite thoroughly. It quickly became clear that no reparations could be wrung from Hitler without reigniting the World War to collect them. In the end, only Finland continued payment and the debt issue faded away, overshadowed by greater problems. When Hitler ceased to pay, a month after MacDonald's Washington visit, he did one of his very few favors for the British and the French by taking the pressure off them. Roosevelt claimed not to have a particularly high opinion of Schacht, and told Morgenthau on May 15 that there was "a very strong possibility" that Germany would go to war.[31] Nearly three years later, in a letter to his ambassador in Berlin, William Dodd, indicating his low opinion of the world banking community as well, Roosevelt wrote: "Germany seems to be staving off actual bankruptcy through the tricky Schacht policies which win him the admiration of the international bankers."[32]

Roosevelt had been considering, and did try his hand at, Wilsonian pacification, with an appeal to fifty-four chiefs of state for a renunciation of aggressive weapons — in particular, warplanes, tanks, and mobile artillery — to ensure the primacy of the defensive in military matters. He endorsed the MacDonald Plan and further proposed a non-aggression pact between all countries. Roosevelt timed his proposal for just before Hitler's address on disarmament and foreign relations to the Reichstag on May 17. Roosevelt's disarmament message, which went out May 16, was along the lines he had explained to Ambassador Lindsay at the end of January. Significantly, Roosevelt already believed, as did his principal military advisor, General MacArthur, the army chief of staff, that aggressive weapons could overwhelm traditional defenses such as fortifications. Unfortunately, the French in particular thought otherwise.

Roosevelt, with Moley, Warburg, O'Connor, and Howe, listened to Hitler's speech in Roosevelt's study in the White House, on May 17. Roosevelt was able to translate some of Hitler's message to his guests. (The official translation came at the end of his speech.)[33] Hitler expressed qualified approval for MacDonald's plan and commended Roosevelt for his "magnanimous" proposal. Hitler called Roosevelt's remarks "a ray of comfort," dismissed war as "unlimited madness," and renounced the "mentality of the last century, which led people to believe that they could make Germans out of Poles and Frenchmen." Hitler offered to dispense with all offensive weapons and to disband his then modest military establishment completely, if neighboring countries would do the same.[34]

Roosevelt's appeal was greeted with almost universal approval. President von Hindenburg of Germany, King Victor Emmanuel of Italy, and Soviet President Kalinin were among those who heartily concurred. Japan's Emperor Hirohito was noncommittal.

Roosevelt backed up his proposal by having the U.S. delegate at the Geneva Disarmament Conference, the versatile Norman Davis, say that should war break out, if the United States believed one side was clearly at fault, it would do nothing to impede the punitive activities of the opponents of the aggressor. This was represented abroad as a departure from the naïve Bryanesque policy of strict neutrality, while inside the United States it was seen as no more than a promise of unarmed moral suasion in egregious cases of unjust war-making. Roosevelt issued a statement the day after his May 16 proposal was published asserting that it didn't constitute a change in the American position, despite Davis's statement. This, too, would become a familiar pattern: a bold initiative followed by a bland assurance that little or nothing had changed. Morgenthau claimed that Roosevelt was so delighted with the reception accorded his proposals that he said: "I think I have averted a war."[35]

Given his thoughts about Hitler and the Japanese, it is impossible that he believed any such thing. Roosevelt may have been indulging in a little bravura with an adulatory Dutchess County neighbor. He was probably staking out a position as peacemaker to impress rather naïve American opinion (at which he apparently succeeded).

The Disarmament Conference continued to be deadlocked, adjourned to the fall, and never achieved anything. In late 1933, Hitler withdrew from the League of Nations and formally renounced the Treaty of Versailles.

IV

THE UNITED STATES had become the world's largest importer, exporter, and investor in the decade after the World War. It had accounted for one-sixth of all exports and one-eighth of the world's imports by 1929. Yet foreign trade was only 5 percent of U.S. gross domestic product, against five times that figure for Britain. Economically, The United States mattered a great deal more to the world than the world did to the United States.[36] This created a deep imbalance in expectations for the World Monetary and Economic Conference, which began in London in 1933, between the United States and almost all other states. Hoover had shared the expectations of the other states because he blamed the Depression on foreign causes. In fact, the Depression was generated in all the industrialized countries, and America exported an exacerbation of it because of Hoover's mistaken deflationary policies, which the conference majority wished to impose on the world.

Roosevelt had always looked with suspicion upon the conference. He considered that Hoover had tried to dodge his own responsibility for the Depression by taking refuge in international factors and a deterministic view of the consequences of the World War. Hoover had tried to propagate the notion that economic conditions were natural phenomena that could not be avoided or resisted any more than could freakish mutations of the climate. Roosevelt also considered that the Europeans regarded the United States as chiefly responsible for the Depression because this excused them from dealing with their own problems. Roosevelt would have less patience with this European reflex than most of his successors.

The conference delegates whom Roosevelt named gave a hint that he didn't take the whole subject seriously. Cordell Hull, James M. Cox, and the chairman of the House Foreign Relations Committee, Samuel McReynolds, were partial or complete free traders. Raymond Moley, Senate Foreign Relations Committee Chairman Key Pittman, and Michigan Republican senator James Couzens were protectionists. Roosevelt had learned from the Versailles fiasco the danger of not involving the Congress in anything it might have to ratify.

The opinions of the other delegate, Ralph Morrison, a large financial contributor to the Democrats put forward by Garner and Farley, were not known and not hinted at in his performance in London. None of these delegates had ever been to an international conference before. Moley called them the "Argonauts" (in search of the golden fleece).[37] The dashing William Bullitt was the executive officer of the committee. He wasn't overly interested in economics and was already rather eccentric. Bullitt, who professed to believe the British had bugged the delegates' living quarters, irritated Ramsay MacDonald by taking the prime minister's secretary out for dinner and trying to elicit state secrets from her under the influence of drink. Pittman was a heavy and often uncontrollable drinker. On one occasion at Claridge's he chased down a corridor with a bowie knife a technical advisor he thought inadequately enthusiastic about silver (which was Pittman's passion as senator from the silver-producing state of Nevada.) The advisor carried a gun thereafter.[38]

The delegation was profoundly divided before it departed American shores. Moley, with Roosevelt's approval, wrote an article debunking tariff reduction and predicting moderate results from the conference. This piece was published without notice to Hull while he was on the high seas. This thoroughly undercut what was left of Hull's position after he had been saddled with such a discordant delegation. The secretary wrote later that he had left America "with the highest of hopes but arrived with empty hands."[39]

The conference aimed to reestablish the gold standard, stabilize the fluctuations between currencies, and reduce tariffs. Tariff levels varied among the main industrial powers from about 30 percent on all imports in the United States to 17 percent in Italy, 12 percent in France and Germany, and only 4 percent in the United Kingdom.

It shortly emerged that there would be great difficulty agreeing on the ratio relationship between the currencies, with or without the use of the gold standard. The British and French were demanding from the opening of the conference that the dollar should be pegged at about $3.50 to the pound sterling. This was absurdly disadvantageous to the United States, because when the conference opened the dollar was trading at $4.18 to the pound.

Roosevelt refused to make any such commitment. The furthest he was prepared to go was an undertaking, revocable at any time, to act unilaterally to prevent the dollar falling below $4.25 to the British pound. Roosevelt strenuously
rebuked a Treasury official who had proposed to stabilize currencies and to
express willingness to return to the gold standard.

About eighty members of the Congress signed a petition asking Roosevelt to
send the radio priest, Father Charles E. Coughlin, to the London Conference to
protect the American people's interest. Fortunately Roosevelt ignored this
request, which if acted upon, might have reduced the conference to an
unseemly shambles. Roosevelt dispatched Moley to join the delegation earlier
than had been foreseen. Moley's views and his proximity to the President were
well known.

Roosevelt himself left Washington by train on June 17, looking more
exhausted than Morgenthau had ever seen him before, with dark half moons
under his eyes, to go to Marion, Massachusetts, on Buzzard's Bay. There he
would board the forty-five-foot schooner *Amberjack II*, which his son James had
chartered, and sail round Cape Cod, along the New England shore, and on to
Campobello Island, which he had not seen since he left it on a stretcher, dysfunctional and in acute pain, twelve years before. It was a less solitary cruise than
that of the previous summer following the Chicago convention. *Amberjack II* was
accompanied by a press ketch, a Secret Service patrol launch, two U.S. Navy
destroyers, the 10,000-ton heavy cruiser U.S.S. *Indianapolis*, and a number of
naval aircraft.

Wildly enthusiastic crowds of more than 250,000 cheered the President in
Boston, where he left his train and rode in an open car through the city and on to
Groton. Here he had a pleasant reunion with his sons Franklin and John and
with his mother. In an improvised chat to the students, he told them that any one
of them could, as he had, with application, change his address from Groton
School to the White House. He then drove to Marion and began his sail. He took
the helm himself all day. Foul weather drove him somewhat off course, but he
came into Nantucket Harbor having impressed the navy and the press with his
nautical skills as he adjusted sail and tacked through the weather. Messages
awaited him from London from his former chief James M. Cox and his advisor
Paul Warburg asking if he would agree to a stabilization of the dollar at around
four dollars to the U.K. pound. He responded by code through one of the destroyers, and then to Washington and on to London, that $4.05 to $4.25 could be
"worth considering."

Roosevelt was proceeding north along the Cape Cod coast when he learned
that Raymond Moley, who was leaving the next day for London, had flown from
Washington to Martha's Vineyard and was asking to see him personally on an
urgent matter. Roosevelt was unlikely to be delighted with this dramatic and
inevitably well-publicized arrival, but anchored his boat, had a destroyer bring
Moley out, and cordially welcomed him aboard. Moley's urgent message was that

Senator Byrnes of South Carolina and the presidential appointments secretary, Marvin McIntyre, thought that it would be a mistake for him to go to London at all—that it would appear to undercut Hull and the delegation and further demoralize them. Roosevelt greeted this concern with a peal of laughter, and wrote out an anodyne message for the White House to issue saying that Moley was merely bringing updated information to the delegation.

The President peered out at the vast Atlantic and told Moley the important mission of the U.S. delegation was to spread his [Roosevelt's] message that prices must rise and that the various governments shouldn't be too much dominated by "banker-influenced cabinets" who overemphasized exchange-rate stability. He wanted to stimulate commodity price increases internationally (Morganthau's latest enthusiasm). It is not now known whether Roosevelt asked what business any of this was of Senator Byrnes' or McIntyre's. Moley gave Roosevelt a paper by Herbert Bayard Swope recommending against too much concern over currency stabilization. Only subsequently, in his memoirs, did Moley imagine the irony of his gift to Roosevelt of such a memorandum. He departed to New York, where he met with Joseph Kennedy, already disgruntled at not having heard from Roosevelt since his inauguration, and especially at not having been named secretary of the Treasury. Kennedy warned Moley to be careful not to annoy Roosevelt by receiving too much publicity, and Moley sailed the next day (on R.M.S. *Olympic,* venerable sister of the *Titanic*), the press having taken note of his theatrical attendance upon the President in his sailboat.

Roosevelt sailed on to Provincetown and then to Gloucester, where Colonel House and Lewis Douglas came aboard briefly, then up the Maine Coast and into Penobscot Bay. On Sunday, June 25, he sent a message via his old friend William Phillips, who was holding the fort at the State Department in the absence of Hull and Moley, and asked that Moley be advised to say no more directly to the press, because he was not a delegate but was now under the secretary of state. This confirmed the timeliness of Kennedy's advice.

Eleanor came aboard for a few minutes at Southwest Harbor. She and Nancy Cook and Marion Dickerman were on their way by car to open the cottage at Campobello just in advance of the President's arrival. Eleanor had had some difficulty getting her bearings in her new role as first lady of the United States. Having agreed to be editor of a new magazine owned by the sensational-tabloid publisher Bernarr Macfadden, to be called *Babies—Just Babies,*" she cancelled the agreement after it was made public and severely ridiculed. It was an odd inspiration, given that she didn't like babies and despised maternity and disliked the act that led to that condition. She similarly abandoned her contract to give radio talks sponsored by a cosmetics firm, after her advice on temperance to young ladies was widely ridiculed and the propriety of the arrangement was widely questioned.

Eleanor had already set a new style at the White House. She arrived on foot for her first visit as wife of the president-elect and traveled as an ordinary passenger, taking taxis and often riding the Fifth Avenue bus in New York. She paid no attention to fashion, had no vanity, was an extremely considerate hostess, and welcomed an immense variety of people into the White House, including the parents of a young hitchhiker to whom she had given a ride. Neither she nor her husband cared about the social or protocol pecking order, and she used her position as White House hostess to introduce large numbers of people of every description in all walks of life to the President. He was generally grateful for this window on the public he would not otherwise have had. She had a housekeeper from Hyde Park, Mrs. Nesbitt, whom the President would have loved to dismiss for unworldliness, but Eleanor insisted on her retention. Eleanor had no interest in food and her menus were notoriously unexciting. But she was gradually beginning to see the potential for her of being the President's wife, especially this president, with his comparative immobility. If the range of Eleanor's socializing sometimes bemused her husband, it flabbergasted her mother-in-law. Sara, observing a number of handicrafts artisans the President's wife had convened at Hyde Park, turned to the nearest recognizable face, Edward J. Flynn, and loudly exclaimed: "Where does Eleanor get all these people?"[40]

She began to travel extensively and drove herself through the grimmest slums of Washington in an open car, frequently inspecting the poorest black districts on foot. She had begun her intense and controversial relationship with Lorena Hickock, an Associated Press wire service reporter assigned to her. This friendship would soon eclipse that with the Misses Cook and Dickerman. "Hick," as Eleanor and everyone else called her, was a discreet and not very active lesbian, but there is no evidence that she and Eleanor ever had a physical relationship, any more than there is regarding Eleanor's other mannish women friends. They had planned a three-week trip together around Quebec's rugged Gaspe Peninsula after the presidential visit to Campobello. Hick gave Eleanor good advice about the media and public relations generally, and Eleanor quickly overcame her initial faux pas and became popular and respected, ultimately internationally.

Roosevelt was delayed by fog and laid up in a Maine cove for two days. While he was becalmed, he learned that the dollar had slipped to the point where a pound sterling was now worth $4.30. Thus the dollar had fallen below the bottom of the range Roosevelt had been prepared to consider defending. Secretary Woodin was ill and the undersecretary of the Treasury, Dean Acheson, speaking for the just-returned banking advisor George Harrison, Budget Director Lewis Douglas, and the ineffable Bernard Baruch, advised the President by cable that the French, Italians, Dutch, Belgians, and Swiss were screaming for unilateral American action—the foreign sale of gold for dollars to prop up the dollar—failing which they might all have to abandon gold completely. Acheson, on behalf of the group he represented, advised against such a course as too potentially depletive of U.S. gold reserves. What was proposed was a loose cooperative arrangement with the British and the French to try to promote stabilization on an ad hoc basis.

The problem of the United States in this conference, as Roosevelt had foreseen, was that the administration's activities to raise commodity prices had enjoyed considerable success, especially in agricultural products. Wheat had risen from thirty cents to over a dollar per bushel. Roosevelt sensed that some degree of inflation was going to be necessary to induce a benign cycle in which economic activity would rise and jobs be created. This was at variance with the conferees' goal of currency stabilization under the discipline of the gold standard, which would preserve sound money for a time but perpetuate the Depression. Roosevelt had tried in his own legislation to blend the proposals of the advocates of traditional sound money with the ideas of the reflationists, though leaning heavily to the latter. He was fundamentally out of sympathy with the banker mentality that put a few percent on the ultimate comparative value of the currency on a par with five times as large a percentage of the work force in long-term unemployment. He had not really reconciled these perspectives in the policy of his own administration, though he had made his usual stylish effort at it, but it would be impossible to finesse these differences in an international conference.

Moley arrived in England on June 27 and the following day gave a generously attended press conference in the presence of the secretary of state, in which he won great admiration for his deference to Hull and his self-deprecatory tone. The following day Roosevelt sent a message to Washington for retransmission to Hull, if Acheson and Baruch didn't object. The President stated that he didn't think it mattered to the United States whether any or all of the petitioning countries abandoned the gold standard, that he had no faith in France's ability to remain on it anyway, and that international stabilization proposals were unlikely to be successful and should be resisted. Acheson didn't think such a message wise or appropriate, so it was not retransmitted and Moley became engaged in intensive stabilization negotiations of the kind that reflected his last-known intimations of Roosevelt's thinking.

On June 29 Roosevelt became exasperated with the marine coastal fog and determined to sail. He did so with remarkable skill, judgment, and recall of the geography and waters he had not seen for twelve years. After nearly ten hours of groping deftly through the mist and tides and currents, he emerged into Passamaquoddy Bay and into brilliant sunlight. His little schooner was greeted by a twenty-one-gun salute from the U.S.S. *Indianapolis*, dozens of yachts, and thousands of people lining the shore and welcoming him back to Campobello. As he approached the pier he shouted greetings by precise name to many of the local people, including some of those who had carried him out of his house and to a special railway car on an improvised stretcher in 1921. It must have been deeply satisfying to him emotionally to return to the scene of the greatest crisis of his life in this magnificent style. His victory over his infirmity was more complete than even he could have imagined. But he remained jovial and unceremonious, as if he had only been away for one season and his health had been completely untroubled.

He spoke to the islanders from the terrace of the yacht club, reflecting that he first came to Campobello "because I was teething forty-nine years ago" and celebrating his recall of how to navigate the Lubec Narrows. He named a couple of local people who had taught him some of the elements of sailing and who were present, and he held out the U.S.-Canadian relationship as a model for the world. He thanked "the Governor . . . [and] Dominion Governor" of New Brunswick (by which he meant, in an unusual slip for him, the premier and lieutenant governor of that province) for their greeting. Then he returned to his house.

There was a picnic on the beach below his house for about a hundred people the next day, June 30. After the picnic as the President was awaiting an important cable from Moley that would be forwarded from Washington to the decoding officer on the *Indianapolis* and then brought ashore, Roosevelt invited up to his house the four reporters who had been on the accompanying boat. They played cards for a while and then, with no warning, he began a one-hour monologue on international economic affairs and told the reporters that his administration would not subscribe to any arrangement that would curtail its economic recovery or facilitate the dumping of foreign goods in the United States.

It was a tremendous scoop, but he tried to keep it an unattributed one. The journalists were understandably unenthusiastic about going with such a story if they were apt to be repudiated. It was agreed that the Campobello byline and the fact that there were four of them gave adequate security. Roosevelt had been irritated that in the last two days mere rumors of a stabilization agreement had caused the dollar to rise by several percent and had caused significant declines on U.S. stock and commodity exchanges. A competent poker player, Roosevelt believed the Europeans were trying to ensnare him in a plan to keep the dollar high and frustrate the recovery he fervently hoped was finally underway in the United States. He found the antics of the Europeans slightly reminiscent of the last-ditch effort to ensnare him in Hoover's failed policies between the 1932 election and his own inauguration four months later.

Roosevelt's guests went to their boat to write and file their stories, and the President convened a cocktail party for his guests, who included Louis Howe, Henry Morgenthau, and Missy LeHand. When they went in to dinner, Eleanor fiercely complained that he was half an hour late. The night before, she had taken him to task in front of the guests for sending Moley to London and undercutting Hull. It was Eleanor at her most harridanly, strident and censorious. It was an embarrassment to their guests and an indignity to her husband on his triumphant return to Campobello. He rebutted her complaints rather curtly.

The balance of the evening proceeded civilly. Morgenthau held forth on his preferred economic theory, propounded by George Warren and Frank Pearson, of raising commodity prices by creating a commodity dollar by buying gold above the current market rate. He had charts and graphs to illustrate his point. (This was an odd inspiration, since Morgenthau had known little of nonagricultural economics.) Moley's cable arrived in the midst of this disquisition and contained a proposal for a joint declaration by countries on and not on the gold standard. With it was delivered a second cable from Baruch, Harrison, and the ailing Woodin urging acceptance of Moley's proposal. (Moley had prevailed upon Baruch and Harrison to go to Woodin's bedside.) Moley had nominated himself to the task of negotiating the agreement between the gold standard adhering and abstaining countries and had arrived at an inoffensive wording that conformed to guidelines Roosevelt had given the delegation and the instructions he had given Moley just before he left New York.

Moley had overconfidently indicated that Roosevelt's approval was a foregone conclusion. He then became acutely anxious as the hours passed with no word from the President. At about midnight on the 30th, suspicious of the Europeans, annoyed with Moley's presumption, impressed by Morgenthau's arguments, and possibly the victim of a garbled transmission from Moley, Roosevelt sent his response out to the *Indianapolis* for retransmission to Washington and on to London. It was mid-morning when it arrived in London, and Moley's recommendation was rejected.

Moley was crestfallen. There could be no misunderstanding that he had been rejected in the most humiliatingly public way before the governments and press of the world. He gamely telegraphed back to Roosevelt: "Personally bow to your judgment with no inconsiderable relief." This was a somewhat pathetic attempt to salvage his relationship with the President. In order to "spare Roosevelt embarrassment," the U.S. delegation in London said only that the President could not agree to the declaration in its present form. Moley, Herbert Bayard Swope, Walter Lippmann, and, in a testimony to Moley's convening power, John Maynard Keynes sat down in Claridge's to prepare a statement that would square the circle of the revolving positions Roosevelt had recently held, from loosely pegging the dollar to a general statement of non-binding purpose. (Roosevelt's statement was fairly close to the memorandum of Swope's that Moley had left with Roosevelt on his sailboat on the way to Campobello.) They produced a statement in the early hours of July 2. Later that day, Roosevelt boarded the *Indianapolis,* his standard was unfurled, another twenty-one-gun salute was fired, and the ship sailed for Annapolis.

Roosevelt wrote out a message for London in the captain's cabin of the *Indianapolis,* which he shared with Howe and Morgenthau and his son Franklin. He wrote: "I would regard it as a catastrophe amounting to world tragedy if the great conference of nations . . . [were to] allow itself to be diverted by the proposal of a purely artificial and temporary experiment affecting the monetary exchange of a few nations only." Roosevelt referred to the European preoccupation with stabilization as a condition precedent to any other agreement as one of the "old fetishes of so-called international bankers." More important was the effort of the individual countries to restore their own economic strength.[41]

Roosevelt's declaration was a bombshell and broke up the London Conference (as the economic summit was also called). The reaction in Europe was outrage. John Maynard Keynes was in a distinct minority when he declared that the U.S. president's action had been "magnificently right." Roosevelt had given Ramsay MacDonald, Edouard Herriot, and Hjalmar Schacht to believe that he would approve some form of stabilization steps and pay some lip service to the value of gold as a reference point for currencies. Most American response to the President's statement was highly positive, though some of the East Coast newspapers were too Atlanticist to accept the President's brusque rebuff. The European fixation on currency stabilization was misplaced.

Moley, scrambling to salvage his own credibility while purporting only to be trying to put the best possible face on Roosevelt's actions, sent the President a message on July 4. "I consider your message Splendid. . . . It was the only way to bring people to their senses," he wrote, adding that the statement was "true, frank and fair." Not all the Americans at the conference were so pleased. When France's Georges Bonnet criticized Roosevelt's position, Cox told him his "words deserve to be carved in marble."[42]

Moley suggested a recess in the conference for from two to ten weeks to hammer Roosevelt's position into resolutions and to replace the existing American delegation with a more suitable and coherent one.

Hull was shown this recommendation of Moley's by the U.S. ambassador in London, Robert Bingham (an early Roosevelt financial backer and proprietor of the *Louisville Courier-Journal*). The recommendation was a serious presumption by Moley, who was only an assistant secretary of state and not officially a conference delegate. Hull exploded with rage, calling Moley a "piss-ant . . . Here he curled up at my feet and let me stroke his head like a hunting dog and then he goes and bites me in the ass!" According to Louis Howe's son, in correspondence with his father, Hull was known at the conference as "Miss Cordelia Dull."[43] Perhaps, but Hull sent a message of his own to Roosevelt July 11 denouncing Moley in terms suggesting that if Moley didn't go, at least from the State Department, Hull would. It could be inferred that Bingham would also resign as ambassador to Great Britain. Roosevelt was rather tired of Moley anyway, and while he had little regard for Hull as a secretary of state, he didn't want him resigning in anger and becoming an enemy. Hull was a well-regarded veteran of both the Senate and the House of Representatives.

Moley returned to Washington July 14, thinking the whole world "believed I had been kicked in the face." He visited Roosevelt in the White House, in the morning while he was still in his bed (from which he conducted a good deal of business). The President greeted him cordially. In the eerie and even sadistic manner Roosevelt often employed, he made no reference to the London incidents at all.[44]

Moley later claimed that only his desire to raise money from some of Roosevelt's friends (Vincent Astor and the Harrimans) for a publishing project prevented him from resigning right there. Moley rejected an offer from Howe to go to Hawaii to study the working of the justice system. But he accepted an offer from Roosevelt in early August that he remain officially at the State Department but go to the Justice Department to suggest ways of reducing the wave of kidnappings that had occurred in the last couple of years. Roosevelt sent him a warm letter of appreciation proclaiming the permanence of their relationship, which of course meant exactly the opposite.

Hull worked very effectively to prevent the London Conference dissolving at once and issuing a statement directly hostile to Roosevelt. He succeeded, and the proceedings continued fairly aimlessly, achieving only a few minor agreements, until adjournment *sine die* and forever, July 27, 1933.

––––––––––

Roosevelt was right that any plan for currency stabilization would not have worked and would have been an effort to bilk the Americans anyway. But he could have agreed to some innocuous text, an economic version of the Kellogg-Briand Pact, and avoided anything harmful to the New Deal.

Instead, acting out domestic political games, he staged a virtual "Day of Dupes" in his own official family and brought completely unnecessary opprobrium down on himself in Europe. It was time to debunk the Hooverspeak that the Depression was inevitable and that only clinging to the gold standard and balancing the budget would solve it. If the major industrial powers had entrenched the gold standard and fixed exchange rates, they would have perpetuated the Depression and strangled any prospect of recovery. But while the economic consequences of Roosevelt's undermining of the London Conference were not negative or durable, there was no reason or excuse for him to have acted in such a contemptuous and capricious manner. Fourteen years after the rejection by the U.S. Congress of the Treaty of Versailles, Roosevelt unwittingly confirmed the Europeans in their predisposed view, which did not altogether abate in the balance of the twentieth century, that the United States was fundamentally unreliable. From Charles de Gaulle suggesting to Roosevelt that he could have prevented the fall of France, to postwar German chancellor Helmut Schmidt blaming Roosevelt for the division of Europe by the Iron Curtain, to millennial European ecologists claiming that the United States was responsible for global warming, the European practice of blaming the United States for almost all the world's ills became ever more predictable.

"In a sober interlude" in London,[45] Key Pittman had arranged for the U.S. government to commit to buy the entire American silver production for the next four years. This was perhaps the most important upshot of the conference. Pittman, who, whatever his limitations, was an astonishingly effective champion of the silver interests of Nevada, persuaded Roosevelt to ratify this agreement not through the Senate but under his authority arising from Senator Thomas's reflation amendment. Roosevelt took this action on December 21, and announced a purchase price twenty-one cents above the market. "Miners shot off revolvers in the streets of Leadville and danced with girls atop the bars of Tonopah."[46] The demagogic radio priest Father Coughlin praised silver as a "gentile metal" and called for the alliance of all Christians against "the god of Gold." His assistant had speculated heavily in silver with the money that flowed into Coughlin's organization, the Radio League of the Little Flower.[47]

In March of 1934, observing the seventy-fourth birthday of the late William Jennings Bryan, the effective founder of political bimetallism, the House of Representatives passed a bill introduced by Martin Dies of Texas providing for the sale of farm surpluses for silver valued above the world price. This pleased the inflationists, the farmers, and the silver lobby, and put Roosevelt on the defensive. He did his best, exposing silver speculators and individually lobbying the principal silver advocates. But finally, in June, he felt obliged to agree to the Silver Purchase Act, which committed the U.S. Treasury to buy silver for up to $1.29 an ounce until it was one-quarter of the country's monetary reserve.

Bryan had won in the end, and there was a historical symmetry in the history of the Democratic Party, as the eastern, sound-dollar Roosevelt enacted the demands of the bimetallists. The cost of this unity was high: over $100 million a year for fifteen years, more than would be paid in the same period for farm price supports, although there were only about five thousand Americans directly engaged in the silver industry. A number of foreign currencies were destabilized and silver was not really monetized. Although Bryan was victorious, his theory was disproved. It was poor economics and not particularly good politics, but it ended the great schism of what had become and would long remain the governing party of the United States.

V

H UGH JOHNSON HAD said of the NIRA: "It will be red fire at first and dead cats afterward. . . . Like mounting the guillotine on the infinitesimal gamble that the axe won't work."[48] Roosevelt and his principal colleagues knew that the sharp rise in stock and commodity prices was a levitation. It was based on inflationary expectations prompted by the partial abandonment of the gold standard and the discretionary reflationary powers voted to the President, supplemented by Roosevelt's infectious optimism. The index of industrial production rose from 56 to 101 from March to July 1933. In the same period farm prices moved from 55 to 87 and the New York Stock Exchange rose 85 percent while the volume of trading rose by 500 percent. There had not been a corresponding increase in full-time equivalent employment. From March to July of 1933 factory production increased by 67 percent but factory employment by only 22 percent, though payrolls increased by about 35 percent. Unemployment did decline markedly from March to October (the American Federation of Labor estimated from 13.7 million to 10.1 million), but this was chiefly due to the requirement of the NRA codes to reduce the working week.

The NRA had successfully countered deflationary pressures, established a national standard of wages and hours, eliminated child labor and some other exploitive conditions, and given work to about two million people. It was a defensible record, particularly opposite Carter Glass's description of it as Hitlerian, and the claim of Joe Martin, the Republican leader in the House, that the NRA was Stalinist.

Hugh Johnson had predicted five million new jobs within a month in July 1933, scaled back to three million in two months, which was technically achieved with the reduction of the workweek. Inventory was being piled up in anticipation of higher prices through inflation, assuring unusual capital gains. There were also from the beginning concerns about the constitutionality of the NIRA—that the licensing power implicit in the administration's ability to give or withhold approval of industry codes might violate the due process provisions in the Fifth and Fourteenth Amendments to the Constitution and be a federal usurpation of the rights of the states.

The basic problem of the NIRA and of the National Recovery Administration (NRA), which implemented it, was that they provided an incentive to raise prices and wages, but raising the two together would not raise employment, shrink unemployment, or raise profits and therefore dividends or investment. There would merely be more money chasing a relatively unchanged quantity of goods and services, a traditional form of inflation but not the most productive form. The NRA was really giving with one hand and taking away with the other. In order to raise prices it discouraged production increases, which was hardly a boon to employment. (The code of the furniture manufacturing industry prohibited the expansion of existing, or construction of new, manufacturing facilities.)

Those who gained from the NRA's operation did so from the production of codes for each industry fixing wages, prices, and working conditions that were more advantageous to ownership or labor than the authors of the legislation had intended, or from simply failing to live up to code obligations. There was a high incidence of both.

There was also an almost impenetrable bureaucratic problem from the beginning, with the NRA lumbered with Industrial, Labor and Consumer Advisory Boards. The first was named by the secretary of commerce and was chaired by Walter Teagle of Standard Oil Company of New Jersey, and included such luminaries as Myron Taylor of U.S. Steel and Gerard Swope of General Electric. The members of the Labor Advisory Board were appointed by the secretary of labor and included William Green of the AFL, John L. Lewis of the United Mine Workers of America, Sidney Hillman of the Amalgamated Clothing Workers, and Rose Schneiderman of the Women's Trade Union League.

The Consumer Advisory Board was an invention of Frances Perkins's and was chaired by her housemate, Mary Rumsey, Averell Harriman's sister, who nominated a number of distinguished academics and activists to the board. The contributions of these three boards immensely added to the confusion of the NRA. (Averell Harriman was New York NRA chairman.) There was also a supposedly supervisory board called the Special Industrial Recovery Board, and after December 1933 a National Emergency Council. It is a sign of the desperation of the times that such a hydra-headed, contradictorily purposed organization enjoyed any credibility at all.

General Hugh Johnson, with Roosevelt's support, determined to move as quickly as possible as NRA administrator in the hope that intense activity would start more money through the system, producing greater demand, a climate of purpose and optimism, and a benign economic cycle. Roosevelt overruled the Special Industrial Recovery Board, which was afraid a massively publicized launch could appear fascistic and embarrass the President. Johnson produced a tremendous public relations campaign in support of the NRA and adopted as the NRA symbol the Navajo thunderbird, henceforth called the Blue Eagle, with an industrial cog in one talon and six thunderbolts in the other. His promotional efforts were modeled on the Victory Bond drives of World War I. The grand launch of the Blue Eagle, an emblem that was plastered and applied all over the country on products and business establishments and advertising with the slogan "We Do Our Part," was on September 13 in New York. Two hundred fifty thousand people, including many popular celebrities, marched for twelve hours down Fifth Avenue, observed by over two million New Yorkers, past a reviewing stand where Governor Lehman, General Johnson, and Averell Harriman waved appreciatively.

The division of the industrial code attribution and job-creation titles of the NIRA also began to seem mistaken, not because Johnson was short-changed but because neither he nor Harold Ickes, responsible for the jobs program, seemed especially well-suited to their tasks. Pyrotechnic, bibulous, and irascible, Johnson was a vital force and a great epigrammatist, but he became progressively more erratic as the wheels gradually came off the NRA in all directions. He was forever raging against "slackers, chiselers, pygmies."

Ickes was a talented and courageous man but was excessively curmudgeonly and extremely cautious: "the incarnation of lonely, righteous, and inextinguishable pugnacity."[49] He was so preoccupied with not wasting money that he moved with the speed of molasses to spend the $3.3 billion that had been allocated to his job-creation activities. The first title of the NIRA was administered by a wild man, the second by a compulsively cautious one, and the two disliked each other intensely.

Resistance by employers to the obligation to accept union adherence caused Johnson and his intimates to modify their views and to accept company unions, the open shop, and management shenanigans to avoid certification. Johnson was no great sympathizer with organized labor and didn't want the impetus of the

NRA squandered in industrial-relations strife. The byzantine procedure was that industries would work out codes of work conditions and pay scales and prices, which first were submitted to the Code Analysis Division of the NRA and then went to a pre-hearing, where the advisory boards could intervene. After this they went to the administrator and then to the President.

A cotton textile code that was rather favorable to management was adopted in late June, the first major breakthrough. Johnson waited impatiently for progress. When little occurred, Johnson produced what he styled the President's Reemployment Agreement, which was sent to every employer in the country. Every signatory became a member pledged to accept NRA standards, especially a thirty-five-to-forty-hour week and a minimum weekly wage of twelve to fifteen dollars until a national code in the particular industry was established.

The tempo of code approvals picked up in July; more than 500 came in in August as the NRA staff was multiplied by ten to process the avalanche of submissions under the President's Reemployment Agreement. The President was signing several industrial codes a week in August and one or two a day through the autumn. Most of the larger codes had to have price-negotiating arrangements so that those who accepted NRA wage increases could meet competition and still be profitable. In late July and early August codes were approved for the shipbuilding, electrical manufacturing, and important parts of the men's clothing industries. Roosevelt went to Hyde Park for August but returned to Washington from the 14th to the 20th to help negotiate oil, steel, coal, and lumber codes. He summoned the chairmen of U.S. Steel (Taylor) and Bethlehem Steel (Roosevelt's World War I acquaintance Charles Schwab), and a procedure was agreed upon whereby the Labor Department would represent the steel industry employees, because the big steel companies refused to negotiate with the union. Frances Perkins took this role very seriously, and toured the steelmaking country of Pennsylvania and neighboring states. She was appalled by what she saw.

Roosevelt leaned heavily on Schwab and Taylor, referring to the gulf between Miss Perkins's findings and the huge salaries and bonuses they paid to themselves. A code was signed that did not achieve union recognition, did allow price fixing, and provided for a forty-hour work week and a forty-cents-an-hour minimum wage.

The coal industry was even more difficult. The majestic John L. Lewis, head of the United Mine Workers, had been a conservative Republican in the twenties and had seen the UMW lose more than three-quarters of the 400,000 members it had had when Lewis took over the union in 1919. (He would continue in that position for forty years.) As soon as the NIRA was adopted, Lewis sent swarms of union organizers into the coal mining areas distributing leaflets saying that "The President Wants You To Join The Union." Strikes broke out across the coalfields, and a miner was killed and many injured in Pennsylvania.

The governor, Theodore and Franklin Roosevelt's friend Gifford Pinchot, called out the National Guard. Roosevelt set up a tribunal chaired by Senator Wagner to arbitrate the coal dispute and summoned the industry leaders. He impressed them with his detailed knowledge of the industry (having lost none of his long-established ability to master the details of a subject quickly). He warned the employers that they were turning the coal fields into a breeding ground for "Communists." A coal industry code was finally agreed in October that accomplished a lot for the UMW in wages, hours, and liberation from company stores and lodging, though it excluded the closed shop. When the Weirton Steel and Budd Manufacturing Companies refused to allow a union secret ballot and were not moved by the Roosevelt cajolery and brow-beating, there were no reprisals.

An automobile industry code was agreed at the end of August that included a clause leaving promotion to management decision on the basis of merit. In March there was a strike in the automobile industry that Roosevelt persuaded the two sides to end. He and Johnson then tried to mediate, meeting alternately with the unions and management and finally producing an agreement that maintained the open shop, the company union, and proportional representation of different unions in the same bargaining unit. Henry Ford completely abstained.

Roosevelt and his underlings were trying to play both sides on the issue of union certification. The President seemed to approve the principle of certification of entire bargaining units when there was a "substantial majority" in favor, in an executive order in February 1934. But a few days later, Johnson clarified that dissenters could stay out of the union or set up another one for a minority in the same bargaining unit.

In fact Roosevelt had little use for most of the labor leaders, whom he thought irresponsible demagogues and leaders of mobs. He was well aware that someone had to defend the working population from the rapacities of the American businessman but he believed he could take better care of the workers without the labor leaders.

The NRA codes generally forbade selling below cost, of which there were many definitions and which was generally impossible to establish anyway. The fact that the NIRA was devoted to the goal, which was largely fulfilled, of raising prices did not prevent Johnson from raging at businessmen to keep prices down "for God's sake!"

VI

THE AGRICULTURAL ADJUSTMENT ACT had a smoother (though far from unruffled) application than the NIRA. But farm prices, which had moved up sharply from early March to early July, abruptly crumbled even more quickly starting in late July as speculative purchasing stopped and the process of disposing of existing or anticipated surplus began. Into the summer of 1933 the United States was awaiting a colossal surplus in almost all agricultural products.

There were 106 million acres producing corn and 40 million producing wheat, and there was an anticipated surplus to requirements on the order of 300 million bushels of wheat, 30 million hogs, and 8 million bales of cotton. Under the AAA plan, the secretary of agriculture would rent the excess acreage and the farmer would be contracted to destroy or otherwise than commercially dispose of the surplus.

The AAA was largely operated by local members of the Extension Service, a federal-state organization connected to the land-grant (agricultural) colleges, which provided an automatic reserve of skilled personnel familiar with local farm conditions and a large number of individual farmers. This connection also had the effect of linking the administration of the AAA to the American Farm Bureau Federation, which had been effectively founded by the Extension Service and represented the more prosperous farmers, not the tenant farmers or poorer farm owners. Within a few days of the promulgation of the AAA, the Extension Service and its affiliates had sent out 22,000 agents in 956 counties to explain the AAA and persuade farmers of its virtues. Within less than a month over one million AAA contracts had been signed. The first farmer to perform his contractual responsibility to eliminate harvestable production was a black cotton farmer from Georgia who was honored by the President in a ceremony on the White House lawn.

The spectacle of destroying tens of millions of bushels of wheat and millions of hogs was a serious public relations challenge in a country with millions of hungry people. Approximately one-tenth of designated disposable surplus was salvaged for redistribution among the needy, an inspired and apparently obvious idea, but one that might not have arisen but for Jerome Frank, who was another of the highly educated people the New Deal had attracted to Washington. Frank was a successful corporate lawyer from Chicago. He had been recruited by Tugwell to be the solicitor for the department, but Farley had vetoed this appointment in the mistaken belief that Frank was the son-in-law of an ancient Tammany foe of his. (Frank's in-laws had been in the Midwest all their lives.)

However, Frank was installed as general counsel for the AAA instead. His presence infuriated the incoming George Peek, who had unsuccessfully litigated with Jerome Frank over the reorganization of Peek's insolvent Moline Plow Company. Peek set out to fire Frank, who roused Tugwell and took the case past the diffident Wallace to Roosevelt. The President imposed Frank on Peek, who responded by bringing in his own lawyer at his own expense and ignoring Frank. Frank brought some exceptional talent into his office, including future presidential candidate Adlai Stevenson, future Supreme Court justice Abe Fortas, and communist sympathizers Alger Hiss and Lee Pressman (who at one point purported to champion the macaroni growers).

It was Jerome Frank, who had gained his position by accident and held on to it with difficulty, who proposed that one-tenth of what was to be destroyed be set aside for distribution by Hopkins as emergency relief. Hopkins liked the idea.

There was considerable public outrage at destroying mountains of food to force up prices, and there was particular sensitivity about destroying baby pigs.

Frank, Tugwell, and Hopkins worked out a plan for a federal Surplus Relief Corporation and took it directly to Hyde Park and presented it to Roosevelt. Roosevelt authorized $75 million in an executive order of September 21, 1933, and broadened the distribution to include surplus clothes. This corporation served as the model for the highly successful Commodity Credit Corporation, which lent money to the farmer at a little above the commodity price, with the crop as collateral. Interest was at 4 percent. The government effectively owned the collateral unless the price went above the loan price, in which case the farmers could sell the collateral on the open market and pay off the loan. It was a classic New Deal experiment born of the creative spontaneity Roosevelt always tried to incite and favor.

By the autumn of 1933 there was a widespread perception, especially in the farm states, that the NRA was largely a government-sanctioned cartel for the benefit of big business, with a slight further incentive to the labor unions but only higher prices for the rural population. The AAA had generated higher farm prices and the mortgage foreclosures on rural homes had been drastically curtailed. But after the crack in farm commodity prices and the stock market at the end of July, the farmers of America were back, many of them, to selling what they produced beneath the cost to them of production. It continued to be a desperate state of affairs. Milo Reno and his Farmers' Holiday Association flared back to life and started sending Roosevelt ultimatums about an imminent farm strike. Roosevelt volunteered to Morgenthau, who was farm credit administrator: "I don't like to have anybody hold a pistol to my head." A delegation from Reno's association was received in Washington by Roosevelt, Wallace, Peek, and Morgenthau and encouraged to exercise their legal right to send in a code for their industry providing the protections they were seeking.

After the governor of North Dakota prohibited sales of wheat at a price below its cost of production, on October 21, 1933, Reno announced an imminent farm strike unless the government approved an agricultural code with a cost-of-production price floor and promised "adequate reflation" of the currency, an end to farm mortgage foreclosures, and dismissal of bankers from control of the country's monetary policy. (Unless Reno was referring to the central bankers rather than lending bankers, they weren't in control of it; but bankers had become emblematic of anti-inflation, gold-oriented monetary views.) "We were promised a new deal. We have the same old stacked deck," Reno said.[50]

Roosevelt, as always, was well aware of the political dangers and was preparing to deal with them. An intellectual civil war had been raging within the administration between the advocates of sound money and an early return to the gold standard, led by Paul Warburg, and the inflationists, now led by Cornell economist George Warren. A monetary advisory committee including Warburg, Lewis Douglas, George Harrison, Professor Sprague, and Assistant Treasury Secretary Dean Acheson reported to Roosevelt in late September. Predictably, the committee made once again the case for gold-backed money in a stable relationship with the other principal currencies.

Roosevelt was concerned that the farmers were now on the verge of open revolt in a way that these prosperous theorists did not understand. The AAA price increases were just starting to come in; the farmers had suffered depressed conditions since the mid-twenties, and many had reached the end of their economic and psychological endurance.

Roosevelt was beginning to believe, in terms that even Reno could agree with, that the greatest obstacle to recovery was a "conspiracy of bankers" staging a capital strike to force him into a sound-money straitjacket. He responded to the report of the monetary committee: "I do not like or approve the report," and added that the authors clearly had no idea how grave the situation was. Roosevelt wrote to Colonel House at this time: "A financial element in the larger centers has owned the government ever since the days of Andrew Jackson—and I am not wholly excepting the Administration of W.W. The country is going through a repetition of Jackson's fight with the Bank of the United States—only on a far bigger and broader basis."[51]

Roosevelt finally determined in early October to act on George Warren's proposal to buy gold above the market price and induce a gentle devaluation of the dollar in that way, but was blocked by the legalistic pettifogging of the assistant secretary of the Treasury, Dean Acheson. Acheson, who was forty in 1933, was an intractable Grotonian alumnus, and with his high intelligence and articulation and great integrity went a caustic arrogance. Despite a lively sense of humor, in the early days of the New Deal, he was a prig and a humbug, opposing the guarantee of bank deposits and the sale of gold. Acheson, a bishop's son, cynical in outlook but righteous in his own conduct, convinced himself that the policy of buying gold above the market price was a violation of the relevant statutes and therefore *ultra vires* to the President. Roosevelt was not one to trouble himself overly about such niceties, and faced with the prospect of the farm states being swept by a revolt that could be a menace to the nation's food supply and a political disaster, he had little time for Acheson's obstructions.

Woodin was desperately ill from inoperable throat cancer and had offered his resignation as secretary of the Treasury, but Roosevelt, who was always particularly supportive of his colleagues in times of illness, asked the secretary just to take a leave of absence. If Acheson, who was the senior functioning official of the department, had adjusted to the times and to the personality of the President, he could have joined the first rank of U.S. public officials fifteen years before he did, and the country would have benefited.

Morgenthau's Farm Credit Administration lawyers, led by the ingenious Herman Oliphant, held that an obscure Civil War statute, coupled with the powers of the executive under the RFC Act and the more recent discretionary powers under a recent amendment to the AAA, gave the President the necessary authority. A method was proposed whereby the RFC would buy the gold and use it as collateral to take loans from the Treasury, which paid for the market gold purchases.

There was a White House meeting October 19, 1933, to thrash out the issues. Acheson argued strenuously for the illegality of the proposal. The RFC and CFA lawyers, led by Oliphant and Solicitor General Stanley Reed, argued the other side, and Roosevelt eventually announced: "I say it's legal." Acheson had stiffly required the written legal opinion of the attorney general, Homer Cummings, and continued to debate with the President, who asked if Acheson didn't "take my word for it that it will be all right?" Acheson rather cheekily reminded him that he, Acheson, would be putting his name to the order, not the President. "That will do!" Roosevelt imperiously commanded, and the meeting broke up.[52]

The departed Raymond Moley loyally reappeared to write a Fireside Chat for Roosevelt, though Moley personally disapproved of the gold-buying policy. The radio address, the fourth of the Fireside series, was delivered on the evening of October 22, 1933. The President reported that millions had gone back to work, that 300,000 had been engaged by the Civilian Conservation Corps, and that large numbers were being taken off the dole and placed in useful public works through various agencies set up under his legislation. He claimed that $2.1 billion of $3.3 billion allocated for these purposes had already been committed, and alleged that dalliance by the states and municipalities was the only reason the full budgeted sum had not yet been committed. In fact, Ickes's prudent dilatoriness probably had more to do with it.

Roosevelt referred to progress in helping people in mortgage arrears and added: "If there is any family in the United States about to lose its home or about to lose its chattels, that family should telegraph at once either to the Farm Credit Administration or to the Home Owners Loan Corporation in Washington requesting their help." This was deft politics as well as sensible economics and sociology.

Roosevelt claimed that farm income had already risen 33 percent from where it had been a year before, but said that since this was an average there were some farmers who were no better off than they had been. He declared: "I am not satisfied with either the amount or the extent of the rise in farm incomes and . . . it is definitely a part of our policy to increase the rise and to extend it to those products which have as yet felt no benefit. If we cannot do this one way we will do it another. Do it, we will."

Roosevelt gave a very positive description of the achievements of the NRA, crediting it with ending child and subsubsistence labor, and he uttered dire warnings to both "big and petty chiselers." He concluded with his determination to get commodity prices up and proposed to do this by continuing to revalue the dollar.

He said, in effect, that he would produce the inflation necessary to revive commodity prices and then impose the currency stabilization that the conservative elements in his administration had been clamoring for. This was reasonable progress from the conundrum he faced when he was elected: how to spend down unemployment and still balance the budget. He had taken the fairly convenient expedient of making those goals sequential: spending, reflation, and pump-priming, followed by stabilization and budget balancing.

He would also seek freer arrangements with other countries after the United States had sufficiently strengthened its own position that its markets and currency could no longer be adversely affected by foreign events over which it had no influence. The free traders were well back in the policy queue with the budget balancers and gold standardists, but their patience would be rewarded, they were assured. In furtherance of all these goals, he would establish "a government market for gold in the United States . . . under the clearly defined authority of existing law. . . . Government credit will be maintained and a sound currency will accompany a rise in the American commodity price level."

This was another artistic political formulation. The President promised a spending solution in the short term and the fulfilment of the objectives of the conservative monetarists in the long term, and claimed unquestionable legal authority for his next reflation move (which the acting Treasury secretary considered illegal).

The gold-price-setting process began with extreme informality, which further affronted Acheson, three days later, on October 25. Morgenthau and Jesse Jones of the RFC came to Roosevelt's bedroom, where he ate his breakfast in bed from a tray. He moved the price of gold up from $29.80 last trade to $31.36. Thereafter changes would be between 10 and 22 cents daily. The goal was to keep moving the price gradually up but not in such jolts as to destabilize the capital markets, and not according to a pattern that could be discerned by speculators.

By mid-November the price of gold had been raised to $33.56 an ounce and the gold value of a dollar had declined from just under 66 cents to 61.6 cents. Roosevelt's methods of calculating the daily fix were too cavalier for his prim and proper neighbor, Morgenthau, much less Acheson (who was extremely witty when his sense of propriety was not affronted). On November 3, Morgenthau asked for more than the usual increase in the gold price and Roosevelt scandalized him by imposing 21 cents because it was three times the lucky number of seven.

Acheson disliked Roosevelt's custom of calling everyone by his first name, of convening senior officials in his bedroom, and of carrying on these meetings while his grandchildren jumped on his bed and sometimes clamped their hands over his mouth while he discussed the price of gold, requiring him to tickle the child gagging him so he could finish his sentence. Acheson wrote many years later that this practice made conversation "intermittent, disjointed, and obscure." He found Roosevelt's methods "condescending" and these sessions in the President's bedroom reminiscent of the famous *levée du roi* of Louis XIV.* Acheson's point was that for Roosevelt to call everyone from his valet to the highest officials of the government by their Christian names reduced everyone to a common level of subordinacy and had monarchical overtones.

He wrote, in retrospect: "It is not gratifying to receive the easy greeting which milord might give a promising stable boy and pull one's forelock in return." Acheson did not like Roosevelt but acknowledged from the start that his "essence was force" and that Roosevelt loved "power and command . . . and packed quite a wallop."[53] When Roosevelt became incensed at leaks to the press claiming dissension within the administration, he unjustly imputed these to Acheson. On October 29 there was a meeting at the White House with a number of Treasury, Federal Reserve, RFC, and Justice Department officials involved in this program, during which Roosevelt darkly stated that anyone "who could not accept his decisions about the gold-buying plan could get out, but no one could stay on and oppose them."[54] Nothing was further said on this occasion, but Woodin, extremely frail, returned briefly to work and told Acheson that he had been asked by the President to obtain the assistant secretary's resignation and that he, Woodin, had tried to resign at the same time.[55]

As a reward for bringing the Warren theory of the commodity dollar to his attention and for generating Herman Oliphant's empowering legal opinion, Roosevelt gave Acheson's position to Morgenthau, who knew less about economics and Treasury matters than Acheson and did not possess Acheson's intelligence or forensic skills. He was, however, malleable, especially to the wishes of Franklin D. Roosevelt. If Acheson had played this differently, he would have won Roosevelt's respect long before he did, would have retained his position, and would probably have succeeded Woodin as secretary. It was unfortunate. Acheson could have been as great a star in Roosevelt's administration as he was in the succeeding one.

Acheson's letter of resignation was civil and respectful, and at Woodin's insistence he came to the ceremony for Morgenthau's swearing-in. Roosevelt was very impressed with this and called Acheson a "real sportsman." He subsequently told people leaving his administration they should learn from Acheson "how to resign like a gentleman."[56] When it came to light that Acheson was innocent of indiscretions and that Lewis Douglas was probably the culprit, Roosevelt regretted his action. Acheson too had second thoughts. Twenty years later he considered his conduct "tinged with stubbornness and lack of imaginative understanding of my own proper role and of the President's perplexities and needs." He was "not at all sure" he had acted correctly.[57]

At the end of the October 29 meeting Roosevelt claimed that if he hadn't repriced gold "we would have had an agrarian revolution in this country."[58] In fact it was a very temporary palliative, and a "puerile" one, thought Frankfurter.[59]

---

* This is a bit exaggerated, since the Sun King even had his court grunt encouragingly as he relieved himself in his opulent chamber pot.

After a few months Roosevelt pegged gold at $35 an ounce, where it remained for forty years. This was on the promulgation of the Gold Reserve Act at the end of January 1934, which put exact but generous limits on the President's power to devalue the dollar. The gold-buying program, despite its trivial results, had been another Rooseveltian masterstroke for taking the wind out of the sails of Milo Reno and his radical Farm Holiday movement at a critical moment. There is no evidence that Roosevelt ever reposed excessive confidence in it, other than as a public-relations gesture.

The governors of Iowa, Minnesota, North Dakota, South Dakota, and Wisconsin came to Washington at the beginning of November 1933, wanting federal support for their demand that farm products not be sold at a price beneath the cost of production. The Surplus Relief Corporation had been buying substantial quantities of wheat, butter, and apples in the open market to try to move up the price of these commodities, with modest success, and then handing over what had been purchased to Hopkins for emergency relief. Roosevelt and Peek appeared to agree with the visiting governors, but Henry Wallace told them that their position was nonsensical, because enforcement of such a price would require the engagement of 500,000 police officers, and that any such pricing system would be a cesspool of corruption.

Roosevelt met with them for a total of four hours, after which, though the governors did not succeed in their original purpose of having an imposed price fixed coercively, four of the five returned impressed by the hearing they had received, by the administration's sensitivity to the issues raised, and by Roosevelt's now legendary charm and grasp of policy detail.

The farm strike spluttered out, and Reno's movement collapsed with it. Roosevelt had narrowly avoided political disaster and a scene of grave disorder in a large part of the country. His political antennae were amazingly finely calibrated to the thoughts and attitudes of the people. The North Dakota governor's embargo on exportation of wheat outside his state, having been unenforceable, was called off in mid-November, and checks for benefit payments from the AAA started to come in in greater amounts as winter wheat production levels were rolled back. Roosevelt was undoubtedly correct that the country had come close to widespread violence in rural areas.

Peek set out again to fire Jerome Frank, but Wallace and Roosevelt, motivated somewhat by Tugwell, thought otherwise and Peek left the AAA instead, to coordinate agricultural exports and, in 1934, to become president of the newly established Export-Import Bank.

Hull was astounded to have this notorious protectionist put in charge of any export activities. But it all seemed to work out amiably enough, until Peek attacked the administration's trade policy as un-American in a speech in New York on November 11. Roosevelt wrote him a sharp rebuke that required and shortly resulted in Peek's resignation. Roosevelt's letter described Peek's speech as "rather silly . . . [and] like a Hearst paper." (Peek told his former boss Baruch that Roosevelt's letter was "kind of mean."[60]) Like so many others who would go through the administration, Peek left as soon as his hour of political utility had passed, unaware of the unseen presidential organization of the sequence of events.[61]

VII

ROOSEVELT EXCHANGED EMBASSIES with the Soviet Union by an agreement signed on November 17, 1933. The Soviets had had an economic office in the United States for some time, and William Bullitt, a dashing adventurer among the wealthy American governmental dilettantes who had married the widow of American romantic Communist John Reed, had, at Roosevelt's instruction, opened discussions on diplomatic recognition through that channel. A detailed agreement had been worked out in Washington with the commissar for foreign affairs, Maxim Litvinov, without much difficulty. Roosevelt and the Soviet President, Mikhail Kalinin, exchanged letters celebrating the opening of relations between "two great republics."

There was the predictable comment in some circles to the effect that this was a conferral of unmerited credibility on a gangster regime. But the administration's claim that it was necessary to have some official relationship with such an important country was practically unanswerable. Roosevelt considered the era of no relations to be aberrant, and as Hitler reasserted German strength it was becoming more hazardous to maintain the Soviet Union in a state of unrelieved isolation.

The Russians had promised religious freedom to Americans resident in the Soviet Union, a trivial concession, and a relaxation of Communist propaganda in the United States, a promise on which they did not deliver. The prediction of Adolf Berle and Gardiner Means that ties with Moscow would yield great and useful economic consequences, a theory to which Roosevelt had never subscribed, proved unfounded. Soviet-American relations would prove useful eventually, however.

As autumn passed into winter at the end of 1933, Roosevelt's exasperation with Ickes' snail's pace at going through his Public Works Administration (PWA), job-creation budget boiled over. After a luncheon talk with Hopkins in early November following a fact-finding trip Hopkins had conducted in the Midwest, Roosevelt determined to reallocate much of this effort from Ickes to Hopkins. At the luncheon, Hopkins told the President they would have to find four million temporary jobs during the winter, and the two men concluded that the program would have to be funded from Ickes' underused budget. Roosevelt sent a delegation of Hopkins, Wallace, and Frances Perkins to advise Ickes of this decision. Ickes took it in uncharacteristic good spirits and the Civil Works Administration was founded by executive order of the President, with the head of the Federal Emergency Relief Administration, Hopkins, as its director.

The CWA was an entirely federal program. Half its workers were taken from the relief rolls and half were needful people who were excused from a means test. Hopkins and his staff showed great ingenuity in devising useful work, at the minimum wage, for over four million people in one month without threatening the jobs of those already employed. In the bitter winter of 1934 the CWA built or upgraded 500,000 miles of roads, 40,000 schools, 3,500 recreational grounds and parks, and 1,000 airfields. It employed 50,000 teachers and sustained or reopened the entire rural school system. Among the prominent buildings the CWA renovated was the Montana State Capitol at Helena, and among those it built was the famous and majestic Cathedral of Learning in Pittsburgh. Without this and other innovative programs, the misery among millions of Americans could have been very severe, and might have led to many deaths and widespread unrest.

Among four of the administration's key figures, Hopkins saw public works as relief for the needy, while Ickes saw them as opportunities for the construction of splendid monuments with great care and economy. Hugh Johnson regarded public works as a stimulant to industry, and Lewis Douglas disapproved of them altogether.[62]

Hopkins returned with supplementary requests to take the program through to the spring of 1934. Roosevelt charged Eleanor's friend Lorena Hickock and the head of the National Emergency Council, Frank Walker, to report on how the CWA was doing in the field, and the reports were uniformly positive. Hopkins's genius and efficiency as a welfare administrator were confirmed on a grand scale. About 80 percent of the one billion dollars spent on the program went to cash salaries, and almost all of that and most of the other 20 percent went directly on to consumer spending. A rough division was worked out that gave Hopkins's agency the short-term work and Ickes the longer-scale projects.

In a fine flourish that would leave a rich artistic heritage, Hopkins created a federal arts program within the CWA, which provided work for 3,000 writers, musicians, sculptors, and painters. The Federal Theatre produced passably good works of Shakespeare, Sinclair Lewis, T.S. Eliot, W.H. Auden, and others. The Federal Art Project engaged a great many aspiring artists of limited ability, but also gave a start to a number of artists who became famous, including William De Kooning and Jackson Pollock. Doubtless there was some waste, and critics were right to object that a great deal of New Deal propaganda was churned out by the artistic beneficiaries and their friends and kindred spirits. But it was a useful program—a blow against philistinism, which customarily flourishes in times of economic hardship, as well as a sage political investment by Roosevelt and his political adjutants.[63] The beneficiaries rendered better service doing useful work in their fields of specialty than they would have repaving roads or replastering school rooms, this measure gained the adherence to the ranks of government supporters of most of the influential cultural community.

Roosevelt always knew that the intellectuals, like the film actors, could be reduced to the status of helpless groupies with a little attention and generosity from a stylish and sympathetic president. When he met the dramatic prodigy

Orson Welles a few years later, he said, almost surely with sincerity: "Orson, you and I are the two best actors in this country." (Welles, captivated, campaigned with him in 1944.) The professional actors rarely had the remotest idea how complete and flamboyant was Roosevelt's masquerade as an almost omniscient leader.

Roosevelt and Hopkins strongly believed in payment for useful work rather than the subsistence dole. This was at some variance to prevailing business opinion, which held that paying rather more for real work created welfare dependency and threatened low wage scales. Roosevelt was concerned to preserve the dignity of work and the habits of paid work uncorrupted by subsidized unemployment. He knew that men would retain greater credibility as heads of families and households if they actually did something rather than merely festering idly while awaiting their welfare checks.

Roosevelt wound down the CWA with the spring of 1934. He was concerned lest a permanent class of relief recipients arise. He was concerned at the cost of the program and did not want to substitute the government for the private sector as the engine for job creation. "We must not take the position that we are going to have permanent depression in this country . . . Nobody is going to starve during the warm weather."[64] This was a glimpse of the true Roosevelt. He was never a bleeding heart.

At the end of 1933, the two-thirds of the country that had never been unemployed but almost all of whom in early 1933 had been afraid of losing their jobs were now, in faithful reflection of their new president, optimistic that the worst was past and that recovery was in progress. Those on the far right looked darkly upon their president as a socialist sympathizer, those on the far left accurately regarded him as an inconstant ally, and both imputed to him a lust for unlimited power. However, the vast army of the center had gained strength at the expense of the extremes and was solidly behind Roosevelt.

He had already written disappointedly to Frankfurter of "the failure of those who have property to realize that I am the best friend the profit system ever had."[65] He should not have been surprised. He well knew the lack of political sophistication of most of America's wealthy and executive classes. He knew that he would have to engage in rhetoric more hair-raising than most of them could possibly abide if he was going to keep the majority of the soft center out of the arms of Huey Long and other populists, and of Norman Thomas and the insidious Communists to the left of him.

His irritation with his natural peers did not alter his perceptive judgment of where the governing majority's hearts and minds were. Like a skillful conductor, he orchestrated approximately equal levels of noise from both ideological poles and repelled trespassers upon his command of the center by whatever means came to hand. Franklin D. Roosevelt had got through his first ten months as president with great style, an elegant, cunning, and popular leader. But behind his inspiriting showmanship, real progress was still tentative and fragile. It was not yet clear whether he would be a great president or merely an agile one.

CHAPTER 8

"Never Let Your Left Hand Know What Your Right Hand Is Doing"

(Franklin D. Roosevelt to Henry Morgenthau, May 1935)

I

THE DISTINGUISHED OXFORD economist John Maynard Keynes, with the encouragement of Felix Frankfurter (who was an academic visitor at Oxford, 1933–1934), wrote a public letter to President Roosevelt that was published in the *New York Times* on December 31, 1933. Keynes expressed admiration for Roosevelt as the only leader who held out legitimate hope for economic improvement without recourse to dictatorship or oppression. Keynes opposed the gold-buying program, which had run its course and had been only a placebo for the militant farmers anyway. He also recommended a vast, debt-financed public works program. Roosevelt wasn't overly impressed with commendations from British (or other, including domestic) academics, but asked Frankfurter to tell Keynes that the public-works budget would be doubled in 1934.*

In the spring of 1934 Frankfurter arranged for Keynes to call upon Roosevelt. Keynes was about to publish his formidable opus *The General Theory of Employment, Interest, and Money,* and had come to the United States to receive an honorary degree from Columbia University. Both men told mutual friends that the meetings between them, on May 28 and 29, had been a huge success, "fascinating and illuminating," said Keynes, "a grand talk" said Roosevelt, both to Frankfurter.[1] But they were not overly convivial. Roosevelt, though he could usually

---

* Roosevelt had commended the auditor general of the Reparations Commission (George Auld) in 1924 for accusing Keynes of hypocrisy when the economist objected to the reparations burden placed on Germany. Roosevelt and Auld thought Keynes's statement just part of British attempts to penetrate German markets.

manage to disguise it, was not especially comfortable with leading academics unless they were completely subservient, like Frankfurter.

Roosevelt was a reasonably though sometimes unrigorously learned man, but he was preeminently a man of action in the Roosevelt tradition. He wasn't a natural admirer of theorists. Keynes had been a fervent public admirer of Roosevelt, but now, face to face, was disappointed that he was not "more literate, economically speaking." He was also prone to judge people by their hands and found Roosevelt's strong and large but lacking finesse, and with "short round nails like a businessman's."[2] Further, the President's hands reminded Keynes of Sir Edward Grey's, and though Grey was generally reckoned an outstanding foreign secretary, he was not respected by Keynes. The interview went well enough socially but did not lead to a lasting relationship, though Keynes continued to give Roosevelt the benefit of his unsolicited advice.

Elevation to the White House of its guiding spirit accomplished wonders for the financial condition of Warm Springs. Henry Doherty, the arthritic chairman of Cities Service, a large oil industry holding company, having been accused of overly aggressive tax avoidance and stock jobbing by the Federal Trade Commission, was in need of some good public relations as well as therapeutic attention. He was approached by Keith Morgan, Roosevelt's Warm Springs fundraiser, and applied his considerable wealth, talents, and influence to the task. An annual fund drive for polio research called the March of Dimes began, and the President's fifty-second birthday, January 30, 1934, was the occasion for 6,000 simultaneous parties all over the country in aid of the Warm Springs Foundation. The President addressed them all by radio at the same time. A powerful group of business leaders was assembled in support of the President's preferred cause, and raised over $1,000,000 on this first campaign. Barely within Roosevelt family memory now were Eleanor's dire warnings that her husband would waste all his parents' money on Warm Springs and would be unable to give his children (who proved not to be very scholarly anyway) a proper education.

His birthday was also the occasion for a meeting of the Cuff Links Club, the supporters from the 1920 vice presidential campaign. It was no longer a stag affair; Eleanor and her Val Kill friends, Anna, Missy LeHand, Grace Tully, Eleanor's secretary Tommy Thompson, and Howe's Rabbit Durand all played key roles. For their first celebration in the White House the club struck a Roman motif, with Roosevelt dressed as Caesar in toga and laurel and the others appropriately costumed in less exalted roles. Even the normally staid Eleanor entered into the spirit of it. There were skits, most of them written by Louis Howe, and improvised songs, and—according to the club's custom—a very late and well-liquefied poker game. (Adolf Berle thereafter addressed his letters to the President to "Dear Caesar" until Roosevelt asked him not to several years later, fearing the press might get hold of such a letter and misconstrue it.)

Criticism of the NRA grew steadily through the winter of 1933–1934. There were great objections to the price-fixing agreements, and the business community was outraged at the collective bargaining rights conferred by Section VII of Title I. Although the government retained its popularity and there was real economic progress, the NRA was generally regarded as a failure by the spring of 1934, almost a year after its passage. Progressives were alienated by the appearance of favoritism to big business and the large labor unions.

In February 1934 Senator Hiram Johnson set up a National Recovery Review Board, which was chaired and dominated by perhaps America's most famous trial lawyer of all time, Clarence Darrow. After the board held public hearings and reviewed a number of the largest codes, Darrow presented his preliminary report in May—an avowedly socialistic document that decried the monopolistic leanings of the code writers and asserted that the NRA oppressed small businesses. A considerable controversy ensued, but Darrow more than held his own in the forum of public relations.

Responding to the widespread view in liberal circles that the NRA was more favorable to big business than to labor, Senator Robert Wagner presented the Labor Disputes Act of 1934 in March. This bill would have banned any management support for company unions and any interference in selection of collective bargaining agents, and would have required negotiation with majority-selected collective bargaining agents. It would also have set up a Labor Relations Board with powers analogous to those of the Federal Trade Commission.

Roosevelt leaned sufficiently on Wagner to secure his acquiescence in the evisceration of what he had originally proposed. Most of the progressive senators, such as La Follette and particularly Bronson Cutting, were in an uproar. Cutting bellowed in Senate debate: "The New Deal is being strangled in the house of its friends." Cutting was generally still a supporter of Roosevelt's programs but regarded the President personally as slippery and duplicitous. His antagonism was heartily reciprocated.

One of the cornerstones of institutional reform in the New Deal, the phase that immediately followed emergency relief, was the regulation of security issues. Roosevelt had never ceased to inveigh against "the money-changers" and like-minded scoundrels, and this was both a symbolic and a substantive opportunity. Ben Cohen, Tommy Corcoran, and James Landis had largely drafted a new securities-regulation bill by the beginning of 1934, which was introduced in the Congress on February 10. (Sam Rayburn was the House floor manager.)* The securities bill required serious descriptions of new issues and timely reporting on financial performance of listed companies, and prohibited dubious stock market practices that enabled insiders to swindle good-faith public investors. It

---

* Dealing with the serried ranks of bright, young, unelected people in the administration, Rayburn was concerned that there not be a Rasputin among them.[3]

established authority over margin requirements and segregated many interlocking financial entities rife with conflicts of interest.

Under intense hostile pressure from the financial industry led by Richard Whitney, who had been such a personality on the floor of the New York Stock Exchange in October 1929 (and who would soon be sent to prison for stock market fraud), the bill was somewhat redrafted by its authors, giving authority over margin requirements to the Federal Reserve, and resubmitted to the Congress accompanied by a forceful message from the President insisting that it be acted upon. (In a recurrent theme, the President then departed for a ten-day fishing cruise as Vincent Astor's guest on the *Nourmahal*.) The Securities and Exchange Act, which has been generally recognized as an intelligent and necessary reform, was signed into law on June 6, 1934.

To administer the new regulations, the law established the Securities and Exchange Commission, with five members appointed by the President. Roosevelt named his five commissioners, including James Landis and Ferdinand Pecora. The big surprise, and an inspired insight, was the chairman, Joseph P. Kennedy. When wails of consternation went up over Kennedy's own stock market skulduggery, Roosevelt breezily replied: "Set a thief to catch a thief."[4] He correctly judged that Kennedy would know all the tricks that the new act was designed to prevent and that he would run the commission honestly. It would also keep the restless and egocentric Kennedy, who had expected to be offered the Treasury, busy.

The Congress passed the Communications Act, establishing the Federal Communications Commission to regulate the radio and telegraph busnesses and new electronic technologies as they came to life. The Railroad Retirement Act provided pensions for railway workers, resolving a vexatious industrial-relations heirloom from the nineteenth century.

Roosevelt, as we have seen, always closely watched those prominent Americans who he thought possessed a dangerous potential for rousing popular support for themselves outside normal democratic politics. Kennedy would be busy for a time with the SEC, and Hearst was still reasonably susceptible to the Roosevelt treatment of flattery and cajolery. Roosevelt extended MacArthur's term as chief of staff of the U.S. Army for another year and then in 1935 would send him to the Philippines to prepare that country for independence with appropriate armed forces. Roosevelt explained to Tugwell: "We must tame these fellows and make them useful to us." He wanted MacArthur and Kennedy where he could keep an eye on them or completely out of the way.[5]

His positive disposition to the general endured despite an apparently acrimonious debate over funding the army. Secretary of War George Dern and MacArthur visited Roosevelt, and MacArthur wrote later (when the other participants were deceased) that "The President turned the full vials of his sarcasm upon me . . . that paralyzing nausea began to creep over me." He claims to have told Roosevelt that when "we [had] lost the next war" and a bayoneted and dying American boy "spat out his last curse, I wanted the name not to be MacArthur, but Roosevelt. The President grew livid. 'You must not talk that way to the President,' he roared."

MacArthur apologized and offered his resignation. Roosevelt responded "with that cool detachment which so reflected his extraordinary self-control, 'Don't be foolish, Douglas; you and the budget must get together on this.' " Roosevelt didn't want to propel MacArthur into the civilian world in this unpromising manner. Even writing twenty years later, the general didn't grasp Roosevelt's political evaluation of him. The general recorded that he "just vomited on the steps of the White House."[6]*

The other suspects identified by Roosevelt as having potential Bonapartist tendencies—Huey Long, John L. Lewis, Colonel McCormick, and Charles A. Lindbergh, the aviator who made the first non-stop solo flight across the Atlantic Ocean—were all circling around and the President was warily watching them. (McCormick was more of a propagandist and king-maker than a rabble-rouser. He spoke often on his radio stations but did not have much taste for direct participation in public life.)

Roosevelt's first exchange of fire with Lindbergh was not a happy one for Roosevelt. Senator Hugo Black of Alabama revealed in early 1934 that the transfer of U.S. airmail contracts from the hell-for-leather aviators of the early twenties to the first airlines, especially TWA (Transcontinental & Western Air, later Trans World Airlines), had cost the taxpayers nearly $50 million in the last four years. Black found that many contracts had been issued in consideration for bribes and that most of the contracts were fraudulent. He so informed the President, who asked the attorney general, Homer Cummings, if a blanket cancellation was justified. When Cummings advised that it was, Roosevelt ignored the advice of the postmaster general, James A. Farley, who asked for a deferral to June, and cancelled the airmail contracts and directed that the Army Air Service (later the Army Air Corps) deliver the mail as of February 19, 1934.

Lindbergh was the highly paid chairman of the TWA technical committee and a popular hero whose celebrity perhaps was matched only by that of the New York Yankee star Babe Ruth. On February 11 Lindbergh sent Roosevelt a telegram that was simultaneously released to the public, accusing the President of unjustly dismissing all the carriers without any due process or any distinction between the guilty and the innocent, and of putting the mails into the hands of army fliers who had inferior machines and maintenance levels and from whose selection tragedy would inevitably result. He proved to be prophetic. By March 10 ten

---

* MacArthur had visited Europe in the autumn of 1932 and reported to Stimson that Stalin had killed all the talented Russian generals and had replaced them with "Jewish Commissars without the brains or requirement for command."[7]

Army Air Service pilots had lost their lives, and the extent of the airmail service was seriously curtailed. The following day Lindbergh met with Secretary of War Dern, who thought they had reached agreement that Lindbergh would serve on a committee that would review the subject. Lindbergh publicly denied this two days later.

Despite the curtailment of service, accidents continued to happen, and two more army aviators died by mid-April. The terms on which the airmail subsidy was paid were drastically revised in the Air Mail Act of 1934, a genuine reform, which Roosevelt signed on June 12. Roosevelt had kept his distance from the issue publicly while Farley and Dern loyally took the heat for him, but it was a setback and an embarrassment. There would be a rematch between Roosevelt and Lindbergh in a few years, on a much larger issue and with a very different result; in the meantime the President looked uneasily upon the popular aviator.

When the congressional session ended, Roosevelt sent congratulatory letters to the senators and congressmen via Vice President Garner and Speaker of the House Henry Rainey (who had succeeded Garner and with whom Roosevelt had first mournfully corresponded over the fate of the Democrats in the twenties). Roosevelt wrote: "This Congress will go down into history as one of large accomplishment for the national good." In a personal side letter to Rainey, he wrote: "It's been a grand session—the best in all our history."[8] Two weeks later, July 1, Roosevelt left for a 14,000-mile trip down the Atlantic coast, through the Panama Canal, to the Hawaiian Islands and back on the U.S.S. *Houston*. (She was a sister of the *Indianapolis* and one of the class of 10,000-ton heavy cruisers that were Roosevelt's preferred means of transport throughout his presidency, in peace and war.)

———————————

There were a number of spectacular labor disputes in early and mid-1934. A Teamsters truck drivers' strike in Minneapolis led to a pitched battle around the city's central market on May 22, 1934, in which two special deputies were killed. This Teamsters local was an avowedly Marxist union—Troskyite, in fact, Stalin then being regarded as insufficiently Marxist. After a hiatus for fruitless negotiation, the strike started up again in July. On July 16, two more people were killed and sixty-seven wounded by gunfire. The governor declared martial law and ruled in this manner for five more weeks, raiding the headquarters of both the strikers and management and arresting a number of hotheads on both sides. Finally a settlement fairly favorable to the strikers was produced by federal mediators, and the city returned to uneasy normalcy in the last days of August.

Even more difficult was the contemporaneous longshoremen's strike in San Francisco, masterminded by the thirty-three-year-old Australian Communist Harry Bridges. The union's principal grievance was the management practice of hourly hiring, with no security at all for anyone, frequent blacklisting, and an atmosphere on San Francisco's Embarcadero of a slave market.

The strike began along the entire Pacific Coast on May 9, 1934. On June 5 the management association declared its intention to hire whomever it wished, to reactivate the West Coast ports. Since this would clearly lead to extensive violence, urgent appeals were made to the President for preventive action. Roosevelt was establishing a National Labor Relations Board under the rubric of the legislation initiated by Senator Wagner, and set up a special board to deal with the longshoremen's strike, consisting of a Roman Catholic archbishop, a distinguished lawyer, and Assistant Labor Secretary McGrady.

When the employers probed the union lines on July 3 there was a prolonged street battle in which scores were injured. The port remained closed through the July 4 holiday. On July 5 a pitched battle raged almost all day, from late morning until well into the evening. Two pickets were killed, scores of people were injured, and there was widespread gunfire for several hours. The governor of California, Republican Frank Merriam, declared martial law and assigned 5,000 National Guardsmen with fixed bayonets to ensure order. Comparative calm descended on the still-closed port, but on the motion of Bridges and his Communist supporters, the unions took the offensive and on July 16 declared a general strike; 130,000 strikers in many industries answered the call. Such a prolonged, widespread, and violent strike in such a civilized city, under Communist auspices, seriously discountenanced the country. The governors of California and Oregon, Senator Hiram Johnson (no mean fire-breather on behalf of labor in his day), and other officials beseeched Roosevelt for enough force to prevent the outbreak of civil war.

Roosevelt would recount later: "A lot of people completely lost their heads and telegraphed me: 'For God's sake, come back; turn the ship around . . . sail into San Francisco Bay all flags flying and guns double shotted, and end the strike.' "[9] The situation was aggravated by Hugh Johnson, embarked on one of his speaking tours, who prevailed upon the University of California at Berkeley to go ahead with a speech of his that the University had tried to cancel, on July 17. The general, at his macho-epigrammatic best, after a reasonably judicious prelude called for the Communist leadership of the strike to be "run out . . . like rats [or else] the people would act, and it would wipe out this subversive element as you clean off a chalk mark on a blackboard with a wet sponge."[10] (Amid squabbling in the NRA, Roosevelt had chosen to retain Johnson, who was much criticized, and he had moved Richberg to the National Emergency Council, replacing the retiring Frank Walker.)

Roosevelt, always unflappable whatever the pressures, remained on the *Houston* fishing and playing cards with his cronies and sending timely, unguent messages back to the protagonists. His judgment of the public mood was exact. Everyone except Hugh Johnson had become frightened by the overheated atmosphere. The Central Labor Council in San Francisco repudiated Bridges, both sides accepted binding arbitration, and the West Coast waterfronts reopened July 27. On October 12 the special board Roosevelt had appointed decreed jointly operated hiring halls, recognition of the union as bargaining agent in the absence of competing claims, and a package of wage, pay, and working conditions improvements. There had been a number of lesser but well-publicized strikes, including ones by New York City's 15,000 taxi drivers and by the famous Waldorf-Astoria Hotel's kitchen and restaurant staff, which paraded up and down Park Avenue implausibly singing the "Internationale."[11] There was a general strike in Terre Haute, Indiana, and a long strike at the Anaconda Copper Mine (the foundation of the Hearst fortune).

In the spring of 1934 the CWA gave way to Hopkins's Federal Emergency Relief Administration, a joint federal-state-administered operation, with less hastily improvised methods and goals than the CWA, which was an emergency creation for the preceding winter. The CWA was providing emergency work and incomes. The FERA aimed to do that but also to relaunch its participants into the private sector. In addition to building 5,000 public buildings (town halls, stupefying numbers of post offices, and so forth) and 7,000 bridges, and executing a great many improvements to park and arable land (without much straying into the forests, the domain of the CCC), the FERA harnessed the talents of white-collar participants. It conducted adult education courses that taught over 1.5 million people to read and write, helped 100,000 people to go to college, and operated large numbers of day-care centers and nursery schools for the children of underprivileged families.

The expression "boondoggle" became current in reference to FERA support for the production of esoteric luxury goods such as woven belts, or for the teaching of calligraphy. This was unjust, because the FERA accepted only means-tested applicants and paid an absolute subsistence $6.50 per week, compared with the CWA's minimum wage of $15.04.

By late summer, the approximately 14 million unemployed of seventeen months before, when Roosevelt had been inaugurated, had been reduced by about 4.5 million by the private sector with the benefit of the shorter work weeks in most of the NRA codes. The ranks of the unemployed had been further diminished by the engagement of 6.5 million of them in the CWA, CCC, PWA, and FERA. The domestic-allotment activities of the AAA and various supplementary measures to raise farm prices and incomes were in place. The banking system was functioning well. The *New York Times* weekly business index was up from 72 in October 1933 to 86 in May 1934. Detroit had twice as many employed people as it had had a year before.[12]

There had been huge gains for participatory democracy; workers and farmers voted in millions on collective agreements, agricultural production restrictions, the establishment of soil conservation districts, and bituminous coal quotas. There were advisory committees for almost everything, including national youth and arts projects. Native people even voted under the Indian Reorganization Act of 1934 on new tribal constitutions.[13] The public mood was becoming steadily more robust.

————————

President Roosevelt returned to the continental United States from his cruise through the Panama Canal and to the Hawaiian Islands on August 3, 1934. The U.S.S. *Houston* entered the mouth of the Columbia River and sailed upriver to the Willamette and then docked at Portland, Oregon.

Roosevelt was greeted by a large portion of the population of Portland with uniform enthusiasm as he drove through the city and to the Bonneville Dam, about one hundred miles to the east. Roosevelt inspected the dam site and spoke to a large crowd there before boarding his train, where he was joined by his wife and three of his sons, and beginning a whistle-stop tour back to the East.

At the Grand Coulee Dam, at Spokane; in the Glacier National Park, in Montana, where his remarks were broadcast to the country; and at the recently built world's largest earthen dam, at Fort Peck, Montana, he focussed on the work of reforestation and of flood and drought control by the Civilian Conservation Corps, especially its 75,000 formerly unemployed corpsmen sprucing up the national parks. The soil of the Great Plains had been terribly eroded by the dust bowl ravages of recent years, and the President's deployment of tens of thousands of the unemployed to engage in works that would enrich the soil and make it more resistant to erosion was a very popular policy in the western states.

When Roosevelt stopped in Wisconsin he made it clear that he would be happy if the La Follettes were elected in that state. Robert (junior) was running for senator and Philip for governor. Roosevelt hoped to encourage in Republican ranks a permanent split of the kind that had riven that party in 1912 between the followers of Theodore Roosevelt and William Howard Taft, ensuring the election of Woodrow Wilson. Roosevelt was trying to cast as wide a net over the voters as he could.

II

ON HIS RETURN to Washington in mid-August 1934, Roosevelt received a visit from Jouett Shouse, the Smith-Raskob party official who six years before had helped lead the party to a position that was in policy terms almost indistinguishable from the Republicans', apart from the question of Prohibition.

Shouse told Roosevelt of the imminent founding of the Liberty League, which he represented as an independent educational organization preaching the eternal American political verities. It was led by Smith, Raskob, John W. Davis, and a number of wealthy businessmen. Raskob had written Shouse shortly after the 1932 convention deploring the fact that the Democratic Party was in the hands of "such radicals as Roosevelt, Huey Long, Hearst, McAdoo and . . . Wheeler."[14] Roosevelt realized immediately that the founders' idea of "education" would be hysterical denigration of him from an arch-capitalist perspective. He was little concerned with this. He had seen the amateurishness of Smith's political judgment when he got outside New York and knew the businessmen involved to be completely inept when they strayed into politics. The Liberty League, Roosevelt told journalists, was like an organization dedicated to the promotion of two of the Ten Commandments.[15]

Roosevelt was more concerned with Huey Long, who had launched his Share Our Wealth Society in 1934. Its motto was "Every man a king," and it proposed a 100 percent tax on individual net worth above $5 million, or 300 times the net worth of American families. Long would propose the same draconian taxation on annual incomes above $1 million, or 300 times the national average. Long calculated that the proceeds of these taxes would provide a $5,000 payoff to every family. He also proposed a guaranteed annual income of at least one-third the national average, a thirty-hour work week, and at least one month a year of holiday. This program was absurdly impractical—the proceeds from the proposed wealth tax would not have raised a fraction of what was required to fund any such program, and such a seizure of private property was grossly unconstitutional. But Roosevelt could see that under Long's skillful guidance such a manifesto could attract many adherents. By early 1935, Long would claim 27,000 of his Share Our Wealth Society clubs, with 7.5 million members.[16] Long had engaged the talented evangelical rabble-rouser Gerald L.K. Smith as his organizer.

Long broke with Roosevelt in the first months of the new administration and lamented: "We took four hundred millions from the soldiers and spent three hundred millions to plant saplings."[17]

Long was "a tousled redhead with a cherubic face, a dimpled chin, and a pug nose." He "had the physique of a Punchinello."[18] He dressed outlandishly, and when he appeared for lunch at Springwood, Sara Delano Roosevelt asked, not especially quietly: "Who is that awful man?" Huey Long had first come to national attention in 1930 when he was excoriated for receiving the German consul in New Orleans and the captain of the visiting German cruiser *Emden* in his pajamas (at the Hotel Roosevelt). Long, then the governor of Louisiana, responded to negative publicity by clambering aboard the *Emden* the next day in tailcoat, striped trousers, and full kit, except a top hat, and ostentatiously bowed and strutted his way around the ship, where he had not been expected.[19]

The visiting Rebecca West said of Huey Long: "In his vitality and his repulsiveness, he was very like Laval" (the greasy, fascistic, Germanophile French premier ultimately executed for treason by France during World War II). Long reminded Rebecca West's companion, H.G. Wells, of "a Winston Churchill who has never been at Harrow."[20] Long had little trouble putting himself at the head of the most visible malcontents in the country.

At about this time, Long informed some of his colleagues in the senatorial cloakroom: "It will not be long until there will be a mob assembling here to hang senators from the rafters of the Senate. I have to determine whether I will stay and be hung with you or go out and lead the mob." *New York Times* reporter Raymond Daniell claimed Long outlined to him how he intended to install himself as dictator of America. Long's hero was Frederick the Great, a surprisingly respectable, cultured, and militarily talented figure to be idolized by America's greatest and cleverest buffoon.[21]

The militant farm leader Milo Reno in the spring of 1935 would introduce Long at the state fair grounds in Des Moines as "the hero whom God in his goodness has vouchsafed to his children." Reno called Roosevelt and his advisors "traitors."[22] This was carrying exuberant fairground oratory further than most Americans found acceptable.

Also at the start of 1934 the gentle sixty-six-year-old Dr. Francis E. Townsend, a retired physician, launched his Townsend Plan, which promised $200 per month for every person in the country sixty years old or more, provided that person retired from active employment and promised to spend the $200 within a month of receiving it. The plan was to be financed by a universal 2 percent sales and goods-and-services tax; it was arithmetical nonsense and would have required millions of enforcement officials to provide authoritarian oversight over much of the whole population. Townsend bravely declared: "I'm not in the least interested in the cost of the plan."[23] Yet by the end of 1934 there were a thousand Townsend clubs across the country with over two million members. Townsend had mobilized the elderly.

Ever alert to what Winston Churchill would describe eleven years later as the "tides and currents" of American opinion, Roosevelt addressed the underlying motivations of the two movements in an extensive message to the Congress on June 8, 1934. The President expressed satisfaction at having "helped to lift agriculture and industry from a condition of utter prostration." He reverted to the Constitution's attribution to the federal government of the duty "to promote the general welfare" in indicating his intention to provide insurance against unemployment and old age and to pay for it on a contributory basis rather than from general tax revenues. He was already building the political ramparts from which it would be possible to repel Huey Long and Francis Townsend.

Father Coughlin had also become hostile by late 1934. An Irish-Canadian immigrant to Michigan, Coughlin had arrived in 1926 at a Detroit radio station as the new parish priest in suburban Royal Oak. A Ku Klux Klan burning cross had been planted in his churchyard, and he offered himself as a Sunday radio commentator.

He was a florid and compelling speaker. His "Golden Hour of the Little Flower" found a receptive, growing audience, and was broadcast on a network that spread throughout the country. By the early thirties he was a national figure. Implausible though it now seems, he had a radio audience of 30 to 45 million people weekly, and for a time received even more mail than the President—up to a million letters a week. He had a staff of 150 to handle his correspondence and affairs.[24]

Some polls indicated that Coughlin was one of the most respected people in the country, and he was for a time its greatest regular radio star. He rebuilt his modest church with the $500,000 per year he received from his admirers, and composed his addresses from an office atop a spiral staircase in the 150-foot steeple of his church.[25] He cleverly constructed his radio addresses to combine homilistic reflections with vivid denunciations of public people of whom he disapproved.

The priest had struck a populist note as the Depression deepened, and focussed much of his anger on the banks. This contributed to the decision of William Paley's CBS to drop him as inflammatory and demagogic, though the public reasons given were less censorious. For a time CBS suffered heavily in comparative ratings, as it replaced Coughlin with the New York Philharmonic Orchestra. When he was governor, Roosevelt, ever alert to every possible source of political support and opposition, had privately expressed his sympathy for Coughlin on his falling-out with CBS.[26] Coughlin had been extremely hostile to Hoover, favorable to Roosevelt, and initially assured his listeners that "Gabriel is over the White House, not Lucifer . . . the New Deal is Christ's Deal."[27]

On November 11, 1934, Coughlin launched the National Union for Social Justice and proclaimed the demise of capitalism. Coughlin upheld what was long the Vatican's espousal of corporatist economics, which was supposed to be a middle way between the evils of uncontrolled mammon (capitalism) and Godless socialism. As economics, it was bunk, but it was dogmatically acceptable. Coughlin's bishop, Michael Gallagher, was friendly with the Hungarian regent, Admiral Miklós Horthy, and with the Austrian chancellor, Englebert Dollfuss, both authoritarian Catholic leaders of fascistic tendencies. Coughlin's Union was pretty muddled, demanding bimetallism and the nationalization of the banks and being ambiguous about civil rights. In March 1935, Coughlin claimed Roosevelt had "out-Hoovered Hoover . . . I will not support a New Deal that protects plutocrats and comforts Communists."*[29]

After the New Deal had eroded extreme farm militancy with mortgage relief, farm price supports, drought control, rural electrification, and other programs, those farmers who were still dissatisfied gravitated toward farm state local parties, especially the Farmer-Labor Party of Minnesota's Governor Floyd Olson and the Wisconsin Progressives of the La Follettes.

---

* One of the few people of any distinction whom Coughlin attracted, and then only briefly, was the eventually eminent architect Philip Johnson. Johnson and a friend went from Harvard to Louisiana to pursue spontaneity and "emotionalism" with Huey Long. When rebuffed by redneck suspicion of the Ivy League, he rebounded to Coughlin, and then ricocheted back into the mainstream.[28]

Roosevelt suavely conciliated Olson, and eventually his entire state party was assimilated to the Democrats and produced one of that party's leading electoral personalities, Vice President and 1968 presidential candidate Hubert Humphrey. Before this denouement occurred, Olson's Farmer-Labor Party officially concluded that: "Capitalism has failed . . . and that . . . all the natural resources, machinery of production, transportation, and communication, shall be owned by the government." Although this was pretty radical stuff, Roosevelt tacitly supported Olson over a conservative Democrat in 1934.

Roosevelt also did his best for the La Follettes, who were essentially prairie cooperativists. They did not understand Marxism, accepted no version of the class system, and disliked Communism's militant atheism and hostility to democracy. The President gave them a free ride in Wisconsin, and they returned as governor (Philip) and senator (Robert) in November 1934. (They were the sons of the 1924 Progressive Party presidential candidate, Robert M. La Follette.)

Another new force in American public life was the movement called End Poverty in California (EPIC), created by the crusading author and journalist Upton Sinclair, who had been an important figure in exposing abuses in the meatpacking and drug industries and elsewhere. A long-serving socialist who was now convinced that change could be effected only through the two major parties, Sinclair became a candidate for the Democratic nomination for governor of California. The Socialist Party leader, Norman Thomas, denounced Sinclair's defection. Sinclair advocated that the state of California buy or rent unused industrial capacity and allow the unemployed to use these facilities to produce for their own needs. It was a combination of traditional socialism and semi-communal cooperativism.

Sinclair was confident that new socialist production-for-use factories would decisively defeat the production-for-profit factories of the old economy. He advocated a 50 percent tax on incomes above $50,000, high inheritance taxes, and high property taxes on large residences. He largely financed his campaign by charging admission to his meetings and selling his manifesto as a little book titled, in part: *How I Ended Poverty: A True Story of the Future.* Sinclair ran strongly from the beginning and in late August outpolled all his rivals combined in the California primary, easily defeating the candidate of William G. McAdoo (who fancied himself the state's Democratic king-maker) and running ahead of Republican governor Frank Merriam in his primary.

After Roosevelt agreed to a "nonpolitical visit" from Sinclair, Sinclair came to Hyde Park on September 4, 1934. He was possibly the most completely and profoundly seduced subject of the mighty Roosevelt charm of all the countless thousands of people who were subjected to it. Sinclair emerged from his two-hour "nonpolitical" meeting in Springwood declaring that he had never enjoyed a conversation so much in his life and that his host was "one of the kindest and most genial and frank and open-minded and lovable men I have ever met."[30] Sinclair mistakenly thought that Roosevelt had promised to endorse him. On his way back to California he stopped in Detroit to pick up the endorsement of Father Coughlin. The socialists and the fascists were now holding hands under the enigmatically smiling countenance of the President. Roosevelt told his wife, in respect of the Sinclair campaign: "1) Say nothing and 2) Do nothing."[31]

Roosevelt declined to play any role in the California election, scandalizing traditional liberals in the state and elsewhere. Since Sinclair was the official Democratic nominee, Roosevelt's reasonable options were circumscribed. Moley blasted Sinclair editorially, which was widely taken as being the President's opinion also and was certainly represented as such by Governor Merriam's campaign. Despite a barrage of importunate telegrams from Sinclair, Roosevelt remained sphynxlike.

The novelist and his EPIC campaign were subjected to a monumental smear job by the major Hollywood studio heads and effectively sandbagged in the last weeks of the campaign. Scruffy and sinister-looking people with heavy beards and thick foreign accents were interviewed on newsreels espousing Sinclair's merits as similar to those of the rulers of Russia. There were fake affidavits published in the newspapers imputing fantastic opinions to Sinclair, whose campaign was virtually boycotted by the California media after Labor Day. A phony poll was published on election eve showing a landslide for Merriam. The Republican state chairman was the movie magnate Louis B. Mayer, who amassed and disbursed a war chest of $10 million, twice what either national campaign had spent in 1932.

Governor Merriam made a deal with the local orthodox Democrats that in exchange for their assistance he would not represent his victory as implying any rejection of the President or the New Deal. Roosevelt continued to keep his distance as he saw the Sinclair candidacy sinking. Merriam won by 1,139,000 to 880,000 for Sinclair and 303,000 for the Progressive, Raymond Haight, whom Mayer had encouraged in order to split the anti-Merriam vote. Merriam had even partially endorsed Francis Townsend's geriatric movement to make such yardage as he could against Sinclair's Santa Claus schemes. Merriam was one of only seven successful Republican candidates for governor, against thirty-nine Democrats and two Progressives.

The politics of California became tremendously confused during and after this egregious contest between an other-worldly naïf and the excesses of cynicism. Journalist George Creel called it a "choice between catalepsy and epilepsy."[32] Roosevelt was unscathed; the greater the fragmentation of the opposition, in California as elsewhere, the easier it was for him to reinforce the center of the political spectrum, leaving only the outlying areas to extremists.

Sinclair returned cheerfully to his books and even wrote a rather good-natured account of his election campaign. Mayer's antics had prompted the adherence to Sinclair of Charlie Chaplin, James Cagney, Jean Harlow, and other actors. Some of the notorious Hollywood Communists of twenty years later were undoubtedly repelled as younger people by the outrageous defamation of Sinclair. ("Production-for-use" concept was mad and if implemented would have led to widespread chaos, but he was a benign and civilized man.)

There was more activity than usual in the United States on the further extremes. The Fascists were led by William Dudley Pelley, a California real estate promoter who had tried his hand at writing screenplays. Pelley was "a little man in his forties with gleaming malignant eyes and a dirty-gray goatee, strutting in silver shirt and riding breeches."[33] The silver shirt was the symbol of the movement, and gave the Silver Legion its name. Pelley claimed that he had died some years before but awakened with the revelation of his political destiny, which he summarized in an article, "Seven Minutes in Eternity." He was a ludicrous figure who never attracted more than a few thousand supporters.

The Deutsch-Amerika Bund, with outright assistance from the German government, appealed to militant German-Americans and Germanophilic Nazis and fared somewhat better, gaining perhaps two hundred thousand enthusiasts.

There was never any significant support for Nazi-emulative politics in the United States. The novelist Sinclair Lewis would arouse the nation with his *It Can't Happen Here*, published in 1935. The inspiration for some of the characters could be identified. Colonel Dewey Haik could have been mistaken for Douglas MacArthur, and Bishop Prang and the League of Forgotten Men could pass for Father Coughlin and the Union for Social Justice. Lewis's book provoked heightened journalistic scrutiny of what motivated offbeat public people and activists, but there was no witch hunt and few witches to hunt.

On the far left, the perennial Socialist leader, Norman Thomas, was to lament, when asked if Roosevelt wasn't carrying out a large part of his program: "Yes, he is carrying it out in a coffin."[34] This was a rare foray into humor for Thomas, whom Arthur Schlesinger accurately described as "too reminiscent of the settlement house, the pulpit, and the college bull session" for American electoral politics.[35]

The Communists were almost as far off the charts as the Nazis. Assaulting capitalism, democracy, and religion as it did, the pathetic little American Communist Party was even more a catspaw of Stalin than the Bund was of Hitler. Only academic foreigners, such as Harold Laski, of the London School of Economics, much respected by American liberals from Felix Frankfurter to the undergraduate John F. Kennedy, took the U.S. Communists and their leader, Earl Browder, seriously. Laski wrote of Browder in 1935: "I miss my guess if the failure of the Roosevelt experiment does not leave him, or some successor, one of the outstanding figures in the American scene." He missed his guess. The young JFK at least had the excuse of being one of Laski's students; there was no such exculpation for Frankfurter.[36]

If Roosevelt had not been making substantial progress with the Depression, such people could have been more of a threat to him. That they became steadily more intemperate only demonstrated the efficacy of Roosevelt's consummate occupation of the political center as he drove all rivals except respectable mainstream Republicans off to bray and snarl on the political fringes.

III

Lewis douglas, whom Roosevelt had regarded as one of the stars of the administration, called on the President at Hyde Park on August 30, 1934, and resigned as budget director. Concerned that the resignation could have a negative impact on the interim elections in November, Roosevelt urged that Douglas stay on until December 1, but he resisted. Douglas was a budget-balancing, hardcurrency gold standardist who could not conscientiously continue in the face of Roosevelt's inflationist policies. He was convinced that natural economic forces would revive the country and that the public-works program was a colossal mistake. He wrote Roosevelt a few days later reiterating his rather dreary refrain that civilization depended on an American balanced budget.[37]

Douglas's economic views were objectively mistaken, but he was an intelligent, industrious, and humane young man who went on to be a distinguished business executive, head of Montreal's McGill University, director of wartime shipping construction, and a very respected ambassador to Great Britain.* He was the best and most persuasive of the economic conservatives, and Roosevelt was temporarily concerned by his defection.†

Roosevelt summoned his Treasury secretary, Henry Morgenthau, and received him while in his bath (another trait he shared with Churchill, the boarding school alumnus's relative lack of physical modesty with other men). On Morgenthau's arrival, the President sat up in his bath and quoted John Paul Jones: "Henry, we have only just begun to fight." He suggested Thomas Corcoran as budget director, but Morgenthau, himself a financial conservative though prepared to compromise, declared Corcoran to be wholly inappropriate and instead nominated Daniel Bell, who was commissioner of accounts in the Treasury. Roosevelt agreed, and the new appointment was announced with Douglas's retirement during the Labor Day weekend, thereby reducing the attention it would receive.

Hugh Johnson had become more and more erratic through 1934, and the NRA was falling apart. Key people were resigning in droves. Business used its pricefixing arrangements but ignored or circumvented the collective-bargaining provi-

---

* It was later alleged that he had some anti-Semitic tendencies and spoke resentfully of the influence of Morganthau, who was in fact a budget balancer.[38]

† The allegation has been made[39] that Douglas was a bigot who blamed fiscal indiscipline on "Hebraic influence" and particularly Morgenthau's "Hebraic arrogance and conceit." This is somewhat implausible, since Douglas, though apparently not a philo-Semite, was a civilized man, and Morgethau and Baruch, as we have seen, were as fiscally conservative as Douglas was.

sions. Labor managed to increase union memberships and enjoyed improved working hours and conditions, but collective bargaining was far from the instant massive accretion of workers' rights that had been anticipated (by labor, though not necessarily by Roosevelt). Johnson had not lost or tempered his tendencies to wild public utterances, prolonged drunken binges, and abrasive relations with colleagues. Roosevelt had asked Berle to look into the state of NRA, a new wrinkle in his intricate methods of keeping on top of his vast bureaucracy. Nothing could be better designed to bring authority back to him than asking his appointees to report on each other's professional performances. Berle was very critical of Johnson.

The subject was complicated by the romantic involvements of both the NRA director and the secretary of the interior, Harold Ickes, with female staff members. Roosevelt himself did not mind. He often found the human vulnerabilities of men endearing and in any case potentially useful to him. And he had had some experience of this himself. But Johnson, responding to the pressure of his office more or less as Baruch had predicted, had submitted emotional verbal and written resignations to the President several times through the summer. Finally, after rejecting these resignation offers, presumably from fear of Johnson's indiscretions if suddenly out of government during a mid-term congressional election campaign, Roosevelt concluded that Johnson was now more trouble than he was worth.

He suggested that Johnson study comparative performances of other advanced industrial countries fighting the Depression. Johnson responded with another histrionic offer of resignation, which Roosevelt accepted warmly and with such diplomacy that Johnson left the administration in good spirits and did not immediately follow Lewis Douglas into the Liberty League or other thickets of opposition.

In fact, Johnson continued for a time as titular head of the NRA, but underlings ran it in direct weekly consultation with the President, while Ickes's old law partner, Donald Richberg, continued to badger Roosevelt with memos asking Johnson's complete removal. Finally, Johnson did retire, with all the theatrics one could have hoped.

On October 1, 1934, he addressed the NRA employees in the auditorium of the Department of Commerce (part of the great monument to himself Herbert Hoover had built). General Johnson made it clear to any doubters that he had succumbed to a terminal case of Potomac Fever. He invoked the "shining name" of Mussolini and spoke of the virtues of the corporate state in a way that not five percent of Americans could have approved. He said that the NRA was "as great a social advance as has occurred on this earth since a gaunt and dusty Jew in Palestine declared, as a new principle in human relationship, 'the Kingdom of Heaven is within you.' " He built to a tremendous, if idiosyncratic, apotheosis by rendering, in Italian, the last words of Madame Butterfly before she committed hara-kiri (awaiting the return of the American naval captain). In a time when Roosevelt, Coughlin, Long, John L. Lewis, and others regularly stirred much of the population with powerful oratory, this was a noteworthy forensic effort that reduced the speaker and most of his audience to torrents of tears.[40]

A reorganization of the NRA followed, in which a council of five was established to run it in place of the autocracy that had prevailed. Roosevelt was becoming suspicious of the aptitude of big businessmen for this kind of work and produced a non-business majority of academics and a labor leader. He had sought the president of the University of Chicago, Robert Hutchins, a candidate of Ickes'. Hutchins obtained the permission of the university to take a leave of absence and accept the post but Richberg, the director, who had come to hate Johnson and led the lynch mob against his former chief, now also went to work against Hutchins. Hutchins would not have been easy to manage, either; he was an extreme controversialist who professed to regard America as a degenerate society. Richberg persuaded the President that business would not accept an altruistic but cranky university president in this role. Roosevelt left Hutchins suspended, expectant but unconfirmed. In some understandable irritation, Hutchins eventually huffily withdrew.

In a rambling Fireside Chat on September 30, 1934, Roosevelt claimed that Johnson had presided brilliantly over the first phase of NRA and that it was now appropriate to move into the second phase, which would highlight institutional changes and enforcement of existing reforms. It was far from his most impressive effort as he explained the shuffling personnel and course corrections.

Roosevelt was finding it increasingly difficult to straddle between capital and labor, and in his September 30 radio address manifested some impatience with business opposition to the New Deal. He kept in touch with many business people but found almost all of them, including Joseph Kennedy, self-seeking and unimaginative.

Roosevelt's political intuition, preternaturally perceptive though it was, was tinged with mild paranoia and hard vindictiveness. It was beginning to tell him that the country's business leadership had recovered enough of its confident aggression to demand that the administration abandon its reformist tendencies and restore as much as possible of the 1920s economy. The President suspected the beginnings of a capital strike encouraged by Douglas. This was unjust to Douglas, who honorably disagreed with Roosevelt, and it partly misjudged the business community, which was neither sufficiently malicious nor uniform of view to conspire against the President. Many business leaders recognized that restoration of the twenties would lead back to economic depression.

Roosevelt was scheduled to address a convention of American bankers on October 24, 1934. His old Columbia professor, Jackson Reynolds, now head of the First National Bank of New York, had to be dissuaded by Morgenthau from referring to Roosevelt's limitations as a law student and making other presumptuous references to the comparative status of the government and the banking community. Both Reynolds's introduction and Roosevelt's address were de-escalated from the lofty disdainful heights they originally would have achieved. Reynolds graciously allowed that the President had "contributed more to rescue and rehabilitate our shattered banking structure than any of us did individually or collectively." The President didn't refer directly to Reynolds's remarks but spoke of "what we call—and accept—as a profit system," and made a reasonable effort at conciliation.[41]

He gave an insight into his thinking with the assertion that he had asked the people to renew their faith in the banks of the country in March of 1933. "They took me at my word. Tonight I ask the bankers of this country to renew their confidence in the people of this country. I hope you will take me at my word." The implication was clear that if the banks and senior businessmen generally didn't join the "army" fighting the retreating Depression, the political atmosphere could become inclement. The New York Times reported that Roosevelt had received "an ovation," but Moley described the atmosphere as "frigid."[42]

The expectations for the interim election were that the normal gains by the party out of office would be repeated, though Jim Farley in the last days of the campaign thought there was a chance of retaining the entire Democratic majorities in the House of Representatives and the Senate. What occurred was a massive vote of confidence in the President and his program. The Democrats picked up nine congressmen and the astounding number of ten senators. They now predominated in the House by 322 to 103 Republicans and ten Progressives and Farmer-Laborites (the latter could normally be relied upon by the Democrats). In the Senate, the Democrats would now have 69, including the newly elected Harry Truman of Missouri, to 27 Republicans, several of whom were in fact Progressives, such as Robert La Follette and George Norris. They and Governor Olson of Minnesota were directly assisted by the Democrats.

The overall election result was everywhere seen as a huge Roosevelt victory. The still generally supportive William Randolph Hearst telegraphed to Roosevelt: "There has been no such popular endorsement since the days of Thomas Jefferson and Andrew Jackson. . . . Your equitable Democratic Administration prolongs indefinitely the life of the Republic. . . . The forgotten man does not forget."[43]

The one disappointment to Roosevelt was the reelection of progressive Republican Bronson Cutting in New Mexico by a very narrow margin. Because of reciprocal extreme personal animosity, Cutting was the only such progressive for whom Roosevelt did not ensure a free ride from the local Democrats. He did his best for Cutting's opponent, Dennis Chavez, even supporting his recount bid. In New York, Roosevelt's old antagonist and Al Smith's protégé, Robert Moses, had declared himself a Republican, been nominated for governor, and lost to Roosevelt's and Smith's anointed successor, Herbert Lehman, by the greatest margin in the history of state elections, almost 850,000 votes. Few results could have been as pleasing to the President.

IV

THE PRESIDENT'S TEAM—or, more accurately, his court—had taken shape fairly coherently. Roosevelt enjoyed duplication and encouraged rivalries, presumably to ensure that he was the font of all power, whether equitable or capricious. Hopkins disliked Ickes for his pettifogging moralism; he called Ickes "the great resigner," and added, "He bores me."[44] Ickes disliked Hopkins for his flippancy and resented his influence with Roosevelt. Both regarded Morgenthau as nervous, too conservative, unqualified for his position, and obsequious to the President. Hopkins and Ickes were highly competent, though Ickes was petulant, self-righteous, and administratively cautious. Both were exceptionally fine public servants, and Roosevelt quickly learned how to get maximum use out of them.

He even tried sometimes to soften the natural rivalry between them, such as by inviting them out on one of his famous fishing trips. With Frances Perkins, the diligent, fearless, and reasonable labor secretary, and with Wallace, Farley, and Howe (and in their ways, Garner and Jesse Jones), they were the main stars of Roosevelt's senior collaborators.

The secretary of agriculture, Henry A. Wallace, was a complicated figure, mystically religious and faddishly scientific. Of erratic judgment and no great political courage, he was yet highly intelligent, imaginative, and generally a distinguished and knowledgeable department head. He was an unabashed liberal, and Roosevelt thought he had possibilities for higher office.

The attorney general, Homer S. Cummings, was a Connecticut Yankee and Yale alumnus, ascetic, spare, and sharp, neither affable nor intellectually original, but a clever and tough lawyer, and a very long-serving backroom influence in the Democratic organization. He lacked the juridical breadth one might wish in an attorney general, but was a cunning and diligent counsel to the President, always ready to execute even his less-distinguished designs.

The political operators were of an unusually high caliber. James A. Farley, postmaster general and party chairman, was a political organizer of legendary talent, though far from a cerebral strategist. Edward J. Flynn was the most enlightened of bosses, honest, learned, and thoughtful.

The great star and guiding light of the Roosevelt inner circle, as he had been for more than twenty years, was Louis McHenry Howe. His health was so fragile and his personality so irascible that he didn't enjoy either the longevity or the social circulation that would have made him more widely appreciated. But he was a political genius and was the only person, except for possibly Hopkins and occasionally Eleanor, who could profoundly influence Franklin D.

Roosevelt. His personality was no less vintage a Damon Runyan creation when Howe and his chief were in the White House than in the decades of striving toward it.

Morgenthau was solid but not brilliant as Treasury secretary, holding the position in part because of Roosevelt's gratitude for the loyalty of Morgenthau and of his father. After his debates with Acheson, Roosevelt was in no mood for insubordination in that office. Morgenthau was a very thorough comptroller, watching the flows of money carefully, and though his instincts were fiscally conservative, he always gave way to the requirements for emergency relief and then military emergency. He was often the butt of Roosevelt's moods and his sometimes nasty sense of humor, but was appreciated for his human qualities. He was, on balance, a more admirable man than a brilliant Treasury secretary. But in the requirements of the times, he was more than adequate.

The vice president, John Nance Garner, was a rough-hewn old Texan who had no interest in his position and had no great regard for the President. He disapproved of much of Roosevelt's program as extravagant and invented by Northeastern big-city intellectuals of little practical experience and an inadequate notion of their own limitations. (His views would be somewhat replicated by his protégé, Sam Rayburn, about the "Best and the Brightest" who came into office a quarter century later with John F. Kennedy. Rayburn would lament that none "of them had ever run for county sheriff.") Garner considered his chief compulsively devious and a snake-oil salesman, though undoubtedly a talented one. He could barely bring himself to call Roosevelt "Mr. President" and generally called him "Captain" instead. He was a formidable and picturesque figure, but not at all a player on this team. Roosevelt took to saying, in cabinet, "We can speak freely; Jack's not here."[45] Roosevelt felt Garner's loyalties were to his friends in the Congress.

Another prominent cabinet member who was a slight disappointment to Roosevelt was the secretary of state, Cordell Hull. Gloomy, sanctimonious, and unimaginative, Hull was frequently passed over as Roosevelt took his own foreign policy decisions. The President did value Hull's popularity in the Congress, where he had served for twenty-four years.

Hull always enjoyed considerable prestige in the country, which respected his judicious and dignified bearing. The secretary of state grandly claimed to be a disciple of "Locke, Milton, Pitt, Burke, Gladstone, and the Lloyd George school."[46] It was generally difficult to find their inspiration in his work at the State Department. Hull resented Roosevelt's manipulation of him but admired Roosevelt's virtuosity and leadership skills.

Jesse Jones, the head of Hoover's Reconstruction Finance Corporation, was a breath of fresh air in that institution. An optimistic and positive Texan, he redefined the RFC from a conservative lender to banks (with inadequate credit safeguards, as the fiasco with Dawes's bank demonstrated) to being an investor in banks and other financial and industrial institutions. A large, tall, blunt, self-made Texas lumberman, banker, and real estate promoter, Jones won the Democratic convention for Houston in 1928 with a check for $100,000 (which he then set about raising back from fellow Texans).[47]

Hoover had brought Jones to Washington in 1932 as an obligatory Democratic member of the RFC board. Jones disagreed with the conservative methods of Eugene Meyer and Ogden Mills and felt the Democratic committee members were condescendingly treated. When placed in charge of the RFC in the new administration, Jones overcame the reluctance of banks to accept a public-sector shareholder by relying on the requirements for the certificate of solvency contained in the emergency banking legislation. By 1935, the RFC had preferred-share investments in half the banks in the country, totalling over one billion dollars. This enabled the guarantee of bank deposits and definitively saved the U.S. banking system in recognizable form.

Roosevelt saw Jones, especially after the departure of Douglas, as the resident conservative in the upper reaches of government. Jones was for private-sector/public-sector cooperation, but was to the right of the administration on the subject of social programs. He favored investment over direct government pump-priming, though he recognized the urgent need for simple, massive relief in the early days of the administration. By 1938, the RFC had invested $10 billion— $4 billion in the financial sector, $1 billion in railways, $1.5 billion in agriculture, and the rest scattered over a great variety of projects and enterprises. Almost all of it was invested wisely.

A star in the early New Deal, Jones was by the end of the thirties out of sympathy with his president and unable to make the adjustment easily from fighting the Depression to preparing to save the world, but his services and talents were very considerable.

The Brain Trust people were not long-term players. Moley had already left, other than for occasional speechwriting assignments. Tugwell was an authoritarian socialist whose ideas would have only limited applicability to America as it was or had any likelihood of becoming. Berle had written Roosevelt's pretentious San Francisco philosophical address in September 1932 and had made a rather sporadic contribution to the administration. Berle was intelligent and his judgment was superior to Tugwell's, but the imbalance between his large ego and somewhat impractical intellect never allowed him to achieve a first-rank position. As years went by, Roosevelt shunted Tugwell and Berle through important but secondary posts, ending with governor of Puerto Rico (Tugwell) and ambassador to Brazil (Berle).

More impressive were the senior legal minds—Frankfurter, Corcoran, Cohen, Landis, Frank, and others. Frankfurter had been one of the country's leading jurisconsults for many years, and if he was a pedantic courtier "upon whom [Roosevelt] could always depend for instant laudatory reassurance,"[48] he was also excessively intelligent, versatile, loyal to Roosevelt, possessed of generally excellent judgment, and ultimately an outstanding Supreme Court justice. Frankfurter had served in Henry Stimson's campaign for governor of New York in 1910, before joining the Taft administration with him when Stimson became secretary of war. He served Newton Baker in that office under President Wilson in the First World War. Frankfurter honeycombed the U.S. government with bright young lawyers for decades, and his protégés swarmed through the New Deal. He had placed Tom Corcoran with Justice Holmes.

Where Brandeis, who continued to be rather active in political circles even while a member of the Supreme Court, was an advocate of small business and labor units, to a point that was almost fetishistic, Frankfurter was a conventional and moderate liberal. He was so shaken by the Depression, however, that he was tempted to join Edmund Wilson in voting for the Communist presidential candidate, William Z. Foster, in 1932. Having long identified Roosevelt as a coming political force, he remained loyal to him when he was nominated and was a frequently consulted advisor throughout his presidency. His extensive correspondence with President Roosevelt oscillated between "Dear Frank" chumminess of olden times and formalistic deference.

With the young Ben Cohen and Rabbi Stephen Wise, Frankfurter had been a member of the American Jewish delegation at the Versailles Conference, seeking a Jewish homeland. He and Brandeis and Cohen were active in these circles for many years, though Brandeis and Frankfurter fell out with the Zionist leader and ultimate first president of Israel, Chaim Weizmann — "Weizie," as Frankfurter called him. It was the proximity of Frankfurter, Cohen, and Brandeis to Roosevelt and their deep involvement in the Zionist cause that apparently convinced Hitler that Roosevelt's was a Jewish-dominated government.

Tommy Corcoran was a congressional advocate and facilitator, a fine legal mind and a sentimental Irishman, passionately devoted to Roosevelt and the New Deal and somewhat undiscriminating in both his causes and his people. Charming and witty, like many of those in the Roosevelt entourage in these difficult but heady times, he tended to be overbearing and to forget that all his influence was derived from the president he served. He was a bantam rooster with the ability to behave like a leprechaun if it suited him. Justice Holmes, in his icy Boston, Unitarian manner described Corcoran as "quite noisy, quite satisfactory, and quite noisy."[49] Moley thought he was "uncomfortably deferential with 'slyly superior eyes above the puckering nose.'"[50] He was called by one insider the "unofficial party whip of the New Deal," and future attorney general and Supreme Court justice Robert Jackson said Corcoran "was leg man for a man who had no legs."[51]

Ben Cohen was a scholarly, shy, brilliant, if painfully idealistic legal mind of the highest ability. He helped stabilize Corcoran's tendency to hero worship and overcommit to people and causes. Corcoran helped Cohen be more gregarious and serviceable and was an antidote to some of his more naïve universalist ideas. A liberal Zionist, Cohen was more a believer in the brotherhood of man than a realist. But he was brilliant, pleasant, and honest, "the intellectual coordinator and keeper of the conscience of the New Deal."[52]

Of those named here, Frankfurter, Ickes, Morgenthau, and Frances Perkins were the only ones who remained in unimpaired function right to the end, and of these only Frankfurter was in a position to give the President any important advice in the latter stages of World War II. When they were no longer useful to Roosevelt, the members of his entourage would usually depart the administration as if through a trap door.

V

ON RETURNING TO Washington from his Thanksgiving holiday at Warm Springs, Roosevelt settled accounts with a redoubtable adversary—H.L. Mencken, the influential and iconoclastic editor, author, and literary and social critic. Mencken had been recruited to roast Roosevelt at the Washington press corps' Gridiron dinner in December 1934. Presumably out of respect for the presidential office as well as the physical presence of its holder—who would have the last word of the evening—Mencken spoke more moderately than he was now in the habit of writing about Roosevelt, though he began, "fellow subjects of the Reich," and said, "Every day in this great country is April Fool Day."[53] Mencken did not mention Roosevelt by name. He had started out supporting the President and liked his style, but quickly came to resent his political agility and regularly denounced him as a slippery posturer.

Roosevelt would not be deterred by Mencken's gentleness on this occasion from returning the fire in Mencken's previous writings. He signalled what was coming with what Mencken had sarcastically described in writing as his "Christian Science smile." Roosevelt referred to the comments of "my old friend Henry Mencken," and then, in a room filled with journalists, began a bitter diatribe against the press, attacking "the stupidity, cowardice, and Philistinism of working newspapermen." He continued to smile beatifically and aroused the mirth of the audience with his versatile intonation as he went on about those "who do not know what a symphony is or a streptococcus" and referring to American journalism as "pathetically feeble and vulgar, and so generally disreputable." Only gradually did it become clear that the entire reflection was a lift from an editorial of Mencken's in the *American Mercury* of more than ten years before. Roosevelt finally, amusingly, identified it as such.

Mencken was sitting with his fellow Marylander, Governor Albert Ritchie (who had received a handful of votes at the Chicago convention). Mencken fumed: "I'll get the son of a bitch. I'll dig the skeletons out of his closet."[54] Even though he knew Roosevelt had the last word, he started to scribble a response but did not get a chance to say it. Roosevelt was wheeled past him at the end of his remarks, which were received with great mirth when he revealed his source. The two shook hands and Mencken gamely said "fair shooting."[55]

[56]Roosevelt was widely deemed to have tamed and chastened Mencken and put him squarely in his place. Harold Ickes wrote that FDR had "smeared Mencken all over."[57]*

In the light of the 1934 election victories, Harry Hopkins determined that there would never be a better time to push the New Deal further. In economic terms, Hopkins favored a reflationary creation of demand in the system through expanded payrolls and consumer spending. And in social terms, emergency relief for millions of unemployed was again required, coupled with social insurance and comprehensive wages-and-hours reform. Roosevelt had already largely come to the same conclusion in a series of White House meetings in late October 1934. He had decided that it was necessary to take the New Deal further to avoid any possibility of being outflanked by Long, Townsend, and Coughlin.

Roosevelt never wavered in his determination to maintain the political center as a position of strength between the radical redistributors and reformers and the left wing of the progressive movement, including Senators Cutting, Borah, Wheeler, and others, on one side, and the conservatives, including the Smith-Raskob Democrats, on the other. Throughout the thirties, this required a good deal of tacking and weaving, activities for which Roosevelt had already demonstrated a remarkable aptitude. By the spring of 1935 he was concerned that Huey Long was making inroads and that his own reformist followers were restless. The President had already given up any hope of coopting Long back into the ranks of the orthodox Democrats and passed over to the first phase of political warmaking. For Roosevelt this meant shutting off the tap of patronage and unleashing tax inspectors and other regulators on opponents.

On Roosevelt's orders, Morgenthau had launched a comprehensive income tax investigation of Huey Long and his senior collaborators, four of whom were indicted by the end of 1934, but not the Kingfish (as Long was called) himself. Roosevelt ordered all agencies to give no aid to Long. The billions that were being spent on emergency unemployment relief largely bypassed Louisiana.

It was easy to underestimate Huey Long because of his outrageous appearance and demeanor, but he was an astute champion of the social underdog in volatile times. He knew that the genteel but incompetent and racist cadres of the old southern aristocracy were an anachronism. He was the leader of the lower-

---

* Roosevelt himself wrote to Arthur Brisbane of the Hearst Corporation that after twenty years of "amusing but cynically rough things" from "Henry" he was "entitled to ten minutes of comeback."[58]

middle class, the working class, and, to an unusual degree for the times, of the African-Americans. Because his appeal was not to regional biases and the ancient southern paranoia that the South had been trampled down unjustly by the Union Army and the carpetbaggers in their train, Long played well to susceptible groups throughout the country.

Roosevelt would respond to the sharers of the wealth with a legislative program that is sometimes called the Second New Deal, which included Social Security, a concept that had its antecedents in American academic circles and popular politics. Various measures had been promoted by different groups since shortly after World War I. Roosevelt established a committee to recommend on this subject in 1934 and initially sought to confine Social Security to insurance for the unemployed. He knew that medical insurance would have no chance against the insuperable animosity of the American Medical Association and did not want to hand his opponents a free shot at a president seeming to stand between the American public and their doctors. (He knew intuitively what some of his successors would learn only after bruising political setbacks.) He also deferred old age security as unsustainably expensive at this time. This was the stance he took in a speech to the National Conference on Economic Security, a group the White House had convened, on November 14, 1934.

That speech was panned as insufficiently ambitious by the *New York Times* and many other press commentators who normally supported the President. Roosevelt had committed the unusual mistake of allowing conventional opinion to get to the left and ahead of him, and let it be known that he had demanded more study from the Committee on Economic Security (Hopkins, Ickes, Morgenthau, Perkins, and Wallace). A mixed plan was eventually proposed combining pay-as-you-go, deferred funding from general revenues, and a partial reserve. Roosevelt sent this plan, covering both unemployment and old-age insurance and recommending increased aid to the states for dependent children and public health assistance, to the Congress on January 17, 1935. Apart from being judged desirable in itself, this was a tactical necessity to repulse the followers of Huey Long and Francis Townsend and to preserve the New Deal and prevent its being kidnapped by radicals or reactionaries.

Response was quite favorable. The far left was scandalized by what it considered excessive timidity in the scope and generosity of the scheme. The right emitted the usual howls of outrage at this extravagant assault on the work ethic, thrift, and fiscal responsibility. After a slightly fumbling start, Roosevelt recovered rapidly and reassembled the grand coalition of the center, extending to the moderate reaches of right and left.

Beyond that, Social Security was an idea whose hour had come. At a time when the United States had been stricken by an economic crisis that had left nearly a third of the country destitute, it gave promise of an imminent time when there would be emergency support for everyone. This measure raised the hope of the nation that it would never again be defenseless against the vagaries of economic fortune, which had shown itself more capricious and dangerous than most Americans had ever imagined possible.

As the new Congress opened in January 1935, Long escalated his conflict with the President and dramatically denounced him in the Senate, claiming that Roosevelt had been elected by progressives like himself and that he had deserted his supporters and become a timid and inept conservative. Roosevelt had just sent a measure to the Senate urging American adherence to the World Court, as both parties had recommended in their 1932 election platforms. Huey Long rallied to the isolationists such as William Borah and Hiram Johnson, and the resistance caught fire, especially when Father Coughlin joined it and urged his vast radio audience to telegraph their senators. (Borah thought the League of Nations "nothing more than a cog in the military machine of Europe.")[59]

More than 50,000 telegrams, almost all of them hostile to court membership, poured in over the next few days. Coughlin attacked the World Court as a device for the expropriation of American sovereignty by international bankers, and named the Rothschilds, the Morgans, the Warburgs, and the Kuhn, Loeb Company. The bill failed to garner its required two-thirds majority in the Senate on January 29, 1935. Roosevelt was annoyed but discreet. He wrote to the nonagenarian Elihu Root, one of the founders of the postwar World Court, a letter criticizing the bill's opponents.* This was a cautionary episode to Roosevelt, who had been ambushed by the enlargement of the coalition of irresponsible radical forces whose emergence he had long foreseen. On February 11, 1935, Long accused James A. Farley of corrupt abuse of his office of postmaster general. The charges were based on fragmentary evidence and were dismissed by the Senate after some inquiry and slight debate.

Long returned to his attack on Farley when he learned of the attempt by Roosevelt the previous year to force Robert Moses out of the chairmanship of the Triborough Bridge Authority, to which the newly elected Mayor Fiorello La Guardia had appointed him. The mayor did not, inexplicably, know of the great hostility between Moses and Roosevelt. Adolf Berle, who had been one of the masterminds of the La Guardia campaign, urged Roosevelt not to force this issue and reminded him, with little respect for the exactness of historical parallels, of Napoleon's murder of the Duc d'Enghien. (Berle's invocation of Caesar and Napoleon in reference to Roosevelt would not have reassured the President about Berle's common touch.) The Triborough Bridge Authority would build a great complex of bridges and roads with PWA grants, ameliorating unemployment and permanently assisting traffic patterns in the nation's largest city.

Following the fiasco of Moses's campaign for governor in 1934, Ickes and Roosevelt had cooked up a directive denying PWA grants to projects within a munici-

---

* Root had been Theodore Roosevelt's secretary of state and had advised Daniels in 1913 not to take FDR into the Navy Department because the Roosevelts always had to lead the parade.

pality in which anyone was both a member of the governing body of the recipient and a public official in the municipality. They meant for this administrative order to apply only to Moses. It did catch someone else, who was assured they would not apply it to him. La Guardia had shown this directive to Moses, who then staged a determined public relations exercise, partially regaining the prestige he had forfeited by his ludicrous gubernatorial campaign. Al Smith entered the fray on behalf of his old protégé, pointing out that the whole Triborough project had been Moses' conception.

Ickes was forced to lie to the press and claim that Roosevelt had never spoken to him about Moses. When Long took up the case and linked it to Farley, it became clear to Roosevelt that this was not the place to give battle against an unimaginable alliance of Long, Coughlin, Moses, Smith, and La Guardia (a staunch Roosevelt ally). This was an inauspicious start to the great contest with Huey Long, and showed Roosevelt to be vindictive as well as uncharacteristically clumsy.

On March 5, 1935, in a broadcast address for *Redbook Magazine*, Hugh Johnson accused Long and Coughlin of being "pied pipers . . . a couple of Catilines" (roughly, the Aaron Burrs of ancient Rome, sinister political outlaws). Johnson imitated Long's redneck accent, tripping erratically over certain consonants, and added that there then "comes burring over the air the dripping brogue of the Irish-Canadian priest . . . musical, blatant bunk from the very rostrum of religion."[60]

This brought Coughlin out into the open as a critic of Roosevelt's administration, though he was still reluctant to attack the President directly. Coughlin claimed Baruch was stopping "a magnificent leader from rescuing a nation still bound to the rock of depression by the chains of economic slavery," as if Roosevelt were the proverbial stooge of Jewish finance.[61] He swore to "confront the Herods by name and by fact, even though my head will be served on a golden platter, even though my body be sawed in twain." Coughlin attacked a number of Jewish international merchant bankers along with Baruch.

Grasping for new material to feed his vast audience every week, Coughlin started to play the anti-Semitic card more flagrantly. He claimed that Alexander Hamilton's real name was Alexander Levine. "One hundred years from today, Washington will be Washingtonski," he warned.[62] Others took up the same cry. Like the eccentric expatriate writer Ezra Pound, Milo Reno had taken to referring to the "Jew Deal." (Pound, in Italy singing the virtues of Fascism, also called it the "Nude Eel.")

With his March 5 speech, Johnson had also inflamed Huey Long, who drawled the next day on the floor of the Senate: "Last night, while I was about to undertake to throw myself into the arms of Morpheus, I thought I heard my name being mentioned over the radio." Long soon moved from the droll tenor of his prelude to a vituperative attack on Johnson, Farley, Roosevelt, and the perceived Fagin-Shylock of America, the inevitable Baruch, before warning his ostensible leader in the Senate, Majority Leader Joe Robinson, "Beware! . . . You will not be here next year!"

This was more than the good-natured Robinson could take. He rose to accuse Long of "egotism, arrogance, and ignorance . . . the ravings of . . . a madman. . . . The manhood in the Senate should assert itself." It did; a number of powerful senators joined in the repulse of the Kingfish of Louisiana.[63] Though substantial numbers of Americans had some reservations about Jews in general,[64] the level of explicit racism attained by Coughlin and Reno—and on this one exceptional occasion, Long—did not resonate well with most Americans.

Long also demanded and received forty-five minutes from NBC to respond to Hugh Johnson, since it had been that network that had broadcast Johnson's speech. Long gave a rather plausible exposition of the Share Our Wealth view of the inequitable distribution of wealth in the United States. He then embarked on a public speaking tour in different parts of the country and attracted large crowds and many adherents despite warnings from the White House to local Democrats to be as inhospitable as possible.

Ickes attempted to be helpful by telling the press April 19 that Huey Long suffered from "halitosis of the intellect . . . presuming Emperor Long has an intellect." Long responded April 22 in the Senate, calling Farley "the Nabob of New York," Ickes "the chinchbug of Chicago," Wallace "Lord Corn-Wallace, the Ignoramus of Iowa," and FDR "Prince Franklin Delay-No Roosevelt, Knight of the *Nourmahal.*"[65] It was entertaining, but most Americans did not like their chief of state subjected to such indignity.

The possibilities of a Long-Coughlin-Townsend-Reno alliance worried Roosevelt's political advisers, such as Farley. An elemental poll ordered by Farley for the Democratic National Committee indicated that Long could take 2.75 million votes, not a decisive total but a potential inconvenience. Some of Farley's campaign specialists feared Long might do substantially better than that. His popularity was not confined to the South, but outside the South was almost entirely among severe Depression victims.[66] Roosevelt himself was confident he could divide, outmaneuver, and confound such an awkward congeries of disaffected hucksters.

Roosevelt gave his first Fireside Chat of 1935 on April 28 and spoke of his legislative program, including Social Security, Senator Robert Wagner's latest labor relations bill, bills to extend elements of the NRA for two years, especially the workfare programs, and bills to eliminate perceived abuses in utility holding companies and to augment federal powers to promote economic growth by modernizing the Federal Reserve. Roosevelt also proposed some tax increases aimed politically at Huey Long. He also planned a regulatory bill for the coal industry that had essentially been written by John L. Lewis, and a bill that purported to shackle weapons and munitions manufacturers. This pandered to the isolationists and pacifists, whose support the President needed to pass the Second New Deal and repulse the extremists of right and left. The President's legislative agenda fulfilled his promise to Ickes and other intimates to "steal Huey's thunder."[67]

On April 29, the day after the Fireside Chat, in a U.S. Chamber of Commerce meeting in Washington, a prominent official of the organization in a welcoming speech accused Roosevelt of attempting to "Sovietize America." Other speakers expressed similar views, and the chamber adopted resolutions opposing the President's entire legislative package.

Despite these misgivings, the President would prevail upon a grumpy Congress to sit in steaming Washington (the Capitol was now partially air conditioned) almost all summer to enact his program.

The Social Security bill was complicated and was financed by a flat levy rather than a progressive tax, the imposition of which would partially arrest the economic recovery in 1937. It was, however, well administered from the beginning by the Social Security Board, presided over by the enlightened Republican former governor of New Hampshire, John G. Winant. At the start, Social Security was not an overly ambitious welfare program. It did not directly combat the problem of the poverty of the aged, since funds had to be taken out of the current earnings of participants and a large reserve built up. Marginal workers, such as farm laborers and domestics, were left out, and the whole concept of health insurance was mentioned as a gleam in the administration's eye, but for another time.

Roosevelt understood the problem of basing the program on employees' contributions but did so for political reasons. The payroll contributions, the President explained, gave "the contributors a legal, moral, and political right to collect their pensions and their unemployment benefits. With those taxes in there, no damn politician can ever scrap my social security program." No one could, and Roosevelt made it clear to intimates that he meant this to be the foundation of a lifelong social insurance system that would coexist with private medicine and provide a safety net without being a health-care cap.[68]

––––––––––

On the evening of May 14, 1935, the President met in the White House with Senators Borah, Costigan, Johnson, La Follette, Norris, and Wheeler, as well as Ickes, Wallace, Frankfurter, and Boston think tank director David Niles (who had suggested such a meeting). The senators expressed their concern that the administration seemed to be running out of steam and that Long was making inroads. They generally felt that it would be impossible to placate the business community, and urged the President to recharge the New Deal. Roosevelt impressed all his visitors with his attentiveness, grasp of the detail of all that was discussed, and judicious responses, and gave them a high comfort level that he intended to do just that, as Frankfurter, having spoken with most of them, advised Roosevelt on May 16. All of them had plenty of experience of his tendency to avoid serious examination of important subjects, but that was not his approach on this occasion.

Missing from the group was Senator Bronson Cutting, who had been invited but was killed in a plane crash over Kansas the day before. He was only forty-seven and was widely mourned. Roosevelt graciously claimed to have been "mighty fond of Bronson," though in fact he detested him. The curious antagonism between them created by their common experience as wealthy Grotonians challenged by infirmity never abated. When his death was announced in the Senate, Norris, Borah, and La Follette wept. His recent opponent, Dennis Chavez, was named to replace Cutting, and Norris, La Follette, Gerald Nye, and Hiram Johnson stalked disapprovingly out of the Senate session when Chavez was introduced.[69]

After Social Security, the second key element of this post-1934 election Second New Deal, which Hopkins had championed, was the Emergency Relief Appropriation Act of 1935. This provided the huge sum of four billion dollars, the largest single appropriation in U.S. history up to that time, for employment in public works of the unemployed, supplementing $880 million that had already been voted. It created a fantastically complicated administrative structure called the Works Progress Administration, which looked at first like a mischievous effort by Roosevelt to turn the abrasive relationship between Ickes and Hopkins into a homicidal one. Three parallel and officially co-equal agencies were set up within the WPA: a Division of Applications and Information, a Works Allotment Division, and a Works Progress Division.

The first agency, headed by the universally popular Frank Walker, would evaluate proposals for the disbursement of works relief money and send them to Works Allotment. Ickes would head Works Allotment, which would consider proposals in "roundtable" meetings attended by two dozen officiators, including representatives not only of almost every government spending department but of organized labor, agricultural associations, the U.S. Conference of Mayors, the American Bankers' Association, and disparate other groups. It was a feeble gesture to both populism and corporatism. This Babel, chaired by Ickes, would make recommendations to the President. Ickes's mental health would at times be impaired by the inevitable mortal bureaucratic combat over budgeting and priorities with Hopkins, who himself developed a duodenal ulcer in the same battles and was never a well man again. The Works Progress Administration was represented as a mere monitoring agency, but Ickes instantly realized that since Hopkins would have the title of administrator, he would, in fact, be directing the entire effort. Ickes's ensuing apoplexy was severe but unavailing.

Roosevelt and the authors of the legislation were careful to propose wage scales that gave the unemployed an incentive to escape the dole of merely subsidized unemployment that the Social Security legislation was establishing without undercutting the bargaining efforts of organized labor. Despite this and the huge Democratic majorities in the Congress, the bill was harassed in its progress through the Senate, especially by Huey Long, who managed by high parliamentary ingenuity to put one amendment through by a margin of one vote that raised pay levels above what the administration could accept. Roosevelt's appreciation of ornithology did not extend to enjoying Long's description of him as a "scrooch owl" rather than a "hoot owl." (The Louisiana legislator explained to the Senate that the former seduced a hen before devouring it, while the latter knocked over the nest and devoured the hen as she descended from the branch.)[70]

The Emergency Relief Appropriation Act was eventually passed after heavy personal lobbying by the President, who then departed on holiday on Astor's *Nourmahal.*

The task of the WPA was to provide work for the unemployed, and Hopkins and his team did this with great imagination. Building on the work of the CWA and the FERA (pp. 315, 324), the WPA built, expanded, or renovated 2,500 hospitals, nearly 4,000 schools, 13,000 parks and playgrounds, 7,800 bridges, and 651,000 miles of road.[71] It restored historic buildings, built some splendid new buildings, and had imaginative programs for blind, handicapped, retarded, and even deranged people.

The National Youth Administration, which shared in the emergency relief budget, put hundreds of thousands of young people to useful work, with enhanced possibilities for vocational or advanced study.

Ickes' PWA, though it received less money and employed less than a third of the people of his rival—Hopkins's WPA—was even more efficient and built many magnificent additions to the fixed assets of the nation. This agency constructed 70 percent of the country's new schools, 65 percent of its courthouses, city halls, and sewage plants, and more than one-third of its hospitals. It was central to the construction of the Triborough Bridge and Lincoln Tunnel in New York, of the elevated highway through the Florida Keys to Key West, and of the monumental buildings and grand parks along the beautiful waterfront of Ickes' native Chicago, and to the dredging of the port of Brownsville, Texas. The PWA also built the aircraft carriers *Yorktown* and *Enterprise* (which would play as decisive a role as any two ships in World War II), many smaller naval vessels, over a hundred military aircraft, and fifty military airfields.[72]

Less successful were the PWA efforts in housing. Roosevelt, seeming to revert to his days at the head of the building trades association, believed the government's role was to encourage the private sector, not to provide housing for large numbers of people. The PWA built about 25,000 units, and the industry only sluggishly revived. The administration would return to this subject in the Third New Deal.

The WPA took in about 3.5 million people. The PWA, CCC, TVA, and other workfare programs accounted for perhaps a little over two million more. The wage scale was very frugal, as low as nineteen dollars per month in parts of the South. Many of the aged and those who were not able-bodied were turned back on the states, which were underendowed fiscally to absorb them and were very uneven in their social programs, ranging from the generous Wisconsin of the La Follettes to poor, miserly, white supremacist Mississippi.[73]

Yet these New Deal relief programs were invaluable. They salvaged the lives of tens of millions from utter misery and hopelessness, endowed the country with a vast infrastructure, and vitalized much of the environment at bargain cost. The 3.5 million or so unemployed (a quarter of the total when the Roosevelt administration entered office) who were left out of these programs were to be sustained by Social Security and absorbed by the eventual general economic recovery.

The last outgrowth of the 1935 Emergency Relief Appropriation Act was the Rural Electrification Administration, one of the most unambiguously successful of all Roosevelt's New Deal initiatives. Roosevelt engaged as administrator a talented Philadelphia engineer, Morris Cooke, whom he had named as a trustee of the New York Power Authority in 1931.

Cooke took as his model electric cooperatives created by the TVA in Mississippi (where 99 percent of farms were not electrified). At the end of 1934 only 11 percent of American farms had electricity. That number rose to almost 50 percent by 1942 and to virtually 100 percent by the end of the forties.[74] Of all Roosevelt's governmental creations, only the Federal Deposit Insurance Corporation (which he had initially opposed) rivaled the REA in the level of its success. Millions of American farmers would not forget that before Roosevelt they illuminated their homes with oil lamps and had no ability to use a home appliance.

In an impetuous move, Roosevelt struck an executive order on May 1, 1935, setting up the Resettlement Administration, which was to resettle poor urban and rural families, and, duplicating the work of a number of other agencies, conduct land-use activities and make agricultural facilitation loans to farmers.

Rexford Tugwell, undersecretary of agriculture, was designated as the head of the new agency. Tugwell had become thoroughly disillusioned with government, and the Resettlement Administration seemed, as much as anything, an attempt by Roosevelt to keep Tugwell and give his socialist nanny-state ideas a laboratory. Tugwell had produced a food-and-drug bill in 1933 that contained a number of rather advanced truth-in-packaging provisions. This had been allowed to languish without coming to the floor of either house of the Congress for two years, with no support from the President.

Tugwell launched his new resettlement occupation with great energy, probably spurred by his conviction that agriculture was a nasty and primitive activity. He aimed to resettle half a million rural families, but in the end (which came for him in less than two years) only 4,500 families had actually been moved—about 20,000 people rather than the astonishing total of two million that was his original goal. He had hoped to buy ten million acres and relieve the inhabitants of barren land

and penurious homesteads, but the rural population, confirming Tugwell's opinion of them as ignorant peasants, were reluctant to be shepherded off the land they knew by professorial planners who despised them. Jerome Frank's directive in favor of the tenant farmers and farm laborers was revoked. These people, who were, in Roosevelt's phrase of 1932, "at the bottom of the economic pyramid," received direct aid from the works relief operations and from unemployment insurance. Agricultural conditions continued to gradually improve, thanks to domestic allotment and anti-drought and flood measures.

One project Tugwell inherited in the Resettlement Administration was Eleanor Roosevelt's brainchild, a cooperative community in West Virginia, of which she was almost as much the patron as her husband was of Warm Springs, though not, as he was, the proprietor. It was a 1,200-acre farm in a depressed area that Eleanor inspired the Interior Department to buy and use to launch the country's pioneer subsistence homestead project. The idea was to evacuate a number of disadvantaged families to the Arthur Farm, which would be renamed Arthurdale, where detached housing would be provided for each family. A factory would be established with a $525,000 WPA grant to make post office supplies, such as letter boxes and mailbags, and a school would be set up on the progressive model of Eleanor and Marion Dickerman's Todhunter.

The school would be directed by Eleanor's friend Elsie Clapp, a follower of the philosopher John Dewey, who would himself be a member of the school's advisory committee. The community would be a mixture of individual and cooperative effort, rural and urban work, and would be self-sufficient. It was to be a prototype for subsistence homesteads all over the country.

A number of problems arose with this plan, which was announced in October 1933. The first was Louis Howe's purchase for it of prefabricated housing originally intended for Cape Cod. He got each house for $1,000, half the budgeted figure, but the foundations were pre-poured to the wrong dimensions, and the houses were inadequate shelter against the rigors of the Appalachian winter and had to be remodeled. This raised their cost to $10,000 each, which put the project budget and the thirty-year homesteader-refinancing schedule under water.

Despite great effort, Eleanor was unable to persuade companies to locate there, and in 1934 the Congress balked at putting money for a post office supply factory into Arthurdale. The President, who might have remembered the skepticism his wife had mistakenly heaped on Warm Springs when he bought it, loyally supported his wife by saying the rising expenses could be justified in a pilot project. Ickes, who rightly feared the imminence of withering publicity, asked what it was a pilot for, since it did not qualify as low-cost housing or an economic initiative worthy of imitation.

The *Saturday Evening Post* produced a mocking exposé of the project in the spring of 1934. Arthurdale would be a terrible albatross for Eleanor. It stumbled on unsatisfactorily into the forties, but welfare dependence, exaggerated expectations, and the lethargy of perceived entitlement would make many of the beneficiaries of her prodigies on their behalf ungrateful, and she became embittered, if not altogether disillusioned. This was one of the more wildly utopian ideas of the New Dealers, some of whom, including Tugwell and Eleanor, came close to giving the regime the appearance of a swarm of amateur tinkerers and meddlers.

Tugwell put great stress on the RA information service, which employed some of the country's promising photographers and produced a vast record (over 250,000 photographs) of the extent of the economic Depression and of the living conditions of Americans generally. It didn't completely insulate the agency or its director from criticism, but it did provide a valuable addition to American visual arts, and virtually invented the documentary.*

But otherwise, Tugwell's laboratory, both in Agriculture and in the Resettlement Administration, produced negligible results. He retired at the start of 1937, grumbling that the New Deal had been reduced to "atomistic progressivism," and took what was left of the respectability of socialist planning with him.† Tugwell retained cordial relations with the President and served as head of a molasses company, as planning director for New York City, and as chancellor of the University of Puerto Rico. Then Roosevelt gave him, in 1941, a more promising laboratory opportunity by naming him governor of Puerto Rico, where he could deal with primitive conditions without having to pay much attention to a constitution or public opinion. Thereafter he returned to academic life.

VI

THE PROSPECTS FOR the New Deal were clouded by the Supreme Court's assault on it. This had begun with the decision January 7, 1935, declaring unconstitutional the section of the NIRA that authorized the President to ban the interstate transportation of oil produced in excess of agreed quotas, as an illegal delegation of legislative powers to the executive. Only Benjamin Cardozo dissented from this judgment. February 18 the Supreme Court produced three five-to-four, ambiguously worded judgments about the abrogation of the obligation to settle demands for payment in gold. This was deemed to be legal in

---

* Among the RA photographers who later became famous were Margaret Bourke-White and the artist Ben Shahn. And among the writers who collaborated with the RA information service in producing memorable and still-consulted books were Erskine Caldwell, Sherwood Anderson, Archibald MacLeish, and James Agee.

† He was by now widely known as "Red Rex," and as the Roosevelt biographer Kenneth Davis somewhat theatrically wrote, there was "a raining down on Tugwell's handsome, unprotected head of such clubs of malicious fury . . . as few men in national public life have ever had to endure."[75]

respect of private contracts as an aspect of congressional control over the currency, but illegal in government contracts as a breach of faith by the government with the people. However, the plaintiff was judged to have failed to prove that damages resulted. On May 6 the Railroad Retirement Act was judged unconstitutional by another five-four majority of the Supreme Court. The Court held that an imposed retirement scheme constituted a confiscation of railway company assets without due process, unjustifiable on grounds of interstate commerce because pensions were too far removed from the real business of running railways.

All of this was fairly ominous, but the Supreme Court fired a thunderbolt on May 27, 1935, with the Schechter case. Four brothers had been convicted of violating the NRA live-poultry code and also of selling food that didn't meet health standards, in their business of selling live chickens for ritualistic killing and consumption for religious purposes by Orthodox Jews in New York. Chief Justice Hughes departed from his usual glacial manner and spoke with great force and animation as he rendered judgment for a unanimous court. The court found that the live-poultry code had been an unconstitutional delegation of powers from the legislature to the executive. The NRA had been unappealably struck down. The Blue Eagle folded its wings and plunged to earth.

Contrary to even his wife's expectations, Roosevelt was not unduly perturbed. He said to Frances Perkins that the NRA had "become a mess," and that aspects of it had been "pretty wrong."[76] He indicated that it had run its course anyway and that he had never wanted to vacate durably the country's anti-trust laws. He told Frankfurter that all he had wanted to retain of the NRA were the wages, hours, collective bargaining, and child labor sections.

Justice Louis Brandeis summoned Corcoran and Cohen to the Supreme Court robing room right after the Schechter decision was brought down. In an act of questionable propriety and considerable presumption, he told them to tell the President that he would have to redesign his entire legislative program. Where Holmes was aquiline, Corcoran thought, "Brandeis appeared a condor — a tall, long-limbed creature with a fleshless beak of a nose and glaring eyes." Standing with outstretched arms as his robe was removed, Corcoran thought him "an avenging angel."[77] "Old Isaiah," as Roosevelt called Brandeis, told the two young men: "We're not going to let this government centralize everything. This is the end." By this time, Brandeis, whatever his other distinctions, had become a pretentious legal and economic atavist. He railed, inter alia, against the automobile industry because he thought Americans should walk more, and urged young men to go to smaller cities in his obsessive pursuit of a simpler world.[78]

Roosevelt eventually concluded, on the advice of Frankfurter and others, that the best response to this new threat was to continue with his legislative plans, as carefully constitutionally formulated as possible. He resolved to challenge the Supreme Court directly by requesting a constitutional amendment or by other means only if the Court made the government's essential economic recovery measures impossible in the eyes of the public generally. To attack the Court now would appear to be petulant.

Though Roosevelt had been spared the challenging task of trying to reform the shambles of the NRA, the implications of the Schechter case would be extremely serious if that decision were replicated in respect of more important measures, such as Social Security, then inching through the Congress.

The President was reasonably jaunty at the start of his usual press conference May 31, 1935. He wasted little time lamenting what he had described less than two years before as the most important legislation in the history of the republic. Undaunted in his love of hyperbole, he yet described the decision as the most important since the (fugitive slave) Dred Scott decision of 1857 (which had helped bring on the Civil War). He assumed a much more grave air when he told the journalists that there appeared to be some question about whether the Supreme Court believed the government had the constitutional authority to wage World War I as comprehensively as it did. He expressed gratitude that the war ended before it could be adjudicated and said, for direct quotation, that this decision had reduced the country to "a horse and buggy era" definition of interstate commerce.

In June 1935 the vast apparatus of the NRA in all its intricacy of boards and agencies was dismantled, leaving only a statistical and information service.

Roosevelt still certainly possessed the upper hand against the Long-Coughlin-Townsend axis and the meddlesome condescensions of the Supreme Court. Whatever the legalities, the justices were goading a dangerous adversary. All the Supreme Court justices except Cardozo had practiced corporate law, and seven of the nine were past seventy. Roosevelt recognized these public relations vulnerabilities much sooner than the judges, who were not accustomed to such considerations, as Brandeis's imperious behavior indicated.

Roosevelt retained the public's confidence as unemployment was now descending fairly steadily in the private sector at the rate of almost 100,000 per month. Most of the remaining unemployed were aided by the many alphabetical workfare programs, and most of the rest were finally about to receive assistance through the Social Security system.

This was a pattern Roosevelt would often repeat as president. He would wait enigmatically until it was clear to him what obstacles could be overcome and which were insurmountable, preserving the ability to marshal public opinion behind him. He would then assault the opponents and obstacles he judged to be assailable, suddenly and with great force.

The apparent but misleading Job-like patience and even inertia he sometimes demonstrated seems to have been learned from observing Woodrow Wilson. He would spring to action with reborn energy and a bully pulpit reminiscent of TR, reinforced with a cunning intuitive and professional calculation of what could be done with public opinion that was unique to him among all American presidents.

The closest Roosevelt came in this period to an exposition of his tactical views and of what he learned from the two outstanding presidents whom he had known well was a letter to Wilson's biographer Ray Stannard Baker on March 20, 1935. He wrote that Baker would "be sympathetic to the view that the public psychology and, for that matter, individual psychology, cannot, because of human weakness, be attuned for long periods of time to a constant repetition of the highest note on the scale.

"Theodore Roosevelt lacked Woodrow Wilson's appeal to the fundamental and failed to stir, as Wilson did, the truly profound moral and social convictions. Wilson, on the other hand, failed where Theodore Roosevelt succeeded, in stirring people to enthusiasm over specific individual events, even though these events may have been superficial in comparison with the fundamentals.

"There is another thought which is involved in continuous leadership — whereas in this country there is a free and sensational Press, people tire of seeing the same name day after day in the important headlines of the papers, and the same voice night after night over the radio. For example, if since last November I had tried to keep up the pace of 1933 and 1934, the inevitable histrionics of the new actors, Long and Coughlin and [Hugh] Johnson, would have turned the eyes of the audience away from the main drama itself. I am inclined to think that in view of the unfolding of the domestic scene and now of the foreign scene, you are right in your thought that the time is soon at hand for a new stimulation of united American action. I am proposing that very thing before the year is out." He did so in fact before it was half out.

He was by this time writing to his cousin and confidante, Margaret Suckley: "It's a little hurricane we're passing through down here — & rather risky for the future of the country, but it's worse in other countries & I'm trying to keep a very tight rein on myself, for the time has not come yet to speak out."[79] A few months later, on September 23, he recounted to the same correspondent Lincoln's reaction on reading some acerbic criticism of himself in the most difficult days of the Civil War: "No matter how philosophical he was in public — those attacks did hurt A. Lincoln . . . because they were repetitions of false or twisted statements. . . . you alone have known that I was a bit 'cast down' these past weeks."[80] It was unusual for Roosevelt to feel as he described and even more unusual for him to admit it to anyone, even Margaret Suckley, who does seem to have been his most intimate conversational companion in 1935.

Roosevelt vetoed another acceleration of veterans' bonuses on May 22, 1935, and intervened heavily to have his veto sustained in the Senate. Before doing this he had horrified Morgenthau by telling him in emphatic terms a few hours apart on the same day why he intended to veto it, and why he might let it go through. He famously told his Treasury secretary, who was an earnest political straight man, that his practice was: "Never let your left hand know what your right hand is doing." When Morgenthau asked which hand he, Morgenthau, was, Roosevelt responded: "My right hand, but I keep my left hand under the table."[81]

Roosevelt drove on through the spring and summer of 1935, pressing his full Second New Deal program.

He was not initially entirely favorable to a bill presented by Senator Wagner that proposed to give the NLRB the authority to define and outlaw unfair labor practices such as oppression of unions, failure to enter into good-faith bargaining, the establishment of sham company unions, and in some cases the importation of replacement workers. The bill, which attracted unprecedented resistance from the business community, made Section 7a of the NIRA a much more tangible reality for organized labor and gave the NLRB enforcement powers similar to those of the Federal Trade Commission.

Despite Roosevelt's serious reservations about unions generally, and his opinion that most union leaders were irresponsible rabble-rousers, he was determined not to be outflanked by Long and his cabal of malcontents, and he believed some modest degree of wealth redistribution was necessary. Without it, the demographic majority would impose themselves on the comfortable minority and a confiscatory regime could result. He had a much greater personal rapport with farm leaders and with reasonably enlightened business leaders than with labor leaders.[82] He knew how insulated the denizens of the boardrooms and great clubs of the principal cities were from the restlessness of the American masses. He also knew how ineffectual they were politically and how incapable they were of defending their own position in a democratic system. It would be Roosevelt, one of them, who would have to prevail in a contest of demagogy with the true enemies of the rich,[83] endure the brickbats of his peers, and make America a land of opportunity for the disadvantaged and a country again safe for the rich. For these reasons, he did put his full weight behind Wagner's bill, and it became law.

The administration's public utilities holding-companies legislation was an attempt to prevent fake financing charges being assessed back to the utility companies and factored into costs and laid off on customers. It was also an attempt to prevent such highly leveraged control of groups of utilities that a precarious Insull-like structure would result. When Roosevelt referred to this bill in his State of the Union message on January 4, 1935, he misread the phrase from his text "abolition of the evil features of holding companies" as "abolition of the evil of holding companies." He explained and corrected the error in the next subsequent press conference, but the suspicion persisted that he had spoken his mind accurately to the Congress.[84] There were more symbolic than practical aspects to it, and opposition was fierce to parts of the bill. Roosevelt sent Senate sponsor Burton Wheeler a letter that was read on the floor of the Senate. It inelegantly stated that removing the most aggressive clauses of the bill would be "wholly contrary to the recommendations of myself."

There was a bruising legislative battle. Senator Hugo Black of Alabama unearthed, among other gems, a utility-backed generation of a nationwide rumor that Roosevelt was insane. The utilities lobby had always before emerged victorious in struggles of this kind but had not encountered such a determined and pow-erful president. Frankfurter eventually produced a compromise that was pre-sented by Senator Alben Barkley of Kentucky: the SEC would abolish by the end of 1939 utilities systems having more than three levels of holding companies, and two-level systems would be permitted only if they could prove their structure con-tributed to operating efficiency. All holding companies became SEC registrants and reporting companies. This bill finally became law on August 26, 1935, and was widely seen as an important reform and a great victory for the President.

The Federal Reserve reform legislation was the creation of Marriner Eccles, a Utah Mormon banker and a Keynesian, although he claimed to have adopted Keynesian views before he had heard of Keynes. Eccles had impressed Rexford Tugwell at a congressional hearing, and Tugwell had introduced him to Morgen-thau. The Treasury secretary broad-mindedly hired him as his assistant, despite his disagreement with Eccles's Keynesianism, and in November 1934 nominated him to fill a vacancy on the Federal Reserve Board. Eccles's bill was a thorough modernization of Wilson's Federal Reserve Act of 1913. It made the Federal Reserve Board more responsive to the public interest and more directly answer-able to the president, gave the board the right to adjust by up to 100 percent reserves required to be maintained against deposits by member banks, and gave the board authority over trading in government-issued securities, removing that function from the private sector. It set up the Federal Open Market Committee with a reduced level of decentralization, and brought all the state banks under Federal Reserve authority by requiring that adherence for eligibility for federal deposit insurance. With this measure, Roosevelt would achieve his objective of federal control over currency and credit. Finally and for the first time, the United States would have a real central bank. The absence of one had contributed to the magnification and export of the Depression in the early thirties.

Ever mindful of Roosevelt's and the late William Woodin's help in reopening his bank two years before, A.P. Giannini, of the Bank of America, was one of the strongest witnesses in favor of the bill before the Senate banking committee. Among the serried ranks of bankers opposing it, mainly on the grounds that it would "politicize the Federal Reserve"—i.e., restrain the absolute liberty of the private banking system that had collapsed in 1933—was former Treasury secretary Ogden Mills, who claimed that the bill would put the country "back 500 years" (i.e., to a period that antedated any recognizable notion of central banking). Carter Glass sent down his own bill, which was reconciled with the administra-tion's, and the fused measure was pushed through by the President on August 24, 1935.

Roosevelt's special tax bill was a conventional "soak the rich" measure, designed as much to shut up Long and Coughlin as to raise revenue. It imposed a substantial federal inheritance tax and gift tax, moved maximum corporate income taxes from 13.75 percent to 16.75 percent and put a surtax on large per-sonal incomes. Hearst became involved because he considered that some of Roosevelt's socialistic oratorical flourishes were directed at him. In his annual message Roosevelt had said, "Americans must forswear that conception of wealth which, through excessive profits, creates undue private power over private affairs and, to our misfortune, over public affairs as well." Hearst responded by unleashing the full fury of America's greatest media company on Roosevelt, who invited the Hearst Corporation's editor-in-chief, E.D. Coblentz, to discuss matter at the White House.

For two years, whenever W.R. Hearst became agitated about administration policy, Roosevelt had invited him to the White House and hosed him down. "The Chief was so charmed and reassured by the President that at an impromptu press conference [after one such meeting] he had nothing but praise for the man and his policies."[85] This interview with Coblentz would be the last of these efforts. Roosevelt could do without having the Hearst newspapers constantly on his back, but he had learned decades before that Hearst wasn't a bad person to run against, either. He may also be assumed to have relished an opportunity to settle accounts after Hearst had publicly embarrassed him in early 1932 with the confection of the Garner candidacy and attack on the other candidates, including Roosevelt, as excessively internationalist.

The meeting with Coblentz was not a great success. The President told Coblentz he was "fighting Communism, Huey Longism, Coughlinism, Townsendism, [and] to save our system, the capitalist system, [and] combat crackpot ideas," it would be necessary to pay some attention to concepts of wealth redistribution and to inconvenience "the forty-six men who are reported to have incomes in excess of one million dollars a year." Coblentz claimed Roosevelt said he would "throw [the 46] to the wolves,"[86] but it is unlikely he would use such an expression, and some of those people were supporters of his. Roosevelt was probably happy enough to bring to an end the publisher's long and preposterous masquerade as the champion of the American working class and force him to reveal himself in his true colors as a reactionary.

In his message accompanying the tax bill Roosevelt had set out, oratorically if not in the radicalism of his proposals, in open competition with Long for the support of those outraged by inequalities of wealth in the country. He wrote (or rather Moley, who didn't agree with a word of it, wrote) that "Our revenue laws have done little to prevent an unjust concentration of wealth and economic power. Inherited economic power is as inconsistent with the ideals of this generation as inherited political power was inconsistent with the ideals of the generation which established our government."[87]

Fiscally, it achieved little, but did provide the political symbolism Roosevelt thought he needed to repulse the barbarians of the unofficial opposition. If Roosevelt had been serious, he would have taxed the middle class, whence most of the government's revenue arises, and used the proceeds to provide more self-help for the poor. Instead, he devised a shabby measure to defend himself against the shabbiest political elements the Great Depression could throw up. Hearst described this as Communism. The White House happily issued a statement on August 15, 1935, quoting from a memo of Coblentz's of eight days earlier: "The Chief [Hearst] instructs that the phrase "SOAK THE SUCCESSFUL" be used in all references to the Administration's tax program . . . also he wants the words 'RAW DEAL' used instead of 'NEW DEAL.' "[88] This was a dramatic change from Hearst's post-electoral laudations of nine months before.[89]

Huey Long was emboldened at one point in the congressional process to claim that Roosevelt wasn't serious about passing the measure, and called him "a liar and a fake," a clear indication that he was rattled by Roosevelt's response to his challenge.* A proposed tax on intercorporate dividends was retained with difficulty, and the graduated corporate income tax was abandoned, replaced by an excess-profits tax. The surtax on high personal incomes skyrocketed to a confiscatory 75 percent, although there were many exonerations and it was essentially political window dressing. As the final bill was read in the Senate, Huey Long "swaggered about, chuckling, pointing to his chest and confiding to other senators that Roosevelt was stealing his program."[90]

The Guffey-Snider Bituminous Coal bill effectively replicated the soft-coal code of the NRA and entrenched it in specific law. John L. Lewis was constantly threatening a nationwide coal strike if this bill weren't passed, and Roosevelt assured him that it would be. To that end the President sent a letter on July 6, 1935, to the chairman of a House of Representatives committee where the bill was bottled up because of fears about its constitutionality. Roosevelt wrote, in words that quickly became controversial and that he regretted as feeding the claims of those who believed he sought to be a dictator: "I hope your committee will not permit doubts about constitutionality, however reasonable, to block the proposed legislation." With a certain amount of friendly persuasion from the White House, the bill went through the Congress and became law at the end of the extended session in late August.

A bill prohibiting munitions exports arose from a series of events that incited public interest in disarmament and pacifism. Gerald Nye, North Dakota's isolationist Republican senator, headed a committee examining the munitions and armaments industries. Everyone from Roosevelt down inveighed against the evils of the armaments makers, who, it was claimed or implied, on no real evidence, not only profited egregiously from war but actively attempted to promote and incite wars.

Roosevelt, climbing aboard this bandwagon and trying to take control of it lest it careen in an undesirable direction, had announced at his December 12, 1934, press conference that "The time has come to take the profit out of war."[91] He then struck a committee that was a catchment for diverse elements: Bernard Baruch,

---

* The pro-administration star of the congressional hearings was Robert Jackson, general counsel of the Internal Revenue Service, whose cogent arguments marked him in Roosevelt's thoughts as a candidate for swift promotion.

General Hugh Johnson, General Douglas MacArthur, George Peek, and a group of cabinet secretaries (including Hull, Morgenthau, Wallace, and Perkins) and less celebrated officials. This group, which by the nature of its membership seemed unlikely to produce a radically pacifist (or even coherent) approach to foreign and security policy, generated a bill from Congressman John McSwain of South Carolina in early 1935. The McSwain bill proposed a freeze on the cost of munitions and armaments at the beginning of any war or foreign emergency, to prevent price-gouging by the suppliers.

Business was relieved at this relatively bland approach, compared with the militant pacifism Nye and his cohorts were clearly stoking up to recommend. The Nye committee investigations were producing some eye-catching testimony. There was testimony that Wilson had lied when he claimed that he had no knowledge of secret Allied treaties before 1919, that Latin American government officials had taken bribes from American arms suppliers, and that U.S. bankers and arms suppliers had influenced American foreign policy, possibly including the decision to go to war.

This was sensational, revisionist, unsubstantiated nonsense, but it resonated well in some circles. Obviously, no special-interest groups had anything to do with the German decision in 1917 to sink any ship apparently bound for an Allied port. And obviously no U.S. administration could acquiesce in the sinking of U.S. flag merchant ships or in the complete abandonment of commercial shipping to accommodate Germany. Wilson (and Roosevelt when his turn came) could not take a less purposeful stance than Jefferson and Madison had taken during the Napoleonic Wars.

It was rumored in the press that the President's managers in the Congress would not approve a continuation of funds for the Nye Committee. Over 150,000 letters and telegrams urging continued funding for Nye's committee poured into the Senate and the White House. Roosevelt, beginning his traditional process of jejune maneuver, had Nye to the White House for a private chat on Boxing Day, 1934. Predictably, the canary (Nye) emerged from his meeting with the presidential cat happily explaining to the press that the Baruch-Johnson-MacArthur committee was intended to strengthen and not supplant the Nye Committee, continued funding for which Roosevelt supported.

At the resumed hearings Nye's committee heard testimony from economic journalist John T. Flynn proposing that in the event of war businessmen in the armaments industry be drafted like servicemen so they would contribute their work to the war effort. Organized labor balked at this, because it feared that the anti-military militants would attempt to conscript the workers at barracks wages also. Roosevelt's agents at the Capitol worked furtively to exploit this fissure. The President had the Nye Committee to the White House on March 19, 1935.

Roosevelt expressed great sympathy for the Flynn views. But he also pointed out that Hitler had, three days before, announced the resumption of conscription and the shredding of important sections of the Versailles Treaty, and that Mussolini was obviously preparing to invade Abyssinia. Roosevelt had originally responded privately to Hitler's move by envisioning a pact between all the countries that surrounded Germany, including Italy and possibly the U.S.S.R., pledging disarmament down to what individual soldiers could carry. Germany would be invited to subscribe to this pact, and if it failed to do so the signatory powers would impose a complete blockade on Germany, which the United States would graciously observe. He took the idea no further than his immediate entourage, since it became instantly clear to him that the proposed co-contractants, with the possible exception of Poland, had no interest in any real challenge to Hitler, and that, on reflection, a U.S. proposal urging a group of European nations to the brink of war without the same step by the United States would be taken seriously by few, least of all by Hitler.

Roosevelt was convinced that Hitler was pathologically and barbarously aggressive, and had been since his installation as German chancellor. He was well in advance of any noteworthy European statesman, including Winston Churchill, in the conviction that Hitler would have to be got rid of if there was to be any assured peace in Europe.

In November, 1933, Ambassador William Dodd in Berlin had sent Roosevelt his summary of Hitler ("less educated, more romantic, with a semi-criminal record"); Goebbels, whom he represented as a xenophobic semicommunist who hated the official Communists ("While Hitler is a fair orator as German oratory goes, Goebbels is a past master"); and Goering, "a more aristocratic and Prussian" war hero. There are inaccuracies; for example, Dodd claimed Hitler received no promotion or decoration in the Great War (he was promoted corporal and awarded two iron crosses). Dodd also represented this threesome as a Roman-style triumvirate, completely underestimating the absolute dictatorship of Hitler. He did, however, accurately conclude that Roosevelt might "see . . . something of the problem you have to deal with."[92]

In May 1935, Dodd, an old Wilsonian who traced all contemporary problems to America's failure to enter the League of Nations, reported to Roosevelt that a prominent German admiral, echoing Schacht six months earlier, had predicted Germany would soon go to war. Dodd reported that Hitler was already remilitarizing the Rhineland by inserting "policemen" there who were in fact trained as soldiers. He also predicted a formal alliance between Germany and Japan aimed at assisting the regional domination of both powers.[93]

On April 1, 1936, Dodd wrote Roosevelt that "Europe can hardly escape [German] domination . . . Japan dominating the Far East and the United States dominating both Americas."[94] On October 19, 1936, Dodd grimly informed Roosevelt: "These dictators mean to dominate Europe and there is a fair chance of their doing it without war." He clearly foresaw appeasement and its consequences.[95] In the April letter he had predicted, two and three years early, the German takeover of Austria and of the Czechs, and of at least part of the Polish Corridor.[96] Dodd found Hitler "such a horror to me, I cannot endure his presence."[97]

He was a prescient, if somewhat dogmatic ambassador, and everything he reported to Roosevelt confirmed the President's preexisting suspicions. (If the British had had such an astute and principled ambassador in Berlin, and Roosevelt had had as capable a pre-war ambassador in London as those accredited by the British to him, the slide into war might have been less inexorable.)*

As the thirties progressed, Roosevelt would play a brilliant and intricate game of awaiting a firming-up of opinion in the countries neighboring Germany that were directly at risk, while gradually painting the American pacifists into the corner of being naïve Hitler dupes or outright Nazi agents. Apart from the numerous isolationists and the few Fascist sympathizers, there was some body of opinion that the Germans, Italians, and Japanese had been shortchanged, and Roosevelt had to take account of this view also, even though he strongly disagreed with it. The outstanding Republican editor William Allen White of Kansas wrote that the United States should convene an international conference at once to meet the legitimate demands of "these underprivileged countries—Germany, Japan, Italy. Are men really Christian sufficiently in their heart of hearts to bring justice to those who are underprivileged?"[99] That a distinguished man like White would so describe the Nazis indicated how implacable a challenge it would be to organize rational American domestic opinion around a policy of preparedness and assistance for those who would resist Hitler and the Japanese.

Roosevelt tried to distract Nye and his colleagues when they visited the White House on March 19 by suggesting they consider how to assure American neutrality in the event of war. Nye happily took up this task and began a massive trespass in the domain of the Senate Foreign Relations Committee, chaired by Senator Key Pittman. The President had hoped this would lead to an intercommittee attrition and squabbling that would drain the momentum of the isolationist peace movement in the Congress. Nye ignored Pittman and on April 1,

---

* Ambassador to Moscow William C. Bullitt encountered Hermann Goering, French Marshal Petain, and former and future premier Pierre Laval at the funeral of Marshal Joseph Pilsudski, one of the heroic founders of Poland, in May 1935. His report to Roosevelt included a humorous description of Goering's girth: "He is at least a yard across the bottom as the crow flies . . . two inches of padding extending each [shoulder] . . . nearly a yard from rear to umbilicus . . . and encases himself in a glove-tight uniform, the effect is novel. . . . He is really the most appalling representative of a nation that I have ever laid eyes on. . . . the Germans will achieve nothing but a series of national disasters until they cease to take the Niebelungenlied seriously."[98]

Bullitt found the seventy-nine-year-old Petain "in great form," keeping a large group "in screams of laughter for half an hour" describing his encounter with Prohibition while visiting America in the twenties. Bullitt returned to Moscow with Soviet foreign minister Litvinov, who professed to believe that Poland expected Japan to attack Russia and then propose, with Germany's blessing, to seize part of the Ukraine, and join in a "German-Hungarian-Polish demolition of Czechoslovakia." This last gloomy prediction would prove insightful.

1935, his committee endorsed the Flynn plan for conscripting everyone into any war effort.

On the eighteenth anniversary of American entry into World War I, April 6, there was a parade against war by 50,000 veterans in Washington, but on April 9 the administration's allies in the House of Representatives pushed through the White House-sponsored McSwain bill, 367 to 15 (freezing the prices of armaments in the event of war). Roosevelt was unenthusiastic about McSwain's bill, but he had to shut down Nye if he was going to have any authority left to deploy American force in the deepening international crisis caused by the dictators.

Nye tried to put through the Senate amendments to the McSwain bill to implement the Flynn and other radical proposals. The majority of the Nye Committee voted for nationalization of the armaments industry, and the committee voted unanimously for Flynn's suggestions. Nye sponsored or encouraged through the summer of 1935 amendments to a pending neutrality bill that would forbid loans to the governments or citizens of any belligerent, forbid arms sales to any warring country, and forbid travel by Americans in war zones. Finally, the embargo on arms sales to belligerents was retained, and Americans would be warned that they would travel at their own risk in war zones.

The bill also set up a National Munitions Control Board to license arms exporters and importers, and restricted the use of American ports by the submarines of belligerents. Strategic raw materials were not affected and Roosevelt managed to restrict the duration of the bill to February 1936—less than six months by the time he signed it, as the Neutrality Act of 1935, on August 31. When he did sign it, it was with an accompanying statement that approved the "wholly excellent" purpose of the legislation but warned that its "inflexible provisions might drag us into war rather than keep us out."

The danger of war between the Great Powers was a good deal more distant than six months, and the Congress couldn't stop sales to countries at war via third parties. And Roosevelt would not be blindsided again by an earnest huckster like Nye.

When the session finally ended, the so-called Second New Deal had been enacted: the Securities Exchange Act, the Social Security Act, Hopkins's gigantic Emergency Relief Appropriations Act (with its rural electrification provisions), Senator Wagner's Labor Relations Act reforms, the Federal Reserve modernization, and the tax and coal legislation. Walter Lippmann wrote of "the most comprehensive program of reform ever achieved in this country in any administration."[100] Republican editor William Allen White wrote that the reforms just adopted were "long past due . . . a belated attempt to bring the American people up to the modern standards of English-speaking peoples."[101]

Arthur Schlesinger wrote that the First New Deal characteristically "told business what it must do; the Second New Deal characteristically told business what it must not do."[102] But neither was principally about business. The First New Deal was an electric jolt, a defibrillation, to produce recovery for the whole economy. The Second New Deal was partly a regulatory regimen to avoid recurrence and partly a disincentive to consider more extreme nostrums proffered by quack-remedy salesmen. Both batches of legislation were adequately successful. In finessing and muscling through such an extensive program over almost a whole fractious summer, Roosevelt had scored another political grand slam. He had demonstrated once again his ability to outmaneuver his opponents and retain the mastery of the political levers in Washington and of the high ground in public opinion across the country.

The President declared himself to Morgenthau completely exhausted, to the point where he would enjoy "sticking pins into people and hurting them." Instead of any macabre divertissement, he boarded the presidential train that had been on its siding awaiting his pleasure for two months and went to Hyde Park for the conventional restorative pleasures of Indian summer on the Hudson.

CHAPTER 9

"Franklin Is on His Own Now"

(Louis Howe shortly before his death, April 1936)

I

RELAXING AT HYDE PARK, Roosevelt concluded that he had adequately undercut Long, Townsend, and Coughlin, and that it was again time to tack to the right and placate sentiment that might be wearied of reform and disconcerted by talk of wealth redistribution. Having armed himself with defenses against the populist demagogues, it was time to repel any invasion from the moderate right by the official Republican opposition. The President offered the prospect of more tranquil government. Roosevelt prevailed upon Moley to prepare a response to an August 26, 1935, letter from publisher Roy Howard, head of the Scripps-Howard chain, an ally against the snarling animosity of Colonel Robert R. McCormick and increasingly the hostility of William Randolph Hearst. Howard had asked in his letter for a respite and expressed the concern that many businessmen thought Roosevelt was anti-business, especially as evidenced by his recently imposed surtax on the wealthy.

Roosevelt, touching up Moley's draft, responded on September 2 that the tax program was "based upon a broad and just social and economic purpose . . . not to destroy wealth, but to create a broader range of opportunity, to restrain the growth of unwholesome and sterile accumulations." He regretted the fact that consumers' taxes had increased as a percentage of national revenue from 30 percent to 60 percent since 1929 and concluded that his reform program "has now achieved substantial completion and the 'breathing spell' of which you speak is here—very decidedly so." The stock market, and Roosevelt's political popularity with many commentators, rose sharply.

The gratuitous reference to accumulation of wealth indicates that he was not entirely tactical, or even vindictive, in his motivations. Roosevelt seems to have subscribed to the faddish thirties notion that wealth creation was "sterile," useless to society, and unjust, as if the economy were a zero-sum game and the well-to-do put their money under their mattresses and no good came of it.

He formulated his squirely prejudices in terms that the working class could support. And he recognized that society would become unstable if too much wealth were concentrated in too few hands. His lack of rapport with most of those in whose hands it would be doubtless sharpened his redistributive motives. He was a precursor of what became, decades later, the social capitalist, and was never an easy target for centrist opponents, constantly placating the sensible majority and isolating the extremes.

But behind both his tactical and strategic political genius lurked some ambition to take wealth from those who had earned it (or their descendants) and spread it around without excessive regard to merit, to assumedly grateful, voting recipients. He underestimated the extent to which the private sector, with the right fiscal and regulatory fine tuning, could achieve the same ends more efficiently. There will always be the unanswerable questions of whether he incited more envy than was politically necessary, even given the appalling economic conditions in which he entered the presidency, and of whether he would have built on the wartime reconciliation with big buisiness that he achieved.

The tendency to antagonize and demonize private wealth never provoked the capital strike Roosevelt's suspicious mind often believed was afoot. But it did make it difficult for all but the most perceptive of the nation's wealthy to appreciate what he had done to preserve the stability of society and make America safe for great "sterile accumulations" of wealth (or even medium-size ones, such as his mother's).

Roosevelt's tussle with the populist mountebanks benefited from unbidden events. On September 8, 1935, Joseph Kennedy came to Hyde Park, and Roosevelt had him telephone Father Charles Coughlin in Royal Oak, Michigan. Kennedy handed the receiver to the President, who said: "Hiya, Padre. Where have you been all the time? I'm lonesome. Come on down and see me."[1] (Roosevelt had not attacked Coughlin publicly. He left that to spokesmen such as Ickes, who considered the Catholic Church a sinister organization anyway and was remarkably effective at it.)

Two hours after this conversation Huey Long was shot by a deranged doctor in a corridor of the Louisiana capitol at Baton Rouge, which Long had built. The assassin was the son-in-law of a political opponent of Long's and was shot dead on the spot by Long's bodyguards. Roosevelt issued a statement beginning "I deeply regret" the attempt on the Kingfish's life, and claiming violence to be "un-American" (not an easy case to make, given its frequent incidence in American life and history).

Huey Long was originally believed to be recovering. But the surgeon had failed to cauterize, and the patient began to bleed to death internally, while Coughlin journeyed by train to see the President (for what turned out to be a cordial but inconsequential visit). Long died in the early hours of September 10,

1935, as Coughlin and Kennedy discovered when Kennedy met the radio priest at the Albany railway station just before dawn on that morning and saw the headlines and heard the newsboys. A reporter asked Coughlin his response, and he said: "The most regrettable thing in modern history."

In fact, Coughlin was almost as little bereaved as Roosevelt. The Kingfish and the priest had been rivals, and their policy ideas, such as they were, were quite divergent. Long was a southern populist champion of the urban and agrarian working classes and petits bourgeois, a proto-Poujadist. Coughlin was an Irish-American neo-Fascist whose appeal was more sectarian and isolationist and ethnic than economic, although he strongly favored a policy of inflation. Coughlin regarded Long's plans as "unspeakable radicalism," and Long, referring to Coughlin's melodious Irish voice and a famous, contemporary, full-figured singer of the day, called Coughlin "a political Kate Smith." Long's last words were "God, don't let me die! I have so much to do!" Huey Long was just forty-two. There was no autopsy, and the rumor circulated, but seems not to be well-founded, that he was assassinated by his own bodyguards.[2] Had Long lived, it is unlikely he would have toppled Roosevelt in 1936 or any other time, but he would have been a significant distraction. Farley thought him good for six million votes in the next presidential election.[3] Even if true, that would not have changed the result. Long was the sort of rumbustious third-party candidate who could disturb American politics between elections, and was one of the most talented of that type in all of the twentieth century. However, events would demonstrate that Franklin D. Roosevelt's hold on the American presidency was now unshakeable.

With the death of Huey Long, his Share Our Wealth movement rapidly came apart. His sidekick, Gerald L.K. Smith, a frequently raving minister from Shreveport, had telegraphed Roosevelt a few days after Long's death, strenuously complaining about "financing potential assassins with government money," scurrilously inciting the inference that he thought Roosevelt might have had something to do with the death of Long. Smith tried to carry on in the shoes of the Kingfish, but the lieutenants in Long's Louisiana machine quickly made their peace with the President and returned to the Democratic fold. This process was widely derided as "the second Louisiana Purchase."[4] This left Smith, who had been engaged for Long's national campaign, footloose. Long's brother, Earl, and his son, Russell, would be the leading politicians in Louisiana for nearly fifty years after the Kingfish's death.

Roosevelt invited Ickes, Hopkins, and Tugwell to Springwood early in September for the division of the huge public works budget. Ickes arrived first, on September 11, complaining to Roosevelt that Hopkins was a "lawless" character who was the greatest threat to the President's reelection. Hopkins and Tugwell and some aides arrived the next day. Hopkins received almost $3 billion, Ickes about $500 million for the PWA, and Tugwell $150 million for the RA (Resettlement Administration). Though so disappointed that he declined to stay for dinner, Ickes was not pyrotechnic and did not, as he often did, threaten to quit the government. (This was not so effective a tactic as Ickes thought, because Roosevelt knew perfectly well how addicted Ickes was to occupying his position and how emotionally dependent he was on the approval of the President. He had put in for Indian Affairs Commissioner when Roosevelt won the election. The Interior Department was a great windfall and he meant to make the most of it.)

Roosevelt tried to cover off another source of frequent irritation on September 13, by having Walter Lippmann to lunch. It was not a huge success. Lippmann, like the late Bronson Cutting, seemed to suffer from intermittent but prolonged and severe bouts of churlish envy of Roosevelt. Lippman was too close to Roosevelt in age and had known him too well in formative moments of Roosevelt's career to revere him as he had TR and Wilson. A few days before his arrival Lippmann had written to a friend that Roosevelt had "a good heart but not a great one," an even more presumptuous assertion than that attributed by Corcoran to Holmes. From the supreme promontory of his post as the nation's leading pundit, Lippmann was "afraid that [Roosevelt] is not thoroughly matured." The Roosevelt charm and personal attention were not completely wasted, however. Lippmann left happy that he and his host were "truly agreed" on important points, though he found Roosevelt tired, "edgy," and lacking his usual self-confidence.*

II

PRESIDENT AND MRS. ROOSEVELT, Hopkins, Ickes, and a presidential staff of seventy left Washington by train for the West Coast on September 26. The President would then embark on U.S.S. *Houston* for the cruise he had not been able to take during the summer. There he would try to impose peace between Harry Hopkins and Harold Ickes, who, with Howe too unwell to exercise his traditional influence, were his two most important lieutenants.

Roosevelt gave three major speeches on his way across the country. At Fremont, Nebraska, on September 28, he told a large agrarian audience that the Farm Credit Administration had saved the homes of half a million farmers by taking over their mortgages. He generally commended his own government's handling of rural issues. On September 30 at Boulder City, Nevada, he dedicated the great Boulder Dam, 726 feet high and holding the largest artificial lake in the

---

* Lippmann was rigorously unimpressed by America's first lady. When Eleanor entered while the men were talking about tax reform, she interjected some ideas that both men considered to be absurd. "Oh Eleanor, shut up! You never understand these things anyway," said Roosevelt, to Walter Lippmann's evident agreement. He later wrote that he came greatly to appreciate Eleanor, but that in those days she blundered irritatingly about "like a goose."[5]

world—sufficient, as Roosevelt pointed out—to cover the state of Connecticut to a depth of ten feet. He exulted in his heartfelt themes of flood control, drought control, and more and cheaper electricity. (This dam, under Republican administrations, and then permanently, would be called Hoover Dam but was currently called Boulder Dam. Roosevelt approved Ickes' restoration of the original name in the thirties.)[6]

The President was warmly greeted by approximately one million people as he took a fifty-mile motor tour of the already sprawling city of Los Angeles October 1. He spoke to 75,000 people at the Los Angeles Coliseum, reminiscing reverently about Woodrow Wilson and claiming the moral and intellectual superiority of liberals.

On October 2, Roosevelt spoke at the San Diego Exposition and remembered that he had been at the previous exposition in that city "twenty long years ago." (It was one of his tired rhetorical flourishes that all references to years gone by were to "long" years, as if the intervening period were almost longer than the calendar indicated because of the travail he and his audience had endured together.)

Roosevelt, Hopkins, Ickes, and some of the President's inner circle boarded the U.S.S. *Houston* and sailed from San Diego later that day, with Eleanor, Missy, and Grace Tully waving from the pier. This ship was now accustomed to the President's requirements. Some brawny seamen were detailed to lift him "as if he were a monstrous infant,"[7] into and out of his fishing launch. There were ramps for his wheelchair, and he used the admiral's bedroom and his sitting room, which was adapted to serve as lounge and dining room for the presidential party. There was a special assignment of a sailor who was an authority on deep-sea fishing. Roosevelt manipulated his fishing rod and reel skillfully, and his massive arms, chest, and shoulders, built up over a decade's exercise to overcome polio, served him well. For such an athletic man prior to the onset of his illness, this was a sport at which he could still excel and relive some of the sporting pleasures of the era before tragedy struck at Campobello in 1921.

Although entrusting himself like a parcel to the hands of others could be dangerous, he showed no concern or even awareness that it was unusual for the holder of his position to be transported in this way. "He commonly talked a steady stream while being carried; he laughed, he joked with those who carried him. . . . Through a marvelous alchemy of character and personality, which included his constant patient good cheer, his joyous openness to experience, his seeming total lack of self-consciousness or sense of embarrassment, he managed to transform personal helplessness into personal power, passive submission into effortless domination. . . . What could have been pity tinged with contempt became an admiration wholly respectful . . . a series of humiliations became for him a series of triumphs."[8]

The *Houston* sailed south past Baja California toward the Panama Canal as Mussolini finally launched his long-threatened invasion of Abyssinia. Robust consideration was given on the *Houston* to how broad an interpretation could be given to the Neutrality Act. Because the United States produced approximately half the world's oil and was a large producer of almost all strategic materials, of most of which Italy was an importer, Roosevelt was minded to over-achieve for the benefit of the pacifists like Senator Nye and define oil, copper, steel, scrap iron, and even cotton as "implements of war," in the parlance of the Neutrality Act.

At the last cabinet meeting before the President left Washington the cautious but righteous Cordell Hull had suggested this, and the concept recurred in the heavily coded signal traffic between Washington and the *Houston*. Roosevelt doubted that he could legally enforce such an interpretation, since American industry was struggling out of depression and eager for export orders at war-inflated prices.

Roosevelt came up with the very questionable notion of "moral embargo," under which there would be voluntary rejection of Italian purchase orders. The President, hardly one to underestimate the avarice and cupidity of American businessmen, could not have believed this idea had any chance of success. He was presumably maneuvering for more flexibility, as he had already asked in the Neutrality Act debate. He would also be demonstrating the unworkability of the existing arrangements and helping to give names and faces to the "war profiteers" he had been haranguing audiences about for several years. He rejected Hopkins's and Ickes' urgings that he return at once to Washington.

Considerable temporary progress was made in Roosevelt's greatest ambition for the trip as Hopkins and Ickes enjoyed a distinct warming of relations. Separated from the official responsibilities that so often brought them into conflicts of budget and jurisdiction, they were able to appreciate each other as capable and entertaining personalities.*

The *Houston* passed Cocos Island, where the original Robinson Crusoe was stranded, as the League of Nations branded Italy the aggressor and began to debate sanctions. Roosevelt caught 109- and 134-pound sailfish, the larger requiring two hours and twenty minutes to reel in. The League was considering asking non-member states for cooperation with the sanctions. Roosevelt approved Hull's asking the League not to request this of the United States because it was legally impossible to comply.

The *Houston* returned via the Panama Canal and the South Atlantic to

---

* Despite this, Ickes would arrange to be called by friendly senators to a committee hearing in May 1936 to give a rather bowdlerized comparative review of the efficiency of his and Hopkins's programs. Roosevelt got wind of this and forbade, at the May 14 cabinet meeting, any provision of statistics to Congress without his express approval. Ickes reacted in his traditional way, writing the President that the PWA had been repudiated and effectively ended, that he no longer had Roosevelt's confidence, and that therefore he must resign. In a handwritten "Dear Old Harold," in point form, Roosevelt rejected the resignation, to Ickes' undoubted relief.[9] Ickes also pursuaded Farley to try to prevent Hopkins from making political speeches until after the 1936 election. Hopkins mentioned this to Roosevelt, who then took Hopkins with him on a tour of the Midwest during which Hopkins spoke often.

Charleston, South Carolina, on October 22, and anchored near Fort Sumter. Roosevelt spoke at the Citadel, the West Point of the South, and then entrained for Washington. The cruise had fully restored his stamina and good spirits. The dark half-moons under his eyes had gone; he was tanned and fit.

As had been anticipated, the "moral embargo" was a fiasco, and no less so after Roosevelt issued a statement October 30 urging the rightful course on his countrymen. The shipments of oil, steel, scrap metal, and copper from the United States to Italy in October 1935 were in each case more than twice the shipments of October 1934. On November 6 the League voted to extend sanctions to oil. Everyone knew that this would be the litmus test of the League of Nations. If the League could not have any impact on Italy, it was unlikely to impose any restraint on a busily rearming Germany or a rampaging Japan.

The unsteady pace of the Italian advance against the primitive and undisciplined Abyssinians confirmed Roosevelt in his low opinion of Italian military capabilities, which dated from his visit to the Italian fleet in 1918. Roosevelt detested Fascism and ardently wanted the attempted conquest to fail, but his entire party, directly and through Farley, was beseeching him to give no comfort to his opponents. They begged the President not to convey the impression that U.S. foreign policy was influenced at all by Geneva or London. Shipments of oil and strategic minerals to Italy increased by the end of 1935 to triple their year-earlier levels. For the first time in seventeen years there was some slight war profiteering in the U.S.

Winston Churchill later wrote: "If ever there was an opportunity to strike a decisive blow in a generous cause with a minimum of risk it was here and now." He too regarded Mussolini as a strutting buffoon who could be brought to heel in a few days by any of the serious powers. American opinion deplored the Italian action but clung to the view that it wasn't America's business. Evil occurred in the world, which was what most of the people in the United States, or their ancestors, had come to the New World to escape. They did not want to be reunited with the world they had left behind for the sake of a Stone Age African despotism, heroic though the Ethiopian (Abyssinian) Emperor Haile Selassie and his countrymen appeared in 1935 and 1936.

Some polling indicated at the end of 1935 that almost half of Americans were in favor of cooperating with the League in sanctions against Italy. Roosevelt knew that the invasion of Abyssinia was, like the outrages of the Japanese in Manchuria, only the sighting shot in the great aggression that was being prepared, that the League of Nations was not a credible organizer of resistance, and that there was no point leading American opinion to a resolute position before the British and French, in particular, had arrived at the same point.

His technique was to assure that no domestic political rival became more credible than he at promising to keep the nation out of war, while maneuvering to achieve greater flexibility to deliver substantial assistance short of war to the powers resisting aggression. It was also his intention, undisclosed but suspected by his enemies, at the right moment and if absolutely necessary to deliver American strength in whatever quantities were necessary to assure the victory of good over evil. Roosevelt did not doubt that any contest involving the Nazis could be so described.

And he didn't want to squander his political capital and the country's unity of opinion or strategic resources on any cause less urgent than the repulse and destruction of Nazism and, to a lesser degree, virulent Japanese imperialism. Though brutal, Mussolini was a sideshow, and an increasingly absurd one at that.

At the end of November 1935, the French and British conveniently validated his caution, double-crossed the outmatched but earnest forces of collective security, and put Abyssinia over the side. The French premier, Pierre Laval, a Fascist sympathizer, and the British foreign secretary, Sir Samuel Hoare, agreed on a plan for acquiescing in the handing over of most of Abyssinia to Italy. Churchill may have been right that stopping Italy might have put a brake on Hitler, but the United States couldn't do it without the British and the French.

The strategic justification for this astonishing capitulation, the Hoare-Laval Pact, was that this would bring Italy into alliance with Britain and France in a defensive ring to contain a resurgent Germany. It was an insane as well as a cowardly move. Public opinion revolted in both countries; Hoare was forced to resign and was replaced by the anti-Fascist Anthony Eden, and Laval's ministry was defeated in parliament and replaced the following month. Italy, which would never have sided against Hitler for long and was of minimal military value anyway, was antagonized by these defections and became more susceptible than ever to Hitler's blandishments.

While this disgraceful charade was convenient to Roosevelt in that it spared him appearing the undercutting force in collective sanctions, it produced such a wave of revulsion against the League and its supporters and against the British and French that the isolationists were more ascendant in the United States than ever. The sentiment in the United States was that if this was the best the forces of collective security could do, it was better to be completely aloof from them and to build "Fortress America" if necessary.

Roosevelt's own ambassador to Italy, Breckinridge Long, was a conservative Marylander who had been an admirer of Mussolini. He was an old loyalist of Roosevelt's, whom the President appreciated for that and for his status as a landed gentleman, but whose political views were incompatible with the President's in several important respects. Long informed Roosevelt in a letter of September 6, 1935, that the Italians were a great threat to the British Empire because "the high state of fanaticism to which they have been worked renders them a very dangerous people."[8] On June 23, 1936, he wrote the President that the Italian conquest of Abyssinia should be recognized, in order to maximize trade with Italy.[10] Roosevelt had already determined to replace Long with his World War I friend and seasoned career diplomat William Phillips, whose views were closer to Dodd's in Berlin. Long also had very esoteric moments, as when he advised Roosevelt at length of a possible return of the Bourbon monarchy in France.[11] "Interesting even though there may not be anything in it," wrote Roosevelt to Hull.[12] (Unfortunately, Long was recalled to the State Department in 1940 as assistant secretary, where he exercised a truly baneful influence over refugee matters [Chapter 14].)

In his annual message of January 3, 1936, Roosevelt warned of growing dangers and cautioned his countrymen and others in the Americas to be prepared to avoid involvement in what appeared to be a slide toward war. As American companies eagerly filled Italian orders, he urged withholding armaments and munitions altogether in the event of an overseas war, and freezing the export of resources and material useful to the prosecution of war at their peacetime levels. As the Neutrality Act expired, Roosevelt got the Foreign Affairs Committee chairman, Senator Key Pittman, to propose a measure that would allow the President discretion to maintain or end exports to belligerents of the commodities Italy had been so eagerly buying.

Senator Gerald Nye countered with a bill making the abolition of such sales to warring powers obligatory. Both bills retained the mandatory wartime suspension of arms and munitions sales. The skirmishing between promoters of the two versions became fierce. Hiram Johnson of California did not want his oil-producing state shackled unfairly; neutrality was fine as long as it didn't cost anything. William E. Borah of Idaho declared, "Neutrality is not synonymous with cowardice," and wanted to continue trading indiscriminately. The immaturity and self-serving hypocrisy of much of what should have been informed American foreign policy opinion, as the war clouds gathered across the seas, did not give President Roosevelt good clay from which to fashion an effective policy. The shambles of the League of Nations controversy in 1919 and the tragedy of Wilson's preferring rejection to compromise had left the people with no precedent to work from, prey to demagogues and posturers of every kind. Roosevelt concluded, as his and Nye's bills competed, that the best he could do was extend the existing law for one year, and this was done.

At the end of February, France ratified the Franco-Soviet mutual-defense pact, which didn't obligate the parties to much but at least reintroduced Russia into the official European equation. Hitler seized upon the pact as a pretext to reoccupy the Rhineland. This was a violation of the Versailles Treaty but also of the Locarno Pact of 1925, under which the Belgians and the French withdrew from the Rhineland and Germany promised to leave it demilitarized. Great Britain and Italy were guarantors of the arrangement. Hitler dispatched only three battalions into the area and falsely claimed that the arrangement between France and the Soviet Union had vitiated the Locarno Pact.

Roosevelt wrote to Margaret Suckley,[13] "The tragedy—deepest part of it—is

Franklin Delano Roosevelt, aged one, on the shoulder of his father, Mr. James, in 1883.

Franklin, aged 5, in a Little Lord Fauntleroy kilt, with his mother, Sara Delano Roosevelt, in 1887.

Franklin, aged 14, photographed by his mother in 1896 in St. Blasien, Germany. On this trip she took him to Wagner's *Ring* cycle at Bayreuth, which fueled his suspicion of German militarism and racial arrogance.

Franklin with his parents in 1899, aged 17.

FDR in 1903, aged 21, a startlingly impressive-looking young man.

FDR's mother and his fiancée, 1904. The marriage created a precarious balance of personalities between the two strong-minded women, with Franklin leaning now toward one, now the other. Note Sara's powerful jaw, which her son inherited and which Jean-Paul Sartre found "alarming" when he met FDR in 1945.

Franklin and Eleanor two months after their marriage, May 1905, at the Hudson valley home of the Delanos, Algonac.

Franklin (wearing TR-style pince nez) in his
first campaign, for the New York State Senate,
in 1910, aged 28, accompanied by Eleanor.

FDR with his cousin
Theodore, the statesman
he admired most, May 4,
1915 (left) and lawyer W.R.
Van Benschoten (center)
during TR's defamation
lawsuit in Syracuse. FDR's
evidence was very helpful
in securing judgment for
TR, and repaid some of the
ex-president's many kind-
nesses to him.

Flag Day. June 14, 1913. From left, Secretary of State and
three-time presidential candidate William Jennings Bryan,
President Woodrow Wilson, and on the right FDR, 31, assistant secretary of the navy, listen to Navy Secretary Josephus
Daniels. Roosevelt thought Bryan a yokel and a demagogue.

President Wilson and Assistant Secretary Roosevelt in a relaxed moment, 1915. Their relations were rarely so convivial.

Tammany Hall boss Charles F. Murphy with FDR, July 4, 1917. FDR had come to Tammany to make peace, but Murphy still told the 1920 Democratic presidential candidate, James M. Cox, when Cox said FDR was his choice for vice president: "The young Roosevelt's no good."

Eleanor's first cousin and Franklin's fifth cousin, Theodore Roosevelt's daughter Alice, c. 1907. Maid of honor at Eleanor and Franklin's wedding, she would nettle the Hyde Park Roosevelts with WASPish wit and indiscretions almost all their lives.

The Democratic nominees of 1920: FDR with Governor James M. Cox of Ohio, August 7. The race was hopeless but Roosevelt built a countrywide political network and called the campaign "a damn fine sail."

One of the most dramatic moments of his life; Roosevelt prepares to return to public life by hobbling to the microphone as 20,000 people silently watch, to nominate Alfred E. Smith for president, June 26, 1924, Madison Square Garden.

With the Democratic candidates for president of 1924 and 1928, John W. Davis and Alfred E. Smith, at Hyde Park, August 7, 1924. Roosevelt's nomination of Smith in June of that year reestablished FDR as the second most important Democrat in New York, after Smith himself.

Roosevelt in 1925, fishing from a canoe at Warm Springs, Georgia, where he went for the thermal waters and bought and developed a polio treatment center. This and the next picture show his atrophied leg muscles. Here, exceptionally, his leg braces are outside his trousers.

At the pool in Warm Springs in 1925. Already his upper arms and torso, compensating for his withered legs, are greatly expanded compared with the photograph of him nine months before at the Democratic Convention.

On horseback with future Democratic Party chairman Edward J. Flynn. This was extremely dangerous, since any movement by the horse could throw Roosevelt to the ground; he had no grip in his legs and was just perched on the saddle.

Roosevelt in 1931 with the flamboyant but corrupt mayor of New York James J. Walker, one of the great personalities of the Roaring Twenties. Roosevelt forced Walker out of office in 1932 and joined with reform Republican mayor Fiorello La Guardia to crush Tammany Hall in 1934.

Roosevelt in general session court in New York, April 29, 1932, defending his superintendent of banking, Joseph A. Broderick, who had been attacked by Tammany. Roosevelt ruthlessly discarded those who were no longer useful, but fiercely protected those who were loyal to him.

Franklin and Eleanor Roosevelt moving awkwardly on a snowy surface, as they leave a church service in Albany six days after his inauguration as governor of New York, January 6, 1929. Roosevelt had to swing each leg, attached to fixed braces, forward from the hip in an exhausting and laborious process. It was like walking on stilts.

Presidential nominee FDR establishes a precedent by flying to Chicago to address the convention, July 2, 1932. Behind him in the car, his indispensable organizers, James A. Farley (top) and Louis McHenry Howe. Howe had written a speech for Roosevelt, which he holds here. Roosevelt read it on his way downtown, while waving to dense crowds, and used one page of it in the introduction to his already prepared speech, which promised "a New Deal for the American people."

FDR campaigns for president in Seattle, September 20, 1932, in a flower-bedecked automobile.

Humorist Will Rogers introduces FDR to 120,000 people at the Los Angeles Olympic Coliseum, September 24, 1932. From the left, FDR, Jimmy Roosevelt (a future candidate for governor of California), Senator and former Treasury secretary and Woodrow Wilson's son-in-law, William Gibbs McAdoo, James A. Farley, and Will Rogers.

Election night, November 8, 1932. "They were the worst of times but he would be president at last." FDR reads President Hoover's telegram of concession to an unenthused Eleanor and their son James (left).

The President-elect arrives at Jackson Memorial Hospital in Miami to visit Chicago's fatally wounded mayor, Anton Cermak, and others shot by anarchist Guiseppe Zangara in an assassination attempt on Roosevelt. FDR had a full night's sleep and never mentioned the incident again.

President Hoover joins the President-elect for the short ride from the White House to the Capitol for Roosevelt's inauguration, March 4, 1933. They scarcely spoke. In a grim reminder of the Depression, there were soldiers and machine gun nests at the entrances to the major federal buildings, for the first time since the Civil War.

Nancy Cook and Eleanor Roosevelt at the furniture workshop they built and operated at Hyde Park (Val-Kill) in 1933. The emblem of adherence to the National Recovery Administration, the core of the New Deal, the Blue Eagle, is on the door.

Ford designed cars for the President with hand-controlled brakes and accelerators. FDR is at the wheel and FDR Jr. beside him. Harry Hopkins and Missy LeHand are in the back seat. Standing from left, the President's assistant, Bill Hassett, Jim Farley, Eleanor, and the financier Bernard Baruch.

The President inspects the Civilian Conservation Corps camp at Big Meadows in the Shenandoah Valley of Virginia, August 12, 1933. From left to right at the table: General Paul Malone; Louis Howe; Interior Secretary Ickes; CCC director Robert Fechner; FDR; Agriculture Secretary Wallace; and his under secretary Rexford Tugwell.

Reviewing the fleet from under one of the main turrets of the U.S.S. *Indianapolis*, New York, May 31, 1934. From left, Labor Secretary Frances Perkins; party chairman James Farley; Navy Secretary Claude Swanson; James Cox; FDR; Secretary of State Cordell Hull.

Eleanor and Franklin on the south lawn of the ancestral home, Springwood, Hyde Park, August 16, 1933. The Hudson River is in the distant background.

The Roosevelts' twenty-ninth wedding anniversary, March 17, 1934; a hug for Eleanor as she returns from Puerto Rico and the Virgin Islands.

The Cufflinks Club was devised after the 1920 vice presidential campaign and met each January 30, on FDR's birthday. Here, in 1934, with a Roman theme, FDR was Caesar, surrounded by "vestal virgins": standing, from the left, Nancy Cook, ER, Marion Dickerman, and ER's secretary, Malvina "Tommy" Thompson. Kneeling, from the left, are secretaries Grace Tully, Missy LeHand, and Margaret "Rabbit" Durand. In the center sits FDR, supposedly ravishing his daughter, Anna.

FDR expertly carved the turkey for the handicapped children at Warm Springs every Thanksgiving from 1926 to 1940.

Relations with General Douglas MacArthur, whom Roosevelt respected as a soldier but regarded as a dangerous political novice, were not always so cordial as this (with Secretary of War George Dern).

Louisiana's governor and senator, Huey P. Long, "the Kingfish." Long was an initial supporter of Roosevelt's but became a bitter and worrisome opponent. His "Share the Wealth" movement was a considerable distraction and his assassination, in September 1935, was not inconvenient to the president.

The Canadian-born radio priest Father Charles E. Coughlin was another Roosevelt supporter who became a vituperative opponent. The Vatican's Secretary of State, Eugenio Cardinel Pacelli, subsequently Pope Pius XII, spent almost the entire 1936 presidential election campaign in the United States and apparently censored Coughlin, whose radio following diminished.

John L. Lewis, leader of the United Mine Workers for forty years, began as a Hoover Republican, became an ardent Roosevelt supporter, and finally became, in Roosevelt's view, more trouble than he was worth.

A powerful and vocal opponent of Roosevelt's throughout almost his entire administration, especially as a spokesman for the isolationists before and after the onset of World War II, was aviator Charles A. Lindbergh, seen here arriving in Germany on October 18, 1937. Roosevelt tarred Lindbergh with the brush of being a Nazi sympathizer and completely outmaneuvered him.

Joseph P. Kennedy, a bad appointment as ambassador to the United Kingdom, is sworn in by Supreme Court Justice Stanley Reed, in 1938.

A grim President and Mrs. Roosevelt and FDR Jr. at the funeral of Louis McHenry Howe, April 22, 1936. FDR asked that the words "Devoted friend, adviser and associate of the President" be put on Howe's gravestone. Howe's widow agreed, but it was not done.

Roosevelt accepts renomination at Franklin Field in Philadelphia, June 27, 1936, before 100,000 people. While approaching the podium, FDR turned to shake hands with the 84-year old poet Edwin Markham, a brace slipped, and he fell down. This was unseen by the public, and his security unit quickly had him back on his feet. Still sorting the scattered pages of his text as he began, he gave one of his greatest speeches, predicting a "Rendezvous with destiny" for the American people.

Roosevelt in his custom-designed Ford, August 27, 1938, at Hyde Park. In the back seat is New York Congresswoman Caroline O'Day; on the running board, New York mayor Fiorello La Guardia; standing (left) Mrs. La Guardia and ER.

FDR in a characteristic pose, cigarette holder at a rakish angle, 1938.

FDR in relaxed mood aboard the presidential yacht *Potomac*, 1937.

Felix Frankfurter (right) at his confirmation hearings as a Supreme Court justice with his personal counsel, Dean Acheson, future secretary of state, with whom Roosevelt had a wary and sometimes abrasive relationship, January 12, 1939.

Large crowds greeted the British king and queen (the queen and ER were in the following car) in Washington and New York. This is Washington, June 8, 1939.

Roosevelt in a rare photograph of him in a wheelchair at Top Cottage, which he designed himself, all on one level. With him are Ruthie Bie, 5, granddaughter of the caretaker at the cottage, and FDR's Scottie, Fala, a gift from his cousin Margaret Suckley, named after a distant Scottish ancestor, February 1941.

that [Germany's] words and signatures are no longer good. If France had a leader whom the people would follow their only course would be to occupy all Germany quickly up to the Rhine—no further. They can do it today—in another year or two Germany will be stronger than they are—and the world can not trust a fully rearmed Germany to stay at peace." Instead, and as Roosevelt feared, in a pattern that was already familiar, France asked Britain for moral support and Britain havered and wobbled. Italy, the other Locarno guarantor, was mired in the bowels of Africa and was in no position to issue warnings to the Germans, who would have ignored them in any case.

Hitler told the Reichstag that he was repossessing German territory to strengthen the country against possible threats from the east. He swore that he had no grievance with Germany's neighbors in the west and implied that he would be their bulwark against the Red menace. "We have no territorial demands to make in Europe! . . . Germany will never break the peace!" he assured the Reichstag and the world. As he had gambled, the Western powers knew they could not really object to Germany's exercising sovereignty over its own territory unless they abandoned all hope that the Nazi regime could be integrated into the community of responsible nations.

This was what distinguished Roosevelt from the temporizers and appeasers in London and Paris and other capitals of democratic states: he had known from the start that Hitler was a compulsive war-maker and a pathological liar and that no durable accommodation could ever be made with him. The ineffectuality of the tepid, verbal Anglo-French response not only strengthened Hitler against his domestic opponents who wanted a more conciliatory foreign policy and enabled him to repossess the region that provided Germany the sinews of war. It confirmed Hitler in his contemptuous view of the Western leaders and incited him to bolder aggressions. All of this was generally foreseen by Roosevelt.

Haile Selassie appeared in person at the League of Nations on June 30. He was disgracefully heckled by Italian and German delegates but persevered with unforgettable dignity. He said: "If a strong government finds that it can with impunity destroy a weak people then the hour has struck for . . . the League of Nations to give its answer in all freedom. God and history will remember your decision. What answer am I to take back to my people?" The answer from the great Western European democracies was the withdrawal of sanctions against Italy and the servile acceptance of Italy's conquest of Abyssinia, which Mussolini's ill-assured armies had finally accomplished. (Italy never did exercise any authority over most of Abyssinia, even after it had occupied the country's cities.)

Again, in one sense, Italy was just doing what the British and French had done for centuries and colonized a country, and Haile Selassie's regime was not as enlightened as his courageous eloquence at Geneva would suggest. But Abyssinia, on Italy's motion, had been a member of the League of Nations, and Italy had deliberately represented its action in that country as a full-fledged military operation and not a colonizing mission. The bloodthirsty zeal with which the Italians celebrated their advantages over this helpless adversary was disgusting. Mussolini's son Vittorio, an aviator, described the bombs he dropped on masses of poorly armed Abyssinian defenders as "red roses" as they burst, and said he had found the incendiary bombing of the Abyssinians "exceptionally good fun."

This did not deter James Michael Curley, Massachusetts governor and frequent Boston mayor, from praising Mussolini at a large meeting in Faneuil Hall as a "defender of peace and Christianity."[14] At about the same time, a much larger crowd led by the much more esteemed Fiorello La Guardia and Al Smith filled Madison Square Garden and judged Hitler guilty of crimes against civilization. African- and Italian-Americans, identifying with different sides in the Abyssinian War, scuffled in large cities, especially at the time of the great black prizefighter Joe Louis's victory over the Italian champion fighter Primo Carnera. And American Jews and their sympathizers became increasingly more alarmed by Hitler's anti-Semitism and strident militarism.

None of these ethnically motivated groups was particularly representative, but the United States, partly because of its complex sociology, had a more fissiparous public opinion than any other important country, and Roosevelt had to organize the consensus that he sought with great care.

The tragic fate of Abyssinia had been sealed for only a couple of weeks when the next eruption occurred, much closer to the home fires of both the aggressors and the appeasers. A revolt of military officers against the newly elected popular-front left-wing government of Spain began in Spanish Morocco July 17, 1936, and spread to the mainland of Spain the next day. A long and horrible civil war, in which a million people would die and almost the entire country would be laid waste, now began. Italy and Germany immediately pledged and began delivering support to the Fascist military rebels (Nationalists) led by General Francisco Franco. Britain declared a policy of complete nonintervention and bullied France, now itself governed by a left-of-center government since the Laval fiasco six months before, into accepting that posture. Germany and Italy purported to agree with the Anglo-French embargo, blockade, and imposition of neutrality, while pouring in aid to Franco and using Spain as an experimental bomber testing area for the German Air Force.

This was the now customary European expedient: The British and French would adopt unctuous and pious positions of principle rather than help a wronged party. The Germans and Italians would purport to share in the fine Anglo-French goals but would make a Swiss cheese out of the embargo they were claiming to help enforce. It was cowardly and treacherous, and made more odious by the affectation of moral high-mindedness.

Roosevelt knew that he would never be able to help or work with such weaklings in any attempted containment of Hitler, so his problem was how to manage the Spanish crisis toward an enhanced foreign policy-making authority for himself. This problem was complicated for Roosevelt by the fact that the Neutrality Act was silent on the subject of civil wars, and by the approaching presidential election. The Spanish Civil War broke out less than a month after Roosevelt's renomination to a second term as president. Rather than run the embargo that the British navy loosely set up around the Iberian peninsula and that the French more or less maintained in the Pyrenees, Roosevelt fell in with the British policy of total nonintervention.

He was not an automatic partisan in a contest between Fascists and Communists, but did identify with the social democratic element of the Republicans (Franco's opponents). Roosevelt allegedly told the Spanish Republican ambassador in Washington, Fernando di los Rios, in the summer of 1936, that he hoped that if Franco was victorious he would "establish a liberal regime."[15] He maintained his ambassador in Madrid, accredited to the Republican government, but when that government asked to buy eight warplanes from the Martin Company, the U.S. administration gently declined to allow the transaction. (The ambassador, the irrepressible historian and editor, Claude Bowers, predicted easy victory for the Republicans if they weren't overwhelmed by German and Italian intervention.)

There was no American national interest in the Spanish conflict, and the U.S.S.R. and Mexico could supply the Republicans if they were prepared to run the blockade, which the British were unlikely to enforce any more bravely against the Soviet Union than against Germany and Italy. If France, now governed by the democratic left, which could easily have assured a Republican victory, was not prepared to do anything, it was asking a lot of the United States to act. To Hitler, the antics of the British and French were yet another confirmation of their contemptible cowardice and naïveté.

Other than in its incitement of Hitler to further aggression, which he would almost certainly have committed anyway, allowing Franco's rebels to win the Spanish Civil War was probably the correct strategic decision for the West, though arrived at accidentally. Franco resisted Hitler's enticements in World War II and maintained a genuine neutrality, unlike the pseudo-neutrality of the Great Powers during the Spanish War. And Franco was very useful in the post-war contest with Soviet Communism. Franco was an unenlightened and repressive Fascist, but he did produce a reasonable level of economic growth, effected a skillful reestablishment of the monarchy, and provided for the posthumous establishment of a well-functioning democracy. He also had a much better record at receiving Jewish fugitives from Nazi oppression than the so-called great Western democracies, including Roosevelt's America.

III

LOUIS MCHENRY HOWE died on April 18, 1936, at Bethesda Naval Hospital in Washington, where he had been since August 1935, when he became too ill to remain in the White House. He was sixty-four and died peacefully in his sleep shortly before midnight while the leader to whose success he had been so indispensable gave an amusing address to the annual Gridiron dinner offered and attended by the White House press corps. Roosevelt had visited his old and intimate friend that day and assured him that, although Howe would not be well enough to attend the convention, he would be consulted on all matters of importance. Howe had wistfully told a recent visitor:* "Franklin is on his own now." The President had visited frequently and Eleanor almost every day. In his last weeks there were intermittent bouts of near-delirium when he would telephone officials and issue preposterous orders in the name of the President. Roosevelt decreed that all such orders should be solicitously received and that only he could revoke them.[16] His death, though long expected, was a heavy blow both to the President and to Mrs. Roosevelt. He had helped them through so many personal and public crises; his devotion was so selfless and unwavering and his judgment so unerring, he was irreplaceable.

Eleanor wrote many years later and after her husband's death: "For one reason and another no one quite filled the void [created by Howe's death], and each one in turn disappeared from the scene, occasionally with a bitterness which I understood but always regretted. There are not many men in this world whose personal ambition is to accomplish things for someone else, and it was some time before a friendship with Harry Hopkins, somewhat different but similar in certain ways, again brought Franklin some of the satisfaction he had known with Louis Howe."[17]

Roosevelt decreed a state funeral in the East Room of the White House, April 21. Flags were lowered on all U.S. government buildings, and a funeral train with President and Mrs. Roosevelt and a large delegation of the administration's highest officials bore Louis Howe's coffin back to Fall River, Massachusetts, for burial. The President stood grimly and thoughtfully for some time at the graveside after the casket was lowered. The *New York Times* correspondent reported that the President "appeared oblivious to everything around him, both during the service and when he returned to his car." Roosevelt asked that Howe's gravestone carry the words "Devoted friend, adviser, and associate of the President." This was agreed to by Howe's widow but did not happen.[18]

Roosevelt had followed Howe's advice when he opened the year with a "fighting" State of the Union speech that was really a campaign address delivered to an astonished but appreciative Congress on January 3, 1936. It was as if Huey Long had not died. Roosevelt declared: "We have earned the hatred of entrenched greed. . . . They seek the restoration of their selfish power. They steal the livery of great national constitutional ideals to serve discredited special interests. . . . The principle that they would instill into government if they succeed in seizing power is well shown by the principles which many of them have instilled into their own affairs: autocracy toward labor, toward stockholders, toward consumers, toward public sentiment. . . . Give them their way and they will take the course of every autocracy of the past—power for themselves, enslavement for the public."

* Fannie Hurst

This was an unprecedentedly partisan message to deliver to the Congress on a traditional occasion, but it was apparently well received by the public, many millions of whom heard it on the radio. It is not absolutely clear what Roosevelt's motive was for such a vituperative outburst, which was sustained throughout the coming campaign. With Long dead there was no particular threat to the President, either from the fringes or from the Republicans. He was certainly miffed that big-business enthusiasm for his administration was not greater, but this was an unlikely cure for that problem.

But it seems that his objective in this provocative outburst was the creation of an imaginary, unnamed (and largely inexistent) scapegoat. He would focus public anger on these imprecise sinister groups as the enemies of progress and those responsible for the incompleteness of the recovery. It continued to be his practice to make outrageous comments of this kind against conjured infestations of opposition but almost never to mention individuals, other than in good-natured ridicule of partisan opponents. In concentrating public anger against unspecified people he served the country as well as himself. In most other advanced countries at this time political leaders showed less restraint, and the name-calling created long-term bitterness and profound fissures in society. Elements of the business community were durably offended by Roosevelt's demagogy, but no one was stigmatized by name and he carried a heavy majority of the public with him.

Three days later, January 6, 1936, the administration's strongest visible opponent, the Supreme Court of the United States, struck again, declaring the pillar of the New Deal's agricultural recovery policy, the Agricultural Adjustment Administration, to be unconstitutional. The judgment was six to three and was not rendered by the chief justice. There were a number of questionable political and business relationships involved in this case. The plaintiff was William M. Butler, former campaign manager for Calvin Coolidge and Republican Party chairman. He was an associate of Frederick H. Prince, one of the nation's greatest financiers and a substantial shareholder in the largest meatpacking businesses, Swift and Armour. It is not improbable that Prince helped Butler with the case, hoping to be rid of the AAA processing tax that was designed to cover the benefit payments that compensated farmers for unused acreage.

Butler's lawyer, George Wharton Pepper, a former Republican senator, was an intimate and almost lifelong friend of Supreme Court Justice Owen Roberts, and had persuaded Coolidge to name Roberts to the bench. Roberts gave the majority opinion, which held that the processing tax was not within the Congress's taxing powers, but was more accurately a regulatory instrument for overwhelming the rights of states to regulate agricultural production. The administration case, argued by Solicitor General Stanley Reed, and the minority of the court, held that it was a simple case of taxation. In his minority dissent, Justice Harlan Fiske Stone commended to Justice Roberts and the majority the possibility that the constitution may "mean what it says: that the power to tax and spend includes the power to relieve a nationwide economic maladjustment by conditional gifts of money." In the circumstances, Roberts should have recused himself.

On February 17, the Supreme Court appeared to uphold the Tennessee Valley Authority, but on a very narrow issue involving the sale of electricity from one dam to the complainant customer. But the Court struck down the Bituminous Coal Conservation Act, which John L. Lewis had written and Roosevelt had forced through nine months before, having written a letter to the Congress urging its passage regardless of constitutional concerns. The Court determined that the wages-and-hours section of the statute was ultra vires to the federal government and struck down the entire statute, even though the labor sections had not yet been drafted precisely and only the price stabilization clauses of the act were in force and their constitutionality was not under attack.

Lewis darkly reflected: "It is a tragic and ominous commentary on our form of government when every decision of the Supreme Court seems designed to fatten capital and starve and destroy labor." On June 1, the Supreme Court lurched further, and declared unconstitutional a New York State minimum wage law for women passed shortly after Franklin Roosevelt had gone to the White House. The law, which at Roosevelt's suggestion had been widely emulated by other states, was deemed to violate requirements for due process.

On advice from Frankfurter and others, Roosevelt had responded with restraint to the Supreme Court's rejection of the NRA, and determined to await events and see if the Court aroused public opinion. Roosevelt had tested the waters, particularly in an article in *Collier's* in the summer of 1935 written by George Creel with the President's anonymous collaboration. He had composed a paragraph that Creel integrated into "his" story envisioning a possible constitutional adjustment of the Supreme Court's position. There had been no response at all. This latest raft of Court interventions, including a state case from a bench that regularly demanded devolution of activity to the states, was apt to raise considerable public concern about an overactive bench usurping legislative and executive functions.

At his press conference of June 2, 1936, Roosevelt dodged a question about the necessity of constitutional change, but urged all Americans to read some of the recent opinions. He said they made it clear that there was a "no-man's land [created by] the present majority of the Court" where government could no longer function. He declined to speculate on what might be done to resolve the problem.

The 1936 session of the Congress was by far the most uneventful since the dreary days of Herbert Hoover. It was largely concerned with replacement of Court-stricken New Deal legislation. The Soil Conservation and Domestic Allotment Act preserved the main purposes of the AAA but dispensed with the processing tax, which had brought it to grief. The new version was much better and less controversially drafted, and passed without difficulty.

Unfortunately, the tax bill that accompanied it to replace the processing tax was much less lucidly composed. Roosevelt was at his imperious, crypto-socialistic worst, in manner reminiscent of Frances Perkins's recollections of his haughtiness twenty-five years before in the New York legislature. The device, on Marriner Eccles's suggestion, that he produced for recovering substitute revenue was a tax on undistributed surplus in corporations.

Roosevelt might have imagined this tax as preferable to many alternatives, socially and otherwise. However, Roosevelt showed no awareness of the fact that it was double taxation. He proposed to tax money in the treasuries of companies that had accumulated as the result of profits on which full taxation had already been paid. Roosevelt couched all this in terms of corporations willfully withholding money from shareholders, as if the corporation had no right to retain any profit and add to its shareholders' equity as a basis upon which to build the business.

He theatrically claimed that billions would "be withheld from stockholders by those in control of those corporations." His performance would have been less irritating if he hadn't masqueraded as a Robin Hood liberating the shareholders' money from the clutches of the avaricious corporate leaders who had gathered the profit in the corporate treasuries. Because personal tax rates were substantially higher than corporate rates, he wanted this money pried loose only so that it could be taxed at full personal rates in the hands of dividend recipients. If he had had any concerns about shareholders' rights and had had any legitimate grievance with the corporate leadership, he would have proposed that tax burdens be reduced on individuals and transferred to corporations. With the addition of some temporary taxes and the softening of objectionable aspects, including the rate of double taxation, the bill was enacted. It was a shabby but minor bit of Huey Long-style grandstanding.

Roosevelt half-heartedly vetoed the perennial veterans' bonus acceleration, this year to be paid in interest-bearing bonds rather than currency. The President did not appear in person to present the veto or fight for it to be upheld. His veto message was a handwritten suggestion that the senators and congressmen read what he had said on the subject the previous year. He knew, in this election year, that his veto would be overridden, and it was. He had made his gesture for fiscal restraint.

The Republican National Convention opened in Cleveland on June 10, 1936. The certain nominee was the governor of Kansas, Alfred M. Landon. He had defeated an incumbent Democrat, Harry Woodring, in 1932, an astonishing feat in a landslide Democratic year, though one altogether due to the vote-splitting of a cranky radio doctor and quack-medicine advocate, John Brinkley. The vote had been 279,000 for Landon, 273,000 for Woodring, and 247,000 for Brinkley. Landon had governed with thoughtfulness and distinction but no great originality, and had been reelected in 1934—another remarkable achievement, since the only other Republican governor in the country to be reelected was the special (in effect, fusion) candidate Governor Frank Merriam of California, who defeated Upton Sinclair.

Landon had made a small fortune in the oil business, had been a Theodore Roosevelt supporter in 1912, and, with Kansas's leading editor, William Allen White, had deserted the Kansas Republicans in 1924 in protest against the prominence in the party of the Ku Klux Klan. He was a sincere and courageous champion of civil liberties, who, demonstrating his attachment to the principle of free speech, graciously introduced Socialist Party leader Norman Thomas when he spoke in Kansas in 1934.

William Randolph Hearst, aggrieved at what he considered Roosevelt's ingratitude and insubordination, started touting Landon as a "Kansas Coolidge" and visited him in Topeka in the autumn of 1935. This encounter was a success, and the Hearst Press made Landon a familiar figure throughout the country. The Republican platform committee produced a document that virtually accused the Roosevelt administration of sodomizing the Constitution, as well as the ethics, character, and liberties of the American people. It promised everything the New Deal had done but said it could better be done by the states.

Landon had tried, without great success, to be a moderating influence. When the convention determined that the wages and working conditions of women and children could be protected within the Constitution despite the Supreme Court's having invalidated the New York State law on the subject just eleven days before, Landon conscientiously telegraphed his preparedness to seek a constitutional amendment if this proved inaccurate. Landon was nominated by acclamation, and he selected as his running mate the publisher of the *Chicago Daily News*, Colonel Frank Knox, who had received some attention as a presidential candidate. Knox, who had been a Rough Rider with Theodore Roosevelt, was the proud possessor of a sombrero allegedly pierced by two bullets while worn by him at San Juan Hill. (Why a serving officer of the United States Army was wearing a sombrero in action remains a mystery.)

Landon was a Middle West, middle-height, middle-aged (forty-eight), moderate man with forgettable features and rimless spectacles, and a flat prairie accent with a slight twang, full of decency and common sense, a good man but in no sense an exceptional or exciting one.*

---

* On May 20 Farley had referred to Landon as "governor of a typical prairie state." This led to great irritation in the Midwest and the White House. An exasperated Roosevelt wrote to him: "I thought we had agreed that any reference to Landon . . . was inadvisable. A good rule . . . is that no section of the country should be spoken of as 'typical' but only with some laudatory adjective." He suggested "one of those splendid prairie states."

The Democratic Convention opened in Philadelphia on June 23, 1936. Farley insisted that it remain five days in session because he wanted the merchants of Philadelphia who had contributed so much to gain the convention in their city to make a profit from their investment with the Democrats. This led to what Oswald Garrison Villard called "the dreariest, dullest, stupidest, loudest, most inane" convention in U.S. history before Roosevelt redeemed it with his acceptance speech.[19]

Eleanor was in another of her distant moods and was writing regularly to Lorena Hickock that she didn't care what the outcome of the election was. Roosevelt paid no more attention to her unsupportive moods than he did to some of her avant-garde economic theories.

As the convention opened, Roosevelt smelt a big victory, and though he missed Louis Howe personally, he had no doubts that he knew how to exploit the opportunity. Unemployment had continued to decline steadily through 1936 at the average rate of about 150,000 jobs per month. It now stood at about sixty percent of the total that had greeted Roosevelt at his inauguration. The number of employed people had increased by about 6 million, from 38 to over 44 million. And the number of unemployed had declined by over 5 million in the same period, from about 13 million to about 8 million.

About 70 percent of the continuing unemployed, or nearly 6 million people, were engaged for at least part of the year by the various alphabetical workfare programs, and most of the rest, about 2.4 million people, did now benefit from federal unemployment assistance. Thus the rate of unemployment as other countries measured it, counting those in the New Deal relief programs as employed, was down to about 5 percent from over 30 percent four years before, and almost no needful person was ineligible for benefit. Farm incomes had recovered significantly, and farm home ownership and rural electrification had made dramatic progress. About 13 million Americans had worked for the relief programs and about half of them had joined or rejoined the permanent labor force.

In the spring of 1936, the *New York Times* business index had risen again to 100 for the first time since 1930. Corporate America, which had run a $2 billion deficit in 1933, showed a $5 billion dollar profit in 1936. In the same period, net farm income quadrupled.[20] These facts counted more heavily with most people than the duel that the President was conducting with the charter members of the Liberty League.

Over four million mortgages had been refinanced by the Home Owners' Loan Corporation, bank deposits were guaranteed, and Social Security provided some assurance for the distant future of a population that had been on the verge of despair four years before. The NRA, despite its chaotic aspects, had raised wages, improved working conditions, and facilitated collective bargaining. In June 1936, a *Fortune* magazine poll indicated that 53 percent of Americans thought the

Depression was over, and all polls showed 60 percent or more of Americans well-satisfied with the President. It had been the greatest reform administration in the country's history, and most of the New Deal's durable changes were popular and uncontested by the Republicans.

The myth has lingered that the New Deal was ineffectual, because progress in private-sector reduction of unemployment was fairly sluggish until late in the thirties. But the Roosevelt administration's policies greatly alleviated the condition of most of the needy and permanently reformed the economic system without greatly disrupting it. The New Deal bears comparison with the performance of other advanced industrial countries and was certainly judged preferable to what was on offer from the domestic opposition.

In addition, Franklin D. Roosevelt was a public personality who intrigued and often raised the spirits of the country. Cultured but not pedantic, irrepressible but not frivolous, grand but not pompous, he appeared an amiable, cunning, well-intentioned but inscrutable and, when necessary, inspiring man. In the magazines and newsreels and on radio, Americans had more exposure to him than to any leader in their history, and the impact of his personality and persuasive talents was very great.

Roosevelt was the issue in the 1936 campaign. He knew and desired that, and, whatever his ancient sniggering foes thought of it, most Americans (and most foreigners) liked and admired him.

The Roosevelt administration's largesse at combating drought and flood and collapsed farm prices had resonated with farmers. The fact that African-Americans, under the orders of both Hopkins and Ickes, with Roosevelt's firm approval, were receiving relief employment at the same rates as whites, albeit most of them in segregated (but not greatly inferior) camps, as well as the recovery program generally, was attracting the black votes away from the party of Lincoln, where it had been for seventy-five years. It now represented about five percent of the total vote (even though the black percentage of the population was double that, reflecting the disenfranchisement of most African-Americans in the southern states.)

Organized labor had made the greatest recruitment progress in its history through the operation of the NRA and the (Wagner) Labor Relations Act. It would do what it could to reelect the President and his party. The Congress of Industrial Organizations split off from the American Federation of Labor in late 1935 and was led by John L. Lewis, David Dubinsky and his Ladies' Garment Workers' Union, Sidney Hillman and his Amalgamated Clothing Workers, and the rubber and textile unions. (With his general disregard for labor leaders, Roosevelt regularly confused Hillman's and Dubinsky's unions, though both were reliable supporters.[21]) Both the big labor confederations strenuously backed the Democrats, with money and election workers. The CIO would contribute an amazing $770,000 to Roosevelt's campaign—$499,000 from Lewis's United Mine Workers, and Lewis had supported Hoover in 1932.

Kentucky's Senator Alben Barkley, a notable orator, gave the keynote address at the Philadelphia convention, which was a salvo across the bow of the Supreme Court. Roosevelt did not choose to refer to the Court but was glad for Barkley to do so. Barkley said: "While anxious farmers ponder their fate, and laboring men scan the heavens for a rainbow of hope, and women and children look in vain for preservation of their lives and health, a voice from the grave at Palo Alto [i.e., Herbert Hoover] shouts 'Thank God for the Supreme Court!' . . . We are at least relieved of the obligation to underwrite the infallibility of the five who prevailed" (in a five-to-four decision). When Barkley rhetorically asked the crowd "Is the Court beyond criticism? May it be regarded as too sacred to be disagreed with?" the crowd responded with a thunderous "No!"

Senate Majority Leader Robinson also defended the President against the Supreme Court. The constitutional implications of these congressional leaders lining up behind the President were serious, and the justices, whatever they thought of the law, should have had a greater sensitivity to political realities, especially a highly intelligent liberal like Brandeis.

For the first time, and by Roosevelt's arrangement, an African-American politician, Congressman Arthur Mitchell of Illinois, addressed the Democratic convention, and praised the President and the benefits of his programs for black people.

Roosevelt's famous convention address was the product of two teams of speechwriters—Moley and Corcoran were one team, Rosenman and the Protestant clergyman Stanley High were the other. Roosevelt and Moley agreed that they could no longer work so intimately together as they had before because of the divergence in their views, Moley moving rightward and Roosevelt drifting slightly left, albeit for tactical reasons. Moley consented to help Corcoran with a draft, and the two pairs of speechwriters came to the White House for dinner on June 24, with the convention at Philadelphia already in progress. High referred humorously to Moley's association with and espousal of the interests of the wealthy. Moley, in the pages of *Today* magazine, had been editorially critical of the President recently, and Roosevelt took up this point. An acrimonious scene ensued.

Rosenman remembered many years later: "For the first and only time in my life, I saw the President forget himself as a gentleman." Missy LeHand, the only other person present, tried to smooth things over without success. The exchanges between Roosevelt and Moley were bitter and sarcastic. Rosenman wrote: "While I knew how deeply Roosevelt had been stung by the unfriendly attacks on his policies by Hugh Johnson and Moley, I thought that his temper and language were particularly unjustified, not only because there were other people present, but because they were all his invited guests. It was an ordeal for all of us." Though there were a few subsequent meetings and a telephone call between Moley and Roosevelt, and Moley downplayed the exchange in his memoirs, this was the sad and undignified end of their relationship. Moley said years later that when he dreamed of Roosevelt, it was of reconciliation.[22] Moley and Corcoran walked together back to the Mayflower Hotel and Moley compared his lot to that of the Earl of Strafford, whom Charles I had permitted Parliament to behead on the charge of loyalty to the king.* "That's what happens with kings—they exact complete loyalty from you but they never can afford to give you complete . . . personal loyalty in return—all promises of kings are presumptive and all of us . . . are presumptively liquidable."[23] Corcoran would learn the same lesson eventually.

The President spoke at Franklin Field in Philadelphia to a crowd of more than 100,000 and a radio audience of many millions. For two hours before the President's speech, the Democratic faithful had been entertained by opera diva Lily Pons and the Philadelphia Symphony Orchestra conducted by Leopold Stokowski.

It was essentially the Rosenman-High version of the speech that was used, though Roosevelt did a good deal of redrafting himself.

When the President moved to greet the eighty-four-year-old poet Edwin Markham, one of his leg braces buckled and the President was sent sprawling to the floor. Surrounded by his entourage, this was not visible to the crowds, and he told his aides to "clean me up." He was quickly back on his feet with a refastened brace. Jimmy Roosevelt retrieved the speech text but had not completed putting the pages in order when his father was introduced (after completing the task of greeting Mr. Markham, who was visibly moved by the President's attention and his courage[24]). The President, ever the unflappable master of the multitask problem, arranged the pages himself as he warmed up the crowd, and he then delivered one of the greatest speeches of his life.

Roosevelt was approaching the high water mark of his posturing as a militant legislative revolutionary, and his principal addresses in this campaign were the main oratorical expressions of that pose. In this speech Roosevelt recited his familiar theme of the original revolution to secure the nation's liberties requiring a bloodless sequel to ensure the people's freedom from the "economic royalists" (Stanley High's phrase). He stretched the direct line from Lexington and Concord and Valley Forge to the New Deal and on to the gathering threat against democracy in the world. As history it was far-fetched, but as politics it was an agile and eloquent performance. Harold Ickes, no mean wordsmith, judged it the greatest political speech he had heard.

"Through new uses of corporations, banks and securities, new machinery of industry and agriculture, of labor and capital—all undreamed of by the Fathers—the whole structure of modern life was impressed into this royal service.

* Like Berle, Moley had a faulty grasp of European history. Strafford beseeched the king to allow him to be executed and Charles shared the same fate nine years later, which was not a fate Moley envisioned for Roosevelt, whose aberrant discourtesy was hardly comparable to decapitation.

"There was no place among this royalty" for anyone but greedy oligarchs. "It was natural and perhaps human that the privileged princes of these new economic dynasties, thirsting for power, reached out for control of government itself. They created a new despotism and wrapped it in the robes of legal sanction. In its service new mercenaries sought to regiment the people, their labor and their property. And as a result the average man once more confronts the problem that faced the Minute Man. . . . For too many of us life was no longer free; liberty no longer real; men could no longer follow the pursuit of happiness.

"Against economic tyranny such as this, the American citizen could appeal only to the organized power of the Government. The collapse of 1929 showed up the despotism for what it was. The election of 1932 was the people's mandate to end it. Under that mandate it is being ended."

He incongruously inserted a reference to faith, hope, and charity from the Corcoran-Moley draft, invoked Dante, and then uttered the phrase, from Tom Corcoran, for which the speech has always been remembered: "There is a mysterious cycle in human events. To some generations much is given. Of other generations much is expected. This generation of Americans has a rendezvous with destiny. . . . Here in America we are waging a great and successful war. It is not alone a war against want and destitution and economic demoralization. . . . It is a war for the survival of democracy." For once, a catchy political phrase proved prophetic. The speaker would make it so.

The politically homeless Gerald L.K. Smith, Father Coughlin, and the rump of Dr. Townsend's sundered movement convened and chose Congressman William Lemke of North Dakota, head of the Nonpartisan League, as the presidential candidate of what was called the Union Party. Coughlin and Townsend personally endorsed Lemke.

Dr. Townsend's geriatric crusade had hit a serious snag with allegations of corruption from his former national publicity director. An antagonistic congressional committee gleefully took this up and washed as much dirty linen as it could find. Nothing was proved against Townsend personally, but his talented partner in his corporate vehicle—Old Age Revolving Pensions, Limited—Robert Clements, a real estate promoter, was shown to have profited amply. Townsend fired Clements and broke with the leader of his congressional support, and his political organization disintegrated. This was an issue on which Republicans and Democrats agreed, and they rivalled each other in the zeal with which they dismembered the prostrate Townsend. The doctor stalked out of the congressional committee hearing room after brutal questioning, in tandem with Gerald L.K. Smith, and was cited for contempt of Congress. In the *Townsend Weekly*, he compared himself with Christ (not unfavorably). He was sentenced to thirty days in prison and spared this indignity only by a last-minute pardon from Roosevelt.[25]

At the Townsendite convention in Cleveland, in July, Coughlin was the big draw. He theatrically took off his clerical collar and jacket and referred to "Franklin Double-Crossing Roosevelt . . . the great betrayer and liar." He blasted the "money changers' servants," going Roosevelt one better. He urged his geriatric listeners to "eradicate the cancerous growths from decadent capitalism." However, a delegate from Oklahoma, Gomer Smith, won the approval of half the hall when he defended Roosevelt as a "church-going, Bible-reading, God-fearing . . . golden-hearted patriot who . . . saved the country from Communism."[26]

Father Coughlin's National Union of Social Justice met in August, but his grand alliance with the other principal malcontents was already in shambles. Coughlin claimed the credit for defeating Hoover, called Roosevelt a Communist, attacked Dr. Townsend and Gerald L.K. Smith, and said that if he didn't bring in at least nine million votes for Lemke he would quit broadcasting. Apart from that boast, he ignored Lemke.

A few days later, on July 28, Coughlin, under orders from his bishop and possibly the Vatican, publicly apologized to the President for calling him a liar and for his "intemperate" remarks generally. Roosevelt made no public comment on either the original outburst or its retraction. Ickes and other members of Roosevelt's inner circle were concerned, but he was not.

On September 14, the country's most powerful Roman Catholic churchman, George Cardinal Mundelein of Chicago, in registering to vote, said his countrymen "should feel extremely grateful for the prosperity, the happiness, and the freedom now abroad in our land. . . . Look at the situation in other countries and compare it to ours." He said that he had instructed his priests to urge their congregations to vote but to give no indication how they thought they should vote. The cardinal had, however, incited a clear inference about his own voting intentions.[27] Roosevelt had cultivated Mundelein from the start of his presidency, having gone to the unprecedented length of congratulating him on his feast day in April, 1933, and he generally showered him with public respect.[28]

Once out on the campaign trail, the overwrought Father Coughlin suffered a further chronic lack of judgment and lapse of self-control. On September 25 in Cincinnati, he described Roosevelt as "anti-God" and implied that recourse to bullets would be permissible to dispose of an "upstart dictator in the United States . . . when the ballot is useless."[29] This was too much for the Holy See and for mainline American Catholic opinion.

The Vatican summoned Coughlin's bishop, Michael Gallagher, to Rome. Gallagher required Coughlin to apologize publicly for calling Roosevelt a "scab president."[30] *Osservatore Romano* accused Coughlin of provoking disrespect for authority. The secretary of state of the Holy See, Eugenio Cardinal Pacelli, subsequently Pope Pius XII, visited the United States for a month in October and November 1936. When he met the press on arrival and from time to time during his visit, he declined comment on Coughlin, and it has never been officially indicated what the Church's second most important official was doing on such an extended visit in the United States during the presidential campaign.* †

Coughlin was rebuked in a radio address on October 9 by a senior Catholic commentator, Msgr. John Ryan, another frequent radio appearer and director of the social action department of the National Catholic Welfare Conference. Speaking on a nationwide broadcast provided by the Democratic National Committee, Ryan rebutted Coughlin's "ugly, cowardly, and flagrant calumnies." He credited the President with "mild installments of too-delayed social justice," pointed out that Roosevelt had received honorary degrees from distinguished Catholic universities such as Notre Dame, and described Coughlin's charge against him of being a Communist as "the silliest, falsest, most cruel, and most unjust accusation ever made against a President in . . . American history."[32]

Coughlin did somewhat moderate his language after these interventions, though he continued to be severely critical of Roosevelt. He had ceased to claim that Lemke would win the election and declared that all he needed was 6 percent of the vote to throw the election into the House of Representatives.[33] (Apart from gratifying his ego, it is not clear why Coughlin thought that would be a positive step, since he professed to find the Republicans as distasteful as the Democrats.)

Roosevelt visited flood-ravaged areas in New England on his way back to Washington from a sailing trip and then gave at Chautauqua, New York, August 14, the most histrionic of all his many denunciations of the evils of war. He said: "I have seen war. I have seen war on land and sea. I have seen blood running from the wounded. I have seen men coughing out their gassed lungs. I have seen the dead in the mud. I have seen cities destroyed. I have seen two hundred limping exhausted men come out of the line—the survivors of a regiment of one thousand that went forward forty-eight hours before. I hate war!" (This was doubtless sincere, but when Roosevelt went on, in the next few years as war drew nearer, to claim to have seen more of war than any other American, it grated on the scores of thousands of Americans who had actually been in action.)

Roosevelt toured drought-stricken states in the Midwest and met with a group of governors of affected states, including Landon, in Des Moines. Landon made a good impression but had nothing like the physical presence or verbal facility of the President. But they got on well. Landon called Roosevelt "a very fine, charming gentleman," and Roosevelt said, "Governor, however this comes out . . . either

---

* It was to this visit that Roosevelt doubtless attributed his entitlement to address the recently elevated Pius XII, in his letter to him of December 23, 1939, with his usual breezy application of the notion of friendship, as "a good friend and an old friend."[31] Roosevelt so described almost everyone, from the generality of the American voters to world figures he scarcely knew, such as the pope, to people he disliked, from H.L. Mencken to Charles de Gaulle.

† Cardinal Pacelli visited the Kennedys at Hyannisport. When he became pope two years later, Rose Kennedy roped off the chair he had sat upon while taking tea; all lesser occupants had become ineligible to sit on it.

you come to see me or I'll come to see you. And . . . don't work too hard!"[34] Roosevelt returned to the White House and gave a Fireside Chat on September 6, on drought and flood control and conservation generally and on the meaning of Labor Day, which fell the next day. He represented it as a national holiday celebrating economic freedom, just as July 4 celebrated civic freedom.

IV

PRESIDENT ROOSEVELT FINALLY opened his campaign for reelection on September 29, 1936, in Syracuse, New York. He was at his most avuncular as he reminded his listeners of conditions in the country when he came to office. This would be one of his most effective refrains as the years of his incumbency accumulated. The reminiscences would become more and more graphic. For this occasion, it was enough to say that "starvation was averted, that homes and farms were saved, that banks were reopened, that industry revived, and that the dangerous forces subversive of our form of government were turned aside." The New Deal, he claimed, had prevented bloody revolution. He rebutted the charge of deficit spending by claiming that it wasn't really conventional spending at all, but "investment" in the human and natural resources and physical plant of the nation, on which there would be a return. This would remain his principal defense against the charges of the budget balancers, especially when they waved at him his famous frugality address made in Pittsburgh in September 1932.

Early in October he made a railway tour of Midwestern states. At Emporia, Kansas, he regretted the absence of William Allen White, whom he described as "a good friend for three-and-one-half years out of every four." But White was there and Roosevelt asked him to come forward, which he did, uttering the line from the famous John Greenleaf Whittier poem about Barbara Frietchie: "Shoot if you must this old gray head." White looked unusually embarrassed standing just beneath the President as Roosevelt continued his whistle-stop talk.

Tom Corcoran was in the presidential party and when Roosevelt asked him one evening on his train if he had learned anything about politics that day, Corcoran responded that every local leader who had boarded the train had departed "with the idea that if you are elected, he would become an assistant secretary of agriculture." Roosevelt replied, amused, that he had not made a "precise promise."[35]

In Chicago on October 14, Roosevelt gave one of his most explicit statements of his belief in free enterprise and of his claim to have saved capitalism and democracy. "The overwhelming majority of businessmen in this country are good citizens, [and not] 'malefactors of great wealth.' . . . Because we cherished our system of private property and free enterprise and were determined to preserve it as the foundation of our traditional American system, we recalled the warning of Thomas Jefferson that 'widespread poverty and concentrated wealth cannot long endure side by side in a democracy.' It was this Administration which saved the system of private property and free enterprise after it had been dragged to the brink of ruin by these same leaders who now try to scare you.

"I believe in individualism. I believe in it in the arts, the sciences and professions. I believe in it in business. I believe in individualism in all of these things—up to the point where the individualist starts to operate at the expense of society."

He retained his domination of the political center; to the conservatives, he was the savior who preserved their society from the extremists. He was no less a savior to the reformers, as the greatest champion they had ever had. By excoriating the exploiters without ever naming them he was performing the confidence trick of swearing vengeance on the wrongdoers without giving anyone the impression of being threatened or accused.

John L. Lewis, in his enthusiasm for Roosevelt, called upon him in his White House office with a check for $250,000 and a photographer to record the occasion. Roosevelt instantly recognized the dangers of this donation and jauntily told Lewis: "No, John, just keep it, and I'll call upon you if and when any small need arises." In the balance of the campaign, the Democrats quietly touched the CIO for more than twice as much money in a series of requests, but Lewis did not have his photographic evidence of the President's debt to him.

Landon had made serious errors, his worst having been his attack on Social Security as being "a cruel hoax." His suggested return to the gold standard wasn't a stroke of tactical genius, either. Landon was getting into the hands of the old Hooverite right, and John G. Winant retired from the Social Security Board to refute Landon's outrageous charges. Winant, as a popular Republican former governor (New Hampshire), was an effective champion of the Social Security centerpiece of the New Deal.

Landon gambled everything on this; just before the end of the campaign he claimed that it would be impossible for the federal government to keep track of everybody and it would be necessary to put dog tags on the whole population. Messages were put into pay envelopes warning workers that their payroll deductions paid to Social Security would disappear and they would receive no return on them.

Roosevelt responded with another of the most powerful speeches of his career in a venue that was already the scene of great personal triumphs—Madison Square Garden in New York City, on October 31, 1936. He went through his refrain of "nine mocking years of the golden calf, three long years of the scourge," and so forth. He enumerated the categories of undesirables: "business and financial monopoly, speculation, reckless banking, class antagonism, sectionalism, war profiteering . . . Never before in all our history have these forces been so united as they are today. They are unanimous in their hate for me and I welcome their hatred." (Prolonged and thunderous applause.)

"I should like to have it said of my first Administration that in it the forces of selfishness and of lust for power met their match. I should like to have it said of my second Administration that in it these forces met their master." A little like the masses in George Orwell's 1984 being stirred to rage against Emmanuel Gold-stein, the crowd in Madison Square Garden was roused to a frenzy of fist-shaking wrath against the unnamed moral outcasts of American society. Roosevelt then shamed the authors of the Social Security scare. "Only desperate men with their backs to the wall would descend so far below the level of decent citizenship." He recounted the lies in the pay envelope misinformation campaign and added: "They are guilty of more than deceit. When they imply" that their entitlements will be "stolen by some future Congress . . . they attack the integrity and honor of the American government itself. Those who suggest that are already aliens to the spirit of American democracy. Let them emigrate and try their lot under some foreign flag in which they have more confidence." He enumerated a long list of policy objectives, interspersing: "For these things, we have only just begun to fight." It was a brilliant performance.

Roosevelt spoke to the nation on election eve from his drawing room at Springwood, but—as he had been four years before—was almost nonpartisan. All polls except one indicated a substantial lead for the incumbents. Roosevelt him-self expected 360 electoral votes to 171 for Landon and thought Farley much too optimistic when he predicted that Roosevelt would carry the whole country except Maine and Vermont.

The nation voted on November 3, 1936, and delivered to Franklin D. Roo-sevelt the greatest victory of modern times. Farley had been right. The President won 46 states with 523 electoral votes to two states for Landon with 8 electoral votes. The popular vote was 27.48 million votes for Roosevelt (61 percent), 16.68 million for Landon (37 percent), and 882,000 for Lemke. Norman Thomas's Socialist vote descended from 900,000 in 1932 to 187,000 in 1936.

Tom Corcoran entertained celebrants at Springwood with his accordion and Irish songs. Although there was never the slightest suspense as the night of the election proceeded, Landon waited until 2 A.M. to send a gracious message, to which Roosevelt responded instantly in the same spirit. W.R. Hearst telephoned Roosevelt on election night and cheerfully acknowledged: "We have been run over by a steamroller." Roosevelt received the call coolly and reported it disparag-ingly to his cabinet. Father Coughlin tersely announced that he accepted the ver-dict and would retire from politics. It is unlikely that this career decision displeased or was entirely independent of the still-visiting Cardinal Pacelli.

―――――――――

Roosevelt's victory was achieved despite the profound misgivings many Ameri-cans felt for Roosevelt's notions of the role of government and of the president. Polling at this time was primitive and unreliable, but according to Gallup, 53 per-cent of Americans considered themselves to be conservative rather than liberal, and 45 percent thought Roosevelt's policies could lead to dictatorship. The majority favored restoring responsibility for social assistance to the states as the economic crisis subsided. There was an inadvertent bias against Roosevelt in the selection of people Gallup canvassed. *Fortune* had been correct in steadily revealing the President's approval rating at 60 percent or more.

American politics were largely recast. The permanent Republican majority that had existed since Lincoln had evaporated. Although Roosevelt's percentage of the popular vote rose 4 percent from 1932 (57 percent to 61 percent), his percentage fell in fourteen states, mainly in the West, and it rose more than the 4 percent national average only in eighteen states, but these included New York, Pennsylvania, Ohio, Michigan, and New Jersey. In New York, the President carried only Albany, of all the counties between New York City and Buffalo, but the tidal wave of votes from the large cities in that and other states provided his huge margin. Roosevelt's percentage of votes went down in the majority of the country's 3,000 counties, though he retained a majority in most of them, but his majorities in the most populous urban districts moved up 6 percent to 57 percent, and to about 70 percent in immigrant and other working-class districts, while his majority in "rural-Yankee" districts declined slightly, to 51 percent. His overall majority was raised above 60 percent by retention of 85 percent of the votes of all kinds in the Old South.

His long-sought coalition of big-city working-class people and rural progressives was taking shape. Of all America's cities with 100,000 people or more, Roosevelt won in 104, Landon only in two.

Both Gallup and Roper indicate that Roosevelt won overwhelmingly among Roman Catholics, Jews, and African-Americans, groups totalling about a third of the electorate, as well as among the traditional southern whites. They also reveal that he barely carried Protestant white America outside the South.

The heavy migration of these large minority groups to the Democrats was a phenomenon Roosevelt had worked hard to achieve. Under the previous three Republican presidents, one out of every twenty-five judicial nominations was offered to a Roman Catholic; under Roosevelt this ratio moved up to approximately their percentage of the whole population: one of four. Roosevelt seemed to take only about 25 percent of northern blacks in 1932 (23 percent in Chicago, against 59 percent of the whites, but in 1936 he more than doubled his percentage of African-American voters in the northern cities while still increasing his percentage of the white voters.[36] Roosevelt carried 80 percent of Harlem, 75 percent of the black districts of Pittsburgh, and 69 percent of the black precincts of Philadelphia.

Fortune magazine, which seems to have had the most sophisticated polling and forecasting of anyone, revealed that 84.7 percent of African-Americans supported Roosevelt by 1938.[37] Eleanor Roosevelt, by her unflagging efforts on behalf of African-Americans, deserved no small credit for this change. The most memorable episode in Eleanor Roosevelt's fifty-year promotion of the rights of African-Americans would come in 1939 when contralto Marian Anderson was prohibited from singing in Constitution Hall. Mrs. Roosevelt publicly resigned from the Daughters of the American Revolution and, with Harold Ickes, organized a concert for Ms. Anderson at the Lincoln Memorial, which was attended by 75,000 people.

Eleanor was less successful in her championship of women. When Roosevelt was asked at a press conference about putting the feminist activist Frances Willard on a postage stamp, he replied: "I have to grant about every one hundredth request that comes from women. That's a fact. I turn down ninety-nine and have to give them something." A woman reporter, Ruby Black, said: "We're listening." The press conference became very jovial; Roosevelt had been pitching to what decades later would be called the chauvinist vote. His record was a great improvement on his predecessors, but far from the equality of opportunity in government that Eleanor Roosevelt and her followers sought. As usual, Roosevelt sought and found the position that would be the most vote-catching, in this case to the female constituency without alienating the traditionalist male (and female) majority.[38]

There is also evidence that Roosevelt's message was well received by more businessmen than had been thought. Apart from Jewish and Roman Catholic businessmen, who tended to adhere to Roosevelt like most of their coreligionists, such as A.P. Giannini of the Bank of America in San Francisco and Edward Filene, the Boston retailer, many businessmen in new industries were Roosevelt supporters. Thomas Watson of IBM (International Business Machines), a company that enjoyed tremendous growth in the thirties, was a strong Roosevelt backer. Just below the most senior levels there was a reform-minded echelon of business people who were very accessible to Roosevelt's appeal.

The 1936 election was another great milestone for Franklin D. Roosevelt; only nine of the thirty men who had preceded him to the presidency had won two consecutive terms (and both of Washington's and one of Monroe's were uncontested). Only three other presidents in the seventy-one years since the Civil War (Grant, McKinley, Wilson) had won two consecutive elections. And no one had ever won such a lopsided victory in a contested presidential election. He was everywhere recognized as a contemporary giant, in the newspapers of his foes, domestic and foreign, and by all reasonably unbiased observers. The *London Times* perceptively described Roosevelt's victory as "a matter of supreme importance at the moment when English-speaking nations are becoming more isolated as the champions of democracy in a world 'blown about by all the winds of doctrine.' "[39] His lifelong skeptics were inaudible.

V

DESPITE THE WIDESPREAD support Roosevelt received in some sections of the business community, the antagonism of most of the more prominent and vocal spokesmen for that community rankled. Roosevelt considered the conventional business lack of appreciation for him and his policies to be spiteful ingratitude and political and economic Neanderthalism. He underestimated the degree to which almost all businessmen hope for ever greater prosperity and imagined that big business was willfully withholding investment to impair economic recovery. He had announced his suspension of the great drive to further reform in his letter to Roy Howard in September 1935. But by May 1936, he was more exasperated than ever, and exclaimed to Moley that business was "a stupid class." [40] "The rich may have thought Roosevelt was betraying his class; but Roosevelt certainly supposed that his class was betraying him."[41] It would require an even greater emergency than the Depression for Roosevelt and the industrial leadership to learn to appreciate each other.

Nothing was more evident of this lack of rapport with elements of the business community than Roosevelt's use of the Internal Revenue Service and the Justice Department to pursue his enemies. This practice did not begin or end with Roosevelt, but as the historian David Burnham, who wrote the authoritative *A Law Unto Itself: Power, Politics, and the IRS*, wrote: "It appears that President Franklin D. Roosevelt may have been the champion abuser."[42] Nor was it confined to use against business people. He unleashed tax inspectors and prosecutors on most of his opponents, including Huey Long, Colonel McCormick, eventually John L. Lewis, and, most celebratedly, Andrew Mellon and Moses Annenberg.

Roosevelt's conduct in this area makes short work of his idolators' presentation of him as a good-natured, long-suffering, Job-like allegorization of indulgence and self-control in the face of endless provocations. Of a piece with his vast repertoire of techniques of duplicity, dissembling, intrigue, and all the political arts from the most to the least salubrious was his capricious use of the tax collection apparatus. In 1934 the Department of Justice sought an indictment of Andrew Mellon, one of the country's greatest industrialists, philanthropists, and Treasury secretaries, who was ultimately ambassador to Great Britain.

A federal grand jury, which is normally rather compliant to the wishes of the Justice Department, found insufficient evidence to charge Mellon with tax fraud. Mellon then applied for a tax refund, and the IRS reopened the case before the Board of Tax Appeals. Henry Morgenthau and his prosecutor in this case, Robert Jackson, held that Mellon should not, as Treasury secretary, have requested advice from his own enforcement officials on tax avoidance and then implemented some of the same methods privately, saving himself an appreciable amount of tax. Even the historian Arthur Schlesinger, who attaches some credence to this view, acknowledges that reviving the prosecution seemed "further evidence of Roosevelt's personal vindictiveness."[43] Schlesinger attributes the Mellon imbroglio to a change of eras, in which the practices of old were no longer acceptable. Unfortunately, the truth is less benign than that.

Mellon had no obligation to pay more tax than the law required and was undoubtedly persecuted as a symbol of the old twenties false boom. As secretary of the Treasury, he had persuaded Congress to reduce the highest personal income tax rate from 50 percent to 20 percent. Since he was in fact innocent, and the appeal of his case produced a mixed judgment but not a criminal finding, the whole proceeding should never have been pursued as it was. Mellon finally visited Roosevelt in 1936 and in a private meeting offered, and the President accepted, the gift to the nation of what became the National Gallery, including Mellon's own collection, which contained a splendid Raphael, twenty-three Rembrandts, seven Vermeers, and many other masterpieces. Mellon died in 1937, aged eighty-two, and the IRS dropped all claims against his estate.

It was generally assumed that a deal was struck between the two men. If so, no one can say that Roosevelt did not strike a good bargain for the country. Nor can we be sure that Mellon would not have endowed the nation with the museum and his collection without IRS harassment. In either case, it was far from a disinterested and fair operation of a state function capable of inflicting terrible abuse on targeted opponents of the regime.

This practice also operated in reverse, of course. Roosevelt intervened to prevent a serious investigation of allegedly improper funding of Congressman Lyndon Johnson's 1941 campaign for the U.S. Senate. The IRS personnel involved were abruptly transferred to other work; a single inspector replaced them and after three days declared there was insufficient evidence to proceed.[44]

Roosevelt punished his enemies and rewarded his friends. There is nothing wrong with that, up to a point, but the capricious persecution of those fully entitled to a presumption of innocence is unedifying and particularly discordant in a statesman who so frequently held himself out, as Roosevelt did, as a champion of natural equity and economic justice. It is a testament to Roosevelt's felicitous personality that while his offenses in this area have been generally overlooked, even by unsupportive biographers, the comparatively minor transgressions of Richard Nixon have been presented to a credulous posterity as monstrous crimes.

The charges against the Philadelphia publisher Moses Annenberg were different, in that there was a well-assembled case of tax evasion and some rather dodgy activity in off-track betting and other matters. There were also in Annenberg's distant past some tenuous underworld connections and the violence of the Chicago newspaper-circulation war of a generation before, which Annenberg had conducted, first for Hearst and then for McCormick. This made him a more vulnerable public relations target than such a pillar of the establishment as Mellon.

The fact remains that Roosevelt, Ickes, Morgenthau, Murphy, and other senior Justice Department officials went after Annenberg because of his fierce attacks in his *Philadelphia Inquirer* on the New Deal and on Roosevelt from 1936 to 1938. (Frank Murphy was then the attorney general.) Once the investigation got going in earnest, and moderate investigators were replaced with more zealous ones, Annenberg was terrified by the specter of a criminal trial and struggled to reingratiate himself with the authorities.

He persuaded the mayor of Chicago, Ed Kelly, whom he had supported in the past; the former governor of Pennsylvania, George Earle, whom he had helped to defeat; and even James A. Farley to intervene with the President. Philadelphian ambassador (to France) William Bullitt and Pennsylvania Senator Joe Guffey were lobbied. Roosevelt raised the matter at the cabinet meeting of December 28, 1938. On May 13, 1939, Ickes recorded that at that week's cabinet meeting, Roosevelt had expressed the supposition that no one at the table had not been approached to try to settle the case. This was not an appropriate forum for a judicial decision.

Roosevelt told Morgenthau: "I want Moe Annenberg for dinner," and Morgenthau replied: "You're going to have him for breakfast—fried."[45] What ensued was rightly described by subsequent reform Philadelphia mayor Richardson Dilworth as a "vendetta." The government prevailed upon AT&T, Western Union, and Illinois Bell to remove the wire service to Annenberg's nationwide betting service to off-track betting establishments. They had and claimed no legal right to do so, but intimidated Annenberg's cocontractants. Roosevelt, Morgenthau, Murphy, and Ickes were unanimous in wanting to send Annenberg to prison. Morgenthau compared him to Al Capone, and Ickes, remembering the rough Chicago circulation wars, compared him to Hitler. Both comparisons were disgracefully intemperate.[46]

A relentless political prosecution was launched, with harassments and charges stirred up in several states and the Annenberg business empire beset at every hand. The charges against Annenberg enveloped his thirty-one-year-old son Walter, against whom there was not a shred of evidence and who was to become a very distinguished publisher, philanthropist, and well-respected ambassador to the United Kingdom. If found guilty, Moses Annenberg would face a sentence of 147 years in prison. He gamely wisecracked that, like Nathan Hale, he had "not enough years to give my country." He was already ill with what proved to be a brain tumor.

The excessive charges and the large number of defendants were a tactic to force a plea bargain on Moses Annenberg, and it worked. Walter Annenberg was discharged, and his father pleaded guilty to a single charge and accepted a custodial sentence. There had been suggestions of a suspended sentence and then of early parole. All of this was forgotten; Roosevelt, Morgenthau, Ickes, and Murphy would not hear of any clemency, even after Annenberg's medical condition had severely deteriorated. They overrode a unanimous verdict from the parole board and requests for commutation from Philadelphia's Joseph Cardinal Dougherty, the judge who had sentenced Annenberg, the entertainer Eddie Cantor, and many prominent businessmen, including the retailer Bernard Gimbel and the film studio boss Jack Warner. Roosevelt personally rejected a plea from Walter Annenberg, delivered by two of his Pennsylvania lieutenants, Matthew McCloskey and David Lawrence.[47]

Annenberg was denigrated by prison guards (at Lewisburg, Pennsylvania) as a Jew, and finally only released in June 1942 because the authorities did not want him to die in custody. His death, a month later, was undoubtedly hastened by poor medical treatment in Lewisburg.[48] Annenberg's last words to his son were "Perhaps my suffering has all been for the purpose of making you a man."[49] Walter Annenberg had the satisfaction of living to a great age and vastly exceeding the detritus of the Roosevelt family in power, prestige, and accomplishments. His loyalty to his father's memory was majestic and unswerving.

That the government had a serious case against Moses Annenberg, unlike their charges against Mellon, does not excuse Roosevelt his insatiable vindictiveness nor liberate him and his entourage from the charge of politicizing the IRS and parts of the federal criminal prosecution service. To give and ask no quarter with political opponents is perfectly acceptable. To use the government's legal enforcement apparatus to terrorize opponents and whitewash supporters while putting on the airs of pristine political virtue is abusive and hypocritical.

The business community, if not the general public, detected some of this, and it aggravated the business-government relationship. A man in Roosevelt's position, enjoying the great power and popularity that he did, diminished his historical status somewhat by failing to be magnanimous to enemies he had crushed, when his political insight, his cultural sense, and even his often kindly nature must have commended that course to him. As we have seen in other matters, sometimes he chose to frighten and torment people, presumably for the exemplary impact such treatment would have on others. This is a well-precedented practice and may sometimes even be necessary. But even if it slightly relieved the frustrations imposed by his physical disability, in so great a leader it is generally unbecoming.

In this respect, Roosevelt's conduct was inferior to that of his greatest contemporaries, the unfailingly generous Winston Churchill and even the world-weary Catholic cynic, Charles de Gaulle. Roosevelt's triumphs might have been even greater and more numerous than they were if he had been able to discard, or disguise completely, what the admiring and rigorous historian William E. Leuchtenburg described as lurking beyond his "agreeable smile and comfortable air . . . the sophisticated Roosevelt with his unsettling and vaguely dishonest charm," and the intermittently vicious instincts that they more or less concealed.[50]

VI

ROOSEVELT DETERMINED TO go personally to the Inter-American Conference for the Maintenance of Peace, which he had proposed the year before to demonstrate the peaceful spirit of the Americas.

He travelled on the U.S.S. *Indianapolis*, reading extensive summaries by Attorney General Homer Cummings of alternative responses to the Supreme Court, and arrived in Rio de Janeiro's magnificent harbor on the morning of November 27, 1936. Roosevelt was impressed at the heavy traffic in the sea lanes and referred somewhat suspiciously to the presence in Caribbean waters of the large airship *Graf Zeppelin* and a pre-war German battleship, though he was put in somewhat better humor when that vessel "fired 21 guns as a salute to my flag."[51] Whatever emphasis he put on being regarded as a good neighbor, Roosevelt never wanted there to be any ambiguity about who held supreme authority in the Americas from pole to pole.

President Roosevelt was greeted by President Getulio Vargas of Brazil, and by tremendous crowds, well over a million shouting greetings to him, some of them referring to the virtues of democracy. A slightly embarrassed Vargas whispered as they drove through Rio de Janeiro in an open car that perhaps Roosevelt had heard that "I am a dictator." Roosevelt continued to wave and smile at the multitude and replied, "Perhaps you have heard that I am one too." He was introduced in the Brazilian Congress as "The Man—the fearless and generous man who is accomplishing and living the most thrilling political experience of modern times."[52]

At least two million Argentinians greeted him when he arrived at Buenos Aires at midday on November 30. His car and path were strewn with flowers, and the Portenos packed the sidewalks and balconies as he passed, shouting their admiration. Roosevelt wrote to James M. Cox that this was the vindication of the Good Neighbor policy, which he credited with turning around Latin American opinion about the United States.

This partially explained his popularity in South America. Here, as elsewhere, Roosevelt was seen as the champion of liberal democracy, as the man who had taken America back from the plump financiers and was showing the world the way to economic justice without forfeiting democracy in the process. He was a compelling figure, especially in Latin America, where he was the first incumbent U.S. president to visit.

The next day, December 1, he opened the conference, which celebrated peace in the Americas, purported to set an example for the world, and resolved to repulse any aggression against any part of the Americas. Resolutions effectively extending the U.S. Neutrality Act to the whole hemisphere were voted down, largely by the intervention of the host, Argentinian foreign minister Saavedra Lamas, who was a supporter of the Republicans in Spain and was not completely won over by the disinterestedness of the Good Neighbor policy. Saavedra Lamas prevailed over Cordell Hull, and the conference did not accomplish much, but it was at least a start at inter-American consultation. Roosevelt received another tremendous welcome at Montevideo, and then the *Indianapolis* sailed north.

Roosevelt stopped at Trinidad on the way home, in the midst of the abdication crisis in Great Britain. There was a shipboard pool, and Roosevelt naturally predicted that Edward VIII would finesse the issue of his romance and marital intentions until his coronation and then marry Mrs. Simpson and make her Duchess of Cornwall rather than queen. He attributed to the king his own tenacity of office and sense of entitlement to rule. He did not win the pool.[53]

The spirits of Roosevelt and his party had been severely dampened by the sudden death from a coronary or a cerebral hemorrhage of Gus Gennerich, Roosevelt's chief security man, upon whom he had come to rely and whom he personally greatly liked. Roosevelt used to try out phrases and ideas on him as an "average American." Gennerich had just had a dance at a nightclub in Buenos Aires, where he was relaxing with some other members of the official party. Only fifty years old, he seemed to die instantly. His personality as well as his courage and competence would be much missed. (When the *Indianapolis* docked at Charleston December 15, Roosevelt canceled any public ceremony and his planned stopover at Warm Springs out of respect for Gennerich. Roosevelt even considered buying Gennerich's farm, where he had intended to retire, and preserving it for Gennerich's son.[54])

When Roosevelt returned to the White House he discovered that Franklin Jr. had been critically ill with a throat infection, but was recovering. His son and namesake was also engaged to the daughter of Pierre S. Du Pont, one of America's wealthiest men and, to FDR's amusement, a founding supporter of the Liberty League.

Just before year-end Roosevelt took on his son James as a secretary, over fierce protestations from Eleanor. She thought Jimmy would be pilloried for nepotism, that his nerves and ulcers might not withstand the pressure, and that he would forfeit the opportunity to forge his own career away from the long shadow of his father. In all this she was right. Compounding the problem was the status of James's wife, Betsy Cushing Roosevelt, who virtually moved into the White House and became the chatelaine during Eleanor's frequent absences. The President found his beautiful and vivacious daughter-in-law very agreeable, and there soon developed an alliance between James and Eleanor in resentment at the excessive congeniality of the relationship between Betsy and FDR.

Roosevelt considered that the economic recovery was now inexorable. Industrial production was almost at 1929 levels, farm income was sharply higher, unemployment was at half the 1933 high and descending steadily, even without the public works programs, and the President planned to accelerate this by encouraging a further-reduced statutory work week, retirement at sixty-five, and more years of schooling for the nation's youth. Roosevelt planned to scale back relief spending and try to balance the budget in 1938, a prospect that excited Morgenthau but horrified Federal Reserve Chairman Marriner Eccles when the three discussed fiscal questions on December 17, 1936. Eccles warned that any such course would start a slide back into depression.

On December 29, Roosevelt issued a statement denouncing an arms exporter who had sold aircraft to the Republican government in Spain, and indicated an intention to broaden the Neutrality Act to include civil wars. Roosevelt's motivation in this case is not obvious but it is discernible. He personally favored the democratic Republicans over their putative Communist and anarchist allies, who were opposed by the American Catholic community, and over Franco's fascist Nationalists. But he knew that the Republicans were dominated by extremists, and he may have seen the dangers of a Republican victory. He assumedly reasoned that there was unlikely to be a civil war in any other country any time soon and that in extending the Neutrality Act to such wars he wasn't giving up much. Franco announced that Roosevelt had behaved "like a true gentleman."[55]

He was finally giving a name and a face to the "war profiteers" whose insidious existence he was endlessly bandying about. Roosevelt knew that the mortal danger came from Nazi Germany and that nothing that happened in Spain was likely to influence matters decisively, especially not the deployment of a few American aircraft, which would immediately be countered by a greater German air presence.

By acting as he did, he gulled some isolationists into thinking he was one of them, which would strengthen his credentials if American intervention in the supreme European conflict really would be necessary for the security of the United States and the future of civilization.

This was another variant on the Roosevelt tactic of enduring some temporary embarrassment for long-term strategic gain. He had distanced himself from the internationalists in early 1932 to placate Hearst, who six months later threw him the nomination. He now had the pleasure of oppressing Hearst fiscally and publicly mocking him (by having Ickes and other administration spokesmen attack him). So he would now seem to toady to the isolationists, in order to make himself more credible to the more moderate of them at the decisive moment upon which all the future would depend. He was playing to the sentiment captured in Senator William E. Borah's assertion that "Neutrality is not synonymous with cowardice" (questionable though that was in Borah's own case). And he was conserving his carefully assembled electoral coalition, as American Catholics were much more hostile to the Spanish Republicans than American Protestants were favorable to them.

Before he could lead a united people into war, as he increasingly feared he would have to do, against what he had long sensed was a mortal evil, he would have to convince a majority of Americans that he was the surest hope for keeping them out of that war. It would be a stern political challenge.

In his own entourage there was some concern that Roosevelt's tidal wave election victory had corroded his customary optimism into overconfidence and that he exaggerated the progress against the Depression. The brilliant and gentle legal expert of the New Deal, Benjamin V. Cohen, feared that the election had "gone to his head,"[56] and the President asserted to intimates that the Depression in America was in inexorable retreat.

Industrial relations were an increasing concern, as labor unions, flexing muscles that had been nourished by the NRA, aggressively pursued some of the nation's largest employers. General Motors, the world's largest automobile company, was struck at the beginning of 1937, with a possibility that all 250,000 workers of that company would soon be on strike or laid off. The technique of the sit-down strike, the occupation of the factory, was catching on and held great potential for the escalation of labor strife. This tactic would obviously turn to chaos any attempt to bring in replacement workers. It also opened the possibility of immense property damage to the employers, and the more flamboyant union spokesmen talked of operating the factories as cooperatives without benefit of management or regard to shareholders. This was nonsense, and it was revolutionary nonsense and not at all the tenor of industrial discourse that the President was trying to promote.

Conditions in Michigan, where the General Motors strike was concentrated, were managed with difficulty by the new governor and former mayor of Detroit, Frank Murphy, whom Roosevelt had already identified with Robert Jackson and a couple of others as rising stars of his party.

The President was cheered loudly and often when he appeared personally at the Congress to give his State of the Union message on January 6, 1937. It was a brief, conciliatory, and upbeat address, with no hint of triumphalism. He was clearly reserving his main oratorical effort for the inauguration, which would this year for the first time be brought forward from March 4 to January 20, under the recently adopted Twentieth Amendment to the Constitution. (This would have spared Roosevelt a good deal of irritating to-ing and fro-ing with Hoover if it had been achieved four years earlier.) Roosevelt also moved the Thanksgiving holiday to help create a maximum shopping period in the month before Christmas.

He said in his address to Congress: "The vital need is not an alteration of our fundamental law, but an increasingly enlightened view with reference to it. Difficulties have grown out of its interpretation; but rightly considered it can be used as an instrument of progress, and not as a device for prevention of action. . . .

"The Judicial branch also is asked by the people to do its part in making democracy successful. We do not ask the Courts to call nonexistent powers into being, but we have a right to expect that conceded powers or those legitimately implied shall be made effective instruments for the common good. . . ." This was a clear warning to the justices seated in front of him. Every critical reference to the Supreme Court brought deafening support from the Congress.

Between the beginning of 1937 and inauguration day, Roosevelt focused on government reorganization. He had long had an exaggerated view of the virtues of planning and was aware of the pandemonium he had imposed on many parts of the government with his endless series of alphabetical agencies attracting bright young people to Washington with overlapping jobs, spewing out money and regulations.

He had set up a committee in 1933 to prepare suggestions for making government more efficient. The four committee members joined the National Planning Board, headed by FDR's favorite adult relative, his uncle Frederic A. Delano. The composition of the group of advisors evolved somewhat, but Louis Brownlow, director of the Public Administration Clearing House and one of Woodrow Wilson's commissioners of the District of Columbia, remained the guiding light throughout.*

In November 1933, Ickes had given Delano a PWA grant to plan a government reorganization, and the work had continued for over three years. An extensive plan had been prepared which Roosevelt had memorized in summary, as was his habit in important matters of advocacy where he relied on his ability to persuade skeptical groups. Roosevelt laid out the plan to the congressional leadership on January 10, 1937.†

The President would have six senior executive assistants to help him with different policy areas; there would be a substantial strengthening of the budget, efficiency research, planning, and personnel services activities of the federal government; the whole new administration would be put on a career basis, and the civil service merit system would be extended throughout it.

The 105 boards, agencies, and other miscellaneous entities that had arisen alongside the traditional departments would be grouped appropriately together under the twelve cabinet secretaries, two of whom would be the newly created secretaries of social welfare and public works. It was proposed to transform the secretary of the interior into the secretary of conservation. An independent auditor general would be appointed, who would report to the Congress and would have full powers of audit throughout the executive branch to monitor performance, expose waste, corruption, and inefficiency, and recommend reforms and improvements.

Moved forward to January 20, the inauguration was bound to be in colder weather. Roosevelt, because of his relative immobility, always had a susceptibility to heavy colds and severe sinus attacks. The doctor assigned him from the navy when he entered the White House, Ross McIntire, had developed a technique for cauterizing the President's sinuses with a thin wire, which relieved pressure

---

* The original committee members were Brownlow; Charles Merriam, chairman of the department of political science at the University of Chicago; Beardsley Ruml, dean of the University of Chicago's social science department; and Guy Moffet, director of the Rockefeller Foundation's Spelman Fund.
† Present were Vice President Garner; the new Speaker of the House (replacing Henry Rainey, who had died), William Bankhead, better known as the father of the waspish and sultry red-haired actress Tallulah Bankhead (see chapter 24); Senate Majority Leader Robinson of Arkansas; the chairman of the Senate Finance Committee, Pat Harrison of Mississippi; and the chairman of the House Appropriations and Ways and Means Committees, James Buchanan of Texas and Robert Doughton of North Carolina.

and hastened recovery. This improvisation was the chief ingredient in McIntire's meteoric rise from lieutenant to rear admiral and surgeon general of the U.S. Navy. McIntire frequently cautioned his patient against the risks of incurring a cold, and inauguration day was another such occasion. Roosevelt continued in 1937, as in 1933, to ignore such advice.

Roosevelt decreed an extensive military parade, but would be deprived of the company of General Douglas MacArthur. He had retired with Roosevelt's approval to the Philippines in 1935 after the expiry of his commission as army chief of staff, which Roosevelt had extended for a year.*

On January 20, 1937, the new army chief of staff, General Malin Craig, stood beside the President. He was not a historical figure to rival those who came before and after him (George C. Marshall), but Roosevelt got on well with him. Roosevelt's only concession to his doctor's advice about the inclement weather was that he rode in a closed car to the religious service that Endicott Peabody conducted for the President and his intimates on inauguration day morning. This year, Peabody did not ask for divine intervention against the dangers of "violence, confusion, and discord," as he had at the service four years before. As Chief Justice Hughes swore him in, Roosevelt tossed his head emphatically and stressed the oath's reference to the Constitution.

He had worked at length with Rosenman, Corcoran, and Richberg on the inaugural address, and wanted to strike a precise tone. He claimed that: "The greatest change we have witnessed has been the change in the moral climate of America. . . . 'For each age is a dream that is dying, or one that is coming to birth.' . . . We have come far from the days of stagnation and despair. Vitality has been preserved. Courage and confidence have been restored. Mental and moral horizons have been extended. . . . To hold to progress today, however, is more difficult. Dulled conscience, irresponsibility, and ruthless self-interest already reappear. . . .

"I see millions of families trying to live on incomes so meager that the pall of family disaster hangs over them day by day. I see millions whose daily lives in city and on farm continue under conditions labeled indecent by a so-called polite society half a century ago.

"I see millions denied education, recreation, and the opportunity to better their lot and the lot of their children. I see millions lacking the means to buy the products of farm and factory and by their poverty denying work and productiveness to many other millions. I see one third of a nation ill-housed, ill-clad, ill-nourished.

"It is not in despair that I paint you that picture. I paint it for you in hope — because the Nation seeing and understanding the injustice in it, proposes to

---

* In 1934 that country had been promised its independence in ten years. MacArthur took over the task of preparing the Philippines militarily for full statehood. He became a local field marshal and designed his famous "scrambled eggs" (of gold decoration) hat.

paint it out. We are determined to make every American citizen the subject of his country's interest and concern; and we will never regard any faithful law-abiding group within our borders as superfluous. The test of our progress is not whether we add more to the abundance of those who have much; it is whether we provide enough for those who have too little."

Four years before, he had concentrated public attention on the economic emergency, which he repeatedly described as equivalent to war. That great struggle had been won. Now he called on those who were comfortable for a general advance to save the one-third of society that had been left behind. The speech was well received. It gave hope to the excluded, such as most of the African-Americans, but gave no rightful offense to the affluent.

———————

By 1937, as had been demonstrated in South America, Franklin D. Roosevelt enjoyed very great prestige not only in every region of the United States but throughout the world. He was the only leader of a major country who appeared decisive, energetic, and benign. The French and British statesmen seemed dyspeptic, ineffective, and unimaginative, as, with few exceptions, they were. The same adjectives could not be applied to Hitler, Mussolini, and Stalin, and they all had their admirers in the Western democracies. But to the great majority in the democratic countries, these were sinister men with blood-stained hands preaching and practicing hatred and violence. There were much-admired leaders in secondary countries but only Roosevelt carried the ideals of Western liberal democracy with the originality, courage, and panache that could universally attract admirers, reassure democratic believers, and refute the widespread theory that democracy was doomed to be surpassed by the Fascists or the Communists.

His splendid appearance, boundless optimism, success at restoring American prosperity and morale, great concern for the disadvantaged, and soaring eloquence were inspiring. He smiled often, but never seemed silly, over-confident, or even unserious. His constantly mobile features were somehow strong and sober, yet cheerful. His gifts as a leader were natural, and his mastery of modern public relations techniques, a skill at which only Hitler among contemporary leaders now rivalled him, made him a unique and heartening figure to countless millions of people all over the world.

᪥

"Save the Constitution From the Court and the Court From Itself"

(Felix Frankfurter, letter to Franklin D. Roosevelt, February 7, 1937)

I

THE LONG-ANTICIPATED confrontation between the President and the Supreme Court was precipitated by Roosevelt at the beginning of February 1937. He had determined not to await passively the Court's pleasure in adjudicating the remaining core of his legislative program. He had asked both Corcoran and Cohen, his most astute legalists, and the canny Yankee attorney general, Homer Cummings, for their suggestions. Corcoran and Cohen were far along with a constitutional amendment proposal that would enable a two-thirds congressional majority, or a simple majority after an intervening election, to overturn Supreme Court invalidations of federal and state legislation.

Cummings produced an alternative proposal. As usual with Roosevelt, both drafting parties worked in total ignorance of the existence of the other. The attorney general's proposal would add a judge for every judge on a federal court who continued beyond a seventieth birthday. No more than a grand total of fifty judges named in this way could serve at any one time, and no more than two at any time on most courts, including the circuit courts of appeals. For the Supreme Court of the United States, however, the ceiling was that the Court was not to exceed fifteen members. This was an attack of astonishing boldness on a venerable institution.

The Court's membership had varied by statute between six and ten from 1789 until fixed at nine in 1869. In 1937, six of its nine members were seventy or over.* Cummings had discovered that Justice James McReynolds, when he was Wilson's attorney general, had proposed a similar measure but it was not taken forward. Despite their service together in the Wilson administration, McReynolds disliked Roosevelt, and it was generally known by Washington insiders, certainly including the President, that McReynolds had sworn he would "never resign as long as that crippled son-of-a-bitch is in the White House."[1] The impact of such sentiments upon Roosevelt may be imagined.

The Corcoran-Cohen plan was cumbrous and would require the very laborious (in this case probably impossible) procedure of securing the approval of thirty-six states necessary for constitutional amendment.

Cummings singled out the Supreme Court for particularly heavy alteration and the aged justices for direct rebuke, including Brandeis, who was a Roosevelt supporter but whom Roosevelt considered a judicial imperialist and a source of foolish economic ideas that distracted many of the intelligent young officeholders who were Brandeis protégés. Roosevelt and Cummings both wanted to address a powerful riposte to an over-mighty Court, and believed they had the approval of the people and the Congress to do it.

The draft legislation was couched in terms to relieve the courts of work overload. No reference was made to any grievance about individual judgments that had been rendered. Roosevelt and Cummings unveiled their plan to Solicitor General Stanley Reed, Samuel Rosenman, and Donald Richberg at lunchtime on January 30, the President's fifty-fifth birthday. The President absented himself from the annual White House birthday March of Dimes luncheon with prominent actors and entertainment industry supporters to chair this session. Nothing but a matter of paramount importance would cause him to miss the outpouring of admiration he always received on these occasions from many of the nation's most prominent film stars, all for the cause he loved most, Warm Springs and the fight against polio. On this day, he greeted the March of Dimes guests briefly, left them downstairs, and joined his cabal in the residential dining room.

Rosenman rewrote the proposed message to the Congress that would accompany the draft legislation. He emphasized the declining powers of judges beyond their seventieth birthdays. He was dismayed by what he called the "too clever" flavor of the Roosevelt-Cummings plan. Rosenman persuaded Roosevelt to accept "A lowered mental or physical vigor leads men to avoid the examination of complicated or changed conditions" and a few similar sentences. He also persuaded him to allow Corcoran and Cohen to look at the suggested legislation on the strict understanding that Cummings would not know that they had been con-

---

* Brandeis (eighty), Willis Van Devanter (seventy-seven), Hughes and McReynolds (seventy-five), George Sutherland (seventy-four), and Pierce Butler (seventy). Benjamin Cardozo was sixty-six, Harlan Stone sixty-four, and Owen Roberts sixty-one.

sulted. Roosevelt's methods of running parallel activities led to absurd and demeaning complexities.

Cohen and Corcoran were horrified. Cohen was without excessive ambition and completely lacking in vindictiveness. He believed passionately in a scholarly, patient approach to the law and jurisprudence. Disappointments such as the onslaught of the Supreme Court should be fought by some combination of action by the states, attrition producing younger judges, and the constitutional amendment procedure. An assault of this kind, under the false pretense of encouraging efficiency, which would establish a dangerous precedent and subordinate the judiciary permanently to the executive, he regarded as a menace to democratic republican traditions. He thought that the legislation was evidence that Roosevelt had been transported by the proportions of his electoral victory.[2]

Corcoran was also a very knowledgeable and distinguished lawyer, but he was an Irish political alley cat and an uncritical, not to say worshipful, follower of Roosevelt's, but he too dissented. In Corcoran's case, there was the additional question of tactics. He had tried to persuade Senator Burton K. Wheeler, who was as annoyed as any member of the Congress by the antics of the Supreme Court, to sponsor a court-packing plan and Wheeler had absolutely refused. Corcoran liked to punish his enemies as much as Roosevelt did, and the President's enemies were his own enemies, but as a serious lawyer he disapproved of this method, and as a professional political operator, he didn't think this initiative would fly.

Roosevelt abandoned the constitutional amendment route as too time-consuming and vulnerable to Republican resistance in enough states to make unachievable the approval by thirty-six states necessary to amend. He abandoned the partial-override legislation as vulnerable to another declaration of unconstitutionality by the existing Court, establishing a stalemate that would immobilize the government of the United States until the undertaker carried off enough of the incumbent bench. In December 1936, he had floated with the friendly journalist George Creel in *Collier's* magazine the idea of "increasing the number of justices so as to permit the appointment of men in tune with the spirit of the age." There had been no reaction whatever in the national media, which emboldened Roosevelt to believe that this approach might not be such an outrage to the country's political sensibilities as most of his advisers thought.

Roosevelt was right to judge the current situation intolerable. The president, the Congress, and the public could not be stalled indefinitely by five or six septuagenarian humbugs snuffling in their dickies in the Supreme Court robing room about antiquarian legal fineries. Columnists Drew Pearson and Robert Allen had helped set the stage for the President with their best-selling book, published in October 1936, *The Nine Old Men*, portraying the Court as palsied and reactionary. That Roosevelt couldn't find a better way of breaking the logjam is also understandable; no better one was obvious.

That he was quite as disingenuous in his pious expressions of helpfulness to reduce the workload of the justices is surprising, because it was bound to undermine the trust most Americans now invested in him. But what was most surprising was that this masterful politician, without rival in all of American history at making the system work as he wished it to, did not manage this bold venture with anything like the skill he habitually showed in even small and uncontroversial matters.

The annual Judiciary Ball was held at the White House February 2, 1937. President Roosevelt was his usual affable self. All the Supreme Court justices except the antisocial Brandeis and the convalescing Stone were present, and the Chief Justice, in particular, reciprocated the President's joviality. Cummings, Rosenman, Reed, and Richberg were also present, and Roosevelt had a drink with them privately before the arrival of nearly a hundred other guests. An unmistakable air of conspiracy united the President, the attorney general, and their intimate collaborators.

Roosevelt and his task force continued to refine the documentation the following day, February 3, and at the end of the afternoon the President issued the unprecedented instruction that the White House staff arrive for work at 6:30 the following morning, and summoned a cabinet meeting for 10 A.M. and a press conference for 11 A.M. The Democratic congressional leaders and the chairmen of the Senate and House Judiciary Committees were invited to join the cabinet meeting. The presidential press and appointments secretaries, Steve Early and Marvin McIntyre, were not told the subject of these unscheduled meetings and were unable to assuage the curiosity of the invitees. By the end of the day Washington insiders knew that a very large shoe was about to drop.

The White House staff had mimeographed reams of material and prepared the attorney general's letter and the presidential message to Congress and a draft for the cabinet, the congressional leaders, and the press by the time Roosevelt began to reveal his plan February 4. He could only give the cabinet and congressional leaders an outline and read a few excerpts, and asked them to leave behind the material before them when they left. It would be personally delivered to them later in the day. He was confident and solicited no questions. He remained exactly one hour and was then wheeled out and to the Oval Office, where he received the press. He displayed no curiosity about the response of his interlocutors; it was an information meeting only.

Roosevelt was a good deal more expansive with the press. He walked them through his bill at length and in considerable good humor. He stressed the question of efficient processing of cases and said that in some jurisdictions "to institute a suit is to embark on a lifelong adventure." Roosevelt read the bill to the reporters, "highspotting" as he put it, certain sections. He pointed out that originally the Supreme Court judges had been somewhat itinerant and had to ride around the district. Having emphasized that that originally meant riding on horseback, he reflected that this was a "pre-horse and buggy court," embellishing on his famous comment of the previous year. He pointed out that 717 of the Supreme Court's 867 petitions for hearings had been rejected in the last year. He referred to the "question of aged or infirm judges—a subject of delicacy and yet one which requires frank discussion."

The President did not refer to the most vexing of the Supreme Court's decisions but did rail against government through "the heavy hand" of injunction, which he said was causing the courts to become "a scattered, loosely organized and slowly operating third house of the National Legislature." This was Roosevelt's academic reasoning: he was not subordinating the judiciary to the executive, he was repulsing a judicial encroachment on the legislature and relying on the legislature to help him do so. The press conference (his 342nd) had its jocular moments, but, following Roosevelt's lengthy recitation, it closed after only a few questions: "Mr. President . . . is this intended to take care of cases where the appointee has lost mental capacity to resign?" (Laughter.) The President: "That is all."

The Judicial Branch Reorganization Plan and accompanying messages were read and distributed in the Congress that afternoon.

Initial reaction to the President's measure contained few surprises. Roosevelt had done Brandeis the courtesy of sending Corcoran to give him notice of it, and Brandeis had naturally expressed "unalterable" opposition, though he did thank the President for forewarning him.[3] The principal southern senators and congressmen, apart from those at the summit of the leadership, Carter Glass and Harry Byrd of Virginia, were opposed. The South had come to regard the Constitution as the guardian of states' rights, in practice of segregation and the unequal treatment of African-Americans, as it had once been a defender of the slaveholding states. The Constitution was and would long remain a partial equalizer for the overwhelming demographic and economic power of the North.

The chairman of the House Judiciary Committee, Hatton Sumners, privately dissented ("Boys, here's where I cash in my chips."[4]) He reserved the right to change his mind without undue public embarrassment and so would say nothing publicly. In a letter to the President he counseled relying on public opinion to change the judges' minds and modestly averred that he was "right as a fox" on the subject.

Senate Majority Leader Robinson and Speaker William Bankhead of Alabama were solidly with the President, but George Norris was discreetly opposed. Roosevelt immediately invited Norris to the White House and had little difficulty persuading the Nebraska progressive, who owed his continued place in the Senate and the fulfilment of his dreams about public ownership of hydroelectricity to Roosevelt, to keep an open mind. Norris was assisted in staying more or less onside by Roosevelt's support of the senator's plan for seven regional authorities modelled on the TVA. (Norris ultimately did not support the bill but defended Roosevelt against the charge of aspiring to be a "dictator, [and] that he is ruthless, hard-hearted, corrupt, ignorant, and sometimes insane."[5])

Press reaction was mixed. Herbert Hoover erupted, accusing Roosevelt of throwing down the mask and revealing his desire to be a dictator. He said the sinister nature of this effort to "pack the court" was revealed by the dishonest manner in which it was disguised. Even sympathetic editorialists were troubled by the disingenuousness of the rationale for the bill. The universally respected moderate Republican editor William Allen White wrote in Kansas's *Emporia Gazette*, February 6, 1937: "Because he is adroit and not forthright, [President Roosevelt] arouses irritating suspicions, probably needlessly, about his ultimate intentions as the leader of his party and the head of Government."

The general expectation was that Roosevelt's magic would work again and he would ram his bill through the Congress. The headline in the *New York Times* declared that the Congress was "expected to approve" it. The list of those the President was expected to name to the Supreme Court was headed by Felix Frankfurter, James M. Landis, Lloyd Garrison, Senator Robert Wagner, and Hatton Sumners.

Frankfurter, whose undoubted brilliance as a jurist was tainted by his relentless truckling to Roosevelt, wrote the President on February 7 and commended him for "the deftness of the general scheme," and asserted that "ways had to be found to save the Constitution from the Court and the Court from itself." He did not express agreement with what Roosevelt had done, confining himself to "deep faith in your instinct to make the wise choice."

Roosevelt responded promptly and laid out the process of elimination by which he arrived at this option. He wrote that the country could not "wait until 1941 or 1942 [for] social and economic national legislation to bring it abreast of the times." He was concerned that returning prosperity had dulled the country's sense of urgency, and repeated his complaint at "the failure of those who have property to realize that I am the best friend the profit system ever had." This was undoubtedly a sincere statement of Roosevelt's view.[6]

From the start, the mail pouring in to senators and congressmen ran at almost eight to one against the bill. Hatton Sumners, while publicly discreet, was lobbying his own House Judiciary Committee against it. Senator Wheeler, one of the most influential progressives, early declared himself against it, and so did normally loyal Democrats Joseph O'Mahoney of Wyoming and Tom Connally of Texas. The early desertion of O'Mahoney and Connally shocked and angered the President.

Wheeler declined personal overtures from the President, including, allegedly, the offer to name one or two of the new Supreme Court Justices. He resisted the President's tangible and intangible charms, rallied western progressives against him, including Gerald Nye, and declared: "A liberal cause was never won by stacking a deck of cards, by stuffing a ballot box, or by packing a court."[7]

The Republicans, who obviously were unanimously opposed, remained silent. They recognized that nothing would unite the Democrats around the President like an attack from the opposition. Landon and even Hoover, after his initial outburst, suppressed their natural urge to attack the court reform bill. Speaker Bankhead and House Majority Leader Sam Rayburn told Roosevelt they could force the bill through the House despite the opposition of Sumners's Judiciary Committee but it would require rough floor management and might imperil the result in the Senate.

Roosevelt then took two tactical decisions with encouragement from Bankhead and Rayburn. They would open the bill in the Senate, where they were confident of having the Judiciary Committee report it out, and Roosevelt would abandon the spurious pretext that he was interested in reducing the judges' workloads and securing swifter justice for the country by adding only a maximum of fifty judges. The President would open a broad attack on the obstreperous, aged, reactionary, usurpatory Supreme Court. He would lead the fight for his bill and would deploy all his vast public prestige to bring the public and the Congress with him. Defectors would be tarred with the brush of reactionary Republicanism. It would be a bare-knuckles fight.

A grand Democratic victory dinner had been planned for March 4, the fourth anniversary of Roosevelt's first inauguration. It was decided to broadcast the dinner live nationally and to follow it with a Fireside Chat to the country on March 9. Cohen, Corcoran, Rosenman, and Richberg worked up drafts of both speeches.

On the evening of March 4, surrounded by the barons of his party and addressing a rabidly partisan audience, Franklin D. Roosevelt carried the battle back into the faces of his opponents. He debunked the argument that what he was proposing was an attack on democracy by invoking the many countries in which democracy had failed because the governments had not responded to desperate economic and social problems.

He recounted the measures that the administration and Congress had taken, and that the people by a vast majority had approved, to alleviate all the ills of the nation—unemployment, floods, drought, destitution, impossible wages and hours and working conditions, child labor, unfair trade practices. He quoted his promises in the late presidential election campaign and at intervals told his audience: "You know who assumed the power to veto, and did veto, that program. . . . Soon the Nation was told by a judicial pronunciamento that although the Federal Government had thus been rendered powerless to touch the problems of hours and wages, the states were equally helpless; and that it pleased the 'personal economic predilections' of a majority of the [Supreme] Court that we live in a Nation where there is no legal power anywhere to deal with its most difficult practical problems—a No Man's Land of final futility.

"I defy anyone to read the [Court's many opinions on New Deal legislation] and tell us exactly what, if anything, we can do for the industrial worker, [farmer, etc.] in this session of the Congress with any reasonable certainty that what we do will not be nullified as unconstitutional. . . . How can we confidently complete the Tennessee Valley project or extend it to the Ohio and other valleys while the lowest courts have not hesitated to paralyze its operations by sweeping injunctions?

"The Ohio River and the Dust Bowl are not conversant with the habits of the Interstate Commerce Clause." He invited the "defeatist lawyers" to give their advice to "sweating men piling sandbags on the levees at Cairo, Illinois. . . .

"If we would keep faith with those who had faith in us, if we would make democracy succeed, I say we must act—now!"

It was a powerful performance that electrified the President's followers and encouraged those who had been unimpressed with his disingenuous launch. The March 9 Fireside Chat was another effective piece of advocacy. The President said that the present Supreme Court "has been acting not as a judicial body but as a policy-making body." He illustrated his point by quoting a number of recent dissenting opinions, including Justice Stone's allegation in the recent New York minimum wage law case that the majority were reading into the Constitution their own "personal economic predilections."

He also quoted Chief Justice Hughes as saying, "We are under a Constitution but the Constitution is what the judges say it is," and then added: "We want a Supreme Court which will do justice under the Constitution—not over it. In our Courts we want a government of laws and not of men."

He ridiculed somewhat histrionically the claim of trying to "pack" the Court. He was seeking not "spineless puppets" but "Justices who will act as Justices and not as legislators.

"This plan of mine is no attack on the Court; it seeks to restore the Court to its rightful and historic place in our system of Constitutional government." He claimed that those advocating constitutional amendment were just trying to mire the country in legal, social, and economic stagnation for their own questionable motives, despite the fact that Cohen and Corcoran were among them.

"The present attempt by those opposed to progress to play upon the fears of danger to personal liberty brings again to mind that crude and cruel strategy tried by that same opposition to frighten the workers of America in a pay envelope propaganda against the Social Security Law. The workers were not fooled by that propaganda then. The people of America will not be fooled by such propaganda now." He was seeking to restore the balance among the three branches of the federal government. "You who know me will accept my solemn assurance that in a world in which democracy is under attack, I seek to make American democracy succeed. You and I will do our part."

This was a high-risk strategy. Comparing the Supreme Court to the Republican scoundrels who produced the pay-envelope scam in the middle of the 1936 election campaign was straining credulity. So was linking his opponents to foreigners who had advocated or passively succumbed to totalitarianism. So was the insinuation that the Court was motivated altogether by partisanship and antiquarian reaction.

There was the usual flood of supportive letters and telegrams to the White House. The polls, which had started out even and then tilted to about a 10 percent lead for the bill's opponents, were brought back to level pegging by the President's speeches, but he would normally expect a more dramatic effect than that. The country did not approve the Court's verdicts but was clearly very uneasy about this degree of interference in the independence of the judiciary. Cummings made an indifferent impression in the Judiciary Committee hearings, harping still on the judges' caseload and excessive dockets.

Corcoran and Roosevelt became concerned that the opposition tactic was to filibuster with lengthy and over-numerous questions, and they abruptly stopped the government's procession of witnesses after two weeks, before half of them had been heard. Roosevelt would gamble on the ability of his supporters to maul opposition witnesses and on his own ability to overcome doubts with further direct appeals to public opinion, though he didn't have many more oratorical guns to fire.

II

ROOSEVELT AND HIS advisers believed that though the senatorial opposition was strong, the Court could be relied upon to blow up its own case by bringing in a new series of verdicts negating the most popular New Deal measures. In the alternative, to save itself the Court would have to undergo a miracle of judicious conversion and stop striking down New Deal measures.

Collusion between the opposition senators and justices reached levels of efficacy that had not been foreseen. Senator Burton Wheeler was friendly personally with Brandeis, who had been a crusader for popular government against what he considered exploitive financial interests for many years before coming to the high court. He continued, through his son-in-law, Paul Raushenbush, a prominent administration legislative draftsman, to have a direct influence on government, particularly playing a role in the writing of the Social Security Act.

Brandeis was also constantly giving advice to Frankfurter, who pipelined it on to Roosevelt, sometimes identifying the originating author and sometimes taking what he fancied to be the credit for himself.

Wheeler, now very disaffected personally from Roosevelt, called on Brandeis at his home on March 20, 1937, and Brandeis prevailed upon him to call the Chief Justice to ask for a letter refuting the claim that the Supreme Court was unable to discharge its workload. Hughes produced such a letter and presented it to Wheeler the next day, March 21, so that it would open the opposition Senate hearings the following day, Monday, March 22. Hughes flatly rejected Roosevelt's claims. He wrote that the rejection of 717 of 867 petitions to be heard in the previous year had nothing to do with workload; that the cases were inadmissible on legal grounds and that no Supreme Court could be accessible to every litigant who wished to appear there. The Chief Justice discounted the possibility of dividing the Court into more panels if there were more judges, on the implausible grounds that the Constitution provided for "a Supreme Court," not several or more highest courts.

Hughes also purported to speak for the entire Court in his letter, although he consulted none of the other justices except Brandeis. This was sharp practice for a rather sanctimonious holder of the nation's supreme juridical office already under attack for usurping the functions of the legislature. This letter did have a dramatic impact, reopening the issue of the President's trustworthiness and therefore of his real motives and jurisdictional ambitions.

Senator Carter Glass responded to the President's March 9 Fireside Chat in a radio address on March 29. Glass was not Roosevelt as an orator and was not especially well known to the public. He was a conservative, illiberal, gold-standard and balanced-budget, segregationist, states' rights Virginian. Yet he was effective in his way. He described Roosevelt's bill as "utterly destitute of moral sensibility . . . [and an] attempt to replace representative government with autocracy."

The most important and unforeseen development in the Supreme Court battle on the day of the Glass radio speech was the Supreme Court's decision completely reversing itself on the matter of state minimum wage laws. The youngest justice, Owen Roberts, a comparative liberal and a protégé of Hughes's, detached himself from the conservatives in the earlier *Morehead v. Tipaldo* case, which had invalidated the New York minimum wage law, and supported the state of Washington's right to impose an identical law in *West Coast Hotel Co. v. Parrish.* This was a 180-degree turn for Roberts from June 1936 to March 1937, and he provided the swing vote on the case. Hughes himself wrote the decision.

Frankfurter, who had straddled with the skill of the agile juridical politician that he was, moved off the fence with this and wrote to Roosevelt March 30: "A blind man ought to see that the Court is in politics, and understand how the Constitution is 'judicially' construed. [Hughes's letter] was a characteristic Hughes performance—part and parcel of that pretended withdrawal from considerations of policy, while trying to shape them, which is the core of the mischief of which the majority have so long been guilty." He expressed "sadness" at the behavior of Brandeis. Frankfurter's assistant, Thomas Powell, felicitously added, "A switch in time saves nine."[8]

The duplicity of the Court and of Hughes in particular was confirmed on April 12, 1937, when the Court reported its verdicts on three cases determining the Wagner Labor Relations Act to be constitutional. The principal case, *NLRB v. Jones and Laughlin Steel,* revealed another complete U-turn by Roberts and Hughes; the Chief Justice deadpanned a dispositive reasoning diametrically opposed to what he and the Court had found the previous year in a practically indistinguishable case.

Roosevelt's position had been slipping in the polls and he was strongly advised at this point to take a compromise. The Supreme Court decisions were generally seen as a victory for him, and the public concern about the intrusion of the Court—and the fate of Social Security and the National Labor Relations Board, in particular—had subsided. The Senate Majority leader, Joe Robinson, allegedly told FDR that he could get two additional justices on the Supreme

Court but not six, but that they would have to move at once. It was also thought by some that if Congress gave the justices a more generous pension, some would be happy to retire. This was conjecture but might have been worth a try.

This is the point at which Roosevelt's tactics become uncharacteristically questionable. He ignored Robinson's advice, told his April 13 press conference that he was continuing to seek passage of his bill without significant amendments, and went on a two-week fishing trip in the Gulf of Mexico on the presidential yacht *Potomac*, leaving his entourage to fend for itself in the troubled waters of Washington.

When he returned to Washington, he invited Robinson, Bankhead, and Sam Rayburn to the White House. The three advised the President on May 14 that there was practically no chance of his bill passing in its present form; they urged him to accept a compromise or leave the bill until the next session, at which time it would be known from further key judgments whether the Supreme Court had gone back to its reactionary ways or was a durably self-reformed institution. The Senate Judiciary Committee was going to report out the bill May 18 with a ten-to-eight recommendation to the full Senate not to approve.

Yet another complexity occurred on May 18: Justice Willis Van Devanter sent Roosevelt notice of his intention to retire from the bench.* Brandeis and Hughes had urged Van Devanter to remain, even though he could no longer write opinions because of a shortening concentration span and physical enfeeblement.[10]

Roosevelt had promised Joe Robinson that he could have the next vacant seat on the Supreme Court, which was the summit of Robinson's ambition and the prospect that had retained his absolute loyalty to the President's program despite his southerner's conservative reservations about many aspects of it.

The resignation of Van Devanter further weakened the argument for the Supreme Court reform bill, because Roosevelt would finally get to name someone to the Court. It also put the President on the horns of a dilemma: if he named Robinson he would get another conservative justice and lose a strong manager in the Senate. If he did not, he would alienate his Senate leader.

Finally, Roosevelt's hand was forced. The President considered the unpromising state of his bill for two weeks, during which Robinson fretted anxiously. Then, on June 3, he called Robinson to the White House, confirmed that he was his nominee to the Supreme Court, and asked for the best compromise possible. Robinson gratefully promised an all-out effort on behalf of a proposal that had already been floating around for some weeks. Initially put forward by Senator Carl Hatch of New Mexico, it allowed the President to name a coadjutor justice for each justice seventy-five or over, with a limit of one such appointment a year

---

* Van Devanter would be missed as much as a character as a jurist. He was a frontiersman who had been chief justice of Wyoming Territory while still in his twenties and had hunted with Buffalo Bill. He became a very successful railway lawyer and was an influential justice whom Taft, when he was the Chief Justice, had called "the Lord Chancellor."[9]

to the Supreme Court. (Cummings's original posturing about reforming the other federal courts had been abandoned months before.)

Roosevelt had delayed too long. Public opinion polls had eroded support of even a compromise measure to about 35 percent. The President's methods had riled many people in Congress, and that institution, which had often smarted under the allegation of being a rubber stamp for the Roosevelt White House, reassured that it was not under attack from the Supreme Court, was in a rebellious mood.

The debacle had spread well beyond the Congress. In order to round up support for his faltering bill, Roosevelt had made what amounted to a Faustian bargain with United Mine Workers' leader John L. Lewis. Lewis had taken to the national airwaves May 14 and denounced the Supreme Court as "a tyrannical and oligarchic tribunal, which arrogates to itself even the power of defying the wishes of the people of the United States. . . . The time of reckoning is . . . at hand." Lewis emphatically supported the President's bill and said that "the future of labor in America is intimately connected with the future of the President's proposal."

The quid pro quo for this endorsement was Roosevelt's policy of official toleration of the technique of the sit-down strike, the illegal occupation by strikers of strike-bound property, with the sometimes explicit threat to operate the assets for the account of the strikers and not the owners. This was lawless Communism, which appalled Roosevelt as much as it did any American capitalist. To have paid this price for the support of so tempestuous a personality for such a questionable piece of legislation as his Supreme Court bill was tactically mad and substantively deeply worrying to his supporters, at the time and in posterity.

Roosevelt professed to believe that labor should learn for itself that the sit-down strike was "damned unpopular. . . . It will take . . . perhaps three years [for the unions to learn that], but that is a short time in the life . . . and education of a nation." It might be, but constitutionally there was no substitute for the President as a teacher. Roosevelt even maneuvered through his loyalists in the Senate to prevent adoption of a measure sponsored by Senator Byrnes of South Carolina condemning the sit-down strike.[11]

The combination of his attempt to pack the Supreme Court and his refusal publicly to attack this Communistic method of labor agitation put his centrist coalition under considerable strain.

John Nance Garner had departed Washington somewhat clangorously June 14, it being well known that he did not approve the Court bill or the way it was being advanced, or the official toleration of the sit-down strike. He went to his home in Uvalde, Texas, and ignored Roosevelt's request for his return. The Senate Judiciary Committee's report on the bill was also published June 14. It was more antagonistic than the White House could have imagined. The bill was described as "a needless, futile, and utterly dangerous abandonment of constitutional principle, [which would] destroy the independence of the judiciary, the only certain shield of individual rights."[12]

The faithful Senator Robinson introduced the compromise Court reform bill on July 2. It was bound to be an uphill fight, and the administration was not pitching in support of this measure as it had in February and March for the original. Robinson had to leave the Senate floor with chest pains July 12 and never returned. He died of a coronary in the early hours of July 14.

The rampaging Burton Wheeler tastelessly demanded that Roosevelt withdraw his bill "lest he appear to be fighting against God." The President wrote July 15 a public letter to the acting majority leader, Alben W. Barkley of Kentucky, condemning the lack of "decency" in the morbid antics of his opponents, without naming his former supporter Wheeler, and asking Barkley to continue the fight. The following day he felt obliged, in the face of the evident impossibility of putting even his watered-down measure across, to accept a further climbdown. A new measure was prepared, which accepted the principle of Court expansion by authorizing the President to appoint one coadjutor justice to the Supreme Court, but not for any justice currently on the bench.

However, the President compounded his former errors by not attending Robinson's funeral in Little Rock and by seeming to have immersed himself in the struggle for the succession to the majority leader by supporting Barkley over his rival, Pat Harrison of Mississippi, who also had been faithful to Roosevelt over many personal philosophical reservations. When Harrison visited the President and angrily accused him of favoritism, Roosevelt denied it and approved a public statement denying it. Since he and his staff had already lobbied a number of senators in favor of Barkley, this fragmented his Democratic support and added to the appearance, which he had earned and acquired throughout this lamentable affair, of inept double-dealing.

Robinson's funeral was on July 18. Garner represented the President, and on the train that brought the large congressional delegation back to Washington, at Roosevelt's request, he carefully canvassed senatorial opinion on what was left of the Supreme Court bill. On July 19, in what must have seemed to him a bloodless reenactment of the end of Julius Caesar, Roosevelt was confronted in that day's newspapers with a hostile column by General Hugh Johnson and an open letter from Governor Lehman to Senator Wagner urging Wagner to vote against the Court bill.

Roosevelt summoned Johnson to the White House and read to him, as if Johnson, the author of the column, were unaware of its contents, the offending statement that Robinson's death spared Robinson the knowledge that Roosevelt had no intention of naming him to the Supreme Court. FDR then, according to what he told Ickes a few days later, as Ickes recorded it in his diary, glared at Johnson and twice called him "a liar, a coward, and a cad." (Not an inaccurate assessment, but the fact of being a cad was scarcely relevant, and Roosevelt wasn't an appropriate source of such criticism.) More to the point, Johnson was a monstrous ingrate who would never have been heard of without Roosevelt's patronage, as well as an often helpless alcoholic. Roosevelt claimed to Ickes, believably, that Johnson then simpered and burst into tears.[13]

Roosevelt didn't, so far as is known, respond to Governor Lehman's gratuitous performance. The Court was no direct concern of the New York governor's, and Lehman owed almost as much for his career to Roosevelt as did Johnson. Frankfurter wrote Roosevelt about Lehman on July 19: "Some things just aren't done — they violate the decencies of human relations and offend the good taste and decorum of friendship."

Roosevelt accepted with equanimity Garner's judgment of July 20: "If you want it with the bark off, you're licked, Cap'n." He asked Garner in perfect composure to wind down the debate with as much dignity as could be salvaged.

Barkley was confirmed as majority leader of the Senate on July 21, but only by a 38–37 margin, and there was great rancor against Roosevelt in the Harrison ranks. However, Barkley owed his job to Roosevelt and did not forget it, at least for a while. (He denied in his memoirs that Roosevelt's influence put him across, but it had influenced more than the one vote that was the margin of victory.[14]) The hideously vexatious Court reform bill was recommitted and the Judiciary Committee produced the final compromise measure, the Judicial Procedure Reform Act of 1937, on July 29.

This measure assured early notice to the federal government of cases with constitutional implications and gave federal government counsel the right to appear in such cases. Appeals in these cases were to be expedited to the Supreme Court. Constitutional injunctions would now require three judges instead of only one and would be limited in duration to sixty days. These were worthwhile changes — "a step in the right direction," said the president — but were not much noticed in the aftermath of the protracted fiasco of Roosevelt's relentlessly bungled management of his original proposal.

That struggle was over but not all its consequences. The Frankenstein's monster of John L. Lewis continued to lurch around the country. When Lewis in his capacity as head of the Committee for Industrial Organization (later the Congress of Industrial Organizations) had seized a General Motors plant in Flint on February 1, 1937, the company secured an eviction order, but the governor of Michigan, Frank Murphy, refused to execute the order. General Motors automobile production was reduced to under 500 per month, and the company negotiated directly with Lewis a collective agreement. The Auto Workers' Union grew between January and September 1937 from 88,000 to 400,000 members. Lewis had further triumphs, including U.S. Steel, RCA, General Electric, and Firestone. But Ford, Goodyear Tire and Rubber, and secondary steel companies such as Republic resisted, and there was considerable violence at several flashpoints — especially Republic's plant in South Chicago on Memorial Day, 1937, when ten strikers were killed by the police.

Roosevelt favored seriously improved working conditions for most of America's workers but didn't like the manipulation of mobs by the labor leaders or any-one (other than benignly and peacefully by elected political leaders, especially himself). He considered the occupation of work sites and incitements to violence to be revolutionary and unacceptable as such, though he regarded some of labor's excesses as having been provoked by management exploitation over a long period.

The South Chicago Memorial Day Massacre, as much of the media called it, caused him at his press conference on June 29 to say of the lawlessness of both sides in the strike: "A plague on both their houses" (from *Romeo and Juliet*). He had come to realize that an alliance with Lewis offended much of labor and almost everyone else, and as his Court bill sank he took his distance from the CIO leader.

Lewis's attack on the constellation of companies around the unyielding Henry Ford, including what was known as "Little Steel" (in comparison with U.S. Steel and Bethlehem Steel), gradually failed over the summer. And Lewis addressed 25 million people by radio September 3, condemning his former patron. Of Roosevelt he said: "It ill behooves one who has supped at labor's table and who has been sheltered in labor's house to curse, with equal fervor and fine impartiality, both labor and its adversaries when they become locked in deadly embrace." It was a magnificent oratorical performance and it was not unwelcome to the President. He was beginning, painstakingly, to recapture the commanding heights of the center of American politics. Such a process would not be assisted by an alliance with a man regarded as a megalomaniac even by many of those who did not consider him an extremist. At his press conference the day after Lewis's speech, Roosevelt said he had no reaction to it.

Roosevelt had set out in February to lead the legislative and executive branches together to repulse the judicial branch of government from a trespass on their prerogatives. By June, having forced retreat on the judiciary, the executive was facing legislative and judicial branches united by a desire to put the executive back in its (co-equal) place. It was yet another flattering reflection on the great talents of the authors of the U.S. Constitution; the system of checks and balances had worked again. It was not such a generous commentary on the (still) legendary political acumen of Franklin D. Roosevelt.

His refusal to compromise promptly when it was obvious that his bill was in difficulty and the opposition was spreading to widely divergent groups appears hubristic as well as inept. True to his customary practice, Roosevelt never even hinted that he might have erred, and claimed that his message of February 5, 1937, was "a turning point in our modern history."

Roosevelt was right when he claimed: "The Court yielded. The Court changed. The Court began to interpret the Constitution instead of torturing it."[15] Since he was correct in this opinion, the question remains of why, after achieving that, he persisted so unsuccessfully to seek further changes in the composition of the Court that he was warned were not achievable.

However, the Court reform saga had been more damaging to Roosevelt in the political class than with the public, whom he never doubted (correctly) still supported him. He got to appoint one new justice and forced the Court to judge his legislation more favorably, thus saving the most popular parts of his reform program. His public speeches on the controversy had been eloquent, and he accepted the final results graciously. The fears of those who thought he was an aspiring dictator had been allayed, though not banished. He remained very popular, unemployment continued to decline through 1937, and those who had earned his animosity would have good reason to be uneasy. The mystery remains of why such a talented leader so mishandled such an important issue.

III

THE ADMINISTRATION'S LEGISLATIVE program had been passed in parts through the spring and summer despite the Court battle. The Bituminous Coal Act restored most of what the Court had struck down with the Guffey Act in 1936. The Bankhead-Jones Farm Tenancy Act advanced low-interest loans to tenant farmers trying to become farm owners. The Trade Agreement Act facilitated trade liberalization agreements of the kind Secretary of State Hull continued to seek (without conspicuous success). The United States Housing Authority was established on a bill presented by Senator Wagner with a budget of $500 million to construct low-rent housing and to pay rent supplements for low-income tenants.

Roosevelt also achieved passage of an anti-tax-avoidance measure. Morgenthau had sent him a letter May 29, 1937, explaining that tax receipts had been $600 million less than had been foreseen because of cunning avoidance measures devised for wealthy Americans by tax specialists. What ensued in the President's message to the Congress, June 1, including the Treasury secretary's letter, was another outburst of Roosevelt's rather quaint, pseudo-religious notions of the moral duty of tax-paying. He asserted: "The decency of American morals is involved. The example of successful tax dodging by a minority of very rich individuals breeds efforts by other people to dodge other laws as well as tax laws.

"It is also a matter of deep regret to know that lawyers of high standing at the Bar not only have advised and are advising their clients to utilize tax avoidance devices, but are actively using these devices in their own personal affairs."

This measure, which closed a number of what subsequently became known as "loopholes," was adopted, but the public discussion revealed the particular combination of naïveté, sanctimony, and political posturing that afflicted Roosevelt on this subject. He morally assimilated legal efforts at tax minimization, the simple effort of a taxpayer to pay the minimum required by law, to lawbreaking. His preoccupation with income inequalities as America and the world struggled with the Depression was understandable, but it is surprising that this champion of constitutional rights, and the rights of property prominent among them, would have no sensitivity to the concept of a citizen's entitlement to retain his income.

He saw no evident philosophical limits to the practice of taking money from people who had earned it, spreading it around the growing apparatus of government, and massaging the remaining proceeds among people who hadn't earned it, on a rather arbitrarily adjudicated basis of merit. The irritation of his political opponents was aggravated by his enjoyment of the vast perquisites of public office at taxpayers' expense.

He told Cummings to prosecute a wealthy person whose taxpaying was illegal — "one son of a bitch," as he said. He had already unsuccessfully persecuted Andrew Mellon. Richard Whitney and Moses Annenberg would be the next prominent targets. Whitney, the confident leader of the market reassurance forces in 1929 and president of the New York Stock Exchange, who led the opposition to the Securities Exchange Act, was exposed as a thief on a large scale after his company went into bankruptcy. He went off to prison as he did everything, with self-possession, even elegance, but is not a particularly sympathetic figure.

In sum, and to borrow a phrase from John L. Lewis, it ill-behooved someone who luxuriated in the public trough and lectured those far more adept at the ways of constructive commerce than he to preach the moral virtues of fiscal self-deprivation while persecuting selected victims. (Other opponents of Roosevelt's, including Colonel McCormick, were constantly being subjected to tax audits, but left no room for even malicious prosecution.)

When J.P. Morgan Jr. said that "Congress should know how to levy taxes, and if it doesn't know how to collect them, a man is a fool to pay taxes," Roosevelt wrote to a friend: "What do you think of JPM's exposition of Christianity the other day? . . . Ask yourself what Christ would say about the American Bench and Bar were he to return today." It is disconcerting to Roosevelt's historical admirers, as it was to many of his contemporaries, that he seems not to have considered that the same exalted judge might also have had some reservations about his own conduct at times. This is not a theological treatise, but the first Christian said nothing about rendering to Caesar more than was his due.

Roosevelt was particularly outraged when a distant cousin, Alexander Forbes, wrote to the *Boston Herald* that the President should consider the contrast between "the sorry spectacle presented by long rows of beneficiaries leaning on their shovels by the hour, at futile projects, and . . . the great universities, museums, and research libraries which have come from the wise and generous giving of such as Morgan."[16]

Roosevelt seems never to have thought through the moral and philosophical implications of some of the political poses that he struck. There was a churlishness that flickered intermittently in his attitude to his economic critics. Psychiatric liberties are hazardous, but some psychological displacements almost certainly were at work, probably originating in the frustrations of his youth at

Groton and in regard to the Porcellian, of his commercial maladroitness, and of his infirmity.

Some of his less admirable tendencies were demonstrated in the massively publicized wedding in the spring of 1937 between FDR Jr. and Ethel DuPont, daughter of one of the President's most rabid wealthy antagonists. Roosevelt behaved like the gentleman that he was, but took an inordinate pleasure among his intimates, some of whom he had had invited to the wedding, in the incongruity of the festivities. He enjoyed the opulent surroundings and celebrations, and according to his son James, "kissed all the bridesmaids."

The Supreme Court nominee Roosevelt eventually put forward to replace Van Devanter was Senator Hugo Black of Alabama, who passed the Senate easily after assuring Senator Borah, who had been delegated to find out, that he was not a member of the Ku Klux Klan.

After his confirmation it came to light in the *Pittsburgh Post Gazette* that Black had been a Klan member as recently as 1923. Black was on holiday in Europe at this time, and he and Roosevelt deferred any comment on the subject until his return to the United States at the end of September. Black addressed a very large radio audience October 1, 1937, and deplored a "planned and concerted" ex parte attack that had been conducted against him. He spoke of his long and warm relations with members of the Alabama Roman Catholic and Jewish communities (but didn't emphasize blacks), said that he had withdrawn from the Klan when he became a U.S. senator, and that he had had no connection with it since. He declined to comment further, and the controversy died.

Roosevelt was by this time on one of his transcontinental rail tours. He had left Hyde Park on September 22, and went through several national parks and much of the country's most magnificent scenery in Washington, Idaho, Montana, and Wyoming. He conspicuously snubbed senators O'Mahoney and Wheeler when he went through their states, though he did appear in public with Borah.

The saga of Burton Wheeler is mysterious. He had been the first senator to declare for Roosevelt as a presidential nominee in 1931 (Chapter 5), and had fought an uphill struggle for progressivism in the Democratic Party for many years. He had been the senior La Follette's Progressive Party vice presidential running mate in the 1924 election against Coolidge and Davis. He found it galling that Roosevelt elevated the southern barons in what was a one-party regime in Dixie—Robinson, Harrison, Byrnes of South Carolina, and others who seemed much less amenable to the President's professed views. And he was annoyed that Key Pittman received all the attention for the success of the silver advocates, for whom he had been a spokesman longer than anyone still active. Wheeler was offended when Roosevelt came through his state (Montana) in 1934 in the middle of a tough reelection battle and did not speak in his favor, or even mention him. He was a natural ally until isolationism became the principal political concern of the country, yet Roosevelt uncharacteristically made no effort to keep him onboard. The Supreme Court battle terminated all but the most formal relationship between them, and that relationship deteriorated a long way even from there.

During the Court battle, Corcoran approached Wheeler and with authorization expressed the President's intention that if the Court were expanded, Roosevelt would put Wheeler on it, "and make up for not appointing him attorney general." (Wheeler had been miffed when the post was offered to fellow Montanan Thomas Walsh.) Wheeler claimed he was only offered a right of participation in selecting the new judges. Corcoran claimed Wheeler went on to suggest that he, Wheeler, had brought Huey Long in for Roosevelt in Chicago in 1932, clinching the nomination, that the President was ungrateful, and that Roosevelt may have been complicit in the assassination of Long. "Now we're going to cut him down to size," said Wheeler. (Corcoran, as we have seen, is not entirely reliable, but neither is Wheeler.)[17]

Roosevelt gave a number of addresses on conservation and social policy themes on his rail tour and returned via North Dakota and Minnesota before giving one of the seminal speeches of his career in Chicago on October 5. This was the "Quarantine" speech, an image prompted by a conversational reflection of Harold Ickes'.* It signaled the beginning of Roosevelt's intricate, almost imperceptible movement toward engagement of the United States in the desperate defense of democracy in the approaching world struggle.

IV

THE PRESIDENT WAS officially in Chicago to dedicate part of the extensive New Deal public works projects that had been completed on Chicago's splendid waterfront. Crowds of astonishing size and enthusiasm, estimated at three-quarters of a million people, cheered him on his one-mile trip in an open automobile from the railway station to the Outer Link Bridge, on Lakeshore Drive near Colonel McCormick's Tribune Tower. This and other large and welcoming crowds he had drawn in his trip across the country demonstrated to him that his popularity with the people had not been seriously shaken by the Supreme Court battle.

The President's foreign policy reflections were timely. The Spanish Civil War had intensified throughout 1937. The rebel Nationalist assault on Madrid had been rebuffed by a hundred Soviet tanks and their crews in late 1936, and a pro-

---

* Ickes had been recovering from a coronary thrombosis, doubtless aggravated by the competition with Hopkins, and Roosevelt had shown great solicitude for him and visited him in the hospital.

longed siege ensued. There were terrible atrocities on both sides throughout Spain. The Nationalists were probably the greater offenders in numbers, but the Republicans engaged in systematic massacres of the Roman Catholic clergy, which understandably inflamed opinion among the 30 million Roman Catholics of the United States, one quarter of the whole population, and probably a third to two-fifths of Roosevelt's reliable voters.

The Nazi aerial destruction of the Spanish town of Guernica, which had no military targets, April 26, 1937, disgusted the world and was immortalized in Pablo Picasso's most famous painting.[18] Fortunately for Roosevelt, who wished to dodge the issue entirely, two-thirds of Americans had no preference between the two sides in the war. Among those who did have a preference, the Republicans were favored by a margin of about five to three, again fortunately, a narrower margin than the proportion of Protestants and Catholics in the country, so not a straight sectarian division. The increasing dependence of the Republicans on the U.S.S.R. and of the Nationalists on Germany and Italy reinforced the neutral distaste of most Americans for both sides.

The British chancellor of the exchequer, Neville Chamberlain, wrote to Henry Morgenthau in March 1937 expressing the hope that the U.S. neutrality legislation would be modified to give the administration more authority to treat aggressor and respondent states unequally. Chamberlain was "profoundly convinced that almost any action common to them both (the U.S. and the U.K.), would go far to restore confidence to the world and avert the menace which now threatens it."[19]

Soon after, Chamberlain replaced Baldwin as prime minister. Roosevelt was pleased, because he assumed that Chamberlain, son and half-brother of forceful statesmen, Joseph and Austen Chamberlain (Roosevelt had met the latter in 1919), would be more purposeful than Baldwin. But he was also concerned that "fundamentally he [Chamberlain] thoroughly dislikes Americans."[20] On May 5, Bullitt, writing from the embassy in Paris, reported that Roosevelt's friend Thomas Lamont had been in Europe, knew Chamberlain well, and said that "if any Englishman was anti-American, Chamberlain was that anti-American Englishman."[21]

Roosevelt was to be disappointed. Chamberlain was anti-American (he regarded many Americans as "cads"). He proved both more egotistical and more gullible than the irresolute cynic Baldwin, who more closely resembled some of the contemporary French politicians. Roosevelt invited Chamberlain to the United States to discuss international affairs shortly after his elevation. Chamberlain deferred this on July 8, through Norman Davis, who was now U.S. ambassador-at-large. Roosevelt wrote back July 28, celebrating purported agreement with Chamberlain on general outlook and renewing his invitation. Chamberlain courteously declined on September 28, 1937, and their relations slowly deteriorated after this.[22]

While in the mood to write to foreign leaders, Roosevelt wrote one of his "My Dear Duce" letters to Mussolini on July 29 — a particularly vacuous example of the genre. He had ignored Mussolini's congratulatory letter on the 1936 election for seven months but now claimed to respond to it. He wrote that he was "confident, my dear Duce, that you share with me the fear that the trend of the present international situation is ominous to peace . . . and . . . that you . . . desire to turn the course of the world toward stabilizing peace." This was a preposterous message to send less than a year after Mussolini had gloried in the slaughter of the Abyssinians and while he had approximately 60,000 (admittedly not very bellicose) soldiers in Spain in defiance of solemn undertakings. Roosevelt wrote of his desire to meet with the Italian leader, adding, "But we both realize the great difficulties that stand in the way—international difficulties as well as the distances of the Atlantic Ocean and the Mediterranean Sea."[23] He could have left his confidence in Mussolini's grasp of elemental geography unspecified.

There was a reason that possessed Roosevelt to write in this platitudinous and absurdly deferential way to Mussolini. Roosevelt hoped there was some chance of detaching him from Hitler. He was also building the record for his own voters. In simulating the wide-eyed earnest of most American discourse on Great Power relations at this time, he was creating a reservoir of trust with the American public.

His countrymen were then almost painfully unworldly in foreign policy matters. The assumption of the popular attitude of innocent benignity might have had some tactical utility in shaping public opinion, but it makes bizarre and disconcerting reading. Four months later, Italy joined the Berlin-Tokyo anti-Communist alliance. This at least disabused Roosevelt of his notion that it was useful to write any more "My Dear Duce" letters.

Roosevelt was successful in carving out greater discretion for himself when the neutrality law came up for renewal in the spring of 1937. He was empowered to require a belligerent to transport in its own vessels what it purchased from the United States and to embargo strategic materials if he judged that doing so could be beneficial to the peace or security of the United States or the lives of its citizens. This change would have enabled him to prevent the direct sale of oil to Italy during the Abyssinian War (though Italy would have procured the oil elsewhere).

Eleanor, as she was wont to do, complicated her husband's life by militating in favor of the Spanish Republicans and identifying with a Republican Basque children's refugee fund that was branded a Communist front by Congressman John McCormack of Boston, a powerful Roosevelt supporter and future Speaker of the House, and by many of the Catholic bishops. The serenity of the Roosevelt marriage was not enhanced by the fact that Roosevelt paid more attention to the Congressman and his clerical allies than to his own wife. When former Spanish Republican premier Juan Negrin came to Washington, the prominent New Deal official Leon Henderson held a stag dinner for him which was attended by Frankfurter, Henry Wallace, Cohen, and Corcoran.[24] Even Senator Gerald Nye, author of the original neutrality legislation, wanted to favor the Spanish Republicans, though obviously at no risk of direct American intervention. Roosevelt realized that only massive foreign intervention (on a scale that only the Germans, Italians, and Soviets would consider) would influence the outcome of the war, and that most of the U.S. debate was symbolic or chimerical.

International conditions darkened further in the summer of 1937 with the renewal of Japanese aggression against China. From July 7 to 10, there was skirmishing around the Marco Polo Bridge a few miles west of Beijing. This quickly turned into a general undeclared war involving around 40 divisions. A further incident at Shanghai August 9 resulted in the death of two Japanese sailors. On August 14, Chinese aircraft inadvertently bombed the international settlement at Shanghai, killing 800 Chinese and 40 foreigners, including three Americans. Roosevelt sent another 1,200 marines to reinforce the 2,200 U.S. military personnel in China in accordance with the treaties made at the time of the Boxer Rebellion in 1900.

On August 17, American civilians were urged to leave China. Roosevelt declined to invoke an embargo because it would clearly be harmful only to China, but on September 14 he did forbid use of U.S. flag ships for transportation of war material to either country. Secretary of State Hull issued the usual calls for peaceful settlement of the problem, with the usual complete absence of any useful response.

These were the circumstances in which Roosevelt spoke to a huge crowd in Chicago and an expectant national radio audience on October 5. The ineffable Colonel McCormick had put up a large sign, visible to Roosevelt and his audience, on the wall of a nearby building he owned, urging skepticism on the President's listeners. Roosevelt ignored it. He said: "The high aspirations expressed in the Briand-Kellogg Peace Pact and the hopes for peace thus raised have of late given way to a haunting fear of calamity. . . . Without a declaration of war and without warning or justification of any kind, civilians, including vast numbers of women and children, are being ruthlessly murdered with bombs from the air. In times of so-called peace, ships are being attacked and sunk by submarines without cause or notice.

"Let no one imagine that America will escape, that America may expect mercy, that this Western hemisphere will not be attacked and that it will continue tranquilly and peacefully to carry on the ethics and arts of civilization. . . . If those days are not to come to pass . . . the peace-loving nations must make a concerted effort to uphold laws and principles on which alone peace can rest secure. . . .

"The peace, the freedom, and the security of ninety per cent of the world is being jeopardized by the remaining ten per cent who are threatening a breakdown of all international order and law. . . . The moral consciousness of the world . . . must be aroused to the cardinal necessity of honoring the sanctity of treaties, of respecting the rights and liberties of others and of putting an end to acts of international aggression.

"It seems to be unfortunately true that the epidemic of world lawlessness is spreading.

"When an epidemic of physical disease starts to spread, the community approves and joins in a quarantine of the patients in order to protect the health of the community against the spread of the disease.

"War is a contagion, whether it be declared or undeclared. It can engulf states remote from the original scene of the hostilities. We are determined to keep out of war, yet we cannot insure ourselves against the disastrous effects of war and the dangers of involvement. We are adopting such measures as will minimize our risk of involvement, but we cannot have complete protection in a world of disorder in which confidence and security have broken down."

This was a giant step beyond the usual well-intentioned pieties about the virtues of peace. It was unspecific and reiterated the inevitable call for avoidance of direct involvement in hostilities. But in the spirit of the President's remarks were an abandonment of isolation, an espousal of collective security, and a preparedness to face down aggressors, peacefully if possible but by force if necessary.

Roosevelt went from his speech to lunch with Chicago's Cardinal Mundelein, and gave him the impression that his notion of "quarantine" stopped short of full sanctions, much less armed intervention.

Friend and foe, in the United States and throughout the world, recognized Roosevelt's address as a matter of immense importance. The *Chicago Tribune* chose to regard it as the impending surrender of American sovereignty to the British. That Roosevelt might be able to conduct international affairs without being completely swindled and turning the United States into a vassal state of grasping foreigners escaped McCormick's imagination.

Relations with McCormick had collapsed since the "Dear Frank"–"Dear Bert" exchange of May 6 and 16, 1933, when the Colonel had invited the President to stay in his home in Chicago and wrote "you are making very good weather of it in the storm." McCormick never had the pretense to pandering to the underprivileged as Hearst had, had never sought serious elective office as Hearst had, and was one of the first and most intractable defectors from the early Roosevelt bandwagon.

The Hearst newspapers would have been expected to take the same line as McCormick's *Chicago Tribune*, but, unbelievably, W.R. Hearst's uncontrollable extravagances as an art collector had driven him to the edge of bankruptcy and he temporarily—to Roosevelt's considerable amusement—lost control of his newspapers, with the result that they became less strident. The *New York Times* considered the speech important, and revealed that the secretary of state was "shocked," had no idea what the President was proposing, and had had no notice of what he intended to say. (Roosevelt rarely bothered to give Hull any notice of important foreign-policy initiatives. Hull was chiefly preoccupied with sending well-intended diplomatic notes and trying, without much success, to reduce trade barriers.) The *Times* of London approved "Mr. Roosevelt's attitude," though the consequent program was not yet discernible.

Roosevelt returned directly to Hyde Park and held a press conference the day after the Chicago speech, on October 6. He declined to elaborate on what he had in mind and declined to agree that his remarks needed to be reconciled with existing neutrality legislation. (Q. "Do you care to amplify your remarks at Chicago, especially where you referred to a possible quarantine?" A. "No.") He knew he was ahead of public and congressional opinion and potentially vulnerable to opposition politicians. At this time he seems not to have been determined to run for an unprecedented third term, though the idea was undoubtedly already in his thoughts.

He had begun the delicate and implacable process of moving ahead of opinion on foreign affairs, then retreating slightly and pulling opinion in behind him before moving ahead of it again. He was at the same time trying to encourage greater boldness by the front-line states, without inciting them to impetuosity on false hopes of what the United States was really prepared to do. He subsequently told Rosenman, of this speech: "It's a terrible thing to look over your shoulder when you're trying to lead—and find no one there."[25] His post bag was heavy and favorable, but the congressional leaders were almost entirely silent, and his equanimity was still recovering from the bruising Supreme Court battle.

Polls showed fairly uniformly a two-to-one opposition to cooperation with the League in sanctions against Japan or the parties in Spain. Roosevelt has been criticized by posterity for not explicitly urging an interventionist policy earlier and rallying public opinion to it. He wasn't confident that a third term could be had on that basis against a credible Republican peace candidate, and he didn't want to replicate any part of Wilson's tragedy in bringing the country to the edge of a new policy and then being repudiated by his successor. He preferred to sound a sort of imprecise international reveille, then deny the noisy concerns of adversaries as irresponsible war-scare tactics, observe a brief period of silence, and then repeat the process. Gradually American opinion would be chivvied toward substantive internationalism.

A conference in Brussels opened November 3 for the purpose of negotiating or even imposing a settlement on the Sino-Japanese dispute, but it broke up in confusion when the Japanese refused to attend. For good measure, it was at this point that Japan and Germany added Italy to their 1936 anti-Comintern pact.

Japan had now seized Shanghai and had laid siege to Nanking, which was being heavily and relentlessly bombed, in a manner that presaged, as Guernica apparently had, German techniques in Europe in less than two years. (Roosevelt predicted to the visiting author H.G. Wells that a new world war would break out in 1941.) On December 11, 1937, the U.S. gunboat *Panay*, anchored in the Yangtze River twenty miles from Nanking, was bombed and sunk by the Japanese, although she was outside the immediate war zone and clearly marked as a

U.S. vessel. Two were killed and thirty wounded. (Film was taken of the attack and rushed to Washington for personal screening by the President and the secretary of state. It confirmed that the hour-long attack was deliberate.) The Japanese also sank two Standard Oil river tankers.

Although the ailing secretary of the navy, Claude Swanson, demanded an immediate declaration of war on Japan, Roosevelt chose to accept the instant and "profound apology" of the Japanese foreign minister. The U.S. ambassador in Tokyo, Joseph Grew, made it clear that the American government had film of the incident and knew that Japanese claims of accidental bombing were outright lies. The United States presented Japan with a bill for the incident of a little over $2 million, which was paid promptly.

V

THROUGHOUT THE AUTUMN there were disturbing evidences of an economic downturn. Roosevelt, in his electoral enthusiasm, had represented and believed that the Depression was in inexorable retreat and that the recovery was now self-sustaining. He had therefore yielded to the pleas of Morgenthau, with which Ickes largely agreed, that emergency relief should be rolled back, because the private sector could now deal with unemployment relatively unassisted. (Ickes was probably more concerned with trimming Hopkins's budget than with policy questions.) Marriner Eccles warned the President that this was mistaken, and that the reduction of this stimulus, the addition to the Social Security rolls, and the collection of the Social Security tax would reduce demand and induce a downward turn in the economic cycle. Roosevelt seemed to promise Eccles, when he spent the weekend at Hyde Park in late October 1937, an increased budget for public and assisted housing and some other ingredients of stimulus. Eccles now became unpleasantly familiar with the Roosevelt practice of "seeming" to promise conflicting things to different people.

Roosevelt "seemed" to confirm his plans for spending resumptions on the afternoon of November 10, but on the evening of the same day the secretary of the Treasury, claiming that every word of his remarks had been cleared with Roosevelt, told an audience of bankers in New York that the administration had decided to make "a determined move toward a balanced budget," and would be reducing spending. (Roosevelt had told him to "turn on the old record of his . . . profound commitment to capitalism.") Eccles wrote, later: "The contradictions between the afternoon and the evening position on November 10 made me wonder if the New Deal was just a political slogan." Roosevelt was able to reassure him, as he generally did all his collaborators. He did act on Eccles's advice eventually, and disappointed the frugal Morgenthau again. But first he gave Morgenthau's proposal a chance to "strip off the bandages, throw away the crutches" (an odd metaphor to use with this president), and determine if the economy "could stand on its own feet."[26]

Evidence of economic deterioration poured in through the autumn. On October 19, the New York Stock Exchange had suffered one of its worst days since 1932 on heavy volume, and there was a good deal of loose reminiscence about the Great Crash. The market stabilized, and the credit conditions, underlying economic conditions, and quality of security issues all made such talk baseless. But it was a disconcerting turn of events and a reversal for the administration. Matters were not helped by Commerce Secretary Roper's saying that the economy was "fundamentally sound." Roosevelt ordered him to avoid "Hooverish" remarks.

Hopkins encouraged Roosevelt to meet with some of the younger members of the administration, who would be more familiar with the lot of the people. He spent all afternoon of November 8 with Lauchlin Currie (presidential assistant), Leon Henderson (chief economic advisor of the WPA), and Isadore Lubin (commissioner of labor statistics). Paul Mazur, a Lehman Brothers partner and friend of Jimmy Roosevelt, was also present. The three government officials recommended a substantial increase in government spending on relief, general purchasing and procurement, and in promotion of residential housing construction. They also recommended retention of the espoused goal of a balanced budget in 1939. The meeting was not decisive.[27]

Unemployment had descended by late spring to about 12 percent, barely a third of the March 1933 percentage, and only about 4 percent when the Hopkins and Ickes job-creation programs are taken into account. But unemployment started to jump in startling increments later in 1937. Although consumer and commodity prices held up well, business activity indices fell by about a third from 1937 to 1938. Where in the spring of 1937 the country had pulled ahead of 1929 output levels, the *New York Times* Weekly Business Index plunged from 110 in August to 85 in December. In the same period, the steel industry went from operating at 80 percent of capacity to 19 percent. The Dow Jones industrial averages of share values, which had descended from 330 in 1929 to 34 in 1933 and had risen to 190 in August 1937, declined in the next two months to 115. If the rate of activity for early 1938 were allowed to continue through the year, the country would lose almost two-thirds of the gains it had made since 1933. The Federal Reserve index in March 1938 was only 15 percent above 1932 levels.[28]

By then, March 1938, the ranks of the unemployed, which, as mentioned, had got down to about 6 million (2 million if the emergency relief workers are counted as employed persons) from a high of around 13 million in early 1933, had ballooned to about 10 million (6 million if the public works employees are deducted).*

---

* The U.S. Bureau of the Census annual figures are here taken as more reliable than those of the AFL and the National Industrial Conference Board. The apparent discrepancies between numbers and percentages arise because members of the armed forces are considered to be employed people but are removed from the work force to calculate the number of unemployed.

The number of employed people peaked at 48 million in 1929, fell to a little over 38 million in 1933, rose to over 46 million in 1937, and slipped again to 43.5 million in 1938. The percentage of unemployed thus increased from its best 1937 figure of 12.5 percent to about 22.5 percent in the spring of 1938. The WPA, PWA, CCC, and the other agencies alleviated the figures by occupying almost three-fifths of the unemployed for substantial parts of the year. And, unlike the conditions of 1933, those of 1938 included direct subsistence relief for most of the other unemployed people.

The country's comparative performance was also suddenly not so presentable. American unemployment levels had gone from half of Britain's in 1929 to nearly twice Britain's in 1933, to about one and one-half times Britain's in early 1937, but were on their way back to more than twice the British levels by early 1938 (again excluding the emergency public works programs). Comparisons with France were even less satisfactory. Both the British and French improved their figures with large rearmament programs in response to the rising war scare in Europe.

Hitler was well along to eliminating German unemployment, but at the expense of accelerated inflation and by recourse to methods that no democracy could possibly accept: conscription of all able-bodied men to the armed forces or the armaments industries and a significant number in what amounted to nonjudicial slave labor. Almost the only advanced country that was performing as sluggishly as the United States in late 1937 was the Netherlands.

None of the other Western democracies provided so much or such original emergency relief employment as the United States did. If these relief workers are considered as employed people, the comparative figures too are substantially improved, even at the end of 1937, when the United States was suffering its relapse, but they were less flattering than they had been.

Roosevelt had called a special session of Congress for November 15, 1937, to clean up the unfinished legislation from the spring session, which had been consumed by the Court reform battle. This session ended December 21, 1937, having accomplished very little, and Roosevelt had to defer his program to 1938. The Congress had been largely distracted by the constitutional amendment proposed by Congressman Louis Ludlow, requiring a declaration of war to be approved by a national referendum other than in the case of a direct attack on the United States. Roosevelt engaged in delaying tactics and surreptitiously had the measure deferred to the next session.

The pressures on him had taken their toll and been compounded by a tooth infection that spread and required surgery and convalescence. He left Washington on his train November 27 for Miami and departed that city on the presidential yacht November 29 for a week's cruising and fishing. It was not as festive an outing as usual, partly for obvious political reasons, partly because of a steady flow of disturbing (and accurate) intelligence about the aggressive designs of the Japanese. Also, Harry Hopkins could not join this trip. His wife had died swiftly of cancer October 6, leaving him and a five-year-old daughter. The President's closest colleague was in an almost inconsolable state.

As 1937 came worryingly to an end, Assistant Attorney General Robert Jackson and Harold Ickes, without an endorsement from the White House, wearied of the Morgenthau ascendancy and got out in front on the recession issue. Jackson gave a radio address written for him by Cohen and Corcoran on December 26. On December 29, he spoke to a large live audience in Philadelphia and espoused the current conspiracy theory, that big business was engaged in a capital strike. He railed against the salaries of the most prominent executives and said the New Deal's only fault was: "It set out a breakfast for the canary and let the cat steal it."

Soon after, Roosevelt told Jackson, "I'm sick of sitting here kissing people's asses to get them to do what they ought to be volunteering for the Republic."[29] Jackson, propelled by Corcoran, was gearing up to run for governor of New York. Jackson thought better of it before he got very far, and was not tempted by elective office again.

On December 27, 1937, the inimitable Ickes claimed that "the sixty families" that supposedly controlled the American private sector had escalated the "irreconcilable conflict" between "the power of money and the power of the democratic instinct." He warned that the country was under threat from "big business fascism."[30] This was unjustifiably inflammatory, but it signaled that the highest ranks of the administration were getting very restive and scouring the horizon for scapegoats. The President was presumably allowing his subalterns to fire a shot across the bows of big business.

Roosevelt's unique nature made him always optimistic about outcomes but always suspicious of the motives of all but a few proven personal loyalists. His concern about a capital strike was inflated by his habitual inability to consider that his own actions could have been mistaken.

In fact, even those businessmen who strongly disliked him desperately hoped for the resumption of economic recovery. At this stage, most assumed that Roosevelt would be gone in two years and that there would be a good chance to have a real change of regime in 1941. (Thomas Lamont, of J.P. Morgan, was one of the few businessmen who confidently assumed Roosevelt would take a third term. He welcomed the prospect and felt that if the country could spend $30 billion fighting Germany in 1917–1918, it could profitably spend $6 billion "to keep people from starving."[31]

Roosevelt had his own ambivalence between Eccles's advocacy of stimulus and Morgenthau's of frugality to thank for the partial economic relapse.

The President started out the New Year with a rather vague State of the Union message January 3, 1938. He didn't mention the economic downturn, which was undeniable and notorious and which his opponents were already calling the

"Roosevelt Recession." He spoke of having raised the country's income from $38 billion in 1932 to $68 billion in 1937 and of its continuing to rise to $90 to $100 billion in the next several years. He scarcely mentioned the legislation that had been held over from the previous year but spoke of his desire to reform certain business practices. In this context he inveighed rather feebly against "tax avoidance . . . investment write-ups . . . [those who] baffle prosecution . . . high pressure salesmanship . . . intimidation of state government." This was not much of a call to arms for a resurgent administration.

The federal welfare system had been rolled back as part of Roosevelt's accommodation of Morgenthau's budget-balancing efforts. The unintended consequences were alarming. In Cleveland in the first week of 1938, 65,000 people on relief went without emergency food and clothing. Goebbels's own *Der Angriff* cited this as proof of the failure of democracy and the superiority of Nazism. Relief rolls skyrocketed in a few months in automobile production centers—194 percent in Toledo, 434 percent in Detroit. St. Louis and Omaha ran through their relief budgets, and Chicago, where relief cases jumped from 50,000 to 120,000 between January and May 1938, was obliged for fiscal reasons to shut all nineteen municipal relief stations.[32]

John Maynard Keynes wrote Roosevelt in late January an unsolicited report card on his performance. He breezily suggested nationalization of all utilities, but failing that, gratuitously reflected that there was nothing to be gained in "chasing the utilities around the lot every other week." Keynes further dilated on the differences between businessmen and politicians, interestingly and not inaccurately, but in a way that would have been more appropriate emanating from, rather than addressed to, the most powerful democratic politician in the world, who had a great deal closer acquaintance with the political and business communities than Keynes did.

Businessmen, Keynes wrote, as if corresponding with one of his students, are "much milder than politicians, at the same time allured and terrified by the glare of publicity, easily persuaded to be 'patriots,' perplexed, bemused, indeed terrified, yet only too anxious to take a cheerful view, vain perhaps, but very unsure of themselves, pathetically responsive to a kind word. You could do anything you liked with them if you would treat them (even the big ones) not as wolves and tigers, but as domestic animals by nature, even though they have been badly brought up and not trained as you would wish."

Keynes made the point that was already being made by Marriner Eccles, that the core of the economic problem was underconsumption and not overproduction. Roosevelt asked Morgenthau for a draft response, which flattered Morgenthau. The resultant letter thanked Keynes for his "pleasant, encouraging . . . interesting" letter.[33]

On January 11, Roosevelt received a number of the country's leading industrialists, including the chairman (for nearly forty years) of General Motors, Alfred P. Sloan; E.T. Weir, of what became the National Steel Company; and Lewis Brown, of Johns Manville (asbestos and base metal mining). On the 17th Roosevelt met with Owen Young, of General Electric; his old friend and former lessee Thomas Lamont, of J.P. Morgan; and John L. Lewis. Both meetings were cordial and seemed to produce a reasonable consensus. Roosevelt's well-known powers of persuasion, his affability, and his detailed knowledge of relevant facts were amply demonstrated and appreciated. (Adolf Berle had arranged the second meeting and was about to take Moley's old position of assistant secretary of state.

Hugh Johnson, now thoroughly antagonistic after his unhappy confrontation with the President in the Supreme Court imbroglio, jubilantly declared: "The Falstaffian army can no longer be kept together and led by a melodious whinny and a winning smile." The author Bernard De Voto, one of Roosevelt's natural supporters, wrote a letter to the historian Garett Mattingly, unpublished for many years, that was indicative of the drift of intelligent sentiment: "Tommy Corcoran's depression is a hell of a lot worse than Hoover's." This was nonsense, but it was dangerous to Roosevelt if allowed to take hold. (It is not clear why De Voto laid the downturn at the door of Corcoran.)[34]

As one Washington columnist put it, though no one in Congress knew what the President's economic policy really was, they knew that "In dry spells, Mr. Roosevelt would go into his tent, make unintelligible noises, and presently there would be rain." In this, the worst dry spell in years, he had neither gone "into his tent [nor reached] for the bag of magic feathers."[35] He was pursuing his standard tactic of waiting until his own thoughts were clear about the way forward and until opinion had formed up behind him awaiting leadership. Then, habitually, he would move decisively.

In early March, Eccles wrote Roosevelt a memorandum warning of "a severe depression" and urged the President to "provide the democratic leadership that will make our system function." He warned of the dangers of Fascism and called for "reflation now."[36] Statistics made Eccles's case for him; he explained to a finally receptive president that a sharp contraction in consumer spending power had coincided with a serious inventory correction and the imposition of comprehensive Social Security taxes. Economic (and political) disaster was at hand unless remedial actions were taken promptly. Harry Hopkins was also an advocate of reviving stimulative emergency relief spending.

Hopkins arrived at Warm Springs on March 30 to discuss the situation with the President. Hopkins had convalesced for several months from a cancer operation, which, coming soon after the death of his wife, had demoralized him and dismayed his chief. Roosevelt had communicated directly with Hopkins's doctors at least once a week since he had taken a leave of absence in December. Hopkins had been told that his chances were two to one his cancer would not recur. Now healthy and energetic, Hopkins had been staying at Joseph Kennedy's house in Palm Beach, and Eleanor, who had known Hopkins before her husband did, was distressed at his hobnobbing with the wealthy. She feared Hopkins would become a frivolous person distracted by the wealthy, as she sternly thought her husband had been.

Hopkins had worked up specific proposals for a massive spending program with Leon Henderson, formerly of the NRA; Beardsley Ruml, an officer of the Macy's department store company and member of the Brownlow committee; and Aubrey Williams, deputy WPA administrator. Hopkins was relieved to find that Roosevelt needed no convincing. He found that the President agreed that his attempted conciliation of business had borne no fruit of "natural recovery" and felt that the "Roosevelt recession" had to be reversed at once, by the only methods that empirically had proved successful up to then. Roosevelt and Hopkins spent a couple of days working out details of an extensive supplementary recovery program.

Morgenthau returned from holiday shortly after Roosevelt and Hopkins. When he heard from Wallace that a resumption of large-scale deficit financing was being planned, he hurried back to Washington, composing a memorandum of his own on the way. He produced a composite plan with moderate initiatives in many different areas, including gold sales, greater government efficiencies, taxes aimed at the sort of speculation Roosevelt had been inveighing against, relatively minor relief spending increases, wages and hours legislation, creation of a transport department, and a few more confidence-building measures toward business.

When he arrived at the White House to present this to Roosevelt and Hopkins he was horrified to hear the plans that were afoot. He thought he had had an undertaking from the President to give deficit reduction a greater chance and was aggrieved that plans had gone so far without any consultation with him or his department. He read his own proposals, which were rather noncommittally received.

Morgenthau was back at the White House April 11, when Roosevelt briefed congressional leaders on the proposed measures, a total supplementary budget of $1.55 billion for the WPA, CCC, and Farm Security Administration. Though not asked to comment, Morgenthau, showing admirable independence if a rather threadbare notion of the Treasury function in a depression, told the group that this would push the 1939 deficit to $3.5 billion. As soon as the congressional leaders had left, Roosevelt exploded, telling Morgenthau that he had been mischievous and obstructionist and that he was wrong to believe that all these decisions had been taken behind his back.

"No use yelling at me," Morgenthau meekly replied to Roosevelt. Morgenthau was back again the next day, April 12, for a conference with Roosevelt, Hopkins, Eccles, Ickes, Hull, Farley, Budget Director Daniel Bell, RFC director Jesse Jones, Jimmy Roosevelt, and Steve Early. Morgenthau had prepared a new proposal for greater gold and silver sales, a further ten percent gold devaluation, the allocation of $500 million of reserves to spending, reduction of bank reserve requirements, and what amounted to outright inflation by effectively printing

$3 billion. Roosevelt and the others commended Morgenthau on his ingenuity and added his suggestions to what they were already intending to do.

Morgenthau thought that he had lost the confidence of his leader, whom he admired with childlike fervor, and he strongly disagreed with the course of action that was about to be adopted. Morgenthau wrote in his diary: "They have just stampeded him during the week that I was away . . . stampeded him like cattle."[37] It wasn't a stampede but a Solomonic progress from deliberation to judgment. (In eight months the Treasury secretary's diarized conception of his leader had evolved from a patient throwing away his crutches to a prodded cow.[38]) He had missed the point.

Morgenthau was back at the White House yet again the next day, April 13, and offered the President his resignation. This was not a juvenile tantrum of the kind that regularly afflicted Ickes. Roosevelt knew how overwrought his old and devoted friend must have been to come to this extremity. Roosevelt thanked Morgenthau for his "grand" performance at Treasury, asked him not to be motivated by "pique," and asked him not to "quit under fire" and bring down the Democratic Party to the benefit of demagogues of the far left and right. It was as much a locker room pep talk as a plea to remain. Morgenthau was almost physically ill and stood his ground with surprising firmness. The meeting was an impasse; Morgenthau claimed he had no choice but to resign, and Roosevelt told him that was impossible and that his resignation was not accepted. At the end of the day, Morgenthau agreed to remain.

The President's economic message, based on a $3.7 billion spending and lending program, was delivered to the Congress the next day, and in the evening of the same day he delivered his first Fireside Chat of 1938, on economic matters. Rosenman, Corcoran, and Hopkins worked on it right up to a few hours before delivery, and Roosevelt was so tired from the week's exertions that he had a nap before speaking to the country. The emergency relief package included $1.4 billion for Hopkins, $1 billion for Ickes, and $300 million for new housing. Both the message to the Congress and the address to the nation laid the blame for the downturn on inventory corrections and the additional stimulus in the previous year from the massive acceleration of veterans' bonuses. This was the end of the respite Roosevelt had promised Roy Howard in September 1935, and this package of measures launched the Third New Deal.

Roosevelt said: "I never forget that I live in a house owned by all of the American people." It was an effective performance, but was criticized by the economically traditional press. The *New York Times* lamented that the "Administration has chosen to pour water down the well instead of mending the pump." The *Times* wanted corporate tax deductions, a rollback of Social Security, and amendment of labor laws to make them less generous to the working class. Roosevelt felt he had done his best to appease business and nothing useful had come from it. He also felt that some modest degree of at least the perception of wealth redistribution was necessary to maintain the stability of the republic. The *Herald Tribune* said the speech "seemed half-hearted in comparison with the . . . supreme confidence of happier days . . . Here was, indeed, a defeated leader."[39]

Roosevelt's plan was eagerly passed by Congress and did have the desired effect. The U.S. economy began a significant revival. By the end of 1938 it had regained at least half of the ground it had lost since 1937. Production increased 28 percent from May 1937 to August 1939. In the same time employment rose by two million, factory payrolls by 26 percent, steel production by 127 percent, and residential construction by 60 percent. Unemployment fell by almost two million, to between 17 percent and 18 percent by the end of the summer of 1939. And of those unemployed, with increased relief appropriations, more than half were once more in the New Deal workfare programs.

The U.S. economic performance was again quite competitive. In August 1939 the American unemployment rate was just under 8 percent, compared with 6 percent in Britain and France, both of which had then cut heavily into unemployment by defense production increases and expansion of the armed forces. The U.S. figure did not count the public sector relief employees as unemployed. (Garner had told Hopkins he objected to the relief recipients being referred to as "clients," because this implied a durable status.[40] The unemployment rate was 11 percent in Canada (which had the economy most similar to that of the United States in the comparative size of sectors) and over 19 percent in the Netherlands. Germany, because of Hitler's militarization of the country, had virtually eliminated unemployment (along with a sound currency, all democratic liberties, and many conventional vestiges of civilization).

By early 1939, Roosevelt could again safely claim to be leading the nation steadily back from the economic abyss to resumed prosperity.

While he had waited almost too long in the chicken game he sometimes played before important policy course corrections, he had in fact waited just long enough to convince most unbiased opinion that the Republican–big-business–Morgenthau–Lewis Douglas and Southern Democrat view of how to end the Depression, by shrinking expenses and restoring the gold standard, could not work, at least until the recovery was complete and solid. Then it might be an appropriate holding pattern to return to, with all the New Deal reforms of banking and credit, tax codes, welfare systems, and securities markets as a safeguard against another crash. But the Morgenthau policy was a possible destination, not a route map for arriving at that destination.

As with the (also costly) gesture to the bimetallists in the Silver Purchase Act of 1934 (Chapter 8), this had been an interlude in which Roosevelt had effectively strengthened his party. Though the policy was not successful, a numerous faction was placated and neutral opinion convinced to follow the President at a time when such an experiment was politically affordable. He had given the budget-balancers a full opportunity—two and one half years from the letter to

Roy Howard in September 1935, and particularly the year from the post-electoral cuts in the relief budget, to the economic message of April 14, 1938, to demonstrate that their policy could succeed.

All but the extreme diehards had to concede that the timing, if not the policy itself, was mistaken, or at least premature, and there was broad support for the President's return to the policy of reflation. An increasingly recalcitrant element of his party (if not Morgenthau himself) was convinced, or at least mollified, and the Roosevelt coalition was strengthened. As often happened during his long preeminence in American politics, he would prove a better judge of the timescales, personalities, and cross-currents of American public life than those who would second-guess him. By this time, he was routinely referred to in the American press, in headlines and cartoons, as "the Champion," or, in prizefighting parlance, just "The Champ." His status grated on many, but few disputed that he had earned it.

VI

A NOTHER SERIOUS DISTRACTION at this time, and a harbinger of the steady approach of the international crisis, was the extended battle over the Ludlow proposal. This urged amendment of the Constitution to require a referendum for a declaration of war. It is illustrative of the fantastic naïveté of the country in foreign policy matters that in 1938 the President would be harassed by any such foolish measure. Roosevelt sent a public letter to Speaker Bankhead stating that while the authors of the idea were sincere, enactment of it would encourage war and incite other countries to believe that they "could violate American rights with impunity." Roosevelt was supported by some sensible Republicans, such as Alfred Landon and Henry Stimson, and the Ludlow Amendment was disposed of, though the vote was close enough, 209 to 188. It is hard in an America that has participated intelligently in world affairs for decades to recreate the profound and prideful lack of foreign policy sophistication of the American voters and many of their representatives in this period.

Roosevelt's problems with the Congress were compounded by the fact that his greatest supporters in domestic affairs tended to be his opponents in foreign policy areas and vice versa. Progressive westerners were reliable voters for his domestic relief and reform measures, but isolationists. Southern Democrats tended to be reactionary and intractable in domestic matters but were much more amenable to America's playing some role in the world and had few pacifistic tendencies. Their internationalism went back to the Confederacy's good relations with Britain, and the southerners always believed in being well-armed.

The most painful illustration of this problem was the long battle over antilynching legislation. Senator Wagner in particular introduced antilynching bills from 1934 to 1937. A majority in the Senate and a larger majority in the House of Representatives approved these bills, but enough southerners could filibuster these measures in the Senate and, with hypocritical Republicans, prevent the qualified majority necessary to impose cloture. In April 1937, as Wagner's current bill was being debated, there was a particularly disgusting murder of two African-Americans who were tortured and burned to death with blow torches in front of a jeering crowd of whites at Duck Hill, Mississippi.

Roosevelt told one of his press conferences in 1935 that he was "absolutely for the objective" of an earlier antilynching bill presented by Wagner and Costigan, and did so again in 1938 during the debates. As with Republicans twenty-five years later, the progressives claimed that such a measure was unconstitutional, as infringing the rights of the states. It was understandable that Southern Democrats, and even conservative Republicans, would embrace such a view. But Borah and Norris and several of the other progressives, who were never reluctant to accept federal government assistance in support of their own legislative hobby horses, and generally, with Hiram Johnson, Nye, and the La Follettes, claimed permanent residence on the moral high ground, also opposed the antilynching bills. Of all the urgent problems Roosevelt had to deal with, the civil rights of black Americans, of whom an average of eighteen were lynched annually in Roosevelt's first seven presidential years, were, tragically, well back in the queue. He would do what he could without reducing his ability to deal with even more threatening issues, particularly the Depression and national security. As an indication of support, and even a portent of the aid he would bring to the cause of the African-Americans when he thought the time right, he encouraged his wife to sit in the galleries of Congress during debate and told the press that in these matters she spoke for both of them.

That respectable, and in most cases civilized, southern legislators would put up such a tenacious battle for what amounted to the right to commit horrible acts of racist homicide is hard to fathom, but is buried in the aftermath of the Civil War. There remained an intense fear and resentment of the liberated slaves and their descendants, and a misplaced pride in resisting the intrusion of "northerners" into the law enforcement and sociology of the South. Wagner's bills would have passed if the President had intervened forcefully. President Roosevelt did not. Wagner's 1937 bill continued intermittently to be debated into 1938, but a six-week filibuster effectively forced Wagner to withdraw the bill February 21, 1938, to permit consideration of emergency relief measures.

Roosevelt's record with the African-Americans was a miraculous improvement on Hoover's. Under Hoover, Gold Star mothers (of sons killed in France in the Great War) sent to France to visit their sons' graves, traveled on separate ships and in inferior accommodation if they were black. Hoover's vice president, Charles Curtis, refused to shake hands with African-American members of a mixed delegation of visitors. There were fifty-seven lynchings of blacks in Hoover's term and no comment from the White House, despite the Republicans' being the party of Lincoln and receiving very few votes in the South anyway. If they had solidified their hold on the African-American vote, it could at least have been of great assistance to them in the more populous northern states.[41]

In these matters, as in aid to the factions in the Spanish Civil War, Roosevelt never lost sight of the order of importance either of desirable objectives or of evils to oppose. To defeat the Ludlow Amendment, to roll back the neutrality legislation, to put through the rearmament plans he was developing, he needed the support of those who would filibuster the antilynching bills. To get emergency relief in amounts adequate to resume the conquest of the Depression, he needed the votes of those who favored the Ludlow Amendment.

He would deal with the evils of the time in the order of their importance. The wonder is not that he failed in a few of his legislative initiatives, but that he succeeded in almost all. A less talented master of the political arts would have been immobilized in such a labyrinthine process.

———————

Almost the only amusement Franklin Roosevelt had in this difficult period resulted from his decision to accommodate Joseph P. Kennedy's ambition, expressed to James Roosevelt, to be ambassador to the Court of St. James (London). The incumbent, Robert Bingham, was unwell and wished to return to the United States. Roosevelt wanted to keep Kennedy occupied, get him out of the country, and repay Chamberlain for the haughty refusal of his invitation to visit the United States. Kennedy, with his bumptious Irish chippiness, Roosevelt reasoned, would certainly be a challenge to the sensibilities of British stuffed shirts. He told Morgenthau he would have his ambassador "watched hourly . . . [and that Kennedy would be] fired . . . the first time he opens his mouth and criticizes me."[42]

For his own amusement he subjected Kennedy to a demeaning charade in the presence of his son James. He told Kennedy to take his trousers down so he could determine if the ambassadorial candidate was too bow-legged to wear the formal attire of knee-britches and silk stockings. Kennedy did this with little hesitation, and Roosevelt (who was not an appropriate judge of other men's legs) pronounced Kennedy's a potential embarrassment to the nation. He regretted that he could not offer him the position. Kennedy responded immediately that he would seek a dispensation to wear striped trousers and a swallow-tail coat if the President would give him the post.

Roosevelt agreed, the British government was certainly not going to sacrifice relations with the United States on such a ridiculous issue, and the appointment of the incandescently unselfconscious Kennedy was made. Roosevelt needed and was entitled to a little entertainment, but he would pay a heavy price for it. The isolationist Kennedy was ultimately widely reckoned to be, along with the Stalin-worshipping Joseph Davies in the Soviet Union, one of the worst diplomatic appointments in the history of the United States.

Roosevelt again brought forward the legislative leftovers from the previous year in the Congress, which had been so disrupted first by the Supreme Court battle and then by the skirmishing with the isolationists over the Ludlow Amendment. A new housing act, building on Senator Wagner's measure of the previous year, was passed in February. The farm bill the 1937 Congress had peevishly failed to pass was adopted in an almost unmodified condition February 18, 1938. This restored the remaining worthwhile aspects of the AAA and entrenched Henry Wallace's notion of the "ever normal granary," reducing cultivation and storing surpluses when appropriate.

Although the liberal Republican senator Charles L. McNary, citing Oliver Wendell Holmes Sr., called Henry Wallace "the autocrat of the breakfast table," the farmers, when consulted in the referenda on marketing quotas, voted in favor by Communist-like majorities: 1,189,000 to 97,000 for the cotton farmers, and 251,000 to 43,000 for the tobacco growers.

Another archconservative Supreme Court justice, George Sutherland, retired in January 1938, and Roosevelt had no difficulty putting Solicitor General Stanley Reed in his place. On March 28, 1938, the Supreme Court, victorious but now chastened and partly renovated, upheld the administration's Public Utilities Holding Company Act.

Roosevelt encountered greater problems with his executive reorganization plans, which had been the issue of the Brownlow committee. Organized labor was afraid that a future president would arbitrarily use his powers to wind down some of the agencies from which the union movement benefited, but was generally at pains to express confidence in the incumbent president. Much of the Roman Catholic hierarchy was opposed to the measure because it feared the creation of a federal department of education and a financial onslaught, under the separation of church and state provisions of the Constitution, against the Catholic school system. For these reasons as well as irritation at Roosevelt's failure to give adequate support to his antilynching bill, Senator Robert Wagner, Roosevelt's ally of twenty-eight years, deserted him on this vote, but it passed the Senate anyway.

In the House of Representatives, new problems arose. Hatton Sumners, whom Roosevelt had ignored and not allowed into the White House for almost a year after the problems over the Court reform measure, said the executive reorganization plan could be reported out of his Judiciary Committee and get through the House only if the proposed new social welfare department were taken out of it and presented separately. There was envy in the House of the power of Harry Hopkins, who was surmised to be the likely first occupant of the post. Roosevelt refused and the bill failed. The President's enemies crowed, the Dow Jones Average rose four per cent, and there was much celebration in the *Chicago Tribune* and like-minded places that the alleged tyranny of Roosevelt was finally ending.

Roosevelt was not overly preoccupied. He could live without the reforms, had every intention of enacting most of them later anyway, and was certainly not prepared to give a posse of reactionary congressmen any authority over who would hold senior positions in his administration. He knew that the odd relatively painless defeat would slake the thirst of those who professed to think the Congress had rolled over too often for the White House. Daniel Roper was about to retire as secretary of commerce, and Roosevelt had it in mind to offer this position to Hopkins.

The last piece of unenacted 1937 legislation was the wages-and-hours bill, which passed in 1938 as the Fair Labor Standards Act. This act banned child labor (as the NIRA had done) and set a forty-hour work week after two years and a twenty-five-cents-per-hour minimum wage, rising to forty cents after six years. Rexford Tugwell's old Food, Drug, and Cosmetics Bill, the first major revision of the 1906 act, also passed, but in less draconian form than Tugwell had demanded. It was a reasonable step forward without shackling the drug companies as Tugwell had proposed.

The reelection campaign of Senator Claude Pepper of Florida was challenged by a conservative Democratic primary opponent, and this contest became more or less of a referendum on the Fair Labor Standards Act and the renewed reform program of the administration generally. Pepper did win, with a large hand from Roosevelt, who authorized Corcoran to raise money for Pepper.

An inordinate amount of attention had been given in this congressional session to Roosevelt's bugbear about distribution of wealth in America, fueled by rumblings about a capital strike and Ickes' panegyrics about the "sixty families" that, in a low mood and under the influence of his current sociological reading, the mercurial interior secretary purported to believe ruled America. One tenth of 1 percent of the corporations owned 52 percent of the national total of corporate assets, 4 percent had 87 percent of the profits. (They did, however, have millions of shareholders.) In 1936, 47 percent of American families made less than $1,000 per year, while the wealthiest 1.5 percent had as much wealth as the 47 percent at the bottom of the economic scale. These figures were in a message Roosevelt sent the Congress April 29, 1938, about monopolies and the concentration of economic power. The President asked for and received $500,000 for "a thorough study of the concentration of economic power." His concern was not just for political appearances but for the continuity of American political institutions.

What ultimately emerged was a slight augmentation of the antimonopoly powers of the Federal Trade Commission.

Also in April, a new party, the National Progressives, was launched by Wisconsin's governor, Philip La Follette. Adolf Berle attended this nativity with Roosevelt's approval. The movement was launched with vague objectives, a Swiss cheese of an election platform, and an emblem (a blue cross in a red field) that struck many observers as fascistic, a cruel irony for such a liberal group. (One writer called it "a circumcised Swastika."[43] Roosevelt wrote to his old friend and ambassador to Italy, William Phillips, after Hitler's state visit to Rome in May 1938: "Most of the country [considers La Follette's party logo] a feeble imitation of the Swastika. All that remains is for some party to adopt a new form of arm salute. I have suggested the raising of both arms over the head, followed by a bow from the waist. At least that would be good for people's figures."[44] Roosevelt correctly anticipated that this ungainly political craft would crash before take-off.

The combination of the 1938 fiscal stimulus measures, the Bituminous Coal Act, the Farm Tenancy Act, Wagner's Housing Act, the restoration of the most successful sections of the AAA, the Fair Labor Standards Act, and the Food and Drug Act constituted the Third New Deal, which was effectively immune from Court interference. Henceforth, as in other countries, national defense would play a steadily more important role in economic development, and in less than two years would provide the Fourth New Deal. Roosevelt would produce his Fifth New Deal in his massive G.I. Bill of Rights for armed forces veterans in 1944.

It was generally agreed that Roosevelt had regained the ground lost in 1937 and that such a reassertion of authority in the midst of a second term was rare and yet another proof of his prowess as an operator of the U.S. political system. Arthur Krock of the *New York Times*, whom Roosevelt detested and rightly suspected of being a paid lackey of Joseph Kennedy, wrote that Roosevelt had achieved "a historic feat" and a "political miracle."[45] This was a representative view in the congressional press gallery.

VII

ON JULY 1, 1938, Roosevelt announced plans for a library at Hyde Park to hold all his papers and various personal collections. This proved a useful initiative, as all subsequent presidents (except, for particular reasons, Richard Nixon, who funded his library from the private sector) have had government-assisted presidential libraries. Some presidents have used their libraries as retirement offices. This step, in the summer of 1938, was seen as evidence that Roosevelt would be retiring in 1941, at the end of his present term.*

No president had completed two consecutive terms in good health and in good standing with the electorate since Andrew Jackson in 1837, and Jackson had then been almost seventy years old. (U.S. Grant could conceivably have been reelected in 1876 to a third term, but that was not clear and his administration was not a success.)

Roosevelt would be ten days short of his fifty-ninth birthday when his term

---

* Eventually, the President's papers would be carefully classified in different levels of accessibility. Roosevelt wrote to Grace Tully that among those that should never be made public were "longhand letters between the King of England and myself [and] between Cardinal Mundelein and myself." (They are now accessible and are not controversial.)

expired. He was popular, likely to be judged a very successful president, and was enjoying himself, and the international situation was likely to create extraordinary circumstances. He spoke of his wish to retire, but declined to rule out consideration of a third term. This was partly because he wanted another term but didn't want to appear to seek it, and partly to preserve his authority from the imputation to him of the status of a "lame duck" waddling into the sunset.

Roosevelt's consideration of this option would have been increased by contemplations of a possible successor. Vice President Garner was completely out of the question. Shortly after Roosevelt returned from a cruise in early May on the heavy cruiser U.S.S. *Philadelphia*, he had a comprehensive discussion about this with Hopkins. He ruled out Hull for age (not to mention boredom), Ickes for belligerency and temperamental instability, and Farley for parochialism; Henry Wallace, Robert La Follette, and Frank Murphy didn't measure up either. (There was some thought of Farley's running for governor of New York, and Roosevelt was prepared, in the light of recent events, to see the back of Lehman, but Farley, postmaster general and party chairman, as president was a hair-raising idea.) Hopkins was clearly the most interesting possibility among cabinet and senior Washington people. Hopkins was flattered and intrigued, as Roosevelt wished him to be, and it was at this point that Roosevelt announced his intention to make Hopkins secretary of commerce.

At about the same time, May 12, 1938 (Hopkins didn't keep the date of his conversation with Roosevelt), the President went over the same ground with Harold Ickes, who was more realistic; he said Roosevelt was irreplaceable and should run again, and agreed with Roosevelt's assessment that he, Ickes, was "too didactic, too likely to blow up." Wallace was judged "aloof." The high commissioner in the Philippines, Paul V. McNutt, had been mentioned, but Roosevelt thought him a reactionary. Robert Jackson was politically inexperienced, Alben Barkley was too long-winded, and so forth.[46]

Neither the congressional leadership nor the Democratic governors yielded a rich harvest of candidates. Just eliminating the southerners (Rayburn), the Roman Catholics (Murphy), and the Jews (Lehman), none of whom could be elected, removed most of the talented people in the wings. Roosevelt had a capable administration but no visible successor. Roosevelt did not want to inflame Ickes' notorious psychosomatic susceptibilities by mentioning Hopkins, who appeared on this early handicapping to be FDR's preferred alternative to himself. (In fact, Ickes and Hopkins were getting on better at this point, but Ickes would never have been able to cope with the thought of President Hopkins.)

The President sat comfortably in his wheelchair, insuperably self-confident, and dismissed all the other possible candidates. Ickes was one of the first to believe that behind all his theatrics, Roosevelt might just wish to remain where he was and break a tradition as old as the republic by seeking a third term as president. All of the visible Republicans, unsurprisingly, seemed to Roosevelt and his inner circle unimaginably unsuitable. (Most of them, at this point, were.

Roosevelt had left few serious Republicans still in high office.) It is the contention of this book that Roosevelt had never had any intention of retiring after two terms if he could present a third term as a matter of duty rather than egotism. This would be a challenge, but not an insurmountable one to such a master politician.

VIII

THE INTERNATIONAL SITUATION had continued to deteriorate throughout this time. Hitler had made covetous advances on Austria in 1934, and the Austrian chancellor, Engelbert Dollfuss, had been murdered, but Mussolini, in the last constructive act of statesmanship of his career, had moved four divisions to the Brenner Pass and Hitler had desisted.

Roosevelt had much more confidence in his old fellow Grotonian and Harvard alumnus and page boy at his wedding, Sumner Welles—undersecretary of state, relative of the firebrand abolitionist Charles Sumner, and descendant of Lincoln's war secretary Gideon Welles—than in the lugubrious Cordell Hull. Welles suggested to Roosevelt a grand conference on the twentieth anniversary of the end of the World War I, November 11, 1938. Roosevelt had said at his press conference the day after the Quarantine speech, October 6, 1937, that nothing was ever achieved by conferences and that he didn't favor one. Yet he found Welles's idea appealing.

He couldn't have imagined such a meeting could succeed, but he must have reasoned that a good-faith chairmanship of such a conference would strengthen his hand among both hawks and doves in his own country. Cordell Hull, Welles's ostensible superior, was horrified at Welles's initiative and did everything possible to stop it.

Roosevelt prepared to send out invitations in January for the November meeting. (The timing was fortuitous also because the conference would come just after the midterm elections, and the prospect of the conference might be more useful electorally than its reality.) The British ambassador in Washington, Sir Ronald Lindsay, recommended a favorable response in transmitting Roosevelt's message to Chamberlain. The British prime minister, however, was rigorously unimpressed. He didn't inform his foreign secretary, Anthony Eden, who was on holiday on the Cote d'Azur. Instead he spoke to the permanent undersecretary at the Foreign Office, Sir Alexander Cadogan, and told him to respond gratefully officially. Chamberlain was in fact opposed to any such meeting and said that Roosevelt's "fantastic" plan "was likely to excite the derision of Germany and Italy."[47]

Cadogan, whom Roosevelt would come to know well, shared the view of Ambassador Lindsay that any opportunity to strengthen relations with the government of the United States should be seized and exploited. Chamberlain was of a different opinion. He was completely preoccupied with his fancied ability to appease Hitler and Mussolini and direct their war-making proclivities away from areas that were strategic to Great Britain. It was a disastrous strategic misconception.

Chamberlain rewrote Cadogan's draft in response to the President in terms that were much haughtier that those with which he declined Roosevelt's invitation to visit the United States the previous year. He thanked Roosevelt for his helpful interest but wrote that the President could inadvertently distract Germany and Italy from the more important matters of the further concessions Chamberlain was about to make preemptively to them. The core of his approach, which he didn't explain in his reply to Roosevelt but which had leaked informally through other contacts, was to offer de jure recognition of the Italian conquest of Abyssinia in exchange for Mussolini's helping to settle Hitler down.

Cadogan, seeing the potential for damage to Anglo-American relations, telephoned Eden and urged his immediate return. Eden arrived the next day and was horrified at his prime minister's ineptitude. He telegraphed Lindsay and tried to reformulate Chamberlain's message in terms that would be less galling to Roosevelt. Roosevelt responded to Chamberlain with undisguised irritation and strongly urged against any such concession as he intended to make to Mussolini. Welles and Hull impressed upon Lindsay the very negative consequences to American opinion if the legitimization of the Abyssinian conquest occurred. Roosevelt agreed to "a short postponement" in launching his initiative, which Chamberlain called a "sulky acquiescence" in his diary.[48] Eden prevailed upon Chamberlain to consult the cabinet, and Chamberlain was persuaded to send a more supportive message to Roosevelt.

On February 11, 1938, Austrian chancellor Kurt Schuschnigg went to Hitler's Alpine retreat at Berchtesgaden. Hitler wanted to discuss "misunderstandings and points of friction." In normal circumstances this need not have been a complicated discussion. Hitler's Nazis had been steadily fomenting violence and unrest in Austria since the failure of the attempted annexation (Anschluss) and the murder of Dolfuss in 1934. Hitler's notion of "discussion" was that he raved, shrieked, screamed in Schuschnigg's face, threatened and verbally abused him for two hours, and then presented a "draft agreement."

This was a remarkable document even by Hitler's notions of how to deal with smaller states. The ban on the Austrian Nazi Party was to be lifted, all Nazi convicts were to be released, and the Austrian Nazi leader Arthur Seyss-Inquart was to become minister of the interior of Austria. Nazis were also to take over the defense and finance ministries and supervise the military and economic integration of Austria into the German Reich. Schuschnigg protested these terms briefly and then surrendered to his psychotic host. Hitler, in the vehemence of his fulminations, allegedly irrigated his chin even if he did not simply foam at the mouth, in a manner well-known in psychiatric hospitals but not in the diplomatic annals of the Great Powers.

Schuschnigg was an ascetic, "colorless and bloodless young man," who wore "a gold cross hanging from one buttonhole and the old Greek sign for Jesus Christ in the other."[49] He returned to Vienna and, trying to retain some vestige of sovereignty, called a referendum for March 13, 1938, in which Austrians would be invited to cast their votes for or against a "free, independent, social, Christian, and united Austria." Hitler was not prepared to tolerate any such popular consultation, and invaded Austria militarily on March 11. His forces encountered no resistance. He entered the country himself in an open car on March 12 and was received with frenzied enthusiasm. When he arrived in Vienna March 14, the delirium of the reception seemed to justify his claims of enthusiasm for a greater German Reich, to which Austria had formally been annexed the day before.

Hitler spoke to a huge and wildly cheering crowd from the balcony of the Imperial Hotel. As a penurious youth he had swept snow from the front steps of that hotel twenty-five years before so the great and lesser nobility and worthies of the fading Habsburg Empire would not find it slippery underfoot at Christmastime. Hitler further celebrated his homecoming with great constabulary efficiency: the Gestapo arrested in one night 66,000 Viennese who did not share in the enthusiasm for the Anschluss. Among them were the psychoanalyst Sigmund Freud and the local head of the Rothschild family. (Both of them were allowed to emigrate.)

Hitler presumably feared that the anti-Anschluss position might have been supported in the plebiscite, but his concern was hard to credit from the enthusiasm of the reception given him. The only possible shadow on his triumphant progress through the country of his birth and childhood was the response of Mussolini, who had stopped the attempted Anschluss four years before. Mussolini gave the takeover his approval, and Hitler expressed undying gratitude. He promised never to forget Mussolini's favor and in this, at least, he was as good as his word.

Cordell Hull gloomily opined, with more accuracy than usual, that Germany was "becoming the colossus of Europe," like Japan in the East, and that "they will try to rule the world."[50]

After the browbeating of Schuschnigg by Hitler at Berchtesgaden, Chamberlain told the House of Commons: "Two statesmen agreed on certain measures for the improvement of relations between their two countries [and] certain domestic changes in one of the countries." Mussolini had not objected to the Berchtesgaden rape of Austria and had expressed no willingness to withdraw any of his approximately 60,000 military personnel from Spain.

Chamberlain's grovelling to Mussolini gave Eden full reason to resign, which he did on February 20, when the prime minister's course was clearly inexorable. Even the recently arrived ambassador Joseph Kennedy wrote from London that the resignation of Eden had been a victory for Germany and Italy.[51]

Eden had also been irritated by Chamberlain's clumsy management of relations with Roosevelt. Thereafter, he became the second most formidable of the parliamentary anti-appeasers after Winston Churchill. Churchill, Eden, Hitler, Mussolini, Roosevelt, and Hull (and, it turned out, Stalin) were all about equally unimpressed with the course on which Chamberlain was now embarked.

Sumner Welles had received the British ambassador, Sir Ronald Lindsay, March 7. He emphatically told Lindsay that the U.S. government would under no circumstances accept to be perceived as considering the efforts of "the British government . . . to find a political appeasement 'to be right.'" Lindsay acknowledged that he and the foreign secretary, Lord Halifax, had "overemphasized" the official silence of the United States government in implying U.S. approval.

The ambassador was shaken by the volume of mail and comment he had received in the United States accusing Britain of propping up the dictators. He assured Welles that the British disliked the dictators but that since the dictators existed, "the only thing to do in order to prevent war is to try and find a basis for peaceful understanding with them." Britain sought a "restoration of confidence and friendship between Italy and England [that] might produce a satisfactory and lasting appeasement in the Mediterranean." Welles assured Roosevelt he had disassociated the President and his administration completely from any such policy.[52]

Roosevelt felt there would be nothing gained in his antagonizing all the major European governments when the Anschluss came, so he made no comment at all on it. His spokesmen refused to be drawn. It was clear that the United States didn't approve this course. But if the countries most directly at risk to Hitler's aggression were not going to object, there was no good purpose in the United States's trying to take a hand in events it could not influence and stirring up domestic opinion in a lost cause.

The President's own view was close to that of his friend John Cudahy, then U.S. minister to the Irish Free State, who wrote him on April 6, 1938, that "Chamberlain's is the most weak, vacillating, humiliating policy England has ever presented. . . . That is the tragedy. There is no leadership to oppose the dictators. Two years ago when Hitler invaded the Rhineland the treaty system was scrapped and there remained only one language they could understand." Cudahy claimed that if the British or French had acted as Roosevelt had "when the *Panay* was sunk, we would have a different picture today. It is not too late even now, but the leadership is not forthcoming."[53]

On the day of Welles's interview with Lindsay, Roosevelt wrote to his old friend and ambassador in Madrid, Claude Bowers, that Chamberlain had determined "to make a great effort with Italy and Germany, even making concessions such as the recognition of the Ethiopian conquest." Bowers had written him on February 20, 1938, denouncing the "brazenly fascistic policy of . . . the utterly stupid Chamberlain who in America would jostle his way into the Liberty League and write the enlightening resolutions of the American Manufacturers Association. . . . Baldwin and Chamberlain have betrayed the democracy of England shamelessly."

In his reply, Roosevelt wrote that if Chamberlain managed to delay war for three years, he would "be hailed as a great leader. If he fails or . . . give[s] too much and receives too little, he will be overthrown. . . . Fundamentally, you and I hate compromise with principle." Five months later, when the appeasement policy was reaching its climax, Roosevelt wrote back to Bowers: "It is amazing and sad to note that so many small nations have lost their confidence in England during the past two or three years."[54]

Chamberlain went ahead with his de jure recognition of the Italian conquest of Abyssinia on April 16, 1938, in the Anglo-Italian Agreement, which achieved nothing for Britain. The spectacle of the British lion, however implausibly personified by the brolly-wielding, homburged Chamberlain, truckling to such a stuffed parody of a leader as Mussolini, disgusted Roosevelt. He wrote back to John Cudahy in Dublin: "Over here there is the same element that exists in London. They would really like me to be a Neville Chamberlain—and if I would, [they would] promise that the market would go up and they would work positively and actively for the resumption of prosperity. But if that were done we would only be breeding more serious trouble four or eight years from now."[*][55]

In response to a congressional request, Roosevelt published the names of countries currently in violation of treaties with the United States. Italy was prominent among them. Chamberlain, and Eden's successor as foreign secretary, Lord Halifax, beseeched Roosevelt for public approval of the Anglo-Italian Agreement. The difference in perspective between Roosevelt and Chamberlain could scarcely be greater, but Roosevelt wanted to preserve what he could of Anglo-American relations until the countries could coordinate their policies, presumably with a more forceful prime minister, or an unrecognizably invigorated Chamberlain. The best Roosevelt could do was a pallid statement of "sympathetic interest" in the Anglo-Italian agreement.

As Roosevelt had believed, the recognition of the Abyssinian takeover was just an *ex gratia* concession to a military power that either Britain or France could have thrashed soundly without difficulty and without a protracted campaign. (Such a comeuppance would have been salutary for Mussolini and cautionary for Hitler. It would have impressed Stalin and assisted Roosevelt in engaging American opinion, and it might have produced an earlier and gentler outcome to the Spanish War.)

Shortly after the Anschluss, the French government of Leon Blum fell and was replaced by an appeasement regime headed by Edouard Daladier, in lockstep with Chamberlain. The Franco Nationalists were now making fairly steady military gains in Spain, and it was possible to envision an outright Fascist conquest of that country. The French and British governments were, as Churchill

---

* He assimilated his domestic conservative Republican critics to British appeasers. He was still preoccupied with the capital strike supposedly conducted by a loose brotherhood of Fascist-sympathizing businessmen. If he had cut taxes as he raised spending, strengthening his stimulus package and not over-targeting the rich, oratorically and fiscally, he would have found out how few his business opponents really were, and that there were virtually no Fascists among them. Much of the senior American business community was politically stupid and economically hidebound, but none of it was unpatriotic, and it almost unanimously favored prosperity and democracy, and disliked Fascism almost as ardently as Roosevelt did.

said at the time, "feeding the crocodiles." (Churchill actually favored Franco over the Republicans, whom he considered Communist-dominated.) Only Roosevelt and possibly Stalin had any disposition to resist Hitler among the leaders of the Great Powers. Stalin was becoming disgusted with the feebleness of the British and the French, and Roosevelt couldn't bring opinion in his country into line until there was some believable resistance to Germany.

It is clear from his diplomatic correspondence that Roosevelt foresaw the course of appeasement, thought it a mistaken effort to buy two or three years peace before Hitler unleashed war, and doubted it would succeed even in that.

IX

ROOSEVELT CONTINUED TO refuse to alter the American abstention from the whole Spanish question. Nye and the others, who thought they were saving the country from war by bottling Roosevelt up in the fetters of absolute neutrality and were now calling for a pro-Republican Spanish policy, had outsmarted themselves, not their president. He knew that American arms would be ineffectual because the Germans would merely insert more arms through the risible British blockade. And he knew how divisive the issue would be on the domestic public consensus he was determined to maintain and build.

Bankhead and Rayburn told him in May 1938 that any move toward the Spanish Republicans would alienate the entire Roman Catholic population of the country. (This was almost certainly true, but they were both Protestants. The President's Roman Catholic allies, like Robert Wagner and John McCormack, and insiders like Corcoran, Farley, Flynn, and Missy LeHand presumably told him the same thing.)* Cardinal Mundelein telephoned Roosevelt to ask that the embargo not be lifted in respect to Spain. Cordell Hull conveniently produced the doctrine that Spain was more than a civil war and so should be subject to an embargo on both sides.[156] Roosevelt knew the risks and rewards in a Spanish intervention were disproportionate, and Nye and his unworldly friends had excused him from having to scramble to avoid an ambush.‡

---

* A minor and peculiar episode in American response to the Spanish war in the spring of 1938 was an attempt by Eleanor's alcoholic brother, Hall, with Eleanor's assistance, to sell 150 mainly used American aircraft to the Spanish Loyalists via the U.S. embassy in Paris. Hall called on the ambassador, now William Bullitt, who sought clarification from Washington and was advised by the State Department that official policy had not changed.
† The son of Arthur Krock, Kennedy friend and *New York Times* columnist, was one of the few American volunteers for Franco.[57]
‡ The role of the Roman Catholic Church in the determination of Roosevelt's policy was a particular irritant to Harold Ickes, whose diary was peppered with anti-papist references. Ickes, a recent widower, married a woman thirty-nine years younger than he (they were sixty-four and twenty-five) at a Presbyterian Church in Dublin on May 24, 1938, having traveled incognito and remaining in his cabin on the magnificent French liner *Normandie*.

Immediately after the Anschluss, there were disgusting stories of persecutions, especially of Jews, in Nazi-occupied Austria. Americans were appalled, but public opinion was not so solicitous that it wanted to open wide the door of entry to America in these difficult times. There was no shortage of anti-Semitism in the United States, including in the State Department, though little of it anywhere in America was of the virulent kind that would approve mistreatment of the property, much less the persons, of Jews.

Roosevelt was always mindful of the need to preserve public support for commitment of his political capital to the ultimate questions of the national interest. He devised a typical method of making a suitable gesture without chipping away any of his broad public support. He called for an international conference and invited thirty-three countries to discuss refugee problems, but emphasized that none would be asked to receive more immigrants than were already permitted under statutes then in place. The conference eventually took place in Evian, but, after a tremendous outpouring of platitudes, did little of tangible help to the victims. Proposing it at all somewhat impressed sympathizers of the persecuted without offending the majority in the United States, which disapproved Hitler's brutality but didn't feel that it was America's obligation to deal with this, yet another evil of the Old World.

Roosevelt had told his ambassador in Berlin, William Dodd, when the extent of the Nazi persecution of the Jews could not have been fully imagined, "We must protect them, and whatever we can do to moderate the general persecution by unofficial and personal influence ought to be done. [But] this is not a governmental affair."[58] He did assist many private channels and had received 30,000 German Jews in the United States from 1933 to 1937, about 5 percent of the total German Jewish population. This total almost tripled before the curtain closed in 1941. On this subject, because of the extreme merit of the cause of the persecuted Jews, Roosevelt went to unusual lengths to reconcile his desire to do right with his determination to maintain his mastery of the domestic political majority.

Roosevelt issued his invitation to the conference on refugees, which he assumed would be largely attended by private sector organizations, from Warm Springs on March 25, 1938. Hitler spoke in Königsberg that same night. Not without a perverted logic, he expressed the hope that those (i.e., Roosevelt) who have "such deep sympathy for these criminals will at least be generous enough to convert this sympathy into practical aid." He claimed to be ready to evacuate the Jews from Germany on "luxury ships." As usual, Hitler had found the soft, flabby, underside of Western democratic moralism.

What Hitler didn't grasp, or if so only partially, was that Roosevelt, in tactical terms, could be just as agile and almost as cynical as he could be himself. Roosevelt sincerely was horrified by Hitler's atrocities, even at this early stage. But he knew that Hitler was a mortal danger who could be defeated only when Western opinion was fully aware of the impossibility of appeasing or reasoning with him.

He knew that he would have to build a righteous consensus, somewhat as Wilson had a generation before against a less obvious and satanic threat. Roosevelt would maintain his liberal credentials, another aspect of the Wilson tradition, but not at the expense of his Bismarckian ability to apply the full measure of American military and industrial power at the decisive point and moment. He would not be drawn prematurely.

Roosevelt would neither become complicit in the Nazi and Fascist crimes by legitimizing or ignoring them, as Chamberlain did, nor commit his country before it was ready, nor commit it on an issue less pressing than national survival and supreme moral legitimacy, as Chamberlain would in 1939. On several occasions over the next three and one-half years, Hitler would think he had exposed Roosevelt as a hypocrite and embarrassed him. But he knew nothing of America, (apart from having devoured Karl May's stories of the Wild West). Hitler didn't realize that every time Roosevelt made a humane or constructive suggestion and Hitler ridiculed him, American opinion firmed up behind the President.

But Roosevelt knew Germany, and he knew something of the mentality of the mad psychopathic demagogue. There were some partial historical precedents to work from. And his formidable political intuition, what Tom Corcoran called his "androgynous" insight, told him practically all he needed to know about Hitler from the start. Hitler compounded his misjudgment of Roosevelt by massively underestimating the military and industrial potential of the United States.

Hitler took Roosevelt for another witless Western idealist, more altruistic and stylish than Chamberlain, but just as weak and gullible, and set at the head of a more powerful but less distinguished country. He realized too late, if ever, that he was dealing with a leader who reciprocated his hatred, matched his cunning, and was implacably determined to be rid of him, an ambition that Hitler never particularly entertained toward Roosevelt. Roosevelt knew from the start, and before Hitler himself did, that Hitler was a menace to him. Roosevelt knew that the world could never be safe for democracy nor America unambiguously the world's most important country while Hitler reigned and Hitlerism flourished. In this, he antedated even Churchill, as the Hitler entry in Churchill's 1937 book, *Great Contemporaries*, makes clear, though by mid-1938 Churchill's and Roosevelt's views of Hitler were almost identical.

As in his manipulation of William Randolph Hearst, of the western progressive isolationists, of the Southern Segregationist Democrats, and of his own budget balancers, in American domestic politics, Roosevelt would protect and build his foreign policy consensus as he had deftly built a new domestic consensus for each phase of the evolving New Deal.

A man of Hitler's political cunning, if he had paid more attention to American affairs, or even listened to his often astute ambassador in Washington, Hans Dieckhoff, would have had some idea of the mortal danger that Roosevelt's

America, uniquely of all the countries in the world, posed to Nazi Germany. He would then, presumably, have behaved more cautiously. Hitler realized only when he was half way to military defeat and personal physical extinction what a threat to him Roosevelt was and always had been. Hitler's defective political judgment in an area where he was usually very astute was probably aggravated by his contempt for Roosevelt's illness and his preoccupation with the presence of Zionist Jews (i.e., Cohen and Frankfurter) in Roosevelt's entourage and "Negroes" on his domestic staff

In general Roosevelt was influenced by no one, only by the impact of events upon his idea of the United States as the world's predestined nation, and of himself as recipient of both a divine and a popular mandate to lead his country to the pinnacle of benign power, where he had always known it belonged. In addition to being almost as objectively good in his purposes—if not always in his methods— as Hitler was evil in his, Roosevelt was as ambitious a visionary and as artistic, if more scrupulous, a Machiavellian as Hitler. In the middle of 1938 these facts were known to, and probably suspected by, no one except the grand and enigmatic occupant of the White House.

PART III

Toward the Rendezvous with Destiny—Undeclared War 1938–1941

CHAPTER II

"I Believe It Is Peace in Our Time"

(Prime Minister Neville Chamberlain on returning from the Munich Conference to Downing Street, September 30, 1938)

I

IN A FIRESIDE chat June 24, 1938, President Roosevelt summarized the accomplishments of the congressional session just ended. He applied his usual hyperbole to the Fair Labor Standards Act, calling it "the most far-reaching, far-sighted program for the benefit of workers ever adopted here or in any other country." The Socialist Party leader Norman Thomas had been prevented from speaking to public meetings in New Jersey by the notorious boss Frank Hague, mayor of Jersey City. Hague, after jumping from Al Smith to Roosevelt following the Chicago convention in 1932, had delivered a great many votes for Roosevelt and been rewarded with a good deal of patronage. But the incidents involving Thomas had so scandalized reasonable opinion that Roosevelt felt obliged to make an unambiguous statement in favor of free speech in this nationwide address.

His most interesting comment was his renewed claim that his Supreme Court initiative had really been a success: "The attitude of the Supreme Court toward constitutional questions is entirely changed [and is] eloquent testimony of a willingness to collaborate with the two other branches of government to make democracy work." The only other reflection of the President's that had any lasting significance was his assertion that "Communism . . . is just as dangerous as Fascism."

Roosevelt also gave notice of his intention to support candidates sympathetic to him and faithful to the 1936 party platform in Democratic primaries. This initiative arose from the "Elimination Committee" led by Hopkins and including

Corcoran, Ickes, and Jimmy Roosevelt.[1] The President departed Washington July 7 for a nine-day campaign trip to stamp out heresies in his own party. He spoke in favor of Senator Robert Bulkley of Ohio and for Alben Barkley of Kentucky, who was facing a tough primary battle. Barkley's defeat would automatically elevate Pat Harrison of Mississippi to the majority leadership of the U.S. Senate. Harrison was a reactionary and a militant white racial supremacist; though he had served the President well in most matters, he resented Roosevelt's support for Barkley over him in the succession to Joe Robinson the year before. (Roosevelt would try to placate Harrison by publicly naming him as one of the founders of the Social Security Act, for which, in fact, he had had little enthusiasm.)

In his concern about the race in Kentucky, Roosevelt made yet another of his dubious bargains with John L. Lewis. Lewis and the CIO supported Barkley in exchange for Roosevelt's support of a CIO man in the Democratic Senate primary in Pennsylvania. Barkley was challenged by perennial Kentucky vote-getter Governor A.B. "Happy" Chandler. Roosevelt employed his customary device of referring to Chandler as "my good friend." As we have seen, he spoke in these terms of almost everybody, from the antagonistic H.L. Mencken to people whom he scarcely knew. To help Barkley along, WPA employees pitched in and worked for him, in an egregious abuse of public-service rules, and undoubtedly at the instigation of the White House. (Barkley, in his memoirs, disputes this. More likely, it occurred without the Senator's having requested it. Roosevelt and his political operatives, led at this point by Corcoran, had a bag of political tricks they dipped into as need arose that would have challenged the imagination, and the ethics, of many beneficiaries.)

Roosevelt moved on to Oklahoma and spoke for Senator Elmer Thomas, and then to Texas. There he spoke for congressmen Maury Maverick, who carried his surname well, to the irritation of John Nance Garner and the other members of the Texas Democratic Establishment, and he spoke for the twenty-nine-year-old Lyndon B. Johnson, who had won a special election to Congress the year before. The tour continued to Colorado and Nevada, where Roosevelt ignored the incumbent senators, Alva Adams and Pat McCarran. Crowds for the President were everywhere large and enthusiastic. The lady in Marietta, Ohio, where the tour began, who knelt and patted the President's footprint in the dust after he had (awkwardly) passed, well represented his reception across the country.[2]

This effort of Roosevelt's at enforcing party discipline ended in California, where the President spoke at the building site of the 1939 Golden Gate International Exposition and crossed for the first time the Golden Gate and Oakland Bay Bridges. He did not endorse his "old friend" William G. McAdoo (whom he had never much appreciated) nor McAdoo's opponent, Sheridan Downey, a California radical in the general tradition of Francis Townsend and Upton Sinclair. Downey's platform was encapsulated in the slogan "$30 every Thursday" (i.e., for every adult male and every unmarried woman).

On July 16, at San Diego, Roosevelt boarded the heavy cruiser U.S.S. *Houston* for a month-long recreational trip down the Mexican coast, through the Panama Canal, and into the Gulf of Mexico. The trip had its usual restorative effect on the Commander in Chief. He took with him a distinguished scientist, Dr. Waldo Schmitt, of the United States Museum of Natural History. The highlights of the trip for Roosevelt were landing a 240-pound shark and Schmitt's discovery of a new palm on Cocos Island, which he named *Rooseveltia frankliniana.*

The President of Mexico, Lazaro Cardenas, a reformer who represented himself as something of a Mexican Roosevelt, had announced March 18 that he was nationalizing foreign oil interests in Mexico. Following a brief strike by Mexican oil workers in 1936, a commission had been established to investigate grievances in the industry and to compare the Mexican and American oil industries. It concluded that Mexican oil workers were more productive and less well paid, and that consequently American and other foreign oil companies were more profitable in Mexico than in the United States.

The companies violently denied the accuracy of the findings and of the suppositions on which the conclusions were based. And Cardenas's methods do not inspire much confidence in the rigor or impartiality of the analysis. The Mexican commission with authority to impose a settlement following the strike decreed a 27 percent wage increase and generous holiday, pension, and other benefits, which were designed to make the companies unprofitable and did so. The companies appealed to the Mexican Supreme Court, which promptly rejected the appeal (it was not a nonpolitical tribunal and Mexico was not really a democratic country).

Cardenas announced his decision in a country-wide radio address, in a manner designed to stir traditional Mexican resentment of foreigners, particularly Americans. The U.S. ambassador to Mexico at the time was none other than Roosevelt's old and much-tried mentor, Josephus Daniels. Cardenas had been sending weapons to the Spanish Republicans, and triumphantly proclaimed that the nationalized oil companies would not be selling to aggressor states as they had been. He reneged on this immediately; Germany, Japan, and Italy were the principal customers from the beginning. These countries paid only about 40 percent in cash and the rest in goods that Mexico would otherwise have bought mainly from the United States.

Roosevelt was concerned that if he muscled Mexico on the issue of compensation it would destroy his Good Neighbor policy, invite foreign mischief in the Americas, and weaken Latin American democracies in favor of local Fascist and Communist elements. But, though he didn't have unlimited sympathy for the oil companies, he couldn't tolerate American property being seized without adequate compensation and didn't want to issue a virtual invitation to all other countries to do the same. He had to walk the line between dollar diplomacy of the jingoistic era and a policy so indulgent it would rightly outrage American industry and public opinion and whet the appetites of leaders of many other countries.

On March 28, Daniels delivered a note of Cordell Hull's to Cardenas in which the secretary of state recognized Mexico's unquestioned right to national-ize industry but asserted as a matter of course, without bluster or threat, that fair value must be paid. This was sufficient for Cardenas, who promptly replied that "His Excellency President Roosevelt [has] won the esteem of the people of Mex-ico [as he] reaffirms . . . the sovereignty of the peoples of this continent." Britain, by contrast, so abrasively handled the question of reparations for the expropria-tions that Mexico broke off diplomatic relations.

Cardenas was so grateful for Roosevelt's suave handling of the affair that he welcomed him to Mexican waters on July 17 by sending a high-level delegation out to the U.S.S. *Houston* to greet the President. FDR had aptly managed the problem, although the negotiations over what constituted fair payment would go on for over six months and strain even Hull's patience.

Roosevelt disembarked from the *Houston* at Pensacola, Florida, on August 9 and proceeded on his train to Warm Springs. He then escalated his campaign for ortho-doxy within his party to an ambitious new level by going to Barnesville, Georgia, on August 11 and urging his "fellow Georgians" to defeat the powerful incumbent, Senator Walter George, and give the Democratic nomination (and automatic elec-tion with it) to the Rooseveltian challenger, U.S. Attorney Lawrence Camp. This was a madcap initiative for so canny a political leader as FDR.

Roosevelt was ostensibly there for the dedication of a new rural electrification project, and both Senator George and Camp, whom the White House had brow-beaten into making the uphill race against him, were present. Roosevelt got to the inevitable reference to "my friend," and then embellished it into a deluxe ver-sion: "I trust and am confident that Senator George and I shall always be good personal friends," the President ritualistically intoned, before asking the voters of Georgia to dump George in favor of Camp. He then turned to shake hands with George. The senator accepted the handshake and then said: "Mr. President, I regret that you have taken the occasion to question my democracy and to attack my record. I want you to know that I accept the challenge." (It would have strained the credulity of even Roosevelt's most adulatory admirers to imagine that Walter George would still be FDR's "personal friend" if he had succeeded in removing George from the U.S. Senate.)

At least in the South, Roosevelt's attempted "purge"—as his opponents described it, to assimilate his behavior to that of Hitler and Stalin (the latter's purges were now in full sanguinary flood)—was designed to remove the most intractable white supremacists. Though it was never presented in this light, there was a commendable element of trying to accelerate the South's evolution to a more racially tolerant society, no longer represented in the United States Senate by people who would consider it a point of honor to filibuster an antilynching bill.

Late in the same day, August 11, Roosevelt spoke to a large crowd from the back of his train at Greenville, South Carolina. Congressman Cotton Ed Smith, who had disapproved of much of Roosevelt's legislation, was under challenge in the primary in his district. He had notoriously said in opposing the Fair Labor Standards Act that a family could live on fifty cents a day. Roosevelt closed out his brief address—saying he wanted to get it in before he finished, "and I believe the train is pulling out in a minute or two" (as if there were the slightest chance that the engineer would lurch out of the station while the President was still speaking from the rear of the train)—with the assertion: "I don't believe any family or man can live on fifty cents a day." This was the extent of his direct intervention against Smith. A purge, to be effective, must be more comprehensively implemented than that.

On returning to Washington, Roosevelt added Congressman John J. O'Connor of New York City to the list of his targets at his press conference on August 16. "Week in and week out O'Connor labors to tear down New Deal strength, pickle New Deal legislation." The day before, he had added Senator Millard Tydings of Maryland to the list of his targets.

On the Labor Day weekend, Roosevelt inconvenienced himself considerably by traveling from Hyde Park to Maryland on his private train and making six speeches around the state against Senator Tydings. This was probably a record for presidential exposure to Maryland. It didn't work. The different primaries in which Roosevelt intervened were held on different dates between July and September and produced a mixed result. Senators Thomas (Oklahoma), Bulkley (Ohio), and Barkley (Kentucky), for whom he had spoken, were reselected as candidates. Congressman Maverick was defeated, but Congressman Lyndon Johnson was renominated. Senator Tydings won by a large margin despite Roosevelt's marathon of speechification on behalf of Tydings's opponent, and Senator Walter George wiped the floor with Roosevelt protégé Lawrence Camp, who came third behind George and the white-trash archsegregationist Eugene Talmadge, who made George seem an allegory for enlightenment in all things.

Cotton Ed Smith, against whom Roosevelt had contributed only one sentence from the back of his railway car, won narrow reelection as congressman from South Carolina. However, a mighty White House effort against Congressman John J. O'Connor in New York (including Corcoran's request, which Henry Morgenthau indignantly rejected, for Internal Revenue agents to be sent out to work and canvass for O'Connor's opponent, James H. Fay) was successful. Roosevelt was not discountenanced by McAdoo's defeat at the hands of Downey, and was pleased at the elevation of Jerry Voorhis as a congressman from suburban Los Angeles. (Having been promoted by Franklin D. Roosevelt, Voorhis would be ousted as congressman by Richard M. Nixon's launch of his political career in 1946.) In sum, Roosevelt's effort at cleansing his party of designated renegades and at supporting loyalists had been about half successful. But it was widely seen, in the words of James A. Farley (whom Roosevelt had dragooned into accompanying him on the anti-Tydings Labor Day weekend trip to Maryland), as "a bust."

Roosevelt was thus generally perceived to have sustained three distinct defeats in eighteen months. He had largely retrieved the Supreme Court fiasco, since the Court had mended its ways and two of its more obdurate members had retired. Though failure to pass legislation based on the Brownlow committee report on executive reorganization was a minor irritant, Roosevelt would revisit the subject, and it was far from a burning issue in the public imagination.

This half-bungled purge was considerably more dramatic. Purges in the late thirties were not image-building activities in a democracy, and this one, coming soon after the Court-packing effort, confirmed the views of those who saw Roosevelt as an aspiring dictator. And it did not enhance Roosevelt's image as the unchallenged heavyweight champion of American politics to have southern feudal lords successfully repulse him. Roosevelt knew that if the spell of a champion is broken, a rockslide of improvident events can ensue. He wasn't at that point, though portents for the off-year elections were not promising, but as he entered the last half of the second term, unprecedented tensions overseas mingled with the first real suspense about a possible presidential third term since the Founding Fathers. Almost everyone sensed that high drama was unfolding in the United States as elsewhere.

II

ROOSEVELT HAD TAKEN his next step after the Quarantine Speech in Chicago in the gradual preparation for America's role in the approaching world crisis in a speech accepting an honorary degree at Queen's University, Kingston, Ontario, Canada, on August 18, 1938. He spoke in favor of his long-standing hobby horse, a St. Lawrence seaway that would harness that mighty river for the production of much more hydroelectric power and canalize it and lesser rivers connecting the Great Lakes, to open up the heart of the continent— including Chicago, Detroit, Cleveland, Buffalo, and Toronto—to large ocean-going vessels, and to the world. Then, in response to the intense war scare that Hitler was then stoking up over the addition of Czechoslovakia's Sudetenland to the Reich, Roosevelt asserted: "The Dominion of Canada is part of the sisterhood of the British Empire. I give to you assurance that the people of the United States will not stand idly by if domination of Canadian soil is threatened by any other empire." The Canadian audience responded with profound appreciation.

The practical relevance of the speech was that a British declaration of war against a European power would almost certainly be followed by a Canadian one, and a Canada in such a war would be a country under threat from overseas. More remotely, since the British Royal Navy had helped enforce the 1823 Monroe Doctrine of noninterference in the Americas, of which these reflections in Kingston, Ontario, were a reaffirmation, the continued strength of the British navy was implicitly being defined as in the U.S. national interest. In comments to the press at his home in Hyde Park the next day, Roosevelt, true to the Chicago

Quarantine speech precedent, denied that he was extending the Monroe Doctrine. Roosevelt was becoming too subtle for the American media, and the reaction was much less energized than after the Chicago speech. But discerning observers detected the trajectory that administration policy was following.

By mid-September, the world was engrossed in the Sudeten crisis, which threatened to bring Europe to war just twenty years after the end of the Great War. Roosevelt participated in the drama peripherally, somewhat distracted by household problems. His son Jimmy, who, as Eleanor had predicted, had not been hugely successful as his father's assistant and had been mercilessly pilloried as a nepotistic cipher of dubious ethics, was laid low by a gastric ulcer that was feared to be malignant. He went to the Mayo Clinic in Rochester, Minnesota, and the President and his entourage arrived there on the presidential train on September 11. Surgery was undertaken that day and there was no malignancy. Jimmy left the Mayo for a convalescence in California with his nurse, Romelle Schneider. He survived and lived to a great age, but he retired from the White House and left his wife, Betsey Cushing Roosevelt, who enchanted the President and disconcerted Eleanor.*

The Nazi leader of Sudetenland, Konrad Henlein, had presented his demands in a speech at Carlsbad on April 24, 1938. The principal one was the ability to establish a Nazi German state in Sudetenland, which had about three million people, about 90 percent of them German-speaking, and an undoubted majority of those Nazis. This state, although Henlein did not say so, would then be able to secede from Czechoslovakia and adhere to Germany.

Neville Chamberlain did not try to preserve the credibility of Anglo-French guaranties of Czechoslovakia. (France had guaranteed that country, and Great Britain was allied to France.) Konrad Henlein visited Paris and London, and shortly after his meeting with Chamberlain, the prime minister had given an interview at the famous Astor estate of Cliveden to the *New York Herald Tribune*. Chamberlain made the point that, given European geography, there was nothing

---

* At the same time, the association between Eleanor and Nancy Cook and Marion Dickerman came to a wrenching end. These two had bitterly resented the arrival of Lorena Hickock in Eleanor's life and her displacement of them. Eleanor had already transformed an unused furniture shop into her own cottage, near but separated from the Val-Kill cottage by a tall fence. With the same ardor with which Eleanor entered into relationships, she brutally terminated them, and there were a number of abrasive scenes as the involvements with Val-Kill Industries and Todhunter School were unwound. The President himself was asked to provide mediating advice on the property disentanglement and did so, but legalities dragged on into the spring of 1939. It is unlikely that he was bereaved at the deemphasis of these mannish women around his house and he never paid much attention to Eleanor when she was in her more vehement moods anyway, but the drama did rile the ambiance at Springwood at a particularly tense time.

Britain, France, or the U.S.S.R. could do to help the Czechs if they were attacked by the Germans. The Czechs would have to accept a Swiss-style cantonal arrangement or cede the Sudetenland to Germany.

Henlein met with Winston Churchill, the veteran statesman now nine years out of office but still an imposing parliamentary figure. Churchill had been in cabinet positions for all but two years between 1905 and 1929, and was a lowering Cassandra full of foreboding. Henlein sketched out to Churchill a plan for local autonomy for the Sudetenlanders, with the Czechs retaining their territorial integrity and control of the frontier fortifications that had consumed much of the new country's defense budget since it had been created by the Treaty of St. Germain in September of 1919. This was acceptable to Churchill and to the Czech ambassador in London, Jan Masaryk. Chamberlain, however, had already undertaken to go further, so there was little incentive for Henlein and his master in Berlin to confine themselves to such terms.

Henlein returned home and immediately began to intensify agitation for his local annexationist and Nazi cause, which led to the deaths of two of his followers on May 20, as the Czech authorities maintained order fearlessly. Czechoslovak President Eduard Beneš immediately ordered a partial mobilization involving 400,000 soldiers. France had reasserted its adherence to its Czech treaty obligations in the waning days of the Leon Blum government of the democratic left in mid-March. Paris and London both warned Berlin that an attack on the Czechs would lead to war, and the U.S.S.R. was making similar noises.

The British ambassador to Berlin, Sir Nevile Henderson, was already awed by the regime to which he was accredited, and presented the official warning as gently as he could: "His Majesty's Government could not guarantee that they would not be forced by events to become themselves involved." From Chamberlain and Henderson, this was uncharacteristically fierce. In the circumstances, Hitler denied any intention of imminent recourse to force and the crisis seemed to subside. To many it appeared that he had backed down as he had under pressure from Mussolini over Anschluss with Austria in 1934. Reports in the world's press that he had been faced down by the likes of Beneš, Daladier, and Chamberlain seriously aggravated Hitler's always neurotically explosive nature. He ordered the immediate preparation of a plan for the invasion of Czechoslovakia, to be ready for implementation in the early autumn of 1938.

Roosevelt's high-strung ambassador in Paris, William Bullitt, had urged Roosevelt to invite Hitler, Mussolini, Daladier, and Chamberlain to The Hague for a conference at which to resolve the crisis peacefully. Roosevelt was always eager to play a role in these matters if a plausible role presented itself, but he balked at convening European leaders at a meeting in Europe where the United States would only be able to repeat unctuously that it would not become seriously involved. In the same measure that he didn't want to inflame the dovecotes of isolationism and pacifism, he didn't want to bring his country and himself into ridicule by playing a role that could not be taken seriously.

In July, Chamberlain sent former cabinet minister Lord Runciman to Czechoslovakia to try to work out a peaceful agreement between Beneš and Henlein. He did so "with the full concurrence of Herr Hitler." Runciman was a mere temporizer, no more disposed to take a stand over the Sudetenland than Chamberlain or Henderson, and he was more of an irritant than anything else.

There was a good deal of activity by dissident German officers, concerned that Hitler was mad and was leading Germany to an unwinnable and completely avoidable war with Britain, France, and possibly the Soviet Union. It will always be a matter of debate how serious these mutinous contemplations were. Doubtless the officers involved were brave and sincere, and doubtless the relentless appeasement of Hitler made their tasks impossible.

But Hitler had an uncanny, almost diabolical skill at outwitting those who would remove him from within. Attempts to blow him up, in the Munich beerhall where his movement was founded, on his aircraft, at his headquarters in East Prussia in 1944, were all foiled by unpredictable last-minute moves by him. He always outsmarted the German officers politically, where the military men were hobbled by their codes of honor and guileless formation. Chamberlain and Daladier have been criticized for not paying more attention to these elements, but they shouldn't be blamed for not attaching too much credit to a shadowy cabal of politically naïve German officer-conspirators.

———————

Churchill wrote Halifax a memorandum on August 31, 1938, urging closer cooperation with the Soviet Union and the United States. He recommended an attempted united front with the French and the Russians, along with at least the benevolent neutrality of the Americans, in dealing with Germany over the Sudeten crisis. On the same day, Roosevelt was working with Morgenthau on a plan to allow the British and French to move gold to the United States, convert it to cash, and purchase war supplies from the United States. This was one of several ways being examined to circumvent the neutrality legislation. A plan was worked out, including restraints on trade with Germany and Italy, but Cordell Hull, who fussed at all times, was dismayed at the effect this might have on his ruling passion of free trade, which was becoming a rather esoteric concern.*

Joseph Kennedy had quickly become friendly with Chamberlain, had expressed understanding of Hitler's "Jewish problem," and was an archappeaser. Roosevelt was aware of his respect for some aspects of Fascism when he appointed him, but assumed his abrasive, bantam rooster preoccupation with his Irish past would prevent him from falling head first into the general feebleness of Chamberlain and his claque. "Who would have thought that the English could take into camp a red-headed Irishman?" Roosevelt asked, adding: "The young man needs

———————

* It was a preoccupation of Joseph Kennedy's too, and one of his highest priorities, assigned him by Roosevelt and Hull, was to negotiate a new and more liberal trade treaty with Britain.

his wrists slapped rather hard." (Kennedy was only six years younger than Roosevelt, but by the middle of his second term, Roosevelt was in avuncular mode with almost everyone. His relative immobility may have encouraged him to put on the conversational airs of someone a generation older than he really was.) Kennedy gave a speech at Aberdeen on September 2 implying that no visible issue in Europe was worth shedding blood over. Hull had required the removal of any references to Czechoslovakia, and both he and Roosevelt were annoyed that Kennedy had given an exclusive advance on the story to the Hearst press.

The British press had reported on September 1 that Halifax had asked Kennedy what America's response would be if Britain did go to war over Czechoslovakia. Roosevelt was outraged that Kennedy hadn't immediately denied that there had been any such conversation. It was obvious to the President that this was an effort to set the United States up: that if Britain went to war it had been pushed into action by the United States, and if it didn't it was because of lack of American support. He reluctantly considered that Kennedy had not blundered into this cul-de-sac but rather had entered it voluntarily to try to restrict Roosevelt's options, "in [Kennedy's] process of playing the Chamberlain game."[3]

The loose cannon in the embassy in London was now one more of the countless moving parts in Roosevelt's great international political puzzle. "Like a hummingbird in flight, Joseph Kennedy had darted about the British capital through the spring of 1938, winning over government officers and financiers; gathering support for his foreign policy views; gauging the possibility of a campaign for the White House. But, unwittingly or not, the hummingbird flitted under a glass dome, and above the dome loomed the omniscient eyes of Franklin Roosevelt. For months the President had known of the gossip that Kennedy was indulging himself in the same denunciations of the President in London that he had in Washington."[4]

Kennedy had performed one useful service for Roosevelt while on home leave in the early summer; he had persuaded Thomas Lamont to secure the deferral of a wage cut at United States Steel that Roosevelt feared would undercut his always tenuous economic recovery. Kennedy had been authorized to offer the incentive of increased government contracts in the event of a deferral of ninety days. The principled Lamont and the U.S. Steel management finally decided to make the deferral unconditionally. Kennedy was one of the few prominent American businessmen who understood how the political mind worked. He was becoming a very troublesome ambassador, but he still had his uses.

Roosevelt's position was extremely delicate. He couldn't altogether disagree with Berle's advice, as assistant secretary of state: "Our emotion is obscuring the fact that were the actor anyone other than Hitler, with his cruelty and anti-Semitic feeling, we would regard this as merely reconstituting the old system, undoing the obviously unsound work of Versailles and generally following the line of historical logic." However, it wasn't anyone but Hitler they were dealing with, and Roosevelt didn't think Hitler was usefully or durably appeasable. He held the Churchill view that the sooner Hitler was resisted the better.[5]

He was also acutely aware that the only way the United States could be brought to do anything seriously useful in the event of Anglo-French resistance would be if Hitler's evil oppressed the American conscience and the Anglo-French leadership inspired American admiration and solidarity. There was no chance of the dithering, anti-American, provincial mediocrity Chamberlain, doing that, with his reedy voice, prominent Adam's apple, and absence of flair or vigor. Even less accessible to American admiration was Daladier—dumpy, cynical, unhygienic, with the stub of an unfiltered Turkish cigarette fastened to his lower lip, and reeking of absinthe as he growled in a heavy Marseillais accent.

There was nothing for it but to bring American opinion along as quickly as Roosevelt could, give the British and French such encouragement to firmness as he plausibly could, and rearm. This last course would at least enable him to bring the country all the way out of the Depression. He could sell the argument that the surest guarantee of American nonparticipation in war was to arm it with deterrent power so that it could protect its hemisphere and give aid to worthy combatants.

Coming to grips with Hitler would be a fate that would await whoever was elected in 1940. Roosevelt's public ambiguity about a third term was already becoming a national guessing game.

Southern conservatives, who didn't like emergency relief, could be persuaded to vote for an expanded defense capacity. Western isolationists, who liked workfare programs but were wary of international involvements, would, for a time, accept massive defense spending in lieu of public works if it were accompanied by perfervid expressions of determination to keep the country out of war.

Starting in mid-1938, the defense budget made inroads on the emergency relief budget, and unemployment accelerated its decline through 1939 and 1940. By election day 1940, it would finally be descending into single figures as a percentage of the work force, and be only about 4 percent if those in the continuing relief programs were considered to be employed people. Unemployment could be seen to be evaporating as the armed forces and defense production industries absorbed huge increases of manpower. (When the Sudeten crisis boiled up in September 1938, the United States had an army of only 176,000, not counting Philippine scouts. This was an absurd and dangerous geopolitical vacuum, and strategy combined with economics to require large accretions of forces.) Unemployment would be eliminated completely while the country was still at peace, in the autumn of 1941.

Complicated and difficult though the times were, Roosevelt saw a method of ending the Depression and becoming the indispensable conservator of peace, even as he made America ready to help subdue a satanic adversary. The gathering crisis did not dim Roosevelt's sense of national or personal destiny.

In September 1938, the deputy chief of staff of the army, General George C. Marshall, approached Harry Hopkins about concentrating some relief work in the production of munitions and small arms. Hopkins readily agreed; production was discreetly begun and steadily increased, and was eventually reckoned to have advanced American preparedness in this area by an entire year when the country finally entered the war. Ultimately and ironically, Roosevelt would complete his defeat of the Depression by methods that, in strictly economic terms, were not unlike those employed by Hitler: defense production and conscription. This beginning was not the least accomplishment of Marshall's remarkable career.

The annual Nazi Party rally at Nuremberg ran for a week from September 6. Sir Nevile Henderson, as catastrophic an appointment to Berlin as Kennedy was to London, was virtually hypnotized by the immense spectacle choreographed by Hitler's architect, Albert Speer, and his propaganda minister, Dr. Joseph Goebbels. Henderson spent the week uncomfortably in a railway car on a siding, passing the days hobnobbing obsequiously with the Nazi leadership.[6] Halifax sent Henderson a message just before Hitler was to speak at the finale of the party meeting, asking that he warn Hitler that the British government would regard any move against Czechoslovakia with the utmost seriousness. This would be construed as a threat of war.

Henderson, instead of carrying out this unusually feisty instruction from his government, executed a supine farce. Because he had no codes or even stationery with him, Henderson tore pages out of the mystery novels he had brought with him as bedtime reading and scribbled on them a message that the first lord of the admiralty, Duff Cooper, described as "hysterical, imploring the government not to insist upon his carrying out these instructions, which he was sure would have the opposite effect to that desired." Henderson sent these pages by private chartered aircraft to London, and the cabinet rescinded its instructions to the ambassador.

In the event, Hitler gave a speech that was rather turgid and inconclusive, though full of threats and grievances, on the evening of September 12. This was the first time that one of Hitler's speeches to a vast live audience had been broadcast in America. Millions of Americans found the German leader's hoarse and bellicose shrieking, interspersed with thunderous shouts of "Sieg heil!" (Hail victory!) from the crowd of approximately one million, very disturbing. New York's mayor, Fiorello H. La Guardia, declared that Hitler had "lost all sense of proportion and reason" and should be locked up.[7]

Roosevelt, according to Hopkins, who was with him in Minnesota awaiting the results of the President's son's surgery, thought war was probably imminent after the two listened to Hitler's speech on the radio. Roosevelt sent Hopkins to the West Coast to make a confidential survey of the country's warplane production potential, because Roosevelt was presciently convinced that air power would be a determining factor in another war between the Great Powers.

The consequence of Hopkins's mission was that Roosevelt began bandying about the necessity of 8,000 warplanes for the U.S. armed forces, to the consternation of the pacifists. Colonel Lindbergh had made a much-publicized visit to Nazi Germany in 1936 as the guest of Hermann Goering, commander of the German Luftwaffe and officially the second person in the regime. Goering had thoroughly brainwashed Lindbergh, convincing him that German aircraft production was ten to forty thousand per year. It seems Lindbergh thought, and convinced the French air minister, Guy La Chambre, at a dinner in Bullitt's embassy in 1938, after Lindbergh had toured Russia and Czechoslovakia, that German aircraft production was about 40,000 annually. In fact, in 1938 and 1939 Germany produced 8,000 warplanes, compared with 11,000 warplanes in Great Britain and about 5,000 in France. (It must be said at least for Chamberlain's government that it produced this increase and that the year before the outbreak of war was not completely wasted.)

Lindbergh returned to Germany in October 1938, and at a dinner at the U.S. embassy Hermann Goering presented him with the highest German honor for foreigners, the service cross of the German eagle with star. Lindbergh had earned it; he had inadvertently disseminated a good deal of Nazi sabre-rattling propaganda in circles little minded to question or resist it, particularly that of the impressionable French air minister.

Senator Gerald Nye publicly grumbled about Roosevelt's advocacy of "undue military preparedness."[8] The President had always known that bringing public and congressional opinion into line with geopolitical realities would be a laborious process.

III

ON SEPTEMBER 13, 1938, a Czech policeman was killed by Nazis in the border town of Eger as he carried out a search order in a hotel where Henlein's people were thought to have stored small arms. A gun battle ensued, in which another policeman and eight armed Nazis were killed. Violence then broke out throughout Sudetenland, and martial law was declared and order restored by the Czech army with professional efficiency.

The German government was predictably outraged. In Rome, the pope, Pius XI, declared that the Holy See "is not for [totalitarianism]. But neither is it for the exact reverse." He solemnly catechized himself in response to the deepening emergency.[9]

Chamberlain had determined to try personal diplomacy. He sent Hitler a message saying: "I propose to come over to see you at once with a view to trying to find a peaceful solution." Hitler's response on receiving this communication was, roughly translated: "This is a bolt from the blue!" ("Ich bin von himmel gefallen.")

Chamberlain, sixty-nine years old and a strange mixture of diffidence and egotism, the colorless but competent political servitor, former Caribbean sisal farmer, and, as Lloyd George had ungenerously put it, "provincial manufacturer of iron bedsteads," set out for Munich. Only his senior civil servant, Sir Horace Wilson, archappeaser and anti-American par excellence, Foreign Office European specialist William Strang, a security person, and a secretary accompanied him. He would rely for translation on Hitler's interpreter, Dr. Paul Schmidt, and on whomever Henderson brought with him. It was a dramatic moment, probably the first in Chamberlain's life, as the little eight-seat commercial aircraft took off from Heston aerodrome with these five passengers and some sandwiches and beverages for the four-hour flight.

The British prime minister was met at Munich airport by Henderson and the German foreign minister, the pompous and incompetent Joachim von Ribbentrop, a former champagne salesman in Canada and ambassador in London. They traveled together to Hitler's mountain retreat at Berchtesgaden. The route into the Alps was shrouded by mist and lined by SS troops, smartly uniformed in black breeches, leather knee boots, and shortish black tunics—a crisply turned-out personification of discipline and authority. Wilson wondered if he and his leader would emerge from this Wagnerian setting alive, but his first impression of the German fuehrer in his brown uniform was of "a draper's assistant." (The year before, Halifax, at a reception, was about to hand Hitler his bowler hat when Ribbentrop forcefully announced "Der Fuehrer.") Wilson went on about Hitler, with unsuspected humor: "I didn't like his eyes. I didn't like his mouth. In fact there wasn't very much I did like about him."[10]

Hitler had no idea what Chamberlain had in mind, and the British and Germans awkwardly exchanged banalities over tea for about twenty minutes before Chamberlain asked for a private meeting. He and his host and the efficient Dr. Schmidt went to Hitler's study. Three hours of unproductive discussion followed. Hitler periodically raged, particularly when Beneš and the Czechs were mentioned. Chamberlain intervened, comically in any less dire circumstances: "This business of the Sudeten Germans isn't really our affair, you know." Another gambit was "Look here, I'm a practical man." Chamberlain returned to London and said to the waiting press only that he and Hitler had had a "frank but friendly talk" and would meet again.

Chamberlain was loudly cheered as he drove from Heston to Downing Street. He told the cabinet that Hitler was "the commonest little dog" but that he, Chamberlain, "got the impression that here was a man who could be relied upon when he had given his word."[11]

Roosevelt, for his part, was disgusted and spoke to Harold Ickes of the British leader having gone "to plead with the ex-corporal, ex-house painter." (Roosevelt could be as much a snob as his analogues in the British upper classes.) "England

and France," said the U.S. president, "during and after this international outrage, will wash the blood from their Judas Iscariot hands."[12] (Was the President or Ickes confusing the betraying apostle with Pontius Pilate?)

Daladier and the even more wobbly foreign minister, Georges Bonnet, came to London on September 18. The British cabinet had been divided between three factions: those, including Halifax, who thought it unjust to hand over hundreds of thousands of non-Germans in Sudetenland and wanted to haggle; those who wanted peace at any price; and the outright resisters, led by Duff Cooper, the first lord of the admiralty. He reminded the cabinet of Britain's longstanding policy of preventing any power from achieving primacy in continental Europe, which now obliged support of the Czechs and the French in league with the Russians.

The French visitors worked out a formula with Chamberlain and Halifax, who quickly overcame his concerns for the Czech minority in the Sudetenland and joined Chamberlain in suppressing the resisters in the cabinet. The Czechs were to yield any part of their country that was more than half German. This would take all Sudetenland, including the fortifications that had been built to defend the country from Germany. Talk of a plebiscite was ended with the French affectation of concern for the integrity of the detritus of Czechoslovakia. They pretended to be concerned that a plebiscite would inspire separatist feeling on the part of the Slovakians and Ruthenians and they would ask for a referendum too. The British and French wrote up their demands of the Czechs in the form of an ultimatum and demanded an immediate reply, since it was envisioned that Chamberlain would return to see Hitler by September 21.

By the afternoon of the 19th, Roosevelt had been accurately informed of the proportions of the proposed abandonment of the ally that France had guaranteed. He summoned the British ambassador, Sir Ronald Lindsay, and warned him that if the isolationist leaders in the Congress learned of what he was about to say, they might attempt to impeach him.* The President described the Anglo-French demands on the Czechs as "the most terrible, remorseless sacrifice" that had ever been asked of any country, and he predicted that the Czechs would have to reject it. He added that if Chamberlain and Daladier were successful in durably placating Hitler with this and imposing it on the Prague government, he would be "the first to cheer." But he doubted that Hitler could be quieted for long by any concessions or that the Czechs could accept this radical dismemberment.

Roosevelt suggested that if Prague did reject the proposal, Britain and France then mobilize, adopt a defensive posture along the Franco-German border (which was precisely what Hitler hoped they would do in the event of war), and, without declaring war, impose an absolute blockade against Germany. Roosevelt recommended that they should then say they were taking this step in the high

---

* The ambassador would have been aware that the possibilities of success in such an endeavor would be nil, but Roosevelt could happily do without the thought's even being voiced.

humanitarian interest of avoidance of casualties, and promised that the United States would observe the blockade and sell war materiel to the Western Allies on favorable terms. Though the President's strategic plan was far-fetched, and it was fanciful to imagine that Hitler wouldn't go to war if subjected to any such blockade, it was an impressive earnest of Roosevelt's desire to be helpful and of his confidence that American opinion could be brought so far as to approve the policy he outlined.[13]

Lindsay transmitted the President's suggestions to his government at once but received no response, even when he sent a follow-up message asking at least for "a friendly expression of appreciation." In London, the British and French ministers discounted Russian aid and considered the United States incapable of any help beyond what Chamberlain called "impotent emotionalism" and mere words.[14] Though Roosevelt's strategic notion was nonsense, his insight into the behavior of the various European leaders—Hitler, Chamberlain, Daladier, and Beneš— was commendably exact, and demonstrated unique familiarity with European affairs by a modern American president.

While London and Paris waited on Beneš, Beneš waited on Moscow for confirmation of Russian support. The Soviet government confirmed late on September 20th that it would go to war with France against Germany, and that it would support a Czech request for League action if France did not honor her treaty obligations. How the U.S.S.R. proposed to conduct such a war, with Poland separating it from Germany, was never clear, and Stalin's good faith was, to say the least, suspect.

This Soviet encouragement, however plausible, and, presumably, a hint of Roosevelt's views, were all Beneš needed to reject the Anglo-French proposals, as Roosevelt had predicted to Lindsay. Beneš also rejected Henlein's call for a plebiscite and proposed instead recourse to an arbitration clause of a 1925 treaty between Czechoslovakia and Germany. Unfortunately, at this point the prime minister of Czechoslovakia, Milan Hodza, snapped, and betrayed his country and his president. He summoned the French ambassador and told him that Beneš had approved his requesting from France an ultimatum that would justify a stand-down by the Czech government.

Thus was squandered the last hope. The Czechs, Russians, British, and French, with the overt but nonbelligerent support of the United States, could conceivably have contained Hitler. The Poles and Hungarians were now demanding the return of their minorities from the beleaguered Czechoslovak state, and Mussolini was loudly proclaiming the virtues of the Hungarian claim. The antics of the Poles were particularly contemptible, because it was well known that they were almost certainly the country on which Hitler would focus next, despite his claim to having "no more territorial ambitions in Europe." Armed with Hodza's request, the British and French governments formulated an ultimatum to Czechoslovakia and delivered it to Beneš the next day. Beneš yielded to the British and French ambassadors. He was broken and exhausted and wept silently, but was majestic in his dignity in the face of this shameful betrayal by those upon whose word he had relied.

IV

THE CZECH GOVERNMENT resigned, replaced under Beneš's continued presidency by a cabinet of "national concentration." Chamberlain returned to Germany the next day, September 22, but only to Cologne, half the flying time from London of Munich; in a somewhat thoughtful gesture, Hitler had come halfway to Bavaria to meet him. The British prime minister was greeted by a guard of honor and a band playing "God Save the King" and was "ferried like an arthritic Rhine maiden across the river"[15] to meet Hitler at Bad Godesberg, in the ancient land of the Lorelei.

From Paris, Ambassador Bullitt wrote Roosevelt that the widespread view in that capital was that the governments were behaving "like little boys doing dirty things behind the barn." Several ministers were threatening to resign. Cadogan wrote in his diary: "How much courage is required to be a coward! We must go on being cowards up to our limit, but not beyond."[16] The British and French governments were clearly close to their limit, elastic though it had been.

Shortly before Chamberlain's arrival at Bad Godesberg, the correspondent and historian William L. Shirer saw Hitler in the Hotel Dreeser and was struck by his dainty, somewhat unmanly gait, a compulsive twitch in his right shoulder and a jerking or flinching in his left leg. The Fuehrer appeared ashen and very fatigued. Shirer had heard and gave some currency to the theory, circulated the night before at the hotel bar, that Hitler periodically hurled himself on the floor and chewed the edge of the carpet. This is, at the least, unsubstantiated. Hitler's behavior was aberrant enough at the best of times without this outlandish embellishment.

Chamberlain arrived and was conducted by Hitler to an upstairs meeting room. They sat opposite each other at the proverbial long green baize-covered table. Chamberlain recounted his difficulties in dealing with the Czechs, French, and his own colleagues, but triumphantly announced that he had secured acceptance of the German leader's demands, that Sudetenland would be handed over without a plebiscite, the process supervised by a three-member commission, and that the French and Soviet treaties with Czechoslovakia would be replaced by an international guarantee of Czechoslovakian neutrality. Hitler, as if not crediting his ears, sought reassurance that the British, French, and Czechs had agreed to the transfer of Sudetenland to Germany. With more than a slight air of satisfaction, Chamberlain smilingly responded that they had.

After a pause of some seconds, Hitler replied: "I am exceedingly sorry, but that is no longer of any use." He credited Chamberlain with achieving more than he, Hitler, would have thought possible, but he had heard of terrible mistreatment of Sudeten Germans, and an immediate solution was required—one that included

Polish and Hungarian participation in the carve-up of the stricken and abandoned Czechoslovak state. Chamberlain was shocked, crestfallen, and angry.
Unlike Hitler the desperate gambler, Roosevelt the seasoned and zestful poker
player, and the inscrutable Stalin, Chamberlain had no talent in face-to-face
meetings for disguising his reaction to people and events.

As Felix Frankfurter's wife Marian recounted to Harold Ickes a few months
later, of the prime minister's response when Kennedy kept noisily calling him
"Neville," "Chamberlain's Adam's apple would work up and down convulsively
three or four times and then he would emit a forced" response. He told Hitler,
rather pathetically, that he had risked his career in these negotiations and had
"actually been booed" on leaving London in the morning.[17] It is fantastic that he
expected Hitler to be impressed or moved by these considerations.

The meeting continued rather abrasively and without agreement, and there
was a further three-hour session in Hitler's suite that night. Hitler handed over a
memorandum of his conditions and eventually, faced with the first resistance he
had seen from Chamberlain, softened his demand for Czech withdrawal from
Sudetenland from forty-eight hours to October 1, which was quite close to the
suggestion Chamberlain had brought with him. A matter of a few days was one of
the few remaining differences between them. It was a difficult meeting. It
became clear to the watching world that the negotiations had broken down when
it was announced that Chamberlain would return to London on the morning of
the 23rd and that the scheduled meeting with Hitler on that day had been cancelled.

On the evening of the 22nd, the American correspondent Edward R. Murrow, of
the Columbia Broadcasting System, gained a live interview with the Czechoslovak
minister in London, Jan Masaryk, son of the founder of his country. Masaryk said:
"I tell you Americans, our powder is dry. As one who has spent many years in America, who knows and loves it, who earned his first dollar in New York City when he
was nineteen years old, as one whose mother was an American and as a citizen of a
small country . . . truth must triumph and will triumph! I salute you, brother democrats." It had a powerful impact on his American listeners.

The diplomatic atmosphere as Chamberlain returned to London was
extremely tense. The press throughout Europe was full of reports of mobilization
and military preparedness in many countries. Ambassador Kennedy responded to
events by inviting Charles A. Lindbergh to London from his temporary home in
Kent, and he arrived September 21. Roosevelt watched Kennedy carefully, like a
man watching an energetic dog digging up around his garden. For the President,
this was a coven of Fascists assembled to cause mischief at a decisive place and
time. Roosevelt had often asserted that Kennedy was a Fascist sympathizer, and
explained to Ickes that Kennedy had advised Roosevelt not to criticize Fascism in
his speeches because he, Kennedy, thought Roosevelt or his successor would
have recourse to that form of government in the United States.[18]

Kennedy and Lindbergh agreed about everything, and Lindbergh's wife,

Anne, a novelist and avowed Fascist sympathizer, found the ambassador "a very nice Irish terrier, wagging his tail."[19] Roosevelt declined Beneš's request that he formally ask Britain and France to stand by Czechoslovakia. Since the United States wasn't prepared to do much beyond sell war materiel at a slightly discounted price, Roosevelt realized he was in no position to be urging other countries into war. He thought he had gone as far as he could in his interview with Lindsay. The President also declined Kennedy's request that Chamberlain be allowed to address the American public directly. Roosevelt was trying to raise American awareness of the implications of the Nazi menace, not anaesthetize the public with a limp espousal of the virtues of appeasement from someone who had shown no great consideration for him.

The British cabinet met September 24 and 25 and was in sharp disagreement. Halifax supported the resisters, led by Duff Cooper. The foreign secretary said that Hitler was "dictating terms . . . as though he had won a war."[20] Daladier and some of his colleagues arrived on the 25th in a more bellicose mood than before, and a stormy session followed. The French supreme army commander, General Maurice Gustave Gamelin, was present, and he confirmed that the French war strategy was a brief and very limited offensive followed by entrenchment in the Maginot Line frontier fortifications for the duration. This was as unaggressive a plan of action as any commander in a comparable position set at the head of formidable armies had ever had. It was a particularly astonishing posture for the successor to Turenne, Conde, Villars, Saxe, Napoleon, and Foch.[*21]

Jan Masaryk informed the British that the Czechs, faced with Hitler's latest demands, preferred to go to war, however unpromising a course that might be, than to submit. The beleaguered and irresolute British and French allies finally agreed on the morning of the 26th that Sir Horace Wilson was to go to see Hitler the next day offering and requesting orderly implementation of the agreed Berchtesgaden terms, failing which France would stand by Czechoslovakia and Britain by France. As this was an ultimatum, Chamberlain meticulously instructed Wilson on how to deliver it, i.e., as unabrasively as possible.

Roosevelt sent messages to the principal players on September 25 asking them to continue negotiations. The following day he sent a further message urging a conference and clearly implying that if war broke out the world would consider Germany responsible. Hitler replied promptly to Roosevelt: "You, Mr. President, when you realize the whole development of the problem from its inception . . . will realize that the German government has truly not been lacking in either patience or a sincere desire for a peaceful understanding."[22] Before a huge crowd at the Berlin Sportspalast on the evening of September 26th Hitler again delivered a speech that was broadcast internationally. He left listeners in some

---

[*] One underwhelmed senior British officer privately called Gamelin "a button-eyed, button-booted, potbellied grocer." Mr. James's friend General McClellan had been a tiger in comparison.

suspense about how he proposed to dismantle Czechoslovakia but not about his intention to do that. Roosevelt wrote to Margaret Suckley: "Did you hear Hitler today, his shrieks, his histrionics, and the effect on the huge audience? They did not applaud—they made noises like animals."[23]

Wilson arrived at Hitler's chancellery on the 27th, mystified at having been chosen for this mission for which he had no apparent qualification. At the mention of the Czechs Hitler went into a tremendous rage, and Wilson was unable to deliver his ultimatum. Hitler ranted and raved to the point that he promised "to smash the Czechs," was indifferent to anything the French and British proposed to do about it, and screamed that they would all be at war within a week.[24] In the circumstances the ultimatum seemed to Wilson superfluous. As far as he could tell, his mission had been unsuccessful.

However, Hitler became aware of other factors more persuasive than the bumbling embassy of Britain's senior civil servant. Roosevelt had had Summer Welles and others labor the German ambassador in Washington, Hans Dieckhoff, with American disapproval of German conduct throughout 1938. Dieckhoff advised Hitler that if Britain went to war for the Czechs, "the whole weight of the United States would be thrown into the scale on the side of Britain." Grand Admiral Raeder warned Hitler that the German Navy (which was a minimal force compared with the British and American navies and modest compared even with those of France and Italy) was in no condition to fight a war. A delegation from the German General Staff expressed a respectful hope for more time to prepare for a conflict with the major powers if there was to be one. Hitler had spent three hours on his balcony on the Wilhelmstrasse on the 26th watching an armored division go by, supposedly on its way to the Czech frontier, and cannot have failed to notice the absence of any public enthusiasm.[25] He began to think relatively conciliatory thoughts.

Chamberlain's thinking was more inexplicable. He had told his inner cabinet September 25 that he had "established some degree of personal influence over Herr Hitler." This "completely horrified" Cadogan, who thought Hitler had "hypnotized" his leader. Cadogan recorded that Chamberlain "was quite calmly for total surrender" (inciting at least historical curiosity about what Chamberlain thought were the practical uses of his newfound influence over Hitler).[26]

On the evening of September 27, 1938, Hitler dictated a relatively civilized message to Chamberlain. The British prime minister had spoken to the nation and the world that afternoon, saying: "How horrible, fantastic, incredible it is that we should be digging trenches and trying on gas masks here because of a quarrel in a faraway country between people of whom we know nothing. . . . If we have to fight, it must be on larger issues than that." If he were "convinced that any nation [sought world domination] through fear of its force, I should feel that it must be resisted. . . . But war is a fearful thing, and we must be very clear, before we embark on it, that it really is the great issues that are at stake."[27]

Roosevelt instructed all his ambassadors to ask the governments they were accredited to for support in requesting that the powers directly involved in the crisis continue negotiations. He sent a further message to Mussolini, who was assumed (because Mussolini routinely claimed it to be so) to have some influence on Hitler.*

British ambassador Lindsay advised his government that he thought Roosevelt would be "disappointed" if there were any settlement on the basis that was apparently being discussed. The President was playing the delicate game of trying to encourage uncourageous men without being able to offer much tangible help, while publicly seeming to be somewhat in step with the general desire for a negotiated compromise. Any such agreement was bound to be favorable to the Germans, because the Sudetenlanders and even Hitler had a legitimate grievance, and Versailles was a very imperfect settlement. But Roosevelt was still hoping for something less than the complete emasculation of Czechoslovakia.

September 28, 1938, was one of the most dramatic days in the history of the British Parliament. A special arrangement was made for immediate transmission to the world of the text of the prime minister's report to Parliament, though not the actual broadcast of his voice. The radio audience was reckoned to be the greatest in the history of the world up to that time, probably more than one hundred million people. In the galleries were the dowager Queen Mary (an unprecedented occurrence), mother of King George VI and King Edward VIII, dressed in black; former prime minister Stanley Baldwin, the archbishop of Canterbury, almost every ambassador accredited to the Court of St. James; and the son of the current U.S. ambassador, the future president, John F. Kennedy. (The whole world would not stand still for a week on the verge of war again until this twenty-one-year-old student, twenty-four years later, ably managed the Cuban missile crisis.)

The prime minister rose to speak at three o'clock in the afternoon and gave an uncontroversial chronology of events leading up to the most recent days. There was absolute silence and almost oppressive attention to his words as he brought his narrative up to date. He had just finished referring to the cables he had sent Hitler and Mussolini the night before when a reply Hitler had dictated the night before and revised and sent that morning, summarizd by Cadogan, was passed along the treasury bench to Chamberlain. In one of history's great theatrical pauses, lasting nearly five minutes, he silently read Cadogan's message and the House of Commons and its galleries maintained a still quiet laden with almost unendurable tension.

In response to Chamberlain's and Roosevelt's messages, Mussolini had telephoned his ambassador in Berlin and told him to seek an immediate audience with the German chancellor and tell him that he (Mussolini) "had been asked to mediate in the Sudeten question. The point of difference is very small. Tell the

---

* Bullitt took this assumption one step further and suggested La Guardia be asked to use his influence on Mussolini. The violently anti-Fascist, half-Jewish mayor of New York had no rapport with Mussolini.[28]

chancellor that I . . . stand behind him. He must decide. Tell him I favor accepting the suggestion." Hitler replied to the Italian ambassador that he accepted the Duce's proposal. Messages were then sent to Chamberlain and Daladier inviting them to Munich the following day, September 29, 1938.[29] This was the message that Chamberlain interrupted his speech to read to himself in the House.

Harold Nicolson wrote: Chamberlain's "whole face, his whole body, seemed to change. . . . All the lines of anxiety and weariness seemed suddenly to have been smoothed out; he appeared ten years younger and triumphant." Finally Chamberlain said: "Herr Hitler has just agreed to postpone his mobilization for twenty-four hours and to meet me in conference with Signor Mussolini and Monsieur Daladier at Munich. I need not say what my answer will be. I will go to see what I can do as a last resort."[30] After a moment of continued silence, the momentum of the unbearable tension of recent days and especially of the last few minutes gave way to tumultuous joy. The House and galleries rose in wild applause and shouts of happiness and relief. Queen Mary wept and silently clasped the hands and forearms of those around her. (She was not normally a demonstrative, much less a tactile, person.) From his exile in Holland, the former German emperor Wilhelm II wrote to Queen Mary, expressing relief and praising Chamberlain. Winston Churchill had entered the chamber "with an air of historic tragedy" and left without congratulating or applauding Chamberlain, saying: "The government had to choose between shame and war. They chose shame and they will get war." Jan Masaryk called upon Chamberlain and Halifax and said: "If you have sacrificed my nation to save the peace of the world, I will be the first to applaud you. But if not, gentlemen, God help your souls."[31]

Roosevelt was relieved, as every other peace-loving person was, though he doubted that the peace would be durable. Given his position and his ambitions to shape American public opinion, it would not have done openly to espouse the same views as Churchill. He sent Chamberlain the splendidly spare and ambiguous message: "Good man."

After World War II, Halifax tried to encourage Chamberlain's widow by claiming this message from Roosevelt came after the Munich conference, as some historians have suggested.[32] FDR had ambivalently worded the message while it was still theoretically possible to hope that what was afoot was something less than the rape of a democratic state that had relied on security guarantees from France, the Soviet Union, and Britain, in exchange for a few months of uneasy peace in which the German war machine would continue to grow. Roosevelt had urged Kennedy months before to "put some metal up Chamberlain's backbone." Instead, his ambassador had gone native and faded into Chamberlain's entourage, and had become an unannounced, indiscreet, and improbable candidate for Roosevelt's job. Roosevelt felt it necessary to tread warily.[33] Now and in the following days he implied no approval of what was coming.

The excitement of some of the President's more demonstrative helpers was palpable. Ambassador Bullitt cabled: "I wish I were in the White House to give you a large kiss on your bald spot."[34] Roosevelt was not in equal transports of joy and was unlikely to have found any element of the ambassador's aspiration agreeable.

The British pound rose thirteen cents against the dollar, and the London Stock Exchange had an influx of buy orders as the British, French, and Italian leaders made their way to Munich. As often happens, the end of the drama was not as gripping as the procession of events leading up to it. The head of the British Foreign Office, Central Europe Division, William Strang, considered the spectacle of Hitler with his "flocks of spruce young SS subalterns in their black uniforms, haughty and punctilious, as though life were a drill," like a teutonic legend of a barbarian chief with his ambitious followers. As if at a Wagnerian opera, Strang had watched at Godesberg as Hitler approached such a group, and saw them leap to their feet in immobilized but galvanized readiness for instruction. Hitler fixed them with his Wotan-like gaze, then turned abruptly away without a word or gesture. Strang always thought Chamberlain naïve and misguided, and he had a better idea of Hitler's character and motives than his chief did.[35]

The conference proceeded for almost sixteen hours without an agenda. Although Hitler was the conference chairman, he didn't have any plan for the meeting except to receive and amplify preemptive concessions. (Mussolini was relatively prominent because he understood the others' languages and was sometimes able to expedite proceedings.) What emerged varied slightly from the Godesberg proposals. There had been no need to go through the agony of apprehension of the last ten days. In fact, Hitler would not have exhausted the patience and credulity of the West so quickly if he had been less bullying and inflexible and had gratefully accepted Chamberlain's proposals at their previous encounter. The Czech withdrawal from the Sudetenland would take place from October 1 to 10 in five stages. As Chamberlain had proposed, an international commission would set the exact frontiers.

Hitler and Mussolini and their large and elegantly uniformed delegations departed when the conference ended, at 2:30 A.M. on September 30th, and left Chamberlain and Daladier to inform the Czechs of the unhappy fate of their gallant country. Daladier poured himself a drink and Chamberlain yawned uncontrollably, in a particularly unattractive lapse of manners, as the Czech representatives, Vojtech Mastny and Hubert Masarik, were read by a junior French official the terms of the agreement that had just been signed. No Czech answer was requested. They were handed a fait accompli. The Czechs wept, and Hubert Masarik said, prophetically and justly: "They don't know what they are doing to us or to themselves."[36] Chamberlain and Daladier and their aides left, leaving the two Czechs eerily alone in the room where the fate of their country had been sealed. These poor, good men were the final players in a macabre and shameful Gothic tragedy.

Franklin D. Roosevelt understood what had happened. He sent a message to Kennedy for transmission to Chamberlain verbally, and forbade Kennedy to give the prime minister a written message, other than one that he would clearly mark as personal and not engaging the President or government of the United States. He forbade Kennedy to imply any official U.S. approval of the Munich arrangements. Roosevelt's verbal message was: "I fully share your hope and belief that there exists today the greatest opportunity in years for the establishment of a new order based on justice and on law."[37] The President could claim to have shared in the spirit of the evanescent deliverance from war without being complicit in what he feared would be a disastrous disappointment. He was still on a tightrope but moving with the agility of the seasoned political acrobat that he was.

After a fitful night's sleep, Chamberlain met privately with Hitler at his Munich residence a little before noon, September 30, 1938. Chamberlain had awakened Strang from a sound sleep after leaving the Czechs the night before and asked him to write up a brief memorandum of agreement about Anglo-German relations, which he wished to discuss with Hitler the next morning when they met without the French or the Italians. Chamberlain, though exhausted, was jovial and optimistic when he attended upon Hitler, and chatted amiably about the four powers resolving the Spanish Civil War and coordinating relations with the U.S.S.R. Something even possessed him to express confidence that Hitler would be "generous" to the Czechs. Hitler, also tired, paid limited attention to Chamberlain's cheerful monologue, according to the only witness, the highly proficient interpreter Paul Schmidt, but interjected "Ja, ja," at intervals. Chamberlain revealed the existence of Strang's brief memorandum, which stated that "the question of Anglo-German relations" was of paramount importance to Europe and that the Anglo-German Naval Agreement of 1935 and "the agreement signed last night [were symbolic of] the desire of our two peoples never to go to war with one another again." It was further agreed that future disagreements would be resolved by "consultation."

Chamberlain asked if Hitler would sign the agreement. "Ja, ja" was the now familiar reply. When did the prime minister wish to do so? "Immediately," said Chamberlain. It was done. Chamberlain departed, lunched happily with his aides, returned to London, and waved this paper aloft at Heston airfield when he arrived to a delirious welcome.[38]

Dense crowds of well-wishers thronged his entire route into central London. The bells of Westminster Abbey pealed joyfully as he came through Parliament Square. He was summoned to Buckingham Palace to receive the congratulations of King George VI, and when he returned to Downing Street he responded to the demand for a speech: "This is the second time in our history that there has come back from Germany to Downing Street a prime minister bringing peace with honor. I believe it is peace in our time."[39] (This was a greater travesty of egocentric revisionism than anything that had preceded it. Disraeli returned from the Congress of Berlin in 1878 having faced Bismarck down and after extracting a remarkable sequence of concessions, including sovereignty over the island of Cyprus, which he hadn't even sought.) Chamberlain had been nine and remembered it.

Chamberlain's greatest error was in overselling the Munich agreement. Everyone knew it had been a cruel and cowardly treatment of the Czechs. Even if it had been peace, there was nothing honorable about it. It was true that Britain and France couldn't go to war against the right of Sudetenlanders to be German, but a gradual arrangement, by which Czechoslovakia retained the frontier fortifications, could have been proposed and defended. Opinion could have been rallied behind it, with Russian support, and possibly that of some of the other eastern European countries that had been looking to the British and French for protection—the Poles, Romanians, and Yugoslavs.

Relations with the Soviet Union, which was eager for an arrangement with the British and French, should have been developed quickly and a Pitt-like effort deployed at coalition-building. If pursued with imagination and energy (not qualities that came often or easily to Chamberlain and Daladier), a plausible containment strategy could have been put in place and Roosevelt would have assisted it as best he could. Instead, Chamberlain acted on a clear preference for Hitler, who was a deadly threat to Britain, over Stalin, who was no threat at all at this point. Chamberlain thus drove Stalin toward Hitler's arms, cast off the Balkan allies to fend for themselves (i.e., submit to German suzerainty), and eagerly helped Hitler destroy Czechoslovakia, a strong and brave democratic ally.

Chamberlain also made it clear that he was more interested in placating Hitler and Mussolini than in tightening relations with Roosevelt, on whose country more prescient people like Churchill and Eden could already see much of Britain's future would depend. A less clear-headed and persevering statesman than Roosevelt would have given up on the British and French and adopted a Fortress America policy. He could easily have asserted U.S. predominance over the Americas and their oceanic approaches and made an amoral but not humiliating demarcation with Germany and Japan, leaving them to squander their resources in the vast morasses of Russia and China. Fortunately, Roosevelt the Anglophile and the strategic student of Admiral Mahan prevailed. He endured Chamberlain's catastrophic misjudgment of appeasement and overlooked his snubs and condescensions. Franklin D. Roosevelt was awaiting a more robust British leadership to work with in an imminent and even more urgent time.

Roosevelt had already begun to act on the strategic imperative that was unique to the United States. Unlike other Great Powers, the United States would not coexist with what it considered potentially lethal threats to its security; it had the power and the will to do the necessary to remove those threats. Even the quasi-pacifist Woodrow Wilson finally determined to help suppress Imperial Germany. Franklin D. Roosevelt was no pacifist and he had come to the same conclusion about Nazi Germany that Wilson had about Imperial Germany.

If Chamberlain had merely said he had followed the national interest, done and hoped for the best, urged vigilance, and left it at that, his fall would not have been so precipitous, nor so unlamented.

In Paris, Daladier, seeing the huge crowds at Le Bourget aerodrome on his return, sent an aide out of the aircraft ahead of him, to be stoned to death first, he joked. When he saw that the crowds were cheering, with commendable Gallic cynicism he said: "The bloody fools!" Chamberlain, intoxicated with his moment of glory, had no such insight.[40]

In Washington, Adolf Berle, the assistant secretary of state, and press secretary Steve Early began to suggest that Roosevelt deserved some credit for what had occurred at Munich, but quickly desisted. Roosevelt wanted no "credit" for what had happened; he only wanted to be able to defend himself against charges, which his domestic opponents would be happy to make, of insufficient enthusiasm for peace.

Roosevelt had already written (September 15, 1938) to his old friend William Phillips, now ambassador to Italy, "of an inevitable conflict within five years," and added: "If we get the idea that the future of our own form of government is threatened by a coalition of European dictators, we might wade in with everything we have to give."[41] He added that "the situation here will be very different from 1914. . . . Ninety percent of our people are definitely anti-German and anti-Italian in sentiment—and incidentally . . . I would strongly encourage their natural sympathy while at the same time avoiding any thought of sending troops to Europe."[42]

He wrote Phillips soon after Munich: "I want you to know that I am not a bit upset over the final result," but it was clear he was referring only to the avoidance of war, in which they felt his message to Mussolini transmitted by Phillips might have played a small part. Roosevelt knew the Sudetenlanders had the right to be Germans, but never approved the complete desertion and dismemberment of Czechoslovakia.[43] To Ambassador Bowers in Madrid, another old friend, Roosevelt went further and wrote that it was "impossible to guess [whether Chamberlain's Munich settlement] would succeed. But fundamentally, you and I hate compromise with principle." (Bowers particularly did as he watched the inexorable approach of Franco's armies.) Roosevelt had written in March 1938 that Chamberlain's appeasement policy was "taking very long chances."[44] Munich strengthened him in that view.

Roosevelt was always enigmatic until he had to take a stand, and then he did so with great determination. From what can be divined from his correspondence and conversation, he thought Munich's success was unlikely, war was inevitable, and eventual American participation in a European war probable. He sought the best possible conditions for that participation, if his fears of Hitler's determination to go to war and threaten American national security (a phrase Roosevelt coined and popularized) proved accurate: these conditions were maximum possible delay, preparedness, and unanimity of public opinion. Roosevelt professed hopefulness but avoided all post-Munich enthusiasm. His forebodings and contingency planning did not abate.

On October 2, Alfred Duff Cooper resigned as first lord of the admiralty and followed Churchill and Eden into distinguished opposition. The same day, Poland, "whose historic inability to manage its domestic and foreign affairs with intelligent morality had contributed greatly to its national misfortunes,"[45] affronted the democratic opinion whose support it would soon desperately need by seizing the Teschen region from the prostrate Czechoslovaks. Hungary too, like the least jackal, but not to be left out after the massacre by the great beast, seized a piece of its mutilated neighbor.

It remained for Winston Churchill, in the House of Commons debate that followed and was essentially a hallelujah chorus for Chamberlain, to utter the most memorable words on Munich. In one of the greatest speeches of his incomparable career, ignoring derisive hoots from the serried benches of government supporters, he said: "We have sustained a total and unmitigated defeat. . . . And do not suppose that this is the end. . . . This is only the first sip, the first foretaste of a bitter cup which will be proffered to us year by year unless, by a supreme recovery of moral health and martial vigor, we arise again and take our stand for freedom as in olden time."[46]

Churchill was more isolated than ever from the respect and confidence of Britain's governing elite. But Franklin D. Roosevelt read these words with great interest. He did not have pleasant memories of his meeting with Churchill in 1919 (of which Churchill had no recollection at all). He told Kennedy, when the ambassador went to take up his post, that Churchill had on that occasion (in a revenance of private schoolyard parlance) been a "stinker." That hardly mattered now, because Roosevelt thought he saw, for the first time, the British leader with whom he could make a holy alliance, informal at first, against the obscene ambitions of Adolf Hitler. Churchill and Roosevelt were arriving at the same conclusion about Hitler by slightly different routes and timetables.

Churchill and Roosevelt had shared in the natural rivalry between British and American Atlanticists. While Roosevelt was always an Anglophile and Churchill was an early and appreciative visitor to the United States, Roosevelt thought British leaders too preoccupied with propping up an illegitimate empire and a stultified class system, and, as we have seen, was by now profoundly exasperated by their obsequious treatment of Hitler and Mussolini.

Churchill in later years largely excised any reflections on the United States that were not florid laudations. He had in fact been naturally resentful of the rise of America and of its erratic policymaking. He had always objected to the Washington Naval Treaty giving the U.S. Navy parity with the Royal Navy after World War I. (Churchill was right in his contention that if Britain had retained more World War I battleships instead of breaking them up under the treaty, they would have been useful in convoying and shore bombardment in World War II.) In June 1927, Churchill complained: "It always seems to be assumed that it is our duty to honour the United States and minister to their vanity. They do nothing for us in return, but exact their last pound of flesh."[47]

As Britain's choice became starker—between alliance with the United States, even in a subordinate role, and a Faustian bargain with Hitler—Churchill overcame his disgruntlement with the Americans. As Roosevelt saw the prolonged Anglo-French dalliance with Hitler, he became nostalgic for a renascent British spirit of imperial confidence. Roosevelt told a group of senators in January 1939 that Hitler was a "wild man" afflicted by "paranoia" and a "Joan of Arc complex . . . [that he was a self-nominated] reincarnation of Julius Caesar and Jesus Christ," and, in sum, "a nut."[48] In these circumstances, the possibilities for Churchill and Roosevelt to get on well with each other grew brighter every week from Munich on.

V

IN THE AFTERMATH of the Munich crisis, Roosevelt placed the first of many supplementary defense production orders, with the approval of the Congress, despite misgivings in some pacifist circles. This initial order was for $500 million and was mainly for new aircraft and warships. Bernard Baruch had been in Europe in the summer of 1938 and returned deeply disturbed by what he had heard of the military imbalance in favor of the Germans and the intensifying persecution of his Jewish kinsmen. Even Baruch, with all his wealth and influence, was unable to secure the evacuation of his relatives from Germany.

Roosevelt had received a visit from the visionary banker Jean Monnet and had subscribed to the idea (originally from Bullitt, of all people) of setting up giant aircraft manufacturing plants in Canada to supply the French Air Force. These would basically be reassembly points for American aircraft to be shipped in parts across the border to Canada, completed, and shipped on to France. On October 16, 1938, Roosevelt met with the vacationing Bullitt, Hopkins, and others, and agreed on a plan to designate substantial portions of the WPA budget to set up aircraft production factories in high unemployment areas and to produce 15,000 planes a year.

Roosevelt now began to receive what shortly became a flood of distinguished European visitors. He had a return visit from Jean Monnet, now head of the French military purchasing mission in America. The President did him the honor of receiving him at Hyde Park. Monnet, one of the most remarkable Europeans of the century, had been in charge of interallied transport and food distribution agencies during and just after the Great War though only in his twenties, and had then been deputy secretary general of the League of Nations. He had also had a distinguished career in finance and would be the founder of Europe's first federal institutions. Roosevelt was impressed by him and promised to expedite sales of aircraft and anything else France wanted, as much as he could.

His old World War I friend Sir Arthur Murray, who had been assistant military attaché in Washington when Roosevelt had been in the Navy Department, and who had been active socially with Roosevelt and Lucy Mercer, called at the White House on October 21. The President gave him an extensive, absolutely private message for Chamberlain and the air minister, Kingsley Wood. Roosevelt knew not to entrust such a message to Kennedy, or even to Lindsay. He wanted Chamberlain to know that in the event of war with the dictators, a contigency he did not think had been rendered implausible by the Munich agreement three weeks before, Britain would have "the industrial resources of the American nation, [to the extent] he, the President could achieve it."

He would be speaking with the Canadian prime minister, Mackenzie King, about his plans for assembling aircraft in Canada from components bought and imported from the United States, and other circumventions of the neutrality laws. Roosevelt fervently believed in the necessity of the Western Allies' achieving air superiority over the Germans and was already envisioning an aircraft construction program that would exceed the most inflated estimates of German production levels the gullible Lindbergh had been induced to accept. Thus, he told Murray, he thought that within one to two years he would be able to offer the British and French up to 20,000 aircraft per year, disassembled but ready for rapid completion in Canadian plants.[49]

He was also already negotiating directly with King George VI the possibility of a visit to the United States the following summer by the British king and queen. He didn't bother to tell his ambassador in London about this, either, which ruffled his feathers considerably when it came to light. Kennedy had given a rabidly pro-appeasement address on the anniversary of the Battle of Trafalgar, October 19. As Kennedy was at pains to make it clear that this was a personal opinion, the State Department did not challenge his text when he submitted it. That the ambassador held such views disconcerted even those who strongly hoped the Munich arrangements would succeed.

None of this would enhance the credibility of Roosevelt's proposals via Murray to Chamberlain. Chamberlain, though Roosevelt regarded him as "slippery," was relatively guileless, as Hitler had been so pleased to discover. He knew nothing of the American Constitution or politics and had difficulty understanding why Roosevelt was using private citizens from Scotland to deliver a message entirely opposite to that publicly expressed by the U.S. ambassador. In any case, in the afterglow of Munich, Chamberlain was still congratulating himself on the triumph of durable peace and had no thoughts of needing 20,000 warplanes a year to repel swarming German aviators. Murray delivered his message in early December, and Chamberlain received it with polite indifference.

Roosevelt moved to counteract the impression made by Kennedy and move his slow campaign to raise American awareness of the importance of developments in Europe, by moving another ratchet up from the "We will not stand idly by" and "Quarantine" speeches. Addressing the Herald Tribune Forum by radio and newsreel, so that it was broadcast and in cinema newsreels throughout the country, the President said: "It is becoming increasingly clear that peace by fear has no higher or more enduring quality than peace by the sword.

"There can be no peace if the reign of law is to be replaced by the recurrent sanctification of sheer force.

"There can be no peace if national policy adopts as a deliberate instrument the threat of war.

"There can be no peace if national policy adopts as a deliberate instrument the dispersion all over the world of millions of helpless and persecuted wanderers with no place to lay their heads.

"There can be no peace if humble men and women are not free to think their own thoughts, express their own feelings, to worship God.

"There can be no peace if economic resources that ought to be devoted to social and economic reconstruction are to be diverted to an intensified competition in armaments which will merely heighten the suspicions and fears and threaten the economic prosperity of each and every nation." (In fact, arms-making was the chief support of such prosperity as most important nations then enjoyed.)

This powerful address was everywhere seen as a rebuke to Kennedy, which it was. The ambassador himself privately called it a "stab in the back." Kennedy's Trafalgar Day address had resonated poorly even in isolationist circles in the United States, because it appeared to include something bordering on admiration for the dictators. Almost all American isolationists disliked the dictators and loved democracy.

Roosevelt had taken relatively little part in the midterm election campaign after his attempt to influence a number of the Democratic congressional primaries. He tried to help Michigan's governor, Frank Murphy, who had been accused of giving aid and comfort to Communists when he declined to execute all the warrants obtained by the auto companies during the 1937 sit-down strikes. An ambitious redbaiting congressman from Texas, Martin Dies, a protégé of John Garner and Sam Rayburn, was chairman of the House Un-American Activities Committee, which examined foreign subversion in the United States. Under his chairmanship, the committee had moved largely away from Fascist to Communist activities.

Dies accepted a good deal of obviously very partisan testimony stigmatizing a number of Roosevelt's protégés, including Frank Murphy. Roosevelt referred to "lurid charges" launched against Murphy, and Dies alleged two weeks later that the PWA had cancelled two projects in his district. When questioned about this by the press, Roosevelt responded: "Ho-hum." He did not always try to disguise his hardball political techniques from the White House press corps, and his candor was appreciated. No great outcry in Dies's favor resulted.[50]

Roosevelt addressed the nation from his home at Hyde Park on November 4, and asked his countrymen not to submit to an interruption of the march of progressive government, as had happened in the Taft interregnum between Theodore Roosevelt and Woodrow Wilson and, he said, the Harding-Coolidge-Hoover era that had separated Wilson from his own administration. "On the eve of another election, I have come home to Hyde Park and am sitting at my own fireside," he began. He was able to assure his listeners that the economic upturn had resumed and that employment had risen 3½ percent in October alone. He directly addressed the New York voters only, and supported Governor Lehman, whom he had now forgiven for his opposition to the Court reform bill, over the rising Republican prosecutor, Thomas E. Dewey.

The President was philosophical and ended on a dignified note of toleration that distinguished America from many countries then torn by racial conflict. "Pick [the candidates you choose to vote for] without regard to race, color, or creed. Some of them may have come of the earliest colonial stock; some of them may have been brought here as children to escape the tyrannies of the Old World. But remember that all of them are good American citizens now." It was homeletic, but it was seemly, and the reference to color was at least a gesture to the long-suffering African-American community as well as the Asians and native people.

Roosevelt knew that the election would be a setback; the Democrats had scored big gains for four straight elections, 1930–1936, and the Republicans were certain to rebound. It was rather worse than he had hoped on election night, November 8. Lehman and Wagner won, but Lehman's majority was reduced by over 90 percent, to just 64,000 out of 4.7 million votes cast, and Dewey became a presidential possibility though he was only thirty-six years old. Another young Republican talent, Harold Stassen, was elected governor of Minnesota, and two Roosevelt protégés, governors Frank Murphy of Michigan and George Earle of Pennsylvania, were both defeated, as was Philip La Follette in his bid for governor of Wisconsin, taking into oblivion with him his new party and his "circumcized swastika" emblem. The Republicans picked up 11 governorships, 8 U.S. Senate seats, and 81 congressional seats, but the Democrats would continue to hold the House, 262 to 169, and the Senate, 69 to 23. (The rest were third-party representatives in both houses.) On the other hand, in California, liberal candidate Culbert Olson defeated the conservative Republican governor, Frank Merriam. The most interesting newcomer would be Ohio senator Robert A. Taft, son of the former president and chief justice, and an isolationist and conservative Republican of a pre-Hoover stripe.

The electorate had moved somewhat to the right and was clearly tiring of the New Deal. Conservative Democrats and Republicans would now be able to stop the President's liberal measures. As he was now turning to the southerners to help him arm America and complete the banishment of unemployment through emphasis on the defense production industry, this was not a great inconvenience for Roosevelt. He would anyway be chiefly preoccupied with foreign affairs, despite public opinion's aversion to foreign involvements. Here the powers of congressional oversight were quite reduced, especially given Roosevelt's talents at dissembling and concealment.

Roosevelt's enemies naturally interpreted the election results as a stinging defeat for the President, and the country was apparently not overly impressed by his recent performance. But he remained very popular, and the economy had resumed its advance. Roosevelt, as always in moments of adversity, was utterly serene and completely free of any sense of self-criticism. He explained in a "Dear Chief" letter to Josephus Daniels, ambassador in Mexico, who had written of his disappointment at the election result, that he was happy to be rid of his former "friend" James Michael Curley of Boston, and of Phil La Follette of Wisconsin. Roosevelt thought that now that the fantasy of a third party was ending, the Progressives would have to come to the Democrats. The President was happy that Frank Hague had been "slapped down" in New Jersey,* and wrote Daniels: "I think we will have less trouble with the next congress than with the last."[52]

VI

W HILE ROOSEVELT WAS crossing the country in July 1938, plumping for his preferred candidates in his desultory purge of congressional candidates, the conference on refugees he had conceived met at Evian-les-Bains, across Lake Geneva from Switzerland. The Swiss declined the "honor" of holding the conference. The new French premier, Edouard Daladier, privately (and accurately) told Chamberlain that Roosevelt was trying "to soothe an aroused public opinion." The French delegate at Evian said that France had accepted 200,000 refugees and couldn't do any more. The British, true to their ancient and durable preference for the cause of the Arabs to that of the Jews, imperiously declared that Palestine could not be discussed.

Arthur James Balfour twenty-one years before, in a pitch for American opinion during the Great War, had promised a Jewish homeland in Palestine, provided nothing be done to "prejudice the civil and religious rights of existing non-Jewish communities in Palestine." The British had effectively almost sold the same real estate twice, to the Jews and the Arabs, and the consequences would weigh ever more heavily on the world throughout the twentieth century and into the twenty-first. The British had approximately 30,000 soldiers in Palestine keeping order. In fact, the opposition of the Arabs, intractable though it was, was a more easily sur-

---

* He may have been "slapped down," but he still kept homes in Florida and Manhattan, plus two in New Jersey, including a fourteen-room apartment in Jersey City, on his $7,500 official salary, and continued as mayor for another nine years, rounding out thirty years in the post and bridging the Wilson and Truman eras.[51]

mounted barrier than the fear of immigration in most Western countries still reeling from the Depression. Admitting those Jews who sought entry to Palestine would have involved Britain in a massive riot-control effort, but would have saved the lives of most people admitted and made for a less vulnerable and tenuous State of Israel when it emerged.

The conduct of the United States and of Franklin D. Roosevelt himself in these matters affords only a limited right to moral superiority toward Britain or any country except Germany and the other persecutors. There was great public revulsion against the mistreatment of the Jews and other groups, especially political dissidents. But in official as in public policy, a virtual firewall was drawn down between sympathy for the victims of these evils of Europe and doing something effective about them. Most Americans wanted to shield their country from all of those evils; most thought that avoidance of European war required avoidance of meddling in any European affairs, including acceptance of large numbers of immigrants.

As he stated in his Königsberg speech in March 1938, Hitler would have been happy to release the German Jews to the Western countries. Their refusal to do other than excoriate Germany without offering real assistance just confirmed Hitler in his largely correct view that most of the Western democracies were led by cowards and hypocrites.

This general subject is one of the most controversial elements of Roosevelt's public record. In this, as in other matters, he had his own judgment of what was possible with American public opinion. He grasped that the brutal mistreatment of Jews and political opponents was a trap Hitler was laying for Western leaders, to make them complicit in his wrongdoing and discredit them before their own publics, or force them into ineffectual action divisive of their domestic public opinion. Hitler knew they couldn't accept and assimilate all these people and so sought to reduce the Western leaders to vapid posturing or mute spectatorship.

Roosevelt devised the stratagem of expressing disapproval but walking the tightrope between American sympathy for the oppressed and fear of immigration in times of high unemployment, by unctuously drawing the curtain between the continents. He was implicitly inciting the inference that the admission of large numbers of immigrants would bring America closer to world conflict. He subtly preyed upon the myth, rooted in the psychology of earlier waves of immigration to the United States, that receiving immigrants on this basis, having been challenged to do so by their oppressor, would shrink the gulf between the source of evil and the place of deliverance.

Roosevelt was convinced from his observations in the Wilson era and since that the sentiment of isolationism was pervasive and had to be broken down by recourse to self-defense rather than compassion. There was a widespread feeling that these were Europe's problems and Europe could solve them and, more self-servingly, those who had left Europe earlier had been rewarded for their foresight; those who had lingered would pay for their lack of it. The endlessly sung patriotic song written during the First World War by Jewish immigrant Irving Berlin, "God Bless America," which often opened public entertainments in the late thirties, contains isolationist advice as well as a request of the Almighty: "As the storm clouds gather across the sea, let us pledge allegiance to the land that is free." Part of FDR's prophetic advocacy of the importance of air power was his conviction that long-range aircraft could threaten America, but that long before they did so, they could be invoked to disturb the complacency of the isolationists.

Roosevelt was not going to be separated from the army of his political supporters by Hitler; in this sense it was a struggle of two surpassingly skillful politicians, only one of whom now really had to be bothered with domestic opinion. There was sympathy for the Chinese victims of the Japanese, but no one, including the Chinese, imagined that the answer was large-scale immigration from China to the United States. This fact encouraged a sense of equivalence in thinking about Europe, despite the racial and numerical differences and the fact that the Jews, unlike the Chinese, had no homeland.

It is still hard to explain Roosevelt's mere acknowledgement, through an aide, of a petition received June 7, 1938, signed by 120,000 sympathizers with the Jews of Germany, proposing that unused immigration quotas from other countries be applied to refugees. Roosevelt received the President's Advisory Committee on Political Refugees on April 13, 1938. It was a group selected by the State Department, which meant that Catholic organizations were overrepresented and Jews underrepresented. (Bernard Baruch and Henry Morgenthau were the Jews' principal spokespeople, but they had never been very active in Jewish causes and were unlikely to say anything Roosevelt couldn't be assumed to agree with.) It was a bland session, and when the group took as its chairman the activist James G. McDonald, former League high commissioner for refugees from Germany, Roosevelt ignored it, though his old "friend" (i.e., almost as much a nemesis) Rabbi Stephen Wise became a member. (The cause was not assisted by Wise's previous testimony to a congressional committee against greater immigration or even assistance for Jewish immigration to Palestine.) This committee was just more window dressing.

Given the political realities, Roosevelt's policy to refugees at this time is defensible if not distinguished. There would soon come a time, when much of the world was at war and Roosevelt was reelected and politically invulnerable, and American unemployment had been eliminated, when he would benefit from no such extenuating circumstance. Then, his conduct, though more generous than it had been, would be subject to more serious controversy.

The very capable former chairman of the United States Steel Corporation, Myron Taylor, was designated head of the American delegation at Evian. The Dutch and the Danes were the moral heroes of the conference, pledging to take all the refugees they could but explaining that since that had been their policy, there wasn't room for many more in their small countries.

Australia had been advertising for immigrants from the United States and Britain, but declined to import a perceived race problem with European Jews. Argentina had already accepted 150 percent of the refugees that the United States had admitted and twice as much as the rest of South America. Brazil, Mexico, the Dominican Republic, Colombia, and Peru, as well as Canada, agreed (Brazil provisionally) to accept some agricultural laborers. This wasn't as implausible as it sounded, since many of the Jews going to Palestine performed this sort of work, and however inexperienced the refugees may have been at farm labor, they proved to be people of incredible determination and ingenuity and generally displayed an aptitude for agriculture.

Taylor said that the Austrian and German quotas for immigration to the United States would be combined, thus not losing any immigrants' places. This total was 27,370 for 1938. In fact, fewer than 18,000 were admitted (including the fifteen-year-old Henry Kissinger, eventually one of America's greatest statesmen). In practice, American consular officials were under orders to be very stingy with visas.

In 1933 and for a couple of years, the German government allowed Germans to leave permanently with the value of 75 percent of their property. This was reduced in the mid-thirties to 15 percent, and in 1938 to 5 percent. These reductions permitted pettifogging U.S. foreign officials to wrap themselves in the concern that the people admitted would become welfare cases. Roosevelt would aggravate matters by asking his director of immigration, Breckinridge Long—a former ambassador to Italy, an anti-Semite, and an admirer of Mussolini—to help Roosevelt depose the incumbent Democratic senator in Maryland. Roosevelt should never have had such an unsuitable person in that post at such a time and should never have indebted himself to Long politically as he did.* Long's baneful influence on refugee matters will be seen in chapter 16.

Colonel McCormick's niece, Anne O'Hare McCormick, wrote at the outset of the conference at Evian: "It is not a question of how many unemployed this country can safely add to its own unemployed millions. It is a test of civilization [against Hitler's] policy of extermination [and] barbarism."[53] Unfortunately Hitler knew otherwise, but he was mistaken in thinking this a permanent condition. Roosevelt would choose the ground where he would settle his inevitable struggle to the death with Hitler. He would not allow Hitler to dissipate Roosevelt's strength in secondary diversions, however heartbreaking the human conditions thus created.

The Evian conference did find place for perhaps 100,000 additional refugees (even a few in Panama, Honduras, Nicaragua, and Costa Rica, which had issued a joint statement that they would accept no "traders or intellectuals," an anti-Semitic euphemism that was not enforced in practice). Evian also set up the Intergovernmental Committee on Refugees in London. It was outside the

---

* Long was a descendant of Buchanan's vice president, John C. Breckinridge, Lincoln and Douglas's pro-slavery opponent in the 1860 presidential election.

League of Nations and was hoped to be less annoying to the German government, given Hitler's hostility to the League. Of course, there was no truth or reason to this pious evasion, and this new committee, yet another bit of window dressing for a problem that required human courage and generosity for anything useful to be accomplished, achieved virtually nothing.

VII

O N NOVEMBER 7, 1938, a Polish Jew in Paris, Herschel Grynszpan, shot and mortally wounded the third secretary of the German embassy in Paris, Ernst von Rath. Grynszpan was outraged at the brutal expulsion from Germany of 10,000 long-resident Polish Jews with nothing but the clothes on their backs and about four dollars each, who were poorly treated by the Poles when they were dumped at the frontier. Goebbels stirred up a mighty wave of anti-Semitic hatred, and Himmler and his deputy, Reinhard Heidrich, instructed the SS all over Germany to take vengeance on the entire Jewish population. Goebbels demanded "spontaneous demonstrations." The result was the infamous "Kristallnacht" (night of broken glass), November 9 to 10, 1938. Scores of Jews were murdered, thousands injured. Two hundred synagogues were burned. Twenty thousand Jews were sent to concentration camps. About 800 Jewish-owned shops were destroyed, nearly as many were looted, a hundred Jewish homes were destroyed. The German government imposed a fine of $400 million on the country's half million Jews, and the victims of the damage were deprived of the benefit of insurance and required to effect all repairs at once at their own expense. A kangaroo court committee headed by Lindbergh's friend Hermann Goering found the Jews totally responsible for the outrages.

Reaction in the United States and most of the world was overwhelming revulsion at the barbarism of the German regime. Roosevelt read a statement to the press November 15. "The news of the past few days from Germany has deeply shocked public opinion in the United States. . . . I myself could scarcely believe that such things could occur in a twentieth century civilization." On Hull's advice, he ordered his ambassador in Germany, Hugh Wilson, home at once for consultation, a less drastic step than permanently withdrawing him but a strong gesture. There would be no U.S. ambassador in Germany again until long after the end of Hitler's Reich—1949—and the setting up of the new Federal Republic of Germany.

To deny Roosevelt the pleasure of expelling the German ambassador, Hitler recalled the perceptive Ambassador Dieckhoff. Dieckhoff made a courtesy farewell call on Hull for "a conversation bordering on the surreal. He complained that an American official had said in a speech that Hitler had killed more people than Charles II, king of England during the Restoration. Dieckhoff demanded an apology for this outrageous slander.

"Hull said he had never thought of Charles II as a particularly notorious killer and asked: 'How many people did Charles Second kill?' Dieckhoff fidgeted, squirmed in his chair and said, 'I'm afraid I don't recall.' With that contribution to diplomacy he left for Berlin," leaving the fine Vanderbilt home of the German ambassador almost empty. There would be no replacement for nine years.*[54]

In London, Chamberlain and his government said nothing, although the British public was just as disgusted by the pogroms as the American people were. When Kennedy, under orders from the State Department, informed the British that failure to comment was causing great animosity to Britain in the United States, Chamberlain made a bland comment that German Jews should be entirely relocated elsewhere, with no hint of where that should be. Palestine was out of the question. The German Jewish population would have been delighted to emigrate en masse, but no country would have more than a few of them, so neither Roosevelt's genuine outrage nor Chamberlain's shameful indifference accomplished much for the victims of the Nazis.

The polls demonstrated the depths of Roosevelt's problem. According to the well-regarded Gallup organization, in November 1938, 94 percent of Americans disapproved of Nazi treatment of Jews, 97 percent disapproved of Nazi treatment of Roman Catholics, and 57 percent approved of President Roosevelt's withdrawal of the United States ambassador to Germany. Organizations ranging from the American Legion to Lewis's CIO strongly supported the President's condemnation of official German anti-Semitism. The President's problem, by Munich, certainly did not consist of any American affection for Hitler. Again according to Gallup, 92 percent of Americans in October 1938 disbelieved that Hitler had no more territorial ambitions, 77 percent thought the demand for annexation of the Sudetenland unjustified, and 60 percent thought the Munich agreement was more likely to lead to war than peace (it is little wonder Roosevelt sought no "credit" for it, since that was his view also). The following month, 61 percent of Americans approved a boycott of German goods. In August 1939, 86 percent opposed Hitler's claim to the Polish Corridor and 88 percent opposed his claim on Danzig. And in October 1939, after the Nazi-Soviet partition of Poland, 78 percent of Americans rejected Hitler's assertion that the "Polish question" had been settled.

The position of Jews in American thinking was more complicated. In July 1939, according to Roper, another respected polling organization, 39 percent of Americans thought Jews should be treated like everyone else in the United States, 10 percent thought they should be deported, 11 percent thought they should be socially segregated, and 32 percent thought they should in certain ways be restricted in the complete access to all American businesses. This clearly indicated that the ancient caricature of the Jew as a dangerous, unethical, or unas-

---

* Charles II, though much defamed by Macaulay, Trevelyan, and the Whig Utilitarian school of British history, was a judicious monarch who showed considerable restraint, given that his father had been put to death by Cromwell in very questionable proceedings.

similable person persisted. In 1938, according to Gallup, 72 percent of Americans opposed allowing an increased number of Jewish exiles from Germany into the United States. When the question was U.S. government financial aid to help Jewish and Roman Catholic refugees from the Nazis to settle in other countries, 52 percent were opposed, though the two communities represented about 25 percent of the whole United States population.

Hard though it is to believe, in 1939, 67 percent of Americans opposed the admission of 10,000 refugee children (religion unspecified, though most respondents doubtless thought they were Jews) into the United States. When they were identified as being mainly Jewish, opposition actually fell to 61 percent, which at least indicated (slowly) rising sympathy for persecuted European Jews. Roosevelt failed in his effort to amend the 1924 Immigration Act to admit Jewish refugee children and in his effort, through intermediaries, to arrange the departure from Germany of 150,000 Jews, financed by an international loan. He has received less credit than he deserved for his efforts.[55]

As late as 1946, when there had been horrifying revelations of the death camps and there was minimal unemployment in the United States, 72 percent opposed allowing more Jewish and other refugees to live in the United States. By 1947, "only" 59 percent of Americans opposed taking Poles, Jews, and other displaced persons into the United States. In 1984, in response to a question about accepting Jews from the Soviet Union facing persecution, 79 percent thought they should be admitted to the United States.[56]

In 1937, according to Gallup, 47 percent of Americans would vote for a Jew for President of the United States if he were otherwise qualified, and 46 percent would not. By 1961, 68 percent would have voted for a qualified Jew for the nation's highest office and 23 percent would not. And in 1987, the corresponding numbers were 82 percent and 10 percent. In 2000 when the Democrats nominated a Jewish candidate for vice president, it had no appreciable impact on voting patterns. In 1938, the climate was quite different.[57]

In the aftermath of Kristallnacht, various methods were proposed for assisting Hitler's victims. Sir Ronald Lindsay called upon Sumner Welles and suggested that the British quota of 65,000 immigrants annually, of which only 4,000 had then been used for 1938, be handed over to Germany. This would effectively triple the German quota. Welles summarily rejected this proposal and gave Lindsay a rather pompous lecture that these quotas were not like transferable invitations in the hands of the recipients. Welles engaged in the further irritating sophistry that the leaders of the American Jewish committee would be the first to object to an expanded Jewish intake, which was almost certainly untrue and in any case irrelevant, since the issue was helping persecuted foreigners, not truckling to domestic minority-group opinion.

On the same day as Lindsay's visit to the White House, November 17, 1938, Frances Perkins, always a reliable source of sensible and humane opinion, visited the President and proposed that the next three years of German quotas be brought forward into one. Roosevelt gently declined, and Miss Perkins emerged from their meeting urging a cautious approach. If the Lindsay and Perkins proposals had been combined, the German quota would have jumped in the year before the war almost tenfold, to about 250,000, which would have been filled if Long's consulates had stopped obstructing applicants. With any such gesture, and in fact a much more modest one, the United States could have bullied the other potential recipient countries, especially the British, as holders of the Palestine Mandate, to take another 250,000, thus saving all the German Jews. This would not have saved Hitler's victims in the countries that he ultimately occupied, but it would have been a magnificent deliverance of a sophisticated population, most of which shortly perished in the most horrible circumstances. The people saved, and the act of receiving them, would have done great honor to America.

What Roosevelt did do was permit the indefinite continuation in the United States of about 15,000 Germans and Austrians, most of them bearers of Austrian passports that would become invalid at the end of 1938, six weeks hence, technically requiring their return to Germany, where, as Roosevelt pointed out to the press: "It is a question of concentration camps, et cetera and so on."[58] This, like the Lindsay and Perkins proposals, was technically illegal, as ultra vires to the President without congressional approval, but that wasn't always much of a deterrent to this president. Among the eminent cultural fugitives from German and Austrian Nazism already or soon to be resident in the United States were Albert Einstein, Kurt Weill, Paul Hindemith, Walter Gropius, George Grosz, Thomas Mann, Lion Feuchtwanger, Bertholt Brecht, Hermann Hesse, Franz Werfel, and many others. Marlene Dietrich had arrived in the twilight of the Weimar Republic.

Joseph Kennedy, trying to recover from the fiasco of his Trafalgar Day speech, took up the comment of Chamberlain about resettling the German Jews, and presented what he self-importantly called the Kennedy Plan for their emigration. The "plan" was nonsense, because there was no suggestion of where they might go to, other than "underpopulated places." These could have been Antarctica, the Sahara, Patagonia, Tibet, "et cetera and so on."

The fatuity of this sort of vague "plan" would be sickeningly demonstrated a few months later, when the "luxury ship" *St. Louis*, to use Hitler's Königsberg terminology of 1937 (chapter 10), sailed from Hamburg in mid-May 1939 with 936 passengers, all but six of them Jewish refugees armed with Cuban entry visas. The president of Cuba, Laredo Bru, had invalidated these visas May 5, before the *St. Louis* sailed, and the ship owner, Hamburg-Amerika Line, had immediately been told of this. As the ship approached, Havana informed the captain of the invalidity of the visas. The captain, Gustav Schroeder, proved a courageous and generous man and did his best for his passengers.

When informed of the Cuban position, one of the passengers suffered a fatal coronary and was buried at sea. Another slashed his wrists and plunged overboard, was rescued, and was admitted to Cuba as a hospital patient. The six non-

Jewish passengers, two returning Cubans and four Spanish tourists, and twenty-two Jews who had more expensive visas were admitted. Apparently the New York Joint Distribution Committee (JDC) had put up the money necessary to buy the more expensive visas and admit all the passengers to Cuba. But the lawyer representing the JDC in Cuba attempted to haggle with the Cuban government, and the government terminated discussions and rejected the refugees.

The lawyer, Lawrence Berenson, a friend of the real power in the country for the next twenty years, Fulgencio Batista, visited President Bru at his country house on June 2. Bru, under the same pressures as Roosevelt and other political leaders, struggling to retain his position in the face of Batista's greater influence, stipulated conditions that had to be accepted and concluded within twenty-four hours. When Berenson, as was the custom in dealing with the Cuban authorities, suggested a small reduction in the quantum for the visas, Bru, having shown what he thought adequate magnanimity for international humanitarian purposes, did the politically expedient thing in the eyes of Cuban opinion, rescinding the offer on June 6 and requiring the *St. Louis* to quit Havana and Cuban waters.

Treasury Secretary Morgenthau intervened with Hull and Welles, hoping to land the refugees in the U.S. Virgin Islands, but Hull discovered that this would be illegal without an act of Congress. Morgenthau had the *St. Louis* shadowed by a Coast Guard cutter, not, as was alleged at the time, to keep the ship's passengers out of the United States, but to be sure of the ship's whereabouts in the event of a breakthrough on admission of its passengers.

Schroeder sailed slowly up the Florida coast. The *St. Louis* became a cause celebre; 734 of the passengers were in quota lines for U.S. entry. Petitions were addressed to Roosevelt from many groups within the United States and from the *St. Louis*'s passengers, who pointed out in their plea that over 400 of their number were women and children. There were many editorials asking Roosevelt to be merciful to these unfortunates. He didn't reply to any of it. Concerned that Hitler's next ploy would be to try to inundate the United States with his indigent and terrified victims, Roosevelt did not alter the challenging means test that Hoover had decreed for immigration candidates, screening out anyone who it seemed could become a welfare case in the United States. And he persisted in regarding the status of the German Jews as not preeminently an American problem to solve, though the Jewish population of the United States was at this time the most numerous in the world except for those of the U.S.S.R. and Poland.

Finally, after extensive diplomatic maneuvering and shameful rejections from many other countries, the admirable performance of Captain Schroeder led to Belgium's admitting the *St. Louis* and its passengers in June. (Tragically, after Belgium was overrun by Germany a year later, many of these fugitives were rounded up by the Nazis and exterminated.) It is hard to understand why Roosevelt did not simply muscle the Cuban president on the issue. Even if his lack of enthusiasm for admitting the *St. Louis*'s passengers to the United States could be understood (with difficulty), he could surely have insisted that Berenson pay up and Bru admit those who had embarked for Cuba in good faith in Hamburg, visas in hand. It must also be said that in the circumstances, the onus was on the JDC to sort it out with the Cuban government when it had the opportunity to do so. The whole episode is a rending human tragedy that reflects no credit on anyone except Captain Schroeder. The liner *Flander* arrived in Havana a few days after the *St. Louis* with 100 refugees carrying fully paid visas. They were admitted to Cuba without controversy.[59] (Batista was no help to Berenson on this matter, but the two remained so close that Berenson accompanied Batista into exile when he was chased out of power by Fidel Castro twenty years later.)

The most sophisticated American opinion was naturally the most enlightened. Roosevelt received a letter in November 1938 from a group of well-known writers calling for liberalization of entry conditions. "We feel that the American people and the American government have no right to remain silent. . . . We feel that it is deeply immoral for the American people to continue to have economic relations with a country that avowedly uses mass murder to solve its economic problems." Among the signers were John Steinbeck, Thornton Wilder, Eugene O'Neill, Robert Sherwood, Pearl Buck, Van Wyck Brooks, Robinson Jeffers, and Dorothy Thompson. This view was publicly supported by many Hollywood stars, including Claudette Colbert, Fred Astaire, and Bette Davis.[60]

Severing trade relations with Germany was one thing. Very different, and practically impossible before the war, was accepting 500,000 fugitives from the Nazis, which, ideally, America should have done, not only on humanitarian grounds but to enrich the human talent pool of the nation.

The United States did admit approximately 50,000 German Jews in the thirteen months between the 1940 election and the U.S. entry into the war. Roosevelt thus overrode the quotas and took in about 15 percent of the Jewish population of Germany in 1933. This was a respectable performance, for which Roosevelt has again received little credit. However, in the light of subsequent horrifying events, he could have done even more when there was no more unemployment in the country and this was the last hope for the targets of Hitler's genocidal ambitions. Although it would have been difficult to circumvent congressional opinion further in the very tense year 1941 when the world hung in the balance, on that issue and at that time Roosevelt should have ignored the polls. This is, however, an opinion furnished retroactively in the knowledge of how America was plunged into the war. Roosevelt was steadily assuming the role of an undeclared combatant against Germany and stretching his constitutional powers to assist Hitler's enemies. Then his desire not to be sidetracked by the question of Germany's oppressed Jews, unforeseeably unspeakable though the evil inflicted on them was, was comprehensible, though unedifying.

Roosevelt should not be censored too severely for not turning his office in 1938 and 1939 into a bully pulpit for the evangelization of America to the virtues of philosemitism. His paramount duty was to conserve the integrality of American moral and political opinion, and to build the nation's industrial and military power in order to exercise a decisive influence on the Manichaean struggle between good and evil political forces that was already underway. That duty was no less a moral and strategic imperative for the fact that Roosevelt, Hitler, and now Churchill were almost the only prominent people in the world, apart from a scattering of intellectuals, who saw what was afoot in anything like these terms.[61]

VIII

W HAT WOULD BECOME a vital and historic relationship between Franklin D. Roosevelt and General George C. Marshall effectively began on November 14, 1938.* Roosevelt had a number of high-ranking civilian and military officials to the White House to discuss implementation of his plans for increasing American air power in a supplementary War Department budgeting request of $500 million he was planning to make to the Congress. The President wanted 20,000 planes and an annual production capacity of 24,000. He did not believe the Congress could be induced to agree to this, so he proposed that half these figures be identified as targets. He said that if the United States had had this level of air power and productive capacity Hitler would have shown more restraint in the last year. He also claimed that the Americas were in greater danger of foreign interference than at any time since Czar Alexander's post-Waterloo Holy Alliance of 1815 led to the proclamation of the Monroe Doctrine to protect the newly independent states of Latin America. Roosevelt exclaimed that the United States must have air power sufficient to defend the hemisphere "from the North Pole to the South Pole." He concluded by asking Marshall, as deputy chief of staff of the army, the man technically responsible for military budget preparation, if he didn't agree that he had made a pretty good case for his program: "Don't you think so, George?"

Marshall demurred. As he later explained privately, he thought there was no attention to ancillary matters—training of pilots, recruitment of technicians, production of ammunition—and he also did not agree that the security vulnerabilities of the Americas were as great as the President had suggested they were. (In fact, as Roosevelt later explained, he didn't believe a word of that either, but didn't want to reveal to such a large group that his real intention was to be able to supply the British and French with enough aircraft to enable them to deter or defeat Hitler.)

Marshall was not used to dealing with such a devious personality as Roosevelt. Nor did Marshall appreciate the President's calling him by his Christian name, since they didn't know each other and it thus seemed unnatural and condescending. Roosevelt was responsible for a vast expansion of the practice of addressing casual acquaintances in formal relationships by their first names. It came naturally to him and was probably a combination of confident affability and occa-

---

* Roosevelt, at the request of General Pershing, with whom Marshall had served in World War I, asked War Secretary Dern to promote Marshall to brigadier in 1935.

sional assumed paternalism, but was certainly not in this case intended to be condescending. On leaving the room on November 14, Marshall was jocularly advised by several of the others present that he was about to be posted to Guam or Alaska. In fact, Roosevelt took no notice of Marshall's dissent.[62]

Most of the advisors were back December 1 with a supplementary defense budget of $1.8 billion, which Roosevelt rejected as politically and fiscally impossible. He demanded that they pay some attention to political feasibility and come back with the best they could do with his $500 million proposal.

The War Department was in a confused state, a condition Roosevelt cultivated. The secretary of war, Harry Woodring (an isolationist who had been appointed assistant secretary after being defeated by Alfred Landon as governor of Kansas in 1932 and promoted on the death of Secretary George Dern in 1936) and his assistant secretary, Louis Johnson, an Atlanticist, were at each other's throats.

Roosevelt on November 20 received a letter from General John J. Pershing that Marshall had put Pershing up to writing, asking for more for the army and effectively less for the Army Air Corps (previously the Army Air Service, soon the Army Air Forces). Roosevelt responded non-committally, not wishing to bring America's greatest war hero into a public debate on military spending.

Roosevelt received an honorary degree at the University of North Carolina on December 5. He pushed his current course of national reconciliation and jauntily told the students: "You have heard for six years that I was about to plunge the nation into war; that you and your little brothers would be sent to the bloody battlefields of Europe, that I was driving the nation into bankruptcy; and that I breakfasted every morning on a dish of grilled millionaire. Actually I am an exceedingly mild-mannered person—a practitioner of peace both domestic and foreign, a believer in the capitalistic system, and for my breakfast, a devotee of scrambled eggs."[63] He was working diligently to cool out the domestic debate and focus attention on foreign dangers. His remarks were received with relief by almost all sections of opinion.

Roosevelt received Anthony Eden at the White House on December 13. The former foreign secretary was on a private visit to make a few speeches. Roosevelt avoided precise discussion of the most pressing foreign policy matters, though they were both opponents of appeasement, but gave his now customary paean to the need for air power.[64]

At the end of 1938, Roosevelt brought some new blood into his government. He permitted Attorney General Homer Cummings to retire, having first asked for his resignation. Cummings was privately held responsible for most of the mistakes in the Court battle. Roosevelt also sent the seventy-one-year-old commerce secretary, Daniel Roper, off to honorable retirement. The outgoing governor of Michigan, election-casualty Frank Murphy, a longstanding Roosevelt favorite, was nominated attorney general, and Harry Hopkins, Roosevelt's secret preferred candidate to replace him in the White House, became secretary of commerce. Both appointments significantly strengthened the cabinet.

Hopkins was sworn in at the White House December 24 and took up his new office two days later, one of his first visitors being his improbable but firm friend, General George C. Marshall. Marshall declined to go over the head of General Malin Craig, the army chief of staff, but initiated the practice of fully informing Hopkins, who, Marshall knew, would know how to deliver any message discreetly to the President. Their initial collaboration over transfer of WPA activity to munitions manufacturing would expand exponentially, because Roosevelt had already concluded that aircraft production had to be expanded by recourse to government-owned plants. Roosevelt initially proposed the establishment of seven large military aircraft production plants on War Department property, which would multiply U.S. aircraft production from 1,200 per year to 10,000, and assured his supporters that "Hopkins could build these plants without cost to the Treasury because it would be work relief which otherwise would have to be provided in any case."[65] The transition of the New Deal into its fourth phase, a massive defense buildup, was under way.

Marshall might have surmised that Hopkins could possibly help him up the last rung of the military ladder when General Craig retired as chief of staff the following year. By that time Roosevelt already had come to appreciate Marshall's outstanding qualities. Apparently thirty-two generals outranked Marshall as possible chiefs of staff, but with application of the long-standing unofficial rule that those who would turn sixty-five in the course of the (normally) four-year commission became ineligible, the number of competitors descended to four. Of these, only one, General Hugh Drum, a friend of James A. Farley, was better known than Marshall. This was one of his problems; Drum's constant self-promotion irritated Roosevelt.* Marshall was supported not only by Hopkins, Craig, and Pershing but by both Woodring and Johnson, though he tried to conceal the support of one from the other, so great was their mutual dislike. (Relations between Hull and Welles in the State Department were almost as strained.)

The relationship between Marshall and Hopkins seemed at first glance the attraction of opposites; the punctilious, ramrod-straight and direct general, and the disheveled, expansive, politically adroit Hopkins. But they pursued similar goals with the same ardor. They were ambitious for themselves and fiercely patriotic. The rest came easily, and Roosevelt, who did not seek solely pliable underlings, came to rely heavily and uniquely on each in his respective sphere.

Marshall's angling for the top position did not drive him to toadying. He never hesitated to contradict Roosevelt (though always very respectfully) on important matters, declined Hopkins's frequent suggestions that he consent to be invited to Hyde Park or Warm Springs, and was always wary of being reduced to a lackey by Roosevelt's legendary and seductive combination of charm and power. He did not even always laugh at Roosevelt's stories, not because he was completely

---

* FDR couldn't resist saying: "I wish he would stop beating his own drum!"

humorless (though humor was far from his most prominent trait) but because of his inflexible integrity.

Marshall initially found Roosevelt's breezy, discursive, self-indulgent manner of conducting meetings unimpressive and a parody of political superficiality. Only gradually did he detect that Roosevelt was a man of great strength, purpose, and, when required, courage. Eventually, between them there developed a relationship sufficiently relaxed that Roosevelt dispensed with tactical circumlocution and Marshall stopped acting as if the slightest informality constituted unethical self-ingratiation. Roosevelt settled on Marshall as chief of staff following discussions with Hopkins at Warm Springs in early April 1939. He became acting chief in July and was formally installed on the fateful first of September, 1939.

IX

I N HIS STATE of the Union message of January 4, 1939, Roosevelt had invoked religious themes to amplify his gradual campaign to raise American consciousness of geopolitical realities. He identified religion with democracy and responsible international behavior. He would have known this to be simplistic. (Germany and especially Italy were dictatorships whose populations were more or less as religiously practicing as the American public, even though their leaders were not.)

"We have learned that God-fearing democracies of the world which observe the sanctity of treaties and good faith in their dealings with other nations cannot safely be indifferent to international lawlessness anywhere.

"We have learned that when we deliberately try to legislate neutrality, our neutrality laws may operate . . . unfairly—may actually give aid to an aggressor and deny it to the victim.

"A strong and united nation may be destroyed if it is unprepared against sudden attack. But even a nation well armed and well organized from a strictly military standpoint may, after a period of time, meet defeat if it is unnerved by self-distrust, endangered by class prejudice, by dissension between capital and labor, by false economy, and by other unsolved social problems at home.

"Our nation's program of social and economic reform is therefore a part of defense, as basic as armaments themselves. . . . Our full energies may now be released to invigorate the processes of recovery in order to preserve our reforms, and to give every man who wants to work a real job at a living wage."

He decried the costs of dictatorship in human liberty and dignity.

"The cost of the blessed right of being able to say what we please. The cost of freedom of religion. The cost of seeing our capital confiscated. The cost of being cast into a concentration camp. The cost of being afraid to walk down the street with the wrong neighbor. The cost of having our children brought up, not as free and dignified human beings, but as pawns molded and enslaved by a machine."

In summary, Roosevelt was saying that religion gave rise to democracy; democracy must be defended. This defense requires both a just society and a well-armed nation. And that defense requires a practical distinction between belligerent dictatorships and peaceful democracies. Respect for God and the national interest require that beleaguered democracies receive assistance short of war from an America unshackled by self-defeating neutrality legislation. And America must be sufficiently armed to render such help while deterring aggression against itself. In the furtherance of all the foregoing, Americans should unite (behind their president), and set aside minor differences about distribution of taxes and benefits.

The nation's enemies were not within, but the ravening dictators abroad. Having avoided the identification of scapegoats for the Depression, other than his mythological litany of monopolists and war profiteers, he was starting to focus America's anger and suspicion on the aggressive foreign dictators. This was a momentous transition and presaged a policy that would decisively influence the course of the world war that was now imminent. This address became known as the "Methods short of war" speech, and was an appropriate and intelligent message for the times.

These times were so treacherous that Roosevelt had to continue a distasteful policy of maneuver in respect to the Spanish war, as he did over the fate of refugees. The division between most conventional American opinion and the militancy of the great majority of the American Roman Catholic community, which was in other respects indistinguishable from Protestant American opinion, cut right across the bedrock of Roosevelt's domestic support, which he was particularly anxious to keep intact for his ultimate showdown with the isolationists. In the autumn of 1938, the departments of state and agriculture and the Red Cross had worked out a scheme for using some of the U.S. agricultural surplus for distribution among famine victims, irrespective of region or faction, in Spain.

Roosevelt helped to set up the Committee for Impartial Relief in Spain, with a blue-ribbon board spanning the political spectrum and the full range from isolationists to internationalists. The U.S. Roman Catholic hierarchy concluded that it was essentially an organization dedicated to helping the Republicans, who had been responsible for the deaths of many thousands of Spanish religious personnel and were violently anticlerical.*

At the very end of 1938, as Franco advanced on Barcelona, a tremendous agitation took place between advocates of lifting and retaining the arms embargo on Spain. Roosevelt's head of his Impartial Relief Committee, George MacDonald, concluded that he had been duped and that the Committee was indeed more or less a Communist front, and resigned.

---

* A particularly unpleasant scene occurred when the government economist and administrator Leon Henderson came to dinner in February 1939, and Eleanor openly scorned her husband's alleged moral cowardice over Spain. In fact, it was not so much cowardice as tactical skill and strategic insight, but accusing her husband of such shortcomings in the presence of a civil servant (or anyone else) was outrageous, and Eleanor Roosevelt at her most tiresome.

Despite the fact that Franco's army in Catalonia was spearheaded by 40,000 Italians who Mussolini pledged were not in Spain at all, Chamberlain and Halifax visited Rome on January 11, 1939, to try again to persuade Mussolini to be a calming influence on Hitler. Chamberlain professed to find it "a very wonderful visit," but it only confirmed the Italian leaders in their low opinion of the British, and the British government in their conviction that Mussolini was now just a posturing, noisy German puppet.

Mussolini was concerned that Chamberlain appeared to be popular with the Roman crowds, but said: "These men are not made of the same stuff as the Francis Drakes and the other magnificent adventurers who created their empire. These, after all, are the tired sons of a long line of rich men and they will lose their empire."[66] (Churchill and Roosevelt might have been inclined to agree with the Duce's disparagements in policy terms. But Chamberlain and Halifax had great physical stamina and took a good deal of outdoor exercise, while Mussolini and Ciano "were chubby, chairbound urbanites, fit only for the sports of the boudoir [if that]. . . . As so often, Mussolini was the principal victim of his own rhetoric."[67]

Roosevelt's struggle to help strengthen the British and French, especially through sale of aircraft, had become his great passion. Pursuant to Jean Monnet's visit, a French team was back in the United States in January 1939, inspecting American aircraft for purchase. Roosevelt himself had to overrule the commander of the Army Air Corps, General H.H. Arnold, and require the French to be given access to the Douglas A-20 bomber. In a test flight in Los Angeles, January 19, the test pilot became overambitious in putting the plane through its paces, with the result that it crashed, the test pilot was killed, and his French passenger, on being pulled from the wreck before it burst into flame, was heard to utter expletives in French. The press discovered and revealed the secret French mission while Arnold was testifying in camera to Nye's Senate Military Affairs Committee.

Arnold had no aptitude for dealing with direct and potentially embarrassing questions, and garrulously babbled forth that the French were thinking of buying the "secret" bomber. It devolved upon Roosevelt, who possessed all the skills at dissembling that Arnold lacked, to bail the government out of potential embarrassment. With Nye threatening to subpoena cabinet members, Roosevelt told his press conference on January 27 that this was a providential development, because the French orders, if they could be landed, would put thousands of people to work and get idle plants functioning, and the order would be finished before the administration's own defense funding requests were authorized and the orders placed. This was not true, and Woodring admitted as much under heavy questioning from Nye and his committee. (The French orders couldn't possibly be completed before the U.S. orders came in. Less than half the French order was filled when war broke out in September.) Morgenthau fared fairly well before the committee discussing trade and financial technicalities.

Roosevelt was at his best. He never had any trouble outwitting the press with a tangled trail of jokes, strained analogies, half-truths, and, if necessary, outright falsehoods. He told Morgenthau and Woodring in the presence of the entire cabinet at its next meeting "to proceed as before [and let the French] buy what they want."[68] U.S. production of aircraft engines almost tripled from mid-1938 to late 1939, and production of airframes more than doubled. Army Air Corps officers who didn't agree with the new policies of supplying the British and the French were apt to be redeployed to distant Pacific islands.[69]

The President had the Senate Military Affairs Committee to the White House on January 31, 1939. He gave a strong exposition of his conception of the strategic interests of the country. His basic premises were that the French Army and British Navy had provided the shield behind which the United States had grown since the Napoleonic Wars to its present greatness. The British and the French were threatened now by an evil and dangerous German regime, and the American national interest required that those countries be supported. The objective was to stay out of war, not get into one, and nothing could be more obvious than that Germany could be a mortal danger to the United States and that the British and French democracies were profoundly friendly countries.

He discussed American political ideas and expressed a determination not to commit the error Jefferson committed with the neutrality legislation of 1807, which responded to British and French embargoes against each other by withdrawing from world commerce altogether. The United States was incomparably stronger now and should have some consciousness of its own strength. The senators should recognize that they all had the same interest, to stay out of war while parrying overseas threats and supporting those threatened by the dictators. He spoke briefly of the Pacific and hoped that the Japanese could be contained by U.S. air and naval installations in the Pacific islands, and referred to "Brother Hitler's" comments on Latin America in his speech marking his sixth anniversary as chancellor the day before. Hitler appeared to claim some interest in political developments there, where among the many Ruritanian military juntas and swaggerers he had some admirers. (Hitler made his first general public threat in this speech to assure "the annihilation of the Jewish race in Europe" in the event of another war.)

In response to a question from Hamilton Lewis of Illinois, Roosevelt launched into his customary refrain about his unique experience of war: "Listen, I probably saw more of the war in Europe than any other living person." This preposterous assertion presumed to place his knowledge above all those who had gone through the entire four years and four months of the war in combat roles.*

---

* He recounted his trip as assistant secretary of the navy for three months in 1918: "I covered the whole coast of France." (There wasn't much war going on there.) "I spent days on the Belgian front, on the British front, on the French front, on the American front. I was an observer in the push up the Veale. I saw the operations in Italy."

He was emphasizing that the United States should do its best short of war for those countries defending themselves from the dictators and also providing the first line of defense against them for the United States. It was not a successful meeting, however. Nye wrote a memo to himself referring to the "so-called democracies." (Did he think Britain and France were dictatorships?) On the way out of the White House, Nye said to the press: "Get the uniforms ready for the boys." The next day in the Senate he deplored the imposition of secrecy on the session. He need not have worried about that, because the *New York Times* ran a full story on the meeting two days following, stating that Roosevelt told the senators they should consider "France as the actual frontier of America in an apparently inevitable showdown between democracies and dictatorships."[70]

This was gratefully received in France and Britain.*

Roosevelt judged that he had to step back from this overexposed position, and at his February 3, 1939, press conference he dismissed the statement about the United States having a "frontier on the Rhine" as "a deliberate lie." Polls generally supported the position he was taking; 65 percent approved the sale of warplanes to Britain and France, 44 percent approved embargoing them to Germany and Italy, and 69 percent favored all aid short of war to the democracies in the event of war.[72]

Franklin D. Roosevelt was now entering the intense phase of the most intricate and important political operation of his presidency. He knew that if he was to take the country through the world crisis, he would have to take a third term and he would have to win it as a virtual conscript to his office in a great emergency rather than as a power-seeker asking a longer incumbency than Washington or Jefferson or Jackson. And he knew that to win a third term, he would have to be the candidate best qualified to keep the country out of war. He would have to sell his emerging policy of peace through strength, to seek peace by preparing for war. This was, also, conveniently, and as has been mentioned, the way to eliminate unemployment and silence the increasing number of people who claimed that the New Deal, whatever its palliative effects and the value of most of its reforms, had not fully delivered the country from the evils of the Depression.

He told a group of Democratic congressmen in early 1939 that armaments production on a grand scale would "mean prosperity for this country and we can't elect the Democratic Party unless we get prosperity . . . Let's be perfectly frank."[73]

---

*The British poet laureate, John Masefield, wrote to Roosevelt's friend Thomas Lamont of J.P. Morgan & Company: "I do not suppose you will ever realize what a profound sensation President Roosevelt's words to the Senators have made throughout Europe. . . . The effect has been so great that I marvel they have not rung the church bells over it. . . . The prestige of America has never stood so high." He wrote that thanks to the U.S. president, there was now "the best chance that the world has ever had of getting a decency to live in, and a Humanity to work for."[71] His judgment was premature but not mistaken.

By the time of his reelection, the European allies would assumedly have produced more determined leadership than Chamberlain and Daladier, leaders capable of galvanizing their own populations from their torpor and assisting Roosevelt in promoting American assistance for the democracies.

Then would come the final act. The Western Allies in World War I, with Russia and Italy on their side, would probably have lost without the intervention of the United States. Roosevelt did not believe that Britain and France, comparatively enfeebled as they were, could prevail over the malignantly reinvigorated Nazi Germany on their own. There was no reason to imagine that Stalin would lift a finger to help them, and Mussolini would do what Hitler told him to do. The Japanese might even be induced to attack Britain and France in the Far East and India.

Roosevelt had recognized from the earliest moments of the Third Reich that Western democracy probably could not coexist with it. He came to believe, by early 1939 at the latest, that the United States would be required as the indispensable force to rid the world of Nazism and that it would then emerge not only as a postisolationist country but as the preeminent nation on earth. Supreme political artist as he was, he cannot have failed, by the beginning of 1939, to have glimpsed this destiny that would carry his country to heights no nation had ever occupied and himself to a position in American history rivaled, if at all, only by Washington and Lincoln.

The reason Roosevelt must have known all this is because there is no other plausible explanation of his conduct as he moved deftly through the world crisis.

British historian D.C. Watt wrote "His personality was overpoweringly regal; his advisers constituted a court rather than a cabinet. His closest supporters and adherents complained that he 'deliberately concealed the processes of his mind,' that he never talked 'frankly, even with the people who were loyal to him.' He displayed to them a mass of conflicting characteristics, not so much ill balanced as constantly shifting in balance."*

Like an agile predator, he knew when to emerge, reveal his design, and execute it. And once determined to lead opinion and implement a policy, he was unflappable, devious, utterly determined, and usually inspiring. Now, in early 1939, his course, though indiscernible to others, was clear to him. It could be summarized in six points. First, he had to complete the conquest of the Depression by arming America. Second, he would arrange a virtual draft to a third term

---

* "Inconsistent in his consistencies, cold and distant behind the apparent warmth of personality with which he could overwhelm even the most hardened visitor, listening always to some private voice whose tones we can recognize but never overhear, and whose advice we can imagine but never verify, his protean, almost chameleonlike changes, his hesitancies, his willingness to leave initiative to others, the freedom with which he abused others for not acting with the strength he was not prepared to display himself, all this is difficult to reconcile with the reputation he has enjoyed as the great leader of the democracies. And yet a great leader he certainly was."[74]

as the candidate of peace through strength. Third, he would complete the acquisition of an overwhelming level of military might. Fourth, and assuming a new world war was already in progress, he would engineer righteous hostilities with Germany and the lesser dictatorships, ensuring that the dictators would be seen as the aggressors. The fifth stage would be winning the war and leading the world to a postimperial Pax Americana, in which, sixth, Woodrow Wilson's goals of safety for democracy and international legality would be established in some sort of American-led international organization. Nothing less or other than these goals can explain Roosevelt's conduct from Munich on. No other American leader has ever conceived such an immensely ambitious plan for making over the world. The few leaders of other countries who were as ambitious—Napoleon, Lenin, Hitler—were not as, or not at all, benign. And no one, benign or otherwise, would be more durably successful in implementing a grand design for reorganizing international relations.

To the extent that other countries would absorb the early brunt of German aggression and endure the casualties of wearing the Nazis down, that would make the achievement of Roosevelt's ultimate goals easier. The less of the ultimate burden that his countrymen had to bear, the better. Thus he told the British ambassador-designate, Lord Lothian, that he was exasperated by the British tendency to despair in the light of the deterioration in relations with Germany since Munich, as Hitler resumed his belligerent threats against Germany's neighbors. Roosevelt wrote to Harvard historian Roger Merriman, who had been corresponding with the noted British historian and Macaulay descendent G.M. Trevelyan, apropos of Lothian (February 15, 1939): "I wish the British would stop this 'we who are about to die salute thee' attitude. . . . I . . . told [Lothian] that just so long as he or Britishers like him took that attitude of complete despair, the British would not be worth saving anyway. What the British need today is . . . not only the desire to save civilization but the continued belief that they can do it. In such an event they will get a lot more support from their American cousins."[75] Roosevelt was a unique combination of soaring idealism in purpose and stark cynicism in method.

Hans Dieckhoff, the German ambassador in Washington up to late 1938, recognized that Roosevelt had a "pathological hatred" of Hitler, and was "Hitler's most dangerous opponent." The President had persuaded the "credulous and mentally dull American people" that Germany was "America's enemy number one." The observant chargé Hans Thomsen headed the embassy after the withdrawal of Dieckhoff. Thomsen constantly warned the Wilhelmstrasse and the Reichsfuehrer himself that Roosevelt sought the "annihilation of Nazi Germany and the nullification of the New Order in Europe." Thomsen also predicted that Roosevelt would, in the event of war, try "creating the conditions for, and a skillful timing of, the entry into the war on their [Germany's enemies'] side." He cleverly foresaw that "Roosevelt will not neglect the possibility that as Supreme Commander of the Armed Forces he has the power to issue orders which in the course of their execution might lead to the creation of a state of war. In the face of this, Congress is powerless." Thomsen told Berlin that Roosevelt had a "pathological hatred" of Hitler and Mussolini, and even predicted that Roosevelt, in furtherance of his goals, might seek a third term as president.[76]

The duel between Roosevelt and Hitler would become increasingly elaborate, like a primeval war dance, until the two mortal enemies came to grips with each other.

———— ⚜ ————

"Mr. Roosevelt, You Perhaps Believe That Your Intervention . . . Can Be Effective Anywhere"

(Adolf Hitler responding to Franklin D. Roosevelt in the German Reichstag, April 28, 1939)

I

ON FEBRUARY 13, 1939, Senator Elbert Thomas of Utah (not to be confused with the silver-promoting Senator Elmer Thomas of Oklahoma) introduced a resolution that would authorize the President to impose an embargo on sales of all strategic items to belligerents, but would also enable him, with congressional approval, to waive the embargo in the case of states that were the victims of aggression. (The debate was largely symbolic, because European and Asian wars were not going to be won or lost on the basis of cash-paid arms sales by the United States.)

This amendment to existing legislation had great and distinguished support; most Americans saw the absurdity and injustice of the existing rules. The amendment was supported editorially by the *New York Times* and by a letter to that newspaper from former Republican secretary of state Henry L. Stimson. Yet Foreign Relations Committee chairman Key Pittman could not stir his committee to consider this or any proposal for revising neutrality legislation. Pittman was a woolly minded and ineffectual drunkard whom Roosevelt periodically bribed by raising the silver price or increasing purchases of silver from his home state of Nevada. He was not as strong as some of the Senate's militant isolationists, such as the rampant megalomaniac William Borah, who had been drinking his own bath-water about being the "Lion of Idaho" for years, or the pestilentially narrow-minded Gerald Nye.

Pittman did produce a proposal similar to Thomas's and advocated it on a nationwide radio broadcast on March 19. Borah responded at once, calling for the extension of an absolute embargo across all possibly relevant materiel. Nye dutifully introduced a conforming bill at once. Roosevelt quietly informed Pittman that he wanted to be rid of the Neutrality Act altogether and not to have it replaced. He added that the cash-and-carry provisions might work with European countries that had foreign exchange reserves and their own merchant ships, but would discriminate against China in its resistance to Japan. The chairman of the Senate Foreign Relations Committee hadn't thought of that. Matters remained where they stood, in a ludicrous time warp, steadily being bypassed by events.

In other respects, the 1939 congressional legislative session dealt fairly satisfactorily with the administration's modest program. The defense appropriation increases went through easily, as did some revisions of the Social Security Act that the government favored. The WPA funding fell short of what the White House requested and the Theater Project, believed to be infested with crypto-communists, was rejected, and this was deemed a setback for Roosevelt personally. Reform of the executive branch, which Roosevelt had been unsuccessfully pushing for two years, finally went through, albeit with a number of unwelcome amendments. The new departments of public works and welfare were not established and the Civil Service Commission was not replaced by a single civil service administrator as had been proposed, but the President was enabled to propose reorganizations, which he promptly and successfully did, consolidating dozens of agencies, bureaus, and commissions under the Bureau of the Budget, the Federal Security Agency, and the Federal Loan Agency.

A devastating amendment to this legislation was narrowly defeated on a second vote, on March 21, when Jim Farley and Steve Early implored Senator Harry Truman of Missouri to return from his home state to vote. Truman did so, flying all night through snowstorms and turbulence, making two unscheduled landings. Truman had been in Missouri supporting his original backer, Boss Tom Pendergast of Kansas City, who had been a big supporter of Roosevelt's, starting at the Madison Square Garden convention of 1924.

Pendergast had also supported Bennett Champ Clark, the other Missouri senator.* Clark was now one of Roosevelt's bitterest isolationist opponents, and Truman suspected the President or his followers of being behind the federal investigation of Pendergast's alleged voting and tax fraud.

Further, Truman had not received the patronage that he felt he should have.

---

* He was the son of the House Speaker who had so closely challenged Woodrow Wilson for the nomination in 1912.

He believed his loyalty had been taken for granted because he was a man of principle and that Clark was receiving inducements that did not succeed in changing his views or his votes, but shortchanged Truman. Truman arrived just a few minutes before the Senate vote, provided the margin of victory, and then telephoned Early at the White House. Harry Truman said: "Well, I'm here, and I damn near got killed getting here by airplane in time to vote, as I did on another occasion. I don't think the bill amounts to a tinker's damn, and I expect to be kicked in the ass just as I have in the past in return for my services." Early asked what Truman would like in return for his support. "I don't want a Goddamned thing. My vote is not for sale. I vote my convictions, just as I always have, but I think the President ought to have the decency to treat me like the Senator from Missouri and not like a Goddamned office boy, and you can tell him what I said. If he wants me to, I'll come down and tell him myself."[1]

The next day, Roosevelt did invite Truman to the White House and placated him by thanking him gratefully for his crucial help. He also impressed Truman with his knowledge of the intricacies of Kansas City machine politics. Roosevelt said that the investigators had his support because the Democratic Party in that city had to be "cleaned up," despite his liking for Pendergast personally. He explained that he was grateful to Pendergast but that if the Democrats became a Tammany-like machine in the big cities throughout the country, the national leadership—i e , Roosevelt—would lose authority, and the party would be discredited, would atrophy, and would become disreputable. He had taken away Tammany's patronage and immunity from prosecution, had humbled Frank Hague in New Jersey, and was not going to become either the creature or the protector of the bosses. Truman the municipal loyalist came face to face with Roosevelt the ruthless reforming pragmatist. This was a turning point in relations between Roosevelt and Truman, and may be taken as the beginning of the trajectory that led to Truman's eventual elevation to the vice presidency, from which office he succeeded Roosevelt as leader of the nation and served as one of its distinguished presidents.

In the long-running question of executive reorganization, as in the reform of the Supreme Court, so in revision of the neutrality laws, Roosevelt would prove indefatigably persevering. The Supreme Court had already come right. Justice Benjamin Cardozo had died in July 1938. It was generally known that Frankfurter was Roosevelt's indisputably qualified candidate as successor. Homer Cummings had argued against Frankfurter, as did some of the President's political advisors, because it was assumed that westerners would object to over-representation from the East. In the Court battle, Roosevelt had spoken against having two judges from the same state, and Frankfurter and Brandeis were both from Massachusetts.

What tipped the balance was a visit from a group of prominent Jews in the late autumn of 1938, including the publisher and principal proprietor of the *New York Times*, Arthur Hays Sulzberger. They urged Roosevelt not to appoint Frankfurter, because this might, in the post-Kristallnacht atmosphere, stir up anti-Semitism in

America by creating the impression of a Jewish entitlement to Supreme Court representation disproportionate to that community's numbers. Roosevelt claimed to have answered noncommittally, but Sulzberger reported that Roosevelt had declared: "I agree with you completely."

Certainly, Roosevelt was unimpressed. He had withdrawn his ambassador from Berlin, repudiated his ambassador in London, denounced the conduct of the German government in terms almost unheard of between countries not at war, and was little inclined to listen to such pusillanimous advice. Frankfurter, when informed of it, was disgusted.[2] Senator George Norris took up the championship of Frankfurter, which assured support from westerners, Roosevelt sent Frankfurter's name to the Judiciary committee on January 5, 1939, and he was confirmed easily, with Dean Acheson as his counsel at the Senate hearings.

There was an extensive and rather abrasive history to the relationship between Roosevelt and the Sulzbergers. The *New York Times* had endorsed Roosevelt in 1932 and 1936 but had attacked him violently over the Court-packing scheme and was generally rather critical. When Adolph S. Ochs, who had been the publisher and the proprietor from 1896 to 1935, and who led the *Times* from obscurity to great influence, died, Roosevelt expected that his estate taxes would end or loosen the Sulzbergers' control of the newspaper. (Arthur H. Sulzberger was Ochs's son-in-law.)

When Ochs died, the Times Company bought the nonvoting shares from the estate, enabling it to pay the death duties while canceling the equity and mitigating dilution to the Sulzbergers' ownership. The resulting debt was in the company and was paid down from operating profits. Mississippi senator Pat Harrison, a thoroughly unreliable source after Roosevelt put Alben Barkley in over Harrison as Senate Majority Leader, claimed to the Sulzbergers that Roosevelt had uttered anti-Semitic remarks about them after the death of Ochs. Seconded by Thomas Lamont and the ever-duplicitous Bernard Baruch, Harrison conveyed to the Sulzbergers that Roosevelt had called their estate planning "a dirty Jewish trick," and had pledged that "When Iphigene [Ochs's daughter and Arthur H. Sulzberger's wife] dies, we will get the *Times*." All of this is possible, but the reporters of the calumny are unreliable, Roosevelt was no anti-Semite, and it was incongruous for this issue to arise over Roosevelt's intended appointment of a second Jewish Supreme Court justice. Iphigene Sulzberger launched a successful peace overture to Roosevelt through Henry Morgenthau Sr.[3]

Justice Brandeis retired in February 1939. Roosevelt sent William O. Douglas's name to the Judiciary Committee on March 20, and he was confirmed without difficulty. Douglas was the forty-year-old Sterling Professor of Law at Yale University, on leave to be the third chairman of the Securities and Exchange Commission. He would serve on the Court with distinction, but not without controversy, through eight presidencies. The Court, with Black, Reed, Frankfurter, and Douglas, had already taken on a coloration agreeable to the President. (This trend would be reinforced in November 1939, when diehard judicial reactionary Pierce

Butler died and Roosevelt named Frank Murphy to replace him. Roosevelt thus named five judges to the high court in less than three years of his second term, having had no vacancies to fill on that bench in all of his first term.)

II

FROM FEBRUARY 18 TO March 3, 1939, Roosevelt was cruising on his favorite warship, U.S.S. *Houston*, in Caribbean waters. He observed a full battle fleet exercise. In January, he had ordered the Pacific Fleet through the Panama Canal and into the Atlantic to conduct an exercise in repelling a trans-Atlantic invasion. The *Houston* took part in the ending phase of the mock battle. This was part of FDR's general plan to break down the complacency of the isolationists and bring Europe's dangers closer to American opinion.

The Commander in Chief always found these activities invigorating. However, the British were alarmed at the aggressiveness of the Japanese, and in the secret back channel that the U.S. and British governments had opened up through the American naval attaché in London (from which, at Roosevelt's direction, Kennedy was excluded), the British expressed a concern that they might have to move part of the Royal Navy's battle fleet to Singapore. This alarmed the French, and Roosevelt, too, was uneasy at leaving the Japanese as the largest battle fleet in the Pacific. At the end of the exercise he ordered the Pacific Fleet back to San Diego, just as Halifax sent Roosevelt a message on April 11 requesting such a move.

Roosevelt treated Cordell Hull's traditional State Department sources with a certain amount of skepticism, if not disdain, but did receive a good deal of intelligence of varying quality from a variety of sources. William Bullitt sent him regular extracts from the findings of the French Deuxieme Bureau. The American ambassador in Warsaw, Anthony J. Drexel Biddle, sent along the findings of Polish intelligence, which contained intermittent insights of value. One of the State Department's German experts, George Messersmith, former consul general in Berlin and minister in Vienna, was in touch with the anti-Hitler opposition in Germany and pipelined what he picked up directly to the President.

The British were in the habit of sharing some intelligence, especially from the Far East, where the two countries clearly had virtually identical interests. Roosevelt also read the reports of American journalists in Europe and sometimes received special briefings from them. He heard a good deal from left-wing Latin American journalists preoccupied with German and Italian infiltration in South America, and there was the newsletter *The Week*, by Communist former London *Times* Washington correspondent Claud Cockburn. (Cockburn had accused Chamberlain of "turning all four cheeks" to Hitler.) When added to the voluminous production of orthodox channels, Roosevelt was unevenly informed, but not underinformed.

On the Ides of March, 1939, the bankruptcy of the Munich arrangements was starkly revealed. The ink was scarcely dry on Chamberlain's famous accord when the German government began agitating against alleged Czech mistreatment of the Slovaks. With the connivance of some Slovak dissidents, the Germans required all sorts of concessions to the Slovaks from the federal state of Czechoslovakia. Then they began again the drumfire of allegations of mistreatment of the German minority in the Czech part of the country. There were 50,000 ethnic Germans in Prague, and Hitler began loudly claiming that Prague had been a German city for a thousand years. Slovakia formally seceded from Czechoslovakia on March 14.

Beneš had retired after the Munich disaster and been replaced by Dr. Emil Hacha, a gentle, kindly, elderly academic. After repeated threats of dire and imminent military intervention, Hitler and his colleagues had reduced the Czech leadership to a state of helpless terror. Hacha was summoned to Berlin March 14. Because his train arrived an hour late, Hitler kept the old gentleman waiting until 1:15 A.M. on the 15th before seeing him. Hacha knew that a German invasion was already underway. In a pathetic effort at ingratiation, the Czechs had already made placatory gestures such as recognizing Franco's government.

Hacha formulated a little plea to Hitler, who was joined by Goering, Ribbentrop, Field Marshal Keitel (the cipher Hitler installed as chief of the German General Staff, although he privately disparaged his intelligence but considered him "loyal as a dog"),[4] the crack foreign ministry negotiator Ernst von Weizsacker (who did the work for the dim-witted and boorish stuffed[brown]shirt, von Ribbentrop), and some lesser officials.

Hitler gave one of his standard tirades, congratulating himself on his patience, which was now exhausted, reciting an endless sequence of spurious grievances, and screaming bloodcurdling threats at his gentle visitor. Hitler then dismissed Hacha and left Goering and von Ribbentrop to bully him. Goering regretted the terrible bombing that he was about to unleash on Prague, but it would be a salutary lesson to the British and the French. Hacha fainted, or suffered a mild coronary, and had to be revived by Hitler's quackish doctor, Theodor Morrell. Hacha telephoned Prague to say there should be no resistance.

But only after Goering and von Ribbentrop had chased him around the table for ninety minutes thrusting a pen into his hand did Hacha finally sign the instrument asking for German entry into the Czech homeland. He did so, it was clear to everyone, because the alternative was the complete "annihilation" of the Czechs, in Hitler's doubtless honest (for once) description. Hitler was so delighted that he erupted into his secretarial pool shortly after 4 A.M., kissed all the secretaries robustly, and disinterestedly told them that he was the greatest German in history.

Germany occupied Bohemia and Moravia in one day. And Hungary, with Hitler's blessing, occupied Ruthenia. A gruesome fate awaited the shamefully discarded Czechs. Roosevelt agreed, and Sumner Welles signed, without any consultation with Hull, whom Roosevelt feared would be too temperate, a statement denouncing "the temporary extinguishment of the liberties of a free and independent people. It is manifest that acts of wanton lawlessness and of arbitrary force are threatening world peace and the very structure of modern civilization."[5]

In contrast, Chamberlain's response was that because Slovakia had seceded the day before, Great Britain was not bound by the guarantee of Czechoslovakia that was part of the Munich agreement. Not even he tried to pretend that there was any validity to the request Hacha had been physically bullied into signing. This latest episode, however, was too much for all Chamberlain's accomplices. Sir Nevile Henderson telegraphed from Berlin that "the cynicism and immorality of the German action defied description," and suggested he be recalled.[6] Cadogan and even Halifax deserted, and Halifax warned the German ambassador, Herbert von Dirksen, in extremely strong terms when the ambassador had the effrontery to call to complain about rude comments that Duff Cooper had made about Hitler.

The Foreign Policy Committee of the British House of Commons now called for conscription, an all-party coalition government of national unity, and alliance with the Soviet Union. Halifax warned Chamberlain that without a serious change of course—which even the London *Times*, whose editor, Geoffrey Dawson, was a prominent member of the Anglo-German Friendship League, was calling for—the government would fall. British opinion had crossed the Rubicon and concluded that war was inevitable and was now the only honorable course. This was the view in the principal Dominions also (Canada and Australia), which would be furnishing large numbers of volunteers in any war. Chamberlain, without a hint of acknowledgement of his own error, effectively announced the end of appeasement in a speech (partly drafted by Halifax) in his home city of Birmingham marking his seventieth birthday on March 17. He reminded his listeners of Hitler's claim that he had had "no further territorial demands in Europe" and of his statement that "We want no Czechs!" Chamberlain claimed that his "heart [went] out in sympathy to the proud brave" Czechs.

Faced with the shambles of his policy, yet still devoted to peace, Chamberlain should have resigned at once, taking the rest of the appeasers with him, and ensured that Churchill, Eden, and Duff Copper were prominent in the new government. This would be the only way of having any deterrent power against Germany. Hitler regarded Chamberlain as a contemptible old weakling masquerading as a serious statesman.

Unfortunately, Chamberlain did not realize this, clung to his office and to his discredited advisors, and then, with Halifax, committed perhaps the most egregious blunder of all. Instead of seeking an alliance with the Soviet Union, which was probably still available and would have been (as it ultimately was) of great military, and probably deterrent, value, the British government judged Poland to be of more military use. The courage of the Poles was beyond question, but their government was a corrupt despotism, and it was a primitive country militarily and otherwise. The Poles themselves considered the U.S.S.R. a more dangerous threat to Poland than Germany was, and this step was a further invitation to Hitler and Stalin to cooperate with each other.

Munich was evil through naïveté. Embracing Poland after betraying Czechoslovakia while, through those two actions, being an uncomprehending cupid to Hitler and Stalin—probably the two most sinister and dangerous leaders in history—must rank as one of the greatest failures of British statesmanship of all time. On March 31, Chamberlain informed the House of Commons that Britain had given Poland a unilateral guarantee.

What was left of peace in Europe now rested on a hair trigger. Hitler, incited by the weakness and gullibility of his interlocutors at Munich, had become addicted to the process he had perfected of crushing small states. He would stalk them, single one out, terrorize it with threats and propaganda, and foment domestic unrest while accusing it of mistreating its local Germans (or Nazis in Austria's case, since the whole population was German-speaking). Next he would agree to accept sufficient concessions to break whatever will to resist remained, while separating the victim completely from any hope of assistance from the virtuous democracies that might have guaranteed it. Then he would brutally devour his prey, further terrorizing his neighbors and whetting his appetite for more.

What Hitler could not understand was that Chamberlain was no longer the personification of Britain, and that his guarantee of Poland, strategically insane though it was, was serious. He was right to question whether Chamberlain himself, if his bluff were called, would really want to go to war over such an onerous obligation, petulantly incurred. But having no grasp whatever of the nature of democracy, he had no notion that this sport of sadistically destroying smaller states with impunity was already over. He could not imagine that the next such initiative would lead to the most apocalyptic war in history, at the end of which much of the world, most of Europe, and almost all of Germany (and his own person) would be ashes. He had one more minor conquest: he seized the largely German Memel from Lithuania on March 23, after the usual forced agreement. Hitler personally arrived seasick on the pocket battleship (armored cruiser) *Deutschland* to lay claim to this latest and last uncontested aggrandizement. He never went to sea again.

III

P RESIDENT ROOSEVELT LEFT Washington on his special train for Warm Springs on March 29. The next day Franco's forces completed their occupation of Madrid and the horrible civil war in Spain was almost over. Approximately one million people died in it, and Spain would be effectively absent from the Western world for decades. Franco, though severe and totalitarian, would achieve considerable economic progress in his thirty-six-year reign, would zealously guard Spain's independence from his former sponsors, and would have a better record in sheltering persecuted Jews than, in Senator Nye's phrase, "the so-called democracies," including Franklin Roosevelt's America.*

Roosevelt lifted the arms embargo on April 1 and extended diplomatic recognition two days later. To assure discretion from Claude Bowers, his old friend and very anti-Franco ambassador to Madrid, Roosevelt had it insinuated that the State Department and not the president had been responsible for the neutral U.S. stance during the war, and hustled Bowers off to Chile as ambassador.[†]

Defeats for the Western democracies were coming in rapid sequence now. Mussolini, feeling left out, seized Albania on April 7. This tiny and primitive state was, in geopolitical terms, a worthless and thankless prize. Senator Borah, at least, was impressed. He exclaimed: "God, what a chance Hitler has! If he only moderates his religious and racial intolerance, he would take his place beside Charlemagne. He has taken Europe without firing a shot."[8]

While returning from Warm Springs, Roosevelt composed a letter he sent to Hitler on April 14, asking him to assure that he had no designs on thirty-one countries (putting Ireland together with Great Britain, to the irritation of Irish premier Eamon De Valera), and including several mandated and colonially governed territories (Palestine, Syria, Egypt). He read this first to a press conference and purported privately to believe that it would "put the dictators on the spot." (An identical letter was sent to Mussolini but by Hull, since the chief of state of Italy was not Mussolini but the king, Victor Emmanuel III. This was intended to be a snub to Mussolini. Relations had descended a long way since the "My Dear Duce" epistolary era.) Roosevelt publicly asked why nations could "find no better methods of realizing their destinies than those which were used by the Huns and Vandals fifteen hundred years ago."[9]

Roosevelt's plan was that the dictators would give a ten-to-twenty-five-year pledge not to attack any of these countries. When the pledges were received, Roosevelt would transmit them to the beneficiaries and organize a conference among all the countries not apparently targeted, with Germany and Italy, to discuss arms limitations and trade liberalization.

He promised that the United States would participate in these discussions and would facilitate substantive "political discussions" where appropriate; that is, where Hitler or Mussolini claimed some "boundary or territorial" grievance or other, the United States would set up but not participate in such political discussions. As always, Roosevelt was at pains to explain to his press conference that this did not constitute an attempt at mediation, only, as he said laboriously, interme-

---

* Finally, Franco would bequeath his country an enlightened monarch and a democracy, and Spain would know her greatest days since the destruction of the Spanish Armada in 1588. But there would be little hint of any of this in the cruel and vengeful repression of former enemies that now afflicted Spain.

† Not much that Bowers saw in Spain or Chile would have reminded him of his study of Jefferson and Hamilton that Roosevelt had reviewed in 1923 (chapter 4).[7]

diation; he was, he said, "the post office, the telegraph office." He sent this message after the absorption of four previously independent countries in the past three years (Abyssinia, Austria, Czechoslovakia, Albania).*

It was, of course, on its face, a mad proposal. The bad faith of the addressees had already been amply demonstrated and hardly needed to be proved again. It could not fail to appear disingenuous and naïve to Hitler and Mussolini. But the point of the letter to Hitler was not to deter, shame, or influence Hitler. Roosevelt said to Morgenthau that the chances that anything useful would come of his initiative were not more than one in five. He said the same to the Canadian prime minister, Mackenzie King, but added: "If we are turned down, the issue becomes clearer and public opinion in your country and mine will be helped."[10] This was the real point of the initiative.

Roosevelt judged that the dictators would ignore, or respond dishonestly, or respond insultingly, or some combination of these, to his message, and further clarify the issues between the democracies and the dictatorships. It also encouraged war-scared Europe to have an American president for the first time since Woodrow Wilson speaking with some moral authority to the world.

Mussolini sarcastically referred to "messiah-like messages" and described the letter as "absurd" but did not otherwise reply, since he would not deign to respond to Hull and had no standing to respond in the king of Italy's place to Roosevelt. Privately, but indiscreetly, he and Goering, who was visiting him, agreed that Roosevelt's polio seemed to be lodging in his brain, and they made fun of what they regarded as his deficient knowledge of geography. Hitler reacted much more forcefully. He saw an opportunity, as he thought, to reply to Roosevelt's provocations, including his imputation to Hitler the month before of lawlessness on a scale that threatened all civilization (after the Prague takeover). From Roosevelt's standpoint, Hitler took the bait (in both senses of the word).

Hitler ordered Ribbentrop to ask the governments named, except for France, Britain, Poland, Syria (which was a French-mandated territory at the time, following the Anglo-French division of the Ottoman Empire in 1919), and Russia whether those countries felt threatened and had authorized this inquiry on their behalf by the President of the United States. All responded in the negative, except Romania and Switzerland, which did not respond at all. All of the remain-

---

* The countries referred to for security guaranties were: "Finland, Estonia, Latvia, Lithuania, Sweden, Norway, Denmark, the Netherlands, Belgium, Great Britain and Ireland, France, Portugal, Spain, Switzerland, Liechtenstein, Luxembourg, Poland, Hungary, Rumania, Yugoslavia, Russia, Bulgaria, Greece, Turkey, Iraq, the Arabias, Syria, Palestine, Egypt, and Iran." Hitler did eventually completely overrun fourteen of the thirty-one named countries (three of which had already been occupied by the U.S.S.R. by German agreement), partially overran two others (Russia and Egypt), completely cowed two others (Bulgaria and Liechtenstein), aerially bombarded Great Britain, and was only prevented from invading it and several of the Middle Eastern countries by heroic British military resistance. And Stalin attacked Finland. So Roosevelt's curiosity was not unfounded.

ing, rather vulnerable countries were in an impossible position and Hitler's game merely illustrated Roosevelt's point. Publicly telling Hitler they felt threatened by him would make matters worse.

Roosevelt was aware of this German initiative and of the imminence of a response from Hitler when he attended the White House correspondents' dinner on April 15. William Allen White presided. As a progressive Republican, he knew and respected but was uneasy about Roosevelt's undoubted magic as a leader. White admired the President's "vast, impudent courage," and his "vivid but constructive imagination," and thought he was a wizard "working a weird spell on a changing world." He knew Roosevelt was far from infallible, but was reassured that "he didn't hesitate in a crisis, that he appeared to be brave, honest, and strong." Nor was he concerned about the charge that Roosevelt aspired to be a dictator: "He laughs too easily," said White; "he is too soft-hearted in many ways."[11]

Thomas Mann, living and touring in the United States and promoting the cause of aid to fugitives from the Nazis, attended the correspondents' dinner, and was impressed by the guest of honor: "Deeply moved by the sight of the genuinely admired President, who gave a brief address at about midnight; gracious and most appealing. His standing up energetically but with effort. His hobbling out, supported by the chief of the Secret Service right beside us. . . . Strong applause for Hull, who has a fine Anglo-Saxon head." Mann had already noted that of all the applause for foreign representatives, the greatest was for the Finn ("because [Finland's] war debts were paid up"), followed by China. Mann certainly recognized at the time that Roosevelt's letter to Hitler was: "A memorable document two-edged. A calculated move for reasons of domestic politics." Mann added: "The large handsome head, often graced with a charming smile, the mellifluous voice, and the total self-confidence captivated the editors. Even hostile observers were taken with the man's commanding personality."[12]

Hitler privately expressed reluctance to reply to a "communication from a creature so contemptible as the present President of the United States."[13] Yet he summoned the Reichstag, with Reichsmarschal Goering in the chair, to hear his internationally broadcast response to Roosevelt, April 28. Roosevelt's expectations of an intemperate reply were fulfilled. Hitler spoke for two hours. This address received the greatest audience of Hitler's career, hundreds of millions of people, including scores of millions in the United States alone.

Hitler opened with his predictable attack upon the Treaty of Versailles. He violently denied that he had any intention of attacking Poland, and then unilaterally revoked the Polish-German ten-year nonaggression pact, which he had promulgated in 1933. His reasoning for this was that in accepting Britain's guarantee, Poland was committing itself to potential belligerency against Germany — i.e., in the sole event of a German attack upon Poland. Hitler considered the assertion of the right of self-defense by a neighboring country to be an outrage.

In the same spirit, Hitler vacated the Anglo-German Naval Agreement of 1935, by which Chamberlain had set such store in his Munich communiqué. Hitler's reasoning was that Britain, by extending a guarantee to Poland, was now embarked on a policy of "encirclement" of Germany. (Germany was not a serious naval threat, other than potentially with submarines, so renouncing the 1935 Naval Agreement achieved nothing useful for Germany.)*

Every observer could see how fraudulent were the pretexts for these moves by Hitler. Hitler then launched into a long and virulent personal attack on Roosevelt. He mocked Roosevelt's having faith in conferences when the United States had declined to join the League of Nations (from which Hitler had withdrawn). Hitler jubilantly reported that none of the countries mentioned by Roosevelt in his "curious telegram" had indicated that it felt threatened by Germany or had authorized the American initiative. Hitler offered to give the assurances Roosevelt suggested if the states themselves expressed a wish for such a guarantee and made "appropriate proposals." He dismissed concerns about any German expansion in the Americas as "rank frauds and gross untruths" inspired by a "stupid imagination." (This was basically true, but the originating imagination was tactically sophisticated, because Roosevelt needed to conjure this threat to generate support for his armament program.)

Hitler concluded with a lengthy screed that was designed to humiliate Roosevelt in the eyes of the world, especially his own people, but that also expressed some of the fuehrer's paranoia and impotent rage at the condescensions, as he considered them to be, of this leader who was beyond Hitler's ability to intimidate or deter. "Mr. Roosevelt, I fully understand that the vastness of your nation and the immense wealth of your country allow you to feel responsible for the history of the whole world and the history of all nations. I, sir, am placed in a much more modest and smaller sphere." He then recited all his achievements in rescuing Germany from chaos, ignominy, disunity, the opprobrium and injustice of Versailles, and the economic depression, emphasizing his achievement in getting all of Germany's seven million unemployed back to work.

This was a sideswipe at the New Deal. Hitler had conscripted everyone to the military or to the armaments industry, thus ending unemployment. As has been recorded, American unemployment, with no such increased defense effort, was 40 percent down from 1933, and 70 percent down if the WPA and CCC programs were considered as employment rather than relief, and was now falling steadily by orthodox measurement. Roosevelt's record was very defensible, particularly in comparison with Hitler's.

"I have reestablished the historic unity of German living space and, Mr. Roosevelt, I have endeavored to attain all this without spilling blood and without bringing to my people and consequently to others, the misery of war. I, who 21

---

* This merely served to irritate the British. Germany had three "pocket battleships," two battle cruisers, and no aircraft carriers, and was building two large, fast battleships (*Bismarck* and *Tirpitz*); the British had three large battle cruisers, twelve battleships, seven aircraft carriers, and seven large, fast battleships, and five large aircraft carriers were under construction.

years ago was an unknown worker and soldier of my people, have attained this, Mr. Roosevelt, by my own energy. . . . You, Mr. President, stepped to the head of one of the largest and wealthiest states in the world." He enumerated various aspects of the bountiful resources of the United States in the most patronizing manner, and as if Roosevelt were unfamiliar with the geography of his own country. "Consequently, you perhaps believe that your intervention and action can be effective anywhere. . . . My world, Mr. Roosevelt, in which Providence has placed me . . . is limited to my people."

Hitler's address was certainly effective in stirring the pride of his own followers and adding to the discomfort of his neighbors. The Reichstag shrieked with laughter, led by the immense Goering, lolling and bouncing with mirth in the speaker's chair, especially as Hitler went through the list of countries in Roosevelt's message. Discriminating listeners could have noted the absence of Hitler's habitual diatribe on the evils of Communism and of the U.S.S.R.

Hitler also apparently pleased some of America's isolationist leaders, such as Senator Hiram Johnson, who wrote to a relative that Hitler had the better of the argument. Johnson, having been closely associated with Theodore Roosevelt and decisively helpful to Woodrow Wilson in 1916, should have known better than to give comfort to Hitler. Less surprising was Senator Gerald Nye's view that Roosevelt had invited "at least part of what [Hitler] said," and "that a reasonable approach to Germany by our government now would invite better understanding." Johnson's and Nye's were not representative views.[14] Most Americans considered that their president's message to Hitler was a "reasonable" inquiry and that Hitler's response was insulting, dishonest, and illustrative of the danger he posed to the peace of Europe.

It was fantastic, but demonstrated the obtuseness of the isolationists that a person in Nye's position could at this point, after Kristallnacht, the rape of Czechoslovakia, and the April 28 Reichstag speech, be asking that Hitler be treated reasonably. Roosevelt's message to Hitler did help establish his bona fides in the eyes of those moderate isolationist Americans who might otherwise be influenced by the ceaseless allegations of warmongering by Borah, Nye, Johnson, Wheeler, and their followers. Roosevelt had already begun to maneuver the militant isolationists into the position where he could tar them with the brush of being Nazi sympathizers. Lindbergh was too fanatical, Borah too egocentric, Nye too narrow-minded, and Hiram Johnson too unworldly to see this trap as the President opened, set, and baited it. Hitler apparently followed fairly carefully the neutrality debate in the United States and convinced himself that there were countervailing forces in the U.S. political system (of which he possessed no understanding whatever) that would contain Roosevelt, despite the warnings of Dieckhoff and Thomsen.

Roosevelt was not playing his constitutional trump cards of presidential authority over foreign affairs at all levels short of formal treaties, and as commander in chief. Garner and other supporters were urging him to use his foreign policy powers, but the President preferred to wait until matters were more urgent and he had more compatible people to deal with in the leading democracies.

Some European historians, especially those generally disposed to discount American statesmen as amateurish, agree with D.C. Watt's lamentation after the April 1939 exchange with Hitler: "It does not bode well for the peace of the world when the President of the United States allows himself to be maneuvered into appearing as an inept and ignorant fool."[15]

Some historians have concluded that Hitler decided on the basis of this exchange with Roosevelt in April 1939 that Roosevelt was as stupid and irresolute as Chamberlain and Daladier.

Most American historians would dissent from Watt and agree with Kenneth Davis's assessment that "Hitler's peroration was an exercise in ironic sarcasm whose heaviness and length seemed grossly excessive to most non-Germans." Hitler was exposed, as never before, in the newsreels and to the ears of the whole world, as mendacious and hypocritical and a dangerous bully to his neighbors. The polls in the United States did not indicate any loss of support for the President. The case cannot be seriously made that this exchange undermined "the peace of the world."[16]

Roosevelt considered the peace of the world to be virtually over, its end awaiting only Hitler's convenience. Roosevelt had to make as clear as possible the distinction between those acting in good will and the evil-doers. He had to separate the inadvertent dupes of Hitler in his own Congress from the majority of American opinion. He had to appear to his country a man of peace, without committing American strength abroad beyond his political authority or to a lost cause, which the failed policies of Chamberlain and Daladier evidently were.

He made useful progress toward the achievement of these objectives. Hitler undoubtedly thought he had done his great rival grievous damage. Roosevelt is not a sure guide, since he never admitted error and was never fazed by a setback, but he was quite satisfied with Hitler's response. To his entourage he expressed relief that his enemy had revealed his nature and ambitions so clearly. To an ever greater number of Americans, Franklin D. Roosevelt was becoming the indispensable president of peace through military and diplomatic strength. Events in Europe were now on an inexorable course. Hitler was already stalking Poland as his next victim. Conditions would certainly deteriorate until the appeasers were replaced and Roosevelt was conscripted by a grateful and apprehensive nation to retain his position. Only then could America play its rightful role in the whole world, and all things would become possible.

IV

IN THE LATE evening of April 17, 1939, the Soviet foreign minister, Maxim Litvinov, had summoned the British ambassador to Moscow and given him a proposal for a tripartite defensive pact between the U.S.S.R., Britain, and

France. Each would be obligated to go to war to support any of the others in case of attack and to defend Poland, Romania, and Greece (to whom the British had also extended their guarantee along with Poland), if any of them were attacked. The British government consulted the Poles and Romanians in a leisurely way, and gave a very tentative and unenthusiastic response on May 8. Stalin, identifying the Jewish Litvinov with what he by then considered the failed policy of approaching the British and French, fired Litvinov on May 3 and replaced him with V.M. Molotov, his stone-faced, almost robotic Old Bolshevist lackey.

Under pressure from the war minister, Leslie Hore-Belisha, who was also a Jew (a fact mentioned here only because of the German habit of imputing discreditable motives and excessive influence to Jewish officials), Great Britain adopted peacetime conscription for the first time in its history, on April 27, 1939. The British government's response to Litvinov's offer of alliance on May 8 was a proposal that the Russians rejected May 11 as unequal. The Russians would have to come more quickly to the assistance of the British and French in case of attack than the Western powers would come to the assistance of the Russians.

Molotov proposed instead a joint immediate mutual defense pact and a joint immediate guarantee of the Baltic and Balkan countries. Even at this late date, such a proposal contained great potential. But when Chamberlain sent a special envoy to Moscow to negotiate in mid-June, it was not Halifax, whom Molotov had invited, nor Eden, who would have been welcome, but the capable but lower-level William Strang.*

Strang, in his own memoirs, was quite pleased with his performance in Moscow, and the draft agreement handed over to the Russians on July 23, 1939, provided for the United Kingdom, the Soviet Union, and France to give "immediately all effective assistance" if any of them were attacked by any other European power, or if Turkey, Greece, Romania, Poland, Belgium, Estonia, Latvia, or Finland were attacked. Lithuania was regarded as a lost cause after Hitler had seized the Memel in March 1939. There was no contemplated protection for Denmark, Norway, the Netherlands, Slovakia, Hungary, or Yugoslavia. "All effective assistance" wasn't defined, either. It is little wonder that Hitler was able to make Stalin a more attractive offer.

Strang essentially defended the whole episode in his memoirs by feebly reminding his readers that the Allies won the war. If the delegation had been led by Halifax or Eden, had referred to war instead of "effective assistance," and had bound the Czechoslovaks (if it had been formulated in time), Romanians, and Yugoslavs (the Little Entente guaranteed, and abandoned, by France) as well as the Poles, something useful might have occurred.[18] This grouping of states, with

---

* Strang should have been sent to advise the chief of mission as he did in the German discussions, in which capacity he would have been valuable, but not to lead the delegation itself. This was a point Churchill made in his memoirs.[17]

whatever support Roosevelt could constitutionally have furnished, might have given Hitler pause, and would certainly have frightened Mussolini.

On April 30, 1939, Roosevelt opened the ambitious New York World's Fair. It contained a number of pleasant hints about the incorporation into daily life in advanced countries of undreamed-of conveniences. There was an intricately planned "Democracity" and General Motors's "Futurama," designed by theater stage designer Norman Bel Geddes. The President's opening remarks were carried on television for the first time, and viewed on grainy pictures on about 200 nine-inch television sets within about fifty miles of the fair site. The Court of Peace was imposing but incongruous. Germany, Spain, and China were absent; the Czech and Albanian flags flew at half-mast.

Roosevelt personally planned to the last detail the visit of the British king and queen to the United States in June. The visit apparently originated as a goodwill trip to Canada by the new monarchs after the rather jarring abdication of Edward VIII to marry the American divorcee Wallis Simpson, in 1936. The Canadian prime minister, W.L. Mackenzie King, had mentioned to Roosevelt the upcoming visit of the British monarch to Canada when Roosevelt visited Canada in August 1938. Roosevelt immediately realized the potential for a royal trip to the United States. He was seeking to raise the popularity in the United States of closer relations with a Britain resistant to Nazi Germany. Nothing could be done to make the inept British political leadership more popular, but Roosevelt thought the young monarch and his queen might perform a public relations coup in the United States.

He must have assumed that it wouldn't do him any political harm either, but he was probably more interested in receiving the king and queen for reasons tinged with snobbery. The correlation of forces between the British Empire and the United States had shifted, but the British king and emperor of India was probably still at the world's highest pinnacle in protocol terms, rivaled only by Roosevelt himself and perhaps by the pope. Roosevelt the descendant of Yankee merchants, Roosevelt the Hudson Valley squire, Roosevelt the politician disparaged by much of America's ostensible aristocracy for his reformist policies could not fail to find the potentialities for such a visit interesting, even piquant.

The British, too, leapt at the opportunity as soon as it was presented. Certainly King George VI and Queen Elizabeth possessed for all of North America the legendary mystique of the British crown, now making its first physical appearance there. How many battles had been fought in its name on that continent, which had produced the epochal schism in the English-speaking world? To anneal this schism, on the eve of gravely apprehended events in Europe, became for both sides the principal purpose of the visit. This would be the most important try at royal diplomacy since King Edward VII's 1903 visit to Paris to seal the Entente Cordiale.

Roosevelt worked out the itinerary and sent it with a personal letter to the king in January 1939. Roosevelt worked through Bullitt and the British ambassador in Paris, to Joseph Kennedy's great and intended irritation when he found out about it. The king and queen entered the United States at Niagara Falls at four o'clock in the afternoon of June 7, were greeted by Secretary of State and Mrs. Hull, and entrained for Washington. The President greeted them at Union Station on the 8th and conducted them to the British Embassy, where they hosted a large garden party on a beautiful but sweltering day. Later, they attended a state dinner at the White House, with after-dinner entertainment from Kate Smith, Marian Anderson, and Lawrence Tibbett. Harold Ickes grumbled to his diary that Roosevelt should have allowed him to air condition the White House as a WPA project in 1933.

Roosevelt's toast began: "In the life of a nation, as in that of an individual, there are occasions that stand out in high relief. Such an occasion is the present one, when the entire United States is welcoming on its soil the King and Queen of Great Britain, of our neighbor Canada, and of all the far-flung British Commonwealth of Nations. It is an occasion for festivities but it is also fitting that we give thanks for the bonds of friendship that link our two peoples."*

The following day, June 9, they went on the presidential yacht up the Potomac to George Washington's house at Mount Vernon, and on the return the king laid a wreath at the Tomb of the Unknown Soldier in the National Cemetery at Arlington, Virginia. The principals traveled to New York on June 10, briefly visited the World's Fair, and then motored up the Hudson to Hyde Park. Their trip from New York to Hyde Park took two hours longer than had been expected because of the huge and enthusiastic crowds that lined the route.

After an informal family dinner at Springwood, the king and the President sat up amiably conversing until 1:30 A.M., when, as was amply publicized, Roosevelt patted the king's knee and said: "Young man, it's time for you to go to bed." The occasion to indulge in avuncularism with the holder of that office would have been deeply gratifying to Roosevelt for several reasons. Not the least would have been Roosevelt's admiration, as one who had mastered disability himself, for a man who had had to work for decades to overcome a speech impediment and had faced up courageously to the exercise of an office he did not seek or want.

The king afterwards appreciatively said: "The President is so easy to get to know and never makes one feel shy." Roosevelt and the king discussed strategic matters quite revealingly. Both thought war was now imminent, though the king, unlike Roosevelt, still thought it might be possible to avoid it. Roosevelt made it clear that

* Roosevelt couldn't bring himself to refer to the Empire, or to the king's status as an emperor, because he disapproved of colonial empires, though not at all of voluntary associations of sovereign countries such as the Commonwealth.

the United States would do what it could to be helpful, and even held out the possibility of it entering the war if London were bombed. The king wrote up extensive notes of the conversation. Roosevelt's comments may even have begun the decline in the king's faith in Chamberlain, though the prime minister retained the monarch's general confidence for another eleven months. The following day, George VI, as supreme governor of the Church of England, accompanied the President and his family to the little St. James Episcopal Church at Hyde Park, where the Roosevelts' minister from Campobello also helped officiate.

They then went on a picnic at Top Cottage, which Roosevelt had designed himself as a retirement hideaway and which was not entirely completed. Many years later Queen Elizabeth told the author that her most frightening experience in the whole period leading up to and during the Second World War was the ride to the picnic. "President Roosevelt drove us in his car that was adapted to his use, requiring great dexterity with his hands. Motorcycle police cleared the road ahead of us but the President pointed out sights, waved his cigarette holder about, turned the wheel, and operated the accelerator and the brake all with his hands. He was conversing more than watching the road and drove at great speed. There were several times when I thought we would go right off the road and tumble down the hills. It was very frightening, but quite exhilarating. It was a relief to get to the picnic."

The king and queen made a great and very positive impression on American opinion. They were not physically imposing people as Franklin D. Roosevelt was, but were regal, gracious, and pleasant looking. The king was rather handsome and the queen quite pretty. There was not a hint of British stiffness, much less condescension. Millions of Americans realized for the first time how close their country really was to Great Britain, especially in a world where strident dictators applying brute force in domestic and international affairs were so prevalent.

The President drove them to the little Hyde Park railway station on the evening of June 11. The crowd, including the chiefs of state of Britain and the United States, sang "Auld Lang Syne," and the whole nation identified with the President when he waved from his car and called out: "Good luck to you! All the luck in the world!"[19] Eleven weeks later, Britain was at war.

V

ONE FINAL EFFORT was made in peacetime to adjust the neutrality legislation that inconvenienced Roosevelt and emboldened Hitler to think that the U.S. president was something of a paper tiger. Sol Bloom, chairman of the House Foreign Relations Committee, had asked to be able to launch an initiative in the House, where the isolationists were not as strong as they were in the Senate. He was a sheet music salesman and real estate developer, a nine-term congressman, and a refreshing, exuberant, somewhat bumptious urban Jewish politician of no particular expertise to chair the committee he did, a position that had come to him entirely through seniority. Speaker Bankhead and Majority Leader Rayburn warned the President that it would be a hard slog, but Roosevelt determined that the international situation was so desperate that the effort had to be made, and promised all-out support from the White House.

The time for studious ambivalence was over. Bloom presented his bill on May 29, 1939. It had been largely written by the State Department and constituted an outright repeal of the Neutrality Act, retaining only cash-and-carry and war zone exclusion provisions of the earlier legislation. Bloom got it through his committee eleven to nine on June 6, and on the floor of the House it was managed by a more diplomatic congressional proceduralist, Luther Johnson of Texas. Johnson and Bloom steered it through immense obstructionist efforts by the isolationists, the most obstreperous being Roosevelt's own congressman at Hyde Park, Hamilton Fish. Fish, on a recount of a vote on another isolationist amendment, secured passage of the amendment by two votes, many administration supporters having left after voting on a show of hands. The President's supporters were unable to remove the amendment, which embargoed arms and ammunition but not items of mixed military and civilian use such as airplanes. One of those voting for the amendment was Eleanor's friend Congresswoman Caroline O'Day of New York, to whom Roosevelt sent a reproachful letter. He wrote: "Our embassies abroad tell us . . . the antiwar nations believe that a definite stimulus has been given Hitler by the vote of the House, and that if war breaks out in Europe . . . an important part of the responsibility will rest on last night's action."[20]

Roosevelt asked the attorney general, Frank Murphy, on July 1 for a report on the extent of his constitutional "duty and obligation to conduct foreign affairs." The Bloom bill, as amended, went to Pittman's committee in the Senate. Even with the usual gesture to Pittman at important moments, an increase in the official price of silver, Pittman was unable to get the bill reported favorably out of his committee, the swing vote being cast by the disgruntled purge survivor Walter George.

In a final effort to pass the bill, damaged though it was by the amendment Fish had sneaked in, Roosevelt had a group of prominent senators to the White House on the evening of July 18 for a convivial session of persuasion. He laid on all the vote-getting allure he had. Drinks all around began proceedings. Present were Borah, Charles McNary of Oregon (the Republican minority leader and a reasonable man whom Roosevelt liked), Atlanticist Republican Warren Austin of Vermont, Majority Leader Barkley, Pittman, Vice President Garner, and Hull.

Roosevelt said that it would be appropriate to open the discussion with a prayer, so great were the implications of what was afoot, though he did not actually offer one. He spoke for an hour with intense eloquence on how America should not be left handcuffed with evil governments apparently about to unleash war on virtuous countries. He handed over to Hull, always popular with the Congress. Hull spoke with great and sincere solemnity. Roosevelt said that the peace of the world was menaced by the views of Nye.

Borah pompously announced that Nye was not alone and that there would be no war in Europe. Borah had an abrasive exchange with Hull about intelligence sources, and Garner canvassed the senators. Only Austin, of the Republicans, spoke strongly for ridding the country of "this impossible Act." Garner concluded: "Well, Captain, we might as well face the facts. You haven't got the votes and that's all there is to it." The intellectual strategic retardation of the leading Republicans is hard to credit in the light of subsequent events. Herbert Hoover continued to proclaim that Nazi Germany could not possibly threaten the United States. He maintained this fatuous position until he finally died in 1964.[21]

As always, Roosevelt's game was complicated. He did not believe that anything the U.S. Congress did would deter or influence Hitler. But he was confident war was about to break out, and was hoping to be able to hang the responsibility for it squarely around the necks of the isolationists. Polls continued to show that two-thirds of Americans favored aid to the Western Allies in the event of war. If Roosevelt had really thought Borah, Nye, Hiram Johnson, and their ilk were destroying the peace of the world, he would have gone to the country with a campaign for support of his policy.

Berle, an isolationist, thought there was a "war party" rising in the administration, led by Ickes, who was constantly writing and giving pro-British, anti-Nazi speeches. Berle, innocent academic as he was, had no idea until many years later how assiduously Roosevelt was encouraging this movement. Roosevelt was already envisioning an alliance in which the United States would take over some of the British bases in the Caribbean. The reciprocal exchanges of naval intelligence had been occurring regularly since they were organized by Roosevelt with the British in January 1938, and were becoming steadily more comprehensive. It was a start to a remarkably complete intelligence exchange that would continue almost uninterruptedly into the next century.

In June 1939, Roosevelt summoned outgoing British ambassador Lindsay and proposed that in the event of war the United States would declare 500 miles of the Western Atlantic a neutral zone. For this purpose, he wanted to lease British air and naval bases in the West Indies and Bermuda. Though astounded at the cavalier manner in which Roosevelt proposed to lease bases from one belligerent to restrict the activities of another belligerent in a purported act of neutrality, Lindsay strongly recommended a positive response to the President's proposal.

Instead, the Foreign Office came back with legalistic pettifogging, internally describing the idea as "hardly within the realm of practical politics."[22] Lindsay presented these legalisms to Roosevelt on July 8, and the President was irritated by what appeared to be a misunderstanding both of his motives and of the "practical politics" of the international climate then sliding toward general war. He persisted, however, convinced that when it came, war would enable him to destroy the credibility of his isolationist opponents in the Congress and strengthen his hand as the conqueror of the Depression, the custodian of peace, and the champion of deterrence and of all aid short of war to the combatant democracies.

By mid-August, discreet navy missions were leasing facilities from Pan American Airways and private individuals in Trinidad, St. Lucia, and Bermuda. Roosevelt was progressively throwing off the shackles of the neutrality legislation.[23]

Hitler had already begun his standard terror campaign against his designated next victim. He was loudly complaining about mistreatment of German minorities in Poland, and was demanding referenda in parts of Poland, the restoration to Germany of the Free City of Danzig (governed by the League of Nations), roads across the Polish Corridor to East Prussia, the annexation of most of Silesia, and other unspecified considerations. He was by now as militant with the Poles as he had been, in their turn, with the Austrians and the Czechs. He did not believe that Chamberlain and Daladier were capable of standing up to him, and couldn't imagine that those who caved in at Munich would actually go to war on the impetuous British guarantee of Poland. Roosevelt was a good deal more worried about another capitulation by the British and the French than he was about a war he now regarded as not only inevitable but even necessary.

The very mention of Roosevelt's name now drove Hitler to paroxysms of rage. Goering dreamed audibly about developing bombers that could attack New York. A press campaign was unleashed in the late spring of 1939 in Germany representing Roosevelt as a Jewish Mason.* Ambassador Dieckhoff had warned Berlin often that "in the next war, it will not be two and a half years before the United States enters; it will be much shorter, much less." Dieckhoff portrayed Roosevelt as "a peculiarly dominating personality" who would bear "a great, if not a decisive, part of the responsibility for the outbreak of the war and the prolongation of the war."[24] Hitler discounted the prospects of American intervention because, he said, "these Jewish Democrats never have shown any determination and will never sacrifice their mammon." Hitler did blame Roosevelt for "opposing economic negotiations between the Reich and the states of South America."[25]

Roosevelt left Washington immediately after the adjournment of Congress, on August 5, went to Hyde Park for a few days, and then departed from New York harbor on a sister of the *Houston*, U.S.S. *Tuscaloosa*, on a cruise to northern waters. The morning of his departure he received a very alarmed call from Bullitt in Paris and checked with Sumner Welles whether it was sensible for him to leave at all. Welles told him he should have two weeks in which to take a holiday. The *Tuscaloosa* stopped briefly at Campobello (which he was never to see again), and proceeded north along the Nova Scotia coast. Welles sent frequent messages summarizing the diplomatic news.

On August 17 Welles reported that the U.S. ambassador in Moscow had cabled that the German ambassador had called upon Molotov and expressed a willingness to have substantive discussions on territorial and other matters and that Molotov had responded that his government would welcome such discussions.

---

* He was indeed a 32nd-degree Mason, having joined the Holland Lodge, Number 8, on February 28, 1911, at Hyde Park.

Roosevelt had already been concerned that Chamberlain would succeed in producing the grand alliance of Hitler and Stalin. Two of his former ambassadors in Moscow, Bullitt and Davies (now mercifully demoted to Brussels), had repeatedly warned that if the British did not pursue discussions vigorously, Russia and Germany could quickly make a pact. Roosevelt did what he could to discourage such a rapprochement by cabling Stalin in August that Hitler was certain to attack Russia once he had conquered France.[26] There wasn't much more Roosevelt could do at this point than warn the dictators and try to encourage the democracies. He was right in both cases but successful with neither.

On August 21 Welles reported that Bullitt's sources estimated that war could begin in the next four or five days and suggested that the President return to Washington. Informed later in the day that Ribbentrop was about to fly to Moscow, Roosevelt ordered *Tuscaloosa* to return to Sandy Hook, New Jersey, where he disembarked and boarded his train for the return to Washington on the evening of August 24.

As he arrived, a ten-year nonaggression pact between Germany and the Soviet Union had just been signed. Stalin toasted Hitler, and Ribbentrop responded with a toast to Stalin at the celebratory dinner.* Germany was now constantly threatening war against Poland. Roosevelt sent messages to Hitler, the king of Italy, and the president of Poland on the evening of August 24 urging avoidance of war, under no illusions that anything useful would result.

———————

At 2:50 A.M., on Friday, September 1, 1939, Franklin D. Roosevelt was awakened when the White House duty officer authorized the switchboard to put through to his bedside an emergency call from Ambassador Bullitt in Paris. Drexel Biddle, the ambassador in Warsaw, had telephoned him, having failed to get through to Washington. The German Army had invaded Poland and the German Air Force had bombed Warsaw. Roosevelt replied to Bullitt: "It's come at last. God help us all."[27]

Roosevelt telephoned Hull, Woodring, Welles, and several others. Messages to Germany, Poland, Great Britain, France, and Italy requesting that they refrain from bombing civilians were sent before any declaration of war had been made. General George C. Marshall, who would be officially installed as chief of staff of the United States Army in a few hours, put all U.S. military forces on war alert. Having aroused his principal subalterns, Roosevelt, showing the iron nerves that never deserted him, went back to sleep for several hours until awakened again by Bullitt at 6:30 A.M. and told that Daladier had just said that France would honor her commitment to Poland and was about to serve an ultimatum on Germany. Roosevelt thanked him for the information and again went effortlessly back to sleep.

* Hitler had Stalin's cigarette air-brushed out of the official German photograph as inappropriate to "a historic agreement between two great nations."

After about three-quarters of an hour, however, night gave way to morning, when a despondent Ambassador Joseph Kennedy called. Kennedy, at the urging of the incorrigible Sir Horace Wilson, with Chamberlain evidently in the background, had been urging Hull and Roosevelt through the last week to put pressure on the Poles to make concessions to Germany. Roosevelt and Hull had flatly refused to do so. Chamberlain had given the insane guarantee to Poland and had straight-armed Stalin, encouraging the Nazi-Soviet Pact. By sheer accident and the force of the British public's sense of national honor, Chamberlain was going to be forced to fight, probably with no greater success than will.

But Roosevelt knew that if British determination were engaged, the military consequences would be formidable, at least eventually. On the morning of September 1, Kennedy foresaw the imminent "end of the world, the end of everything." The following evening, in the weekly White House poker game, Ickes convulsed the President and his other cronies when he deadpanned that Chamberlain had taken Kennedy into his government.[28]

Roosevelt, much more sanguine, and distinctly undismayed at the implosion of the bubble that had been inflated by the Anglo-French appeasers and the American isolationists, tried to invigorate the bedraggled spirits of his ambassador in London. Kennedy subsequently alleged that Britain and France would not have gone to war over Poland without Roosevelt's "constant needling."[29] There is some documentary evidence for this charge. Hull shortly instructed Kennedy not to propose or countenance any end to hostilities that would "make possible the survival of a regime of force and of aggression." (That is, the United States wished the destruction of Nazi Germany.) This message was sent on September 11 while Roosevelt was still piously speaking publicly of neutrality in deed, though certainly not in undisguised preference.

It was an extremely sophisticated and deadly game in which Roosevelt was now well engaged: making placatory proposals to Hitler about arbitration to portray him as vividly as possible as the aggressor, refusing to urge concessions on Poland, encouraging the British and French to stand firm, promising his own citizens he would keep them out of war by propping up the British and French, and discrediting the isolationists as fear-mongers and (for the most part) inadvertent Nazi agents. War greatly enhanced his third-term reelection prospects, but he said nothing of this, wishing neither to become a lame duck on his way out of office nor to launch a presidential campaign prematurely.

His long battle with the isolationists was finally turning in his favor. By late August, polls indicated that those supporting arms sales to Britain and France had risen from 31 percent to 50 percent. (Another poll, however, still had 66 percent of Americans opposing any arms sales to belligerents. The situation was fluid, but flowing Roosevelt's way.)[30] Formerly isolationist congressman John W. Boehme of Indiana sent Roosevelt a telegram on August 30 that he had now been persuaded of the correctness of the President's proposed modifications of neutrality policy.

Roosevelt was chipper at his regular press conference in midmorning on September 1, and was amused when one of the journalists asked if anyone had awakened Senator Borah. The voluble isolationist had gone to Poland Spring, Maine. This intelligence was transmitted to Roosevelt indistinctly and he was briefly emboldened to hope that Borah had gone to Poland: "That would have been news." The President authorized direct quotation of his cautious answer to the question of whether the United States could stay out of the war: "I not only sincerely hope so, but I believe we can. . . . Every effort will be made by the administration so to do."[31]

Roosevelt had told departing Ambassador Lindsay on August 26 that he would delay imposition of the Neutrality Act for a few days to facilitate purchase and removal by the British and French of any war supplies they wanted. He also exhibited "impish glee" in describing how he would delay the departure of German ships but not Allied ones. The President himself had ordered a leisurely search of the great German liner *Bremen* in New York to ensure that there was no contraband aboard that could permit the ship to be transformed at sea into a commerce raider. (Roosevelt had returned from his last trip to Europe on the *Bremen* in 1931.)

There was no comparable harassment of the even greater (Allied) superliners *Normandie* and *Queen Mary*. The *Bremen* did eventually sail when Roosevelt assumed the British would be able to capture or sink her, but she eluded the Royal Navy and sailed to Murmansk, and eventually to Bremerhaven.*

Roosevelt received the new British ambassador, Lord Lothian, who wrote to Halifax on August 31: "There is certainly nothing neutral about the President's personal attitude toward the conflict."[32] Mussolini offered to mediate between Germany and Poland, a suggestion that Roosevelt and other informed observers immediately recognized as the Duce's ducking out on his treaty obligations under the Pact of Steel with Hitler (who hardly had need of him in an assault upon Poland anyway). Chamberlain gave every indication of waffling on his commitment as he twice delayed addressing the House of Commons, and finally gave a rather self-pitying speech on Saturday evening, September 2. The deputy leader of the Labour Party, Arthur Greenwood, with no preparation, rose to reply. As he did so, Conservative traditionalist Leo Amery shouted: "Speak for England, Arthur!" This exhortation enjoyed such instant and universal currency that Robert Boothby, like Amery a flamboyant Churchill supporter, claimed to have uttered it.

Greenwood gave a brief but stirring speech that much better captured the mood of the House and the country than had Chamberlain's pathetic maunderings. "I wonder how long we are prepared to vacillate . . . when Britain and all Britain stands for, and human civilization, are in peril."[33] A thunderous and prolonged ovation greeted Greenwood's remarks, and the government reconvened

---

* The successful flight from the British blockade was unsuccessful in the end, however, because a cabin boy, angry at a box on the ear, set fire to the ship in 1941 and she burned to a wreck.

in another cabinet meeting later in the evening. Pursuant to this meeting, an ulti-matum was issued to Germany at 8 A.M. on Sunday, September 3, requiring assur-ance within three hours that Germany was prepared to begin withdrawing from Poland at once, or Britain would declare war on Germany.

At 11:15 A.M., a tired and dispirited Chamberlain came on the radio and a few hours later addressed Parliament, in each case focusing more on his own disap-pointment than the fact of war. "I have to tell you now that no such assurance has been received [from Germany] and that consequently this country is at war with Germany" were the words with which the world learned that World War II had begun. He clearly described the "bad faith" of the "bad men" that "we will be fighting against." To Parliament he said: "Everything I have worked for, everything I have hoped for, everything I have believed in in my public life has crashed in ruins." In the circumstances, this wasn't really relevant and wasn't an uplifting toc-sin on which to send his people into war. He had gambled, and he had lost.

More hopefully, from Roosevelt's perspective, Chamberlain brought Winston Churchill into the government and the war cabinet after ten years in the back benches, as first lord of the admiralty, in charge of the Royal Navy, Britain's sen-ior service and the position he had held at the outbreak of the First World War. Finally, an advocate of vigorous prosecution of a just war against the unmitigated evil of Nazism was close to the direction of events in Whitehall, hedged about though he was by Chamberlain, Halifax, Sir John Simon, Sir Samuel Hoare, Wilson, and lesser appeasers.

France declared war on Germany a few hours after Britain. The energetic but mercurial Bullitt appeared now to be exerting a considerable influence on Dal-adier, who consulted him on all manner of subjects, generally took the ambas-sador's advice, and even wished to buy a house next to him.[34]

Roosevelt gave a Fireside Chat on the war on the evening of September 3. He recounted the efforts he and his administration had made to avoid war, asserted that "no American has the moral right to profiteer" from the war, and concluded: "This nation will remain a neutral nation, but I can not ask that every American remain neutral in thought as well. Even a neutral has a right to take account of facts. . . . I hope the United States will keep out of this war. I believe that it will. And I give you assurance and reassurance that every effort of your government will be directed toward that end."

This was a considerable evolution from Wilson's unctuous advice to be neu-tral in thought twenty-five years before. And Germany was much more clearly responsible for the outbreak of this war than it had been in 1914.

Roosevelt opened what would be one of history's most important correspon-dences, with Winston Churchill, on September 11, 1939. Twenty years earlier, they had had an unsuccessful meeting that Churchill did not remember, and Churchill had sent Roosevelt, via his son James, a copy of the first volume of his life of his illustrious ancestor the Duke of Marlborough, on October 8, 1933. The inscription, prompted by Churchill's support of the early New Deal, the suspension of the gold standard, and the abolition of Prohibition, was: "To Franklin D. Roosevelt from Winston S. Churchill, With earnest best wishes for the success of the greatest crusade in modern times."

Roosevelt apparently did not respond to the gift then, but did so six years later, on September 11, 1939, when he sent this letter, building to the maximum plausible degree on a very slender previous acquaintance:

> "My dear Churchill,
> "It is because you and I occupied similar positions in the World War that I want you to know how glad I am that you are back again in the Admiralty. Your problems are, I realize, complicated by new factors, but the essential is not very different. What I want you and the Prime Minister to know is that I shall at all times welcome it if you will keep me in touch personally with anything you want me to know about. You can always send sealed letters through your pouch or my pouch.
> "I am glad you did the Marlborough volumes before this thing started— and I much enjoyed reading them.
>
> "With my sincere regards,
Faithfully yours,
Franklin D. Roosevelt"

After speaking with Chamberlain, Churchill responded positively by telephone, and what became an immense correspondence began, initially on very precise intelligence matters. Roosevelt also wrote to Chamberlain, saying: "We shall repeal the arms embargo within the next month." Chamberlain thanked the President for his "sympathetic and encouraging" words.[35]

VI

Roosevelt summoned the Congress to extraordinary session September 21. He was finally going to launch an all-out frontal assault on his isolationist enemies and the Neutrality Act. The President addressed the Congress and the nation that day. He described his problem to William Allen White as being "to get the American people to think of conceivable consequences without scaring the American people into thinking that they are going to be dragged into war."[36] Aid to Britain and France had to be seen to make American participation in war less, rather than more, likely.

To counteract the Republican isolationists, Roosevelt recruited the 1936 candidates of that party, Alfred Landon and Colonel Frank Knox, as well as former secretary of state Henry Stimson, as public advocates of repeal of the Neutrality Act. James B. Conant, of Harvard, and Karl Compton, president of the Massachusetts Institute of Technology, set up a committee to raise support for the President's proposals among the academic community.

William Allen White co-chaired (with the national director of the League of Nations Association, Clark M. Eichelberger) the Non-Partisan Committee for Peace through Revision of the Neutrality Act.* Colonel McCormick's cousin, Captain Joseph Patterson, even brought his *New York Daily News* out in favor of Roosevelt's position on this issue, in apparent deference to the swinging polls, and in unusual disagreement with his cousin and co-owner.

Roosevelt's opponents saw his juggernaut coming and tried to respond with preemptive strikes. Senator Borah spoke over nationwide radio on September 14, but was not the volcanic force he had once been. His voice had lost its strength and he was clearly failing. His credibility had been severely damaged by his mad predictions of continued peace right up to the German invasion of Poland. He used the phrase "imperialist war" in his remarks, in reference to the British and French. This was hardly sustainable: Chamberlain and Daladier could be accused of almost anything except imperialism. Frank Knox followed immediately with a statement and editorial (in his *Chicago Daily News*) severely debunking Borah. Father Coughlin raved and carped as always and still had a sizeable, though reduced, listening audience. But he was thoroughly discredited beyond a thin echelon of susceptible Catholic blue-collar rednecks. More dangerous was the nationally broadcast address of Colonel Charles A. Lindbergh the night after Borah's speech, September 15.

Roosevelt apparently considered muzzling Lindbergh, as he could have done, since the colonel had returned to be a serving officer, but he rejected that as politically dangerous. Lindbergh's friends allege that Roosevelt tried to bribe him with the new position of secretary for air and simultaneously threaten him with a tax audit. Roosevelt was not above either tactic, but each would normally have been more professionally executed than was alleged in this case. It was claimed that Roosevelt's offer and threat were passed to Secretary of War Woodring to General Arnold to Lindbergh's friend Truman Smith. It is not clear that this happened, though the Roosevelt biographer Frank Freidel believed it did, and thought Arnold's views similar to Lindbergh's.[37] Arnold was an isolationist but not a Nazi sympathizer, and he was a loyal officer and not a renegade.

Lindbergh had a huge radio audience when he spoke from the Carlton Hotel in Washington on the evening of September 15. "In times of great emergency, men of the same belief must gather together for mutual counsel and action," he ceremoniously began, and claimed to speak for all those Americans who did not want the United States in the war. "These wars in Europe are not wars in which our civilization is defending itself against some Asiatic intruder. There is no

---

* Among those who joined were Charles Lindbergh's mother-in-law, Mrs. Dwight L. Morrow; Mayor La Guardia, of New York; Henry R. Luce, proprietor of *Time, Life,* and *Fortune* magazines; the theologian Reinhold Niebuhr; the film actors Helen Hayes and Melvyn Douglas; the cultural historian Lewis Mumford; former secretary of state Henry Stimson; and rising young Democrats Paul Douglas, J. William Fulbright, and Adlai E. Stevenson.

Genghis Khan or Xerxes marching against our Western civilization. This is not a question of banding together to defend the white race against foreign invasion. This is simply one more of those age-old struggles within our own family of nations—a quarrel arising from the errors of the last war—from the failure of the victors of that war to follow a consistent policy of fairness or force." He argued against allowing "our sentiment, our pity, our personal feelings of sympathy to obscure the issue." The "issue" was for the United States to "carry on Western civilization" by staying out of war.

Lindbergh denied any qualitative difference between the Nazis and the Western democracies. In asserting that Hitler was not a "Xerxes" and was morally indistinguishable from Chamberlain and Daladier, unimpressive though they were as exemplars of democratic leadership, he committed a disastrous tactical (as well as factual) error. Roosevelt had been eyeing him warily since the fiasco over airmail routes in 1933. Now Roosevelt saw the opportunity to dispense with this dangerous opponent whom he had long considered a Fascist sympathizer.

Public reaction came in to the White House in scores of thousands of letters, telegrams, and telephone messages. There was an overwhelming barrage of criticism of Lindbergh for giving what amounted to a pro-Nazi and overtly racist speech. This was a particularly inept miscue as the sadistic crushing of Polish resistance by the Nazi war machine, replete with news photographs of Jewish families, including young children, being herded out of their homes at gunpoint, unfolded in the newspapers and newsreels of America every day. Lindbergh was also a front for a very disreputable coalition. Pursuant to the Nazi-Soviet Pact, the American far left came to public rallies with the Deutsch-Amerika Bund and other Fascist organizations, making it easier for Roosevelt and the other moderate leaders of both major parties to take aim in one motion against all the extremists of right and left. This was further facilitated a few days later when the secret clauses of the Nazi-Soviet Pact became operative and the Soviet Union stabbed stricken Poland in the back and seized the eastern third of the country, as well as Latvia, Lithuania, and Estonia.

Roosevelt and his advisors—Cohen, Corcoran, Rosenman, Berle, and Hull—worked right up to the deadline on the President's address to the Congress on September 21. The President entered the Capitol grimly and said at the outset of his remarks: "Proceed on the assumption that every member of the Congress and the executive is equally and without reservation in favor of such measures as will protect the neutrality, the safety and the integrity of our country and at the same time keep us out of war. . . . Let no group assume the exclusive label of the 'peace bloc.' We all belong to it." This was another tactical masterpiece; it reduced the isolationists to making completely implausible charges against the administration.

Roosevelt expressed regret that the Neutrality Act of 1935 had been passed by the Congress and signed by him. He chided those who had opposed his efforts to amend or repeal that act earlier in 1939. He declared that the repeal of the act would restore international law as it properly was. He proposed retention of authority to bar American ships and citizens from war zones or require them to enter such zones at their own risk; to bar American citizens from the vessels of belligerents; to require cash-and-carry purchases of American exports by belligerents; and to prohibit war credits to belligerents. He asked the leaders of the two major parties in both houses of the Congress to remain in Washington until the Congress would normally meet in January 1940, so that he could keep them informed and work with them on any contingencies that might arise.

Roosevelt sounded, as Lindbergh had, a note of preserving Western civilization in the Americas. He indulged himself in his happy idyll that the Latin American states were functioning democracies. The fact that most of them were corrupt despotisms run by overdecorated juntas lining their own pockets and blaming everything on the gringos (the United States) seems rarely to have penetrated Roosevelt's public thoughts, though he was well aware of the true political condition of his "sister republics."

The White House was inundated with messages of support. Roosevelt had decisively defeated Lindbergh in the second round of their long dispute. Polls now indicated that 60 percent of Americans supported repeal of the Neutrality Act, and 84 percent favored an Allied victory in the war, against only 2 percent in favor of a German victory (although about 15 percent of Americans could claim German ancestry).[38] On September 28, Pittman was finally able to move the bill out of his committee with a sixteen-to-seven majority for passage. A prolonged and strenuous debate ensued.

The fading Borah spoke October 2, denying that repeal of the Neutrality Act would restore traditional international law. His remarks had little impact. (He would die on January 19, 1940, aged seventy-four.) Stimson informed Hull October 3 of his intention to say in a nationwide broadcast October 5 that repeal was required to assist the democracies against Hitler. Hull was horrified and asked him to put it more subtly. Stimson refused and gave his speech as he had intended. The fact of favoring the democracies over the Nazis was popular in the United States, and the same theme was taken up in a network broadcast by William Allen White in mid-October. Substantial defections were now peeling off the isolationist-pacifist bloc in both houses of Congress. Senator Robert A. Taft of Ohio, an isolationist and a systematic opponent of the President, announced his intention to vote for repeal to assist the democracies against the totalitarian aggressor.

Many Republican businessmen, some of whom expected increased profits from repeal, joined in support of the President, who maintained a discreet silence as the debate raged in Congress and in the media. Roosevelt even deferred a proposed private visit from the British governor general of Canada, Lord Tweedsmuir (the famous novelist John Buchan). Roosevelt was concerned at media interpretation of such a visit until the long-sought legislative change was secured.

On the evening of October 2, Bishop Bernard Sheil of Chicago delivered a radio speech that had largely been written by Tom Corcoran for the President's strongest ally in the Roman Catholic episcopate, the archbishop of Chicago, Cardinal Mundelein. The cardinal had died that morning and would be sorely missed by the President, but the speech given by Sheil on his behalf had considerable impact in Catholic circles. This degree of official Roman Catholic support would have been hard to arrange if Roosevelt had seriously helped the Republicans in the Spanish Civil War. In domestic terms at least, the President's premeditated irresolution over the Spanish War had been politically justified.*

Landon muddied the waters in asking Roosevelt to remove politics from the debate by declaring that he would not be a candidate for reelection in 1940. This was the beginning of what became known to political caricaturists and commentators as the era of Roosevelt as sphinx. (At the Gridiron dinner of the Washington press corps in December 1939, an FDR-faced papier-mâché sphinx eight feet tall and with a long cigarette holder rising from its mouth was the centerpiece of one of the skits. This motif was taken up by cartoonists and was popular with the President, who obtained the Gridiron sphinx for his official library.) The President did not otherwise reply and forbade anyone in his party or administration to respond at all. The subject became the great and overarching question mark of American politics right up to the Democratic nominating convention in July 1940.

Lindbergh gave a second network radio address on October 13, 1939, but attracted a smaller audience and made an even more unfavorable impression than on September 15. He claimed that the war was about the balance of power in Europe and had nothing to do with democracy. "Our bond with Europe is a bond of race and not political ideology. . . . Racial strength is vital—politics is a luxury. If the white race is ever seriously threatened, it may then be time for us to take our part for its protection."

In an article in *Reader's Digest* in November 1939, Lindbergh was more explicit, clearly implying that he favored a Hitler victory as "the strong voice" to defend the white race from the unsalubrious and sinister forces of Asia and Africa—as the "Western Wall of race and arms which can hold back either a Genghis Khan or the infiltration of inferior blood." (Lindbergh did not try to explain the Nazi-Soviet Pact.) This confirmed Roosevelt in his view that Lindbergh was hoping, as were Kennedy, the Duke of Windsor, and other appeasers, for a negotiated peace now that Poland had been crushed and there was no longer an ally for the British and French to claim to defend. Britain and France had scarcely loosed a single war-like act against Germany.

The public battle between Roosevelt and Lindbergh would continue for

---

* So had been the President's deluge of official attention on Mundelein. When the cardinal made a legatory visit to Italy in November 1938, an American naval squadron saluted his arrival at Naples and the U.S. ambassador's private train brought him to Rome, where he had private meetings with Ciano.[39]

another two years, but it was already an unequal contest. Roosevelt routinely referred to Lindbergh in private as a Nazi. Lindbergh was also a malignant proto-type of the opinionated celebrity, a type that would become increasingly familiar in American life: entertainers or sports personalities or cultural figures trying to translate their talent or celebrity in their own fields into positions of political influence, more often than not for the propagation of sophomoric, fatuous, or even seditious views. Roosevelt subjected him to wiretaps, seeking evidence of Nazi connections, but no direct links came to light.[40]

The debate on repeal of the Neutrality Act dragged on through October as the administration poured on the pressure discreetly. Finally, on November 3, Franklin D. Roosevelt won one of the most agreeable of his many victories in Congress. The Senate repealed by a vote of 63 to 30, the House of Representa-tives by 243 to 172. Chamberlain again wrote graciously to Roosevelt "a private line of thanks and congratulations" for America's practical support and "pro-found moral encouragement."[41]

This victory yet contained certain inconveniences. The requirement for other countries to haul away their own cargoes ("cash-and-carry," in Baruch's phrase) and the banning of American shipping from war zones, which Roosevelt defined as almost all of the Atlantic, took American ships off the seas and assisted the Ger-man blockade of Britain "as if all our ships had been torpedoed." In a sense, Kaiser Wilhelm had won, and the isolationists did promote the idea that U.S. intervention in World War I had been prompted by the shadowy but ubiquitous war profiteers.[42]

The President constantly encouraged creative thinking about stretching the revised neutrality rules. He personally favored a proposal from the U.S. Maritime Commission to reflag U.S. merchant ships as Panamanian, without changing their ownership, which would enable them to evade the cash-and-carry provi-sions. William Allen White and Senator Harry Truman both thought this exces-sively devious, though they were very pro-Allied and anti-Nazi. Roosevelt accordingly had this suggestion withdrawn but approved the sale of a number of American merchant ships to British, French, and Belgian buyers.

The United States and Great Britain early worked out a system in which the British inspected U.S. ships before they left American ports and issued them cer-tifications against searches on the high seas. This measure did reduce the volume of incidents that occurred, but there were many irritating episodes of American ships being stopped, shepherded into ports where it was contrary to the revised legislation for them to go, and held there for days or weeks while mail was opened and censored. The State Department protested as little as possible, but Roosevelt eventually wrote Churchill (February 1, 1940) that "the net benefit to your people and France [of detaining and searching these American ships] is hardly worth the definite annoyance caused to us."[43]

The incompetent Polish leaders hadn't mobilized until August 31. Kraków fell September 5. All organized resistance ceased by September 23, though besieged Warsaw held on gallantly until September 27. The 600,000 soldiers in the under-equipped Polish army fought bravely against the 1.2 million superbly equipped Germans, who had an air superiority of seven to one. When the 700,000-man Russian army intervened, they met little resistance. (Yet Chamberlain and Halifax had believed Poland to be a more formidable military power than the Soviet Union.)

With the Soviet occupation of Latvia, Lithuania, and Estonia in the month of September 1939, four more independent countries vanished, in accordance with the Nazi-Soviet Pact. These were added to Abyssinia, Austria, Czechoslovakia, and Albania, which had been trampled down or absorbed between 1935 and 1939. Thirteen million Poles were now in the Soviet Union; 22 million were in Germany, which now comprised over 100 million people, about 15 million more than France and Great Britain combined.

Hitler spoke at the Kroll Opera House, which he generally preferred as a venue to the Reichstag, on October 6, 1939, and made the most conciliatory speech he had uttered since Munich, almost exactly a year before. He expressed the world's need for good relations between Germany and Great Britain, and congratulated himself for not even mentioning Alsace and Lorraine. Since Poland had been eliminated and the chief remaining iniquity of Versailles dealt with, there was no reason for continued war between Germany and Britain and France. "Why should this war in the west be fought?" he asked rhetorically, and there was no shortage of people in London and Paris asking themselves the same question. Hitler preferred the resolution of the "real problems"—armaments, colonies, and the "Jewish problem"—in a conference of Germany, Italy, the U.S.S.R., Great Britain, and France, "after the most thorough preparation." He warned of dire consequences should Churchill and his supporters prevail.

Chamberlain replied in the House of Commons, rejecting Hitler's overture as coming from someone who was untrustworthy and had said nothing about redressing the iniquities inflicted on the Czechs and Poles. Hitler's suggestions were "vague and uncertain." This was quite robust for Chamberlain, but neither the British nor the French were doing anything that indicated they were conducting a war. There was a naval blockade and a slightly accelerated buildup of arms and trained men, but nothing else. This phase was called in the participating countries "the Phony War," "la drole de guerre," and "the sitzkrieg."

There was a slackening in the activities of surface raiders and submarines and there had been, contrary to expectations, no aerial bombardment of the cities of the main combatants, only the hapless Poles. In September 1939, German submarines had sunk an old British aircraft carrier, the *Courageous*, and one old battleship, the *Royal Oak*, when an ingenious U-boat captain penetrated the defenses of the home base of the Royal Navy, at Scapa Flow.

On October 11, Roosevelt's favorite scientist, Dr. Alexander Sachs, had delivered and read aloud to the President a letter from Dr. Albert Einstein, then at Princeton University, another from Dr. Leo Szilard, and an accompanying memo from Sachs himself, simply explaining the significance of the possibilities, destructive and otherwise, of nuclear fission. There was particular reference to the dangers of Germany's developing this potential before the West did. A presidential advisory committee on uranium was established inside the Bureau of Standards. Szilard and Dr. Edward Teller met with it on October 21, but they were greeted with skepticism by their rather pedestrian interlocutors. Roosevelt eventually set up a National Defense Research Committee, which subsumed the uranium advisory committee. The President himself kept a distant eye on this subject but did not really give it much attention until 1941.

VII

SHORTLY AFTER THE Polish carve-up and the Soviet seizure of Latvia, Lithuania, and Estonia, Russia demanded from Finland cessions of the Karelian Peninsula adequate to take Leningrad, the country's historic Romanov capital and second city, out of range of possible artillery fire from Finland. Finland, wary of resisting a German-allied Russia, especially after the fiery demise of Poland, agreed to these terms but not to the additional demand of the lease for thirty years to the Soviet Navy of the port of Hango, at the mouth of the Gulf of Finland. Stalin then raised a mighty propaganda campaign against Finland, a contemptible imitation of Hitler's tactics against the Czechs and the Poles. The Finns held their ground, and the effect was to propel American opinion further toward support of Roosevelt's position of assisting the democracies.

Discussions between Finland and the the Soviet Union broke down November 13, 1939, when the Finns refused to withdraw forces from their border areas unless the Russians did also. Stalin, grossly overconfident and assuming that there would be extensive Finnish defections to a puppet Communist Finnish "government" he had set up on the border, attacked Finland on November 28. He was unpleasantly surprised, as the Finns fought with great courage and ingenuity. It was immediately obvious that the Russian forces were not well trained and were committed with no serious military plan. The Finns, who were well adapted to winter conditions, appeared suddenly out of the northern mists on skis and descended with great effect on the lumbering Russian invaders.

The British and the French, who had responded so sluggishly to comparable outrages perpetrated by the Germans and Italians (though in the case of the Germans, better-executed outrages), became extremely self-righteous and militant. The League of Nations expelled the Soviet Union as "unworthy" of membership on December 14. (Of the Great Powers, only Britain and France now remained, since Germany, Italy, and Japan had all resigned from the League, which the United States had never joined.) The British cabinet lengthily debated a proposal of Churchill's to seize the Norwegian port of Narvik, interdicting the supply of

Scandinavian iron ore and steel to Germany, and advance across Norway and Sweden to assist the Finns against the Russians. Daladier was violently determined to send French forces, which had not fired a shot against their neighboring German opponents, to engage the Russians in Finland. His failure to get approval of this scheme caused the collapse of his government and his replacement by the much more determined and courageous Paul Reynaud, on March 1, 1940.

It was providentially fortunate that Churchill's and Daladier's plans were not implemented. Invading the territory of two neutral states would have muddied the waters on the otherwise clear-cut moral advantage the Allies enjoyed over Germany. By the time any Allied forces could have got to Finland, Stalin had reinforced his units and put them under the command of his most talented generals, Semyon K. Timoshenko and Georgi K. Zhukov (the latter one of the four or five greatest commanders of World War II, of any nationality).

If the Russians hadn't promptly and decisively defeated the Allied expeditionary units that Churchill and Daladier wanted to dispatch, the Germans would have been more than happy to do so, and would almost certainly have intervened against the procession inland from Narvik. Such an action would probably have led to the Soviet Union's joining Germany in war against Britain and France, with incalculably disastrous results. India would have been isolated and the Middle East would almost certainly have been overrun (with the Jews in Palestine delivered over to the genocidal mercies of the Nazis). The pressure on Britain would have been much greater than it actually became before Hitler and Stalin fell out. Finally, the Finnish enterprise would have been such a fiasco that Churchill could not possibly have been elevated to the premiership and emerged as the mighty war leader he became. On such slender threads did civilization hang as 1939 gave way to 1940.

Roosevelt issued the customary ineffectual requests to the aggressor state and on December 1, 1939, expressed "profound shock" over Soviet air and naval bombardment of Finland. He halted the sale of aluminum and molybdenum to the Soviet Union, but had a much greater concern than Churchill or Daladier did about pushing Stalin even further into cooperation with Hitler. The Finns were much commended in the United States as the only World War I debtor that had faithfully paid down its debt. Roosevelt remitted their $235,000 autumn 1939 interest payment and offered them a $10 million credit. He politely declined the request of the Finnish ambassador for substantially more for military purposes. He did ask the congressional leaders on January 16, 1940, to allow the RFC and Export-Import Bank to advance Finland generous credits for non-military purposes. This wasn't a great priority, and the congressional leaders dithered about it until after the Russo-Finnish war had ended.

As always in strategic matters, Roosevelt was absolutely ruthless, as tangibly unsympathetic to the Finns as to the Jewish refugees and the Spanish Republicans and even, in some respects, the black American victims of segregation, though personally he was touched by the fate of all of these. Roosevelt privately referred to the "dreadful rape of Finland" and publicly accused Stalin of "a wanton disregard for law." But apart from a trivial credit for nonmilitary purchases and a resuscitation of his Abyssininan War drivel about a "moral embargo," he didn't actually do anything.

What Hitler in particular failed to distinguish was the difference between Roosevelt's relative inactivity due to the tactical concern not to make Stalin a permanent ally of Hitler, and a reluctance to take hard measures in the national interest, the malaise that afflicted and almost paralyzed Chamberlain. Nothing would distract Roosevelt from strategic priorities, because the fate of all civilization, not just relatively small pockets of victims, was now at stake. Finland would lose territory to the Soviet Union. But Western relations with Russia were preserved, to the irreplaceable profit of the West when the war took turns that Roosevelt sensed but that could not be foreseen exactly.

Roosevelt hoped that the splendid Finnish resistance and Russian caution about completely antagonizing the West and becoming dependent on Hitler would impose some moderation on Stalin, and that he would not try to devour all of Finland. After losing two whole divisions to the Finns and their talent for winter ambush, Stalin pulled back on the Finnish front in mid-January 1940.

Timoshenko and Zhukov regrouped, strengthened the Karelian army, and launched a massive offensive on February 11, beginning with one of the greatest artillery barrages in history. The Finnish positions were breached, and the Finns asked for an armistice on March 11, having lost 25,000 dead in the ranks of their army—one-tenth of their eligible manpower, though barely a tenth of Russian losses. They had fought magnificently and given the Russians a bloody nose, but they couldn't go on. Stalin imposed more severe terms than originally, demanding the cession of 16,000 square miles, including rich nickel mines and the port of Petsamo, and took the thirty-year lease on Hango.

The British had avenged the loss of the battleship *Royal Oak* at Scapa Flow in September with the Battle of the River Plate, December 13, 1939. The pocket battleship *Admiral Graf Spee*, a little over 10,000 tons and with eleven-inch (barrel-diameter) guns in two triple turrets, was discovered in the sea lanes of the south Atlantic by two British light cruisers and one heavy cruiser. The British captains startled the German adversary with their aggressiveness, and the German vessel was significantly damaged. The British heavy cruiser was incapacitated and the others were shot up but still functional. *Graf Spee* sailed into Montevideo, Uruguay.

The United States joined the British and French in insisting on strict neutrality. British intelligence went to work on the local press and convinced gullible or cooperative journalists and other sources that British battleships were now just offshore. The *Graf Spee* would have been promptly dispatched to the bottom by any British capital ship, since they were all more heavily armored and carried six to nine fifteen-inch or sixteen-inch guns. None was, in fact, within hundreds of miles. However, under orders from Hitler, and before a crowd of over half a million on Montevideo's waterfront, including a broadcaster addressing a worldwide listening audience, the *Graf Spee* inched out of harbor and then was scuttled in a spectacular series of self-detonated explosions. Two days later the German captain committed suicide. It was a humiliating defeat for the Germans.

Roosevelt had caused an inter-American conference to adopt generous definitions of territorial waters (in accord with British wishes), which both the British and Germans had violated by conducting a naval battle almost into the roadstead at Montevideo. Formal but very tepid protests were lodged. Churchill sent an appreciative Roosevelt a detailed account of the battle on Christmas Day, 1939.

VIII

Roosevelt's annual message to the Congress, on January 3, 1940, continued the President's high-wire act on the war. "I can understand the feelings of those who warn the nation that they will never again consent to the sending of American youth to fight on the soil of Europe. But, as I remember, nobody has asked them to consent—for nobody expects such an undertaking." He invited his countrymen to reflect on the fact, without telling them exactly what to conclude from it, that "it becomes clearer and clearer that the future world will be a shabby and dangerous place to live in—yes, even for Americans to live in—if it is ruled by force in the hands of a few."

His only legislative requests were for renewal of the Trade Agreements Act, which was expiring in June, and a substantial increase in defense expenditures. The reciprocal trade act, after unexpectedly vigorous debate, was passed in April. The defense request, $1.8 billion, with increases largely paid for by reductions in the public works and relief budgets, was stalled in Congress when overwhelmed by events in Europe. The administration request was then almost doubled, and in the changed circumstances passed easily.

Roosevelt had foreseen this possibility, and when Marriner Eccles, the Federal Reserve chairman, told him that the unemployed were not adequately taken care of, he replied that European events would take care of the unemployed by leading to the expansion and rearming of the U.S. military. These were the initial points of Roosevelt's grand strategy, and he correctly intuited that events would swiftly do his work for him.*

On February 10, 1940, the American Youth Congress came to the White House at Eleanor Roosevelt's invitation, and the President addressed 4,500 young people from the south portico as they stood, huddled and shivering at midday on

---

* In its fatuity, the House of Representatives appropriations committee initially cut General Marshall's request, reducing the army's number of new aircraft from 166 to 58. (This does not count thousands of new aircraft for the Army Air Corps.)

the lawn. This was essentially a Communist front organization, which Eleanor, in her imperishable naïveté, had defended from the allegations of Martin Dies and his House Un-American Activities Committee. The American Youth Congress had faithfully followed instructions from Moscow following the Nazi-Soviet Pact and accused the British, French, and Finns of conducting an imperialist war. Elements of the Youth Congress criticized the administration for building national military preparedness rather than social and relief programs.

Roosevelt's speech was broadcast to the nation. He urged the young people not to "pass resolutions that you haven't thought through." Roosevelt described a resolution passed at a recent AYC meeting that granting aid to Finland was an "attempt to force America into the imperialistic war" against the Soviet Union as "unadulterated twaddle." The young Communists and fellow travelers, to Eleanor's horror, perhaps bemused by the difficulty of the concept of adulterating twaddle, booed the President. He ignored them, other than to imply clearly that they were the robots of Soviet Communist masters, and stated that the "Soviet Union, as everybody who has the courage to face the facts knows, is run by a dictatorship as absolute as any other dictatorship in the world." It had allied itself with another dictatorship and attacked an "infinitesimally small" neighbor of no possible danger, "which seeks only to live in peace as a democracy, and a liberal, forward-looking democracy at that."[44]

The meeting was politically useful to Roosevelt, which is presumably why he allowed the misguided and unmannerly group through the White House gates: it helped to shut up those who were still accusing him of being cozy with the international Left. Their brickbats made a fine counterpoint to Hitler's sarcastic disparagements of April 1939.

On June 3, in the midst of a monumental crisis in the European war, Eleanor brought fifty of these young people back to the White House. Roosevelt met them with courtesy and good humor for three hours, and won Eleanor's admiration, at least, for the patience and rigor of his answers to their questions. It was a more satisfactory meeting than the February encounter. Though many of the youthful questioners were wordy and somewhat strident, they were impressed by Roosevelt's grasp of the issues and were shaken by his concentrated charm.

On February 9, Roosevelt had announced that Undersecretary of State Sumner Welles would visit the principal Western European capitals on a fact-finding mission. When asked if Welles would be empowered to give Roosevelt's or the U.S. government's views on a peace settlement, the President responded: "There you go. Now do not get didactic." Roosevelt had rejected the idea of visiting Russia while it was attacking Finland, and estimated to Welles the chances of his tour's producing a positive result at about one in a thousand. Chamberlain wrote to Roosevelt in early February that the Welles mission was a "potential embarrassment," because it might incite more agitation for a negotiated peace.

Welles arrived in Rome on February 23. He had an extensive session with Mussolini's foreign minister and son-in-law, Count Ciano, who expressed "contempt and hatred" for Ribbentrop and an "underlying antagonism" for Hitler. They then, in company with Roosevelt's friend Ambassador Phillips, met with Mussolini. Welles was shocked by the Duce's flabby and demoralized appearance, though his host perked up when Ciano read a handwritten letter from Roosevelt.* Mussolini evinced intense dislike of the French and British but thought there was a chance of a negotiated peace.

Welles entrained for Berlin, where he was subjected to a two-hour farrago of "misinformation and deliberate lies" by Ribbentrop, delivered with immense "pomposity and absurdity of manner." He had a more rational interview with Hitler on March 2. The fuehrer proclaimed his desire for peace with Britain but professed to be convinced that Britain was determined to destroy Germany. It was almost a Wilhelmine allegation that Britain (and to a lesser extent, France) could not tolerate a strong Germany. Welles also met with Hess and Goering and concluded that there was little chance of movement, other than if Germany were convinced that the United States would join the war to help the British and the French. It was clear that Mussolini had no influence in Berlin whatever.

Welles found Paris very discouraging; anti-Semitism abounded, and the army, cooped up in the Maginot Line, was alleged to be dispirited. London was better, and Chamberlain and Halifax were now quite strenuously anti-Hitler. Morale generally seemed much stronger than in Paris. Welles returned to Rome and found Mussolini much more energetic and nimble than two weeks before. He departed Naples for the United States March 20.[45]

Roosevelt addressed the nation March 16, and squelched reports that he was aiming, through Sumner Welles, to promote a peace that would recognize the ill-gotten gains already made by the dictators. He said: "Today we seek a moral basis for peace. . . . It cannot be a real peace if the fruit of it is oppression, or starvation, or cruelty, or human life dominated by armed camps." It is still not completely clear what Roosevelt was intending to do by sending Welles to Europe, other than enabling him to reinforce his own standing as a man of peace and to be able to claim indiscernible insights into world affairs during the upcoming political campaign.[46]

Hitler knew the United States could be dangerous if France were intact and Russia not reliably attached to Germany, but he was satisfied that Roosevelt couldn't begin seriously arming Germany's opponents for at least a year, that he still had problems with the Congress, and that a third term would not be won easily, even for so successful a master of America's incomprehensible politics. In order to encourage the isolationists, Hitler had given a "very strict order . . . not to do anything or say anything against the United States of America."[47] He wanted to give Roosevelt as little opportunity as possible to turn a European war into a

---

* Welles himself had trouble reading Roosevelt's handwriting, despite a friendship of forty years.

world war, and hoped to have a less antagonistic American leader to deal with in less than a year.

In furtherance of this ambition, the German government produced a "white book" based on captured documents of the Polish foreign ministry. This clearly revealed Drexel Biddle's and Bullitt's activities in 1938 and 1939 to create an "anti-aggressor front" against Germany. Roosevelt had to field questions from the press about the propriety of Bullitt's conduct. The energetic ambassador bailed his chief and himself out by procuring a letter from Daladier, now war minister in Paul Reynaud's new government, stating that over the past two years, "Ambassador Bullitt always said to me that in the case of a European conflict, France should make her decisions knowing that . . . the United States of America would not enter the war."

Roosevelt cabled Bullitt that he was "very much pleased with Daladier's letter of April 4." Roosevelt's domestic opponents, though more suspicious than ever of the President's true intentions, were not prepared to mount an attack upon him based on documents edited and published by Nazi Germany and stolen from the brutally conquered Poles.[48] They rightly judged that Roosevelt's riposte could be eviscerating.

By the time Daladier's words were applied to the domestic controversy in the United States, Germany had overrun Denmark. German soldiers emerged from the holds of merchant ships in Copenhagen harbor and seized the Danish capital. Hitler regarded the formality of declarations of war against harmless and defenseless countries as degenerate bourgeois humbug. There was no real resistance, and a ninth independent country vanished under the hobnailed jackboots of the dictators. The Germans surged on into Norway.

On April 3, the British cabinet, after having been badgered unmercifully for weeks by Churchill, approved his plan for mining the sea routes between Norway, Sweden, and Germany and for Anglo-French landings at Narvik and a number of other Norwegian ports (Stavenger, Bergen, and Trondheim), to stop the supply of Scandinavian steel and iron ore to Germany and forestall a German occupation of Norway, which British intelligence believed was imminent. Despite Churchill's efforts, the British government dithered, concerned about Norway's neutrality and the thought of doing anything energetic. This did not inhibit Chamberlain from telling a partisan Conservative audience on the evening of April 5 that Hitler had "missed the bus." This rivals "peace in our time" as the most unfortunate of all Chamberlain's ill-considered public utterances.

In one of their most impressive military performances to date, the Germans struck at dawn on April 9, landing all along the Norwegian coast from Oslo to Narvik. They managed to effect these landings despite the supremacy of the Royal Navy and its presence near several of the points where the Germans landed. The British Admiralty became concerned about German local air superiority and the vulnerability of the Royal Navy to too heavy an uncontested assault from the Luftwaffe. Even at that, the diminutive German surface fleet lost four cruisers and about a dozen destroyers, including eight sunk by the venerable British battleship *Warspite*, which pursued them up Narvik fjord and sunk them at point-blank range, like shooting fish in a barrel.

These naval successes did not disguise the fiasco of the Allies' on-again, off-again military expedition in Norway; troops were landed but shortly had to be withdrawn. A tenth independent state thus disappeared in four years, assisted in this case by a handful of Norwegian Nazis, including a former Norwegian cabinet minister whose name would become infamous: Vidkun Quisling.

IX

I N LONDON, THE Conservative benches were now extremely restless. It was obvious that the Phony War was ending. A debate on the conduct of the war followed by a confidence motion was set down for May 7 to 10, 1940.

Chamberlain and Halifax, overconfident to the end, hadn't expected the debate "to amount to much." At the prime minister's request, Churchill loyally closed for the government and defended Neville Chamberlain against his critics, who were almost as noisy, though not as numerous, as had been his idolators among the same members of Parliament eighteen months earlier, after Munich. Halifax was shocked at the extent of the animosity to the prime minister, who responded to taunts and jeers with another catastrophic oratorical misjudgment. He pointed out that "I have my friends in the House," which was scarcely the response necessary to rally the regime's remaining supporters in the midst of a historic world crisis.

The debate was eloquent, heartfelt, and vicious in places. World War I hero Sir Roger Keyes appeared in his uniform as a much-decorated admiral of the fleet to denounce the Narvik shambles. Leo Amery quoted Cromwell in his dismissal of the Rump Parliament: "You have sat too long here for any good you have been doing. Depart, I say, and let us have done with you. In the name of God go!" Chamberlain offered Amery his choice between chancellor of the exchequer and foreign secretary, prepared to put even Halifax over the side in these now suddenly desperate circumstances, but Amery would not be bought.

Lloyd George, former wartime prime minister and dean of the House after fifty-two years in Parliament, sarcastically called upon Chamberlain to follow his own call for sacrifice by sacrificing his office. The division revealed the defection of too many Conservative M.P.s for Chamberlain to continue, though the government won by a margin that would have been adequate in peacetime; forty-one government M.P.s voted against their leader and fifty abstained.

The opposition Labour and Liberal parties would not join a national government under Chamberlain's leadership. Halifax, presumably unaware that his own position was about to be "hawked around to safeguard Chamberlain's political future," had met just before the debate started with the prominent Labour politician Herbert Morrison and offered to dismiss Hoare (home secretary), Sir John Simon (chancellor of the exchequer), and Kingsley Wood (lord privy seal), in exchange for Labour's joining Chamberlain's government. Morrison and his colleagues wouldn't have it, and Wood was one of the first prominent deserters from Chamberlain to Churchill.[49] It was an intense conspiratorial atmosphere. Saved only by his inexplicable egotism from feeling the full weight of responsibility for the horrible crisis that was unfolding, but sick and discouraged, Neville Chamberlain tendered his resignation to King George VI on May 10.

Chamberlain recommended, and the king preferred, Lord Halifax as his successor. The leaders of the Labour Party, Clement Attlee, Arthur Greenwood, and Ernest Bevin, made it clear that they would serve under Halifax or Churchill. Halifax professed to believe that he could not serve in that office from the House of Lords; the last prime minister to do so was the Marquis of Salisbury, who retired in 1902. Constitutional arrangements could have been made for him to appear in the House of Commons, but there were other problems. The long-expected German offensive in the west, against the Netherlands, Belgium, Luxembourg, and France, had been unleashed on the morning of May 10, a few hours before Chamberlain's resignation.

Halifax seems to have acknowledged that in these newly more urgent circumstances Churchill was a more appropriate war leader, in whom Parliament, the country, the Empire, France, and the Americans would have greater confidence. Halifax was not much interested in war, had no particular aptitude for it, and had no capacity to stir or uplift the public. Churchill was fascinated by war and knew a good deal about it. Halifax had a stomachache as the debate and its denouement approached; Churchill was, if anything, exhilarated. Halifax knew that if he were prime minister, Churchill would dominate the government anyway, and did not want to be Herbert Asquith to Churchill's David Lloyd George (who had deposed and replaced Asquith in 1916). There was also some question in the minds of the incumbent Tory grandees about Churchill's durability; he was impetuous. Chamberlain was remaining as party leader, and Halifax may have felt that he might have another possibility to take the headship of the government if Churchill's pugnacity were unsuccessful or changing conditions made it inappropriate, but this is conjecture.[50]

On the question on which the whole future of civilization now depended, Churchill had been right and Halifax had been mistaken. The choice was clear. Winston Leonard Spencer Churchill, aged sixty-five and a veteran of thirty-nine years in Parliament and eight different cabinet positions, including chancellor, home secretary, war, the air force, colonies, trade, and the navy in both World Wars, was invested with practically unlimited authority at the head of a national unity government. No one had assumed the great office of prime minister in more dire circumstances, but he did so serenely, his "whole life a preparation for" it. It was the custom in British history to reach for the decisive man when wars with other Great Powers went badly; Pitt in the Seven Years War, Pitt the younger in the Napoleonic Wars (the first two real world wars), Palmerston in the Crimean War, Lloyd George in 1916.

Churchill gave his first address as prime minister on May 13, in Parliament and then to the world by radio. "I have nothing to offer but blood, toil, tears, and sweat.... Our policy is to wage war by sea, land, and air with all our might ... against a monstrous tyranny, never surpassed in the dark, lamentable catalogue of human crime.... Our aim: Victory—victory at all costs, victory in spite of all terror, victory however long and hard the road may be." For everyone but the Nazis and their sympathizers, this was a refreshing change, and for few people more than for the President of the United States.

At last, the leader who would rally the British nation and Commonwealth, uplift the oppressed, and incite the admiration of the American public. Franklin D. Roosevelt would have someone who knew the nature of civilization's enemies and the requirements of mortal combat, with whom he could plan and achieve the repulse of the barbarians.* And with that would come the permanent engagement of the United States in the world and his own historic elevation. The principal combatants in the greatest drama of modern times were all in place: Stalin, Hitler, Roosevelt, and now Churchill.†

---

* Roosevelt's mother, undaunted by her nearly eighty-six years, had visited her sister Dora in Paris in March 1940 and was majestically composed when questioned by a battery of print and newsreel journalists posing questions in both languages. She said in very presentable French that she had every confidence in the French army. On her son's reelection plans, she said only that he had never spoken to her of a third term and looked forward to returning to Hyde Park.[51]

† Already or about to be visible were the two other leading world political figures of the middle half of the twentieth century, Charles de Gaulle, soon to join the Reynaud government, and in the remote fastness of northwest China, fighting both a civil war and, albeit rather desultorily, the Japanese invaders, Mao Tse-tung.

CHAPTER 13

⚜

"They Are Already Almost
at the Boats!"

*(Republican presidential candidate Wendell L. Willkie warning
that if reelected Franklin D. Roosevelt would involve American
young men in a foreign war, October 1940)*

I

SHORTLY BEFORE HE was to retire for the night on May 9, 1940, Roosevelt was advised of the opening of the Blitzkrieg in the west by his ambassador to Belgium, John Cudahy (who had recently replaced Joseph Davies and vacated Dublin). The President telephoned Morgenthau and told him to freeze Belgian, Dutch, and Luxembourg assets in the United States to keep them out of the hands of the Germans. He then retired to a sound sleep, perhaps employing his technique of sleep-inducement: imagining he was a youth riding down the hills at Springwood in a sleigh and repeating the process until overcome by Morpheus.[1]

On the following evening, May 10, Roosevelt addressed the Pan-American Scientific Congress. Before leaving for the address he asked his houseguest, Helen Gahagan Douglas (who ten years later would be defeated for the office of senator from California by the young Richard Nixon), to wait up for him, because he had an important question for her. When he returned to the White House there was a brief telephone call from the newly installed Winston Churchill. Then he put his question to Mrs. Douglas: was it true that the film director Anatole Litvak and the actress Paulette Goddard had made love under the dinner tables at Ciro's? Mrs. Douglas confirmed the story, to Roosevelt's great amusement, and approval.[2]

The conditions on the Western Front deteriorated for the Allies more quickly than anyone, even Hitler, could have imagined. The Germans attacked the Netherlands and Belgium with overwhelming ground assaults, supported by heavy aerial bombardment, including unrestricted bombing of several civilian centers, including Rotterdam. There were also paratroop assaults and diversionary skirmishing to distract the defenders from the real points of principal attack. The Allies had a well-prepared plan for advancing the British Expeditionary Force and the French Northern Army Group into Belgium to assist Belgium's army in the defense of that country. The main French army, on the Eastern Front along the Rhine and in the deep and comprehensive Maginot Line system of frontier fortifications, would continue to be inactive while the battle developed in the north.

The hinge between the eastern and northern army groups was near the French city of Sedan, scene of the decisive German victory in 1870 over Napoleon III in the Franco-Prussian War, which ended the Second French Empire and enabled Bismarck to found the German Empire. Sedan was masked to the east by the Ardennes and Black Forests, which were so densely wooded they were confidently assumed by the French high command to be impenetrable to large military formations. In fact, the forests made excellent camouflage for German movements of tanks and motorized forces.

These poured out of the Ardennes in tremendous force and at great velocity starting May 13 against the weakest part of the French defenses, decimated the units facing them, and wheeled north toward the English Channel, rolling up behind the armies in Belgium and the Netherlands.

This was the exact opposite of the famous World War I Von Schlieffen Plan, in which the German armies were to come through Belgium, north of the main French armies, sweep along the Channel ("Let the last man on the right touch the Channel with his sleeve," said Schlieffen), and wheel south behind and to the west of Paris, enveloping the entire front. Some variant of this was what Gamelin and the British and French general staffs were confidently expecting in the Second World War.

The 1940 German plan, Operation Sicklesweep, chiefly devised by General Erich von Manstein with Hitler's ingenious personal involvement, aimed at squashing the northern Allied armies against the Channel, forcing their surrender, and then, with overwhelming superiority, attacking south while pinning the French army in the Maginot line with light diversionary attacks across the Rhine. It was a brilliant plan, masterfully executed. By May 15 a fifty-mile gap had opened between the eastern and northern army groups, through which a torrent of German armor and infantry was surging. Dutch resistance collapsed in a few days and the Dutch royal family fled into exile. Paul Reynaud telephoned Churchill at 7:30 A.M. on the morning of the 15th and screamed down the telephone: "We are beaten! The road is open to Paris!"[3]

Churchill sent an urgent message to Roosevelt that day: "Although I have changed my office," he said, he was sure the President would wish to continue the exchange. (This indicates that Churchill's telephone call to Roosevelt on the night of May 10 was no more than an exchange of greetings.) "As you are no doubt aware, the scene has darkened swiftly." He described the German technique, which "is making a deep impression upon the French. I think myself the battle on land has only just begun. . . . The small countries are simply smashed up, one by one, like matchwood. We must expect . . . that Mussolini will hurry in to share the loot of civilization. We expect to be attacked here ourselves, both from the air and by parachute and airborne troops in the near future, and are getting ready for them. If necessary, we shall continue the war alone and we are not afraid of that. But I trust you realize, Mr. President, that the voice and force of the United States may count for nothing if they are withheld too long. You may have a completely subjugated, Nazified Europe established with astonishing swiftness, and the weight may be more than we can bear."

Churchill made six requests of Roosevelt: "the loan of forty or fifty of your older destroyers" for one year; several hundred of the latest types of aircraft, to be repaid by those already on order in the United States for Britain's account; anti-aircraft equipment and ammunition, "of which again there will be plenty next year if we are alive to see it"; quantities of steel, given the threat to Britain's traditional iron-ore import sources, to be paid for in cash while possible and on credit after; a visit of a U.S. squadron to Irish ports to remind Germany that Irish neutrality is not so easily violable as that of other small countries; and American attention "to keep the Japanese dog quiet in the Pacific." Churchill offered the United States the use of the Singapore naval base if it needed it.[4]

The situation was more critical than Roosevelt had realized, though the reports from Bullitt and others were extremely worrisome. But Churchill, even in adversity, wrote with a clarity and determination that could not fail to impress an American president who had had only the shilly-shallyings of MacDonald, Baldwin, and Chamberlain from British leaders. That night Harry Hopkins, who had been hospitalized for months until his unusual nutritional problems had been treated, and had only been twice in ten months in his office as commerce secretary, came to the White House for dinner. He felt poorly after dinner and Roosevelt prevailed upon him to stay the night. He would remain for three and a half years.

Roosevelt responded to Churchill May 16. He couldn't agree to the destroyers, which would require an act of Congress, "and I am not certain that it would be wise for that suggestion to be made to the Congress at this moment." However, he wrote that it would take about seven weeks for the ships to be ready for service in the Royal Navy, which indicated that the proposal might have possibilities. He generally agreed on the matters of aircraft, antiaircraft guns, and steel, would think about a naval visit to Ireland, and declined the offer of Singapore. He had moved the U.S. Pacific Fleet from California to the Hawaiian Islands and implied that he thought that sufficient. He concluded: "The best of luck to you."[5]

Churchill went to France to try to buck up Reynaud on May 16. By the 20th, the Allied northern armies were cut off from the south as the great German sweep behind them approached the Channel. Gamelin lasted only ten days as Allied commander and was replaced on the 20th by General Maxime Weygand,

Foch's chief of staff in the great offensive of 1918. But the 84-year-old Marshal Philippe Henri Petain, hero of Verdun but a notorious Fascist sympathizer and defeatist, became Reynaud's vice premier.

Churchill wrote back to Roosevelt on May 20th. Churchill expressed understanding but disappointment on the destroyers, which would be "invaluable" if they arrived in six weeks. He wrote that they were taking out three German planes for every British loss but that the Curtiss P-40 fighters that had been requested were a matter of extreme urgency.

Churchill began to prepare Roosevelt for the worst: "Our intention is whatever happens to fight on to the end in this Island and, provided we can get the help for which we ask, we hope to run them very close in the air battles in view of individual superiority. . . . In no conceivable circumstances will we consent to surrender. If members of the present administration were finished and others came in to parley amid the ruins, you must not be blind to the fact that the sole remaining bargaining counter with Germany would be the fleet, and if this country was left by the United States to its fate no one would have the right to blame those responsible if they made the best terms they could for the surviving inhabitants. Excuse me, Mr. President, putting this nightmare bluntly. Evidently I could not answer for my successors who in utter despair and helplessness might well have to accommodate themselves to the German will. However, there is happily no need at present to dwell upon such ideas."[6] (That, of course, is precisely what he wanted Roosevelt to do.)

Roosevelt had already requested of the Congress, on May 16, supplementary defense spending of $1.4 billion, fully vindicating his assurances to Eccles and Marshall of a few months before that there was no need for a budget battle on behalf of defense or the unemployed because international events would bring the legislators into line. The President went to the Congress in person on that day and was given a tremendous bipartisan ovation on entering. He was uncharacteristically nervous at the beginning of his remarks, fidgeting with his glasses and standing slightly stooped at the podium. Those behind him noticed that his hands shook more than they had noticed before. But his delivery was strong and his message reassuring: his now well-established policy of peace through strength.

Roosevelt startled many to incredulity and some to ridicule when he proposed to increase American aircraft production in the coming year from 12,000 to 50,000. When advised of this, Hitler glibly dismissed this as wildly beyond American capabilities.[7] The production figures ultimately achieved would vastly exceed this and astound the world. Roosevelt concluded that the nation would need "a toughness of moral and physical fiber . . . the characteristics of a free people, a people devoted to the institutions they themselves have built." The senators and congressmen were unanimous in giving him one of the greatest ovations he ever received in the Congress.

Colonel Lindbergh again took to the airwaves on May 26 to dismiss Roosevelt's call for increased aircraft production as "hysterical chatter." This was very odd coming from air power's most consistent American advocate since Colonel Billy Mitchell. On that day, Roosevelt was advised of the proportions of the impending disaster of the British Expeditionary Force—300,000 men, accompanied by about 25,000 French soldiers, steadily hemmed into the small Channel port of Dunkirk. It was estimated that only about 45,000 of them could be evacuated, and Bullitt telegraphed that the balance were expected to be compelled to surrender. He expected the German Army to occupy Paris in about ten days. There were rumors of the imminent surrender of the Belgian Army.

Also on May 26, Roosevelt sent, via Hull and Bullitt, a message to Reynaud and Daladier: "If the worst comes to the worst, we regard the retention of the French fleet as a force in being as vital to the reconstitution of France . . . and as a vital influence toward getting less harsh terms of peace. That means that the French fleet must not be caught bottled up in the Mediterranean. . . . The same thought is being conveyed in the strictest confidence to the British regarding the British fleet." Desperate times produced inelegant overtures from self-interested to hard-pressed statesmen.

Outwardly imperturbable as always as the grim news flooded in, Roosevelt spoke to the nation in support of his defense plans on the evening of May 26. Even more suavely mellifluous than usual, he gave no hint that France, America's oldest ally, was about to collapse and that the British prime minister was envisioning his successors possibly submitting to the Nazi barbarians "among the ruins."

He was even less enlightening about the prospects of a third term as president, which had become a matter of frenzied curiosity in political circles, only a few weeks from the Democratic convention. He did assert, in his most reassuring tones, the need for deterrent force, for defense production to assist those who were fighting democracy's battles, and for retention of all of America's recent social progress and the reinforcement of "the spirit and morale of a free people." He also asked for contributions to the American Red Cross, that it might help the victims of war-torn Europe. An avalanche of contributions to the Red Cross resulted.

The king of the Belgians abruptly surrendered to the Germans unconditionally on May 28, leaving the northern British and French armies even more exposed. They struggled with great skill and tenacity to turn the environs of Dunkirk into a redoubt. The seas were calm and the Royal Navy was unchallengeable in these waters. Heavy insertions of Royal Air Force squadrons, which decisively defeated the Luftwaffe despite being outnumbered, gave the British temporary air superiority over the Dunkirk beaches and approaches. A fleet of about 900 miscellaneous craft had been assembled—yachts, tugs, ferries, and passenger ships—and these moved the stranded soldiers out constantly from May 28 to June 4. An astonishing 340,000 men were rescued, including over 100,000 French. Their equipment was left behind, and the Germans took nearly 40,000 prisoners, but it was an amazing recovery of the cream of the British Army.

The RAF had knocked down four German planes for every loss of their own. Churchill wrote Roosevelt June 1, 1940, asking for 200 aircraft at once: "The courage and success of our pilots against numerical superiority are a guaranty that they will be well used. At the present rate of comparative losses they would account for something like 800 German machines."

The salvation of the expeditionary force had solidified Churchill's control of the government and his uncompromising war policy. The war cabinet consisted of Churchill, Chamberlain, Halifax, Attlee, and Greenwood. The Labour members were noncommittal; Halifax wanted to explore a negotiated peace salvaging British interests and writing off the European continent. Chamberlain, surprisingly and to his credit, was so offended by Hitler's lies and treachery that he supported Churchill. Dunkirk clinched it for the war party. The parliamentary caucus was solidly behind the prime minister and his policy.[8]

Winston Churchill gave one of history's most celebrated speeches to Parliament and the world on June 4. It electrified American opinion and profoundly impressed Franklin Roosevelt. The prime minister warned against giving "to this deliverance the attributes of victory. . . . Wars are not won by evacuations." He did celebrate the victory in the air, which illustrated the difficulty the Germans would have mounting an invasion of the British Isles.

And he offered a fierce, unargumentative pledge: "We shall go on to the end. We shall fight in France, we shall fight in the seas and oceans, we shall fight with growing strength and growing confidence in the air, we shall defend our island, whatever the cost may be. We shall fight on the beaches, we shall fight on the landing grounds, we shall fight in the fields and in the streets, we shall fight in the hills; we shall never surrender, and even if, which I do not for a moment believe, this island or a large part of it were subjugated and starving, then our Empire beyond the seas, armed and guarded by the British Fleet, would carry on the struggle until, in God's good time, the New World, with all its power and might, steps forth to the rescue and the liberation of the Old." (In fact, the international broadcast was given by the exact impersonator Norman Shelley, because Churchill himself, in the throes of the Battle of France, could not spare the time to repeat what he had said in Parliament.[9]

Roosevelt's response was dramatic. He ordered a reluctant War Department (where stubborn officials managed to delay implementation for three weeks until overwhelmed by direct presidential instruction[10] to fill British requests for, and to dispatch at once, 500,000 Enfield rifles, 900 75mm artillery pieces, 50,000 machine guns, 130 million rounds of ammunition, a million artillery shells, and large quantities of high explosives and bombs. The neutrality legislation was circumvented by selling this equipment and ordnance to private corporations, which sold it on at once to the British.[11] Except for tanks, the British Army would be substantially rearmed, albeit with twenty-year-old rifles and field pieces, within six weeks of returning, shorn and waterlogged, from Dunkirk.

On May 28 Roosevelt announced the reactivation of the World War I cabinet committee, the Council of National Defense, and the appointment of an Advisory Commission of the Council. This advisory group inflamed the fears of the most militant liberals in the President's camp, who thought he was becoming too cozy with big business. Among its members were Edward R. Stettinius, chairman of United States Steel; William S. Knudsen, president of General Motors; and Ralph Budd, one of the country's leading railway executives. Roosevelt knew that in the battle for armaments production he would need the country's industrialists. He would return to a reform program eventually, though not one that business objected to, but now the priority was cooperation among business, government, and labor.

On June 10, with the German advance in France apparently irresistible and Paris about to be declared an open city, Mussolini declared war on France and Britain. Churchill privately expressed relief that they had an opponent they would be able to kick hard long before it would be possible to do so to Germany. Reynaud cabled Roosevelt, pledging: "We shall fight in front of Paris, we shall fight behind Paris. . . . and if we should be driven out, we shall establish ourselves in North Africa to continue the fight. . . . May I ask you, Mr. President, to explain all this yourself to your people [and] declare publicly that the United States will give the Allies aid and material support by all means short of an expeditionary force?" Reynaud was somewhat imitating Churchill's prose style, but he could not replicate his governmental unity, the unambiguous determination of the British people, the strength of the British Navy and Air Force, or the protection afforded by the English Channel.

Later that day, Roosevelt gave a long-scheduled commencement address at Thomas Jefferson's University of Virginia at Charlottesville. In the intense circumstances, he was correctly expected to address the world crisis, and the speech was broadcast throughout the world. He referred to "those [Americans] who still hold to the now somewhat obvious delusion that we can permit the United States to become a lone island . . . in a world dominated by the philosophy of force." Such an island would be like a prison whose inhabitants are "handcuffed, hungry, and fed through the bars . . . by the contemptuous, unpitying masters of other continents." Against the advice of the State Department, he retained the description of Mussolini he had composed himself: "On this tenth day of June, 1940, the hand that held the dagger has struck it into the back of its neighbor. . . . In our [new] American unity . . . we will extend to the opponents of force the material resources of this nation."[12]

Mussolini responded to the accusation of back-stabbing with a coarse pun on the Italian meaning of Roosevelt's middle name (of the anus). Churchill wrote, June 11: "We all listened to you last night and were fortified by the grand scope of your declaration." He referred to a "dark but not unhopeful hour . . . The hope with which you inspire [the French] may give them the strength to persevere. . . . Our intention is to have a strong army fighting in France for the campaign of 1941." He mentioned planes again, but particularly emphasized destroyers, reduced in number to thirty to forty and returnable on six months' notice. The "Italian outrage" had brought a hundred more submarines in against the British, possibly based in Spain, Churchill thought. "The ocean traffic by which we live may be strangled. Not a day should be lost. I send you my heartfelt thanks and those of my colleagues for all you are doing and seeking to do for what we now indeed call the common cause."[13]

Churchill wrote again June 12, having just returned from the itinerant French headquarters, which was continually moving south ahead of the invading Germans. "The aged Marshal Petain, who was none too good in April and July, 1918, is, I fear, ready to lend his name and prestige to a treaty of peace for France. Reynaud, on the other hand, is for fighting on, and he has a young general de Gaulle who believes much can be done. Admiral Darlan declares he will send the French fleet to Canada. It would be disastrous if the two big modern ships fell into bad hands."*

Churchill urged Roosevelt to do anything he could to encourage those French who wanted to fight on. "I venture to put this point before you although I know you must understand it as well as I do. Of course I made it clear to the French that we shall continue whatever happened and that we thought Hitler could not win the war or the mastery of the world until he had disposed of us, which has not been found easy in the past." Britain hoped for victory and would do its duty. "If there is anything you can say publicly or privately to the French, now is the time."[14] On the 13th he wrote back that the French had asked for him again. Paris was about to be occupied by the Germans and France had reached the last extremity.

Roosevelt wrote to Reynaud, with a copy to Churchill: "Your message of June 10 has moved me deeply. . . . The magnificent resistance of the French and British armies has profoundly impressed the American people." (This was a liberty with the facts; the rout of the French Army shocked the world, including the United States and particularly its commander in chief.) He urged Reynaud to fight on, promised to redouble all material aid to the Allies, and expressed gratitude at the British determination to fight on in the Empire. "That determination would seem to apply equally to the great French Empire all over the world. Naval power in world affairs still carries the lessons of history, as Admiral Darlan well knows."[15]

This passage has been cited by some[16] as evidence of an obsolete strategic

---

* The battleships *Richelieu* and *Jean Bart* barely escaped the Germans, *Jean Bart* being floated and towed out of the Penhoet fitting-out basin at St. Nazaire as the German Army arrived, and the *Richelieu* hastily leaving Brest. *Jean Bart*, without most of her guns, sailed with uncompleted engines to Casablanca; *Richelieu* went to Dakar.

sense of Roosevelt's based on Mahan. In fact, he was merely trying to encourage Reynaud, extract the French fleet from the debacle, and entice Darlan, whom he knew to be a highly politicized officer. While Roosevelt was impressed with Churchill's fighting spirit, at this point he still thought him an Edwardian gold-standardist Tory, but he told Ickes that Churchill was "the best man England had, even if he was drunk half of [the] time." He rated Britain's chances to Farley at one in three.[17]

Churchill was back to Roosevelt on June 14, immediately on returning from France, and asked that the message to Reynaud be made public. He also told Reynaud that he, Churchill, was convinced that if France remained in the war, the United States would enter it at France's and Britain's side. This was another considerable liberty, since Roosevelt had, as Churchill perfectly well knew, said nothing of the kind. They were both trying to shore up the French to insulate their countries against the Furor Teutonicus and to kill or otherwise detain as many Germans in France as possible for as long as they could. But Roosevelt had never imagined getting involved as a belligerent until attrition had taken its toll on Germany and the United States had armed itself to the teeth. In the summer of 1940, Germany was virtually unbloodied and America chronically under-defended, apart from the U.S. Navy, which most Americans had considered the only armed service they would need. With British war losses, the United States now had the world's largest navy.

Roosevelt replied later on June 14, flatly stating that there could be no consideration of the United States committing to go to war. Without explicitly saying so, both men knew that France was finished. They were chiefly concerned with stretching out the resistance, such as it was, and with keeping the French Navy out of the hands of the Germans.[18]

Churchill cabled back to Roosevelt on the 15th with the most desperate evocation of gruesome possibilities. Hitler might trade the French fleet for retention by France of Alsace-Lorraine. He might trade it for nondestruction of French towns. Churchill, while he would always fight on, again envisioned his government's being replaced by a regime that would buy peace by becoming a German vassal state. If the British, French, Japanese, German, and Italian navies were combined, "overwhelming sea power would be in Hitler's hands." Then Churchill oddly hypothesized: "He might, of course, use it with a merciful moderation. . . . If we go down, you may have a United States of Europe under the Nazi command, far more numerous, far stronger, far better armed than the new world."

He then gave a lengthy summary of the absolute need for thirty-five destroyers immediately, concluding: "We are now faced with the imminent collapse of French resistance and if this occurs the successful defense of this island will be the only hope of averting the collapse of civilization as we define it. We must ask therefore, as a matter of life or death to be reinforced with these destroyers. We will carry out the struggle whatever the odds, but it may well be beyond our resources unless we receive every reinforcement."[19]

Churchill, in office just thirty-six days, was under such strain at this point that even so great a master of the English language was having some difficulty balancing between his indomitable determination to fight to the finish and his alarms that his country could be trodden down and transformed into a sullen German satellite actively participating in a trans-Atlantic assault on America. Roosevelt felt deeply for the British and French leaders who, as he ceaselessly told the lobotomous isolationists in Congress, were the front line of American democracy.

Churchill knew that, even in these fearful days, there was no possibility, without a casus belli and on the verge of an election, of America's declaring war on a rampaging Germany. The geopolitical danger of the whole world's assembling in alliance against the United States was also far-fetched, though it was an understandable gambit for Churchill given Britain's present difficulties. Churchill gave it one more try, late on June 15, writing that he had heard from Reynaud that France's ability to continue in the war depended on a public declaration that the United States would soon be joining the war. Churchill made it clear that this did not mean an expeditionary force, "merely the tremendous moral effect that such an American decision would produce."[20]

Even allowing for the desperate circumstances, these were strange arguments. Great Britain had a far larger navy than Germany and Italy together, and as large as the navies of those countries and France put together. Britain also had the ability, as she shortly demonstrated, to prevent those fleets from concentrating by inflicting grievous damage on the French and Italian navies singly. As Churchill had written Roosevelt and emphasized in his public remarks, the Royal Air Force was likely to be able to hold its own with the Germans, especially over British airspace, where it would have a much greater endurance and downed pilots could be recycled in other planes, while surviving Germans shot down over Britain would become prisoners. This too would soon be demonstrated.*

Finally, the idea of an American statement of intention to declare war, without the likelihood of the early commitment of forces to combat but for moral effect, was, to say the least, bizarre. Yet it demonstrated the degree to which the United States had already become, rivaled only by Germany, the world's preeminent country. Five weeks out of the Phony War, the future of the world was said to depend on American expressions of intent.

On June 16, responding to a French inquiry about seeking German conditions for an armistice, Churchill said that Britain would agree to release France from their reciprocal promise to avoid separate negotiations if France sailed its fleet to British ports and made it clear that Britain had no interest in peace discussions. He also met with Charles de Gaulle—author of France's only victory over Ger-

---

* No Axis submarines operated from Spanish ports. Franco was completely uncooperative with his former allies, and the Italian Navy was ineffectual. In a phrase made famous by the Habsburgs a hundred years before and soon applicable to Franco (and eventually to de Gaulle toward his allies), Spain "would astound the world by its ingratitude."

many in the war to date, a tank action at Abbeville—who had recently been promoted from colonel to general and then to the cabinet as undersecretary of war.

De Gaulle was a fanatical opponent of any notion of negotiation and had come to discuss methods of keeping France in the war. The method arrived at, devised by the fecund and irrepressible Jean Monnet, was federal union between France and Great Britain. On June 16, de Gaulle approved the plan; Churchill and de Gaulle discussed and approved it at lunch at the Carlton Club, Churchill secured its approval from his cabinet, and de Gaulle telephoned it to a jubilant Reynaud, who took it to his cabinet. But it was too late. General Maxime Weygand assured the French government in words Churchill would famously repeat in the Canadian Parliament eighteen months later: "In three weeks England will have her neck wrung like a chicken."

The Reynaud government fell. Petain became prime minister and sued for peace. The following day, June 17, Hull sent a message for the French government to Drexel Biddle, the former ambassador to Poland, now deputy to Bullitt. Bullitt had remained in Paris to try to be a moderating influence on the Germans. The message stated that if the French government should "fail to see that the fleet is kept out of the hands of her opponents, [it] will fatally impair the preservation of the French Empire and the eventual restoration of French independence and autonomy." Should the fleet "be surrendered to Germany, the French government will permanently lose the friendship and good will of the government of the United States." The French cabinet resolved that the fleet would "under no circumstances be turned over to the Germans and if surrender [of it] were part of the German terms, the armistice should be rejected."

France surrendered to Germany on June 22, 1940, on Marshal Foch's railway car in the Compiegne Forest, where the 1918 Armistice had been signed. Hitler personally presided over this, the greatest triumph of his career. He had brought the long struggle between the two countries to the complete submission of France to apparently permanent German domination. More than half of France, including Paris and the entire Atlantic coast, was annexed to Germany. (So were Belgium, the Netherlands, and Luxembourg, bringing to fourteen the number of independent countries eliminated by Hitler, Stalin, and Mussolini in the last four years.) Huge costs and reparations were piled on France, and the unoccupied section of the country was to be a puppet state. The French Navy was to be neutralized but remain in French ports. (In fact, significant units were in British ports and remained there.)

The National Assembly of the Third Republic, born of the courage of the Siege of Paris, which had seen the greatest artistic and literary flowering in French history and got the country through the heroic ordeal of the First World War, ignominiously voted the end of the Third Republic at the Vichy Casino on July 10, 1940. The vestiges of France would be governed in the German interest by the greasy, fascist Quisling, Pierre Laval, in the name of the senescent Petain.

Charles de Gaulle flew to London on June 17, 1940, to found the Free French movement, "carrying with him in his little airplane," as Churchill later wrote, "the honor of France" (so little of it now remained). Churchill gave him the BBC for a broadcast to France, June 18: "France has lost a battle. France has not lost the war," he said, words that would long resonate.

Churchill himself addressed the French, in his heavily accented but comprehensible version of the language: "Good night then. Sleep to gather strength for the morning. For the morning will come. Brightly will it shine on the brave and true, kindly upon all who suffer for the cause, glorious upon the tombs of the heroes. Thus will shine the dawn. Vive la France!"

To the British, the Americans, and the whole world, Churchill said, on June 18, in another Demosthenian oratorical triumph, as France officially quit the war: "Let us brace ourselves to our duties and so bear ourselves that if the British Empire and its Commonwealth should last for a thousand years, men will still say: 'This was their finest hour!' " They did, and it was. Throughout the most daunting period of his premiership, Churchill regularly, in de Gaulle's words, "raised the heavy dough of the English . . . with his infallible eloquence." More than that, he stirred the whole world, especially the United States.

De Gaulle later wrote: "By the light of the thunderbolt the [French] regime was revealed, in its ghastly infirmity, as having no proportion and no relation to the defense, honor, and independence of France."[21]

The Battle of France was over. The Battle of Britain was about to begin. So, in the United States, was one of history's most important election campaigns.

II

ROOSEVELT FINALLY FIRED the secretary of war, Harry Woodring, on June 17, 1940, when Woodring, an isolationist, refused a direct presidential order to transfer a dozen B-17s to Great Britain. Prior to that, Woodring had led the obstruction of Roosevelt's post-Dunkirk shipment of equipment for a new army to Britain.

The internecine squabbling between Woodring and Assistant Secretary Louis Johnson had been destructive and notorious for years. Woodring's isolationism had caused foot-dragging in some areas, and many, including Harold Ickes, had urged Roosevelt to dispense with the secretary. Ickes urged the President to tell Woodring: "It's either Dublin, Ireland [where there was some thought of sending him as ambassador], or Topeka, Kansas, for you [Woodring's home]." "You can't do that sort of thing can you, Mr. President?" "No Harold, I can't," Roosevelt replied.[22]

Roosevelt carefully cultivated the image of a softie who couldn't fire anyone. Edward Flynn, in his memoirs, paints this picture of Roosevelt also. In fact, he disposed of people frequently, sometimes in direct firings, like those of Dean Acheson, Woodring, Attorney General Homer Cummings, or Admiral James O. Richardson, commander of the Pacific Fleet. More often, he discharged people in excruciating, sadistically elaborate plots, from which he derived unseemly amusement. It was part of Roosevelt's ruthless nature that he went to great lengths to disguise it. As Eleanor recognized to her distress, Franklin Roosevelt, beyond a certain point, was icily detached from almost everyone.

It also served Roosevelt's purposes to have his underlings quarreling, and soft-heartedness was a more presentable excuse for this deliberate disorder than a will to domination and love of intrigue which were much closer to the truth. Roosevelt didn't want to remove Woodring before he had to, because he didn't want an embittered insider hitting the trail in an election year accusing him of pushing the country into war. Roosevelt offered Woodring the post of governor of Puerto Rico, but he refused. In the exchange of letters that arose from Roosevelt's request for the secretary's resignation, Roosevelt assured Woodring he would continue what Woodring had described as Roosevelt's "pronounced nonintervention policy."

With the outgoing war secretary as with former French premier Reynaud, Roosevelt would not allow the correspondence to be published. His attempt to hold the center in American politics while defending the national interest abroad had required him to exchange pledges of nonintervention with Woodring while taking intimations of imminent intervention to the edge of a promise of early entry into the war with Reynaud. This was a long and unstable bridge between irreconcilable views, but the fact that Roosevelt could build it at all is another demonstration of his political dexterity.

He also moved out Navy Secretary Charles Edison, who had been doing the job for only a year, knew nothing of naval affairs, and was somewhat ineffective. Roosevelt gave him the Democratic nomination as governor of New Jersey (to clip the wings of Boss Frank Hague). In a cunning political and administrative coup five days before the Republican convention, Roosevelt replaced Woodring and Edison with veteran Republican officeholder Henry Stimson as war secretary and Chicago Daily News publisher and 1936 Republican vice presidential candidate Frank Knox as secretary of the navy.* Both had been friendly with Theodore Roosevelt. Knox was also a direct and antagonistic competitor of Colonel McCormick at the *Tribune* (though not a particularly successful one). Stimson and Knox both believed in going to war to support Britain (as did Ickes and Morgenthau). These appointments, added to Hopkins and Murphy and then Robert Jackson the year before, greatly strengthened Roosevelt's cabinet.

The Stimson nomination had been promoted by Grenville Clark, a fellow junior with Franklin Roosevelt in the law firm Carter, Ledyard, and Milburn, from 1907 to 1910. Clark was now one of New York's leading lawyers and one of the World War I preparedness advocates known collectively as the Plattsburgh Movement, because a group of prominent people set up a training camp for themselves at Plattsburgh after the sinking of the *Lusitania* in 1915. Clark was a

---

* Roosevelt ignored Bullitt's presumptuous request for the navy post, June 7.

friend of Frankfurter's, and the two pressed Stimson on Roosevelt. Roosevelt was receptive partly because of the friendly exchanges he had had with Stimson, then Hoover's secretary of state, when he was president-elect.

Clark also set up an association calling for conscription, the first in peacetime in American history. Inspired by Clark's group, Senator Edward Burke of Nebraska (whom Roosevelt had wished to dispense with in the 1938 purge) and Congressman James Wadsworth of New York introduced what was called a selective service bill, without initial White House sponsorship, on June 20.

The Republican convention opened in Philadelphia on June 24, 1940. The leading contenders were Thomas E. Dewey, New York's dapper, racket-busting, thirty-eight-year-old district attorney; Senator Robert A. Taft of Ohio, fifty; and forty-eight-year-old Wall Street utilities lawyer Wendell L. Willkie, originally of Indiana. It would be the most dramatic convention in the Republican Party since the Taft-Roosevelt battle in 1912. Willkie had been an internationalist Democrat and had gone to the 1932 Democratic convention in Chicago supporting Newton D. Baker. He voted for Roosevelt that year and did not formally become a Republican until March 1939. He even voted for Lehman over Dewey in the close New York gubernatorial contest of 1938. He supported the New Deal welfare and conservation programs and the TVA, though not its power distribution aspects, but he was concerned at the concentration of power in Roosevelt's hands. He considered Roosevelt too prone to aggregate powers for government and himself. Willkie was a large man, slightly uncoordinated and rumpled, with a great shock of tousled hair. He was energetic, ingenuous, and highly intelligent. Roosevelt recognized at once that he would be a much stronger candidate than any previous Republican presidential candidate since Theodore Roosevelt.

Thomas E. Dewey was also a capable, though earnest, public speaker and had an impressive reputation as a successful prosecutor. He had less personality than Willkie and a different style. He was diminutive, natty, and cool; impressive but not so naturally likeable as Willkie. "Dewey always displayed the overly sober mien of a young man to whom success has come too soon."[23] He drank three quarts of water a day, and even to his staff was unwaveringly stiff. Both Willkie and Dewey were internationalists, though Dewey finessed his position to avoid antagonizing the isolationists.

Robert A. Taft, son of the former president and chief justice, was a conservative isolationist. Highly intelligent and well-respected in the Senate, he was shy, unflamboyant, and a monotonous speaker, the quintessence of the politician, like many senior southern senators, who excelled in Congress but was not so saleable to a general electorate for national office.

Willkie had steadily gained prominence as an intellectual businessman, a relative rarity in the United States. He wrote many magazine articles through 1938 and 1939 and often spoke at public meetings on a wide variety of subjects. In a

January 1939 radio debate with the rising star of the New Deal, Deputy Attorney General Robert Jackson, Willkie was generally judged to have won and to have put the case against much of the New Deal very effectively. (This severely jolted Jackson's hopes to succeed Roosevelt, though he did succeed Frank Murphy as attorney general when Murphy went to the Supreme Court in late 1939.) On April 9, 1940, Willkie had scored a triumph when he appeared on the popular radio show *Information Please,* with Clifton Fadiman of *The New Yorker* and four other urbane panelists. Willkie showed himself to be cultured, witty, and charming. He fully held his own in quick and sophisticated repartee with the hosts. (This was before the era of rehearsed soundbites.)

Some of the enlightened Republican publishers, such as Henry Luce (*Time, Life,* and *Fortune*), Gardner and John Cowles (*Look* magazine), and Ogden Reid (*New York Herald Tribune*), began to tout Willkie systematically, and the polls, which in early May had been strongly for Dewey among Republicans, began to move. Willkie clubs arose around the country, and when the candidate came to the convention, he made a huge impression on uncommitted delegates as he lobbied them right up to the opening gavel. He clearly had a much more convivial public personality than Dewey, let alone Taft. The galleries were packed with Willkie supporters, and they rattled the other candidates and the convention organizers by constantly chanting their support of Willkie.

On the first ballot, Dewey led with 360 to Taft's 189 and Willkie's 105. There were hundreds of votes scattered around among favorite son and splinter candidates. On the third ballot Willkie passed Taft into second place, and Dewey's total was declining. On the fourth ballot, with a bandwagon clearly building, Willkie took the lead, and on the sixth ballot won the nomination, in the early morning of June 28, 1940. Republican Senate leader Charles L. McNary of Oregon, a progressive, especially on public control of electricity, but an isolationist, was chosen as candidate for vice president.

Wendell Willkie returned to his home town of Elwood, Indiana, to give his formal acceptance speech to a crowd of 250,000 Hoosiers. It was a spirited effort, but the political sages found it wanting. Norman Thomas, the perennial Socialist candidate who had had his political clothes stolen so often he was in a perpetually indecent electoral state, called it "a synthesis of Guffey's First Reader, the Genealogy of Indiana, the collected speeches of Tom Girdler [Republic Steel chairman], and *The New Republic*."[24]

It was astonishing that Roosevelt had managed up to this point to give no hint of his own intentions. The Republican orators were not sure whether they were watching the departure of a popular president or were about to run against a man they would have to accuse of claiming for himself a greater status and longer tenure of the presidency than anyone in the country's history.

There remains great controversy among historians about when Roosevelt decided to make the race. He had gone to elaborate lengths to discuss retirement plans; he was building his cottage at the top of the hill above Springwood and his official library at Hyde Park. He had discussed with Harry Hopkins buying a Florida Key (Channel Key, between Key Largo and Key West) and operating a fishing retreat there. He had, as always, many ideas. Eleanor thought he was becoming tired and might be happy to retire. Missy LeHand and Ambassador Bullitt were convinced he had suffered a minor heart attack while dining with them in the White House in February. He had told many supposed intimates, such as Morgenthau, on January 24, that he didn't want to run unless "things get very, very much worse in Europe." This could have been his view of the circumstances that would make such a run for a third term explicable, rather than desirable. On January 27, 1940, three days after this comment to Morgenthau, the President signed a contract to write every other week for *Collier's* magazine for three years. Though he was offered more, he refused to surpass $75,000, because he thought it improper for a magazine freelancer to be paid more than the president of the United States.[25] Few of his successors would be so circumspect.

There is no doubt that Roosevelt was sometimes tired. He worked hard and shouldered immense responsibilities. He was fifty-eight, and his infirmity made many things more of a strain for him. His vulnerability to sinus problems was a frequently recurring problem. But he loved his position and had an almost mystical view of where America was going and of his mission to lead it there. He enjoyed Hyde Park and Warm Springs, but he spent a fair amount of time at Hyde Park anyway. Franklin D. Roosevelt was never easy to read; he was a natural dissembler and was proud of his deviousness, not only because he was good at it and it had served him well, but because he was convinced that it was always in a good cause.

He knew Hitler had to be defeated. No scenario for the elimination of Hitler was ever credible without the full involvement of the United States. No real peace was possible while Hitler or any Nazi successor ruled a Greater Germany. Nor could the United States become unquestionably the leading country of the world under the present circumstances. With the crushing of France and the absorption of most of France into Germany along with the Low Countries and half of Scandinavia, the Reich now had a population larger than that of the United States, though barely sixty percent of this population actually spoke German.

If Hitler were allowed to consolidate this position, not only could Germany rival America as an industrial power, but Nazism could more successfully compete with democracy for imitators than it already had. This competition could become bothersome in Latin America, where attachment to democracy was tenuous, and where Hitler and Mussolini had no shortage of swaggering emulators in overstuffed uniforms.

None of this could have been acceptable to Roosevelt. Even if he hadn't enjoyed being president, even if there were a visible successor, even if he had been sanguine on domestic policy grounds about a reoccupation of the White House by the Republicans, Roosevelt would have wished to remain as president to ensure that the United States was not displaced by Germany. And none of these conditions were met. He was overwhelmingly, palpably, infectiously happy to be president. There was no Democratic candidate of the slightest plausibility to replace him.

While Roosevelt respected Willkie and came to admire him, he was convinced that the machinery of any Republican administration, in the executive and the legislative branches, would be in the hands of reactionaries and isolationists capable of a greedy Hardingesque dunciad. This was perhaps ungenerous, but it was his belief. He thought all progressive Republicans were chased out in the end, as had been Theodore Roosevelt, Robert La Follette, George Norris, and, to some extent, even Fiorello La Guardia.* Willkie would have no control over the Republican leaders of Congress.

If Roosevelt had served out his two terms in what his wife was shortly to describe memorably as "ordinary time," he would have found no plausible reason to seek a third term, and would have retired reasonably happily. But from early 1938 on, it was clear that there would be no normality in the times until the forces of malignant abnormality had been defeated.

After the clear proof, as he adduced it, that Hitler was a compulsive aggressor, by early 1939, Roosevelt had no believable intention of retiring on inauguration day, 1941. It was his mission to lead the forces of freedom, to engage America in the world, to make the world safe for democracy, to make democracy fashionable in a post-imperial world, to construct international institutions that would function adequately. To the accomplishment of all of this, Roosevelt believed himself (not without good reason) to be indispensable.

The proof, as nearly as can be found, is in his behavior and in the historical facts. Willkie was an impressive candidate, but neither he nor anyone else could have achieved what Roosevelt did achieve in the coming fifteen months in helping Britain, marshaling American public opinion and building American strength, and edging toward war while always seeming to most of his countrymen, if not to the German and Japanese governments, to be the virtuous innocent.

The whole future of civilization required that it be done. There was no one else who could have done it. If he had truly wanted to retire, he would have stopped talking wistfully about Hyde Park and gone there. That, like the creation of a virtual draft of a reluctant incumbent, was part of the choreography of continuing in office. He would seem to do so out of duty and with some genuine

---

* The argument has even been advanced that he was tempted to retire for a term and then return in 1944. This was no time for any such breather from the presidency; he was not growing younger, and if his cousin's career had taught him anything, it was not to give up an office that you enjoyed and that might be difficult to recapture.[26]

reluctance as well as considerable exhilaration, not, or not mainly, from egotism, self-importance, or inertia. Tactics were devised to complement the facts.

Roosevelt was the only possible candidate to reelect the Democrats. The party was legitimately begging him to run, except for a few deluded seekers who imagined they could replace him—specifically Farley and John Nance Garner. Roosevelt liked Farley, but rightly considered his presidential ambitions absurd. He laughed spontaneously when Farley first told him he aspired to the nomination.

He couldn't abide Garner, a crusty Texan conservative whom he selected in deference to the now semiextinct volcano William Randolph Hearst. (WR had narrowly avoided the receiver but didn't exercise the control over his group that he had done; it had sold off some assets and Hearst was now seventy-seven.) Roosevelt, despite his hearty approval of whiskey and poker, had agreed with John L. Lewis's description of Garner a year before at a Senate committee hearing as "a labor-baiting, poker playing, whiskey drinking, evil old man." He sometimes said at cabinet meetings when Garner was absent: "The vice president's not here; we can speak frankly."[27]

Roosevelt dutifully asked Frankfurter in late June for a paper on whether he should seek a third term, like the chief executive engaging a friendly compensation consultant to recommend his appropriate pay increase. Frankfurter delivered a learned treatise on the President's unavoidable duty to continue. He was a spontaneous overachiever in that he commissioned and sent along, inserted in his own paper, a desperate wail of appeal from the librarian of Congress and unconditional Roosevelt supporter, Archibald MacLeish, that Roosevelt seek a third term.

Winston Churchill played a role, too. Despite Churchill's evident personal resolve, conditions after the fall of France were so daunting, and Churchill's beseechings for an indication of an American readiness to go immediately to war were so impractical, that Roosevelt raised his initial estimate of Britain's ability to carry on the war successfully alone to just 50–50, despite the huge improvement in war-making aptitudes from Chamberlain to Churchill.[28]

But on July 3, 1940, the Royal Navy attacked the French fleet at Oran, Algeria, and demilitarized other French ships at Alexandria. In consequence, all operational French capital ships except the *Richelieu* at Dakar were destroyed, demobilized, or durably put out of action. Roosevelt took this as indicative of Churchill's determination and had no sympathy with the French protests, given their shabby quitting of the war and their failure to give adequate assurance to their former ally that the fleet would not be used against Britain. Roosevelt also noted the tremendous ovation given the British prime minister when he explained the government's action to Parliament.[29]

If Britain were not going to see the war through, there would be little America could do on its own unless it were directly attacked. But a plucky and fierce British underdog led by an eloquent and indomitable fighter was the ally Roosevelt was seeking and not finding from 1935 to May 10, 1940. The British, in de Gaulle's words, as one who had had to make some calculations of his own of Albion's staying power, "led by such a fighter, would certainly not flinch. Mr. Churchill seemed to me equal to the rudest task, provided it also had grandeur."[30]

III

A S PART OF his masquerade that he was essentially accepting a draft out of duty in an international emergency, Roosevelt was not prepared to make or renew the compromises he had struck with the party barons in 1932. Garner would go, Roosevelt would choose the vice presidential nominee, and the party platform would say what the President running on it wanted it to say and neither more nor less. There would be a clear commitment to liberal principles, yet in a tone unfrightening to reasonable members of the business community. There would be a statement of determination to stay out of foreign wars and to assist the democracies in their struggle against dictatorships. There must be a clear statement of the need to arm America and to be prepared to deter aggression and defend legitimate American interests. On the matter of a running mate, he was determined not to throw a bone to the conservatives in the party, who, he thought, didn't believe in what he was trying to do, at least in domestic policy, and probably didn't understand his foreign policy, but were only along for the ride on the great Roosevelt gravy train. The failed purge of 1938 still rankled, and continued.

Exhibiting the weakness he sometimes displayed for unsuitable appointments, especially those designed to affront an annoying constituency, Roosevelt settled on the improbable figure of Agriculture Secretary Henry A. Wallace as vice president. This was as insane a choice as fascistic defeatist Joseph Kennedy for the London embassy, Stalin-dupe Joseph Davies to Moscow, isolationist Woodring in the War Department, anti-allotment, unsuccessful plough-manufacturer George Peek to head AAA, or anti-Semite Breckinridge Long in charge of refugee affairs. Roosevelt's reasoning was that Wallace would help him in the farm states, was a liberal and an internationalist, was an intelligent and imaginative public figure, was healthy and youthful, and was a good writer and public speaker.

That was all right as far as it went, but Wallace was also a faddish mystic, "a wild-eyed fellow," as Farley put it, a sucker for any political or religious idea that popped up, and a person of questionable mental stability. When Roosevelt told Senate Majority Leader and 1940 convention chairman Alben Barkley that he wanted Wallace to add strength in the Corn Belt, where he was "weak," Barkley replied that Wallace "is the reason you're weak in the Corn Belt."[31] Roosevelt, however, had made his decision. The more the organizational conservatives might squawk about Wallace, the more determined the President would be to show that he was the locomotive pulling the entire Democratic Party behind him and this was his decision and no one else's. Of all the hypotheses of American history, a Wallace presidency following the death in office of FDR is one of the more chilling ones.

Jim Farley had declared that he was seeking the Democratic nomination for president. Roosevelt invited him to Hyde Park on Sunday, July 7, 1940, hoping to get him to withdraw. Even at this late date, eight days before the convention opened, Roosevelt was not prepared to tell his party chairman his real intentions. The mad egotism that would have driven an unelected party wheelhorse like Farley to imagine he could assume Roosevelt's position or contest successfully for it against Willkie, as the Depression, the greatest domestic crisis since the Civil War, gave way to the greatest foreign policy crisis since the American Revolution, might justify Roosevelt's discretion. Roosevelt told Farley he didn't want to run again and would tell the convention that. He asked Farley's advice, which was to quote General William Tecumseh Sherman that if nominated he would not run, and if elected he would not serve.

Roosevelt responded that if he were nominated by a genuine draft and elected, he would have no right in these times to decline to serve. Farley did not volunteer to desist from his candidacy and Roosevelt did not say that a draft had already been organized. At one point, Roosevelt lifted his shirt and showed Farley a slight bulge in his chest, which he represented as an enlarged heart, which should have been yet another reason not to be considering Wallace for the vice presidency. Roosevelt and Farley parted cordially, but their relations would not be the same again.

At the Democratic convention, which opened in the Chicago Stadium on July 15, Harry Hopkins occupied the suite in the Blackstone Hotel that had been the original smoke-filled room in which Warren Harding had been selected as Republican candidate for president by the party elders in 1920. Hopkins was representing Roosevelt's interest, and the President had given him a "sincere" note to give to Speaker Bankhead to read to the delegates as keynote speaker on the first night of the convention. It was, as Roosevelt biographer Kenneth Davis well described it, "a typically 'sincere' statement of total untruth."[32]

The statement read: "You and my other close friends [a wild overstatement in Bankhead's case; Roosevelt had no close friends except, up to a point, Hopkins] have known and understood that I have not today and have never had any wish or purpose to remain in the office of President, or indeed anywhere in public office after next January. You know and all my friends know that this is a simple and sincere fact. I want you to repeat this simple and sincere fact to the convention." Hopkins, Chicago's Mayor Kelly, Attorney General Jackson, Senator Byrnes of South Carolina, and others prevailed upon Roosevelt not to add a statement releasing his delegates and also to defer the statement from Bankhead's speech on the 15th of July to Alben Barkley's chairman's speech the following evening.

The President's advisors were concerned that such a statement as Roosevelt had planned, especially releasing the delegates, made on the first night of the convention, might be taken seriously and lead to an open convention (which was, of course, the last thing they wanted). Roosevelt did not think so but deferred to loyalist opinion on site.

Harold Ickes and Frances Perkins detected that many delegates thought they were being treated like pawns in what was assumed to be a stitch-up for Roosevelt's renomination. Perkins and others felt that Farley, a man to whom Roosevelt and the Democratic Party owed much, was being hung out to dry unjustly. This was a little severe, because Farley had to have taken leave of his senses to have sought the office at all. Both Ickes and Perkins thought that Hopkins's high-handed management of Roosevelt's interests was alienating delegates, and Miss Perkins asked the President to come personally to the convention. Ickes thought the same, with 900 delegates "milling around like worried sheep." Roosevelt declined and suggested Eleanor go. "Eleanor always makes people feel right," he said. Roosevelt also, at Frances Perkins's suggestion, telephoned Farley and told him the statement declaring that he did not want another term would be read that evening by Barkley, Farley having noticed its conspicuous absence in Bankhead's remarks, where Roosevelt had told him it would appear.

It was indeed read by Barkley at the end of his spellbinding address on the evening of July 16. Barkley had wound the convention up with a stirring recitation of the achievements of the last eight years and excoriation of the Republicans, without mentioning the President's name. Then in passing and inadvertently, the magic name of the party's most successful leader since Jefferson was mentioned, and the hall erupted in applause and cheers. Barkley was unable to restore order by shouting and banging his gavel, and had to resort to the ruse of calling into the microphone for a doctor, claiming that a woman had been injured in the pro-Roosevelt melee. He then resumed his progress to the peroration, which consisted of his summary of the contents of Roosevelt's message, ending: "He [Roosevelt] wishes in all earnestness and sincerity to make it clear that all the delegates to this convention are free to vote for any candidate. That is the message I bear to you from the President of the United States, our great leader, Franklin Delano Roosevelt." "Any candidate" obviously included the incumbent.

There was complete silence for a few moments. Then the Chicago Democratic machine took over the convention. From the basement a mighty voice bellowed into a microphone connected to all the loudspeakers in the convention hall: "We Want Roosevelt!" This chant was repeated endlessly; every state and city, sequentially, wanted Roosevelt: "Chicago wants Roosevelt!" "New York wants Roosevelt!" etc., peaking every couple of minutes with "The World Wants Roosevelt!" The galleries, packed out by the Kelly organization, exploded in Roosevelt demonstrations. Most of the delegates leapt to their feet, seized the state standards, and began marching around the hall demanding the President's renomination. The bands played "Happy Days Are Here Again" and "Franklin

D. Roosevelt Jones." The demonstration went on for almost an hour; it was obvious that Roosevelt was going to be renominated without significant opposition.

(It emerged that the disembodied voice that whipped up the crowd belonged to Chicago's superintendent of sewers, Thomas D. McGarry, who was thereafter called by Roosevelt's enemies "the voice from the sewers."*)

The following night, July 17, Franklin D. Roosevelt was renominated. There was suspense only on the issue of how many votes would be cast against him, since Hopkins had declared that FDR would decline the nomination if the total were more than 150. (There is no reason to believe that Roosevelt would have done so, though he was so aggravated by the conduct of some of the conservative and isolationist spongers in his party that he might have withdrawn if there were significant opposition, if only to provoke a real draft.) The vote was 946½ for Roosevelt and 148 for all other candidates.[†] Farley graciously moved and gained unanimous acclamation of the nominee. The office wasn't exactly seeking the man, but for Roosevelt's purposes, it was an adequate facsimile of a draft.

A battle took place in the resolutions committee, led by Senators Burton Wheeler, David Walsh, and Bennett Clark and former war secretary Woodring. They demanded an isolationist foreign policy plank. Senator Robert Wagner chaired the committee. The isolationists demanded a statement that the United States would not participate in foreign wars and would not send its armed forces overseas. Roosevelt refused to accept any such thing, because it would be an encouragement to Hitler and the Japanese. Finally, Senator Byrnes arranged a compromise that added "except in case of attack" after the pledge.

There were many contestants for vice president and considerable irritation when Hopkins announced on the morning of July 18 that Wallace was the President's choice. Hopkins had assured Bankhead that the field was open. He, Burton Wheeler, Assistant War Secretary Louis Johnson, Jesse Jones and Sam Rayburn of Texas, Missouri governor Lloyd Stark, and Paul McNutt, former governor of Indiana and governor general of the Philippines, and several lesser figures had all been running. Not only were the other potential candidates displeased by Hopkins's effort to warn them off; Wallace was regarded as an

---

* Twenty-eight years later, when President Lyndon B. Johnson had announced that he would "not seek and will not accept the nomination of my party for another term as your President," six-term Chicago mayor and Democratic Party boss Richard J. Daley offered to stampede the convention in his city to renominate LBJ. He assumed, probably because of his middle-level participation in the 1940 charade of Roosevelt's noncandidacy, that Johnson wished to run again. Johnson declined. Implementing such an offer as Daley's in the chaotic and violent circumstances of the 1968 convention would have been a challenge even for the Daley machine.[33]

† There were 72½ for Farley, 61 for Garner, 5½ for Hull, who was not even nominated, and 9½ for Millard Tydings, who insolently allowed himself to be nominated and denounced Roosevelt for his Supreme Court bill and for his attempt to defeat Tydings in Maryland.

eccentric and unreliable figure and, as Farley said, not really a Democrat. (He had been a Republican most of his life and his father had been agriculture secretary under Harding and Coolidge.)

Eleanor Roosevelt spoke briefly to the convention and was generously received and courteously heard. She said that if her husband, bearing the immense burdens of his office in wartime, "felt that the strain of a third term might be too much . . . and that Mr. Wallace was the man who could carry on best in times such as we were facing," he was surely "entitled to have" Wallace's help. This was, she said, "no ordinary time." Applause was generous, and the convention calmed down. (Though Democrats would not see this, if her husband needed Henry Wallace to help him through a third term, Mrs. Roosevelt had inadvertently given a strong argument for the election of Willkie.)

Paul McNutt and most of the other candidates graciously withdrew as vice presidential candidates in deference to the President's wishes, but Speaker William Bankhead stayed in the race against Wallace. This came to a vote on the evening of July 18. Listening to proceedings by radio in the study upstairs in the White House, Roosevelt became exasperated and set aside the cards he had been using to play solitaire and wrote out a statement to be read to the convention if matters deteriorated. The proposed statement asserted that the Democrats in the twentieth century had won national elections only when they had been "the champions of progressive and liberal policies.... The Democratic Convention, as appears clear from the events of today, is divided on this fundamental issue. Until the Democratic party through this convention makes overwhelmingly clear its stand in favor of social progress and liberalism, and shakes off the shackles . . . fastened upon it by the forces of conservatism, reaction, and appeasement, it will not continue to march to victory."

He accused domestic reactionaries and isolationist appeasers of "the promotion of discord" in the convention. "It is best not to straddle ideals," he wrote, and in order to give the party the right to resolve this contest between what he considered progressive and regressive forces, he was declining the nomination. To his aides in the oval room in the White House, he claimed to be absolutely serious.

He intended to deliver the speech that night if Wallace were not nominated. This was not necessary. The secretary of agriculture trailed in the early stages of the balloting, but was chosen by 628 to 459 for his combined rivals, mainly Bankhead. (Bankhead died September 15, 1940, so his nomination would have caused more chaos, apart from the question of whether Roosevelt would have renounced his own nomination. And if Bankhead had survived as Speaker, this convention would not have improved his relations with the President.)

Eleanor Roosevelt probably spared her husband a great deal of embarrassment at Chicago. If Wallace had lost, the most likely outcome is, considering how attached Roosevelt was to the presidency and what an inveterate poker player he was, that he would have submitted to a real draft after purporting to decline the improvised one. However annoyed some of the rank and file were, they would have prostrated themselves at the feet of their leader had he required it. But his choice of Wallace, like his pursuit of Supreme Court packing and of the 1938 purge in the primaries, showed an inexplicable tenacity over unwise questions touching on his own authority. This came close to damaging his presidency and all he achieved in that office after his first term.

It was as if his endless subtle and discreet calculations drove him to outbursts of frustration that could only be assuaged by reckless gambles of the political capital he had so carefully amassed. The appointments of inappropriate people to important positions, like Joseph Kennedy, were acts of misplaced self-amusement joined to normal human error. This trait of gambling needlessly for minimal or unattainable ends was perverse. It was only good fortune that it did not bring him down. But the disorderly farce in Chicago seems to have cured him of this indisposition. This too was fortunate, because he would hereafter be playing for bigger stakes than ever and his judgment would ramify throughout the world and for many decades.

Roosevelt and his intimates in the White House had sweated through the proceedings in Chicago without air conditioning on a sweltering night, because Roosevelt was concerned about the effect of cool air on his always susceptible sinuses. When Wallace was finally nominated, Hopkins persuaded him not to give the pugnacious reply to his opponents he had planned as an acceptance speech. Roosevelt, soaked in perspiration, went from his study next door to his bedroom, bathed and changed, and appeared refreshed in the White House diplomatic reception room to deliver through a battery of microphones to the convention in Chicago his acceptance of his party's nomination for the third time to the presidency of the United States. The President began speaking at 12:25 A.M. on July 19. Exceptionally, Wallace sat on the dais while the convention listened to Roosevelt address it from the White House, and the vice presidential nominee did not speak to the convention at all.

It was clear at once that the amateurishness and churlishness of recent days, of which the public had only a hint, were over and that the country's heavyweight political champion had reasserted himself. He spoke "with a very full heart" of his ambivalence about running again and the reasons for it. He described "the efforts I made to prevent war from the moment it was threatened. And to restrict the area of carnage . . . in the face of appeaser fifth-columnists who charged me with hysteria and war-mongering." He was determined "to implement the total defense of America," with the help of distinguished and selfless people of all persuasions, "regardless of party, regardless of personal convenience." Some form of "selection by draft" would be necessary.

He then, employing language suggested by Archibald MacLeish in the memo Frankfurter had requested, executed a daring maneuver: "Lying awake, as I have on many nights [unlikely, from what is known of his sleeping habits], I have asked myself whether I have the right as commander in chief of the army and navy, to call on men and women to serve their country or to train themselves to serve and, at the same time, decline to serve my country in my own personal capacity, if I am called upon to do so by the people of my country. . . . The fact which dominates our world is the fact of armed aggression, of successful armed aggression, aimed at the form of government, the kind of society that we in the United States have chosen and established for ourselves. . . . No individual retains or can hope to retain the right of personal choice which free men enjoy in times of peace. . . . Only the people themselves can draft a President. If such a draft should be made upon me, I will, with God's help," etc.

It is a measure of Roosevelt's great prestige and oratorical talent that he managed to put such a pious trumpery over without convulsing the convention and the country in mocking disbelief. Future *Time* magazine editor Hedley Donovan, then of draft age, called it "painful humbuggery,"[34] equating occupancy of the White House to being drafted to boot camp and trained with bayoneted rifle for mortal combat.

He thanked the convention for choosing Wallace, praised his running mate's "practical idealism," and sent "my most affectionate greetings [to] my old friend Jim Farley." (Their friendship was in fact over, and Farley was replaced by Frank Walker as postmaster general and by Ed Flynn as party chairman. Another old comrade of the man "who couldn't bear to fire anyone" bit the dust.)

The campaign "will be different from the usual national campaign," since he would not have the time to electioneer very much or "engage in purely political debate. But I shall never be loath to call the attention of the nation to deliberate or unwitting distortions of fact, which are sometimes made by political candidates."

Roosevelt had already begun to dismiss his isolationist opponents as "appeasers and fifth-columnists," which in practice meant traitors. They would fail to support the heroic defenders of liberty abroad and would leave America defenseless against the barbarous dictators.

One mystified observer at the chaotic proceedings in Chicago was the new deputy ambassador of the Soviet Union, Andrei Gromyko, then on a cross-country tour to familiarize himself with the United States. He found the convention incomprehensible: "One assumed that all the shouting was for the Democrats, but it was impossible to tell in the great roar, which sounded as if an earthquake were approaching. . . . Beyond the yelling and the chaos, however, it was easy to hear the cries of ecstasy every time the name of Roosevelt was mentioned."[35]

IV

THE PRESIDENT WAS bearing down hard on the nexus between eliminating unemployment and building national defense. In his budget message of January 4, 1940, he had described $1.84 billion as "sufficient," and Nye and other congressional termites who complained about an excessive defense effort were nibbling at that when the Nazi hordes swarmed into Norway. With the British army taking to the boats at Dunkirk on May 31, Roosevelt asked Congress for, and promptly received, another $1 billion for defense. On July 10, with the swastika flying from the Eiffel Tower but Churchillian Britain spitting defiance, Roosevelt asked for and again promptly received from the Congress $5 billion, saying in his accompanying message: "The United States . . . must have total defense. We cannot defend ourselves a little here and a little there. We must be able to defend ourselves wholly and at any time." To this end, he laid down eight battleships, twenty-four fleet aircraft carriers (over eighteen months), hundreds of other craft, and 50,000 warplanes, and called for an army of millions of men. (There were at this time only twenty-three operational aircraft carriers in the world, including several small and rudimentary ones. Other countries had approximately ten under construction.)

By the autumn it was clear that Roosevelt's policy of all aid short of war itself was just and sensible, and his argument that this was the only way to strike a blow for democratic civilization while staying out of actual combat was almost irresistible. On October 8, Roosevelt received a supplementary defense authorization for an astounding $9 billion. He was now firmly launched on his plan to build a war machine of unprecedented strength and sophistication.

There remains some dispute about the extent of lingering unemployment in the United States by the autumn of 1940. Even some pro-Roosevelt commentators[36] allege that U.S. unemployment was still between nine and ten million when Roosevelt began his campaign for a third term. The AFL and CIO figures exaggerated the number by divining that millions had given up looking for work. The Bureau of the Census figure for this period is about 5.5 million unemployed, or 11 percent, coming down to 3 million or under 6 percent if those engaged in relief projects are included as employed people.

The Burke-Wadsworth conscription bill passed September 20. It was headed for passage when the election campaign began in earnest about Labor Day, and it would clearly take up another million young men, most of whom the ordinary labor force would have to replace. This would reduce the percentage of unemployed to under 9, and between 3 and 4 if relief workers are included. By election day both figures were down by almost two full points below these.

It is perhaps approximately true that "One-half of the men and two-thirds of the women [who worked in the United States in the summer of 1940] earned less than one thousand dollars a year [and that] only 48,000 taxpayers in a population of 132 million earned more than $2,500 per year."[37] (Forty times as much in the money and purchasing power of sixty years later.)

But the fear of unemployment was over. World War II had enabled Roosevelt to conclude the New Deal in glorious victory. Seven and one-half years after his first inauguration, a broken, defeated, hopeless nation with a collapsed financial system, a dispossessed and migratory farm community, and 33 percent unemployment had almost eliminated unemployment and was preparing to save democracy in the world without having to go to war, merely by going to work as it had desperately wished to do all through the thirties. There was relief in unemployment insurance or workfare for everyone, and job creation was advancing by over 300,000 per month (400,000 in August 1940, 500,000 in September; unemployment was evaporating). There would remain the problems of transferring public sector to private sector employment and raising wages. The country's fear was of foreign war, and Franklin D. Roosevelt, combining the ethical with the expedient as he had a consistent genius to do, was unassailable on this issue.

The polls consistently showed Roosevelt between five and ten points ahead of Willkie through August and September. Most Americans disapproved in principle of the idea of three straight terms for a president. Most thought Willkie would do as well with the economy. But concerns with the New Deal's shortcomings were balanced by its ultimate success and had given way to confidence in Roosevelt as a leader who had tried to keep the peace, had foreseen the dangers of Hitler, had foreseen the resilience of Britain, was right to arm the nation and aid the democracies, and was the best-qualified person to do the right and sensible thing while keeping the nation out of war.

Roosevelt found Willkie likeable, energetic, and, liberal as he was, a difficult opponent to dismiss as one of the reactionary "old guard Republicans in their entrenched positions." But Willkie found Roosevelt hard to attack, too. If he assailed him as too liberal, Roosevelt would hang the Hoover legacy around Willkie's neck. If he attacked from an isolationist perspective, which Willkie personally deplored, Roosevelt would represent him as a Hitler dupe, an appeaser and fifth-columnist. If he attacked Roosevelt for insufficient attention to defense, Roosevelt could skewer him as a warmonger set at the head of a party of purblind Gerald Nye isolationists who had never thought or uttered a word about defense until Hitler's armies goose-stepped down the Champs-Elysees.

In this autumn of the Battle of Britain and the campaign for a third presidential term against an estimable opponent, Franklin D. Roosevelt's political mastery reached its highest point and would remain there for some years.

Hitler had made his long-awaited address to the world July 19. A long motorcade of fanioned automobiles conducted him to the Kroll Opera House in Berlin, where he proposed peace with Britain on the basis of full retention by both Great Britain and Germany of everything they then possessed. All the countries Germany had already conquered were to be conceded permanently to Germany. Hitler called his remarks an "appeal to common sense." He could see "no reason why this war should continue" but warned that if it did, Britain would be needlessly annihilated. He paused dramatically between the conclusion of his summary of recent events and his outline of the possible basis for peace. Churchill listened to the speech on the radio but dismissed it at once as just another act of treachery, containing no worthwhile elements and emanating from an unappeasable psychopath.

Churchill had revived his correspondence with Roosevelt July 31, after a lapse of six weeks following his failure to persuade the President to promise to enter the war in order to help keep France in it. "It has now become most urgent for you to let us have the destroyers, motor boats, and flying boats for which we have asked. . . . Mr. President, with great respect, in the long history of the world, this is something to do now. Large construction is coming to me in 1941, but the crisis will be reached long before 1941. I know you will do all in your power but I feel entitled and bound to put the gravity and urgency of the position before you." He even referred to Kennedy, who was now unrelievedly pessimistic and regretted that Churchill had not taken up Hitler's July 19 proposals, as "a grand help to us and the common cause." Churchill was presumably moved by Kennedy's incessant false claims to proximity to Roosevelt to utter this wild misstatement.[38]

Air activity over Britain had greatly increased after the middle of July, and the strong British performance in the air war as well as the British attack on the French fleet and Churchill's peremptory rejection of Hitler's so-called peace proposal had sharply raised Roosevelt's confidence that Britain was a redoubtable ally. All indications were that the British were continuing to shoot down three to four German planes for every machine of their own that was lost. The German fighters were approximately equal, in quality of planes and airmen, to the British, but the German bombers were sitting ducks once the British defenders got through to them. The sinister Stukas, which had so terrorized the civil populations of Poland, the Low Countries, and France, were decimated by Spitfires and Hurricanes, and after a couple of disastrous days, never returned to British air space.

Churchill's own stature had also risen to almost superhuman proportions. Roosevelt had sent Colonel William Donovan, winner of the Congressional Medal of Honor and former Republican candidate for governor of New York, to Britain in July, and he came back very confident of successful British resistance.[39] He would go on to a remarkable career as Roosevelt's chief of military intelligence. There would never be talk again from Roosevelt about Churchill's drinking habits or even his Tory past.

The whole American public was now much more confident of Britain's staying power, and polls indicated, as soon as the sale of destroyers was mooted publicly, that over 60 percent of Americans agreed to it. Public, congressional, and even high official opinion was evolving rapidly. On June 22, General Marshall and Admiral Harold R. Stark (chief of naval operations) asked the President for a moratorium on arms sales to Britain, following the post-Dunkirk replenishment that had taken away 20 percent of the ammunition and ordnance of the U.S. armed forces. Roosevelt declined, but on July 2 he had no choice but to sign a measure prohibiting such sales unless Marshall or Stark could certify that the military equipment "was not essential for U.S. defense."

On June 25, Gallup indicated that 64 percent of Americans believed that it was more important to stay out of war than to assist Britain. On October 20, 1940, the same polling organization found the division on this question exactly even, at 50–50. On November 19, the balance had shifted to 60–40 that it was more important to help Britain than to stay out of war. The combination of Roosevelt's advocacy, Churchill's eloquence, his countrymen's martial bravery and civilian stoicism, and Hitler's savagery was decisive in moving American opinion.

At a cabinet meeting on August 2, Ickes, Stimson, Wallace, Morgenthau, Knox, and others were strongly in favor of Roosevelt's imaginative idea of trading fifty World War I destroyers for long leases on a series of British bases from Newfoundland to the West Indies. These bases would enable the United States to maintain a very extensive patrol of the western ocean, from which Britain would clearly benefit, since Roosevelt intended, informally, to hand over to the British any information about German submarines that the U.S. Navy could provide. Navy Secretary Knox had discussed the destroyers-for-bases idea with Ambassador Lothian the night before, and Lothian had approved it.

Roosevelt had already effectively declared the first of several huge extensions of territorial waters, from three miles to 200 miles, when he proclaimed a "Neutrality Zone" of 200 miles off the U.S. Atlantic coast in which all submarine and other "suspicious" (i.e., German) ship movements would be "reported in the clear" — i.e., to the Royal Navy. He planned to extend this zone toward the British Isles in large increments.

From the cabinet room on August 2, Roosevelt called William Allen White and asked him to act as a go-between with Willkie and ask Willkie to lobby the Republican senators and congressmen in favor of the destroyers-for-bases deal. Willkie said privately he was for it but couldn't do anything with congressional Republicans. He had no authority over them, was a recent convert to the Republicans, and didn't need a rending struggle with the old guard of his adoptive party now, when he was in hot pursuit of Roosevelt's job. White reported back by cable August 11: "I know there is not two bits of difference between you on the issue pending. But I can't guarantee either of you to the other, which is funny because I admire and respect you both."

Also on August 11, a long letter to the editor appeared in the *New York Times* signed by Dean Acheson and three other prominent lawyers and acquaintances of Roosevelt's stating that he had the constitutional authority under existing statutes to transfer the destroyers to Great Britain by executive order. Attorney General Jackson confirmed this opinion. The group (Acheson, Charles Burlingham, George Rublee, and Thomas Thacher) promised to lobby Willkie not to oppose this step when it was announced, and on August 30 Willkie pledged to offer no opposition.

Roosevelt wrote back to Churchill on August 13 that "it may be possible to furnish to the British Government as immediate assistance at least 50 destroyers," plus motor torpedo boats and flying boats. This aid would be given in exchange for the prime minister's assurance "that in the event that the waters of Great Britain became untenable," the Royal Navy would be sent to other parts of the Empire to continue resistance to the Germans, and not scuttled or surrendered, and in exchange for long-term leases on Newfoundland, Bermudian, and Caribbean naval and air bases.

Churchill replied August 15, accepting Roosevelt's proposal gratefully. "As regards an assurance about the British fleet . . . we intend to fight this out here to the end and none of us would ever buy peace by surrendering or scuttling the fleet. But in any use you may make of this repeated assurance you will please bear in mind the disastrous effect from our point of view and perhaps also from yours, of allowing any impression to grow that we regard the conquest of the British Islands and its naval bases as any other than an impossible contingency. The spirit of our people is splendid. Never have they been so determined. Their confidence in the issue has been enormously and legitimately strengthened by the severe air fighting of the last week."

The Battle of Britain was entering its most crucial phase, as the German Air Force swarmed over British skies all day throughout August, and the entire Royal Air Force was committed to the contest against it. No reserves were retained; every airworthy fighter plane Britain had was engaged.

There was a good deal of back-and-forth debate about the exact nature of the transaction over destroyers and bases. Roosevelt wanted to present it to his people, in the midst of an election, as a shrewd deal: an exchange of some overage ships that had been in mothballs, for excellent strategic bases. This would be inconvenient for Churchill, in the midst of a desperate fight in the skies of England, who wanted to set it up as two friendly acts, lending destroyers and leasing bases, out of solidarity and not in any exact equivalence. A compromise was worked out by the State Department legal section that the Newfoundland bases would be leased out of friendship, and the Caribbean bases leased in exchange for the loan of the destroyers.

This "enabled Marshall and Stark to take deep breaths, cross their fingers, and certify that the destroyers were 'obsolete' and 'useless,'" as required by the July 2 amendment.[40] (Given that they had both asked for suspension of further arms sales to Britain on June 22, there may have been some presidential arm-twisting involved, but neither alleged so in his memoirs.) Roosevelt was conducting a supreme balancing act between the importunings of Churchill, the war scare whipped up by Willkie, and the reticences of his own service chiefs.

Roosevelt had hoped to delay announcing the destroyers agreement until after the selective service bill had passed, but the British ran out of time and could not wait past the beginning of September. So the President announced the agree-

ment to the reporters accompanying him on his train to inspect a restored ordnance factory and other defense installations in West Virginia on September 3.
With more than twenty journalists crowded like sardines into a small compartment on his train, the President engaged in what appeared to be his usual
inflated description of his own measures. He referred to the destroyer deal as "the
most important event in the defense of the U.S. since Thomas Jefferson's
Louisiana Purchase."[41] For once, this may have been accurate, especially since
the Louisiana Purchase had little directly to do with defense, and was simply a
straight accretion of territory, acquired from a friendly power.*

Although Willkie had promised not to attack the deal and issued a statement
supporting it but regretting that it hadn't been shown to the Congress, he soon
fell in behind the Republican congressional leadership and called it "the most
dictatorial and arbitrary act of any President in the history of the United States."[42]
Up to this time Willkie had been launching roundhouse attacks on the New
Deal for failure to eliminate unemployment, and on Roosevelt as an isolationist
for breaking up the London Economic Conference of 1933 and as an appeaser for
being inadequate in his demurral from Munich and insufficiently supportive of
conscription and aid to Britain. He was not making great inroads with this scatter-
gun approach, and Roosevelt's lead was steady through September.

The President's tours of arms and munitions factories and military camps
were in fact campaign trips in every respect and enabled him to wage a vigorous
reelection battle while piously claiming to be above the fray. Willkie was
becoming desperate in his inability to make inroads on Roosevelt's position. The
Republican candidate was trapped between his own convictions, Roosevelt's
record as a reformer, the Hoover legacy, and the congressional Republicans'
narrow-minded isolationism. In his new battle armor, Willkie would concentrate overwhelmingly on his claim that Roosevelt was determined to take the
country to war.

The Republican leaders in the Congress called the destroyer deal "an act of
war." Churchill later wrote that the Germans would have been justified in considering it so, and privately said the same at the time, to emphasize the solidarity
of the United States for the sake of the morale of his own parliamentary colleagues. Churchill was playing the trans-Atlantic solidarity card as strenuously as
he could. He had disconcerted Roosevelt on August 20 when he told Parliament:
"These two great organizations of the English-speaking democracies, the British
Empire and the United States, will have to be somewhat mixed up together in
some of their affairs for mutual and general advantage. . . . I do not view the

---

* Napoleon believed that in making the sale to Jefferson he was helping to create a colossus
that would wrench the leadership of the English-speaking world away from Britain. What he
could not foresee was that the British and Americans would compose their differences and
make the English-speaking peoples much more preeminent in the world than ever.

process with any misgivings. I could not stop it if I wished; no one can stop it. Like the Mississippi, it just keeps rolling along. Let it roll. Let it roll on—full flood, inexorable, irresistible, benignant, to broader lands and happier days."[43] This was a considerable evolution from his interwar complaints about American "vanity" and tendency to "extract the last pound of flesh."[44]

For Roosevelt, this idea of confluence was inconvenient during the election campaign, because it facilitated Republican claims that he was driving the country into war with Germany and, especially for voters of German, Italian, and Irish origin, that he was unduly influenced by the British. "They are already almost at the boats!" Willkie, referring to America's young soldiers, would wail in his hoarse voice, made raspy by his frenetic touring and speaking.

By early September and even before conscription had been passed by the Congress or the destroyers physically handed over to the British, Roosevelt moved to his next initiative in his steady redefinition of neutrality. He ordered Admiral Stark to prepare plans for a greatly expanded neutrality zone, to the 60th meridian, a line from Newfoundland to British Guiana, bounding a section of the Atlantic Ocean a thousand miles wide off the coast of the middle Atlantic and southern states. To Stark's consternation, he received a follow-up note from Berle in the State Department September 27 requesting details of the plan, which he understood had been "thoroughly discussed" with the President.

On October 10, a memo from the President himself arrived expressing irritation at the time it was taking to extend the "Neutrality Zone." Despite being in the middle of an intense election campaign, Roosevelt detailed that he expected the U.S. Navy to have "rushed to completion" a comprehensive patrolling of this vast sweep of the Atlantic, with submarine and other relevant sightings reported uncoded, for the British navy to hear, and added ominously that "loss of contact with surface ships cannot be tolerated."[45] Even as his opponents accused him of leading the nation to war under false political colors, the Commander in Chief was redefining neutrality as systematic hostility to one side while massively arming the other side.

Roosevelt had called the country to a day of prayer on Sunday, September 8, for the deliverance of civilization from the forces of evil. Roosevelt attended the little Episcopal church at Hyde Park with his mother and Princess Martha of Norway, the beautiful and elegant daughter-in-law of the king of Norway, who flattered, doted on, and generally delighted Roosevelt. To Missy LeHand's great irritation, Roosevelt invited her to reside in the White House, an invitation she happily accepted, remaining until she had her own home after about a month. At St. James Episcopal Church, Hyde Park, on September 8, the clergy affirmed: "We are on the brink of the greatest catastrophe of all times. Can the hand of the oppressor be stayed? The President of the United States believes that it can, with God's help. That is why he has called upon us to join today in prayer." Roosevelt was never averse to being proximate to the Almighty, especially during an election campaign.

The British capital was heavily bombed September 7, causing severe damage to "the London that had taken thirty generations a thousand years to build."[46] Throughout August and September, 1940, the RAF lost approximately twelve aircraft per day but only a couple of pilots, but the Germans were losing about thirty aircraft and their entire air crews (dead or captured) every day. As a fillip to British morale and to make a point with the enemy, Churchill ordered air raids by eighty British bombers on Berlin, August 25–29.

This, added to the unsustainable losses the RAF was inflicting on the Luftwaffe, helped cause Goering to abandon daytime raids and shift to massive and indiscriminate nighttime bombing of populated areas. Also, the opposing intelligence services misjudged their adversary. The Germans thought the RAF smaller and technically less capable than it was, and the British thought the German Air Force and aircraft industry stronger than they were. When Goering moved to attacks on populated areas, German intelligence estimated that RAF Fighter Command was down to 177 planes and that Britain had a production of 250 fighters per month. They believed they had inflicted heavier losses than they had and that they had virtually denuded the RAF of fighters. In fact, on September 19, the RAF had 1,084 fighter aircraft in or just entering service, and monthly production (September 7 to October 10) was 428, not counting what might be bought or otherwise provided from the United States.

The British estimated the German front line air force at about 6,000 in August 1940, and annual aircraft production at 24,400. The real figures were respectively 3,000 and 10,247 (for 1940). Between July 10 and October 31, 1940, the RAF lost 915 aircraft, the Luftwaffe 1,733. The kill ratio of three or four to one came down to only two to one for the whole period when the Germans shifted to night raids, after which the losses of aircraft were almost equal, though the German aircrew losses were naturally much heavier than those of the RAF over Britain. The British were producing more planes than they were losing in August, while German losses exceeded their aircraft production prior to the shift to night attacks. If the Germans had continued their precisely targeted daylight attacks, they would have dangerously diminished their air force, and, unlike the British, they could not buy aircraft from the United States or any other worthwhile foreign supplier.[47]

Changing over to night bombing cut German losses, but was the end of any hope of winning the air war. It brought German losses within production figures but made precise bombing of military targets, especially aircraft factories, impossible. The attacks strained but did not break British morale, and it was clear by mid-October that Britain had won the war in her own skies. London was bombed for fifty-seven consecutive nights, and the Parliament buildings were among many famous landmarks severely damaged. After October, both sides effectively controlled their own airspace.

On August 20, 1940, Winston Churchill said of the Royal Air Force Fighter

Comand, in another of his brilliant world broadcasts: "Never in the field of human conflict was so much owed by so many to so few." He claimed the Luftwaffe had outnumbered the RAF by "seven or eight to one." This was a deliberate cultivation of the preferred British status of underdog and a corresponding magnification of the triumph of the British aviators. The official British estimate of the size of the RAF compared with the Luftwaffe was one to three, and the real ratio was two British warplanes to three German.

Churchill knew American politics well enough to know that in giving these inspiriting addresses and announcing a resurrection of his country's military fortunes, he was helping Roosevelt and making the President, in the midst of his reelection campaign, appear both generous and prescient in the eyes of his own voters. Military success sired diplomatic and political success.

Churchill's oratorical powers and the sympathetic reporting of American war correspondents, particularly Edward R. Murrow and William L. Shirer of CBS Radio, Virginia Cowles, and many others, helped to swing American opinion overwhelmingly behind the British. British censors withdrew their normal tight restrictions and cooperated completely with the U.S. networks for radio broadcasts from London, and huge audiences heard the explosion of German bombs and the wail of British air raid and fire engine sirens. Murrow's deep voice and powerful articulation, in particular, presented a clear confrontation between good and evil. Archibald MacLeish wrote: "You burned the City of London in our homes and we felt the flames."[48] *

The British Ministry of Information made a film about "the Blitz" (as the bombing of London was called), entitled *London Can Take It*, which was narrated by the American writer Quentin Reynolds and distributed by Warner Brothers without the real producer's being identified. In this form of disguised war propaganda, this powerful and very professionally put together film was shown in 12,000 American movie theaters and was viewed by over sixty million Americans starting in November 1940. The effect on American opinion was profound.

Churchill undoubtedly spoke for his people when he declared: "We will mete out to the enemy the measure and more than the measure that he has meted out to us." Britain would endure the German air assault with an ever fiercer determination to revisit it upon her enemy. With local air superiority and overwhelming sea superiority, and an army being swiftly reequipped, Britain by late October was no longer in danger of invasion.

The heavy units of the Royal Navy's Home Fleet had been distributed around

---

* In furtherance of the cause of Anglo-American solidarity, Churchill even looked benignly upon a torrid liaison between Murrow, whose wife was in the United States, and his own daughter-in-law, Pamela Churchill, whose husband, Randolph Churchill, was serving abroad. More than fifty years later, Pamela Churchill, as the widow of Roosevelt's friend and supporter Averell Harriman, would be U.S. ambassador to France.

southern ports to intervene in the Channel in the event of an invasion. The Royal Navy's capital ships returned to their more secure base at Scapa Flow in the Orkneys in the late autumn. Hitler had secretly deferred a cross-Channel invasion sine die, October 12, 1940. On October 21, in yet another ringing call to arms broadcast to the world, Winston Churchill permitted himself the reflection: "We are waiting for the long-promised invasion; so are the fishes."

V

T HE SELECTIVE SERVICE ACT was adopted by both houses of Congress in mid-September, after strenuous debate and after Roosevelt's own congressman at Hyde Park, the archisolationist Hamilton Fish, attempted to limit the increase in military personnel to 400,000 and tried for sixty days to make those voluntary enlistments. Senator George Norris claimed that the bill "would change the nature of our citizens." They "would become warlike . . . no doubt . . . would soon be fighting with somebody." Burton Wheeler said the bill would "slit the throat of the last democracy still living."[49]

Willkie supported the bill, but could not carry his party in Congress, most of whom voted against selective service. This confirmed Roosevelt in his view that Willkie, even if a sincere comparative liberal, which he found hard to believe in a securities executive, would be merely a fig leaf for the reactionary, isolationist, and rapacious big business elements that had, in his view, run the Republican party ever since the retirement of his cousin as president in 1909. (He regarded the subsequent Republican presidential candidates up to Willkie as reactionary or inadequate.)

Selective service, like the votes among farmers on reduction of farm production under the AAA, was a great exercise in popular democracy. While all males between twenty-one and thirty-six were required to register and the call-ups would be by national lottery, 6,400 local draft boards would be the final judges of fitness and claims for deferment.[50]

Speaker William Bankhead died September 15. In a grand gesture of reconciliation with some of his congressional dissenters, Roosevelt attended the funeral in Montgomery, Alabama, a few days later.* The talented Sam Rayburn of Texas, House majority leader, became Speaker. The solid John W. McCormack of Massachusetts became majority leader.†

---

* An extremely elaborate wooden platform was built, with ramps up to the top of the steps of the state capitol, so the President's car could bring him up to the level where he could walk straight into the capitol rotunda without the embarrassment of having to be conveyed up stairs in the presence of a large number of witnesses and the news cameras of the nation.

† These two strong figures would between them serve a total of ninety-one years in the House, twenty-seven of them as Speaker (in which office McCormack would follow Rayburn on the latter's death in 1962).

Roosevelt had to reassure the African-American constituency, which had, through New Deal welfare and workfare benefits, largely been won over from the party of Lincoln. At its height, and after Roosevelt had banned, by executive order, discrimination in WPA projects, the WPA was providing income for one million black families, and 300,000 black youths were in the NYA (National Youth Administration, the youth arm of the NRA relief programs and their successors).[51]

Eleanor had addressed the Convention of Sleeping Car Porters on September 16, 1940. This union was founded and led by A. Philip Randolph, one of the ablest and most distinguished black leaders in America. Eleanor arranged for Randolph and two other black leaders, Arnold Hill, formerly of the National Urban League, and Walter White of the National Association for the Advancement of Colored People, to meet the President on September 27.

As the U.S. armed forces expanded rapidly, many African-Americans rallied to the colors, apart from patriotic motives, as a good ticket out of the late Depression. With the U.S. Army at a half million men, less than 1 percent of them were African-American, including only two officers and three chaplains. The country as a whole was 9 percent black. There were four black regiments, only one of them receiving combat training, and not one African-American in the Marine Corps, Tank Corps, Signal Corps, or Army Air Corps. The same week as Eleanor's appearance at Randolph's convention, fifteen black crewmen on the U.S.S. *Philadelphia*, which Roosevelt had commandeered for cruising on occasion, wrote to the *Pittsburgh Courier*, advising other African-Americans not to join the navy so as not to become "sea-going bell hops, chambermaids, and dishwashers." The signatories to this letter expressed the view that no disciplinary action could "possibly surpass the mental cruelty inflicted upon us in this ship." The signers of the letter were thrown into the brig and dishonorably discharged as unfit.

The condition of the African-American members of the armed forces was the principal reason for the September 27 meeting with the President. Also present were Navy Secretary Knox and Assistant War Secretary Patterson. Roosevelt emphasized that the War Department had decreed that the blacks would be put pro rata into all units and that they would be eligible for combat roles. Randolph and the others acknowledged that this was progress but offered a full program of measures to achieve the complete integration of the armed forces. Roosevelt said: "You have got to work into this." Where great controversy impended, his technique was usually gradual. He thought that black and white units would gradually integrate where they were next to each other in combat. He said you couldn't have northern and southern ships, the northern ones being easier to integrate. He did propose bringing black bands onto ships as a form of beginning integration.

Roosevelt promised to be back in touch with the civil rights leaders. He met a stone wall with his military and departmental chiefs. General Marshall said that it was not the time for "critical experiments which would have a highly destructive effect on morale." Knox threatened to resign if he would have to desegregate the navy at the same time he created a two-ocean navy.

With his wife prodding him, Roosevelt prevailed upon the War Department to create black units in every branch of the service and to train African-American aviators. This was further progress, but at a very stately pace, compromised by the President's press secretary, Steve Early, a southern white supremacist and segregationist, who falsely asserted to the press that Randolph, White, and Hill had been satisfied with Roosevelt's efforts and supported continued segregation. The black leaders issued their own release and accused the administration of "a stab in the back" (now a topical metaphor) "of democracy . . . a blow at the patriotism of twelve million Negro citizens."* Walter White wrote to Eleanor Roosevelt, who again brought the issue forcefully before her husband. He issued a statement reassuring the black community that the War Department's position was not necessarily a durable one. In the current world crisis, he wrote, "we dare not confuse the issue of prompt preparedness with a new social experiment, however important and desirable it may be."

African-Americans now accounted for almost 5 percent of the total vote. They tended to vote en bloc in the big northern cities to which they had emigrated and where their vote could be determining of their states' electoral votes. Early's mendacity in the press release had endangered or possibly fragmented what had been considered a reliable constituency. Roosevelt commissioned a little research by Hopkins and learned that the African-American leadership would be mollified by the elevation of Colonel Benjamin C. Davis, the highest-ranking black officer in the armed forces and grandson of a slave, to the rank of general, and by the appointment of William Hastie, dean of the Howard University law school, to the staff of War Secretary Stimson.

The leadership of the black community felt that only by creating some black leadership in the armed forces could a steady force for integration be asserted. Roosevelt agreed to these appointments and Davis was promoted brigadier general and Hastie attached to Stimson. The civil rights leaders and black community press went back to referring constructively to the President.* Stimson wrote Knox that the next time he visited with his black brigadier general he "fully expected to be met with a colored admiral." He thought both promotions a bad mistake and blamed them on "Mrs. Roosevelt's intrusive and impulsive folly." In fact, it was Eleanor Roosevelt at her best.

---

* Roosevelt's efforts with the black vote were not helped when Steve Early kicked a black New York City policeman in the groin at Pennsylvania Station in an argument in the middle of the campaign. Fortunately, the policeman told the press he was a Roosevelt supporter. Early was muzzled and the controversy died.[52]

The day of the meeting with Randolph and the others, the Tripartite Pact was announced between Germany, Japan, and Italy. It pledged the assistance of all if one were attacked by a power not then engaged in the European or Sino-Japanese wars. It was obviously aimed at the United States and was Hitler's diplomatic answer to the sale of destroyers to the British.

VI

THROUGH LATE SEPTEMBER, Roosevelt's campaign appeared unassailable. He was not complacently sitting in the White House but energetically getting round the country, speaking and being seen, but seeing to defense preparedness and not mere politics, though the political effect of his travel was the same. His rearmament program was banishing the last of unemployment.

Willkie did radiate a rough-hewn, benignly ursine Midwestern integrity. The nation liked and admired Roosevelt. He had taken office in terrible times and made them better. He had preserved the honor of his nation through the thirties, unlike the British and French leaders. His physical courage as a man who was assumed to have recovered more fully from polio than he really had was universally respected. And he had often demonstrated moral courage, as one who would ultimately put the national interest ahead of political convenience, currently in the selective service and destroyers-for-bases debates.

Yet there was always discernible in Roosevelt the amiable shaman, the supremely confident and somewhat cynical political wizard of the Hudson Valley nobility who always won in the end by whatever means proved necessary. Most Americans wanted to be led by a winner, but they didn't like to be taken for granted and they wanted their leader's mettle tested, especially as he now asked for a third term. Roosevelt was the supreme progenitor of the political leader the American public would like best as the newsfilm and television age developed, whose photogenic, convivial exterior masked a tough and cunning tactical shell, over a stainless devotion to the founding principles of American democracy and nationhood. In their different ways Dwight D. Eisenhower, John F. Kennedy, and Ronald Reagan (all of whom claimed to have learned a great deal from Roosevelt) would meet these criteria as apparently amicable, tough men, though none as completely as the founder of the genre.

By early October 1940, Willkie, stridently claiming Roosevelt's promise to stay out of war was no more believable than had been his promise to balance the budget, was starting to inch forward in the polls. Roosevelt, ever alert to the slightest currents in American public opinion, began to prepare for a less reserved wind-up to the campaign. His bland and lordly evasions had driven Willkie to a frenzy of travel and oratorical excess, but the race was slowly tightening. Roosevelt, the ne plus ultra of American electoral politics, whose repertoire spanned the highest statesmanship and the lowest chicanery, was preparing an end game that aficionados of practical political science would long remember.

In October Eleanor Roosevelt went to the West Coast to visit her eldest son, Jimmy, who had joined the Marine Corps at San Diego, and her daughter Anna, who had remarried. John Boettiger, Anna's husband, was now the publisher of the *Seattle Post-Intelligencer* and Anna was the associate editor of the women's pages of the newspaper, both appointments made by the proprietor, the indestructible, if mellowing, William Randolph Hearst. Eleanor wrote to her husband that she hoped he would make some political speeches. She was concerned that Willkie was gaining and that Roosevelt's claim that he couldn't spare the time to campaign but could continually travel around the country making what amounted to political speeches disguised as innocuous morale-raisers for munitions workers and military trainees was wearing thin.

The President's entire entourage and his own intuition told him it was time to respond to Willkie, who had barnstormed over 25,000 miles around the country. Ickes, Hopkins, Senator James Byrnes, Justice Hugo Black, and party chairman Ed Flynn were among those who called on the President to enter the battle. There were not three weeks left before the election when the White House announced on October 18 that, provoked by "a systematic program of falsification of fact by the opposition, [the President] has . . . decided to tell the American people what these representations are and will make five speeches between now and election day." In fact, there would be many more than that, as Roosevelt would travel on his train between five major centers for those addresses but would speak constantly at whistle stops and through the press for the balance of the campaign.

Roosevelt was now very close to the realization of his ambitions. He had transformed the United States into a modern state committed to assist the disadvantaged join in the general prosperity. He was very close to a mastery of American public life unexampled in the country's history, to making America the greatest economic and military power in the world, and to engaging it in the world in the triumphant advancement of democracy, the republic's organizing principle, which had not been so threatened in the 175 years since its founding.

Roosevelt's return to the hustings was an instant refreshment to the voting public. He quickly developed a refrain that he had been obliged to enter the campaign to set the record straight: "I cannot say that this is an unpleasant duty. I am an old campaigner and I love a good fight." A good fight it had become.

Willkie and his wife were pelted with eggs in Detroit and Pontiac, and a variety of other fruit in other places, particularly by militantly labor audiences. This sort of incivility usually wins more votes for the target than it loses and probably did in this case. Willkie retained a throat specialist to accompany him (Dr. Harold Barnard) and advise on how to conserve his voice from becoming an incomprehensible croak. Willkie's indomitability and stamina won him a great many admirers.

Roosevelt's first acknowledged campaign speech was in Philadelphia, October

23. He contrasted the achievements of the New Deal, down to the latest gains in employment, with the twelve preceding years of the false and "mocking" worship "of the golden calf" under the Republicans. Most voters well remembered the Great Depression, and Roosevelt had a particular talent for reminding them of it in his rich theatrical voice.*

The Republicans, through less exalted spokesmen than Willkie, had put it about that Roosevelt had made "secret agreements" about getting into the war. Roosevelt responded: "That charge is contrary to every fact, every purpose of the last eight years. . . . It is for peace that I have labored; and it is for peace that I shall labor all the days of my life."

The same night Roosevelt spoke in Philadelphia, Alfred E. Smith set out around New York campaigning for Willkie. Now a distant memory, sixty-seven years old, it is unlikely that he swayed many votes, and his conduct appeared that of a disgruntled former contender rather than the dissent of a serious statesman. Smith was a man of the time of Prohibition, isolation, and the Roaring Twenties. The world had been a simpler place.

Other fading voices were still audible. Father Coughlin railed and raved against Roosevelt and the Jews. His comments had become so tasteless that more and more radio stations discontinued carrying his broadcasts, and his League for Social Justice was disbanded. With regular newsreels and magazine and newspaper pictures and accounts of Nazi atrocities against Jews, and with returning prosperity, anti-Semitism wasn't as saleable as it had been at the bottom of the Depression. Coughlin became part of the background noise as the real issues were debated by more reputable people.

Of the seven prominent men to whom Roosevelt had warily imputed unlimited lust for power and a potential absence of democratic scruple about achieving it, from early in his administration: Huey Long was dead. General Douglas MacArthur was a man on horseback living luxuriously in a hotel in a the semicolonial Philippines. He would be before the American people again, but not in Roosevelt's time. William Randolph Hearst was superannuated and still recovering from his financial crisis. And Colonel Robert R. McCormick had no aptitude for seizing power himself. He would only cheerlead for those in the primary group who did. The other three, CIO leader John L. Lewis, Ambassador Joseph P. Kennedy, and Colonel Charles A. Lindbergh, would play prominent roles in the climax of the 1940 election campaign.

John L. Lewis violently attacked Roosevelt on October 25, before a nationwide

---

* His chief speechwriter, Samuel Rosenman, wrote of "the attractiveness of his voice, its fine shadings and nuances, the infinite variety; he knew how to give it strength, sarcasm, humor, volume, charm, persuasiveness. . . . He read his lines like a finished actor. . . . He had a combination of familiar charm and deep dignity, of camaraderie and majesty."[53]

radio audience of 30 million. Roosevelt had concluded some months before that Lewis had sailed over the bar of megalomania and was a greater vote-getter as an opponent than as an ally, and had taken his distance from him personally. Lewis opposed conscription as an attack on labor and professed to regard the National Defense Advisory Council as a drastic turn to the right, despite the presence on it of Amalgamated Clothing Workers leader Sidney Hillman and the strong labor ally Securities and Exchange Commissioner Leon Henderson.

Roosevelt was slightly startled, however, at Lewis's vehemence, as he listened to the radio in his White House study with Harry Hopkins and Grace Tully. Lewis accused Roosevelt of "overweening, abnormal . . . dictatorial ambitions" and of the intention to lead America to war. "You, who may be about to die in a foreign war, created at the whim of an international meddler, should you salute your Caesar? . . . May I hope that on election day [the mothers of the nation] . . . with the sacred ballot [will] lead the revolt against the candidate who plays at a game that may make cannon fodder of your sons? . . . The President has been scheming for years to involve us in war." He declared that the "reelection of President Roosevelt would be a national evil of the first magnitude." He urged his listeners to vote for Willkie, as a man who "has the common touch . . . He has worked with his hands and has known the pangs of hunger." (If so, it was when he was dieting.)

Lewis concluded that the President could be reelected only if labor supported his reelection. By this reasoning he asked America's workers to "sustain" or "repudiate" Lewis, as if he were running for election, and promised that if Roosevelt were reelected, he, John L. Lewis, would resign as head of the CIO. It did not require a seasoned psychoanalyst to conclude that the CIO leader's perceptions were becoming blurred. Roosevelt's friends in the labor movement were horrified, and rallied to him with great fanfare. Scores of union locals and much of the CIO executive, as well as most other unions, including the American Federation of Labor, repudiated Lewis and excoriated him in terms as vitriolic, if not as picturesque, as those he had employed against Roosevelt.

Hillman visited the White House the next day and found Roosevelt and Hopkins "thoroughly scared."[54] Willkie believed that Roosevelt's gentility was inadvertently "patronizing to John without meaning to be." Lewis was also alleged to be annoyed because he once went to the White House with his wife for tea and was outraged that Mrs. Roosevelt was unable to be present and Missy LeHand, as often happened, substituted for her. This hardly seems justification for such a fierce assault.

Two days after Lewis's violent harangue, Joseph P. Kennedy returned from London via Lisbon on a clipper aircraft. Roosevelt was taking no chances with another defection, which Kennedy, with his customary indiscretion, had been threatening for over a year, as had been reported to Roosevelt on countless occasions. Kennedy was completely discouraged with being out of the traffic between

Churchill and Roosevelt. The ambassador had been contemplating returning for the last year, but once the bombing began in earnest, he didn't want to leave for fear of being branded a coward. This was fine with Roosevelt, who thought London in the Blitz a good place for Kennedy. Kennedy was one of the most prominent Irish-Americans and one of the leading lay Catholics in the country, and a strenuous position by him could affect a strategically relevant number of votes in a close election, in the Irish communities of New York, Boston, Chicago, Philadelphia, and several other large cities.

Kennedy had paid a courtesy call on Neville Chamberlain just before leaving London. Chamberlain was dying of cancer and told the ambassador: "I want to die." In this, at least, he was successful. A couple of weeks later he wrote to his former ambassador in Berlin, Sir Nevile Henderson, that he regretted nothing of his policy to Germany, which had bought time for British military preparations and established an overwhelming moral case for the Allies in the present war. He touchingly added: "I hope you are better, or at least not suffering." Henderson was also a cancer patient and survived Chamberlain by a little over a year.[55] Chamberlain had retired as leader of the British Conservative Party and Lord President of the Council and member of the War Cabinet on September 30 (exactly two years after Munich) because of his illness, and would die November 9, 1940, generously eulogized in Parliament by his successor.

Henry Luce had been expecting Kennedy at his home in Manhattan as soon as Kennedy arrived at La Guardia Field (a flying-boat center at the time). Luce, normally an enlightened Republican, was so convinced an advocate of aid to Britain that he had ceased his criticism of the New Deal and went so far as to declare: "Our job is to help in every way we can . . . to ensure that Franklin Roosevelt shall be justly hailed as America's greatest President." He was determined to do all he could to ensure that: "Roosevelt must succeed where Wilson failed."[56] Luce's newsreel, *The March of Time*, was relentlessly favorable to the President and his pro-British policy, and vividly portrayed the Nazi onslaught on civilized Europe from the skies, on minorities and dissidents, on the innocent populations of conquered countries.

Henry Luce and his wife and others who knew the ambassador believed Kennedy might be about to declare for Willkie when he arrived at New York, October 27. Roosevelt had the same concern. Sumner Welles had promised that Kennedy would be delivered to the White House "before anyone else got at him to talk." When Kennedy emerged from his aircraft, there were two messages for him from Roosevelt, one handwritten and inviting him immediately to dinner in the White House that night. He was still a serving ambassador and could not practically decline.

He was conducted to a special telephone connection and put through at once to the President, who was having lunch in his office with the new House Speaker, Sam Rayburn, and his protégé, Texas Congressman Lyndon B. Johnson. "Ah Joe, it is so good to hear your voice. . . . Come to the White House tonight for a little family dinner. I'm dying to talk to you." At that, Roosevelt looked to his guests, smiled broadly, and made a hand gesture of slitting his throat. A motorcycle escort conducted Mr. and Mrs. Kennedy to an official plane across the tarmac at La Guardia and they were flown as the President's guests to Washington and conducted in an official car to the White House. On the plane to Washington, Mrs. Kennedy reminded her husband that no one would have named a Roman Catholic as ambassador to Great Britain except Roosevelt and that her husband would appear an ingrate to many if he resigned or assisted the President's enemies now. So he would have, and Roosevelt was ready to amplify that contingency: a proverbial last-minute stab in the back from a protégé betraying the leaders and countries by and to whom he was accredited.

Roosevelt and Missy LeHand and Senator Byrnes received the Kennedys. Byrnes and Roosevelt suggested that Kennedy speak in favor of the President's reelection, and Roosevelt devoted considerable attention to Mrs. Kennedy, who had always been particularly susceptible to his legendary charm. Kennedy had wanted a private meeting with Roosevelt, but when it became clear that this would not occur, he deferred all talk of an election speech until he got off his chest what he had come to say. Kennedy complained bitterly of the way he had been treated by the State Department, not informed at all of the destroyers deal, and left out while emissaries like Welles came through London without any consultation with the ambassador.

Roosevelt took up this theme, blasted the "officious men" responsible, and said Kennedy was being charitable. Only the war crisis had prevented Roosevelt from taking draconian measures against these insolent people, he said, and after the election there would be a "good housecleaning" to ensure that old and valued friends and the most important members of the administration like Kennedy were not treated in this way. Roosevelt purported to accept Kennedy's preposterous claims to absolute loyalty, to early and consistent support of the third term, and virtual indispensability to Roosevelt and his family. The whole exchange was an allegorization of self-delusion by Kennedy and of cunning manipulation by Roosevelt.

There has been disagreement ever since this meeting over exactly what happened next. Kennedy claimed that Roosevelt promised his support of Kennedy's elder son's candidacy as governor of Massachusetts in 1942 (unlikely, since he would have been only twenty-six). Future president John F. Kennedy claimed that Roosevelt had dangled the 1944 presidential nomination in front of the ambassador (more likely and quite in character, for the one to make such an outlandish offer and for the other to take it seriously). James Roosevelt said that his father had told Kennedy that he wanted to help Kennedy's sons make their way in politics but that if Kennedy behaved like a "Judas Iscariot," it would be the end of the political prospects of the young Kennedys. (This is quite plausible; although the younger Kennedy and Roosevelt weren't there, their versions seem fairly believable.)

Whatever may have been his enticements, Kennedy agreed to give a pro-Roosevelt speech two nights later, on condition that he pay for it himself, show his remarks beforehand to no one, and say exactly what he chose. Roosevelt happily accepted these conditions and Missy LeHand at once telephoned the Democratic National Committee and in the President's name reserved the October 29 nationwide radio evening time slot for Kennedy.

The next night, October 28, Roosevelt made another of his great quadrennial Madison Square Garden speeches. It was one of his most successful and best-remembered performances. As the tension of the campaign reached its highest intensity, Franklin D. Roosevelt, with the form traditional to champions in every field, became ever more determined and effective. To the 22,000 people inside, 30,000 outside the Garden but listening to loudspeakers, and 40 to 50 million radio listeners, Roosevelt never mentioned Willkie, but dwelt at length and with mordant sarcasm on the reactionary Republican opposition to every reform of the New Deal and every attempt of his administration to assist the forces of democracy in the World War.

He struck upon an oratorical device doubly dangerous because it was ridiculous. He named various Republican legislators, concluding with Congressmen Joe Martin, Bruce Barton, and his personal bete noire and Dutchess County representative, the primitive isolationist Hamilton Fish. Thus, ill-advised votes on many subjects were recited. Desirable things had been done, despite the opposition of Senators Nye, Johnson (Hiram Johnson had just endorsed Willkie), and "now wait"—he paused and smiled—"Congressmen Martin, Barton, and Fish!" He pronounced the words in his broad Ivy League manner: "Mahtin, Bahton," drawling slightly, and then "Fish!" with venomous finality. Once started on this, the crowd took it up. He had only to get to the pause and the crowd roared out the names. It was a simple but brilliant stroke. Willkie, who ascribed most of the excesses of the campaign to the nature of elections, was philosophical. He said later: "When I heard the President hang the isolationist votes of Martin, Barton, and Fish on me . . . I knew I was licked."[57]

At the Chicago convention briefly, and as the Willkie campaign gained ground in the last few weeks, some Democrats had had a glimpse of electoral mortality. Inspired again by the reassertion of their leader's genius for skewering his opponents, they rallied to him with a fervor that only endangered incumbency could produce. (Willkie would have buried any of the Democrats who thought they might take Roosevelt's place—Farley, Garner, etc.—by 5 million votes.)

The next day, October 29, 1940, Mussolini invaded Greece from Albania. After a few months the Italians were thoroughly beaten by the determined Greeks, necessitating Hitler's intervention. On the day of the initial attack, Roosevelt, against the counsel of many of his advisors, personally attended the first selective service draft call by Secretary Stimson. The bowl and cylinders used were those that had been employed in 1917 for the same purpose. And the blindfold that covered Stimson's eyes was from the material that covered the chair on which the signers of the Declaration of Independence had sat. Roosevelt had absolutely refused to be absent for such a momentous event. Whatever the political fallout, Roosevelt refused as cowardly any suggestion to postpone the ceremony until after the election and refused to proceed with it unpublicized. Since all polls indicated general support for the measure, he did not think it overly risky politically. But he considered his presence as commander in chief and principal supporter of the legislation a matter of duty, whatever the political implications. Following the ceremony, he gave a brief radio address to the nation. He referred to the event that had just occurred as a "muster," evoking the citizen-soldier of Revolutionary times.

Then he scored a noteworthy coup and read a letter from the new Roman Catholic archbishop of New York, Francis Spellman. (Spellman would replace Chicago's late Cardinal Mundelein as Roosevelt's best friend in the American Catholic hierarchy. He performed a number of diplomatic missions for Roosevelt during the war. Spellman would be elevated to cardinal at the first consistory after the war and would be probably the most powerful churchman in modern U.S. history.) The Archbishop had written: "It is better to have protection and not need it than to need protection and not have it. . . . We really cannot longer afford to be moles who cannot see, or ostriches who will not see. . . . We Americans want peace and we shall prepare for a peace, but not for a peace whose definition is slavery or death." It wasn't an endorsement of the President specifically, but of his policy, and was thus even more effective, because it avoided the opprobrium a direct partisan recommendation would have attracted. At the most decisive hour, the American Catholic leadership delivered all they had for the President. He could not have asked for more.[58] This was overwhelmingly more important than the demented ravings of Coughlin, and covered off in advance some of the ground to be occupied by the future Cardinal's coreligionist, Joseph Kennedy, later that evening of October 29.

Kennedy gave a gracious and persuasive address: He had just "returned from war-torn Europe to the peaceful shores of our beloved country renewed in my conviction that this country must and will stay out of war." He was confident that both presidential candidates shared this view. "Unfortunately, during this political campaign, there has arisen the charge that the President of the United States is trying to involve this country in the world war. Such a charge is false."

He had often disagreed with the President on some matters, but what employee never disagreed with his employer? It was "later than you think, and too late to train a new President. . . . I have a great stake in this country. My wife and I have given nine hostages to fortune. Our children and your children are more important than anything else in the world. . . . The kind of America that they and their children inherit is of grave concern to us all.

"In the light of these considerations, I believe that Franklin D. Roosevelt should be reelected President of the United States of America."[59]

Kennedy's remarks had a dramatic and positive effect on the Roosevelt campaign, especially because he had been widely expected to denounce the President and endorse Willkie. If there were secret arrangements with Britain that might draw the country into war, surely Kennedy would be aware of them, and his own leanings were well known. (In fact he would have been the last person Roosevelt would have informed, but the country didn't know that.) Willkie considered the speech a damaging blow to his hopes one week before the election. So did the most knowledgeable critic of all, who cabled: "We have all just listened to a grand speech. Many Thanks. Looking forward to seeing you all tomorrow evening. Franklin D. Roosevelt".

Roosevelt's telegram referred to his address in Boston the following night. In fact, Kennedy did not attend, but his son Joe Jr., and his father-in-law, former Boston mayor "Honey Fitz" Fitzgerald (whom the ambassador regularly referred to as "that drunken old bastard") went with the President in his car to the Boston Garden and were with him on the platform.

The same evening, October 30, the last of Roosevelt's unofficial privately designated opponents, Colonel Lindbergh, spoke at Yale University over an extensive radio hookup in his final public campaign assault on the President. Lindbergh gave a lengthy and relatively sober address. He was introduced by the head of the Yale branch of the isolationist organization America First, Kingman Brewster. Brewster was eventually president of Yale University and United States ambassador to the Court of St. James from 1977 to 1981.

Among other young America Firsters were future president Gerald Ford; Chester Bowles, later a liberal senior State Department official; and R. Sargent Shriver, subsequently Joseph Kennedy's son-in-law, U.S. ambassador to France, and Democratic vice presidential candidate in 1972.

Lindbergh began his remarks with a recitation of family history. His father had been chased by Indians as a young man in Minnesota, and it was only ten years after his father's death that Lindbergh had surveyed interhemispheric air routes. The colonel himself had been born one year before the first flight of the Wright Brothers. He criticized his own country for lurching into war in 1917, abandoning Europe and internationalism in 1919, doing nothing as Germany and Italy armed in the thirties, and then deciding to play a role and urging France and Britain into war. There was no policy, he said. "We must decide whether we are going to place our security in the defense of America, or in an attempt to control the affairs of the rest of the world." He left his listeners in no doubt of the course that he favored. This was a reasonable presentation, with no hint of the racist and pro-Nazi reflections of his previous addresses. But he had shot his bolt. His remarks were politely received by his academic and general audiences, but his dissertation on the different air routes to the United States was too esoteric for the grave electoral decision that was imminent.

Lindbergh was vastly overshadowed by the Roosevelt address at Boston shortly afterward. The President had spoken not far from Yale University in New Haven, Connecticut, from his train when it stopped on its way to Boston earlier that day.

He referred to the selective service registration of 16 million American males the day before as a commonplace event. He said: "We have started to train more men not because we expect to use them, but for the same reason your umbrellas are up today—to keep from getting wet." It was a rather anodyne analogy, even by his homespun exegetical methods, on a cold and rainy day in New England.

VII

A S THE PRESIDENTIAL TRAIN proceeded between New York and Boston, there were several whistle stops where Roosevelt emerged and briefly addressed his local partisans. In between stops he sat with Harry Hopkins; his two principal speechwriters, Samuel Rosenman and Robert Sherwood; and his secretaries, Missy LeHand and Grace Tully, working up the final version of the main address in Boston. At each stop, bags of telegrams and letters would be brought aboard from party organizers all around the country. Missy and Grace would sift deftly through them, separating the party elders and V.I.P.s from the commonsensical regulars and from the cranks. The gist of most of the mail was that the President should emphasize that the conscripted young manhood of America would not be sent to war. When he received a cable from Ed Flynn asking for a repetition of the peace plank of the Democratic Party, he asked in some exasperation how often he would have to repeat that. Sherwood responded that he would have to say it "again and again." Roosevelt immediately recognized the potential of that simple phrase if he rolled it off at his most theatrical.

He was less philosophical about beseechings that he assure the parents of draftees that their sons would be housed and fed properly. With London under the Blitz, all continental Europe except Switzerland, Sweden, and what was left of Finland being ground underfoot by a league of malignant dictators, and the Japanese putting vast tracts of Asia to flame and sword, his incredulity that American mothers should be concerned about their sons' diets and shelter was understandable. He consented to a note of reassurance even for them, as if the nation's youth were off on a late autumn portage in the national parks. Obviously his long campaign to teach his countrymen that the world was a dangerous place had made less headway than he might have hoped.

Boston on October 30, 1940, a night when he absolutely had to do well, was another of Roosevelt's memorable campaign addresses: "I can give assurance to the mothers and fathers of America that each and every one of their boys in training will be well housed and well fed. . . . And while I am talking to you fathers and mothers I give one more assurance. I have said this before, but I shall say it again and again and again. Your boys are not going to be sent into any foreign wars." Always before he had added the qualifier "except in case of attack," as the party election platform had stated. He dispensed with that rider on this occasion as superfluous. No one suggested that it would be inappropriate to respond to an attack on the United States. He had explained to Rosenman: "If someone attacks us, it isn't a foreign war, is it? Or do they want me to guarantee that our troops will be sent into battle only in the event of another U.S. Civil War?"[60] Roosevelt was reaching the limits of his patience with the pacifistic irresolution of many of his countrymen.

Listening to Roosevelt on the radio, Willkie exclaimed: "That hypocritical son of a bitch! This is going to beat me!"[61] That was what it was intended to do, but Willkie had obliged Roosevelt to give an unambiguous pledge in the most right-eous terms. (In all of the circumstances, Willkie was hardly in any position to complain of hypocrisy.) On November 2 in Buffalo, New York, Roosevelt said: "Your President says this country is not going to war." With war the overwhelming issue, Willkie, who started out with considerable civility, was reduced to accusing the nation's twice-chosen leader of outright mendacity on an issue of life and death to millions of American families. Some would claim that this pledge would be an albatross around Roosevelt's neck, but he never envisioned asking Congress for a declaration of war against a country that had not initiated hostilities.

At Boston the President trotted out "Martin, Barton, and Fish" a couple of times, to great merriment, and generously thanked Bostonian Joe Kennedy for his endorsement. (Kennedy's much-admired daughter Kathleen, twenty, cabled her father: "The Pres really went to town for you tonight in Boston amidst terrific cheers from the crowd. It's great to be famous—Good night from your fourth hostage.") Roosevelt also pointed out that Britain had ordered 26,000 aircraft from the United States, marrying the nation's military security to its economic well-being.[62]

It had become a very rough campaign, yet there were fears throughout the autumn that it could become worse. From late August on, the President and his senior advisors had been concerned that their opponents would publish a sheaf of letters that the Republicans had got hold of from Henry Wallace to a White Russian mystic and cult leader, Nicholas Roerich. Wallace had employed Roerich in 1934 and 1935 to lead an analysis of drought-resistant soils in Mongolia and Manchuria. Wallace clearly took Roerich's claims to spirituality seriously. The historian Kenneth Davis accurately wrote: "The extravagance of the mystical occult language they employed called into question the mental and emotional stability of the man who wrote them."[63]

David Sarnoff of the Radio Corporation of America had given Roosevelt a recording device, which had been installed under the President's office, with a microphone in his desklamp. It could be turned on when desired by flicking a switch in a left-hand desk drawer. Roosevelt didn't use it much, but it did pick up a conversation with an aide, Lowell Mellett, in late August 1940, when Roosevelt had been advised of the existence of these letters. He immediately responded that if the Republicans "want to play dirty politics . . . some people way down the line [could spread] this story about this gal." He was referring to Irita Van Doren, book reviewer of the *New York Herald Tribune*—"awful nice gal," Roosevelt gallantly allowed—with whom Willkie had been having an affair for years. Mrs. Willkie, from whom the candidate was practically estranged, had rejoined him for the election campaign. In the event, neither set of nasty revelations occurred, which says something creditable about both candidates.

The candidates were coming down to the wire with most polls showing Roosevelt holding a narrow lead. (Gallup had him almost ten points ahead, but indicated that Willkie could win 255 electoral votes, only thirteen short of a majority. Roper had Roosevelt about seven points ahead and also close in the Electoral College. It was a fierce challenge and an implacable defense, for great stakes. They were running about even on economic matters, but Roosevelt had a fifteen-to twenty-point lead in foreign policy, now the greatest issue.

Roosevelt spoke at Cleveland on November 3. Crowds were very large and very generous. Rosenman thought this campaign roundup FDR's greatest speech of all, for professional delivery and originality.[64] He toured around Hyde Park on the day before the election, as he had in all his elections since 1910.

The President gave his quadrennial election-eve fatherly rumination to the country on the evening of November 4. Speaking from his spacious drawing room lined with bookcases and tall chairs, he avoided all partisanship, as was his custom so close to the day of electoral judgment. His goal was always to strike hard but not venomously in domestic affairs; to retain as much leeway as possible to rally the disgruntled; and to reserve politically lethal blows for, under appropriate orders, seconds like Ickes, his own august fingerprints far from the knife.*

On election eve Roosevelt said: "My friends, once more I am in the quiet of my home in Hyde Park on the eve of Election Day I wish to speak to you not of partisan politics but of the nation, the United States of America, to which we all owe such deep and inborn allegiance. As I sit here tonight with my own family, I think of all the other American families—millions of families all through the land, sitting in their own homes. They have eaten their suppers in peace, they will be able to sleep in their homes tonight in peace. Tomorrow they will be free to go out to live their ordinary lives in peace—free to say and do what they wish, free to worship as they please. Tomorrow, of all days, they will be free to choose their own leaders, who, when that choice has been made, become in turn only the instruments to carry out the will of all the people. The opinion of all the people, freely formed and freely expressed . . . is wiser than the opinion of any one man or any small group of men. . . . Your will is a part of the great will of America. Your voice is a part of the great voice of America. And when you and I stand in line tomorrow for our turn at the polls, we are voting equals." (This was an endearing, though an unlikely, prospect.)

---

* In 1936, when Knox, then Landon's vice presidential candidate, declared his "sober and solemn judgment that four more years [of Roosevelt] may destroy our system," Ickes called him "the Paul Revere of doom . . . [who] rides facing the horse's tail."[65] Before the four years were out, the long friendship between Knox, now FDR's navy secretary, and Ickes had been restored at the cabinet table.

He celebrated America and democracy, and did not even ask for the vote of his listeners. It was hard to square this, as he knew and intended it would be, with the febrile imputations to him by his enemies of dictatorial ambitions. President Roosevelt voted with his wife and his mother the next day and serenely awaited the people's verdict.

This did not come as quickly as on the previous two presidential election nights. Family, neighbors, staff members, and friends filled up the reception rooms of the big house at Springwood. Roosevelt himself, accessible to only a few, sat in the small dining room off the family dining room. He listened to the radio, made his own calculations, and had news tape brought to him from wires of the agencies, which flowed on to machines in the dining room. His head of security, Mike Reilly, was at the door of the small dining room to assure that no unauthorized person intruded. Roosevelt was relaxed at first, but after awhile, with no clear indications of a trend, he told Reilly to keep out everyone, even his own family. This didn't discountenance Eleanor in the slightest, but it did annoy Morgenthau, who seemed to some to measure his current status in the country on the frequency of his contacts with the President.

Roosevelt remained alone in the small dining room for about forty minutes, allegedly edgy and perspiring heavily. Distinguished historians have attempted a more comprehensive analysis of what was in his thoughts than could be justified. Roosevelt might have had a bout of indigestion. There was nothing obvious in the results to shock or demoralize him, though Willkie ran somewhat ahead of expectations in the first returns.[66]

The door to the President's vote-counting chamber was reopened at about 11 o'clock, and the occupant was his usual congenial self. By this time, the traditional army of the President's supporters had been heard from in the great cities of the East and Midwest and he had pulled into a clear lead. This held and grew all night; he addressed his neighbors from the portico of his house at midnight, and cautiously expressed hopefulness of the incoming result. He was amused by a child's handpainted sign: "SAFE ON THIRD," and claimed to remember the election of Grover Cleveland in 1884 and to have participated in a similar gathering in the same place to celebrate it. "We are facing difficult days in this country, but I think you will find me in the future just the same Franklin Roosevelt you have known a great many years. . . . My heart has always been here. It always will be."[67]

By 2:30 A.M. it was clear that he had won by about five million votes, ten percent of the highest voting total in the country's history. Roosevelt held about the same 27 million votes he had received in 1936, but Willkie had built Landon's 16 million votes into 22 million. Roosevelt said to Eleanor's young friend Joe Lash: "We seem to have averted a putsch, Joe."[68] Willkie conceded the next morning. Roosevelt had won 449 electoral votes to 82 for Willkie, 38 states to 10. Willkie had put up a tremendous fight, but every time he approached an opening that he might be able to exploit, Roosevelt had closed it.

Roosevelt was too clever ever to appear arrogant to the voters and was a genius at mockery of his opponents. Willkie carried all the baggage of the Hoover Depression and the Nye isolationists, and Roosevelt prevented him from getting clear of it. In the end, the people remembered "Martin, Barton, and Fish" (all three were reelected personally), and had no reason to doubt the President when he told them "again and again and again" that he would keep them out of war.

Although Roosevelt won by five million, it was a close election. In the combination of New York, Pennsylvania, Illinois, Ohio, New Jersey, Massachusetts, Wisconsin, Missouri, and Minnesota, totalling 209 electoral votes, he had only about 52 percent of the votes. Here, the lengths he had gone to in search of the Roman Catholic vote had probably been the greatest single factor in his victory. His cautious policy in respect of the Spanish Civil War, his placation of Mundelein and Spellman, and his reprogramming of Joseph Kennedy had reaped rich rewards. Without these efforts, he would almost certainly have lost some of these states, possibly including New York. These political realities assumed particular importance after the "stab in the back" allegation against Mussolini. Though Italian Americans were generally antifascist, that charge had rankled with many of them as close to an ethnic slur.

Willkie defeated Roosevelt in Michigan, with 19 electoral votes, by 7,000 out of nearly 1.5 million votes cast. Roosevelt won 70 percent of the vote in the South and 59 percent in the country's designated large cities. In the remainder of the country, the proverbially more representative heartland, where 62 percent of the votes were cast, Willkie actually won by 25,000 votes out of 31 million. Roosevelt won the 47 electoral votes of New York State, where both candidates lived, with 52 percent of its votes. But he won 61 percent of the vote in the five boroughs of New York City (which cast 6.5 percent of the country's ballots), but lost 42 percent to 58 percent to Willkie in the balance of the state. It was one of the heaviest voter turnouts of modern times, nearly 80 percent.[69]

With his usual unerring instinct and against the advice of Eleanor, Corcoran, and many others, Roosevelt had moved toward the Republicans with the appointments of Stimson and Knox and a general reconciliation with big business, and had softened the acute partisanship of most of the New Deal. With the world at war Roosevelt tried harder than ever to build a broad national security consensus. There was surely some backlash against the hokiness of the nomination to a third term.

The famous song "This Land is Your Land (from California to the New York Island)" was written in mid-campaign in support of Roosevelt's reelection, by Woody Guthrie. Roosevelt said in one speech in this campaign: "We are going to build a country in which no one is left out," terminology that would be endlessly repeated by his successors.[70] He was striving hard to unite the nation, apart from those whom he classified as Nazi sympathizers. "Roosevelt's brilliant campaign, at once cynical and idealistic, devious and daring, gave our country . . . a leader who seemed more able than his opponents to mobilize its people and in time of crisis produce action toward a unified purpose."[71] So great were the stakes, 1940 was probably an even more important election than 1932, when the country was on the verge of economic and psychological collapse. So great were the obstacles to victory—the two-term tradition, fears of war, lingering hostilities of the Depression, and the force of Willkie's campaign—that this was probably Roosevelt's greatest political victory of all.

Willkie's mighty effort broke the momentum of his career. Disliked by and disliking the conservative Republicans, he became friendlier with his opponent than with his erstwhile followers. But his health and political fortunes began to deteriorate. John L. Lewis resigned as head of the CIO as he promised he would. He came back as head of the United Mine Workers, but never had a fraction of the credibility in the country he had enjoyed through Roosevelt's first two terms. Charles Lindbergh continued to speak to smaller and less respectable audiences about the virtues of isolationism, but he would forever be seen as almost a neo-Nazi.

The congressional results showed little change; the Democrats gained six congressmen and lost three senators. But because the southern Democrats were pro-British and pro-defense, their alliance with the isolationist Republicans had ended, and Roosevelt was again in firm control of the federal government. (There would be 268 Democrats to 167 Republicans in the House and 66 to 30 in the Senate.)

Franklin D. Roosevelt returned to Washington November 8 and received a hero's welcome. Huge crowds greeted him. Hundreds of young people ran after his car and tens of thousands of cheering people lined the streets as he drove from Union Station to the White House. He waved to admirers from the North Portico, with Eleanor and the Wallaces. He had become an institution unto himself, inseparable now from the institution of the presidency.

CHAPTER 14

"Whither Thou Goest, I Go . . . Even to the End"

(Harry L. Hopkins to Prime Minister Winston Churchill, on Roosevelt's policy to Britain, February 1941)

I

ROOSEVELT NOW HAD his mandate to deal with the war. He did not doubt that the world would be much changed in four years and was determined to make it so. Yet he was, according to Felix Frankfurter, "in a deep Lincolnesque mood" facing the approaching war.[1]

Joseph Kennedy called at the White House three days after the election and offered Roosevelt his resignation. Roosevelt accepted but asked that this be kept quiet until his successor was appointed. It was a distinctly cooler meeting than an observer would have been led to expect by the laudations Roosevelt had heaped on the absent Kennedy in the Boston Garden eight days before. Kennedy gave his usual admonition about staying out of the war and the necessity of adopting some fascist methods in American government. Four days later the *Boston Globe* published an interview with Kennedy in which the ambassador claimed that Britain was finished, that Lindbergh was essentially correct, that we had much to learn from the fascists, and that the British were just trying to draw the United States into the war and leave the Americans "holding the bag."

He said similar and even more inflammatory things at a great luncheon for him at Warner Brothers a few days later when he returned to Los Angeles. Louis B. Mayer, Samuel Goldwyn, and Jack Warner were his hosts and the occasion was off the record, but word spread quickly of what Kennedy had said. Douglas Fairbanks Jr. immediately sent Roosevelt an extensive account of it.[2] Kennedy endorsed Lindbergh, appeasement, and some aspects of Fascism, and warned the mainly Jewish film producers and directors to stop producing anti-Nazi films.

Ten days after this, Roosevelt had Kennedy to Hyde Park for the weekend. He arrived Saturday morning. After ten minutes with Kennedy, Roosevelt called Eleanor, asked Kennedy to step out of the room for a moment, and told his wife: "I never want to see that son of a bitch again as long as I live. Take his resignation and get him out of here!" Eleanor, who had rarely seen her husband so angry, reminded him that there were other guests and that the train didn't leave until two. "Then you drive him around Hyde Park, give him a sandwich, and put him on that train!" She gave Kennedy lunch at Val Kill and listened to his monologue about the omnipotence of the German Air Force and related themes. Twenty years later she described this session with Kennedy as "the most dreadful four hours of my life."[3] Considering what her life encompassed and the fact that Eleanor Roosevelt was not known to exaggerate for effect, it must have been a very trying encounter.

Kennedy's written resignation did come in early December. The one shining moment when Roosevelt had needed him was past. Although Kennedy didn't know it, Franklin D. Roosevelt disliked and disdained him, and he would be without political influence, a much-despised though increasingly wealthy figure, until the rise of his talented but tragic sons a generation later.

Roosevelt found waiting for him when he returned to the White House a message from Churchill, who had been relatively silent during the election campaign, except for an exchange about the French fleet. The prime minister wrote, November 6: "I did not think it right for me as a foreigner to express any opinion upon American policies while the election was on, but now I feel you will not mind my saying that I prayed for your success and that I am truly thankful for it. This does not mean that I seek or wish for anything more than the full fair and free play of your mind upon the world issues now at stake in which our two nations have to discharge their respective duties. . . . Things are afoot which will be remembered as long as the English language is spoken in any quarter of the globe, and in expressing the comfort I feel that the people of the United States have once again cast these great burdens upon you, I must avow my sure faith that the lights by which we steer will bring us all safely to anchor."[4]

Churchill resumed his general campaign to represent Britain and the United States as two friendly and fraternal divisions of the same people. Roosevelt would never wholeheartedly enter into quite so intimate a collaboration. Roosevelt strangely did not respond to this message (until it was retransmitted with renewed post-electoral congratulations four years later). It has been suggested that he was miffed at Churchill's failure to repudiate Willkie's quotation of Churchill's criticism of the early New Deal. He may simply have been suspicious of the ingenuous tenor of the message. More likely, he expected to mention it in the regular correspondence, which now picked up again, but forgot to do so.

On December 7, 1940, Churchill sent Roosevelt a long summary of current war conditions. He oddly began by asserting that the "vast majority of American citizens have recorded their conviction that the safety of the United States as well as the future of our two democracies . . . are bound up with the survival of the British Commonwealth of Nations." (It hardly seemed necessary to state that the future of British democracy was.) He held the control of the Pacific Ocean by the U.S. Navy and of the Atlantic Ocean by the Royal Navy to be essential to the interests of both countries. He referred to the immense program of rearmament that Roosevelt had put in hand and for which he had just won his country's approval. "It is our British duty in the common interest as also for our own survival to hold the front and grapple with Nazi power until the preparations of the United States are complete."[5]

He seemed to imply that at that point the United States would enter the war. Britain was unable "to match the immense armies of Germany in any theatre where their main power can be brought to bear. We can however by the use of sea power and air power meet the German armies in the regions where only comparatively small forces can be brought into action." Churchill was particularly concerned to keep the Germans out of Africa and the Middle East.

Churchill referred, again slightly ceremoniously, to the improvements of the war position of Great Britain in the past five months, "fighting alone but with invaluable aid in munitions and in destroyers placed at our disposal by the Great Republic of which you are for the third time chosen Chief." The danger of an invasion of Britain had receded but the new danger for 1941 was strangulation at sea of Britain's ability to feed herself and to transport and maintain armies on the periphery of the Nazi empire to prevent its further expansion. He gave an extensive discussion of naval affairs, expressing concern about the German battleships *Bismarck* and *Tirpitz* when they should be ready, early in the New Year, and still about the French *Richelieu* and *Jean Bart*, and thanked Roosevelt for his strenuous representations to Petain on that subject. Having shot up the Italian fleet at Taranto with torpedo bombers on the night of November 10, Churchill was less concerned about the modern Littorio class battleships, "which will be out of action for a while and anyway . . . are not so dangerous as if they were manned by the Germans." (Unfortunately, the Japanese studied the lessons of Taranto much more closely than the Americans did, although Churchill sent Roosevelt a detailed account of the action. The implications for torpedo attacks on capital ships in confined anchorages would prove historic exactly a year later in the Pacific.)

Churchill invited Roosevelt to uphold "the doctrine of the freedom of the seas from illegal and barbarous warfare in accordance with the decisions reached after the late, Great War, and as freely accepted and defined by Germany in 1935." This would involve a massive U.S. activity maintaining trade with Britain and her affiliates in spite of German submarine and surface raiders. Churchill doubted that this would lead to war, "though probably sea incidents of a dangerous character would from time to time occur." Hitler didn't want to repeat "the Kaiser's mistake. He does not wish to be drawn into war with the United States until he has gravely undermined the power of Great Britain. His maxim is 'one at a time.'

"Failing the above, the gift, loan, or supply of a large number of American vessels of war . . . is indispensable to the maintenance of the Atlantic route." He also asked for the extension of defined American patrolled waters off the Atlantic Coast of the United States and asked the American president to lean on the Irish to allow British use of Irish naval bases and airfields. Churchill's shopping list continued to three million tons of merchant shipping (250 percent of British annual shipbuilding capacity), 2,000 military aircraft per month for an indefinite period, and untold quantities of machine tools, artillery, tanks, vehicles, rifles, small arms, and munitions. "In our heavy need, we call with confidence to the most resourceful technicians in the world. We ask for an unexampled effort.

"Last of all I come to the question of finance. . . . The moment approaches when we shall no longer be able to pay cash for shipping and other supplies. . . . I believe that you will agree that it would be wrong in principle and mutually disadvantageous in effect, if at the height of this struggle, Great Britain were to be divested of all saleable assets so that after victory was won with our blood, civilization saved, and time gained for the United States to be fully armed against all eventualities, we should stand stripped to the bone. Such a course would not be in the moral or economic interests of either of our countries. . . . You may be assured that we shall prove ourselves ready to suffer and sacrifice to the utmost for the Cause, and that we glory in being its champion. The rest we leave to you and to your people, being sure that ways and means will be found which future generations on both sides of the Atlantic will approve and admire.

"If, as I believe, you are convinced, Mr. President, that the defeat of the Nazi and fascist tyranny is a matter of high consequence to the people of the United States and to the Western Hemisphere, you will regard this letter not as an appeal for aid, but as a statement of the minimum action necessary to the achievement of our common purpose.

"I remain, Yours very sincerely, Winston S. Churchill"

Britain was almost out of money and was asking for the sinews of war on a grand scale. In cynical geopolitical terms, considerations of which were rarely far from Roosevelt's thoughts, Britain was a magnificent mercenary for American interests, depleting and wearing down the mortal enemy, paid in materiel, which she claimed would ultimately be paid for in cash. Obviously, he had to supply most of what Churchill asked; the danger of a resurrection of the appeasers and of a dishonorable peace with Hitler was the alternative to helping Churchill and his policy succeed.

If there was no practical alternative, there was certainly no moral one either. Britain and the Commonwealth were carrying the battle for all civilization, and the overwhelming majority of Americans, led in the late election by their president, wished to help them. It is little wonder that Churchill had been praying for

Roosevelt's election victory. Willkie, with the best of intentions, would not have been able to get any significant part of Churchill's wish list through the Congress.

Churchill's letter was delivered to Roosevelt by seaplane as he departed Washington December 3 and sailed on the U.S.S. *Tuscaloosa* in the Caribbean, December 5 to 15. He spent the days fishing, taking the sun, and considering next steps in the great world chess game. Messages too sensitive to be sent or received over the air in coded form, and voluminous correspondence, were transmitted by seaplane at prearranged times and places as the ship stopped in some of the Caribbean islands, at one point for lunch with the new governor of the Bahamas, the Duke of Windsor, formerly King Edward VIII.

Roosevelt realized that Churchill had been waiting for the election before setting out the real proportions of the military and economic problems he faced, and the extent to which the United States could assist. Without consulting with anyone, even Hopkins, who was aboard the *Tuscaloosa*, Roosevelt developed over a few days at sea, reading and re-reading Churchill's letter in his deck chair, the notion that became "Lend-Lease." The idea had been taking shape in his thoughts since his conversation with British ambassador Lindsay shortly before Munich, and he had been aware that Britain would run out of credits eventually.[6]

It was one of the most brilliant ideas of his career, and it changed history. Essentially, the President's concept was that the United States would lend Britain whatever it needed, at no cost, and Britain would repay America in kind, by giving back what it had borrowed, or in other agreed equivalent consideration, when it could. This avoided the disputes about gifts, sales, cash loans, and all the wrangling that had gone on over war debts. Robert Sherwood subsequently wrote: "FDR, a creative artist in politics, had put in his time on this cruise evolving the pattern of a masterpiece."

It was an illustration of Roosevelt's artistic nature; it was a completely original idea that was immediately immune to most of the nasty bickering of the isolationists. At his press conference December 16, Roosevelt disarmed many critics with his example: "Suppose my neighbor's home catches on fire and I have a length of garden hose four or five hundred feet away. If he can take my garden hose and connect it up with his hydrant, I may be able to help put out his fire. Now what do I do? I don't say to him before that operation, 'Neighbor, my garden hose cost me $15, you have to pay me $15 for it.' . . . I don't want $15. I want my garden hose back after the fire is over . . . If it goes through the fire all right, intact, without any damage to it, he gives it back to me and thanks me very much for the use of it." If it were damaged, it could be replaced.

The isolationists made a desperate stand against aid to Britain. But a reelected Roosevelt, lending the military equivalent of garden hose to a valiant and victorious Churchill fighting the Nazi barbarians, outgunned the isolationist opponents who had been plaguing the President's life for five years. Roosevelt was convinced that some of them were abetted by Nazi financial assistance, and that most of the rest were just as dangerous in their naïveté as if they had been German agents. Events and opinion had evolved completely, and pretty much as he had foreseen, since his Quarantine speech in Chicago three years before. Now he was determined to bulldoze the isolationists once and for all. Roosevelt believed that the times and circumstances justified the extreme measure of tarring them all with the brush of Nazi sympathies, no matter how unjust this might be in many individual cases.

The anti-Semite Henry Ford and the Jewish isolationist Lessing Rosenwald joined Lindbergh on the board of the America First Committee, though only briefly. (Rosenwald found the atmosphere uncongenial, and Ford proved too cantankerous to be retained.)[7]

William Allen White, nearly seventy-three and under heavy attack from his isolationist Republican friends, feeling that Roosevelt was going further in extending the outer edges of neutrality than he was comfortable with, retired from the chair of his Committee to Defend America by Aiding the Allies. He had been the direct opponent of Lindbergh, who rejoiced when the publisher Roy Howard printed a letter from White vehemently denying that he was for entry into the war and saying that the motto of his Committee should be: "The Yanks are not coming."

Mayor La Guardia was outraged, and accused White of behaving like Pierre Laval. This was another illustration of Roosevelt's talent in casting a wide enough net to get through each successive electoral challenge and then resuming progress toward his ultimate objective. Lindbergh had been destroyed as a credible public figure; White was burned out. The former was no longer a threat to Roosevelt and the latter was no longer useful to him, but Roosevelt moved inexorably on. "The President uses those who suit his purposes," said Eleanor Roosevelt. "He makes up his own mind and discards people when they no longer serve a purpose of his."[8]

Another who met that fate was Thomas Corcoran, the President's agile fixer for most of his first two terms. Corcoran had offended many in the Congress and many relative conservatives. Now there were abler congressional managers, led by Rayburn, McCormack, Barkley, and Walter George, who proved a much more amenable and competent Senate Foreign Relations Committee chairman than Pittman had been. The New Deal was in abeyance, its institutional reforms unchallenged but its innovative activities suspended. This was the time of the Fourth New Deal, in which jobs were created by rearmament and conscription. Corcoran had been reduced to operating an independent voters for Roosevelt committee during the 1940 election campaign.

Corcoran had been the hatchet man in the surreptitious campaign for renomination to a third term and then, he felt, had been put over the side. Corcoran claimed that Roosevelt and Frankfurter looked down on his wife, Peggy Dowd, who had been his secretary until their wedding in 1939, as socially undistinguished. Corcoran's dispute with Frankfurter was over other things, and it is very unlikely that Roosevelt, always a gentleman in such matters, would have held any such view. Corcoran claimed that Roosevelt had offered his own old position of assistant secretary of the navy. If so, this was a gesture of friendship and would have been a very interesting position, though Corcoran would have been an odd choice given his anti-English views. It is not clear that the offer was made or the subject even raised. Once launched on one of his vendettas, Corcoran was capable of confecting grievances and vengeful calumnies. This is one of the reasons that Corcoran's allegation that Justice Holmes had referred to Franklin Roosevelt as a "second class intellect" should be read with caution.

Whatever the facts, it was a sad end to a close and valuable collaboration. Corcoran flourished in private practice for forty years, but was always embittered by his abrupt departure from the Roosevelt inner circle.[9]

————————

The President took to the airwaves on December 29, 1940, for one of the most famous of all his Fireside Chats. He styled it a talk on "national security," coining and instantly popularizing the phrase. Cinemas, restaurants, and other public places thinned out as nine o'clock, Eastern Time, approached.[10] The whole nation, the whole world, listened. The President declared there was no hope of a negotiated peace with Germany; "a tiger could not be tamed into a kitten by stroking it. There can be no appeasement with ruthlessness. . . . If Britain goes down . . . an unholy alliance" of the dictatorships would continue to pursue world conquest and "all of us in the Americas would be living at the point of a gun. . . . We must become the great arsenal of democracy" (a phrase recommended by Hopkins). "There can be no ultimate peace [with this] gang of outlaws . . . between their philosophy of government and our philosophy of government." The "pious frauds" offered in the name of peace by dupes and agents of the dictators in the American domestic political debate would not distract the United States government. "No dictator, no combination of dictators" would divert or intimidate the government and people of the United States from doing what their national interest and inescapable moral duty required. He called for the "same resolution, the same sense of urgency, the same spirit of patriotism and sacrifice as we would show were we at war . . . I call for this national effort in the name of this nation which we honor and love and which we are proud to serve." It was an unprecedentedly clear statement of America's emerging role in the world.

This address was listened to or read in detail by an astonishing 75 percent of Americans, of whom 61 percent agreed. Letters and telegrams to the White House were running a hundred to one in the President's favor.[11] The nation, Britain and her allies, the oppressed masses of the occupied countries all were electrified by this reaffirmation of purpose by the reelected American president. Winston Churchill promptly wrote him that it was "my duty on behalf of the British Government and indeed the whole British Empire to tell you, Mr. President, how lively is our sense of gratitude and admiration for the memorable declaration which you made to the American people and to the lovers of freedom in all continents. . . . With this trumpet-call we march forward heartened and fortified and with the confidence which you have expressed that in the end all will be well for the English-speaking peoples and those who share their ideals."

As was not infrequently the case, the prime minister's florid Gibbonian prose, applied to matters of alliance, produced an identity of view and condition between Britain and America that was somewhat overstated. But Roosevelt and most Americans profoundly admired the determination of Churchill and the British people and volunteers from the Dominions across the seas to fight as underdogs against an odious tyranny when a relatively painless peace was available. Reporting of the courageous and egalitarian British response to the Blitz helped convince most Americans that Britain was less an empire than a democracy. Roosevelt himself was convinced that a social revolution would occur in Britain as soon as the war was over and that the class system would be radically democratized. Roosevelt had often railed against the "Tory reactionaries" among his Republican opponents. The performance of the Victorian and Edwardian Tories leading Britain's government caused him hereafter to desist from such reflections. What was left of his Yankee reticence about the British evaporated.

Lord Lothian, an exceptionally competent British ambassador, had died December 12, 1940 (because as a Christian Scientist he refused a blood transfusion that undoubtedly would have saved his life). Churchill had sounded out Roosevelt December 14 about Lloyd George as a replacement, and Roosevelt had responded that he "will be entirely agreeable. I knew him in the World War. I assume that over here he will in no way play into the hands of the appeasers."*

Churchill, impressed by Commonwealth reservations and Lloyd George's own, given his seventy-seven years, thought better of the appointment. Instead, on December 21, he proposed Halifax to Roosevelt. "I need not tell you what a loss this is to me personally and to the War Cabinet. [However], it is my duty to place at your side the most eminent of my colleagues."[12]

In fact, Churchill was as delighted to be rid of Halifax, who had been alternately obstreperous, insidious, and duplicitous, as Roosevelt was unenthused to receive him. However, after inflicting Kennedy on the British, Roosevelt was in no position to complain, and Halifax proved a capable if somewhat misanthropic ambassador.

On January 6, 1941, President Roosevelt presented to the Congress his State of the Union message. He made the case for Lend-Lease, building on the fine public response to his December 29 speech. He defined "our national policy" in three goals: "all-inclusive national defense," support of all "those resolute people . . . who are resisting aggression," and a determination not "to acquiesce

---

* The British tended to refer to the Great War. Roosevelt, as part of his campaign against the isolationists, referred to the World War[s], to emphasize the folly of notions of American ability to abstain from Great Power conflicts.

in a peace dictated by aggressors and sponsored by appeasers. We know that enduring peace cannot be bought at the expense of other people's freedom." This speech is best known for its peroration: "In the future days, which we hope to make secure, we look forward to a world founded upon four essential freedoms . . . freedom of speech and expression everywhere in the world; freedom of every person to worship God in his own way, everywhere in the world . . . freedom from want . . . economic understandings which will secure to every nation a healthy peacetime life for its inhabitants—everywhere in the world . . . freedom from fear . . . a worldwide reduction of armaments . . . such . . . that no nation will be in a position to commit an act of physical aggression against any neighbor anywhere in the world. That is no vision of a distant millennium. It is a definite basis for a kind of world attainable in our own time and generation."

This was an uplifting message, but the most important part of the speech was Roosevelt's assertion, which his country has heeded and followed ever since, that: "We must always be wary of those who 'with sounding brass and tinkling cymbal' would preach the 'ism' of appeasement." The refusal of the United States to be an appeasement power, and its accompanying determination under many administrations of both parties to arm itself appropriately, wrought a benign revolution in international affairs. The whole world has been comparatively stabilized by this fundamental American policy Roosevelt enunciated on that day.

The Lend-Lease Bill was drafted quickly by a committee including the legal stars of the New Deal—Felix Frankfurter, though now a Supreme Court Justice, and Ben Cohen. It was initialed within a few minutes on January 7 by Hull, Knox, Stimson, and the President and, styled H.R. 1776 (by the House parliamentarian), was submitted to both houses of Congress by the majority leaders, McCormack and Barkley, on January 10. Former Roosevelt supporter Senator Burton Wheeler of Montana was convinced that Lend-Lease was another shabby deceit of the President's—that the claim of aid to Britain instead of war was false and that Roosevelt's policy was really a disguised gradual descent into the world conflict. On a nationwide broadcast January 12, Wheeler claimed that Lend-Lease would "plow underneath every fourth American boy." Roosevelt responded the next day at his regular press conference that Wheeler's statement was "the most untruthful, the most dastardly, unpatriotic . . . the rottenest thing that has been said in public life in my generation."[13] Wheeler's words were disgraceful, but the underlying concern that Roosevelt was edging closer to war was not unfounded. However, the proposed antidote of denying all aid to Britain and building only a modest defensive capability was morally and strategically insane.

Apart from Willkie, whose support of Lend-Lease was powerful and unwavering, most leading Republicans opposed Bill 1776, including Hoover,* Landon, Dewey, Vandenberg, and Taft. The McCormick and Hearst newspapers were as

---

* Roosevelt had offered Hoover leadership of the refugee and overseas relief effort. Hoover had declined and there was minimal contact between them thereafter.[14]

shrill as they had been at their most frenzied during the New Deal, but the *New York Times*, the *Herald Tribune*, the *Christian Science Monitor*, and many other influential newspapers supported the administration. Polls showed a steady majority behind the President and Lend-Lease, and he answered Churchill's question of when it might pass in a cable January 16, saying that he thought February 15 a realistic date unless there was a Senate filibuster, but that such a stratagem would only cause a "delay." Defeat was not in contemplation; Roosevelt was confident he could break a filibuster if he had to. The balance of power in these matters had shifted decisively since the Battle of Britain and the election.

On May 14, 1935, when Roosevelt wanted to restart his legislative reform program, he had had Borah, Costigan, Hiram Johnson, La Follette, Norris, and Wheeler to the White House for dinner.[15] He tried to purge Walter George in 1938. Borah was dead, but the rest of his former supporters were opponents. George was a powerful, though not cordial, ally. The transition was complete from Depression as the enemy to the Berlin-Tokyo Axis, and from workfare relief to defense as the official scourge of unemployment. Roosevelt the great political navigator had adjusted, apparently effortlessly, to the changing winds, tides, and currents.

Harry Hopkins departed for Britain on January 9, 1941, for a one-month visit as Roosevelt's special envoy. A few weeks later the White House announced that the reform Republican former governor of New Hampshire, John Gilbert Winant, was Roosevelt's choice to replace Kennedy as ambassador to the Court of St. James. This was another clever bipartisan move, like the appointments of Stimson and Knox and Donovan. On January 19, Willkie called at the White House for a very cordial conversation with his recent opponent. Overarching world affairs and some community of views made them rather friendly.*

Willkie, too, was about to depart for Britain, and Roosevelt asked him to "look up" Hopkins. Willkie did not know Hopkins but held the conventional Republican view that he was a shadowy, ubiquitous, cadaverous political fixer, almost a domestic Goebbels. Willkie asked Roosevelt why he kept Hopkins so close to him. The President responded, somewhat insensitively of his friend's fragile physical condition, that he kept "that half-man around because I need him." (Apart from anything else, this was an inappropriate comment for a man in a wheelchair.) Willkie might well some day be president, and he would realize that almost anyone who came to visit him wanted something from him. "You'll learn what a lonely job this is, and you'll discover the need for somebody like Harry Hopkins, who asks for nothing except to serve you." At the end of this agreeable interview Roosevelt asked Willkie to deliver a message to Churchill containing a

---

* Roosevelt had been working on his inaugural address in the cabinet room and received Willkie in his office, where the desk was bare. He hastily demanded a sheaf of "any papers" to spread around the desk so "Wendell" would not think he had nothing to do.[16]

verse from Longfellow. He then wrote it out. It would be the most famous of all the nearly 2,000 messages that passed between them:

"Dear Churchill,
  Wendell Willkie will give you this—He is truly helping to keep politics out over here.
  "I think this verse applies to you people as it does to us:

  " 'Sail on, Oh ship of state! Sail on, Oh Union strong and great,
  Humanity, with all its fears, With all the hopes of future years,
  Is hanging breathless on thy fate.'

"As ever yours, Franklin D. Roosevelt"

The message was dutifully delivered, gratefully received, and read over the international airwaves on February 9. On that occasion, Churchill asked: "What is the answer that I shall give in your name to this great man, the thrice-chosen head of a nation of a hundred and thirty millions?" His immediate answer was: "We shall not fail or falter; we shall not weaken or tire. Neither the sudden shock of battle nor the long-drawn trials of vigilance will wear us down. Give us the tools and we will finish the job." His more reflective answer, a few weeks later (April 27, 1941), was part of the then-famous English poem by Arthur Hugh Clough, "Say Not the Struggle Naught Availeth":

"For while the tired waves, vainly breaking, Seem here no painful inch
    to gain
"Far back through creeks and inlets making, Came silent, flooding in,
    the main,
"And not by eastern windows only. When daylight comes, comes
    in the light,
"In front the sun climbs slow, how slowly, But westward, look,
    the land is bright."[17]

It was fortunate that the Anglo-American world was led by men who so largely personified the civilization they were defending.

On inauguration eve, Churchill cabled Roosevelt that the new and powerful battleship *King George* V would be delivering Halifax to his new post at Annapolis, Chesapeake Bay, January 24, and that the President and anyone designated by him would be welcome to visit the ship. Roosevelt did meet the *King George* V personally, on the presidential yacht *Potomac*, in a gesture of solidarity with Britain. He did not tour the ship, though arrangements had been made for him to do so, but several of his naval staff did, and he gave Lord and Lady Halifax tea on the *Potomac*.

Despite Hopkins's prediction after he met Halifax in early January that he and Roosevelt would get on well because they were both "devout Anglicans," Halifax was mistrustful of Roosevelt, resented his influence on Churchill, and thought him "a very adroit manipulator . . . a little like Lloyd George. You never quite know when you've got him, or whether he will not slip through your fingers."[18] He did not take much advantage, at least in his first year, of the President's invitation to "look him up" (as if the President's whereabouts were a mystery in Washington). Also on board the *King George V* were several senior British military officers who were alleged to be coming to discuss war purchasing. In fact, they were the British members of the secret joint staff talks known as the American-British Conversations, ABC, which lasted two months.

A few days later (January 28, 29), Churchill cabled: "I received Willkie yesterday and was deeply moved by the verse of Longfellow's which you quoted. I shall have it framed as a souvenir of these tremendous days as a mark of our friendly relations which have been built up telegraphically but also telepathically under all the stresses. . . . I am most grateful to you for your splendid reception of Halifax and for all you are doing to secure us timely help. It has been a great pleasure to me to make friends with Hopkins who has been a great comfort and encouragement to everyone he has met. One can easily see why he is so close to you. . . . Many happy returns." (Roosevelt's 59th birthday was January 30, 1941.) Roosevelt's message hangs still in Churchill's bedroom at Chartwell.

Large crowds had cheered the President as he drove to his third induction into the presidency, January 20, faithfully reflecting the Gallup Poll, which showed that his popularity rating was higher, at 71 percent, than at any time since his very first days as president, a remarkable feat for a leader who had established a record for political longevity in uniquely tumultuous times.

Roosevelt's mother, his wife, and seventeen of his children and grandchildren were on the grandstand before the large crowd on Capitol Plaza to observe the ceremony. The President's address, composed initially by congressional librarian Archibald MacLeish but then rather clumsily worked over by less poetic minds, seemed to fall somewhat incoherently on his listeners. Roosevelt spoke forcefully and melodiously as always, and his allegorization of the American people as a body that required more than food and shelter and was most importantly "the spirit—the faith of America," was a perfectly adequate effort. However, it did not have the tremendous impact of his last four major addresses: "Martin, Barton, and Fish," "again and again and again," "the great arsenal of democracy," and "the Four Freedoms," and Roosevelt was disappointed that he hadn't more evidently caught the imagination of his listeners.[19]

II

HEARINGS ON BILL 1776 began in the House Foreign Relations Committee on January 15. Hull, Morgenthau, Stimson, and Knox led off for the administration and made a strong impression. Hull, always popular and respected in the Congress, overcame his irritation that the bill had been composed under the aegis of the Treasury rather than the State Department, and confined himself to a solid, unshakeable statement of the U.S. national interest. He said Lend-Lease was no sure deliverance from war, but "the safest course." The alternative was to hand control of the high seas to "powers bent on a program of unlimited conquest."

Morgenthau, who had been concerned that his testimony would be discounted as emanating from a Jew preoccupied with Nazi anti-Semitism, revealed the figures the British Treasury had given him to justify waiving the long-standing cash-and-carry rules in the sale of armaments to belligerents. There was real concern that Britain would run out of the ability to pay before the bill was adopted. Hull, with his usual tenacity, had privately suggested that Britain put up collateral until Roosevelt pointed out that he wasn't much interested in collecting chunks of India, tenements in Singapore, or primitive tropical islands. Hull was opposed to Morgenthau's revealing so much of Britain's needful condition for fear that it would give comfort to Britain's enemies. Morgenthau emphasized that never before had the government of one country authorized such a revelation of its accounts in the legislature of another country. He was quite effective in defending the financial implications of the proposed arrangements.

Stimson followed and was a very powerful witness. He was a Republican and had been known as a man of unquestioned integrity throughout his public career, which had spanned nearly four decades and seven presidencies. He strongly argued that the proposed measure would be of great benefit to the United States. He debunked the theory that it would strip America in order, militarily, to clothe Britain. He also attacked the claim that the bill conferred dictatorial powers on the President. He had served several presidents in high offices, he explained, and all, certainly including the incumbent, acted with the utmost sobriety and caution in time of war. A "government of law which is so constructed that you cannot trust anybody with power will not survive the test of war."

Navy Secretary Knox followed and did a competent job of explaining the extent of American reliance for its security on the British Navy. He was less effective when pressed hard by hostile questioners and expressed opposition to American armed convoys.*

William Knudsen testified for the administration on technical procurement matters, and a number of private citizens gave valuable testimony for the administration, including Dorothy Thompson, William Bullitt, William Green of the American Federation of Labor, and Averell Harriman's sister-in-law, Mrs. Jay Borden Harriman, who had been minister to Norway when the Germans arrived. Dorothy Thompson gave a vehement and eloquent statement on her detestation of Nazism. Bullitt denounced an American "Maginot Line" mentality with his usual verve. Mrs. Harriman gave a vivid description of the suddenness and brutality of German attack techniques.[20]

---

* Soon after, Knox engaged the young Chicago lawyer Adlai Stevenson, who would twice be the Democratic presidential candidate, as his assistant and legal advisor.

Opposition witnesses were led off by Joseph Kennedy, who appeared January 21. Roosevelt had performed his magic on Kennedy one more time in a ninety-minute meeting at the White House on January 16 (having declared two months before that he wished never to see him again as he banished him from his house). He had heard out all Kennedy's complaints and false professions of undying devotion to the Roosevelt cause yet again. He reminisced, he promised an unspecific pot of golden office and prestige for Kennedy and his sons at the end of the present rainbow, and sent Kennedy on his way in good humor. The former ambassador was a great disappointment to his isolationist sponsors, saying that he couldn't support the bill in its present form because it exempted the Congress from the foreign policy process after passage, but that he did support full aid to Britain.

Roosevelt's son-in-law, John Boettiger, sent Kennedy an appreciative letter shortly after, and Kennedy wrote back sadly expecting to be "a social outcast [to] the Administration." When Boettiger shared this correspondence with his father-in-law, Roosevelt gave one of his most thoughtful explanations of Kennedy's personality: "Joe is and always has been a temperamental Irish boy, terrifically spoiled at an early age by huge financial success; thoroughly patriotic, thoroughly selfish, and thoroughly obsessed with the idea that he must leave each of his nine children with a million dollars apiece. . . . To him, the future of a small capitalist class is safer under a Hitler than under a Churchill. This is subconscious on his part. . . . Sometimes I think I am 200 years older than he is."[21]

Ineffectual as it was, opposition testimony deteriorated from there, apart from the inevitable Colonel Lindbergh. He gave his usual appeal for adequate air defense, which he defined as about 10,000 first-line planes and a sufficient general defense for the Americas but avoidance of any transoceanic capability. The possession of such a capability would, in effect, be a provocation to the Germans and Japanese. He declined to express any preference or recognize any moral distinction between Britain and Germany. This pleased the galleries, which were packed with isolationists.

Norman Thomas, perennial leader of the Socialist Party, testified that Hitler could be brought around by a fine example of noninterventionist social democratic rule in the United States. Robert Maynard Hutchins, president of the University of Chicago, testified that the United States was so corrupt and morally and intellectually sick that it could not possibly give leadership to anyone. The testimony of Thomas and Hutchins was judged unpersuasive. Roosevelt was assumedly confirmed in his decision not to bring Hutchins into his administration.

The House committee went into executive session to take security-classified testimony from Hull and General George Marshall. Hull stressed the likelihood of a revived German attempt at an invasion of Britain in the spring, within ninety days he said, and Marshall spoke of the woefully inadequate state of the U.S. military for the role the country was aspiring to play in the world.

Roosevelt agreed to four innocuous amendments at a White House conference January 27.* The Foreign Affairs Committee reported Bill 1776 out 17 to 8 on January 30, and the whole House of Representatives passed it 260 to 165 on February 8 (236 Democrats and 24 Republicans voted for it and 135 Republicans and 25 Democrats voted against, as did Communist Congressman Vito Marcantonio). This Republican performance, despite Willkie's valiant efforts, and the strong management of Rayburn and McCormack make it clear how accurate Roosevelt's gloomy judgment of his Republican adversaries had been.

Bill 1776 continued to be debated in the Senate, where the anti-Roosevelt conspiratorial historian Charles Beard and *Chicago Tribune* proprietor Robert R. McCormick were among the witnesses. Roosevelt snorted derisively at his February 7 press conference when a *Tribune* reporter asked him about the publisher's testimony. "Did he speak as an expert?" Roosevelt asked mockingly, eliciting the mirth of the working press.[22]

Roosevelt discussed the nomination of John Gilbert Winant as ambassador to Great Britain. He acknowledged that the fact that Winant was a Republican could have been advantageous to his appointment. As if to underscore Winant's worldview, Roosevelt sent Ben Cohen, a social democratic Zionist as well as an outstanding legal mind and draftsman, to London as counsel in the embassy. This gesture was probably not unnoticed by Hitler, who was convinced that Roosevelt's animosity to him was based on saturnine Jewish influences. Winant was a social reformer with a profound altruistic streak, who would be ardent in his support of resistance to the Nazis but not seducible, unlike many of his predecessors in that post, by the British upper classes with the rich blandishments of their stately homes, country sports, and fine pageantry.

Hopkins's trip to Britain was a great success. From the outset he represented his mission as an effort to smooth out any problems between "two prima donnas." (This expression was to achieve considerable currency as the war progressed.) He well knew Roosevelt's ego and had accurate premonitions of Churchill's but believed as passionately as the two principals did in the cause that united them. Hopkins wanted to expedite the Grand Alliance by preparing for a constructive relationship between the two leaders. At their first meeting, according to Churchill's memoirs, Hopkins told his host, in a bomb-damaged and noisy 10 Downing Street, that the "President is determined that we shall win the war together. Make no mistake about it. He has sent me here to tell you that at all

---

* Time limits on the President's ability to authorize initiatives under the bill, non-applicability of the bill to U.S. escorts to convoys (a right the President possessed already as commander in chief), consultation with the military chiefs to avoid the transfer of national security-sensitive material or information to foreign powers, and reports to Congress every ninety days of relevant developments.

costs and by all means, he will carry you through, no matter what happens to him."[23] Hopkins also communicated that Roosevelt wanted a personal meeting with Churchill as soon as practicable. Churchill was grateful for the message and fully reciprocated the desire to meet.

Though Churchill's uncorroborated recollections must occasionally be read with some reservations, this version of events squares well with Roosevelt's gradually revealed grand vision. The first step after his reelection was to ensure that Britain was invulnerable to the threat of invasion. In addition to naval superiority and control of its own airspace, as Churchill eagerly pointed out to Hopkins, Britain now had excellent coastal defenses and twenty-five fully trained and equipped divisions in southern England. The Germans had no possible ability to transport and supply an invasion force of more than a fraction of that size.

Churchill, as he explained to Hopkins, envisioned what amounted to a replay of the Napoleonic Wars more than of the First World War. The British and Americans would underwrite the efforts of the resentful and oppressed European peoples until an adequate coalition was built to topple the German tyrant, preferably with the assistance of the Russians, who had been so instrumental in the ultimate defeat of Napoleon. This war, the British leader said, would "never see great land forces massed against one another."[24]

Here, though Hopkins didn't get into it or even probably altogether grasp it, was the kernel of a major strategic difference between the emerging allies. Roosevelt couldn't go on getting himself reelected indefinitely. America was threatened and, as always when threatened, America's leadership wanted the threat removed, not uneasy coexistence or a generation of intermittent fighting and coalition-building.

Roosevelt was profoundly affected by the crusading spirit with which his country, and the administration in which he had been a middle-echelon participant, had entered the First World War. His utterances about Four Freedoms and a "rendezvous with destiny" were not mere rhetoric. He knew that for Americans to exert themselves internationally, there would have to be a fusion of a practical national interest with an element of idealistic zeal for some new world that had been glimpsed only in dreams.

Roosevelt was about to secure passage of a measure that would enable him to hand over practically unlimited amounts of armaments and materiel to Britain. He was well along in building up American war production to an unheard-of level. And he had extended the "Neutrality Zone"—that is, designated American coastal waters—from three miles in September 1939 to over a thousand miles by November 1940, to 1200 miles in the spring of 1941, to within 400 miles of Scotland in the autumn of 1941. Within this zone, he, as commander in chief, defined American neutrality as doing anything that would assist in the delivery of supplies and people to Britain and in the sinking of German ships. Instead of "cash and carry" it would be Lend-Lease, and the U.S. Navy would work closely with the Royal Navy against a common enemy across most of the Atlantic.

This was virtually the mirror image of Kaiser Wilhelm II's 1917 policy of sinking all ships destined for Allied ports—in fact all ships, since the British naval blockade was impenetrable and the few neutrals largely avoided the high seas. This policy had provoked even the pacifistic Woodrow Wilson to war. Would Hitler prove less resolute? The German dictator had shown great forbearance toward the United States, ignoring provocations from Roosevelt that would have led swiftly to war if they had emanated from a European land power.

Roosevelt could not have expected his policy to be enforced and escalated indefinitely without leading to war with Germany. He had in eighteen months, with the help of British heroism, Churchill's leadership, and Hitler's butchery, brought American public opinion along from opposition to any departure from neutrality to a blank check to the President to give all aid short of war. The trend was obvious. Roosevelt would not want war until the United States was ready, which would require probably another eighteen months to two years. Even then, at the least he would need a full casus belli, and would hope for a partially enervated opponent.

Churchill's fantasy about a twenty-year Napoleonic War would not work for the Americans, who if they went to war wanted it finished promptly. The wild card was the Soviet Union, "a riddle wrapped in a mystery inside an enigma," Churchill called it while still in the Admiralty, in a speech of October 1, 1939. The fact that Russia hadn't plunged into India or toward the Middle East, as Churchill and Roosevelt would have assumed Hitler had encouraged Stalin to do, indicated that Stalin didn't want to move any forces away from his border with Germany. Nor did he wish to do anything that would help remove Britain from the war and eliminate it as a distraction to Hitler. Hopes for eventual Russian collaboration would have been a reason that Roosevelt stubbornly refused to exclude the Soviet Union from Lend-Lease, even under heavy pressure from leading congressional anti-Communists.

Now that Roosevelt was reelected and had extended the U.S. territorial waters almost halfway across the Atlantic Ocean, and Lend-Lease was coming into effect, Hitler had to worry about the possibility of eventually facing the British, Americans, and Russians simultaneously. He must have become convinced by now that, as his embassy in Washington had continually warned him for several years was the case, Roosevelt was dedicated to the destruction of the Nazi regime. The contemplation of that fact, more than any other identifiable consideration, may have caused Hitler, the supreme gambler, to think of a preemptive strike against Russia. If Hitler did nothing while Britain and America became steadily stronger, Stalin would be in a position to blackmail him, an opportunity Stalin would be unlikely to resist. If Hitler struck at the Soviet Union now with overwhelming force, while Britain was still recovering from Dunkirk and the United States was just emerging from pacifist isolationism, Germany might be able to secure a fastness in continental Europe that the British and Americans would be unable to shake or assault for generations.

Like Roosevelt, Hitler knew that any idea of reenacting Pitt's coalition wars against the Third Reich was impractical. Hitler was a totalitarian who crushed and occupied vanquished peoples and left them no room for anything but furtive guerrilla resistance. Napoleon merely defeated his opponents, seized provinces here and there, exacted tribute, and then sought acceptance, even marrying the daughter of the Habsburg emperor. Churchill's strategy was really a placebo to keep up the hopes of the British while they lacked important allies, not a strategic plan to liberate Europe from Hitler and bring about the sort of free world Roosevelt had been inspiring his audiences with for several years. It might have been a variant on his June 1940 request for a promise of war on behalf of France, with assurances that war-making would not really be necessary—that Hitler could be defeated without committing large armies against him. Churchill's respect for the German Army was well-founded, and it is hard to credit that he believed in the feasibility of the war plan that he was advocating.

Churchill, in his talks with Hopkins, set great store by the Turks, but no country contiguous to Germany and its satellites was going to enter voluntarily into conflict with the Reich. This preoccupation with Turkey was another of Churchill's nostrums based on his experience at the British Admiralty, where he had often tried to promote amphibious or diversionary movements on Germany's flanks, from Gallipoli in 1915 to Narvik in 1940. The Central and Eastern European countries had not forgotten what happened when the British induced Romania to declare war on Germany in 1915; all Romania was under German occupation within a few months and remained in that unhappy condition for three years.

Roosevelt didn't expect enlightenment from Hopkins or Willkie on these great strategic questions. He had his own design and kept his own counsel. Hopkins was there to build a relationship and Willkie to build bipartisan American support for it. Churchill had a tremendous impact on Hopkins: "God what a force that man has!" Hopkins exclaimed of him after their first meeting.[25] A few days later, they spent the weekend at the splendid country house Ditchley, which Churchill used when there was bright moonlight and it was thought his official country residence, Chequers, might be vulnerable to German bombing. Churchill painted a picture of a postwar Europe that would be partly federalized under British leadership. Germany and Russia he judged morally incapable of leading Europe. Germany would impose "tyranny and brute force," the Soviet Union "communism and squalor." (The Russians were proficient at tyranny and brute force also.)

Churchill, aware of Hopkins's background as a social welfare administrator, emphasized social and economic goals, including the prime minister's professed intention to provide electricity and running water to "the humble laborer [returning] from his work when the day is done and he sees the smoke curling upwards from [presumably, the chimney of] his cottage home."

When asked what Roosevelt would think of that, Hopkins responded: "Mr. Churchill, I don't give a damn about your cottagers. I've come over here to find out how we can help you beat Hitler." Churchill gave Hopkins a four-hour briefing on the military situation. He took him under his wing for several weeks, visiting the Royal Navy's Home Fleet at Scapa Flow, airfields and aircraft plants, bomb-damaged districts, and weekending at Chequers.*

Hopkins fell somewhat under Churchill's spell, but made an indelible impression himself. Churchill wrote in his memoirs of their "friendship . . . which sailed serenely over all earthquakes and convulsions. He was the most faithful and perfect channel of communication [with Roosevelt], slim, frail, ill, but absolutely glowing with refined comprehension of the Cause. It was to be the defeat, ruin, and slaughter of Hitler, to the exclusion of all other purposes, loyalties, or aims. . . . He was a crumbling lighthouse from which there shone the beams that led great fleets to harbour."[26]

Hopkins was largely engaged in promoting Roosevelt and Churchill to each other in preparation for the Grand Alliance that was being formed by mutual wish, if for slightly different purposes. Midway through his visit, Hopkins wrote to Roosevelt: "The people here are amazing from Churchill down and if courage alone can win—the result will be inevitable. But they need our help desperately and I am sure you will permit nothing to stand in the way. Some of the ministers and underlings are a bit trying but no more than some I have seen [at home]. Churchill is the government in every sense of the word—he controls the grand strategy and often the details—labor trusts him—the army, navy, air force are behind him to a man. The politicians and upper crust pretend to like him. . . . Churchill wants to meet you. . . . I am convinced this meeting . . . is essential, and soon."[27]

Well along in his month-long visit, toward the end of one of the dozens of dinners Churchill tendered him, Hopkins arose and said that he imagined his host was curious about what he would say to President Roosevelt on his return to the United States. "I am going to quote you one verse from the Book of Books: 'Whither thou goest, I will go, and where thou lodgest, I will lodge, thy people shall be my people, and thy God my God!' [and added], even to the end."[28†] Churchill's ability to stir powerful emotions among his listeners was matched by a tendency to emotional response himself. The prime minister wept, silently and without embarrassment. It had been a lonely and a brave struggle, and the prospect of the approaching might of the New World was a vision of inexpressible consolation.

Hopkins told Churchill that there were four distinct blocks of American pub-

---

* There is a marginal difference between the versions of Sir Oliver Lyttleton (trade minister), John Colville (private secretary), and Pamela Harriman (Churchill's daughter-in-law).
† There was disagreement over the venue of this exchange. It certainly was uttered by Hopkins, and Churchill, though neither was a religious man, took it up. This is the version of Sir Charles McMoran Wilson, later Lord Moran, Churchill's doctor[29]; Kenneth Davis has Hopkins saying it in a speech in Glasgow. In either case, it was an apt and moving adaptation of the Book of Ruth.

lic opinion: 10 to 15 percent who were Nazi or Communist sympathizers who sheltered behind Lindbergh, professed neutrality, but wanted a German victory; 15 to 20 percent, represented by Kennedy, who wanted to help Britain but were pessimistic and wanted no risk of American entry into the war; 10 to 15 percent, including Knox, Stimson, and most of the officers, who thought war inevitable and wanted to get on with it; and 50 to 60 percent who wanted to give all possible aid to Britain even if it risked war, but would prefer not to go to war.

Roosevelt was set solidly on top of the majority, was the preferred candidate of the war party, and retained a share of the so-called Kennedy group, and thus the support of about three-quarters of the people, a remarkable achievement in such a complicated situation.[30] Hopkins explained that Roosevelt was more or less in the war party himself, but knew the necessity of leading a united country to what would undoubtedly be a far more costly struggle in human terms than was the U.S. nineteen-month cameo appearance in the First World War.

Hopkins asked Churchill to pitch his February 9 speech, in which he would respond to the Longfellow verse, to make the passage of Lend-Lease easier and to counter the claims of those who said the President was trying to push the United States into war. He gladly did so, read the verse that Willkie had delivered, and made the point that Britain was not seeking manpower but "the tools" of war.

Hopkins departed Britain by plane the night before the prime minister's address, leaving him this note: "My dear Mr. Prime Minister, I shall never forget these days with you—your supreme confidence and will to victory. Britain I have ever liked. I like it the more. As I leave for America tonight I wish you great and good luck—confusion to your enemies—victory for Britain. Ever so cordially, Harry Hopkins"[31].

Willkie would play an important role at this stage also. Not being on an official mission and not a direct conduit to the President, Willkie had more time for a more informal schedule than Hopkins. He made a tremendous impression on the British. He toured bomb-damaged areas of many cities, met with Churchill and all other prominent officials, had extensive intellectual contacts through Harold Laski and Rebecca West, visited countless pubs and stood the habitués to drinks, tried his hand at darts, and even took to the bomb shelters and conversed with ordinary Britons there. The spectacle of his energy, high intelligence, and evident humanity reinforced the war-weary British in their image of Roosevelt's America as a place of boundless, benign, and intelligent strength.

Willkie, too, became convinced that the old class system was crumbling in Britain, that Chamberlain had been motivated to appease in part by a desire to retain a sociological regime that benefited him and his peers. He had been afraid to risk it by doing what national honor required. And this course was only forced upon him eventually by a combination of the brave Tories like Churchill, Eden and Cooper, who put principle ahead of comfort, and the left, the reform conservatives like Leslie Hore-Belisha, and the Labour Party.

The *Times* of London, still edited by the former head of the Anglo-German

Friendship League, Geoffrey Dawson, wrote that Willkie's "sincerity, friendship, boundless energy and radiant high spirits [were] immensely heartening."[32] He was not successful in his visit to Irish prime minister Eamon De Valera and his request that the Irish open some ports and airfields to the British.

Willkie also returned suddenly to the United States on February 9, the day after Hopkins, in order to testify at the Senate hearings on Bill 1776. Less rumpled and tousled than usual, Willkie appeared February 11, before a Senate caucus room packed with 1,200 people. He said that Lend-Lease was not an escalation of the widely supported policy of aid to Britain, merely the logical legalization of it. He held that there was no reason to believe that it would get the United States into war. Rather, it was the last hope for keeping the country out of war.

At one point, in response to a question about the U.S. Navy's providing a naval escort for British convoys, Willkie contradicted Knox's testimony by saying that this could be avoided by giving the British enough destroyers, between five and ten a month. The administration gently let it be known that this was Willkie's own suggestion and not one that would become official policy. (Official policy was to keep expanding the part of the Atlantic that the United States was securing for all purposes, not just for convoys, all in the name of a spurious neutrality.)

The most dramatic segment of Willkie's testimony came when he was questioned about entrusting the great powers of the Lend-Lease bill to President Roosevelt, and various of his colorful strictures against the President in the recent election campaign were quoted to him. He replied: "I tried as hard as I could to defeat Franklin Roosevelt, and I tried not to pull any of my punches. He was elected president. He is my president now." This was not enough for the ineffable Gerald Nye, who pushed Willkie on his prediction a few days before the election that if reelected Roosevelt, on the basis of his past performance, would have the country at war by April 1941. Willkie responded, smiling: "It was a bit of campaign oratory." The room was convulsed in laughter, and Nye was left with his isolationist position in tatters, finally on the verge of decisive defeat by the President. The Republican establishment's detestation of the renegade Willkie knew no bounds. Without elective office, a passing phenomenon, he had virtually read himself out of the Republican Party.

On February 13, 1941, the Senate Foreign Relations Committee, ably chaired by Senator Walter George, reported out the Lend-Lease bill, Bill 1776, 15 to 8. It was almost a straight party vote, though isolationist Democrat Champ Clark and progressive Republican Robert La Follette voted against. On the floor of the Senate the isolationists presented a barrage of amendments but didn't have the votes to sustain a filibuster. A few minor compromise amendments were accepted. The Senate voted the bill through on March 8 by 60 to 31 (50 Democrats and 10 Republicans for, 14 Democrats and 17 Republicans against).

Hopkins telephoned Chequers in the middle of the night (it was a Saturday) and left a message for Churchill. Roosevelt cabled that there would be concurrent action by the House of Representatives (to approve Senate amendments) and signing by him three days later, and added: "Confidentially I hope to send estimates for new orders and purchases under the bill to the House on Wednesday. Best of luck. Roosevelt". Churchill cabled Roosevelt back when he awakened: "Our blessings from the whole of the British Empire go out to you and the American nation for this very present help in time of trouble."[33] Roosevelt's indicated timetable was followed exactly. (The first Lend-Lease shipments—appropriately, given the President's famous illustration of the purpose of the proposal—included 900,000 feet of firehose.)[34]

Speaking in Parliament a few days later, Churchill described Lend-Lease as "the most unsordid act in the history of any nation," and in a special message of March 12 Parliament expressed, on the prime minister's motion, "our deep and respectful appreciation of this monument of generous and far-seeing statesmanship. The most powerful democracy has . . . declared . . . that they will devote their overwhelming industrial and financial strength to insuring the defeat of Nazism. . . . The government and people of the United States have in fact written a new Magna Carta . . . [that not only proclaims] the rights and laws [of] . . . a healthy and advancing civilization . . . but also proclaims by precept and example the duty of free men and free nations . . . to share the responsibility and burden of enforcing them. . . . In the name of all freedom-loving peoples, we offer to the United States our gratitude for her inspiring act of faith."* [35]

Roosevelt responded at the nationally broadcast White House correspondents' dinner on March 14 when he said, to prolonged applause: "In this historic crisis, Britain is blessed with a brilliant and great leader." (Hopkins suggested the flattering remarks about Churchill.)[37] Roosevelt was celebrating not just the passage of a historic act, but his recovery from a tenacious attack of sinus flu, to which he was always vulnerable. The President told the correspondents: "This decision is the end of any attempts at appeasement in our land; the end of urging us to get along with the dictators, the end of compromise with tyranny and the forces of oppression. . . . The great task of this day, the deep duty that rests upon each and every one of us is to move products from the assembly lines of our factories to the battle lines of democracy—now!" Churchill had asked for "the tools [to] finish the job." He would have the tools, but as he and Roosevelt—and Roosevelt's enemies, from Nye and Burton Wheeler to Hitler—knew, the tools alone would not end the war. On March 17, Churchill cabled "congratulations and grateful thanks on your magnificent speech . . . I must also thank you for your most kind and complimentary reference to me."

---

* The colonial secretary, Lord Lloyd, negotiating the bases-and-destroyers deal, became so exasperated with American demands that he told the Foreign Office in March: "These people are gangsters." Churchill told him they could not have a "first class row" with the United States at this point, and Britain yielded.[36]

The Lend-Lease Act was so broad, Hitler now realized that he was effectively, in war production terms, fighting not just the British Commonwealth but also the United States. The Reich propaganda minister, Dr. Josef Goebbels, wrote in his diary: "The Fuehrer finally gave his propagandists permission to attack America. It was high time. Now we shall let rip. Mrs. Roosevelt is shooting her mouth off around the country. If she were my wife, it would be a different story."[38] (A more unlikely match would be extremely difficult to imagine.)

In 1939, Goebbels had told Cornelius Vanderbilt Jr., "When we get good and ready, we will take your impertinent nation from within."[39] This too was Nazi bravura. J. Edgar Hoover's Federal Bureau of Investigation had done a very thorough job of infiltrating American Axis-sympathetic organizations, and they were never very effective at espionage, much less sabotage. Beneath official Nazi disparagements of the United States as a lumpenproletariat infested with subhuman ethnicities, there lurked a recognition by Hitler that this was a country with power of a new magnitude in geopolitical terms, led by a man who from his first days in his country's highest office had been virulently hostile to Nazi Germany. Opposed to appeasement, insusceptible equally to intimidation and blandishments, Franklin D. Roosevelt's America loomed ever larger and darker on Hitler's horizon.

At the same time, Britain had proved insuperable in its island. It was scarcely imaginable that Chamberlain had yielded place to someone so diametrically different as Churchill. And, all the while, there remained the fourth great player, Stalin's Russia, which even at the moment he attacked it, Hitler, like Churchill, described as an unknown quantity. At the height of his power, Hitler's position was much less unshakeable than it at first glance appeared. He could not subdue the British and was almost at war with the Americans. If he had to fight the Russians at the same time, he was doomed.

III

ROOSEVELT LEFT WASHINGTON on March 19 for a ten-day fishing trip off Florida on the presidential yacht *Potomac*. The President didn't want to appropriate his customary heavy cruiser in wartime but the *Potomac* was only a coastal vessel. It was not comfortable in a swell and the last half of the trip, through and back from the Bahamas, was quite rough. Attorney General Robert Jackson pointed out to Interior Secretary Ickes that if the *Potomac* foundered there would be no chance the escorting destroyer could send out lifeboats. Ickes, an inveterate landlubber, wrote furiously in his diary that Roosevelt was taking needless chances with his own security. Roosevelt signed the first appropriations measure, $7 billion, for the Lend-Lease arrangements while on board, March 27. It was flown down for signing because of the urgency of Britain's need, and the courier seaplane landed with difficulty on choppy waters.

In 1941, Lend-Lease furnished just 1 percent of the munitions used by Britain and the Commonwealth, but over the balance of the war it provided for half of Britain's balance-of-payments deficit, relieving Britain of the necessity of covering its defense-related imports with exports. More than $50 billion would be dispensed under Lend-Lease agreements throughout the world up to the end of the war. The importance of this measure was not exaggerated in Churchill's superlatives.[40]

The President delivered a Jackson Day dinner address devoid of partisanship and focused largely on the salubrity of saltwater holidays from his shipboard cabin in Fort Lauderdale harbor on the evening of March 29. Roosevelt met up with his wife shortly after disembarking and they toured the massive Fort Bragg, North Carolina, military installations together. The army had quickly prepared forty-six camps for the reception of initially over a million conscripts. In the course of the war the U.S. War and Navy departments would expropriate over five million acres, a greater area than the Commonwealth of Massachusetts.

On returning to Washington, Roosevelt casually informed his regular press conference that the new Lend-Lease program would be directed by a cabinet committee consisting of Hull, Stimson, Knox, and Morgenthau, and that the secretary of the committee, the chief executive of the whole program in fact, would be Hopkins. This disappointed Morgenthau, who had hoped to control it, but Stimson had sought to wrestle Treasury out of the play, and the President's characteristic compromise was to give it to the official he trusted most (and the only one who knew Churchill and wartime Britain), while throwing scraps to the relevant cabinet members.

Ickes, who was left out entirely, since aid to Britain had absolutely nothing to do with the Interior Department, ungenerously confided to his diary: "Harry has not successfully operated any government enterprise since he came to Washington. People have no confidence in him and I believe justly so." Many did, including Roosevelt and Churchill.[41] Hopkins sent General Hap Arnold of the Army Air Corps to Britain in April to determine Britain's real air needs, because Marshall and others were concerned that Britain would ask for more than she really required.

Hopkins shared Roosevelt's view that the cooperation of the country's big-business executives was crucial to the success of the rearmament and Lend-Lease efforts. Both became increasingly exasperated with the inflexible do-goodism of the inveterate New Dealers, led, in ability to irritate Roosevelt and Hopkins at least, by Eleanor Roosevelt. She had introduced Hopkins to her husband and with Frances Perkins she sponsored him in the administration. She now felt that Hopkins was losing his commitment to social justice and had been somewhat turned, not to say intellectually corrupted, by being the closest confidant of the most powerful man in the world and his principal liaison with Winston Churchill. For his part, Hopkins was actually heard by Sherwood to exclaim in the spring of 1941: "I'm getting sick and tired of having to listen to complaints from those God damn New Dealers!"[42]

The American-British Conversations concluded their first general session, ABC 1, on March 29. They revealed many of the strategic differences between the

British and Americans that would become quite contentious as the Second World War progressed. The major agreement was that both sides considered Germany the principal enemy, regardless of what the Japanese did. There was agreement also between the two sides that it would be desirable, and probably fairly feasible, to knock Italy out of the war with a few well-placed blows.

The Americans declined to do anything that amounted to a rigorous defense of the existing British Empire. Despite the heavy British emphasis on the importance of Singapore, the Americans considered the defense of that city to be an exclusively British matter. The British deluged the discussions with plans for amphibious landings on the periphery of the German-occupied area, aid to resistance movements, and massive bombing campaigns against Germany.

The American representatives did not feel at this point that they had any standing to dispute how the British might like to conduct a war in which the United States was not officially engaged. But they made it clear that in the event of entering the war, the United States would wish to attack Germany as quickly and directly as possible. The President did not endorse or reject the ABC 1 report and Rainbow 5 report derived from it. There was no sequel until General Marshall, having come to understand Roosevelt's operating methods, took it upon himself on June 10 to implement the reports' recommendations of increased coordination. He persuaded Stimson, Knox, and even Hull that the President's failure to reject the reports constituted approval. The principal recommendations and the formal continuation of the talks accordingly proceeded.

———————

The war itself opened 1941 favorably for the democracies. The Greeks had pushed the Italians completely out of their country and had taken about a third of Albania by the end of March. In the same period the British drove the Italians out of the eastern half of Libya, capturing 130,000 Italian soldiers at a cost of only about 2,000 British casualties. In February the British cleared the Italians out of Somaliland and invaded Ethiopia. The tempo of the campaign was determined by the speed with which the British could advance through the rugged terrain. Haile Selassie returned to his country January 20 and reentered his capital to a hero's welcome on May 5, exactly five years after the Italians had seized Addis Ababa. British casualties were minimal, and 200,000 Italian troops abjectly surrendered.

On March 28, the British Mediterranean fleet (led by H.M.S. *Warspite*) in a night action lasting only a few minutes, sank three Italian cruisers and two destroyers off Cape Matapan in rather ignominious circumstances for the Italians, with the loss of only one British aircraft. The Italians were unaware of the proximity of British warships until the Royal Navy turned searchlights on them and fired full salvos at point-blank range.* After being soundly thrashed on land

———

* On the battleship *Valiant*, the searchlights were turned on by the future consort to Queen Elizabeth II, Philip, later Duke of Edinburgh.[43]

and sea, Mussolini offered little more backtalk. Britain's easy victories over the bloated Fascist imposture demonstrated how foolhardy was the Chamberlain-Daladier (and Halifax) policy of appeasing the Duce from 1935 to 1940.

Churchill regularly referred to "this whipped jackal, Mussolini." This condition was useful in itself, but it brought the Germans in to fill the vacuum created by the military implosion of the Italian Fascists. The German Air Force started to appear in strength in the Mediterranean in January 1941, and, flying from Sicily, pounded Malta and was able to cover the movement of a substantial German army to Libya. Under the command of General, subsequently Field Marshal, Erwin Rommel, the Afrika Korps went on the offensive in Libya in mid-March. The British theater commander, General Archibald Wavell, had to maintain substantial forces in Palestine to prevent the Arabs from adhering to the Axis and the Arabs and Jews from erupting in conflict (as they did after the postwar departure of the British). This limited Wavell's ability to respond to Rommel, who soon reversed the Italian retreat.

Hitler had bullied or cajoled Bulgaria, Hungary, and Romania into joining the Tripartite Pact and granting transit rights to the German military. On March 25, in Vienna, Yugoslavia also adhered to the German alliance, through the regent, Prince Paul. Colonel William Donovan, the American intelligence chief who headed up the Office of Strategic Services, forerunner of the Central Intelligence Agency, had visited Belgrade in December 1940 as Roosevelt's personal representative, and promised American Lend-Lease assistance if Yugoslavia did not cave in to German demands. Roosevelt followed up with a letter to the Yugoslavs February 14. (Churchill thanked Roosevelt in a cable of March 10 "for the magnificent work done by Donovan in his prolonged tour of the Balkans and the Middle East. He has carried with him throughout an animating, heart-warming flame."[44])

The British were also very active, and both powers exploited the differences between the principal ethnic groups in the country. The Croatians were pro-German and the Serbs pro-Western. (These stresses too, would explode decades later when the force holding the Yugoslav state, a more artificial Versailles construction than Czechoslovakia, was removed.) After extensive debate, the British War Cabinet decided in early March to run the risk of allowing a German buildup in Libya and began transferring four divisions to help the Greeks against the Italians. Hitler responded like Napoleon when he was told that the British had landed an army in Spain in 1809. It was an almost fatal error by the British, who underestimated Rommel's ability to launch and sustain an offensive. They had become accustomed to routing Italians and were about to rediscover the vagaries of direct land combat with the Germans.

Two days after the regent committed Yugoslavia to the German alliance, acting on the incitement of British and American intelligence, the (mainly Serbian) Yugoslav Army and Air Force staged a bloodless coup, dismissed the regent, installed the seventeen-year-old Prince Peter as king, and repudiated the German alliance. Hitler summoned the German General Staff and demanded a plan for the immediate extinction of Yugoslavia with gratuitous brutality. This plan, which Hitler called "Operation Punishment," was executed with the usual Teutonic martial efficiency beginning April 6, as Yugoslavia was invaded from Austria, Hungary, and Romania by twenty-five German divisions and terrorized from the air. Italian and Hungarian units joined the German assault.

Belgrade was occupied by the Germans on April 13. Yugoslavia surrendered April 17. The Germans moved swiftly to cut off the retreat of the Greek Army from Albania toward Macedonia, and on April 20 the Greek government surrendered, the prime minister having committed suicide in the bravest traditions of ancient Greece. About 45,000 of the 55,000 of Wavell's British and Commonwealth troops in Greece were evacuated by the Royal Navy. Naval losses were heavy, including five hospital ships, for which the Germans showed less than civilized respect.

The Germans finished off this formidable assertion of mastery in the Balkans on May 20, with an airborne invasion of Crete that was successful within two weeks because of overwhelming air superiority, and caused the evacuation of the British and Greek forces, 17,000 soldiers out of the 24,000 defenders of the island. German losses were such that it was almost a Pyrrhic victory. Two more formerly independent countries were thus ground underfoot, bringing the total to sixteen, before the liberation of the first victim, Ethiopia, in early May, brought the net total of occupied countries back to fifteen. Hitler converted three others, Bulgaria, Romania, and Hungary, into semi-self-governing satellites and generally staged a massive show of strength, which cured the Balkans for a time of their ancient tendency to fractiousness.

It also exposed the weakness of the British strategy of amphibious activities, air harassment, and assistance to local insurrections. Britain had again been sent packing from the continent of Europe, taking to the boats with a good deal less dignity even than at Dunkirk. The British now faced a severe threat from the Afrika Korps against the Suez Canal and the whole oil-producing region of the Middle East. The British Mediterranean fleet seemed unable to stop the flow of men and materiel to Rommel. This sequence of reversals reinforced the American conviction that when the time came there would be no alternative to engaging the German Army across the Channel as soon as adequate forces could be assembled for such a challenge, with no illusions about how costly such an encounter would be.

The Germans were also pressing the British very hard on the North Atlantic. German submarines sank 818,000 tons of British shipping in the three months ended May 1, 1941. Britain would not be able to replace these losses, and German submarine construction was increasing more swiftly than the strength of British antisubmarine forces. Hitler further responded to Roosevelt's thousand mile wide "Neutrality Zone" by extending the submarine warfare area to Greenland on

March 25. He did so at the urging of Grand Admiral Erich Raeder, but also for political reasons, to demonstrate that he would not completely ignore Roosevelt's mockery of neutrality.

In these circumstances, Churchill, in his capacity as minister of defense, concluded in a report of March 6 that his country was losing the Battle of the Atlantic. Throughout the late winter and spring of 1941, Churchill was beseeching Roosevelt for further assistance, particularly for American escorts for British convoys. This would not only help vitally in the Battle of the Atlantic. Though this point was never mentioned, it would certainly raise the possibility of a deadly exchange between the United States and Germany.

Assistance was requested with ever greater urgency, in every area, down to the repair of individual ships in American yards. Roosevelt almost always obliged promptly. On March 25, he cabled from the yacht *Potomac:* "Delighted to repair ship you mention [battleship H.M.S. *Malaya*]. Let me know probable port of arrival. Boston, New York and Norfolk available. Will expedite the work. I am getting a week of rest but will return in a few days. All good luck. Roosevelt".[45] Essentially, Britain was valorously and stylishly holding the fort until "the New World stepped forth to the rescue and the liberation of the Old."

The fact was that, brave though they were, the British were a declining power. They could repel or deter invaders from the home islands, but had extreme difficulty retaining the part of their Empire that was within even the distant reach of the Germans, and had almost no capacity to defend themselves simultaneously in the Far East against the Japanese. Without all Roosevelt's direct assistance and aggressive redefinition of "neutrality" in the Atlantic, the United Kingdom would have been strangled. In the battle of the mastodons, Britain, though important and splendid, was slipping to the top of the second rank above Japan, below the German and Soviet masters of the Eurasian heartland, and two rungs below the mighty power of the New World.

American steel production in 1941 was 125 percent of the combined production of Germany, the Soviet Union, Great Britain, and Japan. This figure was replicated or exceeded in every category of strategic manufacturing, from aircraft to shipping. Henceforth, British power and influence would more and more reside in its ability to influence the United States as that country's principal and most compatible, prestigious, and persuasive ally.

The historian Kenneth Davis accurately remarked: "Now as never before in history . . . the fate of Western democracy . . . Western civilization, depended upon the mental operations and decisive will of the President of the United States. Franklin Roosevelt had become the central pivotal figure of the whole free world. Almost his every word, deed, gesture — his every act or refusal of action . . . had worldwide consequence."[46] This was not a daunting prospect to Roosevelt.

Colonel Lindbergh in his public speeches became ever more defeatist about Britain, a position made more plausible by the shambles of the Greek intervention and the retreat that had begun in Libya. Roosevelt, at his press conference on April 25, 1941, had planted a question through his press secretary, Steve Early, about why Lindbergh, as a reserve colonel, had not been called into service. Roosevelt referred to the Copperheads in the Civil War, whom Lincoln had declined to conscript because they were loyalty risks. He also spoke of Thomas Paine's dismissal in the Revolutionary War of the "summer soldiers and sunshine patriots."

The President strongly implied that Lindbergh was a Nazi and a traitor, and Lindbergh responded by publicly retiring from the United States Air Corps Reserve. While he attacked Lindbergh, it served Roosevelt's convenience to have Stimson, Knox, Willkie, Ickes, and even in some measure Hull visibly more hawkish than he was. As always, he screened his relentless progress toward his objective behind the contradictory activities of a variety of other prominent personalities, who were out of, or in a subordinate, office, and could thus be rendered instantly obsolete if necessary.

IV

ON APRIL 29, Churchill sent Roosevelt another in what must have seemed to both of them an endless series of rather importunate letters. He foresaw the attack on Crete, possible airborne German landings in Syria, and pressure on Turkey and Spain to allow passage of German troops, as had been successfully demanded of the Balkan countries, and made another of scores of expressions of concern about Vichy—both the disposition of its navy and the use of French North African air bases by the Germans. He even envisioned a German submarine base at Dakar and a German attempt to seize or use the Azores. Most of his fears proved to be exaggerated.

Roosevelt responded encouragingly on May 1. He cautioned Churchill not to occupy the Azores unless the islands or Portugal itself were about to be invaded by Germany, and to emphasize that the islands would be restored at the end of the war, because "most of Azores are in Western Hemisphere under my longitudinal map reading [making it a Monroe Doctrine question] . . . My thought in regard to Eastern Mediterranean is: you have done not only heroic, but very useful work in Greece and the territorial loss is more than compensated for by necessity for enormous German concentration and resulting enormous German losses in men and material.

"Having sent all men and equipment to Greece you could possibly spare, you have fought a wholly justified delaying action. . . . If additional withdrawals become necessary, they will all be a part of the plan which at this stage of the war, shortens British lines, greatly extends the Axis lines, and compels the enemy to expend great quantities of men and equipment. I am satisfied that both here and in Britain, public opinion is growing to realize that even if you have to withdraw further in the Eastern Mediterranean, you will not allow any great debacle or surrender, and that . . . the naval control of the Indian Ocean and of the Atlantic Ocean will in time win the war."

The President did not think that much could be done with Turkey other than moral suasion, and not even that with Spain, but was more sanguine, with reason as it turned out, than Churchill was about the conduct of both countries.

Roosevelt must have been particularly happy not to have yielded to the entreaties of his wife, the domestic left, and even Senator Nye to help the Spanish Republicans against Franco. Such help would not have changed the military outcome of the civil war and the Republicans were Soviet-dominated anyway, and probably would have been less protective of Spanish sovereignty than Franco was. Hitler had one meeting with Franco and declared afterward that he would rather have all his teeth extracted than negotiate with him again. Had Roosevelt assisted the Republicans during the civil war, Franco might have been more beholden and responsive to Hitler.

Roosevelt didn't think there was "any chance of persuading Vichy to break with the Germans," but thought Vichy would resist German invasion of its colonies as it had the British, and offered to send "two more children's food ships to Marseilles" and some oil and ammunition to Weygand as a quid pro quo. "We think it almost impossible for Germans to reach Dakar over land, especially with what is left of French Army and Navy concentrated there.

"Personally, I am not downcast by more spread of Germany for additional large territories. There is little of raw materials in all of them put together—not enough to maintain or compensate for huge occupation forces. The exception is oil in Mossul and Iraq and I assume production there could be practically destroyed by you in the event of necessity.

"Your talk on Monday was splendid. I expect to go on air within next two weeks. Keep up the good work."[47] (Churchill spoke on April 27 and gave the Clough quotation as his poetic response to Roosevelt's verse from Longfellow.)

This exchange illustrated the contrast between British and American views of colonial outposts. The British tended to regard almost all territory as a matter of prestige and ports and installations on the lifeline to them as strategic points. The Americans regarded almost all of Africa and South Asia as of no geopolitical interest and vastly more trouble than they were worth. And they tended to regard the bases that grew with empire, storied though some of them were, as less indispensable than the British believed. Roosevelt looked with delight at the prospect of Hitler squandering hundreds of thousands of soldiers in garrisons in geopolitically nonsensical places, squatting in deserts, forests, and on mountaintops, patrolling Arab souks and interrogating nomads. Churchill was greatly disquieted by any German expansion at the expense of the British Empire, lest the stability and rationale of the Empire as a whole be put in doubt.

Churchill found Roosevelt's May 1 letter discouraging, because it seemed to him to treat cavalierly the possibility of a German victory in Egypt and throughout the Middle East. He told Winant that he was displeased. He also had a recurrence of the depressive attacks that bothered him all his life—the "black dog," he and his doctor, Wilson, called them. (Wilson wasn't much help, merely ascribing the problem to the "Churchill blood." One thing Churchill, Roosevelt, and Hitler all had in common was the steady receipt of questionable medical advice.)

Churchill replied to Roosevelt on May 3. In his first draft of his letter he went so far as to say that he was "depressed" by Roosevelt's letter but eliminated the sentence in the final version.[48] On the question of the occupation of the Azores, he wrote: "We are far from wishing to add to our territory, but only to preserve our life and perhaps yours." He admonished Roosevelt (who had only been trying to lift Churchill's spirits) not to "be too sure that the consequences of the loss of Egypt and the Middle East would not be grave." (He had "mortal" in the first version but changed it.) The prime minister felt that such a reversal could negatively determine the attitude of Spain, Turkey, Vichy, and Japan.

That Churchill was under almost unbearable pressure was further demonstrated by his request, which he knew to be completely impractical, that the United States declare war on Germany at once, and by his assertion that he would "await with deep anxiety the new broadcast which you contemplate. It may be the supreme turning point."[49] Roosevelt was on the airwaves every few weeks, and his speeches tended, like Churchill's own, to be tours de force that resonated well.* The "turning point" in the war was indeed almost at hand, but it would be provided by a mighty and decisive clash of arms, not by another of Roosevelt's tactical speeches ratcheting up the tension between the United States and Germany.

Roosevelt replied May 10, though he was ill. While in Staunton, Virginia, on May 2, to dedicate Woodrow Wilson's birthplace as a national historic site, he felt distinctly unwell and returned to Washington earlier than had been foreseen. He was diagnosed as suffering from an intestinal disturbance, diastolic hypertension, and extreme iron deficiency due to bleeding hemorrhoids. He received two transfusions and iron injections, and was counseled to rest completely, which he was, for once, happy to do. He barricaded himself in his bedroom until mid-May, considering what to do about accelerating war production and escorting British convoys. Having brought his country's opinion so far, he did not want to run any risk of overstraining his credibility by moving too far ahead of it.

In his May 10 reply, Roosevelt assured Churchill that he "did not intend to minimize in any way the gravity of the [Mediterranean] situation . . . I am well aware of its great strategic importance and I share your anxiety in regard to it. . . . I know your determination to win on that front and we shall do everything we possibly can to help you do it. My previous message merely meant to indicate that should the Mediterranean prove . . . an impossible battleground I do not feel that such fact alone would mean the defeat of our mutual interests. . . . I believe the

---

* Soviet diplomat, long-time foreign minister, and ultimately president Andrei Gromyko, of all people, wrote that Roosevelt "earned the accolade of the National Association of Teachers of Oratory as 'the greatest of all modern American orators.' No other President of the USA that I ever met could compare with Roosevelt in this regard." (He knew ten U.S. presidents; Ronald Reagan might have been a rival.)[50]

outcome of this struggle is going to be decided in the Atlantic and unless Hitler can win there he cannot win anywhere in the world in the end.

"I cannot speak too highly of the admiration which the American people hold toward your generals, admirals, troops, airmen and sailors who fought in Greece and are now fighting in the Mediterranean and Africa. I think the feeling in America is that the effort which your country made to stem the tide in Greece was a worthy effort and the delaying action which you fought there must have greatly weakened the Axis."

Roosevelt acknowledged that while Vichy would not comply beyond the terms of the armistice, neither would it resist German violations of its metropolitan territory. He was still hopeful that Vichy would resist German incursions in its colonies.

The President tried a new tack in reinforcing the morale of his beleaguered ally, by informing him that he was extending "our patrols . . . farther out into the Atlantic," and had "added all of our heavier units of the Coast Guard to . . . the patrol. With this message go my warm personal regards to you."[51]

In fact, Churchill's fortunes did revive somewhat in May, despite the debacle in Crete. On May 7, Churchill won a House of Commons confidence vote, 447 to 3. On May 10, the German deputy fuehrer, Rudolf Hess, parachuted into Scotland on a mysterious mission to arrange peace between Britain and Germany. He was at least partially mad, although Churchill wrote to Roosevelt May 17 that "no ordinary signs of insanity can be detected." He had no mandate from Hitler to do anything, and his peace proposals were delusional, including the requirement of the dismissal of the Churchill government. His defection was a serious embarrassment to Hitler. Hess was one of his oldest collaborators, and Hitler had dictated *Mein Kampf* to Hess while they were in Landsberg Prison together following the abortive Munich putsch of 1923.*

In one of the most dramatic episodes in the entire naval war, the powerful German battleship *Bismarck* sailed through the Straits of Denmark into the Atlantic. When intercepted off Greenland by the famous British battle cruiser *Hood* and the battleship *Prince of Wales*, on May 24, *Bismarck*'s accurate gunnery, at a range of twelve miles, penetrated *Hood*'s deck and blew up her magazines. There were only three survivors out of 1,500 men aboard what had long been the largest and most famous warship in the world. *Hood* suffered from the defects of the battle cruiser design: she was underarmored, and at extended range incoming shot fell

-----

* The psychiatric examination of Hess was essentially an intelligence interrogation. He was sentenced to life imprisonment after the war. No effort was ever made to alleviate or treat his mental illness, and he finally committed suicide in 1987, aged ninety-three, having been the only prisoner in Spandau Prison in Berlin for the preceding twenty-one years. The Soviet Union insisted on retaining him in prison, against the wishes of the Western Allies.

steeply and achieved a great velocity before hitting *Hood*'s relatively thin deck.*
The *Bismarck* shot up and chased off the brand-new battleship *Prince of Wales*
and then resumed her southward course.

This was one of the worst shocks Churchill received in the whole war, but the
Royal Navy recovered quickly, damaged *Bismarck*'s steering gear with an aerial
torpedo, and cornered her May 27. The *Bismarck* was unable to steer for home
and sullenly awaited the arrival of British heavy units like a fighting bull awaiting
its execution after the picadors have done their work. The British battleships *Rodney* and *King George V*, with the commander of the Home Fleet on the bridge,
reduced *Bismarck* to a flaming wreck before cruisers finished her off with torpedoes. In the end, the action was a distinct British victory.

Roosevelt heartily congratulated Churchill that day, May 27, on the sinking of
the *Bismarck*. To support America's ever-expanding neutrality zone, Roosevelt
transferred three battleships, an aircraft carrier, four cruisers, and smaller craft
from the Pacific to the Atlantic in May and June.

Later on May 27 Roosevelt gave the speech that Churchill had hoped would
mark "the turning point." It was a Pan-American Day address, and Roosevelt did
take another step in his carefully calibrated escalation of abrasions with Germany
by proclaiming a "state of unlimited national emergency." He warned in very direst
terms of the dangers of the German submarine campaign, which was generally
taken as a signal that U.S. escorting of convoys was imminent. The President's con
demnation of Nazi Germany, widely broadcast but delivered in person to a group
of Latin American diplomats, many of whom had only an indifferent command of
English and applauded at unpredictable moments, concluded: "The Nazi world
does not recognize any God except Hitler. . . . Will our children, too, wander off
goose-stepping in search of new gods?" He referred in the speech to "the First
[and] Second World Wars," which was not what they were generally called at that
time (the Great War and "the present war" were the usual designations).[52]

Roosevelt also told Churchill on May 27 that 75,000 tons of supplies were on
their way in American ships directly to Egypt (around the Cape of Good Hope),
including 200 tanks and 700 trucks. Churchill thanked Roosevelt the next day:
"We are uplifted and fortified by your memorable declaration and by . . . the
great advance you found it possible to make."

In fact, the emergency declaration did not portend such a change, it merely
succeeded the state of "limited national emergency" that was proclaimed in September 1939, and this had no particular technical significance. Roosevelt's press
conference the next day was disappointing because of the meager substance of
his message. The American freighter *Robin Moor* had been sunk by a German

---

* The problems with the battle cruiser design were demonstrated at the great Battle of Jutland in 1916, where several were sunk. They were built on the principle that "the best armor
is speed," but if the opponent's gunnery was exact, as the Germans' usually was, it was no protection at all.

submarine in the South Atlantic on May 21, in broad daylight and though clearly marked. The U-boat commander showed little concern for the passengers and crew, who drifted in boats on the equatorial ocean for two, to three weeks before being rescued. Yet Roosevelt, contrary to Hopkins's advice, reported this incident quite routinely to the Congress.*

The British occupied Baghdad on May 31, chasing out the pro-German government of Rashid Ali (which Rudolf Hess, as Churchill informed Roosevelt May 17, had insisted be retained). The British invaded Syria June 8, with a supporting contingent from de Gaulle's Free French. Damascus was occupied June 21. A large British convoy got through the Mediterranean to Alexandria, carrying over 300 tanks. General Archibald Wavell, the British Middle East commander, was for a time too distracted by Iraq and Syria to counterattack Rommel. But he had recovered most of his forces from Greece and Crete and resupplied them with the contents of the recent American and British convoys, and seemed better able to hold his position. He launched Operation Battleaxe against Rommel in early June. It was not a success—the battle lines didn't move much and the casualties and prisoners were about equal—but it was at least offensive action. Churchill, changing generals until he found winners, as Lincoln had, retired Wavell and replaced him with the commander of the British Indian Army, Sir Claude Auchinleck, in mid-June 1941. Wavell became viceroy of India.

Hitler at this point had several options: pour into Africa, invade Britain, invade Russia, or sit on his conqueror's laurels. A massive effort in Africa would be difficult, given Turkish and Spanish truculence about granting passage to the German Army and the vulnerability of air and sea supply from Italy. Overrunning those countries would require major dispositions of men and resources and large forces of occupation in constant enervating combat. Invasion of Britain was not a serious option; the RAF and the Royal Navy would obliterate at least three-quarters of any such force and any subsequent supply effort, and the British Army in its coastal defense positions would make short work of survivors. But resting on his laurels was not in character for Hitler. If, at this late stage, he had assumed the personality of Richelieu, Talleyrand, Metternich, or Bismarck, governed more liberally, announced a unilateral deescalation of the war, treated with the countries he had crushed, however one-sidedly in Germany's favor, and become a

---

* Some pro-Roosevelt historians, such as Kenneth Davis, have criticized him for excessive caution, but his technique since the Quarantine speech in Chicago in 1937 had been to push opinion forward oratorically, allow its avant-garde to surge past him, follow opinion cautiously in practice, and keep repeating the process. He was thus a more difficult target for his domestic opponents, the cleverest of whom suspected his game but could never catch him at it. Strangely, King George VI understood Roosevelt's methods better than Churchill did. The king wrote to FDR, June 3, 1941: "I have been so struck by the way you have led public opinion by allowing it to get ahead of you."[53]

believable man of peace with some sense of proportion, it might have worked. But following such a course would have required a total personality transplant, and would have undermined the secret of Hitler's appeal: an absolute dictatorship, savage, disciplined, fearless, full of hate, and sadistically uncompromising. It was an even more impossible scenario than the first two.

That left Russia. Apparently, and by general agreement, any such initiative would be, and was, his undoing. But Hitler was convinced that he would have to deal with the United States as a warring enemy when Roosevelt had finished preparing for war and Germany had been weakened by years of war with the pestilential British. In such circumstances, Stalin could not be trusted not to stab him in the back in exchange for mountains of American money and domination of central Europe. If Hitler could fragment the Soviet Union now, before the United States was ready for war, Roosevelt and Churchill or their successors would be unable to dislodge him from control of the European mainland. And if they did not then make the sort of peace he had offered the year before, dividing the world, after the elimination of Russia, between four powers only—Germany, Great Britain, the United States, and Japan—he could rampage through the Middle East, across North Africa, even into India, using satellite troops such as Romanians and Hungarians and Croatians, even Ukrainians, to do much of the heavy lifting.

It would be an immense gamble, of course, for if he became bogged down in Russia and found himself fighting the Americans at the same time, as well as the British, it would be his turn to be brutally exterminated. Hitler had built his entire career on spectacular gambles, though not when competing with statesmen of the stature of Roosevelt, Churchill, and Stalin, who bore no comparison to the decayed servitors of Munich. He might at least be able to impose a settlement almost as onerous as that he had inflicted on France. Mortally dangerous though an attack on Russia would be, it had a logic.

So also did Roosevelt's strategic reassurance to Churchill on May 1, 1941, that Hitler was becoming overextended by his Balkan and African adventures. Without the British intervention in Greece and the coup in Belgrade, Hitler could have invaded Russia six weeks earlier than he did, with potentially decisive consequences. What appeared to be a British fiasco was a strategic success that arose from a tactical failure.

Roosevelt as a strategist was a talented amateur, with an unfailing intuition in certain areas coupled to a knowledge of his own limitations and excellent judgment of the capacities of senior military personnel. This combination, as well as his mastery of domestic politics and his ability to inspire his people and the world, made him a great war leader.

Stalin had the conventional view. On June 12, 1941, he told his generals: "Germany is busy up to her ears with the war in the west and I am certain Hitler will not risk creating a second front by attacking the Soviet Union. Hitler is not such an idiot."[54]

The tremendous increase in American war production led to an inflammation of industrial relations. The leaders of organized labor professed to believe that the workers were being asked to make sacrifices while executives and shareholders were enriching themselves with returning prosperity. The administration stressed the war emergency and said the unions should be thankful for the end of unemployment, for the Wagner-Connery Labor Relations Act, and for the Fair Wages and Hours Act, and should aid the course of rearmament. The collaboration of all was required, and Roosevelt and his advisors did not want to reopen old problems with big business.

There had been an outcry from labor in early 1941 when the government awarded a $122 million contract to Ford, the greatest union buster of all large American companies, for 4,000 airplane engines. Henry Ford engaged in his usual practices and fired labor organizers on his payroll after he had been passed over for a further contract because he declined even to pledge to observe existing labor laws. The UAW struck Ford in April 1941, but 2,000 black workers, loyal to Henry Ford as a relatively equal-opportunity, antisegregationist employer, remained at work. Considerable violence ensued, some of it stirred up by agents on both sides.*

The company's line was that the strike was Communist-inspired, in obedience to the Nazi-Soviet Pact. Roosevelt declared a policy of "watching and waiting and watching," but his feeling was probably closer to his famous comment on the steel industry of 1937, damning both of them. African-American leader Walter White, who had visited the White House with A. Philip Randolph on September 27, 1940, persuaded the black workers to join the strike. Henry Ford's son, Edsel, then prevailed upon his father to allow collective bargaining and a vote on certification. To the senior Ford's astonishment and disappointment, the employees voted 74 percent to unionize and 70 percent of those voting were for the UAW-CIO.†

Bethlehem Steel Corporation, which had been almost as determined an opponent of union activity as Ford, accepted a National Labor Relations Board arbitration in the early spring of 1941 after Roosevelt declined to use the army against strikers. Complete avoidance of collective bargaining was practically

---

* Eleanor Roosevelt's sources told her, and she told her husband, that Ford's comparative racial tolerance was just a ruse to impede unionization. Henry Ford was a cantankerous and inflexible man. He held many absurd views, such as that milk should be avoided because cows were "lazy." He was extremely hostile to organized labor and was now a militant isolationist, but the fact that he was a comparatively liberal employer of what were then called colored people should not have been negated because of his far from indefensible distaste for the United Auto Workers.

† After Ford's death, in 1947, it was found that his management had been so erratic that, Edsel having predeceased him, Roosevelt felt obliged to muster the founder's grandson, Henry Ford II, only twenty-nine years old, out of military service and urge him to fix up the family business, which he did.

impossible. This undoubtedly led to a more equitable distribution of the wealth generated by the amazing productivity of the American worker. It avoided polarization between management and labor, kept the unions in the hands of comparatively moderate people, and spared the country the class warfare that so scarred the advanced industrial nations of Europe. Thirty years later sclerosis among both management and labor would create a crisis of competitiveness and require the reindustrialization of much of America, but between the Depression and the war, only a clairvoyant could have foreseen that.

Thus encouraged, strikes proliferated in the defense industries. Most controversial was a wildcat in June 1941 at the North American Aviation plant at Ingleside, California, which manufactured vitally needed two-engine bombers. Roosevelt promptly signed an executive order bringing the strike to an end by the insertion of 2,500 soldiers, who stormed out of their trucks and quick-marched the picket line with fixed bayonets, one of which impaled a striker. This had a salutary effect on many union agitators, but there were still sullen unions and some skeptical employers, despite Roosevelt's peace offensive toward big business, until they were all overtaken by events.[55]

The defense production effort had fallen 30 percent behind schedule.

The U.S. private sector was not transferring to war production from consumer goods as swiftly as was necessary to fulfill all the promises to supply the British and Soviets that the President had made. This was partly from governmental confusion, partly from inertia, and partly from lack of enthusiasm for the thin profit margins Roosevelt insisted on for war production, given his long career as an oratorical opponent of war profiteering. To speed up the process he had set up at the end of August 1941 a Supply Priorities and Allocation Board. This new board consisted of Knox; Stimson; Hopkins, as the person in charge of defense aid to the Allies; Henry Wallace, as chairman of the Economic Defense Board; Leon Henderson, as head of the Office of Price Administration; Donald Nelson, as the executive head of the SPAB; and William Knudsen and Sidney Hillman, as cochairmen of the Office of Production Management. This created a further spaghetti bowl of official relationships and chains of authority, in the manner Roosevelt preferred, as a means to retain all authority himself and ensure that his subordinates could not unite for long to frustrate his orders or wishes. It appalled an orthodox administrator like Stimson. Nelson was junior to Knudsen in the OPM but his superior in the SPAB, which was technically the senior agency now.

Leon Henderson, the new head of the Office of Price Administration, was demanding a 50 percent reduction in automobile production to make way for defense needs, but Knudsen was reluctant to try for such a drastic alteration of production schedules. In 1941 the United States produced one million more automobiles than it had in 1939. With Roosevelt's constant inveighings against the evils of war profiteering, there was a great deal more money in civilian automobiles than in Army vehicles or military aircraft. After the horribly depressed thirties, business wished to take advantage of returning prosperity. One of the casualties of this reluctance for a time was the humble landing craft, despite the obvious fact that in the event of war American soldiers would have to debouch on a great many distant and unfriendly shores.[56]

Much of the executive class feared that the drift to war, apart from human costs, would lead to greater unionization and higher taxes. The transmutation of Harry Hopkins from supreme New Dealer to chief Lend-Leaser fanned such fears. Yet the percentage of GDP taken up by defense spending increased from 1.4 in 1939 to 11.2 in 1941, almost all of it paid for from government borrowing rather than taxes. This did complete the evolution of the New Deal to its fourth phase and delivered great benefits to its longstanding opponents. Because of the requirements for maximum efficiency, there was a tremendous gravitation toward concentration of production in big business. The 100 largest companies in the United States produced 30 percent of the country's manufacturing in 1940. In 1943, the same companies' share of twice as large a total of manufacturing was 70 percent.[57]

Roosevelt negotiated with Iceland an invitation to the United States to land troops in that country, and this process began June 10, 1941, relieving the 20,000 British soldiers who had been there since the German occupation of Denmark in April 1940. On June 14 he seized all German and Italian assets in the United States and on June 16 closed all German consulates and agencies. He reported to Churchill on June 17 that the public reaction to these moves, which had been planned for some time,[58] had been "90 percent favorable."

He also, a few days later, issued an executive order barring racial discrimination in defense procurement industries. This was a breakthrough for the African-American leadership, which had, through A. Philip Randolph, been threatening a march of 100,000 black protesters on Washington. Mayor La Guardia of New York, a civil rights activist and ally of Randolph's, deserves more credit than Roosevelt for this unconscionably overdue reform. Roosevelt had been grumbling self-importantly about not negotiating "with a gun at my head"[59] until La Guardia proposed a "formula," which proved to be the executive order that had been sought.*

Missy LeHand had a minor stroke in early June and a severe stroke in mid-June. Missy would never be able to work again. Roosevelt visited her a number of times in Doctors' Hospital. Because she tended to become agitated and even hysterical, he withdrew and returned less and less frequently. Grace Tully took over as chief

---

* When Randolph visited him, Roosevelt, as was his practice with visitors, started out with a charm offensive. His opening gambit was to ask Randolph what class he had been in at Harvard. Unfortunately, Randolph had never attended Harvard University.

secretary, but Missy's incapacitation was the greatest casualty in Roosevelt's official entourage since the death of Louis Howe five years earlier. And it was more of a shock. She was a younger person than Howe, in apparently much better health. While she had been fragile, and had had two breakdowns in the previous fourteen years, she came back well from them, and they didn't seem to affect her physical health. She had been completely devoted to her employer with a passionate, though not necessarily romantic, intensity.*

V

O N JUNE 22, 1941, the "supreme turning point" Churchill had been anxiously looking for, occurred. Without warning, Germany invaded the Soviet Union with 180 divisions. With Operation Barbarossa, Hitler unleashed one of the greatest military operations in the history of the world. When Stalin's foreign minister, Molotov, was handed the declaration of war by the German ambassador, which followed a lengthy recitation of trumped-up grievances, Molotov asked mockingly: "Do you think we deserve all this?"

Hitler had made his supreme gamble. Churchill, after exactly a year since the fall of France, was no longer alone among the major powers in facing the Nazi onslaught. Hitler was not so overconfident at the outset of this campaign as is widely believed. He knew he was taking a tremendous risk, and referred to Russia as like Wagner's "Flying Dutchman," an impenetrable mystery. Germany racked up great advances and bagged well over a million prisoners in the first ten weeks of the campaign. But the Russian armies, despite terrible reversals and the apparent immobilization of Stalin and the high command in the early days, retreated more or less in order, and the lost manpower was easily replaced from the Slavonic and polyglot masses of the Soviet Union. The chief of the German General Staff, General Franz Halder, would record in his diary, August 11, 1941, that the Germans had expected to meet 200 Soviet divisions but had already identified 360.

The vastness of the country quickly absorbed the invading German hordes as they were drawn farther and farther east. Hitler had known, and events confirmed, that the scale, climate, and resistant traditions of the country assured that this would be no case of easily smashing up a victim. It would be a titanic and savage struggle, with no quarter given or asked.

Churchill responded to the German invasion of Russia immediately with supportive comments about the defender. He had been one of the most vociferous anti-Communists in the Western world, since and even before the Bolshevik Rev-

---

* Her only clearly romantic involvement, so far as is known, was with William Bullitt, when he was ambassador to Moscow, 1933–1936. They were apparently engaged for a time in 1936, but this fell through when Missy visited him in Moscow and found that he had a close female companion. The arrangement, which some members of the President's entourage had thought more a power play by the free-wheeling ambassador than a genuine love-match anyway, was called off.

olution. He had been one of the principal advocates of the attempted Western military suppression of the Communists starting in 1919, and had often lamented "the failure to strangle Bolshevism in its cradle." But when he gave a world broadcast on June 23, 1941, though he did not "unsay one word" he had uttered about Communism, he spoke of "ten thousand villages where the means of existence is wrung so hardly from the soil, but where there are still primordial human joys, where maidens laugh and children play." Upon this peasant idyll, the prime minister declared, there had burst "the hideous onslaught [of] the Nazi war machine." He sketched for his listeners "the clanking, stinking tanks . . . dandified, heel-clicking Prussian officers . . . dull, drilled, docile, brutish masses of Hun soldiery." Britain could not fail to give such support as it could to the Soviet Union against "that small group of villainous men who plan, organize, and launch this cataract of horrors upon mankind."[60]

Roosevelt was much more cautious. He said little for some weeks, apart from unfreezing $40 million of Soviet assets in the United States. He told his June 24 press conference that the United States would aid the Soviet Union but dodged the question of whether this would be under the Lend-Lease arrangements. His military advisors thought that Germany would be thoroughly preoccupied for from one to three months, but did not doubt that Germany would overwhelm the Russians. The same group, led by Marshall, were pessimistic about Britain's chances of repelling the German onslaught in the western desert against Egypt.

Roosevelt instinctively had more confidence in the Russians and the British than that. He had written Churchill that he thought Germany was becoming overstretched logistically and that where Germany couldn't cow its opponents or crush them quickly, resistance became steadily more determined. However, he was no admirer of the Soviet regime, as he had often made clear. He was impressed that the Soviet Union had not committed aggressions against other countries, as had Germany, Japan, and Italy (apart from Finland and the small Baltic states that Russia had formerly ruled). He also felt that the universalist views of Communism were less offensive than the genocidal racism of Nazism. And he believed that many ostensible Communist supporters were really social democrats and that democracy would make inroads in Communist regimes as the Western democracies were able to generalize prosperity.

But he thought that Communism was evil nonsense; he was a capitalist, a democrat, and a Christian, and he shared to some degree the general American absence of a natural preference between Hitler and Stalin, as was reflected in his policy during the Spanish Civil War. He had condemned the Russians after their attack on Finland and at his press conference on July 5, 1940, had put the Soviet Union together with Germany and Italy in having abolished democracy by effectively abolishing the courts and legislature.[61]

Roosevelt did not go as far as Senator Harry Truman. Truman said, on June 24, 1941: "If we see that Germany is winning we ought to help Russia, and if Russia is winning we ought to help Germany, and that way let them kill as many as possible."[62] And according to the Gallup organization on July 13, 72 percent of Americans favored a Russian victory and only 4 percent a German one. Communism was not popular, but the Soviet Union was not considered a threat to the United States and Germany was.[63]

Roosevelt wrote to his ambassador in Vichy, Admiral William Leahy, June 26, 1941, that what he called "the Russian diversion . . . will mean the liberation of Europe from Nazi domination—and at the same time I don't think we need worry about any possibility of Russian domination."[64] He believed that Russia was primitive, better at absorbing invasions than conducting them, that Stalin was cautious with other Great Powers, and that Communism was absurd.

When, on May 28, 1941, Halifax and the visiting John Maynard Keynes called upon Roosevelt, the President said that ultimately Europe must be disarmed and that only Britain and the United States must possess serious armed forces. When Keynes asked about the Soviet Union, Roosevelt smiled and replied enigmatically, as was his habit: "Now you are making things difficult."[65] According to Keynes's biographer, Roosevelt later told Archbishop Spellman that Russia would not be easy to contain in postwar Central Europe.[66]

Molotov told the U.S. ambassador in Moscow, Laurence Steinhardt, in early July that the Soviet Union wanted $1.8 billion of war supplies from the United States. But Molotov sardonically allowed that he did not, in fact, expect to get much of it. Roosevelt received the Soviet ambassador, Konstantin Oumansky, July 10, and, ignoring most of the military and political advice he was receiving, promised all that could be provided of Molotov's request, consistent with supplying Britain, and by October 1. He reasoned that Hitler was the primary enemy and that it was illogical to withhold aid to the country that would inflict most of the casualties on the Germans because its regime was distasteful. It was only the second time in 1941 that he had seen Oumansky.

If the Russians had a chance it must be partially because of Western, especially American, aid. If Germany prevailed, it would be, as was Hitler's design, more powerful and dangerous than ever. If it did not and the West had not been helpful to the Russians, Stalin or any successor would have no incentive to be allied to the West or to reject a favorable separate peace with Germany. In that event, all the West would have achieved would be a comparative breathing spell before the reemergence of a strengthened Hitler and a tenaciously persevering Stalin. The problems of dealing with a victorious Soviet Union could not possibly be as difficult as resisting Hitler. As was often the case, Roosevelt's informed intuition was superior to the professional and political advice he was receiving.

The case has been made that Roosevelt paid excessive attention to the slavishly credulous reports from Moscow by Bullit's successor as ambassador, Joseph Davies, 1936 to 1937. This is unlikely, since he moved Davies out quickly to the lesser position of Brussels, and denounced the Stalin regime repeatedly in terms that were not reconcilable with Davies's endless praise of it. Through the thirties Roosevelt had always been irritated that there had been no abatement in anti-

American propaganda from Moscow and no effort at developing a serious commercial relationship, both of which had been promised when diplomatic relations were reopened in 1933.

Roosevelt saw that it was sensible tactics and sound strategy to deal with the inimical Nazi and Soviet regimes sequentially rather than concurrently, which is why he didn't push the Finnish problem too far, unlike Chamberlain, Churchill, and Daladier. Roosevelt also believed that unlike Nazi Germany, the Soviet Union could be tamed without going to war with it. In both of these insights he was correct. The Soviet Union took ten times as many casualties as the British and the Americans combined in subduing Nazi Germany.

———————

Hopkins returned to Britain July 13, 1941, on a fact-finding mission and to arrange the first face-to-face meeting between Churchill and Roosevelt since 1919. In his latest escalation of his creative definition of neutrality, Roosevelt had declared the Western Hemisphere to extend to two hundred miles beyond Iceland and to include the Azores. Most of the North Atlantic was now, effectively, U.S. coastal waters. This was a far more sensible method of helping the British than American escorts for their convoys across the entire ocean. It was a further departure from "cash and carry."

Hopkins had a long meeting with Churchill in the garden at 10 Downing Street on July 16, and again saw a great deal of the prime minister throughout his stay. Hopkins met the Soviet ambassador to London, Adam Maisky, at Churchill's country house, Chequers, on July 19, where Maisky handed over Stalin's response to two personal messages from Churchill. This would be the first of what would be almost three years of demands from Stalin for a second front in northwest Europe. Churchill responded somewhat impatiently to this preposterous request.

Hopkins and Maisky and Winant lunched together at the U.S. Embassy in London on July 22, and Maisky invited Hopkins to Russia. On July 27, Hopkins addressed the British people from Chequers, where Churchill had facilities for such broadcasts. His speech, written by Quentin Reynolds (narrator of the British Ministry of Information's made-for-America film *London Can Take It*), was an excoriation of Nazi Germany that cheered the British and scandalized the isolationists. He had come to Britain in a bomber, he said, accompanied by twenty other bombers that were handed over to the British on landing. Those planes may "tonight be dropping bombs on Brest, on Hamburg, on Berlin, safeguarding our common heritage. Our President is at one with your Prime Minister in his determination to break the ruthless power of that sinful psychopath in Berlin." These were not neutral comments.

Roosevelt had approved Hopkins's trip to Russia, and sent a message for delivery to Stalin. It asked Stalin "to treat Mr. Hopkins with the identical confidence you would feel if you were talking directly to me. He will communicate directly to me the views that you express to him. . . . May I express . . . the great admiration all of us in the United States feel for the superb bravery displayed by the Russian people in the defense of their liberty." (Their resistance to the Germans was stiffening, but whatever they were defending, it was not, in any conventional parlance, liberty.) Fussing to the last about not having a visa, until Winant handed him his passport with a visa in it (the Russians never requested his passport),[67] Hopkins left on July 29. He had a dangerous and uncomfortable twenty-four-hour flight on a Catalina, sitting in the unheated tail-gunner's bubble, to Archangel, went on to Moscow the next day, and went with Ambassador Laurence Steinhardt to meet Stalin in the Kremlin on July 31.

Stalin made a generally good impression upon Hopkins. Unpretentiously dressed in a gray uniform with brightly polished boots and no decorations, broad-shouldered, stocky and muscular, but with tobacco-yellowed teeth and only about five feet, six inches tall, Stalin answered each question frankly, without histrionics, and with no apparent desire for particular effect. It was generally known that he had been seriously shaken by the beginning of the German campaign, and that he took to his dacha in a drunken stupor for several days.

Stalin asked for 20,000 antiaircraft guns, one million rifles, a large consignment of machine guns, and promises of aircraft fuel and of aluminum for aircraft construction. Most important, Stalin conveyed to Hopkins, who faithfully transmitted it to Roosevelt and Churchill, a sense of unruffleable calm and absolute determination. He had taken the full brunt of the Nazi assault for six weeks, but was self-assured and extremely well-informed, and seemed suffused with the ancient unconquerability of Tolstoyan Mother Russia, Georgian Communist though he was.

Hopkins met with Soviet General V.F. Yakovlev to discuss specific military requirements and with Molotov, neither a particularly satisfactory meeting, and again with Stalin. The Soviet leader estimated that the Germans now had 232 divisions in Russia and could commit up to 300. The Russians then had, despite considerable losses, 260 divisions, and could muster the formidable total of 350, nearly seven million men. He thought Germany had started with 30,000 tanks to 24,000 with the Russians, and that both totals had declined, the Russians' more sharply. They could not, at this point, make good all their losses themselves, and would like to build their tanks in the United States. Stalin thought that, in general, Russian tanks were superior to German ones. (He was probably correct; they were certainly superior at that time to American tanks.) The Germans had a slight temporary advantage in the air, but Stalin was confident of redressing that, and of a qualitative superiority over most German aircraft types.

Hopkins's report included a personal evaluation for the President only. In this section, the author gave his instinctive views and also summarized a personal oral message from Stalin for Roosevelt. The Soviet leader claimed that Hitler's weakness lay in the bitter hatred he aroused in the places he had overrun and in the fears of those who might yet be the subjects of German aggression. He claimed (on no evidence that has ever come to light) that the morale of the German Army was low. The masses of the world, including the Soviet Union, "can receive the kind of encouragement and moral strength they need to resist Hitler from only one source, the United States. The world influence of the President and government of the United States is enormous." Stalin cunningly added his requirement for "a minimum moral standard between all nations," in what must have been a direct pitch to Rooseveltian idealism, since he certainly did not believe or practice any such thing. It was obvious to Stalin that the United States was moving inexorably toward war with Germany; why wait any further? This was the same message, delivered more bluntly and less grandiloquently, that Churchill had been expressing for many months.

Stalin said that he would welcome an expeditionary force from the U.S. Army on the Russo-German front, and that it would be welcome to operate autonomously. (It was an interesting concept that no one took seriously except those in Roosevelt's entourage who chose to regard it as evidence of Russian desperation.) Hopkins cabled Roosevelt from the U.S. Embassy in Moscow on August 1, 1941, that he felt "ever so confident about this front, [that] the morale of the population is good, [and that there is] unbounded determination to win."

He was impressed with Stalin as "an intelligent machine," tough, decisive, and efficient. He was rigorously unimpressed with the Communist system. The interpreter for the second session with Stalin had been the former foreign minister, Maxim Litvinov, a Jew whom Stalin had fired when he tired of the antics of Chamberlain and decided to make his peace with Hitler. Hopkins wrote that Litvinov "seemed like a morning coat that had been laid away in mothballs [and] brought out, dusted off." It was obvious to Hopkins, who reported it to Roosevelt with extreme distaste, that Litvinov, who was coldly treated by Stalin, even more than the rest of Stalin's staff, was motivated by sheer terror.

VI

THE GERMAN INVASION of Russia came as a complete shock to the Japanese. The Nazi-Soviet Pact of August 23, 1939, had undercut the former Japanese policy of pusuing a joint German-Japanese anti-Soviet policy and came just as the Russians, under future Marshal Georgi Zhukov, decisively defeated the Japanese in a multi-division "border incident" at Nomonhan. The Japanese government of Prime Minister Kiichiro Hiranuma resigned five days later. Japan then had 850,000 soldiers immersed in the limitless Chinese campaign.

The Japanese adjusted their policy, and their rather industrious foreign minister, Matsuoka, then scampered around Europe trying to organize a full-fledged four-power alliance between the three Axis powers and the Soviet Union. As a first step, he had negotiated a nonaggression pact between the Soviet Union and Japan on April 13, 1941. Stalin thus accepted the Japanese occupation of Manchuria.

The Axis would pay heavily for their failure to coordinate anything between themselves. Hitler was then in the final planning stages of his attack on Russia. If he had taken his Japanese ally at all into his confidence, the pre-Nazi-Soviet Pact policy could have been resuscitated in Tokyo and the Japanese could have pinned down large Soviet forces in the Far East. This would also have sharply reduced their ability to force the United States into war with the Axis.

Given that Hitler realized that attacking Russia was the ultimate gamble of his career, it is not clear why he didn't try to recruit such a well-disposed and formidable ally as Japan. Hitler told Matsuoka in Berlin in April 1941 that relations with the Soviet Union were deteriorating, and showed no interest in the four-power alliance plan, but did nothing to discourage him from concluding his arrangement with Stalin and Molotov, which Matsuoka did on his next stop. Nor is it clear why he made no effort to persuade Tokyo to tear up its nonaggression pact with Stalin in June as he had just done. His failure to secure the collaboration of the Japanese against the Soviet Union must rank as one of Hitler's most serious errors.

The Japanese now moved toward a southern expansionist policy, starting with French Indochina but aiming at the oil resources of the Dutch East Indies (Indonesia). Japan was dependent on American oil for 75 percent of its needs. U.S. oil exports to Japan had been cut back in the summer of 1940 because of the irritation of Roosevelt and his more hard-line cabinet members, Stimson, Ickes, and Morgenthau, at the brutal Japanese aggression in China. Unknown to the President, his officials, starting in July 1940, had denied Japan any export permits for oil. In fact, Roosevelt had wanted only to reduce the flow of oil to a trickle, not stop it.

The origins of the total oil embargo are obscure. On December 14, 1940, the U.S. ambassador to Japan, Joseph Grew, a friend of Roosevelt's from Groton, wrote the President a "Dear Frank" letter stating that "we are bound eventually to come to a head-on clash with Japan."[68] By this time, by an uncharacteristic journey to Canossa, Dean Acheson was about to reinsert himself in the administration. Following his August 1940 letter to the New York Times pointing out that the President had the authority to transfer destroyers to Britain without congressional approval, he wrote a letter to the Baltimore Sun, which the New York Times reprinted on October 2, stating: "Today there is only one test—who can best pilot the ship in this crisis of civilization? . . . The President has met that test. No one can ask more and no one dare ask less."[69]

Roosevelt wrote a letter of thanks to Acheson, and Acheson replied that it was "a joy and a duty . . . to say publicly how essential for our country it is to have you at the helm." Acheson must have been desperate to return to government to resort to this level of obsequiousness to a man he did not like, who had fired him six years before for indiscretions of which he was, in fact, innocent, though he had been impertinent. He had only grumpily supported Roosevelt in 1936. Acheson passes lightly over these events in his memoirs.

Roosevelt invited Acheson to a political strategy session in the White House where Acheson declared that the Democrats were being "too defensive . . . The New Deal and the great horizons it had opened for the common man" (in whose lot Acheson had not previously shown a very lively interest) had to be related to "the dangers threatening freedom everywhere, including in our own land." Roosevelt asked for a written summary of this interesting perspective and Acheson responded with a feisty document urging the linkage of the President's domestic achievements with the need to bring "the might of America to guard the New World from the tragic horror which has engulfed the Old World."[71]

This was good enough for Roosevelt to readmit the penitent Acheson, whose competence had never been in doubt. Shortly after the President's reelection Hull invited Acheson back into government as assistant secretary of state for economic affairs. Acheson was sworn in by Justice Brandeis in the presence of Frankfurter, Attorney General Biddle, and the congressional librarian, Archibald MacLeish, at Brandeis's home on February 1, 1941.[72]

It was in this capacity that Acheson became chairman of the joint Treasury-State-Justice Foreign Funds Control Committee. By October 1940, 83 percent of Americans favored a full embargo against Japan on anything militarily useful, including oil and gasoline. Acheson was a hawk, agreeing with Stimson, Morgenthau, and Ickes on the desirability of a full embargo. Hull, Welles, and Knox were cautious, not wanting war with Japan. Roosevelt didn't want to be excessively distracted by the Pacific, and favored Welles's policy of an embargo on high-octane aviation fuel, which would incapacitate Japan's air capability. He would placate domestic opinion and caution the Japanese, but avoid driving them completely into a corner.

Following the Japanese invasion of southern Indochina at the beginning of July 1941, Roosevelt froze Japanese assets in the United States on July 24, which would further complicate the Japanese purchase of oil or anything else in the United States. The same day, Roosevelt announced the formation of a Philippine army and recalled General Douglas MacArthur to active duty and put him in command of the creation of a serious military force in the Philippines. As field marshal of the Philippines, MacArthur had been shaping up the locals, but this was a vastly enhanced commission. An important part of this plan was to put 165 B-17s, half of America's initial force of the new Flying Fortress bomber, in the Phillipines. Roosevelt allowed himself to be persuaded that the view of his mentor, Admiral Mahan, that the Philippines were indefensible,[73] was no longer necessarily the case in the age of air power. The B-17s could reach the Japanese home islands and would constitute an important strategic ingredient that could alter the traditional equation.

The freeze of Japanese assets was meant to be somewhat flexible. Acheson made it absolute while ostensibly awaiting the elaboration of a precise policy by Hull and Welles. Acheson professed to be waiting for the recommendations of the Export Control Commission and carrying out Welles's wishes in doing nothing until this occurred. Accordingly, all export licenses for Japan for petroleum products were revoked sine die, August 1, 1941, without the President's knowledge, a few days before Roosevelt left Washington for his meeting with Churchill, which was to be in Newfoundland, taking Welles with him.

Later in August, the Export Control Commission advised Acheson and his committee that Japan was entitled to over half a million gallons of gasoline and diesel fuel, and two Japanese tankers were patiently at anchor in San Pedro, California, waiting to be filled. The last sophistry to alight from Acheson's fecund imagination on this subject was: "Whether or not we had a policy, we had a state of affairs," i.e., created by him.[74] (If Acheson had possessed this skill at bureaucratic machinations at the start of the administration, he might by now have been the secretary of state, a post he later occupied with much more acuity and panache than Hull brought to it.) This was how the issue rested until the President returned from his meeting with Winston Churchill.

The rough handling the Japanese had received from the Russians did not raise their prestige in the eyes of the West, especially when contrasted with the brilliant performance of little Finland against the same adversary. The British and the Americans underestimated Japanese capabilities and thought that moving the U.S. Pacific battle fleet from California to Pearl Harbor, supplemented by a capital ship squadron Churchill was planning to send to Singapore, would be a serious deterrent to Japan.

Roosevelt and Churchill were concerned to deter Japan from joining in the attack on Russia. The tide of war could turn against Hitler if Russia could survive the German onslaught, as Hopkins believed. Hopkins was no military genius but was a shrewd judge of men. If the United States were to enter the war, however reluctantly, it should be in time to help the Russians remain in it and survive the German invasion. And it would now, more likely, be through the back door in the Pacific.

Hitler would be bound to join Japan if it attacked the United States. Though he might ignore his treaty obligations, it seemed as likely to Roosevelt that he would honor them in the hope or with the stipulation that Japan would join him against the Russians, even if it meant a partial Japanese withdrawal from China.

More than ever, the conduct of the President of the United States was the key to the war's direction. In these circumstances, the most promising for the Western leaders since the war began, Winston Churchill and Franklin Roosevelt prepared for their first meeting since the brief encounter in 1919 that Roosevelt did not enjoy and Churchill did not remember.

⚜

CHAPTER 15

President Roosevelt Will "Make War without Declaring It"

(Prime Minister Churchill reporting to the War Cabinet after the Argentia Conference with President Roosevelt, August 9 to 12, 1941)

I

OPKINS HAD ANOTHER exhausting and perilous return to Scapa Flow, where the commander in chief of the Home Fleet, Admiral Sir John Tovey, gave him the admiral's cabin on the *Prince of Wales*, blood transfusions, medication, and sedatives for an eighteen-hour sleep. The battleship had just been repaired from the well-placed shots she had received from the *Bismarck* on May 24, following the sinking of the *Hood*.* Churchill and his large party arrived August 4 for their voyage to meet Roosevelt at Placentia Bay, Newfoundland. Churchill signaled to Roosevelt, as they were leaving for the trans-Atlantic crossing: "It is just 27 years ago that the Huns began the last war. We must all make a good job of it this time. Twice ought to be enough."

Roosevelt had already boarded the heavy cruiser *Augusta* and, accompanied by her sister the *Tuscaloosa*, five destroyers, and shortly the venerable battleship *Arkansas*, had started for Newfoundland. Roosevelt had set up an elaborate subterfuge involving his yacht, the *Potomac*, lazing around the Cape Cod Canal and Buzzard's Bay, with one crew member sporting a pince-nez and a cigarette holder, evidently attended by other crew members as he lounged conspicuously and without much pedestrian movement on the upper deck. The yacht issued

---

* *Bismarck*'s gunfire had blown most of the bridge off and shut down two of the *Prince of Wales*'s three main turrets.

regular bulletins that "all on board" were enjoying themselves. Behind this smokescreen, the President made his escape from public and press scrutiny. Both leaders were in high spirits as they sped toward their meeting, eagerly looking forward to meeting with "the one man in the whole free world who was his match in prestige and governing authority, and concerning whom he had intense personal curiosity."[1] Hopkins said that Churchill acted with the shipboard veneration of one who was on his way to "meet God Almighty."[2] (Churchill later wrote that no one had ever studied a mistress as closely as he had studied Roosevelt.)

The original plan had been for an intimate meeting of the two leaders with minimal staff accompaniment. Churchill evinced a desire to bring some of his military and foreign policy advisors, to give a more comprehensive summary of the strategic conditions in which he was operating. Roosevelt quickly decided that staff talks would be useful, under the tutelage of the leaders themselves, to build up relationships that could shortly become crucial, and to take the joint meetings of earlier in the year further. Beyond that, he wanted the British to have a chance to correct the relative pessimism of his own military chiefs over British prospects in the Mediterranean.

It was one of the constants of Roosevelt's adult life that he was often engaged in counteracting the pessimism of others, about polio, economic depression, and world war. In order to ensure surprise, he did not tell his entourage until the very last moment that they were embarking, and not until they were shipboard whom they would be meeting. This was an unnecessarily cavalier treatment of men of the caliber of Generals Marshall and Arnold and Admirals Stark and King. The punctilious Marshall found it especially irritating that they had been given so little time for preparation for comprehensive staff talks and had been forbidden by Roosevelt from telling Stimson and Knox why they were leaving Washington at that time. (Hull had been unwell and was convalescing in Sulphur Springs.)

Churchill brought with him the chief of the Imperial General Staff, Field Marshal Sir John Dill; Vice Air Chief Sir Wilfred Freeman; the First Sea Lord, Admiral of the Fleet Sir Dudley Pound; and the undersecretary of state in the Foreign Office, Sir Alexander Cadogan. He also had with him the popular writers H.V. Morton and Howard Spring to write up the meeting, and photographers to record it. Roosevelt expressed concern about any journalistic presence, and Morton and Spring stayed on British ships and did not publish anything, by agreement, until well after the fact. Roosevelt ordered in American military photographers from the Newfoundland bases to ensure that there would be an American film and pictorial record of the occasion as well as a British one. Hopkins, of course, was also with Churchill and on the way over, as they played backgammon (Churchill lost seven guineas to Hopkins), was grilled constantly by he prime minister about Roosevelt's real views and dispositions. On the last night out, Churchill put himself in the mood by watching the film *Lady Hamilton*, about Admiral Nelson and his paramour, which his entourage thought sentimental pap but which moved the prime minister to tears yet again. The minister of aircraft production, Lord Beaverbrook, a Canadian from near Campobello, New Brunswick, originally, and proprietor of the London *Daily Express*, would join the conference, as would Sumner Welles and Averell Harriman, ordered back from London by Roosevelt.* Roosevelt knew that Churchill would go as far as he could, which would be further than would be politically convenient for Roosevelt, in emphasizing Anglo-American solidarity, or even unity.

Roosevelt's flotilla arrived in the morning of August 7, 1941, in Placentia Bay, at Argentia Harbour. It was a magnificent harbor, with sleek warships, beautiful summer weather, and a dramatic occasion, and the published pictures of it would have a striking effect, as both principals had hoped. The President fished off a small boat along the Newfoundland coast, sending an unidentifiable catch to the Smithsonian for examination. His son Elliott was flying out of Gander, Newfoundland, and was officially commanded to fly down to join him. Ensign Franklin D. Roosevelt Jr. was assistant navigator on the destroyer U.S.S. *Mayrant*, and Admiral King, without the knowledge but to the delight of the Commander in Chief, ordered the *Mayrant* out of Atlantic convoy work to Placentia Bay. Elliott was designated junior military aide, and FDR Jr. junior naval aide, to the President for the conference. Roosevelt had a dry run with his full delegation (except Hopkins) on August 8, but he was more interested in taking the measure of Churchill and his people than setting out an American strategic view, since the United States was officially neutral, however tenuously.

"The huge new H.M.S. *Prince of Wales* escorted by two corvettes came up the harbor" on the morning of August 9, as Roosevelt wrote to his cousin, Margaret Suckley.[4] Harry Hopkins immediately crossed to the *Augusta* and gave his leader a final briefing on Churchill and his state of mind. "After exchanging boarding calls, Winston Churchill came on board *Augusta* at 11 A.M." The national anthems were played, and Churchill handed over a letter of introduction of himself from King George VI to Roosevelt, who received his visitor standing under an awning just below the *Augusta*'s bridge, holding Elliott's upper right arm with his left hand. They "lunched alone, which cut the ice both ways. He is a tremendously vital person. I like him. He reminds me of an English Mayor La Guardia, but don't tell anyone I said that!"[5] La Guardia, a brilliant mayor and a brave and principled man, was a somewhat bumptious and unsophisticated figure to be compared to so great a statesman as Churchill, but Roosevelt was presumably referring to the enthusiasm, physique, energy, and physical mannerisms of the two men.

The two sides assembled at dinner aboard the *Augusta*. Roosevelt placed Churchill at his right, Cadogan at his left, and alternated nationalities and services around the table. Cadogan wrote in his diary that Roosevelt, whom he was

---

* Before leaving Washington, Roosevelt had allegedly questioned Frances Perkins about Churchill, whom she had known distantly as a younger man.[3]

meeting for the first time, "certainly has great, and natural, charm." Harry Hopkins answered questions from the whole table about his visit to Russia and talks with Stalin in a way that convinced the service chiefs that aid would be sent in large quantities to the Russians. There were toasts by Roosevelt of King George VI and by Churchill of Roosevelt, and the British service chiefs, after remarks by Churchill, each gave his view of the state of the war from his own perspective. All spoke well and persuasively. Churchill gave his summary of the war for a group expanded to include the senior officers of the British and American warships in the bay.

Despite what Hopkins had said of the clash of immense armies, now involving over five hundred divisions in Russia, Churchill repeated his theory of mechanized and rapid war conducted at the edges of the Nazi-occupied area, and of bombing, blockade, and assisted insurrection: the Napoleonic Wars with aerial bombing. Roosevelt and Marshall were as skeptical as always that victory could be obtained by any such methods in less than twenty or thirty years, but Churchill did impress the American service chiefs with his determined remarks about the war in the western desert and the approaches to the Suez Canal. Rommel had made minimal headway in the three months since the very rattled Churchill had envisioned the worst in his correspondence with Roosevelt in May. The invasion of Russia and the growing Russian resistance to it had preempted most of Germany's military attention, at the expense of Rommel's Afrika Korps.

If Hitler had been reckless in not coordinating with the Japanese before they signed a nonaggression pact with the Soviet Union, he was even more negligent in allowing Mussolini to blunder into war with Greece. Not only was his ally humiliated by the less numerous but fiercer Greeks. If the Duce had focused instead on trying to put up a better fight against the British in Africa, Germany need never have bothered with Greece at all and could have invaded Russia several weeks earlier.*

For the British, one of the most interesting insights of the Newfoundland meeting was the revelation by Sumner Welles to Alexander Cadogan of the deterioration of relations with Japan. The British were proposing a joint ultimatum to Japan, including the specific mention of Thailand, the invasion of which by the Japanese would be a casus belli. Both sides in these talks knew perfectly well that the likely outcome of such an ultimatum would be to involve the countries in

---

* Nor can the Anglo-American intelligence coup in toppling the regency in Yugoslavia be regarded as the principal cause of all that country's subsequent woes. Yugoslavia lost about 1.6 million war dead between 1941 and 1945 (over 10 percent of the population, the equivalent of 15 million American dead). But the best guess is that the Germans were only responsible for about 600,000 of them. The Serbians, Croatians, Bosnians, Kosovars, Montenegrins, Slovenians, and Macedonians got into the spirit of the times and murdered a million of their fellow Yugoslavs. This might well have happened anyway, whatever regime claimed to govern in Belgrade.

war with Japan, which would presumably make a U.S. declaration of war on Germany easier, if it didn't elicit a declaration of war from Germany on the United States. Welles told Cadogan that since the imposition of the U.S. embargo of scrap metal on Japan in September 1940, and of most oil, two weeks before, with notice of probable tighter sanctions and the freezing of Japanese assets in the United States, he considered war inevitable unless the Japanese abandoned their plans of conquest in East Asia. Welles had said as much to the Japanese minister in Washington.

Roosevelt resisted Churchill's request for an ultimatum, and other demands for a more complete and extensive embargo on exports to Japan. Initially, neither he nor Churchill nor Stalin wanted the United States distracted from the great events in Europe by the need to subdue the Japanese. Gradually, however, Roosevelt concluded that any war with Japan would soon lead to war with Germany as well. American public opinion preferred war with Japan to appeasement of that country by a two-to-one margin in the summer of 1941.[6] Like the British and American leaders, they did not take Japan altogether seriously as a military power.

Roosevelt considered Japan an irritant and a sideshow, but he couldn't keep his country united with him by falling behind robust opinion in reference to Japan as he got ahead of it in respect of Germany. His speeches and the reflections of his spokesmen tended more and more to refer to Japan as effectively a German satellite (though this was nonsense in fact, as Roosevelt knew). Circumstances were obliging Roosevelt to consider that if public opinion, the national interest, and moral duty all required him to deal firmly with the Japanese, this could be a way of entering the war at the head of a united country and at an advantageous time. He was torn between a desire to string out the negotiations with the Japanese government over a relaxation of sanctions and a deescalation of Japan's imperialist activities while he pursued his military buildup, and a concern to come to the aid of the Russians before they were overwhelmed by Germany.

High-level discussions with Japan had begun in March in Washington between Secretary of State Hull and the Japanese special envoy, Admiral Nomura. Japan concluded in August 1941 that it was subject to the complete U.S. oil embargo Churchill had been unsuccessfully asking for, because of Acheson's meticulous refusal of their request for oil export permits.[7]

Roosevelt shortly discovered the excessive zeal of his officials in this matter but was not inclined to alter policy, his own views of how to deal with Japan having evolved. This was a momentous sequence of accident and decision. Roosevelt would lunch with Hull on September 5, 1941, and discuss this issue. Despite his own awareness and the warnings of Hull, Welles, and Grew that a complete oil embargo would lead to war, Roosevelt did not lift the complete embargo Acheson had taken it upon himself to establish as "a state of affairs."

Churchill had prepared a parallel declaration for Japan, to be issued by both his and Roosevelt's government, stating that any further Japanese aggrandizement in the Far East might force the United States to take stern countermeasures that could lead to war. Churchill acknowledges in his memoirs that he underestimated Japan's military power, but he quickly realized in Newfoundland that this could be the best avenue available of getting the United States into the war. Roosevelt gave Churchill to understand that he would add this declaration to what he told Nomura when he returned to Washington. In fact, he did nothing of the kind and added a much more diplomatic and ambiguous note instead. This promised vigilance for American interests and did not refer to other countries and was a disappointment to the British when they learned of it.[8] Roosevelt was now ready to go to or even over the brink with the Japanese, but was not going to guarantee British imperial interests in the Far East.

There was some possibility of moderation with the current Japanese government of Prince Konoye, which appeared to take seriously American demands for a partial Japanese withdrawal in China. All indications were that the Japanese government was in crisis, in a struggle between those who wanted to accommodate the United States and those who wished an early war with the Americans and the British.

On the morning of Sunday, August 10, 1941, one of the most impressive photo opportunities of the war occurred with a divine service on the afterdeck of the *Prince of Wales*. Roosevelt walked a considerable distance, with great but awkward dignity, on his son's arm, past a Royal Marine honor guard. Churchill and Roosevelt sat side by side, under a quadruple turret of fourteen-inch (barrel diameter) guns, and with their service chiefs behind them and approximately 250 American sailors mingled together with the British sailors. Churchill had chosen the stirring hymns "O God Our Help in Ages Past" and "Onward Christian Soldiers." Roosevelt added "Eternal Father, Strong To Save," always evocative at sea. The British and American flags were on the pulpit, and British and American chaplains shared the prayers, which had been approved by Churchill; the readings were also chosen by Churchill, who was not, by most definitions, a practicing Christian. He said he was a "buttress" rather than a "pillar" of the Church of England, supporting it from outside.

From Joshua, the congregation was urged to "Be strong and of good courage." The king, the President, the armed forces, the victims of Nazi and Fascist oppression, and the ability of the supplicants to rise above the spirit of vengeance were all subjects of prayers. Years later Churchill wrote of "the close-packed ranks of British and American sailors . . . sharing the same books and joining fervently in the prayers and hymns familiar to both. . . . Every word seemed to stir the heart. It was a great hour to live."[9]

Roosevelt had added to the spirit of solidarity by delivering to every British sailor a box of tropical fruit, cheese, cigarettes, and other items hard to come by in wartime Britain, "with the compliments of Franklin D. Roosevelt, commander in chief of the United States Navy."

Roosevelt had the tour of the *Prince of Wales* "in my chair," as he wrote to his cousin, that he had not taken of her sister ship *King George V* when she delivered Halifax as ambassador to the United States seven months before. Churchill went ashore in his "romper suit" and rolled large stones down into the water on the rocky shore. Cadogan and Welles conducted their diplomatic talks, the service chiefs theirs, and Hopkins and Churchill's scientific advisor, Lord Cherwell, drifted around between groups, though Hopkins was never far from the two leaders. Except at dinner, when the leading players all reassembled, Churchill and Roosevelt didn't deal with the military and diplomatic working groups. It was agreed that Harriman and Beaverbrook would go to Russia for the conference Hopkins and Stalin had agreed to convene for considering the best allocation of available American resources between the British and the Russians.

In the military sessions of August 11, Marshall strongly and courteously rebutted the British notion of how the war would be conducted. He said that military aircraft were better used in coordination with advancing armies rather than in wasteful and immoral slaughter rained indiscriminately down on civil populations. Who would know better than the British both the evil and the ultimate ineffectiveness of such a policy? Churchill had implied that the United States would be needed as an ally at war chiefly to supply ever greater amounts of materiel, rather than fighting men. He can scarcely have imagined that the American military and civilian leaders would be taken in by that, and Marshall made it clear that the American side believed that Hitler would be defeated only by land forces directly attacking the German heartland, supported by adequately preponderant numbers of aircraft of all types.

Marshall demurred on the importance of the Middle East, thinking the Suez Canal overestimated as an asset in these circumstances. British traffic to and from India couldn't run the gauntlet of the Mediterranean because of the air and submarine dangers, and went around the Cape of Good Hope anyway. The Germans and Italians were not serious maritime powers, so they could not make much use out of the Suez Canal. Given the proportions of the struggle in Russia, a geopolitically important country and one of the world's serious industrial powers, Marshall could not justify the present consecration of resources to the Middle East. Having made his points, Marshall then retreated courteously, saying that the United States was in no position to give the British advice, as the British were "at this business every day—all day," while the Americans were merely noncombatants building up their strength.

Beaverbrook and the director of British purchasing in Washington, Arthur Purvis, had been summoned to Newfoundland. For security reasons, they took separate aircraft from Prestwick. Purvis's crashed shortly after takeoff, killing everyone aboard. A talented and much admired Canadian, his death was described by Churchill as a "grievous loss."

On August 12, Churchill and Roosevelt and their immediate advisors worked much of the day on what became known as the Atlantic Charter. When Beaverbrook arrived on the morning of the 12th, he took an interest in the drafting of the

Atlantic Charter, and objected to the anti-imperial implications of the national self-determination guaranties for the British. The basic document was composed by Churchill, and compromises were required on this section and on the reference to international organizations, which Roosevelt considered still to be politically risky in the United States. He would build a consensus for that too, and outsmart the isolationists yet again, but he couldn't do everything at once.

The Charter renounced territorial claims for the contractants; opposed territorial changes "that do not accord with the freely expressed wishes of the peoples concerned"; respected the right of all peoples to choose their own form of government; sought the restoration of sovereignty to those who "have been forcibly deprived" of it; sought better access by all peoples to trade and raw materials; sought international cooperation and improved standards of living for all peoples; was determined to extinguish Nazi tyranny and sought a world free from fear and want; required freedom of movement on the high seas; and sought disarmament, collective security, and permanent international organizations.

It was an ambitious and, to a war-torn world, an inspiring document. Churchill found the conversion of the United States to the virtues of free trade amusing, given that it had always been exceedingly protectionist.

The Americans were concerned that there be no more secret agreements, as there had been in the First World War, privately carving up territory between individual powers. They were also concerned that they would appear like hypocrites if there were not some likelihood of Dominion status for the component parts of the British Indian Empire. Churchill was prickly on this point and it wasn't much pursued in this conference.

The nationalist politicians of the British Indian subcontinent would seize upon the charter as supportive of their cause or illustrative of British hypocrisy. Churchill assured Parliament that the relevant clause was intended to apply to countries subjugated by the Axis, "a quite separate problem from the progressive evolution of self-governing institutions." Within a few months, however, Roosevelt was publicly asserting that the Charter applied "to the whole world." The willingness of Americans, including their president, to defend Britain against the Nazis would never be allowed to be confused with American defense of the colonial apparatus of the British Empire, though Roosevelt was evasive.[10]

In fact, though it outraged American isolationists as a virtual surrender of sovereignty to the British, and disappointed some of the hard-pressed British as falling far short of the commitment to go to war against Germany they had been seeking from the United States, the Atlantic Charter was a gigantic positive step for the world. The cunning as well as the righteous principles of the two greatest statesmen of the twentieth century had been productively combined. Churchill was normally a reasonably guileless man, but in his pursuit of association with the United States in 1940 and 1941, he was almost fiendishly inventive and persistent. By appealing to Roosevelt's Wilsonian instincts, he had managed a supreme act of solidarity that made the British Empire and the United States and their leaders appear joined at the hip in a common cause. Roosevelt had learned from Wilson's debacle in 1919 to concert war aims with his principal ally in advance, and so to avoid, or at least reduce, postwar squabbling. And he outflanked his isolationist enemies by pledging to produce a world that would make their fears obsolete—a world of peace, collective security, and relative disarmament. In such a world, isolation would be unnecessary and undesirable. The world would, finally, have been made safe for democracy.

Roosevelt, on returning to the United States, went through his customary debriefing of the press to pretend that little had changed and that there had only been a formalization of well-known previous positions, but he and Churchill had agreed to an alliance, albeit an unorthodox one, and had envisioned and begun work on a postwar international organization. Roosevelt told the press at Rockland, Maine, after the Atlantic Charter had been published, August 16, 1941, that there had been "an interchange of views, that's all," and that the country was "no closer to war" (that for indirect quotation).

Hitler recognized the propaganda danger of the Atlantic Charter and forbade Goebbels to publish it. He became more aroused than ever at the collusion of the British and the Americans, and reminded Goebbels of his statement in January 1939, that if the Jews succeeded in provoking a general war, European Jewry would be annihilated. Hitler evidently regarded the liquidation of the European Jews as a deterrent to what he regarded as American war-mongering. This seems to have been connected to Hitler's conviction that Jews dominated the U.S. government.[11]

The Japanese considered the declaration, coupled to Roosevelt's latest antagonistic measures, including, they believed, the total shutdown of access to American oil, to be a virtual declaration of war. It was described in the semiofficial newspaper *Asahi* as a blueprint for Anglo-American world domination and a confirmation of the attempted encirclement of Japan. Consideration of an attack on the Soviet Union was abandoned, as Churchill, Roosevelt, and Stalin had hoped. Japanese expansion would be to the south.[12]

The day the Charter was agreed to, the House of Representative renewed conscription, passing the draft extension bill by only one vote, 203 to 202. The President had Speaker Sam Rayburn to thank for getting it through at all, by gaveling down attempted vote changes and recounts. A good deal of the voting had been tactical and the President, had he lobbied the congressmen personally, doubtless could have secured adoption with minor compromises; as it was, he had to consent not to send draftees out of the hemisphere without congressional approval.

To anyone unfamiliar with the American system, it could have appeared a setback to the President, and this was how it was interpreted in some of the British and foreign press. The vote did illustrate that the isolationist dragon, though consistently confounded and defeated by the President, was not dead. It also demonstrated how quickly the political climate in Washington could deteriorate when

Roosevelt's guiding hand was removed at a critical time for a few weeks. When he had left Washington, he was confident the draft renewal would go through the House without difficulty. Opinion in the country was a good deal more robust than the House of Representatives vote indicated. The Senate, where the measure passed easily, was on this occasion more indicative of popular thinking.

———————

The Atlantic conference ended on the afternoon of August 12, 1941. All had got on well with each other, and both sides were pleased with the results. Churchill and Roosevelt had established an excellent personal rapport. Churchill took his leave of Roosevelt on the *Augusta* very cordially, just before 3:30 in the afternoon. The prime minister received elaborate honors as he went over the side and majestically descended the gangplank. At five o'clock, followed by two corvettes and two American destroyers, including FDR Jr.'s *Mayrant,* the *Prince of Wales* sailed past all the American ships. The American crews were at quarters and lined up on deck as the great battleship bearing its indomitable passenger and his staff steamed for open water. At 5:45, as *Prince of Wales* started accelerating out across the Atlantic, she signaled by flashing light to the American squadron:

"For the President from His Majesty's Government and the British Commonwealth.

"God bless the President and people of the United States. Winston Churchill".

Just "Ten minutes later the *Augusta*, too, stood out of the harbor with our escort, homeward bound."[13]

Churchill was in such high spirits on his way home that when the *Prince of Wales* and her escorts overhauled a large convoy and sailed through it at twenty-six knots, he had the flag signal run up: "Churchill wishes you a pleasant voyage," and stood on the open bridge at the top of the conning tower and received the cheers of the men on ships they passed. He found the whole process so agreeable, he repeated it: he ordered his whole flotilla around and went through the convoy again. When he disembarked from the *Prince of Wales,* he told the ship's company that on their first voyage they had encountered the *Bismarck,* on their second "the illustrious President of the United States."[14]

Churchill would tell his War Cabinet that he and Roosevelt were now "on intimate terms," that Roosevelt "was obviously determined to" enter the war, despite problems in the Congress, which "he did not regard as truly representative of the country." Churchill told his closest colleagues that Roosevelt had said "he would wage war, but not declare it," that he "would become more and more provocative," and that "If the Germans did not like it, they could attack American forces." Churchill said that "everything was to be done to force an incident." One of Churchill's entourage, John Martin, independently confirmed that he had overheard "Roosevelt say that he did not intend to declare war: he intended to wage it."[15]

Churchill had given Roosevelt his customary warning that if Germany vanquished Russia and there were still no sign of American entry into the war, he (Churchill) "would not answer for the consequences." Roosevelt must have become as tired as Churchill himself of this familiar gambit of purposeful British bellicosity followed by dire warnings of enervation or collapse if the United States didn't join Britain in the war. But the prime minister alleged that Roosevelt had "made it clear that he would look for an 'incident' which would justify him in opening hostilities" within the next few months.[16]

Churchill's account was probably fairly accurate, but he would not have noticed, or transmitted, the conditions and qualifications and nuances with which Roosevelt clouded almost everything he said. With Roosevelt, the sure guide of his intentions was to detect the trend of his actions. He had been firm in his skepticism that Hitler could be dealt with other than by ridding the world of him by a war, in which U.S. participation would be necessary for victory, for years. With Hitler embroiled in Russia and the Japanese close to hostilities against the United States, the United States was finally free of unemployment and was within a year or so of becoming an immense military power, with an unprecedented defense production capability and a colossal navy and air force. Roosevelt probably incited Churchill's optimism about the date of American entry into the war, and Churchill would have eagerly accepted the most positive possible interpretation of his words. But all, whether they wished it or not, saw the approach of America's entry into the war.

As Roosevelt was proceeding southwards on his train from Rockland to Washington on August 16, Navy Secretary Knox's personal assistant, Adlai E. Stevenson, clambered aboard at Portland with two urgent messages. Knox had sent him to ask Roosevelt to authorize the nationalization of the giant Kearny, New Jersey, shipyards, which were building about $500 million of naval and merchant marine ships and which had been shut down since August 7, because the union representing the 16,000 workers insisted on a union retention clause in order to give a no-strike pledge for the duration of the emergency. Knox felt that a delay of even one more day was intolerable.

Stevenson also had a message from Admiral Chester W. Nimitz, director of the navy's Bureau of Navigation, who had heard from a "heretofore reliable source" that Stalin had entered into negotiations with Hitler about ending the Russo-German War.

When Stevenson managed to talk his way onto the presidential train and then gain access to Roosevelt, the President was having his dinner with Eleanor, Harry Hopkins, Marvin McIntyre, and Grace Tully. Roosevelt patiently listened to the explanation of the Kearny problem, asked for the papers, said he would look them over that evening, and asked Stevenson to fly back to Washington and arrange for a meeting at the White House the next morning at nine o'clock with Knox, Jackson, and Myron Taylor (former head of U.S. Steel, and now a troubleshooter and Roosevelt's representative to Pope Pius XII), "and you be there too."

When Stevenson said his instructions were to get the order signed that day, Roosevelt assured him it would "work out all right this way."

Stevenson then referred to a message from Admiral Nimitz that he had to deliver to the President alone. When Roosevelt said he didn't think the admiral would mind sharing it with the group of intimates present, Stevenson was reluctant to depart the admiral's requirements and asked if he could write the message on the President's dinner menu. This was done. Roosevelt read it and said: "Adlai, I just don't believe this, do you? I'm not worried at all. Are you worried, Adlai?" Stevenson, severely flustered and disarmed by the President's paternalistic courtesy, said: "I guess not, if you're not, sir." He excused himself and disappeared through the door, but unfortunately the wrong door, and shortly emerged from a cupboard and then departed. We have only Stevenson's authority for this, a man of legendary, self-deprecating wit, who ran two of the most stylish campaigns for the presidency in American history in the fifties. But his account of both his own and Roosevelt's behavior is in character.* [17]

Shortly after his return to Britain, Churchill was able to tell Roosevelt that under British influence the shah of Iran had expelled the entire German community from his country, and accorded transit rights to Britain and the Soviet Union. Churchill declared his intention to improve the railway between the Persian Gulf and the Caspian Sea. This would become a better route for the supply of the Russians than the Murmansk route, which could be mercilessly assaulted by German submarines, surface raiders, and aircraft, and the Vladivostock route, which required redirection across the Siberian land mass and had to take place under the noses of the Japanese.

Churchill allowed to Hopkins in a message of August 28 that there was a "wave of depression" in his cabinet that there had not been more visible progress since the Newfoundland meeting.[18] Observant though Churchill was of Roosevelt, he had not yet grasped his jejune methods of dispensing conflicting intimations and assurances in all directions and advancing imperceptibly within the cloud of incomprehensibility he had created. Churchill liked and had an aptitude for the ruse, but as a great parliamentarian rather than a chief of state, he had little understanding of or patience with dissembling, even from so elegant a stylist as Roosevelt.

As part of his general buildup in favor of his Middle East policy, Churchill informed Roosevelt in a message of September 1 that he intended to send two full divisions, in addition to the 150,000 draftees he had already committed to dispatch, to the Middle East, and he asked for a heavy American sealift capacity for these transfers. Replying on September 5, Roosevelt agreed, and Roosevelt added that he was "delighted that you are going to reinforce the Middle East."[19]

---

* Stevenson subsequently became very friendly with Eleanor Roosevelt, and eulogized her at the Democratic National Convention at Atlantic City, New Jersey, August 27, 1964, which nominated Lyndon B. Johnson for president.

II

ON SEPTEMBER 4, 1941, in the intersection of what Hitler had declared a war zone and Roosevelt had declared part of the Western Hemisphere and part of the U.S. Navy-patrolled "Neutrality Zone" off the coast of Iceland, a German submarine fired torpedoes at an American destroyer, U.S.S. *Greer*, which depth-charged the submarine. The *Greer* was notified of the presence of the submarine by a British aircraft flying from Iceland. In accord with Roosevelt's orders of a year earlier, the *Greer* shadowed the submarine using sonar and radioed its location. A British aircraft then dropped four depth charges, unsuccessfully. The *Greer* continued to maintain contact with the submarine and radio its position, and the submarine, the captain of which may have thought the destroyer had depth-charged his ship, and may not have known it was an American ship, fired two torpedoes at the *Greer*. The *Greer* dodged the torpedoes and then depth-charged the submarine, lost contact with it, rediscovered it, and dropped eleven depth charges on it. None of these connected and the *Greer* resumed its course for Iceland. (The action was not a flattering commentary on the marksmanship of any of the three nationalities involved.)

Between the *Greer* affair and the President's exposé and treatment of it in his planned address to the country about freedom of the seas, the President's family life intruded on the timetable of international events. Time had seemed to stand still for Sara Delano Roosevelt until this summer of 1941, when she had a minor stroke, which did not keep her from Campobello, but slowed her and obliged her, on the request of her son after she initially refused, to accept a full-time nurse. She returned to Hyde Park seeming exhausted, and on September 5, Eleanor, who had no great affection for her mother-in-law, telephoned her husband and expressed concern about his mother's condition and durability. Roosevelt immediately deferred his planned national address on the *Greer* affair and called for his train for that evening. He arrived at Springwood the next morning at 9:30.

The anticipation of her son's visit uplifted her, and she greeted him as jauntily as she could, on a chaise longue in her bedroom. They talked all morning and part of the afternoon about the meeting with Churchill and other goings-on. She had slightly hoped that her son and Churchill might come by Campobello after their meeting, since it wasn't so far from Newfoundland. She seemed better, but at 9:30 in the evening, a blood clot developed in her lung and she sank into a coma. Her son sat with her all night and morning, dozing intermittently in his chair, gazing upon her pallid face, and doubtless recalling the memories of a lifetime, as his mother slowly sank. At noon, September 7, two weeks short of her eighty-seventh birthday, she died. Shortly after, for no apparent reason, the tallest tree at Hyde Park, an ancient and giant oak, broke in the lower trunk and crashed to the ground.

Roosevelt went for a long drive around his estate two days later, driving himself and accompanied by his security chief, Mike Reilly, with whom on this occasion he exchanged not a word. The dowager Mrs. Roosevelt's funeral was in the little Episcopal church in Hyde Park, September 10. She was buried in the churchyard beside her husband, who had died forty-one years before. The President's privacy was respected. He appeared solemn but inscrutable, and left on his private train immediately after to return to Washington. For over a year after, he wore a black armband in mourning.

On his next visit to Hyde Park, Roosevelt was sitting with Grace Tully in his new office in the Franklin D. Roosevelt Library, going through cartons of books and papers that had been shipped from Washington. They came across one they found unfamiliar. As he delved through it, Franklin Roosevelt found, lovingly put away by his mother, his christening dress, baby shoes, a lock of his hair as an infant, and other mementos of his life and the imperishable affections of his mother. There were the letters he had written his parents as a child from Groton, and from Harvard. His mother's adoration of her son was obvious in the selection of articles and in the extreme care with which they were packed. For the only time in the memory of his closest staff, he wept silently, and asked to be left in solitude for a time.

At first the only information Roosevelt had about the *Greer* affair was that a German submarine had fired on an American destroyer, and, as between the two, had initiated action. On the facts, it is hard to conclude that the German ship had commenced aggression. Whether Roosevelt knew that or not, he felt he had provocation for yet another ratchet in the long elevation of American anti-German indignation that he had been masterminding for nearly four years.

He spoke to the nation and the world on September 11, 1941, gave a rather bowdlerized version of events, and, somewhat implausibly in the circumstances, accused the Germans of piracy. He referred to the sinking of the *Robin Moor* and a few other incidents involving merchantmen as "acts of international lawlessness" that, he said, manifested a "Nazi design to abolish the freedom of the seas and to acquire absolute domination and control of these seas for themselves . . . The American people can have no further illusions about it. No tender whisperings of appeasers that Hitler is not interested in the Western Hemisphere, no soporific lullabies that a wide ocean separates us from him, can long have any effect on the hard-headed, far-sighted, and realistic American people. . . . No act of violence, no act of intimidation will keep us from maintaining intact two bulwarks of American defense: first, our line of supply of materiel to the enemies of Hitler; and second, the freedom of our shipping on the high seas. No matter what it takes, no matter what it costs, we will keep open the line of legitimate commerce in these defensive waters. We have sought no shooting war with Hitler. We do not seek it now. . . . But when you see a rattlesnake poised to strike, you don't wait until it has struck before you crush him."

Roosevelt then announced that henceforth the United States Navy, to maintain freedom of the seas, would attack on sight any German or Italian vessel or aircraft "in the waters which we deem necessary for our defense," and would escort and protect the ships of all other countries in those waters. Roosevelt claimed that this action was the result of "months and months of constant thought and anxiety and prayer," and concluded with his customary homily about the "inner strength that comes to a free people conscious of their duty, and . . . righteousness . . . [who will] stand their ground against this latest assault upon their democracy, their sovereignty, and their freedom."* [20]

This was instantly recognized everywhere as a major escalation of the tension between the United States and Germany. Hitler continued to ignore Grand Admiral Raeder's plea for unrestricted submarine warfare against the United States. He said that Russia had to be defeated before he would enter into war with the United States, again confirming that he considered war with Roosevelt inevitable and that he had attacked the Soviet Union to eliminate it before Roosevelt could bring his country into the war. [21]

The President did not explain that he had again extended the area he defined as of national interest, to within 400 miles of Scotland. Escorts began on September 17. The United States Navy was now fully deployed against Germany with what the press called "shoot on sight" orders, in four-fifths of the North Atlantic.

The same night, also to a national radio audience, Charles A. Lindbergh launched an injudicious attack on Roosevelt, the British, and the Jews on behalf of the America First Committee, from Des Moines, Iowa. Lindbergh deplored the anti-Semitism of the Nazi regime, and understood the desire of the American Jews to see that regime defeated, but criticized the American Jews for not realizing that the United States should stay out of the war rather than plunge into it. He said: "Their greatest danger to this country lies in their large ownership and influence in our motion pictures, our press, our radio, and our government." He implied that the administration and Roosevelt personally were puppets of the British and the Jews.

It was a crude exploitation of primitive American fears of foreign colonial and occult influences, and it was a disaster. As admired as Roosevelt's remarks about the *Greer* were, Lindbergh's were roundly condemned as racist incitements unbecoming a person who had been accorded such general public admiration. William Randolph Hearst's newspapers, which would normally have approved an isolationist Lindbergh speech, denounced it in ringing terms. Hearst, though an admirer of Hitler's, who had engaged Hitler and Mussolini (and Churchill) as writers, was also philoSemitic and had tried in personal conversation with Hitler to persuade him of the error of his extreme antagonism to Jews. Lindbergh had played perfectly into Roosevelt's hands, as the President had long been confident he would. Roosevelt considered Lindbergh not only a Nazi sympathizer and a bigot, but a fool, a political naïf who was certain to self-destruct eventually. [22]

An October 5, 1941, Gallup Poll showed that 70 percent of Americans believed

---

* On this same day, September 11, 1941, construction began on the massive new defense headquarters that would be known as the Pentagon.

that it was more important to defeat Hitler than to stay out of war. The badge of bigotry and racism was not one that the great majority of Americans would tolerate. In four years American opinion had evolved from total abstention in overseas conflict to the verge of righteous belligerency. Though Churchill and Hitler, in opposite ways, had greatly contributed to this change, it was preeminently Roosevelt's achievement. At the same time Roosevelt had mightily helped Britain and so disquieted Hitler with the prospect of war with the United States that he hurled his armies into Russia in the hope of victory there before having to face a united Anglo-American enemy. American opinion was much more relaxed about provoking Japan, because it was considered a much less serious potential adversary than Germany and had very few domestic espousers in the United States, where there was a minuscule Japanese community and almost no familiarity with Japanese culture.

Roosevelt, as we have seen, considered Japan a barbarous annoyance but incapable of threatening Western civilization as Germany did. The American public largely embraced the caricature of a bandy-legged, rabbit-toothed little people that might run amok in China but was more adept at the production of paper fans and plastic flowers than at war-making. The Japanese perception of the United States as soft and even cowardly was an even greater underestimation. Each side was about to inflict a rude shock upon the other.

———————

At this point, Beaverbrook and Harriman had just finished their conference on Soviet war supply needs in Moscow with a Stalin who was clearly highly agitated by the onrush towards him of the German Army. Stalin had assured Hopkins in August that the Germans would be held at Kiev, and ordered his armies to "stand and die" if necessary in defense of the Ukrainian capital. The Soviet armies took 350,000 casualties in response to Stalin's orders, but were surrounded, and a further 600,000 surrendered in the biggest single bagging of prisoners in the war, surpassing even the shambles in France the year before. Kiev fell to the Germans September 18, and the barbarities of the occupiers began at once, including the Babi Yar massacre of 34,000 mainly Jewish Ukrainian victims at the end of September.

When Harriman and Beaverbrook were with him at the end of September, Stalin asked for British troops on the Ukrainian front. This was a somewhat less implausible request than his request of Hopkins in August for American troops, since Britain was at least also at war with Germany. But Harriman and Beaverbrook thought they detected signs of depression in Stalin. At this time the German Army was advancing ten miles a day into Russia. When the rains came in early September, the German advance slowed to about five miles per day, but was now only about 150 miles from Moscow.

The outstanding German tank commander, Colonel General Heinz Guderian, wrote: "The war was by now total enough for everyone."[23] He occupied Orel,

200 miles southwest of Moscow, at the beginning of October with such swiftness that the streetcars were still operating as the German armor and motorized infantry rolled in. However, Russian resistance was clearly stiffening. Having taken terrible losses, the Russians had figured out many of the German mobile war tactics and were much cagier opponents than at the outset of hostilities. As the weather worsened, deficiencies emerged in the German kit for insulating their soldiers against the rigors of the Russian climate. This was the mistake of the German General Staff and not Hitler himself. The German Army had adequate supplies of protective clothing for its soldiers against wet and cold weather, but didn't distribute them promptly.

By the time Beaverbrook and Harriman arrived in Moscow, large segments of Soviet industry in western Russia were being disassembled and the factories moved beyond the Urals for reassembly in Asian Russia. Many of the administrative functions of the Soviet government were being transferred 400 miles to the east to Kuybishev.* Even the mummified body of Lenin was removed from its Red Square mausoleum and transported to the east. There was some panic and looting, and several days were required for Stalin's heavy-handed security forces to restore order.[24] Stalin himself and his immediate coterie would remain in Moscow as long as possible and avoid the indignity committed by Reynaud's itinerant regime on the roads from Paris to the Spanish border the year before. In any case, the campaigns were hardly comparable. The Russians had fought with increasing tenacity for three and one-half months and had begun to inflict serious casualties on the Germans. They had lost over one and one half million prisoners to the Germans, but few gave up without a fight and all losses had already been replaced.

Beaverbrook and Harriman's second session with Stalin was very acrimonious, Stalin being inexplicably insulting, given the dire circumstances in which he found himself. It ended happily, with what became the Moscow Protocol, in which the United States promised to ship the Soviet Union a billion dollars of materiel, 1.5 million tons, by June 30, 1942. The British, in a fine gesture, matched the Americans in the most vital areas. Each country promised Stalin 200 planes and 250 tanks per month.[25]

Roosevelt had written Knox and Stimson on July 9 asking for a serious analysis of what would be necessary, in the event of American entry into hostilities, to defeat Germany, Japan, and Italy. SPAB (Supply Priorities and Allocation Board) was useful and intelligent in making this determination. A two-ocean navy, an air force of 50,000 combat aircraft, and an army of six million men were already

---

* A city named after one of the many senior Communist officials Stalin had probably murdered but whose death in 1935 was officially blamed on a stroke.

being planned and built by the President and the service chiefs. Roosevelt received a comprehensive reply to his July 9 request on September 25, from Marshall and Stark. Writing for the joint civilian and military leadership of the War and Navy Departments, they concluded that "If Germany and her European satellites are to be defeated, it will be necessary for the United States to enter the war." The paper came to the same conclusion about the western and southern Pacific, where the colonial and indigenous powers could not stop a Japanese onslaught.

It was expected that $150 billion of war materiel would be required for Allied victory, including the United States, over Germany and Japan, by September 1943. This was no surprise to Roosevelt, but would have been a considerable surprise to many millions of Americans who, only ten months before, took great comfort from the assurance that "Your President says we are not going to war."

War preparations of every kind continued to accelerate throughout the late summer and autumn of 1941, monitored with commendable efficiency by a Senate war-purchasing watchdog committee created and chaired by the rising senator from Missouri, Harry S Truman, and generally referred to as the Truman Committee. Truman kept something of a rod on the backs of the large corporate defense suppliers, but his campaign for a greater participation by small business in war production was not successful. Roosevelt and his senior advisors did not take seriously the decentralization of war production to small enterprises. A number of liberal historians have lamented this lacuna, but Roosevelt was undoubtedly right.

Reorganizing war production along partially decentralized lines would have taken years, multiplied costs, been completely impractical in many cases, and at the least reduced the quality of the production. The Truman Committee was useful at unearthing inefficiencies and corrupt arrangements between the buyers and suppliers, and Roosevelt established the contract-award division of the OPM to discourage the sort of activity the committee steadily brought to light.

On October 9, Roosevelt set up a Top Policy Committee, composed of Marshall, Harvard president James B. Conant, Stimson, Wallace (in his capacity as the only scientist in the cabinet, albeit a plant geneticist), and scientific engineer Vannevar Bush. This committee almost never met, operated in utter secrecy, and essentially provided a cover for scientific exploration under Bush's general direction of the feasibility of a weapon based on a fissionable uranium chain reaction from the splitting of an atom. The Top Policy Committee would report exclusively to the President.

On October 11, 1939, the scientist Leo Szilard had written, and the even more illustrious scientist Albert Einstein had signed, a letter to Roosevelt recommending exploration of the possibility of producing such a weapon. Roosevelt had agreed but progress had been desultory, initially through a committee composed of officials from the ordnance sections of the army and the navy, who regarded any such fantastic operation with more than the usual skepticism of the military toward original thinking. A committee composed entirely of scientists continued the work. Bush, as head of the National Defense Research Committee, had taken over authority for this research. After consultation with his visiting British analogue, Sir Henry Tizard, chairman of the U.K. Committee of Air Defense, Bush determined to recommend to the President an urgent acceleration of efforts toward development of an atomic bomb. He was accompanied by Vice President Wallace when he visited Roosevelt on October 9, 1941, to ask for appropriate funding of this research.

It was mentioned that the Germans were certainly active in this field but that intelligence could not determine how far they had got. Roosevelt departed from his frequent circuitous decision-making methods and even though the research program envisioned would be costly and was highly speculative, determined at once that it must be undertaken. This would prove one of history's most momentous decisions, and the President pondered it for only a few minutes before proceeding. Funding for atomic military research would be put through by Speaker Sam Rayburn, without elaboration, on his certification that he and the President considered it of the utmost national interest and too sensitive to be the subject of any debate, even in camera.*

On the same day, October 9, 1941, Roosevelt sent the Congress a message asking for the arming of merchant shipping and permission for them to deliver cargo to the ports of belligerents. "We will not let Hitler prescribe the waters of the world on which our ships may travel. We cannot permit the affirmative defense of our rights to be annulled and diluted by sections of the Neutrality Act which have no realism in the light of unscrupulous ambitions of madmen. . . . We intend to maintain . . . the freedom of the seas against the domination by any foreign power which has become crazed with a desire to control the world,"[26] he concluded. The next day, October 10, an attempt that had been led by Martin Dies of the House Un-American Activities Committee to bar Lend-Lease aid to Russia was rejected by the House.

A week later, the U.S. destroyer *Kearny* was torpedoed by a German submarine with the loss of eleven crewmen after coming to the aid, with other American ships from Iceland, of an underprotected British convoy attacked by a German submarine wolf pack. Roosevelt pulled out all the stops with a nationally broadcast address on Navy Day, October 27, shouting: "The shooting has started. And history has recorded who fired the first shot. In the long run however, all that

---

* The distinguished journalist David Brinkley recounted Rayburn's avuncular advice to one young congressman to withdraw his request for more particulars. Rayburn suspended proceedings for one minute to ask the congressman to approach the chair. He did so, the conference with the Speaker lasted only a few seconds, and the congressman resumed his place and discontinued his motion.

will matter is who fired the last shot. . . . We Americans have cleared our decks and taken our battle stations." He said that the *Kearny* was "not just a Navy ship. She belongs to every man, woman, and child in this nation." He claimed to have a German map showing South America divided into five German vassal states and including German possession of the Panama Canal. The map was in fact a forgery by British Intelligence. Roosevelt seems not to have known that, but it is academic, since he was, for his own purposes, constantly imputing fantastic ambitions in the Americas to Hitler, and it is not clear how much credence, if any, he attached to these claims.[27] (He hadn't lost his sense of humor; he inscribed a copy of his remarks to Grace Tully: "Fight talk . . . from the coach.")[28]

The next day Roosevelt announced that he was including the Soviet Union in the Lend-Lease program, which would facilitate the commitments Harriman had made to Stalin a few weeks before with Roosevelt's approval. The former head of the United States Steel Corporation, Edward R. Stettinius, was named Lend-Lease administrator on the advice of Harry Hopkins, who was again hospitalized for several weeks with the usual problems of fatigue and dietary insufficiencies.

Three days later, a German submarine torpedoed and sank the American destroyer *Reuben James* off Iceland, where it had been escorting a British convoy, and 115 Americans, including all the ship's officers, were killed. This was the first U.S. warship sunk in World War II. Roosevelt said little, having shot his oratorical bolt on the *Kearny* affair. Even with all these incidents, the Neutrality Act revisions that he had been seeking to arm merchant vessels passed closely enough, 50-37 in the Senate and 212-194 in the House of Representatives with Speaker Rayburn laying on the whips. Neutrality was now a fig leaf, with Roosevelt loudly proclaiming to national audiences that the German chancellor was a "madman" and German and American warships damaging and now sinking each other.

Yet the President was well ahead of Congressional opinion, even if the Congress, according to most polls, seemed to lag public opinion. Roosevelt told the Canadian prime minister, Mackenzie King, that a request for a declaration of war against Germany would be defeated. And he told his press conference, the same day he spoke with King, November 3, 1941, that there was no point in severing diplomatic relations; they could still be useful.[29]

Britain's deputy prime minister and leader of the Labour Party, Clement Attlee, came to New York in October for the rather esoteric purpose of representing Britain at a meeting of the International Labor Organization, one of the few such entities that persevered through the war. The ILO had moved its headquarters from Switzerland to McGill University in Montreal (a university now presided over by Roosevelt's former budget director, Lewis Douglas). This was Attlee's second visit to the United States, the previous one having been in 1907. Attlee, conducted about by Labor Secretary Frances Perkins, went sightseeing and visited naval shipyards and airplane factories. He "was greatly impressed by American efficiency."

Attlee visited Washington and was taken out for a day cruise by the President on his yacht. "He was a charming companion, a brilliant raconteur, and full of ideas. . . . It was clear to me that he thought it was inevitable that the United States would sooner or later have to join Britain in saving civilization. He had no illusions as to the nature of Nazism. I recall particularly how, when we were discussing the probable course of the war, he took down an atlas and, putting his finger on Algiers, said, 'That is where I want to have American troops.' It was a remarkable piece of prevision, especially when one considers how reluctant were the American military authorities to undertake operations in North Africa. But Roosevelt had had experience in the Navy office and his mind took a broad sweep of world strategy."[30]

Roosevelt still had to deal with labor unrest in the autumn of 1941, as the unions agitated for closed-shop agreements that would enable them to keep their positions as bargaining agents in the many industries that were now teeming with newly employed workers toiling to arm America and her allies. A coal strike unleashed by the imperishable John L. Lewis dragged on through most of November, until Roosevelt pushed it into binding arbitration November 22. Lewis did finally win a union shop for the coal mines owned by the steel companies.

Roosevelt also had to mediate personally between the railways and their employees to prevent a strike there. He made it clear throughout that he would not tolerate an interruption of coal production that backed into war production, and would not accept even a day's stoppage of the nation's railroads. It was a matter of such concern that he felt it necessary to reassure Churchill about it on November 25.

John L. Lewis was greatly embittered at Roosevelt's electoral humiliation of him in 1940, which may have influenced his irresponsible industrial relations activity through much of the war. Roosevelt responded in his usual way with relentless Justice Department tax audits of Lewis, and other, lesser harassments. Lewis was invulnerable to such investigations.

III

DISCUSSIONS HAD BEEN desultorily proceeding for some months with the Japanese government of Prince Fumimaro Konoye, who was the leader of the Japanese political faction that wanted to avoid war with the United States. This was one of the few foreign policy areas that Roosevelt was generally content to leave to Hull, who, departing from his usual caution, swaddled himself instead in all his self-righteousness.

With Roosevelt's approval, Hull demanded that Japan withdraw entirely from China, except for Manchuria, where Japan's overlordship would be tolerated, and from Indochina, and renounce its treaty with Germany and Italy, which would bring it into any war that broke out between Germany and the United States. The United States would then fully liberalize trade. This was such an inflexible position that Roosevelt and Hull knew the Japanese could not accept the American demands. Ambassador Grew (a refreshing change from the likes of such incompetent diplomats as Kennedy and Davies and even the able but temperamental Bullitt) continued to counsel comparative moderation. Grew felt that Konoye could gradually bank the fires of Japanese militarism. Roosevelt wasn't interested in Japanese factions; he wanted the world cleansed of the warmongers. But Grew did not know Roosevelt's grand strategic objectives or the evolution of his tactical conceptions of how to achieve them, which in the autumn of 1941 was leaning to entering the war by maneuvering jingoistic Japan into unleashing war on the United States which would then be broadened by Hitler or Roosevelt to include Germany.

Roosevelt had muddied the waters on August 17 by informing Tokyo's new emissary to Washington, Admiral Kichisaburo Nomura, when they met right after the Atlantic conference, that he would be happy to meet with Premier Konoye himself in Juneau or Honolulu if there were reasonable prospects for a successful exchange. This might have deferred the erosion of Konoye's position in Japanese ruling circles, but it could not do more than that if the U.S. administration remained inflexible in all other matters.

Roosevelt was happy enough to hide behind Hull's sanctimonious inflexibility. The secretary of state didn't want war but did not seem to grasp that was where his inflexible attachment to his "Four Principles" would inevitably lead. And he doesn't seem to have understood the implications of Acheson's complete oil embargo. At their luncheon discussion on September 5, it was agreed to retain the full embargo. Unless Roosevelt was playing poker, with a view to trading concessions with Tokyo after the stakes had been raised, the Japanese were certain to take some military action, even if only the seizure of the Dutch East Indian oilfields. The President understood this, but Hull, to judge from his astonishment when war came, did not.

Japan produced only about 10 percent of its oil needs; 15 percent came from Venezuela and Indonesia and about 75 percent from the United States. Roosevelt had effectively stopped all but the domestic Japanese (synthetic) sources. Oil reserves were down to about eighteen months and aviation fuel to about two years. Japan was also facing shortages of other strategic materials, including rubber, bauxite (essential for producing aluminum), and both iron ore and scrap metal, the basis of steel production. Roosevelt knew perfectly well the consequences of turning these screws; Japan would give up her territorial ambitions or attack. With that culture's obsessive preoccupation with perceptions of honor and face-saving, there could be no real doubt which option would prevail. The Japanese Army was screaming for war against the soft and condescending democracies, as it perceived them to be. The Japanese were as unimpressed with the spectacle of British armies being chased into the boats by the Germans from various parts of Europe as the British and Americans were by the defeat of the Japanese by the Russians, who had had such difficulty with tiny Finland.

The Imperial Japanese Navy, having had more exposure to the U.S. and Royal Navies, and with officers who had served as naval attachés in the West, had severe misgivings about any such policy of aggression, especially against the United States. Nomura, an honorable man and retired admiral, now attempted to retire from his special mission, as Roosevelt and Hull discovered from the intelligence service, which had cracked the Japanese code. A joint team of army and navy cryptanalysts puzzled out the Japanese diplomatic code in September 1940; the operation was known as "Magic" and the cryptanalysts as the "magicians." (The army and the navy operated the code-breaking system on alternate days. It was magic that they decrypted anything with this clumsy counterintelligence camel of a method.) The cracking of the code revealed that Nomura described himself in his messages home as "a dead horse," not wishing "to continue this hypocritical existence, deceiving myself and other people."[31]

At an imperial conference on September 6, 1941, the Japanese supreme command decided that plans for war against the United States, Great Britain, and the Netherlands would be completed by October and that if there were no prospect of agreement with the United States by then, the decision to go to war would be taken. There had been an unsuccessful assassination attempt on Konoye on September 18, which had demoralized the premier.

On October 2, 1941, the State Department informed the Japanese that there was no point to a meeting between Roosevelt and Konoye until Japan accepted Hull's "Four Principles"—effectively, withdrawal from Indochina, the Axis, and China except for Manchuria. Konoye was in favor of token army withdrawals from China, but the army minister, Hideki Tojo, was militantly opposed, and on October 17 Konoye's government fell.* Tojo replaced him, while remaining a war minister and as a general on the active list. The incoming government was a fiercely militaristic regime. This clearly presaged the likelihood that hostilities were even more imminent in the Pacific than in the Atlantic.

These developments in Tokyo gravely discountenanced Generalissimo Chiang Kai-shek, leader of China's Nationalist forces, who was already miffed at not having been invited to the Roosevelt-Churchill meeting in Newfoundland. Despite the unimpressive performance of his armed forces against the Japanese and against the Communist Chinese led by Mao Tse-tung, Chiang claimed his status as a fully equal ally to the British, Russians, and Americans. He now asked urgently for direct assistance from the British and Americans to prevent Japan

---

* Konoye played no part in Japanese politics after this, other than in helping to depose Tojo in 1944. When he received a notice from the U.S. occupation authorities in 1946 that he was suspected of being a war criminal, he committed suicide by taking poison. It was an unjust end to a civilized man.

from invading Kunming and cutting the Burma Road. He asked for an American ultimatum to Japan that any such attack would bring the United States into the war against the Japanese, joining a queue where Reynaud, Churchill, and Stalin had preceded him. Roosevelt referred his appeal, and Churchill's retransmission of the requests Chiang had made of him, to his military advisors.

Marshall and Stark responded on November 5 that Chiang Kai-shek's appeal must be denied. They doubted that any such attack by Japan was imminent and thought that in any case an escalation by Japan of its war on China did not justify the United States' going to war. Nor, wrote Marshall and Stark, would an attack on Siberian Russia by Japan. Only Japanese attacks on Singapore and Malaya and Thailand, or the oil-producing areas of the Dutch East Indies, or the approaches to Australia or the United States itself, would justify war with Japan.

Roosevelt replied to Chiang that supplies to him and to the American Volunteer Group, headed by Colonel Claire Chennault, which provided virtually Chiang's only air force, would be increased as much as American, British, and Soviet requirements permitted.

On November 2, a message from the Japanese government to its military high command in China was decoded in Washington and revealed that the imperial government intended to terminate negotiations with the United States November 25 and renew the Tripartite Pact with Germany and Italy for five years the same day.[32] Obviously, unless the United States or Japan drew back from the brink, war was imminent. Roosevelt would not retreat and he was confident the Japanese would not either. So the long and intricate implementation of American semibelligerent "neutrality" was almost certain to bring the country into war at last, possibly in some cooperative Japanese-German offensive. Hitler might have been assumed by Roosevelt to have endured about all he could of American provocations. He apparently considered himself close to victory in Russia.

On November 5, the same day that Marshall and Stark had advised Roosevelt virtually to ignore Chiang Kai-shek's appeal for assistance (which was in any case his inclination), the Japanese government determined to present another suggestion, Plan A, and if not successful, a final Plan B, to the United States. If neither was accepted, the war decision would go to the emperor, with a likely commencement of hostilities in the first week of December. The American Magic code-breaking techniques picked all this up and put it in the hands of the President, the secretary of state, and the military service chiefs before formal delivery of the Plan A message by Nomura.

The commanders of the Japanese fleet had already done a good deal of contingency planning and specialized training. They were assembling plans for an astonishingly daring offensive, fully as ambitious as the German initiatives of 1939, 1940, and 1941. The month of November was all the time they and their zealous comrades in the army needed to prepare a bold plan for a general offensive in the Pacific. They had carefully studied the great British success in striking the Italian fleet with torpedo bombers at Taranto in November 1940.

Meetings of the Roosevelt cabinet, which had been relatively infrequent during the piping days of the New Deal, were now more frequent, as Roosevelt followed all constitutional proprieties at the approach of a historic international crisis. Hull, who was never overly optimistic, was at his gloomiest as he reported on the complete impasse between his intractable demands for a complete Japanese renunciation of aggression and the predictable Japanese response.

When the cabinet met on November 7, Hull stated that Japan could attack at any time in many directions in the Pacific. Roosevelt polled the cabinet on the question of whether the country would support a declaration of war if the Philippines and other U.S.-affiliated territories were not attacked but British and Dutch colonial areas were. All members of the administration thought Congress would give the President a declaration of war if he asked for it but how strong public support would be for the war effort would depend on the circumstances. It was the following week, in the midst of another cabinet meeting, when Hull, who had a slight speech impediment when pronouncing the letter "r," which usually emerged as "w," caused Roosevelt to say to Frances Perkins in an aside: "If Cordell says 'Oh Chwist' again, I'm going to scream. . . . I can't stand profanity with a lisp." Moments of levity were hard to come by in the White House in November of 1941.

Nomura called upon Hull at his Washington home in the Wardman Park Hotel on the evening of November 7 to give him a foretaste of Plan A, of all the contents of which, thanks to the Magic decryption procedures, the secretary of state was already fully aware. November 10, Admiral Nomura called on Roosevelt, who had Hull with him. They went through the motions of having Nomura, whom they both liked personally, lay out Plan A. This consisted of Japanese acceptance of the proverbial Open Door Policy in China and the Pacific, provided it was accepted throughout the whole world as well. This was a far-fetched concept in a world at war, with most of Europe under blockade and a death struggle being waged between German submarine and Allied surface forces, and between German and Soviet land and air forces. Plan A also provided for the withdrawal of Japanese forces from China within two years following the "establishment of peace and order," except for Manchuria, Mongolia, and Hainan Island, where the Japanese would remain for "about 25 years." Nomura was authorized to promise withdrawal from Indochina sometime after the end of hostilities in China. The criteria for "peace and order" and several other key variables were not given, but Roosevelt and Hull were undoubtedly justified in being prepared to fear the worst.

In exchange for these—as they were claimed to be—concessions, the United States was to end all sanctions and bully Chiang Kai-shek into accepting the Japanese-dictated peace, generously rewarding their savage conduct in what Japan referred to officially throughout as the "China incident" (the unprovoked invasion and brutal occupation of almost a million square miles of China). Roosevelt courteously but firmly rejected Plan A. At his home on the evening of

November 7, Hull had asked Nomura to transmit to his government for consideration the possibility of working out a positive relationship with China based on a generous peace and the "moral leadership" (a concept never far from Hull's thoughts) that would accrue to Japan as a result of it.

On November 14 the Americans intercepted a message to Nomura from Tokyo confirming that, in the event of U.S. involvement in a European war, Japan would fulfill "what she understands to be" her treaty obligations. This presumably was meant to indicate that any such involvement would be seized upon by Japan as a pretext for going to war with the United States, but it is not obvious what use the Tokyo authorities expected Nomura to make of it.

On November 17, Saboro Kurusu, formerly ambassador to Germany, arrived to reinforce Nomura, and they made a courtesy call on the President, who was again accompanied by the secretary of state. Kurusu was much shorter than Nomura (the admiral was six feet tall), lacked Nomura's courtly manner and sense of humor, and seemed to Hull shifty eyed behind his thick spectacles. The continuing decryption process confirmed that Nomura was much troubled by his mission and was at heart an honest and rather pacific personality.

Kurusu was a cold and deceitful militarist with overtones of outright racism. After their visit, Roosevelt wrote out for Hull a proposed outline of a plan to defer hostilities in the Pacific. It was a six-month arrangement for what he called a "modus vivendi," in which the United States would reverse to some unspecified degree the cessation of supplies in key areas, especially oil and rice; Japan would send no more military forces to Indochina or Manchuria and would not disturb Thailand or Dutch or British territories; the "Japs" (as Roosevelt, and most Americans, invariably described them) would not invoke the Tripartite Pact if the United States became involved in the European war; and the United States would bring Chinese and Japanese negotiators together but would take no part in the talks.

These ideas were being put into suitable form for presentation to the Japanese emissaries when they returned to the White House with Plan B on November 20. The recipients of the Japanese proposal were, as always, well familiar with its contents in advance of the formal presentation. Under Plan B, neither power would undertake any military action in the Pacific, other than Indochina, where the Japanese forces would be moved from the south to the northern part of that country, and would withdraw entirely when peace was arranged between China and Japan. The United States would open up the Dutch East Indies commercially to Japan and would restore normal commercial relations between the two countries, including providing Japan "a required amount of oil." Something could possibly be made of these suggestions, but the Japanese also required the United States to "refrain from [anything that] will be prejudicial to . . . restoration of general peace between Japan and China." This effectively required Roosevelt to abandon China and endorse in advance whatever terms Japan chose to dictate to the prostrate Chinese.

As American decryption efforts made clear, Tokyo was imposing these inflexible conditions fully recognizing the impossibility of American acceptance. Roosevelt's counterproposal, his "modus vivendi," faithfully reflecting the notes he had written out for Hull after the November 17 meeting with Nomura and Kurusu, was verbally presented to the Japanese representatives November 22.*

Roosevelt also sent the counterproposal to Churchill on November 24, and concluded his message: "Its acceptance or rejection is a matter of internal Japanese politics. I am not very hopeful and we must all be prepared for real trouble, possibly soon."[33] Churchill responded unenthusiastically November 26, professing to be concerned about the "thin diet" afforded Chiang Kai-shek. Churchill had no great regard for Chiang, and did not share Roosevelt's enthusiasm for the potential for China. ("A million pig-tails don't make an army," he gratuitously averred on one occasion. He also referred to the Japanese as "the Wops of the Pacific.")[34]

Indeed, Chiang's regime was corrupt and inept, and the Chinese war effort, other than the sluggish resistance of the numberless masses of the Han Chinese, had not been very effective. But Roosevelt's interest in China was as the champion of non-Caucasian, uncolonized people in the postwar, postimperial international order he contemplated.

With the Germans at the gates of Moscow, Churchill did consider a full Chinese collapse or defection at this point to be, at the least, untimely. Churchill revived his previous proposal of a joint ultimatum, or simultaneous ones by the United States and Great Britain, to Japan that any further aggression would bring dire consequences.

Churchill concluded his November 26 message to Roosevelt: "We feel that the Japanese are most unsure of themselves." The problem was the reverse. (Had the prime minister had the slightest idea of what was about to befall British possessions, interests, and forces in the Far East, he might have been more placatory.)[†]

On verbal receipt of elements of Roosevelt's modus vivendi proposal, Nomura, fully supported by Kurusu, requested an extension of the November 25 deadline from Tokyo. Tojo grudgingly extended it to November 29. The Chinese busily began leaking the President's modus vivendi proposal to the press.[35] Given these

---

* Some of Hull's desk officers had been working up precise plans for the President's modus vivendi. In its details, which were not shown to the Japanese, the American proposal was quite exacting. Japanese forces in Indochina were to be limited to 25,000, petroleum exports would be liberalized only to the extent of civilian requirements, and raw cotton exports would not exceed $600,000 per month, but food and pharmaceutical exports would be rather more generous. Imports by the United States from Japan would not be restricted, provided raw silk comprised two-thirds of the value of such imports. The United States would undertake to approach the British, Australian, and Dutch governments about harmonizing measures with them. The agreement would be for three months, but renewable.

† He produced a draft of the sort of warning he had in mind, after consultation with the Canadian, Australian, New Zealand, and South African governments, on December 7, but was overtaken by events.

indiscretions, Churchill's "lukewarm" response, as the State Department described it, and Chiang's "hysterical" response, as Halifax described it to Sumner Welles, Roosevelt's proposal was not formalized.[36] This constituted something of a bait-and-switch operation, but Tojo probably could not have accepted it, and Roosevelt could not have made it more appetizing to the Japanese. Roosevelt was in any case now ambivalent about whether he wanted war or peace in the Pacific. No such indecision afflicted Churchill, who wanted the U.S. as a combatant however that could be achieved.

IV

IN DECLINING TO reverse the full oil embargo when he learned of it (though he might have feared that a unilateral reversal would have been mistaken for weakness), and again in withdrawing the most moderate proposal he could make to the Japanese, Roosevelt effectively opted for war, and redeemed his pledge to avoid "the 'ism' of appeasement." There is no question of where international law and morality resided in these issues. Japan's invasions of China and Indochina were outrages compounded by atrocities inflicted on the civil populations. Even without the revelations of Magic, Roosevelt would not have been surprised by the Japanese recourse to war.

On November 25, Roosevelt convened a strategy session with Stimson, Knox, Hull, Marshall, and Stark. Stark had met secretly with Nomura at Nomura's request two days before, and Nomura explicitly warned that the Tojo government would go to war if the U.S. did not relax trade restrictions. Nomura said Tojo and his zealous comrades had no idea of the military potential of the United States.[37] The next day Stark sent explicit warnings of imminent danger of war to all naval commanders, including the Atlantic Fleet commander, Admiral Ernest J. King.

Stimson recorded that at the November 25 meeting the President said "that we are likely to be attacked perhaps next Monday, for the Japanese are notorious for making an attack without warning, and the question was . . . how we should maneuver them into the position of firing the first shot without allowing too much danger to ourselves."[38] Roosevelt told Halifax on December 1 that if the British and the Dutch were attacked in the Far East the United States would support them, and he confirmed on December 3 that he meant armed support. This must be true, but at Yalta in 1945 he told Churchill and Stalin that without a direct Japanese attack on American territory, he "would have had great difficulty getting the American people into the war."[39]

Only half of the intended 165 B-17s had been deployed to the Philippines, and the defense of that country would be very difficult. It would depend on the Americans asserting naval superiority, which would be no easy task, given that the Japanese Navy was almost as big as the U.S. Pacific Fleet and would be a serious challenge until Roosevelt's huge naval construction program was completed.

Stark and Marshall pleaded for more time to build up the Philippines and prepare generally for war. Support of the modus vivendi with its renewable three-month arrangements seemed to be the consensus that emerged. Once back at the State Department, however, Hull concluded that he would rather revert to the hard line of his Four Principles. Roosevelt approved of this, and in place of the modus vivendi Hull supervised the drafting of a document that was presented to the Japanese with presidential approval on November 26. By this time Roosevelt had been advised by intelligence of the movement of large troop convoys outward from Japan to unknown destinations.

Roosevelt may have concluded that the Japanese were determined to attack anyway, given intelligence reports, or that further discussion was pointless, or that it was necessary to enter the war at once to prevent the complete discouragement of the Russians and the Chinese.

There was acute Anglo-American fear of a Soviet defeat. The entry of the United States into the war would immeasurably encourage the Russians, as Stalin had told Hopkins in July. With the United States in the war, even the fall of Moscow and Leningrad might not necessarily defeat the Russians, any more than had the fall of Moscow to Napoleon in 1812. Germany, even with Japan, could not defeat the United States, the British Commonwealth, and the Soviet Union together. But if Moscow and Leningrad were overrun and there was no sign of an American entry into combat, there would be little incentive for the Russians to continue serious resistance, if Hitler offered terms no more severe than those he had imposed on France. But if Hitler did knock Stalin out of the war, victory in Europe might require at least 400 divisions and unimaginable numbers of aircraft and ships. The Japanese turn toward the oil fields of Indonesia and other southern targets enabled Stalin to transfer 400,000 soldiers from the Far East to Moscow, providing the margin of victory there.[40] China was much less important, but closer to defeat, than Russia.

The Magic intercepts convinced Roosevelt that Tojo would not accept even a modus vivendi. It was too late for any cooling-off period. The time for such a possibility was when Konoye was still (precariously) in office prior to October 16.

This may have been the most important result of the Atlantic conference in Newfoundland, surpassing even the Atlantic Charter. Roosevelt had arrived at the conference site under the impression that his oil-export policy toward Japan was only a squeeze. He declined Churchill's request for a full oil embargo on Japan, but returned disinclined to relax it at all when he discovered that all oil exports to Japan had, in fact, been suspended. He knew this to be the quickest and surest route to war.

The conditions for going to war are never ideal, but considering all the dangers and possibilities, Roosevelt acquiesced knowingly in a policy that would result in a Japanese attack on the West. In Lincolnian terms, Japan would make war rather than desist from the conquest of its neighbors, the United States would accept war rather than acquiesce in that conquest, and the war came.

Hull's new plan consisted of two parts, the first a benign statement of general principles and the second a list of steps the two governments were going to take. These last included the withdrawal of all Japanese military and constabulary forces from China and Indochina, and the joint pledge not to support in any way any regime in all China except that of Chiang Kai-shek. This was, in effect, an ultimatum that had no chance of acceptance, as its author perfectly well knew.

Despite urgings from his cabinet and from Churchill to try to avoid war in the Pacific, though not at any risk of principle, as Churchill professed to fear even over Roosevelt's modus vivendi points of November 17 and November 22, Roosevelt clearly now considered war inevitable with both Japan and Germany. He still assumed that the two main Axis powers, especially with all their fanfare about renewing their Tripartite Pact, coordinated their actions more closely than they really did.

On November 27 Hull told Stimson that diplomacy had failed; he made no mention of his substitute for the "modus vivendi" proposals delivered the day before and said, according to Stimson's diary: "I have washed my hands of it. It is now in the hands of . . . the Army and Navy."[41] (Both sides were merely going through the motions before embarking on a war to the death.) Full and clear war warnings were again sent out by General Marshall and Admiral Stark to all American military and naval units in the central, southern, and western Pacific. Both messages said that negotiations with Japan had collapsed. The navy said that "an aggressive move by Japan is expected within the next few days."[42] It declared the most probable amphibious targets to be the Philippines, Thailand, Malaya, and Borneo. The army warning was less specific: "Japanese future action unpredictable but hostile action possible at any moment."[43] Marshall was insistent that the Japanese must initiate hostilities.

Roosevelt, who gave no hint, even to intimates, of the tremendous pressure he was under, had had to defer his Thanksgiving visit to Warm Springs, but called for his train and sped south a week late, November 29. He apparently felt that the few days that would be required for the Japanese to reject the final American proposal Hull had formulated might afford him a rest among the Georgia pines and thermal waters he had long found so restorative. He had a belated holiday dinner, attended by the convalescing Missy LeHand, but on receiving an urgent message from Hull requesting his return, he departed after just twenty-four hours and was back in Washington December 1, having spent most of his hoped-for respite on his train.

What had caused Hull to request the President's immediate return to Washington was a speech Tojo had given to a large audience in a public square in Tokyo on the evening of November 30. He accused the United States and Britain of trying to prevent the fulfillment of the Japanese ambitions for an East Asia Co-Prosperity Sphere, which was essentially an attempt to muster racist bigotry in support of rampant Japanese imperialism. "He accused the Anglo-Americans of trying to 'satisfy their greed . . . at the cost of a billion East Asiatic people . . . We must purge this . . . practice from East Asia with a vengeance.' "* [44]

On December 2 Roosevelt asked the Japanese Embassy to explain the massive Japanese troop movements around the western Pacific, and he referred to this inquiry at his press conference in the afternoon of that day. When asked if he had required a response within any fixed time, he dismissed the question as "silly," an unusually tetchy response for these normally very cordial sessions, and added: "We are at peace with Japan. We are asking a perfectly polite question. . . . That's all." He was trying to warn Japan that its movements had not gone undetected and to reinforce an impression of his pacifistic intentions in the eyes of his countrymen, to give him the greatest possible grounds for righteous outrage when the blow fell.

On Saturday, December 6, the British reported that their aerial reconnaissance had found forty-six Japanese troop transports, escorted by a battleship and a number of smaller naval vessels, entering the Gulf of Siam. An attack on Thailand or Malaya and Singapore was obviously imminent. Roosevelt hoped it was Singapore, because it would be much easier to obtain a declaration of war if such an evidently strategic target were involved.[45] On the same day, to prepare American opinion as best he could, the President released the American estimate of 178,000 Japanese soldiers in Indochina, or about seven times what the enfeebled Vichy authorities had agreed to and far more than could be justified by any need except projecting aggression into neighboring states.

He also launched, on December 6, a rather ponderous (because Hull wrote it[46]) message to Japan's Emperor Hirohito. "Almost a century ago the President of the United States addressed to the Emperor of Japan a message extending an offer of friendship of the people of the United States to the people of Japan. That offer was accepted, and in the long period of unbroken peace and friendship which has followed, our respective Nations, through the virtues of their peoples and the wisdom of their rulers, have prospered and have substantially helped humanity," Roosevelt grandiloquently began. He rambled up to recent events with uncharacteristically labored syntax: Japanese forces were present in such large numbers in Indochina "as to create a reasonable doubt on the part of other nations that this continuing concentration . . . is not defensive."

The President concluded with "the fervent hope that Your Majesty may, as I am doing, give thought in this definite emergency to ways of dispelling the dark clouds . . . [recognizing] a sacred duty to restore traditional amity and prevent further death and destruction in the world." Roosevelt knew, and said to intimates, that asking Hirohito at this point to "give thought" to their relations would

---

* In practice, the rule of the Japanese was so brutal and exploitive that it inspired considerable nostalgia for the former Western colonial governors. Had the Japanese ever surged into India, they would have made short work of Gandhi's mad proposal for nonviolent resistance, as Churchill had occasion to point out to Roosevelt.

achieve nothing except the one purpose that motivated him: to build the best possible record for seeking a declaration of war.

Roosevelt planned an address to the Congress on one of the early days of the following week, December 8 or 9, to make the point that an attack on Malaya, Thailand, or the Dutch East Indies constituted an act of war against the United States, so confident was he of impending Japanese aggression.

The Magic decrypting room had been receiving throughout Saturday, December 6, the official Japanese response to Hull's stillborn proposal of November 26. At 9:30 P.M., Roosevelt and Hopkins had absented themselves from a dinner in the White House and were alone in the President's upstairs study. The Japanese response was in fourteen parts, of which only the first thirteen had been transmitted, with instructions to Nomura to await the fourteenth the following day. The President's assistant naval aide, Commander L.R. Schulz, arrived with fifteen typed pages of Magic decryption of the first thirteen points of the Japanese response. He handed them to the President. Roosevelt read them carefully and without comment, and gave them to Hopkins, who did the same. When Hopkins looked up, the President said quietly: "This means war."[47] They gave the fifteen pages back to Schulz, who withdrew.

Roosevelt and Hopkins discussed what more they could do but await the pleasure of the Japanese militarists. Roosevelt was insistent on allowing them the first blow, however destructive. He was altogether concerned with mobilizing domestic opinion. Roosevelt tried to call Admiral Stark, but was advised he was at the National Theatre watching a performance of *The Student Prince*. The President didn't want him paged, because he didn't wish to alarm the house. Although he didn't know where or exactly when Japan would strike, Roosevelt retired on the night of December 6 sure, but unperturbed, that for him and his country, war was finally imminent.

After the proverbial decent interval following the 1940 election, Roosevelt had brought America to the brink of the conflict that only it could win for democracy.

Roosevelt had called himself a "juggler" and was proud (to intimates) of his talents at dissembling and political manipulation. His pride was not misplaced. This had been a supreme act of statesmanship. All was now in place for the events that shaped the balance of the century and the dawn of the third millennium: American engagement in the Far East and Europe, the complete destruction of Nazism and Fascism, the reconstruction of Germany, Japan, and Italy as democracies, an uneven and imperfect but steady increase in the application of international law and institutions, a vast expansion of democratic rule and free market economy in the world, the virtual demise of colonial empires, and a general recognition of the requirement of governments to improve the standard of living of their citizens.

All that remained to be done before this better world could emerge was to obliterate the forces of totalitarian aggression on the battlefields of the world. Roosevelt never underestimated the cost in blood and treasure of doing this, and did not underestimate the Japanese as Churchill did. But he never doubted that the Allies would prevail once the United States was actively among them.

He had himself completely prevented any serious inroads by the Communist and Socialist parties in American politics and trade union organizations, and was confident that Communism would prove a poor competitor for liberal democracy once the world had been cleansed of Nazi and Fascist governments. In these perceptions he would ultimately be proved generally accurate. Roosevelt had predisposed the American public to think in terms of the confrontation of good and evil in the whole world, which proved a useful precedent for the Cold War to come. But to almost everyone but him, the postwar world seemed a long way into a distant future on the night of December 6, 1941.

With the sole possible exception of Abraham Lincoln's conservation of the Union and emancipation of the slaves in the Civil War, Roosevelt's achievement in bringing the United States out of isolation, invaluably supporting the Allies, and engineering entry into the war by becoming a target of Axis aggression, was the greatest feat of any American statesman in the country's history.

Finally, Franklin D. Roosevelt was almost at a summit of historical events equal to his loftiest ambitions. He and his country were about to assume a primary world role as the principal savior of Western Civilization and builder of a new world.

PART IV

Day of Infamy and Years of Courage
1941–1944

CHAPTER 16

⚜

"We Shall Never Cease . . . Until They Have Been Taught a Lesson They and the World Will Never Forget"

*(Prime Minister Winston S. Churchill, addressing
the United States Congress, December 26, 1941)*

I

PRESIDENT ROOSEVELT RECEIVED the decryption of the fourteenth part of the Japanese reply to the last American proposals in his office at 10:30 A.M., Sunday, December 7, 1941. It stated: "Obviously it is the intention of the American Government to conspire with Great Britain and other countries to obstruct Japan's efforts toward the establishment of peace through the creation of a New Order in Asia." (Roosevelt had already famously said, in reference to Hitler's use of the same hackneyed euphemism for outright conquest: "It is not new and it is not order.") The response went on to lament the failure of Japan's good-faith effort "to preserve and promote the peace of the Pacific through cooperation with the American Government," and concluded that there was no point to further negotiations.

Nomura and Kurusu were instructed to give the reply to the U.S. government at exactly one o'clock, Eastern Standard Time. This, too, was disquieting, because it implied coordination with other, presumably military, activity. Hopkins was sitting with Roosevelt in Roosevelt's upstairs study, after lunch at 1:40 P.M., when Navy Secretary Knox telephoned that a radio report had been received that Pearl Harbor was under aerial attack and that this was "no drill." Hopkins was incredulous, and thought it must have been a report from the Philippines retransmitted

683

from Hawaii. Roosevelt disagreed at once; he saw the strategic cleverness of an attack at Pearl Harbor, where it would be less expected and there might be a chance to take out a significant part of the U.S. Pacific Fleet. Roosevelt assumed that after all the interceptions of Japanese cable traffic and all the warnings that had been sent all around the Pacific, the fleet's home base in the theater would be in a high state of preparedness and repulsing the attackers in its air space.

Roosevelt telephoned Hull at a few minutes after two. Nomura and Kurusu were just arriving in Hull's anteroom at the State Department, having requested a delay until they received the fourteenth part of the official message. (Their decoding facilities in the embassy were not as efficient as the U.S. Naval and Army cryptanalysts.) Roosevelt instructed the secretary of state to give no indication that he had any idea what was happening at Pearl Harbor. There was no evidence that the emissaries themselves did, and certainly Nomura did not. Roosevelt told Hull to "receive their reply formally and coolly and bow them out." Hull received them as his chief commanded, left the two Japanese standing while he went through the charade of reading their reply, and then icily addressed Nomura: "I must say that in all my conversations with you in the last nine months I have never uttered one word of untruth. . . . In all my fifty years of public life I have never seen a document that was more crowded with infamous falsehoods and distortions . . . on a scale so huge that I never imagined until today that any government on this planet was capable of uttering them." (This was something of an overstatement; Hull hadn't had much to do with the emissaries of Hitler and Stalin.) He refused to allow the unhappy and honorable Nomura any reply and dismissed his visitors.

While this glacial interview was taking place, Admiral Stark telephoned Roosevelt with the first of many calls he would receive that afternoon indicating the extent of Japanese damage to the U.S. Pacific Fleet and indicating that the attackers had achieved total surprise, that the core of the navy's capital ships had been descended upon like sitting ducks.

Despite this shocking news, Roosevelt was relieved that he had effected entry into the war so unambiguously. There would be a unanimous coalescence of public opinion after such a sneak attack against the United States itself, and it should not be difficult to bring Hitler into his sights as well, even if he did not act in lockstep with his Japanese allies. To Roosevelt the greatest danger had been entry into the war against Japan, and not immediately Germany, with something less than a united public opinion, after provocations directed against secondary targets not clearly related to the United States.

The same confidence instantly uplifted other astute observers, including Winston Churchill, Charles de Gaulle, and even Joseph Stalin, who was now satisfied that the Germans could be held at the gates of Moscow and Leningrad. Hitler and the Japanese had no idea of the overwhelming industrial power of the United States, nor did they apparently grasp that that country could put 12 to 15 million men into the field against them, superbly equipped, skillfully led, and, shortly, adequately battle-tested. In an address to senior Nazis on May 23, 1942, Hitler dismissed Roosevelt's war-production claims, saying that they "could in no way be right."[1] The targets referred to were those announced by Roosevelt in January 1942 of over five times the combined German and Japanese production of every relevant sinew of war, and his targets would, in fact, all be exceeded. Roosevelt, Churchill, de Gaulle, and Stalin, to varying degrees, knew differently, and despite the bad news from Pearl Harbor that day, to them the course of the war was clear. Except for justified nervosity on Stalin's part about what the Germans could yet achieve in a renewed offensive in the spring of 1942, December 7, 1941, was a day of promise and even relief.

Churchill, while dining with Averell Harriman and Ambassador Winant at Chequers, heard a radio news report about the Japanese attack, which was then confirmed by Churchill's butler. Churchill had declared at Mansion House on November 11, 1941, that if Japan attacked the United States, the British declaration of war would come "within the hour." When Churchill left his American guests and went to the office and communications center in his country residence, Winant was afraid he was going to declare war on Japan. He chased after the prime minister and suggested that they get confirmation first. In fact, Churchill went to telephone Roosevelt, not declare war. The President came on the line within a couple of minutes and said: "It's quite true. . . . We're all in the same boat now." Churchill, inexpressibly relieved, said. "This certainly simplifies things. God be with you." He later wrote: "I do not pretend to have measured accurately the martial might of Japan, but now . . . the United States was in the war, up to the neck and in to the death. So we had won after all! Yes, after Dunkirk; after the Fall of France; after the horrible episode of Oran; after the threat of invasion, when, apart from the Air and the Navy, we were an almost unarmed people; after the deadly struggle of the U-boat war—the first Battle of the Atlantic, gained by a hand's breadth; after seventeen months of lonely fighting and nineteen months of my responsibility in dire stress, we had won the war. . . . Britain would live; the Commonwealth of Nations and the Empire would live." (The Empire, as Roosevelt foresaw, did not live long but died a prolonged and mainly peaceful death.) "Once again in our long Island history we should emerge, however mauled or mutilated, safe and victorious. . . . We might not even have to die as individuals. Hitler's fate was sealed. Mussolini's fate was sealed. As for the Japanese, they would be ground to powder. . . . The British Empire, the Soviet Union, and now the United States . . . were twice or even thrice the force of their antagonists.

"Silly people—and there were many, not only in enemy countries—might discount the force of the United States. Some said they were soft . . . would never be united . . . would fool around at a distance [an odd, un-Churchillian choice of words] . . . would never stand blood-letting. Their democracy . . . would paralyze their war effort. . . . Now we would see the weakness of this numerous but remote, wealthy, and talkative [a euphemism for the widespread stereotype of Americans as loud and boastful] people. But I had studied the American Civil War, fought out to the last desperate inch. American blood flowed in my veins. I thought of a remark which Edward Grey had made to me more than thirty years before—that the United States is like 'a gigantic boiler. Once the fire is lighted under it there is no limit to the power it can generate.' Being saturated and satiated with emotion and sensation, I went to bed and slept the sleep of the saved and thankful."[2]

Charles de Gaulle, whose affections for the Americans, and Anglo-Saxons generally, were notoriously less effusive than Winston Churchill's, said: "The war is over. Of course there are years of fighting ahead, but the Germans are beaten." He later wrote: "The attack upon Pearl Harbor hurled America into the war. . . . The colossal war effort [then] mustered . . . rendered victory a certainty."[3]

Churchill's telephone call to Roosevelt came in the midst of a hastily convened meeting of his informal war cabinet—Stimson, Knox, Hull, Marshall, and Stark—which had begun at three o'clock. There was discussion about how to ensure that the Latin American republics fell in behind U.S. policy. There was some to-ing and fro-ing about the timing of the British declaration of war, and Roosevelt, in a message received by Churchill after the British declaration of war had been issued in the morning of December 8, and after Britain too had been attacked by Japan in Malaya and Hong Kong, suggested that the British declaration follow immediately upon the American one. Costa Rica had the honor of being the first country to declare war on Japan, in the evening of December 7.

The full cabinet then met and discussed what Roosevelt should say, the President having already requested a special session of the Congress for 12:30 P.M. on Monday, December 8. Hull wanted a lengthy address, giving the tangled history of Japan's disingenuous negotiations with the United States. Some called for a request for a declaration of war against Germany and Italy as well. Roosevelt listened to the discussion for a few minutes but was completely unswayed by it. He had already determined to seek a declaration against Japan only, to see if Hitler would initiate formal hostilities himself, and he would speak briefly, focusing on the extreme treachery of the Japanese. He would give a lengthier message to the country within a few days. As soon as this meeting ended, Roosevelt dictated his brief war address to Grace Tully. This took only about half an hour, and he made minor revisions in it later.

Bulletins continued to arrive all afternoon and evening on the proportions of the shambles at Pearl Harbor. The scene in the President's study was so confused that Grace Tully, when not typing his war message, was on the telephone in the President's bedroom, taking down from Stark and others the details as they came in of the extent of the losses at Pearl Harbor. She then typed them out, with Roosevelt's military aide and companion, General Edwin "Pa" Watson, looking over her shoulder, and Watson handed the messages to the President. Roosevelt's initial relief gave way to concern at the scale of the setback that had been sustained and anger that Pearl Harbor had been caught unawares. Though tired and somewhat tense, Roosevelt was absolutely calm.

He even thought to order protection for the Japanese Embassy, which he did not want put to sack by angry demonstrators. In midafternoon the White House made telephone contact with the governor of Hawaii, Joseph B. Poindexter, who confirmed the reports Stark had received. While he was on the line, the second wave of Japanese planes came in directly overhead and the governor had to shout to be heard. Roosevelt, hearing the roar of the enemy aircraft in the background, said to his companions: "My God, there's another wave of Jap planes over Hawaii." Stimson and Knox expressed concern about an attack on California and a Japanese invasion.[4]

Congressional leaders arrived about 8:40 P.M.—Speaker Rayburn, Republican leader Joe Martin (of "Martin, Barton, and Fish," but Fish, even in this great emergency, was absolutely barred from the White House), Senate Majority Leader Barkley, Republican Senator and Willkie's vice presidential candidate Charles L. McNary, the raving but civilized isolationist Senator Hiram Johnson, Senator Tom Connally, and Congressman Sol Bloom. Correspondent Richard Strout saw Hiram Johnson "stalk across the little stone stage of the portico, and all the ghosts of isolationism seemed to stalk with him."[5] Roosevelt summarized for them the protracted negotiations and the latest reports on the damage at Pearl Harbor. By this time reports had been received of attacks on Guam, Wake Island, and the Philippines. There were unconfirmed reports of landings on Oahu, but Roosevelt did not refer to them. Roosevelt grimly reported "that we have lost the majority of the battleships there." Connally, in particular, demanded to know why the navy "was asleep." Roosevelt said he did not know, there had certainly been adequate warning. He promised he would find out, but said that this was no time for recriminations. All energy must now be concentrated on bringing the country into war united and stabilizing the military balance as quickly as possible.

Eight of the older American battleships were at Pearl Harbor. The *Pennsylvania*, in dry dock and thus inaccessible to torpedoes, received a bomb hit, but could be ready for action in a few weeks. Four battleships had been in a row, two pairs, side by side, and the rest singly or with smaller craft along side. The inner battleships in the two pairs of ships, *Maryland* and *Tennessee*, had received bomb damage only and could also be back in action within a few weeks. Of the outer ships, *Oklahoma* had capsized and was effectively a total loss, and *West Virginia* had sunk upright after several torpedo hits and skillfully executed counter-flooding to prevent capsizing; she could be refloated but would be out of action for many months. *Arizona* had received a direct bomb hit through the funnel, which blew up the innards of the ship and sank her upright. She was a total loss. *California* had sunk upright and could be brought back to life with many months of work. *Nevada*, in a heroic feat of defiance, had got up steam and got underway during the attack, but had to be beached to avoid any chance of blocking access to the harbor. She would require over a year for recommissioning.

The aircraft carriers based at Pearl Harbor had been out on patrol during the attack and were undamaged. The Japanese also failed to blow up the vast oil and aviation fuel tanks that were right under their bomb sites and would have done tremendous damage to the port. Several lesser ships were sunk and damaged, and 188 American aircraft were destroyed and 159 damaged, almost all of them on their runways. They were conveniently parked there because Hawaii's army commander, General Walter Short, was preoccupied with the possibilities of sabotage and never imagined the possibility of a direct attack on the Hawaiian Islands. There was no truth to the reports of an amphibious invasion, and the Japanese, concerned that their carriers might be discovered and attacked while their planes were off, retired for home waters after two waves and left many targets unscathed. The Japanese lost only 29 of the 343 aircraft that carried out the attacks, and they lost one submarine and two midget submarines. The United States lost 2,403 men killed, 1,102 of those on U.S.S. *Arizona* alone.

The American authorities had learned nothing from the tremendously successful British attack on the Italian battle fleet with torpedo planes at Taranto thirteen months before, when they sank or severely disabled four of the six Italian battleships then operational with minimal losses of comparatively primitive aircraft flown off one carrier, H.M.S. *Illustrious.* Italy had already been at war and was presumed to be in an alert state.

The last warnings sent out from Washington to Pacific installations had arrived late, but there had been a steady stream of warnings for months, and although Hawaii was not thought to be the most likely target, the insouciance of the commanders, General Short and the commander in chief of the Pacific Fleet, Admiral Husband E. Kimmel, were inexplicable. At the least, there should have been torpedo nets out around the battleships, constant air patrolling in daylight hours to a reasonable radius around Oahu, some steam up at all times to facilitate early activation of the fleet, and serious attention to the radar outpost that reported the incoming planes, which were assumed to be new bombers arriving from the United States. (These expected planes arrived a little later, in the midst of the Japanese attack.)

Roosevelt, Stimson, Knox, Stark, and Marshall had every right to expect at least these precautions, which would have very substantially mitigated the damage sustained. One aspect of Roosevelt's well-concealed embarrassment over the debacle was that Kimmel had been appointed by Roosevelt after the President had removed his predecessor, Admiral James O. Richardson. Richardson had objected to Roosevelt's transfer of the Pacific battle fleet from California to Pearl Harbor, where he thought it could be vulnerable. Yet Richardson had also decided torpedo nets were unnecessary at Pearl Harbor, despite Stark's having recommended them. Stark had studied the British attack at Taranto. Richardson dissented from Roosevelt's assertive Japan policy, and had the effrontery to tell the President on July 8, 1940, that "the senior officers of the navy do not have the trust and confidence in the civilian leadership of this country that is essential for a successful prosecution of the war in the Pacific."[6] Roosevelt sacked him on January 5, 1941, and Kimmel was installed as fleet commander on February 1.

On the morning of December 7, the United States had had seventeen battleships, including two, the *North Carolina* and *Washington*, that were new and only just being put into service. Eight more battleships were under construction. Japan had eight battleships, including the just-commissioned *Yamato* and *Musashi*—at 73,000 tons and with nine eighteen-inch (barrel diameter) guns, the largest battleships that would ever be built—and four battle cruisers (faster than most battleships but less heavily armored). Great Britain had three new battleships and three more under construction; ten older battleships, one being extensively refitted; and two battle cruisers—fourteen capital ships in service and three more, two new and one refitted, expected in the next nine months or so. (One modern ship would be completed only at the end of the war.) The Germans were down to one operational battleship (*Tirpitz*, *Bismarck*'s sister ship), two battle cruisers, and two pocket battleships. The Italians had one modern battleship and two older ones operational, but had been rendered gun-shy by the Royal Navy.

In sum, within a few weeks, the U.S. Navy would be minus five of the battleships at Pearl Harbor, two permanently, but would have the two new battleships fully operational, for a full strength of twelve capital ships, the same number as Japan. And four of those under construction would be in service in nine months, bringing the fleet to sixteen battleships. In slightly over two years, the *Nevada*, *California*, and *West Virginia* would be back in service, and the four *Iowa* class battleships, the most powerful in the world except for the *Yamato* and *Musashi*, and a better-balanced, faster, and more technologically advanced design, would be in service, bringing the U.S. battleship fleet to twenty-three.

Even after the debacle at Pearl Harbor, the correlation of forces, with a little juggling, was not too perilous. The British and Americans had twenty-four capital ships in service, with three more due back in service within a month, eleven on the slipways, and four in refitters' yards. The Axis, incapable of moving warships, except submarines, between them, had ten battleships, four battle cruisers, and two pocket battleships operational, two battleships and two battle cruisers under repair, and one battleship under construction. Roosevelt did, however, consider the situation delicate enough to ask Churchill in a cable of December 10 his thoughts about the French fleet (an aircraft carrier, four modern battleships, and two old battleships—scattered in five or six ports on three continents, most in need of repair, and manned by crews whose political preferences were now uncertain).

Battleships were now, as was obvious to everyone and as had been foreseen by Roosevelt, much less important than aircraft carriers, where the Americans retained their nine-to-seven pre-war advantage over Japan. This margin would soon be supplemented by Roosevelt's immense construction program, now including twenty-four aircraft carriers against only five Japanese carriers in builders' yards. Great Britain had nine aircraft carriers, including five large new ships, as well as six under construction, against none in service or projected in the German and Italian navies.

Pearl Harbor produced dreadful and humiliating photographs of grievous damage on Battleship Row, but twenty-year-old, 600-foot-long ships lumbering through the water at twenty or twenty-one knots bristling with naval artillery were not going to determine the outcome of this conflict. Even the splendid *Bismarck* had been doomed by one rickety biplane that jammed its rudders with a torpedo. Old battleships would be useful for escorting convoys and softening up amphibious landing areas only. The naval war would be won by fleet aircraft carriers escorted by fast modern battleships, and by the antisubmarine forces. Pearl Harbor did not reduce the Allied advantage in the first, and the entry of the United States into the war would greatly strengthen the Allied powers in the Battle of the Atlantic, effective immediately.

The strategic balance of forces, as Churchill wrote, was now, instantly, between two and three to one in the Allies' favor, and this margin would rise steadily unless Hitler could knock Russia out of the war in 1942.

Pearl Harbor was as skillfully executed by the Japanese as it was ineptly prepared for by the American theater commanders. Yet the Allied leaders were relieved—even Roosevelt, who had sustained such a serious military reversal that if its full proportions were known, it could have affected his credibility as war leader, at least until the United States had reversed the tide of battle.

The Japanese commander of the expedition, who, like most of the Japanese naval high command, had recommended against war with the United States, was far from jubilant. Admiral Isoroku Yamamoto had spent four years in the United States and knew the temperament and capabilities of the United States well. From 1919 to 1921 Yamamoto was in Boston learning English and studying the application of oil to naval affairs, and from 1926 to 1928 he had been naval attaché in Washington. He was unimpressed with the U.S. Navy, which he regarded as a club for golfers and bridge players, but was greatly impressed by the might and scale of the United States itself. Yamamoto was never optimistic about winning the war he had so auspiciously begun.

In the White House, after dealing with his cabinet and congressional leaders and military advisors, and writing his speech for the following day, Roosevelt had little to do but receive the steady cascade of incoming messages recording the extent of the Japanese offensive and the American lack of preparedness for it. The distinguished American news broadcaster Edward R. Murrow, just back from Britain, and his wife had a longstanding invitation to dinner at the White House on that evening. Roosevelt had wished to hear Murrow's account of life in Britain.

Mrs. Murrow telephoned in midafternoon to confirm that the engagement, in light of events in the Pacific, was off. The Roosevelts wouldn't hear of it. "We still have to eat," said Eleanor. The dinner of the four was very informal, but it occurred as scheduled, consisting mainly of scrambled eggs. After dinner, Mrs. Murrow departed but the President requested that Murrow remain. Several hours later, Murrow was invited back into the President's study with Colonel

William Donovan, who was about to be head of the new intelligence service, the OSS. Sandwiches and beer were served.

It was the shameful destruction of the air force, neatly lined up as if for the convenience of the Japanese intruders, that seemed to upset the Commander in Chief most. "Our planes were destroyed on the ground, by God, on the ground!" he exclaimed, pounding the table. Yet Murrow was impressed with Roosevelt's composure and his ability to look beyond the horrible fiasco of the day toward victory and a reconstructed world.[7] Murrow never violated the President's trust in his discretion. Eleanor, who was often a stern judge of her husband, noted his "deadly calm . . . like an iceberg," especially in contrast to some of those scurrying about him.[8]

As the news came in, large crowds gathered outside the White House fence, illuminated by the floodlights on the façade of the mansion. From time to time, they would burst into "God Bless America," "My Country 'Tis of Thee," "America the Beautiful," or other patriotic songs.[9] Roosevelt retired at about half past midnight and got a full night's sleep, unassisted by medication.

In the late morning of December 8, having revised his manuscript to allow for the latest Japanese landings and air attacks, Roosevelt drove down Pennsylvania Avenue in an open car looking jauntily determined, as if, for all the world, he were coming to remonstrate with the congressional leaders about social legislation or budgetary matters, as he had so often before. When he entered the House chamber, moving slowly and as if on stilts in the center of his entourage, applause was prolonged, thunderous, and unanimous. Even his bitterest opponents now saw him as commander in chief of a wronged, righteous, and vengeful nation. Congressional and public opinion had been galvanized as never before in the nation's history. No previous American war had commanded such universal domestic support. Whatever their tactical success, the Japanese had committed one of the most catastrophic strategic errors in the history of the nation state, surpassing even the Kaiser's 1917 provocation of the United States.

The President's brief and simple address, broadcast throughout the world, was one of the most famous and successful of his career, eloquent and powerfully delivered, capturing exactly the mood of his countrymen and their legislators.

"Yesterday, December 7, 1941—a date which will live in infamy—the United States of America was suddenly and deliberately* attacked by naval and air forces of the Empire of Japan.

"The United States was at peace with that Nation and, at the solicitation of Japan, was still in conversation with its Government and its Emperor,† looking toward the maintenance of peace in the Pacific. Indeed, one hour after Japanese air squadrons had commenced bombing . . . the Japanese . . . delivered . . . a mes-

---

* He meant this in the then-current sense of premeditatedly.
† This was the use he made of his loquacious message to Hirohito forty-eight hours before.

sage [which] contained no threat or hint of war or of armed attack. . . . The Japanese Government has deliberately sought to deceive the United States by false statements and expressions of hope for continued peace."

He referred to "severe damage to American naval and military forces. I regret to tell you that very many American lives have been lost." Roosevelt recited further acts of war: Japanese attacks on American ships "on the high seas between Honolulu and San Francisco," and attacks the previous day and night on Malaya, Hong Kong, Guam, the Philippines, and Wake and Midway Islands.

"Japan has, therefore, undertaken a surprise offensive extending throughout the Pacific area. . . . The people of the United States . . . well understand the implications to the very life and safety of our Nation. . . . Always will our whole Nation remember the character of the onslaught against us.

"No matter how long it may take us to overcome this premeditated invasion, the American people, in their righteous might, will win through to absolute victory. . . . We will not only defend ourselves to the uttermost but will make it very certain that this form of treachery never again endangers us.

"With confidence in our armed forces—with the unbounding* determination of our people—we will gain the inevitable triumph—so help us God." He asked "that the Congress declare that . . . since the unprovoked and dastardly attack by Japan . . . a state of war has existed between the" two countries.

At points in the last series of sentences the President's voice rose to express the fury of the nation, and there were tremendous and sustained emotional blasts of applause at appropriate points. The speech was only twenty-five sentences— about twice as long as Abraham Lincoln's address at Gettysburg—and even with great and frequent applause took less than ten minutes to deliver.

The most durably important line in it was that the United States would "make it very certain that this form of treachery never again endangers us." Roosevelt was committing the country to retention of sufficient deterrent force that no country would again dare to attack it directly. That policy, coupled with his warnings from the same place eleven months earlier against "those who would with sounding brass and tinkling cymbal, preach the 'ism' of appeasement," would provide the basis for American strategic policy into the next millennium.

The country would not appease any country it considered a threat, and maintained a sufficient deterrent force. Unnoticed in the war fervor of the time, these simple principles upheld by all Roosevelt's successors as a fixture of bipartisan American foreign and security policy, would make the Second World War as successful in the achievement of espoused war aims as the First World War had been a failure.

(Toward the end of the twentieth century, terrorist attacks were sometimes launched against the United States, reaching a climax, as of the time of writing,

---

* A curious adjective in the circumstances, perhaps he meant unbounded, but this was the official published version.

in the suicide attacks on the New York World Trade Center and the Pentagon, September 11, 2001, which killed 20 percent more people than the bombing of Pearl Harbor. But no nation would openly be associated with an attack on the United States after Pearl Harbor and its consequences for the Japanese attacker.)

The war resolutions were passed without debate, 82–0 in the Senate and 388–1 in the House of Representatives. The only dissenter was the pacifist congresswoman Jeanette Rankin of Montana, who had also voted against war and in favor of the principle of nonviolence in 1917.

Roosevelt now focused on concentrating national attention on the swiftest possible reversal of the tide of battle, on Japanese treachery rather than American lack of preparedness. His press conference on December 9 was a rather breezy affair, not discernibly different in ambiance from his 679 preceding, peacetime press conferences. He revealed that the Japanese had attacked Clark Field in the Philippines, destroying most of the planes on the runway, despite what had happened the day before in Hawaii. (This would be one of the great controversies in the career of Douglas MacArthur, who as the commanding general of U.S. forces in the Far East was responsible for the defense of the Philippines. Roosevelt referred routinely to war production targets and to SPAB and OPM meetings, and generally exuded confidence at his press conference.

That evening he addressed the nation in the first war Fireside Chat. Apart from urging people not to propagate or believe unsubstantiated war reports and urging everyone to maximum effort, he was chiefly concerned to associate Germany with Japan. More than forty-eight hours had passed since the attack on Pearl Harbor, and although Berlin radio had congratulated Japan on administering such a humiliating comeuppance to the Americans, there was as yet no indication of Hitler's intention to alter his official relationship with the United States. Roosevelt started to prepare his country for a request for a declaration of war against Germany, which he always represented as the satanic motivator and inspiration for the outrages of the Japanese.

"The sudden criminal attacks perpetrated by the Japanese in the Pacific provide the climax of a decade of international immorality," he began.

"Powerful and resourceful gangsters have banded together to make war upon the whole human race. Their challenge has now been flung at the United States of America." He gave a bowdlerized history of U.S.-Japanese relations and recounted the sequence of Axis attacks on unoffending countries, all "without warning," from the Japanese invasion of Manchuria in 1931 through to the immediately preceding days, including all the aggressions of Hitler and Mussolini.

"It is all of one pattern," he concluded. "Remember always that Germany and Italy, regardless of any formal declaration of war, consider themselves at war with the United States at this moment just as much as they consider themselves at war with Britain or Russia." (This was probably true, but Roosevelt was largely responsible for it.) "And Germany puts all the other Republics of the Americas into the same category of enemies. The people of our sister Republics of this hemisphere can be honored by that fact." (A number of them, if consulted, would happily have done without the honor. Argentina did not declare war until 1945.)

The President dodged the question of the extent of damage to the U.S. Navy: "I can tell you frankly that until further surveys are made, I have not sufficient information to state the exact damage which has been done to our naval vessels at Pearl Harbor." This was anything but frank.

He commended the "precious months that were gained" by his policies of cranking up war production and sending all aid short of war to the Allies. "Our policy rested on the fundamental truth that the defense of any country resisting Hitler or Japan was in the long run the defense of our own country. That policy has been justified." So it had, and though he did not go further in this address, now that the isolationists had finally been exposed as the fools (like Nye, Wheeler, Hiram Johnson, and the late William Borah) or knaves (like Lindbergh and even Kennedy) that they were, Roosevelt would derive no small or undeserved pleasure from systematically eviscerating them. The only prominent prewar isolationist who would exercise as much influence after as before the war would be Senator Robert A. Taft of Ohio, and he had cooperated with the President in the repeal of the Neutrality Act.

Ironically, in the light of the future course of the Pacific war, Roosevelt prepared his audience for the fall of further outposts, including Midway Island. He was generally even more eloquent in war than he had been in peace: "The United States does not consider it a sacrifice to do all one can, to give one's best to our Nation, when the Nation is fighting for its existence. . . . It is not a sacrifice for any man, young or old, to be in the Army or Navy of the United States. Rather it is a privilege.

"It is not a sacrifice for the industrialist or the wage earner, the farmer or the shopkeeper, the trainman or the doctor, to pay more taxes, to buy more bonds, to forego extra profits, to work longer or harder at the task for which he is best fitted. Rather is it a privilege. . . .

"And in the difficult hours of this day—through dark days that may be yet to come—we will know that the vast majority of the members of the human race are on our side. Many of them are fighting with us. All of them are praying for us. For in representing our cause, we represent theirs as well—our hope and their hope for liberty under God."*

It was clear from the avalanche of support that flowed into the White House in succeeding days that the country considered itself at war with the Axis and had entire confidence in Roosevelt's leadership. The country, its press, and its politicians from right to left felt that the President had been vindicated as courageous and farseeing, and he retained the adherence of the entire nation as commander in chief in America's greatest crisis since the Civil War.

---

* Words very similar to these would be adapted by General Dwight D. Eisenhower in launching the liberation of Western Europe thirty months later.

II

CHURCHILL BEGAN AN immediate and persistent agitation to come to see Roosevelt. The American leader and his advisors did not want to have to deal with Churchill right away. They well knew his forcefulness as an advocate, and his differences with the American strategic view favoring the earliest possible invasion of Western Europe. The onrush of events had forced an immense burden on the U.S. administration as it set about mobilizing the vast nation for an unlimited commitment to total war. Roosevelt tried politely to defer the British leader with references to his own schedule, then he emphasized questions of safety, though without optimism that it would be persuasive. "I know you will disregard anything I may say to you about the personal risk," he wrote in an unsent draft, December 10. In the message he did send, he asked that Churchill's own safety "be given most careful consideration for the Empire needs you at the helm and we need you there too." Roosevelt liked and admired Churchill and greatly enjoyed their Newfoundland meetings, and when Churchill would not be put off, Roosevelt looked forward to his arrival and was not apprehensive, as were his military advisors.

It was one of the phenomena of their rich relationship that Churchill's diplomatic advisors thought he was dazzled by Roosevelt, by his confidence, by his political authority and dexterity, and by the limitless power of his country. Cadogan thought Churchill "hero-worshipped Roosevelt," and Roosevelt's military (but not his diplomatic) advisors thought their leader was too vulnerable to persuasion by Churchill's florid monologues. Neither group of nervous seconds had much to fear for the independent thinking of their own leaders, though Churchill was always aware of American might. He also deferred somewhat to Roosevelt's status as chief of state as well as head of government and of his mandate as thrice-chosen leader, where Churchill himself had only become leader of his party as Chamberlain was dying and would not lead it to electoral victory until nearly ten years later.

Churchill was so delighted to have America fully engaged in the war that he briefly became more assertive in the tenor of his communications. When asked by one of his collaborators if this was appropriate, he happily responded: "That is the way we talked to her while we were wooing her; now that she is in the harem we talk to her quite differently." In fact, despite the United States' being a newcomer to the conflict, the correlation of forces between Britain and America was such that the deferential tone of the British communications didn't change much. Churchill sailed for the United States on the just-completed battleship *Duke of York*, third of the *King George V* class, December 14, 1941.

Roosevelt concluded his message to Churchill December 10: "The news is bad but it will be better. Warm Regards." The news referred to was the sinking, earlier that day, of the British battle cruiser *Repulse* and of the battleship *Prince of Wales*, sister of the *King George V* and *Duke of York*, by Japanese aircraft off Malaya.

Churchill and Roosevelt had met on the *Prince of Wales* four months before, and Roosevelt well remembered Captain Leach and his senior officers, who had conducted him around the ship in August and went down with her in December.

Prince of Wales and *Repulse* were sent to the Far East with an aircraft carrier that had been delayed because of necessary repairs. They had set out to locate Japanese troop transports, but were returning to Singapore because of the now well-known dangers of operating without air cover, when by chance they were sighted by a Japanese submarine and aircraft. The Britrish squadron weaved desperately but unavailingly. The last signal before the action from the British commander, Admiral Tom Phillips, a former personal aide of Churchill's, was: "We are looking for trouble and expect to find it." Churchill described it as as great a "direct shock" as he received in the entire war. It was another heavy blow, and gave the Japanese a temporary substantial advantage in battleship firepower in the western Pacific, though as they had convincingly demonstrated in the preceding three days, that was no longer the principal criterion for naval power. However, the Allies had to stop losing their great ships in pairs and bunches and land some blows themselves. Churchill and Roosevelt had now both learned that the Japanese were not intimidated by the proximity of Western capital ships sent to impress them.

Roosevelt need not have worried that it would require further ingenuity on his part to go to war directly with Germany. Hitler had been at his Eastern Front headquarters, the so-called Wolf's Lair, at Rastenberg in East Prussia, when the news from Pearl Harbor arrived. He had probably had less notice of it than Roosevelt, and had had to accept failure to conclude the Russian campaign successfully. The German armies were in retreat from Moscow and other salients and had endured nearly 750,000 casualties among the 3.2 million men they had committed to the campaign in June. German arms had not received such a rebuff since the great offensive commanded by Marshal Foch ended the Great War in 1918.

Hitler had indicated when Japanese foreign minister Yosuke Matsuoka visited Berlin in the spring of 1941 that he would join any war between Japan and the United States, however it began. The German ambassador in Tokyo had been asked November 23, 1941, if Germany would join Japan in a war with the United States initiated by Japan. Foreign Minister Ribbentrop had assured the Japanese ambassador to Germany, Hiroshi Oshima, on November 28, that Germany would join such a war promptly. This was obviously with the full authority of the fuehrer. Ribbentrop on December 4, 1941, had presented the Japanese and the Italians with a draft treaty assuring that if one of them went to war with the United States, the others would join in and none would make a separate peace. No quid pro quo was requested in respect of Russia. There wasn't time to sign this treaty, but it expressed Hitler's strategic view.

The strategic reasoning in Berlin was that such a war would enfeeble Britain, because the Japanese would overrun her interests in the Far East and possibly even erupt into India, and that the United States would be entirely engrossed in dealing with Japan and would become, if anything, less of a military nuisance to Germany than she already was. This mad strategic misconception was faithfully recorded in Goebbels's diary: "A complete shift in the general world picture has taken place. The United States will scarcely now be in a position to transport worthwhile material to England let alone the Soviet Union." Hitler expressed similar thoughts to Grand Admiral Erich Raeder on December 12, 1941.[10] Their response could not have been more different to that of Churchill and de Gaulle, and it could not have been more mistaken. When Ribbentrop telephoned Ciano with the news, Ciano did not know why the German foreign minister thought congratulations were in order.[11]

If Hitler had at least required the Japanese to declare war on the Soviet Union and detain some Russian forces in the defense of Vladivostock and Siberia as a quid pro quo for his declaration of war against the United States, he would have either gained an ally against Russia or obliged Roosevelt to obtain a congressional declaration of war against Germany. The Japanese were expecting such a proposal and were relieved when it did not come.[12] Hitler wanted the full energy of the Japanese directed against the British and the Americans (chapter 14), and he wanted to deal with Russia alone.

Hitler wanted to show that he retained the initiative and that he was a declarer, rather than a declaree, of war. The German leaders were delighted with the news of the Japanese success as a distraction from the unsuccessful campaign in Russia.

Hitler had also convinced himself of a romantic martial notion of Japanese invincibility: "We can't lose the war now," he exclaimed. "We now have an ally which has never been conquered in 3,000 years." (He thought it ironic that Germany would assist Japan in destroying "the position of the white race in East Asia" while Britain joined forces with "the Bolshevik swine.")

Hitler had planned a major speech to the Reichstag for December 10, but deferred it to December 11, to prepare and include a diatribe against Roosevelt and a declaration of war on the United States. He also wished to give his and Mussolini's embassies in Washington time to burn their archives. He spoke for ninety minutes, starting at 3 P.M. The first half of his address was as uplifting a summary of the war as he could manage, not omitting the 160,000 battle deaths Germany had already incurred on the Eastern Front. He did not mention the 35,000 missing and the more than half million wounded or prisoners.

The second half of the speech was a splenetic jumble of grievances against Roosevelt personally.[13] In his frenzy Hitler railed against "that man who, while our soldiers are fighting in snow and ice . . . likes to make his chats from the fireside." All his resentments came garrulously out: Roosevelt's prosperous origins compared with his humble ones, Roosevelt's soft war in 1917–1918 compared with his four years in the trenches (collecting two Iron Crosses), Roosevelt's odious speculation and profiteering in the twenties compared with Hitler's virtuous hard work, Roosevelt's alleged inability to resolve the economic Depression compared with Hitler's success, and Roosevelt's recourse, in the light of that failure, to war. Roosevelt was "the main culprit of this war," and he was a stooge for the "entire satanic insidiousness" and "diabolical evil" of the Jews.

He concluded by announcing that Germany and Italy had declared war on the United States. Roosevelt and Churchill were greatly relieved. Hitler's speech was insane, both in its torrent of paranoid resentments and in its strategic misjudgment. Though Goebbels thought it a brilliant speech, no other Germans seemed to be uplifted by the prospect of making war simultaneously on the Americans, British, and Russians. In addition to the imbalance of strategic forces and potential in Germany's disfavor, Hitler, who had so easily outwitted his rivals in Europe in the mid- and late thirties, was no match as a perceptive statesman for Roosevelt, Churchill, or Stalin. He retained his maniacal tenacity and his power to rouse the Germans, but he was now less astute than his rivals.

The evil derangement of his personality became ever more predominant. He privately again declared his determination to annihilate the European Jews because he held the Jews responsible for bringing the United States into the war against him. That the triumph of the "Thousand Year Reich" could be put in doubt at this stage he saw as a Jewish provocation, and pledged a horrible revenge on the Jews within his grasp. Hitler helped to perpetuate the myth that the United States was a Jewish-dominated country, though there is not one scintilla of evidence that Jews exercised any influence on Roosevelt in their capacity as Jews, and though the disposition of lesser figures in the administration was more likely to be hostile than favorable to Jewish influences.

Churchill brought with him on the *Duke of York* Beaverbrook, the supply minister; the First Sea Lord, Admiral Sir Dudley Pound; chief of the air staff, Air Marshal Sir Charles Portal; Field Marshal Dill, who had just been replaced as chief of the Imperial General Staff by General Sir Alan Brooke; Churchill's physician, Sir Charles Wilson; and Lend-Lease coordinator Averell Harriman. Much of the eight-day trip was on stormy seas. This was useful when the *Duke of York* passed within four hundred miles of Brest, a shorter distance than were the *Prince of Wales* and the *Repulse* from the base of the Japanese planes that sank them a few days before. (Presumably, had there been much danger, the battleship would have steered a more northerly course or been escorted by an aircraft carrier until beyond the range of German planes.) A great traffic of messages came in, and once past the Azores Churchill was able to reply by having his messages passed by signal lamp to escorting destroyers, which then fell back a hundred miles or so and radioed them to London before catching up with the flagship again.

Much of the incoming traffic for Churchill was from Eden, who was in

Moscow, standing in for Churchill; the prime minister judged a trip to Washington more urgent and sent Eden to meet with Stalin in his place. Stalin asked Eden for a secret protocol with Britain that would give the Soviet Union East Prussia; the Baltic republics of Latvia, Lithuania, and Estonia; all the territory Stalin had seized from the Finns in the Russo-Finnish War; and the Curzon line, a Soviet-Polish border about two hundred miles to the west of the pre-war border it would replace.

Eden declared that he could not possibly agree to such demands without consulting Churchill and his other senior colleagues and that Churchill would have to consult Roosevelt. When apprised of these developments while on the high seas, Churchill had one of his periodic rages against Stalin. He sent back to London for retransmittal to Eden in Moscow a message that Stalin's demands grossly violated the Atlantic Charter, "to which Stalin has subscribed. There can be no question whatever of our making such an agreement, secret or public, direct or implied, without prior agreement with the U.S." He wanted any such matters deferred to "the Peace Conference when we have won the war." This seemed to scuttle Eden's trip altogether, after an unsatisfactory two-and-one-half-hour meeting with Molotov, but Stalin was more flexible and Eden was able to report to Churchill that his visit had "ended on a friendly note . . . and I am sure the visit has been worthwhile." There had not been any progress in securing a Russian commitment to come early into the war against Japan. Stalin said the forces could not be spared from his western front against Germany, even though he happily recorded that the Germans had been heavily blooded and demoralized as winter closed in upon them.

As he and his party bucketed through the North Atlantic on the *Duke of York*, Churchill wrote out three papers for consideration in Washington, entitled "The Atlantic Front," "The Pacific Front," and "The Campaign of 1943." Their strategic vision was at drastic variance with what had emerged from the Americans in the ABC talks earlier in the year, and substantial elements of them were unrealistic. In the Atlantic Front, Churchill acknowledged that by far the most important event was the repulse of the German invasion of Russia. The Western Allies had no "part to play in this event except to make sure that we send, without fail and punctually, the supplies we have promised. In this way alone shall we hold our influence over Stalin and be able to weave the mighty Russian effort into the general texture of the war."

So intelligent a statesman as Churchill knew that Stalin could not be durably influenced by the mere handing over of supplies. He knew perfectly well that once he had stabilized his front with Hitler, Stalin would make the best deal he could, either with Hitler as he had done in 1939, or with the Western Allies, and that the price for the huge number of casualties he was taking was going to be a massive slice of territory and influence in Eastern Europe, whether Germany yielded it in negotiation or in battle. Stalin would not go on forever taking 90 percent of the casualties of the Allied Big Three just for the honor of being woven "into the general texture of the war." Churchill and Roosevelt must have at least suspected by now that the unwritten arrangement was that Stalin would take most of the casualties and the payoff would come in supplanting German influence in Eastern Europe.

The first challenge for Churchill and Roosevelt would be to keep Stalin from making a separate peace with Hitler, leaving both of the dictators to be contended with, a nightmare scenario. This would have to be avoided by implicitly holding out to Stalin the prospect of a superior Russian position in a Europe in which the three Allied powers would defeat and occupy Germany. The elimination of Germany as a rival and the partial occupation of that country by Russia were greater enticements than Hitler could offer, and only these considerations could prevent a possible separate peace between Stalin and Hitler. The second challenge, when the tide of battle had turned, would be to ensure that the large Communist parties in France and Italy did not topple those countries into the Soviet orbit while Stalin vacuumed up the former German satrapies in the Balkans and Central Europe.

Further along in this paper, Churchill advocated a supreme effort to bring the Vichy authorities to accept a Western takeover of French North Africa. Churchill acknowledged that this would lead to the German occupation of all France, but claimed that this occupation wouldn't be greatly different in practice to government by Vichy. Again, this is an astonishingly implausible view to be entertained by such a great statesman. The Germans, unlike the Petain regime, had an almost unlimited capacity to make their rule more onerous, but even if they didn't, the collaborators in Vichy would rather go on conducting their contemptible, truncated state than do anything that would deprive them even of their masquerade to sovereignty. Taking over French North Africa had strategic virtues as an idea, but Churchill cannot have imagined that the dyspeptic gerontocracy in Vichy would facilitate it.

"The Pacific Front," the unexceptionable second paper, urged the swiftest possible assembly of a stronger naval force than Japan's, which he thought should be possible by May. This was realistic, provided there were no more Pearl Harbor or *Prince of Wales-Repulse* disasters, given the naval construction in hand. This target date, in the event, was missed by only a few weeks. The prime minister warned against an excessive American commitment to the Pacific, especially if huge armies were mustered and not sent into action. He need not have worried, because this was the last thing Roosevelt or Marshall would have considered; their general strategic priority of Germany first as a greater threat than Japan had not been rattled by the unbidden events of the last few days.

The third paper, "The Campaign of 1943," created some further problems. Churchill envisioned incorporating Turkey into the alliance, effectively conscripting it, but gave no hint of how to do this. More important, and faithful yet to his revulsion against a massive confrontation of armies in Western Europe such as had occurred in the previous Great War (and eventually in the Napoleonic and Seven Years Wars too, upon which Churchill partially modeled his strategic conception), the prime minister again professed faith in amphibious action, aid to resistance movements, maritime blockade, and mighty bombing offensives to liberate Western Europe. He foresaw "the liberation of the captive countries of Western and Southern Europe by the landing at suitable points, successively or simultaneously, of British and American armies strong enough to enable the conquered populations to revolt." He proposed landings in "Norway, Denmark, Holland, Belgium, the French Channel coasts and the French Atlantic coasts, as well as in Italy and possibly the Balkans [since the Germans could not] have sufficient troops in each of these countries . . . to cope with both the strength of the liberating forces and the fury of the revolting peoples." He reckoned that forty armored divisions totaling 600,000 men and "another million men of all arms would suffice to wrest enormous territories from Hitler's domination."[14]

Strategically, this was moonshine. The British had taken to the boats at Dunkirk, in Greece, and in Crete. The forces indicated would not have sufficed to hold a beachhead for more than a few days against the Wehrmacht. And the resistance movements, while useful, were incapable of anything beyond harassment. The whole plan begs the idea of what he thought the United States intended to do with its army of 6 million men when it was ready, if he did not want it committed to the Pacific or the European mainland.

The Americans had an altogether different strategic concept. They had gone to war against a serious opponent before only when acts of war had been committed against them. This had been the case, at least as far as American public and political opinion at the time was concerned, in the Revolutionary, 1812, and First and Second World Wars. This had also been the northern view of the U.S. Civil War. (The conflicts with the Mexicans, American Indians, and Spanish were more of the character of adventures than of wars as they were known in the twentieth century.) The United States waged war against a threat or in response to a provocation, not merely for a balance of power or an interest as had constantly occurred in the wars of succession and at other times in Europe. And it waged war for a defined purpose, to be achieved as quickly as possible. American opinion could endure a war of any length or cost, provided every possible effort was being exerted to bring it to a victorious conclusion as swiftly as possible. The Churchillian vision, as outlined in his third paper written on the *Duke of York*, could never have secured the adherence of any American government.

The United States, as had been made clear in the ABC talks, would assemble the necessary force as quickly as possible for a successful assault on Western Europe and drive on into Germany. Air war, the naval blockade, and any assistance that could be furnished by subjugated peoples would be helpful but not decisive. Churchill's aversion to a direct contest with the German Army was understandable after what he had seen in the First World War. Roosevelt had seen it too and was confident that with mechanized units with close air support, as had been the pattern for successful World War II operations up to then (mainly by the Germans), progress could be much faster and less costly in lives than in the Great War. What is less creditable is Churchill's effort in his memoirs to deny that he was ever unenthusiastic about a major cross-Channel invasion. He would try, with all his eloquence and ingenuity, to mire the Allies indefinitely in the Mediterranean, and was advocating incursions into Norway and the Balkans instead of the invasion of France, right up to a few months before the operation was finally launched in 1944.

———————

As Roosevelt awaited his distinguished visitor, he gratefully accepted the pledge of the chairmen of the Democratic and Republican National Committees to avoid normal partisan activities in order to support the national war effort. This would be useful while the United States was on the defensive and until it had assumed the initiative, because it would avoid backbiting and recriminations. Roosevelt could not have believed that any such calm would prevail even through interim, much less presidential, elections.

He also set up a National War Labor Board, and accepted a promise from a conference of labor and industrial leaders to avoid strikes and lockouts and settle differences peacefully. They had been unable to agree on a binding arbitration mechanism, but Roosevelt confidently assumed, generally correctly, that moral suasion, public opinion, executive order, and, if necessary, legislation would keep the country at work.

Roosevelt also appointed Associate Supreme Court Justice Owen Roberts (originally a Republican nominee to the Court) as chairman of a commission that also included two admirals, William H. Standley (former U.S. ambassador to the Soviet Union) and Joseph M. Reeves, and two generals, Frank R. McCoy and Joseph T. McNarney, to investigate what went wrong at Pearl Harbor. (Of the four officers, all were retired except McNarney.) Knox had flown to Pearl Harbor the day of the declaration of war, December 8, and returned with confirmation that the base was completely surprised and that an investigation was warranted. The commission took very extensive testimony from 127 witnesses and reported back promptly, on January 24, 1942. The entire report was published at once. The commission concluded that responsibility lay squarely with Kimmel and Short, who had received adequate warning to have the base on a state of alert with advanced reconnaissance and readiness for defense against any form of intrusion. They had been specifically ordered to coordinate between themselves any matters where their jurisdiction intersected.

This was a fair judgment. Both men were relieved of their commands. Kimmel's place as commander of the Pacific Fleet was taken by Admiral Chester W. Nimitz. Roosevelt had appreciated his work as head of the navy's Board of Navigation, and promoted him over many senior officers, despite a distinct lack of enthusiasm from Admiral Ernest J. King, whom Roosevelt appointed at the same time as commander of the United States Fleet, the navy's highest rank except for the President himself.

King had impressed Roosevelt as a fighting admiral* in the pre-war skirmishing with Germany in the Atlantic, and to reduce jurisdictional overlapping, Admiral Stark had offered his retirement as chief of naval operations. This position was combined with King's, and Stark became commander of the U.S. Navy in Europe, sharing power there with Winant as ambassador and Harriman as U.K. Lend-Lease administrator.

A considerable effort has been made by a variety of historians, ranging from the highly reputable John Toland to scurrilous fiction writers, to promote the theory that Roosevelt knew exactly where and when the December 7 attack was coming, deliberately withheld intelligence from the local commanders, and chose to magnify the damage done by the Japanese in order to inflame domestic opinion in favor of prosecution of the war. This is rivaled only by the most wildly implausible theories of the murder of President Kennedy in 1963 as the most far-fetched conspiracy theory of twentieth century American history. Roosevelt certainly knew he was running a risk, with the Germans as with the Japanese, of pushing them into war against the United States. He was prepared to run that risk because he considered that both were evil regimes and that there could be no peace while such powerful countries were in the hands of dictatorial rulers whose policy was one of practically unlimited military conquest.

He maneuvered the country into war, but a war that resulted from the barbarous militarism of the Japanese imperialists. Though glacially calm, as was his duty, he was as horrified as any American at the failure of his service chiefs at Pearl Harbor to have all their units at action stations when the Japanese arrived overhead. The attack at Pearl Harbor, without prior warning, would have been sufficient for Roosevelt's purposes even if not a single American had been killed. The idea that he would deliberately deceive his own fleet commander, directly causing the unnecessary deaths of thousands of American servicemen and the sinking of five American battleships in order to be sure to whip up enough bellicosity in the American public, is preposterous and has never been supported by a shred of evidence. Any examination of Roosevelt's career reveals a cunning and devious political operator. But there is not a single instance of Roosevelt's being cavalier with the lives of American servicemen. These charges are false and outrageous.

III

THE *DUKE OF YORK* arrived at Hampton Roads on the evening of December 22, 1941. Winston Churchill flew to National Airport, where Franklin D. Roosevelt greeted him, standing upright with his back against his car. The prime minister shook the President's "strong hand with comfort and pleasure." Churchill's doctor, Sir Charles Wilson, commented acerbically in his diary on

---

* Roosevelt told King he had heard that King "shaves every morning with a blowtorch . . . [and] that you cut your toenails with a torpedo net cutter."[15]

the state of Roosevelt's legs. He seemed more struck by this than by what Roosevelt had achieved despite his withered legs and the need to disguise his infirmity. The White House press corps, alerted by press secretary Steve Early, were out in strength for the photo opportunity of the arrival of the prime minister and the President at the White House. Roosevelt, beaming, was almost a head taller than Churchill, glowering, accoutered in his uniform as an elder brother of Trinity House, which maintains the lighthouses around the British Isles. Churchill would reside in the White House for three weeks, except for a foray to address the Canadian Parliament in Ottawa and five days of clandestine vacation in Palm Beach, Florida.

Churchill converted the Monroe Room, where Eleanor Roosevelt had held her press conferences, into a war room, the walls covered with maps of every theater of the world conflict. The White House corridors were infested with officious, scurrying British underlings. Roosevelt was so impressed with Churchill's war room that he set up one of his own in the White House basement opposite the elevator. Churchill's personal habits were a challenge even to the normally resourceful White House staff. He drank heavily at intervals all day long, from sherry in the morning through whiskey at midday, followed by a nap, whiskey in the evening, and tapering off with champagne and brandy before retiring around 3 A.M.

The prime minister accompanied the President at his regular press conference on December 23, 1941. Roosevelt spoke briefly and introduced his guest to field questions; he invited Churchill to stand up. There was polite applause as he did so, but when he stood on his chair to be better seen, in the words of the official account, "loud and spontaneous cheers and applause rang through the room."[16] Churchill was guarded and amusingly evasive, urging, "Don't let us bank on" a collapse of German morale, but accepting happily that, as in 1918, "We may wake up and find we ran short of Huns." In one of his few thoroughly serious responses, he said: "I can't describe the feelings of relief with which I find Russia victorious, the United States and Great Britain standing side by side. It is incredible to anyone who lived through the lonely months of 1940. . . . Thank God." He thought Germany might run short of oil but acknowledged that that was "rather technical for me." Asked if he had "any doubt of the ultimate victory," he replied: "I have no doubt whatever."

The following evening, Christmas Eve, would be the only occasion on which Roosevelt and Churchill would speak publicly from the same platform. Roosevelt said that it was "with particular thoughtfulness of those, our sons and brothers, who serve in our armed forces on land and sea, near and far—those who serve for us and endure for us, that we light our Christmas candles across the continent. . . . We have joined with many other Nations and peoples in a very great cause. . . . One of their greatest leaders stands beside me. He and his people in many parts of the world are having their Christmas trees with their little children around them, just as we do here. He and his people have pointed the way in courage and in sacrifice for the sake of little children everywhere." Then, invoking the most fulsome version of his customary formula, he introduced "my associate, my old and good friend . . . Winston Churchill, Prime Minister of Great Britain."

Winston Churchill, though "far from my country, far from my family, [did not] feel far from home. Whether it be the ties of blood on my mother's side, or the friendships I have developed here over many years of active life, or the commanding sentiment of comradeship in the common cause of great peoples who speak the same language, who kneel at the same altars and, to a very large extent, pursue the same ideals, I can not feel myself a stranger here in the center and at the summit of the United States. . . . Let the children have their night of fun and laughter . . . before we turn again to the stern tasks and formidable years that lie before us, resolved that, by our sacrifice and daring, these same children shall not be robbed of their inheritance or denied their right to live in a free and decent world."

At the reception in the White House Red Room afterward, Eleanor asked her husband if he had telephoned Missy LeHand. Assumedly sensing that Eleanor was motivated by an ambition to be reproachful, he replied that he had not and gratuitously added that he did not intend to call her (in Warm Springs). Mrs. Roosevelt referred to this incident in a letter to her young protégé Joe Lash, and contrasted her "refreshment" from "contact with people she loved" to her husband's total detachment from people around him. According to Lash's diary, Mrs. Roosevelt thought this might make him a better politician and even a greater leader, but she was dismayed that her husband "seemed to have no bond to people," even his own children.[17]

Roosevelt dragged Churchill off to the Foundry Methodist Church, where he heard, for the first time in his life, the hymn "O Little Town of Bethlehem." Roosevelt said: "It is good for Winston to sing hymns with the Methodies," and the prime minister allowed to his doctor that he found it uplifting and restful.[18] Like some subsequent British statesmen sojourning in Washington on urgent business, Churchill was more religiously observant there than at home.

On December 26, "It was with heart-stirrings" that Churchill addressed the Congress. As with his speech to the Canadian Parliament four days later, his remarks were broadcast throughout the world. The prime minister was well aware that some of the senators and congressmen had been very antagonistic to Britain over many years, though the British war effort under Churchill's leadership and the prime minister personally had enjoyed general admiration even from isolationist American legislators. He began by declaring this "experience one of the most moving and thrilling of my life, which is already long and has not been entirely uneventful." He recalled his American ancestors and lamented that his American "mother, whose memory I cherish across the vale of years," had not lived to see this day. His audience was appreciative when he added: "I cannot help reflecting that if my father had been American and my mother British, instead of the other way round, I might have got here on my own."

His summary of the present state of combat dwelt on the rout of the Italians, the successful resistance by the Russians, progress in the Battle of the Atlantic, and his usual promises of imminent victory in Egypt and Libya. Applause was frequent and generous, but came in a great and lengthy crescendo when, after a detailed recitation of the Japanese onslaught, he rhetorically asked, implying as was his wont, intimate Anglo-American fraternity: "What kind of a people do they think we are? Is it possible they do not realize that we shall never cease to persevere against them until they have been taught a lesson that they and the world will never forget?"

He regretted that the United States and Great Britain had drifted apart after the previous World War. There was no apparent unease among the former isolationists in his audience as he speculated that: "Five or six years ago it would have been easy, without shedding a drop of blood, for the United States and Great Britain to have insisted on" German compliance with the Treaty of Versailles. "Prodigious hammer-strokes have been needed to bring us together again, or, if you will allow me . . . he must indeed have a blind soul who cannot see that some great purpose and design is being worked out here below, of which we have the honor to be the faithful servants. . . . I avow my hope and faith, sure and inviolate, that in the days to come the British and American peoples will for their own safety and for the good of all, walk together side by side in majesty, in justice, and in peace." The Congress rose at once and unanimously to give the distinguished visitor a powerful ovation, and the general American response was overwhelmingly favorable. It was a tour de force. When he returned to the White House, Roosevelt, who also had a great deal riding in domestic politics as well as on the battlefields and oceans of the world on the performance of Churchill's Britain, told the prime minister that, as Churchill wrote, he "had done quite well."[19]

Churchill had another conspicuous oratorical success, at the Parliament of Canada, in Ottawa, on December 30. He played the imperial card at least as far as his hosts would have liked, but presumably impressing his American listeners with the proximate reality of the British Commonwealth. He referred to Canada as "the senior Dominion of the Crown" and brought "goodwill and affection from everyone in the motherland," to which, he declared, Canada had "unbreakable ties." He did recognize Canada's "ever-growing friendship and intimate association with the United States." He also referred to Roosevelt, in passing, as "that great man," which brought general spontaneous applause. The prestige of both leaders was very great everywhere in the world except the innermost camps of the enemy.

Because of a beau geste occurrence in the French islands of St. Pierre and Miquelon, off Newfoundland, the most interesting part of Churchill's address in Ottawa dealt with the French world. He made some of his remarks in his heavily accented French, in deference to the one-third of Canadians who were French-speaking, most of whom were unenthusiastic participants in the war. He referred to the "French catastrophe. The French Army collapsed, and the French nation was plunged into utter, and as it has so far proved, irretrievable confusion. . . . It was [the French Government's] duty and it was their interest to go to North Africa, [where] they would have had overwhelming sea power. . . . If they had done this, Italy might have been driven out of the war before the end of 1940, and France would have held her place as a nation in the counsels of the Allies and at the conference table of the victors. But their generals misled them. When I warned them that Britain would fight on alone whatever they did, their generals told the Prime Minister and his divided cabinet, 'In three weeks, England will have her neck wrung like a chicken.' Some chicken! Some neck!"

This famous and felicitous line brought great applause and merriment. Churchill derided "the men of Vichy [who] lay prostrate at the foot of the conqueror. They fawned upon him." He referred admiringly to de Gaulle and his followers: "They have been condemned to death by the men of Vichy, but their names will be held and are being held in increasing respect by nine Frenchmen out of every ten throughout the once happy, smiling land of France."

There was no precedent for the millions of volunteers Canada and the other Dominions had contributed to the British war effort without themselves being under threat (prior, in the case of Australia and New Zealand, to the entry of Japan into the war). Canada certainly had earned a grateful visit from Churchill, but the French dimension was timely and ramified widely.

The incident that had taken place on the islands of St. Pierre and Miquelon illustrated the continuing prostration of France and the difference between Churchill's and Roosevelt's views on how to reassemble the pieces of France. For Churchill, France was eternal, despite the proportions of its defeat in 1940, and would have to be resurrected to help recreate some sort of balance in Europe, against Russia or a post-Nazi Germany, whichever would be the principal power in central and Eastern Europe. Further, those Frenchmen, led by Charles de Gaulle, who fought on, outlawed by official French authorities and risking their lives for human freedom and the liberation of Europe, must be encouraged, especially if there were to be any content to Churchill's plan to help the resistance movements in Nazi-occupied Europe.

For Roosevelt, the collapse of France was so overwhelming, following the procession of ephemeral and ineffectual governments in the interwar years, that he did not really believe France could be resuscitated as an important country. He did not believe in empires anyway, and had no interest in trying to put France back in control of her colonies. Most inexplicably, though he despised the Vichy regime in terms similar to Churchill's, as essentially a wretched gang of traitors prattling on about their honor while betraying their country and its allies, Roosevelt believed that something useful could be achieved by maintaining a full embassy in Vichy and purporting to treat Petain as a serious leader.

The Vichy ambassador in Washington, Gaston Henry-Haye, was a pompous,

loquacious, almost Molieresque caricature of a self-important French haut bourgeois, who had the effrontery, after months of being snubbed by the government
to which he was accredited and by the diplomatic community, to write to Roosevelt comparing his mission to that of Benjamin Franklin in 1776.[20] On Secretary of State Hull's first meeting with him, the secretary lectured the ambassador
about the evils of "Mr. Hitler," as Hull insisted on calling him, and described the
German dictator as "the most devastating and all-pervading conqueror and
destroyer within a thousand years, and we believe there is no geographical limit
whatever to his infamous plans."[21]

The tiny islands of St. Pierre and Miquelon had a population of only 5,000.
Their strategic significance lay in the fact that they had been tyrannically misgov-
erned by Vichy and had a powerful radio transmitter spewing out Axis propaganda that might mislead some French Quebecois; also, it was suspected that
Vichy agents tapped the Western Union telegraph cable that went through St.
Pierre and might be transmitting useful intelligence to the Germans. De Gaulle
wished to take the islands for his own movement and put a stop to all these problems. He advised the British—Eden in fact, who was favorable but felt the Canadians and Americans should be consulted.

The Canadians preferred to do it themselves, but the Americans strongly
desired that Vichy not be disturbed in its possession of the islands at all. De
Gaulle after some uncertainty ordered the insubordinate commander of his minimal naval forces, Admiral Emile Henri Muselier, to take over the islands, which
he did on December 24 without opposition or a single casualty. The admiral had
a cordial interview with the American consul in the islands and assured him that
the islands were now entirely accessible to the Allies. On Christmas Day, a
plebiscite, with the few international observers that could be found in the consulates on the islands monitoring it, declared a 98 percent preference for the Free
French over Vichy. (This was impressive but not as remarkable as the majority of
5,564 to 20 de Gaulle achieved in 1940 in Tahiti, where the population revolted
when the Vichyite governor tried to shut the British consulate.)

The American media, led by the *New York Times*, as well as the British and
Canadian governments, were delighted at de Gaulle's initiative. But Cordell
Hull, showing all his intemperate and misplaced righteousness, rushed back
from holiday on Christmas Eve, spent all Christmas Day on the telephone trying
unsuccessfully to bully veteran Canadian Prime Minister W.L. Mackenzie King
into throwing the Free French out of the islands militarily, and then issued an
irrational communiqué that referred to the "so-called Free French ships," and
called the liberation of the islands "arbitrary" and asked what Canada proposed to
do about it. Hull had accused King of collusion with de Gaulle, and King said he
was departing the next day to join Churchill and Roosevelt and would deal with
it then. The American media violently attacked Hull, the *New York Post* suggesting that it was "treason" to try to give back territory now in Allied hands to a Ger-

man puppet state. Walter Lippmann wrote of "this little, diplomatic Pearl Harbor."[22]

In his memoirs, Churchill gently wrote of Hull over this episode: "He did not seem to me to have full access at the moment to the President. I was struck by the fact that, amid gigantic events, one small incident seemed to dominate his mind." Hull told Churchill his remarks in Ottawa had been "highly incendiary," and pitifully asked for "just a few little words" from the British leader to show that the United States was not "appeasing" Vichy (which, in fact, it was) and was a "friend" of the Free French (which it then was not by any normal definition). "The Prime Minister was not cordial to the suggestion."[23]

Hull cast aspersions on the integrity of Churchill and Mackenzie King. "The President," wrote Churchill, "seemed to me to shrug his shoulders over the whole affair. . . . It did not at all affect our main discussions."[24]

In his memoirs, even with the advantage of hindsight, Hull's account of relations with the French is astonishing. He could not "see any benefit to be derived from recognizing de Gaulle.* Such recognition would have meant the repudiation of our universal policy of noninterference in the internal affairs of another country." The fact of thus preferring a gang of Nazi sympathizers and routed capitulators over courageous and freedom-loving French allies remaining in combat with the enemy did not register with Hull. Describing the existence of Vichy as an "internal affair" suggests that the German invasion of France that created Vichy, and, by the same reasoning, the Japanese attack on Pearl Harbor were merely "internal affairs."

It all blew over in a few weeks, in a deescalating series of memos from Hull to Roosevelt unsuccessfully demanding vengeance on de Gaulle and even Churchill, and an offer of Hull's resignation, which the President brushed off breezily when it was offered.

De Gaulle did not allow his problems with the Americans to prevent his calling on Ambassador Winant, "a diplomat of great intelligence and feeling," and urging the merits of MacArthur, who was slowly losing ground to the Japanese in the Philippines. "As a soldier and an ally, I must tell you that the disappearance of MacArthur would be a great misfortune. There are only a few first class military leaders in our camp. He is one of them. He must not be lost." He asked Winant "to make General de Gaulle's opinion on this subject known to President Roosevelt." There is no record that de Gaulle's advice was taken into account when Roosevelt ordered MacArthur to withdraw from the Philippines to Australia,[26] and MacArthur, whose memoirs were published after de Gaulle's, does not mention the French leader in any context.

---

* The one substantive meeting Hull and de Gaulle had went reasonably well, and de Gaulle described Hull in his memoirs as having "acquitted himself of his crushing task with great conscientiousness and distinction of spirit, somewhat hampered . . . by his summary understanding of what was not American and by Roosevelt's interference in his domain."[25]

The one apparent consequence of Hull's tantrum over St. Pierre and Miquelon was that the Free French were not initially invited to sign the United Nations Declaration that Roosevelt organized for New Year's Day, 1942. This was a tepid statement pledging total war against, and no separate peace with, the Axis powers. Apart from the United States, Great Britain, the Soviet Union, and China, the signatories were the principal Dominions of the British Commonwealth and India, a group of secondary Latin American countries, and some governments in exile—Czechoslovakia, Greece, Luxembourg, Netherlands, Norway, Poland, and Yugoslavia, but not France. This was Roosevelt's only apparent concession to his overwrought secretary of state, but it was unjust and mistaken. Churchill explained in a cable to his deputy prime minister and the leader of the Labour Party, Clement Attlee, that the Declaration could be extended to Free France by side letter, and this information was quickly transmitted to de Gaulle.

The American policy to Vichy was delusional, but de Gaulle's policy of unnecessarily aggravating relations with the world's most powerful country, upon which the liberation of France would chiefly depend, led to mistrust and non-consultation, even in matters of great interest to France, between these long-time allies. From this condition de Gaulle, of necessity, suffered much more than Roosevelt.*

Even if de Gaulle, too, could have handled his early relations with the United States more suavely, this was an area Roosevelt badly misjudged. Although he was reestablishing constructive relations with France in the last year of his life, the United States paid a price through most of the balance of the twentieth century for Roosevelt's reflexive and indiscreet early animosity to de Gaulle.

In a summary to his War Cabinet sent from the White House January 3, 1942, Churchill wrote: "We live here as a big family, in the greatest intimacy and informality, and I have formed the very highest regard and admiration for the President. His breadth of view, resolution, and loyalty to the common cause are beyond all praise. There is not the slightest sign here of worry about the opening

---

* France's relations with the United States were not assisted by the seizure, without any consultation, of the magnificent superliner *Normandie*, which had been idle in New York harbor since August 1939, and her conversion to a troop transport, in the course of which she caught fire in February 1942. The New York Fire Department, failing to distinguish between a ship and a building, poured so much water into the upper decks that she capsized. Generally regarded as the greatest passenger ship of all time (though the *Queen Mary* and *Queen Elizabeth* were certainly rivals), *Normandie* was a total loss. When she was eventually righted, Roosevelt wished to restore the ship, so great was his personal admiration for her, but was finally persuaded that the project was impractical and she was broken up. It would have been a worthwhile investment in Franco-American relations to have restored her.

misfortunes, which are taken as a matter of course and to be retrieved by the marshalling of overwhelming forces of every kind."[27]

On January 6, 1942, Churchill, having suffered chest pains opening a stiff window in his White House bedroom on the night of December 26–27, left clandestinely with his doctor (and accompanied at the outset by General Marshall) for five days of holidays in Palm Beach, Florida.[28] Roosevelt avoided the temptation of deriding that playpen of the rich, which he had never liked. Churchill stayed in the villa of the Lend-Lease administrator and former head of U.S. Steel, Edward Stettinius.*

During his stay in Palm Beach, Churchill learned that the Italians, in their most successful naval operation of the war, had penetrated Alexandria harbor with human torpedoes (i.e., driven by a person seated on the torpedo, whose likelihood of surviving the operation, or at least avoiding capture, was almost nil).

The Italians, in a prodigious act of ingenuity and bravery fully worthy of the other major combatants, put the battleships *Queen Elizabeth* and *Valiant* out of action for some months. The balance of power of the Allied and Axis battle fleets had become precarious. The Axis now had six modern battleships, six old battleships, six battle cruisers, and two pocket battleships in action. A modern battleship and an old one were under repair. The Americans and British combined had four modern battleships, seventeen old battleships, and one battle cruiser. Ten modern battleships were under construction and eight old battleships were under repair. In aircraft carriers, the Allies retained an eighteen-seven lead and had thirty under construction against only four for the Japanese.

On February 12–13, 1942, the German battle cruisers *Scharnhorst* and *Gneisenau*, which had been at Brest, where they constituted a serious threat to the sea lanes, ran the gauntlet of the English Channel and returned to Germany. They weren't much damaged by the shore batteries around Dover, nor by the constant bombardment from British bombers and torpedo planes. It appeared to the world, and was represented by Germany, as a great victory over the British. In fact, both German ships were significantly damaged by mines the British dropped from the air and both were laid up for months, transferring two battle cruisers in the above figures from the active to the repair list. And the whole

---

* His relaxation was disturbed only by the appearance, while he was swimming in the ocean, "of quite a large shark . . . so I stayed in the shallows from then on." When he set out to telephone Wendell Willkie, whose relations with Roosevelt were not so cordial at this point, he did it, as with all his calls from the Stettinius house, via the White House switchboard. There was a mix-up, and when Churchill invited his interlocutor to join him on his train from Florida to Washington, he was greeted with incredulity. He was in fact speaking to Roosevelt, and they quickly ended what had been a rather absurd conversation.[29]

operation, taking the ships away from the dangers of British air raids but far from any quarry in the sea lanes, acknowledged British air and sea power and was a retreat that constituted the first step in the restoration of full Allied naval supremacy.

While Churchill was enjoying his brief break in the Arcadia Conference, as these Roosevelt-Churchill meetings were called, Roosevelt delivered his State of the Union message to the Congress on January 6. He gave his customary eloquent espousal of Allied war aims and the usual denigration of the German and Japanese governments, though he avoided Churchill's ethnic slurs about Huns, which for domestic political reasons would have been inopportune. By far the most important part of his address, provoking perhaps the greatest applause he ever received in his dozens of addresses to the Congress, was when he recounted the war production targets, which he himself had set after consultation with industrial and labor leaders, raising the original estimates of the private sector. Among them, he promised 60,000 aircraft in 1942 and a staggering 125,000, including 100,000 combat aircraft, in 1943; 45,000 tanks in 1942 and 75,000 in 1943; 6,000,000 tons of merchant shipping in 1942 and 10,000,000 tons in 1943. He added in a voice rising in volume and betraying some emotion: "These figures . . . will give the Japanese and the Nazis a little idea of just what they accomplished in the attack at Pearl Harbor." The Congress responded with tumultuous applause that required Speaker Rayburn some time to gavel down.

The conferences between Churchill and Roosevelt continued at an intense pace after Churchill's return to Washington on January 11. There were few disagreements, and a command for the southwest Pacific, called ABDA (Australian, British, Dutch, American), was set up with Field Marshal Archibald Wavell as its head. This structure, which proved awkward, was, however, the genesis of an Anglo-American Combined Chiefs of Staff Committee, which proved hugely effective. That and the United Nations Declaration would emerge as the two main accomplishments of the Arcadia Conference.

The Combined Chiefs of Staff Committee had two headquarters, in Washington principally, where the British were represented by Field Marshal Dill, the just-retired chief of the Imperial General Staff, and in London. The other members of the Committee were Brooke, Pound, and Portal for the British, and Marshall, Arnold, Stark, and King for the Americans. Stark represented the United States in London. Dill was a remarkably effective, diplomatic, and persuasive man, who got on extremely well with the Americans and even struck up a personal friendship with Marshall, who was far from gregarious. When he died in November 1944, Dill was buried in an exalted place in Arlington National Cemetery near Washington, among America's greatest military heroes, an indication of the esteem in which he was held by those to whom he was accredited. Churchill wrote in his memoirs of the joint staff: "There never was a more serviceable war machinery established among allies, and I rejoice that in fact, if not in form, it continues to this day."[30]

The other noteworthy result that emerged from Arcadia was the early dispatch of four American divisions to complete their training in Northern Ireland. This was meant to be a show of deterrent strength to the Germans in respect of the Republic of Ireland, and to the Dublin government of Eamon De Valera himself. Churchill had sent a message the day after Pearl Harbor to the Irish premier, with whom he had long been unfavorably acquainted: "Now is your chance. Now or never! A nation once again!" He had been hoping that De Valera would finally, with the United States in the war, relax his prohibition of the use of Irish bases by the Royal Navy in the struggle against the submarine menace. De Valera was unresponsive. Churchill feared the Germans might land in Ireland and thought the American forces would help deter such a landing. They would also enable the British to send seasoned divisions who were idling in home island defense to the Middle East and Far East. The American deployments began at once.[31]

Roosevelt absented himself from the proceedings of Arcadia for a time on January 13 to set up the War Production Board, which would supersede both the OPM (Office of Production Management) and the SPAB (Supply Priorities and Allocation Board). He appointed Donald Nelson, the quintessential midwestern executive, formerly of the giant retailer Sears, Roebuck, as head of the new agency and, in effect, "war czar." The head of OPM, William Knudsen, agreed to accept appointment as a lieutenant general and a War Department position in army procurement.

The Arcadia Conference ended January 14, an undoubted success, and Churchill emplaned on a Boeing clipper flying boat for Bermuda, where the *Duke of York* and escorting ships awaited the prime minister and his party. Churchill was so anxious to get home and so impressed with the luxurious aircraft that he continued on it the next day. The flight went off course and came perilously close to the French coast near Brest, but did not attract German attention. The plane approached Britain from a different point of the compass than had been expected, causing six Hurricane fighters to scramble. They were quickly reassured and the flight ended uneventfully. Harry Hopkins, who had played a very important role throughout Arcadia, was again at the end of his physical strength and returned to the navy hospital for two weeks, where he was prescribed a strict diet that did replenish his energies as long as he adhered to it.

IV

T HE MILITARY NEWS continued to be adverse. Singapore, which Churchill had never ceased to tout as the supreme pillar of Western interests in the western Pacific, had not been protected from the north. As with the French and the Ardennes, it had been assumed that invasion could not come overland down the Malayan Peninsula. But that is exactly where it did come, and on February 15, 1942, the British garrison of 64,000 men surrendered to the Japanese. This surpassed even the sinking of the *Hood* and of the *Prince of Wales* and *Repulse* as a disaster for Churchill. (He had been chancellor of the exchequer when the defensive facilities of Singapore had been constructed; it is not clear why he was so astonished to learn of their configuration.)

Hong Kong had surrendered on Christmas Day. Manila had fallen January 2, though vigorous resistance in Luzon continued on Bataan. Auchinleck's offensive in the Libyan desert, about which Churchill had been so optimistic in Washington, had fizzled, and by early February the resourceful Rommel had driven Auchinleck back to Tobruk, near the Egyptian border. Japan's attack on the Dutch East Indies proceeded with customary speed and merciless efficiency, and on February 21 Wavell urged dissolution of the ABDA command. Henceforth, MacArthur would be sole commander in the southwest Pacific theatre. (Nimitz would be commander of the central Pacific theater as well as commander in chief of the U.S. Pacific Fleet.)

And from February 27 to March 2, in the Java Sea and Banten Bay, the Allies sustained one of their worst naval defeats of the war. The Japanese sank five Allied cruisers and four destroyers, at minimal cost to themselves. The Allied vessels perished bravely and were outgunned, but it was a severe setback. Among the ships that went down were H.M.S. *Exeter,* one of the victorious cruisers of the Battle of the River Plate against the *Graf Spee* in December 1939, and U.S.S. *Houston,* Roosevelt's favorite ship for cruising, on which he had often sailed and been memorably photographed.

The Americans' defense of the Philippines continued bravely in the face of a fierce and relentless Japanese onslaught. Regarding the destruction of most of the American air forces in the Philippines, including the two squadrons of B-17s on the ground at Clark Field nine hours after the attack at Pearl Harbor, MacArthur lamely claims in his memoirs that he only realized very late that the Japanese attack had been successful, and that his fighters were in the air when the Japanese arrived but the bombers were "slow" taking off.[32] Eisenhower claimed that MacArthur had thought the Philippines' neutrality would be respected. Neither contention is plausible.

When the Japanese attack on the Philippines came, the bombers were supposed to be attacking Formosa, but the mission was canceled. The air forces were supposed to have been dispersed among bases in Mindanao. The local air commander, General Lewis Brereton, was reprimanded for not doing so.* MacArthur was neither blameless nor wholly responsible for the fiasco. But it could not be so easily investigated as Pearl Harbor, where the Japanese came and

---

* MacArthur publicly defended Brereton but privately called him "a bumbling nincompoop." The claim that MacArthur thought the Pearl Harbor attack was by white mercenaries is improbable and unsubstantiated.[33]

went and never returned. In the Philippines, the air raids presaged an invasion, and an inquest would not, to say the least, have been timely. There was confusion between MacArthur, Brereton, and MacArthur's head of intelligence, General Charles Willoughby, and they share responsibility for the fiasco at Clark Field, though MacArthur must take most of it. The B17s would not have slowed the Japanese for long, but it was inexcuseable to lose them on the ground. It was a testimony to MacArthur's talents as a self-publicist that he managed to represent Clark as another Pearl Harbor–type sneak attack.

At his press conference December 9, Roosevelt tried to protect MacArthur by dissembling when asked about this episode. If the Allies had not lost so much firepower at Pearl Harbor, nor lost the Philippine air force, it might have been possible to mount a serious relief mission to the Philippines. The longstanding U.S. strategic judgment, expressed by Admiral Mahan,[34] of which MacArthur was well aware, from his term as army chief of staff from 1930 to 1935, was that the Philippines could not be successfully defended against a full-scale Japanese assault.

Even in the light of the disasters at Pearl Harbor and Clark Field, the loss of the *Prince of Wales* and *Repulse*, and the Italian attack at Alexandria, if the United States and Britain had mustered all their available naval forces in February or March, as MacArthur urged, they might have been able to resupply the Luzon force and provoke a decisive naval battle with the overconfident Japanese. Their chances of losing the battle and most of what was left of their naval strength would have been about 50 percent, especially with the much greater Japanese strength in proximate land-based aircraft, the efficacy of which they had demonstrated in the sinking of *Prince of Wales* and *Repulse*. Yet Roosevelt cannot be blamed for not rolling the dice in this case. It would have been a huge gamble, and the Philippines was not so valuable a prize as to warrant such a risk.[35] Marshall explained in correspondence with MacArthur that he considered the risk in an all-out defense of the Philippines too great. In the circumstances, the principal service MacArthur could perform was to delay an inexorable enemy advance, and he did so brilliantly.

On February 8, 1942, Manuel Quezon, having been sworn in on Corregidor, a rocky island in Manila Bay, for his second term as president of the Philippine Commonwealth, sent an extraordinary message to Roosevelt through army channels, so Stimson, Marshall, and Eisenhower saw it first. Quezon was depressed by the agony of his country, racked by recurrent tuberculosis, and distressed by what he thought was the Anglo-American abandonment of the Philippines in order to gain time to secure the defense of other places in the Pacific for which they cared more. The Japanese prime minister, Hideki Tojo, had offered the Philippines independence, though Quezon, no matter how enervated, should have known to treat such an offer from that source with great skepticism.

Quezon's former secretary, Jorge Vargas, had been set up by the Japanese as a Quisling local government committee chairman, and had been making anti-American comments on the radio and in pamphlets. This had further shaken the embattled Philippine president. Quezon's message proposed that if the United States was not prepared to defend the Philippines adequately, since the Japanese, he thought, were there to displace the Americans rather than to occupy the Philippines specifically, the United States should grant his country full independence and withdraw. The Philippines would then undertake to dismantle all its defensive and military installations and declare its neutrality, and Japan, Quezon piously hoped, would also withdraw.

What made this rather utopian vision more disquieting was that the American civil and military leaders in the Philippines, High Commissioner Francis Sayre (Woodrow Wilson's son-in-law and William G. McAdoo's brother-in-law) and General MacArthur, sent accompanying notes appearing to agree with Quezon. Sayre had simply gone native and unreservedly endorsed Quezon's proposal, if his premise of no early military aid was accurate. MacArthur's was much more guarded. He reviewed the deteriorating military solution and then addressed the question from his perspective as a field commander: "So far as the military angle is concerned, the problem presents itself as to whether the plan of President Quezon might offer the best possible solution of what is about to be a disastrous debacle."

He went on to say that the ultimate status of the Philippines would be unaffected, since it would depend on the outcome of the war (a dubious assertion— the position of the United States in the Philippines would not benefit from bugging out on their protectorate even if it did ultimately win the war). He thought the American hand would be strengthened if the Japanese rejected the proposal and that the Americans would not lose much; and implicitly the men under his command, to whom he had a strong natural loyalty, would be spared the agonies that awaited them in a battle to the death or, for the survivors (presumably, at this point, including himself), in a Japanese prison camp.

In his memoirs, MacArthur, who was certainly not above imaginative historical revisionism, claimed that he "said bluntly that I would not endorse [Quezon's proposals], that there was not the slightest chance of approval by either the United States or Japan." MacArthur further claimed that Quezon agreed with his assessment that there was no chance of acceptance. "But that he felt that only something of an explosive nature could shock Washington into a realization of the importance of the Far East." (This sounds more like a rationale for MacArthur's own unrealistic entreaties for assistance, and twenty years after the fact at that, when Quezon, Roosevelt, Marshall, and Stimson were all dead.)

Marshall and Stimson brought these messages to the White House on February 9 in a state of some concern that the President's political instincts might cloud his strategic judgment in a situation Stimson described as "ghastly in its responsibility and significance." Roosevelt recognized instantly that the whole idea was unthinkable and based on false premises. Japan would have had the Philippines under brutal occupation decades before were it not for the presence of the

United States and the tacit arrangement, going back to his cousin TR's time, that the United States would accept Japanese occupation of Formosa and Japan would not object to the U.S. position in the Philippines.

He agreed with Marshall's assessment that it would be negligently reckless to gamble all the alliance's remaining naval strength on an expedition to the Philippines. It was sad but inescapable that the Philippines continued to be temporarily indefensible. But he knew also that enactment of any such proposal as Quezon's would everywhere be seen as a capitulation by the United States. On reading the messages from Quezon, Sayre, and MacArthur, Roosevelt said at once: "We can't do this at all." Marshall said, "I immediately discarded everything in my mind I had held to his discredit. . . . I decided he was a great man."[36]

Roosevelt cabled back that Filipino units could surrender "when and if in your opinion that course appears necessary. . . . American forces will continue to keep our flag flying in the Philippines so long as there remains any possibility of resistance. . . . The duty and the necessity of resisting Japanese aggression to the last transcends in importance any other obligation now facing us in the Philippines. I therefore give you this most difficult mission in full understanding of the desperate nature to which you may shortly be reduced. The service that you and the American members of your command can render to your country in the titanic struggle now developing is beyond all possibility of appraisement." Quezon replied that he would abide entirely by the U.S. president's wishes, and MacArthur responded: My family "and I have decided that they will share the fate of the garrison. My plans . . . consist in fighting my present battle position in Bataan to destruction and then holding Corregidor in a similar manner. I have not the slightest intention in the world of surrendering or capitulating the Filipino elements of my command."[37]

Neither Washington nor Tokyo had imagined that MacArthur and his successor, General Jonathan Wainwright, could hold out as long as they did. The Bataan forces, starved and disease-ridden because of the tight Japanese sea blockade (though, contrary to then-current mythology, not greatly outnumbered), overwhelmingly outgunned, and under constant air and heavy artillery attack, surrendered April 9, 1942, after a four-month resistance. A skeleton force had already been evacuated to the fortified and tunneled rock of Corregidor, where it held out for another month. The Japanese might, even at this early date, have been raising their early low estimation of the determination of their opponents.

MacArthur finally left, March 10, under a direct presidential order of February 22; he insisted on doing so in a torpedo boat rather than a submarine, to demonstrate the porosity of the Japanese blockade. In fact, there were sightings of the pagoda conning towers of large Japanese warships and perilous passages through minefields, and the general and his wife and infant son were fortunate to make good their escape to Australia. Once arrived there, MacArthur made his theatrical assertion, "I shall return," a promise that encouraged those he had left behind and impressed the public (and was fulfilled) but was so close to a platitude that it was disrespectfully invoked by soldiers going to the latrine for months afterward.

It is not clear why the U.S. Navy did not take off the American forces on Corregidor by submarine instead of leaving the brave and unlucky General Wainwright and his heroic garrison to be captured by the Japanese, who did not observe the Geneva Convention regarding prisoners of war. Of the 70,000 prisoners taken on Bataan and driven on the infamous "Death March" to the prison camp sixty miles away, 16,000 died en route of varying degrees of mistreatment, and 22,000 more died of similar avoidable causes in the first few months of captivity. Some news of the fate of these men leaked out to the West and further intensified the determination of all Americans to crush Japan.

Whatever the reason for not evacuating Wainwright and his garrison, he should not have been left as commander of the entire Philippines, since he was obliged to surrender for all of the archipelago. In fact, the Japanese never subdued the whole country, and guerrilla war was conducted from the jungles until the Japanese themselves were driven out and surrendered nearly three years later. (Then many of their soldiers took to the jungles and conducted guerrilla war, straggling out into the postwar world for decades.)

Roosevelt and MacArthur regarded each other with suspicion, as has been recorded, but they had known each other a long time, and while Roosevelt had reservations about MacArthur's tendencies to be a political general, they shared some characteristics, including courage, physical presence, eloquence, and showmanship.

With Marshall, the rivalry of the generals was stronger. Marshall was an alumnus of the Virginia Military Institute, MacArthur (with the highest graduating scores in its history) of West Point. In the First World War, Marshall had been on Pershing's staff, while MacArthur was a divisional commander and the youngest general in the army. MacArthur disliked Pershing and those around him. He reproached Pershing for many things, including attempting to seduce MacArthur's fiancée, his first wife, Louise Cromwell Brooks, when MacArthur was commandant of West Point in 1921.[38]

Roosevelt and Marshall wished to recognize MacArthur's contribution to the war even at this early date. Despite the shambles at Clark Field, they were impressed by his determination, if necessary, to fight to the death, accompanied by his wife and child. They were grateful for the determination of his resistance to the Japanese onslaught, the first serious opposition on land the Western Allies had mounted against a more powerful German or Japanese foe. It was a particularly refreshing contrast to the collapse at Singapore, a virtual eastern Battle of France in miniature.

Marshall, a man of great ambition but little vanity, opened the process, apparently on his own initiative, of securing MacArthur the Congressional Medal of Honor. He began at the end of January, had sufficient evidence to justify the recommendation at the end of February, wrote a generous citation himself, and sent it to Stimson on March 24. He recommended its approval by the secretary of war because of the positive effect it would have on public and service morale, and "because I am certain General MacArthur is deserving of the honor."[39] Stimson and Roosevelt and the Congress agreed, and Roosevelt announced the award March 25.

Thus MacArthur and his father, General Arthur MacArthur, became the only father and son in history to win the nation's highest decoration for bravery in combat.

MacArthur's most authoritative biographer opined that: "It is regrettable that MacArthur was never fully informed of the roles of Roosevelt and Marshall during this critical period of his career."[40] He was referring to the order to leave the Philippines as well as the Medal of Honor, which MacArthur apparently believed had been demanded by his followers in the Congress. MacArthur's reply to the President and the chief of staff was as gracious as the citation Marshall wrote, and gave the credit for Bataan to the common soldiers.

Roosevelt would continue to be irked by MacArthur's personal propaganda machine, motivated perhaps in part by professional envy, but their relations, though distant, were cordial to the end of Roosevelt's life. MacArthur's appreciation of his old chief in his memoirs was generous: "He had greatly matured [when inaugurated president] since our former days in Washington. His political star had risen to its zenith, but poliomyelitis struck him painfully. He became the leading liberal of the age. Whether his vision of economic and political freedom is within the realm of fruition, only future history can tell. That his means for accomplishment won him the almost idolatrous devotion of an immeasurable following is known to all. That they aroused bitterness and resentment in others is equally true. In my own case, whatever differences arose between us, it never sullied in slightest degree the warmth of my friendship for him."[41] (MacArthur would emulate many of Roosevelt's New Deal measures as military governor of Japan from 1945 to 1951, in which role he would win almost universal admiration as he relaunched what became the second economic power in the world and set a magnificent example of the magnanimity of a justly victorious power.)

Another Allied military rout occurred between February and May 1942, in Burma. The brilliant, irascible, and acerbic American general Joseph "Vinegar Joe" Stilwell was appointed chief of staff to Chiang Kai-shek and commander of the Allied forces in Burma, essentially two Chinese divisions. These units were completely insubordinate, and the situation was compounded by Chiang's meddling and his tenuous grasp of military strategy and Burmese geography. Stilwell eventually became exasperated with the impossible position he was in and conducted a remarkable retreat through mountain jungle, just ahead of the monsoons, of a group of British and American stragglers, miscellaneous Burmese, Chinese, British nurses, and varied ranks. The little group of 114 arrived at Imphal without the loss of a single person.

Stilwell went to Wavell's headquarters at New Delhi. At a press conference he pronounced himself tired of the British habit of describing all retreats as "strategic" and "voluntary" and "glorious." When asked to comment on the remarks of Wavell and General Sir Harold Alexander, he said: "No military commander in history ever made a voluntary withdrawal . . . and there's no such thing as a glorious retreat. All retreats are as ignominious as hell. I claim we got a hell of a licking. We got run out of Burma and it's humiliating as hell."[42] The public loved it, but it didn't do much for inter-Allied relationships, largely because of its accuracy.

He was disgusted by the ineptitude of the British in Burma, which was part of the British Indian Empire, and not convinced that they really favored helping China at all. He was no more impressed with Chiang Kai-shek, whom he considered corrupt, cowardly, and incompetent. Chiang would come to remind him of a famous governor-general of Canton during the Second Opium War, whom the Chinese had memorialized: "He would not fight, he would not make peace, and he would not make a defense. He would not die. He would not surrender and he would not run away."[43] Stilwell was from a zealously Republican family and was not full of admiration for his own commander in chief, about whom some of his diary references were amusingly acidulous. He did enjoy good relations with both MacArthur and Marshall, who enjoyed his respect and appreciated his qualities.

V

ONE OF THE more discreditable episodes in the entire Roosevelt era was the decision, implemented February 19, 1942, to intern the entire Japanese-American population around designated military areas. The ethnic criterion was not mentioned in the enabling executive order—the secretary of war was entitled to remove and detain whom he wished—but this was well known to be aimed at Japanese Americans, who were almost the exclusive subjects of subsequent action. Eleanor Roosevelt had grave misgivings about this action and said so to her husband, who ignored them and asked her not to raise the subject again.[44]

A tremendous campaign arose among unscrupulous California politicians and journalists, fanning and fed by local fears of an imminent Japanese military assault and the myth that there had been any sabotage or even espionage by people of Japanese origins in the events leading up to Pearl Harbor. California's Governor Culbert L. Olson and Attorney General Earl Warren (subsequently a champion of civil rights as Chief Justice of the United States) called publicly upon the War Department to round up the Japanese Americans. There were other respectable sources for this mindless clamoring, such as Walter Lippmann, whose column on February 12, 1942, declared: "It is a fact that communication takes place between the enemy at sea and enemy agents on land." He predicted, with his usual certitude, that coordinated sabotage on a grand scale would occur when "it can be struck with maximum effect." There has never been a scrap of evidence to support that there was any such communication, or any plan for sabotage, or any active Japanese agents on the Pacific coast.

But the climate was charged. On February 26, 1942, Marshall sent Roosevelt a memorandum purporting to believe that Japanese agents had secured fifteen commercial planes that had overflown Los Angeles the previous day "between 3.12 and 4.15 A.M." causing anti-aircraft batteries to fire "1430 rounds . . . Investigation continuing." This bizarre episode was assumed by the chief of staff to have been undertaken "for purposes of spreading alarm." The fact that Marshall sent this report at all indicates that alarm had indeed taken hold. Obviously, no such mission was initiated by the Japanese and the anti-aircraft guns were firing wildly into the night, presumably at civilian aircraft, if at anything at all.[45]

It was convenient to allege collusion between Japan and Hawaiian residents of Japanese ancestry to help explain the complete surprise and the great damage that the Japanese attack achieved there. Pearl Harbor never ceased to be the most important of all American naval bases, and Oahu was swarming with people of Japanese ancestry. There was no detention of these people and no incidents of sabotage nor any known espionage by such people. Japanese Hawaiians were accepted into the American armed forces, where they served in the European theater with distinction (including subsequent long-serving U.S. congressman and senator Daniel Inouye, who lost an arm in Italy).

Attorney General Francis Biddle wrote Roosevelt February 17 warning that there could be race riots because of the incitements of Lippmann and muckraking Hearst columnist Westbrook Pegler, whom he called "armchair strategists and Junior G-Men." Biddle pointed out that the F.B.I. and the War Department believed no sabotage was imminent. J. Edgar Hoover, seventeen years into his forty-eight-year tenure as director of the F.B.I., sent Roosevelt a memo on the night of December 7, 1941, stating that the Bureau had a list of 770 Japanese aliens who would require detention and questioning, which he proposed to arrange as soon as the President had signed the authorization. But Hoover, who was never known as a great civil libertarian, was always opposed to the general roundup of American citizens of Japanese origin, and considered that citizens had to be proceeded against with probable cause, on an individual basis, and with due judicial process.

He has received very little credit from the American left for vastly outperforming their traditional iconic heroes in the Roosevelt administration in this matter, starting with the President himself. Hoover's agents had broken into Japanese consular offices and taken a complete summary of the Japanese spy system in the United States. He was confident that he could deal with it, and did so. The Bureau and army and navy intelligence all agreed that they had destroyed whatever espionage organization Japan had in the United States.

But the regular army, now in charge of defending California since the disappearance of so much of the navy's effectiveness at Pearl Harbor, was in the hands of National Guard officers, who became fixated on the Yellow Peril within. Hoover objected to arbitrary detention of Japanese-Americans on practical as well as civil rights grounds. The Justice Department was opposed for reasons of constitutionality. Roosevelt, like many believers in big liberal government, had never been an overzealous upholder of civil rights. Such people tend to regard civil rights as too often invoked by powerful individuals trying to evade the implications of majority rule. In 1936 he had privately said that "every Japanese [American]" who was seen meeting Japanese ships calling at Pearl Harbor should be inscribed on "a list of those who would be the first to be placed in a concentration camp in the event of trouble."[46]

Biddle allowed that the "constitutional difficulty" had not "plagued" Roosevelt. Stimson, something of a bigot at the best of times, handed the issue to Assistant Secretary of War John J. McCloy, who was relatively enlightened but was prepared to do anything in the name of military necessity. He injudiciously referred to the Constitution as "a scrap of paper" compared with the national interest, in one conversation, February 1, 1942. Stimson had McCloy represent him, as he was happy to do throughout the discussion of the problem.

McCloy and Stimson were distinguished men who fancied themselves upholders of due process, but McCloy began by suggesting a method of removing everyone from sensitive military areas of the West Coast subject to readmission by a screening process. Other American communities farther inland bitterly resisted the arrival of displaced Japanese-Americans in their midst. And the narrow-minded army command in California kept claiming that the amount of processing involved would be impossible. McCloy steadily gave way to the military, even though serious generals who would soon be facing and defeating real enemies, such as Mark Clark (perhaps made more sensitive to confinement of unconvicted people in camps by the fact that he was half Jewish), opposed any such general roundup of the Japanese-Americans.[47]

The measure authorizing the roundup of 110,500 Japanese-Americans, at least 70,000 of them American citizens, Executive Order 9066, was signed by the President February 19, 1942, and permitted the secretary of war "to prescribe military areas . . . from which any and all persons may be excluded." It also gave the War Department the authority to license the "right of any person to enter, remain in, or leave" those prescribed areas. By mid-March, 1942, when McCloy addressed the Japanese American Citizens' League, McCloy had convinced himself that the measure was a benign and painless method of sparing the Japanese-Americans ethnic abuse.*

In his memoirs, Stimson whitewashed the episode by dumping it onto Roosevelt, McCloy, and the generals, and taking refuge in the legitimization by the

---

* This was a little like Herbert Hoover's theory that people sold apples during the Depression because it was a lucrative occupation.

Supreme Court. Stimson, with his collaborator McGeorge Bundy, wrote that "they [presumably the Japanese-Americans themselves] believed in 1947 that the eventual result of this evacuation, in the resettlement of a conspicuous minority in many dispersed communities throughout the country, was to produce a distinctly healthier atmosphere for both Japanese and Americans."[48] By the most self-serving standards of revisionist memoirists, this is an egregious fraud. (Bundy was eventually national security advisor to Presidents Kennedy and Johnson.)

Another prominent American in the permanent odor of sanctity with the American liberal establishment who has much to answer for in this tawdry episode is Justice Felix Frankfurter. He told McCloy, with even more pedantry than usual, in February 1942: "You are dealing with important imponderables, and let me remind you that the fellow who put the term 'imponderables' into the vocabulary of affairs was 'blood and iron' Bismarck." He told McCloy in March 1942 that he was handling the Japanese-American problem with "both wisdom and appropriate hardheadedness."[49] Those who might have hoped that once installed on the Supreme Court, Frankfurter would cease to be an endless source of sycophantic laudations of the powerful were to be disappointed.

In fact, almost all the Japanese-Americans were uprooted and incarcerated with no concern for their civil or property rights and with no evidence whatever of actual or prospective wrongdoing. There was only grandstanding, hysteria, xenophobia, and minor demagogy by lesser officials and some journalists. J. Edgar Hoover kept completely out of the internment operation, and submitted a 480-page report on it in 1943, in which he stated that it was "extremely unfortunate that the Government, the War Relocation Authority, and the public did . . . seize upon what they first believed to be a simple determining factor of loyalty. There actually can only be one efficient method of processing the Japanese for loyalty, which consists of individual, not mass, consideration."[50]

Despite Hoover's opposition, the attorney general, Francis Biddle, much influenced by Stimson's great prestige, experience, and reputation for integrity, gave up without a fight and without telling his own officials that he had defected. He thus, after a promising start, became complicit in one of the shabbiest initiatives of the Roosevelt era. In the Congress the only audible dissent from the internment policy was in the Senate, where only Robert A. Taft of Ohio objected.

The designated targets of this measure were given one week to dispose of their property as they wished, were rounded up in racetracks and fairgrounds and such places, and spent idle days and nights constantly interrupted by searchlights behind watchtowers and barbed wire. This was not comparable to the concentration camps of the Third Reich or the Soviet Gulag, and there was no incidence of brutality or undernourishment, but it was an outrageous way to treat American citizens against whom there was no evidence of wrongdoing and who had been given no access to any aspect of the legal system.

The director of the War Relocation Authority was Milton Eisenhower, Dwight D. Eisenhower's younger brother and former director of the Agriculture Department's information bureau and land-use program. (He was named at the suggestion of General Eisenhower, who was then on Marshall's planning staff.)[51] Milton Eisenhower tried to humanize conditions, emulate the Civilian Conservation Corps, and set up such camps mainly around the western states. He always remembered his attempt to present this approach to a gathering of western governors at Salt Lake City on April 7, 1942, as the most humiliating experience of his life. He had planned for the internees to be free to leave the camps during the day, but the governors would not have any of them in their states other than under constant armed guard. Eisenhower disgustedly resigned in June and was replaced by Dillon Myer, also formerly of the Department of Agriculture, who secured civilian control of the fifteen camps he set up around five western states. There was a substantial improvement in conditions, though life in the camps was extremely monotonous. Roosevelt asked his wife to visit one of the camps, at Gila River, Arizona, in April 1943. Impressed by the ingenuity of the internees and dismayed at the prison camp aspects of their confinement, she intervened with her husband, who, supported by Ickes, asked Stimson to improve conditions. By the end of 1943, between joining the armed forces and obtaining work permits to leave, about a third of the detainees had been liberated from the camps.

In December 1944, the U.S. Supreme Court upheld the constitutionality of all these proceedings, 6–3. Owen Roberts and former Roosevelt attorneys general Robert Jackson and Frank Murphy dissented. Murphy denounced the internment as racist and illegal and found in it "a melancholy resemblance "to the Nazi treatment of the Jews."*

By this time, the Supreme Court was as much of a rubber stamp for Roosevelt as it had been a bugbear to him seven years before; he had appointed seven of its nine members. In his 1950 edition of Roosevelt's public papers for 1942, Samuel Rosenman expressed Roosevelt's recognition that: "To keep a large number of loyal American citizens in concentration camps was certainly not consistent with the principles for which the United States was fighting. There was an obvious inconsistency between the glorious heroism and sacrifices of the Nisei fighting with the American Army overseas and the severe hardships and public opprobrium to which the families of these American Nisei soldiers still in this country were subjected."[52] It was not so obvious that Roosevelt was prepared to do anything about it.

If the military was right about sabotage dangers, Roosevelt didn't want to be responsible for not removing the dangers. We know now that there was no such danger but the President was receiving conflicting advice. His conduct was probably understandable, but it did him no credit. It was a lamentable episode and at

---

* Had he known the full proportions of those latter enormities, he might not have made the comparison. Murphy had attempted to enlist in the armed forces but was declined, because his civilian work as a Supreme Court justice was considered essential.

the least, once the immediate hysteria had subsided, the young, the elderly, the mothers, and carefully screened individual adult males should have been steadily released. The majority were still in detention when the war ended.

Prior to his Fireside Chat of February 23, 1942, the White House announced that the President would be referring to many foreign places and asked the public to have maps to hand. A tremendous demand for maps and atlases inundated the bookstores of the nation. Well over 60 million Americans, over 80 percent of the eligible adult radio audience, were listening as the President spoke. It was another of his acts of political legerdemain. He made the setbacks of more recent days more palatable by comparing them with the long struggle for American independence. He maintained his customary fiction of "speaking with" his audience, as if it were an interactive conversation.

Roosevelt denounced defeatists who mocked the U.S. war effort. There was not much audible defeatist comment in the country at this point (or at any other stage in this war). He was, in fact, skillfully maneuvering critics into the role of defeatists, as he had tarred isolationists as Nazi sympathizers. He side-stepped anticipated criticism with his usual agility.

He explained why defending the Philippines was untenable by reference to maps and referred to the longstanding American military view that it could not be protected if attacked by Japan, other than by eventually subduing Japan itself. He declared that Pearl Harbor had nothing to do with it. "It is that complete encirclement, with control of the air by Japanese land-based aircraft which has prevented us from sending reinforcements." He praised "the defense put up by General MacArthur [which] has magnificently exceeded the previous estimate of endurance; and he and his men are gaining eternal glory therefore."

This geographic and historic exegesis, following by one day his order to MacArthur personally to quit Corregidor, while praising him and giving him the country's highest military honor, were elements, each justifiable in itself, of a plan to exonerate the administration for the loss of the Philippines and downplay the results of the damage to the fleet at Pearl Harbor. "The consequences of the attack on Pearl Harbor, serious as they were, have been wildly exaggerated in other ways. And these exaggerations come originally from Axis propagandists; but they have been repeated, I regret to say, by Americans in and out of public life." He continued, with feigned intimacy: "You and I have the utmost contempt for Americans who, since Pearl Harbor, have whispered or announced 'off the record' that there was no longer any Pacific Fleet—that the Fleet was all sunk or destroyed December 7. . . . Almost every Axis broadcast—Berlin, Rome, Tokyo— directly quotes Americans who, by speech or in the press, make damnable misstatements such as these."

He explained that of all the ships at Pearl Harbor of every category, only three were permanently out of commission. This was true, but glossed over the fact that two of the three were battleships and that three other battleships would be out of action for from eighteen to thirty months.

The President walked his listeners through the map of the Pacific area and praised the country's allies (singling out, among the occupied countries, the Dutch for their valorous performance in the East Indies). He emphasized the principles and objectives of the United Nations: disarmament of aggressors, self-determination of nations and peoples, freedom of speech and religion, and freedom from want and from fear.

"Conquered Nations in Europe know what the yoke of the Nazis is like. And the people of Korea and Manchuria know in their flesh the harsh despotism of Japan." He called upon his listeners to dedicate themselves totally to the war effort. " 'These are the times which try men's souls.' Tom Paine wrote those words on a drumhead by the light of a campfire . . . And General Washington ordered that [they] be read to the men of every regiment in the Continental Army:

" 'The summer soldier and the sunshine patriot will in this crisis shrink from the service of their country; but he that stands by it now, deserves the love and thanks of man and woman. Tyranny, like hell, is not easily conquered; yet we have this consolation with us, that the harder the sacrifice, the more glorious the triumph.' "

It was clear from the avalanche of favorable public and media comment that immediately followed that Roosevelt had scored another popular and tactical triumph. Henceforth, criticism of the administration over aid to the Philippines was muted, even from the political claque of the ever more bemedalled MacArthur, and criticism over Pearl Harbor was nipped in the bud.

The first stage of the impatiently awaited American recovery in the Pacific came on April 18, 1942. In a daring move that was encouraged by Roosevelt himself, the United States bombed Tokyo, Osaka, Kobe, and Nagoya. This was an astonishing development, which intercepted Japanese radio traffic reported in almost hysterical terms. Japanese control of the oceanic approaches to their home islands was such that an aircraft carrier could not have penetrated far enough to launch and take back naval bombers, and the nearest airfields accessible to the United States, in China, were certainly too distant for a return flight by land-based bombers.

Shortly after Pearl Harbor, Roosevelt had asked General Henry (Hap) Arnold, commander of the Army Air Corps, if Japan itself could be bombed. The Japanese moved so swiftly against possible land launch sites that a conventional bombing mission was impossible. Roosevelt asked Admiral King if B-25s could be launched off aircraft carriers, overfly and bomb Japan, and land in China. (King claims that the idea originated with one of his operations officers and the documentary evidence is inconclusive, but Roosevelt certainly promoted the idea.) It was feasible but difficult. The President ordered the mission, and Colonel James Doolittle was appointed to command it. He and his men trained on airfields scaled down to the flight deck of U.S.S. *Hornet,* but did not fly off a carrier deck until the actual mission launch.

Sixteen planes flew off from the new carrier *Hornet*, from two hundred miles farther from Japan than had been anticipated, because of Japanese naval patrols farther out than the navy expected. Despite wet weather and forty-knot winds, Doolittle insisted on proceeding. All sixteen bombers got into the air, and all but one delivered their bomb loads (four 500-lb. bombs each) on designated targets. Most of the planes arrived over unoccupied China at night and couldn't find the prearranged destination, so the crews bailed out. One landed in Russia and two were forced down over Japanese territory; seventy-one of the eighty men in the aircrews survived the mission, four as prisoners of war. The Osaka-destined bombs were dropped instead on Yokohama and Yokosuka, and the twelve planes that attacked Tokyo arrived right after the daily mock air raid was ending, at noon. This lessened the mission's psychological impact but facilitated the planes' escape. About fifty people were killed and one hundred houses damaged in Japanese cities. For this escapade Doolittle, too, won the Congressional Medal of Honor.

On the advice of Samuel Rosenman, Roosevelt responded to press inquiries about the place of origin of the flight by referring to Shangri-la, the magical Himalayan Valley in James Hilton's current novel *Lost Horizon.* The Japanese authorities convinced their own population that the raid was a daredevil stunt, a fluke that could not be repeated, though they cordoned off the damaged areas from public view. But it emboldened American opinion and seems to have played a role in determining Japanese strategy. The Japanese general staff wanted to concentrate its efforts on a drive toward and into Australia. The commanders of the Japanese Combined Fleet, led by Yamamoto, wanted to force a decisive fleet action with the United States Navy, before its construction program could make good the Pearl Harbor losses and open up a big lead in carrier forces.

Yamamoto reasoned that moving toward Oahu, specifically Midway, the westernmost of the Hawaiian Islands, which Yamamoto called the "keyhole" of the Pacific, would force the U.S. Navy to give battle on unfavorable terms. The Doolittle raid helped to resolve this argument in favor of the Yamamoto faction, which argued that no such raid could have been launched if Midway had been in Japanese possession, with air patrols around it interdicting U.S. Fleet moves much west of Hawaii.

Japanese pride had been affronted, just as Hitler's was by Churchill's bomber attack on Berlin in the summer of 1940. That operation helped to turn the Luftwaffe's attention from military targets, especially airfields and aircraft factories, to population centers, especially London.

As the Allies groped their way into the spring of 1942, their fortunes, almost imperceptibly, were starting to turn.

⚜

CHAPTER 17

"Why Are You So Afraid of the Germans? Troops Must Be Blooded in Battle"

*(Joseph Stalin, Marshal and Premier of the Soviet Union,
to British Prime Minister Winston Churchill, the Kremlin,
Moscow, August 12, 1942)*

I

ON THE DOMESTIC front there had been great wariness on the part of the President and the Congress about rationing certain items, especially gasoline and tires, and the Congress passed but the President vetoed a trivial measure to encourage production of synthetic rubber. Roosevelt appointed a committee consisting of the president of Harvard, James B. Conant; the president of the Massachusetts Institute of Technology, Karl T. Compton; and the ubiquitous Bernard Baruch as chairman, to propose what needed to be done about rationing. The committee would report September 10, 1942, and recommend gas rationing, a nationwide speed-limit reduction to thirty-five miles per hour, maximum possible tire recapping, removal of patent restrictions on rubber development, and practical encouragement of synthetic rubber production. The committee recommendations were followed, and by 1945 U.S. synthetic rubber production was as great as the entire world's crude rubber production had been prior to 1939.[1]

On April 27, 1942, Roosevelt presented to the Congress, and the following evening to the country in a Fireside Chat, a comprehensive economic stabilization program. The program consisted of tax increases aimed at holding maximum after-tax income to $25,000 (about thirty times as much in current dollars); a freeze on commercial, farm, and commodity prices and on wages and rents;

intensification of victory bond sales; reduction of consumer credit; and wide-spread rationing of scarce essential commodities.

Roosevelt was obsessed with avoidance of war profiteering and was determined that the entire population should bear the burden of winning the war. "Not all of us can have the privilege of fighting our enemies in distant parts of the world." This program was designed for those lacking that "privilege." The concern was now for inflation and unjust enrichment. Unemployment had descended below 10 percent in the early months of 1940, was below 5 percent by election day of that year, and was almost eliminated by the end of Roosevelt's second term, in January 1941. For the last year it had been about 1 per cent and would go even below that over the next two years. In these circumstances, the dangers of wage and price inflation were great if not closely monitored. Roosevelt's program was generally successful in avoiding these ravages.

The Congress passed his Economic Stabilization Act of 1942 largely as he had drafted it, keeping intact his unprecedented record of success in legislative initiatives.

Among the measures in the act, apart from special taxes and price controls, was the creation of the Office of Economic Stabilization, with the usual rather vague over- and interlap of jurisdiction with other agencies. Roosevelt prevailed upon newly appointed Supreme Court Justice James F. Byrnes to leave the Court and take over the direction of this new agency. Byrnes's office would be only a few feet from the President's, where he was assured high access, and he chose Ben Cohen and the political commentator Samuel Lubell as his assistants. Roosevelt had recommended that Byrnes take a leave of absence from the Supreme Court, but Byrnes "out of propriety," resigned from the court.[2]

One idea that briefly gained currency and was championed by Treasury Secretary Morgenthau was the spending tax. Although this was obviously an insane concept, almost impossible to collect, easy to falsify, and inferior in every respect to a selective sales tax, Roosevelt purported to find it of interest. Morgenthau sent it to the Congress, where it was rejected with contemptuous finality by the Senate Finance Committee. Roosevelt declined to lift a finger to help his Treasury secretary, explaining that he never supported bills before Congress. When Morgenthau politely pointed out the utter mendacity of that remark, Roosevelt explained that he needed "a couple of whipping boys." Morgenthau gloomily allowed that he was "getting plenty of whippings." The act did impose a flat 5 percent "Victory Tax" on all incomes above $12 per week, reduced all exemptions, and increased the number of Americans required to file an income tax return from seven million in 1941 to 42 million in 1942.[3] *

* In 1943 the Congress would remove the $25,000 cap on individual salaries, including the President's own, over his strenuous protestations. In fact, it was a largely symbolic measure, since wealthy people could always arrange to take their incomes by methods other than

In his Fireside Chat, since he had no victories to report, he confined his war summary to the assertion that the Japanese were advancing at tremendous cost and facing fierce resistance, especially in the Philippines. The Doolittle Raid he whimsically referred to as if he knew nothing of it: "It is even reported from Japan that somebody has dropped bombs on Tokyo, and on other principal centers of Japanese war industries. If this be true, it is the first time in history that Japan has suffered such indignities."[4]

There appeared finally to be a glimmer of recognition by Roosevelt that his French policy needed revision. Petain had recently replaced Admiral Darlan, who was anti-British but not pro-Nazi, as premier of the emasculated French state at Vichy, with Pierre Laval, a Quisling, notoriously pro-German in the First World War and steadily more identified with that view between the wars and throughout France's brief participation as a belligerent in the current war. Laval was also evidently corrupt and had visibly enriched himself at the public trough. Roosevelt, on the evening of April 28, 1942, spoke wistfully of "what we used to know as the Republic of France . . . a name and an institution which we hope will soon be restored to full dignity."[5]

"Throughout the Nazi occupation of France, we have hoped for the maintenance of a French government which would strive to regain independence, to reestablish the principles of 'Liberty, Equality, Fraternity,' and to restore the historic culture of France." How he could have expected any such lofty purposes from Petain's wretched band of defeatists and bootlickers has escaped the comprehension of posterity, but Roosevelt now expressed concern "lest those who have recently come to power may seek to force the brave French people into submission to Nazi despotism.

"The United Nations will . . . prevent the use of French territory in any part of the world for military purposes by the Axis powers." (This was all very resonant, but Tunisia was the staging area for Rommel's drive on the Suez Canal, and French Indochina, as he explained in his address of February 23, was a jumping-off point for the Japanese invasion of the Philippines.) "We know how the French people really feel," he assured his listeners, as he explained that virtually all of them realized that the "fight of the United Nations is fundamentally their fight, [for] the restoration of a free and independent France," as against "the slavery that would be imposed by her external enemies and internal traitors."

The replacement of Darlan by Laval caused Roosevelt to recall his ambassador in Vichy, Admiral Leahy, whose life was further confused by the death of his wife in hospital in Vichy. He had a civilized farewell with Petain, Laval, and Darlan; the marshal provided him a private railway car for his wife's remains, and

---

salaries, including dividends, fees, deferred-payment agreements, or even payments in unmonetized consideration. The Congress also declined to act on his taxing proposals, and was more inclined to allow the already huge deficit simply to accumulate, on the theory that it could be worked down, or the country's economy could swiftly grow into it, after the war.

Leahy arrived back in the United States via Madrid, Lisbon, and a Swedish steamer on June 1. Leahy was convinced his embassy had achieved something useful but was under no illusions about the strength, popularity, or friendliness of the Vichy regime. He was particularly contemptuous of their inability even to restore the French Army to the 100,000 men permitted by the surrender agreement with Germany in 1940. Leahy described the current state of the French military as "pathetic."[6] Roosevelt appointed Leahy his military chief of staff in July, which in practice meant an advisory role and chairing meetings of Marshall and King.

As Roosevelt pondered from the trough of the war what the postwar world might look like, he indulged some rather sophomoric notions of how to remake the political map. Next to the continuing imbroglio with de Gaulle and the dalliance with Petain, which Hull never ceased to claim, on no evidence at all, had kept the Germans out of Algeria and Morocco, the clearest evidence of the President's meddlesome woolly mindedness was over India.

Roosevelt the Yankee inherited a good deal of ancient Dutch and American skepticism about the legitimacy and virtue of the British Empire. He was an authentic Anglophile, as long as questions of rivalry between Britain and America did not arise. When they did, the New England merchant rival and the prickly, populist, Jacksonian sides of his nature emerged. Roosevelt did not want to seem to be fighting the Second World War for the retention or reconstruction of colonial empires. He knew that self-determination was the wave of the future, with the setting up of effective international organizations. Woodrow Wilson had been prophetic in his vision but inept at execution. Roosevelt would do much better, but he had moments of ineptitude also.

He had raised the matter of Indian independence with Churchill at the Arcadia conference and received a sustained emotional outburst that caused him to recoil, not a frequent conversational position for Roosevelt. He did not raise it again verbally with Churchill, as the prime minister happily recorded in his memoirs.[7] On February 26, 1942, he asked Harriman to inquire of Churchill what the British government proposed to do about the current political unrest in India. Gandhi, a somewhat saintly and monastic figure, preached civil disobedience and nonviolent resistance to the British, and wished a pacifistic response to the Japanese, even if Japan invaded India. Nehru, his political lieutenant and founder of the Congress Party, favored full resistance to the Japanese but wanted a guarantee of Indian independence. There was considerable unrest in the British Indian empire at this time, just as the Japanese arrived at the gates of that empire in Burma.

Conditions in India were far more complicated than Roosevelt realized, as Churchill was at pains to point out to Harriman. Of the 390 million people in the subcontinent, 255 million were Hindus, over 90 million were Muslims, and the antipathy between them was very severe. The Muslim leader, Mohammed Ali Jinnah, much preferred British rule to absorption in a Hindu-dominated independent India. The Americans, and some Indian nationalists, suspected the British of aggravating these differences in order to retain their control of the whole of the British Indian empire.

Roosevelt professed to believe that a promise of independence would inspire the Indians to a greater war effort. Churchill pointed out that the Muslims provided three-quarters of the Indian soldiers, although they were not one-quarter of the population. He emphasized that Gandhi was a pacifist, which did dismay Roosevelt, who realized that his techniques, derived originally from an essay by Thoreau, could not be used against an uncivilized opponent like Japan. Britain was discountenanced by Gandhi only because it governed with some concern for human decency. Churchill regarded Nehru at this point as a mountebank and rabble-rouser who couldn't be trusted and who didn't speak for most of the Indian people anyway. (Ten years later, Churchill publicly called Nehru "the light of Asia." Both perspectives were exaggerations.)

The empire in India was divided between British India, ruled directly by the British India Office, and comprising about three hundred million people, and the native states, holding nearly 95 million people, ruled indirectly by Britain through treaties with individual Indian princes. Churchill also professed to be concerned about India's 40 million Untouchables, the lowest and poorest socioeconomic caste, who, he said, would be trampled down without mercy in the absence of the British.

On March 4, 1942, Churchill wrote Roosevelt: "We are earnestly considering whether a declaration of dominion status after the war carrying with it if desired the right to secede should be made at this critical juncture. We must not on any account break with the Moslems." He concluded, "Naturally we do not want to throw India into chaos on the eve of invasion," and then enclosed letters supportive of his views from Jinnah, head of the Moslem League, and from the military section of the India Office.

Churchill now embarked on a crash course of educating the President of the United States about the intricacies of the Indian situation. On March 7, he forwarded a letter from the viceroy of India, General Wavell, recommending, for reasons of military performance in the present war only, that the announcement of Dominion status not be made. He followed up later the same day with a further message from Wavell, as well as one from the governor of the Punjab, to the same general effect.

Notwithstanding this effort, Roosevelt sent Churchill March 10 an astonishing cable in which he suggested that India be reconstituted as a temporary Dominion under a regime resembling the American Articles of Confederation, which governed the newly independent colonies very imperfectly from 1783 to 1788 while the Constitution of the United States was being prepared. Roosevelt purported to believe, regardless of the contrary evidence cited to him by Churchill, that promise of imminent independence would improve the fighting quality of the Indian armed forces. He rather disingenuously concluded: "For the love of heaven don't bring me into this, though I do want to be of help. It is, strictly speaking, none of my business." When the message was received by Churchill, he said to his staff that the last comment was the only part of the message he agreed with.

It is fantastic that a man of Roosevelt's intelligence and political sophistication could imagine for a moment that there was the slightest analogy between the thirteen colonies that successfully conducted a seven-year revolt against the British Crown, but that were in all other cultural and political respects British, and the Indian subcontinent, with a population 150 times larger, hugely varied, and largely primitive—teeming masses of peasants in what Gandhi called "the 50,000 dung-heaps of India." Despite his disclaimers, Roosevelt did want Churchill to "bring [him] into this," and offered his services as an impartial mediator. He fancied being the virtual godparent and midwife of the world's largest and newest democracy, while stripping out the torso of the British Empire as he did so.

Churchill was so nonplussed by this message that he did not reply to it at all, though he reproduced it completely in his memoirs and wrote that it "illustrates the difficulties of comparing situations in various centuries and scenes where almost every material fact is totally different." Churchill was endlessly sensible of the wishes and preferences of Roosevelt, as he wrote and as his entourage noticed, often with concern.[8] It must only have been this habit, born not of any natural patience on the part of Winston Churchill but of the indispensable role Franklin D. Roosevelt alone could play in the safe deliverance of Britain from mortal combat, that imposed such restraint upon Churchill.

He must have had immense difficulty resisting the temptation to tell Roosevelt, publicly if necessary, that India would become a self-governing Dominion when the Great Republic of Washington, Jefferson, Lincoln, and the Roosevelts adopted an antilynching law, and could secede altogether from the British connection when African-Americans, now seventy-nine years after their emancipation, were allowed to vote in the southern states.

Instead of any such reply, he sent the prominent Socialist Labor member of the war cabinet, Stafford Cripps, a former ambassador to Moscow and a friend of Gandhi and Nehru, to India to try to find a settlement with the Congress leaders. Cripps arrived in New Delhi March 22, 1942. The Congress Party leadership— Nehru, in consultation with Gandhi in fact—would settle for nothing less than complete and immediate independence. They were prepared to leave a British commander of the armed forces for purposes of defending India, but required control of the defense ministry. Cripps, who accepted the principle of Indian independence unreservedly and was anything but a Churchillian imperialist, concluded that his mission was a complete failure because of Congress's obduracy, and telegraphed Churchill that he was leaving April 12 to return to Britain.

Churchill replied to Cripps thanking him for his effort: "You have done everything in human power and your tenacity, perseverance, and resourcefulness have proved how great was the British desire for a settlement." The letter was designed more for Roosevelt than for Cripps. Roosevelt, not content with his intrusions in this issue up to now, responded very negatively to the failure of the Cripps mission, especially to Churchill's assertion that British and American opinion understood that Indian intransigence was responsible for the breakdown in the talks. He immediately sent Churchill a message to Chequers, which arrived at 3 A.M. for Hopkins, who was visiting for the weekend. Churchill and Hopkins were still up, digestifs in hand, and Hopkins read Roosevelt's message and then handed it to his host. A pyrotechnic scene ensued.

Roosevelt had written: "I am sorry to say that I cannot agree with the point of view set forth in your message to me that public opinion in the United States believes that the negotiations have failed on broad general issues. The general impression here is quite the contrary. The feeling is almost universally held that the deadlock has been caused by the unwillingness of the British Government to concede to the Indians the right of self-government, notwithstanding the willingness of the Indians to entrust technical, military, and naval defense control to the competent British authorities." Roosevelt went on to revive his fatuous suggestion about the American Articles of Confederation and to ask Churchill to prevail upon Cripps to give it one more try on a more flexible basis.

In some respects, Roosevelt was undoubtedly correct. The British rule of nearly 400 million people in the subcontinent, where they never retained more than 100,000 of their own nationals, while a remarkable achievement in colonial management, could not possibly continue. That Churchill was exultant at what he thought to be an adequate level of intransigence by Nehru and Gandhi to break off discussions there can be no doubt. And that Roosevelt better judged American opinion on the subject than Churchill did is certainly also true. But this was not an American matter.

The British were seriously considering new arrangements, and the politics of India were far more complicated and nuanced than Roosevelt seemed to realize. Winston Churchill had carried the torch of human freedom and Western civilization for a long time through very dark days. He was a magnificently courageous and cooperative ally and did not deserve to be beset by this sort of concern at this time and from this source. When Hopkins gave him the letter, the evening continued for another two hours, to 5 A.M., as Churchill stormed around his drawing room fulminating about the implications of what was suggested by Hopkins's chief.

Churchill left it to Hopkins to summarize and transmit his response. It consisted of the statement that if Congress's terms were agreed to, the Indian leadership would withdraw the substantial Indian forces from the Middle East, gravely weakening that front; would negotiate an armistice with Japan; and would rely on the Japanese to assist them while they suppressed the Muslims. He could not imagine what useful purpose would be served by exposing such a profound disagreement between the United States and the United Kingdom at this critical point. But if American opinion was in the state Roosevelt claimed, he, Churchill, would be prepared to resign, and "return to private life," but he would not follow the course recommended by Roosevelt.

On April 12, Churchill wrote Roosevelt that he didn't intend to show the President's letter to his cabinet, because it was marked "personal" and because he was sure the cabinet would agree with him that they could not take "responsibility for the defense of India if everything has again to be thrown into the melting pot at this critical juncture. . . . Anything like a serious difference between you and me would break my heart and surely deeply injure both our countries at the height of this terrible struggle."[9] Finally, even Roosevelt desisted. It was a matter better left to postwar resolution.

––––––––––

Even in the usually unruffled affairs of Canada, Roosevelt demonstrated a rather naïve view of what could be achieved by authoritarian planning. Approximately one-third of the Canadian population was French-speaking, overwhelmingly concentrated in Quebec. These people had effectively been deserted by France at the end of the Seven Years War in 1763. They had sustained their numbers through a high birth rate, not immigration, and had no feelings of affection for the mother country such as inspired many English-speaking Canadians. The response to the outbreak of war had been magnificent from Canadians, who volunteered in great numbers, though Canada itself was not under threat.

Prime Minister Mackenzie King and his Quebec advisors had promoted the compromise that there would be no conscription for overseas service, and the French-Canadians, unconscripted, would support the war effort. By early 1942, the clamor among English-Canadians for conscription was such that King held a referendum on the issue, asking that his government be released from its no-conscription pledge. In English Canada, he was satisfying opinion honorably. In French Canada, he said he was merely asking, as a contingency, for what other government leaders had. "Conscription if necessary, but not necessarily conscription," was his typically ambivalent straddle. Quebec political and Roman Catholic Church leaders warned him that the referendum, in April 1942, would produce problems. (The Church had great influence in Quebec at this time, having assured the survival of French-language education and medical care in that province for nearly 200 years, with little secular assistance, since the defeat of the French in the Seven Years War.) Roosevelt had received the primate of Canada, J.M.R. Cardinal Villeneuve of Quebec, as a favor to Mackenzie King in November 1939.

Roosevelt tried again to assist King, with an address to the Canadian people February 14, 1942: "Yours are the achievements of a great Nation. They require no praise from me—but they get that praise from me nevertheless. I understate the case when I say that we, in this country, contemplating what you have done, and the spirit in which you have done it, are proud to be your neighbors." Despite this support from a prestigious source, English Canada voted 80 percent in favor of King's request in the referendum and French Canada voted 90 percent against. The issue carried, but the division between the founding peoples in Canada could not have been more stark. The English-Canadians had effectively declared that failure to impose conscription would be cowardice. The French indicated that its imposition would be a betrayal.

Shortly after the referendum, Roosevelt wrote King a letter congratulating him on winning the referendum and telling him not to be too concerned about the reticence of his French-speaking compatriots. He reminisced that there had once been a good many French-speaking people in New England, but that they had been assimilated eventually. He went on to say that he would soon be speaking to "our planning people" about the excessive concentrations in certain cities of people of Italian, German, and Jewish origin. He was certainly not disparaging any of these groups, but the thought that he might have imagined that he possessed the power to influence demographic flows on the basis of ethnic origin is disturbing.[10]

Presumably he was just trying to encourage Mackenzie King at a difficult time, and wasn't serious. His letter does reveal, however, a startling ignorance of Canadian affairs from one who spent thirty-six summers of his life in Canada and had returned a number of times since. The Canadian Confederation was essentially an agreement between the English- and French-speaking peoples in the country in 1867 on a basis of official equality, with language rights for both groups guaranteed. This succeeded the United Province Of Canada, 1841–1867, which failed in its avowed purpose of assimilating the French-Canadians. There was no parallel at all with immigration of foreign-language elements to the United States, where the obligation on them to assimilate to the English-speaking country to which they had emigrated was irresistible, and presumably desired. King gave a very circumspect reply to Roosevelt's attempt at cheerfulness.

In other circumstances, nothing much could be read into this. But the combination of the unjust and mistaken French policy, the persistent, well-intentioned, but ill-informed badgering of Churchill about India, and the breezy inanities about Canada does raise important questions. It might indicate that, at best, Roosevelt was having a revenance of the supercilious glibness of his youth that so irritated some of his contemporaries and many of the Oyster Bay relatives.

Such a development, given the immense position Roosevelt now occupied, would be pardonable, though disappointing. At worst, there is the possibility that precisely his position and all the attainments that had put him and kept him in it were starting to impart a false sense of infallibility that could lead to problems. He dropped the India matter, and didn't urge an assimilationist solution for the Quebecois on King again. Problems with France would recur, though he was addressing them in the last days of his presidency. No pattern of flippant superficiality, such as his opponents always claimed to detect, emerged in his behavior at this point or in the balance of the war, though it sometimes crept into his conversation.

But there was still an element of Roosevelt's personality that was self-indulgent, unrigorous, and unbecoming in so distinguished a holder of so great a place of historic trust.

In a "Dear Winston" letter of March 18, 1942, Roosevelt endearingly announced: "Here is a thought from this amateur strategist." After urging Churchill forward in the Near East and India, and promising to hold Australia, he forecast a "more definite plan" for Europe.

"By the time you get this you will have been advised of my talk with Litvinov, and I expect a reply from Stalin shortly. I know you will not mind my being brutally frank when I tell you that I think that I can personally handle Stalin better than either your Foreign Office or my State Department. Stalin hates the guts of all your top people. He thinks he likes me better, and I hope he will continue to do so." In fact, Roosevelt's discussions with Stalin were reasonably successful, but some of Roosevelt's flourishes and presumptions, as recited to Churchill, were gratuitous. In the same letter, he went on to lament the shortcomings of "My Navy" in combating German submarine activity on the U.S. Atlantic coast, before urging Churchill "to take a leaf out of my notebook," and take a long weekend holiday once a month. "I wish you would try it, and I wish you would lay a few bricks or paint another picture."

Churchill graciously replied April 1: "I am so grateful for all your thoughts about my affairs, and personal kindness," but did not reply to the references to Stalin. He suggested he might "propose myself for a weekend and flip over."

Roosevelt had refused to accept Churchill's suggestion of March 7 that the Baltic states of Estonia, Latvia, and Lithuania become part of the Soviet Union. They had been set up following the Treaty of Versailles, having long been ruled by Imperial Russia, and were reoccupied by Stalin in accord with the Nazi-Soviet Pact. Churchill emphasized that it was on this basis that Stalin had acceded to the Atlantic Charter. He cabled Stalin that he had made this recommendation to Roosevelt, who refused, however, to discuss territorial settlements before the end of the war.[11] Churchill had no such inhibitions.

In his April 28 Fireside Chat, Roosevelt started a practice that some of his successors (Reagan and Clinton in particular) would emulate at great length, of singling out individual heroic exploits for public appreciation. He mentioned two such cases on this occasion. These reflections were in refreshing contrast to his remarks at his regular press conference six months before on October 10, 1941, in which he revealed that 50 percent of the two million men who had thus far been called up in the draft had been disqualified as physically, mentally, or educationally unfit. Ten percent had not met fourth grade education standards; more than 10 percent were unfit for dental reasons, 6 percent had inadequate vision, and about 3 percent each suffered muscular, nervous or mental, or hearing problems, or had venereal diseases or hernias, and smaller but appreciable numbers had serious problems with feet or lungs. The Commander in Chief had been disconcerted then and publicly ruminated about a system of compulsory physical checkups, though he acknowledged there could be constitutional problems. A larger draft, military medical and remedial attention, and, almost certainly, somewhat lowered standards produced better results in 1942.

II

A FEW DAYS AFTER Roosevelt's April 28 address, and barely two weeks after Colonel Doolittle's raid on Japan, one of the war's most important naval battles began. The U.S. intelligence units that cracked the Japanese diplomatic code with the Magic system had by now broken into the Japanese naval code as well. (They had not done this prior to Pearl Harbor, contrary to the claims of the conspiracy theorists, but the Japanese fleet signals in the weeks leading to Pearl Harbor were extremely ambiguous even if they had been delivered in the clear.) Before opting for Yamamoto's plan of attacking Midway, the Japanese were still moving south, and thrust into the Coral Sea, between the Papuan Peninsula of New Guinea and the Australian state of Queensland. The Japanese occupied the small island of Tulagi in the Solomons, twenty miles from the larger island of Guadalcanal, on May 3, 1942. The Australians had already pulled out. Admiral Nimitz, advised by Naval Intelligence of the Japanese thrust into the Coral Sea, had assembled a substantial force under Admiral Frank Jack Fletcher, including the aircraft carriers *Yorktown* and *Lexington*, five heavy cruisers, and a variety of lesser craft.

The Battle of Coral Sea began with an attack on Tulagi by planes from the *Yorktown* on May 4, 1942. The battle, the first in the history of the world in which the opposing ships never had sight of each other, continued for four days. Both sides thought they had narrowly won the battle. The Japanese mistakenly believed they had sunk two American aircraft carriers; in fact, they had sunk only one, the *Lexington*, one of the United States' largest, and had damaged the *Yorktown.* But the Americans sank the smaller Japanese carrier *Sohyo*, severely damaged two of the largest carriers, and shot down forty-three Japanese planes and aircrews to thirty-three lost by themselves.

The Japanese withdrew, confident that they would soon return and deal with a less formidable foe, in their inexorable progress toward Australia. As the battle began, General Jonathan Wainwright, unable to hold out any longer against the Japanese, who had landed on Corregidor and captured half of it in desperate hand-to-hand fighting, surrendered. His and the garrison's resistance in the two months since MacArthur's departure had been magnificent. The whole defense of the Philippines, stretched out almost five months, had been a brave feat of arms by the defenders.

Before lunging again at Australia, Yamamoto insisted upon seizing Midway. Plans were put in hand and quickly picked up by American intelligence. The

Yorktown, in an astonishing performance by the dry dock crews at Pearl Harbor, was repaired adequately to sail again in forty-eight hours, not the ninety days originally feared. *Yorktown*, commanded by Fletcher, with escorting vessels, sailed May 29 and joined Admiral Raymond Spruance with *Enterprise* and *Hornet* and escorting vessels. Nimitz approximately equalized the numbers of aircraft on each side by flying in to Midway a large number of planes that would operate against the approaching Japanese from the island.

The Japanese divided their fleet into three forces. A comparatively small one was to bomb the Alaskan port of Dutch Harbor and make a diversionary landing on the barren islands of Attu and Kiska, starting June 3. The main force, commanded by Admiral Nagumo, who had been the fleet commander in the Pearl Harbor action, and spearheaded by four large aircraft carriers, was to attack Midway and land a substantial invasion force, carried on transports. A third force was between the other two, ready to move north if the Americans took the bait and sent their main fleet to the Aleutians, or south if the Americans resisted the bait and gave battle at Midway. Since Nimitz saw the Japanese dispositions because of the Magic decryptions, he ignored the Aleutian diversion and concentrated on Midway. The American fleet, with Fletcher in command, concentrated 200 miles north of the island to intercept the main Japanese force coming from the northwest.

An American reconnaissance plane sighted Nagumo's fleet 180 miles northwest of Midway shortly after dawn on June 3. Nagumo did not believe there were significant U.S. naval units then in the area, because he had sent out seven float planes to do a complete search within 250 miles. One of the planes had been late catapulting off, and the area where Fletcher and Spruance lurked had not been searched when Nagumo launched a large proportion of his planes against Midway. They met stubborn resistance from airborne American defenders. The reception was not at all reminiscent of Pearl Harbor, but most of the attacking planes returned safely to their carriers. Though they had done a good deal of damage, they had not knocked out the runways or destroyed the aircraft flying from the island. A second strike was necessary.

This was the dangerous point in the action, since the planes had to be taken below and reloaded with bombs. If there was a danger of enemy ships in the area, the planes would have to be fitted with torpedoes. Reloading or changing between bomb and torpedo payloads was a time-consuming process; if all the carriers were doing this at the same time, they would be largely or wholly undefended for half an hour or more.

Shortly after Nagumo's planes returned from Midway, he was attacked by twenty-six aircraft from Midway. The attack was unsuccessful, and fifteen of the attackers were shot down. It shook Nagumo's resolve, however. He decided to launch an all-out attack on Midway, having heard no report of American ships in the area. He had retained ninety-three aircraft for potential air defense of his fleet when he sent in the first wave of 108 planes against the island. He now ordered that all the planes that had been loaded with torpedoes (which would be useless in an attack on a land target) be changed to bomb-carrying aircraft and added to the second strike.

While this was in progress, the tardy float plane reported, at about 7:40 A.M., June 4, that it had sighted ten American surface ships. At 7:45 Nagumo ordered that those torpedo-carrying planes that had not yet been changed over to carry bombs be left as they were and brought back on deck to attack enemy ships as soon as the first-strike planes had returned. In response to a direct order to the reconnaissance plane that had sighted the American fleet, he was finally informed at 8:20 A.M. that there did "appear" to be "one" carrier among the U.S. ships. From 8:30 to 9:18, Nagumo's planes from the first strike on Midway were being landed on his flight decks. This was his greatest mistake. He should have kept one of the carriers clear to send up planes to attack the American ships, specifically the one carrier presumed to be among them, or at least to defend the airspace over his ships. Midway would not move as a target and there were still more than twelve hours of daylight. It was ironic that Nagumo had been too cautious in not ordering a further strike against Pearl Harbor on December 7, when its defenses had been decimated, but was impetuous in ordering a second strike against Midway now, despite dangerous movement by the U.S. Navy.

Spruance had launched most of his aircraft from *Enterprise* and *Hornet* against Nagumo at 7 A.M. and at long range, hoping to catch the Japanese recovering aircraft returning from Midway and not suspecting the presence of American carriers. In an all-out gamble, when he saw the Japanese reconnaissance plane, he sent even the thirty-six planes he had retained to cover his ships. As he had been discovered, he assumed it was now a race for each others' carriers. Fletcher had separated himself in *Yorktown*, having had confirmation of only two Japanese carriers in the force Spruance was attacking. At 8:30 A.M., Fletcher sent his torpedo bombers, half his dive bombers, and a few fighters to join Spruance's planes in the attack on the Japanese, retaining the rest of the fighters to protect *Yorktown* should she be discovered.

Nagumo scrambled up some planes as the recovery procedure was being completed shortly after 9:15 A.M. The first American wave, torpedo bombers that had become separated from their escorting fighters, attacked at 9:20. They were not successful, and thirty-five of forty-one were shot down by Nagumo's Zeros, which were thus drawn down almost to water level. This was providentially convenient for the dive bombers, which came in immediately after from a high altitude, braved intense antiaircraft fire, and avenged the American humiliations of the last six months by sinking the three carriers in the main force.

The fourth Japanese carrier sent its planes after the one American carrier believed to be in the area, and eventually found and mortally wounded the gallant *Yorktown*. Nagumo's carrier was among those sunk, and he transferred his flag, in the middle of the action, in a shore launch, to one of the cruisers. Fletcher, in *Yorktown*, was eventually forced to do the same. Midway thus became the second action in history in which the opposing vessels did not see each other, and the first in many decades when both opposing commanders had to transfer their flags to more seaworthy ships. While *Yorktown* was being attacked, the carrier from which the attacking Japanese planes were launched was discovered and sunk by planes from *Enterprise*, depriving the remaining Japanese planes of any landing surface. Japan's entire carrier force for this mission had been destroyed.

Yorktown, derelict but afloat, was taken in tow, but sunk by a Japanese submarine, for whom, inching through the water at two or three knots, she was an irresistible target. Yamamoto abandoned the attempt to take his "keyhole" and retired, decisively defeated. He was afraid that the victorious American carrier aircraft would discover and attack, virtually unopposed, his battleships and troop transports. The Japanese had lost four of their largest aircraft carriers, to only one lost by the Americans, and the Japanese had lost all of their nearly 300 planes and almost all the aircrews, while the United States lost only about 60 aircraft and saved a few of the downed men.

It was a turning point in the Pacific war and was instantly recognized as one by discerning people on both sides of the world conflict. There would be much hard fighting and the Japanese drive on Australia was powerfully resumed, but the United States had defeated its enemy in close combat and had regained a slender superiority in naval strength in the Pacific. A report from a U.S. bomber pilot — "Scratch one flat-top!" — became world-famous.

The Battle of Britain in 1940, the German failure to capture Moscow and Leningrad in 1941, and now Midway in 1942 were dramatic revelations of the limits of Axis power in the air and on land and sea.

The predictions of lack of military aptitudes of American draftees were proved to be unfounded, as Roosevelt and Churchill and de Gaulle (and Yamamoto) knew they would be. Holding on for five months in Bataan and Corregidor and scoring a partial victory in the Coral Sea and a crushing triumph a month later at Midway were impressive performances from a country taken so completely by surprise at the outset of hostilities. It was now only a very short time before the stupefying industrial might of the United States would inundate the battlefields, oceans, and skies of the world. There was consternation in Tokyo. In Washington, and throughout America and the British Commonwealth, the joy was unconfined. Both reactions were justified.

III

B Y THE TIME of Midway, the long-simmering Anglo-American disagreement about the timing of a landing in Western Europe was starting to surface as a major issue. Roosevelt had written Churchill a "Dear Winston" letter April 3, 1942, which accompanied Hopkins and Marshall when they went to London to gain British adherence to the grand strategy Roosevelt and his advisors had worked out. In the April 3 letter, Roosevelt referred to "the establishment of a front to draw off pressure on the Russians, [who] are today killing more Germans and destroying more equipment than you and I put together."

Roosevelt's motive opposite Stalin was not entirely altruistic. All of the Big Three were afraid that the great German drive to the east about to be launched would be one of irresistible force. Hitler knew that everything now depended on his ability to eliminate Stalin before the full weight of the United States was committed to the war. Hitler's position vis-à-vis Stalin was now comparable to Wilhelm's facing Foch and Clemenceau in 1917. Roosevelt didn't want Stalin flattened or resigned to a separate peace with Germany, even on relatively favorable terms. The nightmare scenario, next to outright German victory in the east, was a return to Hitler-Stalin cooperation caused by Stalin's ceasing to believe the British and Americans would land in Western Europe early or numerously enough to help him.

Hopkins and Marshall arrived in London April 8, called upon Churchill, and received an early agreement in principle on a cross-Channel landing. This impressed Hopkins, accustomed to the prime minister's wiles, less than Marshall, who, though suspicious of the British generally, was inclined at this early stage to take Churchill's word at face value. They were back for dinner at Downing Street on the evening of the 8th, and Churchill's discursive treatment of a great miscellany of subjects not germane to the present conflict, such as the U.S. Civil War, kindled fears in Marshall and stoked them up in Hopkins. The deputy prime minister and leader of the Labour Party, Clement Attlee, and the new chief of the Imperial General Staff, General Sir Alan Brooke, were also present. Marshall did not emerge with a high opinion of Brooke, and the reverse was true also, though Brooke was impressed with Marshall's bearing and upright personality.

Hopkins had some concerns that the British, who had feared an excessive American preoccupation with the Japanese in the aftermath of Pearl Harbor, were now themselves too preoccupied with the Pacific theater, eager to preserve their Indian empire and to regain other South Asian and Far Eastern interests. However, he was eventually satisfied at the degree of Churchill's commitment to the cross-Channel invasion, and Hopkins and Marshall returned happily to the United States on April 12. Churchill acknowledges in his memoirs that he was less than candid in these discussions.[12]

In his letter to Roosevelt of April 17, Churchill subordinated the idea of an early attack across the English Channel to the necessity of reinforcing India and the Burma theater, as he put it in that cable, "to prevent a junction of the Japanese and the Germans." This was nonsense; Rommel was being held and Churchill had written many times recently that he did not think Japan capable of erupting into India.

This disparity of purpose was already developing when, in response to Roosevelt's invitation to Stalin, Molotov, on his way to Washington to receive Roosevelt's war plans, stopped in London May 20, 1942. Molotov arrived with a draft treaty giving his country the Nazi-Soviet Pact frontiers. Winant assisted Churchill and Eden in rebutting this, and Eden proposed, and Molotov, after receiving authority from Stalin, accepted, a twenty-year friendship treaty with Great Britain that made no mention of frontiers.

Churchill waffled on the question of an early second front in Western Europe. When pressed by Molotov on what would happen if Russia were overwhelmed by the new German offensive, Churchill dismissed the idea and finally took refuge in his usual pipedream about the blockade, air war, aid to resistance movements, and amphibious landings around the German-occupied perimeter. Molotov must have known this to be a fantasy, but after he had left for Washington, Churchill cabled Roosevelt, May 28: "We made great progress in intimacy and good will." So canny an anti-Communist as Churchill could not have believed that either, so even at this early date an air of make-believe was already enveloping some of the proceedings of the Big Three.

Molotov arrived for his first meeting with Roosevelt at the White House on May 29. Roosevelt found him impenetrably phlegmatic. The usual invincible Roosevelt charm, which Churchill's daughter, Lady Soames, many years later described to this author as "like the beam of a great lighthouse suddenly trained on you," was blunted in this case by translation and by Molotov's stolid personality. Compared with Molotov, the dour General George Marshall "was a riotously entertaining companion."[13] (The ambiance of the visit was not helped by the White House valet's discovery, as he unpacked the Russian foreign minister's luggage, of a revolver in his suitcase.)

Hopkins considered Molotov much more affable than when he had seen him in Moscow. But the initial meeting was frittered in unproductive conversation initiated by Hull over the application of the Geneva Convention to the treatment of German and Russian prisoners of war and a rather naïve offer of State Department good offices in Soviet dealings with Turkey and Iran. Molotov said, from some experience, that there was no point making agreements with Hitler and that his ministry knew more about Russian relations with its ancient neighbors than the State Department did.[14]

The next day, May 30, Molotov met with Roosevelt, Hopkins, Marshall, and King. It was indicative of his current standing that Hull, Molotov's analogue at the head of the State Department, was not invited. Molotov's military advisor had been forced to remain behind in London, where he had broken his knee in an automobile accident. Molotov forcefully asked if there would be a second front in Western Europe in 1942. He expressed the Soviet desire for such an action to draw off forty German divisions from the Russian front. He recognized that this was a British decision principally, because at this stage the British and Canadians would be putting up most of the manpower.

Roosevelt, and probably Molotov, knew that Churchill had no enthusiasm for any such landing for a long time, if ever. The chances of a massacre of Anglo-American-Canadian forces on the beaches were far greater than the possibilities, real though they were, of a decisive German victory in the East. The Germans already had in France forces sufficient to deal with any invasion force the Western Allies could produce in 1942, so the whole discussion was somewhat esoteric.

Roosevelt deferred to Marshall and invited him to answer Molotov's question. Marshall said a second front was being prepared, and Roosevelt then interjected that the United States did expect to create such a front in the current year. Marshall considered this impetuous, since the clear implication was that it would be a landing in northern France, not a coastal raid nor one of Churchill's peripheral distractions. Marshall said the hope was to launch such an attack, forcing a final struggle in the air that the West would win over Germany.

But Marshall cautioned that while there were the men, armor, and aviation for such an invasion, there was not the shipping nor landing craft. (Given the ability of the United States to build in a year ten million tons of merchant shipping, and nearly a million tons of naval shipping, as Roosevelt had announced to Congress January 6, it is mystifying that the construction of simple, small landing craft always loomed as such an obstacle. Marshall alleged that he had to overcome opposition from the navy, both the admirals and the Bureau of Yards and Docks, who wanted real ships and not just landing craft. They looked upon the landing craft as an indulgence of the army. This is one area where it is regrettable that Roosevelt didn't assert presidential authority earlier.)[15]

Roosevelt had a schedule of Lend-Lease materiel that would be produced in the year that would begin July 1, 1942. It comprised eight million tons, but only slightly over half could be delivered to the Soviet Union, said Roosevelt, because of shipping insufficiencies. The following day, Roosevelt clarified that if there were to be a cross-Channel assault, that half would be further reduced and only about 2.5 million tons of Lend-Lease materiel could be delivered to the Soviet Union.

Roosevelt had to break off this meeting with Molotov, Hopkins, and Litvinov to receive the Duke and Duchess of Windsor. (Roosevelt's indulgence of these two is difficult to understand. He suspected the Duke of being an appeaser and a Nazi dupe, he had no regard for people who abdicated, and he once wrote to the well-known journalist Fulton Oursler that he had more respect for the opinions of Oursler's eight-year-old daughter than for those of "little Windsor." The Windsors had, on this occasion, "invited themselves" to Washington. Roosevelt referred to them in a cable to Churchill May 26, as "your Nassau friends."[16]

Molotov became a bit testy, and seemed not to understand the difficulty of shipping millions of tons of tanks, aircraft, munitions, industrial goods, and general supplies, via Murmansk and Iran, from the United States to the Soviet Union. (The United States did deliver to the Soviet Union 13,500 combat aircraft over three years.) When Roosevelt told him he "couldn't have his cake and eat it too," Molotov replied that he would have to have an absolute assurance of a real second front, not merely the President's "expectation" of one. Roosevelt managed to finesse this with a powerful restatement of his expectation, still stopping short of a guarantee.

He also expanded on his plan for a postwar international organization in which the United States, the United Kingdom, the Soviet Union, and China would be the world's "four policemen." This seemed to improve the atmospherics somewhat. Roosevelt certainly knew, and Molotov was almost certainly astute enough to recognize, that there would be no invasion of Western Europe in 1942, but the roundel of comradely assurances continued, and Molotov returned to London on June 4.

Here, Churchill engaged in even more legerdemain than had Roosevelt. He fobbed off on Molotov a promise to invade Western Europe in 1942 unless the likelihood was that any such effort would be a disaster, and so his promise was conditional on such an enterprise's seeming "sound and sensible."[17] Just before Molotov returned to London, Britain launched the first of its thousand bomber raids against a German city—in this case, Cologne, on May 30. (Roosevelt called it "Saturday night's show" in a cable to Churchill June 1.) Fortunes in the air war had turned decisively; it was only twenty months since the most critical phase of the Battle of Britain.

On June 3, Admiral Louis Mountbatten, a protégé of Churchill's whom he had placed in charge of commando operations (and a cousin of King George VI and the Duke of Windsor), traveled to the United States with Generals Arnold, Mark Clark, and Eisenhower. Joint staff talks took place the next day, as news came steadily in of the proportions of the great victory at Midway.

Mountbatten had clearly been designated by Churchill to commence the intricate task of extracting Britain from the obligation to invade Western Europe. He met the President with Hopkins but without, to their chagrin, King or Marshall, for dinner on June 9. Roosevelt expressed great concern about the ability of the Russians to withstand the German offensive that had finally begun, and did not want to accumulate one million U.S. soldiers sitting in the British Isles if there was nothing for them to do. Mountbatten dwelt on the landing craft shortage and the fact that since the Germans already had twenty-five divisions in France the British did not see how a successful landing could be made in 1942, and did not see how the Allied cause, and especially the Russians, would be helped by a bloodbath on the beach followed by a humiliating evacuation. This seems to have been the beginning of a warming up of "Gymnast," an Allied landing in North Africa. Roosevelt said that he was not prepared to send Americans to replace the British as a home guard in England while the British sent all their soldiers to the Near East and India.

Marshall was already irritated that the defeat of the Japanese at Midway, which finished whatever slender hope the enemy had of invading India, had apparently increased the British determination to send forces to that theater. King and MacArthur were calling for a vast addition of U.S. Army forces to drive the Japanese back and liberate the Philippines. At the same time the British, who six months before had been concerned that the United States might feel it had to avenge itself against Japan to the detriment of carrying the war to Germany, were now trying to conduct the war everywhere except across the Channel, against the most vulnerable point of the most formidable enemy.

———————

Churchill cabled Roosevelt on June 13, suggesting that he come to Washington five days later, a proposal Roosevelt was happy to accept. Churchill would bring his new chief of the Imperial General Staff, General Sir Alan Brooke, "whom you have not yet met," he cabled Roosevelt. Churchill told Brooke, on the basis of what Mountbatten had told him, that Roosevelt "was getting a little off the rails."[18] As Churchill and Brooke flew to Washington in one of Roosevelt's splendid clipper flying boats on June 18, the Germans were driving powerfully forward on the southeastern front in Russia, toward the Caucasus oil fields, and in the western desert, where they were approaching the Egyptian border.

Roosevelt was at Hyde Park, and on the morning of June 19 Churchill, with whom the President evidently wished to confer privately, flew to Poughkeepsie, where Roosevelt awaited him at the little aerodrome in his Ford convertible with all manual controls. He gave Churchill a motor tour of his property with the same apparent insouciance toward sharp corners and precipices that had alarmed King George VI and Queen Elizabeth three years before. Churchill admired the great muscularity of Roosevelt's arms and chest, and his host even invited him to test his biceps, assuring the prime minister that the prizefighter Jack Dempsey had been impressed with them. So, he recorded in his memoirs, was Churchill, who had taken virtually no physical exercise for decades. (He said that he occasionally had the urge, but lay down with a snifter of brandy in hand until the urge passed.)

At Hyde Park Roosevelt and Churchill began by discussing atomic developments. It was agreed that the United States and the United Kingdom would share equally in the project. This was a mere semblance, however, as the United States would conduct and pay for the research and manufacture the bombs, should this seem practical.

Churchill presented his views on a 1942 cross-Channel invasion in terms that were virtually unassailable. There was no plan that would lead to anything but a humiliating rout of the Allies, and that would do nothing useful for the Russians. Churchill and Brooke purported to believe that the Russians stood a better chance this year than they had when surprised the year before by an undefeated and unblooded Germany (on land). Churchill suggested that unless the Americans had a plan for an invasion of France that hadn't occurred to the British, they should look at Gymnast—an invasion of French North Africa. (The code words used were "Sledgehammer," for a diversionary or even sacrificial landing in northwest Europe; "Bolero," for such an invasion in 1943; and "Roundup," for the preparations for such a campaign.)

Roosevelt and Churchill returned to Washington on the President's train overnight June 20–21, and Roosevelt arranged for Marshall to join them the following morning. Brooke was immediately overpowered by the mighty charm and gracious confidence of his host, which was amplified in this case by the fact that Roosevelt's father had known Brooke's father and had received him at Hyde Park. As Churchill remarked in his memoirs: "[Roosevelt's] field of interest was always brightened by recollections of his youth."[19] The impression Roosevelt made on such sophisticated people as Brooke at this point in his career was remarkable. His powerful torso and leonine head, in such vivid contrast to his handicap, of which he seemed to take no notice at all, to the point that others were not overly conscious of it; his animated features and strong but melodious voice; the immense wealth and power of his country, already beginning to ride the tide of victory back across the Pacific; and his huge, unprecedented mandate (three terms from the world's largest electorate) and legendary political skill all conferred on him an enormous prestige and power.

To the oppressed and war-ravaged masses of Europe, as to the underprivileged peoples of South America who came out in millions to see him when he visited there in 1936, he was the magical leader of the golden country. Roosevelt wore lightly and unselfconsciously the mantle of the hopes and the great renown he had inspired. He was sometimes flippant, as when he lectured Churchill about India, but his personality never changed with his few confidants. He never showed the slightest interest in office merely for the sake of clinging to it, but was always pursuing new and higher levels of positive government. His remarkable personality was rarely better displayed than on the occasion of this visit from the British prime minister.

In the early afternoon of June 21, as Roosevelt and Churchill were in conversation, Roosevelt was handed a telegram. He glanced at it and gave it without comment to Churchill. Churchill had expected the redoubt of Tobruk, almost on the Libyan-Egyptian border, even though almost surrounded by Rommel, to hold out as it had the previous year, until a counterattack could be launched against the Afrika Korps. The note Roosevelt handed Churchill announced that Tobruk had surrendered to Rommel. The British garrison of 33,000 had surrendered to Rommel's smaller force, giving up, instead of destroying them, vast quantities of oil, gasoline, aviation fuel, and munitions and stores of all kinds.

This was becoming a depressing pattern for Churchill; as with Singapore, there was a great fanfare about the impregnability of an imperial fortress, or, in this case, outpost, and a humiliating and sudden collapse. Churchill and Brooke recounted in their memoirs that they were thunderstruck by this catastrophe and had not considered any such result possible. Churchill wrote: "At Singapore, 85,000 men had surrendered to inferior numbers of Japanese. Now in Tobruk a garrison of [33,000] seasoned soldiers had laid down their arms to perhaps one half of their number. . . . I did not attempt to hide from the President the shock I had received. It was a bitter moment. Defeat is one thing; disgrace is another." The prime minister wrote angrily of British soldiers having "put up their hands." Singapore and Tobruk, he wrote, "had affected the reputation of the British armies."[20]

Roosevelt uttered not a word of criticism or even disappointment and asked immediately: "What can we do to help?" Churchill replied almost as quickly, asking that as many Sherman tanks as possible be shipped at once to the Middle East. This was a new medium tank that had just gone into production, and only a few hundred had been delivered to the U.S. Army. Marshall, whom Roosevelt had sent for, said that it was "a terrible thing to take the weapons out of a soldier's hands," but that the British need was such that it had to be done. Three hundred Shermans and one hundred self-propelled 105-millimeter guns were dispatched in the next few days for Egypt in fast transports, and when one of the ships was torpedoed off Bermuda, Marshall replaced its cargo and sent an even faster cargo ship to assure prompt delivery. This generosity, without a hint of reproach, lack of confidence, or condescension, made an indelible impression on both Churchill and Brooke. "Nothing could exceed the sympathy and chivalry of my two friends," wrote Churchill of Roosevelt and Hopkins.[21] (Marshall's recollections, recounted to his authorized biographer, were that the Sherman tank offer was worked up over meetings in the next two days and was actually first suggested by Marshall himself.)

The reason normally given for Rommel's advance across North Africa at lightning speed was air superiority. If the British could hurl a thousand-bomber raid against a nonmilitary site like Cologne, it is an abiding mystery why they should have had such difficulty providing adequate air support in North Africa.

Churchill swiftly recovered his composure and in the afternoon of June 21, meeting with the larger staffs, made an impassioned plea for an invasion of Morocco and Algeria, as a complement to, and not a substitute for, an early invasion of France. This was seen at once by Marshall and the other Americans as disingenuous; they feared that what was afoot was a prolonged British effort to waste time and resources in the Mediterranean and Indian Oceans and avoid getting to grips with the real enemy. Roosevelt and Marshall, who had resisted the demands of King and MacArthur to give priority to the Pacific, felt let down, because the British strategy seemed to them to be composed of equal parts of fear of directly challenging the German Army and a desire to conscript the United States to help them shore up the extremities of their threadbare Empire.

Churchill claimed that taking North Africa would lead to the fall of Mussolini, confirming Marshall in his fear that this, and not the earliest possible assault on Hitler, was Churchill's real aim. Marshall concluded that Churchill intended to invade Italy, which would draw Hitler into Italy in territory where every advantage was with the defender, that an invasion of France would be delayed sine die, and that, unless Roosevelt forced the issue, it would then be necessary to jettison the cornerstone of their strategy and subdue Japan ahead of Germany. Marshall had been prepared to dispense with Sledgehammer, the diversionary strike in France, in exchange for a British guarantee of a serious invasion of France in 1943. Marshall now felt deceived by Churchill and resurrected Sledgehammer with great energy. It was a potentially dangerous impasse.

Marshall took Churchill and Brooke to watch extensive field exercises by U.S. Army units at Fort Jackson, South Carolina, June 24. The heat reminded Churchill of his army days in India.[22] It was an impressive performance, but the British, while marveling at Marshall's ability to create an army so quickly out of conscripts who had been a rag-tag of file clerks and farmers and factory workers a few months before, did not consider these forces possibly ready to argue the issue with the battle-hardened Germans. They were almost certainly right, just as Marshall had been right that Churchill had misled him. Marshall may have been overambitious about engaging the enemy, but Churchill was too reluctant, and his dissembling antagonized the U.S. chief of staff, who found his own commander in chief's jejuneries challenging enough. The Alliance was starting to show all the problems traditional to coalitions, and it would be up to Roosevelt to sort it out.

Churchill and Brooke returned to the United Kingdom by flying boat June 25, 1942, and Churchill closed out debate on July 2 in a confidence debate in the House of Commons that had been demanded by some opposition M.P.s following the fall of Tobruk. Churchill didn't feel the need to recount what his government had accomplished. Almost all conscient people in the world knew that already. He asked for a vote that did not dismay Britain's allies and provoke rejoicing in Berlin, Tokyo, and Rome. Churchill and his government won by the margin of 475 to 25. He received this cable: "Good for you. Roosevelt".[23]

———

As Churchill bulldogged his way through his third consecutive summer of mortal crisis, Stalin again felt the German noose tighten around his neck. Matters could hardly be as dangerous for Churchill as during the Battle of Britain in 1940 or the shambles in the Balkans and Greece and the inauspicious beginning of the Russo-German War in 1941, while the Battle of the Atlantic raged, but the summer of 1942 was Hitler's supreme offensive effort.

Because of the porosity of American antisubmarine measures along the Atlantic Coast, that area was what Churchill called "a U-boat paradise."[24] The Allies contrived to lose 400,000 tons of shipping in the second week of July alone, but Admiral King was preparing a comprehensive convoy system for coastal waters and there was a reasonable hope that that week was aberrant. The normal rate of loss through the spring, of 600,000 tons per month, was desperately costly but barely sustainable. King, and Stark before him, could have moved more quickly to coastal convoys and the imposition of blackout rules on the Atlantic shore.

Rommel had advanced to within seventy-five miles of Alexandria and was facing the final line of defense of the British in Egypt. In keeping with the well-established practice of the Allied officers consistently underestimating each other, U.S. Army intelligence confidently told Marshall and ultimately Roosevelt that Rommel would be at the Suez Canal in three more weeks. Roosevelt had more faith in the British, and Marshall too was unconvinced, but the situation was so serious that on July 2, Marshall urged Hopkins to ask Roosevelt to prepare the country for Allied defeat in Egypt. Roosevelt wouldn't hear of it and did not feel he needed Marshall's advice on how to maintain public morale.[25] The Suez Canal and with it, to some extent, the British ability to govern India, which was now in a state of partial revolt fomented by Gandhi and Nehru, the oil of the Middle East, and the fate of the religious cradle of the Western and Middle Eastern worlds all hung in the balance. The British had contingency plans to block the Suez Canal so it could not be used for six months if the Germans gained possession of it.

The great German drive into Russia had cleared the defenders out of the Crimea and was surging toward the Caucasus. A collapse on the Russian and Middle Eastern fronts would make it a very long war indeed. There wasn't much chance of Britain's being overrun, as there had been two years before, or even of being starved, as there was the year before. But the Empire was under almost unbearable strain at many points, and Roosevelt and Churchill's Russian ally was approaching the outer limits of his endurance.

It was determined to launch a counteroffensive against the Japanese in the Solomon Islands and New Guinea, to push the enemy back from the approaches to Australia and begin the long drive back toward the Philippines. Roosevelt would not hear of diverting forces from the European to the Pacific theater, as MacArthur was endlessly demanding, but the Solomon and New Guinea actions would consume a lot of attention and resources, including much-needed landing craft.

On July 4, Churchill, having learned that forty A-20 Boston bombers were in Iraq on their way to the Soviet Union, asked Roosevelt if they could be rerouted to Egypt. He expressed a perfect understanding, given the difficulties on the Russian front, if this was impossible, but stated: "our needs are great." Roosevelt consulted Stalin, pointing out that if the battle were lost in Egypt, the entire route of supply of Russia through the Persian Gulf would be lost. Stalin promptly agreed. Roosevelt also rerouted a shipment of bombers bound for Chiang Kai-shek, who was a good deal less philosophical about it than Stalin had been, and required reassurance that the Western Allies took the China theater seriously. (Roosevelt took the theater seriously; he wasn't as convinced about Chiang himself.)

IV

ALL THREE OF the principal Allied leaders showed their mettle in the summer of 1942, as each coped with severe crises. On July 8, the British advised that they would not proceed with Sledgehammer (the diversionary landing in France that had no real hope of success but was designed to force the transfer of German divisions from Russia to the west). It was, as has been recorded, a wildly impractical scheme, as Marshall knew. But the British had, he thought, just a few days before, undertaken to wait until September 1 to decide whether to proceed with it or launch Gymnast (the invasion of French North Africa). Marshall regarded this as a nonsensical plan, because he attached no military value to Algeria and Morocco and wished to fight Germans, not the Vichy French. Field Marshal Sir John Dill delivered this news to Marshall and witnessed the apparently volcanic spectacle of one of Marshall's rages. Marshall implied that he would rather reinforce MacArthur's offensive, which at least was directed at a real enemy, than Gymnast, which he regarded as romantic foolishness designed to lure the United States into the Mediterranean and keep it there.

At a Joint Chiefs of Staff meeting July 10, Marshall secured adoption of a paper for the President proposing that unless the British committed unreservedly to a cross-Channel operation on a convincing scale in 1943, the United States should focus on the war against Japan. Admiral King, who was not greatly better disposed to the British than Admiral Darlan (though he was in all other respects a greatly superior character and probably a more competent admiral other than politically), was delighted at the prospect of pouring forces into the Pacific against the enemy that had done such damage to his navy.

The memo containing the Marshall recommendation was delivered to Roosevelt at Hyde Park July 11. He telephoned Washington and instructed that King and Marshall send him at once their detailed plans for their Pacific alternative. As there were no such plans in existence, its sponsors in waiting were obliged to admit that a great deal of time would be lost transferring men, shipping, and materiel from the eastern Atlantic to the western Pacific.

Roosevelt was shocked by the petulance and the strategic absurdity of the Marshall proposal. He had not lost confidence in his army chief of staff but took the production of such a silly proposal as evidence of the general's great exasperation with the British. He told Marshall on July 14 that he did not approve the Pacific proposal and was sending Marshall and King to London July 16, with Hopkins as a chaperone, to ensure that relations with the British didn't deteriorate further. Roosevelt told Marshall and Stimson, whom Marshall had dragooned to second his reckless proposal, on July 15, that withdrawing from Europe could deliver all of that theater, including the Middle East and North Africa, to Hitler, to whom the defeat of Japan would be irrelevant. Instead of lecturing them to pull themselves together and behave rationally, he expressed great sympathy for the vagaries of coalition planning. Withal, the British were distinguished, brave, and essential allies who were now very stretched, and to give them an ultimatum and threaten to decamp altogether to the Pacific was unthinkable.

He was sending Marshall, Hopkins, and King to London to reach an agreement by which all would abide. They were free to press hard for Sledgehammer (which Churchill, Brooke, Roosevelt, Marshall, and Stimson, all knew to be a bad idea), but failing that they were to agree to some plausible plan that would get American forces into action in this theater against the Germans in 1942. The Middle East and Gymnast were envisioned as alternatives to Sledgehammer, and Gymnast had the advantage of being an all-American operation. The German dimension of it would arise when, as was envisioned, the operations continued through Algeria and into Tunisia, which was the staging area for the German assault on Egypt. The President gave his emissaries one week to reach agreement, a date that was reinforced by Hopkins's planned White House marriage on July 30 to Louise Macy. (Hopkins's previous wife had died in 1937.)

The Americans landed in Scotland on July 18. Churchill had sent his train for them and invited them for the weekend to his country house at Chequers. Marshall disregarded this invitation and required the train to go straight to London, where he met with General Eisenhower, who had already set up an expeditionary forces office in Grosvenor Square, and with some of the British service chiefs. Erupting at this insolence, Churchill screamed down the telephone at a weary and apprehensive Hopkins in Claridge's. Hopkins made a placatory trip to Chequers on Sunday, July 19, and had restored the prime minister's good mood by the end of the day.

Discussions opened under Churchill's chairmanship at 10 Downing Street on July 20 and moved around during the week to Claridge's, to Eisenhower's headquarters on Grosvenor Square, and to Whitehall. On July 24, after a great deal of robust discussion moderated skillfully by Hopkins and stopping short of recriminations, it was agreed that Gymnast, with both Atlantic and Mediterranean amphibious landings, would be launched in October. There was a further recommitment to a cross-Channel invasion of France by July of 1943, though no one seems to have believed that this would prove feasible.

Roosevelt cabled Churchill on July 27: "I cannot help feeling that last week represented a turning point in the whole war." The July 30 meeting concluded that Gymnast would be decided by September 15. Roosevelt read this note and summoned Admiral Leahy, who in addition to being FDR's military chief of staff was now chairman of the Joint Chiefs of Staff, but without direct authority over the constituent forces; he was more of a nonexecutive arbiter between Marshall and King. Roosevelt told him that the decision had already been taken, that Gymnast was on, and that this was final. Marshall still obstructed the preparations, and was as churlish and devious as he had rightly accused the British of being. It would be Marshall's dilatory activities that would delay Gymnast for two weeks after its revised deadline, taking it past the midterm elections and probably causing Roosevelt the loss of twenty congressmen. As election day approached, Roosevelt made no effort to bring the day forward, nor to influence purely military matters at all.

In assuaging the British, hosing down his chief of staff, and producing a military plan that proved to be workable, Roosevelt demonstrated, once again, formidable aptitudes for leadership in the most charged circumstances. He was proving to be one of those rare leaders whose talents are as well deployed and as successful in war as in peace. The same could not be said of Winston Churchill, who was not an unusually imaginative or successful peacetime prime minister, and it is only conjecture that it might be true of Abraham Lincoln.

It was now Churchill's turn to demonstrate, yet again, his undoubted genius as a statesman. Arctic convoy PQ 17 had arrived in Archangel July 14, and only eight ships out of thirty-three ran the gauntlet successfully. As Churchill pointed out to Roosevelt in a cable of that day, nearly 500 of 600 tanks had been lost, and at this time of year, with almost permanent daylight, it was almost impossible to counter the enemy's ability to interdict from the air and with submarines. Churchill proposed to suspend the Arctic convoys and sent Roosevelt a draft of a cable he contemplated sending to Stalin informing him of that unwelcome fact.

In his message to Stalin, Churchill requested three divisions of Poles for Palestine, which Stalin had tentatively offered, despite "the Poles wanting to bring with the troops a considerable mass of their women and children who are largely dependent on the rations of the Polish soldiers." He made his customary hopeful statements about defeating Rommel and concluded: "Believe me, my comrade and friend, there is nothing that is useful and sensible that we and the Americans will not do to help you in your grand struggle."

Roosevelt acknowledged on July 15 that the "message to Stalin is a good one." After discussion with Admiral King, he couldn't take issue with the decision to suspend the convoys, but gently suggested that Americans take over the operation of the railway in Iran, with a view to upgrading it and replacing some of the supplies lost to their Russian ally with the Arctic convoy. Churchill sent the message, to which Stalin reacted very antagonistically on July 28. He suggested that the just-concluded conference with Hopkins, Marshall, and King had determined not to make a serious landing in Western Europe in 1942, which, Stalin said, the Soviet Union "cannot tolerate."[26]

Since Stalin's suspicions were correct, Churchill and Roosevelt considered how to impart this to him without destabilizing their alliance with him, given the desperation of the Russo-German struggle. Churchill had already resolved, as he told Harriman July 24, to go to Moscow and tell Stalin himself that there would be no second front in 1942, but Gymnast instead. He had also resolved to stop in Cairo on the way to Moscow and sack his Middle Eastern commander, Sir Claude Auchinleck, as he had dismissed his predecessor, General Archibald Wavell. For good measure, Churchill decided to try to quell the unrest in India by arresting the Congress leadership, including Gandhi and Nehru.

The War Cabinet approved Churchill's trip to Egypt and Russia July 28, at a meeting attended by King George VI himself (a very rare occurrence). Churchill requested an invitation from Stalin July 28, and indicated a hopefulness about restoring the Arctic convoys in September. (PQ 18 did sail in September, escorted by sixteen destroyers and an aircraft carrier; twenty-seven of thirty-seven ships got through and the convoys were resumed.) Stalin invited him to Moscow at his early convenience July 29. Churchill departed August 2, flying to Gibraltar, and then over Spanish and French Morocco with a fighter escort. Churchill remarked dryly in his memoirs: "It would have been very tiresome to make a forced landing on neutral territory." There were no problems; the fighters retired when darkness fell, and Churchill's four-engine bomber lumbered through the night over the desert and landed at Cairo shortly after dawn on August 4.

Harriman suggested to Eden that he, Harriman, join Churchill to assure Stalin that the British prime minister was not misrepresenting the American position. Eden mentioned this idea to Churchill, who asked Roosevelt to authorize it. The President did so, having initially been skeptical when Harriman suggested it himself. Harriman caught up with Churchill in Cairo, where the prime minister remained with Brooke and the rest of his entourage until August 10. Churchill requested the presence in Cairo of the prime minister of South Africa, Field Marshal Jan Christian Smuts, whom he regarded as one of the wisest and steadiest men he had known, and with whom he had been friendly since they met in the Boer War forty years before. In conference with Brooke and Smuts, Churchill decided to cut the Middle East command in half, having a Near East commander based in Cairo and in charge of Egypt, Palestine, and Syria, and a Middle East commander based in Baghdad and dealing with Iraq and Iran.

The Middle East command would be offered to Auchinleck, and his Eighth Army commander, General Sir Neil Ritchie, was invited to go with Auchinleck. Churchill proposed to give the Near East command to General Sir Harold Alexander, then Eisenhower's chief British colleague in the European command, which would soon be growing by about 80,000 Americans and perhaps 20,000 British and Canadian soldiers per month. The proposed replacement for Alexander in Torch (as Gymnast had been renamed) was General Bernard Law Montgomery, and for Ritchie, General W.H.E. "Straffer" Gott, one of the most successful of the brigade commanders on the western desert.

The War Cabinet balked at the division of the regional command, and Auchinleck didn't want the Baghdad post anyway, and Gott was shot down and killed by a German fighter on August 6, in airspace quite close to that which Churchill had just flown through. Now Alexander was to be Middle East commander, Montgomery Eighth Army commander, and General Kenneth Anderson Eisenhower's chief British subordinate in Torch. When Eisenhower was told in the most laudatory terms of the splendid qualities of this third principal British subordinate in a few days, he remarked that the British Army seemed to have "a lot of Wellingtons."[27] Auchinleck went to India, and all these appointments proved to be very successful. Churchill had had to shuffle his North African generals like Lincoln changing his leading army commanders, but in the one case as in the other, winning combinations were found eventually.

With this work efficiently accomplished, Churchill left Cairo August 10 for Moscow, via Teheran. Here Harriman had preceded him to look at the railway.

As the former chairman of the Union Pacific Railway, he had been designated by Roosevelt to examine the possibilities of moving more supplies to the Russians by this route. Harriman eventually made proposals, especially the use of diesel rather than coal-burning locomotives, that more than doubled shipments by this method, from 3,000 to over 7,000 tons per day.

Cadogan, and Wavell, who spoke Russian, had joined the party, which took off for Moscow in two planes. Churchill and Harriman flew well to the east to avoid the moving battlefront, which was now only thirty-five miles from Stalingrad, and they approached Moscow via Kuibyshev. Churchill would write: "I pondered on my mission to this sullen, sinister, Bolshevik State I had once tried so hard to strangle at its birth, and which, until Hitler appeared, I had regarded as the mortal foe of civilized freedom."

Arriving in the late afternoon of August 12, they were elaborately received at the airport by Molotov, with "a concourse of generals and the entire diplomatic corps," and Churchill was conducted to his guest house, "State Villa No. 7." (He noted when he lowered the car window for some fresh air that the glass was over two inches thick. "This surpassed all records in my experience."[28] The villa had spacious grounds, an extensive bomb shelter eighty feet below the ground, and a pond of tame goldfish that reminded Churchill of his own at Chartwell. "After all necessary immersions and ablutions," Churchill was conducted to "the Kremlin and met for the first time the great Revolutionary Chief and profound Russian statesman and warrior with whom for the next three years I was to be in intimate, rigorous, but always exciting, and at times even genial, association." In addition to the two premiers, Harriman, two interpreters, Molotov, defense commissar Marshal Klimenti Voroshilov, and the British ambassador in Moscow, Sir Archibald Clark Kerr, were present, but no one spoke except Stalin and Churchill (and the interpreters).

It was, as had been anticipated, a difficult session, and it lasted four hours. Churchill began by stating there would be no second front in Europe in 1942. He said that he and Roosevelt did not shrink from losses, but squandering forces on the beachheads of France would not achieve anything for Russia and would weaken the effort planned for the following year; by the spring of 1943, he said, the British and the Americans would have nearly fifty divisions, half of them armor, ready for an invasion of France. (In fact, as we know and Stalin suspected, Churchill was merely trying to defer the cross-Channel landings from year to year, not really committing to a 1943 invasion.) Stalin asked Churchill, "Why are you so afraid of the Germans? . . . Troops must be blooded in battle."[29]

Churchill determinedly parried the skepticism of the coauthor of the Nazi-Soviet Pact and addressed instead a fellow opponent of appeasement. He pointed out why such a landing would be impossible, citing the fact that Hitler had been unable to invade Britain in 1940 as illustrative of the difficulty of cross-Channel landings. Stalin distinguished the two situations by reference to the comparatively greater strength of the Western Allies in 1942, the absorption of Germany's armed strength in Russia, and the difference between the British defending their island in 1940 and the French welcoming liberators in 1942.

The atmosphere improved somewhat when Churchill described in detail the extent of the bombing campaign against Germany. Then he drew a diagram of a crocodile and handed it to Stalin, emphasizing the "soft underbelly," which he represented as the Mediterranean theater. Stalin may have been bemused by the zoological reference; when Churchill emphasized secrecy, Stalin sardonically expressed the hope that the Churchill-Roosevelt war plan would not be revealed in the British popular press. As the atmosphere warmed, Churchill revealed that a second front could and would be launched in French North Africa, in October, it was hoped, less than two months off.

Stalin, though evidently interested, was at first skeptical of this, but soon changed his view and volunteered, with considerable strategic insight, that the landings would assault Rommel in the rear; set the French to fighting the Germans in France, the entire occupation of which was anticipated; probably force Mussolini out of the war; and "overawe" Franco, keeping him neutral. Stalin concluded, implausibly, given his religious views: "May God prosper this undertaking!" fishing a phrase from his distant seminarian past. Stalin too, with nearly 200 German divisions almost at his throat, was showing his mettle as a war leader, whatever his limitations as a humanitarian or cocontractant.

Churchill wrote in his memoirs: "I was deeply impressed with this remarkable statement. It showed the Russian dictator's swift and complete mastery of a problem hitherto novel to him. Very few people alive could have comprehended in so few minutes the reasons which we had all been so busily wrestling with for months." Churchill and Harriman dispute in their memoirs which of them persuaded Stalin of a fifth advantage—that the action would open up the Mediterranean and accelerate the flow of supplies from the West to Russia. Churchill and Stalin parted at midnight, and Churchill reported to the War Cabinet and to Roosevelt that he believed he could "establish a solid and sincere relationship with this man. . . . He knows the worst and we parted in an atmosphere of great good will."[30]

They met again at 11 P.M. in the evening of August 13. (Stalin was even more of a nighthawk than Churchill and as great a consumer of wines and spirits.) Churchill and Harriman again attended upon Stalin and Molotov. Brooke, Cadogan, Wavell, and Air Marshal Sir Arthur Tedder were in the British party. Stalin entered and handed over a written memorandum that was represented as a summary of the previous evening's discussion but was in fact a renewal of the accusation that the British and Americans had betrayed Russia, which had made its plans and counted upon a second front in Europe in 1942. He accused the Western Allies of leaving Russia to fight the Germans and of shortchanging it in supplies, handing over insufficient materiel after helping themselves first.

Churchill resisted the temptation to reply to the taunts, which he could have done with great eloquence and perfect justice. He did pointedly refer to his own

Roosevelt delighted his followers at Madison Square Garden in New York, October 28, 1940, when he attacked isolationist Republican congressmen "Martin, Barton, and Fish."

After perspiring through a long hot evening in the White House, July 19, 1940, because he didn't want air conditioning to inflame his sinuses, the President speaks by radio to the convention that has unspontaneously "drafted" him to a third term in Chicago.

Roosevelt's 1940 Republican opponent, Wendell L. Willkie, a lawyer and utilities executive, returns to his native Elwood, Indiana, to start his campaign. He was a formidable adversary but a friendly one, with whom Roosevelt later considered an alliance between liberal Democrats and Republicans against Southern, segregationist Democrats and conservative Republicans.

The first drawing of the first peacetime Selective Service draft in U.S. history by the new war secretary, Republican Henry L. Stimson, with FDR looking on, October 29, 1940.

Prime Minister Winston Churchill meets President Roosevelt aboard U.S.S. *Augusta*, Placentia Bay, Newfoundland, August 9, 1941. Churchill hands over a letter from King George VI. Roosevelt is supporting himself on the arm of his son Elliott, right.

Divine service on the fan deck of the H.M.S *Prince of Wales*. Winston Churchill wrote: "It was a great hour to live." Roosevelt and Churchill are sitting facing the camera in the lower left, with their service chiefs behind them. The venerable battleship *Arkansas* is in the background.

General George C. Marshall, chief of staff of the U.S. Army and ultimately chairman of the combined Allied military chiefs. He brought the army from 8 to nearly 300 divisions in four years and chose or recommended most of the American senior army commanders, except MacArthur, who was a personal choice of Roosevelt's.

Showing his imperturbability, Roosevelt relaxes in his office after signing the declaration of war against Japan, December 8, 1941. He is surrounded by Congressional leaders of both parties, and shows no sign of concern that one third of his battle fleet had been sunk the day before at Pearl Harbor, a fact that, "frankly," he did not reveal in his Fireside Chat that night.

Joint press conference with Winston Churchill, December 23, 1941. Roosevelt is wearing a black armband in remembrance of his mother, who had died three months before. This was the format for his nearly one thousand press conferences, with the reporters crowded around his desk, notepads and pens in hand. They were no less informal in wartime.

Roosevelt's Fireside Chat on "Progress of the War," February 23, 1942. He was pointing at the map for the benefit of newsreels. He successfully blamed the fiasco at Pearl Harbor on Japanese treachery and the impending loss of the Philippines on inexorable laws of geography. All who dwelt on U.S. losses at Pearl Harbor he categorized as "defeatists," inadvertently serving the enemy.

President Roosevelt watching with Henry J. Kaiser the launch of the merchant ship *Joseph N. Teal* at the Portland, Oregon, shipyard, September 23, 1942. The ship was built up from the keel to launch in ten days. In the following year the United States would build over 11 million tons of merchant and naval shipping.

Driving through the Martin bomber plant, Omaha, Nebraska, to the delight of the workers, very many of them women, April 26, 1943.

Toward the end of his rail tour of munitions factories and military training centers, Roosevelt stopped his train at Uvalde, Texas, September 27, 1942, for a reunion with former vice president John Nance Garner.

Roosevelt speaks at Arlington National Cemetery on Veteran's Day, November 11, 1942, the anniversary of the end of World War I. American and British forces had just landed in Morocco and Algeria and Roosevelt purported to welcome France back to the Allied cause. Beside him is the 82-year-old commander of the American Expeditionary Force in France in World War I, and General George Marshall's great patron, General John J. Pershing.

The Roosevelts' Christmas card, 1942.

1942

WITH CHRISTMAS GREETINGS

AND OUR BEST WISHES

FOR A

HAPPIER NEW YEAR

THE PRESIDENT

AND

MRS. ROOSEVELT

Lunching alfresco at Rabat, Morocco, January 21, 1943, with, from left, General Mark Clark, Harry L. Hopkins (back to camera), and, right, General George S. Patton, whom Roosevelt always liked and encouraged.

Roosevelt and Churchill at the Casablanca conference with French generals Henri Giraud and Charles de Gaulle. Churchill wrote of this contrived meeting: "The pictures of this event can not be viewed, even in the setting of these tragic times, without a laugh."

Churchill insisted Roosevelt see the sun set on the Atlas Mountains from Marakesh. Roosevelt was carried to the top of a tower for this view. The next day, as he watched the president's plane take off, Churchill pronounced Roosevelt "the greatest man I have ever known."

French Admiral Raymond Fenard started as a Vichy spokesman and then became de Gaulle's emissary in Washington. Here on March 19, 1943, he presents Roosevelt with a model of the battleship *Richelieu*, which had spent most of the war at Dakar, the officers and crew receiving bribes and blandishments from both Vichy and de Gaulle.

At "Shangri-La," subsequently Camp David, May 15, 1943. Roosevelt and Churchill take a break in the Trident Conference. Churchill wrote of this try at fishing that Roosevelt "was placed with great care by the side of a pool."

Roosevelt addresses 150,000 people on the grounds in front of the Canadian Parliament buildings, Ottawa, August 25, 1943. (This was half the population of the Ottawa area.)

Roosevelt and Churchill looking at the Pyramids and, as Roosevelt described it, "my friend the Sphinx," November 23, 1943.

Roosevelt with General Dwight D. Eisenhower in Sicily, December 8, 1943, on Roosevelt's way back from the Teheran Conference. Roosevelt had just named Eisenhower commander of the cross-Channel invasion of France planned for six months later.

The long-awaited meeting of the Big Three, at Teheran, November 29, 1943. Stalin is gallantly shaking hands with Churchill's daughter Sarah. Molotov and Averell Harriman are on either side of Sarah Churchill. US Air Corps general H.H. Arnold, British Ambassador to Russia Clark Kerr, and Foreign Secretary Anthony Eden stand behind their leaders.

Charles de Gaulle finally arrives at the White House, July 6, 1944. Roosevelt officially recognized him as leader of all France just seven weeks before millions of French acclaimed his return to liberated Paris. Behind Roosevelt is FDR's daughter, Anna, acting chatelaine in the White House.

Members of the President's War Refugee Board, trying to provide some relief for the victims of Nazi and Japanese persecution: Secretary of War Henry Stimson, Secretary of the Treasury Henry Morgenthau, Secretary of State Cordell Hull, March 21, 1944.

The President is welcomed back to Washington from Teheran by his barons in the Congress, from left, Senate Majority Leader Alben W. Barkley, House Majority Leader John W. McCormack, Vice President Henry Wallace, and House Speaker Sam Rayburn, December 17, 1943.

Admiral Nimitz (commander of the Pacific Fleet and of the central Pacific theater), General MacArthur, and President Roosevelt tour Oahu military installations, July 27, 1944. They were cheered by many thousands of Japanese Hawaiians, though a hundred thousand Japanese-American U.S. citizens, were still confined in camps in the western states, without benefit of trial or any evidence against them.

The President and his chosen successor, vice presidential nominee Harry S Truman, under Andrew Jackson's magnolia tree on the White House lawn, August 18, 1944. Roosevelt had a good opinion of Truman, who respected Roosevelt but resented his hauteur. Roosevelt did little to help Truman prepare for a possible succession.

The Republicans' 42-year old presidential nominee in 1944, Governor Thomas E. Dewey of New York. An able and vigorous young man, he never completely got over being called "the bridegroom on the wedding cake" by Alice Roosevelt Longworth. FDR disparaged his having straddled between the isolationists and supporters of aid to the Allies in 1940-1941, and resented Republican attacks on the President's health.

Another of his greatest rhetorical triumphs: Roosevelt addresses the Teamsters Union, Washington, September 23, 1944, flanked by William Green of the AFL and Daniel Tobin of the Teamsters. Roosevelt mocked Republican claims that he had wasted millions of dollars sending a destroyer to collect his dog, Fala, on an Aleutian Island. "He has not been the same dog since." Dewey was now running for President against the incumbent's dog.

The President, always popular with the film community, who almost unanimously thought him a great leader and a great star and showman, receives a group of actors, artists, and scientists who pledge support, October 5, 1944. Left to right: Van Wyck Brooks, Hannah Dorner, Jo Davidson, Jan Kiepura, Joseph Cotten, Dorothy Gish , and the astronomer Dr. Harlow Shapley.

Three million New Yorkers stood in the rain for up to two hours, on a raw day, October 21, 1944, to see President Roosevelt go by in an open car. He was determined to show he was still fit, and half the population of the nation's largest city (with hundreds of thousands of young men absent in the armed forces) wanted to show their regard for the country's longest-serving president. (Roosevelt is in the second car.)

Roosevelt speaks from his car to 120,000 people at Soldier Field in Chicago, October 28, 1944. His car, illuminated by searchlights, circled the darkened field. It was a dramatic exploitation of the President's popularity.

One more time, as on many previous election nights, Roosevelt received his neighbors on the terrace of his home at Hyde Park. His daughter and his wife stand behind him.

The Big Three at Yalta, February 1945, now ruled the world. Behind Churchill, Roosevelt, and Stalin are their foreign ministers, Eden, Edward Stettinius (Hull had retired), and Molotov. Behind them are Clark Kerr, Sir Alexander Cadogan, and Harriman. There has been great controversy over this conference but the agreements were favorable to the West.

Roosevelt addresses the Congress about the Yalta Conference, March 1, 1945. He was wheeled in and out and apologized "for the unusual posture of sitting down." "Many in the audience felt instinctively that they would never see him there [in the Congress] again," wrote Joseph Alsop.

Roosevelt working on his papers in early April 1945 at his cottage in Warm Springs a few days before his death. He spoke to his intimate companions of retiring after a year or so.

Lucy Mercer Rutherfurd as she appeared when her relationship with Franklin D. Roosevelt was revived in 1941 after a lapse of over twenty years. She saw him often in the last two years of his life and was with him at the end.

The last photograph of Franklin D. Roosevelt, April 11, 1945. He had transferred his irrepressible energy to the once prostrate country whose leadership he had assumed twelve years before. The nation was triumphant but he was exhausted. Yet he was elegant and cheerful and brave until the very end.

Leaving Warm Springs, April 13,
1945. Two million people stood
beside the railway track from
Warm Springs to Washington to
Hyde Park, at all hours, to
glimpse Roosevelt's flag-draped
coffin as it passed in an illuminated observation car.

Most Washingtonians
came out to see the fu-
neral cortege, from
Union Station to the
White House, and back
again, April 14.

Hyde Park, April 15, 1945, Franklin Delano Roosevelt was laid to rest a hundred
yards from where he was born in a little garden beside his parents' house,
where he had played as a child. Seventeen years later, Eleanor joined him.

and his countrymen's experience of facing the full might of German arms. (Stalin always exempted the Royal Air Force from criticism and accused the Royal Navy of excessive caution, while conceding its fighting effectiveness; he reserved his derision for the British Army, which, he said, if ordered to fight the Germans would "find it not so bad.") Churchill said that Britain and the United States had taken their decision and would not change it, and that it was logically unassailable.

He declared that he refrained from a more strenuous refutation of his host's acerbities out of respect for the bravery of the Soviet Army, which, as his host pointed out, was taking 10,000 casualties each day. But Churchill pounded his fist upon the table and delivered, from Brooke's and Harriman's accounts, one of the most powerful monologues of his very long and brilliant career as a forensic orator and debater. In what Harriman called "a magnificent performance," he "poured forth," wrote Brooke, "a wonderful spontaneous oration." The controlled thunder of his impassioned words defeated the British interpreter (whom Churchill fired at the end of the evening), but Stalin's translator, the redoubtable Pavlov, persevered successfully, thus doubtless saving his own life.

Churchill impressed the Soviet dictator, who, as Churchill wrote, was generally not very animated, though unaccustomed to being contradicted. As the British prime minister modestly remembered it, he (Churchill) "exclaimed there was no comradely spirit in [Stalin's] attitude. I had traveled far to establish good working relations. We had done our utmost to help Russia and would continue to do so. We had been left entirely alone against Germany and Italy. Now that the three great nations were allied, victory was certain, provided we did not fall apart, and so forth. I was somewhat animated in this passage."[31]

Stalin suddenly stood up, removed from his mouth the pipe he had been smoking, smiled broadly, raised one hand, and said: "Your words are of no importance. What is important is your spirit." Stalin effectively withdrew his charge of bad faith against Churchill and invited him to dinner the following night. Churchill, irritated by Stalin's brusqueness and having no concern at all for the niceties with such a man, responded with no enthusiasm that he would stay for dinner the following evening, August 14, but would leave at dawn the next day. Stalin, who was apparently enjoying the mighty joust more than his formidable visitor, even though Churchill had clearly got the better of it, asked if he could not stay longer. Churchill replied that he could, if any good would come of it, and agreed to stay until the 16th of August.

Meanwhile, Chiang Kai-shek had written Roosevelt on August 11, and Roosevelt sent on to Churchill on August 14, the Chinese leader's concerns about the arrest and internment of the Indian Congress leaders. Chiang predicted a "disastrous effect." Roosevelt asked: "What do you think?" Churchill responded August 14 from Moscow: "I take it amiss Chiang should seek to make difficulties between us." He pointed out that the decision to arrest the Congress leaders was taken by the executive of twelve, of which eleven were Indian. "All Chiang's talk of Congress leaders wishing us to quit in order that they may help the Allies is eye-wash. . . . It occurred to me that you could remind Chiang that Gandhi was pre-pared to negotiate . . . a free passage for Japanese troops through India, [to facilitate] their joining hands with Hitler."[32] This riposte from the bowels of Rus-sia laid this imperishable bugbear to rest again for a while.

The same day, Roosevelt rather cheerfully thanked Churchill for his encour-aging account of the first evening with Stalin. He was "made very happy by Mr. Stalin's cordiality and understanding of our difficult problems. I wish I could be with you both for that would make the party complete. Give him my warm regards." Roosevelt, acting on Churchill's description, had not the remotest idea of the "raw task" Churchill had undertaken. Stalin wasn't much interested in "warm regards" from Roosevelt or anyone else. Given the desperation of both the Russian and Egyptian fronts, it remains a mystery why Stalin's request for West-ern armies and Roosevelt's offer to Churchill of American soldiers for the Middle East were not taken up. The margin of victory would have been much less nar-row and the political settlement in Europe at the end of the war would probably have been more favorable for the West. As it was, excessive numbers of American, British, and Canadian soldiers festered for many months in Britain waiting for a cross-Channel embarkation that the British wished to defer almost indefinitely.

Churchill cabled Roosevelt a full account of the August 13 encounter, received in Washington August 15. Stalin's memorandum and Churchill's reply were attached. Churchill included the reflections: "He made his salute and held out his hand to me on leaving and I took it. In the public interest I shall go to the dinner tonight. . . . It is my considered opinion that in his heart, so far as he has one, Stalin knows we are right." On the basis of Harriman's and other descrip-tions he had had of Stalin's negotiating techniques, he wrote off the previous evening as histrionics for the benefit of his commissars. Churchill was depressed by Stalin's hostility but rejected Cadogan's suggestion of passing up the next evening's dinner as too great an affront to an indispensable and hard-pressed ally.

According to some accounts, it was a Russian orgy of food and drink for a hun-dred people—the commissars and leading military figures not at the front. There were nineteen courses, four hours at the table, and far too many toasts. According to these sources, Voroshilov and Mikoyan (the veteran trade commissar, not that there was much conventional trade at this time) became extremely drunk. Churchill dismissed these stories as ludicrous exaggerations, and said only forty people were present and the occasion was decorous. Wavell gave a toast in Rus-sian and Stalin's toast included the assertion, meant to be a compliment to Churchill, that the British had defeated the Germans and the Turks at the Dar-danelles in 1915 (a famous but unsuccessful operation which Churchill had spon-sored), but were not aware of this because of faulty intelligence work.[33]

Churchill wrote that the conversation with Stalin was lively. The Russian leader claimed that Lady Astor and George Bernard Shaw had told him when they visited Moscow in the thirties that Churchill was responsible for the Allied intervention against the Bolsheviks after the First World War, but that he was finished politically. Stalin also claimed that he had said that he blamed Lloyd George, that he preferred "a downright enemy to a pretended friend," and that in a crisis he thought the British might bring the "old war horse" [Churchill] back. Churchill claimed that he interrupted to affirm that he did have some responsibility for the intervention, "and I do not wish you to think otherwise. Have you forgiven me?" Stalin, according to Churchill's account, replied: "All that is in the past and the past belongs to God."[34]

When Churchill made his farewells, declining to sit through a lengthy film beginning after 1 A.M., Stalin continued to engage him in cordial conversation and pursued him through the ornate hall, accompanying him the considerable distance to his car. Churchill was still disappointed and had no desire to see Stalin again on this trip, having delivered the message that motivated him to come to Moscow. He felt he had been rebuffed in his desire to have a serious relationship. The staff talks had been cordial but completely unproductive. The Russians just repeated the grievances of their leader, and Brooke didn't believe a word they said about their ability to defend the Caucasus oil fields. Flying at low altitude two days before from Teheran to Moscow, he had looked for evidence of defense construction and found only one half-completed antitank trench. Brooke concluded that the Russians were as likely to lose the Caucasus as American military intelligence thought the British were to lose the Suez Canal. The more optimistic intuition of the three political leaders was, in every case, more accurate than the opinions of professional military advisors.

Churchill went reluctantly to see Stalin at seven o'clock on the evening of August 15, after Ambassador Kerr had beseeched him to request a further meeting. Churchill assured his entourage he would not be more than an hour with Stalin and asked for his dinner to be ready for his return at 8:30. This was not how it turned out. He returned seven hours late, at 3:30 A.M., August 16, after a monumental but rather satisfactory session with Stalin. It started off sluggishly, but when Churchill got up to leave, Stalin invited him to join him at his home for a drink. Churchill did so, and Stalin showed him his modest living quarters, four simple rooms, and introduced his daughter, Svetlana, a shy and attractive redhead, "a nice girl," wrote Churchill (who had red-headed daughters himself).

Churchill stayed for dinner, served by Stalin's ancient housekeeper, and Molotov was summoned and twitted at length by both leaders. Stalin opened and poured his own wine (vintages from the Caucasus), which Churchill considered of good quality, and eventually Cadogan joined the group and a communiqué was very agreeably worked out. Stalin assured Churchill in the utmost confidence that he had prepared a very rude surprise for the German Army in the approaches to the Caucasus. They parted shortly after 3 A.M. At 5:30 A.M. the sixty-seven-year-old British prime minister, showing little of the strain of the monumental encounter that had just ended two hours earlier, and his party emplaned for Teheran, having been ceremoniously seen off by a groggy Molotov. Not having slept at all the night before, Churchill did so on his plane. It was a performance of remarkable stamina and perseverance, and he counted it a definite success. He cabled his thanks to Stalin for his "comradeship and hospitality" from Teheran on August 16 and jauntily concluded: "Give my regards to Molotov."[35]

———————

On August 19, a miniature Sledgehammer was performed by 5,000 Canadians at Dieppe, France. There were 3,700 killed, wounded, or captured in the one-day operation. It was officially claimed that valuable information was ascertained about landing craft types and so forth, but in fact it was a sanguinary fiasco, and a warning of what would happen to anything other than a thoroughly prepared landing in northwest Europe on a massive scale.

The Torch planning was slowed by foot-dragging and hair-splitting from U.S. military staff who had never approved of the operation in the first place, inspired, if not instructed, by Marshall. The designated commander of the operation, General Dwight D. Eisenhower, pursued his task with the conciliatory effectiveness that would serve him well throughout an immensely distinguished career in positions of ever greater responsibility.

Eisenhower, almost fifty-two, from a poor but respectable family that shortly after he was born moved from Texas to Abilene, Kansas, was a West Point graduate who had been a protégé of both MacArthur and Marshall, though he was much more a Marshall loyalist. He was in the Marshall school of the military organizer and soldier diplomat, rather than that of the vain and theatrical but brilliant field and theater commander, MacArthur. Eisenhower's first task was to create an integrated command structure with his British allies, and he succeeded splendidly in doing so. There was no precedent for fusing nationalities together, as Eisenhower did, in layers, as in a "plywood board," as one observer said.[36]

Marshall and his staff insisted that the American forces have a full amphibious exercise, which would delay the landings into November. In one sense, Torch was an inspired option, because the American forces, which had been conscripted and thrown together with considerable ingenuity and great haste, would begin their active military careers attacking Vichy forces, from which less than fierce resistance was anticipated. Roosevelt hoped to vindicate his dubious policy of respectabilizing Vichy by persuading Petain and his ministers that the Torch invasion was in the higher interests of France. It was a tall order, even for a man of Roosevelt's charm and power, to persuade the octogenarian marshal to thank him for taking away most of what was left of his puppet empire. Throwing the new-fledged American army directly against battle-tested Germans would have been very hazardous.

There was an extensive debate between the British and the Americans about whether to make landings in eastern Algeria. The Americans wanted to concentrate on Morocco, with a move into the Mediterranean and western Algeria. The British wanted, and were prepared to provide the manpower for, a move much closer to Tunisia on the eastern border of Algeria, in order to strike as hard as possible at the base of Rommel's Afrika Korps. Churchill, after stopping again in Cairo, returned to London on August 24, and had Eisenhower and his deputy, General Mark Clark, to dinner the following day. He cabled Roosevelt suggesting that the two order a certain date and require the military staffs to work to that timetable. This message to Roosevelt crossed with Marshall's latest plan, which deferred the landings into November, and whittled them down to western Algeria, up to Oran only.

Churchill cabled Roosevelt on August 27: "We are all profoundly disconcerted" by Marshall's latest effort to pare Torch down, if not scrap it altogether. He reminded Roosevelt of the promises he had just made to Stalin about Torch's being a serious diversion for the Germans, and emphasized the principal strategic value of it, to strike Rommel in the back, as Stalin had instantly recognized. It was Churchill's impression that this was Eisenhower's view also, and he requested ("I most earnestly beg") that the American Joint Chiefs of Staff reconsider. Churchill was prepared to provide the manpower for taking eastern Algeria if this was what was required. (Roosevelt had identified Algiers to Clement Attlee as a place where he wished to land American forces just ten months before, six weeks before the U.S. was at war. [37]

Roosevelt had Marshall and Hopkins to lunch at the White House on August 28. Roosevelt summarized his own and Churchill's concerns and listened to Marshall's explanation of the requirement for a proper exercise to train the draftees and of the limits on the resources available, which obliged a retrenchment of the targeted area. Roosevelt left for Shangri-la, a government retreat that had just been built in the Catoctin Mountains. (Roosevelt, having applied this word as the point of origin of the Doolittle raid in April, recycled it. The country home has been better known as Camp David since the mid-fifties, named after David Eisenhower, grandson of the future president and son-in-law of a subsequent president, Richard Nixon.)* There he received Marshall's response to their luncheon meeting, which was an inflexible reaffirmation of the proposal that had so troubled Churchill. Marshall had obtained the agreement of King and Arnold in support of his position.

Roosevelt found Marshall's response substantively and stylistically unacceptable. He had great esteem for his army chief of staff, but was not prepared to have his own concerns and those of the nation's foremost ally so cavalierly disregarded. Hopkins and Roosevelt redrafted Marshall's suggested response to Churchill and now proposed a compromise. They believed that British soldiers in the landings would provoke French resistance, while an exclusively American force might not. The Americans had the resources for only two landings and one of them had to be in the Atlantic, because a line of communications extending inside the

---

* This camp was built on government land in the Catoctins because McIntire declared that the President must have altitude and cooler weather to assist his sinuses in summer. Shangri-la was in these times rather spartan.[38]

Straits of Gibraltar was judged too impetuous. However, a British landing in eastern Algeria one week after the American landings would be acceptable.

Churchill replied September 1 that deferring Algiers could produce a German presence there before an Allied one, and objected to redesigning the plan in a way that was sure to push back the landing date well into November. He wrote that "if we both strip ourselves to the bone, as you say, we could find sufficient naval cover and combat loadings for simultaneous attempts at Casablanca, Oran, and Algiers."

Roosevelt reverted September 2, offering three simultaneous landings, with a mixed American and British force at Algiers and exclusively American forces at Casablanca and Oran. Roosevelt was prepared to tell Vichy that the British forces were merely in transit toward action with German forces in Tunisia. Since the President had shown far too much solicitude for Vichy anyway, this was an elegant solution. Churchill, in the same spirit, wrote on September 5 that the "highly trained" British forces "if convenient . . . can wear your uniform. They will be proud to do so." What Eisenhower sarcastically called the "Trans-Atlantic essay-writing contest" ended with an exuberant exchange of colloquialisms drawn from the recipient's country, Roosevelt writing on September 5, "Hurrah!" and Churchill replying the next day: "Okay full blast."[39]

––––––––––

Roosevelt, in producing a reasonable compromise between his own chiefs of staff and his British and Russian allies, had shown great dexterity. Churchill, after being caught red-handed by Marshall trying to suck the United States into an open-ended commitment to the Mediterranean, had arrested the insurrectionists in India, sacked and upgraded his high command in the Middle East, and carried a message to Stalin that he delivered with unsurpassable persuasive conviction. This was, in the end, a fine hour for him also. And Stalin, despite all his paranoia and morbidity, had shown strategic grasp and admirable composure, given that his country had been torn almost to its vitals by a relentless enemy. All three leaders, as the fortunes of war began to turn, had shown themselves more than fully equal to their great tasks.

The quality of supreme Allied leadership was emerging as another advantage over the Germans and Japanese. Hitler was now mad, though still with occasional flashes of brilliance, and the Japanese leaders, with the partial exception of the emperor, were undistinguished in every respect. And the Grand Alliance was functioning. The Axis was a myth unsupported by any coordination at all between Berlin and Tokyo. Fascist Italy, beaten, sullen, and despised, was now a lead weight around Hitler's ankle.

The world struggle was reaching its most critical phase. The Americans had landed on Guadalcanal, in the Solomon Islands, on August 7, but the Allies had lost four cruisers in the Battle of Savo Island on August 9. The Japanese outmaneuvered and surprised them, and were able to silhouette the Allied ships with starshells and then sink them promptly with well-aimed gunnery.

When MacArthur arrived in Australia in March, that country's defense plan was based on defeating the Japanese in the central Australian outback, the vast, almost unpopulated center of the country. MacArthur rejected this and decreed defense of Australia in New Guinea and the Solomons. The result of the Savo Island defeat was a very tenuous position for the U.S. Marines as they sought to carry out MacArthur's plan.

U.S. naval construction, following the victorious battles of the Coral Sea and Midway, was steadily building a lead over Japan in capital ships and aircraft carriers, which would be unanswerable in the Solomons as elsewhere, if the marines on Guadalcanal could hang on for a little while. (Four new American battleships had already been commissioned since Pearl Harbor. Great Britain would commission two more new battleships and Britain and the United States would each commission a fleet aircraft carrier before the end of 1942.) There would be no Japanese landings in Australia, though Darwin was bombed and there was a good deal of enemy submarine activity around the main ports.

Stalin was preparing his great counterstroke on the southern Russian front. Montgomery was close to launching his counterblow against Rommel, and Torch would introduce American ground forces into the Mediterranean theater and help to collapse the imitating, tottering impostures of both Mussolini and Petain. The next few months could, in Churchill's phrase, provide "the end of the beginning."

___✿___

CHAPTER 18

"He Is the Greatest Man
I Have Ever Known"

*(Winston Churchill describing Franklin D. Roosevelt as he watched
his aircraft take off from Marrakesh at the end of the Casablanca
Conference for his return to the United States, January 26, 1943)*

I

ROOSEVELT HAD Averell Harriman to Shangri-la August 29 and 30, 1942, to receive his impressions of the Moscow discussions between Churchill and Stalin. Harriman expressed great confidence in the ability of the Russians to hold the Germans at Stalingrad and in the Caucasus. He credited Churchill with having delivered the Anglo-American message brilliantly, but noted the difference between Roosevelt's optimism and Churchill's pessimism that the West and the Soviet Union could cooperate after the war. Roosevelt gave Harriman his rather roseate view of these matters in the automobile ride back to Washington on the 30th.*

Roosevelt seems to have risen above most of his grievous misgivings about the Communist system, as they applied to the future of Soviet-American relations. From his remarks to Hariman and many others he seems to have been convinced that atheistic Communism would not stamp out either the ancient religiosity of the Russians or the capitalistic instincts of most people, and that gradually the Communist effort to subvert and proselytize the world would give way to tradi-

---

* The trip was extended to two hours by the thirty-five-mile-per-hour limit Roosevelt had imposed as a rubber conservation measure and abided by himself. In automobiles as on trains, because of his polio, Roosevelt was bounced around at high speeds much more than a person with fully functional leg muscles. He preferred leisurely speeds unless he was driving his own specially adapted car himself, when he was stabilized by gripping the steering wheel and hand controls with his massive upper body strength.

tional Russian imperialism and relative desocialization. He thought Western political life would evolve somewhat toward the social democratic model he had pursued, narrowing the ideological gap between the two systems. He did, as he would make clear to Anthony Eden six months later (next chapter), foresee that the Soviet Union might have to be contained by the West—i.e., the Americans, more or less assisted by a press gang of allies frightened by the Russians. He apparently did not realize how irrelevant any lessening of ostensible ideological differences would be to relations between the Soviet Union and the West.

His poker instincts and skill as a Yankee trader and political cynic always put him on guard against excessive credulity. He was determined to make every effort to produce the best possible outcome in U.S.-Soviet relations, but also to avoid the catastrophic errors of Versailles and of Wilson's bungled ratification effort. Having led his electorate toward war, while Churchill was summoned, unelected, by a desperate Parliament and monarch who had been poorly served, Roosevelt was more conscious of his own domestic and geopolitical strength than Churchill was of the vulnerability of his. Roosevelt could afford a somewhat romanticized view of the potential for relations with Stalin.

To Roosevelt, his allies consisted of a magnificent anachronism (Britain); a brave, gigantic, and primitive political mutant (Russia); and a venerable, potentially formidable representative of the underdeveloped world for which Roosevelt held great hopes (China). France, at this point, was a client state, her status almost as eroded by the passage of time as Spain's. Britain could not possibly maintain her empire, and Russia could not possibly remain forever wedded to the blood-stained heresy of atheistic, totalitarian Communism. Britain would be largely dependent on the United States after the war.

The Soviet Union would need American financial and technical assistance, and China would be a vast, almost helpless dependent of the United States. Only the United States possessed the political and economic system and the scale of nation-state sufficient to influence the entire world decisively. Roosevelt never doubted that that influence was altogether benign; he knew that it was essential to prevent Europe and East Asia from reverting to large-scale war again, and he was sure that it was his destiny to lead America and the world to this great threshold.

He was right, of course, in all these beliefs, and in many respects he saw the postwar world more accurately than Churchill and Stalin. Roosevelt underestimated France's recuperative powers, and de Gaulle would not forget his cavalier treatment at the hands of the Anglo-Saxon leaders, whose responsibility for the deliverance of his country from the Germans he generally acknowledged but also, perversely, resented.

As he aged and wearied, Roosevelt concentrated more on the mighty vision of the world emerging and less on the grubby details of postwar settlement, but he never failed to recognize the necessity of taking France, Germany, Italy, and Japan into the Western, democratic, capitalist orbit, and keeping Soviet territorial gains to secondary geopolitical assets. Behind and along with his vast idealism,

Roosevelt was, in international as in domestic politics, a Machiavellian in method and a cold-eyed realist in the pursuit of his lofty objectives.

Unfortunately, not all Roosevelt's followers and kindred spirits retained the same balanced judgment. Henry Wallace had taken to philosophizing about the evolution of world affairs, mixing science and revelatory religion in a way that brought to mind Jim Farley's description of him in 1940 as "a wild-eyed fellow." Wallace had been going about since May 1942 garrulously explaining his theory that the American, French, German (1848), and Russian Revolutions were all stations on the emancipation of the common man. He implied a close community of view between the United States and the Soviet Union and inveighed against the evils of cartels in such a way as to seem to be attacking the entire U.S. economic system. Roosevelt never commented publicly on his vice president's antics, but obviously took note of his gigantic bound away from the mainstream of American opinion.

Not as other-worldly, but also troublesome, was the performance of the official leader of the Republican Party, Wendell Willkie, with whom Roosevelt had been tinkering with the idea of making common cause. Willkie had asked to make a quasi-official world tour. The lines between when he would be speaking for himself and when for the administration were, as always with Roosevelt, fuzzy, enabling the President to take credit where it suited him and repudiate Willkie where appropriate. The spectacle of the 1940 Republican presidential candidate embarking on a partial mission for Roosevelt was useful to the Democrats, as was Willkie's absence from the United States for almost all of the 1942 midterm election campaign.*

His trip lasted from August 26 to October 14. For the most part it was an effusive, wide-eyed, enthusiastic American discovery of the world, which Wilkie described in a best-seller. For the first two decades after the Second World War this was the attitude of swarms of well-meaning American tourists—large, pleasant, forthright people unwittingly searching for foreigners who would pick their pockets. Willkie attracted attention twice. In Moscow, following a snow job from Stalin at his most persuasive, Willkie declared permanent Russo-American brotherhood and the necessity for an instantaneous second front. Both Churchill and Roosevelt found it necessary to repudiate him gently as straying seriously into matters ultra vires to Willkie and his mandate. Willkie did defend Churchill at a Kremlin banquet from Stalin's charge of stealing 152 Lend-Lease airplanes from him.

In Chungking, where as the sarcastic General Stilwell recorded in his diary, "Willkie is to be smothered by hospitality," Willkie was even more thoroughly brainwashed by Chiang and his attractive and cunning wife. Madame Chiang flirted openly with him and kissed him when he departed. Willkie wanted her to

---

* Willkie flew to Brazil, Gold Coast, Nigeria, Sudan, Egypt, through the Middle East to Russia, and then to China, Siberia, Alaska, Canada, and home.

come with him on his plane and put China's case directly to Roosevelt. She had the presence of mind to decline this invitation, but did come to Washington some months later and made a very positive impression when she addressed Congress. She was a Christian and spoke English very elegantly. At time of writing she is 102 years old and lives in Gramercy Park, in New York City. Only Queen Elizabeth, consort of King George VI, of that vintage and prominence, rivaled her for longevity until she died in April 2002.

Willkie met twice with Chou En-lai, Mao Tse-tung's deputy, and said: "This excellent, sober, and sincere man won my respect as a man of obvious ability." (Chou's ability and sobriety were never in doubt; his sincerity is, at the least, harder to establish.)[1] Willkie was prevailed upon to deliver to Roosevelt a letter from the commander of the Flying Tigers, General Claire Chennault, saying that with 147 aircraft and a transfer of logistical support from the ground to the air war in Burma, he, Chennault, would bring Japan to its knees and end the war within a year. Willkie didn't specifically endorse this proposal, which had been noisily supported by the Chiangs; but in making himself the emissary for it, he enraged Stimson, Marshall, and Stilwell (whom the Chiangs wanted recalled because of his well-founded skepticism about Chiang's aptitude to command the theater, lead the Chinese, or do almost anything else useful). Marshall dismissed Chennault's proposal as "nonsense," which appears to have been Roosevelt's view also.

Willkie also muddied the waters by demanding the immediate end to the British Empire. Roosevelt was not out of sympathy with the idea but, in trying to manage the alliance, was unappreciative of this assault upon a glorious ally in the final weeks before they launched their first joint effort to take the offensive on land against the common enemy. Churchill uttered the famous demurral: "I have not become the King's First Minister in order to preside over the liquidation of the British Empire."[2] Churchill did not deign to mention this episode in his voluminous memoirs.

Willkie's interview with de Gaulle in Beirut was not overly successful, though Willkie disapproved Roosevelt's policy to Vichy. He found the general brilliant but imperious and unrealistic. De Gaulle did not let Willkie off so lightly in his memoirs as Churchill had in his: "Wendell Willkie, who had never been in the Middle East, apparently had made up his mind on every issue. . . . In reference to me he employed the standard malevolent banter in the book that appeared in his name upon his return." De Gaulle thus implied, unfairly, that Willkie wasn't the real author of his book, *One World*, which sold a remarkable two million copies and was generally favorably reviewed as to style and content. De Gaulle alleged that because the French high commissioner in Lebanon had some Empire furniture, "Willkie represented me as aping the Napoleonic style; because I was wearing the officer's standard summer uniform of white linen, he saw an ostentatious parody of Louis XIV; and because one of my men spoke of 'General de Gaulle's mission,' Mr. Willkie hinted that I took myself for Joan of Arc . . . in the summary manner of American public opinion. . . . In this matter, Roosevelt's rival was also his emulator."[3]

From the depths of involuntary exile, de Gaulle was already emboldened to affect a condescension to the American public and its leaders. This was a practice that would be widely and enthusiastically taken up in Europe, as soon as American arms had helped to end the internecine European struggle and permitted its beneficiaries the luxury of such delusions.

Roosevelt could never take his mind entirely off mundane domestic politics. The country was moving toward its first war-time midterm elections since 1918, and the omens for the President's party were not good. Jim Farley, who had implausibly contested the presidential nomination with Roosevelt in 1940 and yielded his party chairmanship to Ed Flynn, continued as New York State Democratic chairman and dreamed and schemed for a partial comeback. Herbert Lehman, despite presidential urgings, declined to run for a fifth term as governor (it had finally become a four-year term in 1938, as Al Smith had long advocated).

Roosevelt had hoped for a Torch invasion in North Africa before election day, and had held up his hands to Marshall in a prayerful attitude that the jump-off date could be before the elections on November 3. When this proved impossible, he did not press Marshall on the date.[4] Roosevelt was always mindful of the mistake Wilson had made with a partisan intervention in the 1918 campaign.

The government faced an electorate made grumpy by rationing and regulations, especially rural voters disgruntled with farm price controls. The country was made more irritable by the sluggish start to the military campaigns.

A low voter turnout was also likely, accentuated by the large numbers of voters working or training in unfamiliar parts of the country or already in the military overseas. And Roosevelt, the Democrats' greatest asset, who always ran well ahead of his party, was not up for reelection.

Roosevelt gave a Fireside Chat on the evening of September 7 on the cost of living. He had received a great deal of conflicting advice about whether to combat inflation by executive order, which he had been voted by Congress the authority to do, or by asking for legislation. Hopkins and price administrator Leon Henderson recommended the latter, but the press had become convinced that he was going to proceed by way of executive order. On September 7 he threw the ball back to the Congress as the course democracy and responsible government required. He showed his customary political astuteness in not taking on himself the entire responsibility for a welter of regulations, but dumping it on the Congress would not (and did not) do wonders for the popularity of Democratic congressional incumbents two months later.

To the farmers, who were the particular target of his anti-inflation concerns, he promised that farm prices in the legislation he proposed, or failing passage, would impose, would be capped during the war but, in contrast to the policy after World War I, would be shored up by floor prices that would protect farm incomes from erosion when the war ended. He concluded with an exhortation to the workers and farmers of the nation to show the same spirit of selflessness as the fighting men of the country.

As a partisan campaign would be inappropriate, Roosevelt determined to visit a large number of war plants and defense sites, starting September 17, with no partisanship and no publicity, until he returned to Washington, when the tour would be greatly publicized. Roosevelt took with him only Eleanor and her secretary, Malvina "Tommy" Thompson; the exotic and diverting Laura Delano (with her blue hair and costume jewelry, she was interested only in show dogs and gossip but amused the President); and Margaret Suckley, who was in charge of the little Scottie, Fala, that she had given Roosevelt. The lawyer Harry Hooker as well as Roosevelt's doctor, Ross McIntire, Steve Early, a few aides, and the three wire service reporters were also along. The reporters were prohibited from filing until after the trip was over, and Roosevelt insisted on seeing everything they wrote. The pretext for this was that it was a national security trip, but everyone knew that the real reason was to facilitate Roosevelt in having the best and greatest possible publicity for his tour when it ended.

The first stop was in Detroit, where Roosevelt and his party drove through a vast Chrysler tank plant that produced thirty Lee tanks a day. The workers were surprised to have the President among them unannounced, but delighted and enthusiastic, as Roosevelt, gratified, remarked to the wire service reporters. They went on to the colossal Willow Run Ford plant for the production of B-24 bombers, allegedly the largest factory in the world, and certainly the main room of the factory was the largest room in the world, a mile long and a quarter-mile wide, shaped like an L to avoid entering Wayne county, where labor rules and municipal taxes were inconvenient. Six concrete runways adjoined the factory; the initial plan had been for the complete manufacture and test flying of aircraft at this one site. An average of over 27,000 workers at a time were employed in the highly automated plant.

Roosevelt toured it with the governor of Michigan, Murray von Waggoner, and with the eighty-year-old Henry Ford, as cantankerous and misguided in many of his views as ever, and his son Edsel. Roosevelt was outwardly friendly to the elder Ford, a virulent and narrow-minded political opponent, but asked him well-informed questions as they went around about the means by which Ford was avoiding the hiring of women, normal wage scales, and so forth. Willow Run never fulfilled the tremendous hype that accompanied its construction, and reverted to being an assembly line, but did produce about 500 Liberator bombers a month, over 8,000 in the last sixteen months of the war.

The President and his party went on to the Great Lakes Naval Training Station in North Chicago, the largest of its kind in the country, training at this point nearly 70,000 candidate navy men at a time. From there the Roosevelt party went to the Allis-Chalmers plant in Milwaukee, now producing turbines and munitions, and then to the Federal Cartridge plant between Minneapolis and St. Paul. Everywhere Roosevelt was greeted with great enthusiasm, and the spirit of each workplace seemed very positive and determined, the more so for the large numbers of women employed in factories for the first time in the United States.

They stopped at a naval training station under construction on a lake in Idaho and then at the Bremerton, Washington, shipyard. Roosevelt toured the Boeing factory in Seattle and jokingly told workers in both places when he addressed them from his car that he wasn't "really here. Pretend for ten days that you haven't seen me." The story suited his political convenience, since the whole idea of a secret trip was a political canard in the first place. News of his presence became so widespread that large crowds cheered the President all along his route as he drove to the Mercer Island residence of his daughter, Anna, and her "mate," as she often called her husband, John Boettiger, for dinner. Eleanor had departed the tour in the Midwest to rejoin it later, and Roosevelt continued down the Pacific coast with his daughter.

Anna was an attractive and charming woman of thirty-six with a quick sense of humor and a delightful manner. She had a bright smile, fine blond hair, and long, shapely legs of the classic American pin-up girl type, set off to best effect as wartime fabric conservation requirements lifted the hems of women with suitable limbs like Anna's above their knees. Anna would gradually take Eleanor's place at the President's side as Mrs. Roosevelt continued her strenuous and valuable tours of the home front and the battlefronts. Jim Farley always felt that Anna had the best political judgment of the President's children, and she was a joy to everyone she encountered.

Anna broke a bottle of champagne over the bow of one of Henry Kaiser's Liberty Ships in the Kaiser shipyard in Portland, Oregon. From laying the keel to launch had required just ten days; most of the ingredients of the ship had been preassembled and inserted in the hull and superstructure as they arose. Kaiser, a "dynamo," as Roosevelt called him, and the shipbuilder (originally yacht builder) Andrew Jackson Higgins were principally responsible for the achievement and the surpassing of Roosevelt's startling requirement of ten million tons of merchant shipping a year. Kaiser's most interesting contribution was the construction of fifty escort carriers—essentially large, modified, 18,000-ton freighters with flat deck tops and somewhat more powerful engines, each carrying approximately thirty aircraft. These ships were invaluable in finally winning the Battle of the Atlantic and in achieving absolute air superiority over Japan and its coastal waters.

Kaiser had become a favorite of Roosevelt's because of his unconventional disrespect for the usual ponderousness of big business and for his contagious and original energy. When U.S. Steel and Bethlehem Steel, irritated at the loss of much of their West Coast shipbuilding business, declined to supply him with steel, Roosevelt was happy to approve Jesse Jones's allocation of RFC funds to assist Kaiser in building the first integrated steel operation in California. (Kaiser's agent on this occasion had been the sans pareil New Deal powerhouse-turned-lobbyist, Thomas G. Corcoran.)

Roosevelt continued to the Mare Island Navy Yard near Oakland, the Oakland naval facilities, the Los Angeles factory of Douglas Aviation, and, in San Diego, the Consolidated aircraft plant, a naval hospital, and a large Marine Corps facility. His train then turned east and proceeded all the way to the dusty little West Texas town of Uvalde, home of Roosevelt's former vice president, John Nance Garner. Two years before, the then-vice president had publicly declined to vote because as a Democrat he could find no true Democrat on the ballot. Roosevelt's entourage was worried that this first meeting since Garner's departure from Washington might be awkward. Roosevelt wondered if there would be crowds at the little station. There weren't. Even Garner himself was late, arriving in an old car he drove himself and bounding aboard the President's railway carriage. "Well God bless you, sir! I'm glad to see you!" Garner shouted as he advanced with outstretched hand. Roosevelt responded in the same spirit: "Gosh, you look well!" They had an amicable, folksy chat, and Roosevelt claimed that Garner supported the position he had taken on inflation and price controls.

Roosevelt's train went on to New Orleans, where he inspected the shipyard of Andrew Jackson Higgins, the chief supplier to the U.S. armed forces of landing craft and other smaller craft, including torpedo boats. Roosevelt was impressed by this yacht builder with many innovative ideas about marine architecture. While he was apparently a less formidable industrialist than Henry Kaiser, he knew more about ships, and Roosevelt found him a refreshing character. Higgins eventually produced over 20,000 landing craft, which brought the Allied soldiers ashore in Italy, France, and across the Pacific.

Roosevelt pronounced himself delighted with the trip and thoroughly relaxed by it. Normally, only a sea voyage could exert such a restorative influence upon him.[5] He returned to Washington October 1.

Roosevelt's long battle with Colonel Robert Rutherford McCormick, proprietor of the *Chicago Tribune* and coproprietor of the *New York Daily News*, spilled into his correspondence with Churchill. The *Tribune* had applied for a license to publish a newspaper for American troops in Britain. Roosevelt cabled Churchill October 6: "Earnestly hope that this application will not be approved. The fact is that it should be turned down on the ground that the Chicago Tribune prints lies and deliberate misrepresentations in lieu of news. . . . You can readily see that I do not trust the Chicago Tribune farther than you can throw a bull." Churchill complied. Relations between Roosevelt and McCormick had deteriorated steadily through the thirties, and Roosevelt had caused the Justice Department to launch an antitrust suit against the *Tribune* in 1941 when McCormick tried to keep the pro-Roosevelt *Chicago Sun-Times*, owned by the Anglophilic retailer Marshal Field III, out of the Associated Press wire service.

Relations between Roosevelt and McCormick struck their nadir when an enterprising *Tribune* war correspondent, traveling on a navy ship in the Pacific, came upon an apparently innocuous record of certain ship movements and included some references to the ships in a story filed and published just before the Battle of Midway. Had the Japanese seen the story they might have surmised that their codes had been cracked by the United States.

Roosevelt exploded and ordered Knox (a rather unsuccessful competitor of McCormick's at the *Chicago Daily News*) to send marines to occupy the Tribune Tower, McCormick's stately Gothic headquarters in Chicago. Roosevelt also ordered the attorney general to charge the colonel with treason. Biddle declined to do this for lack of evidence, and Knox, though he would have been delighted to shut down the *Tribune*, passed the issue back to the attorney general, who claimed there was insufficient evidence for any charge. Roosevelt badgered Biddle into engaging Hoover's attorney general, William Mitchell, as special counsel and sending the matter on a reduced charge to a grand jury.[6]

Two of the *Tribune*'s employees and the *Tribune* itself were the grand jury targets, but it became clear that there was no deliberate breach of security and the respondents were exonerated. McCormick exposed the fact that Knox was taking $60,000 a year as a consultant to his old newspaper, which made a mockery of Roosevelt's call for sacrifice and gave new meaning to war profiteering, and the *Tribune* relentlessly accused Knox and Roosevelt of being negligently responsible for the debacle at Pearl Harbor. Roosevelt had set out to persecute an opponent, albeit an extremely destructive and irascible one, as he had destroyed Moses Annenberg and had tried to destroy Andrew Mellon. It was a discreditable effort and deservedly failed. But Roosevelt cannot be blamed for not wanting the *Tribune* to be the news source for overseas American soldiers. The armed forces set up their own newspaper.

McCormick's cousin, Joseph Patterson, publisher of the *New York Daily News*, who had sometimes been supportive in the run-up to the war, showed up at the White House in the weeks following Pearl Harbor, volunteering any service he could perform for the war effort. Roosevelt told him: "Go back to New York and apologize to your readers."[7] He found useful roles for Wendell Willkie and many other former opponents who he thought had put the national interest first. He never replied to the letters of Herbert Hoover or Joseph Kennedy volunteering their services.

On October 21, Eleanor Roosevelt, accompanied only by "Tommy" Thompson, left the United States for a long-planned visit to London. Their aircraft was detained by bad weather in Ireland, but she was delivered to London's Paddington Station by a combination of special plane and train sent for her by Churchill, and was greeted on arrival by King George VI and Queen Elizabeth, Anthony Eden, and General Eisenhower. She drove with the king and queen to Buckingham Palace, where she was provided a commodious suite. The king and queen had a small dinner for her attended by Prime Minister Churchill and his wife,

Clementine, the Mountbattens, Field Marshal Smuts, Ambassador Winant, and Elliott Roosevelt, now a lieutenant colonel. The film *In Which We Serve*, with Noel Coward allegedly playing Mountbatten as a destroyer captain, was the after-dinner entertainment. When his ship was sunk early in the morning near the end of the film, Coward jauntily praised the virtues of "a swim before breakfast." He played a more credible Mountbatten than Mounbatten himself did.

Eleanor had a tremendous success in Britain, tirelessly touring bomb-damaged areas and American units. She prevailed upon Eisenhower to reduce the incidence of colds and blistered feet by distributing heavier socks, as was suggested to her in a Red Cross dispensary. She traveled around the country, put in sixteen-hour days, and indefatigably cheered up and listened attentively to everyone she met. Socially, she got on better with Ernest Bevin and some of the other Labour Party representatives than with Churchill, with whom she rowed over aid to Republican Spain. She dismissed as irrelevant Churchill's assertion that the Roosevelts and the Churchills would be the first people the Republicans would have decapitated if they had had the chance. Notwithstanding such verbal skirmishing, Churchill telegraphed Roosevelt November 1: "Mrs. Roosevelt has been winning golden opinions here from all for her kindness and her unfailing interest in everything we are doing." In the same message he wrote: "The Battle in Egypt is now rising to its climax, and our hopes are higher than I dare to say." Montgomery was beginning his great counterattack.

When the President arrived at his home poll in Hyde Park on November 3 to vote in the midterm elections, the electoral officer deadpanned: "Name, please?" He responded that he thought "Roosevelt was the name I gave last time." The elections turned up the greatest gains for the Republicans since 1928. They picked up 10 Senate seats and 47 congressmen, but the Democrats still held both houses, 57 to 38 in the Senate, with one Independent, and 222 Democrats to 209 Republicans and three Independents in the House of Representatives. The Republicans had picked up a number of governorships, including Dewey's easy victory in New York, which did virtually seem to assure him the Republican presidential nomination two years hence. Roosevelt was not perturbed. He well knew the fickleness of voters in midterm elections and was confident that in two years he would be the president who had led the nation to victory, or at least to the brink of victory, rather than, as was now the case, the president still trying to overcome Pearl Harbor. He gave no indication, even to intimates, that he was disconcerted in the slightest.

II

THE DAY AFTER the election, November 4, 1942, Churchill cabled Roosevelt a message he had received from General Sir Harold Alexander, the British Middle Eastern commander, reporting a decisive victory at El Alamein, "after twelve days of heavy and violent fighting." Churchill added, doubtless mindful of his many overoptimistic forecasts on this subject in the past: "We are not pro-claiming anything at present." Rommel had been in Germany on sick leave when the battle began, and returned on Hitler's orders to Egypt. He conducted a skillful and tenacious defense but was badly outnumbered and outgunned by General Sir Bernard Montgomery, who was a thorough and determined commander.

Montgomery kept relentless pressure on Rommel, grinding down his tank force, accepting greater losses of equipment as he adeptly used the vast superior-ity of force he had built up, like Grant at Richmond, or Foch in his great offen-sive of 1918, though with far more concern for casualties than Grant and Foch had displayed on those occasions. At the end of the Battle of El Alamein, Rom-mel was reduced to only about thirty tanks and had only about 25,000 soldiers in fighting condition, compared with 600 tanks for Montgomery (including most of the nearly 300 Roosevelt and Marshall had sent him after the fall of Tobruk five months before) and nearly four times as many troops. It was astonishing that Rommel had posed such a mortal threat to the Suez Canal with so small a force.

In the Pacific, though the struggle for Guadalcanal was still desperately con-tested, the U.S. Navy was taking its toll on the Japanese. In the Solomons actions, two Japanese battle cruisers were sunk in the second week of November by new American battleships and other craft. The fourth American aircraft carrier of the war had just been lost (the *Hornet*), a fact that Roosevelt refused as a matter of principle to suppress on the eve of the elections, but the series of new aircraft car-riers Roosevelt had commissioned two and a half years before was now starting to enter service. He had also asserted his knowledge of naval affairs from a lifetime's study and from his service in World War I to order that a class of heavy cruisers be altered on the slipways and completed as aircraft carriers instead. These were the nine ships of the successful *Independence* class, which would be commissioned through 1943, starting on New Year's Day with the *Independence* herself. This was the most intelligent direct intervention of any of the wartime leaders in ship con-struction.

Hornet was lost and the famous carrier *Enterprise* damaged in the Battle of Santa Cruz Island at the end of October 1942. But the Japanese had three carriers severely damaged and lost over 100 aircraft, and henceforth the United States was able to resume supplying the First Marine Division at Guadalcanal and to guar-antee air superiority. The tide had turned in this theater as well by election day, but this fact could not be revealed to the voters without seeming to manipulate news from the war front for partisan purposes, which Roosevelt (in this one area more scrupulous than Abraham Lincoln) refused to do. Fierce fighting contin-ued for another two months before the Japanese were subdued on Guadalcanal.

All eyes were on Stalingrad, except for those knowledgeable few who were concentrating on Morocco and Algeria, for which Allied forces were already embarked. In Stalingrad, the Russian and German armies were locked in desper-ate combat among the ruins of the city, and the Russians had prepared their counterattack on the German flanks that Stalin had mentioned to Churchill, who had transmitted the information to Roosevelt. Like a person being prepared for the guillotine by stretching his neck to receive the blade, the Germans had poured fifteen divisions into the rubble of the city, leaving their flanks largely defended by less determined forces, especially Romanian units that would have preferred to be elsewhere. The German drive to the Caucasus oilfields had been stopped by early February and they were unable to penetrate any of the passes into the mountains, held in strength by the Russian defenders. The prediction of Brooke that the Germans would breach the Russian defenses proved unjustifiably pessimistic. Germany's and Japan's mighty and ferocious offensives were almost spent, as the inexorable force and superior supreme direction of the United Nations came finally, almost a year after Pearl Harbor, to assert themselves.

With the time for Torch approaching, Roosevelt had prepared a letter to Petain that he hoped would placate the marshal as the Americans flooded ashore in Morocco and Algeria and seized control of those territories from Petain's own forces. Roosevelt claimed that the landings were intended to forestall, and assist the French in repulsing, a German invasion of French North Africa. Roosevelt's confidence in his epistolary charm was apparently no less than his faith in his persuasive powers viva voce. He had addressed Petain: "My Dear Old Friend," and closed: "Your friend," true to his practice of applying the word "friend" indiscriminately and with particular warmth to people towards whom he was anything but friendly.

He also absolved Petain of any responsibility for a dishonorable settlement in 1940, "at a time when it was impossible for any of us to foresee the program of systematic plunder which the German Reich would inflict upon the French people." In fact, of course, Roosevelt and probably even Petain and everyone else in the world had foreseen exactly the nature of the German occupation of France, and it is disconcerting that Roosevelt could imagine that even the ancient French marshal could be gulled by this claptrap.

That he foresaw none of the likely effects of such a letter on the British, the Free French, and the French Resistance of all factions confirms how little of his attention he considered France then to be worth. It is disappointing that so astute a judge of politics, including, generally, international political matters, was so dismissive of a country that when liberated was bound to become again one of the most important in Europe and of some potential value to the United States.

Churchill prevailed upon him to remove these professions of friendship, the whitewash of the 1940 surrender, and the President's invocation "as one of your friends and comrades of the great days of 1918." Churchill asked him in a cable of November 2 to remember the "de Gaullists, to whom we have serious obligations," and to "consider toning it down a bit." Roosevelt did so, "so that I am sure it will not offend the friends of France." This was in Roosevelt's response of November 4, just after he had received a further message from Churchill predicting a "decisive victory" in Egypt and pronouncing himself "so glad to see that your news from the Solomons and New Guinea is also so much better."

The following day, November 5, as the troop convoys for Torch passed through the Straits of Gibraltar, Churchill cabled Roosevelt that he was about to tell de Gaulle, on the 6th, of the impending landings and explain that he failed to do so earlier because it was essentially an American operation. He reminded Roosevelt that "I have exchanged letters with him of a solemn kind in 1940 recognizing him as the leader of Free Frenchmen." The prime minister wrote: "I am confident his military honor can be trusted." He added that he was allowing de Gaulle to announce the identity of the "Governor General of Madagascar sometime Friday. This we have been keeping for a consolation prize."

Roosevelt responded just a few minutes after receiving this message that he thought it "inadvisable" to tell de Gaulle anything about it until after the landings were successful, and to tell him that he, Roosevelt, had insisted on complete secrecy for what was an American mission. He blandly told Churchill the Madagascar announcement "will not be of any assistance to Torch and it should be sufficient at the present time to maintain his prestige with his followers."

Roosevelt added that Admiral Leahy agreed with his position, as if this would impress Churchill. Leahy had been just about as inept a judge of French affairs as Joseph Kennedy had of British ones and Joseph Davies of Soviet matters when they represented the United States in those countries. Churchill reluctantly complied with Roosevelt's wishes, though he thought there was little chance of an indiscretion, since "we control all his [de Gaulle's] telegrams outwards." (Churchill should have ignored Roosevelt in this instance, informed de Gaulle, and monitored his outward communications.)

Even more bizarre than the letter to Petain was the proclamation Roosevelt commissioned to the Arab population of North Africa, written for him by OSS Arab intelligence specialists: "O ye beloved sons of the Maghreb . . . We the American holy warriors have arrived . . . to fight the great Jihad of Freedom. . . . We have come to set you free. We have sailed across the great sea. . . . Our fighters swarm across the sands and into the city streets. . . . Light fires on hilltops . . . [Let] the ululation of women be heard in the land. . . . Speak with our fighting men and you will find them pleasing to the eye and gladdening to the heart. . . . If you see our enemies, the Germans or Italians making trouble for us, kill them with knives or with stones. . . . Pray for our success in battle, and help us, and God will help us both. Lo, the day of freedom has come. Roosevelt". It is not clear what, if any, was the impact of this unusual message upon its addressees.[8]

The most frequently encountered player in all the shadowy and often ludicrous maneuverings sponsored by the Americans to reduce the prospects of any real fighting with the French was the diplomat Robert Murphy. He was a likeable and multilingual career foreign service man from Milwaukee who had served as American consul in Munich from 1921 to 1925 and witnessed the birth of the Nazi

Party and Hitler's abortive putsch of 1923, and had served from 1930 to 1940 in the embassy in Paris, latterly as Bullitt's deputy chief of mission. Roosevelt had summoned him to Washington in September 1940 for an intimate discussion of the fragments of the French political world after the fall of France, in the midst of the 1940 presidential election campaign. The President presciently sent him to North Africa as his personal representative to make contact with General Maxime Weygand, who had just been appointed delegate general (governor) of French North Africa, and with the further mission to make contact with all potentially friendly political elements in Tunisia, Algeria, and Morocco, with a view (in Roosevelt's mind) to assisting in bringing the French Empire back into the war on the Allied side.

Murphy entered into discussions with Weygand, who Roosevelt hoped would establish an army in Algeria, resurrect the scattered French Navy, and be persuaded to slough off the feeble authority of Petain and return to the task of putting France in her rightful position among the victors. There resulted the so-called Murphy-Weygand Accord, by which the United States unfroze French assets in America sufficiently for Weygand to buy designated nonstrategic material in the United States, which secured passage for these cargoes through the rigorous British naval blockade. And the United States established extensive intelligence-gathering facilities and personnel in their North African consulates and the right to diplomatic secrecy in communications to the American government, a status not normally available to consular officials.

Weygand was technically only a colonial governor and Murphy officially only a personal representative of a foreign leader. Roosevelt told Murphy at the outset to report directly to him and ignore the State Department, and Sumner Welles confirmed that this was his frequently preferred method of operation.[9]

Roosevelt took no notice of de Gaulle at the time of his interview with Murphy. The fiasco when de Gaulle attempted to rally the Vichyite forces at Dakar in December 1940 had confirmed Roosevelt in his opinions that the Free French were chronically indiscreet and that de Gaulle himself was a somewhat comical mountebank who didn't represent anything. It would be another two years before Roosevelt shared the hopes that Churchill, from the first, and despite their many fierce quarrels (and with stunningly perceptive accuracy as it turned out), reposed in de Gaulle.

Murphy, by a combination of his own surmise and his leader's lack of esteem for de Gaulle, took most of his intelligence from the North African demimonde of Vichyite charlatans and *pied noir* (French colonial) hucksters. There were Gaullists in North Africa from the start, though a minority. De Gaulle was for a long time the only vocal and visible French partisan of uninterrupted and unconditional war against Germany, as opposed to the opportunistic collaborators who were placing bets on both sides in the war. Whatever Roosevelt or anyone else might think of de Gaulle, as the progress of Allied arms accelerated, de Gaulle was automatically legitimized as having been right, both morally and politically, from the start. Oddly, Roosevelt misjudged the de Gaulle phenomenon because he was too cynical. He had known many French politicians and considered practically all of them after Clemenceau to be, at best, Cartesian rationalists who could justify any duplicity or, at worst, morally bankrupt cynics of no courage or loyalty, even to France herself. Thus, he was unable to recognize de Gaulle, until very late in their relationship, as the brave, if inflexible, patriot and brilliant political operator that he was, and ultimately a statesman of great stature.

One of those with whom Murphy was unfortunately impressed was the wealthy collaborator and political and financial scoundrel Jacques Lemaigre-Dubreuil. Lemaigre-Dubreuil convinced Murphy that the French military figure the Americans were seeking to rally the Vichy forces in North Africa when the Allies landed was General Henri Giraud, a hero of the suppression of the Moroccan rebellion of the twenties and a recent escapee from Nazi imprisonment following his capture in 1940.

Even Hitler, who was no great respecter of the French military, had considerable esteem for Giraud. When he escaped German captivity in April 1942, Hitler said, in conversation with some of his ministers: "We must do everything possible to recapture this man. As far as I know, he is a general of great ability and energy, who might well join the opposition forces of de Gaulle and even take command of them. . . . I see in the escape of this general, to whom every possibility had been granted to alleviate the burden of his captivity, a significant pointer to the real attitude of the French toward us." Hitler seemed surprised at the thought that the French might lack affection for the Germans and that Giraud would prefer his own home to a comfortable prison cell. Hitler went on to claim that when a final peace was signed with France, Germany, "if we are to retain the hegemony of the continent . . . must retain strong-points on what was formerly the French Atlantic coast, [and] the old Kingdom of Burgundy . . . from time immemorial German soil, which the French seized from us at the time of our weakness." (Despite his concern, Hitler did nothing to recapture Giraud from Vichy France in the ensuing six months, and his version of ancient history is naturally very contestable.)[10]

General Weygand had been recalled by Petain as governor of French North Africa at German insistence in November 1941, having rebuffed overtures from Churchill and revealed himself as what everyone except Roosevelt knew him to be, an unscrupulous defeatist and a discredit to the great name of Marshal Foch. (It was his proximity to Foch, the greatest French Army commander since Napoleon, that was the key to Weygand's subsequent prominence; he was a totem, briefly reminding his countrymen of the greatest and most decisive moments of World War I.)

After Murphy's visit to Washington in mid-September, he called upon Eisenhower, General Mark Clark, Harriman, and Winant in Britain. Murphy traveled disguised as a general himself, and touted Giraud as a man who could assure the absence of resistance to the Anglo-American landings if he were given a suitably prominent position. After a further visit to Washington, Murphy returned to

Algiers in mid-October. As it was obvious even to the French who formerly enthusiastically collaborated with their Nazi conquerors that the Allies were now likely to win the war, Murphy's anteroom was crowded with those professing undying loyalty to the Allied cause and a huge capacity to deliver French political support. Weygand's replacement as governor of North Africa, Admiral Raymond Fenard, professed to represent the devious commander of the French Navy and former Vichy prime minister, Admiral Jean-Francois Darlan. The commander of the French Army in the Algiers area, General Charles-Emmanuel Mast, told Murphy that he, Mast, had been designated as Giraud's personal representative in Algeria.

The generals and admirals were doing what French generals and admirals have generally done (best) in times of political uncertainty—engaging in febrile and utterly unprincipled political maneuvers. Darlan's reputation was largely based on his ability before the war to gain the political support for building up the French Navy to the greatest comparative strength it had enjoyed since Trafalgar. It was in 1939 about two-fifths of the size of the British or American navies and considerably more powerful than those of Germany or Italy. In addition to being premier at Vichy, he had been minister of defense and of the interior. Though he was fired to make way for a return by the unspeakable Laval in mid-1942, whereupon he discreetly declared his preparedness to work with the Allies, he was the designated heir to Petain, should anything (such as exhausted longevity) befall the eighty-six-year-old marshal.

Roosevelt's policy toward Vichy was now thoroughly unpopular in the United States and Britain. Roosevelt thought he saw in Darlan the possibility of turning his shabby courtship of Vichy to account after all. Eisenhower, with the approval of London and Washington, devised a plan for securing the collaboration of Darlan and Giraud. Eisenhower would soon prove to be endowed with surpassing diplomatic and political skills, but this foray into French factional politics mired him in the lowest form of political skullduggery. The Giraud forces resented Darlan, ostensibly because of his Vichyite record, but also largely because of fear of loss of influence in post-invasion North Africa, when Darlan could offer the French Navy as an inducement to the Allies for favors, regardless of whether he could actually deliver it.

Murphy arranged a highly secret and dramatic meeting near Algiers on October 22, 1942, attended by Mast and Mark Clark, who arrived in Algeria by submarine. At one point, Clark and his party had to hide in what he assured Eisenhower in his report of the operation was an "empty" wine cellar. Clark, dubbed "the American Eagle" by Churchill because of his aquiline nose, was a canny and competent general who could hold his own with the political lowlifes who abounded in the French armed forces, and especially in the French Empire in such fluid times. It was not generally known that Clark was half-Jewish (his mother's name was Becky Ezekiel), and the generally anti-Semitic Vichyites, facing the end of their disreputable regime, didn't focus on the point.

Even Eisenhower professed curiosity to Patton about whether Clark was a Jew, during a luncheon at Gibraltar on November 17, though his curiosity was innocent. Patton, almost as caustic a diarist and correspondent as Stilwell, wrote that "Ike lives in the middle of the Rock in great danger." He complained of the presence of the British governor of Gibraltar, whom he described in his diary as "an old fart in shorts with skinny red legs."[11] Patton would always have a problem with most of the English whom he worked with, especially Montgomery and Brooke, and vice versa. (He wasn't always an uncritical admirer of Eisenhower, either.)

Eisenhower had imposed upon Murphy and Clark the strict order to give no hint of the imminence of the Allied landings, so the politicized French senior officer corps and colonial administrators plunged into their orgy of scheming and double-dealing with the further encouragement of thinking they had an almost unlimited time for haggling, bluffing, and political mendicancy. The American representatives were also to finesse the question of French authority post-landing, so Clark told Mast that authority would be handed over to the combined Giraud-Darlan tandem "as soon as possible" after the landings. Mast railed furiously against any Darlan presence in the command structure and purported implausibly to believe that the French Navy would do what the army in North Africa did, regardless of what Darlan and the other admirals told it to do.

An urgent message was dispatched to Giraud that the landings were a good deal closer to hand than he had thought, and he replied angrily, amplifying Mast's self-righteous histrionics, that this was impossible, because he was building a pro-Allied network in France and would not be ready until at least November 20. Whatever the limitations of Roosevelt's French policy, and it was seriously misguided, it had at least honeycombed the prostrate country and its colonial adjuncts with feverish conspiracy, almost all of it completely self-interested. The only elements who believed in anything more exalted than where they would be sitting when the murderous game of musical chairs ended were the Gaullists and the Communists, though Giraud, a far-from-brilliant man, was at least a sincere patriot. Murphy was now getting seriously out of his depth and urgently begged Roosevelt, with a copy to Eisenhower, November 1, for a two-week delay in the landings, failing which a "catastrophe" impended.[12]

Eisenhower received this request in London before Roosevelt did in Hyde Park. With his forces now on the high seas on their way to their landing points, Eisenhower, though not untempted by apoplexy, demonstrated the sangfroid under stress that would serve him and the Western alliance so well in all the great command positions he would hold. He sent a message to Marshall rejecting any such suggestion and asking Marshall to represent his views to the President. Roosevelt received the request from Murphy before hearing from Marshall, and instantly instructed Leahy to reject Murphy's request and order Murphy to do his best with the factions he was then trying to bring into line.

Murphy now sent the contemptible Lemaigre-Dubreuil back to Giraud promising him supreme command, not when, as Clark had suggested, the beachheads were consolidated but, and on his own insufficient authority, as soon as Giraud arrived in Algeria.

This was almost as evasive as Clark's answer to General Mast, but at least caused Giraud to abandon his request for a delay and to make a Scarlet Pimpernel departure from France. He went surreptitiously to the coast, embarked in a rowboat with muffled oars, and was taken aboard a British submarine, though not without a brief, unscheduled dunking in the Mediterranean, fully dressed and without a change of clothes. To assuage French sensibilities, the British submarine was disguised as an American vessel, by having an ostensibly American captain welcome him aboard. The ship, with difficulty, made a rendezvous with a flying boat that conveyed Giraud and three aides to Gibraltar, where Eisenhower (to Patton's irritation) now had his headquarters in what he called a "dungeon" buried in the base of the Rock. Giraud had expected to go to Algeria but was advised in flight that it would be prudent to work out exact arrangements with the Allied commander first. He arrived in the afternoon of November 7. The landings were only twelve hours away.

Giraud announced his arrival in Eisenhower's subterranean command room: "General Giraud has arrived. General Giraud is ready to assume command of the operation." Fortunately, Eisenhower didn't understand French, but he soon grasped the kernel of Giraud's message. The French general's dignity and sense of self were unshaken by the fact that he was dressed in a civilian suit that had become misshapen and discolored by his immersion in the Mediterranean the night before. Eisenhower had been warned by political advisors that Giraud "had some seriously mistaken notions of what his role in the enterprise was to be."[13] Eisenhower was then obliged to waste most of the evening run-up to the supreme moment of his life to date in a robotically repetitive argument with Giraud. The French general impressed Eisenhower by his resolution, integrity, and dignity, if not his subtlety of mind or grasp of military and political realities, and continuously repeated that he must have command of the operation, as Murphy had promised.

Eisenhower repeated endlessly, trying to put it slightly differently at each retelling, that Giraud could not command an operation in which he might have to order attacks on his own countrymen. "There is not a single Frenchman in the allied command and ... the enemy, if any, is French," Eisenhower wearily repeated ad nauseam.[14] The interpreter finally became worn down by this dialectical attrition, and the versatile "American Eagle," whose French was indifferent, took over. Eisenhower finally rather bluntly told Giraud that the operation would proceed no matter what Giraud did and that he was about to squander his opportunity to play an important role in history. After seven hours Giraud retired, announcing that "General Giraud will be a spectator."

The next morning, with the Torch landings successfully underway against little initial resistance, Giraud was in better spirits and told Eisenhower he would do as asked. Eisenhower promised him that if he rallied French support for the landings, Giraud would be treated as the administrator of French North Africa, pending a permanent political arrangement.

———————

In Shangri-la, Roosevelt had only Grace Tully, Margaret Suckley and a couple of her nieces, Hopkins and his new wife, and a naval aide to dinner. For once, he was tense. The President had been almost constantly on the telephone all afternoon, though only Hopkins and Miss Tully among his guests knew the subject of these urgent exchanges. Not long after dinner, Grace Tully handed him the telephone, saying it was the War Department. Roosevelt almost always had some tremor in his hands, but it was more noticeable as he took the telephone now. The landings had begun, casualties were light. "Thank God! Thank God! That sounds grand. Congratulations." It wouldn't satisfy Stalin's exhortation to "blood your troops" (which, as we know, in his parlance meant a staggering 10,000 casualties per day), but Americans were finally engaged in the trans-Atlantic theater. And they were taking the offensive as they had just started to do on Guadalcanal.

Roosevelt had insisted on this operation against the advice of Marshall, King, and Arnold, and a fiasco would have been disastrous in many ways, not least to his own moral authority with his service chiefs. That it appeared to be unfolding well was an immense and justified relief. Complete tactical surprise was achieved, because the Axis, Vichy, and even Spanish intelligence had all assumed that the huge and heavily escorted convoys that went through the Straits of Gibraltar were destined for Malta.

Roosevelt returned to Washington by car from the Catoctin Mountain camp on Sunday afternoon, November 8. He was so composed by the positive news that he slept in the car until Margaret Suckley awakened him as they approached the Washington suburbs. She thought it unseemly for the President to be seen asleep in his car on a day of great importance. He had sent a message, in his accented but elegant French, that had been prerecorded and broadcast as the landings took place. He had evoked what Churchill in his memoirs called "the rather tired glories of 1918," emphasized how well he had known and admired France personally ("your farms, your villages, and your cities"), emphasized the shared history and values of France and America, and promised an immediate Allied departure as soon as the territories were secure from German and Italian threat. It was a stirring, a rather debonair, and even a believable performance, resonantly concluding: "Vive la France eternelle!"

When he returned to the White House, however, he found Petain's predictably aggrieved reply, with the usual humbug of the defeated and the dishonorable about "honor" in all its contortions. "You should know that I would keep my word." He accused the United States of a "cruel initiative," and promised that "we shall defend ourselves." Such might have been his order, but Petain's author-ity in North Africa, tenuous from the start, evaporated quickly with the arrival of scores of thousands of British and American soldiers.

More successful were Roosevelt's messages to Franco and to Portugal's presi-dent (Salazar was the prime minister), both of whom responded immediately, thanking him for his courtesy and all but welcoming the United States military to the area. If Roosevelt's French policy was still hard to defend or even explain, his refusal to be drawn into the coalition against Franco during the Spanish Civil War now looked more sensible than ever.

Churchill and de Gaulle had an uneasy but in some respects noble interview on November 8. Churchill reiterated that he would always place preeminent emphasis on the American alliance, but that he would never desert de Gaulle as the "man of destiny" for France, as he had described him at their first meeting in the desperate springtime of 1940. De Gaulle urged Churchill to speak for Europe and professed astonishment that Roosevelt had even delayed the BBC's broad-casting of de Gaulle's proposed address to the North Africans (which proved to be eloquent, disinterested, and entirely helpful to the Allies). De Gaulle expressed awareness that he didn't control the BBC, but sarcastically reflected that he hadn't realized that Churchill didn't either. These and similar conversations would still be reverberating twenty and twenty-five years later, long after Roo-sevelt and Churchill had gone but de Gaulle soldiered on.

De Gaulle welcomed Giraud as a brave and patriotic man and assured Churchill that he would cooperate with him entirely. The mention of Darlan caused the conversation to take a very difficult turn, however. De Gaulle said to Churchill and the next day to Roosevelt via Admiral Stark that there was no pos-sibility of agreement between the Free French and Darlan or any other represen-tative of Vichy. Roosevelt was consulted about a Gaullist mission to Algiers and posed no objections. The mission took place in December and reached an instant and complete impasse with the Vichyites.

Churchill expressed private agreement with de Gaulle's views on the Darlan arrangements; he ascribed the problem to the vagaries of an alliance and assured de Gaulle that it was not a durable association.

The invasion force had encountered good luck in a calmer sea than usual for November off Morocco, and General George S. Patton led his men ashore safely. There was strenuous but brief resistance near Casablanca. Further resistance to the American forces as they proceeded toward Casablanca was subdued by Pat-ton as he prepared a massive naval artillery and aerial bombing assault on the city. The American capability was highlighted by the new U.S. battleship *Massa-chusetts* shooting up the French battleship that had been such a source of con-cern since 1940, the *Jean Bart* (sister of the *Richelieu,* which was still sitting in Dakar with a crew divided between followers of Petain and those of de Gaulle, receiving cash bribes from both and closely observing the fortunes of both as if watching a horse race). The *Jean Bart* had only one quadruple turret of fifteen-inch-barrel-diameter guns, couldn't leave the jetty, and was silenced and left sagging against the pier in a thoroughly battered condition after some well-placed gunnery from the American vessel, which carried nine sixteen-inch guns.*

III

THE FRENCH COMMANDER in Morocco, General Auguste Paul Noguès, faithful to the practice of 1940, having put up what he fancied to be an "honorable" resistance, ceased firing, and Patton, the most colorful American field commander since George Armstrong Custer (and infinitely more successful), took effective control of Morocco. Noguès later unashamedly told an American interviewer that he had given up the fight after conferring with the local German representative, who advised him that his position was hopeless. Noguès reproached the German for having left Vichy insufficiently armed to defend itself.[15]

In Oran and Algiers there was virtually no resistance; Murphy's efforts had prepared a good deal of useful pro-Allied activity in Algiers, where the radio station and airfields were quickly in friendly hands. In many respects the operation had been as much opera bouffe as military execution, but it had come off well, and the arrival of the Americans in the Mediterranean sounded the death knell for the Afrika Korps, Mussolini, and Petain.

The absurd aspects of the operation did not end with the landings. Murphy called upon General Alphonse Juin, commander of land forces in Algeria and Mast's superior. He roused him from a sound sleep to tell him as he sat in his drawing room in pink pajamas that French North Africa was being liberated by 500,000 American soldiers, a considerable liberty with both words and numbers.[16] Juin said that he personally would favor such an action but that Darlan was

---

* The world's first effort at covenanted arms control was the Washington Naval Disarmament Conference and Treaty of 1922, establishing quotas and displacement ceilings for battleships and aircraft carriers and a sixteen-inch limit on battleship gun barrel diameters. Displacements were not to exceed 35,000 tons for battleships and 27,000 tons for aircraft carriers. Allowable total tonnages for the contracting powers in battleships and carriers were 525,000 and 135,000 for the Americans and British, 315,000 and 81,000 for Japan, and 175,000 and 60,000 for France and Italy, and were not to be built for ten years. Germany, under the Treaty of Versailles, was not to have warships exceeding 10,000 tons, but this was varied in agreements with the British, and by unilateral action by Hitler. When battleship construction was resumed, the results were the American *Washington* and *South Dakota* (including *Massachusetts*) classes, totaling six ships; the British *King George V* class (five ships including also *Prince of Wales* and *Duke of York*); the French *Richelieu* and *Jean Bart* (and two others projected but not completed); the Italian *Littorio* and three others, of which only two were built; and the German *Bismarck* and *Tirpitz* (and two others projected but not built). They were all interesting and apparently successful designs, revealing much of the personalities of their nationalities. The French and Italian ships were the most elegant and original

now in Algiers and had the supreme authority. They telephoned him, and Darlan, likewise awakened, arrived twenty minutes later, peevish, furtive, and thoroughly unprepossessing. He responded very negatively, raging at the British and the Americans, and was skeptical that any such invasion was really in progress. Darlan did agree to send Petain a message summarizing the situation and asking for a free hand to deal with it. By this time Murphy's contacts had surrounded Juin's villa and refused to let anyone in or out. But Murphy's vice consul was permitted to take Darlan's message to Petain to French naval headquarters in Algiers for transmission to Vichy.

Murphy's operatives were shortly chased away by Juin's security unit, and Murphy was arrested when he went into the garden for some fresh air in the middle of the night. Petain did not respond to Darlan's original or subsequent messages, and in midafternoon of November 9, Darlan released Murphy as American forces poured into Algiers itself. Darlan ordered Noguès to cease resistance in Morocco and authorized Juin to surrender only Algiers to the Americans, no other part of Algeria. This was completely spurious for several reasons. Darlan was surrendering, not Juin. And the Americans had already occupied most of the city, except that two-thirds of the forces were in fact British and not American (fully justifying Churchill's claims of the relative ease of capture of the city by British soldiers against the reservations of Marshall). Darlan and Juin themselves thus became wards and prisoners of the United States, and the Allies could take as much of Algeria as they wished, as all the parties to this trumpery fully realized.

Eisenhower broadcast that morning that Giraud would shortly become the leading figure in North Africa, and Giraud broadcast shortly after, demanding that the French cease resisting the invaders. His remarks, to the perplexity of Murphy and Eisenhower, had no discernible impact. Giraud flew that afternoon to Algiers, but roused no popular interest and had to go into hiding to avoid arrest by the Fenard-Darlan-Juin elements. Clark arrived a few hours after Giraud and was almost killed by a German aircraft plummeting to ground after being felled by antiaircraft fire. In his manner, the American Eagle, who detested even relatively straightforward American politics, much less the mess of French eels he encountered in this operation, was rather effective in the ensuing discussions. He

---

(especially the French), the Germans the best engineered, the British the least preoccupied with appearance, the Americans the best-balanced design.

Demonstrating the great difficulty of arms control verification, all of the ships exceeded the 35,000-ton limit. The Western powers cheated less egregiously than the Axis countries. The Japanese showed the greatest integrity, in that they renounced the treaty and built the *Yamato* and *Musashi* at 73,000 tons each. The fact that treaty compliance in huge ships that required three years to construct could not be verified was not a good augury for arms control efforts for the last quarter of the twentieth century.

had none of Murphy's deference to these people, had a short temper, and clearly possessed an ever greater superiority in the correlation of forces. He was outraged at the hollowness of Giraud's claims to popular support.

Clark met on the morning of November 10 with Darlan, Fenard, and Juin. Clark demanded a cease-fire order at once, and professed contempt for the suggestion that there was any purpose in waiting for Petain, since the United States had finally broken off all relations with Vichy after Petain's rejection of Roosevelt's message. Clark pounded the table and told Darlan that if he didn't comply within thirty minutes, he, the American Eagle, would take him into "protective custody" and get Giraud to issue the cease-fire order. Darlan was too astute for this and told Clark that no one would pay any attention to anything Giraud did.

One of Clark's staff, Colonel Benjamin Dickson, instructed the captain of the guard around Darlan's villa that Darlan was "a short, bald-headed, pink-faced, needle-nosed, sharp-chinned little weasel. If he tries to get away in uniform or in civilian clothes, he is to be shot."[17]

Further table-pounding by Clark and sophistical evasions by Darlan continued until Clark's rages became so apparently reflective of his intentions that Darlan overcame his attachment to his solemn oath to Petain (who had fired him and for whom in fact he now had little respect, much less affection). Darlan wrote up a cease-fire order that he would claim to issue in Petain's name, an outright imposture and forgery, activities not customarily found in the officers' code of ethics. Darlan was to take over the administration "in the name of the Marshal." This, of course, was nonsense, since he was effectively already in American custody and if he possessed any authority it would come from Eisenhower and Roosevelt and Churchill, not from Petain.

This agreement shocked American and British opinion and left intact many reprehensible Vichy laws, including the repression of Jews and political opponents, and prison camps not greatly more humane than the German ones upon which they were modeled, though they were certainly not extermination camps. Clark should have simply enforced his protective custody of Darlan and issued whatever orders he wanted in Darlan's, or even Petain's, name. Better still would have been for Roosevelt to reconsider his low opinion of de Gaulle. Clark had reserved the right for Eisenhower to alter political arrangements, and the infamies Vichy imposed on North Africa were, in fact, almost over.

Clark had bullied Darlan into ordering the French governor of Tunisia, Admiral Jean Esteva, to resist the Germans, who were using Tunisian airfields to supply the Afrika Korps. Rommel would soon be in full retreat toward Tunisia, Montgomery at his nimble heels. Darlan, released by Clark as part of their arrangement, revoked—or, as he claimed, suspended—his order to Esteva. This produced one of the American Eagle's supreme theatrical moments. Advised of Darlan's action at five o'clock in the morning, it was his turn to summon Darlan and Juin and receive them in his pajamas. He informed them without bluster or preamble that if they did not immediately reinstate the order to Esteva to resist the Germans in Tunisia, he, Clark, would put them both at once before a firing squad. Darlan found this persuasive and reinstated the order to Esteva.*

The commander at Dizerte, Admiral Louis Derrien, wrote in his diary: "November 8 we fight everybody. November 9, we fight the Germans. November 10 we fight nobody. November 10 (noon), we fight the Germans. November 11 (night) we fight nobody."[19] The humiliation of France was almost, but not quite, complete.

The French North African leaders preferred the Allies to the Germans and recognized that the tide of war was shifting. Nor did they have any great regard for Petain. But they had the idea, so typical of the pusillanimous legalism of the late-thirties French officer class, that if they avoided a violation of the 1940 "Armistice" with Germany, Germany might not occupy Vichy France.

It should by now have been as clear to them as it was to de Gaulle that any distinction between Vichy and outright German occupation was technical sophistry and that this was France's opportunity to rejoin the Allies. Darlan asked Clark to await the arrival from Morocco of Noguès, whom Petain purported to have put in charge of French forces in North Africa. Darlan was fired by Petain as navy minister, having declared himself a prisoner of the Americans, and had no longer any authority to command the fleet. He had missed his great opportunity to be useful to France. He should have ordered the fleet out of Toulon as soon as he learned of the landings in North Africa, even if it only cruised to Dakar to join the *Richelieu*. It could then have rallied intact to de Gaulle.

Laval had rushed off to see Hitler to try to forestall the occupation of Vichy France. The Germans invaded Vichy France anyway on November 10, 1942, which gave Darlan all the justification he felt he needed to desert Petain. When Noguès arrived in Algiers on November 12 to exercise the authority Petain had conferred upon him, the American Eagle, who had had more than was good for his blood pressure and vital organs of these political French officers, refused to see him.

Clark did convene Darlan and other principals on November 12, insisted that Giraud be put at the head of French volunteers to fight the Axis—a force the United States would equip and pay—and confirmed Darlan, Noguès, Chatel, and Esteva as governors of North Africa and the constituent units of Morocco, Algeria, and Tunisia respectively. Eisenhower had launched the attack eastward from Algiers toward Tunisia under the command of the British general Kenneth Anderson, a bold move in the circumstances. Eisenhower and the commander of the British Mediterranean Fleet, Admiral Andrew B. Cunningham, flew from Gibraltar to Algiers on November 13. Eisenhower confirmed the existing agreement with

---

* According to Clark biographer Martin Blumenson, the general's threat may not have been so explicit, but his views were indisputably sharply formulated. (Blumenson's claim that Clark and Darlan "became friends" was an overstatement.)[18]

Darlan, but he and practically all the American participants took their distance from it for the rest of their careers, both as professionals and memoirists. Eisenhower did manfully produce a persuasive explanation of it at the time, that even Churchill, who had publicly attacked Darlan in the same terms as Laval, described as "ably expressed."[20] Eisenhower need not have been quite so embarrassed.

Essentially, Roosevelt and Hull, being opposed to de Gaulle, and with the objectives of avoiding casualties and undercutting the Germans in Tunisia as quickly as possible, and with the further objective of increasing antagonism between Germany and metropolitan France, chose to deal with whoever could speak for the military and bureaucratic apparatus in place in North Africa. For these purposes, Darlan was the best available interlocutor. He knew the vanity and avarice of the Vichy colonial officer class, since he himself personified it. They were chiefly interested in position, pay, pensions, and other perquisites, which Darlan secured for them. The anti-Semitic attitudes and decrees of Vichy were popular with the Muslim majority. The Americans made it clear throughout that any arrangements were transitory; the Americans didn't care how the French political factions sorted themselves out until much later.

The fundamental error was not to have supported de Gaulle from the start, though even this would not have provided an easy life.

It must also be said, however, that the failure of the Roosevelt policy toward de Gaulle only became obvious long after Roosevelt was dead and the war was over and France had moved forward two Republics in its syncopated political chronology. Roosevelt was correct that de Gaulle would not succeed in replacing internecine political chaos after World War II with what de Gaulle himself described as "the spirit of union, energy, and sacrifice." He did so only after 1958, when he was summoned to power, wrote a new constitution, and severed France's 130-year connection with Algeria. These were distant and esoteric matters in the autumn of 1942.

Darlan probably made the success of Torch somewhat easier. Darlan's beloved son, Alain, had just been afflicted with poliomyelitis while conducting espionage for his father in Tunisia, disguised as a traveling salesman. Roosevelt launched one of his customary charm offensives and offered to accommodate Alain at Warm Springs. It was to visit his son that Darlan had happened to be in Algeria when the Allies landed. This was an affecting and genuine gesture by the President that was gratefully considered by Darlan in December. But Roosevelt was under no illusions whatever about Darlan's true nature and value.

Roosevelt had fallen into the irritating habit of referring to de Gaulle, Darlan, and Giraud, as "three . . . prima donnas," his own underlings having resurrected two of them.*

---

* Roosevelt became fond of this expression in reference to de Gaulle, but it was introduced into the discourse of top-level American officials by Hopkins in reference to Churchill and Roosevelt himself (chapter 14).

Roosevelt cabled Churchill that "I wholly agree that we must prevent rivalry between the French Émigré factions," but it was a bit late for that, and he seemed to be rather bemused at puppeteering among the politicized French military, though he claimed the "Darlan business . . . naturally disturbed me as much as it did you." If so, only when the political backlash hit him, in the pages of the *New York Times* and other reputable and friendly newspapers. He then advised Eisenhower, through Marshall, that he considered Darlan a Fascist and a Nazi collaborator who could not be "kept in civil power any longer than is necessary."[21] He denounced Darlan to his cabinet as a "skunk."

De Gaulle, on a return visit to Downing Street on November 16, had advised Churchill unhistrionically that if the French came to believe that their liberation consisted of elevation for Darlan and his ilk, Stalin would be the only victor in the war.[22] Secretary of War Stimson, learning of Wendell Willkie's intention to blast the Darlan arrangement as a cynical betrayal in a major address, persuaded his fellow Republican not to attack the President in this way. This obtained only a brief respite for the administration, however; Willkie regularly denounced the Darlan arrangement with tongue and pen through December. So did Walter Lippmann, who had been a de Gaulle admirer from the beginning and remained so to the end of the general's life. On November 17, 1942, Lippmann accused Roosevelt of propping up a "Quisling" in North Africa.

Finally, on that day, Roosevelt issued a statement saying that he had "accepted General Eisenhower's political arrangements made . . . as a temporary expedient, justified solely by the stress of battle." He reiterated that the direction of liberated France would be entrusted to whomever the French people freely chose, and stated that he had demanded the immediate abrogation of all Nazi-inspired laws and regulations in French North Africa. In fact, some of the anti-Semitic decrees were temporarily retained to appease the Muslim Arab population, though it could be claimed that they were not Nazi-inspired, that the morally palsied men of Vichy conceived them without foreign assistance. A good deal of the opprobrium that should have been directed at Roosevelt was thus absorbed by the military, as the Commander in Chief inelegantly dumped it into the lap of the innocent Eisenhower. And the apparently incorrigible Cordell Hull had witlessly and conveniently attracted the rest of the fire by proclaiming that the Darlan agreement had vindicated his shabby Vichy policy. (In fact, Hull came to his senses in French policy before Roosevelt did.) Murphy, more than anyone else, confected this malodorous Algerian political bouillabaisse.

Eisenhower demonstrated his own political talents by accepting the poisoned chalice abruptly handed him by Roosevelt and imposing censorship on political reporting from North Africa. This was recognized, even by Eisenhower after the fact, as a mistake, but it shut down the immediate criticism. At the same time he made discreet overtures to de Gaulle, whom, he claimed in his postwar memoirs, he swiftly recognized as the most popular and legitimate figure in the eyes of the French North African majority.[23]

Roosevelt and Churchill had hoped that Darlan could snatch the much-discussed French fleet out of Toulon before the arrival of the Germans in that port, and galvanize other units, including the *Richelieu* at Dakar and the aircraft carrier *Bearn* in Martinique. Had he done so this would have given the Allies four additional modern battleships, two older but serviceable ones, the *Bearn*, a large sea plane tender, twelve cruisers, and a significant number of lesser craft. They were all well-designed ships and would have provided a useful, though at this point hardly decisive, boost to Allied naval strength. They would have gone some distance to justifying the legitimization of Darlan and, more important, they would have given France a greater sense of participation in the successful outcome of the war.

As it was, Darlan, having been officially stripped of command of the navy by Petain, "invited" the French Fleet to cross to Algeria from Toulon when the Germans approached that city. But the local commander, Admiral Jean de Laborde, a rival of Darlan's who shared his Anglophobia, scuttled the fleet instead, including three battleships and ten cruisers. It was, as de Gaulle wrote, "the most pitiful and sterile suicide imaginable. . . . I was reduced to . . . receiving by telephone the British Prime Minister's nobly expressed but secretly complacent condolences." (Churchill was almost certainly genuine and not at all "complacent.")*

With the collapse in 1940, the French fleet had been the greatest remaining geopolitical asset the stricken country possessed. Opportunity knocked for Darlan from Pearl Harbor to Torch, but he didn't recognize it.

Unlike de Gaulle, who detected and bravely and brilliantly pursued an intersecting path for himself back to his subjugated country, Darlan squandered his asset, his moment in world history, his possibility for great service to France. As de Gaulle wrote: "Like other notorious afflictions that had rained down upon France, Admiral Darlan's faults, the sad fate of our fleet and the fathomless wound inflicted upon the spirit of our sailors were the consequences of a long disease of the state."[25]

Winston Churchill, more detached and perhaps unduly generous, wrote that Darlan "showed himself a man of force and decision who did not fully comprehend the moral significance of much that he did. Ambition stimulated his errors. . . . He brought to the Anglo-American Allies exactly what they needed, namely, a French voice which all French officers and officials in this vast theatre . . . would obey. He struck his final blow for us, and it is not for those who benefited enormously from his accession to our side to revile his memory."[26]

The *Richelieu* and the *Bearn* did soon rally to the Free French, as did the old

---

* By the generous standards of his memoirs, this was an uncharacteristically bilious reflection by de Gaulle. Churchill was an authentic Francophile and, as he styled himself in his correspondence with Roosevelt, "a former naval person" who could not have failed to regret the needless destruction of a proud and potentially useful fleet.[24]

battleship *Lorraine*, and de Gaulle gradually, painfully, began to assemble the instances of a great nation at war for its life, and for the civilization to which it had made a huge contribution. De Gaulle was not to be spared further controversy about using Allied assistance to bribe sailors on the *Richelieu* (outbidding Vichy for the loyalties of the same men). Some of the shipboard maneuverings were almost worthy in their cynicism, if not their scale or sophistication, of the vessel's namesake.

At a luncheon December 23 with Eisenhower, Murphy, Clark, and Admiral Cunningham, Clark told Darlan he was welcome to accompany his son to Warm Springs if he wished, but that he should retire from his present functions. Darlan had outlived his usefulness to the Allies in Algeria. Darlan indicated that he would be happy to go, leaving matters to Giraud. "He likes it here and I don't," he said.[27]

After this lunch, Darlan confidentially told Murphy there were four plots to assassinate him. He seemed to seek reassurance that the Americans weren't involved in any of them. In fact, Darlan had become completely submissive to the Americans, their military success and Clark's threat to shoot him having apparently had a salutary consequence, and Eisenhower was grateful to Darlan for his halcyon effect on the cauldron of French colonial and military politics.[28]

On Christmas Eve afternoon, Darlan, returning to his office from a prolonged lunch, was shot and killed on the stairway of the Palais d'Ete by an alleged Gaullist-Royalist (no coloration or tendency was then unusual in what was left of French politics), Fernand Bonnier de la Chappelle.

Bonnier signed a confession, apparently without coercion, implicating Henri d'Astier de la Vigerie, a royalist conspirator and brother of de Gaulle's recent emissary to Algiers (in the visit Roosevelt and Churchill authorized). D'Astier (the brother of de Gaulle's emissary) had allegedly persuaded Bonnier to act, but was never charged or officially connected to the murder. The emissary, Francois d'Astier de la Vigerie, one of de Gaulle's confidants, whom Darlan had tried to exclude from Algeria, and who ignored Darlan when they met after Churchill and Roosevelt approved his visit, returned to London on December 24 and predicted Darlan would soon vanish.[29] (The third d'Astier brother, Emmanuel, was a resistance hero; they were nephews of an illustrious cardinal and worthy scions of a distinguished family.)

The assassin, Bonnier, just twenty years old, was given a drumhead, in camera, military trial, with counsel but without recorder, and was executed by firing squad at dawn on December 26, Christmas having been spent in desperate appeals. The resident d'Astier and the official Bourbon pretender to the long-vacant throne of France, the Count of Paris, asked Noguès and Giraud for a deferral of Bonnier's execution, inciting the inference that the confused youth who had killed Darlan was more of a royalist than a Gaullist. Noguès denied jurisdiction and Giraud quoted the Bible about "an eye for an eye." He similarly rejected the Count's imperious suggestion that the general hand over control of the regime in Algiers to him as Bourbon claimant to the crown of France in this somber period of eclipse of the French Republic. The Count was so disgusted by Giraud's impudence in refusing his proposal to hand over the government to him that he perversely declared himself tempted by republicanism.[30] Apart from being fatuous in itself, the Count's proposal ignored the fact that Roosevelt and Eisenhower, not Giraud or any other Frenchman, now ruled in Algiers.

In the course of Christmas Day, Roosevelt, through a cable from Leahy, appointed Giraud Darlan's successor as high commissioner in Algiers. Eisenhower, Anderson having been unsuccessful in his effort to capture Tunis before the retreating Germans arrived there, drove back from the front all night to Algiers and helped persuade Giraud to take the post. Giraud had only wanted a military command, but allowed himself to be seduced by the prospects of high office, in the well-established French military tradition. He quickly revoked all Vichy's oppressive and anti-Semitic laws.

De Gaulle, Eisenhower, Churchill, and Clark all refer to the murder of Darlan as suspicious, though all were relieved at his removal, "an act of providence," in the words of the American Eagle. The admiral received a grandiose funeral. Eisenhower, Clark, Cunningham (probably Britain's greatest admiral since Nelson and a man who had developed a professional respect for the deceased), Giraud, and the bemedalled representatives of Vichy and the Gaullists saluted Darlan's coffin as it was carried out of the Algiers Cathedral on December 26. Winston Churchill graciously wrote: "Let him rest in peace, and let us all be thankful we have never had to face the trials under which he broke."[31] It was a melancholy end to an unsavory association.

———————

Churchill, faithful to his word to de Gaulle, began at once to organize a fusion of the interests of de Gaulle and Giraud, without, for once, giving timely notice of the fact to his American ally, to whom, as de Gaulle had pointedly remarked, he had the almost unbroken habit of great deference.

Roosevelt had addressed the nation on November 17, a few days after Churchill had spoken of "not the beginning of the end, but . . . perhaps, the end of the beginning." The President, noting developments in the Pacific, in Russia, and in Africa, referred to "the turning point of the war" having been reached, but as "no time for exaltation. There is no time now for anything but fighting and working to win." Eleanor Roosevelt had written her friend Lorena Hickock in October that Stalingrad made her feel "ashamed," because of the absence of a Western Front. If she had reflected on the fact that the war would not have begun without the Nazi-Soviet Pact of 1939 she might have found it easier to contain her attacks of self-reproach. The great counterattack at Stalingrad was launched November 19 and 20; the Russians knifed through the supporting Romanian divisions, though they put up a respectable fight, and severed the German Sixth

Army in Stalingrad, approximately 300,000 men, from the main body of the German Wehrmacht in Russia.

Had Hitler been prepared to countenance a tactical retreat, most of his army in Stalingrad could still have been saved. The fuehrer considered all retreat to be cowardice and demanded a fight to the death. That is what occurred. Field Marshal Erich von Manstein, the chief architect of the masterly German plan for the conquest of France in 1940, one of the world's greatest World War II generals, and probably Germany's greatest, launched a counterattack that came to within thirty-five miles of Stalingrad by December 16. Manstein begged Hitler to allow his commander in Stalingrad, von Paulus, to stage a breakout.

Even at this point, most of the Sixth Army might have been saved and Germany could have had the morale boost of a sort of terrestrial Dunkirk, the deliverance of a trapped army. Hitler, again, would not hear of it, and Manstein's outnumbered forces fell back. By the end of 1942, the German Sixth Army, like the Afrika Korps, and the Japanese forces on Guadalcanal, was doomed. Barely a year after Pearl Harbor, the Germans and the Japanese had been forced into permanent retreat.

IV

ROOSEVELT AND CHURCHILL stoked up enthusiasm for an early meeting of the three principal Allies. Roosevelt had proposed staff talks, but Churchill thought only a summit meeting would produce executable decisions. Roosevelt agreed and turned to consideration of sites; he judged Iceland and Alaska too cold for a winter meeting and Khartoum or another oasis unacceptable because of mosquitoes.[32] Stalin declined Roosevelt's invitation, because he could not separate himself from his armies during the winter offensive. He proposed that they try to resolve matters by correspondence, and reaffirmed his presumption that the Western Allies would honor their promise to invade Western Europe by the spring of 1943. Roosevelt proposed to Churchill that the two of them meet, though he was at least as interested in getting away from Washington and in being the first president in the country's history to inspect American combat forces overseas. A site near Casablanca was eventually agreed for mid-January 1943.

There was not a Christmas tree lighting ceremony at the White House in 1942, for a combination of symbolic, conservation, and security reasons, and the President gave a sober Christmas wartime message to the nation. On New Year's Eve, the Hopkinses, the Morgenthaus, the Rosenmans, the Sherwoods, and the crown prince and princess of Norway dined at the White House with President and Mrs. Roosevelt. After dinner, the party previewed a movie, one that was well-chosen not only because it became one of the most famous and popular films of all time but because of recent events and of the President's itinerary in the next few weeks: *Casablanca*, with Humphrey Bogart, Ingrid Bergman, and Claude Raines. Raines, in his superb performance as a Vichy police chief, must have reminded Roosevelt of a benign version of many of the people his generals and diplomats had been dealing with in the same part of the world.*

At midnight, the President offered his customary toast to the United States of America, and added: "and to the victory of the United Nations."[33] A slightly different version has the second toast as "The United Nations," not referring to victory specifically, followed by a third toast from Eleanor to family and friends elsewhere, and by FDR's toast to "the person who makes it possible for the President to carry on," referring touchingly to his wife.[34]

Roosevelt delivered the most conciliatory message of any he ever gave to the Congress in his State of the Union address on January 7, 1943. He reviewed the progress of the war and prophesied some goals for the peace. "The Axis powers knew that they must win the war in 1942—or eventually lose everything. I do not need to tell you that our enemies did not win the war in 1942." He celebrated the "heroic people of China—that great people whose ideals of peace are so closely akin to our own" (a cultural insight that would be lost sight of over the next several decades). He spoke glowingly of the North African invasion, not only invoking "what Mr. Churchill well described as 'the under-belly of the Axis,' " but claiming the Allies had prevented thereby a German invasion of Latin America across the South Atlantic from West Africa. Roosevelt knew this to be a preposterous strategic concept. But he wanted to bolster the "Germany first" policy. (It had been Roosevelt who had assured Churchill seven months before that the Germans could not get to Dakar, much less South America.)

The President promised that in 1943 the Allies would strike at Hitler, but declined to specify whether the blow might come in Norway, the Low Countries, France, Sardinia, Sicily, the Balkans, or Poland—all of which he mentioned—or any combination of them. He celebrated the mighty feat of war production that had been achieved, surpassing most of the targets that domestic critics (and Hitler himself) had claimed were wildly unattainable. The U.S. armed forces had grown from two to seven million and would continue to grow at the same pace in the current year, with vastly increased overseas deployments. He praised the Allies, including "those Frenchmen who, since the dark days of June, 1940, have been fighting valiantly for the liberation of their stricken country." He did not, however, refer to any French leader by name, as he did to Churchill, Stalin, and Chiang.

Roosevelt admonished the Congress and the nation that the young men and women of America were not toiling and risking their lives to return to a jobless future and to restore an unjust world. He emphasized his enumeration in 1941 of

---

* Raines expressed shock that there was gambling in Humphrey Bogart's nightclub before being handed his own winnings, and gave the famous order to "Round up the usual suspects," after witnessing Bogart murder a German officer. (Both Bogart and Raines were public political supporters of Roosevelt's.)

freedom from want and fear and said the American people "expect the opportunity to work, to run their farms, their stores, to earn decent wages. They are eager to face the risks inherent in our system of free enterprise.

"They do not want a postwar America which suffers from undernourishment or slums—or the dole. They want no get-rich-quick era of bogus 'prosperity' which will end for them in selling apples on a street corner, as happened after the bursting of the boom in 1929." Even in the depths of the war while espousing a bipartisan pursuit of victory, Roosevelt never yielded the commanding political heights of the country's ambitions for progress and security. He concluded his remarks: "The spirit of this Nation is strong—the faith of this Nation is eternal."

The President began an elaborate departure procedure at midnight, January 9, going north on his train from Washington, as if to Hyde Park, turning in Baltimore in the dead of night and going to Miami, where he emplaned for Casablanca, via Brazil and West Africa. He had his clipper fly over the Citadel of Haiti, which he had visited in 1917. At Bathurst, Gambia, he spent the night on the cruiser Memphis, which was in the harbor, and had a tour of the town, an old slave-trading port. He described it as a "pestiferous hole" and expressed gratitude in private correspondence[35] that his country had never acquired an empire (much as he had wished it otherwise when younger, and not counting the Philippines and Puerto Rico, of course). He was impressed with the British colonial governor, but was reinforced in his view of the impermanence, unprofitability, and illegitimacy of imperial occupation.

Roosevelt arrived at the conference site on the afternoon of January 14 and was soon visited by Churchill. Both men were in high good spirits and had a preprandial drink. They stayed in the Anfa Hotel compound, having comfortable villas only fifty yards apart. Roosevelt was accompanied by Hopkins, and he summoned to Casablanca his sons Elliott and Franklin Jr. and Hopkins's son Robert, who was a military photographer in Tunisia. The hotel and its outbuildings overlooked the Atlantic and were defended by Patton with hundreds of soldiers and massed anti-aircraft batteries. Patton claimed to be nervous about German air raids, but the nearest German airfield was many hundreds of miles away, the Allies had overwhelming air superiority, and the meeting had been heavily shrouded in secrecy.

Roosevelt invited the principal members of the delegations, which had preceded the leaders to Casablanca, to dine with him on the 14th. The American party was Roosevelt and sons, Hopkins, Harriman, Marshall, King, and Arnold. The British were Churchill, Brooke, Pound, Portal, and Mountbatten. Eisenhower, Clark, Leahy, Dill, Alexander, and Air Marshal Tedder were also at the conference, though not at the opening dinner. This was a most convivial affair, reduced to candlelight by an air raid warning, which the diners otherwise ignored. According to Brooke, the highlight was Admiral King, well into his cups, "more and more pompous, and with a thick voice and many gesticulations," telling Roosevelt how to organize French North Africa politically. Churchill, who didn't realize how intoxicated King was, took issue with him. "Most amusing to watch," wrote Brooke in his diary, as something of a connoisseur of such occasions. (Unsurprisingly, King makes no mention at all of this exchange in his own memoirs.)

January 15 and 16 were consumed by staff talks. Churchill and Roosevelt conferred mainly with their own entourages and about their decision to invite de Gaulle and Giraud to join them. Churchill wanted, as he had indicated to de Gaulle in the latter phases of the dalliance with Darlan, to combine the efforts of the two generals. In effect, for these purposes, Churchill was de Gaulle's sponsor and Roosevelt Giraud's, though they had determined not to be drawn into internecine French émigré disputes.

De Gaulle declined Churchill's invitation to Casablanca twice, and Roosevelt alleged in correspondence to Margaret Suckley that he suggested that Churchill threaten to cut off the source of his money if he didn't appear.[36] Churchill does not refer to quite so crass a threat, and de Gaulle himself only wrote: "Without paying much attention to the threats in [Churchill's] message, which, after many such experiences, no longer affected me very strongly," he decided that the war and the current condition of France required him to meet the Anglo-American leaders, Roosevelt for the first time.[37]

While this visit was being prepared (Giraud accepted Roosevelt's invitation promptly), the staff chiefs fought out the issue of whether to proceed next to invade Sicily, as most of the British high command favored, or Sardinia, as was proposed by Mountbatten, or northern France, as the Americans wished. Marshall, unfazed by having stepped down from his plane at Casablanca in antimosquito gear, veiled hat and gloves, which he quickly discarded when greeted by British officers wearing short trousers, led the argument for the Americans, who were against wasting any more effort in the Mediterranean after clearing the Axis out of Africa.[38]

Brooke recorded in his diary the laborious work in bringing the Americans around, as if building a ship model or climbing a mountain, a matter of inevitable outcome—the U.S. view being, implicitly, the amateurism of newcomers. Brooke was also unimpressed with King's request for a sharply increased dedication of resources to the Pacific theater.[39] Marshall presumably produced this diversion to keep current his threat to redeploy to the Pacific if the British insisted too sternly on squandering resources in a secondary theater and deferring indefinitely the cross-Channel effort.

It was obvious to all the Americans that movement in Italy would be slow, owing to terrain that gave the advantage to the defender, and that the prize was secondary. The Americans did not doubt that with sufficient forces—i.e., a concentration of everything available for the West European theater—a successful war of maneuver, bearing no resemblance to the sanguinary trench actions of World War I that so traumatized the British, including Churchill, could be successfully conducted in northern France and into Germany. It was a vigorous debate.

The Americans had no interest in getting rid of Mussolini, now an extinct volcano, despised in his own country and scarcely still capable even of bluster. It was agreed that any invasion of Italy would bring the Germans into the peninsula. Mountbatten's idea of Sardinia was quickly dismissed by almost everyone else of both nationalities as a strategically irrelevant island. Sicily at least led to Italy, Sardinia led only to Corsica. Marshall was prepared to accept Sicily, as a spillway for the troops that would have chased the Germans and Italians out of North Africa, if it stopped there, but not as a mere conduit to becoming mired for years in Italy.

Roosevelt and Marshall's problem was that as long as the British had the majority of the men, ships, and aircraft in the European theater, which would be the case for another year (including the Canadians with the British, although they were rarely consulted on such matters), Churchill could always claim preeminence in decision-making. This condition obtained despite Roosevelt's complete solidarity with his own staff chiefs that the British vision of war with Germany of blockade, aerial bombing, aid to indigenous resistance movements, and amphibious irritants around the periphery of German-occupied Europe was an impractical route to victory.

The Americans all thought such a vision a recipe for a prolonged stalemate that could be rendered virtually permanent by resumption of a separate peace and continental demarcation between Germany and Russia. No one expected Stalin, almost indifferent to casualties though he apparently was, to go on indefinitely with Russia alone enduring 90 percent of the bloodletting sustained by the Big Three Allies.

In practice, the United States would be able to require a cross-Channel invasion only when it was able to provide most of the forces for it. The only way to accelerate the timetable of U.S. preeminence in Europe was to divert some of the flow of men and materiel from the Pacific.

Of all the versions of historical revisionism that endlessly arise over World War II, one of the most interesting is that Casablanca should have launched a countdown to an invasion of northwest Europe in 1943. The threat to the Suez Canal, Middle Eastern oil, and Palestine was over with El Alamein. The German forces in Tunisia, though heavily reinforced by Hitler, were doomed. They could have been contained in Tunisia and strangled by the application of air and sea power.

The usual excuses for delaying the cross-Channel invasion—inability to get the men to England, shortage of landing craft, insufficient air superiority, lack of experienced soldiers, excessive German strength in northern France—are not entirely convincing. The eventual invasion plan, named "Overlord," that was successfully executed in 1944 allowed for eight divisions to be put ashore on

D-Day and twenty-two more divisions within thirty-five days, and between two and three divisions per week thereafter until Germany had been defeated. In March 1943 there were nearly forty divisions in Britain.

The Allies had less shipping at the end of 1942 than they had had at the beginning of the year, though new shipping construction was now pulling ahead of U-boat sinkings. (Soldiers were transported in liners that were too fast for U-boats. The largest, *Queen Elizabeth* and *Queen Mary*, could carry almost a whole division each.)

The United States Army had grown from thirty-seven trained divisions on entry into the war to seventy-three trained divisions at the time of the North African landings almost a year later, and would have 120 divisions by the summer of 1943 and 220 divisions a year later. The British Commonwealth would have approximately seventy-five combat divisions by the summer of 1943. The required Overlord force levels could have been met, and probably delivered to England.

They particularly could have been met if the British and Americans had facilitated the regeneration of the French Army, which numbered 300,000 in North Africa. Even if 50,000 would have had to be mustered out for reasons of political incompatibility, another ten divisions could swiftly have been assembled from this force. The Free French fought with distinction in Africa, Italy, France, and Germany. The Americans were prepared to equip these forces on the understanding that Giraud would command them, but the British, Brooke in particular, wanted them as support forces in noncombat roles only.[40]

They should have been placed under de Gaulle's command. This step might also have instilled in de Gaulle an enhanced sense of gratitude to his allies and greater national self-confidence, the absence of which characteristics in France would be troublesome to the British and Americans for decades to come.

Roosevelt always intellectually dominated the Canadian premier, Mackenzie King, who was anxious to get Canadian forces into action. If he had lobbied King, Roosevelt probably could have detached Canada from the Mediterranean policy. Interspersing experienced and inexperienced soldiers, as long as they were all adequately trained and the officers were capable, would have produced competent armies. One of the central problems was that while Churchill and Brooke feared the German Army, Brooke—but not Churchill—mistakenly doubted the battle-worthiness of Marshall's mass-produced American armies.

German forces in France increased from forty-nine divisions in the summer of 1943 to fifty-seven divisions in June 1944, though those divisions were smaller because of the losses they had sustained, so the comparative strength was probably not much changed year over year. Von Rundstedt and Rommel greatly strengthened the Atlantic Wall in the year before D-Day.

The landing craft problem has long been a mystery. The U.S. Navy did not particularly like these vessels, because they were more army than navy ships. And the naval high command, especially Admiral King, allocated most of them to the

Pacific war, which was almost entirely amphibious operations and largely a naval war. The admiral's preferences are understandable, but given the agreed Allied policy of defeating Germany first, Roosevelt should have overruled King.

American public opinion demanded an aggressive policy against Japan, and Roosevelt had to keep one eye on the 1944 elections. But after Midway and the injection of increasing numbers of the ships Roosevelt had laid down in 1940, it should have been possible to direct more men and landing craft to the European theater. By the summer of 1943 the United States Navy had twice as many battleships and three times as many aircraft carriers as Japan. In May 1944, the United States had 31,000 landing craft, but only 2,500 assigned to D-Day. Two-thirds of the landing craft on that occasion were provided by the British.

It would have been a daring move, but the Western Allies could have managed a cross-Channel invasion in August or September 1943. They could have bypassed Sicily or invaded Sicily even before the final German surrender in Tunisia. The sea invasion force that assaulted Sicily in July 1943 was actually slightly larger than that deployed at Normandy eleven months later. And the Allies took fewer casualties securing the bridgehead in Normandy in 1944 than they did at Salerno, near Naples, in 1943.[41]

Marshall was right that Torch was intended by the British to lead to almost endless involvement in the Mediterranean, but the United States did not have to, and ultimately did not, acquiesce in this. Churchill privately acknowledged that he was trying to ensnare the U.S. in the Mediterranean, and was hoping that the formula "in for a penny, in for a pound," would prevail.[42] In order to impose a swifter timetable and overcome Churchill's and Brooke's resistance to Overlord, Roosevelt would have had to scale back Pacific operations from the twin parallel offensives of Nimitz in the central Pacific and MacArthur in the southwest Pacific.

This would have brought with it certain political problems. But Roosevelt mastered all political problems. MacArthur would have stirred up his claque in the Congress and the press, unless he were placated by promotion. The two Pacific theaters could have been combined and awarded to him. Nimitz could have been promoted to King's position of chief of naval operations, where he would undoubtedly have been an improvement. King had more bellicosity than intelligence or judgment, while Nimitz was one of history's great admirals. As will be discussed in chapter 20, when the Overlord commander was named, MacArthur could even have been given command of the cross-Channel operation.

Whether commanded by Eisenhower or MacArthur, an August or September 1943 invasion of northern France, if it had been decided upon at Casablanca, would probably have shortened the European war by six to nine months and have left the Russians well to the east of where they ended the war. Failing this, as an alternative to Italy, the Allies might even have done well to consider accepting Stalin's request to participate on the Eastern Front and might have salvaged some of the Balkans from Russian control. With all that said, Roosevelt's lack of enthusiasm for having a fierce battle with the British, much of his own high command, and a large segment of domestic political and congressional opinion over grand strategy at this time is understandable.

The objectives that were agreed upon at Casablanca—clearing the entire North African coast, invading Sicily, and trying to eliminate Mussolini—were reasonable, if not very imaginative. But they were important and they were achieved.

On January 18, 1943, Brooke and Marshall again went head to head in strong disagreement over these basic strategic questions for hours of highly articulate, intense discussion. The full staffs of both sides were present, but the government heads were absent. Brooke objected to the implicit American threat to concentrate on the Pacific and Marshall responded that the British wanted to squander time and resources in the Mediterranean, where no real damage could be done to the Germans, while slowly building an invasion army in Britain that would be wholly inactive, until the far-off day when the British decided it was of adequate strength to cross the Channel. The United States, Marshall declared, would rather use those forces in the Pacific than have them spend endless months in barracks in Britain.

King kept interjecting the need to assure continued progress in the Pacific and accused the British of trying to starve him of the forces necessary to avoid disaster there. Marshall and Brooke tried to agree on the extent of desirable advance in the Pacific and reasonable force ceilings for that theater. But it was Dill, a conciliator of immense ability, universally trusted, who mediated an agreement. The compromise finalized on the morning of January 19, 1943, was that the recapture of Burma and a southwest Pacific offensive to Rabaul and on into the Marshall and Caroline Islands would be conducted with whatever means could be spared without compromising the objective of defeating Germany first. Sicily would be attacked, since the forces to do so were nearby and it would at least provide a distraction to the Germans.

A cross-Channel landing would be conducted as soon as possible, but the unofficial view arose and gained currency, supplemented by Eisenhower's view, which he expressed at Casablanca, that the forces necessary for success could not be assembled until mid-1944. In all of the circumstances, Roosevelt deferred to this opinion. This may possibly have been the second-best strategy, but it wasn't bad strategy, as long as the Americans could bring the British into a cross-Channel invasion before Stalin and Hitler made a separate peace or Stalin seized most of Europe.

The British were delighted with the result of the Brooke-Marshall discussion, most elements of which were unveiled on the evening of the 18th at a dinner of Roosevelt's where the combined staffs were all present. The President called upon Marshall to speak for the Combined Chiefs and he deferred to Brooke. The exchanges that had occurred, though often difficult, were always the civil exchanges of people who spoke the same language and were fighting the same enemies, and now Brooke handled his task with diplomacy.

Brooke found the Americans "difficult though charming people to work with." He said that Marshall had "practically no strategic vision," and that "his thoughts revolve around the creation of forces and not on their employment." He found Patton, the area commander, a "swashbuckling personality . . . a dashing, courageous, wild and unbalanced leader, good for operations requiring thrust and push but at a loss in any operation requiring skill and judgment." Time would prove both opinions ungenerous.[43]

Brooke's skepticism about the size and quality of the forces that Marshall would be able to deploy, and about the rapidity with which they would become battleworthy, was unfortunate but understandable. In the same way, it was difficult for people from other countries to grasp the extent of American war production capabilities, although the British, in particular, were beginning to have considerable exposure to it. A fully mobilized America operated on a scale the world had not seen before.

On January 17, Patton gave Roosevelt a tour of some of the recent sites of military action, including the contested landings at Port Lyautey. Roosevelt laid wreaths on graves, greeted soldiers, and went as far as Rabat. The U.S. Army lined the entire route, eighty-five miles. Everywhere, American servicemen were astounded and delighted to see him.

Roosevelt and Churchill had an agreeable private dinner that night.* Roosevelt's sons embarked on a rather uninhibited tour of the highlights of Casablanca's nightlife, with which they regaled their delighted father on their return. On the evening of January 18, Roosevelt had the sultan of Morocco to dinner with Churchill. But the evening was not entirely successful, because Roosevelt referred several times to the imminent disappearance of colonial empires, a nettlesome point to the prime minister, and to de Gaulle, when he learned of it.

V

THE ARRIVAL OF Giraud and de Gaulle announced the next phase of the conference. De Gaulle objected to being behind barbed wire, heavily guarded, with American soldiers even performing the domestic tasks.† The arrival

---

* The only shortcoming was that Churchill ran out of cigars and all that could be found was a package of White Owls sent to an aide of Patton's by the soldier's wife. Churchill put his first White Owl out after one puff. Churchill incidentally reinforced the famous claim of Woodrow Wilson's vice president, T.R. Marshall, that "What America needs is a good five-cent cigar."

† It is unlikely that any GI would have prevented the general from making his own bed or cleaning his own lavatory had he wished to do so.

of France's greatest leader since Napoleon did not eliminate the farcical elements of the discussions of French affairs.

De Gaulle had no difficulty establishing an intellectual domination over Giraud. At one point, after Giraud had recounted to him and others the gripping tale of his escape from German captivity, de Gaulle asked him to tell the story of how he became a German prisoner in the first place. (As Brooke wrote, Darlan was able but without integrity; Giraud had integrity but was unintelligent; de Gaulle possessed integrity and high intelligence but was an impossible and dictatorial personality.[44])

Future prime minister Harold MacMillan arranged for de Gaulle to visit Churchill, to whom de Gaulle railed against being "surrounded, on French territory, by American bayonets." He dismissed out of hand Churchill's proposal for a French National Committee of equal presidents, including de Gaulle, Giraud, the North African governors, and others. De Gaulle even accused Churchill of unilaterally devaluing the French currency.

De Gaulle went on to meet Roosevelt. "We spent an hour together on the same couch. . . . [Though] Roosevelt affected to be alone in my company, I noticed shadows at the rear of a balcony and saw curtains moving in the corners," producing "a strange . . . atmosphere." De Gaulle claimed Harry Hopkins and secretaries were secretly listening. It was Roosevelt's security detail behind the curtain, with drawn guns, because it seemed to Mike Reilly that his handicapped chief was having a dispute in a foreign language with an able-bodied man six-and-a-half-feet tall.[45] Patton had a low opinion of the Secret Service detail, calling them "a bunch of cheap detectives, always smelling of drink."[46]

Despite these absurd atmospherics, Churchill wrote of the general's first meeting with Roosevelt: "To my relief they got on unexpectedly well. The President was attracted by 'the spiritual look in his eyes.' "[47] De Gaulle's analysis of Roosevelt also had perceptive elements: "Franklin Roosevelt was governed by the loftiest ambitions. His intelligence, his knowledge and his audacity gave him the ability, the powerful state of which he was the leader afforded him the means, and the war offered him the occasion to realize them. . . . The United States, delighting in her resources, feeling that she no longer had within herself sufficient scope for her energies, wishing to help those who were in misery or bondage the world over, yielded in her turn to that taste for intervention in which the instinct for domination cloaked itself. It was precisely this tendency that President Roosevelt espoused. He had therefore done everything to enable his country to take part in the world conflict. He was now fulfilling his destiny, impelled as he was by the secret admonition of death." (De Gaulle would eventually learn something of the same race that statesmen sometimes run between their own time and events they can't entirely control.)

These reflections contain several questionable psychological liberties, compounded by de Gaulle's claim that Roosevelt had insisted on "an American peace," which Roosevelt would "dictate . . . and that France, in particular, should recognize him as its savior and its arbiter." De Gaulle completely failed to grasp the facts that only America's presence in Europe and the Far East could win the present war, prevent a major war thereafter, and advance the cause of liberal civilization and democratic government. He seems not to have seriously considered the undoubted fact that this, rather than a will to rule the world (though Roosevelt was not entirely immune to such temptations), was the American leader's principal motive. De Gaulle claimed that "the fact that France was reviving in the heat of battle" (of which there was little perceptible evidence) "as a sovereign and independent nation, thwarted his intentions."

There was perhaps some truth to this, but de Gaulle went too far when he claimed that: "Diligent at charming others, but hampered deep within himself by the painful infirmity against which he struggled so valiantly, Roosevelt was sensitive to partisan reproaches and gibes. Yet it was precisely his policy to General de Gaulle that aroused the fiercest controversies in America." Roosevelt was in fact rarely bothered by criticism, and after Hull's fiasco with St. Pierre and Miquelon and the sojourn with Darlan, France wasn't an issue in the United States.

More accurate was de Gaulle's observation: "Like any star performer he was touchy as to the roles that fell to other actors. In short, beneath his patrician mask of courtesy, Roosevelt regarded me without benevolence. . . . Nevertheless . . . realizing that a clash would lead to nothing, for the sake of the future, we [knew that] each had much to gain by getting along together." (De Gaulle preceded Roosevelt by at least a year in that realization, and the risks of a severe dispute were hardly equally distributed between them. France was awaiting American-led liberation, not the other way around.)

A good deal of discussion ensued between de Gaulle and Giraud over Churchill's French National Committee plan, which Roosevelt had endorsed. De Gaulle rejected it, as he did when variations, drafted by Churchill and Roosevelt or by their aides and instantly accepted by Giraud, were presented to him, despite intense lobbying from Murphy and MacMillan. (De Gaulle had a very limited regard for Murphy and mixed feelings about MacMillan; their relationship would be long and complicated.)

Inevitably, Churchill asked to see de Gaulle. This encounter "was characterized on his part [Churchill's] by extreme acrimony." There was an "ungracious . . . furious scene; the Prime Minister showered me with bitter reproaches in which I could see nothing but an alibi for his own embarrassment."

On to Roosevelt. "My reception at his hands was a skillful one—that is, kind and sorrowful." Roosevelt said: "In human affairs, the public must be offered a drama." A de Gaulle-Giraud meeting in the presence of Churchill and himself, de Gaulle claimed Roosevelt said, with a joint communiqué, no matter how vague, "would produce the dramatic effect we need."[48] To a man of de Gaulle's vanity and vulnerability, this was a demonstration of Roosevelt's great talents as a negotiator.

"Let me handle it," de Gaulle claimed he replied. All the Americans, British, and French of all factions then poured in, and Churchill "loudly reiterated his diatribe against me with the evident intention of flattering Roosevelt's somewhat disappointed vanity. The latter affected to pay no attention." Roosevelt asked de Gaulle if he would be photographed with Giraud, which de Gaulle was happy to do, and if he would shake hands with him for the cameras. "I shall do that for you," de Gaulle responded in English (a language he barely, and almost never, spoke). "Then Mr. Roosevelt, delighted, had himself carried into the garden . . . where innumerable cameras" would portray the "deus ex machina in the person of the President," who had created this apparent reconciliation.

De Gaulle drew up a brief declaration, stating that he and Giraud had met, affirmed their "faith in the victory of France and in the triumph of human liberties," and announced the establishment of a permanent liaison between themselves. Both signed, and the communiqué was issued without being shown to the Allies. In his fashion, de Gaulle had made his point.

Churchill recalled it, naturally, a bit differently, and wrote that Giraud and de Gaulle were "made to sit in a row," and "forced" to shake hands. "The pictures of this event can not be viewed, even in the setting of these tragic times without a laugh."[49]

Fierce and frequent though their disputes were, Churchill and de Gaulle were reciprocally generous in their memoirs. Churchill wrote of his Casablanca encounters with de Gaulle: "I had continuous difficulties and many sharp antagonisms with him. There was however a dominant element in our relationship. I could not regard him as representing captive and prostrate France. . . . I knew he was no friend of England. But I always recognized in him the spirit and conception which, across the pages of history, the word 'France' would ever proclaim. I understood and admired, while I resented, his arrogant demeanour. Here he was—a refugee, an exile from his country under sentence of death, in a position entirely dependent on the good will of the British government and now of the United States. . . . Never mind; he defied all. Always, even when he was behaving his worst, he seemed to express the personality of France—a great nation, with all its pride, authority, and ambition."

Churchill, long a leader of the pro-French faction in British public life and a promoter of the Entente Cordiale from the beginning, a romantic personality, could appreciate de Gaulle in a way that Roosevelt did not. Roosevelt, a worldly and civilized man, appreciated France culturally and geographically (and spoke French better than Churchill did), and came to respect de Gaulle as a brave and clever political operator. From Casablanca, however, he wrote to Margaret Suckley: "De Gaulle a headache. One day he thinks he's Jeanne d'Arc; the next he's Georges Clemenceau!"[50]

It was after the choreographed handshake and the departure of the Frenchmen, while Churchill and Roosevelt were conducting a press conference, that the most controversial aspect of the Casablanca conference occurred. Roosevelt volunteered that the commanding general of the Grand Army of the Republic in the U.S. Civil War, U.S. Grant, was often referred to as Unconditional Surrender Grant, and that the Allies insisted on unconditional surrender from their enemies in this war. It has generally been represented that this was a spontaneous inspiration of Roosevelt's, after consultation with no one, and that it was a serious tactical error, because it provoked the Germans and Japanese to fight more tenaciously.

The facts are more complicated. A State Department committee on postwar policy chaired by the imperishable Norman Davis suggested to the President in mid-1942 enunciation of unconditional surrender as an objective in regard to Germany and Japan, but not Italy. On January 7, 1943, the day of the State of the Union message and just before the departure of the military chiefs for Casablanca, Roosevelt met with his military advisors and asked their opinion of an unconditional surrender statement as an outcome of the upcoming talks. The President, not so much solicitous of Stalin's "feelings," as many of his critics have claimed, but concerned for Stalin's morale as a combat warrior, suggested it might raise the credibility of the Western Allies as full-scale participants in the land war against Germany, especially since a further deferral of the cross-Channel landings to 1944 seemed increasingly possible.

Roosevelt raised the matter socially with Churchill, who approved it, and raised it more formally in detailed discussions at Casablanca. Churchill consulted the War Cabinet by cable about it January 20, and received no demurral. His subsequent claim to have been astonished when Roosevelt popped this on the press January 24 was, as Churchill generously stated in his memoirs, mistaken.[51] So was Roosevelt's own statement that the press conference statement was spontaneous, in that he was referring to the timing of the announcement, not the prior consideration of the policy.

Also mistaken was the claim of Ernest Bevin (a member of the War Cabinet and postwar foreign secretary) in 1949 that the War Cabinet was not consulted.[52] General Marshall initially claimed that he had first heard of it at Casablanca, but then amended his recollections when reminded of the January 7 discussion. Marshall felt that the declaration was desirable as an encouragement to Stalin as well as to the occupied countries, and was helpful to Allied morale generally. He and Roosevelt, impressed by the manner in which Hitler had been able to convince a large number of Germans that Wilson and Foch had swindled Germany into the 1918 Armistice and that Germany had not been defeated at all, believed that some such Allied declaration was necessary now.[53]

As Churchill points out in his memoirs, the exclusion of Italy from the unconditional surrender requirement undoubtedly contributed to its early collapse and to the deposing of Mussolini, which occurred six months after Casablanca. Subsequent statements by Roosevelt and Churchill made it clear that unconditional surrender was only required of the Nazis and of the current Japanese rulers. It was clear that some negotiation would be possible with more respectable elements, and the settlement with post-Mussolini Italy made that clearer.

"Unconditional surrender" may have caused the Nazis and Japanese extremists to fight with enhanced desperation, though that has not been proved, but it encouraged the forces of dissent in both countries, ultimately including the emperor of Japan. Those who tried to murder Hitler as the war continued to close in on the Axis were well aware of the possibility of doing better for Germany than unconditional surrender. In general, the attacks on Roosevelt in this case were unfair. The claims of some historians that the "unconditional surrender" requirement greatly prolonged the war (and even, according to one otherwise serious historian, produced the Ardennes offensive in 1944) are unsustainable.[54] The policy was justifiable, and both the prior consultation and the subsequent refinement of it were adequate.

The Casablanca Conference ended January 24, 1943, and was generally judged a solid success. Churchill entreated Roosevelt: "You cannot come all this way to North Africa without seeing Marrakesh. Let us spend two days there. I must be with you when you see the sunset on the snows of the Atlas Mountains."[55] This was agreed and the two motored the next day the five hours to Marrakesh, again the entire route lined by "many thousand American troops . . . and aeroplanes circled ceaselessly overhead."[56] A luxurious Marrakesh villa had been lent to the U.S. vice consul, Kenneth Pendar, by a Mrs. Taylor, an American but an arch-Republican and implacable political foe of the President. She had lent her house to the U.S. government when the war started and she returned to the United States, but had stipulated that it not be used by President Roosevelt, whose visit to Marrakesh only an authentic clairvoyant could have guessed. Pendar was aware of Mrs. Taylor's stipulation but wisely ignored the unenforceable restriction.

Mike Reilly and another aide carried Roosevelt to the top of a tower in the villa to view the sunset. Wilson, Churchill's doctor, unfailingly noted, as the President was conveyed up the steep steps, that his legs were "dangling like the limbs of a ventriloquist's dummy."[57] The panorama of the Atlas Mountains as the sun descended behind them was a memorable sight and it was a poignant moment.

The two leaders had a very convivial closing dinner in Mrs. Taylor's forbidden villa, and made their farewells. Some American black soldiers entertained the leaders by singing, and Churchill was impressed with the American words to "Danny Boy," the British words to "Londonderry Air" being rather banal. Roosevelt's plane was to take off the next morning at 7:30 on its circuitous return to the United States. According to Churchill, although they had parted the night before, "he came round in the morning on the way to the aeroplane to say another good bye. I was in bed but would not hear of letting him go to the airfield alone." Churchill claimed he put on his siren suit, zippered up the front, but onlookers allege he was in his red dragon dressing gown and velvet slippers.* "I drove with him to the airfield, and went on the plane and saw him, comfortably settled down, greatly admiring his courage under all his physical disabilities and feeling very anxious about the hazards he had to undertake. These aeroplane journeys had to be taken as a matter of course during the war. None the less I always regarded them as dangerous excursions." To Wilson, Churchill had said: "I love these Americans. They have behaved so generously."

As the President's majestic clipper gathered speed on the runway and got determinedly into the air, Winston Churchill grasped Pendar's arm and said: "If anything happened to that man, I couldn't stand it. He is the truest friend; he has the farthest vision; he is the greatest man I have ever known."[58]

Winston Churchill returned to the Villa Taylor in Marrakesh for another day's conference and correspondence with colleagues. He painted "from the tower the only picture I ever attempted during the war." He later gave it to Roosevelt. When Eleanor inherited it, she gave it to their son Elliott, who sold it for a risible sum to a woman in Iowa, in the very bowels of America.[†]

---

* That the prime minister was probably in his dressing gown was appropriate, given how much recent North African history had been accomplished by Juin, Mark Clark, and Darlan when similarly accoutered.

† It was eventually sold to a private collector in New York, where it remains.[59]

CHAPTER 19

⚜

"Roosevelt Recognized the Importance of Capturing Berlin as Both a Political and a Psychological Factor"

(U.S. Army Chief of Staff General George C. Marshall's comment on Roosevelt's strategic objectives to General Albert Wedemeyer, August 25, 1943)

I

ROOSEVELT RETRACED HIS steps, flying to Bathurst, Gambia, where he arrived with a slight fever. He again slept on the *Memphis*, and went up the Gambia River the next day on a tugboat, impressed again by the poverty and insalubrity of this misbegotten colonial outpost. On his return to Bathurst he told reporters, accurately, but without a surfeit of prescience, that Africa would be a problem for a long time. On January 28, 1943, he flew to Monrovia, Liberia, and had lunch with the president of that country, Edwin Barclay. Liberia had been set up to receive emancipated American slaves wishing to return to Africa as free men.

The capital was named after President James Monroe, and the country after the liberty of the early inhabitants, but there had not been many takers at the outset and fewer since, and the whole concept had not been a huge success. This had been a great disappointment to Henry Clay and other great mid-nineteenth century American political figures who long thrashed about looking for a compromise resolution of the problem of slavery. Roosevelt's presence had astounded the natives as he drove through the city, as he had in Gambia, and he was very warmly received by U.S. (African-American) troops whom he reviewed in Liberia.

Roosevelt crossed the South Atlantic and conferred at length with Brazilian President Getulio Vargas, on board a U.S. destroyer in Recife. He flew on to Florida and entrained for Washington, arriving in the evening of January 31, the day after his sixty-first birthday. He felt fluish, which confined him for part of February, and which he blamed on Gambia.[1]

On his first night back in the White House, Roosevelt had dinner with his daughter, Anna, and her husband, John Boettiger, who was already showing some signs of the temperamental instability that would ultimately drive him to suicide. When Boettiger expressed a desire to attend such a meeting as his father-in-law had just returned from, as Anna's brothers had done, Roosevelt abruptly debunked the idea by pointing out that he wasn't in uniform. This was all Boettiger needed to enlist, writing to his long-standing acquaintance, General Dwight D. Eisenhower, to facilitate this.[2]

Roosevelt and Churchill had approved a letter to Stalin, cheerfully outlining all the helpful things they were going to do to assist Russia in defeating Hitler, but omitting any mention of a full second front. They did not dare to describe the forecast takeover of Sicily as something that would take any pressure off the Russian front. Stalin replied January 30 asking when they expected to open the second front. Churchill replied on behalf of both addressees of Stalin's eminently reasonable request, after two weeks. Churchill and Roosevelt, who contributed some editorial flourishes, resorted to outright falsehoods, a hazardous course in an alliance.

On behalf of both leaders, Churchill promised the expulsion of the Axis from Africa by April, the seizure of Sicily by July, a subsequent move in the eastern Mediterranean, probably the Dodecanese, and a cross-Channel attack in August or September, provided "limiting factors" could be surmounted. These were shipping and landing craft availability and the state of German defenses. None of these reasons, as was discussed in chapter 18, was plausible, especially not to Stalin. The authors and their military chiefs doubted the feasibility of any such timetable, and Churchill and the British high command were in fact opposed to a cross-Channel landing unless the Germans had been almost completely enfeebled. Churchill's message to Stalin, which Roosevelt expressly asked be identified as approved by him also, was sent on February 10, 1943.

Stalin replied February 16 with his usual, and for once justified, skepticism. Stalin objected to the delay in clearing the Germans out of Africa, from December to April, and claimed that twenty-seven German divisions had been moved to the Russian front, so that the Anglo-American activities were not drawing off, but adding to, German strength in the east.

Stalin ominously added: "I must give a most emphatic warning, in the interest of our common cause, of the grave danger with which further delay in opening a second front in France is fraught." The Soviet leader was deliberately unspecific about the danger, as between military reversals and a separate peace with Hitler. But the danger of a military collapse, after the great victory at Stalingrad, was much reduced. And the concern of the ever-paranoid Stalin that he was just being used to enervate Germany while enduring an unlimited bloodbath himself could quite comprehensibly drive him to compose his differences with Hitler on a basis of much greater strength than when he negotiated the Non-Aggression Pact of 1939.

Roosevelt and Churchill now had to keep Stalin in the war, taking as many of the casualties as they could safely expect him to endure, while they mounted an operation in Europe that would convince Stalin the West would do its part to subdue Germany and enable some Russian penetration of central Europe. This was not a goal that could be achieved by the British flim-flam of milling endlessly about in the Mediterranean.

Obviously, Stalin would have to be compensated for doing most of the fighting, but the effort would be to reward him in Eastern Europe with secondary geopolitical acquests.

Churchill proposed to Roosevelt the wording of a reply to Stalin March 4. Churchill slightly sheepishly ascribed the delay in Tunisia to greater German strength than had been foreseen, and added a bit self-consciously: "We thought you would like to know those details of the story although it is on a small scale compared with the tremendous operations over which you are presiding." Churchill thought the Germans had transferred only about twelve divisions to the Russian front, net of those that had been withdrawn from that front. He hedged more in this message than the previous one on the cross-Channel operation. He stressed the shipping problems and raised the clear possibility of no cross-Channel landing in the current year and concluded on the familiar theme: "A premature attack with insufficient forces would merely lead to a bloody repulse and a great triumph for the enemy."[3]

Roosevelt replied March 5 to Churchill, apologizing for not having sent him his own reply to Stalin of February 22, which was shorter and less defensive than Churchill's, perhaps because of the gigantic scale of American supplies to Russia, which gave Roosevelt a comparative moral advantage. Both correspondents showered Stalin with compliments on the valor of Russia's "heroic army." Roosevelt concluded: "You may be sure that the American war effort will be projected onto the Continent of Europe at as early a date subsequent to success in North Africa as transportation facilities can be provided by our maximum effort."

Churchill had contracted pneumonia when back in London, and Roosevelt was still suffering from what he invariably called the "grippe," a multipurpose umbrella description for all his ailments, from sinusitis to anemia, bleeding hemorrhoids, and irregular cardiological phenomena.

Hitler had belatedly decided to put up a spirited struggle in Africa. Having starved Rommel when he was only a hundred miles from the Suez Canal and could have gone a long way to winning the war, Hitler now poured in 110,000 first-class soldiers to fight it out in Tunisia, where his army was surrounded and subject to unanswerable attack from superior Allied sea and air forces. In late

February, Rommel pounced on a new American army at the Kasserine Pass, mauling it badly and taking several thousand prisoners before being forced to withdraw. The Americans fought with adequate bravery but evident inexperience. The Second Corps commander, General Lloyd Fredendall, was removed, one of the few American military leaders of the war to suffer that fate, and was replaced by the ferocious General George S. Patton, who quickly began to shape up his new command. The Kasserine Pass affair confirmed German and British skeptics about the quality of American troops and commanders. This would be a swiftly passing perception. (They had behaved less ignominiously then the British at Tobruk a year before.) Marshall and Eisenhower rejected suggestions that Patton's army be withdrawn for more training or dispersed among other units.

The tide turned steadily in Tunisia, with the Americans playing their part with ever-greater confidence. Rommel, ill, left his command in mid-March and never returned to Africa. Although the battle in Tunisia was delayed in final outcome until May 13, the bag at the end of it was 275,000 prisoners, half of them German, a victory not greatly smaller in scope than Stalingrad, and encompassing the clearing of an entire continent. This campaign proved a perfect testing ground for the incoming Americans, as they graduated from the half-hearted opposition of Vichy forces to unambiguous but not very warlike Italians, before facing real Germans. And for the first time a Free French corps made a significant contribution to a successful action. This made relations with de Gaulle more important than the parlor game farce Roosevelt had been conducting.

Relations with Stalin had taken a further setback at the end of March when Churchill, with Roosevelt's approval, had again suspended Arctic convoys as too vulnerable to aircraft, submarines, and surface raiders in the almost day-long light of the Arctic summer. Stalin described this as "catastrophic,"[4] but in the light of developing events in Tunisia, spared Churchill his customary implicit threat of military collapse or a separate peace with Hitler. The fact that Churchill and Roosevelt had "blooded" their soldiers and killed and captured a large number of Germans impressed Stalin and left him somewhat reinvigorated as an ally. It was another strategic disaster for Hitler, who inserted far too many forces, much too late, into the theater, and then convinced himself that he had forestalled an invasion of Europe and the collapse of Italy. He had done neither.

II

H ITLER HAD LOST over half a million of his best soldiers in the last four months. From approximately this point on, at the latest, he must have known that total, crushing defeat awaited him, culminating in his execution by his enemies, if he did not cheat them of that pleasure by committing suicide first.

For the past year Hitler had cranked up the liquidation, the outright mass murder, of Jews to a paramount objective. Many aspects of this horrible act will never be resolved. This vast purge is widely regarded as the greatest single act of evil in all of recorded history, though not without rivals, including Stalin's destruction of the Kulaks and his monstrous liquidations of the thirties. There is no sensible explanation of what motivated Hitler to such hostility to the Jews. He is forthright, in *Mein Kampf* and elsewhere, in falsely accusing the German Jewish community, about 600,000 in 1932, and less than 1 percent of the World War I and interwar German population, of betraying the country in the First World War. Since there is not one scintilla of evidence to support such a charge, it is not likely that Hitler actually believed it, at least initially.

He did convince himself that the Jews owed their loyalty to their tribe or cult and not to Germany or other nation states. And he tended to impute any lack of cooperation with his wishes as Germany's leader on the part of other countries to the manipulations of an international Jewish conspiracy. Knowing nothing of the United States, he conjured a lurid picture of a physically defective Roosevelt manipulated by Baruch, Frankfurter, Morgenthau, Brandeis, Cohen, and the other prominent Jews in his entourage, possibly reinforcing the President's susceptibilities by using the "Negro" household staff at the White House to medicate him according to the wishes of the rabbinical masters.

When he finally realized that Roosevelt was not just another Chamberlain, Hitler was unable to imagine anyone but a Jew or someone directed by Jews to be capable of the depths of Roosevelt's cunning and determination. It was consistent with his blustery dismissals of America for Hitler to impute Roosevelt's hatred of him to saturnine Hebraic influences.

Hitler had said on January 30, 1939, "If the international Jewish financiers . . . again succeed in plunging the nations into a world war the result will be . . . the annihilation of the Jewish race throughout Europe." He repeated these words, almost textually, at least five times before the war actually began. He apparently defined a world war as one in which the United States participated. And he delayed fully trying to implement his grim promise until the conflict with America had begun and the war had turned against him with his repulse at the gates of Moscow and Leningrad. Although he declared war on the United States, it was, he believed, with some reason, forced upon him by Roosevelt.

He had tried, with the threat of massive pogroms in Europe, to deter the American Jewish conspirators that he apparently believed were bedevilling him, and now he would show he was not bluffing. He repeated this intention to Goebbels right after Pearl Harbor.

Hitler's allegation of the machinations of Jewish finance driving Roosevelt to greater and greater provocations of Nazi Germany from 1939 to the end of 1941 formed the core of his ravingly incoherent declaration of war on the United States, on December 11, 1941. And the policy of exterminating the Jews, as opposed to merely grossly mistreating them, was secretly adopted at the Wannsee conference, chaired by Reinhard Heidrich, assisted by Adolf Eichmann, on January 20, 1942, six weeks after Germany had declared war on the United States.

The greatest part of the tragedy was that from 1933 to 1938 Jews had been free to leave Germany, with a diminishing share of their financial resources. After the Kristallnacht, in 1938, they could still leave, with difficulty. This became even more difficult after the start of World War II, in 1939. We have reviewed the extent of anti-Semitism in the United States. Though virtually all Americans were disgusted by the German pogroms (chapter 12), there was little enthusiasm for increased immigration.

Roosevelt never wavered in his determination to marshal American opinion against Hitler in all the barbarous implications of his regime. He wished to bring the decisive weight of the United States to bear against Nazism in its entirety, not just against individual outrages such as the mistreatment of Jews. The organization of American public policy was Roosevelt's domain and he would not allow anyone to divert him. He would then turn the full might of his nation to the elimination of Hitler, not just the mitigation of individual policies of Hitler. He refused to be distracted by the policy cul-de-sacs that arose in the late thirties. With the Spanish Civil War, as with the plight of the Jews and the Soviet attack on Finland, and even the proponents of antilynching legislation in the U.S. Congress, whose southern opponents were essential to his rearmament program, he could have squandered some, even much, of the moral integrality of the nation that he was carefully assembling to overwhelm the isolationists.

At the time of Roosevelt's third-term electoral victory in November 1940, Hitler had occupied most of Europe and had reasonable expectations of winning the war. The conventional wisdom is that this is when he moved to exterminate the Jews.[5] But it is more probable that he resolved to impose his infamous "final solution" later, when contemplating the, as he thought, Jewish achievement in creating a "world war"—i.e., one involving America. His genocidal zeal increased with the increasing possibility and then likelihood of his defeat, after Pearl Harbor and the failure of his 1941 offensive in Russia.

The period from November 1940 to the American entry into the war in December 1941—with Roosevelt reelected, unemployment banished, Churchill and Britain popular in the United States—was a thirteen-month window when it would have been possible for Roosevelt to rescue large numbers of Jews at little domestic political risk. He should have developed a dramatic plan to resettle Jews, not only in the United States but throughout neutral countries on an assisted basis. The fact that the Nazi government of Germany always denied that the death camps were anything other than labor camps, and denied that they were carrying out liquidations of Jews or others, indicated a recognition of the enormity of their actions and a possibility of pursuing some other method of resolving official antipathy to Jews, such as evacuation, as Hitler had suggested in his Königsberg speech in 1938 (chapter 10), when he offered to send them away on "luxury ships." (These were available, since most of the great French, German, and Italian liners were idle after June 1940.)

Hitler had pledged to get rid of the Jews in Europe, but refused ever to acknowledge publicly that he was prepared to murder them all, even when he had almost done so. A plan to evacuate them might have been welcome.

————————

In fairness to Roosevelt, it was hard to imagine that the culture of Goethe and Beethoven would systematically murder, as quickly as possible, six million Jews, three million Soviet prisoners of war, three-quarters of a million gypsies, and over two million miscellaneous opponents. Even allowing for the enormity of Hitler's "soul-destroying hatred," in Churchill's phrase, it was hard to believe that he would aggravate a severe labor shortage by murdering such vast numbers of potentially useful, not to mention innocent, people.

It should also be reemphasized that Roosevelt did try to lift the 1924 Immigration Act quotas, though he did not put his full political weight behind the effort. It was a little like his sending Eleanor to sit in the congressional galleries when antilynching bills were being debated, to show moral, if not fully engaged, support. The Roosevelt administration did ultimately admit 15 percent of the original Jewish population of Germany, about 90,000 people. This was a defensible record, and better than Roosevelt usually gets credit for. But it would have been better with more sympathetic people in direct charge of implementing his refugee policy.

The principal influence here, and an important part of the problem, was the assistant secretary of state responsible for refugees, Breckinridge Long. He was an old friend of Roosevelt's, a strong financial supporter whom Roosevelt had named his first ambassador to Italy, and in other respects an adequate occupant of his post. But he was a catastrophic incumbent at this time, as much a misfit as Joseph Kennedy or Joseph Davies had been in the diplomatic service. Long was a southern gentlemanly bigot who mourned the decline of the country squirearchy and looked upon most Jews as grubby and distasteful.

In his memoirs, Long passes lightly over this whole subject, but there are adequate hints of his attitude. He disapproved Roosevelt's "stab in the back" speech against Mussolini at the University of Virginia in June 1940, because he feared Americans could become "champions of a defeated cause."[6] He bought fairly far into the just-returned Joseph Kennedy's emphatic prophecy of British defeat and the need for a settlement with the Nazis.[7] He tended to see the refugee population as heavily composed of Nazi infiltrators, and the flow of refugees as a regrettable source of foreign exchange for the German government ($235,000 per week, although it was Jewish and other relief agencies that paid for the visas and ship passages).[8]

His dislike of the "sanctimonious" Rabbi Wise (and the Roman Catholic archbishop of New Orleans[9]) is understandable, but Long always resented the Jewish and Catholic leaders. "Each one of these men, hates me."[10] That they did is hardly surprising either, but Long believed they were always trying to "embarrass" him, strain "the spirit . . . if not the letter of the [excessively restrictive immigration] law"[11] and assert a false and universal right of anyone to enter the United States.

In the summer of 1940, Long triumphantly wrote in a memo to subsequent assistant secretary James Dunn and to former Brain Truster Adolf Berle: "We can delay and effectively stop [indefinitely] the number of immigrants into the United States . . . by simply advising our consulates to put every obstacle in the way and to require additional evidence and to resort to various administrative devices which would postpone and postpone and postpone and postpone and postpone the granting of the visas."[12]

Roosevelt could not have been unaware of Long's unsuitability to this post, especially after the memo to Dunn and Berle, and there is no excuse for his retention of him in it. He had got rid of Davies and Kennedy (and his "friend" Joseph Cudahy, who proved to be a chronic isolationist) as soon as practicable, but indulged Long and his systematic bigotry. That he did so is possibly Roosevelt's greatest failure as president.

That Roosevelt retained the loyalty of both Wise and Long attests to his political dexterity, but by 1942, the loyalty of the first was a badge of honor, that of the second almost of dishonor.

At the time when Roosevelt could have done most for the European Jews, when Hitler still hoped not to go to war with him, Roosevelt had no reason to believe that the Nazi crimes would achieve proportions remotely resembling those that were ultimately committed. And Roosevelt had no idea how or when, or even with certainty if, America would go to war, having just promised his faithful and credulous voters he was determined to keep the country out of war.

As the decision to exterminate every Jew in Europe, and millions of other innocents, was only taken at Wannsee in January 1942, when all doors had been closed, the sequence and timing of the escalation of evil were important elements of this unspeakable tragedy.

Once Hitler had furtively determined to murder those whom he regarded as enemies within his grasp, the infernal tragedy possessed a horrible, mechanical logic. It was almost insusceptible to outside influence.

Despite Germany's efforts to suppress information about its mass-murder policies, evidence of them trickled steadily out to the West. A report came from the Polish government in exile in June 1942 that 750,000 Polish Jews (one-quarter of the total pre-war Jewish population of the country) had been killed. When Roosevelt's old sometime ally from New York politics, Rabbi Stephen Wise, head of the American Jewish Congress, prevailed upon Justice Felix Frankfurter to visit and remonstrate with the President in September 1942, Roosevelt blandly assured him that he thought most of the deportations of Jews were for forced labor rather than extermination. He must have known this to be untrue, and was either trying not to disconcert his old "friend" or was inexplicably reluctant to take the issue on fully.[13]

Roosevelt repeatedly attacked and denounced Hitler's anti-Semitism, and racism generally, all through the thirties, and with particular vehemence from Kristallnacht on. Noting that up to 40 percent of Americans had some anti-Semitic impulses, he cast a wider net, deservedly, since Jews were not Hitler's only victims: half the victims of the death camps were non-Jews. On August 21, 1942, he made the first of several formal statements promising severe justice for the authors of "barbarous crimes," which he forcefully alleged were occurring on a scale without historical precedent.

Roosevelt received a report from the Swiss representative of the World Jewish Congress, Gerard Riegner, as well as a statement forwarded by A.J. Drexel Biddle, now ambassador to the governments in exile in London, from a Czechoslovakian official, Ernest Frischer, detailing the proportions of Nazi extermination of Jews and others that had already been achieved. The Riegner document reached Rabbi Wise via the British consul in Geneva, because the transmission from the American consulate had been suppressed by the State Department.

Rabbi Wise was desperately concerned when he received the Riegner report, but agreed on September 3, 1942, to Sumner Welles's telephone request of him not to release the Riegner report to the press until the State Department had verified it. While this process ran its unconscionably lengthy course, the United Kingdom government was waiting to make a joint statement with the U.S. government about postwar trial of those guilty of war crimes and crimes against humanity. Roosevelt intermittently promised retribution on war criminals and persecutors of the innocent beginning in 1941, and on March 21, 1944, he described the persecution of the European Jews as "one of the blackest crimes in all history. . . . All who share the guilt shall share the punishment."

There had been a good deal of foot-dragging in Long's section of the State Department about this too, despite the vigorous sponsorship of the idea by Ambassador John G. Winant, with the support of Harry Hopkins. Finally on October 4, 1942, Winant transmitted a message from Foreign Secretary Eden that a Parliamentary debate on the subject that had been twice postponed would not be delayed again and would start October 7. If the United States had not been heard from by then, the United Kingdom would have to proclaim its own policy in respect of the punishment of such crimes. This had the desired effect; the message was given to the President himself, who suggested only two slight changes and invited the British to issue a statement on behalf of both governments establishing a War Crimes Commission.

On November 24, 1942, Welles urgently invited Rabbi Wise to Washington and there handed him information confirming that the Riegner report was accurate, and that the Nazis were undoubtedly engaged in the liquidation of very large numbers of Jews and others. Welles declined to make the information public officially, but invited Wise to do so. Why Welles, presumably with the support of the President, since he rarely dealt with his nominal superior, Cordell Hull, because of their mutual detestation, would not publish these monstrous facts officially was not explained then, nor since. Welles mentioned nothing about this subject in his memoirs.

Rabbi Wise held a press conference on the evening of November 24 and laid out the facts, including the Nazi murder to date of two million Jews. Jewish spokesmen rarely mentioned, then or subsequently, the huge numbers of non-Jewish victims of the Nazis, thus missing an opportunity to assemble a broader coalition of outrage against the Nazi atrocities, and forfeiting a greater degree of solidarity with the oppressed nationalities of Europe after the war. Virtually monopolizing the Holocaust was a tactical error, at the time and thereafter.

Wise's press conference was not particularly well publicized in the United States. He did better with a Day of Mourning and Prayer December 2, partly because of the support of Mayor La Guardia. Half a million New York workers stopped on the job for ten minutes, though they added ten minutes to their following work day to avoid the charge of obstructing the war effort.

Wise requested a meeting with the President, which was accorded six days later, December 8. The Rabbi and four other prominent members of the American Jewish community attended upon the President for thirty minutes. Wise read a two-page statement by the temporary committee he had established about this emergency calling for "immediate action." He then gave Roosevelt a twenty-page summary of the information they had about the liquidations and beseeched Roosevelt to call the world's attention to these unimaginable crimes.

The President replied that the U.S. government was unfortunately aware of the truthfulness of Wise's statement. (The Rabbi's information had been publicly corroborated by Roosevelt's personal ambassador to the Holy See, Myron Taylor, former head of the United States Steel Corporation. The Vatican's information was extensive and supported the other reports that had been received.) President Roosevelt asked Rabbi Wise and his companions to write any statement they wished on his behalf condemning the atrocities and promised to endorse it sight unseen. He invited them, in effect, to write his statement for him, and asked for their recommendations for action. They had none. Roosevelt expressed complete understanding of this: "We are dealing with an insane man. Hitler and the group around him represent . . . a national psychopathic case. We cannot act toward them by normal means."[14]

This was the kernel of the problem. There wasn't much the Allied leaders could do. Roosevelt and Churchill repeatedly denounced the barbarism of the Nazis—"racial arrogances," in one of Roosevelt's phrases, "made more sinister and more protracted by the lights of perverted science," in one of Churchill's. Even Pius XII—who has been much criticized, not entirely unjustly, for not going further—though effectively a German captive in Rome, condemned official racial persecution in his Christmas message of 1942. He had always detested the Nazis, and though he was more preoccupied with the Communists, had been the author of

Pius XI's 1938 encyclical condemning racism, "Mit Brennende Sorge" ("With Burning Sorrow"—rendered in German to aim it clearly at the Nazis).

Similar historic arguments have taken place over the failure of the Allies to bomb the rail lines to the death camps, especially Auschwitz, even though Churchill ordered that they be bombed on July 20, 1944. (The RAF then asked the Polish government in exile for a topographical map, which was eventually produced. Churchill assumed his order had been carried out, as his orders usually were, but, lacking follow-up from him, the RAF did each day what the military high command required. The rail approaches to Auschwitz were never bombed.) In a message of March 21, 1944, Roosevelt went so far as to ask "the free peoples of Europe and Asia temporarily to open their frontiers to all victims of oppression. We shall find havens of refuge for them and we shall find the means for their maintenance and support until the tyrant is driven from their homelands and they may return." Even at this late date, the President was not throwing open the doors of America, other than as a temporary refuge.

Roosevelt seemed to promise action in his message of March 21, 1944: "Insofar as the necessity of military operations permit, this government will use all means at its command to aid the escape of the intended victims of the Nazi and Jap executioner." No military measures resulted. But it is not clear that much would have been accomplished if the camps or railways to them had been bombed. Track can be quickly relaid. There was such a huge population of prisoners at Auschwitz and the other main death camps that the Germans would certainly not have run out of victims to gas or otherwise kill while the railroad was repaired, and it is not clear that many lives would have been spared.

There would have been a symbolic value in showing Allied concern. As the Germans were denying that they were exterminating millions of people, such bombing might have imposed some slight caution on them. Assistant Secretary of War John McCloy, like Stimson, was rigid in his attachment to the principle of saving the victims by winning the war, and claimed that D-Day could have been delayed by bombing the camps. This could not be true; if the Allies could send a thousand bombers over German cities, they could spare up to twenty for intermittent attacks on death camps and their rail connections.

Having denied for over forty years that the matter was ever raised directly with Roosevelt, an aged McCloy claimed Roosevelt had personally vetoed such a mission. There is real doubt about McCloy's believability in this case, especially since he must have tired of being reviled as uninterested in the Jewish victims of the Nazis and in the Japanese-Americans whose incarceration he had promoted. According to McCloy, Roosevelt was afraid that the Allies would be blamed for joining in the killing of the victims[15] if they bombed any part of the camps themselves. Eisenhower believed that attacking the death camps would be a distraction to the war effort. None of them understood the scope of the crime.

If Roosevelt had decided as McCloy claimed, he would have been unlikely to give his March 21, 1944, hint at military action. More likely is that he wasn't directly asked and didn't think to order such an action, unlike Churchill, who was directly asked but whose order was not carried out.

Even at the very end, and to people close to the scene of the crimes, the dimensions of the Nazi atrocities were unbelievable. The newsreels of General Patton and General Eisenhower touring the death camp at Buchenwald, after Patton's U.S. Third Army had liberated it, show them to be visibly shaken. Eisenhower wrote in his memoirs: "Up to that time I had known about it only generally or through secondary sources. I am certain . . . that I have never . . . experienced an equal sense of shock."[16] This visit occurred on the day after the death of Roosevelt, who died unenlightened of the full proportions of Nazi barbarism. Eisenhower required photographers, journalists, and legislators to record the scenes at all the camps liberated by his armies, so the extent of Nazi evil could never be disputed. He considered one of the most moving moments of his life the sight of scarcely living cadavers saluting him bravely as he passed, wearing the five-star insignia of supreme commander of the Allied armies.

When Patton forced the entire adult population of the town neighboring the Ohrdruf death camp to come through the camp, almost all were speechless with horror, though they were well aware of the camp's existence and of Hitler's rhetorical reflections on Jews and other designated enemies. They had seen long trains of cattle cars packed with victims enter the camp, and never saw any inmates leave the camp. Many vomited uncontrollably at the sight of the cadavers, skulls, dental fillings, personal effects such as children's shoes, ovens, gas chambers, and skeletons, living and dead. General Patton himself was physically ill.[17]

The mayor of Ohrdruf and his wife committed suicide, from guilt and shame at their association by proximity with satanic human wickedness. It is easy to blame the leaders of that time for not having done more, sooner, to help Hitler's victims. It is impossible to recreate exactly their circumstances. The Nazis' genocidal fiendishness rose steadily as their own doom approached, yet the only truly effective way to help the victims was to destroy the Nazis.

If Roosevelt and Churchill had realized the centralized manner of the German liquidations of the innocent, they would surely have ordered a systematic campaign of bombing the gas chambers and enclosures and rail approaches to the main camps. Even when they learned something of the scale of the massacres, they assumed that the victims were being killed in their homes, in prisons, in countless camps, not with such focused efficiency.

Roosevelt, Churchill, and the pope—possibly even Breckinridge Long, if he had known what was really happening, and it was disgraceful that he wasn't much more aware than he was—were horrified. The pope and those acting in his name and with his general approval saved hundreds of thousands of lives. The pope himself sheltered many of the Jews of Rome, whose chief rabbi converted to Catholicism after the war. His successor as pope, Angelo Roncalli (John XXIII), saved tens of thousands of Jews as pro-nuncio in Istanbul by issuing visas to all who asked for them. The Hungarian bishops, including future cardinal Joseph

Mindszenty, secured a deferral of Nazi plans for destruction of Jews in that country by condemning and forcing the postponement of the confinement of the Hungarian Jewish population in ghettoes, saving tens of thousands of them. Yet the pope surely should have condemned this monstrous evil far more explicitly and repeatedly than he did, even if, as he feared, it would have led to fiercer reprisals and the suppression of the Church's ability to render the assistance that it did.

When the Dutch Catholic bishops spoke out against Nazi anti-Semitic decrees in 1941, the occupiers extended their dragnet to formerly Jewish Christians, including Edith Stein, who was gassed at Auschwitz and eventually canonized by Pope John Paul II. It is easy from the comfortable perspective of a subsequent era to offer such views, but in the face of the greatest moral crisis in the history of the modern world, the leader of the premier Christian church and the Western Allied leaders should have emphasized the Nazi atrocities more than they did.

They should have done so even if it meant captivity or martyrdom for the pope and even greater bloodletting among those under Nazi occupation. At the very least, all Vatican officials, whatever their concerns about Communism, which on balance was no greater an antichrist than the Nazis, should have been as helpful as possible to the persecuted. There were too many failures of Christian moral duty in high places, as when the secretary of state of the Holy See, Cardinal Maglione, told Roncalli that nothing more could be done to assist Jews in reaching Palestine. In these terrible times, even some church leaders became relatively inured to the climate of inhumanity.[18]

Of course Roosevelt spoke the truth when he told Rabbi Wise that Hitler and his collaborators were criminally diseased madmen. Precisely because the western Allies did not make more of an issue of the Nazi atrocities, powerless as they were to render direct assistance to the victims, Goebbels recorded in his diary, on December 13, 1942, "I believe both the British and the Americans are happy that we are exterminating the Jewish riff-raff."[19] This doesn't square with Hitler's view that Roosevelt was a puppet of the Zionist elders, or with Nazi denials of the exterminations in progress, but it illustrates Roosevelt's point that the German leaders could not be dealt with in any normal way. They could only be defeated and killed—or, if captured, tried and, in most cases, executed—and abominated for all posterity as illustrative of man's capacity for evil.

Roosevelt and Churchill promised vengeance, and judicial vengeance was visited upon those proved guilty. Their greatest service, by 1942 and 1943, was to win the war. They did a noble job of that.

Twelve million souls perished in the Nazi death camps, including six million Jews, half the entire world population of that ancient and gifted people. Yet civilization survived, including Jewish civilization and German civilization. The Jews, the perennially, and ultimately tragically, stateless people, acquired a state, and turned it into a flourishing democracy, albeit a country severely contested by its Arab neighbors into the next millennium.

And Germany, too late unified, ambivalent about whether it was an eastward- or westward-facing nation, insecure but incapable of addressing its insecurities without oppressing its neighbors, as European statesmen from Richelieu to Napoleon and Metternich had realized, finally became a secure, stable, prosperous, Western democracy. Winston Churchill and Franklin D. Roosevelt and others should have done more to help the Nazis' victims. That they did not does not minimize what they did accomplish for those victims. And it does not seriously diminish the fact that they delivered most of the world, including the Jews and the Germans, from evil.

III

FRANKLIN D. ROOSEVELT returned from the Casablanca Conference at the beginning of February 1943, to a Washington where there was still plenty of irritating, backbiting domestic politics to deal with. John L. Lewis in particular, among American labor leaders, having permanently reduced his moral and practical authority with his attack on Roosevelt's bid for reelection in 1940, was continuously chipping away at wage scales. Roosevelt had brought many audiences to their feet in indignation against (nameless) bloated capitalists fattening their wallets with the profits of war; he had more difficulty coping with labor leaders who continuously held war production to ransom with work stoppages while unctuously professing complete solidarity with the nation's war effort.

The miners began straggling out in scattered strikes in April 1943, despite Roosevelt's public appeals to them to remain loyal to him rather than Lewis, as they had in the 1940 election. The President moved to seize the mines, and addressed a Fireside Chat directly to the mine workers on May 2, 1943, even though they had already committed to return to work, pending arbitration. He pulled out all the patriotic stops. He declared that any interruption of the nation's coal supply "would involve a gamble with the lives of American soldiers and sailors and the future security of our whole people." He cited many miners and sons of miners who had been wounded and decorated. "The toughness of your sons in our armed forces is not surprising. They come of fine, rugged stock." He expressed confidence that the strike would end promptly.

When the War Labor Board declined the miners' demand for a pay boost, however, the miners struck again, despite the exhortations of the Commander in Chief. Lewis "recommended" that his workers return to work, but so tepidly that it was a phony exercise. The Justice Department was arresting strikers in significant numbers, and Congress passed, over the President's veto, the Smith-Connally bill restricting the right to strike. Roosevelt's principal grounds for the veto was that it purported to supersede the unions' no-strike pledge. Always ingenious, even when seriously exasperated, the President ordered a waiver of age exemptions in the draft and the conscription of miners from thirty-eight to forty-five years of age. He offered more pay for an increased work week. This, and a renewed seizure of the mines in the autumn, after a summer hiatus, brought most of the miners back to work. It had become a personal grudge match between Roosevelt and Lewis, to which Roosevelt brought his full bag of tricks, including renewed harassment of Lewis from the Internal Revenue Service.

There were similar problems in the railroad industry, where there was a good deal less unity on the union side. Roosevelt himself tried to arbitrate this problem just before Christmas 1943. Finally, at the very end of the year and after General Marshall had threatened to resign, blaming railway strikers, the President ordered Stimson to take over the railroads by the War Department, and personally arbitrated a settlement. There were similar problems in the rubber and other industries. The cumbrous arbitration machinery was rarely adequate, and much of Roosevelt's time was taken up in these matters. His haphazard organizational methods, setting up overlapping boards and agencies, assuring squabbling among underlings and constant reference to him as the font of all authority, was becoming inefficient and oppressive of him, given the vast scale of the war effort.

There was a move to resuscitate the War Mobilization Board, put it on top of Nelson's Office of Production Management, and give it to the timeless and almost inevitable Bernard Baruch, who had directed the same entity under President Wilson. After cranking Baruch up for such a role, and causing him to consult his doctor, Roosevelt inexplicably, presumably on the advice of Hopkins, thought better of it and ignored Barnuch's purported acceptance of the post. James Byrnes and his small staff headed by Benjamin Cohen would add the War Mobilization responsibilities to the Economic Stabilization position. Fred M. Vinson, former congressman, Byrnes's assistant, and future Chief Justice of the United States, took over the Economic Stabilization job.

Roosevelt's love of feuding between underlings produced more than he had bargained for in the spring of 1943, when Vice President Henry Wallace and Commerce Secretary Jesse Jones, the ultraliberal and ultraconservative of the administration, crossed swords over Wallace's position as head of the Bureau of Economic Warfare, which wanted to fund two programs for experimental rubber production in Haiti and Africa. Such a fierce dispute arose between Wallace and Jones that Roosevelt collapsed Wallace's BEW, put it into an Office of Economic Warfare with control of its own budget, along with the Export-Import Bank and the rubber and petroleum administrative apparatus, and gave the direction of it to Leo Crowley.

He also sent around a message to all agency heads requiring that any interagency disputes that they couldn't solve themselves be referred to Byrnes or him. He asked that with any release of a public statement about such an internecine dispute, "you send to me a letter of resignation." This snap of the whip seemed to improve coordination somewhat for a while. "A little rivalry is stimulating, you know,"[20] Roosevelt said to Frances Perkins.

Roosevelt's erratic methods were often the despair of his more orthodox underlings, such as Stimson. Roosevelt had a wide range of interests and was constantly asking about details of every department in an unpredictable way that was designed to keep middle as well as senior echelon people on their toes. And while access to him was limited, it was also unpredictable. He accepted the requests of some trusted subordinates, especially Hopkins, about those whom he should meet, and often reached well down in every department to receive detailed information about specific matters. His methods may have been maddening, but they were certainly broadly successful.

Welles was finally forced out of office by Bullitt in 1943, after Bullitt had circulated a description of Welles intoxicated on a rail trip in September 1940 returning from Speaker William Bankhead's funeral in Alabama. Welles had made indecent advances on a black railway porter, who had complained to his employer. Roosevelt received a report about it from J. Edgar Hoover shortly after the fact at the end of 1940 and simply ignored it. He had assigned a bodyguard to Welles to ensure that there was no possible repetition, and blamed it on a freakish combination of medicine and alcohol. Welles himself had no recollection of the incident. On April 23, 1941, Bullitt had demanded of Roosevelt that Welles be fired as a degenerate and a security risk to blackmail as well as a depressant to department morale. Roosevelt refused and never had as favorable or close a relationship with Bullitt again. But the former ambassador's insinuations against him finally demoralized Sumner Welles, and he retired in September 1943.

Roosevelt had difficulty moving any domestic legislation other than mere maintenance of the status quo during wartime, especially after the return of a more conservative Congress in the 1942 midterm elections. However, with his usual resourcefulness, he devised a method for stampeding the reluctant legislators: everything was to be presented as a veterans' measure. The President had established a committee in November 1942 to produce recommendations for a program of benefits for demobilized veterans to relaunch them into civilian life at the end of the war. By the summer of 1943, the administration's recommendations were almost ready for unveiling: assistance for a year's education, and where an aptitude seemed to exist, for years of education equal to the number of years of military service, up to four years. There would also be special provision for unemployment and medical insurance, veterans' hospitals, and aid to home, farm, and business ownership. This would prove one of the greatest and most important and successful of all Roosevelt's initiatives and would effectively be the Fifth and posthumous New Deal (after the Hundred Days of 1933, its resumption around Social Security in 1935, the return to Keynesian pump-priming in 1938, and the massive defense buildup of 1940–1941).*

Another area where there was appreciable progress, largely due to the efforts of Eleanor Roosevelt, was day care. By 1945 there were 19 million working women

---

* Roosevelt had expressed mock outrage to Frances Perkins when reading of the Beveridge Plan for "cradle to grave" insurance in mid-1943. He said he had been speaking of such a program for many years.[21]

in the United States, one-third of them with children under the age of fourteen, and Mrs. Roosevelt was the strongest, and one of the earliest, voices against the dangers of child neglect and severe resulting war industrial work losses. She prevailed upon a readily persuadable Henry Kaiser to establish a splendidly large and imaginative day care center in Portland to serve the 4,000 working mothers he employed there. This proved a very successful pilot, and by the summer of 1945 more than 4.5 million children were in assisted day care, almost all of it private sector initiatives.[22]

Eleanor Roosevelt also played an important and entirely admirable role in improving the lot of African-American servicemen. The beautiful and talented black singer Lena Horne concluded that German prisoners of war had a better chance of hearing her when she performed than her own people in the U.S. armed forces did. Eleanor received a great quantity of information about the segregation of African-American servicemen and bombarded General Marshall with such a volume of questions and suggestions on the subject that he ultimately had to engage two assistants just to deal with that one important correspondent.

On March 10, 1943, the War Department officially abolished separately designated "white" and "colored only" recreational and other facilities, though this did not apply to transport, which, as in the civil rights movement that began to gain national attention a decade later, was a flashpoint. There also continued to be recreational areas designated by number or named otherwise than by pigmentation but having the same effect. But this was distinct progress, and again, Mrs. Roosevelt's role in it was vital and entirely constructive.

She also played a role in having the 99th Pursuit Squadron sent into action. This was the first unit of black combat pilots, which had been set up in response to litigation, and had been massively trained for many months but not moved from Tuskegee Air Field. Eleanor Roosevelt, having been appealed to by the director at Tuskegee, wrote forcefully to War Secretary Stimson. This certainly influenced the departure of the 99th, on April 15, 1943, for Africa. In the balance of the war, the 99th had an extremely distinguished record, destroying 111 enemy aircraft in the air and at least 150 on the ground, never losing a bomber it was escorting, and earning 100 Distinguished Flying Crosses in 1,578 combat missions in North Africa, Italy, and northwest Europe. This was another important milestone in the complete emancipation of African-Americans from the long bondage of segregation.

The summer of 1943 witnessed the worst eruptions of racial violence in the United States since shortly after the First World War. At the end of May 1943, eleven African-Americans were injured in Mobile, Alabama, when skilled black welders were integrated with white welders in the city's shipyards. In mid-June there were widespread racial incidents in Los Angeles involving Hispanic Americans, in which dozens of them were beaten and publicly humiliated. On June 20, a race riot erupted in Detroit that raged for three days, until the governor of Michigan finally acknowledged that he could not restore order and asked for federal help. Roosevelt immediately dispatched nearly 4,000 soldiers, who stopped the violence promptly but after thirty-four people had been killed, twenty-five of them black, and including one black and one white medical doctor and several women. Nearly a thousand people were injured. There were racial disturbances in Harlem and Newark, and a black man was dragged from a jail in Florida and lynched.

Roosevelt perfectly well knew, without his wife's reminding him, that this was not America the Beautiful, or antics worthy of a land that was free and a home to brave people. As the African-Americans slowly emerged from the twilight of segregation, following what Lincoln called the "bondman's 250 years of unrequited toil," frictions were inevitable, especially as impatient African-Americans met and rivaled poor whites who regarded a primitive notion of racial superiority as their greatest safeguard against falling back into Depression-era poverty. The adjustment of America to complete desegregation, the acceptance of the equality of the African-American by whites, and the renunciation of the victim culture by the descendants of the slaves would require all the rest of the twentieth century and more to accomplish. The process accelerated under Roosevelt by the establishment of equality of social benefit and then in the military, and in the treatment of veterans in what became the G.I. Bill of Rights.

Roosevelt wished to take it further if he could emancipate himself from the power of the segregationist southern congressional political leaders. To this end he envisioned an alliance with the Willkie Republicans, but neither he nor Willkie lived to consummate such an arrangement, and this long and painful battle really began in earnest only in the middle of the following decade.[*]

IV

WINSTON CHURCHILL SENT his foreign secretary, Anthony Eden, to see Roosevelt in March 1943 for a first talk about postwar arrangements. Eden had his first meeting with the President March 13, and a further extensive discussion with him on the Ides of March. Hopkins and Winant were present for the first meeting, and only Hopkins on the 15th. Eden also had an extensive talk with Cordell Hull, who felt he had been very harshly judged in his efforts to make something out of relations with the French. Eden explained that the British approved a contact with Vichy but were strongly loyal to the French who had not accepted defeat, who remained faithful to the Alliance, however obstreperous they might be, and that the British public detested Petain and his followers as cowardly and dishonorable.[23]

Roosevelt had a range of ideas about France, from disquieting to fantastic. He

---

[*] It would be 1965 before then president and former Roosevelt acolyte Lyndon Johnson would pass the landmark Civil Rights Act of 1964.

felt that the liberating armies in France should govern the country for an indefinite period, and should deal with separate local authorities in France and its widely dispersed colonies. "It seemed to me that Roosevelt wanted to hold the strings of France's future in his own hands so that he could decide that country's fate," Eden wrote.[24] Roosevelt further entertained some disturbing ideas about making a country he called Wallonia out of the French part of Belgium, Luxembourg, Alsace-Lorraine, and part of northern France. This was like, and may have been inspired by, Richelieu and Napoleon's carving out independent German Rhineland states. Their motives in wishing to weaken Germany were obvious enough, but what Roosevelt thought he would accomplish by imposing himself on the French and fragmenting that country was incomprehensible to Eden and remains so. "I poured water, I hope politely, and the President did not revert to the subject."[25]

Roosevelt also considered the merits of separating the Serbs from the Croatians and Slovenians. Eden replied that in principle "I disliked the idea of multiplying smaller states . . . that we should aim at grouping. I could not see any better solution for the future of either the Croats or the Slovenes than forming some union with the Serbs." Given the eventual disintegration of Yugoslavia, Roosevelt's vision was clearer.

The largest part of the discussions was taken up with Russia. Roosevelt was quite pragmatic about Poland. He had no objection to the Curzon Line, moving the border of the Soviet Union well to the west, and compensating Poland by awarding it East Prussia. "In any event Britain, the United States and Russia should decide at the appropriate time what was a just solution, and Poland would have to accept." Roosevelt had no problem with Russia's going back to its former border with Finland before the Russo-German War. He didn't even object to Russia's taking back the Baltic states of Estonia, Latvia, and Lithuania, though he hoped there might be a referendum, even a rigged one, to improve appearances for international, especially American, opinion.[26]

Roosevelt didn't see much point in trying to force Russia out of former parts of its own territory of which it would be in full military possession when the war ended. (The Baltic countries had been part of Russia for over two hundred years before enjoying twenty years of interwar independence.) Roosevelt thought that if Stalin wouldn't go through some sort of a plebiscite, even a burlesque of one, then some concessions should be extracted from him in return for recognition of the takeover in the Baltic countries.

Roosevelt was under no illusion that there was a substantial possibility that Stalin desired to "overrun and communize" the whole continent of Europe.[27] Eden said that it would make matters no worse by trying to work with Stalin, even if these were his objectives, and that it was difficult to discern to what extent his policy was Russian and to what extent Communist. (Neither statesman considered either likely motivation particularly benign.)

Roosevelt favored the dismemberment of Germany and the tripartite policing of all Europe by the main Allies. Eden urged the distinction between faultless occupied countries they were all pledged to liberate and those that were, or had been, enemies. The foreign secretary also parried a suggestion for the virtual disarmament of all Europe except for the forces of the principal Allies, because disarming friendly and neutral states would "present obvious difficulty . . . but I did not take the idea as a serious proposal and it passed with little comment."

In sum, Roosevelt was not naïve about Russia, was not overly sentimental about Eastern Europe, expected Russia to be compensated for having paid such a terrible price in blood and treasure in winning the war, and was determined that the United States would emerge permanently from isolationism and play a leading role in the whole world. But he was also, at least tentatively, indulging his taste for flippant treatment of greatly complicated questions, as he had for a time with India. Eden had an exceptional insight; he had enjoyed "the exercise of the President's charm and the play of his lively mind," but found the conversations "perplexing. Roosevelt was familiar with the history and geography of Europe. Perhaps his hobby of stamp-collecting had helped him to this knowledge, but the academic yet sweeping opinions which he built upon it were alarming in their cheerful fecklessness. He seemed to see himself disposing of the fate of many lands, allied no less than enemy. He did all this with so much grace that it was not easy to dissent. Yet it was too like a conjuror, skillfully juggling with balls of dynamite, whose nature he failed to understand."

There was, at this early stage of postwar discussion, indeed something of the stamp collector in Roosevelt's approach. He mused on detaching and reattaching faraway places to each other. What was important was that the United States not be threatened, that it be engaged in the world through a righteous and legitimate international framework, and that it be ready to act preemptively against a threat. The power of liberal democracy and humane capitalism must be visible for the whole world to see and emulate. An attempt must be made to bring Russia to the high table of world governance, but its misguided totalitarian system must be encouraged on the pathways of social democracy and not let loose on the most geopolitically important parts of Western Europe.

It was not an unsound vision, but the supreme confidence of its author and the benignly capricious way in which he moved from place to place (like a stamp collector, "from Ruthenia to . . . peanuts," as he said to Hopkins[28]), serious and flippant opinions mixed together, could well have been "perplexing" to a conventional Old World foreign minister like Eden, from an important but not unlimitedly powerful country.

The Jefferson Memorial had been a special project of Roosevelt's, and he persevered with it even when women threatened to chain themselves to cherry trees that had to be removed to make way for the monument. Roosevelt deadpanned that the government could remove the trees with cranes and replant them with the women continuously chained to them, transporting women and trees with equal safety and comfort to new sites. He opened the memorial April 13, 1943, emphasizing as timely in current circumstances Jefferson's assertion: "I have sworn upon the altar of God, eternal hostility against every form of tyranny over the mind of man." The Jefferson Memorial joined the famous obelisk to George Washington and the colonnaded Lincoln Memorial as the only presidential monuments in Washington. The next presidential memorial opened in Washington would be fifty-five years later, and only about a mile away across the Tidal Basin from Jefferson's, to Franklin Delano Roosevelt.

Later on April 13, Roosevelt left on a sixteen-day tour of military facilities. His wife reluctantly remained behind to be with their daughter, Anna, whose husband had abruptly left the job of publishing the Hearst newspaper in Seattle to her while he went off to North Africa in a military role, arranged for him by General Eisenhower. Margaret Suckley and Laura Delano accompanied the President, along with Grace Tully, Dr. (now Rear Admiral) McIntire, Steve Early, and Basil O'Connor. Eleanor and her assistant, Malvina "Tommy" Thompson, joined the tour in progress. Tommy Thompson found the rather preposterous Laura Delano "imperious" as well as banal; she brought a dog along on the train journey with her, and never failed to describe the dog's accomplishment of physiological and biological needs at each stop.[29]

The tour proceeded to the Parris Island Marine boot camp in South Carolina, immense Fort Benning in Georgia, and the Women's Army Auxiliary Corps camp at Fort Oglethorpe, Georgia. The Roosevelts visited with Elliott's wife and children in Fort Worth, Texas, dined with the President and Señora Camacho of Mexico in Monterrey, and went on to the naval cadet camp at Corpus Christi. The tour more or less concluded, before returning to Washington, at Fort Riley, Kansas, which had been in continuous operation since 1852, when Kansas was still a territory in the great slavery controversies before the Civil War.

Everywhere Roosevelt was gratified at the tremendous and visible progress of the American recruiting and training process. There was an abundance of armaments, instead of men training with wooden guns, truncated hockey sticks, toilet plungers, and the like. And the trainees were fit and tough compared with the rather well-upholstered first wave that Roosevelt had seen three years before. He saw a great range of activities—parachuting, dive-bombing, target practice with a variety of weapons. The Great Arsenal of Democracy was well along to putting in the field General Marshall's army of 6 million soldiers and 2.5 million airmen, as well as a navy of 5 million sailors and half a million marines trained, equipped, motivated, and led by an outstanding officer corps.

Roosevelt, in the aftermath of his discussions with Anthony Eden in March, had decided to try to arrange a personal meeting with Stalin, and resorted to the dubious tactic of sending a message with former ambassador Joseph Davies, whom the historian James MacGregor Burns charitably describes as "an old favorite with the Kremlin."[30]

In his message to Stalin, Roosevelt proposed a number of places where they might meet, as he had to Churchill in December 1942, but rejected Khartoum for the same reason as he had in December (mosquitoes). He also ruled out Iceland, not because of the cold, as he had with Churchill, but because "quite frankly" . . . it would be "difficult not to invite Prime Minister Churchill at the same time." He proposed instead one side or the other of the Bering Strait for a two-party meeting and promised that he would bring only Hopkins, an interpreter, and a stenographer.

This was an absolutely mad enterprise as well as a completely unethical one; Churchill had earned the right, after all he and his countrymen and the Commonwealth Dominions had done to hold the fort against Hitler and Mussolini, not to be treated like a penurious and boring relative at a family council. Roosevelt's initiative appears to have been grounded in the fatuous notion that Stalin would have visceral objections to Churchill as a traditional British imperialist and anti-Bolshevik, but would be well-disposed to Roosevelt as a social democrat. It was understandable that Roosevelt had not grasped what only became clear in the times of Presidents Richard Nixon and Ronald Reagan, that authentic Communists preferred American leaders of the unambiguous right, capable of delivering American opinion as a whole, rather than center-left do-gooders.

Roosevelt, as we have seen, was more tactically than viscerally a man of the center left and just as Machiavellian as Hitler or Stalin at times, though, unlike them, he had a proper humanitarian concern for the consequences of his actions, no matter how casual he sometimes was about the probity of his methods. Nor, as he had just made clear to Eden, was Roosevelt blind to the possibilities that Stalin was a rabid imperialist of Russian tradition as well as a Communist world revolutionary. He wanted to inflict on Stalin the ravages of respectability. Roosevelt's pursuit of the American national interest, though always couched for domestic consumption in the most altruistic terms, was, to the chagrin of de Gaulle and others, relentless and immensely ambitious.

In the President's desire to expose Stalin to his charm and to his great power in the world, Roosevelt, perhaps betraying a little of what de Gaulle sensed in him — a race against death for the achievement of the supreme and durable world settlement that only he had the position and genius to produce — sometimes appeared overeager.

Next to the incomparable power of America, industrially and in the ever-growing might of its land and air and naval forces, and the mystique of its bountiful democracy, of which Roosevelt was long the personification, the close but uneven British alliance was Roosevelt's greatest geopolitical asset. What, Stalin must have wondered, did Roosevelt think he was achieving by affecting a distaste for the ally that he had sustained even while Stalin was in uneasy alliance with Hitler? It was this sort of posturing that caused Stalin to ask Gromyko, when he became the ambassador in Washington, if Roosevelt was "intelligent." Gromyko, by then schooled in the mastery of Roosevelt over the complexities of American opinion and politics, replied that he was undoubtedly very intelligent. Davies returned to Washington in mid-May.

While Davies was on his way to Moscow to try to set up the Soviet-American Summit, Churchill, unaware of the desire of his great ally to meet Stalin without him, was speeding toward the United States on the great liner *Queen Mary*, with 5,000 German prisoners of war below decks. They got no glimpse of their illustrious fellow passenger and his large entourage. Churchill, coming to concert the next phase of war plans, sent cheerful messages to Roosevelt and Stalin from the ship, which was escorted part of the way by a British cruiser and aircraft carrier and was then picked up by a squadron of American cruisers and destroyers.*

General Marshall and the other American staff chiefs were determined to be ready, as they weren't at Arcadia and Casablanca, with detailed and sequential arguments for the British. The strategic bifurcation between the two sides, especially as it applied to the Mediterranean and cross-Channel operations, could not be deferred much longer and had to be resolved.

V

WHAT BECAME KNOWN as the Trident Conference opened at the White House on May 12, 1943. Roosevelt brought the session to order with a gracious reflection on what had occurred since the meeting there a year before. Then there had been great concern about Tobruk and the Torch operation had been conceived, which was now about to culminate in the surrender of all remaining Axis forces in Africa. The now traditional strategic disagreement between the Allies opened early. Churchill declared his support of a cross-Channel operation eventually, but pressed for further action in the Mediterranean.

He thought that the attack across the Channel should be launched as soon as there were "reasonable prospects of success." But "Churchill predicated reasonable success on the virtual internal collapse of Germany." He held out the prospect of the imminent collapse of Italy, which "would cause a chill of loneliness [to settle] over the German people and might be the beginning of their doom."[31] He thought Italy the most attainable prize and the greatest assistance the Western allies could offer the Russians. Roosevelt was in general more concerned than Churchill with keeping Stalin in the war.

---

* Considerable effort was expended to confuse the ship's crew and maintenance workers about the purpose of the trip. Signs were put up in Dutch, to make it seem the queen of the Netherlands might be on board, and superfluous ramps were put down to incite the thought that the *Queen Mary* might be going to fetch Roosevelt.

Vigorously prompted by Marshall and Stimson, Roosevelt "feared that this meant a lengthy pecking away at the fringes of Europe." Roosevelt required a definite and prompt timetable for a return to Western Europe by the spring of 1944. Apart from other considerations, he would have to face the voters in November 1944, and could not defer elections indefinitely as could Churchill. He did not mention this at Trident, but the American people would want to see substantial progress in Europe before reelecting the commander in chief.

Marshall spoke for the amassing in Great Britain of the forces necessary to cross the Channel in adequate strength, and agreed with the Joint Strategic Survey Committee's recent findings that air superiority over and around the landing sites would reduce the strength of land forces required. Marshall advocated a landing in France of twenty-nine divisions, and severe application of air power in Central Europe, including against the oil fields at Ploesti, Romania.

This was a much more organized and aggressive stance than the British had been accustomed to from the Americans. Brooke, off guard, but as convinced as always of the strategic naïveté of the Americans, emphasized the inexperience of Allied troops, lack of manpower, and lesser problems, and rhapsodized in the contemporary British manner about the Mediterranean. Marshall joined the issue and declared that these operations, as the British were well aware, always took longer than had been foreseen and that invading Italy would create "a vacuum" that would suck in Allied forces through 1944. If the British "were committed to the Mediterranean, except for air alone, it meant a prolonged struggle and one which was not acceptable to the United States."[32] Marshall, Leahy, and King all sounded the familiar refrain that if the British weren't prepared to commit to the initiatives that alone would achieve the agreed goal of defeating Germany first, the United States preferred to deploy its forces in the Pacific and in the Burma theater to keep China in the war.

Brooke replied that nothing could be done in France until 1945 or 1946 because "in previous wars there had always been some 80 French divisions on our side." This was a very lame argument, because the United States was offering all the manpower necessary to make up for the French. This exchange is absent from Brooke's diaries, indicating he had thought better of it. The chief of the Imperial General Staff could not have required three whole years to appreciate the strategic implications of the defeat of France. (Particularly as he had opposed rearming the French North African Army.) Brooke merely retained the pained forbearance of the patient tutor with slow and unruly charges.

Matters had reached an impasse when there was a weekend adjournment. Churchill went with the Roosevelts and Hopkins to Shangri-la. They passed through the town of Frederick, near Gettysburg, and Churchill impressed his hosts by reciting the famous poem about Barbara Frietschie: "Shoot if you must this old grey head, But spare your country's flag, she said." The President worked on his stamp collection and fished. "He was placed with great care by the side of a pool," Churchill wrote.[33] It was a relaxing respite for both leaders.

Marshall took the military staffs to Colonial Williamsburg, a magnificent restoration by the Rockefeller family, and John D. Rockefeller II organized a sumptuous weekend for them. Brooke indulged his favorite hobby of bird watching. Others walked, golfed, played croquet, and swam. The lunches and dinners were opulent, some of the ingredients brought from the Rockefeller estate at Pocantico (thirty miles down the Hudson River from Hyde Park) by Rockefeller's butler. Admiral of the Fleet Sir Dudley Pound became lost in the maze.

The normally austere General Marshall verged on gregariousness and played a tune on an antique spinet. Air Marshal Sir Charles Portal, given rather larger bathing trunks than needed, dove into the swimming pool at such velocity that he emerged without them. Brooke was impressed by the divine service he attended at Williamsburg: "All women beautifully turned out, no poverty and all well educated." Gradually, subtly, the barriers between the Allies were coming down.

The conference resumed May 17, and the outline of a compromise emerged. A cross-Channel assault could be mounted in the spring of 1944, and this would be assisted, not retarded, by an invasion of Italy. The Allies would undertake to provide the resources of all kinds necessary for such an attack, but sufficient resources would remain in the Mediterranean to invade Italy, draw off German units from France to Italy, rid Europe of Mussolini, and provide substantial early relief for the Russians. Brooke made a powerful case that such an action would distract the Germans while the French invasion was prepared. The compromise that started to take definite shape May 19 was the commitment to the spring, 1944, French invasion; the approval of the operations following the conquest of Sicily best calculated to knock Italy out of the war and pin down German forces; and agreement that four American and three British divisions would be ready for transfer from the Mediterranean to Britain from November 1, 1943, on, at Marshall's request.

Winston Churchill again addressed the U.S. Congress, on May 19, and his remarks were again broadcast throughout the world. He reported to his appreciative live audience that "The African excursions of the two Dictators have cost their countries in killed and captured, 950,000 soldiers," and expressed his gratitude, in reference to Africa and Stalingrad, for "the military intuition of Corporal Hitler."

The conference moved on to the Pacific, Burma, and China. King did not act in lockstep with Marshall and called for an increased effort in the Pacific. American naval construction and the U.S. Navy's defeat of its Japanese rival at Midway and elsewhere had given King the scepter of the seas. A vague formula for according the Pacific every resource that wasn't necessary to the achievement of the "Germany first" policy was agreed.

The decision had been taken at Casablanca to attempt the recapture of all Burma, but General Wavell, who was present at Trident, had little faith in his own plan to accomplish that and Churchill had no faith in it at all. The Americans at Trident demanded that a serious effort be made to lift the siege of China.

Churchill expressed forceful opposition to anything "silly" just to please Chiang Kai-shek (for whom he had, on occasion, declared a disingenuous solicitude).

General Joseph Stilwell, a China expert and a legendarily fierce soldier, who despised Chiang Kai-shek as a crook and an incompetent, sought to open the land route to China to strengthen the Chinese in their land struggle with Japan and gain access to Chinese airfields from which the Allied air forces could bomb Japan. In the staff meetings, the British refrain was "can't, can't, can't." Stilwell took a particular dislike to Brooke, whom Stilwell's biographer describes rather ungenerously as "a small, dark, unamiable man who disliked Americans and vice versa."[34]

Brooke reciprocated in his diaries, describing Stilwell as "a strange character," whose nickname, Vinegar Joe, "suited him admirably. . . . Except for the fact that he was a stout-hearted fighter, suitable to lead a brigade of Chinese scallywags, I could see no qualities in him. . . . [He was] nothing more than a hopeless crank."[35] Brooke accused him of "a deep rooted hatred of anybody or anything British." Brooke imputed all Stilwell's failings to Marshall, who championed him. (Stilwell and Brooke agreed at least on their views of Chiang.)

Marshall defended Stilwell as "a fighter" and contrasted him to the local British "set of commanders who had no fighting instincts, [and] were soft and useless."[36]

Stilwell recorded that at Trident it was "hard to say my piece," but Marshall was disappointed that he didn't argue his corner better.[37] In order to keep China in the war as well as to develop its immense potential as a fighting ally, Stilwell not only argued for the opening of an overland supply route to China but also made a strong case for a great air transport commitment. Roosevelt and Churchill agreed to Stilwell's goals to get 7,000 tons of supplies per month by air to China and to reopen the overland route to that country. It was delegated to the relevant staffs to work up and return with a plan for how to do so.

Stilwell's efforts were complicated by the political lobbying of General Claire Chennault, a megalomaniac who made MacArthur, de Gaulle, Patton, and Montgomery seem like self-effacing cloistered monks. But Chennault, the founder of the volunteer group known as the Flying Tigers, was a brave and effective aviator and a protégé of Chiang and Mme. Chiang. Stilwell told Roosevelt that Chennault was "probably a tactical genius" but had been "for many years a paid employee of the Chinese government."[38] In February, Roosevelt had taken the advice of Hopkins and supported the Chiang-Chennault plan for air war, despite the Marshall-Stilwell warning that if at all successful, the air war would attract a Japanese offensive against the airfields and there would be a ground war anyway, for which the Chinese were not prepared. Hopkins was a man of great ability, but not in military matters; in this case, he proposed supporting the political leader of the majority of the Chinese as the best hope the West had. This was what Marshall and Stilwell were trying to put right at Trident, because they favored a militarily sensible plan and not a political wish list.

But neither Churchill nor Roosevelt, despite the support of Marshall and King for Stilwell, were convinced of the Chinese vision. Roosevelt was the pioneer of the treatment of China as a potential great power, where Churchill thought it a vast degenerate peasantry. Roosevelt romanticized the Oriental past of his family (while ignoring its enrichment in the opium trade) and celebrated the American championship of the "Open Door" policy.

As usual, Roosevelt had rather exaggerated views of the popularity of America and of its virtue compared with the colonial powers. He constantly compared America's intended grant of independence to the Philippines and benign government of Puerto Rico (now ruled by the old Brain Truster Rexford Tugwell after a brief stint by Admiral Leahy, before his dispatch to Vichy)* with what he considered the misgovernment of Indochina by the French. In urging another fate for Indochina than reversion to French colonial rule, Roosevelt uttered one of his many prescient suggestions for the postwar world.

As part of his back-burner crusade against colonialism, Roosevelt had sent his old friend William Phillips, unemployed since the closing of the embassy in Rome, to India as his special representative. His reports were very discouraging about the mounting incredulity of the educated Indians concerning the real purposes of the Atlantic Charter and the inflexibility of the British governors. When the viceroy, Lord Linlithgow, refused to permit a meeting between Phillips and Gandhi, his mission ended. This was shabby treatment by the British of a distinguished American emissary. It was a credit to Roosevelt that he did not allow this incident to intrude upon his good relations with Churchill.

Roosevelt had successfully asked the Senate to ratify a treaty renouncing extraterritorial rights in China and the Chinese exclusion laws severely restricting Chinese immigration. The Senate did so and the British followed on the first point, and Chiang Kai-shek expressed China's gratitude and solidarity with the Allies. His own position, however, was tenuous. By mid-1943, Mao Tse-tung's Communists controlled 150,000 square miles and about 50 million Chinese (of a total population of 400 million).

Neither Chiang nor Mao was making any real contribution to fighting the Japanese, but Stilwell believed the Chinese army, with enough resources and himself as the real commander in the name of the indolent generalissimo (G'mo, as Stilwell called him, when not referring to him simply as "Peanut"), could achieve great things. But Stilwell was a disputatious figure and he did bear his nickname (Vinegar Joe) much better than his surname. When Roosevelt, in an informal session at Trident, asked Stilwell and Chennault what they thought of Chiang,

---

* A candidate to succeed Leahy, but vetoed by Ickes, was the Interior Department's territories and islands commissioner, Ernest Gruening. Roosevelt then appointed Gruening governor of Alaska, and he remained there, ending his career after Alaskan statehood as U.S. senator and an early opponent of the Vietnam War.

Stilwell replied: "He's a vacillating, tricky, undependable old scoundrel who never keeps his word." Chennault immediately responded that the "Generalissimo is one of the two or three greatest military and political leaders in the world today. He has never broken a promise or commitment made to me."

Roosevelt's life during Trident was complicated by the fact that Mme. Chiang turned up without an invitation and "to Roosevelt's vexation had resumed residence in the White House."[39] From this august place, she telephoned around Washington officialdom, badgering people with her husband's interests. A more conventional intervention was made by T.V. Soong, the Chinese ambassador and Chiang in-law, who told the conference that China would make a separate peace with Japan if a serious effort were not made for the relief of China. Roosevelt and Churchill were not overly intimidated, though Roosevelt "told the conference" he did not think the Allies should "be put in the position of being responsible for the collapse of China."

The President's problem was that while he envisioned China as a Great Power leading Asia out of colonialism, he recognized that Chiang was unlikely to lead it there. Nor could Roosevelt do much with Mao Tse-tung, since he preferred non-Communists to Communists and any liaison with him would drive Chiang into the arms of the Japanese. It was the ultimate Chinese puzzle, but the time to deal with Mao Tse-tung and Chou Enlai would have been right after the Japanese surrender at the end of the war. The consequence of not doing so was that there was no worthwhile relationship between the United States and China until five presidencies after Roosevelt's, when Richard Nixon visited Mao and Chou in 1972.

Madame Chiang was an exotic figure at this and subsequent conferences. Though not beautiful, she was "gifted with great charm and gracefulness, every small movement of hers arrested and pleased the eye. For instance, at one critical moment her closely clinging . . . dress of black satin with yellow chrysanthemums displayed a slit which extended to her hip bone and exposed one of the most shapely of legs." (This was Brooke's demure description of her performance at the Cairo Conference in November 1943.)[40] She had an excellent figure and a feline appeal that was conspicuous in these all-male conferences. Roosevelt, always somewhat susceptible to female charms and wiles (not having been showered with them by Eleanor, whatever her other merits), especially enjoyed Madame Chiang's description of Wendell Willkie as an "adolescent," while he, Roosevelt, was "sophisticated."[41] Willkie's "adolescent" qualities, as has been recorded, didn't inhibit Mme. Chiang from charming him too, including her ostentatious kissing of Willkie when they parted.

One Pacific development Roosevelt had particularly welcomed was the shooting down of Admiral Isoroku Yamamoto at Bougainville on April 18, 1943. American code-breakers learned the timetable of his inspection trip, and Nimitz specifically authorized his interception. Despite his initial caution after Pearl Harbor, Yamamoto was misinterpreted as saying that he would dictate peace terms in the White House. Roosevelt wrote out for Leahy a mock letter of condolence to "Dear Widow Yamamoto," showing how searing he still considered Pearl Harbor: "Time is a great leveler and somehow I never expected to see the old boy at the White House anyway."[42]*

When the conference ended, Churchill insisted that Marshall come with him to Algiers to discuss Mediterranean strategy with Eisenhower, who he thought was more sympathetic to British views. Marshall, who had been planning a trip to the Pacific to visit Nimitz and MacArthur, felt he had no option but to agree, and they emplaned May 26 in one of the luxurious flying boats directly from the Potomac River. The President saw the British delegation and his chief of staff off in person, returning Churchill's favor at Marrakesh four months before.

VI

STILL UNSETTLED WAS the advice to Stalin that the full-scale invasion of Western Europe had been further delayed from the autumn of 1943 target date notionally agreed to at Casablanca. Churchill and Roosevelt had tried without much success to work out a letter to Stalin. "Two of the most gifted expositors in the world at this moment were reduced to stammering schoolboys making a confession." They gave up at 2:00 A.M. on the 26th and left it to Marshall to make something of their heavily interlineated drafts, which he did on Churchill's plane later that morning.[43]

The British were pleased that the Americans had not tried to shut down the Mediterranean; the Americans were pleased that they had a date and critical path for a cross-Channel invasion. There was some reciprocal underestimation and mistrust at the staff level, but the principals, ably assisted by the emollient Hopkins and Dill, had performed admirably, even if, as Brooke felt, Churchill "pushed strategic flexibility to the point of chaos."[44] Roosevelt cabled Churchill when he had arrived in Algiers: "I miss you much. It was a highly successful meeting in every way."[45]

Roosevelt waited a week and then sent the agreed message over his own name only to Stalin, the deferral of the invasion of France buried near the end. Surprisingly little was made in the message of the impending invasion of Italy, which was probable but not completely agreed to, but which might have seemed more impressive to Stalin as a commitment to a vigorous war policy by his Western Allies. As it was, Stalin dismissed any such step in advance as inadequate. Marshall's summary emphasized the usual points and added the objectives of bringing Turkey into the war and preparing the Free French forces in North Africa to participate in the liberation of Western Europe.

---

* This refers to a letter Yamamoto sent to a friend saying the United States would only surrender if terms could be dictated from the White House. It was published in a misleading way indicating that he expected this to occur, when he had been writing pessimistically, but Roosevelt didn't know that.

Meanwhile, Joseph Davies had returned from his ludicrous mission to Stalin, pleased with his success at breaking down the Kremlin leader's suspicions. He gave Stalin a copy of the movie *Mission to Moscow,* depicting Davies' slavish worship of Stalin when ambassador there.[46] Stalin would meet Roosevelt at Fairbanks, Alaska, in July or August. In his reply to Roosevelt's Trident summary, June 11, Stalin, as was now his habit, enumerated every previous promised date for the opening of the Western Front and dismissed the actions in Africa and the proposed strategic bombing campaign as unacceptable substitutes. And he cabled a few days later that he could not meet Roosevelt after all.

Stalin, who had awarded himself the title of marshal after the Stalingrad victory, which he had had little personally to do with, had an extensive catalogue of grievances. He sometimes bordered on self-righteousness about the Soviet-Polish border, laying claim to the fruits of the Nazi-Soviet Pact while blaming it on the cowardice of Chamberlain and Daladier. He occasionally put on the airs of the aggrieved over the nonrecognition of what he had gouged from the Finns. He had dissolved the Comintern in deference to Anglo-American wishes, though in fact, international Communist subversion and espionage barely abated. And although he obviously had no concern for casualties, he was beginning to become histrionic on the subject.

His real concern was that the British and Americans would promote an indefinite enervating war between the Germans and the Russians. As an angry gesture Stalin withdrew Maisky from London and Litvinov from Washington.

After Roosevelt and Churchill communicated with each other, Roosevelt replied to Stalin June 14, and Churchill did on June 20. Both expressed understanding of the Soviet leader's "disappointment" but were rightly unapologetic about the war effort each was exerting in the common cause. Both proposed an early tripartite meeting, and Churchill implied that the defeat of the Axis in Africa had denied the Germans the ability to launch another serious summer offensive in Russia.

There was a further disagreeable exchange between Stalin and Churchill, and Churchill advised Roosevelt June 28 that although the relative inactivity on the Eastern Front "is not necessarily due only to our Mediterranean activities [contrary to what he had implied to Stalin in his letter eight days before] no decisive volte-face is pending in Russia"—i.e., a separate peace with Hitler.[47]

The thought was very much in the minds of both leaders, but they correctly calculated where Stalin's rational self-interest lay. As long as there was a live possibility of crushing Germany, obtaining a Russian zone of occupation in that country, and supplanting German influence in Eastern and central Europe, all of which required the British and Americans to attack Germany in the west, Stalin would stay with the Allies, but not if he concluded that they were merely promoting the Russo-German War and not really trying to defeat Germany themselves.

As Roosevelt and Churchill suspected, Hitler and Stalin had already tested the waters of reconciliation. There is no evidence to support the assertion of the British historian B.H. Liddell-Hart that Molotov and Ribbentrop met at Kirovo-grad in June 1943. That account is almost certainly false.[48] However, Peter Kleist, a German diplomat who frequently visited Sweden because he was repatriating Swedes from the Baltic states, did receive an overture from Edgar Klaus, an international businessman of uncertain nationality, on behalf of Soviet under foreign minister Alexandrov. Klaus claimed that the Russians were disaffected with the Western Allies and were interested in pursuing a return to the 1939 frontiers. (This would leave Germany in control of Latvia, Lithuania, and Estonia.) Hitler dismissed this as "Jewish provocation."[49]

A few days later, July 5, Hitler launched his great tank offensive against the Russians at Kursk. It was a catastrophic failure, and Ribbentrop, who had opposed the invasion of Russia in the first place, reactivated the Kleist-Klaus discussions. The two met in Stockholm on September 4 and 8. The Russians were still interested, but the correlation of forces had changed and they now wanted the frontiers of 1914 and the dismissal of Ribbentrop (as Stalin had dismissed Litvinov as relations with Hitler had warmed in 1939).

Vladimir Dekanozov, the Soviet deputy foreign minister, would be in Stockholm September 12 to 16 and was authorized to meet with Kleist. The Western Allies invaded Italy on September 8 and Italy had quit the Axis. So Ribbentrop beseeched Hitler to permit the discussions to proceed, despite the stipulated requirement for his own departure. Hitler considered it, and when Mussolini arrived, sprung from captivity by German paratroopers, Hitler said he was considering settling with Russia. But a couple of days later he again declined to authorize substantive talks. He explained to Ribbentrop: "If I settled with Russia today, I would only come to blows with her again tomorrow. I just can't help it."[50]

We have only Ribbentrop's very unreliable word for this last quotation from Hitler. Hitler did send Kleist back to Stockholm after all, but he was informed by Klaus on September 28 that the Soviets were no longer interested. Stalin informed the Americans of these contacts, representing them as an entirely German initiative. The long-sought meeting of Churchill, Roosevelt, and Stalin had now been tentatively scheduled for two months hence, and this was a useful hint for Stalin to drop.

It is impossible to determine how serious these feelers were, but the familiar methods of Stalin and Hitler prevent us from ruling out a possible separate peace, as Churchill and Roosevelt both knew. If the Germans had won at Kursk and started to push the Russians back again, Stalin would probably have been receptive, but Hitler might have been more emboldened than ever, at least for a time. However, Churchill and Roosevelt didn't have an unlimited time to demonstrate their seriousness as allies to Stalin.

Churchill had been advised verbally by Roosevelt of his suggestion of a Roosevelt-Stalin meeting, and he wrote: "I shall not seek to deter you if you can get him to come."

Some Western historians hold out this delay in opening up the Western Front as the start of the Cold War,[51] but the West had made Russian survival possible; Africa and Italy were significant attritions of German strength, and the air war over Germany was militarily useful, as Stalin eventually acknowledged. With the summer of 1943 and the failure of the Germans to renew their advance against Russia, so weakened had they become by their recent defeats and so powerful now was the Red Army, Stalin became more consolable about the delay of the invasion of France. The scramble for the principal geopolitical assets of Europe was already beginning. This started the Cold War. The Alliance was held together by the necessity of self-interest, not by any great community of interest between the British and Americans and the Russians, or even an identity of view between the Americans and the British.

The discussions between Marshall and Churchill on their way to Algiers via Gibraltar were largely taken up with red herrings that Marshall devised to keep off the subject of an invasion of Italy until he had spoken to Eisenhower. The upshot of the Algiers meetings was an agreement on the invasion of Sicily and the consultation with Eisenhower, as theater commander, about what to do after that. General Sir Bernard Montgomery made a presentation on the proposed action in Sicily. This was the first exposure to him of Marshall and a number of the other Americans, and it was not a satisfactory encounter. Brooke took the side of the Americans, and both he and Marshall found Montgomery's gamecock manner unfortunate.[52] This was an accurate foretaste of what was to come.

VII

THE U.S. SEVENTH Army under General Patton and the British Eighth Army under General Montgomery came ashore in eastern and southeastern Sicily on July 10, 1943. Churchill had cabled Roosevelt July 6, 1943: "It is lovely working with you. Everyone here would like a joint message."[53] A statement mainly composed by Roosevelt but to which Churchill also contributed was issued on behalf of both leaders to the Italian people. It referred to the "shameful leadership" of Mussolini and credited the Italians with having fought "courageously" but said they had been "betrayed and abandoned by the Germans . . . on every battlefield." It was only by disowning "Germany and your own false and corrupt leaders" . . . by consulting your own "self-respect and your own interests" that "national dignity, security, and peace" could be restored. "The time has come for you to decide whether Italians will die for Mussolini and Hitler, or live for Italy and for civilization."

In the battle around Kursk, July 5 to July 13, one of the greatest tank encounters in history, the Soviets defeated the Germans in the air as well as on the ground, and Hitler blamed the Allied invasion of Sicily. He publicly said that this required the transfer of several armored divisions. This was a decisive turn and the end of Germany's systematic offensive in Russia. This was the end of Stalin's ability to claim that his allies weren't engaging Germany on the ground. Apart from occasional spasmodic outbursts, Germany would be in retreat on the Eastern Front for two years, all the way to Berlin.

Patton and Montgomery, with overwhelming air and sea superiority, handled their forces with great skill, clearing the German and Italian forces out of Sicily by August 17. The Allies sustained 20,000 casualties; the Germans had 12,000 dead and captured, and the Italians, who were now completely crumbling, took 147,000 casualties, mainly prisoners.

Mussolini was sacked by his Fascist Grand Council, even his son-in-law and foreign minister, Galeazzo Ciano, voting against him. The next day, July 26, Victor Emmanuel, who had never liked Mussolini and had endured his condescensions for twenty-one years, dismissed him, and the duce was taken from the Quirinal Palace in an ambulance for confinement in a police barracks. Roosevelt privately lamented that the U.S. Office of War Information had just described Victor Emmanuel in a broadcast as a "moronic little king," since he was showing some pluck. (Though there seems to be some evidence that he was also removing plunder to Switzerland. The Italian monarch was only five feet, two inches tall.)

The king called upon Mussolini's former chief of staff, Marshal Pietro Badoglio, to become prime minister. There was some political controversy reminiscent of the furor over Darlan, because the American press wanted to know if the king would be retained. Roosevelt explained that it was not clear that Victor Emmanuel had ever been a Fascist, and that the United Nations were committed to determination of such issues which could not be accomplished in Italy overnight.

Roosevelt addressed the nation in a Fireside Chat on July 28. "The massed angered forces of humanity are on the march." He reviewed the impressive progress of the war and celebrated the fall of Mussolini and "the criminal, corrupt, Fascist regime, [which] . . . will be brought to book and punished for their crimes against humanity. We will permit no vestige of Fascism to remain."

He outlined what became the G.I. Bill of Rights and promised that the armed forces would not "be demobilized into an environment of inflation and unemployment." He reciprocated the frequent public compliments to him by the British prime minister when he said: "The dauntless fighting spirit of the British people in this war has been expressed in the words and deeds of Winston Churchill—and the world knows how the American people feel about him."

The distinguished Canadian-born novelist Saul Bellow recalled "walking eastward on the Chicago Midway on a summer evening. The light held after nine o'clock and the ground was covered with clover." Under the elms, "drivers had pulled over, parking bumper to bumper, and turned on their radios to hear Roosevelt. They had rolled down the windows and opened the car doors. Everywhere the same voice, its odd Eastern accent which from anyone else would have irritated Midwesterners. You could follow without missing a single word as you strolled by. You felt joined to these unknown drivers . . . not so much considering the President's words as affirming the rightness of his tone and taking assurance from it."[54] After more than ten years at the headship of the nation, Franklin D. Roosevelt had crafted what he called on his induction into office "the warm courage of national unity."* The United States that had been so dispirited and poor when Roosevelt assumed its leadership was now a mighty engine for universal goals of human freedom and general prosperity. The great Roosevelt magic now uplifted all mankind.

It quickly became clear that Italy's new government intended to leave the war and negotiate peace on any terms it could get with the British and Americans. It only slowly dawned on the British high command that the Germans would strenuously defend the country, mountain by mountain and river by river. The theory of the soft underbelly was correct in political terms, but as a glance at a topographical map would demonstrate, it was anything but soft militarily.

Advances in radar and in destroyer, frigate, and corvette construction, and British cracking of German naval code had sharply reduced the depredations of German U-boats, and the number of German submarines being sunk rose steadily through 1943 and was the subject of a good deal of gratified correspondence between Churchill and Roosevelt. Like the wars in Russia, the Mediterranean theater, and the Pacific, the Battle of the Atlantic had turned decisively in the Allies' favor.

VIII

BY THE TIME resistance ceased in Sicily, Roosevelt and Churchill were again meeting, in Quebec City, at what was called the Quadrant Conference. There was a good deal of backing and filling about the status of Canada at the conference. King George VI purported to invite both leaders to use the summer residence of the governor general of Canada at the Quebec Citadel. Churchill opposed any particular role apart from presence at plenary sessions and photo opportunities for long-serving Canadian Prime Minister Mackenzie King.

He was ostensibly concerned not to start an agitation by the other Dominions. This was absurd, because Canadian participation would only be as the host country, and Roosevelt and Churchill would not be journeying during the war to confer in Australia, New Zealand, or South Africa. As with India and other matters, Churchill was trying to retain the pretense that Britain's writ still governed in Canada. Roosevelt knew better, but he had his own reasons for confining King to a well-publicized but substantively minor role: he was concerned that the Brazilians and Mexicans would request a place at such a conference. This too was preposterous, since the two countries together did not contribute ten percent of the

---

* A phrase that would be used in 2001 by President George W. Bush in reference to terrorist attacks on the United States.

forces to the war effort that Canada did, and they started much later. Roosevelt resorted to his customary formula of letting down a petitioner, by referring to Mackenzie King in a cable to Churchill on July 24, 1943, as "one of my oldest personal friends." Roosevelt did, after proclaiming this ancient friendship to Churchill, invite King to call him "Franklin," but King was so uncomfortable with that degree of informality that he became flustered even writing it.

Roosevelt was absent on a fishing trip on Manitoulin Island on the Canadian part of Lake Huron for the first week in August while Churchill made a very fast passage to Halifax on the *Queen Mary*, arriving by train with his daughter Mary at Hyde Park on August 12. An apparently becalmed Stalin, justly pleased with the Kursk outcome, wrote Churchill August 10, congratulating the British and Americans on the elimination of Mussolini, and proposing an early tripartite summit meeting with full staffs (while still dickering with the Germans at Stockholm). As usual, he was unable to leave his own theater for more than a week and left it to his acting ambassadors, Gromyko and Gousev, to work out the details of the meeting with the British and Americans, because his ambassadors were still on compulsory home leave over the deferral of the cross-Channel invasion to 1944. Churchill replied from the Citadel of Quebec reciprocating congratulations.

It was certainly time for such a meeting. The Allies were now riding a tide of victory on and over every continent and ocean. Unimaginable prodigies of war production and inexhaustible reserves of manpower were pouring into the war every month on the Allied side, but the alliance was in disarray. Churchill and Roosevelt would be in conference together for much of the balance of 1943.

Despite the Trident agreement on Overlord (the cross-Channel invasion scheduled for the spring of 1944), the Americans received the distinct impression at Quadrant that Churchill was still angling for alternatives. He tried to revive a Norwegian operation, which Brooke and the other British staff chiefs rejected as vehemently as the Americans did, as a peripheral area that would not threaten the Germans and would waste forces on a vulnerable military sideshow. Quadrant was another stormy conference. Brooke took the position that an Italian operation in Italy itself was essential to creating the conditions necessary for Overlord.

Marshall was profoundly skeptical. He expressed a complete willingness to exploit weaknesses swiftly in Italy and take as much of the country as could be had cheaply, but not to the point of putting Overlord in doubt. Brooke then gave his lecture on the theme that the greater the Italian operation was, the easier Overlord would be, as if defense in rugged territory (Italy) required as much manpower as repulsing an amphibious assault on a fortified sea wall (France), and as if there were no such thing as interior lines—i.e., the Germans could transfer forces between France and Italy much more easily than the Allies could.

Marshall, according to a now well-rehearsed script, said that if the American forces accumulating in Britain were going to wait indefinitely, they would be redeployed not to the Mediterranean, where the British wanted to commit them to mountain excursions in Italy and the Balkans, but to the Pacific, where, implicitly, there would be no debate with the British about how they were employed.

August 15 was made more unpleasant for Brooke because he knew that Roosevelt, assured by Marshall and Stimson that by the spring of 1944 the United States would have the preponderance of the forces necessary, could require that the cross-Channel Overlord operation have an American commander. Stimson, who had just visited Churchill, told Roosevelt: "The shadows of Passchendaele and Dunkerque hung too heavily over the British. They were giving it [the cross-Channel operation] only lip service. . . . They still felt that Germany could be beaten by attrition but that sort of pin-prick warfare would never fool Stalin."[55] This, said Stimson, made an American commander for Overlord essential. "We cannot rationally hope to come to grips with our German enemy under a British commander," he said.

On that morning Roosevelt was offered that position by Churchill in anticipation of a request by Roosevelt, though Churchill implied to Brooke that Roosevelt had demanded it.[56] Not the least irony of these Byzantine tractations was that if Brooke, to whom Churchill had promised command of Overlord, had actually believed in it and shown some enthusiasm for it and had been less committed to the Mediterranean, he might have commanded Overlord.

A lesser irony was that in the spring of 1944, the Americans did not have the preponderance of the forces in the invasion after all. The Americans had only 45 percent of the forces, though their percentage grew rapidly as the Expeditionary Force grew in France and Germany to nearly 100 divisions over the next nine months, almost 70 of them American.

It was assumed by the British that Marshall would be the Overlord commander, Eisenhower would take Marshall's place as chief of staff, Montgomery would become head of the British Overlord contingent, Alexander would take over as commander in Italy, and Britain's Maitland Wilson would be Mediterranean commander. As a consolation prize, a Southeast Asia (Burma) theater would be set up with a British commander. Marshall objected so violently to Air Chief Marshal Sir Sholto Douglas as anti-American (though he subsequently admitted he was acting on hearsay) that Mountbatten was chosen instead.

Brooke thought Mountbatten unfit to command more than a destroyer, a vain though dashing careerist, but Churchill wished to befriend the son of the admiral he had had to demote at the start of the First World War because his family name was then Battenberg and he was regarded as unacceptably German.[57]

The gap between the British and Americans was narrowed at the Quadrant Conference on August 16th, through what amounted to a consciousness-raising session initiated by Brooke. He noted that the Americans did not believe that the British were whole-hearted about Overlord and that the British feared that the Americans were so fixated on it that they would proceed regardless of the strategic circumstances of the spring of 1944. Marshall acknowledged that the Americans were unconvinced that the British had really committed to Overlord, which Brooke admitted, but blamed it all on Churchill for constantly dragging in red herrings about ridiculous operations like Norway.

Brooke acknowledged that American concerns were understandable and said he would attempt to allay them, and volunteered that the Americans had shown great flexibility in their attitude to the Mediterranean.[58] In his memoirs, Brooke grudgingly records progress but ascribes it to his going over the merits of the Mediterranean plan virtually in monosyllables and with examples adapted to the mind of a child of ten. He was deeply exasperated at the end of the session.

The ice broke on the 17th of August just before Roosevelt's arrival, so the Combined Chiefs were able to give their leaders a reasonably complete agreement. The Americans effectively accepted the reasserted British commitment to Overlord, and accepted that Italy would be useful in the diversion of German forces from defense against it; uncertainty remained regarding the extent of forces necessary to commit to Italy as the Allies approached Rome, as against the value of sending such reinforcements to Overlord. A general principle of professional evaluation of effectiveness of reinforcements was agreed on', after many alarms and excursions about Norway and a Churchill suggestion, enthusiastically taken up by the Americans, of increasing the strength of the Overlord invasion force by 25 percent.[59]

It was an agreeable leitmotif at this stage to hear overtures from Badoglio for surrender. Victor Emmanuel III was making it clear through his channels that he was all that stood between Italy and Communism. Churchill, a monarchist, tended to believe this, and Roosevelt, who was just as emphatic in saying that a Communist takeover in Italy had to be prevented at all costs, thought any recognition of the monarchy would have to be provisional upon an ultimate referendum.

It is surprising that Brooke and Churchill, in all the fecundity of their imaginations in finding arguments in favor of the Italian operation, didn't seize upon prevention of a Communist takeover as one of them. Certainly Roosevelt peremptorily rejected Stalin's request for a seat on the Italian occupying authority when he made it a few months later.[60]

The Americans particularly noted the deteriorating attitude of the Russians. Marshall remarked that where they had previously been insistent on more help and an early second front, they were now reverting to a suspicious antagonism. On August 23, 1943, Roosevelt said he wanted provision for an emergency entry into the continent and stressed the need for the Western Allies to enter Berlin at the same time as the Russians. Brooke assured him that such contingency plans were already being prepared. It was already being contemplated that once the Western Allies were installed across the Channel, the Germans might fight much more strenuously against the Russians than in the west, enabling a more rapid advance toward the heartland of Europe by the Americans, British, and Canadians than by the Russians.

Given the postwar posturings by British military and civilian leaders that they had sounded the alarm about Russia to deaf, inert, and naïve American analogues, it is noteworthy that at Quadrant this was a subject exclusively raised by the American side. It was clearly in the minds of Roosevelt and Marshall that the way to take as much of Europe as possible back for the West was the earliest and heaviest possible implementation of Overlord. Floundering about in Norway, in the boot of Italy, and among the "sheepstealers" (as Bismarck had habitually called the inhabitants of the Balkans) would have merely opened the highway to Paris and the English Channel to the Red Army.

The ferocity of the Russo-German War had been so great, with ultimately nearly 5 million prisoners of war murdered by the two sides combined, in addition to several million military and many million more civilian deaths, the Germans could rightly assume, once it was clear to them that the war was lost, that their best chance lay in surrendering in the west, benefiting from the Geneva Convention rules, which in general Germany had abided by with Western Allied prisoners, and delivering Germany, France, and Italy into the hands of the Western powers. This was the supreme political prize of the war, and Roosevelt, Churchill, and Stalin were already focused on it. The British did not emphasize this point at this stage, but according to Marshall (who was an unusually reliable recollector of events), "Roosevelt recognized the importance of capturing Berlin as both a political and psychological factor."[61]

The conference slowly improved in ambiance after the rocky start by the military chiefs, and was highlighted by a few unforeseeable divertissements. One was Mountbatten's demonstration of the reinforcing powers of an armor additive while proposing aircraft carriers made of ice. Two blocks of ice were placed at the end of one of the conference rooms in the stately Chateau Frontenac Hotel (a magnificent building that looks down on lower town Quebec and a broad and winding reach of the vast St. Lawrence). Mountbatten then took out a revolver and said he would demonstrate his point, the additive he was championing having been placed in one of the blocks of ice but not the other. The first shot shattered the unfortified ice and showered the eminent onlookers with shards and splinters. The second ricocheted off the ice and passed between the legs of the distinguished onlookers, narrowly avoiding a grievous injury, which would have been a historic low point in Allied conferencing and a unique war wound, if not a less-than-glorious fatality, for an exalted officer.

As it was, the lesser officers and officials in the anterooms became alarmed that the Brooke-Marshall disputes might have boiled over into direct exchange of gunfire, even a duel.[62] Mountbatten's proposal and the method of advocacy were so eccentric that the whole episode was like an isolated happening with no preamble and no sequel, though some must have wondered at the general equilibrium of the new Southeast Asia theater commander. (Aircraft carriers made of ice in such a tropical theater as Mountbatten was about to take over would have provided Britain revenge of a sort against ice for the loss of the R.M.S. *Titanic*.)

The more exotic figure of Orde Wingate, guerrilla warrior and founder of the Chindits, pioneer of deep-penetration paratroop forces operating in the enemy's rear in Burma, arrived in Quebec in Churchill's entourage. He made an excellent impression on the Americans. In general the Americans liked unambiguous fighting generals and disliked British widdering and procrastinating. Wingate always enjoyed the full patronage of Marshall, as did, generally, Patton and Stilwell. Swift agreement was achieved to give Wingate everything he asked for the conduct of the war in Burma.

Brooke was more than usually displeased with Churchill at the end of Quadrant: "a peevish temperamental prima donna of a prime minister, suspicious to the very limits of imagination, always fearing a military combination of effort against political dominance."[63] (The Americans might have been mollified to learn that the British chief of staff was as severe in his strictness on his own leader as on them.)

IX

MONTGOMERY BEGAN THE invasion of Italy September 3, 1943. Later the same day, the Italian authorities signed surrender terms in an olive grove in Syracuse, Italy. The Rome-Berlin Axis had been formally broken. The terms and even the act of the signing of this instrument were kept secret, as the Germans suspiciously encircled Rome. The king and Badoglio escaped to Brindisi, while the derelict Mussolini was shunted about like a malignant Infant of Prague from Rome to Ponza to La Maddalena to a mountain resort in the Abruzzi, in central Italy.

The Allies had planned an amphibious landing at Salerno, thirty miles south of Naples, as well as dropping an airborne division near Rome. On the 8th of September Badoglio signaled that the airfields that had been intended for the airborne landings were now in German hands. It was determined to proceed with the Salerno landings while the forces that had attacked across the straits from Sicily mopped up the heel and toe of Italy. The airborne landings near Rome were cancelled. The Italian fleet sailed from Genoa, La Spezia, and Taranto on the night of September 8, 1943, for Malta. German planes flying from French airfields attacked the Italian fleet and sank the modern battleship *Roma* with a glider bomb (a large semi-rocket), with extensive loss of life, including the fleet commander, Admiral Carlo Bergamini. This was on September 9, 1943, the day the surrender was announced to a generally relieved Italian public.

As Winston Churchill wrote, "On the morning of the 10th the [Italian Fleet was] met at sea by British forces, including the [famous and successful battleships] *Warspite* and *Valiant*, which had so often sought [it] before under different circumstances, and escorted to Malta."[64] It was still a sizeable fleet, including four powerful battleships, which thus passed into Allied hands. Churchill, always as magnanimous in victory as he was implacable in adversity, and a lover of Italy whatever his hatred of Mussolini, ordered Admiral Cunningham to receive the Italian Fleet "in kindly and generous manner," given that it had "scrupulously fulfilled armistice conditions and sustained the revengeful attack of the Germans." He even directed that "Films should be taken . . . of surrender of Italian Fleet, their courteous reception by the British, and kindly treatment of wounded, etc." He intended these for showing in Italy to begin rebuilding relations at once with that country.

The Allied landings and advances were initially virtually unopposed, but heavy fighting began shortly after the troops came ashore at Salerno. Otto Skorzeny, Hitler's paratroop commander, led ninety men on a mission to collect Mussolini from his mountain confinement. Skorzeny brushed aside the carabinieri and whisked the fallen duce to Munich for yet another interview with Hitler, a reunion attended by much less grandiosity than many of their previous theatrical encounters. Mussolini was established at Salo, on the shores of Lake Garda, as figurehead ruler of a Nazi puppet regime, with less authority and a good deal less credibility than Petain.

Mussolini sat grimly and obediently in Salo. Victor Emmanuel III and Badoglio sat in Brindisi, as Churchill wrote, "under the eyes of the [Anglo-American] Allied Commission, and with no effective authority beyond the boundaries of the administrative building of the town."[65]

Churchill remained throughout these developments in the White House, conferring with Roosevelt, the generally pleasing atmosphere dampened only by the fact that his First Sea Lord, Admiral Sir Dudley Pound, took a stroke, and had to retire at once from his post. Roosevelt was conferenced out by September 9, and left the White House and returned to Hyde Park. He urged Churchill to remain as long as he wanted and use the White House as his own headquarters. The President wouldn't hear of the prime minister's returning to his own (commodious, Lutyens-designed) embassy.

Churchill gave new meaning to the legend of the English houseguest and after a brief hiatus convened another conference in the White House, September 11, attended by Marshall, Leahy, King, Arnold, Harriman, Hopkins, Dill, and Ismay. Arnold reported that there were now 3,000 Allied aircraft in the new Italian theater, more aircraft than in the entire German Air Force. It was agreed to accelerate the insertion of divisions into Italy to clear the enemy out of Naples and move toward Rome as quickly as possible. (Naples became the first large Western European city to be liberated from Axis occupation, October 1, 1943.)

There was relatively little rivalry or friction between Roosevelt and Churchill. Their mutual regard was very great. Roosevelt never felt overawed by Churchill's fluency or reservoir of information. As Eleanor, often her husband's sternest critic, though not an unalloyed admirer of the whiskey-swilling Tory prime minister either, wrote of Churchill in a letter to Joe Lash: "He is always using quotations and can quote endless poetry," yet neither Churchill, nor Beaverbrook (who offered to help Anna Roosevelt Boettiger with her newspaper), nor anyone else has "the geographic knowledge, nor the all around historical knowledge and grasp of the whole picture today which our own raconteur has and he can outtalk them all too."[66]

Roosevelt did find Churchill's visits exhausting, as did the White House staff, given the prime minister's prodigious alcoholic consumption and unusual hours. After Trident and Quadrant, Roosevelt went to Hyde Park mainly to recuperate from the rigors of entertaining so absorbing though welcome a visitor.

Winston Churchill left Washington by train on September 12, stopped briefly at Hyde Park to make his farewells to the President, proceeded on to Halifax, and embarked at once on Britain's only surviving battle cruiser, the swift and graceful H.M.S. *Renown,* for the journey home. He and Roosevelt had just received an exceedingly respectful message from Stalin congratulating them on the Italian surrender and the Naples landing (as he called it). Winning the war would now be costly but straightforward, depending mainly on a successful Overlord vigorously pursued. Winning the peace would be the supreme challenge of these great protagonists.

CHAPTER 20

"Always the Underdog . . . I Am Sick at Heart at the Mistakes and Lost Opportunities That Are So Prevalent"

(General Douglas MacArthur writing to General Bonner F. Fellers, June 18, 1943)

I

As THE MILITARY tide flowed more heavily in the Allies' favor through 1943, this year of almost constant conferences struggled with the end-game strategy and the jockeying for postwar position. Casablanca, Trident, and Quadrant, Eden's visit to Roosevelt in March, Stimson's to Churchill in July, the Churchill-Roosevelt talks before and after Quadrant, Churchill's North African discussions with Marshall and Eisenhower, and foreign ministers' meeting in October in Moscow had prepared the way for the long-awaited meeting of the western Allied leaders with Stalin. This was arranged for Teheran in late November, and was to be preceded and followed by discussions between Churchill, Roosevelt, and Chiang Kai-shek.

Roosevelt pushed through his postwar veterans' legislation in October—the last and most indisputably benign of the five phases of the New Deal, which ensured that the best of its spirit survived the terrible crucible of war. But Roosevelt was almost completely preoccupied by questions of war and peace. Stalin's abrupt withdrawal of his ambassadors from Washington and London following the Trident decision to delay the cross-Channel assault to 1944 had seemed ominously like the preamble to the Nazi-Soviet Pact, though Gromyko and Feodore Gousev were upgraded in their places. Stalin's nightmare had been that Hitler would be got rid of by the Germans and the Western Allies would then make a separate peace with Germany. The Anglo-American nightmare was that Stalin would resurrect such a peace with Hitler still in place. As the Russians began to roll the Germans back, even through the summer in 1943, their enthusiasm for a second front visibly declined.

Stalin's foreign vice-commissar, Alexander Korneichuk, told the correspondent Alexander Werth that it might be preferable not to have a second front until 1944 at the earliest, in order to facilitate the greatest possible Soviet penetration of the heart of Europe. Even before the Western landings in France, there was the Soviet concern (which proved not to be unfounded) that Germany would cave in on the west while fighting with desperate tenacity in the east.[1]

Stalin sought to take all he could as a prize of war before returning to Communist revolutionary and subversive activity after the war, Marxism's credibility heavily reinforced by the universally esteemed heroism of the Red Army (though it is far from clear that Stalin was much of a Marxist believer himself). Churchill sought to preserve what he could of the British Empire, and to conserve perceived influence through an unusually intimate alliance with the United States. Roosevelt had to complete the process of committing America to world involvement. After his close observation of the careers of Theodore Roosevelt and Woodrow Wilson, he thought this could best be done in an apparently idealistic framework. He had gradually built the United Nations from a slogan into a concept for an updated Wilsonian organization to preserve peace and promote progressive government. Roosevelt considered Communism a brutal and bad system, and was confident that intelligent and humane, liberal, capitalist democracy would easily prevail over it.

He was also convinced that imperialism generally was doomed. Roosevelt thought that sophisticated colonial entities like India should quickly become self-governing. Others, like Indochina, should be in limited-duration transitional trusteeships. And more primitive areas, like much of sub-Saharan Africa, should be started on what would be a long process of preparation for independence. Roosevelt was an authentic Anglophile, and liked and respected Churchill, but they were now seeking somewhat different ends. Roosevelt feared (again with good reason) that Communism could have considerable appeal to colonized peoples. As we have seen, unlike Churchill, he also thought Stalin could be prevented from surging to the English Channel or recomposing his differences with Germany only by a prompt Anglo-American invasion of Western Europe. Churchill, though largely resigned to Overlord, continued to be tempted by strategically nonsensical alternatives involving Norway, Turkey, and Slovenia.

On Veterans Day, November 11, 1943, President Roosevelt, with the war and navy secretaries, attended at the Tomb of the Unknown Soldier at Arlington. Unusually, Roosevelt did not give an address and did not speak to the press. This was his last appearance in Washington for several weeks. That evening, with Hopkins, Leahy, and McIntire, he drove in a motorcade of White House cars to

Quantico, Virginia, boarded the presidential yacht *Potomac*, and sailed to Chesapeake Bay. On the morning of November 12, the *Potomac* came alongside the mighty, 45,000-ton, newly commissioned battleship *Iowa*. A ramp was installed between the unequal decks of the two vessels, and in the calm of the bay the Commander in Chief was wheeled aboard his newest and largest warship. Roosevelt ordered that there be no official ceremony for his arrival. Marshall, King, and Arnold were already aboard. *Potomac* continued to fly the presidential standard and simulated a leisure cruise in coastal waters. The *Iowa* refueled at Hampton Roads, adding several feet to her draught, with which she would not have been able to clear the bottom of Chesapeake Bay.

Roosevelt, who had certain nautical superstitions, asked the captain of the *Iowa* not to sail until midnight, when it would be Saturday, because sailors traditionally considered Friday an unlucky day to start a cruise. The *Iowa* was bound for Oran, Algeria, and Roosevelt would go on by air to conferences in Cairo and Teheran. From the first, Roosevelt ignored Navy General Orders No. 99, adopted July 1, 1914, when he was assistant secretary, banning alcoholic beverages from U.S. Navy ships. He exempted his party and himself. *Iowa* was escorted by three destroyers, pursued an anti–U boat zig-zag course, and had one-third of her crew at battle stations at all times.

On the first page of a diary he kept of the voyage, Roosevelt recorded that *Iowa* and her sister *New Jersey* (other sisters *Missouri* and *Wisconsin* would only be completed in 1944) were "the largest battleships in the world." This demonstrated the shortcomings of U.S. Naval intelligence, because the Japanese *Yamato* and *Musashi* were more than 25,000 tons heavier, more thickly armored, and more powerfully gunned, though the faster *Iowas* would still have been formidable combatants for the giant Japanese ships had they ever exchanged fire, especially given generally more accurate American gunnery.

The trip across the Atlantic was uneventful except for an accidental scare on November 14, caused by a torpedo launch from an escorting destroyer that would have hit the *Iowa* if evasive action had not been not taken. A demonstration of *Iowa*'s antiaircraft potential was in progress and Roosevelt and his entourage were sitting with cotton stuffed in their ears watching "the curtain of fire" when the destroyer *William D. Porter* signaled: "Torpedo is coming your way!" There quickly followed a further message: "Torpedo may be ours!" Someone had forgotten to remove a primer from the torpedo-launching firing lock and the firing device had been activated inadvertently. In practicing a torpedo attack without actually firing any torpedoes, the *Iowa* had been the notional target (a practice that was discontinued). The *Iowa*'s captain ordered a sharp acceleration from twenty-four to thirty-three knots and a turn to starboard to present less of a target to the incoming torpedo, which passed astern as a result and detonated noisily in the choppiness of the battleship's wake. Had the torpedo struck, it would certainly not have sunk the flagship, but might have slowed it, introduced water into the anti-torpedo layer between armored hulls, and generally been an embarrassment.

King was so humiliated by the episode that he initially placed the whole crew of the *Porter* under notional arrest, then wished to court martial the captain, but Roosevelt, who had his valet move his wheelchair closer to the rail so he could see the approaching torpedo, insisted that no disciplinary action be taken, provided the fleet commander was confident there would be no repetition.[2]

Churchill had also left on the twelfth, again on the battle cruiser *Renown*, which conveyed him to Gibraltar, where the *Renown* had for several years been the flagship of the local fleet, the famous "Force H," including the aircraft carrier *Ark Royal*, which had operated in the Atlantic and the Mediterranean with great success. The prime minister was fluish and remained in his cabin. He took to his bed in the governor's house at Malta, where the *Renown* docked after Gibraltar and Algiers. Churchill became so irritated with noisy Maltese boulevardiers on the sidewalk below his window that he hurled open the window one day in a state of partial undress and bellowed at the astonished strollers below: "Go away, will you? Please go away and do not make so much noise." He also complained about the mooing of the governor's cows.[3]

Churchill summoned Brooke and the other service chiefs around his Malta bedside on November 18. Brooke was concerned about what he called "new feelings of spitefulness" about the Americans. The United States now had over 10.5 million men under arms, compared with British and Empire forces of about 9 million, and the gap was growing each month as Marshall continued to generate first-class units out of the instant conjuration of masses of conscripted warriors. The moment Roosevelt and Marshall had patiently awaited for the first eighteen months of America's participation in the war had come, when Roosevelt could assert himself and demand a greater degree of British accommodation to the American strategic vision.

Churchill sensed what was coming and raged to Brooke and the others in "a long tirade on the evils of the Americans." He claimed that he was going to threaten to withdraw support from the cross-Channel operation if the Americans were not more supportive of his Mediterranean plans, and if the Americans then threatened to decamp to the Pacific he would invite them to do so.[4] Brooke was confident Churchill would not follow through on such a mad whim, but still found it disquieting. Matters had taken a strange turn when Brooke was intervening with Churchill on behalf of the Americans.

Roosevelt's service chiefs presented the President with a paper that opposed carrying war in the Balkans beyond air and sea supply of local resistance units and bombing, and opposed any diversion of forces—even if Churchill could wheedle the Turks into the war on the Allied side—that would retard the date and scale of Overlord. To this Roosevelt declared, "Amen!" and initialed the paper, saying that it should be given to the British and adhered to, whatever the ally's objections.[5]

Roosevelt had initially opposed agreeing to a westward movement of the Russo-Polish border, or a reincorporation of Estonia, Latvia, and Lithuania into the Soviet Union. As we have seen, he prevented the British from agreeing to these matters with Molotov when the Soviet foreign minister was in London in May 1942. By March 1943, when Eden visited Roosevelt in Washington, the President was prepared to accept the Curzon Line (coincidentally, approximately the line of demarcation in the Nazi-Soviet Pact of 1941). He was also prepared for the Russians to take over Königsberg, though most of East Prussia would go to Poland. He would also concede the inevitable with the Baltic states, though he would still have preferred some sort of referendum, however spurious. This forlorn wish revealed Roosevelt's incomprehension of Stalin's conviction of Soviet entitlement to virtually the full borders of Imperial Russia.

A few days after returning from his mission to Moscow during the Trident Conference in May 1943, Joseph Davies had gone to Mexico to speak to the Soviet ambassador to that country, Konstantin Oumansky, whom Davies knew well and who was thought to have some influence on Stalin. Oumansky had formerly been ambassador in Washington. As Oumansky reported it to Davies, who faithfully transmitted it to Roosevelt,* Stalin regarded Churchill as irrationally anti-Soviet, and was concerned that he might have a Mephistophelean influence on Roosevelt. He was disconcerted about these recurring Anglo-American conferences arriving at decisions important to the Soviet Union, in which Stalin was never consulted.

Oumansky told Davies that Stalin was concerned that any meeting with Churchill and Roosevelt would be a stitch-up, in which he would face a solid wall of prearranged Anglo-American positions. This was one of the reasons why he had been so obstreperous about arranging the meeting, and had refused to come any closer to the Western leaders than Teheran. They had invited him to Scapa Flow, Cairo, Khartoum, and even Basra (Iraq), and a desert place where they would set up, as Churchill cabled Roosevelt, quoting the Bible, "three tabernacles."

Stalin drearily refused, even after Roosevelt unwisely explained that he couldn't be more than ten days' distance from Washington because of the necessity of signing legislation. Stalin knew this to be false, since the President's authority was obviously sufficient to achieve a dispensation from any such footling rules. Stalin would not go beyond Teheran, though he was prepared to send Molotov and some generals to Cairo. Finally, Roosevelt agreed to come to Teheran, and the destination was agreed just as he was departing Washington. He laboriously explained to Stalin that he had had to reconstrue the Constitution to permit such a prolonged absence (as if Stalin had ever evinced the slightest interest in any country's constitutional niceties, including his own).

Roosevelt had even asked Cordell Hull, at the foreign ministers' meeting in Moscow beginning October 19, 1943, to make his case with Stalin for a more convenient meeting site. Hull did so, unsuccessfully, but did elicit a promise from Stalin to enter the war against Japan after the defeat of Germany. A European Advisory Commission was also established by the Big Three at the Moscow meet-

---

* Davies sometimes signed off his letters to Roosevelt "Affectionate and devoted greetings to Mrs. Roosevelt and your wonderful self."[6]

ing to decide all matters to do with the occupation of Germany. Apart from that, Hull was reduced to spending most of his time invoking U.S. constitutional trivia in support of Roosevelt's desire not to appear to be going cap in hand to see the Soviet leader on his own doorstep. Hull wrote that Roosevelt looked "forward to his meeting with Stalin with the enthusiasm of a boy." This eagerness was unrequited. Stalin watched the approach of his allies with suspicion. And he never attached the slightest credence to what he thought the pious bunkum about the United Nations. The divergences between the British and the Americans, and Western Allies and the Russians, had already begun.

Roosevelt reconvened his service chiefs in a shipboard conference on the *Iowa* not unlike those Churchill had often held on the vessels that had carried him and his colleagues to meet the Americans. The Joint Chiefs presented the President with their views on occupation zones of Germany. So drastically had the tide of battle turned that such considerations were certainly not premature. Britain had already tentatively proposed that the United States occupy France and southern Germany and the British would occupy northwest Germany. Roosevelt had no interest in occupying France, which he regarded as a "British baby," and ascribed the occupation of all of it to Britain, as if Britain or the United States had any right, desire, or capacity to occupy their ostensible ally for any length of time. Roosevelt also wished to give Britain responsibility for Luxembourg, Belgium, Baden, and Württemberg. He drew three lines across a map he tore out of a *National Geographic* magazine and declared he would resist the British effort to put the Americans in southern Germany.

Roosevelt thought it possible there would be "a railroad invasion of Germany with little or no fighting." Two years of intense warfare all over the world had not blunted his optimism. Marshall and others pointed out to the Commander in Chief that the Americans would have to advance into Europe and eastward into Germany to the right of the British for logistical reasons. They started from camps to the west of the British in southern England. The two army groups could not diagonally crisscross as they traversed the English Channel on D-Day. Nor could they change places in the face of the enemy and on the point of crossing the Rhine.

Roosevelt suspected the motives of the British in trying to shunt the Americans into Bavaria, and paid little attention to Marshall's comments about rationalizing lines of communications. He was generally prepared to support Marshall in his military dispositions but paid no attention to him at all where politics, foreign or domestic, were involved. The British and Americans understood from the start that the U.S.S.R. would occupy northeastern Germany, but Roosevelt wanted American forces in Berlin as soon as possible. He said there would "definitely be a race for Berlin" and the United States must get there ahead of the Russians. Whatever his hopes for his meeting with Stalin, he was under no illusions at all about the geopolitical stakes the Allies were playing for. Hopkins suggested the United States be ready to put an airborne division directly into Berlin as soon as the Germans seemed to have weakened sufficiently to make such an action feasible. Roosevelt said he expected to retain an occupation army in Europe of one million men for up to two years. He did not say how quickly or to what level it would recede after that.[7]

Rough agendas were drawn up for proposed separate meetings in Cairo with the Chinese and with the British, and then in Teheran with the British and the Russians. Roosevelt would give Chiang only the vaguest outline of proposed Allied activities in and around China, because of fear of Chinese indiscretions. He would not accept an American sphere of influence in some unremitting place such as the Balkans. Roosevelt was determined not to allow the United States to fall into the traditional European practice at the end of wars of the Great Powers carving up for their own account miscellaneous interests and responsibilities having nothing to do with their direct national interest.

He was confident the United States had outgrown isolationism. But he believed the American people preferred to operate in an international organization in a coherent and legally defensible way. The United States could not be, or behave like, other Great Powers, and to the extent that the world appeared to be organized in a civil, lawful way, it would be less forbidding to those Americans who wished to abstain from it.

Roosevelt's fear was that now that the Russians were only sixty miles from the Polish border and forty miles from Romania, they would agitate for the Balkan campaign that Churchill had been advocating. This would shuffle the British and Americans into Romania, Hungary, and Slovakia and possibly consign the heart of Western Europe to the Russians, who could arrive, red banners flying, at the English Channel.

In planning ahead for discussions with Stalin, Roosevelt went over proposals governing collaboration in strategic bombing, American use of Soviet air bases, preliminary ideas on spheres of occupation in Germany, policies toward Sweden and Turkey, and disposition of the Italian fleet and merchant shipping. Roosevelt was prepared to give Russia one-third of the Italian ships as an act of goodwill. Anglo-American merchant shipping construction now exceeded requirements.

Roosevelt intended to ignore agendas in discussions with Stalin. He was much more concerned with a general session enabling him to evaluate whether anything constructive or durable could be arranged with the Russian dictator. As Lord Keynes had discovered in Washington, Roosevelt was far from being "an automatic supporter of the Soviet Union," though he had acknowledged to Cardinal Spellman that Eastern Europe was likely to be dominated, at least for a time, by the Soviet Union.[8]

II

THERE WAS A flurry of concern about press leaks in the United States of an impending conference in Cairo, and Roosevelt recommended a change to Khartoum (Sudan), while Eisenhower suggested Malta. Churchill, who was still in Malta, said it was completely inadequate, and Eisenhower reverted to Cairo, promising additional air cover if it was necessary.

On the afternoon of November 19, 1943, the *Iowa* rendezvoused with a further escort group of a cruiser and five destroyers (three of them British), increased speed to twenty-seven knots, and went to general quarters as the flotilla passed through the Strait of Gibraltar. Roosevelt subsequently wrote that he had seen the "loom" of the Rock.

Iowa anchored in Oran harbor at 8:09 A.M. on November 20, the largest ship ever to have entered that port. Roosevelt went ashore at once in a whale boat that was lowered into the water by a davit, accompanied by his wheelchair. He and his party got into a long motorcade and drove at speed with a heavy escort through streets well-lined with U.S. soldiers and military police facing both ways, to the airport, where they took off at once in several aircraft, again well-escorted by fighter planes, for Tunis.

After a somewhat turbulent flight of three and a half hours, the presidential party landed near Tunis, and Roosevelt went to the Casa Blanca, well-named, as he wrote, which served as Eisenhower's residence. He caught up on official business; toured the ruins of Carthage and a recent battlefield, where Eisenhower showed him how the action had unfolded; had a nearby picnic lunch; and dined with his sons Elliott, who commanded a local photo reconnaissance wing, and Franklin Jr. He left on the evening of November 21 in a transport plane that had been modified to make it more comfortable for Hopkins and him and flew overnight to Cairo, approaching from the south so that he could get a good view of the Nile, the Pyramids, and, as he called it, "my friend the Sphinx."[9]

Chiang Kai-shek and his wife had arrived at Cairo November 20, and Mme. Chiang attracted a large crowd while driving through Cairo to a hairdresser, thus upsetting the extensive efforts that had been expended to tighten security. Winston Churchill arrived on H.M.S. *Renown* at Alexandria and flew to the compound of the Mena House Hotel near Cairo, which had been very heavily reinforced and guarded for the conference. On the afternoon of November 22, Roosevelt and Churchill drove out to the Pyramids and the Sphinx.

The Sextant Conference, as the meeting in Cairo was called, opened on the morning of November 23 in the Mena House Hotel, with Madame Chiang, at her lissome best in a tight, slit satin skirt, accompanying her husband to meet Churchill and Roosevelt and their senior advisors and military chiefs.

Roosevelt asked Mountbatten, as theater commander, to sketch out his plans for the next year, which he did with his usual flair and confidence, envisioning the complete expulsion of the Japanese from Burma. Chiang then called for extensive naval support along the Burma coast and fell into unequal debate with Churchill, who explained that since the naval units would be operating thousands of miles from their bases, the sort of support he was seeking would be very difficult. Roosevelt eventually changed the subject.

Brooke welcomed Chiang's generals to the Combined Chiefs' meeting and invited them to comment on the plans Mountbatten had summarized, which had been given to them for their consideration. (The British were the hosts in Egypt, so Brooke took the chair of the Combined Chiefs.)

Accounts differ of what happened next. Brooke records that when he introduced the Chinese, a "ghastly silence" ensued, and the Chinese said they wanted to listen to the deliberations. Brooke said the deliberations had been completed. He suggested that the Chinese withdraw and study the plans further, and that British and American officers would be attached to them to explain details, should they wish. When they shuffled out, Brooke and Marshall agreed that this had been a "waste of time," and Brooke, not uncharacteristically, blamed it all on the Americans for attaching such credence to Chiang in the first place.

Stilwell thought that Brooke had introduced the Chinese with great condescension and had insulted them. He, Stilwell, had been prevented from speaking for them by an order from "Peanut" (Chiang). Stilwell referred a couple of times in this section of his diary to Roosevelt as "Rubberlegs," a particularly tasteless comment, even when made to himself.[10]

Roosevelt had lost most of whatever confidence he had had in Chiang. He described Chiang to Sumner Welles as "highly temperamental," was disgusted by his "corruption and inefficiency, [and] . . . apparent lack of sympathy for the abject misery of the masses of the Chinese people," but felt that "badly as his troops were fighting," there was no option but to support the Chiangs. (Whenever Chiang spoke at the sessions, his general-interpreter translated, but the graceful and very fluent Madame then sprang to her feet and undertook to transmit "the Generalissimo's full meaning." Brooke wrote that they were never sure whether they were hearing from Chiang or his wife.[11]

Stilwell regarded Brooke as a racist who disparaged the Chinese on those grounds alone, which is surely unfair. Brooke had a view of Chiang similar to Stilwell's, for similar reasons, though he had not met him before. Brooke thought Chiang a cross, physically, between a "pine marten and a ferret . . . [with] a shrewd foxy sort of face," but with "no grasp of the war" or anything else except how to pick the pockets of the West. Brooke's disparagements of Chiang would not have surprised or offended Roosevelt. Roosevelt correctly foresaw that China would be a postwar major power, was well aware of Chiang's shortcomings, but had no other candidate to support in China at this time.

He tried to make Cairo a success for Chiang and to strengthen his hand opposite the Japanese and the Communists. To this end, he undertook that the United States would equip from sixty to ninety Chinese divisions. He stuck (at this point) to his commitment to take the Andaman Islands, as a staging area for increased air and naval activity in support of Burma.

Roosevelt wanted to encourage the Chinese armies, because they had to some degree returned to active combat with the Japanese in the Chungking area. They were tying down a significant number of Japanese soldiers, however ineptly.

There were also some concerns of China's seeking a separate peace with Japan, but Roosevelt discounted this, because the only way China could regain Manchuria and Formosa was through Allied victory over Japan. So the likelihood of any such defection was even less with the Chinese than with the Russians, now that victory was in sight.

The Andaman project, code-named "Buccaneer," quickly led to the first of several serious disputes between the British and the Americans. Even though Stilwell regarded Buccaneer and Mountbatten's planned Burmese offensive as "abortions," because they did not "lead anywhere," Roosevelt thought it important to show activity and enable Chiang not to return empty-handed.

The British, it emerged on November 23, opposed Buccaneer. The afternoon Combined Chiefs session on that day, before the fiasco of the Chinese generals, became very heated when Brooke made it clear that he would rather scrap Buccaneer and consecrate the forces required for it to fight Churchill's current hobby horse, Rhodes. (Churchill was convinced that seizing the island of Rhodes would help bring Turkey into the war on the side of the Allies.) Brooke and the other British service chiefs didn't much care for this project either, but preferred it to the Andamans and were in any case loyal to their chief. An acrimonious scene developed between Brooke on one side and Marshall and King on the other. Stilwell only wished King "had socked him [Brooke]."[12]

Churchill launched his argument in favor of Rhodes that evening and the following day, November 24. As was his custom when trying to make inroads on the Americans, he tried a private softening-up meeting with Marshall, whose influence on Roosevelt, though far from infallible, was well-known to Churchill. He had the chairman of the Combined Allied Military Chiefs and chief of staff of the now immense U.S. Army to dinner on November 23. Marshall found it the usual impressive demonstration of the prime minister's articulation, erudition, charm, stamina, memory, and capacity for drink. The occasion continued until 2 A.M. When Marshall mentioned that he had been reading the addresses of William Pitt on the crossing from the United States, Churchill strode about the drawing room of his villa reciting extensive lapidary tracts of Pitt the Elder's most celebrated orations.[13] Marshall, who was not easily impressed, was always impressed by Churchill, and certainly was on this occasion.

The next morning Churchill convened the Combined Chiefs and put the Rhodes operation forcefully before them, making his claim that such an action would bring Turkey into the war.* (This was constantly invoked by the British as

---

* Eden had just met with officials from the Turkish foreign ministry. They had been completely unmoved by his exhortations to join the war, including his promises of massive air support and assurances that the Germans were too stretched to attack Turkey by land. Churchill records in his memoirs: "Considering what had been happening under their eyes in the Aegean, the Turks can hardly be blamed for their caution," referring to the campaign in Greece and Crete in 1941, and the recent German expulsion of the British from two of the lesser Dodecanese Islands.[14]

a certain consequence of relatively minor initiatives, but not one scrap of evidence has ever come to light to indicate that Turkey had any intention of entering the war at any useful date under any circumstances.)

The conference temperature quickly escalated as the merits of the Rhodes scheme were debated. Finally, according to Marshall, Churchill, defiantly holding his own lapels, "his spit curls hung down . . . said: 'His Majesty's Government can't have its troops standing idle. Muskets must flame.' I [Marshall] said 'God forbid if I should try to dictate but . . . not one American soldier is going to die on that Goddamned beach.' Churchill never held this against me, but Ismay had to stay up with him all night."[15]

Churchill's summary of the war was jubilant about progress in Africa, Russia, and the Pacific, but ascribed "disappointments" in Italy to insufficient commitments of manpower. The Americans avoided references to the "soft underbelly," but Churchill revealed his concern that Britain had only sixteen divisions it could commit to Overlord, and would not be able to replace losses. The consequences of defeat would be catastrophic, because British manpower had reached its outer limits. Roosevelt recited the huge manpower figures already attained and still to be achieved by the United States Army and Navy.

Throughout November 24 and 25 Chiang overplayed his hand and irritated everybody by agreeing to proposals after lengthy haggling and then reneging and demanding more concessions. The British thought he should be sent packing. The Americans, exasperated by him but mindful of China's potential, all thought the effort to keep him in the Alliance justified.

The sessions of the afternoon of November 25 were adjourned to celebrate the American Thanksgiving holiday. There was a service at the Cairo Anglican (Episcopalian) Cathedral, which Brooke regarded as "a sad fiasco and abominably badly run from the prereservation of seats to the Bishop's sermon. . . . I was in a cold sweat of agony throughout."*[16]

In the evening the service chiefs had a very convivial party, during which the preceding acerbities were forgotten, while Roosevelt entertained Churchill and Eden to dinner, with his son Elliott, his son-in-law John Boettiger, Churchill's daughter Sarah, Hopkins and his son, and his closest staff.

Churchill remembered it as a "pleasant and peaceful feast. . . . The President carved for all with masterly indefatigable skill." Churchill was impressed that there appeared to be turkey for every American serviceman everywhere in the world. "Speeches were made of warm and intimate friendship. For a couple of hours we cast care aside. I have never seen the President more gay" (traditional meaning of affable, obviously). A dance followed, but since Sarah was the only

---

* Brooke seems to have specialized in his diary in critiques of divine services and the appearance of women of suspect virtue; he rarely commented on anyone's wife in what appeared to be a normally functioning marriage, but he was full of prurient observations on those in irregular relationships.

woman present, Churchill dutifully danced a cakewalk with Roosevelt's military assistant, General Edwin "Pa" Watson. Roosevelt sang the U.S. Marine Corps anthem, accompanied by a military band. "This jolly evening and the spectacle of the President carving up the turkeys stand out in my mind among the most agreeable features of the halt at Cairo."[17] Churchill's memoirs make no mention of the altercation with Marshall.

Churchill had sought, but did not get, a candid, one-on-one session with Roosevelt to prepare for Stalin. He was reduced, as Eden wrote, to having to "play the role of courtier and seize opportunities as and when they arose. I am amazed at the patience with which he does this."[18] Eden and Churchill agreed that Roosevelt was "a charming country gentleman," but they were beginning to sound like Brooke in their impatience with his discursive methods.

The afternoon of November 26 produced what Brooke called "the father and mother of a row" with Marshall over Buccaneer, which Brooke urged be postponed to concentrate on defeating Germany. They went to executive session without the relatively junior staff, and comparative calm returned. Brooke had touched a sensitive nerve by inadvertently giving the Americans to believe that the British considered the Asian and Pacific theaters to be insignificant.

There was a tea party by the Chiangs, which Brooke predictably, though probably accurately, considered "a dismal show."

Roosevelt had met with a group of Egyptian notables, including the prime minister, the exiled kings of Greece and Yugoslavia and their prime ministers, and the American ambassadors to Turkey, the U.S.S.R., and Egypt. Roosevelt, unlike Churchill, counted Sextant a success, leading to "a good announcement" about China.[19] The Cairo proceedings were adjourned, and almost the entire British and American delegations left shortly after dawn on November 27 to make their appointment with the marshal-premier of the Soviet Union at Teheran.

III

THERE HAD BEEN considerable controversy about Roosevelt's route to Teheran and about his accommodation there. After the thoroughly unsatisfactory negotiations over the site of the conference, in which Stalin refused to accommodate the President in the slightest degree, the White House sent General Patrick Hurley and the President's security chief, Mike Reilly, to Teheran to reinforce the minister there, Louis Dreyfus, and to advise on methods of travel and on residence during the meetings. Hurley, who had been Hoover's war secretary, was a rather unsubtle soldier who had some value as a Republican serving the administration. But his counsel was almost always mistaken, from Iran to Vietnam. His real importance was his role as an insurance policy for Roosevelt against his ancient foes on the Republican right, not the wisdom of his advice.

There was a variety of air and rail approaches. The President's physician, Dr. (now Admiral) McIntire, suggested rail, because flight at 16,000 feet could be hazardous to Roosevelt's sinuses and to his cardiological and pulmonary well-being. Reilly reported that the trains traveled through uncontrolled areas open to rebellious tribes and German paratroopers, through scores of tunnels vulnerable to saboteurs, and that the tracks reached a height of 8,000 feet—and that that, not 16,000, was the required flight altitude. From Cairo, the President would fly, even though aircraft then were much less well pressurized than in more recent times.

The U.S. mission in Teheran was across town from the Russian and British embassies, which were side by side. As none of the three leaders was a host in Teheran, the conference site would have to rotate among them. Teheran did not have roads to take dignitaries swiftly or easily between different parts of the city. Reilly and Hurley advised that there could be security problems commuting from the U.S. legation. Both Stalin and Churchill invited Roosevelt to stay in their embassies, after Roosevelt had asked Stalin for his advice in arrangements. Andrei Vyshinsky, the vicious prosecutor in Stalin's thirties show trials, visited Roosevelt in Cairo November 23 and invited him to stay in the Soviet embassy. Reilly and Hurley inspected the accommodation and found it very commodious, but Roosevelt initially declined both Churchill's and Stalin's invitations.

Roosevelt flew over the Suez Canal, Jerusalem, and Bethlehem, which the pilot circled to give him a good view, and Roosevelt wrote: "Everything very bare looking—and I don't want Palestine as my homeland."[20] They flew east over Baghdad and landed at Teheran at 3 P.M., November 27.

Roosevelt went for the first night to the U.S. legation. He wrote in his diary of Teheran: "This is a very dirty place—great poverty."[21] Dreyfus, his minister, had been denied by Hurley the right to meet the President at the airport and had been expelled from his own legation to make way for the President. Only Hopkins, Leahy, Roosevelt's son-in-law, John Boettiger, and another admiral stayed with Roosevelt. The others were a few miles away at the Persian Gulf command center. A special ramp had been installed to facilitate Roosevelt's entry in his wheelchair. Unfortunately, the ramp covered the only access to the legation's liquor storage room and the Americans had to borrow eight cases of whiskey from their British colleagues. This amused the British, who felt somewhat snubbed that Roosevelt had declined their invitation to stay in the British embassy.

Roosevelt proceeded through streets heavily guarded by his soldiers and Secret Service men in a swiftly moving motorcade. Stalin had already arrived, in what seems to have been the only air journey of his life. The Red Army had provided massive security along his route into the city from the airport. Churchill did not benefit from the same preparations. Eden arrived ahead of him and was spirited off in the midst of Persian cavalry. He made good progress until the gates of the British embassy, where a peasant and his donkey blocked the entrance. Churchill moved through sparsely protected streets and through ever thicker crowds until his car was stopped completely by the throngs for several minutes. "I grinned at the crowd and on the whole they grinned at me," he wrote.[22]

After the Russians claimed to have discovered a plot to assassinate all three leaders as they traveled to and from the distant American legation, Roosevelt determined to accept the invitation of the Russians to stay in their embassy. Roosevelt feared that if he stayed in the British embassy it would enflame Stalin's paranoia about an Anglo-American conspiracy. The British embassy was much smaller and more crowded than the Soviet building and Reilly recommended the Russian option on logistical and security grounds.

Roosevelt moved to the Soviet embassy in the morning of November 28. A decoy motorcade on a grand scale left the U.S. legation, complete with a look-alike FDR in fedora and cape and brandishing a cigarette holder.[23] Shortly after, Roosevelt and his intimates left the back door in a single car that sped through the streets almost unescorted. The President found this derring-do exhilarating. Soon after he arrived and took possession of the rooms that had been offered to him, a message arrived that Stalin wished to call on him. His interpreter, Charles Bohlen, who would become one of the nation's most distinguished foreign service officers and was then deputy head of the Soviet desk at the State Department, was sent for. He had interpreted for Hull at the foreign ministers' conference in Moscow in the summer, and Hull recommended him to Roosevelt.

A few minutes later, Stalin and his interpreter, V.N. Pavlov, arrived. The Soviet leader was unprepossessing and self-conscious. He wore a mustard-colored uniform and large shiny boots, and had the Order of Lenin on his chest. He stood only five feet four inches, and had a pockmarked face, a luxuriant and unruly moustache, stained and broken teeth, and a slightly deformed left arm. He had brown eyes and a full head of grey hair. The contrast between him and the elegant, debonair American president in a blue suit in his wheelchair, with his leonine bearing, could scarcely have been greater. But they were now the two most powerful men in the world, and the future of the world lay to a great extent between them.

"Hello, Marshal Stalin," said Roosevelt in the disarming manner with which a great many were now familiar. Stalin apologized for coming so soon to see FDR but said he was just doing his duty as host. Roosevelt thanked him for his hospitality and expressed entire satisfaction with the arrangements. Stalin offered his visitor a cigarette, but Roosevelt preferred to continue with his American cigarettes. It was agreed there would not be a rigid agenda—a tour of political matters, a summary of events on the various fronts for which all of the delegations could speak, and discussion of how to draw German divisions away from Western Europe for Anglo-American Western Front in a few months.

Roosevelt dangled before Stalin the prospect of giving the Soviet Union a large number of what would be surplus U.S. merchant vessels after the war. Stalin was appreciative and promised to share Soviet natural resources with the West. Roosevelt mentioned his talks with Chiang and his intention to equip sixty Chinese divisions. (He had told Chiang up to ninety.) Stalin dismissed the battlefield performance of the Chinese Army and blamed their leaders. Stalin referred to the situation in Lebanon; de Gaulle's Free French had reoccupied the country, but when the local parliament voted for an end to Lebanon's colonial status, de Gaulle had suspended the Lebanese constitution, until Roosevelt had insisted it be restored. Roosevelt, predictably, blamed the whole problem on de Gaulle. Stalin said that de Gaulle was an authentic representative of the soul of France but was completely out of touch with physical France under Petain, which had served the Nazis and must be punished. De Gaulle, acting as if at the head of a great state, was "unrealistic in his political activities," said Stalin.

Roosevelt claimed that no Frenchman over forty years of age should be allowed into government. He told Stalin that he took issue with Churchill's eagerness for the rapid rehabilitation of France. Roosevelt believed that purging the country of rotten elements would be a time-consuming task. Stalin undoubtedly saw de Gaulle as the principal barrier to a Communist takeover of France. Roosevelt saw him as a potential rallying point for resistance to American leadership of Western Europe. Both were right, but Roosevelt still had not figured out, as Churchill had, that the price of keeping the Communists out of control in France and of resurrecting a powerful French Army quickly could be tolerating a more independent France than was convenient to Roosevelt.

Roosevelt and Stalin agreed that Indochina should not be restored to France and that this and other colonies should become trusteeships and prepared for eventual independence — in twenty or thirty years, Roosevelt thought in the case of Indochina.

Roosevelt strayed into a discussion of India and said that nothing could be done with Churchill on the subject, since he was deferring it to the end of the war, but that eventually he would like to discuss it with Stalin. He implied that he thought there might be something to learn from the Russians in how to develop India. Stalin would not take the bait and said that India's castes and cultures made it very complicated.

In the most important exchange of the entire conference Stalin confirmed to Roosevelt that his preference, among the different strategic alternatives favored by Roosevelt and Churchill, continued to be an Anglo-American invasion of northern France. This enabled Roosevelt to enlist Stalin to help him bring Churchill fully on side with Overlord, and to nail it down once and for all.

It was time to start the plenary session. It had been an agreeable conversation with Stalin, and Roosevelt pronounced himself to his entourage and to his son Elliott as well-pleased with this first meeting. He claimed to like Stalin, which meant that Stalin must have made an even greater effort to be pleasant than had Roosevelt, to whom such conduct came much more naturally.[24] Churchill and Roosevelt had not spoken seriously since Cairo, and nothing had been done to narrow the gap between their military staffs. Churchill had a severe cold and sore throat, and felt the Aegean was being ignored and the eastern Mediterranean shortchanged because of Overlord, an operation about which he was haunted by morbid fears.

Stalin didn't share any of Roosevelt's idealistic concerns about how the world would be organized, and apparently assumed they were just a smokescreen for devious capitalistic machinations. He also assumed that Britain and America would take over whatever territories they desired as prizes of war, dressing it up in whatever unctuous pieties of "trusteeship" or a "civilizing mission" that they found convenient. Stalin was prepared to embrace words like "freedom" and "democracy," but he certainly did not mean by them what his interlocutors did and he never had the slightest intention of making his definitions conform to theirs.

———————

It subsequently came to light that all the Soviet servants taking care of the President and others in his rooms were NKVD agents. It was obvious they were carrying weapons and assumed by Roosevelt and his staff that they were eavesdropping and probably recording American conversations. Roosevelt didn't care. He was well aware of the nature of Soviet Communism. But he thought it worthwhile to try to develop a normal relationship with Stalin. If Roosevelt's conversations were overheard, it might assist as a confidence-building measure in the overwrought minds of his hosts.[25] In fact, to some extent this is what occurred. Stalin instructed the son of his much-feared police minister, Lavrenti Beria, to take on the "mission which is delicate and morally reprehensible" of listening to and reporting in great detail Roosevelt's conversations with his own staff and Churchill. "I must know everything in detail," said Stalin to young Sergo Beria. Stalin justified his action by saying that "it is now that the question of a second front will be settled. I know that Churchill is against it. It is important that the Americans support us in this matter."

Stalin questioned young Beria closely on the exact words and tone of voice of Roosevelt in his assertions on various subjects. He surmised that Roosevelt knew he was being bugged but seemed to speak quite uninhibitedly anyway.[26] Roosevelt always spoke positively of both Stalin and Churchill to his staff, at least in Teheran, and Stalin, according to Sergo Beria, was eventually grateful for Roosevelt's apparent goodwill. He was suspicious of Churchill, who was more antagonistic to Stalin in his views but generally more deferential in person than Roosevelt.

Beria claimed that he heard Churchill "beg Roosevelt not to commit himself to" Stalin on a date for the cross-Channel landing.[27] This is plausible. Roosevelt was not prepared to be pushed by Churchill into a premature confrontation with Stalin, and he was not prepared to commit American strength and prestige to trying to hold the British Empire together. Beria claims that when Leahy urged Roosevelt to take a firmer line toward Stalin, Roosevelt replied: "I am pursuing this line because I think it is more advantageous. We are not going to pull the chestnuts out of the fire for the British."[28]

There is no suggestion that Churchill and Roosevelt discussed details of postwar relations with the Soviet Union within earshot of Stalin's eavesdroppers. But some of Roosevelt's key objectives—Soviet entry into the war against Japan and creation of the international organization he sought—could be achieved only at the very end of hostilities in Europe, when American strength (conventional and atomic) would be reaching its height.

Roosevelt was probably excessively mindful of Oumansky's claim to Davies that Stalin believed Roosevelt and Churchill had rehearsed a complete unity of view. Since Roosevelt differed with Churchill on a number of important matters, he thought this point worth making to Stalin.

Roosevelt had had no briefings from the State Department on the Soviet Union. He had prepared some military proposals and had a clear idea of political matters that would be discussed. He had little use for the State Department anyway, and felt that if this meeting was to be a success, it would depend on the emergence of some personal rapport between Stalin and himself, and the beginning of a Russian view that respectability and a great role in the world cooperatively with the Western Allies was preferable to resumed revolutionary militancy.

Roosevelt hoped Stalin would prove "getatable," as Harry Hopkins later put it. Stalin had said to Churchill in Moscow in August 1942 (chapter 12) that he liked "a downright enemy better than a pretending friend." He probably thought Roosevelt a "pretending friend." Stalin told the Yugoslav Communist politician Milo van Djilas in 1944: "Churchill would pick your pocket for a kopeck. Roosevelt is not like that. He dips in his hand only for bigger coins."

IV

ROOSEVELT PRESIDED OVER the initial session, on November 28, and "looked very much like the kind rich uncle paying a visit to his poorer relations."[29] Roosevelt welcomed "new members of the family circle," referring to the Russians. He urged everyone to speak freely and reiterated the assurance of discretion. Churchill said the three represented "the greatest concentration of worldly power that had ever been seen in the history of mankind," and urged them all to use it to shorten the war and strengthen the peace. Stalin then said in his opening remarks that they had been "pampered by history" in having been accorded such an opportunity and that they must seize it.

Roosevelt opened with a military summary from the American standpoint, including the Pacific, before turning to "the most important theater, Europe." He cast the die inexorably on Overlord, blamed delays on landing craft, and emphasized that since the English Channel was such a "disagreeable body of water," it could not be traversed before May 1.

Stalin was rightly skeptical about the landing-craft excuse. Roosevelt said that, for manpower reasons, the British and Americans were in the position of having to choose between the cross-Channel operation and a large-scale operation in the Mediterranean. The President said he would seek the advice of Stalin and Voroshilov on which operation would be of greater assistance to the Russians.

Voroshilov, an uneducated old Bolshevik soldier, had been a loyal Stalin subaltern during the civil war and occupied a position analogous to those of Marshall
and Brooke. He was an unqualified political general, totally out of his depth in
these meetings. Roosevelt, by assuring himself in advance of Stalin's support for
Overlord and establishing the criterion of assistance to Russia for choosing
between Overlord and the Mediterranean, had stacked the deck in favor of the
cross-Channel option. He declared his own support for Overlord.

Stalin started by confirming what he had told Hull in Moscow in August, that
the Soviet Union would join the war against Japan as soon as possible after the
defeat of Germany. It was one of the ironies of these meetings that Roosevelt was
concerned to lure Stalin into the Pacific War, when Stalin's fear was that the
Americans would win the war before Russia could enter it and undo the Treaty of
Portsmouth, by which Roosevelt's cousin Theodore had brokered the end to the
Russo-Japanese War in 1905 (and won the Nobel Peace Prize).

Stalin then cogently and heavily supported the American strategic view of
Western Europe. He remarked that the Russian general Aleksandr Suvorov had
discovered in 1799 the impossibility of invading Germany across or through the
Alps from Italy. He said the Italian campaign was of secondary value to the Russians and was useful chiefly for opening up the Mediterranean to greater shipments of supplies to the Soviet Union. He was confident that Hitler would try to
tie down as many Allied divisions as possible in Italy, where there could be no
decisive outcome. Turkey would be a welcome addition to the Allies, but the
Balkans were a long way from the heart of Germany and were rugged country. A
Balkan campaign would be preferable to squandering forces in Italy, but: "We
Russians believe that the best result would be yielded by a blow at the enemy in
northern or northwestern France. . . . Germany's weakest spot is France. The
Germans will fight like devils to prevent such an attack."[30]

This was a decisive intervention. Churchill followed and confirmed his commitment to Overlord, but added, as he had in Cairo, that after the initial commitment of sixteen British divisions, the British would have no more manpower to
insert on that front, all its resources being engaged elsewhere. The Americans
and Russians were still calling up, equipping, and sending into the line apparently inexhaustible reserves of manpower, but the British Empire had reached
the outer limits of its means.

The reason for this is not obvious. Apart from the Muslims, who provided
three-quarters of the British Indian Army, though they made up only one-fourth
of India's population, Gandhi had demotivated much of the rest of the subcontinent from any martial inclinations. But Britain, the Dominions, and the more
advanced colonies could still have furnished about four million soldiers, two-
thirds of the total manpower of the U.S. Army, excluding the air corps. Though
British Commonwealth forces were widely scattered from Burma to India to Iraq,
Palestine, and Italy, Churchill could have scraped together more forces for Overlord, and eventually did produce several divisions more than he had promised.

No comprehensible purpose was served by Churchill's declaration of comparative military poverty.

The Overlord force would also have nineteen American divisions, for an initial strength of thirty-five divisions, equivalent in numbers of men to about forty German divisions. If the initial landings were successful, practically unlimited forces would be poured into France, but not by Britain. And as France was cleared, French forces in large numbers would quickly reappear on the Western Front.

Churchill was confident Rome would be captured in the next two months.* Churchill proposed halting just north of Rome and then opening up a third front in southern France or at the northern head of the Adriatic, advancing toward the Danube and assisting Tito and his partisans against the German occupiers of Yugoslavia. Churchill sketched in the most attractive terms the possibilities for bringing Turkey into the war and the benefits that would result, envisioning a domino theory involving Romania, Bulgaria, Hungary, and Greece.

Churchill asked Stalin for his advice and Stalin questioned him closely about the implications of each step. After several minutes back and forth Stalin declared: "It would be a mistake to disperse forces by sending part to Turkey and elsewhere and part to southern France. The best course would be to make Overlord the basic operation for 1944 and, once Rome had been captured, to send all available forces to southern France. These forces could then join hands with the Overlord forces when the invasion is launched. France is the weakest spot on the German front." Stalin did not believe that Turkey would join the war.

Churchill became almost plaintive. He had thought Russia wanted Turkey in the war. The British leader was concerned about six months of inactivity between the fall of Rome and Overlord. Stalin replied that they should dispense with Rome, stop in Italy where they were, and provide ten divisions from Italy for an invasion of southern France two months before Overlord, which would assure the success of the cross-Channel operation. Churchill, placed sorely on the defensive, said that the airfields north of Rome were essential for the comprehensive aerial bombardment of Germany, and failure to take Rome would "be regarded on all sides as a crashing defeat and the British Parliament would not tolerate the idea for a moment."

Stalin didn't directly reply to this last point, but with Churchill as with Roosevelt, he considered these governmental niceties mere humbug; Churchill, after all he had done to save and lead Britain and its empire, would no more be thrown out by his parliament for not taking Rome than Roosevelt would be impeached for signing a few legislative bills a few days late because of being in

---

* He had an unfortunate habit of overoptimistic predictions at these conferences, as in his previous conference comments on Singapore and Tobruk. Rome would not be cleared of the Germans, despite the fact that there was almost no fighting within the city, for over six months.

Teheran. He was astounded at the feebleness of imagination of such eminent statesmen in invoking such implausible arguments with him, like underperforming schoolboys claiming the cat had eaten their homework.

On the subject of Rome, it is not clear whether Stalin wanted northern Italy left unoccupied by the Western armies because he thought the local Communists had a better possibility to succeed there than in France, or whether his ancient dislike of the Roman Catholic Church led him to desire that the pope continue to be in the hands of the Germans for as long as possible, thus reducing his moral credibility, or both.

Roosevelt suggested staff work begin at once on a plan for the invasion of southern France. Roosevelt declared his opposition to any delay in Overlord for any reason. Churchill declined to commit to "sacrifice the activities of . . . twenty British and Commonwealth divisions [in the Mediterranean], merely in order to keep the exact date of May 1 for Overlord."

For the British prime minister, it had been a dispiriting retreat from distracting the Americans with alternatives to Overlord, to facing down U.S. threats to redeploy to the Pacific, to trying to delay the operation by mousetrapping the Americans in peripheral operations that would be more consumptive of manpower than had been foreseen, to facing a solid wall of insistence on Overlord from the Americans and the Russians, both of which had become greater powers in the world than Britain in the last three years. The fact is that Britain could have put more manpower into Overlord if Churchill had believed in it, and he would have had a stronger hand to play with his allies if he had taken this tack rather than promoting alternatives in Turkey and Norway and the Balkans and claiming he was at the end of his resources.

Churchill asked for further consideration of Mediterranean alternatives and of the possibilities for Turkish involvement. Roosevelt agreed, and Stalin undertook to provide some generals to join Marshall and Brooke and their colleagues in staff talks. Stalin said that all neutrals looked upon belligerents "as fools," and Roosevelt expressed the fear that bringing Turkey into the war would require such a payoff in warplanes, tanks, and other military equipment that it would imperil the timing of Overlord. He undertook to try to persuade the president of Turkey to join the Allies but was not optimistic about it. Churchill said he considered the Turks to be "crazy." Stalin responded that they might be and that the Russians had had much experience of that temperament, but that some people preferred to remain "crazy." The meeting adjourned, and the Russians served refreshments.

———————

For the British it had been a very unsatisfactory start. The divisions between the British and American strategic concepts were laid bare for the delectation of the Russian monster. Stalin had shown himself in his second meeting with Churchill and his first meeting with Roosevelt to be extremely astute, forceful, and strategically sophisticated. Stalin was trying to make the greatest legitimized accretion of territory and people by military means in history. Churchill was trying to maintain an increasingly ramshackle empire, retain influence with the United States, and set about building some Western European counterweight to the approaching Soviet Russian juggernaut.

Roosevelt wanted to confine Stalin to Eastern Europe and to bring the United States into its rightful place in the world. He believed this had to be done in the framework of an international organization that would confound the fears of the isolationists. He would carry his cousin Theodore's famous "Big Stick" inside an updated version of Wilson's forum of nations. Within this framework he wanted America's preeminence. This is essentially what occurred, especially after the end of the Cold War in the 1990s. He knew the British Empire and other empires were doomed and didn't want Stalin vacuuming up all the gratitude of the emancipated colonial masses. He was determined to lead a liberal democratic, social capitalist, secular but Christian coalition. Roosevelt had no doubt such a grouping would be seen as preferable to any Communist alternative. He hoped to convince Stalin that his best course was cooperation with such a force.

In these circumstances, the heroic and magnificent Winston Churchill was somewhat sluggish. He had wanted to concert with Roosevelt that very morning of November 28 on a plan to delay Overlord and send "two or three divisions" into the Aegean. Roosevelt, knowing the purpose, was not prepared to go around this track again, and declined to meet with him. This was discourteous as well as mistaken; they might have been able to resolve their differences without inviting Stalin's arbitration. If Roosevelt had forcefully restated the necessity of an early Overlord, and of not seeming disunited in Stalin's presence, Churchill might have come around. Roosevelt should always have been accessible to Churchill.

There now began two lengthy processes that attended Western deliberations for decades after. The British immediately concluded that Roosevelt had been entirely duped by Stalin. This would be an allegation in which Roosevelt's domestic opponents would be only too happy to join soon enough. The British imperialists, right-wing U.S. Republicans, and anti-American Western Europeans, uncoordinated among themselves, would taint his reputation for a long time with the accusation of naïve subservience to Stalin. And the British would see the first glimmerings of the foreign policy alternatives that would tantalize them for many years: to continue to ally themselves closely to the United States, albeit in a subordinate position, yet often an influential one, or to throw in their lot with the Europeans and try to maximize their influence in what would become "an ever closer Union" (in European Union 1990s parlance).

The British leadership was generally incapable of considering that Roosevelt might be correct strategically—that France should be invaded as quickly as possible and the Western Allies move as quickly as they could toward the heartland of Europe, and not fritter away their resources in secondary theaters. Brooke knew as well as Marshall did that the Rhodes plan made little sense, but he couldn't, even as a memoirist or a historian, break ranks and make the obvious connection that in these matters the Americans had been right from the start, even if optimistic about timing.

Brooke, in his diary for November 28, 1943, refers to the struggle with the Americans about how to prevent the Russians from seizing an uncomfortably large portion of Europe. The debate was not over the end but the means, Brooke rigorously adhering to the British line of an approach through the Balkans and the Adriatic and the Americans to their aproach through France. Brooke ascribes Stalin's support of the American position to a cynical desire to see the British and Americans mired in Dunkirks and Dieppes as the Red Army swept westward. This was his explanation of Stalin's support for these "strategical misconceptions." Brooke may have been right that Stalin believed Overlord and Anvil would fail, distract the Germans, and facilitate his advance. If so, both the British and Soviet views would be proved mistaken.[31] Brooke sounded the British party line in his diary: "The conference is over when it has only just begun. Stalin has got the President in his pocket."[32]

The fact is that Roosevelt was the only one of the Big Three who had what could ultimately be considered an acceptable strategic view. Only the form of government and economic life he championed, led forcefully but unjingoistically by the United States, could contain, and eventually strangle, Communism. As was often the case with Roosevelt, his political intuition was exact. As was occasionally also the case, his methods were incoherent. His practice, when in uncharted areas, was to pursue simultaneous parallel or even contradictory courses until he had a clear idea of the preferable alternative. Except for the Battle of Britain emergency, when events required decisive action, and even then he disguised his ultimate ambitions in 1940–1941, his elaboration of foreign policy was not unlike the confusing development of the New Deal.

The British inflated Stalin into a satanic statesman of gigantic capacities, as they anointed themselves the only people capable of dealing with him successfully. Stalin anticipated discussion about joining the war against Japan, but not that he would be brought into Anglo-American staff talks about what beaches to land on in Western Europe. This was why he had no serious generals present.*[33]

Churchill, in his recollections, largely avoided direct criticism of Roosevelt, though implying that the end-of-war arrangements went badly. Churchill toiled against the charge of trying to avoid Overlord. "It has become a legend in America that I strove to prevent the cross-Channel enterprise . . . and . . . to lure the Allies into some mass invasion of the Balkans, or a large-scale campaign in the Eastern Mediterranean, which would effectively kill it." Any such claim would be "nonsense."[34] But he did seek to defer Overlord until an uncertain date when German resistance would be sure to have eroded. This was a consequence of

---

* Marshall and Arnold were not present at the opening session, because they had been inadvertently misled by Roosevelt about the time of the meeting and were on a sight-seeing tour.

Churchill's profound wariness of the German Army, a legacy of the First World War. Churchill's concern for another bloodbath in northern France and possibly even another Dunkirk was the fear that dared not speak its name.

The product of Roosevelt's insistence on not conveying the impression of Anglo-American collusion to Stalin, and of Churchill's being so determined to delay Overlord almost sine die, was that Stalin became the virtual arbiter between the two. Having been obliged by the shilly-shallying of the British to recruit Stalin to help produce a prompt Overlord, Roosevelt was actually assisted by Stalin's cynicism. It is hard to think of any other motive that would have caused Stalin to endorse the proposal that would prove least helpful to the achievement of his own postwar designs to move as far westward in Europe as possible.

If Stalin had supported Churchill's Mediterranean escapades, he could have made matters difficult for Roosevelt and delayed Overlord, and would probably have ended the war occupying more of Germany than he did. On the other hand, if Overlord had been determined at Casablanca and carried out in September 1943, the Western Allies would have had a much stronger hand to play at Teheran. The conferees were now playing poker for very high stakes, and in the Overlord round, Roosevelt won the hand. He has received insufficient credit for it.

Roosevelt's strategic and political vision was perceptive; Stalin's was exclusively avaricious; Churchill's was astute but nostalgic.

———————

On the evening of November 28, 1943, Roosevelt had the principals to his rooms for dinner. The stoves and even the cooking and eating utensils had been taken out of the kitchen in his section of the Soviet embassy. The U.S. Persian Gulf Command at Fort Amirabad several miles away hastily brought in what was necessary, with the Filipino cooks who served on the presidential yacht *Potomac*, and whom Roosevelt had brought in his party. It started out as a more successful meeting than the awkward plenary session that preceded it.

In keeping with his desire to make it as much a family occasion as possible, Roosevelt mixed the drinks for his guests, as he did every night in "the children's hour" in the White House. He was proud of his proficiency with a cocktail shaker, but his drinks were almost universally unappreciated. He customarily made martinis with large quantities of both sweet and dry vermouth. When Roosevelt mixed such a drink for Stalin and asked what he thought of it, Stalin thoughtfully replied: "Well, all right, but it is cold on the stomach." Like most of his countrymen, Stalin preferred vodka neat and Caucasus wines with dinner.

Stalin held forth at length on his views of France and Germany. He wanted both countries laid low, and for these purposes, he made little distinction between the two. "The entire French ruling class is rotten to the core, and delivered France over to the Germans and . . . in fact, France is now helping our enemies." Churchill, ever loyal to the Entente Cordiale, in his career as in his sensibilities, replied that he could not imagine a "civilized world without a flourishing and lively France." Stalin, unencumbered by ever having set foot in France, said that "France could be a charming and pleasant country but could not be allowed to play any important role in the immediate postwar world."

One of the last things Stalin wanted was a revived French Army of over 100 divisions as part of a Western counterweight to the Red Army in Central Europe. Stalin wanted Germany severely occupied, dismembered, and closely and permanently monitored so that no possibility of war-making could arise in the future.

He found Churchill's and Roosevelt's proposed measures to ensure peace inadequate. He referred to an episode he had witnessed in Leipzig in 1907 when German workers were unable to attend a Communist mass meeting because their tickets permitting them to leave the railroad station had not been punched. Given that they were there to promote a world revolution, Stalin professed to have found that the inability of his German comrades to face the wrath of a ticket collector deprived them of any credibility as revolutionaries. He regarded the Germans as dangerous robots if programmed by the wrong people.

Stalin did complain about the demand for unconditional surrender, claiming it enflamed German resistance. Roosevelt found this nettlesome, since it was largely to placate and reassure Stalin that he had adopted this position in the first place. Roosevelt demurred, but changed the subject to postwar discouragement of German aggression.

Roosevelt referred to Hitler's mental instability and Stalin replied that "only a very able man could accomplish what Hitler had done in solidifying the German people, whatever we think of his methods." (Hitler and Stalin continued to speak rather well of each other to the end. On July 22, 1942, Hitler had said to his aides: "Stalin must command our unconditional respect. In his own way he is a hell of a fellow."[35] They didn't regard each other's murderous proclivities as particularly unusual or unattractive.)

Stalin advocated the Oder River as the western border of Poland. Moving millions of Poles and Germans westward as Poland was redefined hundreds of miles to the west of where it had been would cause serious dislocations in Europe, but Stalin was happy to inflict them to secure his country.

Roosevelt explained that he favored a form of trusteeship for the approaches to the Kiel Canal, which would be part of an international state, with guaranteed free passage to ships of all nationalities through the canal. Stalin received a mistaken translation and thought Roosevelt was advocating an international state for Estonia, Latvia, and Lithuania. He heatedly replied that these Baltic states had already been popularly consulted and had chosen reintegration into the Soviet Union.

Roosevelt now suddenly began to perspire heavily, turned very pale, and ultimately attained almost a green hue. Hopkins took charge and had him wheeled out of the room and examined by his doctor. McIntire reported that the President was suffering only from indigestion, and required only rest; his patient retired for the evening. Even though McIntire reassured the other guests, Roosevelt's indisposition cast something of a pall over the festivities.

Stalin and Churchill repaired to a sofa in a neighboring room, unaccompanied by the Americans. Churchill told Stalin that they had to keep the peace for at least fifty years. Britain, Russia, and America would have to keep in close alignment hereafter, he said.

Stalin required the dismemberment of Germany, as Richelieu had done 300 years before. Churchill proposed taking away German armaments and aviation industries. This was not enough for Stalin, who said furniture and watch factories could make war materiel. Stalin said that when he interviewed German prisoners of war, as he did occasionally, and asked working-class Germans why they fought and committed atrocities for the Nazis, such as raping and pillaging, and received the response that they were merely following orders, he had those prisoners shot.[36] He turned to his fear that the Germans were irrational, mechanical, war-making beasts. Churchill distinguished between the Germans and their leaders. The German people could be reformed with "a generation of self-sacrificing, toil, and education."[37] It seemed to Stalin, with some reason, that Churchill was as wary of the Russians as of the Germans.

Churchill favored Poland's moving entirely to the west, yielding territory to the Soviet Union, and being compensated with territory from Germany. He acknowledged that Poland would inevitably be, at least for a time, under the overwhelming influence of the Russians. Churchill drew out for Stalin his proposed Polish frontiers with matchsticks on a table. Stalin appreciated this but kept harping on the failure of the Western powers to enforce and secure the 1919 settlement of World War I. Churchill ascribed all the failures of the 1919 agreement to the desertion of the United States and the complete exclusion of the Soviet Union from the Treaty of Versailles.

At the end of these conversations, Churchill triumphantly declared that God was on the side of the Allies. "At least I have done my best to make him a faithful ally." Smiling broadly, Stalin exclaimed, "And the Devil is on my side. Everyone knows that the Devil is a Communist, and God, no doubt, is a good conservative."[38] (Churchill was probably no more religious than Stalin. He was probably a deist. Stalin, though he despised religion, revered his mother's religiosity and was rather superstitious himself.) Churchill had been very forthcoming in this conversation and Stalin rather mysterious, though cordial, and the two had got on well. It had been a lively and discursive evening.

V

THE NEXT DAY, before the second plenary meeting, Leahy, Marshall, Brooke, and Portal met with Voroshilov in what was supposed to be a detailed military staff meeting. Brooke made a spirited effort to recapture ground lost by the British the day before.

Portal commented on the air war, saying that the intense bombing of Germany required that the Germans concentrate about 1,700 fighters in Germany, leaving only about 750 planes for other fronts.

Voroshilov questioned Brooke closely about the British view of Overlord and questioned the British commitment to the operation. Brooke struggled not to lose his fiery temper as Voroshilov laboriously lectured him on the similarity between crossing the Channel and crossing a large European river, and he described the application of machine gun and mortar fire, as if Brooke were unfamiliar with such operations. Marshall joined in supporting the British position that crossing the English Channel was not like crossing a river. Voroshilov wound up, full of uninformed conceit and condescension. Stalin, satisfied of Anglo-American seriousness about Overlord, determined that there was no need for another such meeting, a decision Brooke, Portal, Marshall, and Leahy received with considerable relief.

Roosevelt had fully recovered overnight, but he again declined Churchill's invitation to a private lunch before the second plenary session. "That's not like him," said an uncomfortable Churchill.[39] Roosevelt didn't want to feed Stalin's paranoia about Anglo-American agreement, didn't want to lock horns with Churchill's elegantly phrased dilatoriness again, and didn't want to say anything within earshot of his NKVD agent servants in the Soviet embassy.[40] This was, again, shabby treatment of his greatest ally, who had always shown him every courtesy. They could have had complete privacy from Soviet espionage by going across the street to Churchill's embassy.

Roosevelt sent Harriman to request another private meeting with Stalin, and held a short meeting with his own chiefs of staff. Stalin arrived for the private session with Roosevelt at 2:45. Roosevelt gave him four papers, describing each as he did so: a laudatory report about Tito and his Yugoslav partisans from an American officer who had spent six months with the partisans; a memorandum about American use of Russian airfields for bombing Germany and better exchange of weather information and the like; and two memoranda about the conduct of the war against Japan and American use of Russian naval bases and airfields against that country. The Soviet entry into the Japanese war should enter the planning stage he said, and attempts to work out such details through the American military mission in Moscow had not led to any substantive discussions thus far.

Stalin promised to take up these questions directly with Harriman, who was just beginning as U.S. ambassador in Moscow, but little resulted from such exchanges. No discussion of the Japanese war ever occurred, and by the time the Soviet Union entered that war, there was little left to do and no need for conversation about Russian bases. Stalin did authorize shuttle bombing of Germany from Russian bases from June to September 1944, but not after Overlord had overwhelmingly succeeded and Russian forces had penetrated well into Eastern Europe. (This may indicate that Stalin did not wish to assist progress on the Western Front.)

After Stalin declined to raise any questions or concerns of his own, Roosevelt unveiled his plan for a postwar international organization.*

Stalin doubted that China would be a very powerful state after the war and proposed a European committee and another for the Far East, with the Big Three on both. Roosevelt again mired Stalin in the minutiae of what the U.S. Congress could be persuaded to approve in terms of commitment to multilateral organizations. Any such talk of limits to what he could get from his legislators was an unwise profession of weakness. It was fortunate that Stalin didn't believe any of it.

Roosevelt proposed a two-tier method of dealing with international crises: quarantine, and, if necessary, isolation, bombardment, and even invasion by the four policemen. In proposing to take this prerogative of intervention upon the Big Four powers, Roosevelt was resurrecting the post-Napoleonic Holy Alliance, albeit with a liberal rather than a reactionary purpose.

Stalin returned to his bugbear of the previous evening—the prevention of German aggression. He expected Germany to revive within fifteen or twenty years and considered the organization the President envisioned quite inadequate to contain it. He believed certain strong points in and around Germany had to be permanently occupied. Roosevelt concurred. Roosevelt had claimed that he had urged France to close the Suez Canal during the Abyssinian War, which, he said, the four policemen would accomplish.†

The cordial but noncommittal conversation ended, and the two leaders attended the ceremony of the handing over by Churchill to Stalin of the Sword of Stalingrad, a splendid ornate sword with silver handle and Persian lamb grip, ordered by King George VI for presentation to the people of Stalingrad. On the handle, in Russian and English, was the inscription: "To the steelhearted citizens of Stalingrad, the gift of King George VI, in token of the homage of the British people." There were British and Soviet honor guards, national anthems, a few words of presentation from Churchill and of appreciation by Stalin, who handed the sword on to Voroshilov. It fell out of its scabbard and Voroshilov caught it just before it hit the floor.

When the second plenary session began, with Roosevelt again in the chair, Stalin demanded insistently to know who would command Overlord. Roosevelt said

* There would be thirty-five members of the United Nations, with an executive committee of ten states: the United States, the United Kingdom, the Soviet Union, and China as permanent members, along with two states from Europe, one from Latin America, one from the Middle East, one from the Far East, and one British Dominion.

The executive committee would deal with nonmilitary questions. Military questions and matters of enforcement of international law would be in the hands of what Roosevelt called "the four policemen," the Big Three and China.

† There is no evidence that he did anything of the kind, and in any case France had no control over the canal, being only a minority shareholder in the Suez Canal Company.

that that had not been determined, which Stalin interpreted as meaning that there was no assurance that there would be such an operation. He felt that the absence of someone with "the moral and military responsibility for Overlord" meant that it was "just so much talk."[41] Churchill eventually intervened that it would be an American, to be agreed by the Western Allies, and that his name would be announced within two weeks. This seemed to quiet Stalin.

In response to Churchill's familiar concerns, Stalin again treated the capture of Rome, aid to the Yugoslav partisans, and the possible entry into the war of Turkey as matters of little importance. He emphasized the importance of Overlord and did not want to hear of its postponement. Roosevelt intervened and essentially agreed with Stalin.

At no time did Stalin object to the six-month delay, as he had to the initial deferral from 1942, when he raged at any postponement as cowardice or treachery. This was another indication that he was now probably more concerned with getting as great a head start as possible in the race to central Europe.

Churchill reverted to the agreement at the Moscow Conference that the success of Overlord depended on a reduction of German fighter strength in the area of the invasion; German reserves in the area could not exceed twelve divisions, and the Germans should not have the potential for reinforcements of more than fifteen divisions in the first sixty days of Overlord. The prime minister represented that what he was advocating would achieve those goals. There was discussion of referring matters to military staffs and to the foreign ministers, and impatient questions from Stalin about how long the conference was expected to continue; he said the leaders themselves should promptly decide the date of Overlord, its commander, and the southern France diversionary invasion. Churchill insisted the military and foreign ministers' committees should meet.

Stalin pointedly asked if Britain was really committed to Overlord. Churchill growled back that it was if the Moscow Conference criteria were met. There was considerable tension now, and Roosevelt suggested adjournment. It had not been a satisfactory meeting. Churchill had been overpowered in argument and Roosevelt obliged to side with the Russians. Observers agreed that the Soviet leader's performance had been impressive. General H. H. Arnold wrote that he was "fearless, brilliant, quick . . . of repartee—a great leader, [with the] courage of his convictions . . . bold, humorous, half-scathing." Ismay found him "inscrutable . . . quiet . . . direct and decided." Brooke, who built up Stalin as much as Montgomery had built up Rommel, claimed that Stalin had a "military brain of the very highest caliber." Marshall found that Stalin was "a very astute negotiator," with "a dry wit," and that he "was a rough SOB." Cunningham and King were also impressed.[42] Stalin was cool and calm, spare of words, often ironic, and doodled wolf heads on a pad of paper. These became the most desired souvenirs of the conference.[43]

Stalin had the advantage of demanding specific performance of what the Allies had promised; Churchill was persisting in championship of a military plan that could not possibly keep the alliance together, and Roosevelt, in his enthusiasm for an early Overlord and for his international organization, was prepared to be fairly accommodating on most other matters. Churchill took the lead from Roosevelt in moving Poland to the west.

Churchill was shocked to encounter opposition to his strategic ideas, not of the urbane, gentlemanly Rooseveltian kind, but the blunt cynicism of an old Bolshevik who had made his way in the world by methods infinitely less suave and civilized than those that had been employed by his two Western analogues. The prime minister went once again to the end of the limb, advocating the Aegean plan that the Americans and his own advisors disagreed with, and instead of being coaxed back by his friend, the "country gentleman" from Hyde Park, he found that the branch was hacked off by Stalin with sturdy Caucasian strokes.

The dinner on November 29 was a Bacchanalian occasion that approached a rout. Stalin was the host, and an NKVD major general, six feet, four inches tall and dressed as a footman, stood behind the host all evening. Stalin made frequent, rather sarcastic references to Churchill, reasonably good humored, but also, in his sinister fashion, rather barbed. Stalin acknowledged that the Soviet Army had been unprepared for the Finns at the start of the Russo-German War, but asserted that it had become "a genuinely good army."[44] He reverted to his particular preoccupation of Germany and its ability to rise again as a militarist country. He declared that 50,000 to 100,000 German officers should be summarily shot at the end of the war. Churchill said Britain would never tolerate such an outrage. Stalin generously reduced the number to 50,000. Churchill heatedly replied: "I would rather be taken out in the garden here and now and be shot myself than sully my own and my country's honor by such infamy." Roosevelt interjected with an attempt at levity, and suggested only 49,000. Eden tried to deescalate the tension by suggesting it was all a joke, and then Stalin canvassed the table for everyone's view of how many German officers should be executed.

Earlier in the evening, an NKVD officer had pointed out Roosevelt's rambunctious son Elliott to Stalin, and the Soviet leader had insisted he join the official dinner. When Stalin's inquiry of the guests got to Elliott, he arose, somewhat waterlogged with Russian champagne, and asserted that the question was "academic. . . . When our armies start rolling in from the West and your armies are still coming from the East, we'll be solving the whole thing, won't we? Russian, British and American soldiers will settle the issue for most of those 50,000 in battle, and I hope [for] . . . many hundreds of thousands more Nazis as well." Stalin rose from his chair and came over to Elliott and put his arm appreciatively around his shoulder as he started to sit down. Churchill was outraged. He bellowed at Elliott: "Are you interested in damaging relations between the Allies? . . . How can you dare such a thing?" (Churchill wrote in his memoirs that Elliott had "given a highly coloured and extremely misleading account" of the exchange. Churchill wrote that young Roosevelt had stood up spontaneously and had made a "speech saying how cordially he agreed with Marshal Stalin's plan and how sure he was that the United States Army would support it. At this intrusion I got up and left." Winston Churchill is a more credible memoirist than the louche ne'er-do-well Elliott Roosevelt.[45] Churchill never invited Elliott to Chequers again, as he had been in the habit of doing. Eden, Cadogan, Bohlen, and Harriman did not mention the incident in their memoirs.

With this, Churchill, followed by Eden, went out into the garden. He was not long there when a pair of powerful hands were clamped on his shoulders. He turned round to find a beaming Stalin, accompanied by a beaming Molotov. Stalin assured Churchill it was all a joke, but given his blood-stained record, Churchill can be forgiven for not having taken it as one. They stood with an arm on each other's shoulder, and then Stalin and Molotov brought Churchill and Eden back into the party, amidst Stalin's jocularities about Churchill's being a lover of Germans, and raking up the previous night's theme that the Devil was a Communist and, said Stalin, "my friend God is a conservative."

There was a further embrace. The British ambassador in Moscow, Sir Archibald Clark Kerr, subsequently wrote that he wished he had "a record of what was said, that people might know what piffle great men sometimes talk." Churchill wrote: "Stalin has a very captivating manner when he chooses to use it, and I never saw him do so to such an extent as at this moment."[46]

As normal conversation resumed, there was further discussion about what points to occupy to deter a revival of German militarism. Churchill, irritated by Roosevelt's silence while Stalin had been goading him, said that Britain sought no accretions of territory, nor would it surrender any "without war," particularly Singapore and Hong Kong. Some areas in the Empire, he said, might be given independence, "entirely by Great Britain herself, in accordance with her own moral precepts."

Roosevelt said nothing, but Stalin complimented Churchill on Britain's splendid fight in the war and said it had earned an accretion to the British Empire. When Churchill asked Stalin what territories he aspired to, Stalin declined to answer but ominously stated: "When the time comes, we will speak."[47]

Stalin said that before Munich he had never believed the Czechoslovaks would fight. When he and Churchill got round to Churchill's early opposition to the spread of Bolshevism, Stalin said he "need not have worried quite so much as we Russians have discovered that it is not quite so easy to set up Communist regimes."

The evening concluded with an astonishing scene at the British embassy across the road from the Russians. Churchill and Eden had wanted some fresh air, and walked the few hundred yards from the Russian embassy, laughing and occasionally bursting into a few bars of song. The prime minister's car had returned through the main gate, and the sentries assumed he had been in it. When he knocked at the gate, the responding soldier required some persuasion that this was not a prank.

Eventually, after Churchill had reached a state of some audible annoyance, he was admitted to his embassy and held forth to his doctor, Moran, in very gloomy tones. (Dr. Wilson had become Lord Moran. Churchill made his doctor a peer while Roosevelt made his, McIntire, an admiral.) Churchill contemplated war with Russia and even the complete destruction of the human species. He told Moran that Roosevelt had said that Churchill could lose the next election but that he, Roosevelt, would be reelected, and claimed that Hopkins had thought Roosevelt's interventions had been inept. (It is unlikely Hopkins would have spoken of his chief in such terms. Nor is there any evidence that such criticisms would be justified. But if Roosevelt made that dual electoral prediction, it was accurate, as his electoral predictions usually were.)[48]

VI

NOVEMBER 30, THE third full day of the Teheran Conference, was Winston Churchill's 69th birthday, and he had arranged to be the host at dinner that night. The Anglo-American Combined Chiefs of Staff met in the morning under orders from Churchill and Roosevelt to fix a date for Overlord, as Stalin had demanded. It was agreed that they would undertake to launch the cross-Channel invasion by June 1, 1944, if the Soviets would undertake to launch a general offensive in the east by the same date to prevent German forces from being transferred from that front to France. Simultaneously, or slightly later, there would be an invasion of southern France, contingent upon adequate numbers of landing craft being left in the Mediterranean.

It was agreed that sixty-eight of the landing craft required for Overlord would remain in the Mediterranean until January 15, 1944. Mediterranean operations, apart from the southern French landings, would be confined to Italy and aid to the Yugoslav partisans. Activities in the Aegean were conditional on Turkey's entering the war first and dependent on being able to scrape up the necessary landing craft.

Finally the die was cast.

Roosevelt went to the post exchange that had been set up in the Russian embassy for the benefit of tourists (who were not numerous at this time) and bought Winston Churchill a birthday present, a kashan bowl. On his return to his rooms, Roosevelt received a visit from the young shah of Iran. There had been a considerable protocol concern about the shah's insistence that Roosevelt stay in "one or all" of his palaces, and about the shah's tenacious insistence that Roosevelt pay him a return visit.

This was a lofty position to be taken by the twenty-four-year-old emperor of a country that was in fact occupied by the three countries whose leaders had chosen to meet in Teheran (without consulting the local emperor about it). The meeting with the shah lasted about twenty minutes, and Roosevelt had his son Elliott with him. The President held forth on the merits of reforestation, having noted the barrenness of much of the country as he flew in to Teheran. He agreed with the young shah that Iran's resources should be protected from foreign pillagers, though he did not specifically subscribe to his complaints about the British oil and mining companies in the country. (The shah presumably changed his tune somewhat when he crossed the street to meet with Winston Churchill a few minutes later.)

The shah later wrote that Roosevelt had seemed "in the long tradition of distinguished westerners who have become enraptured with my country and culture." There is no evidence that Roosevelt was impressed in the slightest by Iran, but he would be the first of eight U.S. presidents whom the shah would know and deal with, as he became a steadily more important political figure in the Cold War, before his reign crumbled in the late seventies.

Churchill met privately with Stalin at midday. "The fact that . . . [Roosevelt] had avoided ever seeing me alone since we left Cairo, in spite of our hitherto intimate relations and the way in which our vital affairs were interwoven," caused him to seek a personal interview with Stalin.[49] Churchill was concerned that the British attitude to Overlord was being misrepresented. He told Stalin that the British had the preponderance of forces in the Mediterranean, and he was promoting that theater not to delay Overlord, but to keep his forces occupied and to ensure that the British were pulling their weight in the war. He further stated that any delay was not caused by him, but by the Americans' asking the British to carry out the amphibious invasion of the Andaman Islands, "Buccaneer," in accord with Roosevelt's promise to Chiang Kai-shek.

Churchill explained that he had agreed that Roosevelt should name an American commander for Overlord, and that when he did, he, Churchill, would name a Mediterranean commander. Churchill explained that Britain would be contributing 500,000 of her finest battle-tested troops, 4,000 front-line aircraft, and the entire Home Fleet of the Royal Navy (the second largest fleet in the world after the U.S. Pacific Fleet) to Overlord. The United States, the Battle of the Atlantic having been won, would send 150,000 soldiers per month to Britain.

Even when trying to convince Stalin that he wasn't dragging his feet on Overlord, Churchill could only bring himself to say that if the Red Army attacked, "we held them [the Germans] in Italy, and possibly the Turks came into the war, then I thought we could win." This wasn't a very convincing endorsement, and it invited Stalin to exploit the differences between the British and American positions. However, Stalin never tried to do so. He seems to have thought the Anglo-American frictions a fraud designed to confuse him.

Roosevelt, Churchill, and Stalin lunched alone, apart from interpreters, in Roosevelt's rooms. Roosevelt read to Stalin the determination of the Combined Chiefs to invade northern France by June 1, and southern France then or soon after, provided the Soviet Army launched a serious offensive against the Germans by the same date. Stalin expressed pleasure at the decision, and promised the desired offensive. They had a pleasant talk, agreeing on the independence of Korea and the restoration to China of Formosa, Manchuria, and the Pescadores.

They also agreed on the right of Russia to access to unspecified warm-water ports, and to unfettered passage of the Dardanelles and the Kiel Canal. Roosevelt promised to reveal the identity of the commander of Overlord within four days, but after he and Churchill would have returned to Cairo.

The third plenary conference convened that afternoon and had none of the tension or abrasion of the previous sessions, the Overlord decision having been inexorably taken. The most memorable phrase to come from the Teheran Conference was uttered by Churchill on this day, after Stalin had given a dissertation on how they deceived the Germans by moving in vast numbers of dummy tanks and airfields and by intense decoy radio traffic, while preparing for real offensives in great secrecy elsewhere. "Truth," said Winston Churchill, "deserves a bodyguard of lies." It was an amicable session.

Churchill's birthday dinner in the British embassy was a grand affair, undimmed by Stalin's bodyguard's collaring and sticking a gun into the ribs of the valet who tried to take Stalin's cape, and by the waiter's dumping a platter of ice cream onto Stalin's interpreter as he translated one of Stalin's toasts. (The unflappable Pavlov didn't miss a word from his master's voice as a glacial mass of ice cream cascaded down on his head and shoulders and shoes: "Mr. Stalin says . . .") Churchill said early on that they would observe the Russian rule that anyone who wished to make a toast was free to do so at any time. This led to the predictable endless sequence of minor speeches. Roosevelt graciously toasted Brooke, mentioning that their fathers had been friends. When Stalin commented that Brooke didn't like the Russians, Brooke got to his feet and offered a toast (quoted very extensively in his memoirs) to the effect that that was mere deception, as in the bodyguard of lies, and that he liked and admired the Russians. The waspish Brooke was certainly not above flattery, as his generous diary description of his own eloquence demonstrates, but Stalin seemed to enjoy the response (according to Churchill).[50] All three leaders gave eloquent improvised addresses.

Churchill concluded with a toast to his principal guests, but Stalin insisted on raising his glass to Roosevelt and American war production, expressing particular admiration for the astonishing American production of 10,000 aircraft per month, more than three times the Soviet production. (Even in his compliment to Roosevelt, Stalin considerably exaggerated Soviet aircraft production.) Roosevelt then spoke, referring to the joke Churchill had made about Britain becoming "pink." He said the United Nations were "a rainbow . . . that traditional symbol of hope." It was an unoriginal and even trite pastoral metaphor, but it came well from the senior member of the group, in power and in protocol, in the mellifluous voice that on this historic Persian night, as always, seemed no less confident for emanating from a man in a wheelchair. And it seemed appropriate enough to the chief participants. After extensive birthday greetings for the British prime minister, the marathon party ended at 2 A.M., December 1, 1943.

The military part of the Teheran Conference was over and the generals and admirals departed for Cairo, with a day's stopover for sightseeing in Jerusalem. Brooke, in particular, was relieved to be done with the politicians. Roosevelt's purpose in making the arduous journey to Teheran, to break the ice with Stalin, had not been fulfilled, and he now embarked on one of the more controversial enterprises of his career. He later said to Frances Perkins: "I had stayed at his embassy, gone to his dinners, been introduced to his ministers and generals. He was correct, stiff, solemn, not smiling, nothing human to get hold of. If it was all going to be official paper work, there was no sense in my having made this long journey. I had come there to accommodate Stalin. I felt pretty discouraged because I was making no personal headway. What we were doing could have been done by the foreign ministers." (What had been agreed was well beyond the authority of foreign ministers.)

Roosevelt recalled that after buying some gifts and souvenirs where he had bought Churchill's birthday present, he had encountered Churchill on his way to the plenary session at noon on November 30. "I said, 'Winston, I hope you won't be sore at me for what I am going to do.' Winston just shifted his cigar and grunted. I must say he behaved decently afterward."[51] Roosevelt started his escalated charm offensive with Stalin with chummy intimacy and then whispered, "Winston is cranky this morning, he got up on the wrong side of the bed."

Roosevelt's account to Frances Perkins of this dubious endeavor continued: "A vague smile passed over Stalin's eyes, and I decided I was on the right track. As soon as I sat down at the conference table, I began to tease Churchill about his Britishness, about John Bull, about his cigars, about his habits. It began to register with Stalin. Winston got red and scowled, and the more he did so, the more Stalin smiled. Finally Stalin broke into a deep hearty guffaw, and for the first time in three days I saw light. I kept it up until Stalin was laughing with me, and it was then I called him 'Uncle Joe.' He would have thought me fresh the day before, but that day he laughed and came over and shook my hand. From that time on our relations were personal, and Stalin himself indulged in occasional witticism. The ice was broken and we talked like men and brothers."[52]

Roosevelt undoubtedly embellished this account. We have only Miss Perkins's word for it. Churchill makes no mention of any such tack by Roosevelt. Nor do Bohlen, Eden, or Harriman. If anything so puerile and egregious as Frances Perkins claimed Roosevelt proudly described had actually happened, it would have been commented on by other participants. Since Miss Perkins is generally a reliable source, the exaggeration in the story is almost certainly Roosevelt's. So the damage to Roosevelt's reputation should be that he ever thought it appropriate or self-serving to have given such a fraudulent account to a valued colleague, not that he had actually demeaned himself and provoked a great ally and admirer by tweaking Churchill to pander to Stalin. It is particularly alarming to imagine that Roosevelt was ever concerned at being thought "fresh" by Stalin.

Roosevelt set great and justified store by his talents at ingratiation, persuasion, and guile. It is understandable that he found Stalin annoyingly impervious to such wiles. And though he apparently did pay some attention to the Oumansky version of Stalin's view of the Roosevelt-Churchill relationship, as recounted by Davies, it is not believable that he went nearly as far as the Perkins account suggests.

As Walter Lippmann said, since Roosevelt never trusted anybody, it is unlikely that he trusted Stalin, of whom he had been very critical prior to the Russo-German war. That Roosevelt wanted to charm Stalin does not imply that Stalin charmed or deceived Roosevelt in the slightest. It merely meant that Roosevelt set out to enlist Stalin wholeheartedly in his designs for the world, employing methods that had generally succeeded before—a mixture of America's might and his own negotiating techniques—and was less than completely successful. He was not, however, altogether unsuccessful.

VII

THE POLITICAL MEETING on December 1 dealt with Turkey, Finland, Poland, and Germany. Churchill rhapsodized about the benefits of getting Turkey into the war, and volunteered to go to Ankara and paint a dark picture of what would happen to Turkish interests if it did not join the Allies. The only decision taken was to invite the Turkish president, Ismet Inonu, Kemal Ataturk's successor, to meet Roosevelt and Churchill and a representative of the Soviet government in Cairo in a few days. Churchill had unrealistic notions of the ease of replicating the feat of persuasion in the present war that British and French statesmen had achieved in bringing Romania and Italy into the First World War. He even envisioned persuading Sweden to join the Allies. Churchill's enthusiasm for the possibility of cajoling or dragooning other powers into war with Germany was inexplicable. It was also unseemly, given his own reluctance to return in force to the beaches from which his army had been evacuated in 1940.

Stalin and Molotov made it clear that they expected an enhanced status in the administration of the Dardanelles in exchange for any Russian aid to Turkey.

Roosevelt raised the issue of Finland during lunch, asking what the United States could do to extract Finland from the war. Stalin said he had already been approached by the Swedish foreign minister on this subject, but that he suspected the Finns were still hoping for a German victory. Churchill said that he had sympathized with the Finns but considered their joining Hitler's attack on Russia disgraceful. The Swedish foreign minister had told Stalin the Finns feared the Russians wanted to repossess Finland as a province. Churchill said that the sea lanes to Leningrad had to be secure, but that Finland must remain independent. Stalin claimed to have no designs on the country at all, beyond certain extensions of the 1940 borders in Russia's favor as well as an indemnity for the damage the Finns had caused Russia. Churchill said Finland was too poor to provide more than lumber as an indemnity.

Roosevelt concluded that he should ask the Finns to negotiate directly with the Russians, which was acceptable to Stalin, though he doubted that much would be accomplished by it. What he stated to be his final conditions were the restoration of the 1940 border but exchanging Petsamo for Hango, reparations of half the damage caused Russia by the Finns (as calculated by Stalin), Helsinki's absolute break with Germany, and the expulsion of Germans from Finland.

The leaders adjourned briefly, and Roosevelt asked to see Stalin privately. They met at 3:20 P.M. with Molotov and Harriman and the interpreters, Bohlen and Pavlov. Roosevelt expressed his concern to Stalin about the sensibilities of American voters of Polish, Lithuanian, Estonian, and Latvian extraction. He said there were six or seven million Polish-Americans. He said he personally approved moving the Polish borders 250 miles to the west, rewarding and securing the Soviet Union and punishing the Germans. But he could make no declarative statement about it, either in the conference proceedings or publicly thereafter, until after the U.S. election eleven months off. Stalin expressed understanding of the President's dilemma, though what he really thought of it is conjecture. Roosevelt's invocation of domestic political concerns is not a matter he should have got into with Stalin at all.

Stalin was less indulgent when Roosevelt again suggested some sort of a referendum in the Baltic states, even if a rather pro forma affair. Czarist Russia, from Peter the Great on, said Stalin, had occupied these places, and the British and Americans had never asked for any kind of a referendum in the Baltic provinces while they were allied with the Romanovs (which the United States never was, to Wilson's great relief [chapter 2]).

In fact, Roosevelt opted out of the Polish political discussion not so much because he was so concerned with Polish-American votes, since he could almost certainly corral them no matter what he did with Stalin, though he was mindful of them, but because he wanted to defer such considerations as long as possible.

He was confident that Overlord and its aftermath would clear France and most of Germany before the Russians could arrive there. The British-led army plodding up Italy would secure that country to the West. Britain, France, Italy, most of Germany restored to the West—given that Western democracy had been pushed almost completely out of Europe three years before, this would be a considerable achievement.

And Roosevelt continued to believe that there was a possibility to induce Stalin into the camp of the respectable and law-abiding nations. Finally, if the worst occurred and Stalin simply occupied Poland more or less as Hitler had, the less Roosevelt had had to do with the Polish discussions at Teheran, the better.

The final session of the Teheran Conference was brought to order by Roosevelt at six o'clock that evening. There was a robust discussion about the disposition of Italian naval and merchant vessels, though both Churchill and Roosevelt pronounced themselves in favor of handing over a battleship, other vessels, and sizeable quantities of merchant shipping to the Soviet Union. Churchill and Roosevelt promised to deliver the ships by January 1944, but Churchill cautioned that it would have to be handled carefully, because the Italians were performing a number of useful services for the Allies, and if this were managed too brusquely, they might rebel and scuttle their ships in the French manner. It was a cat-and-mouse operation, said Churchill, a cat owner.* In fact, Stalin was trying to collect reparations before the war was over, and a controversy would continue on this subject between the principal Allies through 1944. Eventually, the Russians were given the battleship *Giulio Cesare* and lent the old British battleship *Royal Sovereign.*

At last the subject of Polish government was addressed. Roosevelt hoped Stalin would restore relations with the London government. It was obvious that this would be difficult, because Stalin claimed that the London Polish government was killing partisans—i.e., Communists—in Poland. Here, as in China and Yugoslavia, France and Italy, there were competing Communist and non-Communist administrations or shadow governments, and sorting it all out would prove immensely complicated.

Churchill declared Britain's interest, since it was in defense of Poland that Britain had gone to war. He expressed astonishment at Chamberlain's having capitulated over Czechoslovakia, which was a much better prospect, and then having committed Britain to Poland, and he understood Stalin's policy in 1939, given the spinelessness of the British and French. But it was important, said the prime minister, for Poland to emerge secure and strong from the horrible ordeal of being trampled down under the German and Russian armies.

Stalin launched into a tirade against the exiled Polish government and complained that Churchill had spoken the day before of giving the Poles a fait accompli, but now spoke of negotiation. (Churchill, as Stalin was well aware, had suggested a fait accompli over Poland's borders, not over her status as an independent country.)

A lengthy digression now occurred over Poland's proposed borders with Germany and the Soviet Union: the Oder-Neisse Line, the Curzon Line, and, as Eden pointedly called it, the "Ribbentrop-Molotov" Line. ("Call it whatever you want," said Stalin.)[53] Maps were got out, and conferees milled about in groups. Churchill eventually generated some enthusiasm, as he recorded in his memoirs, for explaining to the Poles that they were giving up marshland to the Soviet Union and being compensated with superior arable and mineral-rich land from Germany. Stalin said he had no desire to take over large numbers of Poles. Roo-

* And his cat had the same name as one of his battleships, Rodney. Lady Soames (Mr. Churchill's daughter) surmises that this was a cat from the Admiralty and so not named by Churchill himself.

sevelt, as he had indicated to Stalin earlier in the afternoon would be the case, said little.

When a consensus emerged about moving Poland to the west, leaving the exact demarcations essentially to the British and Russians to work out, and imposing it on the Poles, Roosevelt raised the question of Germany. Roosevelt again said that Germany had been safer when it was divided into 107 principalities, as it was under the German policies of Richelieu and Metternich.

Churchill, remembering the Prussian-dominated German general staff of Bismarck's time, bought into the legend that the Prussians were responsible for German militarism, and wanted that region separated from the rest of Germany. This was an obsolete notion. Many prominent Prussians were a good deal more appalled by the excesses of Hitler than comparable people in some other German regions. Hitler had not done well in Prussia when he still held elections. What the Allies were suppressing was not Prussian militarism but Nazi criminality.

Roosevelt's plan was that Germany, after yielding large tracts of territory to Poland, and East Prussia to the Soviet Union, should be divided into five independent states and two international areas governed by the United Nations. The U.N. trusteeships would be Hamburg and the Kiel Canal, and the Ruhr and the Saar Basin. Prussia, Saxony, Bavaria, Hanover with the northwest of Germany and a state grouping Hesse, Westphalia, and the southern Rhine, would be the five constituent states. Churchill wanted to separate Prussia and treat it harshly, and attach Bavaria, Saxony, and the rest of southern Germany to a "Danubian Confederacy," which would be a partial revival of the Austro-Hungarian and Holy Roman Empires—a catchment, a "cowlike" confederation, he called it, for many groups and irredentisms in central Europe.

Stalin was closer to Roosevelt's idea and thought Churchill's might provide a matrix for a resurrection of German militarism. He warned that all Germans fought "like devils, as the British and American armies would soon learn. Only the Austrians, when surrendering, shout 'I'm Austrian.'" Austria, Hungary, Romania, and Bulgaria could continue as independent states, but Germany should be broken up and not readmitted to a larger grouping. Roosevelt accurately stated that there was little difference between Prussia and the other areas of Germany, and Churchill, having championed the separation of Prussia and Bavaria, acknowledged that dividing Germany could just create the ambition of the parts of the country to reunite again. He suggested it be their goal to keep Germany divided for fifty years; beyond that was not realistic. (This proved to be remarkably farsighted, though not along the exact lines he advocated.)

In one of his greatest contributions to the conference, Churchill insisted that Austria be treated as a separate and independent country, the first of Hitler's victims rather than a cradle of Nazism, with joint Allied occupation zones. This was agreed and ultimately saved Austria the fate of the postwar satellite countries.

VIII

THE WESTERN ALLIES, and ultimately the peoples of central Europe, paid a price for the delay of Overlord into 1944, as Roosevelt and Marshall had feared. The great Russian victories at Stalingrad and Kursk had given Stalin an advantage over the British and Americans. El Alamein was a trivial operation in comparison, though strategically important. Largely because of Churchill and Brooke's aversion to full combat with the main German army, the Western Allies were still unproven, at the end of 1943, by the greatest litmus test of the war. At the time of Teheran, they had not met the Germans in force in Europe successfully, and the Russians certainly had. Now, to ensure success, they were asking Stalin to mount a general offensive to coincide with Overlord.

Stalin then held the best bargaining position of the Big Three at Teheran, unless Roosevelt had wished to invoke his status as the war supplier of the alliance. Stalin was obviously going to want to influence the government of Poland, and preventing that influence from becoming complete domination might not be possible.

The great strategic contest now fully under way was for Germany. As in the Thirty Years War, the Seven Years War, and through most of the Napoleonic Wars, the struggle for Germany would determine who really won the war. As was made clear at Trident and Quadrant, and again on the way to Cairo, Roosevelt and Churchill both wanted the Western Allies to occupy Berlin.

When Yalta came round fourteen months later, the Russian tactical advantage had been reduced by the great victories of the British and Americans on the Western Front. This surge in the fortunes of the Western Allies had been made possible by the Overlord decision, which was the principal outcome at Teheran.

In fact, as we have seen, if Stalin had not been so morbidly suspicious of his allies that he required the Overlord decision at Teheran, and had played along with Churchill, they might have got it deferred again and Stalin would have ended up with most of Germany, with absolute control of Austria, Greece, Denmark, and Yugoslavia, and with a better chance of a neutral or subservient or even Communist-dominated France and Italy. In all of the circumstances at Teheran, Stalin had a good conference and Roosevelt a successful one, and Churchill, in losing his principal argument, felt he had done poorly, though he denied this in his memoirs. He was well-served by the decision he had opposed and had some important successes, particularly over Austria. All three had shown their usual impressive powers of personality and articulation.

Brooke's poor view of Teheran, as an opponent of an early Overlord, is understandable, though mistaken. Montgomery's is not understandable, given that he was the field commander of Overlord.

The final event of the Teheran Conference was the dinner hosted by Stalin on December 1. It was chiefly concerned with approving a private summary of agreed points, particular declarations, and a public communiqué. In addition to the agreements on Overlord and a simultaneous Russian offensive in the east, Polish borders, and Russian participation in the Pacific war, there was a bland declaration on Iran.

Roosevelt was quite interested in the possibilities for Iran of an aid program and a generalized notion of his Good Neighbor policy that had been such a public relations coup in Latin America. Stalin had called upon the shah for ninety minutes November 30; he had been "particularly polite and well-mannered and he seemed intent on making a good impression on me," wrote the shah.[54] Stalin was also the only one of the three visiting leaders who called upon the monarch of the host country, instead of the other way round.

Stalin offered the shah twenty T-34 tanks and twenty modern airplanes, the merest foretaste of the vast military capacity the shah would buy as decades passed. A competition between the Russians and Americans for influence in Iran, where the British were regarded as exploiters, had already begun. (Nearly sixty years later, the Shahbanou, Fara Diba, the shah's last wife, told me: "We didn't like the British, but it was hard not to be impressed with Mr. Churchill.")

The contest between the Soviet Union and the United States in Iran would be an unequal one, because of America's greater means, development expertise, and relatively disinterested motives. The United States already had a mission in Iran dispensing development aid and forming necessary public services.*

The official communiqué declared the responsibility of the conferees to create a peace that would "command the good will of the overwhelming mass of the peoples of the world, and banish the scourge and terror of war for many generations." They pledged to enlist the whole world to the elimination of "tyranny, slavery, oppression, and intolerance," and claimed to leave Teheran "friends in fact, in spirit, and in purpose."

Roosevelt left the Soviet embassy immediately after dinner and drove to Camp Amiribad a few miles away. He addressed the hospital patients and workers and the soldiers of that camp the next morning, drove to the airfield, and took off for Cairo. He landed at 4 P.M. on December 2 and had a convivial dinner with Churchill. The British were horrified at the American plan to leave Cairo December 5 or 6. Brooke furiously wrote in his diary that the Americans had been "wasting all our time with Chiang Kai-shek and Stalin before we had settled any points with them. . . . It all looks like some of the worst sharp practice that I have seen for some time."[55] This was Brooke's usual exaggeration. Roosevelt had already been away for three weeks and he was still a long way from home, and

----

* Among the latter was a successful effort to organize a local police force, headed by Colonel H. Norman Schwarzkopf, former head of the New Jersey State Police and father of the commander of the American-led action against Iraq in 1990–1991.

time spent in discussion with Stalin, though it might be fruitless, was hardly wasted.

The debate about Operation Buccaneer, the amphibious landing in the Andaman Islands at the head of the Bay of Bengal, which Roosevelt had promised Chiang Kai-shek, began where it had left off when the British and American conferees had removed from Cairo to Teheran.

Faced with fierce British opposition, Roosevelt determined on December 5 that Buccaneer was impractical. He told his staff chiefs to cease arguing for it. The British were undoubtedly right. It was a far greater effort than Chiang deserved.

Turkish president Ismet Inonu arrived in Cairo that day. He was a wily negotiator and made it clear that he could not consider bringing his country into the war without massive military assistance, which, as he doubtless knew, the Allies would not find it convenient to give. Vyshinsky, whom Stalin had deputed to represent him in these talks, failed for logistical reasons to arrive, so the Soviet Union was unrepresented.

Roosevelt deferred his departure while he and Churchill continued to press Inonu. Churchill turned his great powers of argument on the Turkish leader, but he refused to be drawn. Roosevelt, never having believed in this project, was relatively aloof, and Inonu's requests for military aid received an evasive response from the Allied leaders. Inonu was in fact far more concerned with the power of Russia than with Germany (with good reason).

Churchill and Eden saw Inonu to the airport, and the Turkish president embraced and kissed Churchill before boarding his plane. "Did you see, Ismet kissed me?" said Churchill to Eden, who replied that that was all they had got out of him.*

IX

EARLY ON THE morning of December 7, Churchill and Roosevelt made their farewells at the Cairo airport and the President took off for Tunis, flying over the battlefields of the Eighth Army and the Afrika Korps. General Eisenhower met him at Tunis and conducted him to the Villa Casa Blanca, where he had stayed on his way to Cairo and Teheran. Roosevelt had asked Marshall what he next wanted to do professionally, and Marshall declined to express a preference between commanding Overlord and continuing as chief of staff. This was a customarily selfless act by Marshall, who would have preferred the Overlord theater command but didn't feel his own desires should influence the Commander in Chief.

---

* Turkey would join the war sixteen months later, at the last possible moment to be considered part of the United Nations, long after it would have any military impact. Inonu would explain to his colleagues then that he had taken that measure "to ensure that Turkey is at the table and not on the menu."

Roosevelt then said that he could not "sleep at ease if you were out of Washington."[56] Roosevelt informed Eisenhower shortly after arriving in Tunis that he would be the Overlord commander. "Well Ike, you'd better start packing," he said in greeting.[57]

In some respects, the best choice for Overlord would have been MacArthur, the West's greatest military strategist, as even Brooke and de Gaulle admitted. Roosevelt, unlike his successor as president, had the moral authority and self-confidence to control him.

MacArthur would have been popular with the Russians. As a theater commander, even in retreat in the Philippines, MacArthur always conducted his own foreign policy and had set out to entice the Russians into the war against Japan even before he fetched up in Corregidor. On the anniversary of the Red Army in February 1942, MacArthur had sent Stalin the astonishing and much-publicized message: "The hopes of civilization rest on the worthy banners of the courageous Red Army. . . . The scale and grandeur of [the] smashing counterattack [at the gates of Moscow and Leningrad] mark it as the greatest military achievement in all history."[58] Yet militant anti-Communist that he was, MacArthur probably would have been much bolder than Eisenhower in occupying territory at the end of the war in Europe. (He threatened to jail any Russians who turned up in Japan.)

America's greatest battlefield commander, thorough in tactics and frequently possessed of strategic genius, MacArthur was an inspiring leader and an imaginative theater commander. Logically, since this was the most important theater (as Roosevelt had just confirmed at Teheran), it should have had the Allies' most experienced amphibious general and greatest army group commander. MacArthur's elevation would have been welcomed by de Gaulle. His grandiose but brilliant personality would have commanded more respect from Montgomery than did the capable but cautious soldier-diplomat Eisenhower. He was a more brilliant but less stable and not necessarily a more compelling personality than Eisenhower.

MacArthur would most likely have produced a Manstein Plan in reverse and bypassed Paris and the Low Countries, knifing between them directly to the Ruhr and the heart of Germany, with Patton the tip of the lance. He would likely have produced an obverse blitzkrieg and not have bothered with a continuous front such as Eisenhower devised, where each nationality had its own command. It should not, in the abstract, have taken six months, as it did, to get from the liberation of Paris to the crossing of the Rhine.

If at Casablanca it had been determined that Overlord should occur in September 1943 and MacArthur had been given command of it, it would probably not have been much riskier than it proved to be, and there is some hypothetical possibility that the Western Allies would have arrived on the Rhine more than a year earlier than they did, at the time of the Teheran Conference and at about the same time or even before the Soviet armies arrived on the Vistula. It would then have been possible to reconstitute Poland, Hungary, and Czechoslovakia as neutral states, as Finland and Austria were, and possibly to have reduced the likelihood of the Cold War. That the Western Allies achieved 80 percent or 90 percent of what might have been possible is far from a discreditable performance, but it left 50 million Eastern Europeans languishing under the Soviet jackboot for forty-five years.

This promotion to Overlord would have ended MacArthur's ceaseless agitations for more forces in the Pacific, which would have made it easier to load forces into Europe and leave Japan to the navy and marines and accelerated island hopping. It would also have ended MacArthur's status as a sulking outsider to the main war theaters. He wrote, just a few months before Teheran and seven months after taking to the offensive following the victory at Guadalcanal, to an intimate old comrade in arms: "It has been a desperate time for me . . . always the underdog . . . destruction just around the corner . . . I am sick at heart at the mistakes and lost opportunities that are so prevalent."[59] (He had not been an underdog for almost the last year, and took personally the fact that New Guinea was of less geopolitical importance than France or Germany.) MacArthur was a high-strung, high-maintenance commander, unlike Eisenhower, who was equable and steady. But MacArthur possessed genius where Eisenhower was at the highest level of conventional competence.

There would have been political difficulties as well, because MacArthur's ego could not have been restrained from immersion in the presidential selection process—i.e., of himself. Roosevelt, as we have seen, was aware of MacArthur's political susceptibilities, but, as we will see in the next section, considered him almost as complete, though not as odious, a political incompetent as Lindbergh, Kennedy, Hearst, McCormick, and John L. Lewis. Roosevelt could undoubtedly have managed MacArthur, as he managed or outwitted, or otherwise used and/or disposed of the others, and of all who would be his domestic political rivals.

As it turned out, Roosevelt was designating not only the commander of history's greatest military operation with Overlord, but a future president of the United States. Eisenhower executed that office with distinction, if not with unlimited imagination. MacArthur, though ten years older than Eisenhower, had more obvious political ambitions and considerably more presentational flair and oratorical ability. But the thought of him in the nation's supreme office, as Roosevelt always recognized, was disquieting. MacArthur's record leaves room for real concern about how he would have performed without any check on his vainglory from any superior.

There is no evidence that MacArthur was ever considered for command of Overlord or that Roosevelt had any thought that Eisenhower would one day be a candidate for president. But it may have occurred to him that success in Overlord could, as had so often been the case with military distinction in American history, from Washington to Theodore Roosevelt, lead to high political office. If Roosevelt had only been naming a theater commander, MacArthur could have been a better choice. But in choosing a national hero capable of election to the White House, Eisenhower was clearly the better choice, Marshall (who would never have sought elective office) having been judged indispensable where he was.

If Marshall had had Overlord and Eisenhower had become army chief of staff, which was what the British had expected, they would doubtless both have performed capably, but not necessarily better than in the roles they did fill.

This is all hazardous conjecture, justified at all only because of the implications of an alternate scenario. As with the strategic decision at Casablanca not to press all-out for a 1943 cross-Channel invasion, Roosevelt's personnel choice may or may not have been the very best possible, but it was a very good choice, and the safest one. Eisenhower admirably fulfilled his mandate to defeat Germany, as MacArthur fulfilled his in the Pacific, and Marshall his as, in Churchill's phrase (coined for Carnot in the French Revolution), "the organizer of victory." And all went on to further great achievement in civilian office, until, in MacArthur's case, he carried insubordination to a subsequent president to intolerable extremes.

X

SENIOR ALLIED THOUGHTS on the organization of Germany, the most important of all postwar subjects, were already beginning to evolve. The foreign ministers' conference at Moscow in October 1943 had set up, on Eden's motion, the European Advisory Commission, to work up plans for Germany. The British had in mind a broad remit; Roosevelt wanted to defer as much as possible to the end of the war, when he calculated Western bargaining strength would be greatest. The EAC was confined to surrender terms and enforcement and zones of occupation in Germany. The EAC would meet in London, be chaired by the Foreign Office's Sir William Strang, and be further composed of the American and Soviet ambassadors, John Winant and Feodor Gousev. (Strang had accompanied Chamberlain to Munich and led the unsuccessful British discussions with the Soviet Union in the summer of 1939.)

Winant knew that he was really taking his orders directly from Roosevelt, although Hull and the State Department assumed they were instructing Winant. And Winant knew that Roosevelt had not told Hull much about what happened at Teheran, or what his own views about the future of Germany were. Roosevelt never even gave Hull the minutes of the Teheran proceedings, and the State Department began sending Winant conventional plans for a democratized, but integral Germany, which the ambassador ignored.

Roosevelt impressed Eisenhower, at Tunis and after, as astonishingly knowledgeable about geography, confident of his ability to deal with the Russians, and initially minded to divide Germany into autonomous units that would conform to the three occupation zones, after rethinking his more atomized division into five states and two international zones. Having just been invested as supreme commander of the Western Allied armies, Eisenhower strongly recommended a single military government for the whole of Germany, as a framework for containing Soviet influence. It is difficult to imagine how he figured this out, since the strength and size of the Red Army would make the Soviets preeminent over the West in the government of all Germany. Roosevelt discounted this advice, and Eisenhower found the President "almost an egomaniac in his belief in his own wisdom."[60]

Roosevelt was hoping the Western Allies would make a lightning advance in Germany, take Berlin, and trade Stalin influence in Germany and severe measures for the pacification of that country, as well as prodigious economic assistance to rebuild the ravaged Soviet Union, in exchange for civilized Russian behavior in Poland and the rest of Eastern Europe.

(In Washington ten days later, Roosevelt, through Stimson, began to let it be known that there should be three German occupation zones governed separately. There would obviously be a good deal of cooperation between the British and the Americans. The European Advisory Commission (EAC) would take up the boundaries of the occupation zones early in 1944. Roosevelt had committed his views to the National Geographic map he had touched up with his staff while conferring on the *Iowa* on the way to Teheran. He had mapped out his occupation ambition, including American occupation of Berlin. Beyond that and until his wishes could be realized by Eisenhower's armies, he wanted the EAC to stall. However, the British and the Russians had other ideas, and from those ideas postwar Europe began to take shape.)

Roosevelt had dinner in Tunis on December 7 with Eisenhower, General Carl Spaatz (air force commander in North Africa), and his son Elliott and his squadron. The waiters were Italian prisoners of war. Roosevelt spoke to them and diarized, "like 9/10ths of all the wops, [they] are crazy to come to the U.S. for good."[61]

For safety reasons, Eisenhower, Leahy, and security chief Mike Reilly dissuaded Roosevelt from going to Naples to review and encourage American soldiers and airmen, so he went instead to Malta on December 8. He reviewed British units that had defended the gallant island and then flew to Palermo, where he met with Generals Mark Clark and George S. Patton, encouraging the latter following the famous reprimand Patton received from Eisenhower for slapping a soldier claiming to suffer from battle fatigue. Patton was grateful for the support of Roosevelt and Hopkins. There was a strong rapport between the most pugnacious and colorful of all America's generals and the protean but severely handicapped Commander in Chief. When Patton had called on him at the White House on October 21, 1942, just before setting out on the Torch landings, Patton had said: "I will leave the beaches either a conqueror or a corpse." Roosevelt wrote: "Patton is a joy."[62]

Roosevelt returned to Tunis late on December 8, having greatly heartened American soldiers by turning up to review them in what had recently been a combat zone. Hitler and Stalin, despite being able-bodied and relatively proximate to the war fronts, were almost never seen by their soldiers. Even Churchill rarely got as close to combat as Roosevelt did on this occasion. Constitutionally, Roosevelt was like a king and a prime minister combined. He had held his position as long as many of his young draftees could remember. His presence uplifted the soldiers and sailors and impressed the nation.

On the morning of December 9, President Roosevelt and his party took off from Tunis for Dakar. Roosevelt recorded of the flight: "hour after hour of desert . . . I am so bored I could shriek. At last we saw the Atlantic and the good old *Iowa* in the outer harbor."[63]*

Iowa stood now where for three years the *Richelieu* had been idle, her officers and crew subjected to the competing blandishments of Vichy and de Gaulle. Now the flagship of the Free French Navy, *Richelieu* had gone to New York to be refitted for active service at last. From his reading of Mahan forty years before, Roosevelt had always been curious to see Dakar, the strategic trans-Atlantic harbor closest to the Americas. The Free French insisted on having the honor of conveying the President of the United States to his battleship. Within an hour of his boarding, *Iowa* and her escorting destroyers were under way.

It was a restful and uneventful crossing. *Iowa* entered Chesapeake Bay in the afternoon of December 16. Roosevelt gave the crew of the *Iowa* a speech on the quarterdeck before leaving the ship. He made fun of Harry Hopkins and General Edwin "Pa" Watson for coming up the gangplank on their hands and knees at Dakar, and then stated that they had to "eliminate from the human race nations like Germany and Japan." He reviewed the progress of the war in the two years since Pearl Harbor, and closed: "And so good-bye for awhile. I hope that I will have another cruise on this ship. Meanwhile, good luck, and remember that I am with you in spirit, each and every one of you."[64] He transferred to the *Potomac* and was back in the White House on December 17th. He had traveled almost 17,500 miles, a considerable feat for a man in his physical condition. The cabinet, the congressional leaders, and the entire White House staff were on hand in the diplomatic reception room to welcome him back.

Public and journalistic response to the Teheran meeting and communiqué were almost universally positive, from the *New York Times* to the crew of the mer-

---

* It was illustrative of America's now overwhelming naval superiority over Japan that since dropping him off at Oran, the *Iowa* had made a goodwill visit to Brazil and then waited at Freetown, Sierra Leone, to take the President home, rather than hastening into combat. She had spent several months prior to this trip at Iceland, awaiting a sortie by the *Turpitz*, to meet that ship as the ill-fated H.M.S. *Hood* had met *Turpitz*'s sister, the *Bismarck*. Aficionados of the big-gun ships have always regretted that this single ship combat never occurred. Given her superior firepower, size, and speed, the advantage would have to be given to the *Iowa*, but it would have been a Homeric contest.

chantman S.S. *George Woodward*, which telegraphed the congratulatory malapropism on the "stupendous task . . . [the leaders] have undertaken to obliviate the fascist powers [which] will be immortalized in the future pages of history."[65] Soviet press references to the Western Allies now became much more favorable than they ever had been before. This was the first multilateral summit conference of Allies since Versailles, and it electrified the world. Yet Stalin's private suspicions of the reliability of his allies persisted. To exiled Czech leader Eduard Beneš, and to Russia's most illustrious soldier, Marshal Georgi Zhukov, Stalin expressed lingering doubts about whether the Western Allies really would frontally attack Germany.[66]

Goebbels and Hitler agreed that there was no reason not to publish the Teheran Conference communiqué in Germany, sufficiently unimpressed with it were they. They had anticipated some propaganda pitch to the German public. Instead they got a promise of the impending severe and overwhelming defeat and punishment of Germany. Goebbels had written in his diary, December 7: "Everybody is tense and full of expectation. As a result there is very little news, because the entire world news machinery is geared to the Teheran communiqué," but when it was issued, the Reich propaganda minister found it "neither fish nor fowl."[67]

What a change there was from the cocksure swaggering of the Nuremberg rallies of just five years before. Now, Goebbels and Hitler knew they were hunted men, exterminating the European Jews before they themselves were exterminated, helping to spread the myth that Churchill and Roosevelt were naïve to have anything to do with Stalin. Despite all their barbarity, they still posed as defenders of Western civilization against the savage hordes of Asiatic Bolshevism.

Once back in the White House, Roosevelt was reluctant to speak too freely to Eleanor and Anna about his "Odyssey," because they had both wished to accompany him. He found Eleanor's bombardment of him with incessant questions irritating.[68] Eventually he regaled intimates with splendid anecdotes about the rich personalities and exotic settings and great events of the last few weeks. Anna, upon whom her father doted (even more than fathers usually do on daughters), had a natural talent that her mother almost totally lacked for drawing her father out. Attractive, bright, sexy, a spirited raconteur with a hearty laugh, Anna knew exactly how to relax her father with amusing gossip, which he always enjoyed.

On the morning of December 18, she breakfasted with him in his bedroom, and told him stories of the romantic and sexual pursuits of her brothers Elliott and Franklin Jr. Elliott was violently in love with the actress Faye Emerson, and FDR Jr. fancied General Eisenhower's young English female driver, Kay Summersby. President Roosevelt had met Miss Summersby when he visited Eisenhower in Tunis on his way to Teheran, and had had dinner and a picnic lunch with her. He concluded, with his, as Tom Corcoran had called it, almost androgynous intuition, that the general and his chauffeuse were sleeping together. There was no place for his son on the fringes of the Supreme Allied Commander's romantic life. (Ambassador Winant, following in the fine tradition of Edward R. Murrow and Pamela Churchill, was conducting a torrid liaison with Sarah Churchill, the prime minister's daughter, upon which Mr. Churchill, an indulgent father and a full-service ally, smiled benignly.)

Harry Hopkins finally moved out of the White House on December 21, 1943, and moved into a home with his new wife in Georgetown. His departure, following that of Missy LeHand and the death of Louis Howe, made the White House and the business of being president a good deal gloomier for Roosevelt. He had little difficulty persuading his daughter to retire from the Seattle newspaper and join him as a chatelaine and general helper in the White House, starting in January 1944. He promised to take her with him on his next overseas trip to a summit conference.

For the first time during his presidency, Roosevelt and his wife spent Christmas in Hyde Park and had Anna, FDR Jr., and John with them. It was a serene and pleasant holiday after a strenuous year of great achievement. Victory was in sight, and all was now a countdown to the opening of the Western Front. Roosevelt returned to Washington from Hyde Park on December 27.

He had another attack of the "grippe." He had also, at his daughter's insistence, reinforced his medical team with an authentic cardiologist, Dr. Howard Bruenn, who described his condition as "upper respiratory infections . . . occasional bouts of abdominal distress and distension, accompanied by profuse perspiration . . . influenza . . . unusual and undue fatigue."[69] Churchill had been unwell too, and Roosevelt invited his radio listeners to pray for the recovery of the prime minister.*

On December 26, 1943, the German battle cruiser *Scharnhorst*, which had been a source of much concern as an Atlantic surface raider earlier in the war, was cornered off the North Cape of Norway by the more powerful H.M.S. *Duke of York* and escorting vessels. *Scharnhorst* was decisively defeated and sent to the bottom of the Arctic Ocean by the British battleship's superior range and firepower. Hitler himself, anxiously listening to radio transmissions, had the disagreeable experience of hearing *Duke of York*'s signal officer, on behalf of the fleet commander (Admiral Bruce Fraser), ordering: "Destroyers, finish her off with torpedoes." The Soviet press drily reported that *Scharnhorst* had been added to the German underseas fleet. Roosevelt cabled his congratulations to Churchill.[71] The *Tirpitz*, harassed in its fjord constantly by British aircraft and even submarines, and the *Scharnhorst*'s sister, *Gneisenau*, were the only heavy surface units left to the Axis in European waters. The Royal Navy alone had fifteen capi-

---

* "The heartfelt prayers of all of us have been with this great citizen of the world in his recent serious illness."[70]

tal ships in the North Atlantic and Mediterranean. All the surviving French and Italian naval units were now in the hands of the Allies.

Churchill convalesced from his pneumonia in Marrakesh, where he stayed in a fine villa, heavily protected by units of the U.S. Army. He cabled Roosevelt on December 30 that he had on the same day received congratulations on his medical recovery from General Franco and Marshal Tito. Roosevelt cabled back an indication of his continuing views of the political extremes of right and left: "I suggest that on New Year's Day you invite the two gentlemen who congratulated you, then lock them up in the top of the tower where we saw the sunset and tell them you will stay at the bottom to see whether the black or the red throws the other one over the battlement."[72] Roosevelt continued to see little moral distinction between fascists and communists. Franco and Tito would rule their countries with unwavering firmness and some success (measured otherwise than by democratic criteria) for over thirty years.

On December 28, Roosevelt had told his last press conference of the year that the country had turned from "Dr. New Deal to Dr. Win the War." In fact, as we have seen, the second doctor banished the last of the Depression while preparing for the war. But Roosevelt had never lost sight of the need for postwar America to be an equitable and prosperous as well as a grateful country to which the millions of victorious servicemen overseas would return. The G.I. Bill of Rights was just the first step in this program.

These were his thoughts as 1943 ebbed away and the year of conferences gave way to the long-awaited year of liberation.

PART V

Pax Americana

1944–

CHAPTER 21

⚜

"OK, Let's Go"

*(General Dwight D. Eisenhower ordering that poor weather be
ignored and the invasion of Western Europe by two million men,
with 4,500 ships and 12,000 aircraft, be launched,
twenty-seven hours later, June 4, 1944)*

I

THE ARRIVAL OF Anna Roosevelt as a helper and substitute chatelaine and companion to her father in the White House in January 1944 represented Franklin D. Roosevelt's final attempt to recreate the vivacity and intimacy of the early Roosevelt presidency. In those early days, Louis Howe, covered with cigarette ashes and swearing profusely, lurked like an animated cadaver in the Lincoln bedroom. Anna's children got into bed with their grandfather while he was setting the gold price with the ramrod-stiff Dean Acheson and others, placing their hands over his mouth as he was pronouncing world-consequential decisions. Acheson compared these sessions to the *levee du roi* of Louis XIV, but the Sun King's levees were both more grandiose and more mundane. The court grunted encouragingly while the King had a bowel movement. Roosevelt at least spared his treasury officials any such *son et lumiere*.

In those days, Missy LeHand roamed about in her dressing gown, and Eleanor's large friend Lorena Hickock wandered around after the first lady "like a St. Bernard." There were "the colorful aides with Runyanesque nicknames. And above it all had been FDR himself, orchestrating events like Prospero on his enchanted island."[1]

Louis Howe had died in 1936 and Jimmy Roosevelt and his charming first wife had moved in. The President invited controversy and resentment by first naming Jimmy a lieutenant colonel in the Marine Corps so he could accompany his father to South America as a military aide. Jimmy had been involved in some questionable financial schemes, and sections of the press that were hostile to his father gave him a very rough ride. Jimmy was a good deal more sensitive than his rhinoceros-hided parents and was afflicted with severe ulcers in 1938 (chapter 11); when his marriage broke up and he moved on, he returned to questionable business practices. He replaced the wife on whom his father doted, Betsy Cushing, with his nurse at the Mayo Clinic, where his father was visiting him during the Munich crisis in October 1938. Betsy's popularity with the President stirred the envy of Jimmy and Eleanor; she was of the family that married into the Astors, Whitneys, and Paleys as well as the Roosevelts. FDR was seriously annoyed at the end of that marriage, though not at most of the many other marital crackups endured by his offspring. Harry Hopkins lived in the White House for over a year after remarrying, but now he had gone.

From time to time Roosevelt tried to reinflate his marriage as a fully functioning relationship. There was no doubt of Eleanor's intelligence and competence and, if committed to something, her constancy. She rendered him great service, and in these war years travelled unceasingly to inspect far-flung facilities and encourage the fighting men overseas. She was a benign and indomitable force, but was far from a perfect spouse. Hectoring, insensitive, resentful, and generally humorless, she effectively rebuffed her husband's sporadic efforts to breathe new life into their marriage. At the end of 1936 she had written to a friend: "I realize more and more that FDR is a great man and he is nice to me but as a person I'm a stranger and I don't want to be anything else."[2] They got on well enough most of the time but never lost the genius for quickly and profoundly irritating each other.

The President kept in his desk drawer a poem someone had sent him about Eleanor which scanned like Poe's famous "The Raven": "And despite her global milling, Of the voice there is no stilling, With its platitudes galore, As it rushes on advising, Criticizing and chastising, Moralizing, patronizing, Paralyzing—ever more, Advertising Eleanor."[3]

Eleanor was far to the left of Franklin, wore her heart on her sleeve, was gulled by almost any faddish leftist cause that came along, but courageously joined many of the greatest and most difficult causes early, such as civil rights for African-Americans. Thus she was a tireless advocate of aid to Russia and an apologist for the domestic left. But her harebrained causes were not confined to the far left. Soon after Pearl Harbor she wrote out a memo for her husband that planes should be filled with hornets, wasps, and bees and emptied near enemy lines to torment German and Japanese soldiers. The Commander in Chief replied that Eleanor's correspondent had a "bee in his bonnet."[4] Much of the time she thought Franklin and his friends frivolous, and he thought her and her entourage tedious. Neither was altogether mistaken.

Hopkins, the President's closest collaborator, was not frivolous, but Eleanor resented his hedonism, tendency to excessive drinking, love of horse racing, and proximity to her husband. She thought he had in some ways betrayed his roots as a social worker. In a sense little had changed since the Roosevelts' initial stint in

Washington, when he was a young social lion and she was steeped in her own earnest and was much mocked by the glamorous Alice.

The constituency of the Roosevelt family continued to be sharply divided between the Hyde Park and Oyster Bay branches.

Alice's behavior finally exceeded the bounds of what Franklin Roosevelt was prepared to tolerate. He was never concerned about her rather slatternly and semi-public liaison with Senator William E. Borah, the domestic progressive but fervent isolationist, and a bête noire of FDR's. Alice had a notoriously open-plan marriage with Congressman, eventually Speaker, Nicholas Longworth of Cincinati, or "Cinci-nasty," as Alice called it. (Longworth died in 1931.) Alice was known in gossip columns as "Aurora Borah Alice." When at the height of the affair she gave birth to a daughter, her husband, who was a considerable philanderer himself, as well as a prodigious drinker, declined to agree to name the infant "Deborah," as Alice outrageously suggested.

She went on to controversial relationships with two others of her cousin's most prominent enemies, John L. Lewis and Burton Wheeler. Lewis responded to Roosevelt's unleashing of his politicized Justice Department on him with illegal, not to mention unpatriotic, shipyard, automobile, and coal strikes. It was Wheeler, an early Roosevelt supporter, who claimed before Pearl Harbor that FDR would "kill one in four American boys" by departing the confines of Borah's and Wheeler's isolationism. For Alice to get so involved with a sequence of such strident and purblind isolationists raises questions about her romantic motives.

FDR was also prepared to overlook Alice's ostentatious hostility to the New Deal. She festooned herself with gold jewelry at a White House party immediately after the United States departed the gold standard, made frequent references to "getting the pants off Eleanor and onto Franklin," reflected sarcastically on the President's infirmity, never failed to describe Eleanor as a lesbian, and imitated Eleanor's weak chin and buck teeth, even once in the White House at Eleanor's own suggestion.

At first Eleanor tried to discourage Alice from coming to the White House if she didn't enjoy it. "I never want you to come unless you want to come," she wrote. Alice was not to be got rid of that easily. "I adore coming to the White House," she replied, and she let it be known that "there was always a sufficient number of people who didn't like Franklin and hovered around me."[5] But FDR drew the line at her antics with America First. Alice remained prominently in its ranks even after Lindbergh's anti-Semitic speech in Des Moines drove out the other respectable supporters. Alice was left in league with the Silver Shirts, the Deutsch Amerika Bund, Father Coughlin, and the incorrigible Lindbergh. Even Hearst and McCormick had bolted.

The last straw fell when Alice was asked what she thought of her cousin's seeking a third term as president. She snapped: "I'd rather vote for Hitler." FDR said: "I don't want anything to do with that damned woman again," and banned her from the White House.

Alice commented: "They might have said, 'Look here you miserable woman, of course you feel upset because you hoped your brother Ted would finally achieve the presidency and now he hasn't. But after all, here we are. Come if it amuses you.' But they took it all seriously. They took the meanness in the spirit in which it was meant." Ted's disappointments as an office-seeker were hardly an excuse for Alice's conduct. Alice finally allowed, when her cousin was at the height of his powers as a war leader, that after all her malicious jokes at Franklin's expense, "the joke was on us."[6]

She does seem to have played at least a cameo role in the resumption of relations between FDR and Lucy Mercer Rutherfurd. This began in 1941. Lucy had written Franklin a couple of letters in the twenties and had famously attended his presidential inaugurations, watching from a distance from official limousines. She seems to have come to the White House for dinner on August 1, 1941, and from time to time thereafter.[7] The retirement of Missy LeHand, who disapproved of any such relationship, and the heavy travelling schedule of Eleanor facilitated the resumed friendship. Their meetings became quite frequent, and Grace Tully knew to put Mrs. Rutherfurd through when she called, using the name Mrs. Paul Johnson. The old attraction between them was undimmed by time (twenty-two years), had perhaps even been strengthened by enforced absence. Lucy was as gracious, attractive, witty, and full of empathy for Franklin, with all the burdens of his years and office, as ever, and he responded to her as delightedly as ever. They went for drives in the Virginia countryside together. Anna became a go-between and even a chaperone. She was always convinced of the innocence of this revived companionship for her lonely and heavily burdened father.

Alice had always liked Lucy, and she generally approved of infidelity, not that this reprise would necessarily qualify as such, but it was at least a revenant from when Franklin had lived dangerously a whole generation before. It seems also that Alice despised Eleanor even more than she resented Franklin. Her role in this matter was, in any case, peripheral.

Out of respect for TR and for the enduring bonds of family, Franklin and Eleanor Roosevelt maintained some ties with the other Oyster Bay Roosevelts even through these difficult times. The TR branch was overwhelmed by envious stupefaction at the unexampled triumph of their supposedly lightweight cousin, and even more at the rise to great prominence and public esteem in her own right of TR's homely niece and goddaughter. Alice tried to write a newspaper column, to compete with Eleanor's popular and successful "My Day," but, wit though she was, it didn't work. She had plenty of caustic bons mots, but couldn't string together enough consecutive sentences about real subjects to make a go of it.

Theodore Roosevelt Jr.—Ted, as he was known—after serving as governor of Puerto Rico and the Philippines, with distinction in both cases, settled down to a life of muted sour grapes in resentful opposition to his all-conquering cousin. When the war came in 1939, he played a prominent part in America First. As has been described, this group was infested with less-considerable figures than Ted

Roosevelt and was completely outmaneuvered and discredited as a virtual Nazi-Soviet front by the President.

In the parlance of FDR's "Great Arsenal of Democracy" Fireside Chat of December 29, 1940, Ted Roosevelt had become a purveyor of the "pious frauds" that served the interests of the dictators in the American domestic political discussion. All those who knew the Roosevelts knew that Franklin had won another victory; his stance against the Nazis much more closely approached that which President Theodore Roosevelt would have adopted than did Ted and Alice's mindless and spiteful isolationism. " 'Anything to annoy Franklin,' said Alice."[8]

This was not the least of Franklin D. Roosevelt's innumerable successes. He was the true continuator of his illustrious namesake, not just in the nation's greatest office but in character and bearing through the world crisis. It is hard to avoid the impression that some of his relatives were isolationists mainly because they did not want their cousin to have the honor of leading the nation to victory in history's greatest war. Their frustration was aggravated by the knowledge of their own irrelevance to the vast affairs that Franklin was now directing with such deftness and courage, qualities they had long professed to believe he did not possess.

The antics of Ted and Alice split the Oyster Bay Roosevelts, as their brother Kermit, an alcoholic torn between a wife and a mistress, enlisted in the British Army and resigned from membership in the Republican Party. He was eventually designated as an expedition leader in Winston Churchill's quixotic mission to fight in Finland against the Russians. He lunched with Winston Churchill on March 5, 1940, at the Admiralty and was able to enlighten Churchill that the reason his father had not liked Churchill was that he had not stood up when ladies came into the room when he visited the then New York governor in 1900.[9]

Fortunately for the world, it was too late for Finland, so war was avoided between Russia and Britain and France. Instead Kermit floundered with the rest of the British forces in Norway, and eventually shipped out to North Africa. Early in 1941, he was mustered honorably out of the British Army on medical grounds (his alcoholically enlarged liver alarmed the doctors), was returned to the United States, and was confined to a rehabilitation hospital by his brother Archie, as Eleanor's father had been by TR.

———————

At the same time, complexities of relations among the Hyde Park Roosevelts themselves abated somewhat.

The President's only daughter, Anna, was from all accounts a delightful person, attractive, vivacious, intelligent, and unpretentious. She seems to have been universally popular, though she, too, had her marital problems. After the temperamental instability of her second husband, John Boettiger, caused that marriage to unravel, she had a successful and durable marriage with Dr. James Halsted.

As for the President's four sons, the war brought some order into what had been unruly lives. All four served in the armed forces and did honor to the family military tradition (a tradition going back only to TR, to be sure; FDR and Mr. James, as has been recounted, had never fired a shot in anger). Jimmy was a marine, Elliott was in dangerous air reconnaissance for the air force; Franklin and John were in the navy. All were good officers. Before the war, all four of them were somewhat self-indulgent, though John, the youngest, much less than the others. They were brought up in the comfortable means and famous name of their family, and, as they entered or approached manhood, in the atmosphere of the ever greater power and prestige of their father.

The marriage between Franklin and Eleanor had been largely dysfunctional at least since the First World War, and this led to extensive ambiguity in Franklin and Eleanor's parental performance. Eleanor became thoroughly pre-occupied with her causes, and although always dutiful, was rarely a warm person other than with chosen, not begotten, companions. The Roosevelt children thought that Eleanor's search for protégés, like Joseph P. Lash and others in the left-wing American Youth Congress, was an attempt to redress her shortcomings as a parent.[10]

Franklin had mastered early the fatherly appearances, carving the Thanksgiving turkey, taking his sons sailing, making familial allusions in his speeches, gathering all about him on Christmas Eve for a flamboyant reading of Dickens's *A Christmas Carol*. But he revealed nothing of himself to anyone, and certainly not to his sons, and between his political career and his crusade to recover from his illness sufficiently to relaunch his career he had little time to be the doting father he implicitly pretended to be before the public.

The Roosevelt boys grew up, as one writer noticed, to fulfill the famous passage from Fitzgerald's *The Great Gatsby*: "They were careless people. . . . They smashed up things and creatures and then retreated back into their vast carelessness, or whatever it was that kept them together, and let other people clean up the mess they had made."[11] The war redeemed them from this undistinguished regimen. But when the war ended, their father would be dead and the world less indulgent of their carelessness. Life would be less interesting without the overpowering presence of their father as the most powerful and publicized man in the world.

Elliott had always been the most troublesome. He had at first refused to go to college, having disconcerted Dr. Peabody by the roughness with which he contested school sports at Groton. Peabody had described Elliott to FDR as "a fierce player who does not care particularly whether he hurts people or not."[12]

As an adult, Elliott had drifted to Texas, fell into the company of right-wing oil-men and ranchers who disapproved politically of his father. Elliott shamelessly used his position to put rich Texans in touch with the President all through the thirties. At a personal level, especially with women, he was rather louche and inconstant.

Eleanor was horrified at Elliott's behavior and often felt guilty about it. FDR found Elliott's insouciance and immorality interesting, even fascinating, and looked upon Elliott with some professional curiosity. The President was widely regarded as a political trickster, just as at Groton and Harvard he had been considered a little slippery. He was a great and intuitive student of what could be done tactically without surrendering a plausible claim to high moral ground. He had frequently stretched this process to its outer limits, as when he claimed in 1940 that he didn't want to be reelected but could not conscientiously avoid a draft, any more than could the nation's young conscripts. Elliott had a much more cynical notion than his father of how much latitude he could take in any situation without becoming completely outrageous. He sometimes misjudged this and went too far, unlike his father, who had an unfailing precision in these and other matters.

As one chronicler of the Roosevelts put it, Elliott "was the id of the family — the one who understood most clearly the nature of the 'deal' Franklin and Eleanor had made. What he had seen exonerated him in advance, he seemed to believe, for whatever he did or said later on."[13] Elliott considered his father to be, in large measure, an elegant hustler, misleading the country about the extent of his illness; convincing the left he was one of them, when he wanted to make the country safe for the squire of Hyde Park; holding himself out as the defender of the patrician classes, when he in fact regarded them as idiots politically. Elliott certainly realized that at bottom his father was a patriot, and a sincere advocate of help for the disadvantaged and of the right of the successful to enjoy the fruits of their work. But Elliott, other than when put to the test in the war, was a cynic. His father, who was no stranger to that sentiment, felt the restraint of political acceptability and had a core of genuine belief, but was bemused by Elliott's uninhibited self-absorption.

On graduating from Groton in 1928, Elliott and some friends had shipped out along the Gulf of Mexico on a coastal steamer. Discontented with life in the boiler room, he rushed from dockside in Baytown to Houston to the Democratic convention to assist his father in nominating, as he had four years before in Madison Square Garden, Al Smith for president. He went to a university preparatory school in Philadelphia, followed by Princeton. While there he became a baseball player for a semi-professional team in Brooklyn. This led to new complications at Princeton and he left, never to return to college, which had never enthused him anyway, without having completed a course.

Like his brothers, Elliott had been sent out west for a summer, in the TR tradition, to experience the wide open spaces of Wyoming. He became an extremely skilled rodeo performer, using the show name Robinson. In 1929, when his rodeo came to Madison Square Garden, Governor and Mrs. Roosevelt attended and saw young "Robinson" gored, only subsequently realizing that it was Elliott who had been injured (though not too seriously).[14]

Elliott joined an advertising firm and through this connection became the chauffeur of E.L. Cord, the illustrious automobile designer. On one occasion he was apprehended driving Mr. Cord's Duesenberg at an excessive speed, but, on examination of his license establishing him as the governor's son, was given a motorcycle escort into Manhattan.

Elliott's first marriage, to Betty Donner, a prominent Philadelphia heiress, started to breakdown shortly after the honeymoon in 1932. He dumped her at the White House with their infant child and drove west after ten months. His wife admirably gave back to Eleanor a pearl necklace, correctly surmising she would not see her husband again. When he arrived in Little Rock, Arkansas, Elliott was out of money and, invoking the standard Roosevelt procedure, made a collect call to his father. It was soon after FDR's inauguration, and the President came bubbling on to the line asking: "How are you, Bunny?" Elliott was asking for a wire transfer of money. Roosevelt counted out the coins in his pocket and said: "I have only eight dollars myself and I've just shut down the banks. I suggest you stop at some prosperous farmer's house and perhaps earn enough money to continue your trip."[15]

Elliott was feted by the Texas oil rich in Dallas, and shown a large distillery in Mexico that had been set up awaiting the repeal of Prohibition. He continued to California, where William Randolph Hearst offered him the position of aviation editor of the *Los Angeles Examiner*. As with his subsequent offer of the publisher's chair to John Boettiger and Anna Roosevelt, this seems to have been a hedge move by Hearst to retain some entrée to the White House, whose chief occupant he had substantially alienated.

The pattern of the great crackup of Roosevelt marriages had already begun. Curtis Dall, Anna's first husband, a gloomy and reactionary stockbroker whom Anna had embraced to escape the tense atmosphere of her parents' house, was despised by the whole family, including his own children. The Dalls's son eventually changed his name to Curtis Roosevelt. This marriage ended in divorce, to the relief of all participants and onlookers, after a few years. The President and Eleanor were happy to facilitate Anna's intermarital affair with her second husband, John Boettiger, providing cover for trysts in a way that was somewhat morally audacious for the time.

The President sent Anna to try to talk Elliott out of so swiftly divorcing his first wife, but it was unavailing. He divorced Betty Donner in Reno and married Ruth Googins of Texas at once. FDR retaliated at the rejection of his matrimonial advice by what became the time-honored formula of banning the wrongdoer from family Christmas celebrations. This was the doghouse and most of the children suffered it at one time or another, but FDR always brought them back into the fold by some act of reconciliation. It was an itinerant court, Franklin and Eleanor at the center, lent dignity and significance by their importance as well as their demeanor, not by the virtue or brilliance of the young people rotating and ricocheting almost aimlessly around them.

Jimmy was endlessly involved in dubious insurance deals that regularly percolated into the seamier aspects of news reporting. Elliott was more imaginative, becoming a go-between in the shadowy sale of Fokker military aircraft, disguised as civil airliners, to the Soviet Union. This was steering a little close to the wind at a time when the President had a denunciation of war profiteering as a staple of his standard political stump speech. Roosevelt forbade Elliott to go to Russia, and the deal fell through, because the Russians balked at the price. Elliott went on to be Hearst's director of radio operations, in which capacity he took to the airwaves denouncing New Deal measures. His father rose above this irritant as he had risen above so many others. Elliott did provide the useful service of introducing the oilmen Sid Richardson and Clint Murchison to the President. They raised and contributed large sums for his 1936 reelection campaign, hoping to persuade him of the inadvisability of reducing the oil depletion allowance and of the protective tariff against Argentinean beef. They were partially successful.

When the Hearst Corporation wobbled under the weight of the founder's extravagance in 1937, Elliot sought to buy a group of Hearst's radio stations and form them into the Texas State Network. (This was part of his quest to be "a really big man," as Elliot put it, an ambition he never attained.) In pursuit of this deal, Elliot sought a $200,000 loan from John Hartford, the head of the Great Atlantic and Pacific Tea Company (A&P). Elliot telephoned his father from Hartford's office and then handed the phone to Hartford, who was trying to avoid a chain-store tax that would be costly to his business. The President, far too canny to realize what was afoot, hoped Hartford would be helpful to Elliot, because it sounded like a sound venture. (This was one area, as we have seen, where FDR's judgment was not reliable.) When this deal, like most of the Roosevelt sons' commercial brainwaves, hit the wall, Roosevelt intervened with Jesse Jones, the Secretary of Commerce, who persuaded Hartford to accept a 2 percent payback on his loan. Hartford could only say that he had not wished to displease the President, not that he had been promised anything as a quid pro quo for helping Elliot.[16] Whatever the pretensions to being "big," the decisive moments were usually engineered by Mr. President through the vast and complicated web of his contacts. At the Democratic Convention in Chicago in 1940, Elliott became a dupe of the stop-Wallace forces and was cranking up to nominate his benefactor Jesse Jones as vice president when Eleanor descended upon this little insurrection and told Elliott, as if addressing a six-year-old, not to defy his father any further. Elliott desisted.

Shortly after the convention, Elliott, convinced that American participation in the war was imminent, joined the Army Air Corps, becoming a captain. At his thirtieth birthday party his father toasted him as "the first of the family to think seriously and soberly enough about the threat to America to join the country's Armed Services. We're all very proud of him and I'm the proudest." That Elliott made it so quickly to the rank of captain stirred considerable controversy. Cousin Ted, still a partisan conspicuously available for office-seeking at this point, included in his speeches the assertion that Eleanor's favorite song was "I Didn't Raise My Son to be a Private." Amid the controversy, "I Want to Be a Captain Too Clubs" sprang up around the country under the aegis of the Republican Party.[17] Ted was outraged that Franklin put on the airs of great familiarity with the horrors of war when he had not had much exposure to them in 1917 and 1918. His irritation was compounded by his (probably well-founded) conviction of his cousin's insincerity in claiming to be trying to keep the nation out of war now.

Young Franklin would career rather insouciantly through careers and marriages, the first nuptials being the famous wedding with Ethel DuPont. Franklin had had the wildest school and university years, suffering from what one family historian called "narcissism and almost pathological carelessness." He punched photographers and broke their cameras and was a formidable partygoer. At one point he moved into the White House with Ethel but had the White House staff arrange dalliances with other female houseguests, reducing Ethel to a pathetic, underdressed wanderer, distractedly prowling the White House corridors. The President called her "our hot house flower."[18]

John was more restrained, lived quietly in Boston, married young and discreetly, and almost anonymously took his first job as a sales clerk at Filene's department store. He made a better fist than his brothers of carving out a stable and independent life for himself. He secretly apostatized politically, but made no reference to the fact, even within his family, while his father lived.

Elliott's next wife, after Ruth Googins, would be Faye Emerson, whom he met under the auspices of Howard Hughes. Elliott came home on leave in the summer of 1943 and was sent to Los Angeles to inspect Hughes's D-2 aircraft as a possible new reconnaissance aircraft. Hughes, a film mogul as well as an aviator and designer and manufacturer of airplanes, assigned Faye Emerson to the President's son as a business promotion measure. Elliott's infidelities while overseas had already been publicized in the U.S. press, and his wife, Ruth, seriously disconcerted, had gone to the President to talk about it. He told her: "Things happen in war and this is nothing to worry about."[19] He knew his second son better than to have believed that himself.

Elliott sent a friend who was preceding him on home leave to call upon his wife and placate her. His friend had an accident on landing at San Antonio and was hospitalized, where Ruth visited him. These two then fell in love, which assisted Elliott in his spurious claim that he, the gallant airman overseas, was the wronged party. Elliott did recommend the Hughes plane; the War Department bought it, and Elliott married Faye Emerson in November 1944.[20] This marriage lasted less than four years, and Faye tried to commit suicide before it ended. (John Boettiger and Ethel DuPont, when no longer Roosevelt in-laws, did commit suicide.) The five Roosevelt children would ultimately have nineteen spouses. The war, while it did not drastically curtail their romantic activities, did impose some comparative decorum on the professional careers of the President's sons.

The Oyster Bay Roosevelts were not the only segment of U.S. opinion that felt that the young Hyde Park Roosevelts were besmirching the family name with financial skullduggery, wanton and scandalous romantic exploits, and nepotistic preferments. (Given Alice's peccadilloes, Oyster Bay did not qualify as high moral ground matrimonially, but her brothers worked themselves up to a commanding height of sanctimony anyway.) Franklin and Eleanor sailed serenely above it, concerned parents when that was called for, as with Jimmy's potentially cancerous ulcer when they trooped to the Mayo Clinic in 1938, but long-suffering, publicly uncomplaining parents, implicitly sharing the nation's disappointment, conspicuous in the dignity of their own behavior, at other times.

The Oyster Bay relatives were not without their problems, either. Cousin Kermit did not survive the war. He became something of a personality in Anchorage, Alaska, a little like Eleanor's father when he was banished by TR to North Carolina in 1894, and, like Eleanor's father, was alcoholic and depressive. He killed himself with his service revolver on June 3, 1943. Franklin and Eleanor did their best in all respects for his widow and had her often to the White House.

Ted had a braver war and a seemlier end. He finally realized (unlike his sister) that America First was a ragtag bunch of Nazi and Communist sympathizers and naïve isolationists, and retired from it in the spring of 1941. He requested from General Marshall, and received from the reserves, posting to active duty as a regimental infantry commander. He served with distinction in Sicily and finally, after lobbying General Eisenhower personally, in the manner of his family (they generally ignored their cousin but badgered his senior commanders), became the oldest American soldier active in combat in the cross-Channel invasion.

He and his son Quentin would also be the only American father and son in that invasion. In Normandy as he had in Sicily, Ted came ashore with a cane because of arthritis in one hip. He would be completely impervious to heavy fire all about him and be an inspiration to his men. On the day of the invasion he was under constant machine-gun fire for several hours as he conducted his men in small groups to more secure positions. General Omar N. Bradley would rate the performance of Theodore Roosevelt Jr. on D-Day the greatest act of bravery he had ever witnessed in a long and very distinguished career that ultimately raised him to the highest rank, General of the Army.

Once installed in Normandy, Ted Roosevelt was temporary military governor of Cherbourg, and was raised to the rank of major general and division commander in the field by Eisenhower, but before learning of his promotion he died in his sleep of a heart attack. He was only fifty-seven. He was buried in the little town of Sainte Mere Eglise, and had six generals among his pallbearers, including Omar Bradley, George S. Patton, and Lawton Collins. The military band played the apt and stirring hymn "The Son of God Goes Forth to War." He was, along with Douglas MacArthur, the most decorated officer to serve in the United

States Army in World War II, having ultimately received every ground forces combat medal.

General Eisenhower, seconded by General Marshall, and with the strong encouragement of the President, recommended a much-deserved posthumous Congressional Medal of Honor for Ted Roosevelt, the supreme recognition of conspicuous valor, which Theodore Roosevelt Sr. had unsuccessfully aspired to win.* The Congress unanimously approved the award, and the citation began: "For gallantry and intrepidity at the risk of his life and beyond the call of duty," and ended: "He . . . contributed substantially to the successful establishment of the beachhead in France."

The President gave the medal to Ted Roosevelt's widow, also an Eleanor Roosevelt, at the White House, September 22, 1944. He spoke nothing but the truth when he said: "His father would have been proudest."[21] His cousin was a most deserving recipient, but it was still a generous act by the Commander in Chief and head of the family.

As the distinguished *New Yorker* writer A.J. Liebling wrote, TR had been "a dilettante soldier but a first class politician; his son was a dilettante politician and a first class soldier."[22]

TR's other surviving son, Archie, also prevailed upon General Marshall, after the United States entered the war, to send him to a combat theater, and Marshall entrusted him to MacArthur, who had once been TR's military aide. In the noblest tradition of his family, Archie was seriously wounded. He was the only American serviceman to suffer a 100 percent disability in both world wars. He was invalided home from the Pacific, and while beseeching his cousin and Marshall and others for reassignment to combat, he suffered a relapse into tropical malaria that he had contracted while serving under MacArthur. After recovering, he called upon the President at the White House in the autumn of 1944. It was, FDR wrote to Archie's wife, a "nice chat." As he was leaving his cousin's office, Archie saw a crumpled pack of cigarettes and gave Franklin his metal cigarette package holder that he had carried all around the Pacific. The President found this an affecting gesture, though he returned it to Archie's wife. "I want you and the children to have it. But do not, for heaven's sake let him know that I have given it to you," he wrote. He and Archie maintained a very amicable and witty correspondence thereafter. "It marked a moment of partial closure in the long conflict between the Roosevelt branches."[23] The President and the chief of staff were corresponding about how to get Archie back into the war in relative safety right up to FDR's own death.

Franklin D. Roosevelt had well learned the lessons of the pettiness of President Wilson's rejection of TR's attempt to join the war actively in 1917. He rel-

---

* President Theodore Roosevelt was ultimately awarded the medal of honor seventy-five years posthumously. The Roosevelts thus joined the MacArthurs as the only father and son winners of the country's highest military honor.

ished the status his office conferred as paterfamilias. Next to the presidency itself, FDR almost surely considered that the greatest honor he received was recognition, however grudging or entwined with political success, as the head of twentieth century America's greatest public family. Whatever he thought of his cousins or they of him, they were courageous and patriotic, as were his own sons. In this cause, he was determined, whatever Alice's antics, that there would be no spitefulness, no pettifogging, and no settling of ancient scores. Aware of his cousins' importunings of the chief of staff and theater commanders, President Roosevelt discreetly asked that his relatives be accommodated as much as possible in their desire to serve the nation in mortal combat.

II

THE PRESIDENT DELIVERED his 1944 State of the Union message on January 11. He did not follow the format of the previous year and give an uncontroversial call to arms. In domestic as in international affairs, as victory came almost within reach of the Allied armies and naval and air fleets, Roosevelt paid greater attention to the shape of the postwar world. The stirrings of such thoughts would also have been encouraged by the fact that it was an election year. Roosevelt never seriously considered, or pretended to consider, not running for a fourth term. The same reasoning he had employed in 1940 was essentially unaltered, and having gone through the charade of being drafted like the conscripts of Selective Service, he did not feel any need to repeat that refrain in 1944.

There was a powerful argument, going back to Abraham Lincoln in 1864, not to "change horses in the middle of the stream." Roosevelt would not be easy to attack as a war leader. His pre-Pearl Harbor support of the Allies was unassailable, as was his massive defense production program in 1940 and 1941. From five months after the initial Japanese attack, the American war effort had been almost uniformly successful. The principal military and civilian leaders Roosevelt had assembled were demonstrably competent and included a number of outstanding men who, then or subsequently, achieved world historic stature, such as Marshall, MacArthur, Eisenhower, Nimitz, Patton, Truman, Acheson, Adlai Stevenson, and arguably Stimson and Hopkins.

The only threats to Roosevelt's continued incumbency were his health—the perception that he lacked the stamina to finish his work—and the difficulty of getting out the colossal military vote of over ten million, most of them scattered in combat zones at the ends of the earth. Roosevelt had admirably deceived his countrymen for many years about the extent of his disability. He now proposed to put on a grand display of physical and intellectual robustness to undercut any concerns about his physical fitness for office. And he would make himself the unchallengeable champion of the fighting man, not only for his own sake but for the great majority of the public who were wholly devoted to the cause of the American soldier, sailor, and airman overseas. His motive was not exclusively electoral. He had a passionate conviction that the nation's youth must be relaunched into a just and prosperous America.

The January 11 address contained a powerful statement of the President's claim for reelection and plan for postwar America. As was his custom, he deftly combined matters of national interest with simple political expediency and staked out an aggressive position while his opponents were still in complete disarray. New York's forty-two-year-old governor, Thomas E. Dewey, was assumed to be the likely candidate of the Republicans, navigating between Willkie and his "One World" internationalist liberals and Robert A. Taft and his isolationist conservatives.

Roosevelt sent his message to the Congress but read it in a Fireside Chat that night, explaining that he was just recovering from the flu. He recorded his displeasure on "returning from my journeyings . . . to find faulty perspectives in Washington." These consisted of many forms of complacency and lassitude: "bickerings, self-seeking partisanship, stoppages of work, inflation, business as usual, politics as usual, luxury as usual."[24] He reminded his listeners of "the lessons of 1918. In the summer of that year the tide turned in favor of the Allies. But this government did not relax. In fact our national effort was stepped up. . . . The President called for 'force to the utmost. . . .' And in November, only three months later, Germany surrendered. That is the way to fight and win a war—all out—and not with half an eye on the battlefronts abroad and the other eye and a half on personal, selfish, or political interests here at home." (Some of his successors, especially Lyndon Johnson in Vietnam, would have profited from remembering the wisdom of this admonition.)

In order to galvanize the whole country to the supreme and equitable burden-sharing of ultimate victory, he proposed "a realistic tax law which will tax all unreasonable profits . . . and reduce the ultimate cost of the war to our sons and daughters." He proposed to fight his ancient bugbear of war profiteering by continuing the law for the renegotiation of war contracts, and called for a "cost of food law," would provide reasonable prices for the farmer and the consumer. He asked for reenactment of the October 1942 stabilization statute, without which "the country might just as well expect price chaos by summer." And he repeated his familiar request for a national service law, which would enable the conscription of people to domestic tasks on the basis of need and would eliminate practically all work stoppages. "National service is the most democratic way to wage a war. Like selective service for the armed forces, it rests on the obligation of each citizen to serve his nation to his utmost where he is best qualified."

This was a comprehensive program and it possessed considerable merit, but it also demonstrated the extent to which Roosevelt had forgotten the virtues of the free market as a determinant of supply and demand. Fixing all prices, conscripting the entire work force, and decreeing what the government would pay for whatever it wanted could conceptually be justified in the war emergency, and there were bad private sector practices the President rightly wished to avoid. But he obviously had no idea in the world of what a vast, cumbrous, arbitrary mass of rules and regulators he wished to rivet onto the back of the nation. To him, "these five measures together form a just and equitable whole." Theoretically, perhaps; implementation would have been quite a challenge, as cool heads in the Congress realized.

In the United States as in Great Britain and Canada, the war had restored prosperity after the free market had failed in the early thirties, and there was no consensus about how fully or soon the free market should be restored. It would be to America's advantage that the congressional leaders favored an early restoration of the private sector in all its spontaneity. The United States thus enjoyed a greater and swifter return of postwar prosperity than any other major country. Roosevelt had more faith in centralized planning than was justified in peacetime.

The President raised the voting problem in his address, castigating those who would leave the administration of the election in the armed forces to the forty-eight states' statutes, which the armed forces would be unable to implement. He was the champion of the interests of the fighting men, in combat and when they returned, and particularly he was the champion of their right to vote. "No amount of legalistic argument can becloud this issue in the eyes of the ten million American citizens [affected]. Surely the signers of the Constitution did not intend a document which even in wartime would be construed to take away the franchise of any of those who are fighting to preserve the Constitution itself." It was a powerful argument.

The problem he had was that the southern Democrats feared that the measure Roosevelt proposed would vacate the poll tax and other spurious measures invoked in the South to prevent African-Americans from voting, and the Republicans suspected that the great majority of the military personnel would vote for the Commander in Chief, especially after his G.I. Bill of Rights was adopted. It was a shabby alliance. They controlled the Congress between them and Roosevelt couldn't attack them with the vehemence he would wish—he didn't want to split his party, because he still could work with southern Democrats on most issues.

The southern Democrats feared that if African-Americans voted freely, they would never be docile again, and they would begin by deposing a large number of bigoted incumbents. Their fear was well-founded, but the answer, as the President knew and frequently stated, was a more liberal policy, not an entrenchment of oppression. Though Roosevelt didn't focus on the civil rights aspect of the dispute directly, he referred repeatedly to the right of all citizens to vote. It was the beginning of the end for the solid Democratic South and for the exclusion of African-Americans from full citizenship, but the end would be another twenty years coming.

Roosevelt gave the outline of his postwar program as a "Second Bill of Rights." The inalienable political rights on which the Republic was founded had, as the economy had expanded and become more complicated, "proved inadequate to assure us equality in the pursuit of happiness . . . 'Necessitous men are not free men.' People who are hungry and out of a job are the stuff of which dictatorships are made." The rights that he wished to have proclaimed were: a "useful and remunerative job," earning power sufficient "to provide adequate food and clothing and recreation," returns to the farmer "which will give him and his family a decent living," freedom to all businessmen from unfair competition and foreign and domestic monopoly, decent housing, medical care, education, and "protection from the economic fears of old age, sickness, accident, and unemployment," for every family and individual in the country, irrespective, the President portentously emphasized, of race and creed.

Even after eleven years in office, Franklin D. Roosevelt was no mere servitor; his proposals were ambitious and highly marketable politically. "America's own rightful place in the world depends in large part upon how fully these and similar rights have been carried into practice for our citizens. For unless there is security here at home, there cannot be lasting peace in the world." The New Deal and winning the war were complementary objectives, and world peace depended on America's equitable prosperity and moral credibility as a just society. Isolationism, laissez-faire economics, and racial segregation would all be endangered political species in postwar America.

The President presented his radical program in dramatic terms. Where the first Bill of Rights had been for the citizens opposite their government, Roosevelt was proclaiming a Bill of Rights to be enacted by the government in favor of the citizens, "positive liberty through government" rather than "negative liberties against government."[25] Failure to enact it would mean that "even though we shall have conquered our enemies on the battlefield abroad, we shall have yielded to the spirit of Fascism here at home. . . . Our fighting men abroad—and their families at home, expect such a program and have the right to insist upon it. It is to their demands that this Government should pay heed rather than to the whining demands of selfish pressure groups who seek to feather their nests while young Americans are dying. . . . For America in this war, there is only one front. There is one line of unity which extends from the hearts of the people at home to the men of our attacking forces in our farthest outposts. When we speak of our total effort, we speak of the factory and the field and the mine, as well as of the battleground—we speak of the soldier and the civilian, the citizen and his Government.

"Each and every one of us has a solemn obligation under God to serve this Nation in its most critical hour—to keep this nation great—to make this Nation greater in a better world."

This stentorian call to arms fell on cloth ears in the Congress but resonated powerfully in the country. The Congress finally passed a feeble federal measure for overseas voting by the armed forces, which Roosevelt did not veto or sign, and thus it became law eventually. As a result of it, about 85,000 men voted, barely 1 percent of what would have been the ordinary turnout.

First thing every Monday morning that Congress was in session and that he was in Washington, Roosevelt continued to meet in his bedroom with the Democratic congressional leaders. He was in bed and Vice President Wallace, Speaker Rayburn, Senate Majority Leader Barkley, and House Majority Leader McCormack gathered round his bedside to discuss strategy for the legislative program. At one such session in February 1944 he ignored the advice of three of his visitors and vetoed what he considered a completely insufficient tax bill. Only Wallace supported the President in the veto.[26] Roosevelt objected in his veto message that he had asked Congress for a tax bill that would add $10.5 billion to annual revenues and had received a bill that provided net increases of only about 10 percent of that figure. He described the measure adopted as more of a tax relief bill and an inequitable one at that, favoring various interests championed by the logrolling regional barons of the Congress.

Barkley was outraged at the sarcastic tenor of the President's message. He was an accomplished, if loquacious, public speaker and a Paducah, Kentucky, political wheel horse who had served thirty-two years in the Congress, including the last seven challenging years as majority leader. He was not at ease with Roosevelt's high-handed, urbane, and idiosyncratic methods of managing relations between the executive and legislative branches.

Barkley revolted against Roosevelt and denounced the President's veto as, among other transgressions, "a calculated and deliberate assault upon the legislative integrity of every member of Congress." Roosevelt, at Hyde Park, was completely unconcerned, and wrote a conciliatory letter. The President's veto was overridden, the congressional barons had their moment of rebellious enthusiasm, and Roosevelt had made his populist gesture.

The Congress chose to increase borrowings required by conducting the war rather than follow Roosevelt's ideal of equitable fiscal sacrifice until victory was achieved. (Passage of the tax bill saved the President personally, as a tree farmer, $3,000 a year that he would have foregone under his own proposal.[27])

During the same month, Roosevelt received a visit from members of the Negro Newspaper Publishers Association. There was a lengthy recitation of well-founded grievances about discrimination in the armed forces. Roosevelt complimented his visitors on their statement. "It is perfectly true, there is definite discrimination in the treatment of the colored . . . troops. . . . And you are up against it, as you know perfectly well. . . . The trouble lies fundamentally in the attitude of certain white people—officers down the line who haven't got much more education, many of them, than the colored troops. . . . You know the kind of person it is. We all do. We don't have to do more than think of a great many people that we know. And it has become not a question of orders—they are repeated fairly often. . . . It's a question of the personality of the individual. And we are up against it, absolutely up against it."[28]

Roosevelt could have been talking about his own press secretary, Stephen Early, a southern white supremacist. The President saw the problem and there was no doubt where his sympathies were, but he judged it too dangerous at this point to break up his party over this issue (or any other). His preferred method was effectively by stealth: his benefit programs were color-blind, and there had been great advances by African-Americans in the military. The G.I. Bill of Rights would make no racial distinctions. He was certain that returning black soldiers and sailors and airmen could not and would not be treated with the condescension and brutality that they had known before. It would be a very long struggle.

The only fast track he could see was the fusion between liberal Democrats and reform Republicans, once cured of their isolationist tendencies. This was the great project he had wished to bruit with Wendell Willkie. Willkie was imploding as a political force, and the true face of the Republican Party was somewhere between Thomas E. Dewey and Robert A. Taft. When the war was over and the times were better and the idea had, with some leadership, come of age, Roosevelt might have been prepared to lead this crusade too, but not now, in the middle of a war, with everything on a knife edge.

III

SINCE ROOSEVELT, for reasons he had explained at Teheran (somewhat pusillanimous and disbelieved by Stalin though they were), declined to become directly involved in shaping postwar Poland, Churchill took on the thankless and laborious task of trying to broker an arrangement between Stalin and the Poles.

Churchill and Eden had the leaders of the Polish government in exile in London to Chequers for a strenuous session on February 6, 1944. The Poles were led by their prime minister, Stanislaw Mikolajczyk. Churchill, at the request of the London Poles, had sent a telegram to Stalin January 28 putting certain questions to him, and had received satisfactory answers from him through the British ambassador in Moscow, to whom Stalin had granted an interview four days before. The ambassador, Sir Archibald Clark Kerr, reported that Stalin guaranteed a "free and independent Poland, as much so as Czechoslovakia, and he would not try to influence either country's choice of government." He also promised a formal Soviet guarantee if this were requested, complete assistance in expelling the Germans from Poland, freedom of movement back to Poland of Poles who found themselves in the Soviet Union under the frontiers agreed at Teheran, and a full right of return of the exiles to set up a broad-based government in Poland. Stalin had sent Churchill a cable the day before, complaining of anti-Russian comments by Polish émigré officials, including General Wladyslaw

Anders, commander of Polish forces in the Middle East and Italy. But Churchill, in sending Stalin's message to Roosevelt, described it as "by no means devoid of hope," having described Clark Kerr's interview as "encouraging."[29]

Stalin had claimed that the Poles had ordered their courageous and numerous underground in Poland not to cooperate with the Russians. Mikolajczyk denied this and said he had shown the British his instructions, which were never to oppose the Russians, and to cooperate wholeheartedly with them as soon as relations were normalized between Moscow and the London Poles. This was the only card the Polish exiles had to play, but they were holding out for better terms than so skilled and ruthless a poker player as Stalin was prepared to concede. Mikolajczyk pointed out that the Polish underground was prepared to come into the open and attack the Germans with all its strength in cooperation with the Russians, but contingent on maintaining their own organization independently of the Polish units that had been formed in Russia, and contingent upon acceptance of frontiers less generous to the Soviet Union than those that had been agreed at Teheran. Mikolajczyk objected that the Russians had already clandestinely set up in Warsaw a Peasants' Party in opposition to the London government. Churchill pointed out on many occasions throughout the afternoon that if agreement were not reached, Stalin would occupy all of Poland and impose whatever he wished on the prostrate country. The Poles wrangled at length about Lvov, which they opposed handing over to the Russians, and they disputed the exact demarcation of the Curzon Line, the proposed border between Poland and the Soviet Union.

Churchill remonstrated fiercely with them that Poland had lost its independence 150 years before, except for the brief interlude between the world wars, and that though the Polish soldiers and airmen then in England "had made themselves both loved and respected," one of three things would happen: an agreement would be reached between the Russians, Poles, and British; an agreement would be reached between the British and Russians alone and implemented by the Russians with the approval of the Western Allies; or nothing would be agreed, "while the Russian steamroller moved over Poland, a Communist Government was set up in Warsaw and the present Polish Government was left powerless to do anything but make its protests to the world at large."[30]

Further debate ensued over the proposed eastern border of Poland, but Mikolajczyk claimed that what was really at stake was the independence of Poland. He was obviously right, as Churchill repeatedly recognized during the conversation, but the Poles had no bargaining position. Churchill emphasized that their best and only hope was an agreement that Britain and the United States would then try to make the subject of specific performance by Stalin. Unfortunately, showing the stubbornness of his people, which, as Churchill pointed out, had caused immeasurable tragedies to be brought down on Poland over centuries, Mikolajczyk clung to his version of the Curzon Line. Churchill warned that "Poland had taken many wrong turns in her history and that a refusal now might be the most fatal and disastrous of all."[31] The meeting, of which Churchill furnished Roosevelt an exhaustive account (from which these quotations are drawn), concluded with Churchill's saying that he would advise Stalin that the Poles considered their previous position on Poland's borders to be "alterable," that they would consider broadening their government, and that Poland would then be "a strong, free, independent state."[32] Churchill said he could get Stalin's commitment to this, but he could not have been optimistic about his ability to deliver Stalin's compliance with an agreement guaranteeing Polish independence. It also seems that Roosevelt's complete abstention from any of these discussions was not based on fears of the Polish vote in the upcoming American elections but on the recognition that the only possible mitigation of Stalin's conduct in Poland would be the ability of the Western Allies to trade something else for Soviet moderation toward the Poles. There would be no shortage of enticements that could be used in horse-trading with Stalin, starting with money. Stimson's notes on an extensive strategic exchange between him and Roosevelt in August 1944 clearly state that the possibility of atomic power, in both its civilian and military applications, could help achieve "the necessity of bringing Russia . . . into the fold of Christian civilization."[33]

In early 1944, a pre-Overlord, pre-atomic age, all that the champions of Poland had with which to deter or persuade Stalin was the collaboration of the Polish underground with the Russian "liberators" and the goodwill of the Western Allies. Stalin did not care about casualties in Poland and was therefore not much concerned with the help of the Polish underground. He knew that the anti-Nazi resistance could just as easily be anti-Russian and that if the Germans killed them all it could make his own designs easier to achieve. In Stalin's sinister mind, goodwill had no value.

Roosevelt hoped that a year later the British and Americans would hold most of Germany and Western Europe and possibly possess atomic power as well as unlimited resources of all kinds. Then, an imaginative combination of sticks and carrots wielded and proffered by him in the apotheosis of his talents at personal diplomacy might yield better results than Churchill's present admirable but thankless efforts. For whatever combination of reasons, Roosevelt's acute political intuition warned him to steer as clear as he could of these discussions, at least in their early stages.

He had explained his position at some length to Churchill in a cable of February 7, 1944. "I recognize that because of treaty obligations with both sides you are more directly concerned with the immediate issues between the USSR and Poland. Our primary concern is the potential danger of this situation to the essential unity which was so successfully established at Moscow and Teheran. It is for this reason that I have confined the official action of this Government to a tender of good offices looking towards the resumption of relations between Poland and the Soviet Union." Roosevelt enclosed the text of a lengthy message he had just sent Stalin on the subject, asking avoidance of words or any "unilateral act [which could] transform this special question into one adversely affecting the larger issues of future international collaboration . . . I feel I should ill serve our common interest if I failed to bring these facts to your attention."[34] Churchill, tellingly, glosses over these discussions completely in his memoirs, making no reference to Polish matters between the Teheran Conference at the beginning of December 1943 and the arrival of the Russians on the Polish border in March 1944.

Stalin was quite relaxed about giving guarantees of Polish independence that neither Churchill nor Roosevelt, much less the Poles themselves, thought worthy of the slightest credence. But such declarations could have, as they eventually did, considerable value in the forum of world opinion, and especially domestic opinion in the United States and the United Kingdom and the other Western countries, in mobilizing resistance to Soviet advances in Europe.

Churchill reported to Roosevelt on February 21, 1944, that Mikolajczyk and his colleagues had gone as far as they could, without the support of most of the parties they were supposedly representing, in saying they agreed to Churchill's February 6 proposals, and hoped they could bring their coalition partners and supporters into line if Stalin agreed. Churchill cabled Stalin February 20 that the Poles had made substantial concessions. Ambassador Clark Kerr was directed to seek a meeting with Stalin and narrow the gap between him and the Poles.

Roosevelt congratulated Churchill and sent a message to Stalin supporting Churchill's proposals and saying that their acceptance would expedite defeat of Germany and assure the assistance of the Polish underground.[35]

Stalin received Clark Kerr February 29, 1944. "It was not a pleasant talk," reported the ambassador at once to Churchill, who forwarded his extensive cable immediately to Roosevelt. Stalin "dismissed with a snigger . . . snorted," and otherwise brushed aside claims that the Poles were accommodating him. He was well aware of the fissures in the Polish factions and the lack of clarity in Mikolajczyk's supposed acceptance of his terms. Stalin purported to blame the Poles for stirring up a rift between Russia and its principal allies and asserted that "the Russians and British shed their blood while the Poles sat on [Eden's] back or hid behind Churchill's." When asked for "constructive suggestions," Stalin said he insisted on the Curzon Line and removal of designated anti-Soviet elements from the putative Polish government. He said he would accept two Americans, whom he named, one of them a Polish-American priest and certainly not a Communist, to illustrate his broadmindedness. Prior to the Allied Overlord landings, Stalin was at some pains not to antagonize the British and Americans completely. Clark Kerr described it as a "dreary and exasperating conversation."[36]

Stalin formally and succinctly replied to Churchill on March 4, 1944, writing that the "solution of the question of Soviet-Polish relations has not yet matured." Churchill forwarded this "most discouraging" response to Roosevelt at once, though Stalin claimed to have already communicated it to Roosevelt. "Not yet mature" was Stalin's euphemistic way of saying that he would set up a puppet regime in Poland when he had commenced occupation of that country.

Churchill replied to Stalin March 7, playing the only real card he had: "Force can achieve much but force supported by the goodwill of the world can achieve more." He hinted that the issue could produce a rift with the Western Allies. Churchill advised Roosevelt March 21 that he would shortly be reporting to Parliament that the Russo-Polish discussions had "broken down, that we continue to recognize the Polish Government, with whom we have been in continuous relations since the invasion of Poland in 1939 [by Hitler and Stalin], that we now consider all questions of territorial change must await the armistice or peace conferences of the victorious powers, and that in the meantime we can recognize no forcible transferences of territory."[37]

Roosevelt responded the next day, detaching himself thoroughly from the discussions by referring to "the Anglo-Soviet disagreement about Poland," and adding: "I hope your strategy will accomplish the best possible advantage to both of us."[38] He had already advised Churchill in a cable of March 16 that he thought the whole Polish matter can "well be laid aside . . . we can well let nature take its course." He knew as certainly as Churchill and Stalin what would be the verdict of "nature" in this case. So matters were left for some months.

Unless some higher considerations could be brought to bear on Stalin by Roosevelt when the Western Allies had acquired a stronger position in the European theater, Poland's fate was sealed, as Churchill had explicitly explained to Mikolajczyk at Chequers on February 6. He informed Stalin, via Clark Kerr April 1 that: "His Majesty's Government can only retire from the ungrateful role of mediator and announce their failure."[39] Also on April 1, Churchill cabled Roosevelt, with a copy of his note to Stalin, the hope that Stalin's "bark may be worse than [his] bite and that [the Russians] have a great desire not to separate themselves from their British and American allies. Their conduct about Finland has been temperate and their attitude towards Rumania and Bulgaria seems to be helpful."[40]

Discussions of Italian affairs also took a lot of Churchill's and Roosevelt's attention in the early months of 1944, as their armies advanced at a snail's pace up the Italian peninsula. The Anzio landings in Italy, near Rome, took place January 22. Churchill described this as a "cat-claw" and professed his customary confidence, as with all diversionary operations, that great things would result from it, possibly including the general destruction of the German army in Italy. Nothing of the kind occurred. Field Marshal Kesselring deftly redeployed his army and almost drove the invaders into the sea. They hung on desperately, but were stalled in a narrow perimeter while the forces advancing up the Italian peninsula were stalled before Monte Cassino. Churchill, instead of coming to the conclusion that Italy was not propitious country for an offensive, as could be deduced from a glance at a topographical map, now began the predicted (by Roosevelt and his military advisors) agitation for cancellation of Anvil, the southern France invasion that had been agreed to with Stalin at Teheran, in favor of a further buildup in Italy.

Eisenhower, consulted by Roosevelt and Marshall, demonstrating his remarkable qualities as a soldier-diplomat, managed a partial increase in the resources available for Italy but only slightly deferred Anvil, not sufficiently to require approval from Stalin. Roosevelt warily declined Churchill's proposal for a Combined Chiefs of Staff meeting to discuss allocation of resources in the Mediterranean in a cable of February 9. He envisioned an initial five- to seven-division landing for Overlord and an opening two-division landing for Anvil.

A good-natured and at times rather entertaining tug of war continued through this time between Churchill and Roosevelt over the composition of the Italian government. Roosevelt wanted to dispense with the king, Victor Emmanuel, and the new prime minister, Marshal Pietro Badoglio, as soon as possible. Roosevelt considered them both too tainted by association with Mussolini, and he wanted to introduce six anti-Fascist, non-Communist parties into the government that was advancing slowly in the baggage train of the Allied armies in Italy. Churchill was particularly mistrustful of Count Carlo Sforza, an opposition figure who eventually became one of Western Europe's most distinguished postwar foreign ministers.

The tables had turned since Algiers, where Roosevelt was flippant about fraternizing with Darlan. Here, he was squeamish about association with people not greatly, if at all, more presentable, and Churchill was the champion of expediency.

In a message to Roosevelt on February 13 Churchill explained the rationale for his Italian policy. Victor Emmanuel and Badoglio were the legal government, with whom peace had been contracted. "This Italian Government is tame and completely in our hands. It will obey our directions far more than any other that we may laboriously constitute . . . out of the worn out debris of political parties, none of whom have the slightest title by election or prescription. A new Italian Government will have to make its reputation with the Italian people by standing up to us." He recounted his "strong support" over Darlan, about which the State Department now seemed "rueful . . . Looking back upon it, I consider [our policy] was right. Several thousand British and American soldiers are alive today because of it and it got us Dakar" (and the famous battleship *Richelieu*).[41]

Roosevelt was concerned that the Allies not become discredited by associating with unregenerate Fascists and give a postwar advantage to the Communists in Italy. He rejected Stalin's effort to gain a seat on the Italian Control Commission, and was interested in resuscitating the democratic political parties of Italy as soon as possible. Roosevelt was back March 7, suggesting a "Lieutenant of the Realm" in Italy following the king's abdication, and he suggested the respected quasi-socialist philosopher Benedetto Croce. Roosevelt was concerned that the Allies might be reduced to quelling pro-democratic demonstrations by force.[42] Roosevelt was impatient: "The political situation in Italy has developed rapidly . . . the military situation has not kept pace." Stalin had sent an ambassador to Badoglio, furnishing the hard-pressed Churchill with another argument against the "ambitious windbags," as he called the Italian politicians. He privately reiterated the hope of keeping "that old trickster Sforza out or in a minor position."[43]

Churchill's immovability on this subject was almost perverse. Once the Italian campaign was thoroughly bogged down, there was no possible military advantage to continuing with Victor Emmanuel and Badoglio, and they were a political liability. Churchill the convinced monarchist would have done better to promote the cause of Victor Emmanuel's son, Umberto, from the start.

Compromise with Roosevelt and others was achieved when the king did abdicate in favor of Umberto on April 12, 1944, and Badoglio brought Croce, Sforza, and the Communist leader Palmiro Togliatti into his cabinet as ministers without portfolio. Badoglio continued as prime minister and minister of foreign affairs until the fall of Rome in June, when he retired. His remarkable career had spanned victory at Monte Sabotino, defeat at Caporetto and victory at Vittorio Veneto in the First World War, the Italian embassy in Rio de Janeiro, the governorships of Libya and Ethiopia, and two stints as chief of the Italian general staff. The second term abruptly ended when he resigned in protest over Mussolini's invasion of Greece, though it is not clear whether his demurral was moral or expedient, though he had always opposed the operation. He was the sort of sly survivor Churchill tended to like, and he probably served the Allies as well as had Darlan, without having been tainted by treason or having failed to deliver his country's navy, unlike Darlan in both respects.

————

There were other abrasions between Roosevelt and Churchill, on matters of Britain's dollar reserves and the oil rights of both countries in the Middle East. There was a division in the U.S. administration between Morgenthau and other Treasury officials, who were concerned that there could be a congressional backlash at a time Lend-Lease was shipping consumer goods to Britain, if Britain's dollar reserves rose above a billion dollars. They were well above that in the spring of 1944 and the fear was expressed in the Congress that Britain was effectively picking America's pocket. Reduction of Lend-Lease aid would force Britain to spend these balances, and it was at the Lend-Lease level that these questions were argued in the Congress. Roosevelt managed to keep the lid on it, but any airing of the question aroused Churchill's unease.

In cable exchanges of February 22 and 24 and March 3, Roosevelt tried to lay to rest British concerns that the United States was, as he wrote, "making sheeps' eyes" at British oil rights in Iran and Iraq, and sought assurance that Britain was not trying to "horn in on" American oil rights in Saudi Arabia. The required assurances were reciprocally given, but the strategic jockeying had already begun between the oil companies and junior government commercial officials of both countries.

Another area of minor disagreement between the British and the Americans was in Yugoslavia. The British mission to Yugoslavia's partisan resistance forces, led by Marshal Josip Broz Tito, included the swashbuckling brigadier and M.P. Fitzroy Maclean, the illustrious and sardonic novelist Evelyn Waugh, and Churchill's raffish son, Randolph.*

Churchill was a monarchist in Yugoslavia as in Italy, and favored the restoration of the Serbian king, Peter II. The king's defense minister, General Draza Mihailovich, had fought the Germans less than he had fought some of the non-Serbian factions in Yugoslavia. Tito was a Croatian Communist, though not a slavish follower of Stalin, and would not tolerate a monarchy, especially a Serbian one. This cauldron possessed all the potential for disaster proper to the Balkans.

Roosevelt, conforming more to his performance with Darlan and less to his continuing objections to Badoglio, moderately favored the king, but was more interested in promoting a common front between Tito and Mihailovich against the Germans. This was not practical, but neither was Churchill's plan for Tito to serve King Peter while Mihailovich was put over the side. Churchill deserted Mihailovich and endorsed Tito, although the king told him Tito would never work with a monarch. And Churchill asked Roosevelt on April 6 not to send a mission to Mihailovich.[44]

Roosevelt agreed two days later to cancel the OSS mission[45] and contentedly left it to Churchill thereafter to sort out the conflicting factions and interests in that country. Tito would impose a thirty-five-year lid on Yugoslavia, following which it disintegrated and erupted, drawing in the Americans and the British and many other countries.

Overshadowing everything all through these months was the approach of Overlord. Winston Churchill, perhaps somewhat defensively, given the stubbornness and ingenuity of his resistance to the cross-Channel invasion and the disappointing progress in his preferred theater of Italy, steadily volunteered to Roosevelt his mounting enthusiasm as D-Day approached. He concluded his cable to Roosevelt of March 18, 1944 (which was mainly about Turkish matters): "I am hardening for OVERLORD as the time gets nearer." On April 1 he similarly concluded: "I have seen a lot of your splendid troops over here lately. As you

---

* Waugh and Churchill were friends, but when Churchill had a cancer checkup in England many years later and a biopsy recorded a benign tumor, Waugh wrote in his diary that the medical profession could be relied upon to find and remove "the one part of Randolph that wasn't malignant." They were an improbable pair to be bucketing about the Balkans on behalf of His Majesty's Government. They enlivened their time there with the outrageous canard that Tito was, in fact, a woman. This was debunked when Tito, in the presence of a British delegation, went for a swim in the Adriatic in an exiguous bathing suit.

know I harden for it the nearer I get to it. Eisenhower is a very large man." (Merchant shipping losses in the battle of the Atlantic had declined from 659,500 tons in February 1942 to 378,400 tons in February 1943, and to 70,000 tons in February 1944. The Allies were sinking more U-boats than they were losing merchantmen and the Americans were delivering almost two whole divisions per week to the United Kingdom. These developments completely exceeded German expectations, which invariably underestimated U.S. military capacities. It is little wonder Churchill had encountered American forces in the home islands.[46]

And on April 12, Churchill again wrote Roosevelt: "I am becoming very hard set upon OVERLORD." He had spoken to a group of British and American generals of his "confidence in the result of this extraordinary but magnificent operation . . . I do not agree with the loose talk which has been going on on both sides of the Atlantic about the undue heavy casualties which we shall sustain. In my view it is the Germans who will suffer very heavy casualties when our band of brothers gets among them."[47] "I'm glad you feel hardened about OVERLORD," Roosevelt had already replied appreciatively, March 20.[48]

Frictions inevitably arose, especially over the widening difference between the Rooseveltian postimperialist, liberal, ostensibly benign method of meeting postwar Communism and the Churchillian, imperial, and confrontational method. But both policies were based on a swift revival of France, Germany, and Italy, and the two leaders made the effort to ensure that their personal relations were excellent. They exchanged photographs and paintings (Churchill hung the painting of Roosevelt in his bedroom in his home at Chartwell). Churchill expressed great sympathy on the death of Harry Hopkins's younger son Stephen, who was killed in action in the Pacific war, aged only eighteen, and on the death from a coronary of Secretary of the Navy Frank Knox, April 28, 1944.[49] (He was replaced by his talented undersecretary, James V. Forrestal.) For Harry Hopkins, Churchill had inscribed on parchment and sent to him the lines from the last scene of Macbeth: "Your son, my lord, has paid a soldier's debt; He only liv'd but till he was a man; The which no sooner had his prowess confirm'd In the unshrinking station where he fought, But like a man he died."[50] Churchill had great fondness and respect for Hopkins, "one of the paladins," and saw him as a powerful supporter of the Anglo-American alliance. Winston Churchill was always at his very best in times of great strain, sorrow, and poignancy, when his culture, fortitude, and magnanimity conjoined.

———

The Joint Chiefs of Staff had urged Roosevelt to amend his unconditional surrender policy, because they thought it was serving the Nazis by encouraging a more tenacious resistance. Intelligence reported that German propaganda was representing this requirement as a determination to destroy Germany. Roosevelt declined to alter it, at least publicly, because he was concerned that it would arouse Russian suspicions that such a change signaled a first step in seeking a negotiated peace. Once possessed of any such idea, Stalin could probably be relied upon to seek the same objective and to get there first. Roosevelt did tell Hull that there was room for varied application of the principle. He tried to send the message that the requirement of unconditional surrender could be varied if the Nazis were dispensed with and replaced by a respectable German government. He believed that the treatment of the post-Mussolini Italian government demonstrated that.

Reports of Nazi atrocities, especially against Jews, and of Japanese outrages were becoming steadily more persistent in the opening months of 1944. Morgenthau took up this cause and raised it strenuously with Hull. He directly accused Breckinridge Long of being anti-Semitic, which Long denied (unconvincingly), and he commissioned a report from Randolph Paul, the able general counsel of the U.S. Treasury. Paul charged that the State Department had not only failed to do what it could to help the Jews of Europe but had set out to obstruct private-sector efforts to help them.

Morgenthau, Paul, and the Treasury's foreign funds director, John Pehle, attended upon the President in January 1944, and impressed him by the vehemence and logic of their arguments. Roosevelt put up a partial defense of Breckinridge Long by pointing out that many of the people who had been personally championed by Rabbi Stephen Wise had turned out to be "bad people." He agreed with most of what his visitors told him, and after discussion between Morgenthau and Undersecretary of State Edward Stettinius, the War Refugee Board was set up, with Pehle as acting director. Hull, faced with the likely proportions of the problem, reverted to the righteous old judge he was and supported the new initiative, as did Stettinius. Stimson was a strong supporter.

Roosevelt was well aware of Arab opposition to the continued arrival of large numbers of Jews in Palestine, and of British reservations also, largely because of concern for their relations with the Arabs. But he determined to act, initially by setting up refugee centers in the United States. He accepted 1,000 Jewish refugees from Italy and placed them in a camp in Oswego, New York, and announced his plan after the fact to the Congress.

On March 21, he issued his statement on German and Japanese war crimes (chapter 19). These barbarities were denounced generally, including incidents in specific European and Chinese cities and savage mistreatment of prisoners of war. Then: "In one of the blackest crimes of all history . . . the wholesale systematic murder of the Jews of Europe goes on unabated every hour. As a result of the events of the last few days hundreds of thousands of Jews, who while living under persecution have at least found a haven from death in Hungary and the Balkans, are now threatened with annihilation as Hitler's forces descend more heavily upon these lands. . . . The United Nations have made it clear that they will pursue the guilty and deliver them up in order that justice be done. That warning applies not only to the leaders but also to their functionaries and subordinates in Germany and in satellite countries. All who knowingly take part in the deportation of Jews to their death in Poland or Norwegians and French to their death in Germany are equally guilty with the executioner. All who share the guilt will share the punishment.

"Hitler is committing these crimes against humanity in the name of the German people. I ask every German and every man everywhere under Nazi domination to show the world by his action that in his heart he does not share these insane criminal desires. Let him hide these pursued victims, help them to get over their borders, and do what he can to save them from the Nazi hangman. . . . Until the victory that is now assured is won, the United States will persevere in its efforts to rescue the victims of brutality of the Nazis and the Japs. . . . In the name of justice and humanity let all freedom-loving people rally to this righteous undertaking." It was late, but it was still useful. It is clear from this statement that Roosevelt envisioned the Jewish survivors returning to the countries where they had been oppressed, once liberal regimes had been established there, since he asked unoccupied countries of Europe and Asia "temporarily to open their frontiers to all victims of oppression" and promised to provide for their maintenance. Portugal, Spain, Sweden, Turkey, and the Vatican City had distinguished to good records in this area, unlike Switzerland, but they could only palliate slightly the Nazi horrors. Roosevelt was well aware of the problems of a Jewish state in Palestine. Although this was one of those many issues that he judged were better tackled closer to the day when they had to be determined, his early leanings were to a multicultural state including a haven and welcome for Jews, rather than a Jewish homeland as such, at least in the Middle East. He had proposed a Jewish domain in Ethiopia, and wrote to Mussolini about it in late 1938. Mussolini replied on January 11, 1939, that "The general attitude of Jewish circles toward Italy is not such as to make it advisable for the Italian Government to receive on any of its territory large numbers of Jewish immigrants." Mussolini advocated the "creation in some part of the world of a true and proper Jewish state," although he regarded the resettlement of Jews in Palestine as having "failed on account of historic conditions which were absolutely unfavorable."[51] The Ethiopia idea was not pursued. By the time Roosevelt met Haile Selassie in 1945, it was not a live option.

IV

THE EUROPEAN ADVISORY COMMISSION (EAC), set up in the aftermath of the Moscow foreign ministers' conference in October 1943, was intended by Roosevelt (chapter 19) to get the Russians accustomed to collegial action with the British and Americans, and beyond that to stall until the Western armies were successfully landed in northwest Europe and proceeding toward central Germany. Winant, the American representative, wrote FDR that no "commission created by governments for a serious purpose has had less support from the governments creating it . . . in recorded history" than the EAC.*[52]

Winant received a steady flow of suggestions from the State Department for the reconstruction of Germany on orthodox lines and in its pre-war borders, but with limits on war-making capacities. Hull had no idea even of the frontier changes agreed at Teheran. So the charade of showering Winant with earnest proposals for postwar Germany that Winant knew had not been approved by the President and were made in complete ignorance of what had already been accepted at Teheran, including the radical shift of the Russian and Polish borders to the west, continued. None of these motions saw the light of day at the EAC.

Sir William Strang, the British delegate, and host-chairman of the EAC, had other instructions and ambitions, though Churchill too largely ignored the commission. At the January 14, 1944, session of the EAC, Strang tabled a comprehensive British proposal that was somewhat less ambitious for the West than what Roosevelt had marked down on his National Geographic map on U.S.S. *Iowa* on the way to the Teheran Conference, in that Berlin was embedded 110 miles within the Soviet zone, rather than at the intersection of Western and Soviet zones, as Roosevelt had intended.

It has come to light since the end of the Cold War that Stalin envisioned at this time a Soviet zone that would go only to the Elbe, but it is not clear how definite this limitation on Soviet ambitions was. If the British and Americans had not landed in Normandy, cleared France, and advanced into Germany, Stalin would presumably have raised his sights.[53] Stalin's advisors wished to accept Strang's plan, but Stalin initially refused. His views of what would be achievable and desirable in Germany were presumably evolving.

Winant presented the American proposal, based on what Roosevelt had stipulated on the *Iowa* on the way to Teheran. This gave the United States 46 percent of Germany, the Soviet Union 20 percent, and Britain 34 percent. Gousev indignantly rejected this as presumptuous for a country whose only troops in Europe were in Italy and not overly numerous nor rapidly advancing there.[54] As late as August 12, 1944, ten weeks after the Allied landings in France, Winant told Morgenthau, visiting England, that he had no idea what Roosevelt's intentions were for postwar Germany.[55]

By then, the British and Russians had agreed and put through the EAC, to Roosevelt's "irritation,"[56] and over Winant's objections, a modified version of Strang's original proposal. This divided pre-war Germany into three approximately equal zones, and left Berlin well within the Soviet zone, but with a three-power Allied Control Commission governing the city. Strang's plan did not initially guarantee Western access to Berlin.

On balance, Strang unfortunately kept intact his record of participation in

* Roosevelt rebuffed Morgenthau's bid to name his aide, Lauchlin Currie, as U.S. delegate on the EAC to promote Morgenthau's vision of a harsh peace with Germany.

unsuccessful foreign initiatives, which began with Munich and crested in the Anglo-Soviet talks of 1939. It is a mystery why the pre-war German borders were used by the EAC for demarcation of occupation zones, since Teheran had approved the Oder-Neisse, or Molotov-Ribbentrop, Line, which put much of the Soviet zone of Germany in Poland. This presumably implies that Stalin was more concerned with grinding the Poles underfoot than with Germany, but that would have been uncharacteristic strategic shortsightedness, and was superfluous anyway, because much of the German population of the designated Russian sector fled westwards, transporting Germany literally on the feet of its inhabitants into the Western world. In promoting this migration, and making Germany part of the West at last, Strang's achievement was considerable, if inadvertent.

In another sense, Strang had gained a diplomatic triumph for Britain, since Overlord had not occurred and at the end of the European war Britain's forces equalled barely a quarter of American forces in Germany and not 10 percent of Russia's. This is presumably the reason why Churchill, Eden, and Cadogan protected Strang in their memoirs. They don't mention Strang in this context, barely mention his commission, and don't refer to the EAC German demarcation. It is not easy to explain why the American memoirists were as restrained, other than that Eisenhower and Truman seemed more interested in aspersing each other than in any lèse-majesté to the great prestige of Winston Churchill.

But Roosevelt's policy of awaiting the final position of the Allied armies would undoubtedly have been preferable. His premonitions of rapid Western advances proved accurate, compared with the sluggish and sanguinary progress of the Russians in the east and to British nightmares of a bloodbath on the beaches or in static war in northern France. What was, as will be discussed in the last chapters of this book, rendered absolutely egregious by Strang's initiative was the complaint of Churchill's more vocal espousers that Eisenhower should have ignored the EAC agreement and taken territory pledged to Russia as a result of Strang's initiative.

In his memoirs, Strang presents the British case for its conduct on the EAC as best he can. He is reduced to the po-faced confection that "There was still some doubt whether (in spite of what Stalin may have said on a convivial occasion in October 1943) the Soviet armies would cross the German frontier, and whether they would not stand fast there, having expelled the enemy from their soil and that of their neighbours, and leave the Western Allies to finish off the war."[57] Doubt in Strang's mind, perhaps, but in no one else's.

Strang claimed: "Our anxieties" on this subject "are illustrated by Churchill's obvious relief" at the Soviet offensive in October 1944. In fact, while Strang was voting with the Russians to bring them within one hundred miles of the Rhine, Churchill was already expressing alarm to Roosevelt about the possible penetration of Western Europe by the Red Army.

Strang defends the zones as "fair," as if that were a legitimate criterion in such circumstances. His second line of defense of the demarcation of zones of occupation is that it "was in line with the desire of our military authorities, who had pre-occupations about postwar shortages of manpower, not to take on a larger zone of occupation than need be." He might have checked this assertion out with Montgomery, the British deputy allied supreme commander, who was screaming for more German territory to occupy, especially Berlin. Montgomery never ceased, to his last breath decades later, to blame the Americans for the expansion of the Soviet occupation zone, which was in fact achieved by Strang's proposal, over American objections.

Finally, Strang claims that there would not have been any Western zones in Berlin without the EAC division. In fact, as Montgomery and the American generals for once agreed, the Western armies would have occupied Berlin, and could have offered the Soviets office space only, had they so wished and not already been committed otherwise in the EAC.

V

THE AMERICANS WERE now advancing steadily westwards in the Pacific along parallel lines, MacArthur in New Guinea and the Solomons, Nimitz in the central Pacific through the Marshall and Caroline Islands. Both campaigns were conducted with great skill. Landings were effected with high efficiency, and both theater commanders bypassed the largest pockets of Japanese forces. MacArthur swept past and ignored 250,000 Japanese soldiers at Rabaul, leaving them isolated, helpless, and starving as he drove inexorably back toward the Philippines, as he had prophesied when he left Corregidor two years before.

The superiority of the United States Navy was now practically unassailable, and U.S. aircraft production and pilot training enabled the United States to turn even small islands into powerful air bases. Apart from mass suicide air attacks and defenses to the death of every approach, there was no sustainable Japanese resistance strategy to the inexorable might of vengeful America.

Starting in the last week in February 1944, the Royal and U.S. Air Forces had been sending almost 4,000 bombers over Germany on clear days, pounding German defense plants. At night they bombed German cities indiscriminately, with devastating effect. There would be no more hesitation in razing Dresden to the ground in February 1945 than the Americans had in incinerating most of Tokyo and other large Japanese cities starting two months later. Churchill and Roosevelt had promised severe punishment to the civil populations of both countries.

The bombers over Germany were now escorted by long-range Thunderbolt and Mosquito fighters that reduced losses to about 5 percent of the bombers or less, down from ten times as great a percentage the previous year. These raids took a heavy toll among the Luftwaffe defenders, and damaged or destroyed almost 70 percent of Germany's aircraft manufacturing capacity. Absolute air superiority would be required for Overlord, and heavy raids on Germany through March, April, and May 1944 helped achieve it, though the Germans showed their customary determination and ingenuity in decentralizing, camouflaging, and rebuilding their aircraft industry.

This period was the most challenging to Roosevelt's health in his eleven years in the White House. Ever since his return from Teheran he had suffered from a lingering, intermittent flu, causing frequent headaches and fevers. He slept poorly, and was constantly tired. Eleanor rarely noticed such things and was constantly travelling anyway, but Anna and Grace Tully did notice, and Anna asked Admiral McIntire, the President's physician, for his evaluation. "I didn't think he really knew what he was talking about," she said later.[58]

On March 27, 1944, Roosevelt was examined by Dr. Howard Bruenn, a navy heart specialist, and by others, at Bethesda Naval Hospital. Roosevelt showed up jovially for his examination and submitted to it, but, as was his custom, never showed the slightest curiosity about his condition. Bruenn diagnosed hypertension and congestive heart failure. He found the heart dangerously enlarged at the left ventricle—a dilated aorta and engorged pulmonary vessels. Bruenn prescribed digitalis and a weight-loss program, less smoking, only one cocktail a day, ten hours sleep per day, including a nap after meals, and an immediate and prolonged rest. The President had a systolic murmur and seemed to have almost permanent bronchitis. His blood pressure was erratic and at times worrisome.

Three days into his new regime, Roosevelt's color was better, his chest was clear, and improvement continued, but the murmur did not vanish and his blood pressure did not immediately stabilize. After two weeks, his heart had largely returned to normal size and he slept normally. Reporters noted that his color, alertness, and spirits seemed much improved. Since Roosevelt asked his doctors nothing about his state of health, the doctors—navy men, who apart from McIntire hadn't known him before—did not take it upon themselves to tell the Commander in Chief about his condition.

It was assumed that McIntire, who did know the patient and was trusted by him because of the improvement he had wrought in Roosevelt's sinus condition, would tell him the facts. There is no evidence that he did so.

For the first time, the health of the President was becoming the greatest obstacle to the achievement of his lofty ambitions. He had a domestic consensus for the role of the state as he had redefined it. Economic depression was now just a dim and bitter memory, and most Americans gave their long-serving president most of the credit for their deliverance from it. The war was clearly going well and should end victoriously in 1945 or 1946, and there was an emerging consensus on some elements of the peace. There would be an international organization, and the isolationists were discredited and defeated. If the invasion of France were successful, Western Europe would be in the hands of the British and Americans. Roosevelt did not underestimate the difficulties of separating the Europeans from their colonial empires, but knew it would happen.

He was well aware of the possibility of competition with the Communists for preeminence in the postwar world but was convinced that atheistic Marxist dictatorship did not pose a serious rivalry to enlightened social market democracy for the hearts and minds of the world. And the democratic West would start out with vastly more geopolitical power. His general plan was to face Stalin with an overwhelming military, economic, cultural, and public relations superiority at the disposition of the American-led West, and make a sincere and flattering offer of reasonable cooperation. Given the condition of the world just three and four years before, this was a remarkable evolution.

But a race was now developing between the unfolding of events, more or less as Roosevelt had wished, foreseen, and even ordered them, and his own physical and intellectual stamina and capacity to remain in command of events. As with his polio, the question would be not only the practical matter of his strength and serviceability, but also his ability to project strength and competence to the public and the world, whatever the facts. The immediate remedial steps stabilized his condition, but before long, liver spots appeared on his face and the dark half moons below his eyes that had occurred in times of fatigue for many years became fairly constant.

On seeing him after an absence of some months Elliott could not disguise his shock at his father's appearance. Noticing Elliott's discomfort, FDR said: "Well, what did you expect?"[59] His hands shook more than ever when he lit a cigarette, and his shoulders had become slightly stooped. He appeared somewhat gaunt, but that was partly in response to his loss of weight, from 188 to 165 pounds, an appropriate weight given that there was only skin and bone in his legs.

For the moment, Roosevelt elected to go on a prolonged holiday at Bernard Baruch's grand and secluded house in South Carolina, which he called "Hobcaw Barony." He wrote to Churchill March 20: "I am very angry with myself. The old attack of grippe having hung on and on, leaving me with an intermittent temperature, Ross decided about a week ago that it is necessary for me to take a complete rest of about two or three weeks in a suitable climate which I am definitely planning to do beginning at the end of this month. I see no way out and I am furious."[60] Roosevelt represented every indisposition from heart disease to bleeding hemorrhoids as "the grippe." His general campaign of misinformation about his condition began, logically, with his principal ally.

The administration had observed the beginning of its twelfth year on March 4 with a reception for two hundred of the old stalwarts as well as the new military and naval personnel. The ageless (in fact eighty-six-year-old) Dr. Endicott Peabody came and asked God's blessing yet again "on Thy servant Franklin." Their relationship had taken unimaginable turns since young Roosevelt had arrived at Groton forty-eight years before.

Al Smith had turned seventy at the very end of 1943, and Roosevelt sent him a gracious note and received an appreciative reply. Smith had lost his bitterness at the man he had underestimated, who had replaced him in Albany and then at the Democratic National Convention, and had gone on to do things Smith would concede were beyond his aspirations. To his family, "his soul serene, all passion spent," he remembered "Dear Frank" as he had first known him thirty-five years before: "He was the kindest man you ever met, but don't get in his way."[61]

Anna was doing admirably as White House chatelaine and was a great joy to her father, as bright, attractive, and attentive daughters always are to their fathers. She learned shorthand in her spare time, and cheerfully said: "It was immaterial to me whether my job was helping to plan the 1944 campaign, pouring tea for General de Gaulle, or filling Father's empty cigarette case."[62] Lucy Mercer Rutherfurd's fairly frequent visits were a further encouragement. Eleanor's tireless touring around the battle theaters and all over the home front were an invaluable service to the country, but she was little direct help to her husband, wrestling with the problems of the world as medical limitations closed in on him.

The President was at Baruch's estate in South Carolina from April 9 to May 7, 1944, slept twelve hours a day, got a good deal of sun, and escalated his resumed relations with Lucy Mercer Rutherfurd, who spent the winters in Aiken (140 miles away), and whose husband had just died after a long illness. (It was only after the onset of Mr. Rutherford's incapacitating illness that relations between Lucy and the President were resumed in 1941. By all accounts, Lucy cared admirably for her husband all through these years.) She came to lunch at Hobcaw on the day of Navy Secretary Knox's death. Shortly after lunch, Roosevelt suffered severe abdominal pain and a throbbing sensation. Bruenn and McIntire had both accompanied him, and Bruenn gave a tentative diagnosis of gallstones. He gave the President an injection of codeine to get him through comments about Knox to the accompanying press (who were quartered eight miles away and didn't bother him during his stay). Roosevelt invoked medical grounds not to go to the funeral and remained another week with Baruch.

The principal diversion provided by the news while the President was on holiday was the occupation of Montgomery Ward, the great Chicago mail order house, by the army. A strike had broken out, following a longstanding refusal by the management to recognize the union or hold a serious vote on certification. Roosevelt ordered the end of the strike, and the strikers complied. He also called for cooperation with a War Labor Board order to hold a fair unionization vote among the employees, but the company refused.

Attorney General Francis Biddle argued against Stimson, who wanted nothing to do with it, that a military takeover was justified because most of Montgomery Ward's customers were farmers, whose output was vital to the war effort. Roosevelt sided with Biddle, and the troops (whom Roosevelt had wanted to deploy against Colonel McCormick and the *Chicago Tribune*) went in with fixed bayonets. When the company chairman, Sewell Avery, refused to move, two soldiers locked arms to make a chair under him, while two others walked behind, providing a back for the improvised chair, and the four soldiers carried the solemn, expressionless Avery out of the building and gently deposited him on the sidewalk. (This was how Roosevelt himself was often carried.)

The resulting news photos were professionally judged the best of the year. Avery denounced Biddle, who supervised the operation in person: "To hell with the government, you New Dealer!" It was good theater and Roosevelt was vastly entertained, but there was a good deal of criticism, including from Walter Lippmann and the *Washington Post*, that it was an excessive use of force and improper deployment of the military.[63]

On May 8, President Roosevelt returned from South Carolina to Washington, where the highest circles of government were now in an unbearably tense count-down to D-Day. The *New York Times* welcomed him back with an editorial cele-brating his holiday from "the almost overwhelming burdens his office forces him to carry. He earned every hour of it."[64] Roosevelt had intended to travel to England to be with Churchill when the expedition was launched, but medical advice was to pass on such a strenuous trip.

VI

THE PERENNIAL PROBLEM of relations with de Gaulle was never absent for long. Harold Macmillan opined: "I have never seen a man at once so ungra-cious and so sentimental. . . . the smallest act of courtesy or special kindness touches him with a deep emotion. . . . The terrible mixture of inferiority complex and spiritual pride are characteristic of the sad situation into which France has fallen. I have often felt that the problems here could not be dealt with by politi-cians. They are rather problems for the professional psychiatrist."[65]

By the end of 1943 relations had apparently improved, and de Gaulle and Churchill had a rather agreeable meeting at Marrakesh, where Churchill was recuperating from pneumonia contracted on the way back from Cairo and Teheran. Churchill's attitude to de Gaulle was a good deal subtler than Roo-sevelt's. As the observant Harold Macmillan put it: "He feels about de Gaulle like a man who has quarreled with his son. He will cut him off with a shilling. But in his heart he would kill the fatted calf if only the prodigal would confess his faults and take his orders obediently in future."[66] Following the Marrakesh meeting, Churchill described de Gaulle as "un grand animal" (a great beast). Eisenhower had grown more appreciative of him also, and found de Gaulle easier to work with than Giraud.[67] Difficult though de Gaulle was, time spent with him gradu-ally raised one's opinion of him.

It has entered history that Leahy advised Roosevelt that Petain should be relied on as the Frenchman most likely to be of help to the Allied armies of liberation in France in 1944. This is based on Halifax's reporting to Eden that McCloy had told him this was Leahy's opinion.[68] Such a message could easily have been garbled in transmission, deliberately or otherwise, considering the personalities involved. Leahy's advice from Vichy had been almost wholly wrong and the entire mission was dishonorable, though the admiral was not to blame for that; Roosevelt and Hull were. But it is not likely that at this very late date even Leahy imagined that Petain could be of any use to the Allies, or would have any wish to be.

The difficulties with de Gaulle had led, at the approach of D-Day, to a ludicrous impasse: Churchill had arranged for General Leclerc's Free French armored division to be part of the liberating force, but only to land in France in August, and de Gaulle was given no official prior advice of the landings, though he knew they were imminent. The Free French mission in London was headed by General Pierre Koenig, who had led his men across the Sahara to participate successfully in the defeat of the Afrika Korps, but Koenig remained in Algiers. Because Roosevelt forbade Eisenhower to have substantive political talks with de Gaulle, de Gaulle forbade Koenig to discuss political matters with Eisenhower. It was now obvious to everyone except Roosevelt, and perhaps Leahy, that de Gaulle was the government in waiting of France (even Hull had seen this light). This fatuous state of affairs continued while Roosevelt and de Gaulle went through yet another diplomatic two-step prior to meeting. De Gaulle refused to come to Washington unless invited as head of a provisional government. Roosevelt refused to invite him in this capacity, or to go further than confirming that he would receive de Gaulle if he chose to come to Washington.

Becoming even more exasperated with his Anglo-Saxon allies than he habitually was, de Gaulle made a speech in Algiers in which he criticized Churchill and Roosevelt for ignoring the government of France and envisioned an alliance between France and "dear Russia." Roosevelt had asked Churchill that if de Gaulle were invited to London, he be detained in Britain until the landings had commenced. Roosevelt's extreme unreasonableness on this subject at this late date is disconcerting. He was probably the world's most accomplished political manipulator, with a remarkable intuitive and practical insight into political men and events. His irritation at de Gaulle's obduracy and even ingratitude is understandable; his misjudgment of the strength of de Gaulle's position among the French is not.

Churchill was grilled in Parliament as the anomaly of the Anglo-American position became ever more conspicuous, and he wrote to Roosevelt on May 26, 1944, that "we should be in a difficulty if it were thought that more British and American blood was being spilt because we had not got the French national spirit working with us . . . and after all it is very difficult to cut the French out of the liberation of France."[69]

Churchill had feared bombing the French railways and other targets likely to result in civilian casualties, as the military commanders had requested, because of the possible effects on Anglo-French relations. Roosevelt had no such qualms. Unlike Churchill, he had not forgiven the French for what he considered their cowardly behavior in 1940, and he authorized whatever bombing the military wished to conduct in France without any great effort to square it with Churchill. Having wanted to invade France at least nine months earlier, Roosevelt wasn't prepared to countenance anything less than a maximum effort now. And he wasn't prepared to risk the life of one American, British, or Canadian soldier for the sensibilities of the French public.[70]

Roosevelt testily replied to Churchill's May 26 cable the next day: "I am hopeful that your conversations with General de Gaulle will result in inducing him to actually assist in the liberation of France without being imposed by us on the French people as their Government." De Gaulle's own version of these tortuous events shows that with Churchill's desertion from the American line, Roosevelt was finally, majestically, changing course: "Roosevelt decided it was time to indicate the beginning of a policy of resipiscence. But . . . he had chosen a rather circuitous path by which to apprise me of it."[71] Admiral Fenard, head of de Gaulle's naval mission in Washington (whom we last saw unsuccessfully urging patience on General Mark Clark in Algiers) "arrived in great haste," carrying an informal invitation from Roosevelt. Because of all the sensibilities involved, it must remain, said the envoy, a matter of discretion from whom the initiative originated. "I could not despise the desire which [Roosevelt] himself formally expressed. . . . But effusion was not called for," wrote de Gaulle with his usual asperity.[72]

"The President's behavior completed my enlightenment," he wrote, that his long struggle for recognition of himself and of the independence of France would end victoriously. Roosevelt had declined Churchill's request to send a cabinet-level official to discuss political matters with de Gaulle, and sent only Marshall, who was authorized to deal only with military questions, which Eisenhower was perfectly competent to deal with unaided.

De Gaulle had relaxed his longstanding ban on receiving the British ambassador—Duff Cooper, who had replaced Macmillan—because Cooper had indicated "a new orientation." (It was, as Churchill appreciated, in its way magnificent that de Gaulle could sit in Algiers, which the British and Americans had reclaimed from the palsied and bloodstained hands of Vichy with no help from de Gaulle, and refuse to receive the British ambassador.) Undersecretary of War John McCloy wrote Roosevelt a memo on June 1 debunking press reports that de Gaulle would soon be negotiating fiscal matters with Churchill. (This might have been expected to rouse the curiosity of the Germans.) McCloy reminded Roosevelt (via General Watson, who was asked to transmit the memo) that special currency for the invasion forces had been decided "many months ago . . . with rates of exchange agreed on."[73]

A letter from Churchill inviting de Gaulle to Britain was delivered in Algiers on June 2, followed the next day by Churchill's own plane to bring him to Britain. De Gaulle arrived June 4 and went at once to Churchill's invasion headquarters, a private train near Portsmouth, from which, Churchill had cabled Roosevelt, "there are wonderful sights to see with all these thousands of vessels."[74] (The invasion fleet consisted of 4,500 ships, screened by 12,000 aircraft. It was to be the greatest military operation in the history of the world.)

Churchill loved his train, but his entourage was less enthusiastic. It had only one bath, which the prime minister, according to Eden, occupied more or less perpetually, and one telephone, which was in constant use by Churchill's chief of staff, General Ismay. De Gaulle arrived here on June 4 and was greeted by Churchill with literally outstretched arms. De Gaulle was cool in this moment of vindication.[75] The South African leader, Field Marshal Jan Smuts, was present, despite having recently announced that since France was no longer a Great Power, she should seek membership in the British Commonwealth.

According to de Gaulle, "Churchill immediately showed his steel." He recounted the gigantic proportions of what was afoot and expressed pride in Britain's part in it, especially the predominance, as always in English Channel operations over many centuries, of the Royal Navy. De Gaulle, and his account is corroborated by others, "expressed my admiration to the Prime Minister; that Great Britain, after so many ordeals so valiantly endured and thanks to which she had saved Europe," would be the base and co-originator of such a mighty and noble enterprise. This " 'was the striking justification of the courageous policy which [Mr. Churchill himself] had personified since the war's darkest days. . . . France was proud to be in the line of attack, in spite of everything, at the side of the Allies for the liberation of Europe.' At this moment, a similar flood of esteem and friendship carried away everyone present."

Unfortunately, matters then deteriorated from this high plateau. After de Gaulle had agreed to speak in French through the BBC to France, Churchill urged that they try to achieve a political understanding, for which de Gaulle could then seek Roosevelt's approval when he went to Washington. Given Churchill's sensitivity to the French, it is surprising that he didn't present his proposal more enticingly. The problem was compounded by the remark of the labor minister, Ernest Bevin, that the British Labour Party would be "hurt" if de Gaulle did not go to Washington. De Gaulle erupted: "Hurt! Has France not been hurt?" He recounted how he had attempted to open political discussions for nearly two years and been rebuffed by Roosevelt.

The Allies were liberators and welcomed as such, but he spoke for France, and everyone except Roosevelt and, ostensibly, Churchill, knew it. De Gaulle objected that Eisenhower was about to commence an occupation of parts of France that, for all the attention paid to the representatives of legitimate French opinion, would be like the occupation of an enemy country. He added, in reference to the plan for the issuance by the Supreme Allied Commander of special money for use in France: "Allez, faites la guerre avec votre fausse monnaie!" (Go and make war with your counterfeit money.)*

Churchill then uttered the portentous statement that would reverberate in relations between France, Britain, and the United States for a great many years—that whenever faced with a dispute between France and America, Britain would side with America. He would pass over it lightly in his memoirs. Eden was appalled and Bevin demurred, but de Gaulle resignedly expressed his understanding of his host's perspective. Churchill toasted: "De Gaulle, who never accepted defeat." De Gaulle responded: "To England, to victory, to Europe."

Churchill had pierced the heart of the matter. He loved France and disliked but admired and respected de Gaulle, but he loved America more. And he saw influence in and support from Washington as the greatest and most durable pillar of British strength in the world. After what the Anglo-American alliance had achieved in the last four years, and was about to attempt, it would have been unnatural for him to think otherwise. If he regarded France, as personified by de Gaulle, as a beloved but difficult relative, America was an inseparable, if benignly domineering, spouse.

For de Gaulle, there was an underappreciated relative's craving for the approval, or at least the notice, of mighty America and its august, now almost omnipotent (but physically fragile) president. There was also the flickering but imperishable hope that Britain would opt for Europe and not for subordinacy to America in an Anglo-Saxon arrangement.

Churchill was the disappointed benefactor and uncle to de Gaulle, yet showing flashes of appreciation for him; de Gaulle the insecure claimant on Churchill's attention, teased but ultimately, on the great occasions, passed over by Churchill in favor of Roosevelt. Roosevelt was the irritated wealthy relative, slightly disdainful and insufficiently sympathetic, but evidently favoring the venerable and deferential Churchill to the odd and inflexible de Gaulle. Roosevelt liked and respected Churchill, though he regarded him as a splendid anachronism, and was just coming to recognize that he had underestimated de Gaulle, disagreeable though he was. But he considered both Britain and France to be in

---

* McCloy summarized the Churchill-de Gaulle conversations for Roosevelt in a memo of June 10 and reported that de Gaulle "was in a very arrogant and belligerent mood and it was quite apparent that the matter of the currency had been grasped by him and his supporters in England as the touchstone of the whole political recognition issue." McCloy described discussions with de Gaulle's commissioner for finance, Pierre Mendes-France (subsequently prime minister), and his financial negotiator, Herve Alphand (eventually, nearly twenty years later, de Gaulle's ambassador in Washington). It had been agreed that de Gaulle's people could monitor the issuance of the special currency, and thus judge the accretion in France's money supply. McCloy reflected the usual American outrage at de Gaulle's inflexibility, but did warn Roosevelt of the proportions of Churchill's problem. Large sections of parliamentary opinion and many members of the cabinet wanted immediate recognition of de Gaulle and the Free French: "The emotionalism which had been turned on in this subject might result in a crisis in the government."[76]

inexorable decline, Britain less steeply and with her honor inspiringly enhanced, France rather discreditably.

They were all great leaders at one of the supreme and sublime moments of world history. Doubtless their relations would have been settled more satisfactorily if it had been vouchsafed to them to remain at the head of their peoples for a few more consecutive years. All three would be gone in eighteen months, Roosevelt forever. Their successors, less talented than themselves, would work it out eventually.

The immediate problem, as Eisenhower pointed out to Churchill and Roosevelt on June 3, was that he was about to invade France to liberate its people without the official approval of the one person who commanded any useful military support in that country. De Gaulle went on from his lunch with Churchill to a briefing from Eisenhower. The rough weather threatened a postponement of the invasion because of the difficulty of landing troops in such conditions. This caused the supreme commander, as de Gaulle put it, "the severest perplexity."[77] De Gaulle, when asked, said he would support any decision of Eisenhower's but urged him not to delay, "which would prolong the moral tension of the executants and compromise secrecy."[78] (Given his own well-earned reputation for indiscretion, this reasoning was piquant.) Any delay would, for reasons of tide and moonlight, have to be for at least two weeks.

De Gaulle disapproved of Eisenhower's proposed statement to the peoples of Western Europe. He felt that the statement, composed in Washington, treated France as a conquered country, while other subjugated nations were soon to be liberated ones. De Gaulle was advised the next day that it was too late to change anything in the material that was about to be rained down on the heads of the populace. The Allies had such an immense supply of aircraft and aircrews, there were sufficient of them to drop pamphlets all over Western Europe.

———————

On June 3, Eisenhower had declared a one-day delay in the invasion, to June 6. The decision was tentative. Millions waited to know when they were to be hurled into mortal combat. Churchill, in "an agony of uncertainty,"[79] returned to London, and felt "chilled" as he told Eden, when de Gaulle declined his offer of a lift and said he would prefer to return to London with French officers. Roosevelt had gone to Charlottesville, Virginia, on Friday, June 2, to spend the weekend with his military aide, General Edwin "Pa" Watson. He was accompanied by his daughter, Anna, and her husband, John Boettiger. He worked with them on an outline of his remarks for D-Day night. They suggested it be in the form of a prayer, and Roosevelt took up this theme.

Churchill, having returned to London, cabled Roosevelt on Sunday, June 4: "Our friendship is my greatest stand-by amid the ever-increasing complications of this exacting war. . . . How I wish you were here."[80] Roosevelt, as always, was icily composed. His serenity, Eleanor believed, derived from his polio, which had taught him that when there was nothing that could be done to alleviate tension, it had to be ignored.[81]

All waited for the decision of the Supreme Allied Commander, to invade or postpone. Having gathered his combined staffs, after canvassing weather predictions of a slight improvement and all other factors, General Dwight D. Eisenhower, at about 4 A.M. on June 5, 1944, uttered the deceptively mundane words to the assembled officers: "OK, let's go." The mighty invasion apparatus was thrown into action; eight divisions would hit the Normandy beaches starting twenty-six hours later, followed by scores of further divisions as they could be delivered, conveyed and covered by immense sea and air armadas.

The tension on June 5 was increased by de Gaulle's refusal to broadcast to the French, in protest against the dropping on France of the proclamation that called upon the French to accept Eisenhower as the country's civil authority and said nothing of de Gaulle or the Free French National Committee. For good measure, de Gaulle pulled two hundred French liaison officers who were to accompany the liberating forces, because there had been no agreement on their political status. Churchill exploded and said that if this decision stood, he would have nothing further to do with de Gaulle. Marshall, who was in England, also exploded, and said: "No sons of Iowa will fight to put up statues of de Gaulle in France."[82] (History took its course: many sons of Iowa died, and many statues of de Gaulle were erected.)

De Gaulle's ambassador to London, Pierre Vienot, shuttled back and forth between the Foreign Office and de Gaulle's temporary residence at the Connaught Hotel. De Gaulle was in as great a rage as his English hosts. The Washington invitation was a trap: "They're out to get me, but no one will!" and so forth. Vienot sought out Eden after 1 A.M., and found him at Churchill's bedside. The prime minister, on one of the most intense evenings of his life, had had a good deal to drink and had retired earlier than usual. Vienot claimed that there was merely a misunderstanding and that de Gaulle would speak on the radio. Churchill, from under the covers, poured forth a torrent of abuse, accusing the general of "treachery in battle. . . ." He claimed de Gaulle failed to understand or appreciate the monstrous sacrifice of young British, Canadians, and Americans who were going to die for France. Churchill's harangue continued for nearly two hours. Vienot finally said he would not be spoken to in this way and left at 3 A.M. Churchill then awakened an aide and shouted down the telephone to him that de Gaulle should be forcibly conducted to a plane and returned to Algiers, adding in a magnificent Churchillian flourish, "in chains if necessary. He must not be allowed to reenter France." The aide found this scenario so disconcerting, he ignored it and went uneasily back to sleep, as if after a nightmare. As D-Day dawned, there was disarray among the avenging Allies.

When Vienot reported all this to de Gaulle, the general, placated by inflicting such an uncontrollable and sleep-depriving rage on Churchill, was calm and satisfied, and promised to speak on the radio and permit the political liaison officials to go with the invading armies. These had already embarked. Paratroopers had already begun landing in the German rear areas.

Rome had just finally fallen to the Allies, and in Washington Roosevelt had just addressed the nation and the world. Unaware of the pyrotechnics in the British prime minister's bedroom, inscrutable and unruffleable, the President rejoiced: "The first of the Axis capitals is now in our hands." He paid tribute to "the gallant Canadians, the fighting New Zealanders . . . the courageous French and French Moroccans, the South Africans, the Poles, and the East Indians," as well as to the British and Americans. "Ever since before the days of the Caesars, Rome has stood as a symbol of authority. Rome was the Republic. Rome was the Empire, Rome was . . . the Catholic Church. And Rome was the capital of a united Italy." He glossed over the Fascist period as one of enslavement and praised the "great sons of the Italian people—Galileo and Marconi, Michelangelo and Dante— and that fearless discoverer who typifies the courage of Italy, Christopher Columbus." He welcomed Italy back into the civilized world.

The official announcement of the invasion of Western Europe was made at 3:32 A.M., Eastern Time, June 6, 1944. Eisenhower's order of the day was read over the air: "Soldiers, Sailors, and Airmen of the Allied Expeditionary Force, you are about to embark on the great crusade toward which we have striven these many months." He reassured his forces that "much has happened" since the Nazi triumphs of 1940 and 1941, though the enemy was "battle-hardened and will fight savagely." But: "The tide has turned! I have full confidence in your courage, devotion to duty, and skill in battle. We will accept nothing less than full victory."

De Gaulle issued a statement announcing that he was in this "old and dear England," having rhetorically asked, with a humorous insight few would have suspected: "How could I not be here?" He again refused to see the British ambassador and declined to submit his proposed address to France to the British in advance. Churchill concluded that he had no choice but to let the general speak, and if his remarks were too abominable, to cut off his microphone in mid-speech. (The thought of such a fiasco, even at this remove, is hard to grasp.)

In the event, General de Gaulle spoke with an eloquence and power that were unusual even for this master of the French language and culture and national psychology. "The supreme battle has been joined. For the sons of France, wherever they are, whatever they are, the simple and sacred duty is to fight the enemy by every means in their power." He reserved all authority over French civil affairs to the government of France, by which he unambiguously meant the Free French National Committee presided over by himself. "From behind the cloud so heavy with our blood and our tears, the sun of our greatness is now reappearing." He was generous to his Allied comrades in arms.

Churchill, listening like the people of France, live on his radio to his rebarbative guest, ready at the outset at any moment to stop transmission of the general's broadcast, was profoundly moved, not for the last time, by de Gaulle, even unto tears. When Ismay looked at him incredulously, Churchill bellowed at him: "You great tub of lard! Have you no sentiment?"[83]

VII

ROOSEVELT RETIRED at midnight, aware the landings were underway. Eleanor was too keyed up to sleep, so the White House switchboard put General Marshall's call from England, when it came in at 3 A.M., through to her and she awakened the President. He put on his old gray sweater, propped himself up in bed, and remained steadily on the telephone for nearly six hours. Marshall reported that while there had been heavier resistance than anticipated at Omaha Beach, most of the men on all five beaches (Omaha and Utah for the Americans, Gold and Sword for the British, Juno for the Canadians) were moving steadily ashore and inland. Roosevelt ordered the switchboard at 4 A.M. to call the entire White House staff in to work at once. Throughout the United States, church bells and school bells pealed and factory whistles blew all morning. Huge crowds, tense and excited, gathered in all public places. The churches and synagogues were full all day and in succeeding days throughout the country. Special services were run almost continuously in places of worship of all denominations throughout the United States in favor of the cross-Channel operation.

On D-Day morning, Roosevelt met congressional leaders at 9:50 and military leaders at 11:30. Winston Churchill telephoned, very cheerfully, shortly after noon. The news from the beachhead, though fragmentary, was encouraging by the time Roosevelt had lunch with his daughter under the magnolia tree planted on the White House lawn when Andrew Jackson was president. By the time he met the press at 4 P.M., his office jammed with more reporters than it had ever contained before, indications were that the Allies had taken over 6,000 casualties, with many "little paroxysms of red foam" where soldiers were killed in the water.[84] But that was less than had been foreseen. The President, jovial and happy, told the reporters that they knew just about as much as he did, and revealed that the date had been chosen at Teheran. When asked about the importance of individual landing dates, he asked the questioning reporter if he had ever crossed the English Channel, and said, as if giving holiday travel advice: "Roughness in the English Channel has always been considered by travelers one of the greatest trials of life."

In the course of the day Roosevelt brought himself to send de Gaulle a message saying that should the general come to Washington in July, he would be delighted to receive him. He also sent Churchill the unusual D-Day present of two electric typewriters, because "I am informed that you liked the type script of a letter recently sent you by General McNarney."[85] It was a remarkable achievement that he managed to retain any semblance of business as usual on this June 6 of 1944.

He spoke to the nation and the world in the evening. His remarks are generally regarded by aficionados of Roosevelt oratory as rivaled only by his first inaugural address as the greatest and most effective speech he ever gave. It was, as Anna had suggested, ostensibly a prayer, and it was as a prosperous, respectful, but not overly pious Christian head of a great family that Roosevelt called all those in his charge to ask the mercy of a just Providence for the great undertaking of that day.

"Last night, when I spoke with you about the fall of Rome, I knew at that moment that troops of the United States and our Allies were crossing the Channel in another and greater operation. It has come to pass with success thus far.

"Almighty God; Our sons, pride of our Nation, this day have set upon a mighty endeavor, a struggle to preserve our Republic, our religion, our civilization, and to set free a suffering humanity.

"Lead them straight and true; give strength to their arms, stoutness to their hearts, steadfastness in their faith.

"Their road will be long and hard. For the enemy is strong. He may hurl back our forces. Success may not come with rushing speed but we shall return again and again; and we know that by Thy grace, and by the righteousness of our cause, our sons will triumph.

"They will be sore tried, by night and by day, without rest—until the victory is won. The darkness will be rent by noise and flame. Men's souls will be shaken with the violences of war.

"For these men are lately drawn from the ways of peace. They fight not for the lust of conquest. They fight to end conquest. They fight to liberate. They fight to let justice arise, and tolerance and good will among all Thy people. They yearn but for the end of battle, for their return to the haven of home. Some will never return. Embrace these Father, and receive them, Thy heroic servants, into Thy kingdom.

"And for us at home—fathers, mothers, children, wives, sisters, and brothers of brave men overseas—whose thoughts and prayers are ever with them—help us, Almighty God, to rededicate ourselves in renewed faith in Thee in this hour of great sacrifice. . . .

"And let our hearts be stout, to wait out the long travail, to bear sorrows that may come, to impart our courage unto our sons, wheresoever they may be. . . . Let not the impacts of temporary events, of temporal matters of but fleeting moment—let not these deter us in our unconquerable purpose.

"With Thy blessing, we shall prevail over the unholy forces of our enemy. Help us to conquer the apostles of greed and of racial arrogancies. Lead us to the saving of our country, and . . . a sure peace—a peace invulnerable to the schemings of unworthy men. And a peace that will let all men live in freedom, reaping the just rewards of their honest toil."

This was a psychological master stroke, gravely but firmly delivered. The grandeur of the occasion was such that Roosevelt was justified in invoking the assistance of the just God most Americans have always thought looked over their country, for their fighting sons, "pride of our Nation," and the united crusade for a better world, "invulnerable to the schemings of unworthy men."

He spoke with the determination of a commander in chief, the wariness of a father of soldiers and sailors, the moral conviction of the leader of a great and righteous cause. He successfully combined the roles of military leader and high secular episcopacy. If attempted on a less solemn occasion, or with less virtuosity, in a way that bore any hint of presumption, his speech would have been a disaster. As it was, the President stirred the nation and enlisted the adherence and earned the gratitude of a unanimous people and much of the world. As Samuel Rosenman said, his remarks could not have been more different from those Hitler would have uttered had he been announcing his invasion of Britain.

The *New York Times* editorialized the next day: "We have come to the hour for which we were born. . . . We go forth to meet the supreme test of our arms and our souls, the test of the maturity of our faith in ourselves and in mankind."[86]

Hitler gave his usual order that his commanders resist to the death and liquidate the beachhead. This, he mused happily, would deny reelection to Roosevelt, who, "with luck, would end up somewhere in jail."[87] Churchill would be washed up also, and the Western powers would be disabused of any notion of invading France for a very long time.

Overwhelming air and sea superiority made it difficult for German counterattacks to take hold. Hitler held back some of his armor units, thinking that Patton, the Western general the Germans feared most, who had been detained in Britain as a decoy, would land at Calais. Eisenhower's selection of Normandy as a landing site was extremely astute, and it thoroughly confused and surprised the Germans. There was fierce fighting in the bocage hedge country of the Norman interior, but it became clearer each day, and certain within ten days, that the Normandy landings had torn too great a hole in Hitler's "Atlantic Wall" to be closed. Within three weeks, more than a million men, 172,000 vehicles, and nearly 600,000 tons of supplies of all kinds had been landed.

Rommel and the theater commander, Field Marshal von Rundstedt, told Hitler by June 17 that it would be impossible to contain the Allies in their beachhead. Allied air power prevented the Germans from massing such armor as they had for a counterattack. Montgomery, in tactical command of the Allied forces under Eisenhower, forced the Germans to commit their strength piecemeal. Rundstedt had said privately that all Hitler's bravura about Fortress Europa was "humbug." By the end of June, the Allied penetration was sixty miles wide and up to twenty miles deep. Rundstedt was replaced by Kluge on July 3, 1944.

The balance of power had again changed, and the British and Americans, fortified by a reviving if obstreperous France, were in a race with the Russians for Berlin. These were intense hours for Churchill and de Gaulle, returning to

France with emotions that were almost inexpressible even for these masters of tongue and pen. And Roosevelt's power in the world, and moral authority as leader of what had been an economically and psychologically shattered and purposeless country when he assumed its headship eleven years before, was approaching heights never approached in the history of the nation-state.

Tempered by personal ordeal, long travail, and world crisis, Roosevelt yet seemed cheerful and relaxed when he judged it possible to return to Hyde Park for a break on June 15. He organized picnics, worked on his stamp collection, kept in intimate touch with the Western Front, but seemed for all the world a man unshaken by the great events in which he was such a consummate protagonist.

✲

CHAPTER 22

"It Was Difficult to Contradict This Artist, This Seducer"

(General Charles de Gaulle's description of his conversations with President Roosevelt at the White House, July 6–8, 1944)

I

THE EXILED PRIME MINISTER of Poland, Wladislaw Mikolajczyk, had arrived in Washington just before D-Day, and Roosevelt responded to Churchill's request to see him and thus encourage Stalin to believe that the Americans, too, cared about Poland. Roosevelt seems to have confined the two days of meetings to generalities, and in his toast at the state dinner he tendered to his Polish visitors, he referred to having scrutinized sixteen different maps of Poland. He said that when his guest and he were young men there was no independent Poland, and that when he as a youth had traveled in Europe, there was much less antagonism between nationalities than in the years since 1914. He was presumably hinting that the Poles should be aware of the tenuousness of their position and rely on a European spirit. This was not the message Mikolajczyk had come to hear, and he was not impressed by Roosevelt's recitation, which Churchill had already given, of Stalin's pledge to a free and independent Poland. It was a cordial but unspecific meeting. Mikolajczyk had no public meetings and minimal contact with the U.S. media.

Roosevelt asked Stalin to see Mikolajczyk. Stalin had launched the general offensive he had promised to synchronize with Overlord on June 23, moving a million men forward on a front of 450 miles in Belarus. The Red Army captured a large number of Germans, cleared the enemy out of Minsk, and surged on into Poland, occupying Lublin and Brest-Litovsk (where Leon Trotsky had agreed to Russia's departure from World War I in 1917). At this point Stalin moved his hand-chosen Polish committee into Lublin and replied to Churchill and Roosevelt that the London government had proved "ephemeral and impotent" and he would see Mikolajczyk only if it were arranged through the Polish National Committee he had set up.

Polish-American editors were expressing grave concern about the status of Poland, and Roosevelt did tell intimates that Poles were a far more coherent voting block than Jews, Italians, Irish, Germans, or other ethnic minorities among the American voters. Obviously, these people could not be allowed to dictate policy to the U.S. government. They didn't vote mainly on overseas issues and were generally Roosevelt loyalists anyway. But the conundrum of the Poles and the Russians, while not a determining fact in Roosevelt's taking his distance from the Polish issue, was another reason Roosevelt wanted to defer definitive discussions on Poland until after the election, when, in any event, the Western Allies would have a stronger negotiating position.

Roosevelt was not an unlimited admirer of Poland's pre-war performance: a corrupt, anti-Semitic despotism that leapt on Hitler's bandwagon at Munich just before Hitler turned on Poland. Britain and France and Canada had gone to war for Poland, but the United States had not.

In his ultimate goal of a just world led by an equitable and morally distinguished America, Roosevelt knew never to lose control of the majority of American opinion, unlike his greatest democratic contemporaries, Churchill and de Gaulle, who at times suffered spectacular rejections from their electorates. And the interplay of Roosevelt's unusual cunning, intuition, and idealism always told him the weight to attach to different elements in moral and strategic crises and the sequence in which to tackle them. He had known in 1933 when to move to avoid violence in the American farm states, and in 1938 when to move back to Keynesian economics before the "Roosevelt Recession" took hold of the economy, the voters, and his historical record. And he had known in 1940 when he had to risk everything, including war and reelection, to help the Churchillian war party against the Nazis and the domestic British appeasers.

Unfortunately for suffering Poland, he also knew that its turn had not yet come. He sought nothing less than the salvation of all peoples, but he knew that they could not all be saved at once, nor always at the time their need was greatest. Realism and benevolence coexisted in his thoughts, but realism almost always prevailed.

As unyielding as Stalin was about Poland, he was prompt and generous in his comments on Overlord and the strategic bombing campaign that had preceded it. He credited the latter with having wrought havoc in German war industries, and issued a public statement at the end of June praising the "brilliant successes" of General Eisenhower's forces. "The history of war does not know of another undertaking comparable to it for breadth of conception, grandeur of scale, and mastery of execution."[1] This was nothing less than the truth, from a source not given to hyperbole in praise of others.

If Brooke was right and Stalin had supported Overlord because he didn't believe it would succeed, other than in weakening Germany and facilitating the Russian penetration of Europe, Stalin must have been astonished. If the Western Allies had still been fidgeting in the Mediterranean as Churchill and Brooke had wished, they would have had no credibility with Stalin at all.

As the Republican National Convention approached, to choose an opponent to Roosevelt for the fourth time, the ineffable General Douglas MacArthur had let it be known, first through a letter to a Nebraska Congressman and then in a letter to the influential Senator Arthur Vandenburg of Michigan, that he was available. To Vandenberg he wrote that he could not campaign from his present geographic and official position, but that he would submit to the popular will if drafted. Suggesting he might continue in his command while running against the Commander in Chief was a bit rich even for MacArthur, but Roosevelt had taken his measure many years before and knew how to deal with him.

He convened MacArthur and Nimitz at a conference in Honolulu on July 26, 1944, and had his records scoured for some of the general's more glaring vulnerabilities. One in particular that he recalled and got to hand was a transcript of a conversation MacArthur had had with Admiral Thomas Hart a week before Pearl Harbor. The general had then stated that if attacked he could defend the Philippines from the Japanese without further reinforcement. "My greatest security lies in the inability of our enemy to launch his air attack on our islands."[2]

By setting the Honolulu meeting, Roosevelt was holding out the possibility of giving MacArthur the supreme military and psychological opportunity of his life by overruling the navy and authorizing the invasion of the Philippines. He was also dragooning him into a political photo opportunity of his own after both parties would have nominated their candidates.

Nimitz and (especially) King wanted to bypass the Philippines and keep taking smaller islands, approaching Japan closely enough to hammer the home islands with island- and carrier-based bombers. They then envisioned an invasion of Formosa and amphibious attacks on Japanese positions in China and on Japan itself from Iwo Jima, Formosa, and Okinawa. They considered the Philippines a waste of time and manpower and a publicity stunt for MacArthur's benefit, given his connection to that country.

Roosevelt sought to confuse the grandiose general between alternative military and political paths to glory. But in the off chance that he was nominated and accused Roosevelt of insufficiently purposeful war leadership, the President was ready to expose MacArthur's overconfidence and self-indulgence, and did not think the general's vanity could survive the intense scrutiny and combat of an American presidential election campaign. Roosevelt was always confident that if MacArthur ever threw down the mask and ran for Roosevelt's job, he would prove as clumsy and inept a political strategist and tactician as he was usually an agile military one.

Roosevelt could at many times have hampered MacArthur's career, including over the Clark Field debacle in 1941, and the astonishing gift to MacArthur by Philippine President Quezon of $500,000 from his country's treasury in January 1942 (when the general was making $33,000 a year as a soldier, and was retreating through Bataan). It was a gift in recognition of MacArthur's military services to the Philippines. But accepting it was a serious impropriety for a serving U.S. officer, and Roosevelt presumably acquiesced in it only to give himself future leverage over MacArthur if he needed it.[3] Revelation of this transaction would have done terrible damage to any MacArthur campaign, particularly given Roosevelt's matchless talents at political denigration.

While Roosevelt had long recognized MacArthur's narcissistic and antidemocratic tendencies, he had also regarded him as a convenient opponent of last resort on the far right. Roosevelt believed MacArthur a capable general, certainly, and accepted his request to be brought back to active duty in the summer of 1941, and ordered him out of Corregidor in 1942 to save him as a theater commander for the Allies. But he also helped him remain the darling of the Republican right.

Subsequent events would indicate that Roosevelt's judgment was correct, as it almost always was in tactical political matters. As one knowledgeable historian wrote: "MacArthur's endless teeterings on the edge of insubordination bothered Roosevelt not in the slightest. There was nothing in the General's character patterns that did not suit the President's need for an idol his enemies could worship at without damaging him, so long as MacArthur was fighting a war within the Roosevelt consensus. This resonant figurehead was a political hopeless cause, and the more of Roosevelt's opponents who could be persuaded to join it, the safer the President became from serious attack."[4]

Roosevelt had effortlessly made a MacArthur presidential campaign very improbable, but the Republican Party made his preparations superfluous. They ignored the general, dispensed with Willkie, and, as Roosevelt had anticipated, gave their nomination to Governor Thomas E. Dewey of New York. The Republican candidate for vice president was Governor John Bricker of Ohio, an amiable and photogenic figure of no remarkable qualities.

Dewey was the sort of Republican for whom Roosevelt had a visceral dislike. Cold, precise, and humorless, though eloquent, intelligent, and efficient, Dewey had placed himself ambiguously between the reactionaries and liberals in his party. Alice Roosevelt Longworth, in what must have been almost the only favor she ever did for FDR, greatly damaged the natty but diminutive Dewey by calling him "the bridegroom on the wedding cake." The Republican convention, which met in Chicago in the last week in June, attempted to ignore the Depression and even the war and focus exclusively on the postwar reconversion to a peacetime economy. Dewey was only forty-two, and laid great stress on his youthfulness and energy, implicitly contrasting Roosevelt's age and tiredness, which was again becoming evident.

Roosevelt's doctor, Admiral McIntire, had spoken bluntly, for once, to his patient, and told him to get smaller suits and shirts, because the suit he was wearing was so loose and oversized that it "hung on him like a bat." He told the President that he could serve another term in office if he could cut his workload in half.[5] Roosevelt's closest collaborators, such as Grace Tully, frequently noted that he nodded off at his desk and sometimes lost his train of thought in mid-sentence, but he could always rally for an important meeting and be the same dauntless and sparkling personality, charming, confident, and jut-jawed as ever.

Wendell Willkie had run for nomination again, oblivious of the hatred of him in the Republican professional organization as an ex-Democrat of doubtful loyalty who had hijacked the party in 1940 and been a divisive force in it since. He was well to the left of his party, had become an internationalist beyond anything Roosevelt advocated, and was regarded by many rank-and-file Republicans as a world federalist apt, if nominated, to give his acceptance speech in Esperanto. His campaign was extremely inept. When introduced at one meeting as an "ingrate" in the run-up to the Wisconsin primary, Willkie had dismissed his audience as "a bunch of political liabilities," possibly an exact analysis but an eccentric solicitation of support.

Roosevelt had it in mind to recruit Willkie to the administration as he had Stimson and the late Frank Knox in 1940, and Donovan, Winant, Stettinius, and Hurley, and to bring the Republican progressives across. His ultimate dream was to be able to dispense with the segregationist southern Democratic bosses and congressional committee chairmen without losing control of the Congress, but that would be a project as complicated as defeating the isolationists had been.

Former Pennsylvania governor and conservationist Gifford Pinchot, a friend of President Theodore Roosevelt, came to see FDR as an emissary of Willkie's in late June and bruited this possibility, as well as a possible third party, like TR's Bull Moose movement, which Pinchot had helped organize in 1912. Roosevelt said to Judge Samuel Rosenman: "I think the time has come for the Democratic Party to get rid of its reactionary elements in the South and to attract to it the liberals of the Republican Party. . . . We ought to have two real parties—one liberal and the other conservative. As it is now, each party is split by dissenters."[6]

The President was interested in Pinchot's overture and had Rosenman meet privately with Willkie in the St. Regis Hotel in New York on July 5, 1944.[7] Willkie was very positive about the possibilities of cooperation, and it was agreed that nothing would be said about it until after the election. Roosevelt wrote to Willkie on July 13, as he left for the West Coast and Hawaii, and Willkie asked the 1920 Democratic presidential candidate, James M. Cox, on August 2, to be his go-between with Roosevelt. However, a comedy of errors among the White House staff, of leaks, denials, and unattributable retractions of denials, caused Willkie to become suspicious that he was being used to divide the Republicans. He had been interested in a third political party, which also would have interested Roosevelt, because any such schism in Republican ranks not only would have confirmed the Democrats in office for an indefinite period but would have enabled him to take a very strong line with recalcitrant Democrats. His grand design, however, remained a general realignment between liberals and conservatives, which would have to await the election.

Most unfortunately, Willkie, a vital but curiously vulnerable man, would die of a coronary, aged fifty-two, on October 8, 1944, creating one of the great might-have-beens of U.S. history. Willkie felt his recent political rejection very keenly. Apart from preliminary discussions with Roosevelt, with whom he dealt warily because of the President's legendary political cunning, he had only just begun to plan his political future. Had his physical health been more robust, he would surely have been a durable rather than a meteoric figure. His moment of national and international prominence had been brief and brilliant.*

Alfred E. Smith had died just four days before, aged seventy-one. They were two of the most admired unsuccessful candidates for president of the twentieth century (along with William Jennings Bryan and Adlai E. Stevenson). Both were generously eulogized and given prodigious obsequies. Franklin D. Roosevelt made gracious statements about both. He described Smith as "frank, friendly, warm-hearted" and Willkie as "earnest, honest, and whole-souled," and praised the courage and integrity of both. In Willkie's case, the President said: "Courage—which was his dominating trait—prompted him more than once to stand alone and to challenge . . . powerful interests within his own party."[8] Had it not been for Roosevelt's own invincibility, both Smith and Willkie might have been president, and both would probably have done honor to the office.

The G.I. Bill of Rights was signed into law after a lengthy congressional passage in an elaborate ceremony on June 22, 1944, the President using ten pens, so he could hand them out as souvenirs. In 1940, a year in college had cost the average annual wage; the G.I. Bill made a college education accessible to veterans, and more than two million of them took advantage of it. In the late forties, half the male university students in the United States were veterans subsidized by this measure. It was arguably, even ahead of the TVA and the Federal Deposit Insurance Corporation, the most indisputably successful measure of the entire Roosevelt presidency, and was entirely his original conception and his achievement.[9]

----

* His 1940 running mate, Senator Charles McNary, had died in February 1944. So if Willkie had won the 1940 election, his term would have been finished by whomever he had appointed secretary of state (the sequence of presidential succession at the time).

By means of it the American working class gained a massive accretion of professional status and income earning capacity, and African-Americans took a long step toward real equality. This would be the Fifth, last, and posthumous New Deal.

———————

Robust discussion began in mid-June 1944 between Churchill and Roosevelt over the future of Anvil, the invasion of southern France. In what would be the last of these endless agitations about the Mediterranean, Churchill asked that the five to seven divisions that were to be extracted from Italy to be landed in France be retained for a push through Italy and into Austria, or even for another amphibious end run up the Adriatic and through Churchill's chimerical Ljubljana Gap into Austria and Bohemia. Eisenhower was convinced that Anvil would lead to a very rapid advance up the Rhone, forcing the Germans quickly back to the Rhine, and enabling his forces to invade Germany at about the end of the year. Eisenhower cabled Marshall June 20: "Wandering off overland via Trieste to Ljubljana is to indulge in conjecture to an unwarranted degree."[10]

Only Eisenhower's immense respect for Churchill could have motivated him to put the point so understatedly. The American general staff, and the President himself, thought that Italy had shown itself to be an unfruitful area of combat, and an attempt to go through the Alps into Austria, Hungary, and Bohemia was a much less promising strategic notion, given the ruggedness of the terrain and the secondary strategic value of those areas, than plunging into Germany at the earliest opportunity, and taking as much of that most important country as possible from under the nose of the advancing Russian bear.

There was a certain amount of skirmishing between Churchill and Roosevelt over this issue, and then Churchill seriously exploded on June 28, 1944, and sent Roosevelt a lengthy memo. He clung to his old fondness for Italy and professed to believe that a great breakthrough was at hand there, as he had been predicting for almost a year. He disparaged the possibility of an early landing in the south of France, and predicted that if it were attempted, the Germans would withdraw a comparable level of force from Italy and intercept and destroy the Anvil army as it progressed up the Rhone, or at best, produce "a costly stalemate." He dismissed the quality of the French forces involved, for implicitly racial reasons (they were Moroccans), but lamented their departure from Italy all the same.

He even pandered to Roosevelt's views of de Gaulle, from which Churchill rightly dissented, by predicting that transferring two French divisions to France would assist de Gaulle's takeover of France. In accord with his customary practice, Churchill suggested preferable alternatives that he knew to be wholly impractical, such as seizing Bordeaux and other Bay of Biscay ports to facilitate the delivery of American troops directly to France without having to come via Britain. (If they could land directly, tanks and all, they might as well come to Cherbourg; Bordeaux was a complete red herring at this point.)

But Churchill persisted in regarding Anvil as "bleak and sterile," partly because of its distance from Bordeaux, as if Bordeaux had ever been a chief objective in any scenario. It was the large city in France most remote from Germany, and possessed no strategic value at all. Churchill flatly stated that Anvil, as conceived, could not "directly influence the present battle in 1944."[11] His real objection, of course, was none of the preceding nonsense; it was the reduction of a British command to feed an American one. This is a comprehensible concern, but the real source of it was Churchill's strategic error in devoting so many resources to the Mediterranean in the first place, in resisting Overlord so stubbornly, and in not seeing that Roosevelt, with Stalin's assistance, would force the issue.

The prime minister was splendid at all times, but he was far from strategically infallible, and because of his distaste for Overlord, Britain's role became relatively, and prematurely, marginalized. He had written to his wife not long before: "Undoubtedly I feel much pain when I see our armies so much smaller than theirs [the Americans]. It has always been my wish to keep equal, but how can you do that against so mighty a nation and a population nearly three times our own?"[12] He narrowed the gap by claiming all Commonwealth forces for Britain, but by this time American manpower numbers, supplemented by overwhelming U.S. defense production, conferred an unchallengeable supremacy upon that country.

Roosevelt replied to Churchill on June 29 with a comprehensive memo on which the chiefs of staff had advised. Roosevelt denied that there was any shortage of troops or supplies for Eisenhower as a result of Anvil, and said that anything further he might ask for would be supplied at once from the United States. "My interest and hopes center on defeating the Germans in front of Eisenhower and driving on into Germany, rather than on limiting this action for the purpose of staging a full major effort in Italy. . . . We can—and Wilson [the British commander in the Mediterranean] confirms this, immediately withdraw five divisions [three U.S. and two French] from Italy for Anvil. The remaining 21 divisions plus numerous separate brigades will certainly provide Alexander with adequate ground superiority."

He wrote that "the probable duration of a campaign to debouch from the Ljubljana Gap into Slovenia and Hungary" would be excessive. "The difficulties in this advance would seem far to exceed those pictured by you in the Rhone Valley, ignoring the effect of organized resistance groups in France and the proximity to Overlord forces. . . . I cannot agree to the employment of U.S. troops against Istria and into the Balkans, nor can I see the French agreeing to such use of French troops.

"The Toulon area [is] most suitable. The Rhone corridor has its limitations, but it is better than Ljubljana and is certainly far better than the terrain over which we have been fighting in Italy. I am impressed by Eisenhower's statement that Anvil is of transcendent importance. . . .

"At Teheran we agreed upon a definite plan of attack. That plan has gone well so far. Nothing has occurred to require any change. Now that we are fully involved in our major blow, history will never forgive us if we lose precious time and lives by indecision and debate. My dear friend, I beg you, let us go ahead with our plan.

"Finally, for purely political consideration over here I would never survive even a slight setback in Overlord if it were known that fairly large forces had been diverted to the Balkans."

Contrary to some subsequent historical opinion, all evidence is that Stalin didn't enter into American calculations at all; Roosevelt and his general staff and the theater commander thought Churchill's plan an ill-advised enterprise for military reasons and Anvil a promising initiative for the same reasons.[13]

Churchill's initial reaction to Roosevelt's dissent was a cable threatening to resign and including the assertions: "The whole campaign in Italy is being ruined . . . simply for the amount of damage that 10 divisions . . . the French almost entirely black . . . can do advancing up the Rhone Valley almost five months hence." Moroccans, Arabs, are not generally considered to be black, and this was an inappropriate reflection from a man with two million East Indians under arms, addressing himself to the commander in chief of armed forces that did include a million African-Americans, both groups, like the Moroccans, serving with distinction.

Churchill's own staff had its doubts about "Armpit," as the Ljubljana Gap project was called (a likely sign that Brooke and his colleagues weren't entirely serious about it). Brooke, Portal, and Cunningham, seeing Churchill was inclined to have a major confrontation with Roosevelt on the issue, persuaded him that it wasn't worth breaking up the Alliance. They agreed Anvil was foolish, and developed some fatuous surmise that it was based on American domestic politics, but felt they had to go along with it in the higher Allied interest.[14]

Churchill did reply, July 1, more in sorrow than in anger. He wrote at length, beginning: "We are deeply grieved by your telegram." He stated that Montgomery believed it would take ninety days for Anvil to influence Overlord. (The real delay would be about two weeks; Montgomery's views on this subject were even more ludicrous than Churchill's but were based on simple anti-Americanism.) The prime minister forlornly concluded: "What can I do Mr. President, when your chiefs of staff insist on casting aside our Italian offensive campaign, with all its dazzling possibilities, relieving Hitler of all his anxieties in the Po Basin? . . . If you leave all our hopes . . . dashed to the ground, His Majesty's Government, on the advice of their Chiefs of Staff, must enter a solemn protest. . . . It is with the greatest sorrow that I write to you in this sense. But I am sure that if we could have met, as I so frequently proposed, we should have reached a happy agreement. I send you every personal good wish. However we may differ on the conduct of the war, my personal gratitude for your kindness to me and for all you have done for the cause of freedom will never be diminished."

Roosevelt responded within a few hours in conciliatory manner: "I deeply appreciate your clear exposition of your feelings and views," but declined to alter his decision. The forces were withdrawn from Italy, Churchill tried as late as August 4 to redirect the landings to Britanny, and Roosevelt again politely declined, on August 8.[15] Anvil, renamed Dragoon, was launched on schedule on August 15, 1944, with Churchill in person watching from the destroyer H.M.S. *Kimberley*. He wrote of this in his memoirs: "I had at least done the civil thing to Anvil, and indeed I thought it was a good thing I was near the scene to show the interest I took in it."[16]

Roosevelt wrote Churchill on September 3 of "the great Allied success in southern France."[17] The American and French force met the Allied armies that had landed in northern France near Dijon on September 11, and were engaging the German armies on the ancient Franco-German frontier near Belfort on September 14. Among the serving officers in the French divisions was William Bullitt, having been denied entry into the U.S. Army, having unsuccessfully offered himself as mayor of Philadelphia, and having been virtually ostracized by Roosevelt for the role he played in ending Sumner Welles's career.

The swift progress of the Allied southern army had been as the Americans predicted. They cut off and captured nearly 100,000 German soldiers in southwestern France, and their arrival made possible the double envelopment of the Ruhr and facilitated the seizure of most of Germany while the Russians were still on the outskirts of Berlin in early 1945. Roosevelt and his advisors were substantially vindicated. In fact, since the United States was then delivering two divisions per week to northern France, it was possible to carry out Dragoon without denuding the army in Italy, where progress continued.

The Italian front moved swiftly for a brief period and then, as had been foreseen, more slowly. As a platform for a breakthrough into the heart of Europe, it did not succeed and never justified Churchill's hopes and claims. As a steady drain on German strength, it was a success, and did keep large German units from Russia and the Western Front. It became a catchment for forces from the four corners of the earth as crack American, British, Canadian, and French divisions were withdrawn and sent elsewhere. They were replaced by Italians, the Japanese-American 442nd regimental combat team, a Jewish brigade, Brazilians, Gurkhas, Indians, Moroccans, Newfoundlanders, New Zealanders, Poles, and South Africans. All fought well, but coordination and even dietary logistics were difficult. The Jews fought under the Jewish flag (later adopted by Israel), a gesture of encouragement to the Jews by Churchill with Roosevelt's blessing, but against the wishes of his Foreign Office, which feared Arab reactions, because the soldiers were mainly from Palestine. Churchill, like Roosevelt, was a Zionist sympathizer, especially in this terrible and tragic time for the Jewish people.[18]

If Churchill and the British Chiefs of Staff exaggerated what was possible in Italy, they should not be denied credit for causing the undernourishment of

Hitler's Atlantic Wall and for furnishing in Italy a magnificent attack point for much of the British and Americans' most effective bombing of central Germany.

Alexander and Clark and their men have probably not received sufficient credit for what they accomplished. As the official history of the U.S. Military Academy (West Point) states: "In no small way, Italy was to Hitler as Spain was to Napoleon—an 'ulcer' steadily draining away strength from a weakening empire."[19] The Allied clearance of almost all Italy may well also have prevented a Communist takeover of that vital country.

II

THE LONG-AWAITED, tortuously prepared visit of Charles de Gaulle to Washington began on July 6, 1944.* He arrived on an aircraft Roosevelt had sent for him. "Franklin Roosevelt greeted me at the door of the White House, all smiles and cordiality." Anna accompanied her father and graciously poured tea. (Roosevelt allegedly suggested Vichy water for Leahy.[21]) De Gaulle also had discussions with Roosevelt's senior civilian and military colleagues, including Hull, who had had a complete change of heart and was very agreeable, Marshall ("a bold organizer but reserved interlocutor"), and Leahy ("astonished by the events that had defied his counsels . . . but persisting in his prejudices"). As always over this long era in Washington, de Gaulle wrote, "Roosevelt's glittering personality" predominated.

This was de Gaulle's first visit to the United States. (He would return to visit Roosevelt's five immediate successors, including being among the most prominent mourners at the funerals of Kennedy and Eisenhower.) On this occasion, he dutifully went to the Tomb of the Unknown Soldier at Arlington and to George Washington's house at Mount Vernon, and visited General Pershing, then eighty-three, in a nearby military hospital. When Pershing asked after his "old friend, Marshal Petain," de Gaulle dryly responded: "The last time I saw him, he was well."

"During five days in the capital," de Gaulle wrote, revealing the envy that has

---

* Marshall sent Roosevelt an extensive memo about de Gaulle's visit on July 4. There had been considerable progress on most issues. The principal remaining one was that de Gaulle, supported by the British, wanted use of French forces to be agreed intergovernmentally, as was the case between the British and Americans. The American position had been that this was a matter for the supreme theater commanders, Eisenhower and Alexander, and eventually MacArthur, to decide. Marshall wrote, with the peculiar insensitivity of talented American officials on this matter, like McCloy: "The Joint Chiefs of Staff insist that the method of employment of French troops (as is the case with other Allied forces, Canadian, Australian, New Zealand, Polish) is a responsibility of the Supreme Commander[s]." De Gaulle's desire to be treated differently to the British Dominions and the London Poles, especially in operations in France, where he was contributing ten divisions, was not unreasonable.[20]

not ceased to be a large part of European political analysis of the United States, "I observed with admiration the flood of confidence that sustained the American elite and discovered how becoming optimism is to those who can afford it. President Roosevelt, of course, did not doubt for a moment that he could." Roosevelt acknowledged that isolationism was "a great error," and he now envisioned what his visitor described as a "permanent system of intervention that he intended to institute by international law." His proposed international organization, de Gaulle concluded, "would have to involve the installation of American forces on bases distributed throughout the world," including on French territory. De Gaulle plainly saw that the proposed Big Four would in fact be, in the case of the Chinese and to a large extent the British, clients of the United States, and that the forty or fifty smaller countries would be highly susceptible to American influence — financial, military, and otherwise.

It also clearly emerged that, since Roosevelt was going to sponsor the independence of virtually every colony in the world, these new fledgling states would be dependent on and grateful for the generosity of the United States. It was in this intricate web of impressionable countries organized and orchestrated from Washington that Roosevelt, as de Gaulle perceived it, intended to involve the Soviet Union. By a subtle combination of flattery, largesse, and overwhelming power, the United States would engage the Soviets in this system "that would contain their ambitions."

"As was only human, [Roosevelt's] will to power cloaked itself in idealism." The fact that there might be a real element of idealism in the President's motives was implicitly dismissed with vintage Gallic cynicism. Roosevelt did not explain his plans by "setting forth principles, nor as a politician who flatters passions and interests. It was by light touches that he sketched in his notions, and so skillfully that it was difficult to contradict this artist, this seducer." This did not deter de Gaulle, according to his own retroactive account (which is not altogether credible), from explaining to his host that his proposals "risked endangering the Western world."

De Gaulle then enunciated what became the basic canons of the foreign policy of France and its acolytes in Europe, Africa, and the Middle East, in the Fifth French Republic, which de Gaulle eventually founded fourteen years later. The chief tenet of that policy was, and remains more than forty years into the Fifth Republic, that American power in the world is too great and that it is France's destiny to lead the counter forces of loyal opposition. De Gaulle conceived that France, though an unshakeable fundamental ally of the United States, is an essential force in preventing American hegemony from completely homogenizing the world along American-imitative lines, poorly adapted to other cultures.

The companion theory was that Roosevelt failed to notice, and effectively legitimized, the encroachment of the Soviet Union on central Europe. The myth arose, fanned by British and European anti-Americans and eventually by the McCarthyite Republicans of the United States itself, that Roosevelt had imperiled the West by his naïve assumption that Stalin could be transformed into a passive social democrat by being drawn into the United Nations organization. They imputed to Roosevelt the view that Stalin could be defanged, like a dangerous criminal rendered harmless by being seated in a kindergarten. De Gaulle was one of the earliest, most consistent, and most effective propagators of this spurious version of events.

De Gaulle's theory, which he claimed to have expressed to Roosevelt, was that the President was implicitly conceding Stalin more of Europe than was justified to achieve his agreement to the United Nations international organization. He also claimed that he suggested China could take a radical turn and be less docile than it then was, and that in encouraging hasty decolonization, the United States was creating a host of immature and unstable countries, little prepared for nationhood.

All of this section of de Gaulle's recollections must be read with great caution. Roosevelt was as aware as de Gaulle of the limitations of Chiang Kai-shek, and was well aware of the inroads that had been made by Mao Tse-tung. He had proposed, in respect of Indochina and other colonies, an extended transition to sovereignty. Roosevelt was no partisan of instant nationhood for a mass of primitive, tribal colonies. He favored an unexploitive, internationalized process of trusteeship, qualifying countries as sovereign nations as quickly as practicable, but not prematurely. When de Gaulle set up the French Community fourteen years later, it bore some resemblance to what Roosevelt proposed. Nor, at this time, did Roosevelt propose to retain any thing like the military presence abroad that was eventually, under subsequent U.S. presidents, judged necessary.

The immense success of the United States, and its comparatively slight direct exposure to the ravages of war, aroused first the importunity and then the envy of the suffering masses of Europe and Asia. They had reached pathetically out to America like starving mendicants begging scraps from a passing millionaire (like Reynaud asking Roosevelt for aircraft in 1940). Once the war was over and the crisis had subsided, joined by some of Roosevelt's rancorous domestic opponents, they blamed the United States for almost all shortcomings in the world.

De Gaulle claims that he lectured Roosevelt on the importance of the West, by which he really meant Europe, though it is unlikely that Roosevelt was in need of such enlightenment. "If it regains its balance, the rest of the world, whether it wishes to or not, will take it for an example. If it declines, barbarism will ultimately sweep everything away." De Gaulle was grateful for the American army of liberation and for the material assistance the United States was about to extend to France, "but it is in the political realm that she must recover her vigor, her self-reliance, and consequently, her role. How can she do this . . . if the settlement of the war definitively imposes upon her the psychology of the vanquished?" The general was trying to repeal the consequences of 1940, and objecting to the exclusion of France from the Big Four.

"Roosevelt's powerful mind was open to these considerations." (In fact,

France was admitted to what became the Big Five and regained all her territories except Syria and Lebanon.) De Gaulle acknowledged that Roosevelt was in fact an admirer of France, "or at least of the notion of it he had once been able to conceive." He attributed the subsidence of this Francophilia of the President's to his extreme disappointment and irritation at "yesterday's disaster among us and . . . the mediocre reaction" of many Frenchmen, including most that Roosevelt knew personally.

Roosevelt paid homage to de Gaulle personally for his courage and steadfastness, but was unconvinced that France had so swiftly recovered the spirit and character of a great nation and a Great Power in the world. He lamented that before the war he had sometimes been unable to remember the name of the incumbent leaders of the Third Republic's revolving-door governments. The President admitted uncertainty that de Gaulle would be successful in introducing a new political era in a country whose political life had so severely atrophied after the First World War, and had been unstable for 130 years prior to that.

De Gaulle, describing the exchange for posterity, casuistically wrote: "It would have been easy but pointless to remind Roosevelt how much America's voluntary isolationism had counted in our discouragement," after the First World war and in the collapse in the Second. He would have known better than to try such a spurious line of reasoning on Roosevelt. Roosevelt would have had no difficulty pointing out to the general that the United States was not responsible for the putrefaction of the pride, principle, resistance to evil, and will to national life to which France had succumbed in 1940.

De Gaulle began the process of building an elaborate mythology for many of the policies he would ultimately pursue, by claiming that these conversations with Roosevelt, as if they had come as a revelation, "proved to me that, in foreign affairs, logic and sentiment do not weigh heavily in comparison with the realities of power; that what matters is what one takes and what one can hold on to; that to regain her place, France must count only on herself." Roosevelt replied, when de Gaulle told him this: "We shall do what we can. But it is true that to serve France, no one can replace the French people."[22]

De Gaulle knew better than anyone how shameful France's performance had been between 1940 and 1944. The godfather and namesake of his son Philippe, Marshal Petain, had sentenced de Gaulle to death in absentia for refusing to surrender to the Germans. Cowardice, spitefulness, the ancient bigotry of the French officer class, the cynical avarice of much of the haute bourgeoisie, and the Cartesian hypocrisy of many of the intelligentsia were crucifying burdens to de Gaulle throughout his brilliant public career of more than thirty years. He famously loved France but did not much care for the French.

He admired Great Britain and particularly admired Churchill, and never understated his gratitude to the British and their wartime leader. But just as Churchill respected de Gaulle as the incarnation of French patriotism, he resented him for his uncooperativeness, the very posture de Gaulle felt compelled to assume by the inherent comparative weakness of his position. De Gaulle was trying to achieve recognition as a full-fledged ally. Churchill was trying to exact his due as a guardian and liberator, and to maintain his relations with the United States that aroused the general's jealousy. Churchill's exasperation with de Gaulle was tempered by his respect for the permanence and place of France, which only de Gaulle could assure. If there was to be any balance in Europe opposite the Germans or, after they were subdued, the Russians, it had to rest on the revival of France and of the Anglo-French alliance, and there was no one other than de Gaulle with whom to achieve this.

The equation became more complicated with the United States. Roosevelt admired France and was reasonably familiar with its language and culture. As de Gaulle detected, this intensified his disgust in 1940 and thereafter. He wanted France to revive because he had had affection for the country, not, unlike Churchill and de Gaulle himself, because he thought it necessary to the equilibrium of the world. This made it more annoying for him when the resurrection of France took the form of slights to the Anglo-Saxon powers that were putting France back on its feet.

De Gaulle respected and admired the limitless power of the United States but felt he had to demonstrate his and his country's importance to gain America's respect. Until that event occurred, he never gave up hope that Britain would cease to be an automatic ally of the United States and would lend its power and prestige to a policy of a Europe independent of the United States.

Churchill was convinced for obvious reasons that the alliance with America was the cornerstone of Britain's national interest in foreign policy. In the world wars and the Cold War, the United States was an indispensable and irreplaceable ally to Britain. So, what Churchill wanted from France, the solidarity of an ally, leavened by appropriate gratitude, de Gaulle could furnish only if America accepted France as an equal ally to Great Britain, a status it had not earned; or, failing that, if Britain broke ranks with the United States, which has rarely been a sensible policy for Britain since the end of the U.S. Civil War.

De Gaulle could get the respect he required for a satisfactory relationship with the United States only by impressing that country with the geopolitical importance of France, and this could be done only in negative terms, by being an irritant, at which de Gaulle's proficiency was conceded by all.

The rest of Charles de Gaulle's long career would be devoted to this end: to establishing France in the place it had briefly enjoyed with Clemenceau, in a grand alliance with the United States and Great Britain. When he returned to office in 1958 and his wartime comrades Dwight D. Eisenhower and Harold Macmillan were at the head of their countries, he would propose a tripartite leadership group for the North Atlantic alliance that was formed after the war. It was declined, in part out of concern for the sensibilities of the other countries, especially Germany; in part because, as Roosevelt had felt in 1944, it wasn't clear that France had regained any such status.

In sum, de Gaulle aspired to an alliance of equals with the Anglo-Saxons. Unable to achieve it from the Americans, he attempted to raise Europe on a course that professed friendship for the United States and was with it in decisive hours such as the Cuban missile crisis in 1962, but was intended to be a rivalry more than an alliance most of the time.

Almost everything he wrote about his relations with Roosevelt reflects this perspective. He did not seriously believe that Roosevelt was unaware of the menace posed by Stalin; the problem was that Roosevelt just wasn't asking de Gaulle to play a central role in the postwar architecture. Roosevelt's greatest foreign policy error wasn't his handling of Stalin, which was not particularly unsuccessful. It was his reflexive hostility to de Gaulle and his lateness in getting over it.

At the state luncheon he tendered de Gaulle on July 7, 1944, Roosevelt excoriated the "troublemakers" who claimed there was a problem between de Gaulle and himself. "There are no great problems between the French and the Americans, or between General de Gaulle and myself. They are all working out awfully well, without exception." He proposed two toasts, one to the accelerated liberation of France and one to "General de Gaulle, our friend." (This, we have seen, was always a dubious categorization when uttered by Roosevelt.) He praised France, yearned for its liberation, and foresaw its full revival "to something even more appealing, something even greater than before this war."

Roosevelt gave his visitor a photograph of himself signed: "To General de Gaulle, who is my friend." It remained ever after, and remains yet, in the general's library at his home at Colombey-les-Deux-Eglises.*

At a personal level, the July 1944 trip was a clear success for de Gaulle and a partial one for Roosevelt, because he had finally put relations with France on a proper footing, from which great things were possible. He had moved to make amends. De Gaulle was still prickly, and cited in his memoirs an indiscretion of Roosevelt's shortly afterwards—a statement that de Gaulle was "essentially an egotist." Though, if Roosevelt actually said it, it was an uncharacteristic lapse, this wasn't such a horrible, nor inaccurate, allegation. De Gaulle proceeded on to New York, where La Guardia arranged a tremendous reception for him, and then to "the beloved and courageous country" Canada. This was a fair but bizarre description, given the damage de Gaulle tried to inflict decades later on that unoffending country, France's co-liberator, which on the whole had treated its French-speaking minority generously.

Two months later, in Quebec, when Churchill railed against de Gaulle, "The President mentioned that he and de Gaulle were now friends," though he added that in a year de Gaulle would either be President of France or a prisoner in the Bastille.[23] Mackenzie King seemed to be the only other contemporary statesman who noticed the flippancy with which Roosevelt bandied about

---

* Also displayed are similar photographs of many other statesmen, including Eisenhower, Truman, (President) Kennedy, Nixon, Churchill, King George VI, and Pope Pius XII.

claims of friendship. King wrote in his diary during the 1944 Quebec conference of the President's references to his great friendship with King George VI and Queen Elizabeth: "It seemed to me . . . that language was very loosely used. There was the closest friendship with everyone"—the king, Churchill, Mackenzie King, the Canadian governor general. "Rather a lack of discrimination," King wrote. This was a bold foray for Mackenzie King, who was exaggeratedly deferential to Roosevelt, even in his diary.[24]

Roosevelt cabled Churchill that "the visit has gone off very well," and confirmed his acceptance of the French Committee of National Liberation (de Gaulle) as the "temporary de facto authority for civilian administration in France." His only conditions, that this not impede Eisenhower's ability to fight the war and not prevent the French people's being consulted in free elections as soon as practical, were not, and would never have been, an obstacle for de Gaulle.

De Gaulle was not as stand-offish and resistant to the charms and powers of Roosevelt at the time as he claims in his memoirs. De Gaulle wrote Roosevelt on August 14 of the "admiration and gratitude with which Frenchmen are following the magnificent operations of the armies of Eisenhower, Bradley, and Patton." He looked forward to the "honor and pleasure" of being able "to carry further the unforgettable conversations" of Washington. The general aired the same themes in a letter of September 13, 1944, offering the "most hearty and sincere" congratulations on the "recent successes of the Allied armies."[25]

A word must be included about the role of Leahy in the development of Roosevelt's French policy. Leahy's views of de Gaulle were consistently mistaken. He refused to believe that de Gaulle represented anything, where Churchill recognized at once that he personified the eternal spirit of France. Leahy was incapable of such insights. Leahy had ignored the resistants who had called on him in his early days at Vichy,[26] claimed, on the basis of no knowledge at all, that de Gaulle's political views were identical to Petain's,[27] urged Roosevelt to delay a visit from de Gaulle,[28] and helpfully refused Britain's request that de Gaulle's governor of French Guiana be transported by the Americans to that colony. He even accused the British of making trouble for the United States by promoting de Gaulle's hopes.

When de Gaulle finally did come to Washington, Leahy acknowledged that he "made a very good impression . . . including on myself. I had a better opinion of him after talking with him." (He might have been better qualified to carry out his task at Vichy and continue to advise the President on French matters after leaving there if he had taken the trouble to meet de Gaulle at any time in the preceding four years.) "I remained unconvinced that he and his Committee of Liberation necessarily represented the form of government that the people of France wished to have after their nation's liberation from the Nazis."[29] This is an outrageous series of assertions from someone who assumed de Gaulle was a semi-Fascist and refused to inform himself or be confused by readily available facts.

A year later, at the time of the Potsdam Conference, with de Gaulle governing in Paris in exemplary democratic manner, Leahy wrote of "this vain Frenchman who suffered acutely from a blindness to the present helplessness of his country and from a severe oversupply of national pride."[30] De Gaulle's problem was not unawareness of the erosion of France's position in the world since 1940, but chronic, almost obsessive consciousness of it.

Leahy even held de Gaulle responsible for confusion in postwar French politics by refusing Petain's offer of a direct handover of official leadership. Leahy actually considered de Gaulle unreasonable in August 1944, with much of France liberated and the Germans in full retreat, in not recognizing Vichy as the source of his authority.[31] Leahy couldn't bring himself to refer to the delirious reception de Gaulle was given by liberated Parisians two weeks after this generous offer by the marshal.

De Gaulle must have enjoyed Roosevelt's Bastille Day message, July 14, 1944. The President of the United States celebrated the solidarity of the Americans, British, Canadians, and French as liberators of France and of Italy, "in traditional unity . . . I look forward that the French people on July 14, 1945, will celebrate their great national fete on French soil, liberated alike from the invader and from the puppets of Vichy." Rising majestically above the attentions he had heaped on the "puppets," Roosevelt delighted in the "indissoluble unity and the deep friendship of the American and French peoples."

III

THE EVENING of Roosevelt's final meeting with de Gaulle in the afternoon of July 8, 1944, the President went in his clearly identified car to 2238 Q Street in Georgetown and collected, with Anna's approval, Lucy Mercer Rutherfurd. They drove through Washington, as they had done more than a quarter century before, but in the conspicuous manner in which the President traveled in the capital. And with Anna, who instantly liked Lucy (and must have remembered her slightly from her adolescence), they had a quiet and pleasant dinner in the White House. The next day, they drove to Shangri-la. Anna was constantly concerned at her father's state of fatigue, and though she knew that her mother would be devastated if she learned that her father's liaison with Lucy had started up again, she saw what a positive effect Lucy had on FDR. They would meet again at the end of August, when Roosevelt diverted his train to stop near Lucy's New Jersey house, when he was on his way to Hyde Park for the Labor Day weekend.[32]

A leading authority on the complicated relationship between Franklin and Eleanor Roosevelt wrote: "Were Lucy and Roosevelt lovers at this point? It is impossible to know, though, given the state of Roosevelt's health, doubt remains. Still, even if they did not share the same bed, it is reasonable to imagine that there was a pleasing sexuality in their friendship."[33]

The only suspense at the Democratic National Convention, which opened in Chicago on July 19, was who the vice presidential nominee would be. With Roosevelt's physical condition sometimes less than reassuring, this was not an unimportant question. The Democrats had not taken to Henry Wallace. He was judged strident, far too left for the mainstream, eccentric in many of his views, uncooperative with the congressional leadership, and a moralistic obstructionist in all questions involving patronage and party matters generally. Roosevelt rather liked him and found the controversy he aroused endearing. Wallace was a good deal more loyal to Roosevelt personally than Garner had been. The President casually let slip in the presence of a reporter that he would be happy to keep things as they were.

This was sufficient for Ed Flynn, representing the party organizers, to call on the President and remonstrate with him on Wallace's shortcomings. Flynn had retired as party chairman to become ambassador to Australia the year before, but withdrew his name from the Senate when his confirmation process provoked excessive partisan controversy. He would continue as head of the Democratic Party in the Bronx until his death in 1961, probably the most learned and reflective of the Democratic Party's many urban barons.

Roosevelt did not put up a tenacious defense for retention of his running mate. With the Republicans having effectively disqualified most of the armed forces from voting, this election could be closer than the previous three, and Roosevelt did not want another wrenching split over Wallace, as had occurred in the test of strength at the convention in 1940.

Wallace was also the victim of a systematic sandbag job in the President's entourage, as well as a comprehensive security challenge presented by J. Edgar Hoover and lesser officials. Edwin Pauley, the treasurer of the Democratic National Committee and a wealthy oilman from California, was one of the leaders of the dump Wallace movement. He made an arrangement with General Watson, who also disapproved of Wallace and was one of the President's closest cronies, that anti-Wallace figures would be admitted to the President's office in droves and supporters would, as far as possible, be barred, in the several months prior to the convention.[34]

Hoover's F.B.I. had labeled Wallace a security risk. Wallace had spoken in Los Angeles on February 4, 1944, at a union meeting, presided over by the film actor Edward G. Robinson and deemed by the Bureau to be a Communist meeting. Roosevelt was skeptical about this, since Wallace had said nothing inflammatory himself. But after a trip to South America that Roosevelt had sent Wallace on (there was little else for him to do except go on goodwill visits), Hoover had written Attorney General Francis Biddle that the vice president "is being unknowingly influenced by Bolivian Communists." This was apparently the transmission of information about insalubrious working conditions in the tin mines of that country, and was probably a truthful account. Roosevelt was too sophisticated not to recognize a smear campaign, and was well aware of the paranoiac tendencies of the director of the F.B.I. However, Roosevelt, at this stage in his career and in the evolution of world affairs, did not wish to have to defend himself from a terrier like Dewey on the charge that his vice president was an agent of Stalin's.[35]

Virtually Wallace's only defender apart from the party's official left wing, such as Senators Joe Guffey and Claude Pepper and the labor leader Sidney Hillman, predictably, was Eleanor Roosevelt. Mrs. Roosevelt did not in the slightest disapprove of Wallace's socialistic views, and was little concerned with the practicalities of reelection. On July 6 Roosevelt told Morgenthau that Eleanor was lobbying him on Wallace's behalf. Morgenthau strenuously counseled the President otherwise. The unspoken thought in the minds of all those seeking the vice presidency, or promoting or assailing those who were, was that Franklin D. Roosevelt was almost certainly an unbeatable candidate, but did not look like a man who could physically survive another four years in that office.

Roosevelt had implied to some intimates that he didn't need the presidency as much as the presidency needed him.[36] This and other reflections indicate that by this time Roosevelt intermittently had become a bit truculent, a symptom of tiredness and of the arteriosclerosis that at least lightly affected him. In any case, he sometimes, and for the first time, seemed to suffer the crotchetiness of the prematurely aged, a man worn down beyond his years by great office and infirmity. (Arteriosclerosis had been diagnosed but was very difficult to measure, and McIntire and Bruenn and others on the President's medical team were uncertain of its gravity, since their patient still functioned well most of the time.)

Never had the stakes for the vice presidential nomination seemed greater. And never did an incumbent president treat the issue of the choice of his running mate more casually or duplicitously.

Wallace returned from his 27,000-mile trip to Russia and China on July 10. Time was closing in, because the President was leaving Washington for Hawaii and Alaska for a month in a few days, and the Democratic convention would open on July 19. At Roosevelt's request, Rosenman and Ickes called on Wallace to advise him that he would not be renominated. Wallace declined to discuss the matter; he would be reporting to the President on his trip at 4:30 that day and would speak of renomination only to him. They discussed his trip for two hours, and then Roosevelt raised the vice presidency and said that Wallace was his own choice but that all the advice he was getting was that Wallace would cost them one to three million votes. Wallace gallantly said that if Roosevelt could find someone who brought more to the party than he, "By all means take him."[37] Roosevelt professed to be unable to bear the thought of the ridicule and brickbats that would come down on Wallace and his family if his name were put up and rejected. "Think of the catcalls and jeers," he said to his vice president, who volunteered that he could endure such things and was more concerned about the future of their party and country. Roosevelt invited him back for lunch the next day.

When Wallace returned it was with a folio of Mongolian postage stamps and an Uzbecki bathrobe he had bought for the President on his trip. He asked the President for a statement of endorsement for renomination and had a somewhat self-serving suggested wording. Roosevelt went over the convention vote with him state by state, demonstrating again his encyclopedic knowledge of the composition of his party's organization. He told Wallace that many regarded him as a Communist, and mentioned the slogan that had been mistakenly attributed to him: that he "wanted to give a quart of milk to every Hottentot." The discussion was adjourned after the President assured the vice president that he always defended Wallace against his critics. Wallace was invited back again to lunch in two days' time, July 13. Roosevelt was evasive, but Wallace subsequently claimed to believe Roosevelt would support him.[38]

Roosevelt's announcement of his candidacy for a fourth term was in a letter to party chairman Robert Hannegan that day, July 11. It contained several rather strained passages: "It is perhaps unnecessary to say that I have thought only of the good of the American people. . . . All that is within me cries to go back to my home on the Hudson River." However, the "Nation has been attacked and . . . its future existence and the future existence of our chosen method of government are at stake. . . . Therefore, reluctantly but as a good soldier, I repeat that I will accept and serve in the office, if I am so ordered by the Commander in Chief of us all — the sovereign people of the United States."

In his conversation with Ed Flynn that had stoked up the discussions about Wallace and a replacement, the President had asked about William O. Douglas, now of the Supreme Court, and former Securities and Exchange Commission chairman. The President was not in favor of James Byrnes or Alben Barkley. He wasn't particularly impressed with Barkley's performance as Senate majority leader, especially after his revolt on the tax bill. Apart from that, Roosevelt didn't want a southerner. The South was safely in his column anyway. As Barkley recorded in his memoirs, the dispute over the tax bill "did more than any other event of my career to keep me from becoming President."[39] Roosevelt knew that the race issue was looming in the Democratic Party and in the country, and was wary of being too closely identified with southern whites.

Dewey was a popular incumbent governor of New York, and though Roosevelt was generally reckoned to be unbeatable in his home state, it was feared that a vice presidential candidate unpopular with African-Americans could cost up to 200,000 votes in New York, clouding the prospects in that state.

By the end of the war, the number of African-Americans employed in manufacturing had risen from 1.4 million to over two million; those in unions had risen by 700,000, and the number employed in war production had risen as a percentage of the total from 2.5 percent to 10 percent, almost their percentage of the population as a whole. The black percentage of federal employees in Washington rose from 8.4 percent to 19 percent and there was much upward mobility in the nature of black employment in the private and public sectors.[40] The black community was stirring. It was, at long last, a start.

Byrnes, in addition to being a well-known segregationist, had also left the Roman Catholic Church when he married a Presbyterian, thus potentially alienating both Roman Catholic voters and the most suspicious and virulent of the anti-Catholics who would not accept the grace of his conversion. And there was the added problem that Byrnes had been running, virtually openly, for Roosevelt's job, and professing some entitlement to it, having served as almost a deputy president in administrative terms for the last two years, in his role as director of the Office of Economic Stabilization. Roosevelt did not like this degree of presumption from subordinates, and sent Leo Crowley, the custodian of alien property and a Democratic Party insider, to tell Byrnes he would not be president. This was a sequencing question, because Roosevelt knew he would shortly be sending someone else to tell Byrnes he would not be vice president either. Byrnes had given up the Senate to go to the Supreme Court and the Court to serve at the President's pleasure, and though he had performed capably, he had come close to incurring the President's displeasure.

Byrnes telephoned Roosevelt after receiving Crowley's visit and would not be put off by his usual unguent evasions. Then, and in a subsequent written message, Roosevelt expressed great admiration for Byrnes but asked him to desist from his vocalized ambition to be president. Byrnes did so, but his relations with the President were compromised on both sides.[41]

Roosevelt met on the evening of July 11 with Robert Hannegan and other party bosses, including Chicago's Mayor Edward Kelly, Ed Flynn, Postmaster General Frank Walker, party treasurer Edwin Pauley, and party organizer and fundraiser and future head of the RFC George Allen, as well as Anna and her husband, to discuss the vice presidency. Every name that had been mentioned for the vice presidency was reviewed. Wallace was scarcely mentioned and had no supporters in the group. "Roosevelt offered him no defense."[42] Roosevelt was reminded that he had encouraged many who were now rejected: Wallace, Byrnes, Barkley, Douglas, even Cordell Hull (now on another of his moral crusades, breaking off diplomatic relations with the Finns and trying to bully the British into doing so with Argentina, which still had a neo-Fascist government). Apart from their other failings, Hull and Barkley were both older than Roosevelt. Sam Rayburn, Ambassador Winant, Henry Kaiser, and Paul McNutt, administrator of the Federal Security Agency, had also all been encouraged by Roosevelt to think about it, though there is little evidence that any of this last group did so.

Some others, however, didn't need much encouragement, but none of these found favor with the group meeting July 11 in the White House. The Texas delegation to the convention had split, because there had been some anti–fourth term sentiment in that state, which sank any consideration of Rayburn, who was anyway too valuable as Speaker of the House (and where he remained, a mighty Washington fixture for nearly twenty more years). Hull was not a serious suggestion; Roosevelt was already planning to disembark him and Jesse Jones, who was not blameless in the Texas embarrassment, from the cabinet and replace them with younger blood.

Roosevelt's championship of Douglas was not a huge success with this group. The President, in playful mood, said that Douglas had led his law class at Columbia, which had included Thomas E. Dewey; had done well as a Yale law professor, at the S.E.C., and on the bench; had had experience as a logger; was a good poker player and raconteur, especially of dirty jokes; and looked youthful and appealing, with tousled hair that fell forward over his forehead. The President thought he had a politically useful "Boy Scout" quality.[43] All the men present were in shirtsleeves on a stifling Washington summer evening, and this idea was allowed to die in warm silence. (Roosevelt was so enervated, he could hardly turn the wheels on his chair.)[44]

Hannegan suggested fellow Missourian Senator Harry S Truman. Truman had a good record as a senator, was incorruptible, despite his long association with the Pendergast machine in Kansas City, and was popular and ideologically acceptable—a reformer but a moderate. Everyone was thinned out of the running except Truman and, in deference to the man who had the deciding vote, Douglas. Roosevelt sent for a Congressional Directory to determine Truman's age, which was sixty. He then told the group that they appeared to favor Truman, and that that was fine with him. Harry Truman and some historians[45] have asserted that Roosevelt wrote on an envelope near the end of the discussion, to Hannegan: "Bob, it's Truman. FDR".[46] The bosses seemed to think they had it for Truman, but Walker urged Hannegan to get it more precisely in writing. Hannegan dashed back upstairs and asked the President to specify in writing what position he had in mind for Truman. Roosevelt did so. He wrote that he would be happy to run with Douglas or Truman.[47]

All had forgotten that Truman had pledged to place Byrnes's name in nomination. The universally popular Frank Walker accepted the task of standing down Byrnes yet again. Byrnes was incredulous, given the support he had received from the President. When Byrnes besieged Roosevelt, the President blandly told him that Douglas and Truman were not his preferences but those of the group with whom he met. He told him by all means to run if he wished.

Byrnes asked Truman to confirm his support, alleging he had the encouragement of the President. Truman happily agreed. This became a matter of public dispute between them ten years later, Byrnes claiming to have been let down and Truman alleging that Byrnes had misled him. Truman is more believable, but it could have been a legitimate misunderstanding.

Hannegan tried to talk Wallace out of running, but Wallace said he would desist only if Roosevelt asked him to withdraw. All the party bosses were sandbagging the vice president in off-the-record press briefings.

When Wallace came back for lunch July 13, Roosevelt promised to send a letter to the convention chairman, Senator Samuel Jackson, saying that if he were a delegate he would vote for Wallace, but that the choice was the convention's. He mentioned Wallace's problems and referred to the conversations he had had with party elders two nights before. Wallace again manfully said that if that was the President's view, "I will withdraw at once."[48] Instead of taking this selfless offer, which he described as "mighty sweet," out of the transports of concern for the embarrassment to Wallace's family if he lost at the convention, which he had emphasized two days before, Roosevelt, who knew his vice president was going to be blackballed, said he didn't know what the public view was. To be confident of it himself, he would have to "drive among the farmers in Dutchess County."

Instead, after shaking hands warmly and reiterating that he hoped it would be "the same team again," Roosevelt added, ominously, that if Wallace did not succeed in Chicago, "we will have a job for you in world economic affairs." This was the President's subtle method of warning Wallace that he was finished, as Rosenman and Ickes had told him three days before. Wallace had served twelve years in Roosevelt's cabinet. Anyone more worldly than the earnest vice president would have taken this as a political death warrant and withdrawn.

Roosevelt thought he had given Wallace all the warning he should have needed. His letter to the convention began "I like him and I respect him and he is my personal friend" (the inevitable kiss of death). Beyond this point, FDR was going to be an amused spectator. The thought of the gullible, faddish, cryptosocialist Wallace, the "wild-eyed fellow," as Jim Farley had called him four years before, getting anywhere near the White House other than as an occasional social visitor, is a chilling one.

Wallace apologists point to his good position in the polls and public support of his trips to Asia, but the public didn't know him as the Democratic bosses, skilled judges of political horseflesh, did.[49] Roosevelt was inviting the bosses to elect their candidate, exactly what he had refused to do in 1940. The political journalist and novelist Allen Drury called this process in his diary "perhaps the coldest and cruelest brush-off in all the long Roosevelt career."[50]

Roosevelt should have had more curiosity about his own health and more respect for the continuity of what he had labored to achieve, in America and in the world, than to treat his succession so lightly. For once, the party bosses came to the rescue of the Western world. Sadistic magisterial puppeteering was one of the handicapped President's chief amusements (and possibly psychological displacements), but not one of his most admirable traits.

His letter was too ambiguous to please the bosses. But the almost somnambulant Wallace was dumbfounded when the President's letter was read. He had been expecting an endorsement, and privately ascribed Roosevelt's behavior to an insufficient blood supply to his brain. His mind "was a sick mind," he said, referring to physiology, not psychiatry. Wallace had offered three times to withdraw. Roosevelt had no such excuse as Wallace offered. His intelligence hadn't deteriorated, but his cynicism had no more abated than had Wallace's impenetrable political innocence.

Roosevelt departed for the Far West, on his way to meet with MacArthur and Nimitz, on July 17, and ordered that the train should proceed slowly enough that he would arrive in California only when the balloting was over. Far from being too preoccupied with the war to visit the convention that would nominate him to a fourth term, he simply could not be bothered any more with the squalling and puling of political conventions.

When the President's train stopped briefly in Chicago, Hannegan and Mayor Kelly clambered aboard and asked the President for help in unraveling the chaos over the vice presidential nomination. After they met for an hour, Hannegan emerged and asked Grace Tully to retype the note expressing pleasure at the thought of having either Douglas or Truman as a running mate. Hannegan assured her that the President authorized that the sequence should be Truman and then Douglas, contrary to the alphabetical order he had followed in what he had written out at the White House on July 11.

Wallace claimed Hannegan had bullied Roosevelt: "When a man who means business . . . was talking that way to the President, the feminine side of the President would succumb to the dominant Hannegan," Wallace ludicrously reminisced. Hannegan was a forty-one-year-old provincial political wheel horse who had no capacity whatever to intimidate the world's most powerful officeholder, an almost certainly invincible candidate for reelection.

The revised statement by the President created the impression that Truman was the President's preference, since his name came before Douglas's. By such threads would history unfold. Roosevelt must have been convinced of Truman's superior merits, given that Douglas was a political novice then on a hiking holiday in the Oregon Cascades and inaccessible. It is not plausible that Hannegan misled the president's secretary, as some have suggested,[51] into reversing the order of the two preferred candidates.

Grace Tully's assistant, Dorothy Brady, typed the letter. Neither Grace Tully nor Roosevelt nor anyone else involved ever suggested skullduggery by Hannegan. Truman was obviously the better-qualified candidate. What is most likely is that Roosevelt accommodated that fact in his typed note to Hannegan but didn't wish to exclude Douglas entirely. This swung the convention and changed history.[52]

Having sown confusion and resentment but, with the strenuous connivance of Hannegan, having also effectively made Truman the frontrunner for the nomination, President Roosevelt continued on to San Diego in his armor-plated train. A good deal of backing and filling continued in Chicago. Roosevelt had thrown a sop to the left by famously saying, "Clear it with Sidney [Hillman]," in reference to the vice presidency and any other important matter. This was the same Hillman to whom Roosevelt had promised the position of wartime labor coordinator and then decided not to create the position and left Hillman uninformed and awaiting a call that never came.*

Hillman was for Wallace. Roosevelt had effectively vetoed Wallace. Hannegan orchestrated an early move for Byrnes, who was strongly opposed by Hillman (on ideological grounds; religion seems to have had nothing to do with it). Hannegan then rallied Hillman to Truman, and the Byrnes campaign disintegrated. All this maneuvering took place in the fetid back rooms of the Chicago convention hotels while the President's train rolled westwards.

Hannegan, Kelly, Flynn, and Walker telephoned the President on his train near El Paso late on July 17. Roosevelt concluded that the farce had to end. He spoke last to Walker and said finally: "Frank, go all out for Truman."[53]

The next morning, Truman breakfasted with Hillman and asked Hillman's support for Byrnes. Hillman said he was for Truman as vice president. Wallace imputes this to Hillman's opportunism and inconsistency.[54] It was really Hillman's getting behind the President's own choice.

Though unconvinced that Roosevelt wanted him as vice president or that he wanted the position himself, Truman asked Byrnes to release him from his pledge to nominate him, which Byrnes did. Byrnes then wrote a letter withdrawing as a candidate and left Chicago with more dignity but not greatly more enlightenment about Byzantine Rooseveltian political realities than Wallace, who only arrived in Chicago on July 19, after Byrnes had left. Wallace had become more erratic than ever, physically assaulting an unoffending photographer who took his picture July 18 in the lobby of the Wardman Park Hotel, where the vice president (and also the secretary of state) lived in Washington.[55] Wallace perservered on in Chicago in a doomed cause.

The pro-Wallace historians and anti-Roosevelt memoirists like Jim Farley claim that Barkley was ready to decline to renominate the President.[56] Barkley acknowledges[57] that he was sufficiently irritated at the treatment of Byrnes (but not of Wallace) that he considered altering his speech, but decided against it. There was no thought of not renominating the President, which would have been an act of political suicide by Barkley.

In the frenzied atmosphere of the convention, many of these politicians seemed momentarily to forget that they had only one candidate who could defeat Dewey, that he was supported by 95 percent of the delegates, and that he was the country's greatest leader since Lincoln. Roosevelt had given the convention the

* He treated the president of the University of Chicago, Robert Hutchins, in the same way after preparing him for the succession to General Hugh Johnson's position at the NRA in 1935. He did the same to Bernard Baruch in regard to the directorship of the Office of Economic Stabilization, putting in Byrnes instead. There was plenty of precedent for his bizarre treatment of Wallace.

chance in 1944 to choose a vice president, having been criticized for forcing Wallace on his party in 1940. In the President's absence from Chicago, the children were squabbling for control of the kindergarten.

In the President's traveling party were Eleanor and her secretary, Tommy Thompson, Rosenman, Watson, Dr. Bruenn, Grace Tully, and Dorothy Brady. As they moved at a stately pace, he had a leisurely and agreeable time with Eleanor. Their relations were at a steady and rather convivial level, though he looked to Anna and Lucy and Margaret Suckley and Laura Delano for light-hearted, humorous, and relaxing companionship. The President arrived in San Diego on July 20.

On that day, a group of disaffected German officers, with the support of Field Marshal Erwin Rommel, attempted to kill Hitler at his eastern headquarters at Rastenberg. With the uncanny sense of self-preservation that delivered him from many such plots, Hitler moved around the large map table where they were plotting the military campaigns just before the explosion of the bomb that had been left beside him in a briefcase. Some were killed, but that the world might be spared nothing, the fuehrer survived. He was dazed, twitching, with an incapacitated right arm, and with, as he said, "a bottom like an East African baboon," but not seriously injured. He was even more crazed than ever, and wrought a horrible vengeance on all suspects. Rommel, out of deference to his service and reputation, was spared a more gruesome end and only forced to take poison. He was given a full military funeral, and his part in the plot was not publicly revealed. This was the last opportunity to avoid a severe division of Europe and the murder of two million more innocents, more than half of them Jews.

On the afternoon of the 20th the party bosses, still floundering in Chicago, telephoned Roosevelt and asked him to persuade Truman to accept the vice presidential nomination. Roosevelt's personal intervention was necessary even for the accomplishment of mundane tasks. Roosevelt told Hannegan to tell Truman, who was beside him and overheard the President,[58] "that if he wants to break up the Democratic Party in the middle of the war and maybe lose that war, that's up to him." Truman, who had honestly said he wasn't interested in the post, relented.*[59]

The President was advised formally of his renomination without opposition and addressed the convention from the observation car of his train, now in the San Diego naval base, on the evening of July 20, 1944. "I have already indicated to you why I accept the nomination that you have offered me—in spite of my desire

---

* Truman eventually rewarded Hannegan with the position of postmaster general, in which capacity he played a cameo role in U.S. folkloric history by being mentioned in the popular film *Miracle on 34th Street*. Truman also rewarded Byrnes for his trouble by making him secretary of state, but soon tired of him, as Roosevelt did, and replaced him in that post with General Marshall.

to retire to the quiet of private life," he began. "Today Oklahoma and California are being defended in Normandy and on Saipan; and they must be defended there—for what happens in Normandy and Saipan vitally affects the security and well-being of every human being in Oklahoma and California." (Saipan, one of the Mariana Islands, was cleared of Japanese by Nimitz's marines in June and July 1944, in a bloody engagement.)

"The isolationists and ostriches who plagued our thinking before Pearl Harbor are becoming slowly extinct. . . . All nations of the world . . . will have to play their appropriate part in keeping the peace by force." (This was a robust concept for which he had not secured any other foreign leader's agreement.) He defined the country's task in the next four years: "First, to win the war—to win the war fast, to win it overpoweringly. Second, to form worldwide international organizations, and to arrange to use the armed forces of the sovereign nations of the world to make another war impossible within the foreseeable future. And third, to build an economy for our returning veterans and for all Americans—which will provide employment and provide decent standards of living."

He launched a preemptive strike on the age issue by saying that the people would have to decide if they wished to "turn over this worldwide job to inexperienced or immature hands, to those who opposed Lend-Lease and international cooperation against the forces of aggression and tyranny, until they could read the polls of popular sentiment . . . to entrust [it] to those who offered the veterans of the last war breadlines and apple-selling and who finally led the American people down to the abyss of 1932." The Republicans could not have imagined that their task in unseating the incumbent would be an easy one. However, an unfortunate photograph of a haggard-looking Roosevelt giving his acceptance speech went out on the wires.

On the morning of the 21st, Roosevelt was going to review an amphibious landing exercise in Oceanside, when he was stricken with acute stomach pains. He called for his son Jimmy (Eleanor having departed for Los Angeles), and asked him to help him out of bed so he could lie flat on the floor. He forbade him to call the doctor, claiming these were only pains of indigestion due to eating too quickly. "For perhaps ten minutes, Father lay on the floor of the railroad car, his eyes closed, his face drawn, his powerful torso occasionally convulsed as the waves of pain stabbed him."[60] After a few more minutes the spasms stopped, his color returned, and he asked his son to help him up, and proceeded in an open car to watch the military exercise.

In Chicago, there had been one final outburst of chaos after the President's speech. When Wallace seconded Roosevelt's nomination, there was a tremendous demonstration for Wallace, and the great pipe organ in the Chicago Stadium played "Iowa, That's Where the Tall Corn Grows" in his honor. Hannegan and Kelly with difficulty had managed to get the convention adjourned on the night of July 20, though a large part of the hall was clamoring for Wallace. The beleaguered vice president's biographers claim that Kelly had dispatched one of his city workers with an axe to shut down the great Chicago Stadium organ.[61] On the morning of the 21st the convention reopened with the bosses and Truman lined up behind the President. It was at this point that he was closeted in his railway car recovering from his angina attack and receiving bulletins about the attempted coup in Berlin.

On the first ballot, Wallace led Truman 429 1/2 to 319 1/2, with 427 votes scattered among other candidates. On the second ballot, after Hannegan, Pauley, and the bosses had done their work, the rank and file fell in contentedly, as they were unable to do in 1940, and Truman swept the convention 1031 to 105. Eleanor pronounced herself "sick about the whole business." She thought it "bad politics [and] disloyal," though she understood Truman was "a good man."[62]

Joseph P. Kennedy, rarely a reliable source, would write in his diary for distribution to his family that on October 29, 1944, he met with Truman and Hannegan in Boston, and that both men "believe Roosevelt won't live long, particularly Hannegan. . . . They felt that Truman will be President and will kick out all these incompetents and Jews out of Washington and ask fellows like myself and others to come back and run the government. Truman assured me that that is what he would do. He said that he disliked Mrs. Roosevelt very much . . . I state again—both Truman and Hannegan discussed what they would do when the President died."[63] It is very unlikely that Hannegan, and almost inconceivable that Truman, would have said anything remotely resembling what Kennedy recounted. Truman frequently engaged in routine anti-Semitic reflections but was sympathetic to persecuted Jews and would be the virtual godfather to the new State of Israel. He also admired Mrs. Roosevelt.*

IV

ROOSEVELT LEFT SAN DIEGO on the new heavy cruiser U.S.S. *Baltimore* at midnight on the 21st, a Friday, in keeping with his reluctance to start a sea voyage on a Friday. He was on the high seas before the convention ended. He arrived at Pearl Harbor on July 26 after an agreeable voyage. The many ships of the Pacific Fleet had all hands on deck in review formation as the Commander in Chief's flagship and her escorts came into port.

Admiral Chester W. Nimitz, commander in chief of the Pacific Fleet and of the Central Pacific Area, came on board with his staff. There was convivial conversation, and Roosevelt expressed curiosity about the whereabouts of MacArthur. A siren was heard and a large open car pulled up at dockside with the general sitting in the back seat in a leather flight jacket and his familiar self-designed hat, combining the regalia of a U.S. general (four stars and about to be

---

* Kennedy was shocked by the President's appearance when he visited him at the White House on October 26, 1944. He also thought Roosevelt's memory had deteriorated; "his memory was his next greatest asset to his charm."[64]

five, when that rank was created) and a Philippine field marshal. Roosevelt had not seen MacArthur, who moved to Manila in 1935, when he retired as army chief of staff, for seven years.

The Pacific war had gone almost unbrokenly well after the turning of the tide at Midway in the central Pacific and at Guadalcanal and the Solomon Islands in the southwest Pacific. Both MacArthur and Nimitz proved themselves theater commanders of great skill as they proceeded westwards and northwestwards across the Pacific toward Japan.

Nimitz had launched his drive in the Gilbert Islands, particularly the hard-fought action on Tarawa, in November 1943; moved on into the Marshall Islands, to Kwajalein and Eniwetok, in January and February 1944; and then into the Marianas, to Saipan, Tinian, and Guam, in June and July. These islands were 1,600 miles from Japan, and could serve as bases for the new B-29s the United States was now producing in large quantities.

Japanese resistance was even fiercer than usual at Saipan. The Japanese had installed 45,000 defenders and the Americans attacked with 125,000 men. Savage fighting continued for weeks, as every square foot was defended. The Japanese refused ever to surrender—they had to be killed or seriously wounded. Finally, the Japanese leapt from cliffs into the ocean to their deaths or retreated into caves, where they were pursued with flame-throwers and incinerated or asphyxiated.

This movement 1,500 miles toward the Japanese home islands in nine months smoked out the Japanese Navy, which had struggled to rebuild its carrier forces after Midway, converting battleships and uncompleted liners to aircraft carriers and frantically training air crews. The Japanese emperor, Hirohito himself, ordered that Saipan be held, and the Japanese Navy sailed against the Americans in the midst of the Saipan action with nine aircraft carriers, five battleships, and a large number of smaller craft. Japanese Vice Admiral Jisaburo Ozawa had 430 carrier aircraft. He met U.S. Admiral Raymond Spruance, commanding a significantly larger force, in the Battle of the Philippine Sea, starting June 18, 1944. It was an uneven match; in addition to greater numbers, the Americans now also had qualitative superiority in aircraft and better-trained pilots. The United States Navy scored one of its greatest victories, sinking three Japanese aircraft carriers and destroying almost 400 Japanese warplanes as well as smashing up Japanese airfields on neighboring islands, all with minor losses to itself. Hirohito had ordered the attack to avoid the prospect of bombs falling on Tokyo. He and his subjects were now going to become very accustomed to the presence of American aircraft overhead, and they would not be dropping leaflets.

After clearing the Solomons, MacArthur moved almost a thousand miles from point to point along the northern shore of New Guinea and on to Morotai, almost the last stop before the Philippines, from January to September 1944. His forces had just reached the end of New Guinea when he arrived at Pearl Harbor on July 26. MacArthur said to his entourage (Marshall had observed during a visit some months before that MacArthur didn't have a mere "staff," saying, "General, it is a court") that he was annoyed about being used as a second in Roosevelt's reelection campaign. Given his own penchant for public relations, this concern was bizarre. MacArthur professed privately to be appalled at the President's physical appearance, though his wit, powers of concentration, and fluency seemed unimpaired.[65]

The purpose of the meeting in Honolulu was to determine where to go next. The central Pacific thrust was clearly toward Iwo Jima and Okinawa, the nearest islands to Japan, but the issue between the navy and the army, or more accurately between King, with Nimitz arguing the case for him, and MacArthur was whether to move on Formosa, as the navy suggested, or the Philippines. Nimitz put the Formosa case crisply on King's behalf, since Roosevelt did not bring King, Marshall, or Arnold, but only Leahy with him. But Nimitz was not personally convinced of the Formosa argument.

The argument in favor of Formosa was that it was nearer to Japan than the Philippines and would enable direct aerial intervention against the Japanese in China, strengthening Chiang Kai-shek as well as adding to the American potential for inflicting damage on the Japanese. It would facilitate interdiction of shipment of oil, tin, rubber, and other vital resources to Japan. This would bypass the Philippines and approach Japan through the central Pacific only, virtually shutting down MacArthur's theater.

The arguments against the Formosa option, apart from advocacy of the Philippines as preferable, were that it would involve a more extensive land war than would be possible until the end of the European war, that it was too distant an amphibious target from the launching base, and that it would be extremely hazardous with the Japanese still in control of the Philippines. Further, recent Japanese advances against the Chinese made Formosa's practical utility for intervening in the war in China less valuable.

MacArthur made an eloquent argument for the Philippines. He expressed the above reservations about Formosa, made the point that the Philippines was a less risky target, and mentioned that it was the repossession of American territory, the fulfillment of a promise to the Filipinos, and the liberation of many thousands of American prisoners, providing they had survived the barbarities of Japanese prison camps. Australia was understood not to favor an exclusive concentration on the central Pacific, and MacArthur emphasized the danger of too great a reliance on carrier-based aircraft to the comparative exclusion of land-based ones. The aircraft carriers could still conceivably be vulnerable, especially in the midst of amphibious action, and they were a finite aerodrome, while unlimited numbers of aircraft could be launched from land bases, which would not be available for an attack on Formosa. MacArthur expressed concern about opinion in Asia if it appeared the United States was not interested in liberating the Philippines, which had been a loyal friend. He emphasized that the Filipinos would rise in support of an invasion, where the Formosans, after fifty years of Japanese rule, would not.

From all accounts, Roosevelt handled the meeting with great finesse and tact. Hereafter, accounts vary, and have to be weighed carefully, since no written account was kept. MacArthur claims that he privately warned Roosevelt: "If your decision be to bypass the Philippines and leave its millions of wards of the United States and thousands of internees to languish in agony and despair—I dare to say that the American people would be so aroused that they would register most complete resentment against you at the polls this fall." The general claimed that with the benefit of this insight, Roosevelt assured him: "We will not bypass the Philippines. Carry on your existing plans. And may God protect you." (The distinguished historians James MacGregor Burns,[66] Doris Kearns Goodwin,[67] and Eric Larrabee[68] all reprint this version.)

Since these remarks were allegedly uttered by MacArthur and Roosevelt outside the earshot of anyone else, and were written by MacArthur after Roosevelt had died, Nimitz's version must be much closer to the facts. He recalled MacArthur saying: "You cannot abandon 17 million loyal Filipino Christians to the Japanese in favor of first liberating Formosa and returning it to China. American public opinion will condemn you, Mr. President, and it will be justified." This is fairly presumptuous by the standards of any serving American officer except MacArthur, but could be taken as considered professional advice as well as an insight from an aspiring politician and an old acquaintance. Roosevelt gave no such response as MacArthur claimed, and as always with those seeking his help, left the general in hopeful suspense. The official process was that Leahy prepared a summary that Roosevelt approved, and Marshall and King were required to make a recommendation.

Roosevelt does seem to have anticipated his adjudication of the King-Marshall disagreement (Marshall supported MacArthur on this issue). Roosevelt wrote MacArthur on August 9 ("Dear Douglas"), while still on his way back to Washington: "As soon as I get back, I will push on that plan for I am convinced that as a whole it is logical and can be done." He added that "to see you again gave me a particular happiness. Personally, I wished much in Honolulu that you and I could swap places—and personally I have a hunch that you would make more of a go as President than I would as general in the retaking of the Philippines."[69] Roosevelt wrote generously to all his senior commanders, and MacArthur had earned his praise, but this effusion was piquant, given Roosevelt's awareness of and disdain for MacArthur's political ambitions.

As it was, the Philippine invasion was launched only two weeks before the election, and it would not have been possible to raise the failure of the Roosevelt administration to liberate the Philippines up to that date before the election. King was obdurate despite MacArthur's persuasive efforts. Roosevelt decided for MacArthur on the national honor argument and because he thought it was useful to keep the twin parallel ladders toward Japan, in the central and in the southwestern Pacific. Sending out troop transports for a Japan invasion force involving two to three million men from Okinawa, 350 miles through the Ryukyus, and Iwo Jima, across 600 miles of open ocean, with no prospect of an alternate route, would have been very dangerous when an alternative could be obtained. Waiting six more months for atomic testing would have been irresponsible, and even cowardly. Formosa was judged, almost certainly correctly, to be too hazardous. In retrospect, with the knowledge of the power of the atomic bomb, the Philippines might have been a superfluous operation, but at the time it was almost certainly the correct decision. It was arrived at by intelligent analysis by detached commanders, not as a result of MacArthur's political saber-rattling.

Nimitz, because he was less flamboyant than MacArthur and never held great civilian offices as MacArthur (in Japan), Eisenhower, and Marshall did, is comparatively less known. He is generally revered as probably America's greatest admiral and, along with Britain's Andrew Cunningham, one of the two greatest admirals of the Second World War. White-haired, blue-eyed, trim and undemonstrative, Nimitz, like most American admirals, was born far from the sea, in Fredericksburg, Texas, where his originally German family owned the Nimitz Hotel. He spoke German and liked dogs, the game of horseshoes, and classical music. He had long impressed Roosevelt, not least when in early 1941 he declined the navy's second-highest post, commander in chief, U.S. Fleet, because he felt that in being promoted over a large number of senior officers he would stir up a good deal of resentment and internecine strife.

Nine days after Pearl Harbor, when Knox returned from the scene of the debacle and told the President that Kimmel was too compromised by what had happened, Roosevelt responded: "Tell Nimitz to get the hell out to Pearl and stay there 'til the war is won!"[70] This is pretty much what happened. Nimitz's promotion of officers in his command, especially Admiral Raymond Spruance, had been exemplary. He got on reasonably well with MacArthur, which was sometimes challenging, and he had an unbroken series of successes, from Coral Sea and Midway, for which he denied any credit for himself, on through the Solomons, Gilberts, Marshalls, Marianas, Palaus, the Philippine Sea, Iwo Jima, and Okinawa.

It is said of Spruance that as a fleet commander, at Midway, the Philippine Sea, Leyte Gulf, and in between, he never made a mistake.[71] Nor did Nimitz. "To say that Roosevelt appointed Nimitz and Nimitz appointed Spruance is to say much of what needs to be said about the way the war was fought in the Pacific hemisphere."[72]

Nimitz hosted a luncheon at the end of the formal meetings in Honolulu. Roosevelt had three martinis before lunch, and one of the host's aides counted 146 stars on the collars of the 36 men seated, led by MacArthur, Nimitz, Leahy, and Halsey. Nimitz was astounded that Roosevelt's security chief, Mike Reilly, and his men, commanding a group of SeaBees, had uprooted palms and built a ramp to allow the President direct access to the Pacific Fleet and theater commander's office. They had rebuilt and widened the door to the admiral's bathroom to enable entry by the President's wheelchair. Reilly's crew had repainted swiftly and speed-dried the makeover with blowtorches, an impetuous undertaking for any work crew less skilled. "Nimitz hardly recognized his quarters."[73]

On July 27, after the strategic discussion and debate, Roosevelt, MacArthur, Nimitz, and Leahy toured Oahu in an open car. Given the scores of thousands of mainland Japanese-Americans who were still interned, while there had been no such action taken in Hawaii, this was a bold move from a security standpoint. It should also have reminded the President of what an outrage the detention of the mainland Japanese-Americans had been. The President and his party were greeted by thousands of cheering Hawaiians and a great many saluting servicemen. Demonstrations were put on for the President by the army, navy and marines. He noted the contrast from his last visit, ten years before, when there had been a military display in which most of the tanks and trucks had broken down.

At a military hospital on July 28, Roosevelt had himself wheeled through all the wards where there were soldiers, sailors, and airmen who had suffered an amputation. He had a Secret Service man wheel him slowly past every bed where someone had lost an arm or leg, and spoke with many of the injured veterans. Rosenman wrote: "It affected us all very deeply."*[74] Rosenman records that he had never seen the President so close to tears as on that day in Hawaii when he toured the hospital.[76]

———————

A few hours later, Roosevelt and his party boarded the *Baltimore* and sailed out of Pearl Harbor for Alaska. The trip had been justifiable, to enable the President to make an informed determination of the best course to pursue in finishing the Pacific war. It would have been irresponsible to summon MacArthur and Nimitz away from their commands back to the United States, and there was no method as effective as personal exposition in evaluating the opposing arguments.

While Roosevelt was on the vast Pacific, sailing northeastwards through rising seas, Missy LeHand went to her local cinema in Boston with her sister and a friend. She was so disturbed by the haggard appearance of President Roosevelt in a newsreel of the San Diego proceedings that when she returned home, she sought out old photo albums, became agitated, suffered a series of strokes through the night, was taken in an ambulance to Charles Naval Hospital, and died there in the morning of July 31. Missy was only forty-five. The White House

---

* The only other occasion when he had not disguised his handicap at all was in 1936 at Howard University, an African-American institution whose rector, Mordecai Johnson, asked the President to allow the students to appreciate his handicap, that they might realize that they, too, could do anything. He allowed himself to be lifted from his car and walked awkwardly to the podium.[75]

cabled the President. He issued a statement referring to "memories of more than a score of years of devoted service. . . . Faithful and painstaking, with a charm of manner inspired by tact and kindness of heart, she was utterly selfless in her devotion to duty."

Missy was given a prodigious funeral in her parish church, presided over by the future cardinal and archbishop of Boston, Bishop Richard J. Cushing. Mrs. Roosevelt, Joseph P. Kennedy (who had once questioned the propriety of Missy's relations with the President), and James A. Farley led the mourners. Insiders like Harold Ickes and observers including Arthur Krock considered that the departure from the White House of Missy, following by a few years the death of Louis Howe, deprived the President of his closest, most trusted, and most astute advisors. The President would not have disagreed. As Krock wrote, "Missy's death severs a shining link between these grim times and the exciting days when the New Deal and the administration were young."[77] Roosevelt ordered a navy transport to be named after her, and sent a message to the ship's launching, March 27, 1945: "Mrs. Roosevelt and I send warm greetings to all who attend the launching of the S.S. *Marguerite A. LeHand* in the hope that a craft which bears so honored a name will make a safe journey and will always find a peaceful harbor. Franklin D. Roosevelt".[78]

The *Baltimore* and its escorts reached the Aleutian island of Adak on August 3, 1944. Roosevelt was not speaking entirely in jest when he said to the officers and men of the naval air station: "I like your food. I like your climate." He had a vision of Alaska as the last frontier of America, and likened Alaskan waters to those he knew best, off Maine and New Brunswick. He transferred to a destroyer, a modest and crowded ship to bear so exalted a passenger, and proceeded in foggy weather down the Pacific coast to Bremerton, Washington.

There, on August 12, he spoke to 10,000 shipyard workers from a podium set upon the foredeck of his destroyer. It was an ill-conceived plan. Roosevelt had not stood in his braces for over a year and as he had lost weight, on doctors' orders, they no longer fitted well. A considerable wind blew up, and he had trouble controlling the pages of his text on the podium. He was standing at a slight angle on the sloping deck, and with the slippage in the loose braces, he had to grasp the lectern with both hands. The wind that threatened his pages also rocked the ship. The challenge was distracting, and was compounded by severe chest pains that extended to both shoulders.

In a monumental display of self-control, he persevered with his speech, despite acute discomfort, heavy perspiration, and concerns about losing his balance or even his consciousness, not to mention his text. Rosenman, in annotating Roosevelt's speeches and public papers, wrote of this occasion: "The pain of the braces, the feeling of insecurity, and the other adverse circumstances [angina] combined to make the President's delivery hesitant, halting, and ineffective. The reaction of the audience—which the President was always quick to sense during the delivery of a speech—was so unfavorable that it only served to make the President's delivery worse. The reaction of the entire country to this speech was very bad." (It was broadcast to the country as a report on his trip to Hawaii.) "Even some of the President's best friends and most loyal supporters began to whisper to each other that they were afraid the old master had lost his touch, that his days of campaigning must be over and that he would be a sorry spectacle in the coming campaign against the young, virile, Governor of New York." Once again, one last time, Franklin D. Roosevelt would confound his enemies and inspire his supporters.

Roosevelt gamely finished his address, a remarkable achievement in the circumstances, and hobbled back to the destroyer captain's cabin and collapsed into a chair. Bruenn cleared out everyone, including Anna, who had flown to join her father for the train trip home. An electrocardiogram and white blood count, administered at once, revealed nothing worrisome, but the President was instructed, and agreed, to rest all the way back to Washington, where he arrived on August 15.

Strangely, almost the only flattering comment Roosevelt's Bremerton speech received was from Charles de Gaulle, writing from Algiers on August 14. The general claimed to have "listened with great interest to the fine speech you have just made."[79]

Despite the President's immense popularity with the working press, with the American public, and in the world, where he was now generally revered as a great and golden incarnation of a mystical, quasi-Biblical Balm of America, Franklin D. Roosevelt resented press curiosity about his infirmity and his medical condition generally. He had dodged or blunted the intrusiveness of the journalists for twenty years, and said to Mike Reilly, his chief of security, of the latest burst of unfounded rumors: "Those newspapermen are a bunch of God-damned ghouls."[80]

V

THE POSTWAR CONDITION of German-occupied Europe loomed ever larger in the concerns of Churchill and Roosevelt as the Allied armies closed in on the Reich from east and west and south. Churchill cabled Roosevelt August 17 to tell him that he was preparing a rapid deployment force to occupy Athens as soon as the Germans withdrew, to prevent Greece from being taken over by Communists. The State Department was at this time advising Roosevelt that if the monarchy were retained in Greece, as Churchill favored, the Communists would prevail. Churchill volunteered in his August 17 message that the Greeks would have to decide whether they wanted a monarchy or a republic when the country was cleared of invaders, but that he was assuming the legitimacy of the monarchy ad interim. Roosevelt ignored the State Department (as he usually did) and messaged back his agreement with Churchill on August 26.

Developments in Poland were reaching a critical stage as the Red Army moved across the country. Mikolajczyk had a relatively cordial meeting with Stalin in Moscow on August 10, in the course of which Stalin repeated that he would make no effort to communize Poland. Stalin pledged to help any Polish rising and discounted any thought of a Communist Germany, saying that "Communism was no more fit for Germany than a saddle for a cow." This encouraged Mikolajcszyk, as he told British ambassador Clark Kerr. The ambassador summarized the Polish leader's visit to Churchill, who forwarded his message to Roosevelt as he received it, August 11.

The joy at Stalin's remarks proved premature. On August 18, Stalin cabled Churchill dissociating the Soviet Union from the "reckless and terrible adventure" of the Warsaw uprising. The Polish underground had risen in Warsaw and was bravely challenging the Germans for control of the city, on the assumption that the Russians, on the other side of the Vistula, would help the uprising. Stalin claimed to Churchill that he had initially dropped "arms intensively in the Warsaw sector," but on further consideration, regarded it as ill-considered and needlessly destructive to the population, and objected that the uprising had begun without any consultation with his government.

The same day, Churchill cabled Roosevelt that the "glorious and gigantic victories" of the Allied armies in France could "far exceed in scale anything that the Russians have done on any particular occasion." He thought that Stalin would accordingly "have some respect for what we say so long as it is plain and simple. It is quite possible Stalin would not resent it but even if he did we are nations serv ing high causes and must give true counsels towards world peace." At this point the Western armies in Europe were only about 40 percent of the numbers of the Red Army, and the disparity in casualties they had endured was immense. The Anglo-American hand was obviously strengthened opposite Stalin, but it wasn't clear how this could immediately help Poland. It was, however, a stirring confirmation of the value of Overlord by the long-skeptical Churchill.

Roosevelt proposed the next day to send a joint message with Churchill to Stalin asking for all possible aid to the Warsaw Poles, "thinking of world opinion if the Warsaw Poles are in effect abandoned." Roosevelt thought the Warsaw uprising was probably a doomed cause and didn't want to destroy relations with the Soviet Union over it, but the scale of Stalin's cynicism in encouraging the revolt and then standing aside while the Nazis slaughtered the Polish patriots was a grim augury.

Churchill instantly agreed and sent Stalin Roosevelt's message with his own name added to it. He also sent Roosevelt a reference to the longstanding Soviet practice of broadcasting incitements to the Poles to rise up against the Nazis, which they were now doing. On August 20, the Soviet assistant foreign minister, Andrei Vyshinsky, sent a message to Churchill assuring him that the Soviet government had no objection to having British and American aircraft drop supplies to the Poles but did not want those planes to go on to land in the Soviet Union, "since the Soviet government do not wish to associate themselves either directly or indirectly with the adventure in Warsaw."

Churchill was still in the Mediterranean, having seen the launch of Anvil (Dragoon) on the 15th. He wrote Roosevelt, also on August 20, congratulating him on the appearance of his soldiers and oddly adding: "We are most grateful for your help." Four days later he cabled back that the message had been intended for the President of Brazil. "The cipher people had apparently not realized there was any other president in the world."[81]

Eleanor unearthed and gave to her husband a memo written by Churchill in 1919 when he was secretary for war and air and an advocate of, as he later put it, "strangling Bolshevism in its cradle." Eleanor added: "It is not surprising if Mr. Stalin is slow to forget!" The thought that Churchill might have been correct in 1919 didn't occur to Eleanor Roosevelt until some years later, when "Mr. Stalin's" nature was much clearer to her.

Roosevelt's attitude was not greatly more positive to Communism as a system than was Churchill's. Roosevelt was a more religious man than Churchill and more of a respecter of capitalism, since it was so much more a part of the political culture of the United States, even if he was in domestic matters slightly to the left of Churchill (but only slightly). He thus found Marxism thoroughly abhorrent, to the point where he had the utmost difficulty taking it altogether seriously as political science.

The result was that while he disapproved of Communism as much as Churchill did, he was less afraid of it. He was convinced that progressive democratic government would easily be seen as preferable in every way to Communism, as long as the West did not become mired in lost causes such as the defense of untenable imperial commitments. He discreetly responded to Churchill's increasingly alarmed cables, August 23, 1944: "We must continue to hope for agreement by the Soviet to our desire to assist the Poles in Warsaw."[82]

Churchill had sent Roosevelt a candid and moving eyewitness description of the suppression of the uprising. He sent it also to the Soviet ambassador in London. The same day Stalin sent Roosevelt a message calling the leaders of the uprising "power-seeking criminals," and blamed them for endangering the civil population of Warsaw. The United States had succeeded in negotiating landing rights at three Ukrainian airfields, but Molotov informed Harriman on August 17 that these bases would no longer be accessible to Western aircraft.[83] Roosevelt confirmed to Churchill August 24: "Stalin's reply of August 23 to our joint message about the Warsaw Poles is far from encouraging." Churchill wrote Roosevelt August 25, enclosing a proposed message to Stalin, and added to Roosevelt that the planes should be sent whatever Stalin said: "I cannot conceive that he [Stalin] would maltreat or detain them [the aircrews]." Roosevelt demurred August 26: "I do not consider it advantageous to the long range general war prospect for me to join with you in the proposed message." He encouraged Churchill to send any message he wanted to Stalin on his own account.[84]

Churchill sent Stalin a stern message on September 4. He found "it hard to understand your government's refusal to take account of the obligations of the British and American Governments to help the Poles in Warsaw. Your Government's action in preventing this help being sent seems to us at variance with the spirit of Allied cooperation to which you and we attach so much importance both for the present and the future." The prime minister wanted to stop the convoys to Russia but was persuaded by the Foreign Office that doing so would cause even greater vengeance to be wrought on the Poles.[85]

In an accompanying message to Roosevelt, Churchill wrote that he and his cabinet were "deeply disturbed at the position in Warsaw and at the far reaching effect on future relations with Russia of Stalin's refusal of airfield facilities. . . . [He again asked Roosevelt] to order unauthorized landing on Soviet airfields of aircraft parachuting aid to the Warsaw uprising. I cannot think that the Russians could reject this fait accompli." Churchill also included a heart-rending letter to the pope from the women of Warsaw.

Roosevelt replied September 5 that according to his "office of Military Intelligence . . . the fighting Poles have departed from Warsaw and . . . the Germans are in full control. . . . The problem of relief for the Poles in Warsaw has therefore unfortunately been solved by delay and by German action and there now appears to be nothing we can do to assist them. I have long been deeply distressed by our inability to give adequate assistance to the heroic defenders of Warsaw and I hope that we may together still be able to help Poland be among the victors in this war with the Nazis."[86] This was rather disingenuous; "the fighting Poles" only "departed" Warsaw when the Russians finally arrived and generously facilitated the disposal of the 200,000 corpses of brave Varsovians, one-fifth of the city's total population.

On September 9, while still denouncing the "Warsaw adventure," the Soviet government indicated that it would cooperate in aiding the Polish underground. There were further delays caused by bad weather, but American planes did drop supplies to the Poles from 104 bombers that flew on to Soviet airfields on September 18. The Soviet Air Force dropped some supplies to the Poles for several days beginning September 13 and the Soviet Army advanced to the Praga suburb, but no farther. The Russians, as Churchill wrote, "wished to have the non-Communist Poles destroyed to the full, but also to keep alive the idea that they were going to their rescue."[87] But Warsaw had already been largely and brutally crushed, while, as the women wrote to the pope (who did not need much encouragement to take a dim view of Stalin), the Red Army remained "at the gates of Warsaw [and had] not advanced a step."

Premier Mikolajczyk reported to Churchill October 2 that the Poles were about to surrender to the Germans in Warsaw. The resistance of the Polish capital was one of the most heroic episodes of the entire war, in the same category of unlimited valor as the revolt of the Warsaw Ghetto the year before, when a small number of lightly armed Jews held the German occupiers at bay more than ten times as long as the resistance of the Kingdom of Denmark endured in 1940, and more than a quarter of the time of the great French Republic's resistance a few weeks later, between the German attack on May 10 and the French surrender June 18. Warsaw in 1944 had held out three weeks longer than France in 1940 and four weeks longer than Poland itself in 1939.

The Poles, of whatever faith, were invariably difficult and invariably brave. As Winston Churchill recorded in his memoirs, one of the last broadcasts from Warsaw before the Germans briefly reimposed their authority concluded: "This is the stark truth. We were treated worse than Hitler's satellites. . . . May God, who is just, pass judgment on the terrible injustice suffered by the Polish nation, and may He punish accordingly all those who are guilty. Your heroes are the soldiers whose only weapons against tanks, planes, and guns were their revolvers and bottles filled with petrol . . . the women who tended the wounded, carried messages under fire . . . and who soothed and comforted the dying . . . the children who went on quietly playing among the smouldering ruins. These are the people of Warsaw.

"Immortal is the nation that can muster such universal heroism. For those who have died have conquered, and those who live on will fight on, will conquer and again bear witness that Poland lives when the Poles live."

Churchill commented: "These words are indelible."[88] They fought 60 days, lost 15,000 of the 40,000 Polish Underground Army, and inflicted 26,000 casualties on the German Army. Churchill, still seething with well-founded outrage when he published his memoirs ten years later, wrote: "When the Russians entered the city three months later they found little but shattered streets and the unburied dead. Such was their liberation of Poland, where they now rule. But this cannot be the end of the story."[89] It assuredly was not.

Churchill professed to Cadogan to be ready to go "to the verge of war" with Russia over Poland.[90] What Churchill really meant was that he was prepared to urge such a policy on the United States, and that is eventually what happened, without much urging from him. The United States and Great Britain and their reliable allies were on the verge of war with Russia for decades. In the end, after forty-five years, their victory would be complete. Poland and all Eastern Europe would be free, without another major war.

VI

POLAND RECEDED AS an issue for a time, but the Western leaders had had a bitter foretaste of what Soviet occupation of Eastern Europe could involve. Churchill's rage is commendable, and even now seems much more appropriate than Roosevelt's glacial calm. However, there was nothing that could be done for

Poland except trade better treatment for that benighted country for something within the gift of the Allies that Stalin would want more than to oppress Poles. In this sense, Roosevelt was correct; blowing up the relationship with Stalin, such as it was, could foreclose the real horse-trading that might be possible if the Western Allies could proceed swiftly enough to the center of Europe.

Stalin feared Germany as much as Churchill had, and since most of Germany would be in Anglo-American hands, it would be up to Churchill and Roosevelt (or in fact their successors) whether Germany would rise again or not. Roosevelt hoped that it might be possible to trade on Stalin's fear of Germany and possible desire for respectability as well as economic assistance to secure civilized Russian behavior in Eastern Europe. If atomic developments were successful, that would further strengthen America's bargaining position opposite the Russians.

There is an element of reasonable supposition in this estimation of Roosevelt's intentions, but it is the only interpretation that squares with his expressed views and usual methods. The imputation to him of terminal naiveté, indifference, or intellectual enfeeblement is not consistent with indisputable facts.

Churchill's and Roosevelt's armies were approaching the Rhine and were two-thirds of the way up the Italian peninsula. They were prepared to snatch Greece and possibly Yugoslavia almost from Stalin's jaw. On August 25 Charles de Gaulle returned to Paris and the following day was given an unforgettable reception by millions of Parisians as he walked down the Champs Élysées. Serried ranks of French officialdom, including many Gaullists of very recent date, gathered to march with him from the Arc de Triomphe. "One step behind, please, gentlemen," said de Gaulle, as he set off down the great boulevard to the delirious adulation of the liberated masses of the French capital. Roosevelt had sorted out his relations with the general just in time. If recognition were still being withheld as this mighty confirmation of the general's legitimacy occurred, it would have been a sorely embarrassing state of affairs. As it was, de Gaulle, vested finally with the instances of a state, quickly reconstructed the French Army with American equipment, and was slightly less prickly than he had been. And he thoroughly outmaneuvered the French Communists.

On his first full day back in Paris, de Gaulle began the fabrication of the myth of France as a victorious power. He implied in his public remarks at the Hotel de Ville that France had largely liberated itself, that resistance had never ceased or been extinguished. It was as if there had never been an armistice nor a regime at Vichy. This was the start of the effort not only to expunge the shame of 1940, but to present France as a much stronger and more recently and uniformly glorious country than it was.

The tenets of Gaullism were already discernible. The British and Americans could not have won without the Russians, to whom they abandoned Eastern Europe, having excluded France from the peace conferences where France would have defended Eastern Europe. If Britain would detach itself from America and Russia would dispense with Communism, Gaullist France would coordinate the British, Russians, and Germans and lead Europe back to preeminence in the world. Even without the British, a French-led Western Europe could hold the balance of power between the Soviet Union and the "Anglo-Saxons." From this early date, de Gaulle's alliance with the British and Americans was relaunched as a rivalry. So it would remain as long as he and his followers were directing French foreign policy. Given the limitations of France's population, resources, and political credibility, it was an aggregation of confidence tricks, but de Gaulle himself by his stature and ingenuity would briefly give it some currency twenty years later when the United States was distracted by the war in Vietnam.

Gaullism was always a luxury created and preserved by the umbrella of American protection.

In furtherance of Roosevelt's plan to enable himself to play the German card with Russia, he broadly endorsed Treasury Secretary Henry Morgenthau's plan for the radical de-Nazification and deindustrialization of Germany. This was a prospect that he believed Stalin would pay for. This was the way to help the Poles, not by blustering as 360 Russian divisions swarmed across Eastern Europe. The U.S. Army, in contemplation of occupying Germany, had a general plan for weeding the military out of the government of Germany. The State Department had a plan for eliminating and replacing "German economic self-sufficiency for war [with] an economy which can be integrated into an interdependent world economy."[91] Neither Hull nor Stimson had known what went on at Teheran or at the European Advisory Commission, so Winant had ignored their suggestions.

Roosevelt encouraged the Morgenthau plan, but he never really believed in anything so contra-historical as the transformation of Germany into 70 million shepherds, apple cultivators, and poultry farmers. Morgenthau's plan also decreed that German "archcriminals" be arbitrarily designated, rounded up, and "put to death forthwith by firing squads," with no pretense of even military judicial process. This was a pretty feisty revival of Old Testament justice for the normally rather mild Treasury secretary. There was no chance Churchill or Roosevelt could agree to this either. The appeal of the plan was as a carrot to dangle in front of Stalin.

The struggle in Roosevelt's entourage over postwar treatment of Germany produced another epic yet often farcical battle among courtiers and senior officials. Morgenthau, convinced of the inbred evil and compulsive bellicosity of the German people, was seconded to some degree by Hopkins, who aspired to govern occupied Germany, and to some extent by Eleanor Roosevelt. Stimson and McCloy were wildly opposed to the Morgenthau plan and keenly felt the need for a reconstructed Germany to be integrated into the civilized world and not harshly treated as it had been after 1918, which largely contributed to World War II. Hull began in some sympathy with Morgenthau but quickly shifted to stern opposition when he got a good look at the Morgenthau plan. Anna Roosevelt was distinctly cool to Morgenthau, and when the Treasury secretary played his last card and camped outside the President's private office in his residential quarters, Anna, on instruction, grasped his forearm and conducted him to the elevator with the assurance that her father did not wish to see him.[92]

Morgenthau had visited Britain in August 1944 to consider postwar Lend-Lease requirements and economic relations generally. When he reported to Roosevelt that Britain was "bankrupt" and that Churchill would lose the election, Roosevelt said that in that case, he would "buy it" (Britain). Mrs. Clementine Churchill conducted Morgenthau on a tour of air raid shelters (Britain was then dodging the V-1 rockets). She pronounced her guest "a funny, vague old thing," not obviously competent to operate a "whelk stall" (be a street vendor). This was a little harsh. Morgenthau gave a speech from London to both countries, largely written by Robert Sherwood and Edward R. Murrow, that advocated severe treatment of Germany.

To the considerable irritation of Churchill and Roosevelt, Morgenthau wheedled out of Eden the minutes of the Teheran meeting, which Eden didn't feel he could withhold, since he sought Morgenthau's assistance in Lend-Lease and other economic matters. Eden, not conversant with Roosevelt's idiosyncratic methods, had apparently not considered that the President would not have shared the Teheran proceedings with his senior colleagues as Churchill, under the requirements of cabinet government, had done. Morgenthau misread the inconclusive talk about partitioning Germany that went on at Teheran to mean that this course had been decided upon. Having been rather placid about mistreatment of the European Jews in the thirties, he now launched himself on a holy crusade to achieve a Carthaginian peace against the German genocidists.

When Morgenthau returned to Washington, he stirred up Hull and Hopkins. Roosevelt urged Hopkins to get Stimson to calm Morgenthau down. All were on the President's Germany subcommittee of the cabinet and were shortly at each other's throats. The Morgenthau faction began leaking their version of events to the columnist Drew Pearson, and the Stimsonites, whose ranks were shortly reinforced by the supposedly nonpolitical Justice Felix Frankfurter, replied with systematic leaks to the columnist and Kennedy payee Arthur Krock. Morgenthau attacked Hopkins to Eleanor Roosevelt for exchanging private cables with Churchill and attacked Stimson to Roosevelt as someone who had been too close to Hoover. (Roosevelt's own preferred conduit of leaks to the press was the columnist and broadcaster Walter Winchell, a fiercely supportive Roosevelt idolator, who received a steady stream of tips from Stephen Early and other presidential assistants.)

Roosevelt watched all this with some bemusement until, at the start of another presidential election campaign, he decided it was getting out of hand and demanded the protagonists show more discretion. Throughout he claimed to be more or less on the side of whichever faction was being given his audience. Frankfurter, the cleverest of the faction heads, was right when he assured Stimson that Roosevelt could not possibly be serious about Morgenthau's proposals for Germany and that Stimson should not be too concerned with them.[93]

Roosevelt would not allow Morgenthau to set an exchange rate for American occupation soldiers trading dollars into Deutschemarks. "Nothing doing," said the President realistically. The soldiers could work out their own exchange rate in free-market transactions with the locals (from the position of strength of heavily armed occupiers) as they went along, he said.[94]

Roosevelt deadpanned to Morgenthau that the key to any peace imposed on Germany must be to prevent the Germans from having any aircraft, "even a glider," and his old bugbear of preventing the Germans from donning uniforms and marching. He affected to believe that the Germans were a nation of self-mobilizing robots who, if allowed to wear uniforms, would stage endless parades until they marched into the territory of their neighbors. It was a caricature like Churchill's professed belief that the Prussian Junkers had transformed Germany into a warrior state. In fact, Churchill sometimes claimed to be almost back to his post-World War I view: "Kill the Bolshie; kiss the Hun," in accord with Britain's centuries-old policy of opposing continental Europe's strongest power.[95]

Roosevelt would decide later whether to rebuild Germany as a counterweight to the Russians or suppress the Germans within humane limits, in exchange for good Soviet behavior. (On September 29, 1944, Roosevelt told Hull: "In their occupied territory, [the Soviets] will do more or less what they wish."[96] On September 13, at Quebec, Roosevelt gave Morgenthau a telegram he had just received from Harriman in Moscow, who said that the Russians "are trying to force us and the British to accept all Soviet policies, backed by the strength and prestige of the Red Army," and would, if allowed, "become a world bully.")[97]

In the first of his Germany committee meetings that he attended in person, Roosevelt commended the utility of soup kitchens to feed the Germans and actually claimed that it would be wholesome and useful to deny Germans modern plumbing and require them to use outhouses, as he claimed to have done himself as a youth. One of Morgenthau's aides, Herbert Gaston, asked later if this was the President's plan for pacifying Germany, to strip the plumbing out of the Ruhr rather than the heavy industry.[98] It remains a mystery how Roosevelt or any of his interlocutors managed to conduct such a surrealistically jocular discussion with any apparent seriousness. Stimson, whose sense of humor was not extensive, abruptly denounced Morgenthau's proposal to turn the Ruhr into an "ash heap" and declared German industry "a gift of nature" that was essential to resuscitating postwar prosperity.[99] Roosevelt agreed with Stimson and dissolved the Germany committee after just one month and four rather absurd sittings.

VII

THE DAY OF ROOSEVELT'S resigned last reply on Poland, Churchill and his party sailed for Halifax on the *Queen Mary* from the Clyde for a second conference in Quebec with Roosevelt and their staffs, which it was agreed would be called Octagon. In order to maintain what Roosevelt knew to be the fiction that Churchill was the host at the governor general of Canada's summer residence, the Citadel of Quebec, Churchill wished to get to Quebec ahead of Roosevelt to receive him. Roosevelt advanced his timetable, called for his train earlier than he had originally planned, and greeted Churchill at Quebec's Wolfe's Cove railway station when the prime minister's special train from Halifax arrived, September 11.

Mackenzie King never ceased to promote Canada's independent identity, but found both leaders implicitly skeptical. He thought "The President was rather assuming he was in his own country."[100]

Octagon opened on the morning of September 13. Roosevelt asked Churchill to start the session, and he gave a very upbeat summary of the military situation in all theaters. Churchill graciously "congratulated the United States Chiefs of Staff on the gratifying results of 'Dragoon.' It seemed that eighty or ninety thousand German prisoners had already been captured, and the south and western parts of France were being systematically cleared of the enemy."[101] It was hard to believe that only three months before, Churchill had been contemplating resigning his office in protest against Anvil (Dragoon), and just a few weeks before had been advocating rerouting it to Brittany

Churchill also generously acknowledged that the offensive was continuing in Italy, the campaign he had claimed three months before had been "ruined" by Anvil-Dragoon. He obtained American approval to retain some landing craft in the Mediterranean, in case an amphibious move against Trieste and Fiume and "a right-handed movement to give Germany a stab in the Adriatic armpit," with a drive on to Vienna, might prove opportune. (A stab in the armpit was not quite as alluring as an attack on the soft underbelly, but the prime minister was giving the German anatomy a workout.) He emphasized "the dangerous spread of Soviet influence" in the Balkans, and certainly received no demurral from Roosevelt or his senior advisors.

Churchill proposed taking Rangoon and driving the Japanese out of Burma, and congratulated the Americans on Stilwell's victories there. He again thanked the United States for its immense contribution to the impending crushing defeat of Germany and said that the British Empire, no less affronted by Japanese treachery and aggression than was the United States, desired to play its full part in the defeat of Japan. He offered twelve divisions, starting as soon as Germany was defeated, added to the sixteen British Empire divisions already in Southeast Asia. And he offered immediately a large contingent of bombers from the Royal Air Force, and a large part of the Royal Navy, a mighty fleet, exceeded only by the U.S. Navy and larger than any fleet in the world had been at the start of the war.

Roosevelt accepted the offer of the British Navy (overruling King, who always regarded the British with suspicion). He gave a confident but sober summary from the American perspective, and there were no substantive differences between the two sides. There had been a great evolution in the spirit of these meetings since the Arcadia Conference in Washington in December 1941. Initially, the British came better prepared and equipped with all their experience of the war going back to September 1939. There had been a compromise over Torch and indecisive tussles about Overlord, until the deployed strength of the United States was such that it was able to impose its will, with Stalin's help, at Teheran. Torch, Overlord, and Anvil-Dragoon had all been great successes, Italy a success but a laborious one, and the power, competence, judgment, and experience of the Americans were such that there was little disposition among the British to argue with them.

It was clearly a meeting between a senior and a junior partner, though a very convivial one. There were no material differences about postwar matters. This was the first wartime conference where all the news was good; Eisenhower, Alexander, MacArthur, Nimitz, and Mountbatten, and Stilwell and (Field Marshal Sir William) Slim in Burma, were all making excellent progress. But both Churchill and Roosevelt warned that the Germans would stage one more great battle in the west, to try to hold their frontiers.

Poland, where the struggle continued hopelessly in Warsaw through September, was little mentioned. (Marshall and Arnold caucused privately and authorized an airdrop, though they knew these were not particularly accurate.[102] Churchill did succeed in reviving, for one final levitation, the possibility of an amphibious assault at the northern end of the Adriatic. There was vague talk of a thrust toward Vienna, even though his own staff thought this impossible.[103] According to Brooke, Churchill claimed: "We have two main objectives, first an advance on Vienna; secondly the capture of Singapore!" There were no military plans for either.

Churchill was concerned, as he acknowledged in his memoirs, that Britain would seem not to have pulled her weight in the Pacific war. "We had to regain on the field of battle our rightful possessions in the Far East, and not have them handed back to us at the peace table."[104] This raised the specter of colonialism again. When he wrote: "Singapore must be redeemed and Malaya freed," he meant, of course, restored to British rule.[105] Britain had 160,000 prisoners of war and civilian interns in Japanese camps, and had lost more war dead in the theater than the Americans at this point, though this balance would tip sharply in the last year of the Pacific war. The British had no experience opposing the Japanese in the approaches to their home islands and so placed less importance than the Americans did on bringing the Russians into the final attack on Japan, where one million casualties were anticipated. Large units of the Royal Navy could be sent at once to the Pacific. The last dangerous Axis surface ship left in Europe, *Bismarck*'s sister, the *Tirpitz*, would be destroyed, capsized by several British 5.5-ton bombs on November 12, 1944.

Churchill initially denounced Morgenthau's plan for Germany in such strictures at Quebec that Morgenthau was unable to sleep the night after Churchill's blast. The Treasury secretary said, "I have never had such a verbal lashing in my life," and suspected Roosevelt of enlisting Churchill to slap down the secretary for him (such was the conspiratorial ambiance of the Roosevelt court). Churchill exclaimed that he would not be "chained to a dead German."[106] He was already remarking to friends that he did "not want to be left alone in Europe with the Bear."[107] He wanted French and post-Nazi German accompaniment.

Churchill started out thinking the Americans conceived the Morgenthau plan as a substitute for postwar aid to Britain. Churchill discovered that it was intended by Roosevelt to be a tactical chip opposite Stalin and that British acceptance of it would facilitate American generosity in providing postwar economic assistance to Britain.

Having attacked the plan initially as "unnatural, unchristian, and unnecessary" (a perfectly accurate judgment, but Morgenthau made no pretense to Christianity), Churchill declared that he had been "converted" on September 16. The prime minister warmed up to greater enthusiasm for the plan than Roosevelt, the original sponsor, who never really took it seriously other than to get Stalin's attention.[108] Churchill delegated his scientific and industrial advisor, Frederick A. Lindemann (Lord Cherwell), to work with Morgenthau on modifications to the plan.

Cherwell and Morgenthau, both anti-Germans of German ancestry (though Lindemann seems not to have had Jewish ancestors), got on well, and Cherwell and Churchill rewrote Morgenthau's memorandum, keeping many of its features but not pledging to a dismemberment of Germany or the dismantling of the Ruhr.

This was a conspicuous service furnished to the alliance by Churchill, as it effectively deescalated the squabbling among Morgenthau and Stimson and Hull. In this partly emasculated form, Morgenthau's plan survived for a time, but was of more use to Goebbels in warning his countrymen of the consequences of Allied victory than in Western discussions with Stalin. It was an entertaining sideshow but amateurish geopolitics.

Churchill claimed in his memoirs that he had agreed to the Morgenthau plan reluctantly. In fact, he seems to have yielded to Cherwell's counsel that if the Morgenthau plan were implemented, British industry could replace Germany as a supplier of a vast range of sophisticated industrial products. Roosevelt completely disavowed Morgenthau's plan in conversation with Stimson on October 3.[109] The generally unreliable Joseph Kennedy wrote that on October 26 Roosevelt debunked the plan and said: "I don't know anybody who has less political sense than Henry." In this case, though some allowance should made for Kennedy's anti-Semitism, his account is plausible.[110]

The Americans overcame their reluctance to accept southern Germany as an occupation zone by taking the ports of Bremen and Bremerhaven as an enclave in the British zone, so their communications with the United States would not be through France, a thought that worried the Americans. Roosevelt told Hull that the United States would have to retain troops in Europe for an indefinite future, contrary to the posture he generally assumed publicly and with foreigners (except de Gaulle).

Churchill was particularly concerned to assure continuation of Lend-Lease, and at one point, as Roosevelt chatted discursively before signing the enabling document, Churchill asked if he was "to get on my hind legs, and beg like Fala" [the President's ubiquitous dog].[111]

(Roosevelt later overcame skepticism in parts of his administration, and ignored the hostility of elements in the Congress, to agree continuation of Lend-Lease to Britain, and promised $6 billion in aid in the first postwar year. He appears to have been subtly reminding Churchill of the economic correlation of forces between them, but after this foreplay he responded generously and routed the domestic critics. At immediately subsequent meetings in Hyde Park, Roosevelt also agreed to share fully with the British "in developing [atomic energy] for military and commercial purposes.")

Roosevelt and Churchill agreed to grant Italy greater self-government and to extend aid to the country through the United Nations Rehabilitation and Relief Administration for the reconstruction of the economy. It may be reasonably assumed that Roosevelt had one eye on the imminent U.S. elections in this decision. The leaders were united in their determination to keep the Communists out of governmental influence in Italy, and Roosevelt was already delighted with the ostentatiously pro-American government of Premier Ivanoe Bonomi. (This would be the first of many postwar European governments essentially run from the U.S. embassy.)

Even Brooke was relatively magnanimous in his diary comments, with only a few exceptions, touching on the "ghastly hypocrisy" of official banquets, the "boring and . . . charming" personality of Marshall (unlike Roosevelt, who was "very pleasant and easy to talk to"), and the time-consuming automobile ride (of one minute in fact) between the Chateau Frontenac Hotel and the Quebec Citadel, where Churchill and Roosevelt stayed.[112]

Churchill was concerned at the decline in Roosevelt's appearance and good health, and asked McIntire about it. McIntire assured him the President's health was fine. Churchill responded: "With all my heart I hope so. We cannot have anything happen to that man."[113] On the evening of September 18, Roosevelt had selected the film *Wilson*, about the former president, for after-dinner entertainment. This was a production with which Wendell Willkie had been associated as one of the film's promoters. Willkie was then hospitalized and died less than three weeks later. As Wilson's health and political fortunes collapsed on screen, Churchill became uneasy at the portent and left the room. Roosevelt exclaimed: "By God, that's not going to happen to me!"[114]

Churchill and Roosevelt had been accompanied by their wives, and Churchill by his daughter Mary also. The ineffable Mackenzie King, now almost twenty years the Canadian prime minister, was much in evidence in Quebec, insinuating himself into the front pages of the world press in joint photographs. In addition, the notables of French Quebec had to be taken into account. Churchill attended a Quebec cabinet meeting, presided over by French Canada's most formidable leader in twenty-five years, and King's most dangerous opponent, Premier Maurice Duplessis.*

The Roman Catholic archbishop of Quebec and primate of Canada, who had played an important role in maintaining French-Canadian support for the war effort, J.-M. Rodrigue Cardinal Villeneuve, was deferentially received by the leaders, and Churchill and Roosevelt were loudly cheered by heavy crowds as they went through the city. Quebec had had no shortage of Petainists and Anglophobes, but by this stage in the war, especially after de Gaulle's dramatic return to Paris three weeks before, local opinion had solidified behind the impending Allied victory.

The British prime minister remained a few days in Quebec after the conference, attending to Canadian sensibilities after Roosevelt had returned to Hyde Park. Then Churchill, too, entrained for Hyde Park. Harry Hopkins was invited to Hyde Park at Churchill's request, and Churchill noted with sadness the decline in Hopkins's medical and political fortunes. Hopkins "explained to me his altered position. He had declined in the favour of the President. There was a curious incident at luncheon, when he arrived a few minutes late and the President did not even greet him." The atmosphere warmed, Hopkins had his usual positive impact on relations between the two, and "In two days it seemed to be like old times." But Hopkins told him: "You must know that I am not what I was."[115]

Roosevelt had not accepted Hopkins's departure from the White House, even though it was for the unexceptionable excuse of marriage, and at that he had remained over a year in the White House with his new bride. Despite all they had been through together, Roosevelt largely dispensed with him. "There was no open breach between them," Sherwood, Hopkins's biographer, correctly wrote, and Hopkins did make a partial comeback as Roosevelt's chief advisor. But that was the point—he was discarded without any breach, just as Corcoran had been, and just as Moley and Farley had been after a breach.

Churchill was still not altogether aware of the extent to which Roosevelt, quite unlike himself, could be utterly unsentimental. Roosevelt's objectives were almost always benign, but his techniques, while bloodless, were not always much less ruthless, devious, and cynical than Hitler's or Stalin's. Churchill, though capable of rascality, and often enjoying a ruse, was quintessentially a man of principle—a rebel within the British upper classes, but a subscriber to the rules of the

---

* Duplessis was portrayed briefly in the famous film *Rosemarie*, with Nelson Eddy and Jeanette MacDonald.

British public school, the British Army and Royal Navy, the London clubs, and above all, Parliament, where he had sat for forty-three years. He was an imperial Tory in the world, a progressive Tory in home affairs, and, above all and almost all the time, a fearless if sometimes self-indulgent man of integrity.

Roosevelt had equally strong and distinguished objectives and had a more perceptive and less romantic view of the world than Churchill. Churchill, whose power was derived from disparate forces of empire and alliance, was continually engaged in gathering those forces together. Speaking for a mighty and unitary nation that he had led to the forefront of world affairs, Roosevelt had the perspective of someone who was almost omnipotent. This sensation of his own matchless strength was doubtless augmented rather than diminished by his triumph over both the practical problems and public appearance of infirmity. And Roosevelt had enjoyed phenomenal electoral success, unlike Churchill, whose standing with the voters was usually precarious throughout his career.

Beyond that, Roosevelt had never thought the rules applied to him. Perhaps because of the constant doting attention of his mother, coupled with his own cunning analysis of the vagaries of human nature, refined by the rebuffs of Groton and Harvard, he had early developed the technique of masquerading as a faithful adherent to the governing system while always looking for the main chance. Endicott Peabody and the admissions committee of the Porcellian detected this, but Roosevelt refined his presentation and evoked his political career to a broader and less discriminating jury of peers, the American electorate. This was not like applying for membership in a club, which doesn't have to accept new members. The political offices had to be filled. Unlike candidates for membership in a club or fraternity, one candidate had to win (and only one could win). And the voters were more open-minded, more impressionable, less exigent, than the authorities of elite schools and university fraternities.

Roosevelt maintained, particularly in the run-up to an election, the pretense of being the loyal subject of the popular will. Now, the whole world and all history were his stages and whole countries and large parts of continents hung in the balance. Roosevelt knew to retain the fidelity of his countrymen by dressing his actions in the most indefectible idealism, and this was not a complete imposture. Roosevelt sought peace and progress and was not, contrary to de Gaulle's insinuations, an American imperialist. But he knew there was no precedent for a war-free world without an American presence in Europe and East Asia, and that that presence had been essential to the satisfactory outcome of the two world wars. In a race to finish his work before his life ended, Franklin D. Roosevelt would not scruple to discard individuals and trade nationalities in the pursuit of a world where peace would reign and America would be preeminent. Sentiment was not absent in his thoughts, but it did not weigh heavily either.

De Gaulle, having, as he put it himself, "rejected the dictates of a false discipline," had defied his own country, swum against a crushing tide of malevolent events, and astounded his benefactors by his ingratitude. He had had to make up his own rulebook as he went along, and detected this aspect of Roosevelt more clearly than Churchill did. Hitler judged from Roosevelt's rhetoric, augmented by his own distaste for the handicapped and his own racial bigotry, and realized too late that Roosevelt was not another weak and gullible democratic leader, havering and prattling about peace and justice. Stalin detected as soon as he met Roosevelt that he was a subtle operator; he would, if necessary, let Poland go by the boards, at least for a time, until he had a practical remedy to its plight, to pursue the world he wanted to organize and lead, as he had done with Spain and the Jews. These were epochal personalities, high stakes, stirring times.

———————

The Roosevelts had the Duke of Windsor (the Duchess was undergoing surgery in New York) to lunch with the Churchills at Hyde Park, although the President had no great regard for the former king, whose interest Churchill had championed eight years before. Roosevelt does seem to have enjoyed the company of European royalty, not, for the most part, because of their stimulating conversation or worldly importance, so presumably for psychosociological reasons.

The prime minister and his party left Hyde Park on the evening of September 19 for New York, where the R.M.S. *Queen Mary* had come to collect them. With 9,000 American soldiers also on board, they returned comfortably on the great liner to the Clyde, leaving their host to pursue his reelection. Before doing so, Roosevelt went to sleep right after the Churchills' departure, shortly after 7 P.M., and slept for over twelve hours. He always found Churchill's visits enjoyable but strenuous.[116] Then he rose, practiced walking with his braces for almost the first time in over a year, mindful of the nearly catastrophic speech at Bremerton, and returned to Washington to seek yet another mandate as head of the American people.[117]

꙳

CHAPTER 23

"Where Is Task Force 34, the World Wonders?"

*(Signal of Admiral Chester W. Nimitz, commander in chief,
U.S. Pacific Fleet, to Admiral William F. Halsey, commander,
U.S. Third Fleet, Battle of Leyte Gulf October 25, 1944)*

I

THE PRESIDENT'S HEALTH was becoming ever more precarious. His mental powers were strong but his intellectual stamina had declined so that he could now work hard for only about four hours a day. He concentrated almost all his energies on postwar settlements. At no time did he appear to expect great difficulty winning the 1944 election, although he said to a few visitors that there might be a problem. He detested Dewey as a self-righteous upstart who had straddled on the greatest issue of the generation, aid to the Allies in 1940–1941, and whose entire campaign was a denigration of Roosevelt's physical condition, the wages of long years of service correcting, as Roosevelt would have it, the horrible mistakes of the Republicans.

Unfortunately, the whole Roosevelt team was getting very tired, not just Hopkins. Hull was even more tired, boring, and unimaginative than ever. He had declined in advance to go to the 1944 Quebec Conference (Octagon), and then complained after the fact, when he learned that Morgenthau and Eden attended. Stimson was still sensible, but seventy-eight years old and weakening. Ickes and Perkins remained the strongest of the continuing cabinet members, but their positions, Interior and Labor, were not particularly important in wartime.

The best and strongest of the group would prove to be the newest, Harry Truman, the vice presidential nominee, but no one knew this and he was not consulted on any serious matters. Roosevelt had him to lunch under the Andrew Jackson magnolia tree on the south lawn of the White House on August 18, 1944, and told him that after all the progress of the last twelve years, what was needed was a period of digestion, and that he wanted a successor who would be "slightly right of center."[1] Roosevelt knew how great the impact of the G.I. Bill of Rights would be and knew that the next great domestic battle would be for the civil rights of the African-Americans. He had packed the administration with Republicans (Stimson, Knox, Donovan, Winant, Hurley, Stettinius, and soon the young Nelson Rockefeller), valued the contribution of big business to the war effort, and got on better with business people than with the labor leaders, not only the megalomaniacal John L. Lewis but the hectoring Sidney Hillman.

Roosevelt's desire to pry loose the Willkie Republicans and overwhelm the southern reactionaries was a logical sequel to how he had enlisted the Southern Democrats to overpower the isolationist progressives in the late thirties, and the same progressives to outvote the conservative Republicans and Southern Democrats in the early thirties. He saw in Truman a solid liberal, but a tough and realistic pragmatist. It is not clear that Roosevelt already envisioned not finishing his fourth term. He may have, or he may have thought of Truman as his electoral successor in 1948. As always with Roosevelt, only the general outlines of what he thought can be discerned from the conflicting signals he sent in all directions and only his deeds are a guide to his thoughts—not, as with more direct leaders (such as Truman), the other way round.

As Roosevelt had foreseen, Dewey's aggressiveness had left the Republicans overexposed, and it would give him great pleasure to set the record straight. He knew that while rebutting Republican charges he would have to put on a spirited display of physical vigor to dispose of the one dangerous Republican claim: that Roosevelt was not physically up to another term as president. Roosevelt had told Mackenzie King, when he met him and Churchill at Quebec on September 10, 1944, that he was "far from sure of the results" of the election, though Churchill was confident Roosevelt would be reelected. Otherwise, "It would be ingratitude itself." Churchill would learn how strong that trait could be in an electorate ten months later.[2]

A major address to launch the President's reelection campaign had long been scheduled for the evening of September 23, in the Statler Hotel in Washington. It was a labor gathering brought together under the aegis of what then rejoiced in the name of the International Brotherhood of Teamsters, Chauffeurs, Warehousemen and Helpers of America (before that union developed severe problems of respectability). Anna Roosevelt Boettiger, who had been with him for the regrettable speech at Bremerton, sat nervously with Samuel Rosenman, who had collaborated with the President in writing the Teamsters' speech. They were a few tables from the speaker.

Because the necessary muscles had been underused there was some doubt about whether Roosevelt could still walk with braces. His professional medical advice was to stick to his wheelchair. He set out to establish that he could still walk, with braces. But to the Teamsters, Roosevelt elected to give his remarks sitting, to concentrate entirely on his carefully crafted text and minimize risks of another disappointment. The country had been so accustomed to his oratorical tours de force that two Bremertons back to back would be extremely damaging to his reelection prospects.

Concern over the rumors that had circulated about his health caused the public to listen to this speech in unusually great numbers. His versatile, sonorous, and powerful voice had been familiar to it since his Happy Warrior speech of twenty years before. His major addresses had been one of the nation's longest running entertainments, usually pulling huge audiences, over most of that time. He did not disappoint his countrymen on this night; it was one of his greatest and most famous political speeches of all. He showed and communicated what is called in sport the pride of champions. FDR was reverently introduced by the leader of the Teamsters, Daniel Tobin. Waves of thunderous applause rolled around the room as Roosevelt tossed his head smilingly in the confident manner that had long uplifted his followers and infuriated his opponents.

"Well," he finally began, as if at a family gathering, "here we are together again—after four years, and what years they have been! You know, I am actually four years older, which is a fact that seems to annoy some people. In fact, in the mathematical field, there are millions of Americans who are more than eleven years older than when we started in to clear up the mess that was dumped into our laps in 1933." He deprecated those who "When votes are at stake . . . suddenly discover that they really love labor and that they are anxious to protect labor from its old friends. . . .

"The whole purpose of Republican oratory these days seems to be to switch labels. The object is to persuade the American people that the Democratic Party was responsible for the 1929 crash and the Depression, and that the Republican Party was responsible for all social progress under the New Deal.

"Now imitation may be the sincerest form of flattery—but I am afraid that in this case it is the most obvious common or garden variety of fraud." He credited "enlightened, liberal elements" of the Republicans with trying to get the party "in step with the forward march of American progress. But [they] were not able to drive the Old Guard Republicans from their entrenched positions.

"Can the Old Guard pass itself off as the New Deal? I think not.

"We have all seen many marvelous stunts in the circus but no performing elephant could turn a hand-spring without falling flat on its back." (Roosevelt was always adept at typecasting conservative Republicans as absurd and desperate defenders of overwhelmed battlements, as if fighting to the death for the prerogatives of the Flat Earth Society. This was one of many irritants that upset his social peers. The elephant, of course, was and remains the Republican Party symbol.)

"Words come easily, but they do not change the record. You are, most of you, old enough to remember what things were like . . . in 1932.

"You remember the closed banks and the breadlines and the starvation wages; the foreclosures of homes and farms, and the bankruptcies of business; the 'Hoovervilles,' and the young men and women of the Nation facing a hopeless, jobless, future; the closed factories and mines and mills; the ruined and abandoned farms; the stalled railroads and the empty docks; the blank despair of a whole Nation—and the utter impotence of the Federal Government.

"You remember the long, hard road, with its gains and its setbacks, that we have traveled together ever since those days.

"Now there are some politicians who do not remember that far back, and there are some who remember but find it convenient to forget. No, the record is not to be washed away that easily. . . .

"But perhaps the most ridiculous of these campaign falsifications is the one that this Administration failed to prepare for the war that was coming. I doubt whether even Goebbels would have tried that one. For even he would never have dared hope that the voters of America had already forgotten that many of the Republican leaders in the Congress and outside the Congress tried to thwart and block nearly every attempt that this administration made to warn our people and arm our Nation."

Then came a thrust doubly dangerous because of its ridiculous character, which Roosevelt had been preparing for weeks—the successor to "Martin, Barton, and Fish" of 1940. Republican congressman Harold Knutson of Minnesota was the author of the charge Roosevelt now rebutted, but the President implicitly hung it around Dewey's neck.

"These Republican leaders have not been content with attacks on me, or my wife, or on my sons. No, not content with that, they now include my little dog, Fala. Well, of course, I don't resent attacks, and my family doesn't resent attacks, but Fala does resent attacks. You know, Fala is Scottish, and being a Scottie, as soon as he learned that the Republican fiction writers in Congress and out had concocted a story that I had left him behind on the Aleutian Islands and had sent a destroyer back to find him—at a cost to the taxpayers of two or three or eight or twenty million dollars—his Scotch soul was furious. He has not been the same dog since. I am accustomed to hearing malicious falsehoods about myself—such as that old worm-eaten chestnut that I have represented myself as indispensable." (To raise it as he did, was to imply that he was indispensable, which in fact he had been through much of his presidency, especially the last four years.) "But I think I have a right to resent, to object to libelous statements about my dog. . . ."

Admiral Leahy, on behalf of the navy, officially confirmed to Speaker Rayburn and Majority Leader McCormick that the charge was unfounded.[3] Though the Republican candidate had had nothing to do with this charge, his campaign had been so strident and hostile that a great many Americans resented it, and were pleased also by the relatively good humored tenor of the President's response.[4] The mystery is why Dewey did not do a better job of distancing himself from the original accusation.

"I think that the victory of the American people and their allies in this war will be far more than a victory against Fascism and reaction and the dead hand of despotism of the past. The victory of the American people and their allies in this war will be a victory for democracy. It will constitute such an affirmation of the strength and power and vitality of government by the people as history has never before witnessed.

"And so my friends . . . we move forward, with God's help, to the greatest epoch of free achievement by free men that the world has ever known."

Rosenman, who was hardly impartial, wrote in the edition of Roosevelt's public papers where the speech was published that its effect "was smashing. . . . The Teamsters' Union address left no doubt in the minds of the President's friends, and his enemies, that he had lost none of his skill as a campaigner and political speaker." The speech was rendered with the greatest verbal flamboyance, animated, ironic, mocking, inspiring. Most of the sentences quoted here brought great applause, and where appropriate, uproarious laughter. It became an emotional meeting; the Democrats were inexpressibly relieved that their leader still had the magic. At his best, as on this night, he was an almost hypnotic speaker. Rosenman wrote: "There were tears in the eyes of many, including his daughter Anna."[5]

Time magazine reported: "The Champ had swung a full roundhouse blow. And it was plain to the newsmen on the Dewey Special that the challenger had been hit hard—as plain as when a boxer drops his gloves and his eyes glaze."[6]

In historic fact, as most Americans knew, Roosevelt had, in his fashion, defeated the Depression he inherited from the Republicans. He had been right in his attacks on the isolationists, in his aid to the democracies, and in his rearmament program in the two years before Pearl Harbor. And he had led the nation and the alliance with great skill back to the Rhine and the approaches to Japan several thousand miles to the west of the Hawaiian Islands. And Dewey was now running against the President's dog. It was a great tour de force for Fala's owner. Even the acidulous Cadogan, still in the United States, who had heard it on the radio, was impressed: "Very good electioneering stuff."[7] Roosevelt returned to Hyde Park and left Dewey to shadowbox with himself and bark back at Fala.

Roosevelt gave a Fireside Chat from the White House on October 5, devoted to urging people to vote, denying that there were Communists in his government, and presenting a golden vision of the postwar world he was laboring to build. Apart from the suggestion that he was not physically up to executing his office, Roosevelt's greatest concern in the election was the fear that in preventing millions of members of the armed forces from voting, the Republicans and southern Democrats had disenfranchised many more Democrats than Republicans and made the race narrower than it should have been, given the government's outstanding record.

It was to combat this that he took to the airwaves on October 5, ostensibly on an almost nonpartisan basis, to urge his listeners to be sure to vote, as a "sacred right and duty." He went further: "The right to vote must be open to our citizens irrespective of race, color, or creed—without tax or artificial restriction of any kind. The sooner we get to that basis of political equality, the better it will be for the country as a whole." This was a direct assault upon the voting system throughout the southern states, where the African-Americans were prevented from voting by a morass of racist restrictions, starting with the poll tax. Roosevelt clearly envisioned a showdown with the rednecks of the south when the war was over. Now that he had routed and disgraced the isolationists, he was unlikely to need the votes of the southern congressional barons as much as he had in the three years before Pearl Harbor.

With the same tactical skill with which he had used the war scare to rearm and complete the economic recovery, he used war production and the G.I. Bill of Rights to raise working-, lower-middle-class, and rural living standards and to assault racial and economic discrimination against African-Americans. The southern Democrats had effectively deserted the national leadership and revealed that they prized the retention of the white supremacist post-slavery system in the southern states above reelection of the party's president. The entire antiquarian, segregationist political structure of the South had begun to collapse, and the altogether desirable process that would take another thirty years to complete, the provision of a vote and equal opportunity for all, was clearly coming. "They are, of course, perfectly happy to let you vote, unless you happen to be a member of the Army or Navy or Marine Corps overseas, in which case they have made it pretty hard for you to vote at all," he had said to the Teamsters. In that speech and elsewhere he said: "There are some candidates who think they may have a chance of election if only the total vote is small enough."

In the same spirit of supposed nonpartisanship, in his October 5 address he declared: "The Allied Armies under General Eisenhower have waged during the past four months one of the most brilliant campaigns in military history." This was not an unfounded assertion, and he may reasonably have assumed that the commander in chief would get some of the credit for the operation. Having championed Overlord as he had, he deserved some.

A group of Republicans in the Congress had sent out a document under their free congressional postage (franking) privilege that alleged the Roosevelt administration was effectively a Communist front. The President's rejoinder was: "I have never sought, and do not welcome the support of any person or group committed to Communism, Fascism, or any other foreign ideology which would undermine the American system of government, or the American system of free competitive enterprise and private property.

"That does not in the least interfere with [our] firm and friendly relationship . . . with the people of the Soviet Union. The kind of economy that suits the Russian people, I take it is their own affair."

Again he stated that after the war: "We must and I hope we will, continue to be united with our allies in a powerful world organization which is ready and able to keep the peace — if necessary by force." This continued to be a more precise and activist version of the mandate of the United Nations organization than anyone but Roosevelt was at this point espousing. He wasn't just advocating the end of American isolationism. In terms that had so alarmed de Gaulle, he was claiming an American-led worldwide right and duty of peace enforcement.

For a nationally broadcast speech just a month before the election, his remarks were pretty bland. Roosevelt was trying to be above the fray, standing as a virtual father of the nation, having led his people out of the economic wilderness through the fires of war, to the very verge of peace and prosperity.

II

CHURCHILL, WATCHING THE ADVANCE of the Red Army into central Europe with mounting concern, determined to try personal diplomacy with Stalin to reduce possible frictions. He and Anthony Eden flew to Moscow, arriving October 9. Bohlen, Hopkins, and Roosevelt became uneasy about what Churchill might agree to with Stalin, and Roosevelt cabled both leaders on October 5, asking that Harriman be present at the sessions and stressing that the United States considered the meeting a preliminary to a tripartite meeting in a few months, which was to be held in the Crimea. Roosevelt thus declined to be bound by whatever was agreed between Churchill and Stalin. Churchill rather grumpily did not specifically reply, while Stalin cabled October 8 that he was "puzzled," having assumed that Churchill was bringing whatever had been agreed on at Quebec and was speaking for Roosevelt as well as himself. He philosophically concluded, "This supposition . . . does not seem to correspond to reality."[8] At this late stage in the war the Americans were more concerned about what the British might concede to the Russians than the British were about American intentions. The legitimacy of the American concern has been somewhat obscured by concerted historical revisionism.

Churchill and Eden met with Stalin and Molotov at 10 P.M. on the evening of their arrival. It was agreed to invite the Polish prime minister, Mikolajczyk, and two of his colleagues to join the conversations at once. Churchill had written to Mikolajczyk, in terms reminiscent of those he employed with de Gaulle in trying to entice him to Casablanca, that failure to come would be an affront to Britain and "would relieve us of further responsibility towards the London Polish Committee."[9]

Undeterred by Roosevelt's words of caution, Churchill said to Stalin: "Let us settle about our affairs in the Balkans. Your armies are in Romania and Bulgaria. We have interests, missions, and agents there. Don't let us get at cross-purposes in small ways." He suggested that in Romania Russia have 90 percent of the influence and all others, including Britain, 10 percent; that Britain have 90 percent in Greece; and that they have 50 percent each in Yugoslavia. While this was being translated for Stalin, Churchill wrote it out on a half sheet of paper, adding a 50-50 percent in Hungary and 75-25 in Russia's favor in Bulgaria. Churchill passed Stalin the paper. "There was a slight pause. Then [Stalin] took his blue pencil and made a large tick upon it, and passed it back to us. It was all settled in no more time than it takes to set down."

Somewhat self-consciously, in his memoirs Churchill added: "Of course we had long and anxiously considered our point, and were only dealing with immediate wartime arrangements. All larger questions were reserved on both sides for what we then hoped would be a peace table when the war was won." This is implausible. Churchill had been rightly decrying the steady encroachment on central Europe of the Red Army; especially eight days after the extinguishing of the heroic uprising in Warsaw, Churchill cannot have entertained any illusions about the likelihood of Stalin's relinquishing control of Romania and Bulgaria. As if to make this point, he continued in his memoirs: "After this there was a long silence. The penciled paper lay in the centre of the table. At length I said: 'Might it not be thought rather cynical if it seemed we had disposed of these issues, so fateful to millions of people, in such an offhand manner? Let us burn the paper.' 'No, you keep it,' said Stalin."

If it had been an arrangement for only a few months, it would not have been "fateful to millions," and he would probably not have suggested burning the paper. In fact, he had not struck a bad bargain. If the West had succeeded in parity with Russia in Hungary, the painful events of 1956 in that country would not have occurred and Hungary's life would have been incomparably more agreeable in the years following the war. In subsequent meetings in the same conference, Eden conceded Molotov 75 percent in Hungary to 25 percent for the Western powers. Even this would have been an improvement on the 100 to 0 that swiftly came to pass while Stalin ignored his undertakings, seized all of Hungary, and stoked up a civil war in Greece, challenging Churchill and the Americans there.

Harriman got a fairly clear understanding of what had occurred when Churchill produced what he called his "naughty document," and communicated this to Roosevelt. Despite his public objections to spheres of influence, and the idealistic widderings of Hull and the rest of the State Department, Roosevelt well knew their necessity and was staking out some for his own country (e.g., Italy).[10] He regretted Churchill's concessions, declined to legitimize them, but recognized their reflection of current military realities.

Churchill never told Roosevelt specifically what had occurred. Instead (without Stalin's involvement), he cabled, also on the 11th: "We have found an extraordinary atmosphere of goodwill here. . . . It is absolutely necessary we should try to get a common mind about the Balkans, so that we may prevent civil war breaking out in several countries when probably you and I would be in sympathy with one side and U.J. with the other."

"U.J." is Uncle Joe; it is distressing that Stalin should still be referred to in this way between Churchill and Roosevelt even after his tacit collusion with the Nazis to suppress the Warsaw uprising.

In his conference summary on October 18, Churchill, still in Moscow, wrote to Roosevelt: "Arrangements made about Balkans are, I am sure, the best that are possible. Coupled with our successful military action recently we should now be able to save Greece and, I have no doubt that agreement to pursue a fifty-fifty joint policy in Yugoslavia will be the best solution for our difficulties. . . . The Russians are insistent on their ascendancy in Romania and Bulgaria as the Black Sea countries."

All of this was true but disingenuous, because Churchill put on a quite different guise in his subsequent, still extensive, career as an active statesman and historian. He not only took the lead in indicating the Western Allies would acquiesce in the Soviet satellization of Romania, Bulgaria, Poland, and Hungary. He pretended to be the defender of those countries. These arrangements left Roosevelt with even less bargaining position than he would have had with Stalin over Eastern Europe.

Churchill had insisted at Octagon (Quebec), and Hyde Park afterward, that no mention be made to the Russians of atomic development, and Roosevelt agreed to this. If Churchill at this point had started bandying about the imminent existence of these weapons while he was in Moscow, it might have imparted some sense of sobriety of ambition, or at least cautious suspicion, to Stalin, whose espionage service would not yet have given him much hint of their development.

In resumé, if Churchill had not delayed Overlord with his excursions in the Mediterranean and all the nonsense about a soft underbelly and a Ljubljana Gap, the Czechs and Hungarians would have been delivered from Stalin's tender mercies, and virtually all Germany would have been in the hands of the British and Americans. If the British had not voted with the Russians at the European Advisory Commission on German occupation zones, it would have been possible for the Western Allies to get all the way to Berlin, as Roosevelt, no less than Churchill, had always wanted to do.

Barring the success of a trade-off with Stalin between treatment of Eastern Europe and that of Germany, lubricated by financial assistance, only the fate of Czechoslovakia was really still a matter of suspense when Churchill left Moscow on October 19, 1944.

And Churchill was certainly not hoodwinked. When the competing Polish groups arrived, the Lublin Committee, as Churchill wrote, "were mere pawns of Russia. They had learned and rehearsed their part so well that even their masters evidently felt they were overdoing it. For instance, M. Bierut, the leader, spoke in these terms: 'We are here to demand on behalf of Poland that Lvov shall belong to Russia. This is the will of the Polish people.' When this had been translated into English and Russian, I looked at Stalin and saw an understanding twinkle in his expressive eyes, as much as to say: 'What about that for our Soviet teaching?' "

Before the arrival of the Poles, Churchill, whose eloquent championship of the Warsaw underground at the time and in his memoirs has been noted, made some particularly unfortunate comments about the Polish underground commander, General Tadeusz Bor, to the effect that he would no longer be an irritant to the Russians, because "the Germans are looking after him" (i.e., torturing him). He effectively threw in the towel on behalf of the London Poles, agreeing that they were "unwise." They were, and they didn't have much bargaining power even before they compounded their problems with their diplomatic maladroitness. And Stalin had a point when he said that Poles were so quarrelsome that even an individual Pole, if left alone, would "quarrel with himself through sheer boredom."[11] But the Poles deserved better than to be handed over to their Russian occupiers so furtively and cavalierly.

The conversations between the two Polish factions achieved nothing useful, and a bland communiqué was issued saying that differences were being narrowed. As the Soviet zone of occupation in Germany had been defined by the European Advisory Commission along pre-Teheran lines, including about 40 percent of postwar Poland, which would be taken from Germany as Poland moved westwards to the Oder-Neisse line, the EAC gave a chunk of Poland to Russia to hand over to Poland on terms it alone would determine. Again, these arrangements reflected the facts on the ground.

Stalin had, however, outsmarted himself. As most Germans would flee on foot and in cart before the Red Army, not only did the Soviet occupation zone of Germany become largely a Polish occupation zone, but the German population of central Europe was driven into the arms of the advancing Western armies. In securing his hold on Poland, Stalin was trading Poles for Germans. He would gain a sullen Poland, but a new Germany, physically and politically of the West, and under Anglo-American tutelage, would rise again.

The only other important subject, the Soviet intention to enter the war against Japan as soon as Germany was disposed of, was reaffirmed. As had become clear at Teheran, this was no triumph of diplomacy, because Stalin wanted to add territory in the Far East, on the heels of his great accretions in Europe. It would have been difficult to keep him out of the war in the Far East. What would have been a diplomatic achievement would have been the Soviet invasion of Japan itself, had that been necessary. To keep that prospect alive was worth the concession of a few remote territories Stalin would have taken under any circumstances, whatever the Japanese, Chinese, and Americans thought of it. "This [visit to Moscow] was not Mr. Churchill's finest hour."[12] It is little wonder that Stalin, in his enthusiasm for the concessions made to him, took the unusual step of going to the airport to see Churchill off.

Although it would have been better if Churchill had not gone to Moscow at all in the autumn of 1944, even ten years later he referred to the great ovation he and Stalin had received on the evening of October 14 when they attended the Bolshoi ballet and opera. And he wrote of this trip: "There is no doubt that in our narrow circle we talked with an ease, freedom, and cordiality never before attained between our two countries. Stalin made several expressions of personal regard which I feel sure were sincere."[13] They probably were sincere; Stalin always admired Churchill (not an unrequited respect), but they were also tactical and did not translate into any flexibility on Stalin's part in the great matters at issue between them.

III

A LENGTHY DRAMA in Sino-American relations was also grinding to a climax. The singular personalities of Chiang Kai-shek and the caustic four-star chief of the U.S. mission in China, chief of staff to Chiang and commander of the Allied armies in China, General "Vinegar Joe" Stilwell, finally came to a complete breach, and the catalyst was the normally diplomatic General Marshall. Stilwell had reported to the Joint Chiefs that Chiang refused to do anything. Chiang was determined to conserve his meager resources while the Japanese and Americans settled the issue between them. Stilwell and Marshall demanded that he do something to contribute to the liberation of occupied China. Roosevelt was (correctly) convinced of China's potential as a Great Power and so would not just abandon China, having elevated it to the status of a major ally.

Chiang's position may have been comprehensible up to a point, but since it was now obvious the Americans would defeat the Japanese, the best Chiang could do would be to undertake military action to make himself look victorious opposite Mao's Chinese Communist rivals, who were also almost inactive against the Japanese (despite an elaborate subsequent contrary mythology).

At a party for Mme. Chiang at the end of June, Chiang publicly denied there had been any infidelity by his wife or himself, which amused the small Western press contingent, because their marriage was a rather open-plan arrangement.[14] Mme. remained away for over a year, which deprived Chiang of an advisor who understood Western thinking and might have smoothed relations. At the Quebec Octagon Conference, Churchill and Roosevelt determined that there was nothing to be done except keep China nominally in the war. The Americans knew that Mao Tse-tung and Chou En-lai were considerably more energetic than Chiang, but it was as disagreeable to Roosevelt as to Churchill to support a Communist takeover of any country, though Roosevelt wished to pursue discussions with Mao. Chiang, in his weakness, had a certain strength, in that there was no viable alternative to him in the calculations of the Western powers.

Chiang sent a telegram to the U.S. Joint Chiefs, which Marshall summarized at Octagon, threatening not to lift a finger to break the blockade of China by Japan. Thorough man as he always was, Marshall had a proposed reply to hand, which was a 600-word "note" from Roosevelt that "adopted the tone of a headmaster to a sullen and incorrigible schoolboy."[15] Roosevelt (i.e., Marshall) would tell Chiang that his actions squandered the courage of all who had actually fought to defend China, that Chiang was fulfilling the wishes of the enemy, that air supply to China would be jeopardized, and that: "For this you must yourself be prepared to accept the consequences and assume the personal responsibility." It was a completely justified assertion. Roosevelt and Marshall were thoroughly exasperated with Chiang.

Stilwell was jubilant to receive such a communication and threw all caution to the winds by deciding to bypass the normal channels and deliver it himself to Chiang. "The harpoon hit the little bugger right in the solar plexus and went right through him." Writing a jig of joy to his wife, Stilwell resorted to doggerel: "The little bastard shivered, And lost the power of speech, His face turned green and quivered, As he struggled not to screech. For all my weary battles, For all my hours of woe, At last I've had my innings, And laid the Peanut low."[16]

Stilwell's jubilation was premature. Chiang, incompetent and contemptible though he was, knew that if he didn't get rid of Stilwell now, the next American initiative might well be to impose Mao on him as an ostensible ally. Chiang imperturbably executed one of his most incompetent army commanders, and Stilwell undertook to try to negotiate a new cooperative arrangement with Mao Tse-tung.

When Patrick Hurley, the rather inept diplomatic emissary of Roosevelt to Chiang, went to propose this initiative on September 23, Chiang startled the emissary and demanded the recall of Stilwell. Chiang at least had firmness of intention opposite his ally, if not toward his foreign enemy. He realized the mortal threat to himself and gambled that the Americans would not transfer their allegiance to the Communists and would not, in the face of the Japanese and in the midst of a presidential election, admit complete failure in the theater.

Roosevelt had unfortunately made this theater a catchment for displaced officials and had the deracinated Donald Nelson, rendered virtually redundant by James Byrnes, wandering rather aimlessly about China giving economic advice, whether solicited or otherwise. Chiang took advantage of this situation by inviting Nelson to take over reconstruction of the postwar Chinese economy: "I will unconditionally invest in you all China's economic powers." Roosevelt, the supreme practitioner of the flattery of sidetracked officials, was not impressed with this initiative. He had abolished the unequal treaties between the United States and China. Chiang, though grateful for the renunciation of extrality and the Exclusion Act, was fighting for his life, and claimed that the September 16 note from Roosevelt was a new infringement on Chinese sovereignty.

Harry Hopkins revealed to Chiang's brother-in-law, visiting Washington, that in a matter of the sovereign rights of China, Roosevelt would reluctantly accept the recall of Stilwell. This was another illustration, along with his poor advice about continuing to withhold full recognition from de Gaulle, that Hopkins, after all the buffetings of his medical condition and fluctuations in his standing with his patron, had lost some of his acuity of judgment, and therefore his utility to

Roosevelt. Stilwell wrote in his diary: "If Old Softy gives in on this . . . the Peanut will be out of control from now on."[17] So he was. Chiang's misjudgments were henceforth self-destructive.

Marshall drafted what he called "a sharp rejoinder," but Roosevelt declined to send it. The United States did not want to give up on China completely. Marshall did draft a compromise that was the essence of Roosevelt's reply to Chiang on October 5. Stilwell would no longer be the Lend-Lease administrator in China, nor any longer Chiang's chief of staff, but would continue to command the Chinese forces in Burma and Yunnan. Chiang declined this and demanded Stilwell's recall. Roosevelt reasoned that it was impossible to foist upon an ally a general the ally refused to work with and so Stilwell had to go.

At this point, it was probably the correct decision. There was general agreement on the point made by one of the leaders of the U.S. civilian mission in China that "We must not indefinitely underwrite a politically bankrupt regime."[18] Probably the best course would have been to open serious negotiations with Mao Tse-tung and Chou En-lai as soon as the U.S. election was over a few weeks later. Instead, the next phase of American policy that now began was to try to bring Chiang and Mao together. This was impossible, and was soon found to be so.

Assisting the Communists in effectively ceasing to be Communists and integrating China into the world would be an exacting process. This somewhat resembled Roosevelt's intended policy to the Soviet Union. More than twenty-five years would have to go by before President Richard Nixon would pick up the threads of America's China policy where Roosevelt's successor would leave them.

Marshall, wary of Stilwell's penchant for controversy, hustled him out of Chungking and back to Washington, keeping him away from the press. He promised to do his best to find him a suitable position, but there were no American armies now in need of a four-star general, and Marshall judged it inappropriate to make so eminent an officer a mere divisional commander, as Stilwell had requested. Stilwell did meet Roosevelt once more, on March 8, 1945. Roosevelt had approved a British decoration that Churchill had wanted to give him, as well as further recognition from his own government. The President was never influenced by Stilwell's lack of enthusiasm for him, which he was too astute and well informed not to have detected. Stilwell thought the President looked unwell when they met in March, but actually was impressed with what he said, "as if, now close to the weary end, he had felt for a brief moment a ray of the Roosevelt charm."[19]

IV

THE LONG-AWAITED United States liberation of the Philippines was launched on October 20, 1944, as four divisions, commanded by General MacArthur and escorted by vast sea and air forces, landed in Leyte Gulf in the central Philippines. Six more divisions were quickly introduced. In the succeeding days one of history's great naval battles, the final throw of the Imperial Japanese Combined Fleet, the Battle of Leyte Gulf, took place in several proximate approaches to the landing site on Leyte. U.S. Rangers landed on islands on the eastern side of Leyte Gulf October 17 and 18, and MacArthur's main force achieved complete surprise when it came ashore on the 20th.

Before a massed battery of photographers, General MacArthur walked ashore, followed by a diminutive President Sergio Osmena (who had succeeded to the post on the death of Manuel Quezon a few months before). The landing was successful. From his beachhead MacArthur spoke to the Philippine people with unfeigned emotion: "People of the Philippines, I have returned! . . . Rally to me! Let the indomitable spirit of Bataan and Corregidor lead on. As the lines of battle roll forward to bring you within the zone of operations, rise and strike! . . . For your homes and hearths strike! In the name of your sacred dead, strike!" His bloodcurdling message concluded: "Let no heart be faint. Let every arm be steeled. The guidance of divine God points the way. Follow in His name to the Holy Grail of righteous victory!"[20] Though it was the last objective on MacArthur's mind, the landing was not unhelpful to the Commander in Chief's reelection campaign.

The campaign on Leyte would be largely over by Christmas. It did not furnish all the air bases the Americans had been seeking for the main assault on Luzon, but it did inflict 70,000 casualties on the Japanese, to 15,584 American casualties. And it did bring out the Japanese Navy for a decisive engagement. The Leyte invasion placed a scythe of American occupation squarely between Mindanao in the south and Luzon in the north of the Philippines. The main attack on Luzon would begin at Lingayen Gulf on January 9, 1945.

The great naval battle began on October 23, 1944. Because the Japanese had taken such a mauling in the carrier battles of the last two and a half years, they had to rely on land-based aircraft to deal with overwhelming American superiority in carrier forces. The commander of the U.S. Third Fleet, Admiral William F. Halsey, had smashed up Japanese airfields on Luzon and Formosa in September and October, and the Americans were assured of air superiority regardless of the activities of the Japanese land-based air forces, which now included a large number of trained suicide pilots, Kamikazes, about to make their first real appearance in the Pacific war.

The American naval forces were divided into two groups. Halsey's Third Fleet, under Nimitz's overall control, had six large carriers, six light carriers, six new battleships (including two of the *Iowa's* sisters), 15 cruisers, and 58 destroyers. The Seventh Fleet under Vice Admiral Thomas C. Kinkaid, but under the ultimate command of MacArthur, had 16 light carriers, six old but renovated battleships (five of them had been at Pearl Harbor and two, *California* and *West Virginia*, had been sunk upright in shallow water there), 11 cruisers, and 86 destroyers. Halsey was east and west of Leyte, protecting the landing site and looking for the enemy. Kinkaid was providing close-in support for the landing site.

The Japanese divided their forces into three main groups. The so-called Main Body, with two battleships, four carriers, three cruisers, and eight destroyers, was a decoy force under Vice Admiral Jisaburo Ozawa, and was to pass under Halsey's nose and lure him to the north. The Japanese carriers had few planes on them, and all these ships were to be sacrificed to draw the Third Fleet away from the landing area. The First Attack Force, under Vice Admiral Takeo Kurita, had five battleships, including the giant *Yamato* and *Musashi*, 12 cruisers, and 15 destroyers. What was called C Force, under Vice Admiral Shoji Nishimura, and the smaller Second Attack Force, had two battleships, four cruisers, and four destroyers. While the Main Body lured Halsey's Third Fleet north, the First Attack Force was to come through the San Bernardino Strait northwest of the landing beaches, and C Force and the Second Attack Force were to come through the Surigao Strait southwest of the landing area. All these forces were to converge at the beachhead and dispose of the Seventh Fleet and destroy MacArthur's transports and landing site.

It was a complicated plan with a lot of moving parts. Two of Kinkaid's submarines sank two of the First Attack Force's heavy cruisers on October 23. Halsey then swept the seas and found and attacked both the First Attack Force and C Force, and sank the great battleship *Musashi* (with seventeen direct bomb hits and nineteen torpedo hits) and damaged other ships in both forces. Kurita briefly reversed course, causing Halsey to believe that Ozawa's Main Body was now the main threat. He took the bait and took off after the decoy force.

Kinkaid believed Halsey was covering the San Bernardino Strait, and sent all six of his reconditioned battleships to the Surigao Strait to await C Force. The six battleships stood at the head of the strait, moving back and forth at a stately five knots, and on the two sides of the strait, as Nishimura sped up it, were thirty American torpedo boats, about twenty destroyers, and seven cruisers. As one of the American officers remarked of the Japanese: "Their strategy and intelligence seemed to be inversely proportional to their courage."[21]

Nishimura beat off the torpedo boats, but the destroyers sank one of his battleships and damaged several other ships with a dense accumulation of well-aimed torpedoes. The cruisers added to the carnage, and only three Japanese ships, including Nishimura's flagship, the battleship *Yamashiro*, came within range of the American battleships. They were dispatched in a tremendous torrent of 16-, 14-, 8-, and 6-inch naval gunfire. *Yamashiro*, majestic to the end with its lofty pagoda superstructure, disintegrated into sections that exploded and capsized after receiving perhaps fifty or sixty direct heavy hits in barely a minute. The Second Attack Force, only six ships, started up the strait a few minutes after the death of Nishimura and his squadron, glimpsed some of the eerie wreckage of their unfortunate comrades, and prudently withdrew, departing from the usual near-suicidal Japanese practice.

As Halsey, contrary to the advice of his group commanders, raced north, Kurita erupted into the approaches to Leyte Gulf, which was protected only by escort carriers, destroyers, and destroyer escorts, under the command of Rear Admiral Clifton A. Sprague. In the circumstances, with heavy shells landing all around his vulnerable little ships, Sprague retired, made smoke, and sent all his planes to harass the enemy. Roosevelt, shortly after Pearl Harbor, had engaged the historian Samuel Eliot Morison to write the history of the U.S. Navy in the war and gave him the rank of rear admiral. Morison wrote of this engagement: "The most admirable thing was the way everything we had, afloat or airborne, went baldheaded for the enemy."[22] (Morison's splendid history is one of the many kindnesses Roosevelt extended to his favorite service.)

A rain squall came to the rescue of Sprague's carriers for a quarter hour, in which they changed course, and all other craft carried out a spirited torpedo attack on the Japanese heavy ships, laming a cruiser and several destroyers. As one particularly heroic American destroyer, the *Johnston*, went down under fire from battleships and cruisers, one Japanese destroyer commander was seen on his bridge saluting his gallant adversary. *Johnston* had fought so aggressively, charging the Japanese fleet even when her torpedoes had been spent, the Japanese recorded her sinking as that of a heavy cruiser.

At Pearl Harbor, Nimitz, Halsey's commander, gradually came to the realization that Halsey had taken his whole fleet after Ozawa, rather than leaving the battleships to guard the invasion force, covered by the aircraft from Sprague's escort carriers. Obscure phrases were dropped into American messages to confuse Japanese decoders. This was Balaklava Day, so Nimitz's signals officer adapted from Tennyson's "The Charge of the Light Brigade" as the nonsensical end to messages that day: "the world wonders." Nimitz sent Halsey the signal: "Where, repeat where, is Task Force 34, the world wonders." (Task Force 34 was Halsey's fast battleships.) When this signal reached Halsey's flagship, *New Jersey*, the decoding ensign thought the phrase might be part of the real message and left it in. Halsey threw his hat on the deck and became incoherent with rage at what he thought to be Nimitz's sarcasm. In response to Ozawa's mocking signal, *en clair*, "Where is the American Fleet," Halsey had just replied by sending Ozawa his latitude and longitude. Receiving Nimitz's message, he now angrily turned his entire fleet toward San Bernardino Strait. But his carrier commander, Vice Admiral Marc Mitscher, launched his planes against Ozawa's decoy force and sank all four of the Japanese carriers in the Main Body, in what became known as the Battle of Cape Engano.

Kurita, who had little that was substantial standing between him and the American beachhead, was convinced by the vehemence of the American attack that he was dealing with fleet carriers and that the American battle fleet must be close at hand. He was being relentlessly attacked by American aircraft. The Americans had sent a tremendous traffic of clear messages full of bravura, Kurita was aware that Nishimura had been wiped out the night before, and, confused in the tumult of battle and unaware of how close he was to doing real damage, he abruptly turned again and withdrew in late morning of October 25. One of

Sprague's signalmen magnificently shouted: "Goddammit, boys, they're getting away!"[23] Sprague, in his report of the action, ascribed survival to "our successful smokescreen, our torpedo counterattack, continuous harassment of enemy by bomb, torpedo and strafing air attacks, timely maneuvers, and the definite partiality of Almighty God."[24]

If Kurita had pressed his attack, he would have sunk MacArthur's transports and done considerable damage to the beachhead, but he would have been intercepted by Halsey and most or all of his force would have been lost. For all the Japanese Navy achieved in the rest of the war, it would have been worth it for the Japanese. It would not have slowed the American progress across the Pacific very much and would not have enabled the Japanese to repel the invasion of the Philippines, but they would have had more to show for their losses. These were disastrous; Japan lost four aircraft carriers, three battleships, ten cruisers, and nine destroyers, to American losses of three light carriers and three destroyers. The Japanese Navy was finished as a fighting force, and would never directly challenge the United States Navy again.

Halsey signaled Nimitz at the end of the eventful 25th of October: "The Japanese Navy has been beaten and routed and broken by the Third and Seventh Fleets."[25] Roosevelt gave the same message to his press conference the following day. On October 27, Churchill asked Roosevelt if he would object to the publication of his succeeding message: "Pray accept my most sincere congratulations . . . on the brilliant and massive victory gained by the sea and air forces of the United States over the Japanese in the recent heavy battles." It was ten days before the election and Roosevelt replied immediately: "I will be much pleased if you should make public the message."[26]

V

BY THIS TIME, Roosevelt had put his election campaign into high gear. Dewey had made the mistake of charging that Roosevelt had short-changed MacArthur in men and aircraft. This was a difficult charge to sustain with MacArthur returning to the Philippines. Roosevelt's physical fitness was the only argument the Republicans had left. He set out to demolish this argument with a strenuous display of campaigning energy.

On Saturday, October 21, 1944, the President toured the four largest boroughs of New York City in an open car. The tour had been heavily publicized, and large crowds were expected to come out to greet him. There was a steady cold rain and the temperature was only 40 degrees Fahrenheit. This deterred neither the population nor the President, who declined McIntire's advice to put the convertible top up on the elegant green presidential Packard. The tour began in Brooklyn, proceeded fifty miles through Queens, the Bronx, and Manhattan, and lasted four hours. Roosevelt discarded his navy cape and smiled and waved throughout.

He stopped at Ebbets Field, home of the Brooklyn Dodgers, and received a tremendous ovation as he stood and hobbled toward a lectern near second base. He made the point that he could still walk in his braces, a considerable feat after more than a year, given his other preoccupations. He made a gracious reference to the home team and then spoke on behalf of Senator Robert Wagner, his political ally for most of the previous thirty-four years, since they first met in Albany. He moved on to a Coast Guard garage, where he was able to change, out of view of the public but without getting out of the car, into a dry suit and continue the tour. Queens and the Bronx followed, and then, in Manhattan, Harlem, Broadway, and the garment workers' district. An estimated three million New Yorkers, nearly half the whole population of the city at the time, with hundreds of thousands of servicemen away, came out to see the President on this inclement day, and stood several—often many—deep, all along his route, many for hours.

Besides attesting to the President's vigor, the tour testified to his mighty prestige and magic personality. Seven percent of the total vote would be cast in New York City, a greater percentage than ever before or since.[27] "The polyglot masses were . . . celebrating [Roosevelt's forthcoming political victory], but even more, they were, with a sense of wonderment and exultation beginning to understand that their country—the country which had seemed ruined and stagnant just eleven years before—was now the most powerful and prosperous and beneficent country in the world."[28] They wished to pay homage to the man who had led them from the brink of despair to the verge of triumph.

The President concluded the tour at Eleanor's apartment on Washington Square, where he had three glasses of bourbon, lunch, a nap, a hot bath, and another complete change of clothes.[29]

That evening he spoke to 2,000 members of the Foreign Policy Association in the grand ballroom of the Waldorf Astoria Hotel, on Park Avenue. He lambasted the Republicans as isolationists who had even prevented adherence to the World Court, as advocates of high tariffs, and as Russophobes, who by nonrecognition of the Soviet Union would have made cooperation to win the war impossible.

He recounted the meeting in the summer of 1939 with Borah and others, when Borah explained that there would be no war and he would block revision of the Neutrality Law, a few weeks before Hitler's attack on Poland.

He went through his standard routine of referring to sensible Republicans, and cited "our great Secretary of War, Henry Stimson," who was sitting near him. However, "the majority of the Republican members of the Congress voted . . . against the Selective Service Law of 1940 . . . against repeal of the arms embargo in 1939 . . . against the Lend-Lease Law in 1941; and they voted in August 1941 against extension of the Selective Service," and would have demobilized the army four months before Pearl Harbor.

He excoriated Senator Gerald Nye and Congressmen Joseph W. Martin and Hamilton Fish (survivors of 'Martin, Barton, and Fish'), each of whom would hold positions of great influence if the Republicans won control of the Congress. He declared himself "proud of the fact that this Administration does not have the support of the isolationist press. You know, for about half a century I have been accustomed to naming names. I mean specifically . . . McCormick-Patterson-Gannett and Hearst."

As was now his custom, he asserted that the "[Security, as it became] Council of the United Nations must have the power to act quickly and decisively to keep the peace by force, if necessary." He referred to Germany as "that tragic nation that has sown the wind and is reaping the whirlwind . . . I should be false to the very foundations of my religious and political convictions if I should ever relinquish the hope—or even the faith—that in all peoples, without exception, there live some instinct for truth, some attraction toward justice, some passion for peace—buried as they may be in the German case under a brutal regime. We bring no charge against the German race as such, for we cannot believe that God has eternally condemned any race of humanity." He praised the German-Americans, promised stern punishment for the Nazis, and declared that the Germans would have "to earn their way back into the fellowship of peace-loving and law-abiding nations. And in their climb up that steep road, we shall certainly see to it that they are not encumbered by having to carry guns. . . .

"This generation must act not only for itself, but as a trustee for all those who fell in the last War—a part of their mission unfulfilled. . . . I do not exaggerate that mission. We are not fighting for, and we shall not attain a Utopia." Roosevelt signaled, even in a foreign policy speech, as he had so often in recent times, that the issue of discrimination against African-Americans would have to be addressed.

It was a forceful and successful speech. The Republicans had been guilty as charged. Many might be inclined to forgive them the Depression. But the prewar policy that effectively favored Hitler and the Japanese was too recent, the combat with those states too intense, for that to be overlooked.

Roosevelt returned to Hyde Park on his train, which was parked in the subbasement of the Waldorf Astoria, just a few blocks north of Grand Central Station. He remained a few days there and then sallied forth again, to Shibe Park in Philadelphia on October 27. Before he spoke he drove around the city for two hours in an open car, waving at large and friendly crowds as he had in New York. The weather was again wet and cool, but he took no notice of it as he spoke to the large crowd. It was Navy Day, so named in honor of Theodore Roosevelt's birthday (he would have been eighty-six that day). Philadelphia, the site of one of the country's largest naval bases, was a good place to play one of the incumbent Roosevelt's trump political cards as commander in chief. "I think that Theodore Roosevelt would be happy and proud to know that our American fleet today is greater than all the other navies of the world put together. And when I say all the navies, I am including what was—until three days ago—the Japanese fleet." This was, naturally, a popular line.

"The record will show that when we were attacked in December, 1941, we had already made tremendous progress toward building the greatest war machine the world has ever known. . . . Every battleship in [Halsey's] fleet was authorized between 1933 and 1938. Construction had begun on all of those battleships by September, 1940. . . . All of the aircraft carriers in that fleet had been authorized by the present Administration before Pearl Harbor, and half of them were actually under construction before Pearl Harbor." All but two of Halsey's cruisers were also authorized between 1933 and 1940. "Less than three months before Hitler launched his murderous assault, the Republicans in the House of Representatives voted 144–8 in favor of cutting the appropriations for the Army Air Corps. I often think how Hitler and Hirohito must have laughed in those days. But they are not laughing now."

Roosevelt dredged up a report of MacArthur's to the secretary of war in 1943 praising administration preparedness for war. MacArthur must have found this particularly galling, since he had been feeding complaints about his treatment to the Republican candidate, but he was in no position to elaborate on the report cited here, from the midst of the Philippine campaign.

Roosevelt went on the next day to Chicago and spoke to over 100,000 partisans from his car in Soldier Field, America's largest stadium. In an entry worthy of some of Hitler's spectacles, he circled the field in his car, illuminated by powerful searchlights with the rest of the stadium in darkness. The Republican orators, according to Roosevelt, "say in effect, just this: 'Those incompetent blunderers and bunglers in Washington have passed a lot of excellent laws about social security and labor and farm relief and soil conservation—and many others—and we promise that if elected, we will not change any of them.

"And they . . . say, 'Those same quarrelsome, tired old men . . . have built the greatest war machine the world has ever known, which is fighting its way to victory;' and . . . 'If you elect us, we promise not to change any of that either.'

" 'Therefore,' say these Republican orators, 'it is time for a change.' They also say, in effect, 'Those inefficient and worn-out crackpots have really begun to lay the foundations of a lasting world peace. If you elect us, we will not change any of that either. But,' they whisper, 'we'll do it in such a way that we don't lose the support even of Gerald Nye or Gerald Smith' [Huey Long's successor], 'and this is very important—we won't lose the support of any isolationist campaign contributor. . . . Why, we will be able to satisfy even the Chicago Tribune.' "

Speaking in the home of the Chicago Bears football team, he said that "our gigantic fleet . . . has just driven through for another touchdown," an unusually awkward metaphor for him.

In Chicago Roosevelt focused more on his economic record: "By 1940 . . . we had increased our employment by ten million workers. We had converted a corporate loss of five and one-half billion dollars in 1932, to a corporate profit [after taxes] of nearly five billion dollars in 1940." He responded effectively to the Republican claims that the New Deal had been unsuccessful, a hazardous allegation for the Republicans, given their own record preceding the New Deal.

The President spoke by radio from the White House on November 2, and lamented his inability to travel to Cleveland and Detroit and other centers, which he blamed on pressures of war. He celebrated the combat war effort and recited a large number of countries with whose leaders he had conferred, emphasizing the smaller ones, especially some of the governments in exile, and first among them were those with the most sizeable ethnic communities in the United States. The defined objective was to act worthily of the nation's fighting sons. The postwar task was to "build a better America than we have ever known. If in the next few years we can start that job right, then you and I know that we have kept faith with our boys—we have helped them to win a total victory."

With over fifty journalists and actor Orson Welles on his train, he proceeded to Boston, bringing local political panjandrums aboard between whistle stops, listening delightedly to the gossip and flattering them with his attention and with joint photographs from the rear platform of his train car (called the *Ferdinand Magellan*) for the local press. This had been one of Roosevelt's most effective techniques since his campaign for the vice presidency in 1920.

He spoke to over 40,000 in Fenway Park on November 4. Frank Sinatra, one of Roosevelt's many admirers in the entertainment world, opened the gathering by singing "America." Sinatra's Christian name was Francis, but his son, Frank Sinatra Jr., was named Franklin after the President. The combination of Roosevelt's flair, charm, position, reform-mindedness, and political invincibility seduced almost all of the Hollywood community in 1944 as in his previous presidential elections.

In 1944 Hollywood joined with writers and scientists in a splendidly organized umbrella organization called Arts and Sciences for Roosevelt. Its letterhead* was so extensive that it filled an entire page. This group (which included a number of non-Americans), with Hollywood's customary energy, doubly energized by such an infusion from heavy units of the intellectual community, fanned out across the country, were constantly in the press and on radio, and delivered a message uniformly helpful to the President. Roosevelt thanked many of them individually for their support, in writing, but did not otherwise pay a great deal of attention to this famous and influential claque.[30]

Roosevelt was delighted when Morgenthau recruited Orson Welles to sell Victory Bonds on newsreels and on the radio. He told the Treasury secretary to per-

---

* Among the names on the letterhead were: Jo Davidson, Fredric March, Larry Adler, Talullah Bankhead, Ethel Barrymore, William Rose Benét, Thomas Hart Benton, Leonard Bernstein, Henry Seidel Canby, Eddie Cantor, Bennett Cerf, Aaron Copland, George Cukor, Agnes De Mille, John Dewey, W.E.B. DuBois, Will Durant, Albert Einstein, Clifton Fadiman, Edna Ferber, Jose Ferrer, Ruth Gordon, Oscar Hammerstein, Moss Hart, Lillian Hellman, George Jessel, George Kaufman, Hellen Keller, Gene Kelly, Otto Klemperer, Sinclair Lewis, Thomas Mann, Karl Menninger, Yehudi Menuhin, Clifford Odets, Dorothy Parker, Wilfred Pelletier, Jerome Robbins, Paul Robeson, Richard Rodgers, Carl Sandburg, Joseph M. Schenk, James Thurber, Michael Todd, Louis Untermeyer, Mark Van Doren, Max Weber, Orson Welles, Franz Werfel, and Monty Woolley.

suade Welles to repeat the accomplishment of his 1938 radio program, "War of the Worlds," which had, as the President said, "scared the pants off a lot of people."[31] Welles wrote Roosevelt after the 1944 campaign: "I count my small part in this last campaign as the highest privilege of my life, and our visit on the train as the richest experience."[32]

Roosevelt possessed an almost irresistible attraction for most celebrities, especially those with any artistic talent. To a few, such as the novelist Ernest Hemingway, he seemed a stylized, Ivy League posturer, though Hemingway did not question Roosevelt's greatness as a leader and was much impressed by Eleanor.

Roosevelt got on well with most of America's other great writers. The New Deal programs for impecunious writers and artists in the thirties, which so irritated the Republican right, had won the adherence of the cultural community and materially helped many. John Steinbeck's greatest work, *The Grapes of Wrath*, was essentially propaganda for the New Deal, as was the film version of it starring Henry Fonda. Steinbeck, who eventually won the Nobel Prize, said of Roosevelt that he "loved the man." He sometimes requested appointments with Roosevelt, once in 1943 to share his brainwave for how to win the war by deluging Germany with counterfeit money. Roosevelt knew the political value of such people and heard him out indulgently. He wrote Steinbeck a congratulatory letter when the author's son was born. ("I learned the grand news of Tom's arrival."[33])

Another Nobel Prize–winning novelist, Sinclair Lewis, started out regarding both Roosevelt and Hoover as "fatheads" in 1932, graduated to calling Roosevelt and Willkie "stuffed shirts" in 1940, but gave a radio address for Roosevelt just before the 1940 election. Lewis also gave a supporting speech for Roosevelt at the 1944 Democratic convention, and grieved profoundly when the President died.[34]

John P. Marquand, a long-standing "Non New Dealer," America First supporter, and lifelong Republican, finally voted for Roosevelt in 1944. Long after Roosevelt died, Marquand could not "forget the courage or the high quality of the leadership he gave us." However, Marquand did become impatient when Robert Sherwood made Roosevelt's "deceits and contrivances seem noble and Christ-like, as one of the palace guard should."[35]

America's greatest playwright, Eugene O'Neill, though he took no direct part in politics, was won over by WPA assistance to writers. He supported the New Deal, and thought Roosevelt a "great democratic leader" whose electoral success he welcomed.[36] Even the crusty Mississippian William Faulkner respected Roosevelt, though he named two of his mules "Eleanor Roosevelt" and "Jim Farley."[37]

Roosevelt knew how to flatter, cajole, and dazzle the writers as well as he did the film stars. And he used the Communist and fellow-traveling writers to good effect during the war, as when he sent Lillian Hellman to Russia for three months in 1944 to cement cultural relations at the same time that he was rallying Marquand and other diehard conservative Republicans. Beyond his policies, his personality, and his power, Roosevelt possessed the qualities of a great star on a dramatic mission that enlisted almost all those who detected his artistic virtuosity.

In Boston, Roosevelt evoked the memory of the recently deceased Al Smith, who carried Massachusetts in his campaign for the presidency in 1928, and subtly cited Smith about himself and his physical condition. He recalled that in 1928, when Roosevelt was running to succeed Al Smith as governor of New York, Smith had said, "You don't have to be an acrobat," and a few months earlier, Al Smith had visited him in the White House and said, "It is perfectly evident that you don't have to be an acrobat to be President either."

Robert E. Sherwood, who had accompanied Roosevelt to Boston in the campaign of 1940, urged the President to refer in his address to the earlier occasion when he had promised no participation in war. Roosevelt was happy to do so. "We got into this war because we were attacked by the Japanese—and because their Axis partners, Hitler's Germany and Mussolini's Italy, declared war on us. I am sure that any real American—any real red-blooded American—would have chosen, as this Government did, to fight when our own soil was made the object of a sneak attack." Then, defiantly repeating, to great applause, the same formula he had famously used four years before, he said, "As for myself, under the same circumstances, I would choose to do the same thing—again and again and again." He delighted in quoting "a Republican candidate" whom he did not name, though everyone knew he meant Dewey, who had accused Roosevelt of such subversive incompetence that "the Communists are seizing control of the New Deal, through which they aim to control the Government of the United States. . . . However, on that very same day," the same candidate said that "with Republican victory in November, 'we can end one-man government, and we can forever remove the threat of monarchy in the United States.' Now really, which is it, Communism or monarchy?"[38]

As for the vice presidential candidate, Harry Truman wrote: "The campaign of 1944 was the easiest in which I ever participated. The Republican candidates never had a chance."[39] Truman had an extensive election tour and found the President's prestige overwhelming.

Roosevelt had certainly debunked the claims of those who said he was physically decrepit. Unlike many of the reporters and Secret Service men who provided his security, he had not contracted a cold in extensive open-car motor tours of New York and Philadelphia. His hustings performance had been vigorous and eloquent. He had infected the legions of his followers with his optimism, tickled their sense of humor, and stirred the patriotic susceptibilities of the nation one more time.

On election eve, November 6, as on previous corresponding quadrennial occasions, he spoke to the country from his home, Springwood. "As we sit quietly this evening in our home at Hyde Park, our thoughts, like those of millions of other Americans, are most deeply concerned with the well-being of all our American fighting men. We are thinking of our own sons—all of them far away from home—and of our neighbors' sons and the sons of our friends.

"I do not want to talk to you tonight of partisan politics. The political battle is finished. Our task now is to face the future as a militant and a united people. . . . Twice in twenty-five years our people have had to put on a brave, smiling front as they have suffered the anxiety and agony of war. No one wants to endure that suffering again." He concluded with a prayer that had been sent him not long before by Bishop Angus Dun of Washington. This increased frequency of Roosevelt's evident religiosity may have been a response to the war and its Manichaean character, or may have been inspired by intimations of his own mortality, or may even have been tactical. It was difficult to accuse of dictatorial or messianic ambitions someone leading the country in prayer.

He ended: "Enable us to guard for the least among us the freedom we covet for ourselves; make us ill-content with the inequalities of opportunity which still prevail among us. Preserve our union against all the divisions of race and class which threaten it." This was, among other things, yet another warning that the inequality of the African-Americans had to be ended.

Election night, November 7, the Morgenthaus, the Watsons, Rosenman, Sherwood, Grace Tully, Early, and his assistant Bill Hassett joined the President and Mrs. Roosevelt, Laura Delano, Margaret Suckley, and Marion Dickerman at Springwood. The journalist Merriman Smith referred amusedly to "arty old ladies in tweed, or evening gowns of two decades before."[40] Roosevelt, amiable and composed, sat with his long tally sheets as results came in on the large radio, on a primitive television set, and on the newswires clicking in the dining room. Anna sat in what had been Missy's place, beside her father.

Roosevelt's confidence was justified. Shortly after ten o'clock, the thundering tidal wave of Roosevelt's support from the great cities began to pull him ahead of Dewey. It was the closest of his four elections, because with more than 10 million servicemen away from home and over 90 percent of these effectively disenfranchised, the vote total went down. Roosevelt won 25.6 million votes to 22 million for Dewey, a very respectable showing by the Republican challenger. In percentage terms, it was 53.8 percent to 46 percent. If the eleven states of the old South are taken out, Roosevelt's margin was only 1,500,000, though his plurality almost undoubtedly would have been over five million and on the scale of the victory over Willkie if the servicemen had been able to vote in representative numbers.

Roosevelt carried 36 states with 432 electoral votes to 12 states with 99 electoral votes for his opponent. Dewey won the Dakotas, Nebraska, Kansas, Iowa, Wisconsin, Ohio, Indiana, Wyoming, Colorado, Maine, and Vermont. Roosevelt lost some support among the farmers, aggrieved at farm price supports they thought insufficient (as part of his campaign against inflation). This toppled most of the farm states over to Dewey. Roosevelt was more popular with the CIO union workers than with those of the AF of L, despite the antics of the subsiding but unextinguished John L. Lewis. All surveys indicate that the President kept intact his Catholic, Jewish, and African-American voting blocks as well as a substantial lead among religious nonpractitioners. Middle and high church, prosperous Protestants, his own native group, continued to be his weakest electoral area and divided narrowly.

Roosevelt received the customary torchlight parade of well-wishers on his verandah shortly after midnight. He singled out a few neighbors, reminisced, and said: "It looks as if I will have to come back here on a train from Washington for four more years. . . . It will always be worth it. And so I am glad to be here on this election day again. I might say again and again and again! But I'll be perfectly happy to come back here for good, as you all know. I don't have to tell you that."

Roosevelt was resorting to nostalgia quite frequently now. He had had an almost imperceptible transition from the dynamic young President of the New Deal, to the serene reigning President of the pre- and early war years, to the wise and benign elder statesman preparing to reconstruct the world, though he was now only sixty-two. His illness and his political longevity combined to give him the aura of the sage before his time. Though Washington, Jefferson, and to a degree Jackson were legendary figures in a primitive pre-electronic era when the United States was a small country, none of them in his own lifetime and certainly none of the other twenty-seven men who had preceded the incumbent, even Lincoln or TR, remotely approached Roosevelt in the length or depth of the impact of his personality (as opposed to legend) on the consciousness of the American public. To the world beyond, those men had been distantly known, and Woodrow Wilson had passed meteorically across the sky. The other previous American presidents had had no currency at all outside official circles. Franklin D. Roosevelt was an unprecedented phenomenon.

It was a considerable achievement for Dewey, a forty-two-year-old freshman governor and former district attorney, to have come as close as he did to such an eminent leader and consummate politician. But to win a fourth consecutive presidential election made the incumbent an even more incomparable figure in the political annals of the country than he had already been. He was the champion to the end.

Dewey did not concede until after 3 A.M. Roosevelt then sent him a perfunctory telegram and retired, saying of Dewey to his assistant, Bill Hassett: "I still think he's a son-of-a-bitch."[41] Dewey's very courteous handwritten message arrived several days later and received a more appreciative reply.[42] Senator Gerald Nye, to Roosevelt's great joy, was defeated. Robert Wagner, Claude Pepper, Elbert Thomas, and Alben Barkley were among those reelected. Among those elected for the first time to the Senate were Wayne Morse and J. William Fulbright, and to the House of Representatives Adam Clayton Powell of Harlem. Morse and Fulbright would be among the leading opponents of the Vietnam War twenty and twenty-five years later, as it was conducted by President Lyndon B. Johnson. Fulbright would be the mentor of future president William Jefferson Clinton.

The Democrats narrowly reinforced their control of both houses of the Congress, but the ability of the conservative Republicans and southern Democrats together to obstruct the President's program continued.

Among those who sent Roosevelt congratulations were Churchill, Stalin, Mao Tse-tung,[43] de Gaulle, and Pope Pius XII, all of his most important contemporaries except Hitler. Churchill wrote: "I always said that a great people could be trusted to stand by the pilot who had weathered the storm. It is an indescribable relief to me that our comradeship will continue and will help to bring the world out of misery." As Roosevelt had never acknowledged Churchill's congratulatory message of November 1940, Churchill retransmitted it, saying much of it "is true today." In that message, Churchill had written: "I prayed for your success and am truly thankful for it. . . . Things are afoot which will be remembered as long as the English language is spoken in any quarter of the globe. . . . I must avow my sure faith that the lights by which we steer will bring us all safely to anchor."[44] Roosevelt thanked the prime minister, and assured him that he had not forgotten the earlier message.[45]

The President's train returned him to Washington's Union Station on November 10. Roosevelt again drove in an open car, with Wallace and Truman. Thirty thousand people had gathered in the rain to greet him in front of the railway station, and he addressed them briefly from his car, reassuring the country that he did not intend to be President for life (a reference to his political ambitions, not his health). He reminisced for a moment on how the city had changed since he had first come there during the first administration of President Cleveland nearly sixty years before. Federal employees had been given the day off, and more than 300,000 lined Pennsylvania Avenue as the President's motorcade, escorted by a large phalanx of motorcycle policemen, swept up Pennsylvania Avenue to the White House. Roosevelt held a press conference, where one of the questions was whether he intended to run for reelection in 1948.[46]

VI

NOW REINSTALLED IN PARIS, de Gaulle set out to put his tempestuous relations with Churchill on a sound footing and to make yet another play for Churchill's affections for his European vocation, as opposed to his status as junior ally of the United States. He had invited the British prime minister to come to Paris for Armistice Day, the November 11 anniversary of the imposition of Foch's peace terms in 1918. Churchill had maintained his acceptance in principle of this invitation, even though many at a lengthy cabinet meeting advised against the trip. Resigned in advance to a disagreeable session but inspired by his love of France and awareness of the necessity of France as an important component in a resurrected Europe, Churchill went, taking Mrs. Churchill, Eden, and Duff Cooper with him. But de Gaulle, too, rose above recent and current differences and determined to express his gratitude to Churchill for all that the British had done for France. He was also launching the long Gaullist campaign to wean Britain away from America, which would be punctuated over the decades by spiteful acts of resentment at the continuing Anglo-American "special relationship."

De Gaulle greeted the Churchills most courteously at Orly airfield with a full honor guard and conducted them to their Paris residence, the Quai d'Orsay, the French foreign ministry. The Germans had occupied the building for four years and Churchill slept in the bed that had been used by Goering on his visits, conducted with the chief purpose of looting works of art for the Reichsmarschall's own collection. "Everything was mounted and serviced magnificently," wrote Churchill, "and inside the palace it was difficult to believe that my last meeting there . . . with Reynaud's government and General Gamelin in May 1940 was anything but a bad dream."[47]

The next morning at 11 A.M., the exact anniversary of the Armistice, de Gaulle and Churchill rode "in an open car across the Seine and through the Place de la Concorde, with a splendid escort of Gardes Republicaines . . . a brilliant spectacle," breastplates shining in the bright sunlight. "The whole of the famous avenue of the Champs Élysées was crowded with Parisians and lined with troops. Every window was filled with spectators and decorated with flags. We proceeded through wildly cheering multitudes to the Arc de Triomphe, where we both laid wreaths on the tomb of the Unknown Warrior." Then, "the General and I walked together, followed by a concourse of the leading figures of French public life, for half a mile down the highway I knew so well. . . . A splendid march past of French and British troops" followed. De Gaulle told the bandmaster to play the anthem of the French Army, "Le Pere la Victoire," "In honor of Mr. Churchill," he said in English, a language with which he was not really familiar. "And it was only justice," de Gaulle wrote later. Then Churchill "laid a wreath beneath the statue of Clemenceau, who was much in my thoughts on this moving occasion," he wrote in his memoirs.[48]

De Gaulle rose near the end of the large luncheon he held in Churchill's honor at the Ministry of War. "As everyone knows, Paris, France, and the French government have had to get through some quite difficult moments since the last time these distinguished visitors favored us with their presence in this capital. We never doubted that those cruel days would pass. But the truth is that they would not have passed without the unconquerable heroism of the British people and Dominions, under precisely the impulse and inspiration of those whom we honor today. No French man or woman is not touched to the depths of their hearts and souls by that fact."

De Gaulle dryly doubted that "M. Hitler's" Reich would last 1,000 years but confidently stated that the memory of Britain's invincible courage and that of its great leader in the present war would. His toast was to King George VI and the British people, and above all, "to a great statesman and a great man, whom I shall always be proud to call my comrade, my mentor, and my friend, the Right Honorable Winston Churchill." The toast was drunk and was lengthily applauded.

Churchill was flabbergasted, and with tears in his eyes quietly took a few moments to compose his thoughts and arose a minute later. "For more than thirty years I have defended the cause of friendship, of comradeship, and of alliance between France and Great Britain. I have never deviated from that policy throughout the whole of my life. For so many years past have our two nations shared the glories of western Europe that they have become indispensable to each other." He expressed his gratitude at returning "to Paris, this brilliant star shining above the world." He reminisced at having been in Paris on Bastille Day, 1939, and having seen a formidable parade of the French Army on the Champs Élysées that day. "How many dangers and sorrows have we not had to get through since then, and how many dear friends have been lost, on both sides of our Channel? Yet what memories remain with us today? One night in October, 1940, during the worst raids on London, I did not fear to address the French people in French and tell them that the day would come when France would again take her place among the great nations and play her part as a champion of liberty and independence.

"I would be lacking in truthfulness and gratitude if I failed to pay tribute to the capital part that General de Gaulle has played in the transformation which has brought us . . . to a new era of vision and greatness." It was de Gaulle's turn — and he was a good deal more impassive than Churchill — to be visibly, though discreetly, moved. The two leaders stood together as the room, including Marshal Foch's venerable widow, rose and cheered and applauded for several minutes.[49]

Churchill and de Gaulle went to see the starting point of a French offensive against the Germans in eastern France. "The French soldiers seemed in the highest spirits. They marched past in great style and sang famous songs with moving enthusiasm. . . . Dinner was pleasant and interesting. I was struck by the awe and even apprehension, with which half a dozen high generals treated de Gaulle in spite of the fact that he had only one star on his uniform and they had lots."[50] De Gaulle had transcended rank. Churchill cabled Roosevelt a very positive description of his visit. It was fantastic that, only two years before, Roosevelt had equated de Gaulle to Giraud, much less Darlan, and that Leahy considered his political views indistinguishable from Petain's.

The President departed Washington for Warm Springs, his first real visit there since before Pearl Harbor, on November 27, 1944. He would resume his traditional Thanksgiving dinner with other polio patients and was looking forward to the comparative rest. It was a successful visit. Laura Delano, Margaret Suckley, and Lucy Mercer Rutherfurd were there with him, and gave the sort of companionship—light, indulgent, and supportive—that never came easily to Eleanor, who tended to be relentless and argumentative. The President slept in, dealt with his correspondence, swam and sunned in the afternoon, or drove in his modified Ford convertible, license plate FDR-1, over the hills and through the forests of the area. He drove Lucy around, becoming agreeably reacquainted with her, sometimes without even a distant Secret Service escort.

On Saturday, December 6, the President and Lucy drove to Roosevelt's favorite local prospect, Dowdell's Knob, where the panorama was always splendid and inspiriting. Roosevelt expatiated on postwar problems, interspersing his reflections with comments about trees or other objects in view. When Lucy later described this to Roosevelt's daughter, Anna, she said: "I realized Mother was not capable of giving him this—just listening. And of course this is why I was able to fill in for a year and a half, because I could listen."[51]

Cordell Hull, unwell, had retired after nearly twelve years as secretary of state. Roosevelt appointed his assistant secretary, Edward Stettinius, former Lend-Lease administrator and head of U.S. Steel, to replace Hull. Roosevelt's colleagues were appalled at the appointment of someone generally regarded as a lightweight for such a position at such a time. Morgenthau considered Stettinius a "clerk," McCloy thought him, in Menckenese, a Rotarian, while Ickes considered him merely a "backslapper."[52] These views were somewhat harsh. The new secretary of state was a competent man who had performed well in a number of important positions. He was popular and impressive in appearance. Roosevelt didn't need a Talleyrand for foreign affairs; he needed someone who would help assemble support for a bipartisan foreign policy.

Stettinius was another Republican, in the tradition of Stimson et al., and a sop to big business as well. He was a good tactical choice, as long as the President himself was making the foreign policy decisions. He had much less stature than Hull or Stimson, who had been secretary of state under Hoover, or than Charles Evans Hughes and Frank Kellogg before him, or than Byrnes, Marshall, Acheson, and Dulles, who followed Stettinius. It was a measure of Roosevelt's determination to bring the Republicans into the United Nations and avoid the horrible mistakes of Wilson at the end of World War I that he now had Republican secretaries of state and war.

Stettinius scandalized Eleanor and other New Dealers with the appointment of his deputies: Nelson Rockefeller; Joseph Grew, the former able ambassador to Japan; Texas commodities dealer William Clayton, and James Dunn, a croquet-playing career diplomat who severely galled Eleanor by having favored Franco in the Spanish Civil War. At least two of these, Rockefeller and Dunn, were Republicans. Roosevelt stayed above the fray and ignored the protestations, including Eleanor's. "Father hung up the phone on Mother" when she called him in Warm Springs to protest, Anna reported.[53] In fact, Stettinius's candidates were better choices than he was himself.

Almost every day, blissfully unaware of her husband's dalliances with Lucy,

Eleanor bombarded Franklin with some policy question by cable or letter. Roosevelt and Churchill had one of their sharpest exchanges over the status of Count Sforza. The British considered him a double-dealing, grandstanding political opportunist, and removed him from the Italian government. The State Department then issued a statement on December 5, disassociating the United States from the British position and describing the matter as an internal Italian question. Churchill cabled Roosevelt the following day that he would have to deal with questions in Parliament about the American rebuke, and would have to do so quite bluntly.

"I feel entitled to remind you that on every single occasion in the course of this war I have loyally tried to support any statements to which you were personally committed." He cited the imbroglio over Darlan as an example. "I do not remember anything that the State Department has ever said about Russia or about any other allied state comparable to this document with which Mr. Stettinius has inaugurated his assumption of office." Churchill regarded Sforza's status as preeminently a British matter because of overall British command in the Mediterranean.[54]

As always when Churchill was seriously riled, Roosevelt responded within a couple of hours: "I deplore any offense which the press release may have given you personally. . . . While military operations continue, Italy is an area of combined Anglo-American responsibility. . . . This move (the purge of Sforza) was made without prior consultation with us in any quarter and it is quite contrary to the policy which we have tried to follow in Italy." Sforza was back in government in a few months.

———————

By this time, Charles de Gaulle had taken his quest for restoration of France's status as a great power to Moscow. He wrote of his host as a man without "illusions, pity, sincerity, [who saw] in each man an obstacle or a threat, [and] was all strategy, suspicion, stubbornness . . . and totalitarian rigor, bringing to bear a superhuman boldness and guile, subjugating or liquidating all others.

"Stalin regarded his country as more mysterious, mightier, and more durable than any theory, any regime. He loved it, in his way. Russia herself accepted him as a Czar during a terrible epoch. . . . His fortune was to have found a people so vital and so patient that the worst servitudes did not paralyze them, a soil full of such resources that the most terrible destruction and waste could not exhaust it, and allies without whom he could not have conquered his adversary but who would not have triumphed without him."

This last reflection was the first hint of de Gaulle's great effort twenty years later to hold the balance of power between the Soviet and American blocs. In fact, the British and Americans could have defeated Germany without Russia, and would have done so, even without atomic weapons. But they would have had to finish off Japan first, and then concentrate all their forces, as many as 450 divisions and unimaginable numbers of aircraft and ships, in the European theater.

The war would have continued to 1948 or 1949, but there would have been no Cold War after it.

It suited de Gaulle's purposes to foster the illusion of American limitations, in order to enhance the role he could play. If the strongest powers are believed to be less strong than they are, the secondary powers become more important. If the second power is encouraged to believe it is almost as strong as the first, the tertiary powers become more influential. Considering where he started on June 18, 1940, de Gaulle parlayed his unexciting geopolitical cards into a formidable position, but it was largely illusory.

"During the fifteen or so hours . . . of my interviews with Stalin, I discerned the outlines of his ambitious and cryptic policy. . . . So fierce was his passion that it often gleamed through this armor, not without a kind of sinister charm."

When Stalin mentioned the French Communist leader, Maurice Thorez, he said: " 'In my opinion he is a good Frenchman. If I were in your place, I would not put him in prison.' He added, with a smile, 'At least, not right away!' "

At these meetings, Stalin was trying to make a Franco-Soviet security pact conditional on French recognition of the Lublin Committee as the government of Poland. Stalin claimed to de Gaulle that "agents of the government in London [Mikolajczyk] were responsible for the failure of the Warsaw insurrection." De Gaulle drew him out on the eastern and Balkan countries. They would be "democratic," but would "receive the deserved punishment. . . . It was evident that the Soviets were resolved to deal just as they chose with the states and territories occupied or about to be occupied by their forces. There was therefore every reason to expect, on their part, a terrible political oppression in Central and Balkan Europe. It appeared that in this regard, Moscow put no credence in any determined opposition from Washington and London."

De Gaulle revealed his own proposals for postwar Germany: everything west of the Rhine would be separated from Germany and would be autonomous, and there would be international control of the Ruhr, Germany's industrial heartland.

De Gaulle consented to meet with the Lublin Committee, but "was not greatly impressed with" them. De Gaulle also met with Harriman, who allegedly told him: "For our part, we Americans have decided to behave with the Russians as if we trusted them." That certainly did not mean that they did trust them, as Harriman's dispatches to Roosevelt demonstrated and as de Gaulle knew, but de Gaulle, for his own purposes, pretended that this was exactly what it did mean.

Discussions were still deadlocked on the last night of the visit. Stalin invited the French to "an overpowering banquet. The Russians around the table, watchful and constrained in manner, never took their eyes from [Stalin]. On their part, manifest submission and apprehensiveness; on his, concentrated vigilance and authority."

Then Stalin got into the toasts. After dealing with the foreigners, including Roosevelt and Churchill in absentia, "Thirty times Stalin stood up to drink to the health of those Russians present. To Novikov, chief of staff of the Air Force, he said: 'You are the one who uses our planes. If you use them badly, you know what's in store for you. . . . There he is! That is the supply director. It is his job to bring men and material to the front. He'd better do his best. Otherwise he'll be hanged for it—that's the custom in our country.' . . . This tragicomic scene could have no other purpose than to impress the French by displaying Soviet might and the domination of the man at its head. But having witnessed it, I was all the less inclined to lend my support to the sacrifice of Poland."

De Gaulle continued to stonewall, and Stalin exclaimed, to Molotov's visible discomfort: "Ah, these diplomats! What chatterers! There's only one way to shut them up—cut them all down with a machine gun! Someone get me one." They then watched "an extremely conformist and quite naïve" film about the Russo-German war. As it made no mention of the Nazi-Soviet pact of 1939, de Gaulle commented on its stark variance from the facts at the outset of the conflict. De Gaulle left, but eventually, in the middle of the night, there was movement. Stalin agreed to the security pact if France would send someone to meet with the Lublin Committee. As this did not imply recognition, de Gaulle agreed, and returned to the Kremlin at 4 A.M. The party he had left four hours before was still in progress. The pact was signed and Stalin announced another banquet, which de Gaulle politely declined. "Stalin was a good sport. . . . He complimented me." He expressed pity for Hitler, "a poor wretch who won't escape from this one. . . . The farewells on his part assumed an effusive quality," though he declined to commit to come to Paris on grounds of age. Stalin turned to his translator and said: "You know too much! I'd better send you to Siberia." On this lugubrious note, de Gaulle departed.[55] Stalin's version of the meeting, to Churchill and Roosevelt seven weeks later, was a good deal less colorful, and he professed not to be overly impressed with France or de Gaulle.

Churchill had wished to transform the Franco-Soviet pact into a tripartite pact with Great Britain, and so cabled to Stalin and de Gaulle in the midst of their meetings. But de Gaulle declined this initiative until he had ironed out certain issues with the British, especially in the Middle East and in policy to Germany.

By December 1944, the Soviet design for Eastern Europe was obvious, and any material derogation from it would be difficult, given the personality and ambitions of the Soviet leader. Only Roosevelt, with the full panoply of American wealth and power, had any possibility of ameliorating what de Gaulle correctly foresaw as an iron-fisted suppression of the East European nationalities.

The Gaullist fantasy had begun that France had lost a battle but was a victorious power in the war, was the true champion of the European states between the Anglo-Saxons and the Russians, would embrace the Anglo-Saxons when appropriate, as fellow democrats, and the Russians, when possible, as fellow Europeans. He attempted to translate his exclusion from the Great Power conferences at the end of the war, which deeply irritated him at the time, and which he misrepresented as sellouts to Stalin, as a moral advantage to him. And he remained completely oblivious of the fact that Stalin was using his discussions with deGaulle and the agreement reached at the end of them as a spurious argument in favor of Anglo-American recognition of the Lublin Poles, whose legitimacy de Gaulle professed thereafter to have resisted.

The postwar world had already begun, at least politically. The Americans had all the power, but would use it only when they themselves were threatened, as in the two world wars and the Cold War to come. They would not risk too much for nonstrategic areas like Poland. This left U.S. and, to a degree, British policy vulnerable to de Gaulle's posturings at times. (Vietnam would be an aberration, where the Americans didn't at first take North Vietnam seriously, and didn't really know what they were getting into, and didn't prepare it constitutionally or prosecute it with a will to win. The mistakes began with Patrick Hurley, but Roosevelt and his immediate successors would have avoided that morass.)

The British had their European moments, but as Churchill had bluntly told de Gaulle in June 1944, Britain's primary loyalty was to the American alliance. The Russians were as great a menace as Nazi Germany but less reckless, and de Gaulle always professed to see, beneath the pretensions of Communist universalism, the soul of Mother Russia, a great power spanning Europe and Asia.

There was among Churchill, de Gaulle, and Stalin the solidarity of European statesmen who had been through the rigors of war in their own countries, unlike the American leaders. With de Gaulle even more than with Churchill, there was a certain identification with Stalin as men who had been at close quarters with a mortal enemy and whose nations had been in the grips of war up to their vitals. The comparative detachment, vast resources, and unquenchable optimism of Roosevelt and his countrymen, while inspiring, was less familiar to Churchill and de Gaulle than Stalin's grim determination, leavened, as both Churchill and de Gaulle record, by his witty, though often gruesome, sense of humor.

In some respects, the essence of America was to be un-European, as the millions who had fled to America from Europe had wished. As de Gaulle wrote, "France is at the end of a continent, Britain is an island, America another world." Roosevelt's task was to preserve popular concepts of Americanism while convincing his countrymen of the necessity of staying engaged in Europe as well as East Asia for reasons of self-defense, to prevent threats to America from arising there. Precisely the differences of scale and general optimism that astounded and buoyed America's European allies during the war would often be disturbing to America's postwar allies, and for many decades. Winston Churchill, half-American, pro-American, and well travelled in the United States, would be more unambiguously supportive of the United States than most of his successors, but no less pro-French for that.

The necessity for Roosevelt to dress everything in idealistic terms for the benefit of his electors and legislators was also disconcerting to Churchill and de Gaulle. Churchill never seems to have recognized the extent to which this was tactical, while de Gaulle appears to have thought it almost entirely tactical and to have underestimated Roosevelt's sincerity. Both had trouble with Roosevelt's singular fusion of feline characteristics, cynical impulses, devious methods, and exalted aims. His illness contributed to his starkly realistic view of the world, but also to his conviction that anything was possible. Thus his goals were more virtuous than those of the old imperial Tory, Churchill, and the cynical Cartesian Gallican, de Gaulle. But his political ethics were inferior to Churchill's and almost as amoral as de Gaulle's. It is difficult to imagine Roosevelt, if he were in Churchill's position in 1941, risking so much to assist the Greeks. But it is impossible to imagine him, if he were in de Gaulle's position, trying to break up Canada, which had helped liberate France, as de Gaulle did in 1967.

At one level, and the most important one, Roosevelt, Churchill, and de Gaulle were Christians (though Churchill "had a problem with worship," as his daughter Mary put it to me many years later), democrats, and civilized men. Each was an evocator and a voice of the culture and ethos of the West. At a secondary level, de Gaulle and Churchill saw in Stalin a European who had fought for his and his country's life, whose cynicism, while less creditable than what de Gaulle called "Roosevelt's vast idealism," was more diverting and exotic, and was less demanding to keep up with. Churchill was less stoical than the world-weary Catholic rationalist, de Gaulle.

Oddly, and partly for the same reasons, Roosevelt was a good deal less impressed with Stalin personally than Churchill and de Gaulle were. He always regarded him as a clever and tough but rather unprepossessing little man. Though, for a time after Yalta, Roosevelt did claim to appreciate Stalin's sense of humor, and as with anyone who apparently deferred to him, Roosevelt professed some friendly feelings for Stalin.[56] Of course Roosevelt was also very late in appreciating de Gaulle's qualities, and though a great admirer of Churchill, who worked very hard on the relationship with Roosevelt, he was never overpowered by Churchill, as both de Gaulle and Stalin were on occasion.

Roosevelt thought he was "pushing Winston uphill in a wheel barrow" over India and other colonial matters. Churchill thought he was guiding and chaperoning the United States into the great world. De Gaulle was trying to earn American respect by being a nuisance on such a scale that they would have to deal with him as a serious figure. Stalin did not care about anyone or anything except seizing all the territory his armies could reach where the British and the Americans had not preceded him. The Russian Bear, confined for centuries, saw its cage door open and was lumbering into Central Europe.

VII

P RESIDENT ROOSEVELT RETURNED to Washington from Warm Springs on December 16, just as Hitler made the last great play of his life, an attack toward the Belgian coast that became known as the Battle of the Ardennes, or of the Bulge. It had been prepared with great care and secrecy, even from his general officers. Two Panzer armies of Germany's best and most battle-tested soldiers were launched through the Ardennes toward Antwerp, in a smaller-scale reenactment of the great sweep to Dunkirk of 1940. The Germans waited for bad weather to reduce the importance of the Allies' air advantage.

The initial attack, against some of the most thinly held areas and inexperienced troops of the American army under General Omar Bradley, moved about fifty miles northwestwards in the first ten days of the attack, to Christmas Day, and barricaded an American division into the town of Bastogne. Hitler's plan had counted on overrunning American fuel depots to keep his own armor supplied, but the Germans did not capture any American depots. Eisenhower, made wary by intelligence reports, had positioned his depots well behind his lines. He has received little credit for this tactical insight.

Eisenhower, admirably cool throughout the action, committed his strategic reserve to Bradley, especially two famous airborne divisions (82nd and 101st), and gave Montgomery, commander of the northern army group, direction of the northernmost American divisions. Nine thousand Americans were forced to surrender in southeastern Belgium, the second largest American surrender in history after Bataan. It was a tense time, but Roosevelt, as always, was completely calm and businesslike, following the minutest movement of forces from the map room in the basement of the White House. Though there had been hopes for a German collapse as the hopelessness of their position became obvious, both Roosevelt and Churchill had predicted at Octagon a final German counteroffensive in the west.

Patton, at the southern hinge of the German attack, pivoted the U.S. Third Army northwards and attacked toward Bastogne on December 22. Four days later he had relieved the city. It was one of the most brilliant moments of his remarkable career. Montgomery, after meticulous preparations, counterattacked in strength from the north on January 2, 1945. The German salient was relentlessly beaten back, assisted by tremendous air strength that came increasingly into play as the weather lifted after Christmas.

When Stimson reported to Roosevelt on the last day of the year that the Germans had killed more than a score of American prisoners at Malmedy, Roosevelt coolly responded: "It will only serve to make our troops feel about the Germans as they . . . feel about the Japs."[57]

The Germans took 120,000 casualties in the Battle of the Ardennes, compared with about 90,000 for the Allies, more than two-thirds of them American. Hitler also lost about a third of his air force, over 1,500 planes. He could not remain in the war for more than another few months. In transferring much of the Ardennes force to the west and losing it, Hitler denied himself any possibility of resisting the Russians in the east, and he stalled the progress of the Western Allies by about six weeks. This, unforeseeably, made the future for the Eastern European countries even bleaker, since it assisted the Russian advance while retarding the progress of the Western Allies. The Allies resumed their advance toward Germany in fierce skirmishing immediately west of the Rhine through January. They reached the Rhine in February and crossed it in early March.

This sequence highlighted the reservations about Eisenhower's theater battle plan. It should not have taken six months from the liberation of Paris to the crossing of the Rhine. The British and Patton were calling for a decisive stroke, instead of a solid front from the sea to the Swiss border. If properly executed, such a stroke would have sliced through into the heart of Germany, prevented the organization of the Ardennes offensive, shortened the European war, and led to the Western liberation of Prague and the capture of Berlin. Hence the consideration of alternative expeditionary force commanders in chapter 20. MacArthur and Marshall were the only candidates of the required stature and Marshall was an unknown quantity as a theater commander. With that said, Eisenhower did receive the unconditional German surrender a year ahead of the original schedule. He coordinated difficult subordinates and conflicting national sensibilities with exquisite tact, and he administered occupied areas judiciously. His performance was distinguished in execution, but it lacked genius in conception, unlike some of MacArthur's campaigns.

Senator Burton Wheeler, unsubdued by the many defeats he had suffered at Roosevelt's hands, demanded, in the midst of the Battle of the Bulge, an end to the requirement for unconditional surrender and to the quest for "vengeance" on Germany. He wanted an early departure from Europe, which he called "a seething furnace of fratricide, civil war, murder, disease and starvation." This was judged an inappropriate comment in the midst of the Ardennes battle, and Roosevelt publicly ignored Wheeler, his first senatorial supporter and now, since the death of Borah, his bitterest critic in the Senate. After his claim in 1940 that Roosevelt's pro-British policy would kill one-quarter of young American manhood, Wheeler's credibility outside his home state of Montana was not high.

In the most testing moments of the Battle of the Ardennes, African-American soldiers who had been confined to maintenance jobs were invited to volunteer for combat. About 4,000 did so and fought with great distinction. They went back to their segregated units when the crisis passed, but the success of the experiment changed the attitudes of a great many of the white soldiers. It was another step forward for the patient black population of America.[58]

Christmas of 1944 for the Roosevelts was at Hyde Park. Most of the grandchildren were there, along with Anna and her husband, Franklin Jr.'s wife, and Elliott and his new wife, Faye Emerson, whom Eleanor (accurately) considered only "a passing house guest."[59] Everything was as it had always been, including FDR's flamboyant recitation of Dickens's *A Christmas Carol,* improvising a different voice for all the characters.

The President briefly addressed the nation by radio from his home on Christmas Eve. His statement confirmed the now established trend of increasing religiosity in his public remarks. Of course, a Christmas Eve address always had some religious content, especially during wartime, but Roosevelt was sounding more and more like a man using religion to prepare himself calmly for a supreme personal crisis.

"It is not easy to say 'Merry Christmas' . . . tonight to our armed forces at their battle stations all over the world—or to our allies who fight by their side. . . . [Yet] the Christmas spirit lives tonight in the bitter cold of the front lines in Europe and in the heat of the jungles and swamps of Burma and the Pacific Islands." Our fighting men "know the determination of all right-thinking people and Nations, that Christmases such as those that we have known in these years of world tragedy shall not come again to beset the souls of the children of God. . . . We pray that God will protect our gallant men and women in the uniforms of the United Nations—that He will receive into His infinite grace those who make their supreme sacrifice in the cause of righteousness, in the cause of love of Him and his teachings." These last he interpreted as a peace of universal and durable brotherhood.

The President was coming perilously close to sanctimony. He was approaching fervor in his internationalism, prefiguring a sort of Götterdämmerung for the disbelievers and an apotheosis for himself as high priest. There is no reason to believe that his increasing spirituality offended opinion in the country, or was much noticed at the time, but because it didn't serve any political purpose, it indicates that such thoughts, presumably in contemplation of his own mortality, were increasingly on his mind.

On Christmas night, Roosevelt sat with his son Elliott beside the fireplace in his bedroom and talked about reviving his relations with his wife. He spoke warmly of her and was hopeful that their life could be reconstructed.

When this was reported to her by Anna, Eleanor smiled and said she shared the hope. Yet when Eleanor asked her husband to take her with him to the upcoming conference in the Crimea with Stalin and Churchill, he declined, preferring Anna, and having already promised to invite Anna when he enticed her into the White House the year before. That he would prefer Anna is not surprising—she was such an enjoyable, attentive, attractive companion. But if Roosevelt was serious about stoking up relations with Eleanor, this was a peculiar way to do it. It was not only a rebuff but an implicit statement of preference of the company of his daughter over that of his wife. It could not fail to be hurtful to Eleanor. There was so much scar tissue on this relationship by now that unraveling the grievances of the two protagonists and restoring some degree of real cordiality would be a time-consuming task. And they did not have much time. He should have taken both to Yalta.

There was also the impediment of Roosevelt's flourishing revival of relations with Lucy. If Eleanor had had the least notion that her husband was driving around Washington and the back hills of Georgia with Mrs. Rutherfurd, and even stopping the presidential train in New Jersey to see her on his way to Hyde Park, her reaction would have been pyrotechnic. It was as if Franklin Roosevelt, as in 1917 and 1918, had simply suspended judgment and begun to behave in an irresponsible manner. However, with his mother, who had threatened to disinherit him, dead, and having successfully faced the voters for the last time, he had little left to fear except controversy. He probably also sensed that the end was near and he wanted to know again the pleasures of the companion he had loved, while seeking the best possible reconciliation with his wife of forty years.

The President's health was a real cause for concern to his family and close collaborators in the opening weeks of 1945. Some days he would seem solid and alert, color good, the usual animated and witty conversationalist. A few hours later, he could have a gray, ashen pallor, almost blue lips, severe shaking in his hands, glassy eyes, and a slack jaw. Frances Perkins said that he seemed like "an invalid who had been allowed to see guests for the first time and the guests had stayed too long."[60] One day, Senator Frank Maloney of Connecticut, an old friend and ally of Roosevelt's, came to see the President. Roosevelt looked vaguely and blankly at him, and Maloney rushed out, fearful that the President had taken a stroke. "Pa" Watson sent him back in, saying that FDR would come around. This is what happened; Roosevelt became very affable and was completely sensible.[61]

But there were many warnings. McIntire, as always, represented that with a little rest, Roosevelt would be fine and live to the normal actuarial age. Bruenn was much more cautious. To those with some right to know, he said that the President's cardiovascular condition was such that his life was precarious. He could live for years, or expire at any moment. The latter was more likely.

Roosevelt gave a somewhat condensed version of his State of the Union message to the country over the radio on January 6, 1945. He celebrated the victory in the Battle of the Ardennes, the hardest fighting the U.S. Army had engaged in yet in Europe, except for D-Day on Omaha Beach. As in his corresponding address of a year earlier, he dwelt at surprising length on the need, as he saw it, for a national service law. This was a peculiar preoccupation, demonstrating his exaggerated interest at this point in authoritarian regulation.

A national service law would be like conscription for nonmilitary work. He claimed that such a law would "assure that we have the right numbers of workers in the right place at the right times," would "provide supreme proof to all our fighting men that we are giving them . . . our total effort," and would be the final, unequivocal answer to the "Nazi and the Japanese [hope] that we may become halfhearted about this war, and that they can get from us a negotiated peace."

A national service law might have been useful for ironing out the comparatively few industrial relations problems that arose, and even for allocation of manpower. But it was also very authoritarian and would have entailed a colossal bureaucracy to administer, and the same ends could have been achieved without conscripting the entire work force, which now included twenty million women. And the two last reasons were absurd; the fighting men knew there was a mighty effort on the home front. Germany had been hammered to rubble; scarcely one brick stood upon another throughout the country's large cities, and Japan was starting to become acquainted with the same condition. The enemy had no illusions about a negotiated peace. In any case, the proposal had no chance of success, and the President's preoccupation with it is somewhat mystifying.

Barely three weeks before he was to meet Stalin and Churchill, he hinted in his State of the Union message at his mounting concern over the fate of the Eastern European countries. "I must admit concern about many situations—the Greek and Polish for example. But those situations are not as easy or as simple as some . . . would have us believe. We have obligations, not necessarily legal, to the exiled governments, to the underground leaders, and to our major Allies who came much nearer the shadows than we did." He reiterated the Allies' pledge to "respect the right of all peoples to choose the form of government under which they will live. . . . Until conditions permit a genuine expression of the people's will, we and our Allies have a duty, which we cannot ignore, to use our influence to the end that no temporary or provisional authorities in the liberated countries block the eventual exercise of the peoples' right freely to choose" their government. Roosevelt undoubtedly knew by this time that there were bound to be some robust disagreements with Stalin over timing and over some of the definitions of democratic institutions.

The American invasion of the main Philippine island of Luzon and the march on Manila began on January 9. Manila, almost as battered as German or Russian cities had been, would only be cleared of the enemy in late February, and the Philippine fighting would continue in underpopulated areas until the end of the war as a whole.

The Americans lost 14,000 dead and 48,000 wounded in the liberation of the Philippines, but they eliminated an entire Japanese army group of 450,000 (killed, wounded, captured, or driven into the jungles and scattered), won the great naval victory at Leyte Gulf, and destroyed at least a thousand Japanese aircraft. At the end of the war the Philippines was becoming "the England of the Pacific" as a staging area for the invasion of Japan.[62] All in all, MacArthur's advocacy of this campaign was justified, his conduct of the campaign was exceptionally capable, and Roosevelt's endorsement of his proposal of it was correct.

For his inauguration to a fourth term on January 20, Roosevelt reduced the budget for the ceremony by about 90 percent and moved it from the steps of the Capitol to a portico of the White House. He had all of his grandchildren present, all staying in the vastly overcrowded White House, another likely indication of his recognition of a weakening grip on life. The quadrennial religious service—Dr. Peabody having died aged eighty-six—was organized by the young curate of St. John's Church, Howard Johnson, whom Eleanor Roosevelt had introduced to her husband and who had fired in Roosevelt an interest in the Danish philosopher Søren Kierkegaard.

It was from Kierkegaard that Roosevelt professed to have discovered how people could be so evil as the Nazis. Johnson inserted in the service "The Prayer for Our Enemies," written at the beginning of the war by the archbishop of Canterbury, William Temple. Though Johnson was advised that the President would never agree to such a prayer, he pronounced the idea "Very good—I like it."[63]

The service was held at the White House, because the Secret Service asked that the President not go to a public church in wartime. Roosevelt made a point of greeting all the invitees singly as they left. When Frances Perkins, aware that he was about to depart for a summit conference, said: "I hope everything will be all right," he replied: "You'd better pray for me, Frances." The labor secretary considered his courtesy, his politeness to others, even uninteresting people, and his interest in having people actively pray for him to be manifestations of a simple and unaffected Christianity, the faith of his fathers. Roosevelt did know a great many hymns, psalms, and passages from the King James Bible and the Book of Common Prayer, and they appeared to be a considerable cultural and psychological comfort to him.

Roosevelt requested the presence of his eldest son, Jimmy, whose arm he had grasped during all previous inaugurations. His address was barely 500 words and consisted of a reassertion of well-known goals. He unselfconsciously quoted "my old schoolmaster, Dr. Peabody." Roosevelt seemed to be oblivious of the fact that 99 percent of Americans had schoolteachers, not the masters of the private schools.

Peabody's moment of immortality was the statement the President attributed to him that day: "The great fact to remember is that the trend of civilization is forever upward; that a line drawn through the middle of the peaks and the valleys of the centuries always has an upward trend." This was Roosevelt's fundamental belief, simply reasserted. He believed in progress, and believed he had accomplished some.

He quoted Emerson: "The only way to have a friend is to be one"—a hazardous sentiment with which to set off to bargain with Stalin, but Roosevelt was rarely as full of good will as he seemed. He knew better than anyone how generous the United States had been to Russia. If his protestations of good-neighborliness to Latin America were in large measure a public relations operation, his aid to Stalin was vital and indispensable, as Stalin had acknowledged at Teheran. Roosevelt was prepared to continue and expand that aid in exchange, along with other considerations, for good behavior in Eastern Europe.

He knew that difficult negotiations with Stalin lay ahead and he was preparing his countrymen, if needs must, for a strong line against Russian territorial gluttony. The struggle with the isolationists had been long and intricate. Debriefing the Soviet apologists, if it proved necessary, starting with his own wife, would be less complicated, and the dangers of appeasement of dictators were now generally acknowledged. Roosevelt was undoubtedly sincere in seeking agreement with Stalin, but the first precautionary step was to lay claim to the high ground of the potentially wronged party. For these purposes, Emerson was a good place to start.

After all he had said about Communism, his recognition of Stalin's brutal treatment of the Finns and the Warsaw uprising, his frequent references to the inadvisability of letting Stalin too far into Western Europe, his desire to get to Berlin ahead of the Russians, the concern he had expressed to everyone from Eden to King George VI to Keynes to Spellman about the possibility of a problem with Stalin, and his agreement with Stimson on the possible utility of atomic weapons in bringing Russia into the "Christian" world, Roosevelt certainly knew that cooperation with Russia might prove impossible. In a few months, Roosevelt would recognize Stalin's bad faith without surprise or even disillusionment.*

The President concluded his inaugural address, as was usually the case these

---

* He had frequently denounced the Soviet regime as qualitatively indistinguishable from Hitler's prior to Russian entry into the war, and said as much in his comments to George VI at Hyde Park in 1939 and in his letter to Pius XII of September 3, 1941. Roosevelt considered Pius XII's anti-Communism one of the pope's most admirable traits. Like most civilized Western leaders, the Pope had no affection for either contending totalitarianism, though, unlike Roosevelt, he found the Communist anti-Christ more obnoxious than the Nazi "pagans," as he described them to Joseph Kennedy in April, 1939.[64]

Roosevelt wrote to the pope in his September 1941 letter: "Russia is governed by a dictatorship, as rigid in its manner of being as is the dictatorship in Germany. I believe, however, that this Russian dictatorship is less dangerous to the safety of other nations than is the German form of dictatorship. The only weapon which the Russian dictatorship uses outside of its own borders is communist propaganda which I, of course, recognize has in the past been utilized for the purpose of breaking down the form of government in other countries, religious belief, et cetera. Germany, however, not only has utilized, but is utilizing, this kind of propaganda as well, and has also undertaken the employment of every form of military aggression outside of its borders for the purpose of world conquest by force of arms and by force of propaganda. I believe that the survival of Russia is less dangerous to religion, to the church as such, and to humanity in general than would be the survival of the German form of dictatorship."

He urged that all American religious leaders, and implicitly the Holy See, "should recognize these facts clearly and should not close their eyes to these basic questions and by their present attitude . . . directly assist Germany in her present objectives." Since Stalin, for his own purposes, had dragged out the Russian Orthodox patriarch to demand the repulse of the Germans, Roosevelt held out to the pope some possibility of improving religious freedom in Russia.

The pope was not buying much of it. The pope responded vaguely on September 20, 1941—in fact dodged the question completely, not even mentioning Germany or Russia, but congratulating Roosevelt on "the magnificent assistance which the American people have given . . . demonstrating once again a charitable understanding of the needs of their suffering fellow-men and a noble desire to alleviate their misery."[65]

last months, with words of supplication, for "vision . . . a better life for ourselves and for all our fellow men—and to the achievement of His will to peace on earth." Never in all their history had the American people been called to place their faith in divine Providence with such zeal and frequency by their leader.

Molotov had asked Harriman as early as September 1941 if Roosevelt, being an intelligent man, really was as religious as he appeared, or whether it was all for political purposes.[66]

Following the inauguration ceremony, there was a luncheon reception for 2,000 people in the White House. As the *New York Times* had reported that morning, Roosevelt had had a dispute with his unimaginative and inflexible cook, Mrs. Nesbitt, who had been protected by Eleanor for years, despite her dull and unappetizing cuisine and insubordinate manner. He had wished chicken a la king, but she insisted on chicken salad and made a poor job of that. He had joked to Grace Tully and to Anna in the run-up to the election that he wanted to win the election in order to fire Mrs. Nesbitt. (She outlasted him in the White House, but only by a few days.)

Just before facing the throng of inaugural celebrants, Roosevelt had another angina attack, as at San Diego and Bremerton, though somewhat less severe. "Jimmy, I can't take this unless you give me a stiff drink. You'd better make it straight." His son brought him a half tumbler of whiskey; the President drank it as if it were a soft drink, and then attended the reception, a considerable feat of self-control. Greeting hundreds of guests while suffering the pains of angina and grappling with crutches demonstrated once again his demiurgic powers of concentration and physical courage. In the circumstances, his ecclesiastical preoccupations are not altogether surprising.

One of the guests was Mrs. Woodrow Wilson, who had never forgiven Roosevelt for, as she claimed, stealing from her a desk from the liner *George Washington*, on which Wilson had written much of his World War I peace plans. It was not really a just charge. Daniels had given him the desk, but that had not prevented Mrs. Wilson from calling him "a common thief." Mrs. Wilson had thought Roosevelt "socially wonderful" in the Wilson administration. Like many others, she had thought him "more charming than able, but I changed my mind because the rude discipline of polio changed him."[67] Mrs. Wilson expressed her concern to Frances Perkins. "Oh, it frightened me. He looks exactly as my husband did when he went into his decline."[68] Roosevelt appeared only briefly at the large reception and then repaired to the Red Room, where he had his lunch with Princess Martha of Norway (his favorite of his many royal acquaintances because of her beauty and vivacious manner) and a few comparative intimates.

Two days later, on January 22, 1945, Roosevelt sailed with Anna, General Watson, Admiral Leahy, Justice Byrnes, and his doctors and other aides on the heavy cruiser U.S.S. *Quincy* for Malta, on the way to the Crimea and the second

wartime meeting of the Big Three, at Yalta. He took Byrnes as a conciliatory gesture, to assuage him after his rather shabby treatment as a potential vice presidential candidate, and after passing over him as secretary of state in favor of the less
talented Stettinius.[69] At his last cabinet meeting before departure, Roosevelt told
the ranking remaining cabinet member, Morgenthau, to convene a cabinet
meeting in his absence whenever he felt like doing so.[70] This, too, was a stark
contrast with Wilson's obsession after his stroke that only he could convene the
cabinet.

It was a restful trip, though Roosevelt never felt "slept out," despite ten hours
of sleep per day. Roosevelt took the captain's quarters, because he liked to be on
the starboard side of the ship. The admiral's quarters would normally have gone
to Leahy but were awarded by the President to his daughter, because if she slept
below decks she might distract the men and inhibit them from being underdressed in leisure hours.[71] (Given her pulchritude, the distraction would have
been considerable, though doubtless not unwelcome.)

Shortly after they started out from the great naval base at Newport News, Roosevelt pointed out part of the Virginia shore and offhandedly said to Anna that
that was where Lucy had grown up. Roosevelt relaxed and took the sun, and often
stared into the distance with the wistful look that was where his countenance usually settled in his latter years, if he was not closely engrossed in conversation or
engaged in pleasurable pastimes.

It was at moments such as these that the relentless and hugely successful struggle of his life became visible, covered over as it usually was by his jut-jawed, head-
tossing joviality. To what extent Roosevelt's confident cheerfulness was a tactic,
and to what extent it came naturally is difficult to discern. He was of an optimistic
nature and had achieved so much against such improbable odds that his positive
demeanor was not an affectation. But as he entered the winter of his days, he
knew that his ability to control events was limited, and felicity yielded to urgency,
fatigue, and otherworldly contemplation.

He was no less attractive for that. Still distinguished in appearance, though
thinner and more vulnerable, still a magnetic personality and seeming more seasoned and dignified for the attrition of life and limb that he had endured, his confidence appeared more measured and earned than in his younger days. As his
physical strength ebbed, his powers in the world reached a height that has rarely,
if ever, been approached by any other person.

CHAPTER 24

"In His Sensitive Hands Lay Much of the World's Fate"

*(British Foreign Secretary Anthony Eden, describing
President Roosevelt's arrival in the Grand Harbour at Malta,
on his way to the Yalta Conference, February 2, 1945)*

I

ON JANUARY 30, 1945, Roosevelt celebrated his 63rd birthday on ship-board. Eleanor had dutifully gone around on his birthday night to the March of Dimes parties raising money for polio treatment and research.

These March of Dimes parties were also one of Roosevelt's methods of drawing in the stars of America's entertainment community. Almost all of them recognized that he was the greatest American star and performer of all, rivalled only by Churchill as the world's preeminent personality. Many, as we have seen, like Orson Welles, Frank Sinatra, Myrna Loy, and Al Jolson, and all those mentioned in the 1940 campaign, most of whom were back in 1944, campaigned for him. And on these March of Dimes nights at the White House, as in the early NRA days and the parades and parties in ceremonies of the Blue Eagle, most of Hollywood was delighted to be associated with a president who was such a master showman in a good cause.

Joe E. Brown, Gene Kelly, Jane Wyman (wife of future president Ronald Reagan), Danny Kaye, Alan Ladd, Veronica Lake, and Victor Borge were among the show business people present at the White House on January 30. Eleanor graciously gave them a tour of the family quarters, including the President's private office, even opening up the desk drawer to reveal his memorabilia. Few entertainers could resist the double-barrelled charm of the President and Mrs. Roosevelt.

For his birthday, on the U.S.S. *Quincy*, Anna gave Roosevelt a package of gadgets from Lucy Rutherfurd and Margaret Suckley (a windproof cigarette lighter, a room thermometer, a comb, and so forth), and arranged for a series of five birthday cakes. Each cake represented a presidential election, and the fifth was a little cake with "1948?" on it in icing. The President received a cable from Eleanor on his birthday, but about Henry Wallace. Roosevelt had fulfilled his promise to Wallace, who, after he was dumped as vice president by the Democratic convention, was asked what job he would like. When Wallace expressed a desire to be secretary of commerce, Roosevelt removed Jesse Jones, whom he now considered cantankerous and somewhat reactionary, to open the place for Wallace. Roosevelt offered Jones an ambassadorship, but this did not appeal to him. (Jones said of Roosevelt, "[He is a] hypocrite . . . lacking in character, but you just can't help liking that fellow!" This wasn't ungenerous for someone who had just been fired, joining the long list of people dispensed with by a leader who supposedly had an aversion to dismissing people.[1])

Eleanor hectored her husband to get behind the Wallace commerce nomination, but there wasn't much he could do about it at this remove. It was, in fact, unthinkable that the President's nominee, and a former vice president of the United States at that, would not be confirmed, and he was, though not without difficulty and after a slight statutory reduction in the prerogatives of the Commerce Department.[2] These confirmation problems are a fair indication of Wallace's ineptitude at senatorial relations.

On the morning of February 1, on a bright, calm day, the *Quincy*, flying the presidential standard, glided into the Grand Harbour at Valetta, Malta. Anthony Eden had been awakened by his ship's band, busily practicing "The Star Spangled Banner." "At half past nine President Roosevelt's cruiser hove in sight," Eden wrote in his memoirs. "As the great warship sailed into the battered harbour every vessel was manned, every roof and vantage point crammed with spectators. While the bands played and amid so much that reeked of war, on the bridge, just discernible to the naked eye, sat one civilian figure. In his sensitive hands lay much of the world's fate. All heads were turned his way and a sudden quietness fell. It was one of those moments when all seems to stand still and one is conscious of a mark in history."[3]

Winston Churchill came aboard the *Quincy*. The two leaders had a very pleasant conversation. Churchill wrote back to his wife: "My friend has arrived in the best of health and spirits. Everything going well." They dined together that evening and the following evening, though little that was substantive was discussed, to Eden's consternation.[4] They transferred to their planes in the late evening of February 2. Twenty aircraft were required to take the Anglo-American party of 700 to the Crimea. They took off at ten-minute intervals for over three hours and flew through the night toward Yalta.

Roosevelt arrived at Saki, in the Crimea, on his personal aircraft, the *Sacred Cow*, shortly after noon, February 3, having picked up a fighter escort when approaching Greece and for the rest of the trip. They had carefully skirted Crete, still under German occupation and with a German air presence based on the island. Roosevelt's doctor would have preferred avoiding air travel, but the Dardanelles were judged unsafe, because the President's ship would have been in narrow waters and well within German air strike capacity.[5]

Sacred Cow, so named by the White House press corps, was the first of the presidential aircraft, with four engines, a fitted bedroom and bathroom, and an elevator for the President in his wheelchair.

Churchill thought the Crimea an absurd location for the conference: "We could not have found a worse place if we had spent ten years on research," he said.[6]

Churchill recorded that when "Roosevelt was carried down the lift from the 'Sacred Cow' he looked frail and ill."[7] Stalin had not yet arrived in the Crimea, and the arriving visitors to Russia were greeted by Molotov. Roosevelt, seated bareheaded in an open jeep in subfreezing weather, with Churchill and Molotov walking beside him, reviewed a goose-stepping Russian honor guard. There followed a six-hour drive to Yalta, where the climate was much more salubrious.

Beria's son Sergo was again, as at Teheran, entrusted with recording from bugging devices, and reporting personally to Stalin the contents of conversations between the Allied participants. Young Beria, reflecting the cynicism of his elders, purported to find Churchill's conduct on arrival in the Crimea "comical. . . . He went up to the guard of honor and looked each soldier in the eyes with a stupefied air, as though he had just landed among extraterrestrials." He and his young comrades insolently claimed to regard Churchill as a "poodle wagging his tail around Stalin." But, "When I saw Roosevelt, I was struck by the dignity of his entourage and by the care taken of their disabled President by his bodyguards. It was obvious that they loved him. One had only to observe the way they put him in his car, doing everything to conceal his infirmity. Even the [loutish] guards who accompanied me noticed this and refrained from making jokes about the American President."[8]

Roosevelt and the principal members of his party stayed at the Livadia Palace, the former winter resort of the last Czar, Nicholas II. Stalin and Molotov were in the nearby Yusupov Palace, and Churchill and his party were five miles away in the Vorontsov Villa, which had been designed by a British Victorian architect. The Germans had been chased out of the area only about eight months before, and the war damage, including looting, was severe. The only vestiges of the Czar's furnishings in the Livadia were two paintings in Roosevelt's bedroom. Romanian prisoners of war had replanted the garden in the last few weeks, and the interior of the palace was adequate except for the shortage of bathrooms. The senior delegation members didn't do badly, but there were sixteen colonels in one bedroom, and thirty-five officers to a bathroom. All of these had to shave from buckets by their cots.[9]

The ambiance at Livadia was not helped by the attempt of a Soviet intelligence officer to grope Anna Roosevelt. Her father described the wrongdoer as "a most sinister appearing pest," reminiscent of some "big businessmen" he had known.[10]

Stalin arrived at Yalta February 4, having come most of the way by train. The Soviet leader called on Churchill in a large black Lend-Lease Packard.[11] At least all the nonsense about avoiding the appearance of excessive Anglo-American solidarity was over and the three leaders interacted reasonably spontaneously, despite the British concern about insufficient bilateral meetings with the Americans. Stalin told Churchill that Hitler's Ardennes offensive had been "a stupid maneuvre . . . done for prestige." He thought the best German generals had quit or been fired, except for Guderian, "and he was an adventurer." Churchill showed Stalin his portable map room, and Stalin, reversing his advice at Teheran, suggested (according to Churchill's recollection) the removal of some divisions from Italy and their redeployment to Yugoslavia and toward Vienna.[12] At this stage this would have been such an absurd waste of manpower that Stalin's motives in suggesting it, as usual and as Brooke had mentioned at Teheran, were open to question.

Stalin then called on Roosevelt, accompanied by Molotov. Stettinius, who had not met him before, thought the "Marshal, with his powerful head and shoulders set on a stocky body, radiated an impression of great strength."[13] Roosevelt said there was betting on his ship on the way across the Atlantic over whether the Russians would capture Berlin before the Americans liberated Manila. Roosevelt knew this to be nonsense, because the fall of Manila was imminent. Seeing the German devastation of the Crimea, Roosevelt said, caused him to hope Stalin would again propose the execution of 50,000 German officers. The two leaders discussed de Gaulle. Stalin said that he had not found de Gaulle a "very complicated person." Roosevelt told the imperishable story that de Gaulle had told him he considered himself the spiritual successor to Joan of Arc and the secular successor to Clemenceau. He had rather overused this yarn.

Roosevelt said he had favored a French occupation zone only "out of kindness." In fact, Roosevelt was now persuaded by Churchill's argument that a revived France would be a useful bulwark against their glorious Russian ally.

Stalin gave completely different accounts to Churchill and Roosevelt of conditions on part of the Eastern Front. He told Churchill that the Red Army would soon be in Berlin, and told Roosevelt that the Oder line would be hard to cross. This may have contributed to the different British and American perspectives on Berlin. While the leaders were at Yalta, the Russians did cross the Oder and found little resistance initially beyond it. Stalin telephoned Zhukov from Yalta and ordered him not to advance, but to clear the "Baltic balcony" to his right first. This was a great missed opportunity, but may have reflected his remarks to Roosevelt about the difficulty of taking Berlin.[14]

Roosevelt's interpreter was again, as at Teheran, Charles Bohlen, assistant to the secretary of state and now head of the department's Russian desk. As the only chief of state in the group, Roosevelt was again the host at all plenary sessions, which were held in his residence, in the Czar's former ballroom, in deference to Roosevelt's physical convenience. Roosevelt was also the only one of the three leaders in civilian attire, as Churchill and Stalin affected military uniforms (an unprecedented costume in the modern history of British prime ministers). Toasts were regularly proposed to Roosevelt, King George VI, and Stalin's fig-leaf chief of state, President Mikhail Kalinin, who had held the honorific post with what Stalin considered commendable anonymity since 1922. In order to attract as little notice as possible to his condition, Roosevelt arrived early for most sessions and was seated at the table when the other delegations entered.

II

THE FIRST PLENARY SESSION opened shortly after five o'clock in the afternoon of February 4, 1945. The general procedure at the conference was that the Combined Chiefs of Staff (British and American) met in the mornings, under the joint chairmanship of Marshall and Brooke. There followed a meeting of the Combined Chiefs with the senior Soviet military staff, the first instance of such close cooperation between all three principal Allies. At lunchtime the foreign ministers met, and there were simultaneous meetings of the heads of government, with their military staffs or with each other. Plenary sessions began at 4 or 5 o'clock and proceeded to about 7:30 or 8. Dinner followed, the usual sumptuous, loquacious, well-lubricated Russian affairs, alternating with nights off for quiet dinners of delegations or bilateral groups.

Stettinius, Harriman, and Roosevelt agreed that there were eight major subjects to address: general postwar organization; an emergency European high commission to administer liberated and conquered territory ad interim; political and economic treatment of Germany; Poland; the Allied Control Commissions in Romania, Hungary, and Bulgaria; Iran; China, especially the desirability of ending the Chinese civil war between Chiang and Mao; and Soviet entry into and ambitions for the Pacific war.

At the first plenary meeting, Roosevelt gave an opening homily, and Soviet General Antonov presented a very detailed summary of the Eastern Front, which had now moved well into Germany and twenty-five kilometers into postwar Germany, as it had been redefined at Teheran. Marshall followed with a comprehensive summary of the Western Front. The Allies now had about eighty divisions on that front and were continuing to add two per week, and had thirty-two divisions in Italy and ten other divisions in the Mediterranean. (Roosevelt told Stimson: "Churchill is always a disperser."[15] Marshall estimated that Allied bombing, some of the most effective launched from Italian airfields, had eliminated 80 percent of German oil production and supplies, and much of its tank, aircraft, and artillery production facilities. There were about 13,000 Allied tanks and 13,000 aircraft in the west (including Italy) and equal numbers in the east, against fewer than 4,000 tanks and aircraft in the hands of the Germans on both fronts combined. Given the extent to which they were outnumbered and outgunned, not to mention the dubious moral premises for their war effort, the performance of the German armed forces continued to be remarkable, perhaps even more so as defeat impended than it had been in victory.

There were now only about thirty or thirty-five German submarines operating in the Atlantic, only about one-fifth of the former total, and the Western leaders thought these came from Kiel and Hamburg, Danzig having just been vacated by the German Navy. New German submarines, equipped with the snorkel apparatus, did not have to surface to recirculate air and recharge batteries, and were much less vulnerable than earlier types of submarines had been at the height of the Battle of the Atlantic. The Germans were also desperately trying to deploy more Messerschmitt 262 jet fighters and V-2 rockets. The 262s had been active for almost a year in small numbers and the V-2s since September 1944. Advanced weapons were Hitler's last hope.

There was an approximate equality of manpower between the Germans and the Allies in France and Italy, but the Russians had a superiority of nearly 100 divisions over the Germans on the Eastern Front, and more than 20 in Poland and pre-war Germany alone.[16]

At the end of the first meeting Stalin went directly to the lavatory and inadvertently eluded his two NKVD guards, whose perplexity verged on hysteria and inspired some mirth from Western observers by the time the Russian leader emerged from the palace men's room two minutes later.[17]

At the dinner following the first plenary session, all was conviviality. Stalin betrayed some concern that the proposed international organization gave equality to the great and small powers. He was prepared to do his part to keep the peace, but the Soviet Union had not fought through to this point, he said, in order to have parity in the counsels of the world with Albania. When Bohlen mentioned the importance of public opinion in the United States, Vyshinsky, Molotov's assistant foreign commissar and former prosecutor in Stalin's show trials in the thirties, said that the American people "should learn to obey their leaders." Bohlen said he would enjoy the spectacle of Vyshinsky telling them so, and the Russian said he would be glad to visit the United States bearing that message. Stettinius noticed that at important meetings such as this, Stalin drank half his glass of vodka and "when he thought no one was watching, surreptitiously poured water into the glass."[18] Among the toasts on this occasion was Churchill's to "the proletarian masses of the world."[19]

III

ON FEBRUARY 5, 1945, Manila was captured by the United States and reentered by MacArthur (who was disappointed to find that the well-known Japanese respect for him as an orientalist and a great commander had not deterred them from ransacking his suite in the Manila Hotel). At the foreign ministers' luncheon at Yalta on that day, a fulsome toast was proposed by Molotov to this latest Allied victory.

At this session, Stettinius dangled explicitly before Molotov the economic administration of Germany and extraction of reparations from that country, without any mention at this stage of a quid pro quo in Soviet accommodation of Western ambitions for the peace settlement.

The second plenary session of the Yalta Conference opened at 4 o'clock that afternoon and lasted four hours. The pre-agreed agenda was Germany, and Roosevelt in his introduction observed that the occupation zones had been determined by the European Advisory Commission ratified by Octagon at Quebec, on September 12, 1944. There remained the question of France, as an occupying power and a member of the control machinery that would be set up over Germany.

Stalin wanted to know if Roosevelt and Churchill still adhered to the principle of the dismemberment of Germany as had been suggested at Teheran by both of them. Roosevelt implied that the dismemberment might arise from the existence of the different occupation zones—i.e., each occupying power could operate its zone as virtually a colonial satrapy in Germany. At Teheran Roosevelt had suggested dividing Germany into five sections, and if France had an occupation zone, as Churchill, with Roosevelt's approval, proposed, there would be four such pieces of Germany, after its eastern areas had been severed and given to Poland and the Soviet Union, plus four Allied zones in Austria.

Churchill adhered to his doubly antiquarian notion of separating Prussia, as if it really were the unique source of German militarism, and reconstituting the western and southern German-speaking areas as a state based on Vienna, recreating notions of a central (Habsburg-style) European empire or confederation, a concept that both Roosevelt and Stalin disapproved of, though for different reasons. Roosevelt thought the idea impractical, Stalin thought it feasible but undesirable; he preferred a slew of vulnerable little states.

Churchill said the dismemberment of Germany would require a good deal more study. Stalin, not to be easily deflected, suggested acceptance of the principle of German dismemberment, a foreign ministers' commission to work out the details, and addition, though not publicly, to the unconditional surrender terms of a requirement that Germany be dismembered, with the details unspecified. Dismemberment in principle was accepted, but nothing but eventual further negotiation was envisioned as a sequel.

A lengthy discussion of a French zone followed. Churchill explained that he considered France essential to ensuring that Germany did not rise up yet again and assault those now closing in on it, and that if the United States were not to remain durably in Europe with large forces, Britain would need France to help her provide armies of occupation, enforcement, and deterrence in Germany. Churchill said that the French zone would come exclusively out of the British, and possibly the American, zone and that it need not affect the Russians at all.

Stalin objected to any sharing of the control function among four powers. He did not consider that France had made a serious contribution to winning the war, and was concerned about a precedent that would excite the appetites of the lesser countries on Germany's borders. Stalin said he respected France but that France now had only eight divisions in the war, compared with twelve for Yugoslavia and thirteen for the Lublin Poles (he didn't mention ten more for the London Poles).

He explained that de Gaulle had told him when he visited Moscow a couple of months before that he intended for France to occupy Germany up to a stretch of the Rhine (as Roosevelt had said in private correspondence that France had to do in 1936 when Hitler had remilitarized the Rhineland).[20]

It became obvious that Stalin was far more implacably opposed to any political progress for France even than Roosevelt was, much less Churchill, despite de Gaulle's posturings about "dear Russia." It was also clear that his chief interest in making any agreement at all with de Gaulle in December 1944 had been to pretend that doing so conferred the legitimacy of precedent on the Lublin Committee. This was piquant: that the august and theatrical figure of de Gaulle would be employed by Stalin opposite two leaders whose Job-like patience de Gaulle had sorely tried, to justify recognition of a Communist puppet regime in Poland, which de Gaulle himself had peremptorily dismissed as without any legitimacy.

De Gaulle was talented enough at making the lives of Roosevelt and Churchill difficult without being duped by Stalin and held up in support of the desertion of the non-Communist Poles. The anti-Communist Poles were precisely the cause that he sincerely believed and never ceased to proclaim he had been more tenacious in defending than Roosevelt and Churchill had been.

Even when he wrote his memoirs nearly ten years later, de Gaulle thought he had been striking a blow for Polish independence in Moscow in December 1944. In fact, he had been creating an argument for Stalin to claim, as he endlessly did during the Yalta Conference, that the Lublin Committee had more legitimacy than de Gaulle, because its leaders had remained in Poland in the underground during the German occupation, while Mikolajczyk and de Gaulle were, said Stalin, sitting in London in comparative luxury and safety. Stalin went so far as to compare the Lublin Poles, as agrarian reformers, with de Gaulle, who, he said, had done nothing "to arouse popular enthusiasm."

Despite de Gaulle's grandstanding as a truer champion of Eastern Europe against the Communists than Roosevelt and Churchill, he was in fact illustrating the failure of the frequent future French policy, other than in international crises, of equivocation between the Kremlin and the Anglo-Saxons. Churchill was an ally of France; Roosevelt was at least benevolently disposed. Stalin's duplicity in these matters, if not his wickedness, exceeded even de Gaulle's apprehensions.

Roosevelt said that he did not envision the United States maintaining sizeable forces in Europe for much more than two or three years, though he had already acknowledged to de Gaulle in Washington in July 1944 that U.S. forces would probably have to be maintained in Europe and in the Far East, at least partly to counterbalance Soviet forces in central Europe and trans-Siberian Russia. And in that period of continued American military presence in Europe, Roosevelt expected to retain a million American soldiers there. Roosevelt whetted Stalin's appetite, and his indication of early withdrawal of forces from Europe ranks with Churchill's profession at Teheran to be unable to supply more than sixteen divisions to Overlord as a preemptive expression of comparative weakness to a dangerous interlocutor. Roosevelt would have done better to tell Stalin he would maintain forces in Europe and de-emphasize this to de Gaulle, instead of the other way round.

Churchill said France had great experience dealing with Germany and was a historic naval power, and that Great Britain did not "want to bear the whole weight of an attack by Germany in the future."[21] In fact, of course, as he often said privately, he didn't want to be left alone in Europe with "the Bear." Roosevelt supported a zone of occupation for France, but not for any other country apart from the Big Three.

Churchill acknowledged that "France had not been much help in the war . . . [but] the destiny of great nations was not decided by the temporary state of their technical apparatus," a reference to France's 1940 deficiency in tanks and warplanes.[22] Churchill did not want to contemplate the appearance of a German army across the Channel again, he said, and needed the resuscitated French to ensure it did not happen. He implicitly demurred, with Roosevelt's evident concurrence, from Stalin's Carthaginian peace plans for Germany, and the implications of German survival as an important country could not have been lost on Stalin. The Morgenthau plan and the sort of thinking that had inspired it was not in evidence on the Western side, but treatment of Germany was already emerging as the great Anglo-American bargaining chip with Stalin in Europe. Churchill wanted France and a de-Nazified Germany rebuilt as a bulwark against Russia, convinced that Stalin would take all he could get in Europe. Roosevelt would adopt the Churchill position if Stalin behaved as Churchill expected, but would trade some level of pacification of Germany and economic assistance to the Soviet Union for good behavior in Eastern Europe.

During this session, Hopkins reminded Roosevelt that France was already (just) on the European Advisory Committee (as he called it), and urged him to agree to a French zone and defer the Control Commission question.

Hopkins had stopped in London and Paris on the way to Yalta at Roosevelt's request. De Gaulle was not particularly grateful to learn from Hopkins that France was going to receive an occupation zone, and he declined to subscribe to anything that might be agreed at Yalta without seeing it in advance. He did agree in principle to see Roosevelt on the President's way home from Yalta.

Roosevelt initially agreed with Churchill that France should have her zone but with Stalin that France should not be on the Allied Control Commission. Eden pointed out that there was no question of any other power having an occupation zone and that it would be impossible to have a French occupation zone but no French presence on the Control Commission. Eden added that it was also academic, since de Gaulle would not accept the one without the other, nor, he implied, should he. Stalin suggested referring this matter to the foreign ministers, and this was done. Stalin undoubtedly found Roosevelt a disappointment in these French matters. He was playing to Roosevelt's well-known aversion to de Gaulle, reviving the Teheran discussion about purging French public life as thoroughly as German.

The conference moved on to reparations. The former Soviet ambassador in London, Ivan Maisky, outlined his country's view of reparations. Stalin, not surprisingly, had an extreme hair shirt in mind for the Germans. The proposal was for two categories of what Stalin and his acolytes loosely called reparations. First, there would be, over two years, the systematic removal from Germany of physical assets—factories, machine tools, railway locomotives and rolling stock, and so forth—and second was a program of ten yearly payments in kind.

The Soviet intention was to take away 80 percent of German heavy industry, including steel, electrical power, and chemical industries. Industries of war production such as aviation and synthetic oil refining should be removed 100 percent. Maisky had his Morgenthau-like moments; he called for Anglo-American-Soviet representatives on the board of directors of every German company capable of war-useful activity for a prolonged period, and a system of division of reparations entitlement based on contribution to Allied victory and on the extent of German-originated war damage. By these criteria, though the calculation was never formally made, the Soviet Union would receive 80 percent or more of the benefit, and there would be a token for Britain and crumbs for everyone else among Hitler's long list of victims.

A smaller country like Poland, which had suffered horrible devastation and the deaths of millions (thanks in part, no one directly pointed out, to the Nazi-Soviet Pact) would get little, since that country, though it fought with magnificent heroism, was insufficiently powerful to make a great contribution to victory.

Maisky did express the expectation of ten billion dollars of the payments in kind for the Soviet Union. This invoice hung heavy in the air at Livadia Palace.

Churchill spoke of the failure of reparations after World War I and the absurd situation by which the United States lent Germany the money to pay the French and British and the entire economic system eventually collapsed, bringing Hitler to power and the descent to the present terrible war. He offered a few historical embellishments, dismissing the amount of reparations after Versailles as only two billion pounds, which was, at the time, in fact, ten billion dollars. And he spoke of Britain's having "taken some old Atlantic liners from the Germans, who had immediately proceeded on credit to build new and better ships."*

---

* In fact, the world's three largest and newest liners were seized (*Imperator, Vaterland,* and *Bismarck*) in 1919 and renamed *Berengaria* (replacing the torpedoed *Lusitania*), *Leviathan* (an outright gift to the Americans, who had never had a large liner before), and *Majestic*

Churchill said that the "fantastic" dreams of reparations in 1919 had proved to be a "myth." He was concerned that Germany would be so overburdened that the country could collapse, leaving the Allies with the choice of allowing millions of Germans to starve, or paying to save them from the reparations they themselves would then have imposed. Britain needed to export to pay for the food it had to import, and it could not export profitably to destitute countries. It was a good primer on basic capitalism for the world's leading avowed Marxist. Churchill concluded that if you "wanted the horse to pull the wagon you had to give it fodder sometimes." Stalin replied that you also had to be careful "the horse didn't kick you."

Roosevelt said that the United States had lost ten billion dollars in loans and assets consequent upon the loans to finance reparations and related transactions in and after the First World War. His country would seize all German property then in the United States and not return it as had happened in 1919, but he had no interest in the "capital, factories, or equipment" of Germany and "did not wish to have to contemplate the necessity of helping the Germans to keep from starving."[23] Roosevelt didn't want the German standard of living to exceed the Soviet, at least initially, and some transfer of resources was appropriate, but not on such a scale that Germany became "a burden to the world." Roosevelt saw no possibility that reparations would seriously alleviate the desolation of war. U.S. economic assistance was the second bargaining counter, after the organization of Germany, in the Western leaders' postwar relations with Stalin.

General William Donovan and his staff in the Office of Strategic Services had prepared some background material for a possible economic aid package for post-war Russia. Donovan's study estimated that the Soviet Union had lost one-quarter of its fixed capital in 1937 prices, or about $16 billion of value, as well as $4 billion of manufacturing inventory and personal property. An aid proposal of $6 billion for the Soviet Union was being prepared. Roosevelt wanted the Soviet Union to receive aid from the United States while Germany was rebuilt as a Western democratic state; he did not want Stalin putting Russia back on its economic feet by crushing the life and sucking the blood out of Germany.

The main strategic issues were now emerging. On the one side, Soviet treatment in practice of occupied countries where Stalin had pledged to establish free, independent, and democratic states with elections based on universal suffrage and secret ballot. On the other, Anglo-American treatment of and eco-

(replacing *Titanic*'s mined sister *Britannic*). *Berengaria* and *Majestic*, as Churchill and Roosevelt well knew, continued as the flagships of the British merchant marine for over fifteen years, long after the commissioning of the new German *Bremen* and *Europa*, and until the magnificent French *Normandie* compelled the British to build history's other 1,000-foot, 80,000-ton liners, *Queen Mary* and *Queen Elizabeth*. For most of the twentieth century these great liners were primary exhibits of national pride and prestige for the British, French, Germans, and Italians, and even the Dutch and the Canadians, which is the only reason they have been given attention here.

nomic aid to the majority of the former Germany, a country that still frightened even Stalin, despite his bold talk that the 250-year war between the Teutons and the Slavs had been won by the Slavs. The options for Germany ranged from partial pastoralization (Morgenthau) and severe economic punishment (though not as severe as Stalin wished), if Russia dealt equitably with Eastern Europe, to fast-track rebirth as a major industrial power integrated into the West, if Stalin enslaved Eastern Europe. (All the industrial heartland and almost 80 percent of the German people would be in Western hands.)

As has been mentioned, in shifting Poland so far to the west, Stalin was delivering much of his German zone to Poland (albeit a Poland he intended to dominate), and in the same measure that that increased his influence over Poland, much of which was an official Soviet occupation zone, it caused millions of Germans to flee further west and assured an ever greater portion of the German population for the Western occupied zones. The lot of the Poles was onerous, but it was a good strategic trade for the Western Allies, because Germany was delivered definitively into their hands, as Roosevelt had advocated since Trident nearly two years before (chapter 19). Poland was an uncooperative protectorate of the Russians and (West) Germany became a strong ally of the British and Americans.

Eventually, Roosevelt delicately asked what distinction Stalin made between the reparations policy and the occupation zones themselves, and Stalin replied that there was no such distinction. Though no one bothered to elaborate, it thus became clear that Stalin purported to expect the Americans, British, and French to strip their sections of Germany to the bone for the benefit of the Russians. Even Stalin must now have realized that Churchill, de Gaulle, and Roosevelt were not going to do anything of the kind, at least not without some practical modifications to his emerging occupation policy in Eastern Europe and some incentive from him to their own national interests.

Maisky fought his corner gamely, saying that Anglo-American lending practices had assisted the Germans to evade reparations after the First World War, and that payments in kind would avoid the problem of money transfers—i.e., the Russians would tear the crops from German granaries and the products from German assembly lines. The world's second greatest industrial power would become a pro bono supplement to the sluggish production levels of Stalin's command economy. Maisky claimed he was only seeking from Germany about 10 percent of the present U.S. budget and six months of current British war expenditures, and that German light industry and agriculture could function adequately. There was no thought of starving the Germans, but they had no right to a higher standard of living than central Europe. Maisky attempted the imposition of Communist leveling of economic benefit, irrespective of comparative efficacy and diligence between Germany and its neighbors.

Churchill moved for the traditional reference to a subcommittee, and this was agreed and the meeting adjourned.

IV

THE THIRD PLENARY SESSION began at 4 P.M., February 6. Roosevelt, in opening in support of the (recently concluded) Dumbarton Oaks agreements over what would become the United Nations organization, espoused the same goal Churchill had enunciated to Stalin when he visited Moscow in October 1944, to maintain the peace for at least fifty years. This was a surprisingly unambitious goal, given that the peace had lasted for twenty-one years between the world wars, despite the ineffectuality of the West and the militarism of the dictators. Stalin took up the same objective, and fifty years of peace became a conference shibboleth.

Stettinius outlined the Dumbarton Oaks agreements, emphasizing the absolute requirement of unanimity between the Great Powers in general, and in key areas in the new organization, including admission and expulsion of members, election of the secretary general, and enforcement of the peace. Stalin was concerned about the ability of other countries to complain about the conduct of the Great Powers and force a vote in which those powers would be excluded. Churchill reassured him and gave illustrative examples involving China's complaining about Hong Kong and Egypt's about the Suez Canal, none of which would be accepted.

Stalin finally volunteered that the manner in which Britain and France had caused the Soviet Union to be expelled from the League of Nations in December 1939 still annoyed him and that he didn't want any possibility of a repetition. Churchill replied that at the time, during the Soviet war with Finland, "the British and French Governments were very, very angry at the Soviet Union," and that no such thing could occur under the proposed arrangements. He observed the conference practice of not referring to the Nazi-Soviet Pact or to Stalin's aggression against Finland.

The subject moved to the vexed question of Poland. Roosevelt introduced the subject with qualified approval of the westward move of Poland to between the Curzon Line, which cut near the center of pre-1939 Poland, and the Oder-Neisse Line, currently well inside Germany. (There were eastern and western Neisse Rivers and between them lived several million Germans. The Russians invariably claimed the western Neisse and the British and Americans, strongly led in this by Churchill, only offered the eastern Neisse line.) Roosevelt asked for some Soviet concession to Poland, particularly Lvov and the oil production around it.

As a governing mechanism for Poland, until free elections could be held, Roosevelt suggested a Presidential Council, on which the five recognized non-Fascist and anti-Nazi parties would be represented. This would bring the Lublin and London Poles in under the same umbrella. He emphasized that Poland must be encouraged to have the most cooperative relations with the Soviet Union. Roosevelt said he had a very high opinion of Mikolajczyk, who was currently out of the government in exile. In the usual disputatious way of the Poles, he had been judged by his colleagues to be too accommodating of the Soviet Union, which now occupied almost all of Poland and was, to say the least, difficult not to accommodate.

Churchill spoke in the same manner. He was prepared to support the Curzon Line even without any concession to the Poles such as Lvov, though such a gesture "by the mighty Soviet Union . . . this act of magnanimity would be acclaimed and admired." He too had a high opinion of Mikolajczyk, and although his country had no direct interest in Poland, it was for Poland that Britain, France, and the Dominions had gone to war, and it was a matter of honor that Poland should have a democratic choice of government and end the war "mistress in her own house and captain of her own soul." Stalin requested a ten-minute intermission.

When the conference reconvened, Stalin delivered his well-rehearsed speech on Poland. He recognized Churchill's point of honor and shared the desire that Poland be strong and free, and he wished to make amends for Russia's having historically "committed many sins against the Poles."[24] But for his country, Poland was a corridor for invasion and had been used as such for centuries. This, he said, was "a matter of life and death." He was having nothing of the Churchillian theory of magnanimity. He pointed out that Curzon and Clemenceau had drawn up the so-called Curzon Line, which Lenin had not wanted to accept as insufficiently generous to Russia. Was he to return to Moscow conceding that Curzon and Clemenceau were better defenders of the Russian interest than he, Stalin, was?

He purported to make a great sacrifice by being prepared to shed his army's blood to advance the Polish border farther into Germany, as if he were fighting for the Poles rather than to seize as much German territory for himself as possible. No one mentioned, though all were perfectly aware, that since the European Advisory Commission's delineation of occupation zones in Germany was agreed in the spring of 1944 and ratified by the British and Americans in September 1944, more than a third of the reconstituted Poland, the territory between the pre-war western border of Poland and either definition of the Oder-Neisse Line, was a Russian occupation zone ostensibly of Germany. It was as if all three leaders were conducting an elaborate charade that each, and particularly Stalin, would only do what the others accepted.

Stalin wryly commented that he was frequently called a dictator but was enough of a democrat to wish to have Polish participation in the composition of a Polish government. He implied that his opinion of Mikolajczyk had gone up since he was deposed by the other London Poles, but he accused the London Polish government of opposing any agreement with any other elements and of being violently anti-Russian. Stalin claimed that they had been responsible for the murder of 212 liberating Russian soldiers and were conducting guerrilla operations against the Russians who had delivered them from the Germans. He declared that it was intolerable to have hostile activity in his rear in Poland, and defended the Lublin government as popular, patriotic, and respected. (The Russians had initiated the actions, rooting out armed, non-Communist Poles and killing them, as Churchill and Roosevelt had been advised by the London Poles.)

It may have been a reflection of his own pride as an old Bolshevik who had remained in Russia until the Revolution of 1917 while Lenin, Trotsky, and others were in exile, but Stalin set great store by the fact that the Lublin Poles had remained in Poland throughout the German occupation, in underground activities. He acknowledged that they were not particularly intelligent, but held them out as exemplary in other ways (by which he meant, but did not say, slavishly subservient to him).

He concluded with his carefully developed—as he thought it to be, clinching—trump card, that the Warsaw Poles had as much legitimacy as de Gaulle, whom he had recognized. Churchill and Roosevelt consistently ignored the comparisons with de Gaulle as absurd.

The distinguished historian Anthony Beevor holds that Stalin was trying to promote a comparison between Polish harassment of Red Army supply lines and the French Communists not harassing the Western Allies. This is implausible, because a Communist attack on Eisenhower's rear area would have completely doomed the French Communists and broken up the alliance. Beevor thinks Stalin was implying that he wanted to extend to Poland and France the spheres-of-influence agreement he had made with Churchill in Moscow the previous October, but he acknowledges that neither Churchill nor Roosevelt "decoded" any such message.[25]

Churchill drew nearer to the crux of the problem when he squarely told Stalin that he did not believe that the Lublin Poles (the Western leaders pointedly declined to call them the Warsaw Poles) represented more than a third of the Polish population (i.e., the Communists in that very Catholic country), and did not believe that it was the policy of those directed by the London Poles to harass the Red Army. Wrongdoers should be punished, but the destiny of Poland, the prime minister forcefully stated, could not be determined on the basis of unrepresentative incidents. The conference adjourned until the following day.

V

THE FOREIGN MINISTERS, Eden, Molotov, and Stettinius, were now having large numbers of complex issues dumped in their laps at the end of each plenary session, so for the balance of the meetings at Yalta their proceedings assumed more importance than usual for foreign ministers. At their session at the Yusupov Palace (the Russian residence), beginning at noon on February 7, Vyshinski, Cadogan, and Freeman Matthews, U.S. undersecretary of state for Europe, were delegated to redraft the document of surrender by Germany to include an unspecific reference to the dismemberment of Germany. This was accepted by the chiefs of government later in the day.

The foreign ministers wrestled with the status of France; it was agreed that

France could have an occupation zone, but the question of a place on the Control Commission was passed back to the chiefs of government. Maisky provided a substantiation of his reparations claims that consisted of the usual nonsensical Marxist concept of deductions of asset value in a zero-sum game. German national wealth before the war was calculated at $125 billion; 40 percent had been destroyed by the war, and about 30 percent of what was left was judged to be mobile. The Soviet Union was proposing to remove "only" slightly less than half of that. The Reparations Commission was to be set up at once and sit in Moscow.

The fourth plenary session opened at four o'clock in the afternoon. It was devoted to trying to make progress on issues that had already been under discussion. Churchill stated emphatically that France should have an occupation zone and a place on the Control Commission. This was again deferred. No one at the conference told Stalin, though his sources in Paris may have, that Hopkins had already promised de Gaulle an occupation zone. Again, as the French zone would be carved exclusively from Western territory, there was an air of unreality in the discussions. Stalin could prevent the Western Allies from doing what they proposed with the French only by breaking up the Control Commission, since de Gaulle would not, as Eden had pointed out, accept responsibility for a zone in Germany without a place on the Commission.

The conference circled round to Poland. Roosevelt had sent Stalin a letter suggesting that two representatives of the Lublin Committee and two other representatives of other Polish factions should be invited to the conference at once and asked to settle the terms of an interim government. Roosevelt had suggested two professors and the bishop of Cracow and another distinguished Pole as possible non-Lublin candidates for the Provisional Government. Stalin said that he had tried to reach the Lublin Poles by telephone but that they were not available in Cracow. He doubted if any credible delegation of Poles could be produced to the present conference quickly enough, but said that Molotov had worked up a counterproposal to the President's letter and that this was now being typed.

The subject moved to the international organization. The Roosevelt-Churchill proposals of the previous day, including Churchill's reassurances about Hong Kong and Egypt, were accepted. Stalin raised again the desire for the constituent Soviet republics to have votes in the general assembly. He acknowledged that it would be unworkable for all sixteen of the so-called republics to be represented, so he had scaled his request back to a total of three votes.

Roosevelt was grateful for the acceptance of his general proposals and non-committal about the multi-vote suggestion for the Soviet Union. He subjected the conference to a rambling disquisition on the comparative size and population of states, including Brazil, Canada, Haiti, Cuba, and others, all facts well known to his interlocutors and of questionable relevance. Though coherent, this was one of the few signs that were ever observable at Yalta that Roosevelt's intellectual acuity had begun to fluctuate. He declined to consider the obvious but unspoken fact that most of the Latin American countries would vote as the United States wished, at least as faithfully as the Commonwealth countries would follow Britain.

Churchill gave his "heartfelt thanks" for the Soviet response, and was more positive about the several Soviet votes than Roosevelt had been because he effectively accepted some technical equivalence between the Soviet republics and the Dominions. He had what proved to be a rather outworn notion of the fealty of the Dominions. Roosevelt, who knew Canada well from his thirty-five summers at Campobello, knew better but remained silent. Churchill took the occasion to say what a magnificent contribution the Dominions had made in the war, having entered the conflict alongside Britain, although they knew "full well the weakness" of Britain and "knew they could not often be consulted on major matters." He could not agree to any diminution of their status and understood the Soviet desire for a greater voice. His heart went "out to mighty Russia, which, though bleeding, is beating down the tyrants in her path." He went so far as to ask Roosevelt not to reject the Soviet request.

There was inconclusive discussion about an organizing conference for the international structure that was under discussion, and Iran was referred to the foreign ministers for a durable arrangement to succeed the present joint occupation, and distribution of oil rights.

By now, Molotov's proposals for Poland were ready. He proposed the Curzon Line in the east, with divergences of from five to eight kilometers in Poland's favor, the westernmost definition of the Oder-Neisse Line in the west, the addition to the Polish Provisional Government of some "democratic émigré" individuals, the recognition of this government by all the Allies, and the earliest possible elections. Molotov, Harriman, and Clark Kerr were to be designated as a committee to recommend enlargement of the Provisional Government.

Roosevelt responded positively but objected to the word "émigré" as pejorative. Churchill was also upbeat, disliked the word "émigré" as inappropriate, and cautioned against moving Poland so far west that "the Polish goose [be] so full of German food that it gets indigestion." There appeared to be eight million Germans in the areas being awarded to the Poles, but Stalin claimed most of them had already fled westward to get away from the Red Army (with good reason, it must be said). It was agreed that progress was being made and the meeting adjourned.

VI

At the foreign ministers' meeting at midday February 8, at the British villa, Eden declared the British in favor of Molotov's request for three votes for the Soviet Union in the general assembly of the world organization. Like his leader, Eden hoped that Britain would maintain influence over the Dominions and could not conscientiously object to three Russian votes. (In fact, India was more of a concern to the Americans and Russians as a captive British vote, but like a number of other sensibilities of the conferring powers, this subject was never directly raised at any level of the conference.) Molotov wanted time to consider Iranian matters, since the questions of oil concessions in particular were too complex for swift resolution.

Roosevelt and Stalin met just before the day's plenary session. Roosevelt said that with the fall of Manila, the United States was closing in on Japan and would want to use air bases in Siberia and extreme eastern Russia to prepare for its final assault. Stalin had no objection to this. Stalin said he hoped the United States would, as Stettinius had indicated to Molotov, make some merchant shipping available to the Soviet Union after the war. Roosevelt replied that he would be happy to do so and thought that the British would also, and added that he hoped "the Soviet Union would interest itself in a large way in the shipping game."

Roosevelt encouraged anything that would reduce Russian isolationism and paranoia, and a new merchant fleet became another card in his hand to encourage reasonable Soviet behavior. Stalin took this occasion to tell Roosevelt how brilliant a scheme he had considered Lend-Lease to be as a flexible form of assistance that did not embarrass the recipient, and one that had greatly shortened the war. Roosevelt did not disagree, and told Stalin how the idea had come to him on a recreational cruise on one of his warships.

Stalin was probably sincere (and it was an inspired idea), but he had taken the trouble to stimulate Roosevelt's vanity, a gambit against which the President was usually fairly vigilant (as he always had been with Churchill). Stettinius recollected that Stalin went out of his way to agree with Roosevelt. Contrary to the general mythology, Stalin recognized the correlation of forces and was much more apparently accommodating of Roosevelt than Roosevelt was of him.[26]

With this preamble, Stalin stated his price for coming in against the Japanese. He wanted back everything that had been lost to the Japanese in the war of 1904–1905 — specifically southern Sakhalin, the Kurile Islands (which had in fact been ceded by peaceful agreement in 1875), control of the port of Dairen in Manchuria, and control of the Manchurian railways. Roosevelt balked at these last points and said that it would have to be joint control with China, or the Chinese would rightly see the arrangement as a return of colonialism.

He was determined to achieve recognition of China as a Great Power, even if Chiang didn't ultimately make the cut as China's leader. And he could not do this by writing off chunks of China to one of its former neocolonial masters. Dairen would be internationalized, but Port Arthur, as a Soviet naval base, would have to be a long-term Soviet lease. With these modifications, which were worked out between Molotov and Harriman, but with Roosevelt proving completely inflexible on his basic points, the leaders reached agreement.

Indeed it was not an excessive consideration for Stalin to exact for the assistance the Soviet Union could bring to the defeat of Japan. This prospect greatly relieved the U.S. Joint Chiefs of Staff, who rightly had visions of casualties in Japan vastly exceeding those on the Western Front in Europe, unless there was confirmation that the atomic bomb was militarily useable. Many have lamented that any consideration had to be paid to bring the Russians into that war, given that the atomic bomb made Russian presence unnecessary. The atomic bomb was not successfully tested until ten weeks after the end of the war in Europe (July 17, 1945). And the United States would take 80,000 casualties capturing the small islands of Iwo Jima and Okinawa alone.

What Russia received for its efforts in the Far East was not particularly significant, and if there had been no atomic development, nor any agreement with Stalin to enter the Pacific war, he would have taken the Kuriles, southern Sakhalin, and the Manchurian railways with access to Port Arthur and Dairen anyway, without assisting in the defeat of Japan. The criticism of Roosevelt on this issue is completely spurious; he did a better job, by refusing neocolonial arrangements that Stalin had requested, of defending China's interest than that country could have done for itself.

One of the reasons Roosevelt didn't take an even stronger line with Stalin at Yalta, as Stettinius recalled, was that Roosevelt's military chiefs put the President "under immense pressure . . . to bring Russia into the Far Eastern war. At this time the atomic bomb was still an unknown quantity, and our setback in the Battle of the Bulge was fresh in the minds of all. We had not as yet crossed the Rhine. No one knew how long the European War would last nor how great the casualties would be."[27]

Roosevelt would inform Chiang Kai-shek of these arrangements with Stalin in due course, but did not want to do so yet, because of the notorious indiscretion of the Chinese government. When Roosevelt said that he had been trying to keep China alive, Stalin responded that China would live but that it needed new leaders. Roosevelt said the United States was trying to promote cooperation between the Communists and the Kuomintang and were finding Mao Tse-tung easier to deal with than Chiang.

Stalin showed no preference for Mao Tse-tung over Chiang Kai-shek, because he wanted a vulnerable, even a prostrate China over which to assert Soviet claims. He and Roosevelt both knew that Mao would be a good deal more forceful a Chinese nationalist than Chiang. Geopolitical realism easily prevailed over ideology in Stalin's case and idealism in Roosevelt's.

Given his statement to Stalin at Teheran that Indian independence might require modernization of that society with some possible recourse to Russian methods, it is not unlikely that Roosevelt would have been prepared to entertain an accommodation of Mao Tse-tung, if his Communism could have been mitigated. But Roosevelt could not ditch Chiang while they were all at war with the Japanese. The perceptive Bohlen thought that the remarks about possible utilization of some Communist techniques in India indicated Roosevelt's rather sanguine view of the nature of Communism. Since his comments on Stalin's regime were consistent and well-known and were never positive, it is just as likely that they indicate a desire to be placatory in a broader interest, and leave Stalin with the impression that Roosevelt had a good deal more respect for Communism than he really did. It is unlikely that Roosevelt would have gone very far into the brave new postwar world towing the dead weight of Chiang Kai-shek behind him (chapter 23).

As the diplomatic and presidential historian Robert Dallek remarked: "Since Stalin apparently feared a [renewed] Chinese civil war as likely to destroy the Communists and put the Nationalists in a position to resist Soviet claims in Manchuria and Outer Mongolia or give the Communists a victory that could also produce a challenge to Soviet border claims and to Soviet leadership of Communist movements around the world, [Stalin] was entirely ready to agree" to support a coalition regime. Roosevelt was interested in building up China as a counterweight to Russia in Asia and a reorganized and thoroughly chastised Germany as a counterweight to Russia in Western Europe.[28]

Roosevelt also promoted his idea of trusteeships in place of colonial regimes. He thought this the best solution for Korea, and suggested in private conversations with Stalin on February 8 that the trusteeship powers be the Soviet Union, the United States, and China. He acknowledged that it was a delicate matter not putting the British on such a panel, but the British were not active in that area. Stalin agreed that it was awkward and joked that Churchill might "kill us." He agreed that Britain was not a strong guarantor in that region.

Roosevelt had a trusteeship in mind for Indochina also. De Gaulle had asked for shipping to send a force of French reoccupation there, but Roosevelt had so far professed to be unable to spare the shipping. He said that the American experience in the Philippines had been that fifty years was required to prepare such a country for independence. Stalin said that Britain had lost Burma through reliance on Indochina and that he considered Indochina a very important area.

This was a more prescient remark than Roosevelt's WASPY condescension that the Indochinese, like the Burmese and Javanese, were diminutive and unwarlike. In the whole history of these conferences and in the light of events twenty years later, this was the most fatuous comment Roosevelt uttered.

Replacing French colonial governance with a fifty-year American-sponsored trusteeship was not necessarily a dizzying leap forward for the independence party in Indochina. Stalin confined himself to the well-founded hope that the Indochina trusteeship would endure a good deal less than fifty years.

———————

Roosevelt and Stalin terminated their meeting to reconvene in the fifth plenary session in the afternoon. The foreign ministers had agreed to hold the United Nations Conference on the proposed world organization on April 25, 1945, in the United States. Stalin pointed out that ten of the proposed invitees were countries that did not have diplomatic relations with the Soviet Union. He would find it strange to try to build future world security with countries that did not wish to have any relations with the Soviet Union. Roosevelt said that most of them would like to exchange embassies with Moscow, though a couple were so heavily influenced by the Roman Catholic Church's official position that this was inhibiting; in any case, he said, the "Soviet Union had sat down with these states at the Bretton Woods [international financial] and UNRRA conferences."

Stalin was opposed to admitting as founders countries that had not declared war on the Nazis, or had done so for exclusively opportunistic reasons and had made no real contribution to the war. Roosevelt said that they really had to accept those who had declared war, whether they had made a serious contribution or not. He suggested March 1, 1945, just three weeks hence, as the cut-off date for a declaration of war on Germany (he couldn't stipulate war against Japan as well, since the Soviet Union would not meet that criterion).

This was agreed, and Churchill added that it would be demoralizing to the Germans to face a sudden avalanche of declarations of war, albeit from remote and militarily insignificant states. The acceptability of various individual countries was discussed. Egypt and Turkey were acceptable, Ireland was not, and Denmark would have to await liberation. It had been overrun so precipitately, in one night, that the only government in exile was a consular minister in Washington.

The subject moved back to Poland. All three powers had now submitted different papers to the conference on this subject. Churchill and Roosevelt confirmed to Stalin that recognition by their governments of a new Polish government would result in the transfer to that government of all the assets of the London Poles. Roosevelt had suggested a provisional government led by two of the Lublin Poles and two others; Molotov replied that three of the Lublin committee and two others might be appropriate. The world's most powerful statesmen were now down to very simple arithmetic.

Churchill attempted to reinforce Roosevelt by giving yet another soliloquy, no less eloquent than the many that had preceded it, on Poland's contribution to the war. Churchill restated Britain's refusal to desert the government it had given refuge to when Poland was overrun in 1939, stubborn and foolish though that government often was.

Churchill thought it "frightfully important" that agreement should be reached and signed on the Polish question. Stalin, understandably, was not so concerned about agreement. He claimed the ancient animosity between Poles and Russians had been replaced by the goodwill due to a liberator. And he trotted out, yet again, his canard about de Gaulle and his failure to "arouse popular enthusiasm" among the French, unlike Lublin, which had instituted land reform—specifically, the confiscation of the estates of the upper and middle classes and anyone whom it pleased the regime to consider as "émigrés." (Churchill and Roosevelt did not ask Stalin what he thought motivated the millions of cheering Parisians who greeted de Gaulle at the Liberation, August 26, 1944, or how Stalin had furthered the liberation of Poland by facilitating the suppression of the Warsaw uprising.)

In response to a question from Roosevelt, Stalin estimated that elections in

Poland could be held within a month. There was some skepticism about this among the British and Americans, but it at least demonstrated a sensitivity on Stalin's part to the time scale for any internationally recognized Lublin-dominated regime. The issue was now ostensibly a narrow one and was again sent back to the foreign ministers.

Stalin inquired what was holding up the proclamation of a unified government in Yugoslavia and wanted to know what was happening in Greece. Churchill responded that Britain favored two small amendments to the agreement that had been worked out for a regency in Yugoslavia, between Subasic (the British-sponsored regent) and Tito. This was part of what the Americans rightly saw as Churchill's chimerical pursuit of a constitutional monarchic regency with a Communist head of government (Tito) who would soon possess all military authority in the kingdom. The Russians knew as well as the Americans how little was the prospect of success for such an arrangement. Churchill said that "If Marshal Stalin said two words to Tito, the matter would be settled." Stalin commented that "Tito is a proud man . . . and might resent advice." (Stalin would find out how proud in three years, when Tito sent the Russians packing.) Churchill replied that he thought "Marshal Stalin could risk this." Stalin assured Churchill that he was "not afraid" of Tito, and the fifth plenary session adjourned.

Roosevelt circulated a response to Molotov's 3-2 Polish formula suggesting a new committee of six: two from Lublin; Mikolajczyk and another Londoner; and the bishop of Cracow (Msgr. Sapieha) and the well-regarded non-Communist and anti-Fascist, Vicente Witos.

That evening, a very festive dinner took place, which all the principal figures attended except for King and Marshall. Anna Roosevelt Boettiger, Sarah Churchill (Oliver), and Averell Harriman's daughter Kathleen (who had had a torrid affair with FDR Jr., as Anna was told by Harry Hopkins and jubilantly told her father),[29] were the women present. Edward J. Flynn, former Democratic Party chairman, who had been brought to the conference by Roosevelt to try to improve relations between the Kremlin and the Vatican and was going on to Rome for a papal audience, attended the dinner. So did Stalin's much-feared police minister, Lavrenti Beria. Roosevelt asked Stalin who he was and was somewhat taken aback when Stalin said of Beria: "That's my Himmler."

There is some dispute about whether Stalin ever moved off his preoccupation with ruling an ever greater tyranny. There is limited evidence that he was slightly affected by the tremendous impulse to comradeship at this decisive moment. Those who believe they saw a glimmer of humanity in Stalin's behavior point to this dinner.

There were forty-five toasts, and Stalin was in "high spirits," according to Bohlen. He proposed a toast to Prime Minister Churchill, whom he described as "the bravest governmental figure in the world. Due in large measure to Mr.

Churchill's courage and staunchness, England, when she stood alone, divided the might of Hitlerite Germany at a time when the rest of Europe was falling flat on its face before Hitler. Great Britain, under Mr. Churchill's leadership, carried on the fight alone irrespective of existing or potential allies. I know of few examples in history where the courage of one man has been so important to the future history of the world. I drink to Prime Minister Winston Churchill, my fighting friend and a brave man."

Churchill replied with his toast to Stalin: "The mighty leader of a mighty nation, which took the full shock of the German war machine, broke its back and drove the tyrants from her soil. I know that in peace no less than in war, Marshal Stalin will continue to lead his people from success to success."

Stalin then proposed the health of the President of the United States. He said that he and Churchill had had relatively simple decisions, because Hitler's aggressions obliged them to fight for their very existence. However, the leader of the United States "was not seriously threatened with invasion, but he had a broader conception of his national interest and even though his country was not directly imperiled, he has been the chief forger of the implements that have led to the mobilization of the world against Hitler." He made particular reference to Lend-Lease and implied that Roosevelt had initiated hostilities with Hitler.

Roosevelt replied that the atmosphere that evening was like that in a "family gathering . . . and that though each of the national leaders present is pursuing the interests of his people in a different way, we are all dedicated to providing all the people of the world a glimpse of opportunity and hope." Much remained to be done, but the proportion of the world's people who had no prospect of opportunity and no hope for anything beyond brief subsistence was steadily declining. Their objective was and must always remain "the possibility of security and well-being for every person in the world."

Roosevelt hoped that Stalin was warming to the role of being one of the world's most powerful men, fully accepted in the world's highest political councils, an astonishing change from his pre-war role as pariah and dreaded revolutionary. This had been somewhat the role he had played all his life—misfit, nihilist, and shadowy outsider, as a failed seminarian and amid more flamboyant and intellectually modish figures in Lenin's entourage, an underestimated ogre who ultimately frightened even Lenin and murdered Trotsky and most of the other old comrades.

"It was as if, for a moment, Stalin really did look upon the other two as allies, fellow members of the Big Three, as if that inferiority complex which is the source of Russian chauvinism and insecurity had lifted for a moment and he realized that his country truly was a superpower, with a rightful place at the top table, and as if, briefly, that new realization mellowed him and made him adopt something close to the language of a statesman."[30] This was Roosevelt's primary hope, that Stalin would succumb to the temptations of being a figure of stability and gradually a reliable associate in the governance of the whole world. He had inducements, as well as the fact of American strength to fall back on, if Stalin proved incorrigible. The ambiance was further improved when Roosevelt generously had the body and family of the recently deceased Soviet ambassador to Mexico, Konstantin Oumansky, flown back to the U.S.S.R. on an American aircraft.[31]

Roosevelt must have hoped that the positive option had a possibility of success when Stalin rose at this dinner and said, with apparent emotion: "I am talking as an old man, that is why I am talking so much, but I want to drink to our alliance, that it should not lose its character of intimacy, its free expression of views. In the history of diplomacy I know of no such close alliance of three great powers as this. . . . I propose a toast to the firmness of our three power alliance. May it be strong and stable, may we be as frank as possible." Winston Churchill rose to state that that was his hope also.[32]

VII

S HORTLY AFTER THE OPENING of the sixth plenary session, February 9, an absurd leitmotif was introduced into the proceedings when Churchill "interrupted with great vigor" Stettinius's discussion of trusteeships, saying that "he did not agree with one single word of this report. . . . Under no circumstances would he ever consent to forty or fifty nations thrusting interfering fingers into the life's existence of the British Empire. As long as he was Minister, he would never yield one scrap of their heritage. He continued in this vein for some minutes," although Roosevelt asked him to allow Stettinius to finish his explanation. Stalin, highly amused at this disarray among his visitors, "got up from his chair, walked up and down, beamed, and at intervals, broke into applause."[33] Churchill asked how Stalin would feel if the Crimea were declared to be internationalized as a summer resort. The parallel was preposterous but Stalin jovially volunteered to give the Crimea as a permanent meeting place between the three Great Powers.

Eventually, with Roosevelt gently calling Churchill to order, Stettinius was able to explain "that this reference to the creation of machinery [of trusteeships] was not intended to refer to the British Empire." It had to do with "dependent areas taken from the enemy," especially Japan and Vichy. Churchill's acute sensitivity was rather revealing.

The conference discussed Yugoslavia. The proposed British amendments were accepted. Any former officials who had not collaborated with the Germans were to be included as members of the anti-Fascist Yugoslav Vetch (Communist committee of local government). All their legislative initiatives were asked to be confirmed. Stalin agreed, "and as a man of my word, I will not go back on it." He did not waste the conference's time with further references to Tito's national or ethnic pride.[34] An adjournment of half an hour followed to permit consideration of the latest versions of the Polish formulations.

Roosevelt reopened discussion and proposed the reference to the Warsaw regime be changed from "Provisional Government" to "the Government now operating in Poland." He emphasized that the people of the United States, and especially the six million of them of Polish ancestry, attached great importance to the assurance of democratic processes to determine the government of Poland.

Churchill agreed with Roosevelt, but went further and asked Stalin's assistance in mitigating the excesses of Polish internecine hatreds, which, he understood, now extended to a promise by the Lublin Poles to try to punish those who had risen against the Nazis in Warsaw in the autumn of 1944. Churchill asked, without a trace of irony, that these points be considered "with Marshal Stalin's usual patience and kindness." Churchill, of all people, given his well-known concerns about the Soviets, could have been in no doubt of the outcome of any adjudication by that arbiter and by those criteria.

Churchill then asked the acceptance of uniform standards for the much bandied-about definition of free elections. He asked for international observers in Poland, which he promised would be welcome in Greece and, he was sure the Americans would agree (as they did), in Italy.

Stalin attempted to muddy the waters with comparisons with Egypt, where the king, the egregious dissolute Farouk, had clumsily manipulated elections. Stalin tried to establish a relationship between the level of literacy and the credibility of elections, and spuriously implied that his point was made by the inability of Churchill and Eden to give precise answers to his questions about literacy levels in Egypt.

Churchill wanted to be able to assure his parliament in good conscience that the Polish elections, when they came, would amount to something as an expression of popular will. Stalin was like a Cheshire cat fondling the canary between his paws, but masquerading to the other felines that he was motivated by notions of animal rights, not hunger, much less sadism or gluttony. He praised the Poles for once, for all their quarrelsomeness, as the people who had produced Copernicus, an example of free thinking he professed to admire.

Stalin now claimed to support the American-drafted Declaration on Liberated Europe, but asked that in the case of liberated countries everywhere, preeminence be given to those who had "taken an active part in the struggle against the German invaders." This had the effect he had desired of smoking out Churchill again. Behind the pristine American shield of universal self-determination, Churchill was concerned that these reflections should not apply to the British Empire, many parts of which were not fully independent but had made an admirable contribution to victory. Stalin, when trapped in evasions or untruths, routinely tweaked Churchill by mischievously implying that the British Empire was scarcely distinguishable from the conquests of the Axis, in that its inhabitants too sought independence and had earned it. His point having been made, Stalin happily gave Churchill the sought-for assurance, since he had no more interest in Gambia and British Guyana than Roosevelt did.

Churchill said he had given Wendell Willkie a copy of his statement on the subject of the compliance of the British Empire to the democratic rules of the Atlantic Charter. Roosevelt interjected, to considerable amusement, to ask if this had caused Willkie's premature death.

Stalin volunteered that he had "complete confidence in British policy in Greece," but conspicuously failed to take up Churchill's suggestion of election observers for Greece and Poland—not a happy portent for the incipient "free, independent, and democratic" Poland.

Churchill had been insistent on continuing until agreement had been reached on all points, and was startled when Roosevelt announced that he had to leave Yalta on February 11 to make scheduled appointments with the kings of Egypt and Saudi Arabia and the emperor of Ethiopia. This set off alarm bells in the British camp, as if the President of the United States had no right to meet these people without a British chaperone.

Obviously, these three potentates were insignificant compared with Churchill and Stalin, but Roosevelt thought that the major points had been resolved as much as they could be.

After an inconclusive discussion about war criminals, the conference adjourned to what was scheduled to be its final session. The foreign ministers met with great assiduity, starting at 10:30 P.M., February 9, and reconvened in the morning, noon, afternoon, and evening of the following day to clean up their masters' leavings.

VIII

THE SEVENTH PLENARY SESSION of the Yalta Conference opened at 4 P.M. on February 10. Roosevelt announced that he had changed his mind about France and that that country, having been conceded an occupation zone in Germany, could not, as Churchill and Eden had pointed out, and as Hopkins had effectively promised de Gaulle ten days before, be denied a place on the Allied Control Commission for Germany, but that there would be no further countries as zone holders or candidates for membership on the Commission. Roosevelt's only word of explanation for the evolution of his views was that it would be easier to deal with France (for which read de Gaulle) in, rather than outside, the arrangements being concluded.

Roosevelt had actually come to this conclusion many weeks before, but chose to defer it until Stalin's attitude became clear. On hearing Roosevelt's views, Stalin good-naturedly declared, "I surrender," and France became one of the four occupying and Control Commission powers in Germany, one of the five permanent Security Council members of the intended world organization, and one of the convening powers at its founding conference in April. This was no small achievement for de Gaulle, who four years before had been an obscure fugitive under sentence of death commanding a few thousand refugees bankrolled (frugally) by Churchill.

It was also a distinct Western victory. Given Stalin's ever more obvious postwar ambitions, and de Gaulle's disinclination to be even as accommodating to Stalin as he was to Churchill and Roosevelt, this added another comparative bulwark of Western and democratic values to the supreme councils of the world.[35]

Reparations were vigorously debated next and finally Stalin achieved agreement only for the very bland formulation that it was "agreed that Germany must pay compensation for the damages caused to the Allied nations as a result of the war, and that the Moscow commission be instructed to consider the amount of the damages."[36] This was after Hopkins had handed up to Roosevelt a note saying: "The Russians have given in so much at this conference that I don't think we should let them down. . . . Simply say it is all referred to the Reparations Commission."[37] In fact, and ironically, considering future interpretations, Stalin had indeed given ground on almost every point. The Russians always considered Hopkins friendly to their cause, as Churchill considered him friendly to Britain's interest. (Henry Wallace, by contrast, the Russians regarded as "an imbecile.")[38]

Stalin took the opportunity to militate against the closing of the Dardanelles to Russia. "It is impossible to accept a situation in which Turkey has a hand on Russia's throat," he said. Roosevelt commended to Stalin the virtues of trying to have a frontier with Turkey like that of the United States with Canada. Given the endless Russo-Turkish wars over many centuries, this was as ridiculous a parallel as Stalin's between the Lublin puppets and de Gaulle, or Roosevelt's 1942 inspiration of a comparison between India and revolutionary America.

Churchill pointed out that Stalin had been invited at Teheran to present a view on this subject in writing and had not done so. He added a note of levity by remarking that he had done his best to open up the Dardanelles to the Russians in the First World War and had been fired and disgraced for his trouble, but was an unimpeachable partisan of the cause. Stalin said that Churchill had withdrawn prematurely—that the Turks had been on the verge of surrender (a generous view for which there is no historical support).

The best that could be done on the question of Polish frontiers was the Curzon Line, with minor variations in Poland's favor in the east and "substantial accessions of territory in the North and West." When Molotov attempted to interject in favor of Poland's "ancient frontiers in East Prussia and on the Oder," Roosevelt asked how ancient these claims were. Molotov waffled and obviously hadn't any idea, and Roosevelt warned that the espousal of such criteria might lead the British to demand the return of the United States to the British Crown. Stalin did his best to rescue his foreign commissar, and the conference ended, apart from the drafting committees, which were to report after dinner.

The conference closing dinner, February 10, was just the government heads, foreign ministers, and interpreters. The three leaders philosophized about the

nature of government. Roosevelt said that the United States before his first presidential election had been on the verge of "revolution because the people
lacked food, clothing and shelter," but that he had addressed "their primary
needs . . . and there is now little problem in regard to social disorder in the
United States."[39] Roosevelt then felt moved to propose a toast to Churchill. Roosevelt had been "twenty-eight years old when I entered political life but even at
that time Mr. Churchill had had long experience in the service of his country.
He had been in and out of government for many, many years," rendering great
service in both capacities. Referring to his opposition to Munich, Roosevelt
wasn't sure that Churchill had not given even greater service out of office,
"since he had forced the people to think."

Stalin professed to regard left and right as parliamentary terms and claimed to
be unable to understand why Daladier, an ostensible "radical socialist," had dissolved the trade unions while Churchill, a Tory, had not bothered them. In yet
another act of self-enforced discretion, neither Roosevelt nor Churchill pointed
out that the Communist unions Daladier dissolved were agitating for withdrawal
from the war against Germany in 1939, under orders from Stalin, while the
British labor movement was solid behind the war effort. Roosevelt instead disparaged the chaos of French politics, remarking that that country had had eighteen
political parties at the end of the Third Republic and that he had once had to correspond with three different French premiers in the same week. De Gaulle, Roosevelt said, had assured him he would change all that. Churchill said that Stalin
had a better system with only one party, and Stalin acknowledged that this "was a
great convenience."

In one of the most interesting exchanges of the conference, Stalin referred to
the Jewish problem. Without animosity he said that the Jews were natural
traders—that when his government had tried to concentrate them in the region
of Virovidzhan, they had all scattered to the cities within a few years, despite an
undoubted gift for agriculture that the Jews had demonstrated in places in the
Soviet Union. (In fact, the Soviet government forcibly dispersed them.) Roosevelt, having said that he was going to meet Ibn Saud and Farouk and Haile
Selassie, largely to discuss a homeland for the Jews, declared himself unequivo-
cally to be a Zionist, and asked Stalin if he shared that position, as Churchill was
known to do. Stalin said that he was a Zionist in principle but recognized the difficulty of the problem. Thus, unknown to those most directly engaged, at this
most tragic time in all the history of that ancient people and all its sorrows, the
prospects for a Jewish state were brightening, endorsed, at least in principle, by
the world's three most powerful statesmen.

Stalin volunteered, in what seems to have been his only mention of it at Yalta,
that he never would have signed the Nazi-Soviet Pact if it had not been for the
Munich agreement and the Polish-German Treaty of 1934.

In a fine democratic gesture, Stalin toasted the interpreters, after first consulting Churchill's translator, Major A. H. Birse. Stalin's ability to charm the British,

which rarely failed with Brooke and Cadogan, certainly extended to the lower ranks, and Birse's breathless recitation of it, like Brooke's of his toast to Stalin at Teheran, illustrates the greater susceptibility of all but the most pro-American British to the blandishments of the Russians than to what many of them thought the excessive familiarity and confidence of the Americans. As Stalin offered his toast to the interpreters, Churchill added, in a parody of Karl Marx that amused the Russians as much as the others: "Interpreters of the world unite! You have nothing to lose but your audience!"[40]

Birse excitedly wrote: "To me, a small cog in the machinery, he [Stalin] was amiable, friendly, and considerate. . . . There was something in his personality which revealed preeminence, a grasp of the essentials, an alert mind." This was in contrast to Roosevelt, who he had the insolence to imply was a backslapper, a particularly inapt reflection given Roosevelt's chairbound disability.[41]

As for Cadogan, he seemed to dislike virtually everyone except possibly his own wife, though he acknowledged Roosevelt's charm. With the ineffable arrogance of the senior permanent civil servant, he disparaged all elected and appointed officials as mere fronts for those who, he thought, did both the creative and the practical work. After dismissing Churchill as a "silly old man . . . plunged into a long harangue about World Organization, knowing nothing whatever of what he was talking about and making complete nonsense of the whole thing,"[42] Cadogan confided (February 8, 1945) to his diary his worshipful admiration of Stalin. "I must say I think Uncle Joe much the most impressive of the three men. He is very quiet and restrained. . . . The President flapped about and the P.M. boomed, but Joe just sat taking it all in and being rather amused. When he did chip in, he never used a superfluous word, and spoke very much to the point." The fact that Stalin shot most of Cadogan's Russian analogues more or less for sport, was the coauthor of the Nazi-Soviet pact, and was guilty of the deaths of over 20 million of his completely innocent countrymen, while his own prime minister and Roosevelt had saved Western civilization, did not weigh heavily on Cadogan's reflections as a diarist.

IX

THERE WAS A FINAL supplementary plenary session at noon February 11, to go over the proposed communiqué and secret protocols of the conference, which had been the subject of intense specialist work over the previous twenty-four hours, followed by a luncheon and a foreign ministers' meeting.

The conference communiqué was released to the world press in the name of the three principals and on behalf of their governments on February 12.

Section I dealt with the defeat of Germany and concluded: "Nazi Germany is doomed. The German people will only make the cost of their defeat heavier to themselves by attempting to continue a hopeless resistance."

Section II outlined the occupation of Germany and confirmed the invitation to France to take an occupation zone and join the Control Commission. "It is our inflexible purpose to destroy German militarism and Nazism and to insure that Germany will never again be able to disturb the peace of the world." The German general staff would be dissolved and war criminals punished. "All Nazi and militarist influences [would be expunged] from the cultural and economic life of the German People."

Section III promised reparations through "compensation . . . in kind to the greatest extent possible." The reparations commission was referred to without elaboration.

Section IV convened the World Organizational Conference on behalf of all five powers for San Francisco, April 25, 1945. Stettinius was proud of having settled on San Francisco as a location, on awakening in the dead of night after many other cities had been rejected by Roosevelt as inappropriate. Stettinius had visions of the famous sites of San Francisco and concluded that it would meet the convenience of Pacific countries, and would cause the others to "travel through the United States and see for themselves its magnificence, greatness, and power. I recall now, for instance, Molotov's remark after he had been across San Francisco Bay to visit shipyards that he was at last beginning to understand the greatness of America."[43]

Section V was the Declaration on Liberated Europe, built upon the Atlantic Charter principle of "the right of all peoples to choose the form of government under which they will live." It promised to assist the people of liberated Europe "to establish conditions of internal peace; emergency measures to . . . carry out for the relief of distressed peoples; to form interim governments "broadly representative of all democratic elements in the population and pledged to the earliest possible establishment through free elections of governments responsive to the will of the people and to facilitate where necessary the holding of such elections." The three powers reserved collectively to themselves the right to impose democratic solutions, as defined, on liberated areas.

Section VI (Poland) promised "a strong, free, independent, and democratic Poland . . . and a new Polish Provisional Government of National Unity," composed of existing and additional democratic groups. "This new government shall be pledged to the holding of free and unfettered elections as soon as possible on the basis of universal suffrage and secret ballot. . . . All democratic and anti-Nazi parties shall have the right to take part and to put forward candidates."

Section VII dealt with Yugoslavia. Churchill won his two points: Tito and Subasic (the regent) were urged to put into effect at once the agreement between them brokered by the British.

Section VIII promised meetings of the three foreign ministers every three to four months for an indefinite period, and Section IX was a statement of "Unity for Peace as for War." Unity was held to be "a sacred obligation," in order that "the highest aspiration of humanity be realized—a secure and lasting peace which will, in the words of the Atlantic Charter, 'afford assurance that all the men in all the lands may live out their lives in freedom from fear and from want.'

"Victory in this war and establishment of the proposed international organization will provide the greatest opportunity in all history to create in the years to come the conditions for such a peace."

There were further protocols covering treatment of war criminals, the proposed easing of the Montreux Convention to permit the Soviet Union freer passage through the Dardanelles in and out of the Black Sea, a nonbinding guideline on reparations somewhat watered down from Maisky's draconian suggestions, and an accord on treatment of prisoners of war and displaced civilians. This last measure entailed the return of all such nationals to their country of origin. As many Russians had in fact fled the Soviet Union, their return proved to be controversial. This problem had not been foreseen, and thousands of Russian anti-Communists were handed over to Stalin's agents for summary execution or imprisonment.

"It has been calculated that by the end of the war there were more than one million . . . Soviet volunteers serving in German Army or SS units," as well as a large number of civilian fugitives not implicated in association with the Nazis. "It was inconceivable that Stalin would permit treason on such a scale to go unpunished or allow [these people] to remain at liberty beyond his frontiers." The agreement provided for the return of all Soviet citizens in liberated countries, military or civilian. "Whereas the Americans were prepared to treat these as Germans [or whatever], should they resist repatriation, the British were not . . . and implemented the policy of repatriation with a zeal beyond the call of duty, even though the Foreign Office soon realized that batches of returnees were being shot at their disembarkation points. 'We shall only get into the most hopeless muddle if we decide cases of this nature on humanitarian grounds.' "[44]

There was the further secret agreement, not made public for two years, of the Soviet undertaking to enter the war against Japan within "two or three months after Germany has surrendered and the war in Europe has terminated." The consideration for this, revoking the Japanese gains of the Russo-Japanese War, were as Roosevelt and Stalin had agreed between them on February 8. This agreement was consigned to Roosevelt's safe in the White House, and only a few of the most senior government officials in the three countries were aware of it. The British, especially Eden, were miffed at having had no part in the negotiation, but the Americans were conducting more than 90 percent of the war against Japan, upon which the return to Britain of Singapore, Hong Kong, and Malaya, which had been none too gloriously forfeited, depended, and Churchill wisely declined to make an issue of it. The British at this point had little idea of what it was like to fight the Japanese near their home islands, where no Japanese soldier or airman would accept to be taken alive.

Notes were also exchanged between Churchill and Roosevelt ("My dear Franklin") and Roosevelt and Stalin, assuring that should domestic political difficulties arise with the United States having only one vote while the Soviet Union, Ukraine, and White Russia all had votes, and the British Dominions had votes, both leaders would support the attribution to the United States of three votes in the new world organization.

The three leaders signed the Conference Declaration and protocols, and the Yalta Conference ended after lunch, at 3:45 P.M., Sunday, February 11, 1945. Roosevelt said to Stalin: "We will meet again soon, in Berlin."[45] The leaders made their farewells most cordially and dispersed by automobile. Roosevelt and his daughter drove eighty miles to Sevastopol, past the site of the Charge of the Light Brigade at Balaklava, and boarded the American maintenance vessel *Catoctin* in Sevastopol harbor. The damage to the city from the prolonged actions with the Germans was very severe. On the morning of February 12, Roosevelt and his daughter and other members of his party drove to Saki, boarded the *Sacred Cow*, and flew to Egypt.

X

I N ALL HISTORY, only the Congress of Vienna in 1815 ending the Napoleonic Wars and the Conference at Versailles in 1919 at the end of the First World War are more famous among war-end summit meetings than the Yalta Conference of 1945. The Congress of Vienna is generally thought to have been a reasonable success, because there was no general war for almost a century afterwards. The Versailles Conference's ultimate failure is usually ascribed to the defection to isolationism of the United States, the exclusion of the new Russian government, and the unfairness of the treaty's terms on Germany. Yalta, however, is notorious. It is widely regarded as an instance of shameful surrender to the lurid appetites of an evil dictator.

As late as the spring of 2001, the president of the United States, George W. Bush, told cheering thousands in Warsaw that there must be: "No more Munichs; no more Yaltas!" as if there were any similarity between them. President Bush is something of a Roosevelt admirer and yet he implied that Yalta was a shaming giveaway of Poland to the Soviet Union, and thousands of Poles approved the reference (overlooking Poland's disgraceful role at the time of Munich).

Initially, Yalta was seen to be a fair agreement or a Western victory, since Roosevelt and Churchill apparently achieved their objectives. Then the conventional wisdom proclaimed the victory of Stalin over the Western leaders. Churchill did not altogether discourage his admirers from suggesting that he had fought valiantly against the tendency of Roosevelt to give away Eastern Europe to Stalin.

Churchill's acquiescence in the Soviet takeover of Romania, Bulgaria, Hungary, and (to some degree) Poland to Stalin in Moscow in October 1944, is, as we have seen, described as a "temporary measure" in his memoirs. As the prime minister well knew, this was not the basis on which spheres of influence were determined, and particularly not with Stalin. Churchill purported to see himself, as he had in writing about Teheran, as a "British donkey" between the American buffalo and the Russian bear, but "I'm the only one who knows the way home."[46] All three leaders knew where they wanted to go and how to get there.

The facts, by the opening of the Yalta Conference, as has been recounted, were that almost a third of postwar Poland was in the EAC-designated Soviet

German occupation zone and almost all of pre-war Poland was occupied by the Red Army. Churchill had acknowledged Russian control of Romania, Bulgaria, and Hungary, and the British had voted with the Russians at the European Advisory Commission to divide pre-war Germany into approximately equal sections, though with the westward movement of Poland this would leave most of postwar Germany in Western hands but Russia within one hundred miles of the Rhine in one place. This unsatisfactory decision had soured Roosevelt on the EAC, which, he felt, "had not been a success."[47]

The official British version of all this was essentially flimflam, because Churchill refers rarely to the commission in his memoirs, describing it as the European Advisory Council at one point[48] (Hopkins called it the Advisory Committee in his note to Roosevelt at Yalta.) No one seemed to take it adequately seriously. Cadogan wrote that the commission received only "the most lukewarm American support" and that "Churchill appears not to have understood in time what was going on in the Commission."[49]

The British leaders then systematically blamed the Americans for allowing the Russians so far into Europe. Some, though not Churchill, reviled Roosevelt, Truman, Marshall, and Eisenhower for not tearing up the occupation zone agreements the British had themselves sponsored and having an immediate, massive confrontation with Stalin. Such a confrontation would have taken place before the development of atomic weapons and while Stalin possessed numerically superior forces in the theater. (It might still have been successful, but the conditions for initiating such a showdown were far from ideal.)

One of the chief propagandists of the disgruntled British imperialist school was Arthur Bryant, the initial annotator and editor of Sir Alan Brooke's diaries. He subtitled his chapter on Yalta with Roosevelt's alleged remark: "Of one thing I am certain, Stalin is not an imperialist."[50] He does not attribute the statement any more precisely, but implies that Brooke claimed to have heard Roosevelt say it. There is no reason to believe that Roosevelt held any such opinion. What he did believe and often stated, as has been mentioned, was that Stalin would be cautious about unleashing aggressive wars potentially involving other major powers, unlike Hitler, whom Roosevelt had considered a compulsive warmonger from the beginning of his regime. In both of these opinions, Roosevelt's judgment was accurate.* (Brooke considered the Yalta Conference "as satisfactory as could be hoped for, and certainly most friendly."[51])

Britain's leading fighting general (along with Slim), Bernard L. Montgomery, an Americophobe of the old school, violently objected to the southern French

---

* Bryant was himself a semireformed Fascist, who in 1940 produced a book he later went to great lengths to suppress entitled *Unfinished Victory*. The victory was Hitler's, and, undeterred by the fact that Britain was then at war with Germany, Bryant praised the fuehrer's "Cromwellian" qualities. He is not a natural source for an assessment of Roosevelt's war aims and negotiating record.

landings in August 1944,[52] many years after it had become clear to everyone else, most conspicuously Churchill, that they had been a valuable success.

He overlooked the foot-dragging of the British over crossing the Channel. He lamented that the Anvil-Dragoon operation had "removed ten divisions from Italy and thus made it impossible for an offensive from that country to be developed northwards through the Ljubljana Gap towards Vienna."[53]

Montgomery, pretending to be majestically oblivious of the fact that the British had joined the Russians in forcing on the Americans in early 1944 the ultimate German occupation zones, called in late 1944 for a concentration on the Ruhr and a drive on Berlin. Montgomery also stoked up the Stalin myth, crediting the Russian leader with "an amazing strategical sense."[54] Stalin's intelligence and formidability are beyond question, but he was a peer in the company of the other leading political figures of the century and not a Brobdingnagian phenomenon (as his unheroic initial response to the German invasion of 1941 demonstrated).

"Roosevelt," Montgomery had the effrontery to write, "never seemed to me to be clear about what he was fighting for. . . . [Stalin] had no difficulty fooling Roosevelt."[55]

Montgomery even censored Churchill: "The leaders of the democratic nations behaved to the communist dictator at Yalta much as their despised predecessors had to the Nazi dictator at Munich. They persuaded themselves that Stalin was a gentleman, and agreed to the partition of Germany. But by this time there was nothing else they could do. Stalin had outwitted his allies; he had won the peace for Russia at Teheran."[56] Though false, this general view has received widespread acceptance.

———

Next to the theory that Roosevelt was simply swindled at Yalta is the theory that he was mentally and physically incompetent to conduct such negotiations. Churchill had his daughter Sarah with him at Malta and Yalta, and she was shocked by Roosevelt's appearance ("the terrible change in him"), but came gradually not to notice, because of his "bright charm . . . and brave expansive heart."[57] Eden thought Roosevelt "looks considerably older since Quebec. He gives the impression of failing powers."[58] Yet he told Stettinius, whom the British seemed to like (having found the solemn Hull heavy going, not that Roosevelt allowed him very often to deal directly with America's principal ally), that the "President looked better, seemed much calmer and more relaxed than when he had last seen him . . . that he was in particularly fine shape."[59] Cadogan was quite positive about Roosevelt's apparent condition in his diary and to Eden,[60] but told Stettinius he was "shocked at the President's appearance."[61] The robustness of his appearance seemed to fluctuate rapidly, as some of his entourage attested.

There was no suggestion by anyone, British or American, of President Roosevelt's mental powers having diminished until the fiction writers went to work after Yalta. Harriman found Roosevelt "worn, wasted . . . but alert."[62] James

Byrnes, who traveled with him on the *Quincy*, was well aware that Roosevelt did not appear robust, but would "marvel" at his mastery and presentation of material throughout the conference.[63] Stettinius pronounced his chief "steady, patient, kind, sympathetic, but determined" at Yalta. "The President's ability to participate on fully equal terms day after day in the grueling give-and-take at the conference table with such powerful associates as Churchill and Stalin" was a definitive answer to the sensational "stories . . . without foundation" that circulated about his health.[64]

The theory of Roosevelt's being physically and intellectually unfit for his task at Yalta, apart from some disconcerting photographs, comes chiefly from an alleged statement of Hopkins's to Halifax after Roosevelt's death that Roosevelt didn't follow more than half of what was said there. Neither Hopkins nor Halifax can be trusted here. Hopkins's son Robert was present as a military photographer at Yalta, and has authorized me to say that Roosevelt was alert at all times and that his father made no such statement. If Hopkins said anything remotely like this, he could have been motivated by spite at his decline in Roosevelt's favor, or by a desire to inflate his own role at Yalta.

Halifax only floated this story after Hopkins and Roosevelt were dead. The former archappeaser, who was rusticated to Washington to get him out of the War Cabinet, must be treated with great skepticism. As with Corcoran's unsubstantiated claim that Justice Holmes had described FDR as a second-class intellect and Bryant's assertion that Roosevelt was sure Stalin was not an imperialist, we are dealing with posthumous hearsay from dubiously motivated people (squarely contradicted in this case) citing a suspect source. Halifax is also the source, quoting McCloy, of the claim that Leahy recommended concerting D-Day with Petain. There has never been one word of corroboration of this, and McCloy lived on for forty years. The malice of the imperialist U.K. Tory appeasers didn't yield much to the McCarthyite Republicans or dyed-in-the-wool Gaullists.

The Halifax-Hopkins account doesn't square with the theory of Leahy, who despite his relentless misjudgment of French affairs was far from a stupid man or a toady, that Roosevelt often dominated in the proceedings at Yalta.[65] Bohlen, interpreter and Russian expert, and ultimately one of America's greatest diplomats, thought Roosevelt at Yalta mentally and psychologically not affected by his physical decline, "mentally sharp [and] effective" at all important times.

Any such claim as that imputed to Hopkins is incongruous, given that Hopkins represented the conference as a clear success and a vindication for the American position. Churchill's lugubrious and indiscreet doctor, Lord Moran, confidently announced that Roosevelt would be the first of the Big Three to die. "He is a very sick man. He has all the symptoms of hardening of the arteries of the brain in an advanced stage, so that I give him only a few months to live."[66] Hopkins, who came to Malta on Stettinius's plane, collapsed in a cot the whole way, became alarmed when he saw Roosevelt, and fearing irresolution at the full conference, urged Anna Roosevelt to ensure that her father concerted his position with Churchill. "The President, he ranted, had asked for this job, and was going to have to take the responsibility of seeing it through. Anna calmed him down."[67]

The problem here was that Moran's comments on Hopkins were not much more encouraging: Hopkins seemed "only half in this world. . . . His skin was a yellow-white membrane stretched tight over the bones."[68] Hopkins had also suffered a return of dysentery and was drinking far too much, as Stettinius and Anna discussed with concern before the group left Malta.[69] Hopkins would attend the plenary meetings, sitting behind Roosevelt and sending up generally useful notes. He took his meals in his room and received visitors there, but had only a fraction of his former energy. His performance was somewhat reminiscent of Louis Howe's at the Chicago convention of 1932, though less influential. Hopkins, a slender man at all times, lost eighteen pounds during the conference.[70]

The diplomatic historian Warren Kimball has convincingly made the point that neither Roosevelt's cardiological problems, pulmonary weakness, high blood pressure, anemia, bleeding hemorrhoids, sinusitis, and other lesser difficulties, nor Churchill's angina, minor strokes, intermittent pneumonia, excessive drinking, and other concerns affected their performance as statesmen. Roosevelt sometimes suffered an insufficient blood supply to the brain, a result of several of the problems enumerated, which caused "occasional periods of forgetfulness, a condition called secondary metabolic encephalopathy," which led to "the slack-jawed, gape-mouthed FDR" who appeared in some Yalta photographs.

"Roosevelt was unquestionably ill at Yalta," Kimball writes, "exhausted by the physical and mental stress of wartime leadership and the cumulative debilitating effects of his paralysis. . . . But, as with Churchill, illness and tiredness did not determine his policies. Whether or not Roosevelt knew how ill he was is likewise a red herring. Nothing he did at Yalta or immediately afterward altered the approach he had taken throughout the war, an approach toward a postwar settlement that, by the time of the Yalta talks, had been outlined in some detail."[71] Roosevelt did suffer from alternating strong and weak heartbeats for several days, which worried Dr. Bruenn but did not affect his performance.[72] This view is uncontradicted by any credible evidence from any of the other sources that have garrulously opined on this subject.

William Bullitt became more erratic than ever following his loss of influence after forcing Sumner Welles out of government. He fathered the claim that Roosevelt had a hunch that if he gave Stalin "everything I possibly can and ask for nothing in return . . . he won't try to annex anything and will work with me for a world of democracy and peace." There are extensive records of Roosevelt's entire relationship with Stalin. All the correspondence is preserved, and all the discussions at their only meetings, at Teheran and Yalta, were translated and recorded in writing. None of it supports the conclusion that Roosevelt did more than try the olive branch with Stalin, at no geopolitical cost to the West, while fully aware of the strong possibility that relations would break down, and while preparing for that eventuality also.*

It is inconceivable that Roosevelt would have said anything so foolish as Bullitt claims, and he never in his dealings with Stalin did give him anything without requiring a quid pro quo, as Hopkins pointed out had occurred at Yalta, in his memo to Roosevelt at the end of that conference.

XI

THE PROBLEM IN ROOSEVELT'S RELATIONS with Stalin was not Roosevelt's gifts to Stalin, but Stalin's broken promises. The historian Robert Conquest, generally a critic of Roosevelt's performance at Yalta, does affirm that by late March 1945, just six weeks after the end of the Yalta Conference, Roosevelt realized that cooperation with Stalin was impossible.

None of the critics has ever shed any light on what they expected Roosevelt to do to push Stalin back within his own borders, after Strang had given him half of Poland and a chunk of Germany and Churchill had legitimized Soviet preeminence in Bulgaria, Romania, and Hungary (all of which in strictly military terms the Red Army had largely earned).

There is no doubt that Roosevelt's optimism and faith in his own power and personality, and general fatigue, caused him to invest more hope in a positive outcome of his dealings with Stalin than was justified. But if he had not tried that option it would have been very difficult to sustain Western opinion through the Cold War.

The best-qualified commentator on Roosevelt's relations with Stalin was probably Charles Bohlen, advisor to all Presidents from Roosevelt to Nixon and eventual ambassador to the Soviet Union, and to France after de Gaulle's creation of the Fifth Republic. Bohlen has a little of the unelected official's disapproval of the political leader, though he is more indulgent than Acheson and far from terminally afflicted by it as was Cadogan. Bohlen nowhere hints that Roosevelt was intellectually inadequate to his task at Teheran or Yalta, nor that he gave away too much. Bohlen did believe that Roosevelt's knowledge of the fraudulence of the 1917 Bolshevik Revolution was sketchy and that he was too generous in his interpretation of it.[74] He also did "not think Roosevelt had any real comprehension of the great gulf that separated a Bolshevik from a non-Bolshevik, and particularly from an American. . . . What he did not understand was that Stalin's enmity was based on profound ideological convictions."

---

* Bullitt sent Roosevelt an extensive warning against Stalin's expansionist tendencies in a memo of August 11, 1943. It was a prescient document. Roosevelt's response is not recorded.[73]

Bohlen is surely right. But Roosevelt was almost as suspicious by nature as Stalin was. His great façade of goodwill was composed of natural optimism and self-confidence, lofty objectives, and a poker player's talent at inscrutability, behind which he conducted an always complicated range of tactics and strategies to achieve his ends.

Bohlen recorded that "Stalin did have a regard for Roosevelt, and on a number of occasions at the wartime conferences I saw the Marshal show genuine feeling for the President. He rarely argued with Roosevelt. . . . I do think Stalin respected Roosevelt as a man who genuinely believed in democratic liberalism, [although] Stalin obviously did not agree with or even understand democratic liberalism. . . . On balance, I think he had a higher regard for Roosevelt than he did for Churchill."[75]

Gromyko confirms the same point, that Stalin respected Churchill but liked and admired Roosevelt.[76] (Gromyko's memoirs are frequently inaccurate where Soviet motives and policy are described, but may be believable on this point.) Gromyko claims that at one point in the Yalta Conference, when Roosevelt was supposedly unwell and very tired, Stalin said of Roosevelt contemplatively to Molotov and Gromyko, while filling his pipe on the stair landing, "Why did nature have to punish him so?"[77]

Stalin was certainly capable of being agreeable and entertaining. Churchill and Roosevelt even claimed to like Stalin.[78] None of this conviviality implies the gullibility or subservience of any of these men.

The intervention of Russia in the war against Japan would have been extremely useful if the atomic experiments had not produced a militarily useful weapon. Wars can not be conducted on the supposition of scientific miracles.

The core of the Yalta agreement was two propositions. In the first, Stalin accepted the world organization. Giving it a good launch provided Roosevelt the ultimate political framework for leading his country permanently out of isolation and into the world. Isolationists could not object to full American participation in the world that was being created in San Francisco. For these purposes, even a brief semblance of unity among the Big Three was invaluable to Roosevelt in engaging America in the world.

The second proposition was that despite the strictures of Section II against German sovereignty, if Stalin didn't deliver on Sections V and VI on behalf of Liberated Europe, and specifically Poland, Churchill and Roosevelt could de-Nazify Germany and rearm it as an ally of theirs, along with a reinvigorated France and other Western-liberated European countries.

Heavy reparations and the radical dismemberment of Germany, both of which Stalin had sought, had essentially been rejected, apart from the German territory that was being awarded to Poland and to Russian occupation. If Stalin wanted money, he would have to get it from the United States and pay for it, at least in behavioral terms, rather than engaging his allies to help him pillage Germany for his benefit, as he had asked.

If Stalin did deliver on Sections V and VI, Section II would be honored, there would be modest reparations, and Roosevelt would advance Russia a $6 billion economic recovery package and give Russia a sizeable merchant marine of super-fluous Liberty ships and Italian vessels. He might even consider atomic coopera-tion for peaceful purposes, as he indicated in conversation with the nuclear physicist Niels Bohr in 1944.

The issue of whether the British and Americans' (and France's) foremost ally would be Germany or Russia would be determined by whether Stalin could resist the temptations of enslaving Eastern Europe.

Had the United States been constructively involved in the world in the previ-ous forty years, it is very unlikely that either world war would have occurred. Henceforth the United States would be constructively involved and there would be no major war for many more than the fifty years the Yalta principals claimed to be hoping for. The United Nations, as it became, has not justified the hopes invested in it. But as a Wilsonian framework it provided America's permanent passport out of isolation, which produced a decisive and almost wholly positive influence on the future of the world. Roosevelt assumed that the Latin Ameri-cans, the British Dominions, and grateful emancipated colonies would provide a durable majority for Anglo-American plans. This proved to be the case for about twenty-five years.

With the Declaration on Liberated Europe, Roosevelt had succeeded in his secondary objective of putting the onus for any shortfall in its enactment squarely on the Soviet Union. If the maintenance of peace in the world was going to require a constant and credible American presence, as its absence earlier in the century indicated would be the case, Roosevelt and his successors would have to have an unquestionable moral right and a clear national interest to exercise that deterrent capacity.

At Yalta the United States and its leader achieved virtually everything they sought. If the agreement had been adhered to, it would have been a triumph of diplomacy. That this proved not to be the case was because of the noncompli-ance of the Soviet Union with the agreements. The forty-five-year Cold War ensued, which had many vicissitudes, but never was a shot fired between the Soviet and Western forces, and eventually the Western victory in the Second World War was completed with the total disintegration of the Soviet Union.

Yalta's critics would bewail the fate of what became the satellite countries. None of these peoples except the Czechoslovaks had had any distinction at self-government, and the Poles, in particular, had operated a corrupt, viciously anti-Semitic, obtuse, and not very democratic regime. The peoples in these countries suffered an unkind fate, but geography assured them of that, and the political sci-ence of those countries had been harsh throughout their histories. Only the Czechs and the Poles had shown any political affinity for the Western powers in the latter pre-war years. Ultimately, forty-five years later, the Declarations on Lib-erated Europe and on Poland would be implemented.

Because of lurid allegations by McCarthyite Republicans in the early fifties, a word must be said about Alger Hiss, who attended the Yalta Conference as a junior State Department official specializing in international organizations. Hiss was eventually revealed as a former member of a Communist espionage ring in the United States and was convicted of perjury on the dogged examination of Congressman Richard Nixon. Roosevelt had never met Hiss before Yalta, and never spent one minute alone with him at Yalta, according to Bohlen, who was with Roosevelt throughout as interpreter and counselor in Soviet matters. Hiss's chief contribution at the conference was a sensibly reasoned argument against giving the Soviet Union three votes in the international organization. In this as in all other matters, while he was competent and unexceptionable in his functions, Hiss had no influence whatever on Roosevelt or American policy at Yalta.*

Roosevelt had always felt that there was a susceptibility in Stalin to deal honorably with an American leader who was not a traditional European imperialist. This was the basis for his famous message to Churchill of March 18, 1942: "I know you will not mind my being brutally frank when I tell you that I think I can personally handle Stalin better than either your Foreign Office or my State Department. Stalin hates the guts of all your top people. He thinks he likes me better, and I hope he will continue to."

This was certainly nonsense. Stalin didn't particularly like anyone, despite giving Bohlen and Gromyko the impression that he liked Roosevelt. He appreciated Roosevelt's power and doubtless noted his human qualities, as he did Churchill's, de Gaulle's, and even Hitler's. (In Hitler's case, he saw genius, energy, and determination, and the aptitudes of an inspirational leader. Their mutual admiration was striking. They seem to have been virtually oblivious of each other's evils.) And Stalin had no great objection to imperialists, as he clearly said at Teheran (being one himself).

But the context of Roosevelt's comments on how the British and Americans should deal with Stalin was a lengthy, candid, thoroughly amicable "Dear Winston" letter suggesting a sensible division of effort between them. It was not, as it is often represented, a profession of slavish alignment with Stalin and against Churchill.

According to Frances Perkins, Roosevelt also told a cabinet meeting shortly after coming back from Yalta that he thought there was "something else in [Stalin] besides this revolutionist Bolshevist thing." He connected it to the "priesthood," for which Stalin had briefly been an unenthusiastic and unsuccessful student. Roosevelt oddly mused that this might have communicated something to Stalin of the "way in which a Christian gentleman[79] should behave."[80]

As with other one-line fragments from Roosevelt's reflections on this and some

---

* The last Communist president of Poland, General Wojciech Jaruzelski, told a visiting, mainly American delegation, including the author, in 1990, that the free elections promised at Yalta for Poland were about to take place. He was under no illusions about the likely performance of the Communists; they received 8 percent of the vote.

other subjects, there is not a shred of evidence that Roosevelt thought Christian decency predominated in Stalin's character, or that he let his guard down in his dealings with him.

Admiral Leahy said of the Polish section of the Yalta Declaration: "Mr. President, this is so elastic that the Russians can stretch it all the way from Yalta to Washington without ever technically breaking it." Roosevelt replied: "Bill, I know it. But it's the best I can do for Poland at this time." These are not the words of a naïve and euphoric peacemaker like Wilson after Versailles or Chamberlain after Munich. In Roosevelt's reply there was a grasp of strategy and of negotiations to come, preferably when the United States would be the world's only atomic power (with Britain progressing behind).

To Adolf Berle, the old Brain Truster now in the State Department (about to be ambassador to Brazil), Roosevelt said of Yalta: "I didn't say the result was good. I said it was the best I could do."[81] He told Margaret Suckley Yalta "had turned out better than he dared hope for,"[82] but there is no evidence that he shared the mercurial Hopkins's belief that "this was the dawn of the new day we had all been praying for and talking about for so many years. We were absolutely certain that we had won the first great victory of the peace—and by 'we' I mean all of us, the whole civilized human race. The Russians had proved that they could be reasonable and far-seeing. . . . we could live with them and get along with them peacefully for as far into the future as any of us could imagine."[83]

What most of the critics would fail to recognize was that the agreements of that conference secured the one ingredient that assured world peace and the ultimate liberation of Eastern Europe, including the peoples of the Soviet Union itself. With Yalta came the relentless pressure throughout the world of American military, economic, and cultural might in favor of democracy, the market economy, and the liberal state.

Roosevelt did not gamble the national interest, the cause of the democracies, or the great sacrifices of the American armed forces on the proposition that Stalin would quickly evolve into a fully house-trained partner for peace. If necessary, the Soviet Union could be contained, as Roosevelt had correctly implied to Pius XII when he wrote him that it was a cautious country in its relations with the other Great Powers. Except for the brief impetuosity of the Cuban Missile Crisis in 1962, it continued to be so to the end.

As ambassadors in Moscow, after the catastrophic Davies (whom Truman briefly and unfortunately reactivated a few months later, sending him to see a rigorously unreceptive Churchill), Roosevelt sent William Standley and Averell Harriman, determined skeptics. According to Dallek, he did so "partly to provide a contrary perspective to the wartime euphoria about Russia."[84]

"No one could deny Stalin 'a wide military and political glacis on his Western frontier . . . except at the cost of another war, which was unthinkable . . . and since public questions about postwar Soviet intentions would have shattered wartime unity at home and with the Russians, Roosevelt endorsed the new dimensions of Soviet power, in the hope that it would encourage future friend-ship with the West. . . . At the same time, however, he acted to limit the expansion of Russian power in 1945 by refusing to share the secret of the atomic bomb, agreeing to station American troops in southern Germany, endorsing Churchill's arrangements for the Balkans (Greece and Yugoslavia)," acquiring "American naval bases in the Pacific and the Atlantic, and encouraging the illusion of China as a great power . . . as an [eventual] political counterweight to the USSR. . . . Mindful that any emphasis on this kind of 'realpolitik' might weaken American public resolve to play an enduring role in world affairs, Roosevelt made these actions the hidden side of his diplomacy."[85] It was also consistent when he spoke in the last weeks of his life of becoming "tougher [with Russia] than has heretofore appeared advantageous to the war effort."[86]

Dallek believed that "had he lived . . . his greater prestige [than Truman's] and reputation as an advocate of Soviet-American friendship would have made it easier for him than for Truman to muster public support for a hard line."[87] This echoes Bohlen's comment: "Given great prestige and his reputation for dealing fairly with Stalin, Roosevelt would have been in a position to have adopted a much firmer line toward the Soviet Union—as I am confident he would have—with a much greater degree of public acceptance than Truman did."[88]

Roosevelt "was a world figure of monumental proportions. Roosevelt's strength in dealing with foreign leaders stemmed from his enormous popularity throughout the world, even in countries he had never been in . . . and the aura of the office was always around him. . . . Certainly the Kremlin had considerable respect for Roosevelt, in a large measure because they understood what a powerful figure he was in the entire Western world. Since the Russians always respect power, whatever its source, this might have made Stalin somewhat more careful with Roosevelt than he was with Truman."[89]

As the Roosevelt biographer Sanche de Gramont (Ted Morgan) wrote: "Yalta was a defeat for the Soviets, and they so regarded it. What they won at the negotiating table their armies already possessed. If Yalta was a sell-out, why did [Stalin] go to such lengths to violate the agreement?" He cited a War Department memo of April 3, 1945, referring to "very big concessions" by the Russians at Yalta in conceding anything about "liberated areas adjacent to Russia . . . [as Stalin] had it in his power to merely sit tight and force the Lublin Government down our throat."[90] Stalin did just that, of course, but in making the ostensible concession on treatment of Poland and Liberated Europe, he forced himself to break his word in order to subdue Polish independence, aroused American moral indignation, and facilitated an American-led containment policy that ultimately caused the Soviet Union to implode. Without the Yalta agreement, any such policy by the United States could have been a hard domestic political sell.

Winston Churchill had come to Yalta seeking a resurrected balance of power in Europe among Britain, France, and a de-Nazified Germany, which would, with American assistance, bar the way westwards to the Russian Bear.

Joseph Stalin, it soon became clear, had no interest in accepting the olive branch the Western leaders proffered at Yalta. His strategic genius was endlessly proclaimed by the anti-Roosevelt choristers, including their British contingent. But in opening the Cold War, Stalin would commit the greatest strategic blunder of the twentieth century, except for the German recourse to unrestricted submarine warfare in 1917 and the Japanese attack on Pearl Harbor. If Stalin had taken what was on offer, the Soviet Union would have survived and evolved more or less as Roosevelt had hoped, and as post-Soviet Russia has evolved. And it would have retained more influence in Eastern Europe at the end of the century than Russia has had since the collapse of the Soviet empire. (And if Stalin had not been co-opted by Roosevelt at Teheran into supporting Overlord, he would have ended the war well to the west of where he did.)

Franklin Roosevelt, at Yalta and elsewhere, after the fortunes of war turned in favor of the Allies, sought a favorable imbalance of power, to America's permanent advantage, either as a country whose preeminence would obviate traditional alliances, or as leader of an unassailably strong Western alliance. The latter occurred, but after the end of the Cold War nearly fifty years later, something closer to the former began to develop.

Both Churchill and Roosevelt carried visceral aversions from their experiences in World War I. Churchill had his abhorrence of becoming locked in ground combat with the German Army in France and Flanders, which made him reticent about the Normandy landings. Roosevelt was fanatically determined not to make the mistakes of Woodrow Wilson. That is why he wanted the United Nations agreed on before the end of the war, packed his administration with Republicans, and sent to the San Francisco organizing conference a large congressional delegation composed of Democrats and Republicans equally, despite the current Democratic preponderance. He enlisted or neutralized most other Republicans, and isolated the isolationists — Wheeler and Hiram Johnson were braying to themselves. Roosevelt's determination to secure the peace was the reason he was partially indulgent of Stalin until he was sure of his domestic political constituency and the efficacy of atomic weapons, in order then to make the best deal he could with the Soviet Union.

XII

PRESIDENT ROOSEVELT AND HIS DAUGHTER regained the U.S.S. *Quincy* in the Great Bitter Lake in the Suez Canal. Here Roosevelt received his three potentates. First came Farouk, incongruously dressed in an admiral's uniform. Roosevelt advised him to grow more cotton and gave him a twin-engined transport. Haile Selassie, a much-admired figure after his disgraceful treatment at the hands of Mussolini and the appeasers, came aboard and talked about the disposition of former Italian colonies. He was particularly interested in Italian Somaliland and Eritrea, which adjoined his country. Roosevelt gave him four armored reconnaissance cars.

The Ruritanian character of the President's trip reached a climax when Ibn Saud "hove to in full regalia on the deck of an American destroyer, which had picked him up at Jiddah along with his rugs, sheep, awnings, charcoal cooking buckets, holy water, and a retinue of royal relatives, guards, valets, food tasters, servers of ceremonial coffee . . . and miscellaneous slaves."[91] The king had numerous wives and forty-two sons and sometimes offered family members as gifts to acquaintances he found agreeable. His principal interests were women, prayer, and perfume. He suffered from poor eyesight due to cataracts, and was lame. He complimented Roosevelt on his wheelchair, thinking it an example of American efficiency to spare unwanted exercise. Roosevelt gave him several wheelchairs, and gave him an aircraft as well.

After a pleasant discussion about oil and reforestation, Roosevelt got to the point and asked Ibn Saud to approve of the admission of more Jews to Palestine. The king of Saudi Arabia was militant in his refusal. He denounced the Jews as successful in converting desert to arable land only because of the generosity of American and British Jews. He claimed the Palestinian Jewish brigade was fighting Arabs and not Germans (which would have been difficult in Italy, where most of the Palestine Jewish soldiers were deployed and fought with distinction). Ibn Saud said that the Arabs would all rise in permanent combat before they would admit more Jews.

Roosevelt reasoned that the Jews were only a small percentage of the Arab population, but the king was immoveable. He professed to regard the alleged murder of three million Polish Jews not as an argument for a Jewish homeland in the Middle East, but as proof that space had been freed up in Poland for three million more Jews. He evinced no sympathy whatever for the plight of the Jewish victims of the Nazis and their collaborators. Roosevelt returned to the subject several times without success. Roosevelt was appalled at the proportions of Ibn Saud's antipathy to the Jews, though he found him in other ways rather entertaining. Roosevelt was unshaken in his conviction that the Jews needed and deserved a homeland and that Palestine was the logical place for it. He could scarcely fail to realize that placating the Arabs would be a complicated and exacting process.

The Jewish-Arab problem, like the Chinese civil war (which was about to resume), the governance of Eastern Europe, and decolonization would have to be addressed after the present war was over. All would be intractable, but Roosevelt, after the struggle and triumph of the last twelve years, and disposing more power and moral authority than anyone since Napoleon, thought almost anything was possible. Dashingly dressed himself in his naval cape as he received his visitors on the gun deck of the *Quincy*, he cordially saw Ibn Saud off and the *Quincy* sailed to Alexandria. Roosevelt wrote to Margaret Suckley of his meeting with Ibn Saud: "Whole party was a scream!"[92]

Here Churchill came aboard and the two leaders had a pleasant lunch. Both were pleased with the results of the Yalta Conference, but they agreed that vigilance would be required and that the peace would be very challenging.

Churchill was accompanied by his son, Randolph, and daughter Sarah, Roosevelt by his daughter. Harry Hopkins and Ambassador John Winant were also present.

Roosevelt liked and admired Churchill as much as ever, but wearied of his Gibbonian rhetorical excesses, which he saw more and more as a cover for the threadbare condition of the British Empire. Roosevelt would have had even greater respect for Churchill if the prime minister had recognized that Britain's imperial position was unsustainable and had applied his genius to a new strategy to perpetuate his country's influence, based on Europe, the Commonwealth, and the special relationship with the United States.

Churchill conveyed to him the impression of trying to command the retirement of irresistible forces, instead of exploiting them. In an off-the-record briefing with the three wire service reporters accompanying him on the *Quincy*, February 23, he described Churchill in questions of empire as "mid-Victorian. . . . Dear old Winston will never learn on that point." He said his trusteeship proposals "might bust up their Empire."

As Stettinius recorded in his diaries, Roosevelt had the problem with Churchill that his "early fascination with him had declined, and there was an increasing divergence in their desires for the postwar world."[93]

For his part, Churchill may have resented the steady accretion of comparative and absolute American power, pro- and part American though he was. The rise of America, though it brought salvation, also brought the relative marginalization of Britain since the great days of 1940 and 1941, when Winston Churchill and his people held the key to the world's future.

Yet Roosevelt and Churchill knew each other well, were liberal patricians, saviors of their countries and of their shared civilization. They were united by reciprocal admiration and had scaled history's greatest heights. Their alliance was fading somewhat, but their friendship, like a good and durable marriage, though less exuberant than in years past, was profound and vital.

"The President seemed placid and frail. I felt that he had a slender contact with life. I was not to see him again. We bade affectionate farewells."[94] The *Quincy* weighed anchor and sailed for Algiers shortly after the prime minister and his party were piped over the side.

This was not the only affecting leave-taking on this voyage. On leaving Alexandria, Harry Hopkins was even more drained than Roosevelt, and could scarcely function. And General Edwin "Pa" Watson, a loyal, beloved, poker-playing crony of the President's, who had ignored doctors' advice and accompanied his chief to Yalta exclusively out of loyalty, took a stroke the day after leaving Alexandria and was in a coma when the *Quincy* arrived in Algiers. Roosevelt arranged for the *Quincy*'s Roman Catholic chaplain to receive Watson into the Catholic Church, because it was Roosevelt's understanding that this had been Watson's intention. His wife was a Roman Catholic and Watson had been considering converting for a long time. It was a thoughtful gesture by Roosevelt to his stricken friend.[95]

Hopkins was too sick to continue and left the ship at Algiers to go with Bohlen to Marrakesh, to recuperate before flying back to the United States. Roosevelt, with Watson at death's door and feeling none too well himself, felt that Hopkins was deserting him, and their farewells were perfunctory.[96] They, too, were not to meet again. Considering their magnificent association through many domestic and foreign crises, it was an unseemly ending, though neither would have known how close the end was. Two days out of Algiers Watson died. Rosenman, who boarded the _Quincy_ at Algiers to help Roosevelt with his congressional address on Yalta, wrote: "It was a sorry ship."[97]

The ship had initially been scheduled to stop at Algiers, to enable Roosevelt to meet de Gaulle. The general, already sensing discord among the British and Americans and the Russians, assumed his new status as an occupying power in Germany and cofounder of the world organization, and declined to be convoked by a visiting dignitary on French soil again. It may have reminded him of his humiliating summons to Casablanca, but this was a considerable provocation, given that there were now seventy American divisions in France completing the clearing of that country of invaders (and only eight French divisions). Churchill's doctor, Moran, whose diaries are almost as reliable a source of causticity as Brooke's or Stilwell's or Ickes' referred to de Gaulle's performance in declining to meet Roosevelt as an act of "debauchery" and even of "buffoonery."[98]

De Gaulle had had to endure some uncalled-for irritations from Roosevelt, but he fully repaid those slights with this very public snub. Roosevelt was now set on the course of rallying France all the way into the Western camp, and while he could have done without de Gaulle personally, he recognized the general's indispensability to a swift revival of France. Coexisting with his idealistic goals was Roosevelt's unswerving realism in political method. He told his grandson he had lost a political skirmish to de Gaulle and was quite philosophical. He made not even a private reference to de Gaulle's insult and told all who asked that his relations with the general were excellent.

Two days after the Yalta Conference had ended, on February 13, 1945, the Red Army captured Budapest amidst a terrible climax of massacres and destruction by both sides, and the RAF fire-bombed Dresden, razing most of the beautiful and militarily insignificant capital of Saxony to the ground. Scores of thousands of innocent people perished, including a great many helpless refugees of various nationalities fleeing the moving warfront. It was probably, morally, the most dubious of Churchill's initiatives, but the RAF was acting on Soviet intelligence claims that large troop trains were moving through Dresden delivering soldiers to fight the Russians. The Germans had invented the concept of total war in Europe; it was late for them to complain of its consequences, though that did not prevent Goebbels, in particular, from doing so.

Rosenman had hoped to disembark at Gibraltar, having worked up a text for the President, who had promised to address Congress as soon as he returned, but the President was clearly shaken by the death of Watson and the departure of Hopkins, so Rosenman remained on *Quincy*. Steve Early also left at Algiers, but that had been foreseen; but it might have contributed to Roosevelt's sense of loneliness. Rosenman was "disheartened" by the deterioration in Roosevelt's physical appearance in just the month that he had been away. "I had never seen him look so tired. He had lost a great deal more weight; he was listless and apparently uninterested in conversation—he was all burnt out."[99] Almost a week passed before Rosenman could get Roosevelt to focus on his speech.

Roosevelt remained in bed most of each morning, reading books or official reports. He usually lunched with Anna and Leahy and Rosenman, "and then he would go above to sit with his daughter on the top deck in the sun, quietly reading or just smoking and staring at the horizon. Sometimes Admiral Leahy and I went above to join him. Most frequently we left him alone with his book—and his thoughts."[100] He would take a nap when the sun started to set, have his usual cocktail hour, have dinner in his cabin, and then the presidential party would watch a film in Leahy's cabin.

Rosenman wrote a speech on the basis of what Leahy told him about Yalta and the documents Bohlen had shown him before leaving the ship and conducting Hopkins to Marrakesh. The speech was the subject of serious activity on the last day at sea.

Immediately on reaching Hampton Roads on February 27, the official party transferred to the President's train and went directly to Washington. The next day was General Watson's funeral at Arlington National Cemetery, and on March 1 the President addressed a special joint session of the Congress. It was his first physical appearance at the Capitol in two years. His remarks were broadcast throughout the world.

This too was a poignant occasion. For the first time, the President entered the Congress in his wheelchair, still the simple Hyde Park kitchen chair with no arms and small wheels and no cushion. His supporters and his adversaries could see his vulnerability and his courage. The supreme champion of American politics was not only human, he was a severely disadvantaged man as he led the nation from the depths of poverty and insularity to prosperity and victory.

Roosevelt apologized "for the unusual posture of sitting down during the presentation of what I want to say," and gave a fairly faithful recitation of the Yalta proceedings. He pressed his mopping-up attack on his isolationist foes. He said that the question of whether Yalta was a success "lies to a great extent in your hands. For unless you here in the halls of the American Congress . . . give [this agreement] your active support, the meeting will not have produced lasting results."

He responded to those who had questioned his health and stamina: "I am returning from this trip . . . refreshed and inspired. I was well the entire time. I was not ill for a second, until I arrived back in Washington, and there I heard all of the rumors which had occurred in my absence."

Roosevelt claimed that the Big Three had developed "a greater facility in negotiating with each other, that augurs well for the peace of the world." He vigorously defended his insistence on unconditional surrender: "It means the end of Nazism. It means the end of the Nazi Party—and of all its barbaric laws and institutions. . . . It means for the Nazi war criminals a punishment that is speedy and just—and severe." It was clear enough from the July 20, 1944, plot against Hitler that the plotters knew the unconditional surrender applied to the Nazis, not to respectable Germans who would depose the Nazis. Nazi decrees of drastic severity in the prosecution of the war had more to do with maintaining German resolve than with FDR's policy of requiring unconditional surrender.

Roosevelt recounted the terrible destruction wrought by the Germans in the Crimea, and made something of the fact that the Communists had turned the Czar's palace in which he had stayed into a worker's resort, and that the Nazis had seized it for one of their generals. He professed to be scandalized at this, but he must have realized that Eisenhower, MacArthur, and Patton did not bivouac in pup tents and cardboard and corrugated metal sheds either.

He took the unusual step of concealing the multiple Soviet voting right, and emphasized the difference of his approach from Woodrow Wilson's. "This time we are not making the mistake of waiting until the end of the war to set up the machinery of peace. . . . The Senate and House of Representatives will both be represented at the San Francisco Conference . . . [with] an equal number of Republican and Democratic members."

He laid great stress on the Declarations on Liberated Europe and Poland and the commitment to democracy, referring to Lublin as "practically in Russia," to minimize its character. He was unprecedentedly conciliatory to de Gaulle: "No one should detract from the recognition that was accorded [at Yalta] to [France's] role in the future of Europe and the future of the world."

Not wishing to ignore the Japanese, he referred to the invasion of Iwo Jima in overwhelming force on February 19.

He claimed to have learned more about the Jewish-Arab problem from five minutes with Ibn Saud "than I could have learned in the exchange of two or three dozen letters." Even Rosenman criticized this, but it was probably true, because Ibn Saud demonstrated the depths of Arab hostility to the Jews.[101]

His delivery had been uneven and discursive, with a good deal of recourse to ad lib reflections. Acheson, who was present, wrote: "It was an invalid's voice." (He had been an invalid for twenty-four years.) But Frances Perkins thought the President's delivery quite forceful. There is no dispute that Roosevelt gave his peroration in a clear and determined voice that recaptured some of his old authority. "There can be no middle ground here. We shall have to take the responsibility for world collaboration, or we shall have to bear the responsibility for another world conflict. . . .

"Twenty-five years ago, American fighting men looked to the statesmen of the world to finish the work of peace for which they fought and suffered. We failed them then. We cannot fail them again, and expect the world again to survive. I know I don't want to live to see another war." (His gaunt appearance left little room for concern on that point.)

"The Crimea Conference was a successful effort by the three leading Nations to find a common ground for peace. It ought to spell the end of the system of unilateral action, the exclusive alliances, the spheres of influence, the balances of power, and all the other expedients that have been tried for centuries—and have always failed."

He knew this to be nonsense as he said it. Six weeks before, he had told an influential bipartisan group of senators that spheres of influence were unfortunately very much alive and that the American sphere, though he declined to regard it as such, was immense. His method for ending the concept of a balance of power was that he knew and intended that the United States should replace it with an imbalance of power—that America would have such power in the world that no other combination of states could counterbalance it.

Roosevelt knew he had won the greatest victory of all. The United States would enter the world through his universal organization for peace. If the hopes he had just expressed were dashed, it would be because of Stalin's bad faith.

Either way, he was likely to win. America was engaged, and her power would ultimately be irresistible. And Franklin D. Roosevelt was chiefly responsible for both these facts. The isolationists were almost finished. Five years before, he had tarred them with the brush of Nazi sympathies. In this most uneven rematch, he held them potentially accountable in advance for a failed peace and all the tragedy of another war. America was supreme. After Britain bravely held the fort and with Russia taking most of the casualties, America had led the world to the brink of victory in a just war. It would do so again in pursuit of a just peace, as leader of a universal organization or as organizer of an insuperable alliance. If Stalin forced the latter course upon America, there would be many anxious moments, as there had been in pursuit of victory in World War II. A high level of statesmanship would be required, and generally would be provided, by most of Roosevelt's successors.

Applause was generous when the President concluded his address. As he was wheeled out of the chamber, columnist Joseph Alsop later wrote, "Many in the audience felt instinctively that they would never see him there again."[102] It was a startling thought, so great and so prolonged had been his political mastery of Washington. A jaunty and brave death's head in an elegant dark-blue suit, he was a handsome and compelling figure yet, as he was propelled away in his wheeled, spartan, kitchen chair.

His victory was made more complete by showing his supporters and opponents, for the first time on this last occasion, just how great were the obstacles he had had to overcome personally in leading the nation and the world so far. All might marvel at his physical fragility, his followers in heightened admiration and his detractors in accentuated frustration. None could doubt the proportions of his achievement, as a leader and as a man.

❧

CHAPTER 25

"His Voice Is Silent But His Courage Is Not Spent"

(President Harry S Truman proclaiming a national day of mourning for Franklin Delano Roosevelt, April 13, 1945)

I

IT DID NOT TAKE LONG for Stalin to demonstrate a greater interest in the ruthless imposition of Soviet Communist rule over occupied territory than in cooperation with his allies. The Russians dragged their feet over military agreements, retarded the formation of the German Control Commission, made a mockery of the Declaration on Liberated Europe in Romania initially and then elsewhere, and were profoundly uncooperative about Poland. In preliminary examinations by the U.S. Army Air Corps of possible bases near Budapest, the Russians took so long to authorize their use that the subject eventually became superfluous. They were even difficult over reciprocal treatment and return of prisoners of war with their Western allies.[1]

The Russian delegates expected in London to help prepare the Allied Control Commission for Germany did not arrive, to Ambassador Gousev's evident embarrassment.

In Romania, the Russians refused to call a meeting of the Allied Control Commission, and on February 27, 1945, Vyshinsky, whose presence anywhere was an unfavorable augury, arrived in Bucharest, forced the king to appoint a Communist government, and ignored American and British protests about violations of the Yalta agreement.

Molotov presented a list of non-Lublin Poles who would be accepted in the new government, which so far included only one of the names Roosevelt had suggested. Molotov rejected Mikolajczyk and made it clear that the Soviet definition of a reorganized Polish government was the addition of a few tokens to the Lublin Committee.

Churchill had addressed Parliament about Yalta two days before Roosevelt spoke to the Congress on the same subject. He said, on February 27: "Marshal Stalin and the Soviet leaders wish to live in honourable friendship and equality with the Western democracies. I feel also that their word is their bond. I know of no Government which stands to its obligations, even in its own despite, more solidly than the Russian Soviet Government. I decline absolutely to embark here on a discussion about Russian good faith. It is quite evident that these matters touch the whole future of the world."[2]

Churchill was reluctant to become too militant about Romania, because he was concerned that would cause Stalin to jettison his few obligations on the "naughty" piece of paper agreed in Moscow between them in November 1944 and increase support for anti-British groups in Greece.

Churchill was, however, prepared to become fairly robust about Poland, and warned Roosevelt that it could appear that they had signed "a fraudulent prospectus" on that subject. "I think you will agree with me that far more than the case of Poland is involved. I feel that this is the test case between us and the Russians of the meaning which is to be attached to such terms as Democracy, Sovereignty, Independence, Representative Government and free and unfettered elections."[3] This was March 8, 1945, nine days after the prime minister had assured Parliament that Stalin's word was his bond and that his government was one of the most honorable in the world.

Churchill followed with a lengthy message March 10 detailing the systematic Soviet oppression of Poland by the NKVD and other outrageous flouting of the Yalta Declaration on Poland.

Roosevelt replied March 11. "I am fully determined, as I know you are, not to let the good decisions we reached at the Crimea slip through our hands and will certainly do everything I can to hold Stalin to their honest fulfillment." He said Harriman was taking up Romania with Molotov: "It is obvious that the Russians have installed a minority government of their own choosing, but apart from the reasons you mentioned in your message, Romania is not a good place for a test case." Roosevelt was presumably referring to Churchill's gift of Romania to Stalin in November 1944. Roosevelt also cited the legitimate need of the Russians to have their military rear area clear, though he acknowledged that this excuse was being outrageously abused by the Russians.

Regarding Poland, he said, "I most certainly agree that we must stand firm on the right interpretation of the Crimean decision. You are quite correct in assuming that neither the Government nor the people of this country will support participation in a fraud or a mere whitewash of the Lublin Government and the solution must be as we envisaged it at Yalta." He recommended it be dealt with by both countries at the ambassadorial level before they dealt with Stalin themselves, "particularly since there is no question of either of our Governments yielding to Molotov's interpretation."

He followed the next day with a reply to Churchill's detailed cable of Soviet abuses in Poland on March 10. He wrote of an "urgent necessity of our taking every practicable means of accomplishing the corrective measures in Poland" agreed at Yalta. "When and if it should become necessary because of failure of the Ambassadors" (Harriman and Clark Kerr), appeal would be made to "Stalin for relief for the oppressed inhabitants of Poland."[4]

Churchill returned to the charge March 13 with another lengthy cable. He resorted to a technique from earlier in the war of claiming that in response to parliamentary questioning, he would have to reveal a difference in view between the British and U.S. governments, "and if we get out of step, the doom of Poland is sealed."[5] The danger was that he would have to admit "a great failure and an utter breakdown of what was settled at Yalta, but that we British have not the necessary strength to carry the matter further and that the limits of our capacity to act have been reached."

Roosevelt replied March 15 that he saw no divergence whatever, only a slight difference in tactics. He wanted the ambassadors to do what they could before he and Churchill addressed Stalin directly, and pointed out that Harriman had not yet made his representations, because Churchill had asked that his initiative be upheld pending an agreed approach at the head-of-government level. In this as in the whole flurry of messages back and forth on this subject from mid-March to mid-April, there is no absence of realism and determination on Roosevelt's part. Churchill responded March 16 "most relieved that you do not feel that there is any fundamental divergence between us and agree that our differences are only about tactics."[6] The two leaders confirmed full agreement on the ambassadorial message to Molotov in messages of March 18 and 19.

It was another of the post-Yalta myths that some serious difference of opinion developed between Churchill and Roosevelt over the conduct of the Russians in Eastern Europe. There is no documentary or serious anecdotal support for that view.

Contrary to Bruenn and McIntire's advice that he could survive a full fourth term if he cut his work load in half and avoided strains and tensions as much as possible (a ludicrous prescription for the holder of his office in such times), Roosevelt, after his five-week absence overseas, took up a hectic schedule. He worked full days, with a great many visitors, and the early monitoring of the Yalta agreements required a good deal of attention.

On March 9, at the end of his regular press conference, he enjoyed a little badinage in his passable French with a group of visiting French journalists. It was another part of his campaign of reconciliation with France. He poured cold water on the theory that there was the slightest problem between de Gaulle and himself, and denied that there was any problem over the non-meeting at Algiers; a contretemps of no significance, he called it. The redoubtable communist existentialist Jean-Paul Sartre, implausibly representing the conservative newspaper *Le Figaro*, was thoroughly captivated. Though he found Roosevelt's powerful jaw "alarming" in its potential belligerency, Roosevelt's prestige, power, and charm were such that Sartre excitedly wrote: "[The President] smiled at us and spoke to us in his deep slow voice. . . . What is most striking is the profoundly human charm of his long face, at once sensitive and strong." This encounter alone justified his entire trip around the United States, Sartre wrote.[7]

With the French reporters, Roosevelt conveniently transported a number of touring memories of his childhood and adolescence from Germany to France. He claimed that all suggestions of *froideur* between de Gaulle and himself were the invention of the press. "We are great friends," he said. (At his press conference on March 20, reporters noted that Roosevelt had to lock his elbow in his desk drawer to steady his hand sufficiently to light a cigarette.[8])

That evening the timeless Mackenzie King came to dinner with the Roosevelts. He was concerned by Roosevelt's appearance and repetition of two anecdotes told a few hours before. Eleanor and Anna were clearly worried about him.

"He looked very much older; face very much thinner, particularly the lower part. . . . When I went over and shook hands with him, I bent over and kissed him on the cheek. He turned it toward me for the purpose." But after a few hours King felt less concerned about him. "He is consolidating into a man of different size and shape, looking more like President Wilson; his front features thinner in the lower part of his face." (Mackenzie King was an authority on the occupants of the White House; he knew all nine from Theodore Roosevelt to Dwight D. Eisenhower.) King also felt that Roosevelt's right eye was clearer than his left, and that the President had "the tendency to credit himself with the initiation in many things." King ascribed this to the excessive power now exercised by Roosevelt, Churchill, and Stalin, but he was hardly exempt from the same charge himself, in his occult way and more modest sphere. In fact, Roosevelt had had this habit of exaggerating his role, taking undeserved credit, denying error, and self-serving invention since he was a boy. Only at the very height of his intellectual and political powers, when plausible exaggeration of his activities would have been a challenge and was scarcely necessary, did this habit abate at all. Now, as his life ebbed, this unattractive but more or less innocuous habit arose again.[9]

Roosevelt told King he was planning to go to Europe in June, to stay with the king and queen of Great Britain at Buckingham Palace, address Parliament, visit Churchill at Chequers, visit Queen Wilhelmina of the Netherlands and possibly de Gaulle in Paris, and to inspect victorious troops and recent battlefields. Churchill predicted to Rosenman that the British people would give him "the greatest reception ever accorded to any human being" since Napoleonic times.

"It will come genuinely and spontaneously from the hearts of the British people; they all love him for what he has done to save them from destruction," and give them a sense of security for their future.[10]

Lucy Rutherfurd was in Washington the week beginning March 12. The President picked her up and went for a drive in the Virginia countryside with her, in the familiar presidential limousine with the glass partition up between the driver and the rear of the car, and with a Secret Service car behind. It is astonishing that these excursions attracted no publicity and were never reported to Eleanor. The President's car, generally with its escort security car, ignoring stoplights and traffic regulations, was well known and did not move about unobtrusively. That evening, Lucy and Anna and her husband had a relaxed dinner with the President. It was the same group the following night, with the addition of the inevitable Mackenzie King. Roosevelt referred to Lucy as a "relative," and King found her "a very lovely woman and of great charm." The prime minister, a bachelor with an eccentric heterosexual romantic life, a fixation on his deceased mother, and a reliance on seers and obscurantist spiritualists, diarized that Lucy had "an exceptionally fine character." He evidently did not have the faintest idea of the history or intimacy of his host's relationship with her.

The following day, Lucy and Anna lunched with the President, and that night Roosevelt and Lucy dined alone. Eleanor returned on March 15, and two days later they celebrated their fortieth wedding anniversary with a luncheon and a small dinner. Anna and her husband attended both, along with, at lunch, the Morgenthaus and FDR's old law partner Harry Hooker, and at dinner, Dutch Princess Juliana, Assistant Secretary of State (and future vice president) Nelson A. Rockefeller, the Canadian minister (whose son was a fellow polio victim and who was a trustee of the Warm Springs Foundation) Leighton McCarthy, and Justice Robert Jackson, whose wife told him, on the way home: "We won't have Mr. Roosevelt with us very long."[11] Eleanor departed Washington March 19 and Lucy was back for a drive in the country with the President the same day, dinner with him and the social chameleons Anna and her husband that night, and tea in the President's study March 20.

There was some concern, articulated by Jonathan Daniels, son of the President's old chief, whom he had engaged on his staff, that Anna and her husband were trying to set up a sort of "regency." According to the historian Michael Beschloss, Anna had been concerned when James Dunn had secured the President's signature on a paper effectively revoking the Morgenthau plan. Her concern was based on her father's apparent unawareness of the contents of what he had signed. Anna was unfamiliar with her father's well-established technique of seeming to agree with everyone, no matter how kaleidoscopic the range of positions he seemed to be endorsing, until he was ready to act. Morgenthau's plan was a dead letter and there was no reason not to endorse Dunn's paper. Roosevelt signed a draft by Rockefeller of an invitation to Argentina to join the United

Nations. Rockefeller was unaware of the conditions established at Yalta for such membership. Bohlen and Breckinridge Long caught it, but the President's inattention was worrisome.[12]

According to Daniels, Anna was trying to restrict access to her father in a way that, he wrote, reminded him of Edith Bolling Wilson. This was exaggerated by Beschloss; Anna was only trying to shield her father from unnecessary visitors. Wilson had been completely incapacitated and could think straight for only a few minutes at a time, and even then was completely unreasonable. Filial concern does not make the President a vegetable or the daughter a Lady Macbeth, and undue credence should not be attached to alarmist opinions on this subject.[13]

The annual White House press corps dinner was March 21. The distinguished political journalist and novelist Allen Drury noted that Roosevelt seemed somewhat vague at times, had gape-mouthed moments during which he stared rather uncomprehendingly at the crowded ballroom, but most of the time was alert and animated. When his time to speak came at the end of the evening, he rose as always to the occasion. He had often given the humorous concluding address at these dinners before. This night, Danny Kaye, Jimmy Durante, and Fanny Brice provided the entertainment. Roosevelt mocked the platitudinous: "We all love humanity; you love humanity; I love humanity." In furtherance of humanity, "I will give you a headline story: 'I am calling off the press conference for tomorrow morning.' "[14] He transferred back to his wheelchair as the applause rose. And as he was wheeled out, Allen Drury wrote in his diary, "He acknowledged [the applause] with the old familiar gesture, so that the last we saw of Franklin Roosevelt was the head going up with a toss, the smile breaking out, the hand uplifted and waving in the old, familiar way."[15]

President and Mrs. Roosevelt departed for Hyde Park March 24. For the first time, Roosevelt was happy to have his wife drive him in his car around the estate while he sat beside her. Normally, he had insisted on taking the wheel and demonstrating his great skill, as he did when carving a turkey, or even signing his confident, flamboyant autograph, as a defiance of his infirmity. (His signature, too, had become cramped and hesitant, as of mid-1944, but this was allegedly because of a stiffness in his thumb.)

———————

Six weeks after the close of the Yalta Conference, it was clear that Stalin was in massive default of many of his obligations. On March 23, Roosevelt told Anna Rosenberg: "We can't do business with Stalin. He has broken every one of the promises he made at Yalta."[16] Robert Conquest duly remarked that this wasn't quite accurate, because Stalin would still find others to break.

There were no more fatuities about the effects on Stalin's character of his brief study of the priesthood. On March 29 Roosevelt told Anne O'Hare McCormick of the *New York Times* that either Stalin was dishonest or was no longer in control of the Soviet government. Churchill and Hopkins had both alluded to pressures and rivals that Stalin had to deal with, but Stalin's dictatorship had been stable through the tumultuous and sanguinary events of the thirties; it could certainly not be shaken now, after Russia's greatest military victory since the repulse of Napoleon.

Churchill wrote Roosevelt on March 27, recording that Molotov had flatly rejected every one of the points raised by ambassadors Harriman and Clark Kerr. The Russians were clinging to the absolute legitimacy of Lublin. Molotov wouldn't hear of observers in Poland, despite having finally offered access to them, and nothing was done to organize an election. "It is as plain as a pike staff that his tactics are to drag the business out while the Lublin Committee consolidate their power. . . . There seems to be only one possible alternative to confessing our total failure. That alternative is to stand by our interpretation of the Yalta declaration."[17]

It is not at all clear why Churchill thought a direct approach to Stalin might work; Stalin would not be more forthcoming than Molotov, since Molotov only held his job because of his slavish obedience to every capricious whim of Stalin's. Churchill asked what the prospects would be of success for the world organization. Would he not have to reveal to Parliament that "we shall be building the whole structure of future world peace on foundations of sand?"

Roosevelt sent Churchill an exchange he had had with Stalin March 24 and 27, in which he had asked Stalin to send Molotov to San Francisco and Stalin politely but firmly declined to do so because the Supreme Soviet had been convened "on request of the deputies" (as if they had the slightest influence on the calling of the so-called Soviet parliament—this must have been Stalin's parody of the constitutional obscurities Churchill and Roosevelt had tried to foist upon him).

Roosevelt further sent Churchill extensive cables March 29, agreeing with Churchill's concern. He was "watching with anxiety" the behavior of the Russians, "acutely aware of the dangers . . . [for] future world cooperation. . . . For our part (and I know for yours) we intend to shirk no responsibility which we have assumed under [the Yalta] decisions." He agreed it was time to speak frankly to Stalin. He enclosed a proposed letter to Stalin that was clear but polite. Churchill proposed a few points of elaboration in what he described as Roosevelt's "grave and weighty document." Roosevelt accepted these and sent the message. Churchill sent Roosevelt his own, forceful message to Stalin before dispatching it. Roosevelt agreed with it, and Churchill replied April 1: "I am delighted with our being in such perfect step. I have bunged off [mine] to the Bear." "The Bear" was preferable to the quasi-affectionate "Uncle Joe," which was now phased out. Churchill gave the impression of being almost as relieved to be in full agreement with Roosevelt as he was disconcerted by Stalin's defection from his obligations. Roosevelt responded to Churchill in a very conciliatory message on April 4.

Roosevelt was playing for time. He didn't want the founding euphoria of the world organization to deteriorate before his country had formally committed to it and the Senate had ratified. This was the swiftest way to involve America in the world so that a betrayal by Stalin would raise the wrathful determination of the American public to protect those who would otherwise be vulnerable to the gluttony of the Bear. Of course, he was also hoping for atomic developments that would implicitly strengthen his hand in any showdown with Stalin.

He was already encountering reluctance in the scientific community, from Albert Einstein, Robert Oppenheimer, Leo Szilard, and Niels Bohr, to any exclusive national or binational (with Britain) use of atomic energy, beyond winning the war.* He dealt with it in his usual manner of noncommittally conveying to the scientists the impression of agreement, at least philosophically. None of them had had any experience of negotiating with so subtle and elusive a person as Roosevelt, and all seemed pleased. Some, in their naïveté, may have imagined that they had some proprietary rights over nuclear fission, although they were all effectively employees of, or had done contract work for, the U.S. government.

Stalin would by now have detected that the United States would never go back into isolation, and that there would be no general dismemberment of Germany nor any heavy reparations. Germany would thus remain a powerful country in the hands of the Western Allies. Stalin might now have foreseen that the Americans and British, de Gaulle and Pius XII would among them defeat the Communists in Italy and France, the Russophobia of the Turks would be mobilized, Churchill would deliver Greece, and Spain could be added to an American-led and infinitely more powerful revival of the Anti-Comintern Pact (founded by Japan and Germany). He could have avoided most of it by adhering to the Yalta agreements, or at least appearing to until the Americans had largely departed Europe. Instead, he launched Russia into a competition that it could not win and that Communism could not survive.

As part of the move to coordinate more closely between the Western and Eastern Front high commands, Eisenhower had been authorized at Yalta to communicate directly with the Soviet high command. Eisenhower did so on March 28, indicating a drive toward Leipzig and the foreclosure of any German retreat toward a "Bavarian redoubt" (that Hitler and some of his spokesmen had been loudly envisioning). This, to the irritation of the British, left Berlin to the Russians, despite Roosevelt's longstanding view that that city should be taken by the Western Allies, which had been superseded by the September 12, 1944, demarcation of German occupation zones.

This was Eisenhower's point, that since the occupation zones had been estab-

---

* Einstein sent him a letter supporting, and asking him to see, Szilard, on March 25. Roosevelt delegated the meeting to Byrnes.[18]

lished already, he did not see the utility of losing the lives of American, British, Canadian, and French soldiers for territory that would be handed back to the Russians under the EAC occupation zones agreement. Stalin replied to Eisenhower, via the American military mission in Moscow, implying that he had no great interest in Berlin either, while in fact launching a mighty offensive to take the city.[19]

Churchill objected to letting pass the opportunity to advance as far eastwards as possible, and though he did not specifically urge Roosevelt to refuse to return the territory that would thus be occupied from the Russian zone by the Western powers, that was obviously his idea, and he did urge this course on Truman a few weeks later. Any such step at this point would have put the more positive interpretation of the world organization over the side and would have caused Roosevelt and his successor some difficulty with the isolationists, who were otherwise now on the ropes.

In his memoirs, Eisenhower rather over-virtuously remarked: "The Prime Minister knew, of course, that regardless of the distance the Allies might advance to the eastward, he and the President had already agreed that the British and American occupation zones would be limited on the east by a line two hundred miles west of Berlin. Consequently, his great insistence on using all our resources in the hope of assuring the arrival of the Western Allies in Berlin ahead of the Russians must have been based on the conviction that great prestige and influence for the Western Allies would later derive from this achievement." General Bradley's view was that taking Berlin would lead to 100,000 Western casualties, a "pretty stiff price" for temporary "prestige."[20] Bradley was certainly exaggerating. It cost the Russians many more casualties than that, but resistance in the west would have been less determined.

Eisenhower himself, to use his own parlance, "knew, of course," that what Churchill had in mind was not taking Berlin or any other territory and returning it to the Russians, but keeping it from them. (All the American leaders showed great forbearance in not reminding Churchill and the British that they had joined the Russians in imposing these occupation zones that they now wished to ignore.) Eisenhower was right to avoid political questions and confine himself to military ones, but not, in his memoirs, unctuously to claim that this continued to be a purely military question.[21]

On receiving a copy of Eisenhower's letter to Stalin, Churchill erupted and bombarded Marshall and Roosevelt with demands to move to the east as quickly as possible. Eisenhower responded on March 30 that he was "completely in the dark as to what the protests" of the British are about, and that he was "merely following the principle that Field Marshal Brooke has always shouted to me . . . to concentrate on one major thrust."[22] It was on receiving Eisenhower's message that Stalin launched his final offensive against Berlin.

Marshall was close to the mark when he told his semiofficial biographer: "We had a Republican Party that had been out of power for a long time. They had built up a great deal of feeling towards Mr. Roosevelt and there was some Democratic assistance to it, I believe." Yalta, he said, had "become so much a political . . . discussion." He was critical of Leahy and King for claiming to have advocated a more robust policy to Russia than they actually did.[23]

Churchill would tell Truman in a cable of April 18, 1945, that this was "part of broad strategy and could not be left out of war plans . . ." As for the occupation zones, Churchill expressed his willingness to adhere to them, but pointed out that this matter would come up only after V-E Day (the term for Allied victory in Europe was already in use) and that there would be problems to discuss with the Russians. According to Truman, Churchill added (a bit late in the circumstances) that the "occupation zones had been decided in some haste . . . at a time when no one could foresee our great advances in Germany."

Roosevelt had some idea of them, yet he has borne the blame for insufficient optimism over the attainable limits of the eastward advance of Eisenhower's armies. Because he died abruptly, he didn't have the ability Churchill, Truman, and Eisenhower enjoyed to the full, of writing self-exonerating memoirs. Marshall, as the only one of them never to seek elective office, was more objective in his recollections.

Truman wrote ten years later: "I could see no valid reason for questioning an agreement on which we were so clearly committed, nor could I see any useful purpose in interfering with successful military operations." He also quoted Eisenhower, by this time a domestic political opponent, that if the Russians "should serve notice that they intend to push directly ahead to the limits of their occupational zone, the American forces are going to be badly embarrassed."

This was an unbecomingly defeatist attitude for the Supreme Allied Commander in Western Europe. The Soviet Union had nearly three times as many divisions as Eisenhower, but if the German prisoners of war in the west who were untainted politically had been remobilized and given their surrendered weapons back, as Stalin would have feared, and if the reequipment of the French Army had been accelerated and both forces added to Eisenhower's command, and all supplies from the United States to Russia had been cut off, the balance of power would have shifted decisively against Russia within a couple of months.

This would have revived the isolationists to some extent, and raised huge risks, but Eisenhower had no business straying into political interpretations, having meticulously avoided them up to then.

Eisenhower's concern about blundering accidentally into war with Russia was understandable but exaggerated. He wrote on April 5 to the Combined and British Chiefs of Staff, "We have already had minor incidents due to air contact, which have been magnified and have resulted in recriminations." He thought it of the "utmost importance" to "safeguard us against more serious incidents in the future."[24]

One event that has never been explained, other than by the fear of inadvertent conflict with the Soviet union, was Eisenhower's failure to follow up on Patton's early penetration of Czechoslovakia. At the least, he could have taken the Czech part of the country, leaving Slovakia to the Russians. Czechoslovakia was not governed by any EAC agreements, nor by the Churchill-Stalin accord of October 1944.

Eisenhower was plausibly concerned that the Russians might get to the Danish peninsula ahead of the Americans and precede the Western Allies into Scandinavia.[25] Harry Hopkins later put it about that General William H. Simpson, who would have spearheaded a drive for Berlin from the west, had outrun his communications, but this was a complete fiction and Hopkins knew nothing about military matters.

A guileless and forthright man from Missouri, Truman could scarcely have been more different from his predecessor, or his interlocutors, Churchill and Stalin.[26] Truman was far less mischievous in his treatment of the Yalta myth than Churchill, and about on a level with Eisenhower. He never acknowledged that he could have taken more territory, hung on to it until the atomic tests, and then dealt from greater strength with Stalin.

It was not an adequate response to refer these questions to Marshall, who deferred to Eisenhower, who did not see it as his role to contemplate violating the agreed occupation zones, a strategic judgment well beyond his remit. This was a political and not a military decision, and Truman and Marshall should not have referred it to Eisenhower at all. The new president's position was complicated by the fact that Churchill had no plan except asking the Americans to take what they could and be militant with the Russians, since Britain, he acknowledged, did not have the power to do so itself.

Eisenhower's fuzziness on these strategic questions is illustrated by a conversation he had with Patton at dinner on April 12, 1945. Eisenhower said: "From a tactical point of view it is highly inadvisable to take Berlin and I hope political influence won't cause me to take the city. It has no tactical or strategic value and would place upon American forces the burden of caring for thousands and thousands of Germans, displaced persons and Allied prisoners of war."[27] Patton remonstrated with him forcefully. It was a few minutes after this exchange that the generals learned of Roosevelt's death.

If Eisenhower had known of the Russian default on Yalta promises and the possible revocation of the occupation zones by the West, or even of the possible imminent existence of atomic weapons, he might have thought differently. Truman and Marshall passed the decision to Eisenhower without giving him the background to enable him to make an informed decision.

Even without following Churchill's importunings to move on Berlin, the Western Allies seized a good deal of territory that had been designated for Soviet occupation, and did not relinquish it until June 11, 1945, more than a month after the German surrender. The British and Americans were still at that time trying to bring the Soviet Union into the war against Japan, and the atomic bomb would not be tested for another five weeks. For these reasons, Truman declined Churchill's urgings that these lands be retained as a deliberate bargaining counter beyond June 11.

Truman should have retained them. That this was not done was not Roosevelt's responsibility. Yet Truman is not greatly to be faulted; he was new to the position, with no background in these matters, and was receiving conflicting advice from different and distinguished sources. He learned quickly.

It became convenient for the British High Tories, the U.S. Republican right, and the Gaullist upholders of the unreliability of the Anglo-Saxons as defenders of Europe all to blame the Soviet presence in central Europe on Roosevelt. De Gaulle further joined in the partial laundering of Churchill's role, as part of his intermittent overture to Britain to ally itself with Europe (led by France), rather than America. If Churchill could be reclaimed for Europe and not abandoned as an icon of Anglo-Americanism, he could unwittingly serve de Gaulle's cause. Thus, the Gaullist, Euro-anti-American version of events was that Churchill the semi-European tried and failed to reason with the indifferent, inept Americans.

The Yalta myth, made more believable by Roosevelt's evidently declining health and early death and the supposedly Mephistophelean presence of Alger Hiss at the Conference, miraculously arose to serve Roosevelt's detractors.

Too much is made by some historians of the fact that many of the messages from Roosevelt to Churchill at this stage were written by Leahy and Bohlen. All were approved by the President with or without modification. The more important ones were composed by him personally. No message would have been sent in Roosevelt's name to Churchill or Stalin without Roosevelt's seeing it. The distinction of exact authorship is immaterial.

II

ROOSEVELT RETURNED BRIEFLY to Washington from Hyde Park and then departed for Warm Springs on a restorative trip, arriving March 30. His security chief, Mike Reilly, usually found it easy to transfer him to another chair—for example from his train to a car—as Roosevelt propelled himself with his powerful arms and chest muscles. On this occasion, on arriving at Warm Springs he was "dead weight" and Reilly had to move his entire 160 pounds (down from 185 pounds and very little of it accounted for by his legs). His head lolled and onlookers were momentarily concerned.[28] Only once before, when he returned from Teheran, had Reilly found him so listless. Once in his car, however, he happily took the wheel himself and drove from the little railway station to the "Winter White House." He told Daisy Suckley his ambition was to "sleep and sleep and sleep."[29] His assistant, William Hassett, said to Dr. Bruenn on March 30: "He is slipping away from us, and no earthly power can keep him here." (Bruenn told Miss Suckley: "Like all people who work with this man, I love him.")[30]

On April 1, 1945, the second greatest amphibious operation of the Second World War, the American invasion of Okinawa, in the Ryukyus, only 350 miles from Japan, began. (Though Sicily involved more landing craft, it engaged fewer naval and air forces than Normandy and Okinawa. The opening bombardment included the full fire of an unprecedented seventeen American battleships.) It was a fierce action, lasting almost three months and costing 49,000 American casualties (12,500 dead) and about 117,000 Japanese casualties, including 110,000 dead, because of the Japanese determination to fight to the end. The Japanese also lost nearly 8,000 aircraft, many of them second-rate machines piloted by suicide-aspirants.

The British didn't understand the costliness of assaulting Japan, and the importance of bringing in the Russians, because they had had little contact with the self-destrucive ferocity the Japanese displayed as their homeland was approached.

By this time, Nimitz's U.S. Pacific Fleet, including those units under MacArthur's control, had achieved gigantic proportions: over 20 battleships, about 25 fleet carriers and as many as 70 escort carriers, 50 cruisers, and many hundreds of destroyers, frigates, smaller craft and maintenance vessels. The fleet carried over 4,000 aircraft and sometimes took over 400,000 sailors to sea at one time in the great operations in the last phases of the Pacific war.

During this same week, complex relations with the Soviet Union were muddied further by an overture from a German officer on Kesselring's staff in the German army in Italy who inquired whether a surrender there could be brokered for more favorable treatment for the units involved. When Stalin heard something of this, his paranoia fused with his tactical cunning and he purported to have uncovered a shameful act of backstabbing by the British and Americans.

Roosevelt and Stalin had an extensive exchange April 3 and 4 about the talks that took place in Berne, Switzerland, led by SS General Karl Wolff and U.S. intelligence director Allen Dulles. Roosevelt did not answer Stalin's question of why no Soviet representative was invited to join the Allied side in the conversations, other than to imply that had the discussions proceeded, the Soviets would have been brought into the talks. Wolff could not deliver any significant part of the German Army, and the conversations did not get very far. It was left with Wolff invited to contact Field Marshal Alexander if he had any serious proposals to make.*

Curiosity on Stalin's part is understandable, especially since Churchill would have liked to do exactly what Stalin accused his allies of planning: rush through the passes into Austria and Hungary, filling a vacuum. But Stalin's allegation of Western collusion in strengthening German resistance against the Russians was unfounded. Stalin imputed to others motives that would have governed his own actions were he in their place.

---

* Roosevelt was initially made aware of the overture by a memo from the acting secretary of state, Joseph Grew, on March 10, enclosing an intelligence report that represented it as a far-fetched initiative.[31]

Roosevelt concluded his April 4 letter to Stalin (which he undoubtedly composed himself): "It would be one of the great tragedies of history if at the very moment of the victory, now within our grasp, such mistrust, such lack of faith [as Stalin had just shown], should prejudice the entire undertaking after the colossal losses of life, materiel, and treasure involved. Frankly, I cannot avoid a feeling of bitter resentment toward your informers, whoever they are, for such vile misrepresentations of my actions or those of my trusted subordinates."[32] He effectively accused Stalin of having been duped by the German propaganda apparatus, which was now desperately seeking to promote conflict between the Russians and the Western Allies.

Churchill was back to Roosevelt April 5, urging an ever harder line verbally, since he had no practical suggestions for raising the ante with Stalin other than to redirect forces toward Berlin. He was concerned—unnecessarily, as it turned out—that Stalin would deny the Western Allies access to their zones of occupation in Austria.

Churchill sent a message of his own to Stalin pointing out that the British ambassador in Moscow had given Molotov reasonably timely disclosure of what was afoot in Berne and joining himself to Roosevelt's retort "to the charges which are made in your message to the President of April 3rd, which also asperse His Majesty's Government."

The issue died, but Roosevelt sent a further update of his views to Churchill April 6: "I am pleased with your very clear, strong, message to Stalin. We must not permit anybody to entertain a false impression that we are afraid. Our Armies will in a very few days be in a position that will permit us to become 'tougher' than has heretofore appeared advantageous to the war effort."

It is impossible to be confident of exactly what Roosevelt had in mind, but he was certainly well aware that Stalin was in default of his undertakings, and it was not in his nature passively to allow people to get the better of him and to trample brave and unfortunate victims underfoot as they did so, especially when he was in possession of such immense power of all kinds.

He had been steadfast in his support of Marshall and Eisenhower, but, as Kimball mentions,[33] this was the first evidence that he was preparing to put postwar geopolitics ahead of strictly military considerations in his direct dealing with Stalin. He was a poker player of some panache, and he might well have been veering toward the Churchill view that the Western Allies should take as much as they could and take their time handing over territory to the Soviet Union for its occupation zone in Germany, until there was specific performance from the Russians on the Declarations on Liberated Europe and on Poland.

This would have been entirely consistent with Roosevelt's policy in assembling a bargaining position in Western and central Europe before seeking a final resolution of outstanding matters with Stalin. He would try to avoid a public break with Stalin until after the world organization and its umbrella of commitments to benign goals had been set up, and America had subscribed to its formal debut as a postisolationist country. He would try to defer the thorniest matters to the next summit conference, in July 1945, when the atomic bomb would have been tested. As has been recounted, his last words to Stalin at Yalta were: "We will meet again soon in Berlin."[34] But Roosevelt would not throw in a winning hand in the face of gross provocation, and Stalin's behavior was now close to that.

Roosevelt followed up in the same vein April 8, writing Churchill that in view of developments, he did not choose to send an economic mission to Russia to discuss economic assistance. He didn't think a bilateral commission would be appropriate either (i.e., aid to Britain but not Russia), because he did not wish the United States to be the party that was vacating the Yalta agreements: "We must be careful not to do anything that would weaken the effectiveness of our efforts to get the Russians to honor those decisions on their side." In this concern, he was following the lead of Woodrow Wilson in 1917, who wanted to go to war "with clean hands." Roosevelt knew that if what became the Cold War began, there would be no shortage of people claiming the West instigated it, if great care were not taken to put the onus entirely on Stalin.

On April 10 Roosevelt wrote Churchill: "We shall have to consider most carefully the implications of Stalin's attitude and what is to be our next step. I shall, of course, take no action of any kind, nor make any statement without consulting you, and I know you will do the same."[35] (Margaret Suckley records that Roosevelt himself dictated the response to Churchill on this day.[36] He had told her that he did not have faith in Stalin but thought there was a possibility of working out a "practical" arrangement with him.)[37]

This traffic between the British and American leaders about relations with Stalin reached a supreme climax on April 11, when Churchill sent Roosevelt six cables and Roosevelt responded with three. Churchill enclosed Stalin's message to him partially retracting the Berne allegations: "Neither I nor Molotov had any intention of 'blackening' anyone. . . . If, however, you are going to regard every frank statement of mine as offensive, it will make this kind of communication very difficult. I can assure you that I had and have no intention of offending anyone." Churchill commented to Roosevelt: "I have a feeling that this is about the best we are going to get out of them, and certainly it is as near as they can get to an apology." Stalin did accuse his allies of contemplating treachery and desertion. Not even he could have imagined that such allegations were inoffensive, particularly to men who had gone to such lengths to win his goodwill.

Stalin had also written Churchill that if Mikolajczyk was prepared to accept the Yalta settlement, "I should be ready to use my influence with the Provisional Polish Government to make them withdraw their objections to inviting" him for consultations on the composition of the new Polish government. Churchill overoptimistically wrote Roosevelt that this statement, "if seriously intended, would be important." It was neither, as soon became obvious.

Roosevelt replied: "I would minimize the general Soviet problem as much as possible because these problems, in one form or another, seem to arise every day and most of them straighten out as in the case of the Berne meeting. We must be firm, however, and our course thus far is correct."

This was Roosevelt's last known word on the subject, and reflected his confidence that a strong line against Stalin's treating his Yalta commitments with complete contempt would prevent an early public breach with the Soviet Union. Three more months would be needed to test atomic weapons and get the United Nations launched. If atomic weapons did not work, three to six months would be needed to subdue Japan, even with full Soviet assistance.

It will always remain a moot point how Roosevelt and Stalin would have reacted to each other had Roosevelt survived his last term as president.

Churchill contributed appreciably to the Yalta myth by writing in his memoirs and stating elsewhere that Roosevelt's declining health was responsible for the descent of what he later called the Iron Curtain across the middle of Europe. "We can now see the deadly hiatus which existed between the fading of President Roosevelt's strength and the growth of President Truman's grip of the vast world problem. In this melancholy void, one President could not act and the other could not know."

Churchill knew generally why Roosevelt wanted the world organization launched and atomic weapons tested before any showdown with Stalin. He also knew that Roosevelt was prepared to demand a reasonable level of apparent compliance from Stalin even before these milestones were reached, and that until they were, the correlation of forces, as Eisenhower remarked, were disadvantageous for the sort of confrontation Churchill was urging the United States to enter into with Stalin. It has never been explained exactly why Churchill thought this was the best time to have a showdown with Stalin. Nor did he state what role, after all his pleas, at Teheran and subsequently, of British military limitations, he intended to play in such a contest himself. After Strang's performance on the EAC, which could not have been unauthorized, though Churchill, Eden, and Cadogan admit to no hand in it, there is an unseemly element of posturing, as well as historical injustice in the officially propagated and widely received British version of these events.

Churchill himself was never called properly to account for handing Stalin Romania, Bulgaria, and Hungary on the "naughty" piece of paper, and accepting with unbecoming callousness the Nazi-Soviet cooperation in the German suppression of the Warsaw uprising, though he gave Stalin nothing he would not have taken anyway, and possibly saved Greece from the Communists. (More accurately, he deferred a Communist takeover until Truman could durably save Greece from the Communists.)

On April 13, Stettinius gave Truman a summary of relations with all the principal countries. These faithfully represented the final policy positions of the Roosevelt administration. While Churchill "fully shares" the American interpretation of Yalta, "he is inclined to press this position with the Russians with what we consider unnecessary rigidity as to detail."

With France, "the best interests of the United States require every effort . . . to assist France, morally as well as physically, to regain her strength and influence." The French government and people, because of the shambles in 1940, "are at present unduly preoccupied . . . with questions of national prestige." It was U.S. policy to "treat France . . . on the basis of her potential (rather than present) power and influence. . . . De Gaulle has recently stated his appreciation of the necessity for the closest possible cooperation between France and the United States."

As for the Soviet Union, "Since the Yalta Conference the Soviet Government has taken a firm and uncompromising position on nearly every major question," which he enumerated, especially Poland and Liberated areas. "They have asked for a large postwar credit," which Roosevelt had withheld.

Poland: "Highly unsatisfactory with the Soviet authorities consistently sabotaging . . . implementation" of Yalta agreements. (Interestingly, Stettinius thought this a domestic as well as an international problem.)

The Russians were in complete default of their obligations for collective governance in Hungary, Romania, and Bulgaria.

There was no agreement, though discussions were continuing, "on the treatment of Germany during the period of military government."

In Italy, the United States was having difficulty with both the Russians and the British, who wanted to retain that country in its "anomaly of . . . a dual status as active cobelligerent and as defeated enemy." The United States rightly wanted Italy admitted to the United Nations at once. Britain's reticence was understandable at a human level, since Britain and France had been the victims, as Roosevelt memorably declared, of Mussolini's stab in the back, but the British position was politically impractical.[38]

The magic of Warm Springs seemed to work on Roosevelt in April 1945 as it often had before. After a few days he was no longer gray and torpid; his color and his appetite returned and he gained some weight and animation, although his blood pressure continued to fluctuate. He was stronger in the mornings and evenings, often wearying in the afternoon. In the mornings he worked on his correspondence and other papers at a table in front of his fireplace; after lunch he would deal with dictation with Grace Tully or Dorothy Brady on the terrace of his little antebellum-style home. Most afternoons, he would sleep for about an hour and then drive in the surrounding country with Laura Delano and Margaret Suckley, and with Lucy Mercer Rutherfurd, when she arrived at Warm Springs at Anna's invitation on her father's behalf on April 9. "The days flowed peacefully by," said Daisy Suckley, years later.

She wrote in her diary on April 6 that FDR thought he could "retire by next year" after a year of the new international organization, with the United States launched in the world. "I don't believe he thinks he will be able to carry on. . . . If he cannot physically carry on, he will have to resign." If he wasn't "filling his job, far better, to hand it over," she wrote, and enjoy a few happy retirement years.[39]

Walter Lippmann, the nation's premier political columnist, had known Roosevelt for more than thirty years. He found the appearance and rumors of the President's deteriorating health alarming, and decided to write a tribute to him while Roosevelt could still read it. He did read it, appreciatively, when it was published on April 7, 1945. "His estimate of the vital interests of the United States has been accurate and far-sighted," Lippmann wrote. "He has served these interests with audacity and patience, shrewdly and with calculation, and he has led this country out of the greatest peril in which it has ever been to the highest point of security, influence, and respect which it has ever attained."[40]

On April 9, Roosevelt and Daisy set out in the President's car, with a security escort, to meet Lucy's car, "on and on, away from the sun, scanning every car that headed toward us, imagining it was slowing up," Daisy wrote.[41] (This was an astonishing foray for the world's most important statesman at this stage of the war and his career. It is hard to imagine Churchill or de Gaulle, much less Stalin or Hitler, embarking on such a mission. It was more like an initiative of a love-sick teenager.) Lucy was travelling with the portrait painter Elizabeth Shoumatoff. Their encounter occurred eighty-five miles from Warm Springs, at Manchester, Georgia, where the President stopped for a Coca-Cola. The arriving ladies transferred to the presidential car.[42]

On April 11, 1945, after his vigorous exchange of cables with Churchill, Roosevelt had dictated changes to Robert Sherwood's draft of a Jefferson Day address. It was an impassioned plea for peace, ending: "The only limit to our realization of tomorrow will be our doubts of today. Let us move forward with strong and active faith." The speech was to be given a few days later.

Then he went for a drive with his three accompanying ladies to his favorite picnic spot and scenic lookout in the area, Dowdell's Knob, which he had visited the previous day with Lucy and Fala alone. This, wrote Daisy, had been "the best thing he could do. They sat in the sun talking, for over an hour, and he came back with a good tan."[43]

He would have remembered on these visits that this was always the place to which he had brought demoralized polio sufferers from his sanitarium in the twenties to be encouraged by the beautiful panorama. He had come here himself countless times over the past twenty years to consider the steep trajectory of his own career. In these inspiriting surroundings and in this convivial company, perhaps he took a moment to reflect on how he had changed his country and the world since his first visit here. According to his companions, he did again find the venue, with its memories and prospects, serene and revivifying.

That evening, Henry Morgenthau came to dinner, still pressing his fantasy of the pastoralization of Germany. Morgenthau claimed Roosevelt said he was "with you 100 percent." With Roosevelt, that meant about as much as a claim of friendship, as Morgenthau had learned long before. The Treasury secretary recorded that Roosevelt's hands shook so severely he almost knocked over the cocktail glasses while pouring drinks. The President was constantly "confusing names," and Morgenthau was "in agony watching him" move from his wheel-chair to his chair at the dinner table.

The secretary assailed the State Department officials who wanted to recon-struct Germany, with particular reference to Eleanor's bugbear, Assistant Secre-tary James Dunn. Roosevelt defended Dunn, apparently not miffed by Dunn's promotion of his own paper for the reconstruction of Germany.[44]

Morgenthau left after dinner, with FDR and the ladies "sitting around laugh-ing and chatting, and I must say the President seemed to be happy and enjoying himself."[45]

Given how friendly Morgenthau and his wife were with Eleanor, it was incau-tious to have him to dinner with Lucy. Roosevelt must have been almost ready to unveil this surprise for his wife, having resented her absolute prohibition of con-tact, as she thought, for twenty-seven years. Anna recalled that at Yalta there had been no letters from her mother and that her father's only comments on Eleanor had been when he "griped about her attitudes towards things he's done and peo-ple he likes."[46]

Bruenn had recorded in late March that the President's blood pressure had jumped fifty points in a forty-five-minute conversation with Eleanor. He remained polite, repeating at intervals: "I'm sorry, Eleanor, but I can't do it." (She was asking for increased assistance to the Yugoslav Partisans.) "The veins stood out on his forehead."[47] But however difficult Eleanor might continue to be for him, time had shifted the balance to Franklin, and there was not much that Eleanor could do if he chose to frequent Lucy. With his mother dead and no thought of facing the voters again, Roosevelt had relative freedom of action at last in his romantic relationships. Daisy Suckley certainly recorded Lucy's presence at Warm Springs as if there were nothing controversial about it.

The following day, he was working on papers in the late morning, while Lucy's friend Elizabeth Shoumatoff* painted his portrait. As a Russian, she won-dered if Roosevelt had liked Stalin. He said that he had but thought Stalin had poisoned his wife.[50] Ms. Shoumatoff complimented him on his improved color. (This proved to be a symptom of an impending arterial crisis.) He was wearing an elegant, double-breasted grey suit and a crimson tie. Lucy, Laura, and Daisy were all with the President in the drawing room of his little house. Daisy was crocheting. Laura was arranging flowers, and left the room briefly. Lucy was admiring the artist's subject, as she had, from near and far, for more than thirty

---

* Ms. Shoumatoff wrote of Mrs. Rutherfurd: "Lucy was very feminine, she had no extraordi-nary intellect, but she possessed the most idealistic, almost naïve, mind, with a really unselfish, understanding heart."[48] Daisy wrote, possibly with a slight tinge of jealousy: "Lucy is such a lovely person, but she seems so very immature—like a character out of a book."[49] The contrast with Eleanor was profound.

years. Bill Hassett came and went with papers to sign and read, and found Mrs. Shoumatoff's presence annoying. "Here's where I make a law," said the President with a flourish as he signed an act of Congress.*

The houseboy was laying the table for lunch. The President looked at his watch at 1 P.M. and said the portrait session would have to end in fifteen minutes. Almost at the end of that time, "F[ranklin] seemed to be looking for something, his head forward, his hands fumbling." Daisy approached until her face was only a foot from the President's and asked if had dropped his cigarette. He put his left hand up to the back of his head, and said, "distinctly, but so low that I don't think anyone else heard it: 'I have a terrific pain in the back of my head.' "[51] Daisy advised him to put his head back.

"Lucy, something has happened!" said Mrs. Shoumatoff.[52] Lucy and Laura, who had returned to the room, tilted the President's chair back while Daisy telephoned for Dr. Bruenn. The butler and the President's valet, Arthur Prettyman, with the help of the women, carried him to his bed in the next room. As they did so, he was understood by Laura Delano to say, only semiconsciously: "Be careful." These were his last words.

Daisy held the President's right hand. Laura fanned him and monitored his heart. Lucy put camphor under his nostrils. "Two or three times he rolled his head from side to side, opened his eyes," wrote Daisy, but "I could see no sign of recognition in those eyes."[53] He lapsed into complete unconsciousness.† Grace Tully arrived and prayed silently. Elizabeth Shoumatoff folded up her paints, and she and Lucy hurriedly packed and left for Aiken, South Carolina, in less than an hour.

Bruenn arrived, shooed out the women, and helped the butler and the valet get the President into his pajamas. He gave some injections, but knew at once that his patient had suffered a cerebral hemorrhage and must have sustained serious brain damage. The President's breathing was loud and became labored. Bill Hassett entered the bedroom and later remembered that the President's eyes were closed and mouth open, "the awful breathing. . . . But the Greek nose and the noble forehead were as grand as ever. I knew I should not see him again."[54]

His breathing stopped abruptly at 3:35 P.M., April 12, 1945, as Dr. James Paullin, an Atlanta specialist who had been one of the group of doctors who examined him at Bethesda in March 1944, arrived at the Little White House. Bruenn was speaking by telephone to McIntire in Washington and asked him to hold the line as he and Paullin rushed to the bedside. Even an injection of adrenalin directly into the heart was unavailing. Franklin Delano Roosevelt died in his

---

* A few days before, FDR had signed his acceptance of James Byrnes's resignation as head of the Office of War Mobilization. The trip to Yalta had not placated Byrnes; his peevishness at not being invited to the opening dinner had irritated the President. Byrnes was replaced by the future Chief Justice Fred M. Vinson.
† The book at the President's bedside, eerily perhaps, was *Six Feet of Earth.*

own bed among his most cherished companions. Mercifully, for one who had cheerfully borne so much pain for so long, at the end he suffered little conscious discomfort and no apparent fear or unnerving mortal premonitions.* He had faced his approaching end with rising spirituality but with nonchalant stoicism.

He would not suffer the indignity of Woodrow Wilson, neither the bitterness of an ultimate defeat nor a prolonged terminal illness. To America and the world, he seemed to have fallen like one of his 13 million soldiers, sailors, and airmen. Having been embarrassed for more than twenty-five years at never having been in a real uniform in time of war, he would have been especially proud that his name, as commander in chief of the mighty and victorious armed forces of the United States, headed the following day's official list of American war dead.

III

MCINTIRE HAD CALLED Eleanor shortly after her husband's initial attack and said that he had "fainted." In his inimitable manner, the doctor who had certified that Roosevelt was perfectly fit to seek and serve a fourth term as President† told her that he was "not alarmed," but that she should get ready to come to Warm Springs that evening.[58] (She had volunteered in advance to come with her husband, but since Anna, unable to come herself, had already arranged for Lucy to be there, FDR had gently dissuaded his wife.) Eleanor had asked if she should cancel her 4 P.M. speaking engagement at the Sulgrave Club. McIntire had urged her to continue with it, because otherwise alarm would be generated.[59]

Hassett called Stephen Early, which is how the news of the death of the President first reached Washington. Eleanor gave a short speech to the Sulgrave Club and resumed her place next to Mrs. Woodrow Wilson to hear the performance of the distinguished pianist Evelyn Tyner. In the midst of it she was called out for an urgent telephone call from the White House. It was Early, who sounded agitated, and stressed that it was very important that she return at once to the White House. "Nevertheless, the amenities had to be observed," she subsequently wrote with a sense of decorum that even now, as she suspected, her late husband would have admired.

---

* McIntire later wrote that "Coughing spells racked [Roosevelt] by day and broke his rest at night" for the last sixteen months of his life after returning from Teheran. "His heart, of course, became a subject of concern, because of his continual coughing."[55] He had a post-Teheran bout of influenza and "experienced several attacks of acute respiratory infection."[56] "It is reasonable to conclude from the available evidence that a lifelong series of sieges of the common cold, sinusitis, pharyngitis, tonsillitis, laryngitis, tracheitis, bronchitis, influenza, and pneumonia could very well have been among the factors contributing" to his death.[57]

† It would have been a sacrifice for McIntire to urge retirement on the President. There were no other vice admirals in the Bureau of Medicine and Surgery, and he would have been relocated and demoted.

She returned to hear the rest of Miss Tyner's piece and then made her apologies, explaining that she had been called back to the White House. She left amid generous applause and had a tense ride home, "with clenched hands. . . . In my heart I knew what had happened, but one does not actually formulate these terrible thoughts until they are spoken." Early and McIntire were in her sitting room and spoke the dreaded words.[60]

Anna, who was visiting her sick son at Bethesda Hospital, was collected and returned to the White House without being told why, having been advised earlier by McIntire that her father had suffered a "collapse," which the admiral represented at first as medically insignificant. Her mother had already donned a black dress, called for Vice President Truman, and sent a message to her sons that their father had "slept away," an expression from Victorian times that was not strictly true. "He did his job to the end, as he would expect you to do." (If she had known that he had spent his last conscious moments and days with her ancient rival, albeit chaperoned by cousins, she might not have commended his example so heartily.) Eleanor even telephoned the hospital in Florida where the wife of Treasury Secretary Morgenthau was convalescing and asked that her radio be disconnected that she not receive too severe a shock.[61]

Vice President Truman had been having a post-session drink with the "Board of Education," a group of cronies at the summit of the Democratic Party leadership in the Congress, who met in a hideaway room of Speaker Sam Rayburn's. Invitations were cherished, and confined to Rayburn's closest friends and some promising young people invited as an act of recognition from time to time. On this day, only Rayburn, House parliamentarian Lewis Deschler, and White House congressional liaison James Barnes were present when Truman arrived a few minutes after five o'clock. Rayburn told Truman, at Deschler's prompting, that the President's press secretary, Steve Early, had asked that he call at once. Truman poured himself a glass of bourbon from the Speaker's private stock and returned Early's call. In a constricted voice, Early asked Truman to come at once to the White House. Truman said he would be right over, put down the telephone and his drink, and said: "Jesus Christ and General Jackson!" He reached for his broad-brimmed white hat, encountered Congressman Lyndon Johnson on the way out, and was driven at speed to the White House.[62]

Harry Truman arrived there at 5:30. The country had been without a president for two hours, and without a president capable of functioning for over four hours, but only a handful of people knew it. Mrs. Roosevelt said: "Harry, the President is dead." After a few moments to absorb the news and its implications, Truman asked if there was anything he could do for her. She asked if there was anything she could do for him, "for you are the one in trouble now." She said she was planning to go to Warm Springs, and asked if it was appropriate still for her to use a government plane. He assured her that she should.

Stettinius arrived, tears streaming down his face. As the senior cabinet member by traditional rank except for Truman, and the coordinator of changes of office by virtue of the technical powers of the secretary of state, he advised that the cabinet was being assembled for the swearing-in of the new president at 7 P.M. Most of the cabinet members were present when the Chief Justice, Harlan Stone, administered the oath to Harry S Truman as the thirty-second man to hold the office of president of the United States.

Eleanor Roosevelt departed the White House shortly after the swearing-in of her husband's successor. (Had she been listened to, Henry Wallace, who three years later made himself the instrument of a coalition of American Communists and fellow travelers to run as a third-party presidential candidate, would now be president.) The public announcement of Roosevelt's death had finally been made, and Eleanor graciously spoke to a group of White House employees and journalists before getting into her car.

Eleanor Roosevelt arrived at Warm Springs just before midnight. She came to the Little White House, embraced Daisy, Laura, and Grace, who had been awaiting her, and asked each of them to describe exactly what had happened. Laura's turn came last, and she casually revealed that FDR had been sitting for a portrait while reading correspondence and papers, that the artist was a friend of Lucy Mercer Rutherfurd, and that Lucy also was present and had been staying as the President's guest at Warm Springs (in a nearby cottage). There was apparently no effort by the three women to coordinate their stories; Daisy Suckley and Grace Tully made no mention of the portrait or the other two ladies present. Laura Delano was a rather ludicrous figure, preoccupied with her dogs, attention-seeking with her blue hair, outlandish dress, and profusion of costume jewelry. FDR seems to have found her entertaining, though she was not a soulmate and correspondent like Daisy, much less a romantic involvement and highly accomplished woman like Lucy.

Eleanor Roosevelt was thoroughly composed throughout this intense afternoon and evening, and her dignity did not desert her now. Heavy and humiliating as it was to be told that her cousins and daughter (as she instantly deduced) were involved in a conspiracy to withhold from her the virtual double romantic life of her husband of forty years, she remained collected. She then went into his bedroom, closing the door behind her. She remained alone with the mortal remains of her husband for five minutes.

Eleanor emerged, outwardly unperturbed, and resumed her calm interrogation of Laura, who was only too pleased to explain the frequency of the contacts between FDR and Lucy, and to incite the newly minted widow's worst fears about the depth and duration of her husband's infidelity and the extent of the group privy to his indiscretions.[63]

Eleanor returned to the bedroom and selected the clothes for her husband to be dressed in for the last time; a double-breasted blue suit, white shirt, blue-and-white tie. Arthur Prettyman dressed the body and combed his employer's hair. He was still a fine-looking man when carried back into the living room and placed in his casket. "Oh, he was handsome," said the maid, Lizzie McDuffie. "You wouldn't have thought he had a day's illness."[64] Eleanor Roosevelt, having sustained two tremendous shocks within a few hours, showed superhuman self-control.

On the morning of April 13, 1945, thousands of Georgians crowded around the little Warm Springs railway station. Mrs. Roosevelt had asked General Marshall to take charge of arrangements, which he did with his unvarying efficiency. An honor guard from Fort Benning, Georgia, provided a military farewell and a military band played dirges. A large number of the townsfolk and visitors wept. Among those in the honor guard was the nineteen-year-old volunteer soldier and future star of American conservative politics and writing William F. Buckley.

The presidential train had been modified by the placing of a raised catafalque in a parlor car that would permit the flag-draped coffin of the President to be seen by onlookers as the train proceeded northwards. It was illuminated at night and could be seen from a great distance. The train moved slowly out and continued sedately along the 800-mile journey to Washington. Eleanor took to her bed but did not sleep much through the night of April 13–14, and with her blinds up watched in amazement at the numbers and solemnity of ordinary people as the funeral train passed. Over two million people came to the edge of the tracks to witness the last voyage of the nation's longest-serving leader. At crossroads, on rural railway platforms, in the fields, in hamlets, at all hours of the day and night, huge numbers of people stood in reverent silence, except for the church choirs that showed up and sang "Rock of Ages," "Abide With Me," "Nearer My God To Thee," and other stirring hymns where the train stopped briefly for replenishment of water or stores.

The train arrived at Washington's Union Station in the morning of April 14, and was met by President Truman, the cabinet, the Joint Chiefs of Staff, and representatives of the Congress and the judiciary. Dense and silent crowds lined the great avenues as the funeral cortege proceeded to the White House. The coffin was on a horse-drawn caisson followed by a riderless but fully bridled horse with reversed stirrups, traditionally symbolic of the fallen warrior. In between ceremonial military overflights and the funeral music of a marching band, the sobbing of scores of thousands of onlookers was all that was audible over the clatter of the horses' hooves.

The coffin entered the White House through the main door and was carried to the East Room. Eleanor asked that the coffin be reopened, and for a few minutes "alone with my husband." She gently transferred a gold band from her finger to her husband's, and very calmly left the room. The coffin was sealed and not opened again. Eleanor then went to the residential part of the White House and confronted Anna in the most forceful and aggrieved terms. Anna defended herself as having responded to her father's wishes at a time when he was bearing crushing responsibilities, was suffering declining health, was alone because his wife was often away, and was seeking what appeared to be only innocent companionship. Though there was no outward sign of it, their relations were strained for some time afterwards.

(Eventually even Eleanor and Lucy were reconciled, when Mrs. Roosevelt had Daisy Suckley send Lucy a watercolor of FDR by Elizabeth Shoumatoff, and Lucy replied with great elegance.[65] Lucy herself would die in 1948, aged only fifty-seven, a little like the Empress Josephine, not long after the end of the love of her life. Mrs. Roosevelt soldiered on into the sixties, to the age of seventy-eight, in the pursuit of good and often noble causes.)

The White House funeral was at 4 P.M., April 14, and was attended by all of official Washington, military and civilian, executive, congressional, and judicial. The senior representatives of American allies were the irrepressible Mackenzie King, British Foreign Secretary Anthony Eden, and Soviet Ambassador Andrei Gromyko.

Churchill arranged to go, and decided not to only at the last moment. There has never been any believable explanation for why he did not. He told the king and Hopkins that he didn't wish to leave with many ministers already out of the country. This was clearly a pretext. An emotional man of powerful loyalties, Churchill wept copiously at Roosevelt's memorial service. He may have been afraid of being overtaken by one of his depressive attacks if he flew sixteen hours to see the man with whom he had saved and rebuilt the world lowered into the ground. He should have gone, as Halifax urged him to do, not only for historic reasons but to concert policy with Truman, whom he shortly found a staunch kindred spirit opposite the Russians. If he had attended Roosevelt's funeral, he and Truman might have made common cause against Stalin earlier.[66]

The White House ceremony was brief and simple, beginning with the fine hymn "Faith of our Fathers," and including a short reading from the deceased's first inaugural address. While many, including the cadaverous Harry Hopkins, wept uncontrollably, Eleanor Roosevelt remained completely calm. Her only betrayal of grief through these freighted days was on the train from Warm Springs to Washington when her voice broke slightly as she asked Grace Tully if her husband had ever made any request to her about his funeral arrangements.

President Roosevelt left the White House for the last time that evening, and his coffin was reloaded onto his train and conveyed through the night to Hyde Park. Anna was assigned her father's old bedroom on his train but was unable to sleep. "All night I sat at the edge of that berth and watched the people who had come to see the train pass by. There were little children, fathers, grandparents. They were there . . . at all hours during that long night."[67]

The coffin was again placed on a caisson and borne up the hill to Springwood by a fine team of horses. There was a slightly smaller official group of mourners than at the White House, and a large number of the President's neighbors of every social and economic stratum. The seventy-eight-year-old Episcopalian minister of St. James, where Franklin Roosevelt and his father before him had been vestrymen, presided with elegant simplicity. An honor guard of scarlet-caped cadets from nearby West Point fired three volleys. Fala barked after each one. (In subsequent years, whenever important visitors with accompanying police sirens, such as Churchill, de Gaulle, Eisenhower, or Truman arrived to lay wreaths on Roosevelt's grave and pay their respects to Mrs. Roosevelt, Fala jumped up excitedly at the sound of the approaching sirens, as if his master were returning at last.)

It was a fine spring day; the lilacs were out and the birds were singing. The grave had been dug by the local people who normally did such work, including the Roosevelts' senior tenant farmer, Moses Smith, who had performed the same service as gravedigger for Mr. James forty-five years before, and had known Franklin all his life. Franklin Delano Roosevelt was buried near the main house in a little garden where he had played as a child. The crowd dispersed. Eleanor Roosevelt wore a brooch her husband had given her as a wedding present forty years earlier. She was the last to leave the graveside.

Roosevelt had stipulated that his gravestone should bear only his name and the years of his birth and death. Seventeen years later, Eleanor joined him.

The world was stupefied by the sudden demise of its most famous and important inhabitant.* Even bitter domestic enemies such as Colonel McCormick treated Roosevelt's death with the respect due an epochal event. Admirers like the writer Studs Terkel burst into tears and remained generally in that condition for days. "I can't stop crying. Everybody is crying."[69] Republican Senate leader Robert A. Taft, a strenuous partisan opponent and continuator of all the antagonism between the Tafts and the Roosevelts, said that the late President was "the greatest figure of our time at the very climax of his career. [His death] shocks the world to which his words and actions were more important than those of any other man."[70]

His own followers were almost inconsolable. Alben Barkley, with whom he had had his differences, spoke of "one of the worst tragedies that ever happened."[71] Roosevelt's colleagues in government, even those who found his methods exasperating, were severely shaken by his death. Morgenthau, Ickes, Perkins, even Wallace, and conspicuously Hopkins, recorded their distress. Stimson wrote in his diary: "With all his idiosyncrasies our Chief was a very kindly and friendly man and his humor and pleasantry had always been the life of Cabinet meetings.

---

* The President's estate was eventually valued at $1,943,888.[68] His stamp collection was sold for $213,000. His heirs waived their life interest and Springwood was combined with the FDR Library as a national historic site. Eleanor bought Val Kill and Campobello, but both became historic sites following her death in 1962. The estate paid about $400,000 in taxes, including $50,000 divided between New York State, Canada, New Brunswick, and the District of Columbia. Roosevelt had put some of his papers under a time seal and permanently forbade publication of some others. Those from the White House Map Room were "impounded by President Truman in the interest of national security."

I think every one of us felt keenly the loss of a real personal friend. I know I did. I have never concealed the fact that I regarded his administrative procedures as disorderly, but his foreign policy was always founded on great foresight and keenness of vision, and at this period of great confusion of ideas in this country, the loss of leadership will be most serious." President Truman, in proclaiming a national day of mourning, wrote: "Though his voice is silent, his courage is not spent."[72]

Dean Acheson, the former assistant secretary of the treasury and of state, whom Roosevelt had been about to appoint as solicitor general of the United States, had also had disputes with Roosevelt and been dismissed from his government in 1934 (chapter 7). He shared the incomprehension of political leaders endemic in certain types of unelected officials. He wasn't as ulcerous or cynical as Cadogan but shared some attitudes with him. Acheson was astounded at how dazed the people standing outside the White House appeared. He hadn't realized that for millions, Roosevelt was like "a parent," he wrote to his son, serving in the Pacific.

"Large crowds came and stood in front of the White House. There was nothing to see and I'm sure they did not expect to see anything. They merely stood in a lost sort of way. One felt as though the city had vanished, leaving its inhabitants to wander about bewildered, looking for a familiar landmark. . . . Something which had filled all lives was gone."[73]

Acheson had squared his inflexible reaction to Roosevelt's unorthodox methods with the formula that his attitude toward him "was one of admiration without affection. . . . The President could relax over his poker parties and enjoy Tom Corcoran's accordion, he could and did call everyone from his valet to the Secretary of State by his first name," treating him, Acheson felt, like "a promising stable boy."

Roosevelt's "responses seemed too quick; his reasons too facile for considered judgment; one could not tell what lay beneath them. He remained a formidable man, a leader who won admiration and respect. In others, he inspired far more, affection and devotion."[74] This analysis is largely true; Roosevelt was facile, enigmatic, ruthless, and eerily detached from other people, other than collectively or superficially.*

Acheson's view conforms somewhat with Bohlen's, though Bohlen was a more

---

* But Acheson's comment also says a good deal about Acheson, a stiff, inhibited, and righteous Grotonian, though an able public servant and capable secretary of state under Truman. In his memoirs, Acheson conceives a fraternity of principled men, headed by Churchill and Truman, with Marshall and himself in close support and Roosevelt excluded. Acheson was more critical of Endicott Peabody than Roosevelt was. But Acheson, unlike Roosevelt, was hobbled by Peabody's priggishness, and by the sanctimony of his father, an Episcopal bishop, neither of which he ever entirely outgrew. By selective treatment in his memoirs of his rather obsequious return to office under Roosevelt, in 1941, Acheson seems embarrassed at his general mismanagement of his relations with Roosevelt.

affable personality. Having written that Roosevelt was a great man, Bohlen went on: "I cannot say Roosevelt was a likeable man. . . . Among those who worked with him in the White House for long periods of time, there was real affection for him, but not the kind of human feeling that springs from personal love."[75]

Probably only Lucy Rutherfurd and perhaps Margaret Suckley—and Anna, in the manner of fathers and daughters—had a relationship of outright love with Franklin D. Roosevelt. No one now knows how his illness and his office escalated his natural sense of detachment. Mostly he seems to have enjoyed the singularity of his position, though there were signs of loneliness in his correspondence and in his last years with Lucy. He was not speaking entirely in jest when, flying over the Nile near Cairo in October 1943, he looked down and said: "Ah, my friend the Sphinx." Of all the skits and caricatures of him by the Washington press corps, the portrayal of him as a sphinx was his favorite.

These characteristics may have added to his talents as a statesman. His detachment was probably as much of an asset as his impersonality was a limitation. He understood people and was even more popular with masses of them than with individuals, and this was one of the secrets of his immense success as politician and leader.

He said: "I am like a cat. I make a quick stroke, and then I relax."[76] This is a particularly revealing statement, since Roosevelt was not a cat owner but a dog owner, and went to great lengths to present himself as a traditional, altruistic country gentleman, entirely masculine and rather straightforward. Behind this façade lurked a feline personality, a complete loner, except for a coterie of female listeners—Missy, Lucy, Daisy, Laura, eventually Anna—to all of whom, as far as is known, he revealed little of himself, but was affectionate. Corcoran spoke of his "androgynous" personality. Henry Wallace finally figured out, after being dumped as vice president, that "He doesn't know any man and no man knows him. Even his own family doesn't know anything about him." Anna confirmed that this was true.[77]

There were moments, with Lucy and Daisy, when he appeared to seek a relationship of confidence, when he exposed his sensitivities to extreme controversy and reminisced quite personally. And with Missy and Lucy, in his presidential years, no one knows how far relations went in any respect, although his revived relations with Lucy were necessarily circumscribed and lasted only two years. With no one else, apparently including his wife and sons, was he at all revealing about himself, always remaining behind his public mask of imperturbable patrician cheerfulness. Neither the correspondence with Margaret Suckley, nor, so far as is known, his conversations with Lucy Rutherfurd, touched upon his goals and methods as a statesman other than in a general way. Nor is there any evidence he discussed his illness with anyone except doctors, and with them only rarely after the mid-twenties.

He knew he was like a cat not because he had studied cats or owned them but because he was aware that in his cunning, concentration, and self-absorption, he had the character of one. This is a very tentative conjecture, but part of his love of dogs may well have been that their uncomplicated loyalty was such a refreshing contrast to his own reasoning processes and to the nature of most of those with whom he dealt—an interspecies attraction of opposites. These factors also raised his appreciation of unconditional loyalists like Ickes and Morgenthau (to whom he described himself as "a juggler"—of a piece with being a sphinx and a cat).

In Moscow, Averell Harriman learned of his leader's death at 3 A.M. Knowing Stalin's nocturnal habits, he dressed and went to the Kremlin and advised the Soviet dictator. For once, Stalin appeared genuinely shaken, "deeply distressed," as Harriman wrote, and held the ambassador's outstretched hand for half a minute. He then asked a long sequence of questions about the circumstances of Roosevelt's death, and the next morning sent a personal message to the State Department recommending an autopsy to determine if the President had been poisoned. Harriman suggested that Molotov represent the Soviet Union at the United Nations meeting in San Francisco, out of respect for the deceased President. Stalin instantly agreed, overcoming his previous reticences about Molotov's high parliamentary duties.

De Gaulle subsequently claimed that "it was with all my heart that I saluted his memory with regret and admiration," though his reaction at the time was less effusive, and he did not encourage a memorial service for Roosevelt such as the splendid ceremony at St. Paul's Cathedral in London, attended by the entire royal family, government, and leadership of the United Kingdom.

Radio Tokyo, surprisingly, announced Roosevelt's death soberly, and played funeral music, "in honor of the passing of a great man," whom the Japanese credited with "the Americans' advantageous position today."[78] In Berlin, however, the official radio rejoiced. Goebbels, informed of Roosevelt's death upon returning to his ministry (which, like much of Berlin, was in flames from another RAF bombing), called delightedly for champagne. The Reich propaganda minister congratulated Hitler, seeing a parallel with the death of the Russian empress when Frederick the Great was hard-pressed in the Seven Years War. The stars, he said, proclaimed the turning point in the war. In his order of the day to the German Army of April 14, Hitler declared that German fortunes would revive, because "Fate has removed the greatest war criminal of all time."[79] The Nazi finance minister, Schwerin von Krosigk, a Rhodes Scholar, wrote in his diary: "This was the Angel of History! We felt its wings flutter through the room." It is an indication of the psychotic surrealism of life in the bowels of the Reichschancellery if these militant atheists were now taking refuge in the perceived proximity of angels.[80]

The British custom is for all party leaders to speak in Parliament on the death of an exalted figure. In this case, in deference to the coalition government that united all elements of national politics and the close relationship the President had had with the prime minister, Mr. Churchill was asked to give a principal address for both houses of Parliament, all parties, the entire nation, and the whole Empire. Parliament had adjourned April 13 after a session of just eight minutes, out of respect for the late President. It reconvened, packed out to the steps and doors and with full galleries to hear Churchill's tribute in the afternoon of April 17. Officially, it was an address to the king asking that Parliament's sympathies be expressed by His Majesty in the royal message to the government and people of the United States.

After briefly describing the history and extent of his relations with Roosevelt, Churchill said: "I conceived an admiration for him as a statesman, a man of affairs, and a war leader. I felt the utmost confidence in his upright, inspiring character and outlook, and a personal regard—affection I must say—for him beyond my power to express today. His love of his own country, his respect for its constitution, his power of gauging the tides and currents of its mobile public opinion, were always evident, but added to these [was] . . . that generous heart which was always stirred to anger and to action by spectacles of aggression and oppression by the strong against the weak. It is indeed a loss, a bitter loss to humanity, that [that heart] is stilled forever.

"President Roosevelt's affliction lay heavily upon him. It was a marvel that he bore up against it through all the many years of tumult and storm. Not one man in ten millions, stricken and crippled as he was, would have attempted to plunge into a life of physical and mental exertion and of hard, ceaseless political controversy. Not one in ten millions would have tried, not one in a generation would have succeeded, not only in entering this sphere, not only in acting vehemently in it, but in becoming indisputable master of the scene . . . [through an] extraordinary effort of the spirit over the flesh, of will-power over physical infirmity.

"There is no doubt that the President foresaw the great dangers closing in upon the pre-war world with far more prescience than most well-informed people on either side of the Atlantic. . . . There was never a moment's doubt . . . upon which side his sympathies lay. . . . He and . . . vast numbers of his countrymen . . . felt the Blitz of the stern winter of 1940–41 . . . as much as any of us did, and perhaps more indeed, for imagination is often more torturing than reality. There is no doubt that the bearing of the British, and above all of the Londoners, kindled fires in American bosoms far harder to quench than the conflagrations from which we were suffering. . . .

"He devised the extraordinary measure of assistance called Lend-Lease, which will stand forth as the most unselfish and unsordid financial act of any country in all history." Following the "act of treachery and greed" of Japan, said the prime minister, "both our countries were in arms" together.

After recounting the progress of the war: "At Yalta I noticed that the President was ailing. His captivating smile, his gay and charming manner, had not deserted him, but his face had a transparency, an air of purification, and often there was a far-away look in his eyes. When I took my leave of him in Alexandria harbour I must confess that I had an indefinable sense of fear that his health and his strength were on the ebb. But nothing altered his inflexible sense of duty. To the end he faced his innumerable tasks unflinching. . . .

"What an enviable death was his! He had brought the country through the worst of its perils and the heaviest of its toils. Victory had cast its sure and steady beam upon him.

"In the days of peace he had broadened and stabilized the foundation of American life and union. In war he had raised the strength, might, and glory of the great Republic to a height never attained by any nation in history. . . .

"All this was no more than worldly power and grandeur, had it not been that the causes of human freedom and social justice, to which so much of his life had been given, added a luster [to him and his achievements] which will long be discernible among men. . . .

"For us it remains only to say that in Franklin Roosevelt there died the greatest American friend we have ever known, and the greatest champion of freedom who has ever brought help and comfort from the New World to the Old."

The prime minister's address was received with profound but sober approval and his motion was unanimously adopted. He said little of Roosevelt's performance in the last two years as peace was being planned. But these were fluid and charged issues still, which make the rest of his tribute to Roosevelt as rebuilder of his nation, author of Lend-Lease, and conqueror of his illness, even more powerful.

Winston Churchill wrote with his customary generosity and eloquence to Mrs. Roosevelt, President Truman, and Harry Hopkins. He was one of the sponsors of the project to raise up a statue to Roosevelt in Grosvenor Square in front of the United States Embassy.

In his supporting remarks for this project in Parliament, Churchill declared that Roosevelt was the greatest of all American leaders, because if he had failed, Western civilization would have been enslaved, whereas the consequences of the failure of Washington or Lincoln would have been confined to America.

Engraved on the base of the Roosevelt statue in Grosvenor Square is the fact that contributions to it were of small sums, in order to permit people from "every walk of life throughout the United Kingdom" to honour this great friend of Britain. The statue was unveiled on the third anniversary of the President's death by Mrs. Roosevelt, in the presence of the king and queen and all the leaders of British public life.

Fifty years after his death, there was a small but distinguishedly attended service of remembrance at the statue, in which a well-spoken clergyman intoned that those present were gathered "to observe the anniversary of the death and give thanks for the life of Franklin Delano Roosevelt, President of the United States, leader of the Allied nations in the Second World War, and champion of the rights and dignity of all men."

There is nothing remotely resembling a precedent in British history for so elegiacal a tribute to any deceased foreign leader. The British, and Winston Churchill in particular, perceived before anyone how preeminent a titan of the twentieth century Roosevelt was. The British had endured the agony of importuning American assistance in two world wars; they knew how great a difference would be made by American engagement in the world in support of democracy, the rule of law, and Western values generally.

The British had come to realize that without the United States' consistent involvement in the maintenance of the peace and the reinforcement of the democratic countries, everything would be at risk every generation. With it, there would be a measure of security and the possibility of gradually evangelizing the world to Western political and economic concepts, in the absence of a competitively effective system devised elsewhere.

IV

IT IS THE CONTENTION of this book that Franklin D. Roosevelt was the most important person of the twentieth century, because of his achievements as one of America's greatest presidents and its most accomplished leader since Lincoln. This greatness rests on seven achievements.

First, he was, with Winston Churchill, the co-savior of Western civilization. He persuaded his countrymen to assist their natural allies in 1940 in order to stay out of war themselves. In order to see out the war emergency, he professed to be drafted to an unprecedented extension of his presidential tenure. Having pledged to avoid war by helping Britain and the Dominions fight for the common cause, his progressive provocations of the Axis, lawful and benign as they were, were almost artistically executed. Britain could not have remained in the war without his support. He extended U.S. territorial waters 1,800 miles out into the Atlantic and attacked German ships when they were detected, and imposed on Japan an embargo on the sinews of war—oil and scrap metal. This made it almost certain that America would be attacked. He knew this to be the only method of winning the war for the West, and the Japanese, German, and Italian governments, in their aggressive stupidity, played into his hands.

With the help of the eloquence and courage of Churchill and the British and of the revulsion against Hitler's inhumanity, Roosevelt led American opinion from profound isolationism in 1937 to accepting war rather than an Axis victory in 1941, even before Pearl Harbor galvanized the nation. This was arguably the greatest political tour de force in the history of democratic government, as even Stalin recognized in his main toast to Roosevelt at Teheran. His technique of getting ahead of public opinion, pulling it partly behind him while denying his views had evolved, allowing a brief respite and then moving again, was conceived and perfected in this period.

This anchoring of the United States in the world was Franklin D. Roosevelt's second great achievement. His permanent defeat of the isolationists by representing them as Hitler dupes before the war, who would bring the world to war again if heeded in 1945, and by placating them with an international organization designed to make the world seem less dangerous, was the greatest achievement for world stability since the Battle of Waterloo.

The reason the second half of the twentieth century was so greatly more successful than the first half was precisely because of the stabilizing power of the United States, providing deterrence and containment in Europe and the Far East. In the postwar world in which Roosevelt had conditioned America to play its full part, the Soviet Union gradually crumbled, without a major war. And China, whose status as a Great Power Roosevelt was the first important foreign leader to champion, developed a capitalist growth economy, and progressed syncopatedly toward greater political liberalism.

Roosevelt's third great achievement was the reinvention of the American state. Before bringing the United States out of the immaturity of isolation and into the world where it could defend its interests and assume its responsibilities, Roosevelt had to bring the United States out of the Great Depression. In doing so, he involved the government in many areas where its presence had been limited or non-existent — industrial recovery, reflation, large-scale workfare programs, Social Security, reform of financial institutions, rural electrification, flood and drought control, stabilization of farm production and prices, conservation, refinancing of home mortgages and farm loans, reform of working conditions, public sector development and distribution of hydroelectric power, generous treatment of veterans, as well as the repeal of Prohibition.

The New Deal was certainly not an unqualified success. The initial core of the program, the National Industrial Recovery Act and the Agricultural Adjustment Act, were successful to only a limited extent. But most of the programs in the areas enumerated were overwhelmingly successful. By later standards, the New Deal was passing but not brilliant economics. As crisis management and preservation of a civil society, it was a masterly success. Only a leader of immense political dexterity could have presented such a smorgasbord as a coherent program and retained political capital while sorting out conflicting policies. There were many useful innovations, including the application of participatory democracy in crop production restraint programs, and the great scope of workfare projects, from theater companies to the preservation of the whooping crane.

The collective effect of these measures gradually alleviated the Depression in America and prevented a recurrence of a similar catastrophe.

Roosevelt redefined American government as the conservator of last resort not only of public order but of national confidence, and of at least a minimalist concept of social justice. He restored the confidence of Americans in their country, and in their government as a vital and active promoter of an equitable society, and a corrective to economic and natural disasters. No other American president has had anything remotely like as important a reform record.

Roosevelt stole the arguments of the left, enacted very diluted legislative versions of them, and deprived the left of any possibility of political success. It was not just a witticism when Socialist Party leader Norman Thomas said that Roosevelt was carrying out the Socialist Party's program — "in a coffin."

By channeling all the public's resentment at the consequences of the Great Depression into an impersonal cul-de-sac, Roosevelt preserved the moral integrality of the nation so he could focus alarm and moral outrage on America's real enemies: the conquering foreign dictators. He was both the savior of American capitalism and the foremost reformer in the country's history. Thus did he deliver the country from overexposure to the extremes of right and left. American capitalism ceased to be a menace to itself and became an unambiguous engine to greater and better-distributed national prosperity.

It was illustrative of Roosevelt's singular political genius that he completed the recovery from the Depression by accelerating rearmament to prepare the country for world war. It was the tactical triumph of using the fear of one enemy (Hitler and the Japanese) to rout another (domestic unemployment and underproduction), thus preparing the military defeat of the first. His political legerdemain was so refined that no one realized what he was doing, and his mastery of the scene, as Churchill called it in his eulogy, was such that he confided in no one as he engineered this maneuver. He began the complete emancipation of African-Americans in the same way, using the exigencies of depression relief and the nascent welfare system and then the war to start them up the long ladder to equality of opportunity.

In this third achievement, overcoming the Depression and partially reforming the economic and social system, Franklin D. Roosevelt preserved or restored the good name of democratic government. In the thirties, Roosevelt's was the only democratic government of an important country with any panache, and the only one that actually uplifted the people. This was due to the originality of its programs, and even more to his magnetic personality.

He was also the only leader of a very important country between the mid-thirties and 1940 not ultimately to be ashamed of: neither a dictator nor an appeaser of dictators. Churchill and many others helped to give democracy an overwhelming legitimacy. But in the daunting years from 1933 to 1940 this heavy responsibility rested lightly on the massive shoulders of Franklin D. Roosevelt almost alone.

Roosevelt's fourth great achievement was that he was an almost uniformly successful war leader, far more so than Washington, Madison, Lincoln, or Wilson. (The Indian, Mexican, and Spanish Wars don't bear comparison.) After the initial fiasco at Pearl Harbor, where the local commanders had badly let the country down, and except for the momentary setbacks in the Philippines and at the Kasserine Pass and Savo Island and Java Sea, American forces were almost never defeated, even when, as in early actions like the Coral Sea and Midway, they were heavily outnumbered.

His strategic insights were almost always accurate, even though he made no pretense to being a military strategist, and he harassed his commanders much less than did Churchill, let alone Stalin and Hitler. His command appointments were excellent. Marshall, Nimitz, MacArthur, and King were personal choices of Roosevelt's, and Eisenhower was agreed to on Marshall's recommendation. All performed well; most performed brilliantly.

He never wavered on the Germany-first strategy, even on the day of Pearl Harbor. He was an early champion of air power, massively augmenting aircraft production and aircraft carrier construction, and he personally ordered the successful conversion of nine heavy cruisers on the slipways to aircraft carriers, over some reluctance from the Navy Department, vitally accelerating American naval victory in the Pacific.

Roosevelt insisted, against professional advice, on the Doolittle air raid on Tokyo, a bold stroke that, though this was not foreseen, contributed to the great victory at Midway. He conceived of and required the very successful Torch landings in North Africa, over the objections of his own military advisors, especially Marshall. He was absolutely correct in insisting upon an early cross-Channel invasion as the only means of defeating Nazi Germany in a timely manner, of ensuring that there would be no separate peace between Hitler and Stalin, and of giving the West its best chance of preventing a Soviet takeover of Germany and even France. He insisted on the Anvil invasion of southern France, over fierce resistance from the British, and was vindicated, as Churchill, in contrast to the intractable Montgomery, graciously acknowledged at the second Quebec Conference and in his memoirs. He was almost certainly correct in ordering the Philippine invasion, about which Marshall and King were divided. And his experience as assistant secretary of the navy in the First World War had taught him the value of planning for the next war boldly and not on the basis of the preceding one.

From 1940 to 1945, the United States amply fulfilled Roosevelt's exhortation to be the "Great Arsenal of Democracy." It produced 300,000 warplanes, two million trucks, over 100,000 tanks, nearly forty million tons of naval and merchant shipping, over twenty million rifles and pistols and machine guns. As Stalin acknowledged at Teheran, American war production made an indispensable and immense contribution to victory. And it was achieved in a fine and relatively unabrasive partnership between the private and public sectors and business and labor that augured well for the administration's postwar relations with business.

At times of supreme crisis—Pearl Harbor, D-Day, the Battle of the Ardennes—

Roosevelt was imperturbable, and he was admired by all his subordinates, even MacArthur and conspicuously Patton. The only exception was the cantankerous Stilwell.*

At the border between political and military strategy, his acute intuition was his sure guide. It enabled him to judge how long Stalin could be left to take 90 percent of the casualties, as among the Big Three, before he might be tempted to compose his differences with Hitler, as he had done in 1939; and how long the British and Americans could operate on the periphery of the main theater before moving to assure that most of geopolitically useful Europe was in their hands and not Russia's. The management of relations with Stalin and Churchill in these matters, apart from the purely military elements, required almost preternatural insight and finesse.

This led to Roosevelt's fifth great achievement: his creation of the circumstances that enabled his postwar successors to complete the Allied victory in World War II, liberate Eastern Europe, and make the world safe for democracy at last. He had done what he reasonably could to bring Stalin into the fold of responsible world leaders. He played a decisive role, with Churchill, in limiting Russian and domestic Communist influence in postwar Italy and France, and focused from early 1943 on occupying as much of Germany as possible until the British and Russians, for reasons that have been explained, determined the zones of occupation in Germany. He, no less than Churchill, always recognized the danger of letting Russia into Western Europe.

While representing a swift postwar departure of American forces from Europe as likely, he prepared for an occupation of a large part of Germany for an indefinite period. He moved decisively to develop atomic weapons. And he was the principal creator of the United Nations, a framework for international cooperation and, to a very limited extent, world government, that could operate according to the wishes of the Allies, if they remained united (as during the Gulf War of 1990–1991). He would have been appalled at the degeneration of the United Nations into a Western-bashing forum for Third World dictators that it has largely become. The Latin American "Good Neighbors," British Dominions, and emerging colonies were supposed to assure the British and Americans a durable majority and multilateral legitimacy. They did, for a generation. These two developments, for which Roosevelt was ultimately responsible—the nuclear age and the United Nations organization—offered the world at the time he died an ultimate conceptual Manichaean alternative between Armageddon and cooperation.

Roosevelt saw that empires would crumble, though Churchill and de Gaulle

---

* Roosevelt appreciated Stilwell despite the lack of rapport between them. And even Stilwell was warming to Roosevelt after their last meeting (chapter 23).

(despite his subsequent rationalizations) dissented. He foresaw both the possibility of rivalry with Communism and Communism's ultimate failure. And he saw the potential for China and India. His trusteeship proposal for preparing under-developed colonies for independence wasn't taken up, but would almost certainly have been more successful than the many colonial wars that occurred, and the indiscriminate granting of independence to scores of primitive colonies, many of which became failed states. If his successors had studied his views on Indochina, the Vietnam debacle would have been avoided.

In ending American isolation, leading the admission or readmission of France, Germany, Italy, and Japan to the West, and staking out the moral high ground opposite Russia through the Yalta declarations on Poland and Liberated Europe, Roosevelt created the principal elements for victory in the Cold War. If he had been ambivalent about imperialism, had not forced Stalin, when the Russian leader subjugated Eastern Europe, to violate agreements with the Western Allies and arouse American political and public opinion, and had not drawn the United States into an international organization even before the war ended, Stalin might have been able to snaffle up Eastern Europe without bringing an unwinnable war of containment and ideological and military competition down upon himself. In such circumstances, the Soviet era, in Russia and its satellites, could have been very prolonged.

This fifth great achievement of Roosevelt's has been obscured by the Yalta myth. Starting the Cold War, as has been mentioned, was a catastrophic mistake by Stalin, but the shock of the breakup of the Grand Alliance and the revelation of Stalin as a double-dealing enemy created the opportunity for the systematic defamation of Roosevelt. The deceased President became a catchment for the evasions of the complicit and for the demagogy of the unscrupulous, or merely of the uninformed.

Completing Western Allied victory in World War II by almost bloodlessly defeating the Soviet Union required great skill and perseverance from many of Roosevelt's successors and many Allied statesmen. But the West always held the advantage in this contest.

Most of the key American figures in the Cold War were Roosevelt's protégés, or at least emulators, who learned much from him. This was directly the case with Truman, Eisenhower, Marshall, Acheson, and Lyndon Johnson; and indirectly with Kennedy and with other younger men who did not know Roosevelt but served in junior military ranks in World War II and studied him, such as Nixon, Kissinger, Ford, Reagan, and George Bush Sr.

———

Churchill's setback in the 1945 British election highlighted Roosevelt's sixth claim to greatness—his unmatched mastery of the American political system. Churchill had never led a political party in a general election before, and Britain had not had an election since 1935. Roosevelt faced the voters twice during the war and never lost touch with American opinion. This may partially explain why Churchill believed until the end of 1943, if not later, in a war of attrition.

Roosevelt well knew the public's impatience, but the world was astounded by Churchill's electoral defeat, though Roosevelt, as he warned Churchill at Teheran, would not have been. De Gaulle would generously and fairly write: "[Winston Churchill's] personality, identified with a magnificent enterprise, his countenance, etched by the fires and frosts of great events, were no longer adequate to the era of mediocrity."*[81]

Stalin, who in July 1945 must have been consolable to see the back of Churchill when he abruptly left the Potsdam Conference, said that "Western democracy must be a wretched system if it could exchange a great man like Churchill for Attlee."[83]

Churchill himself initially envied Roosevelt his death while undefeated but soon said that if the people wanted Attlee, they could have him, and that that was why Britain had fought and won the war."[84]

Roosevelt never had to think in such terms, so sure was he of his ability to keep the public's approval. Remote and unrepresentative of the country though he was in his tastes and manner, he was an intuitive and tactical political genius and an electrifying political personality.

In twelve years as president, Roosevelt's only significant political defeats were on the Supreme Court packing bill and his attempted party purge in 1938. These are minor (and temporary) setbacks against an avalanche of electoral and legislative success with nothing slightly resembling a precedent or a sequel in American history, nor, probably, in any other of the great democracies.

Lyndon Johnson had great legislative success, with more ambiguous practical consequences, apart from civil rights, but couldn't carry public opinion very far. Ronald Reagan could stir and shape national opinion and was an important president, but his entire program was essentially tax reduction and simplification and an arms buildup. Roosevelt governed more than four years longer, far more radically and in much more complicated times than Reagan.

Roosevelt was a master of every aspect of American politics. He knew how to maneuver with the congressional leaders, how to mobilize public opinion, how to frame and time legislation, how to take care of the machine captains and ward heelers. He had an uncanny intuition of where public opinion was and where and how fast it could be led.

He was cautious and at times, occasionally pusillanimous, vindictive, or sim-

---

* Eleanor Roosevelt, who disapproved of Churchill's drinking and his Toryism, graciously wrote in her newspaper column: "No one in the British Empire, nor in the United States, who heard his brave words after Dunkirk, will ever feel anything but the deepest respect and gratitude and affection for Mr. Churchill, the man and the war leader."[82]

ply mistaken. But his shortcomings are vastly outweighed by the countless times he moved opinion, cajoled the Congress, and achieved what had not been thought possible in good or great and often vital causes.

His record of four consecutive presidential election victories, his seven consecutive congressional election victories, the huge crowds that always came out to see and cheer him throughout his long reign, attest incontrovertibly to his genius at operating every lever of the vast and intricate political machinery of the United States. His insight into common men was the more remarkable because he was certainly not one of them, and never pretended for an instant that he was.

Rather, he presented himself as a constructive aristocrat, though, as Acheson pointed out, of the European, not the bourgeois British, variety.[85] He had the nobility of spirit and outlook becoming to the scion of a famous family, but without the effete snobbery, idleness, or venality the public often impute to the hereditary rich.

He was unfailingly courteous, and sincerely considerate of the disadvantaged. He could set almost anyone at his ease, but struck some other gentlemen, such as Dean Acheson, and some people of other backgrounds, like Ernest Hemingway, as presumptuous and condescending by his familiarity, which, because of his office, could not be contradicted or reciprocated.

But to the overwhelming majority of people of every description, his personality, on encountering it, was, as Churchill said, "like opening your first bottle of champagne."[86] Since he was not altogether close to anyone, but generally well disposed to most people, he was completely independent of individual relationships but had a clear idea of how to appeal to masses of people. Thomas Mann, as we have seen (chapter 12), was captivated by him—his combination of power, sensitivity, and physical vulnerability, his liberality in an age of dictators, and the immense popularity he had earned in his own country. Mann wrote: "When I left the White House after my first visit (June 30, 1935), I knew Hitler was lost. . . . I shall be eternally grateful to Roosevelt, the born and conscious enemy of the Infamous One, for having maneuvered his all-important country into the war with consummate skill."[87] This general view was shared by people all over the world who saw him as the shining hope for liberation, peace, and justice. They were not wrong, and despite some disappointments, he did not fail them.

He also had great style. His powerful, handsome, animated appearance, cigarette holder at a rakish upward angle, flamboyant gestures, hearty and contagious laugh, skill at repartee, and evident love of his work and his job, made him an irresistible personality. Even some of his sartorial flourishes, the fold in his hat, his naval cape, a walking stick, were widely emulated. His idea of how to be president was to be himself. He loved virtually every aspect of the job, and felt he held it by a unique combination of personal determination, popular adherence, and natural right, even predestination. He could not conceive that everyone would not like to be president.

He became and long remained the most publicized and visible person in the world, though rivalled in this at times by Hitler and Churchill. His confidence, flair, and sure judgment of occasion caused him never in over twelve years to embarrass himself publicly. His physical presence, eloquence, and command of his position and tasks were all, and at all times, impressive. This conferred upon him a unique status as a public personality.

He was always confident but never vain or apparently domineering, and rarely ill-tempered. His position and the stylish, supremely confident way he filled it made FDR an unrivalled personality in the United States throughout his presidential years.

He was a natural leader. As Isaiah Berlin wrote, all through the terrible years of his presidency, he never once appeared to experience a moment of fear.[88] This impression is not contradicted in his correspondence or the memoirs and recollections of his closest collaborators and family. He is alleged to have said: "If you have spent six months on your back trying to move one toe, nothing seems difficult."

He was a phenomenon, and as in other fields, it was difficult to know when his unfailing intuition left off and cunning analysis began. He was a brilliant phrase-maker and epigrammatist, often finding the expression that would electrify the country: "a New Deal for the American people. . . . Nothing to fear but fear itself. . . . The good neighbor . . . rendezvous with destiny . . . one third of a nation . . . the dagger struck into the back of its neighbor . . . the great arsenal of democracy . . . the day of infamy." When pressed, as on D-Day, he could rise to heights of Lincolnian eloquence.

He kept his own counsel politically after Louis Howe's death, and was in little need of anyone else's, as he demonstrated when he dispensed with Jim Farley and then Ed Flynn as party chairman. In this field, as he outwitted first the conservatives and then the isolationists, he didn't need advisors, only executants.

He led a steady progression from the depths of the Depression to postwar optimism and prosperity, each step accomplished with an almost imperceptible shuffling of the domestic political deck. Like that of a great acrobat, Roosevelt's virtuosity and ultimate success became obvious only when his performance was over and he had left the stage. The change in America and the world from when he entered office to when he departed it, largely traceable to his conduct of the U.S. presidency, was from night to day.

It would be astonishing, given his Protean attainments, if Franklin Roosevelt were not the repository of remarkable human qualities. His achievement in triumphing over polio while disguising its effects has been amply recounted. That he could not stand for more than about forty-five minutes at a time after 1921 and "walked" with extreme awkwardness, as if on stilts, yet managed to project the impression of great strength and vigor, is astonishing, even allowing for the cooperativeness of the press. This was an era when a physical handicap was perceived as an electoral liability. No one can know to what solitudes, renunciations, and inhibitions he was subjected, and what feats of will and courage were necessary to surmount them.

Winston Churchill, in his eulogy, said that not one man in a generation in Roosevelt's physical condition could have made himself "indisputable master of the scene." He could have added that in all history no one else, building upon the power of the country he resurrected, and which quadrennially renewed its support of him, so transcended his illness and projected his personality and ideals that they positively touched the life of virtually every person in the world.

This is submitted as Franklin D. Roosevelt's seventh great achievement—not only the courage and determination to prevail over his disability while disguising its extent, but the implications of his triumph for all who strive against heavy odds, whether medically afflicted or not. The importance of his example is immeasurable and almost inexpressible, but it is real to anyone who considers it, even so inhumane a person as Stalin (as he showed in his reflections on Roosevelt's condition to Gromyko at Yalta).

Roosevelt would have been particularly gratified when, on the tenth anniversary of his death, his old law partner Basil O'Connor announced at Warm Springs the development of the Salk vaccine, which prevented polio and won the Nobel Prize for its discoverer. This was Roosevelt's ultimate victory over his illness and would not have occurred, at least until decades later, without him, so successful were his fundraising efforts. For years after his death the Warm Springs Foundation met with Roosevelt's chair unoccupied, in silent memory of the founder.[89]

V

FRANKLIN D. ROOSEVELT was an educated man, urbane and endowed with a remarkable memory. He was too much of an intellectual dilettante to master many whole subjects, but had a plentiful insight, and vivid curiosity. His intuition, energy, and confidence gave him a vast reach over almost all matters with which his office brought him into contact. He was a widely read man, and read retentively with great speed. To Eleanor's astonishment, he read at least the central parts of the 400,000-word novel *Gone With the Wind* in a "very short time" sufficiently to answer his wife's detailed questions about it.[90]

As someone who spent virtually his entire adult life recuperating from illness or in high public office, his knowledge of many fields, apart from personal areas of specialization, tended to be sufficient for him to keep his officials on their toes, rather than a profound expertise. He had, as Eden observed, something of the eclectic and arbitrary mind of a stamp collector, coupled to the cunning of the schemer and the ambitions of a genuine altruist. Out of this mélange of knowledge and insights emerged a general plan for making the world a better place. He implemented the plan, and in general it has worked.

Winston Churchill was a great man who, once Britain's survival was assured, was dedicated to the preservation of an empire that could not possibly be held together. His service as co-savior of the West was beyond estimation, and he was in some respects a more attractive personality than Roosevelt. He possessed greater integrity, and greater culture (but not by a wide margin), and had a more generous nature than Roosevelt. Despite his moodiness and indifferent manners at times, he was probably more companionable than Roosevelt once matters progressed much beyond the superficialities of the card table or the fishing party. Like de Gaulle and unlike Roosevelt, Churchill was a brilliant and prolific writer.

After his inspirational performance from 1940 to 1942, Churchill gradually marginalized himself through his Mediterranean strategy, with its illusory "soft underbelly" and "armpit" the (Ljubljana Gap), and through his chimerical preoccupations with peripheral places such as Norway, Turkey, Rhodes, and even Sumatra.

He faced the voters in 1945 without an imaginative plan for either domestic or foreign affairs. There was nothing like Roosevelt's G.I. Bill of Rights for the exhausted, class-riven British people, who held the Conservatives responsible more for Baldwin and Chamberlain than for Churchill's great war coalition leadership. There was no vision in foreign affairs except growing wariness of the Russians and clinging to empire. Churchill's prestige in Europe was immense. If he had developed a plan for a British-led economic and even political confederation of Western Europe, instead of investing unjustifiable faith in the Commonwealth and Empire, the European Community and Union would not have developed along the socialistic and somewhat anti-British, anti-American lines that it has. His postwar premiership would have been one of great achievement rather than an anticlimactic Indian summer.

Charles de Gaulle did magnificently with only the romanticized spirit and a few vestiges of France to start from, but he was an ungenerous man (other than in his memoirs). He was doomed by the prickliness of his own nature and his search for vengeance on his own liberators to spend the rest of his career trying to take greater grandeur for his country and himself than they really deserved. In furtherance of these goals, he engaged in a number of shabby political maneuvers, such as his attempt to break up the Canadian Confederation in 1967, and to truckle rather egregiously to Arab Israelophobia once he had extricated France from Algeria. He could not escape the consequences of the battles of the Plains of Abraham and of Waterloo, which left the world with ultimately twenty times as many English-speaking as French-speaking people, and confined France's empire to Britain's leavings.

To propagate his myth of French triumphalism, de Gaulle could accept little blame for France. He held that American isolationism was responsible for the Fall of France in 1940 and British-American lassitude for the postwar division of Europe, and that American policy in Vietnam was responsible for the student uprising and general strike in France in 1968. And he could distribute little credit to others in World War II, apart from Churchill's unique contribution, the exertions of Allied warriors, and the production of U.S. defense factories.

De Gaulle rendered great service to France, and it was a service to the world to restore France as a politically serious country. But his means, ends, and breadth of spirit were too circumscribed to make him a full rival to Roosevelt and Churchill, either in his comparative historic importance or as a man commanding the admiration of enlightened posterity. After Roosevelt and Churchill saved civilization, de Gaulle redeemed France, not least by his artistic and inveterate myth-making. Neither the roles nor the personalities were comparable.

Stalin was a clever and relentless dictator, but also a paranoid butcher of tens of millions of innocent people. Apart from that, greed and cynicism distorted his strategic judgment. They drove him to a competition with the United States that Soviet Russia could not win, when he could have had respectability, generous redevelopment assistance, continued alliance with the British and Americans, and a relationship with the East European countries somewhat like that of the United States with its smaller hemispheric neighbors.

Instead, he doomed his country to ultimate disintegration and his political philosophy, which it is hard to believe he really took seriously, to extinction. In his obligatory interpretive book on Lenin, Stalin implausibly exclaimed: "Let us have done with this rubbish of a state!" This is precisely what happened, but not as a practicing Marxist or traditional Russian nationalist would have wished.[91]

Hitler was a destructive and eventually self-destructive force. He was an almost unbelievedly satanic figure, though a formidable and persuasive one. To have transformed the nation of Beethoven and Goethe into a militarist battering ram to be hurled by him at the gates of civilization was a remarkable, though horrifying, accomplishment. Hitler's greatness was in his nihilism and monstrousness. He was a powerful force, an evil man, and, as the military historian John Keegan has written, a false hero.[92] He bears some comparison with Stalin, who had less panache but better judgment than Hitler, and was one of history's most important figures, though his psychotic wickedness denies him comparison with democracy's great leaders.

Of these five principal Western political leaders (accepting Stalin as a man of the West), Roosevelt was the only one with a strategic vision that was substantially vindicated in the fifty years following the Second World War, though de Gaulle and Churchill still have, as they deserve to have, many espousers.

When Roosevelt assumed the presidency, as Eleanor Roosevelt remarked,[93] the United States was in the depths of economic and psychological depression, but he was vital and irrepressible. Gradually, Roosevelt suffused the government and the country with his determination and optimism. And when, in his fourth term, he had transferred all his strength to the nation he served, and was worn down, and he died, the United States had a high and fixed purpose in the world, and enjoyed unexampled prosperity—more than twice as great as when he entered office and more generously distributed. It exercised a military, economic, popular cultural, and moral influence in the world unprecedented in the history of the nation-state, and had triumphed over every foreign and domestic enemy.

American capitalism was no longer a self-destructive force, and the foundations were laid for the final emancipation of the African-Americans. Apart from his indulgence of high taxes to deal with the economic and war emergencies, Roosevelt's successors have retained virtually all his reforms, no matter how strenuously some resisted them when they were introduced.

Franklin Roosevelt's place in American history is with George Washington and Abraham Lincoln. Few now dispute that in saving American democracy and capitalism from the Great Depression, and bringing America to the rescue and then the durable protection of the civilized world, Franklin Delano Roosevelt belongs in the same pantheon as the father of the country and the savior of the Union and emancipator of the slaves.

A.J.P. Taylor was right to credit Roosevelt with strategic genius but exaggerated when he wrote that "of the great men at the top, Roosevelt was the only one who knew what he was doing; he made the United States the greatest power in the world at virtually no cost."[94] All the principal leaders had clear objectives, and nearly three hundred thousand American war dead and three hundred billion dollars were a heavy cost, if modest compared with what had afflicted some other countries, and to what the cost of defeat would have been.

Because Franklin D. Roosevelt rescued America from the Depression, it could then lead the democracies to victory in war. Roosevelt created the circumstances in which America and the other democracies could win the peace and lead the world to a happier time than it had ever known before. America and its allies would promote human rights and the economics of generally distributed wealth everywhere in the world. To remake the world was a vast ambition that is still unfolding. Winston Churchill was prophetic when he said in his eulogy that the consequences of Franklin Roosevelt's astonishing life "will long be discernible among men."

Notes

KEY TO ABBREVIATIONS

ASNP	Assistant Secretary of the Navy Papers
FDRL	Franklin D. Roosevelt Library
GP	General Papers
GPNY	Governors Papers—New York
OF	Office File
PCA	Personal Collection of Author
PF	Personal File
PL	Elliott Roosevelt, editor, Personal Letters of Franklin D. Roosevelt, 1917–1945
PPA	Samuel I. Rosenman, editor, Public Papers and Addresses of Franklin D. Roosevelt
PPF	President's Personal File
PSF	President's Secretary's File
RFBPP	Roosevelt Family, Business, and Personal Papers
RFP	Roosevelt Family Papers
RP	Roosevelt Papers
RSSP	Roosevelt State Senator Papers

Any of FDR's public addresses or press conferences that are not otherwise attributed can be found in the appropriate annual volume and at the indicated date in the Public Papers and Addresses.

CHAPTER I

1. FDRL, RFBPP, Box 8, James Roosevelt entry in Sara Roosevelt diary, 30/1/82.
2. Letter to Margaret Suckley, personal collection of author, 28/10/33. Description of trees: FDRL, PPF 1820, letter of transfer of deed to U.S. government, 23/7/39.
3. FDRL, PPF 2313, letter of 7/3/35.
4. FDRL, Frederic Delano Papers; Eleanor Roosevelt, On My Own, p. 31, Time, 3/1/38.
5. FDRL, RFBPP, — James II, Box 52.
6. FDR to Margaret Suckley, 15/10/41, Elliott Roosevelt, ed., PL, vol. IV, p. 1224.
7. FDRL, PPF #3012, letter from FDR to Roy Nichols, 14/11/35.
8. Geoffrey Ward, Before the Trumpet, vol. I, pp. 38, 41.
9. Ibid., p. 35.

10. Ibid., p. 14; Clara Steeholm, *The House at Hyde Park*, p. 57.

11. Frank Freidel, *F.D.R.*, vol. I, *The Apprenticeship*, p. 10.

12. Ibid.

13. Eleanor Roosevelt, *My Day*, compilation of columns, 1938, p. 41.

14. R.J.C. Burton, "A Noble Passage to China: Myth and Memory in FDR's Family History," *Prologue*, Fall 1999, pp. 159–189.

15. Ibid., p. 91.

16. Rita Halle Kleeman, *Gracious Lady*, p. 83.

17. Ibid., pp. 102–103.

18. Ward, p. 104; Nora Ferdon, *Franklin Roosevelt: A Biological Interpretation of His Childhood and Youth*, p. 143.

19. *New York World*, 7/10/80.

20. FDRL, RFP, Sara Roosevelt diary, 19/3/82.

21. Ward, p. 111.

22. Constance Drexel, unpublished letters of FDR to his French governess, *Parents*, vol. XXVI, September 1951, PPF #119.

23. Ibid., p. 83.

24. Ward, p. 112, cites Sara Roosevelt, *My Boy Franklin*, and Kleeman, *Gracious Lady*, pp. 128–131.

25. Ward, p. 125.

26. Ibid., p. 111.

27. Ibid., p. 113; FDRL, RFP, Sara Roosevelt diary, 18/6/82, p. 20.

28. Sara Roosevelt diary, pp. 18, 33; Kleeman, p. 172.

29. Freidel, p. 24.

30. Ward, p. 114.

31. FDRL, RFP, Sara Roosevelt diary, March 1885, pp. 32–33.

32. Ward, pp. 115–116; Freidel, p. 22; Kleeman, pp. 52–53; Ernest K. Lindley, *Franklin D. Roosevelt: A Career in Progressive Democracy*, p. 47.

33. Sara Roosevelt diary, pp. 20–21; I, p. 24.

34. FDRL, speech to Hudson River nurses, 10/9/37; Steeholm, p. 57.

35. Kleeman, p. 134; Freidel, p. 24.

36. Ward, p. 141.

37. Ibid., p. 154.

38. Kleeman, p. 146; San Diego Union, 14/4/14; Ward, p. 124.

39. Ward, p. 130.

40. FDRL, RFP, Sara Roosevelt diary, 5/11/89–7/1/90, pp. 50–51.

41. Ibid., p. 63; Kleeman, p. 192.

42. Freidel, p. 7.

43. *New York Times*, 17/1/33; I, p. 20.

44. Samuel I. Roseman, *Working with Roosevelt*, pp. 44–45, 560.

45. William D. Hassett, *Off the Record with F.D.R.*, p. 9.

46. Ross T. McIntire, *White House Physician*, pp. 78–79.

47. Freidel, p. 27; Kleeman, pp. 147, 177.

48. W.J. Stewart and Charyle C. Pollard, *Franklin D. Roosevelt, Collector*.

49. Freidel, p. 46; inscribed copies FDRL.

50. D. Brinkley and D.R. Foley-Crowther, eds., *Atlantic Charter*, pp. 34–35; Gaddis Smith, *Roosevelt, the Sea, and International Security*.

51. *Philadelphia Record*, 6/14/13; Freidel, p. 29.

52. August Kubizek, *Young Hitler*, p. 118; Ian Kershaw, *Hitler*, vol. I, *Hubris, 1889–1936*, p. 610.

53. Freidel, p. 34; Kleeman, p. 166.

54. Frank D. Ashburn, *Peabody of Groton*, p. 341.

55. Ward, p. 97.

56. Ibid., p. 119.

57. Ibid., pp. 120–121, 335–336; Francis Biddle, Roosevelt's attorney general forty years later, did not recall him as a tenor.

58. *New York Times*, 3/6/34; original source George Biddle, "As I Remember Groton School," *Harper's*, August 1939.

59. Harriman quote: Ward, p. 189; Freidel, p. 41; Acheson quote: David Acheson, *Acheson Country*, pp. 163–164.

60. PL, p. 315.

61. Ibid., p. 207; Sara Roosevelt diary, pp. 42–45.

62. PL, pp. 332–334; Ward, p. 203; Kenneth S. Davis, *FDR*, vol. 1, *The Beckoning of Destiny, 1882–1928*, p. 125; Freidel, pp. 49–50.

63. PL, p. 392; Davis, p. 125; Ward, p. 204.

64. Ward, p. 203.

65. PL, p. 392.

66. George Biddle, *An American Artist's Story*, p. 67; Ward, p. 207.

67. Ward, p. 207, told to Geoffrey Ward by Franklin D. Roosevelt Jr.

68. PL, pp. 212, 213, 298, 396, 397; Davis, p. 120.

69. Davis, p. 405.

70. Ward, p. 222.

71. Kleeman, pp. 201–202.

72. Ward, p. 225.

73. Arthur M. Schlesinger Jr., *The Age of Roosevelt*, vol. 2, *The Coming of the New Deal: 1933–1935*, p. 557.

74. Kleeman, pp. 215–216; PL, p. 458.

75. PL, pp. 467–468.

76. Freidel, pp. 55–56; FDRL, general correspondence, letter to Michael Hennessey, 22/10/31; *New York Telegram*, 30/11/13.

77. Ward, pp. 235–238, from interview of James Roosevelt by Geoffrey Ward.

78. *Harvard Crimson*, 4/11/03, p. 1.

79. *Harvard Alumni Bulletin*, 28/4/45, pp. 47, 444.

80. Ibid., editorial comment.

81. FDRL, RFP, Sara Roosevelt diary, p. 59.

82. PL, pp. 245, 366, 437; Freidel, p. 49; Ward, p. 29.

83. Ward, pp. 253–254.

84. Ibid.; Freidel, p. 65.

85. Ward, p. 255, from Geoffrey Ward's interviews with Mrs. Sohier's descendants.

86. Kleeman, p. 233.

87. All these episodes from Eleanor's early years are recounted, inter alia, in Ward, chap. 7, pp. 258–313.
88. Eleanor Roosevelt, *This Is My Story (TIMS)*, p. 104; Kleeman, pp.172–173; Freidel, p. 25.
89. PL, p. 510; Freidel, p. 63.
90. Rexford G. Tugwell, *The Democratic Roosevelt*, pp. 31–32.
91. Eleanor Roosevelt, *TIMS*, pp. 149–150.
92. Kleeman, p. 244; Lindley, p. 68; Freidel, p. 78; Ward, p. 340.
93. Ward, p. 319.
94. PPA, 1944–1945, pp. 46–47; S. Jackson, *Caruso*, p. 110; Ward, pp. 328–329.
95. Kleeman, pp. 235, 240.
96. FDRL, RFP, TR to FDR and TR to ER, 29/11/04.
97. Eleanor Roosevelt, *TIMS*, p. 123; TR letter to FDR, PCA, 18/5/17.
98. Ward, p. 339.
99. Ibid., p. 116.
100. Ibid., p. 117.
101. Ibid.

CHAPTER 2

1. PL, vol. II, p. 7.
2. Eleanor Roosevelt, *This Is My Story (TIMS)*, p. 35.
3. Ibid., p. 148.
4. Geoffrey Ward, *A First Class Temperament*, vol. II, p. 28.
5. Eleanor Roosevelt, *TIMS*, p. 125.
6. PL, vol. II, p. 127.
7. Ward, p. 24.
8. Ibid., p. 28.
9. Kenneth S. Davis, *FDR*, vol. I, *The Beckoning of Destiny, 1882–1928*, p. 195; Eleanor Roosevelt, *TIMS*, pp. 104, 137.
10. PL, vol. II, p. 80.
11. Ibid., p. 38.
12. Eleanor Roosevelt, *TIMS*, p. 151.
13. Bernard Asbell, *Mother & Daughter: The Letters of Eleanor and Anna Roosevelt*, p. 20.
14. James Roosevelt and Sydney Shalett, *Affectionately, F.D.R.: A Son's Story of a Lonely Man*, p. 20.
15. Frances Perkins, *The Roosevelt I Knew*, p. 63.
16. Eleanor Roosevelt, *TIMS*, pp. 149–150.
17. Davis, p. 201; Ward, p. 96.
18. Eleanor Roosevelt, *TIMS*, pp. 157–158.
19. Ward, p. 64.
20. Noel F. Busch, *What Manner of Man*, pp. 74–75.
21. Richard Harity and Ralph G. Martin, *The Human Side of FDR*; Davis, p. 213.
22. Grenville Clark, *Harvard Alumni Bulletin*, vol. 47, 28/4/45, p. 452; R.D. Graff, R. Ginna, R. Butterfield, *FDR*, p. 46.
23. PL, vol. II, pp. 141–145.

24. Eleanor Roosevelt, *TIMS*, p. 165.
25. FDRL, RFP, Eleanor Roosevelt to FDR, summer 1909; Ward, p. 99.
26. FDRL, Palmer-Mack, small collections, interview of 1/2/49; Frank Freidel, *Franklin D. Roosevelt*, vol. I, *The Apprenticeship*, p. 87; Ward, p. 101; Davis, p. 221.
27. *Letters to Anna Roosevelt Cowles*, p. 289, TR to ARC, 10/8/10.
28. FDRL, PPF 1009.
29. FDRL, Mylod Papers, F. Kennen Moody dissertation, p. 216.
30. FDRL, R. Graff Papers, Interview with Eleanor Roosevelt, Reel 2, p. 15.
31. Eleanor Roosevelt, *TIMS*, p. 167.
32. *Poughkeepsie Eagle*, 11/11/10, p. 3.
33. Edmund R. Terry, "The Insurgents at Albany," *The Independent*, 7/9/11, p. 538.
34. FDRL, Roosevelt State Senator Papers, FDR to D. Blagden, 21/2/12, FDR to J.P. Chamberlin, 29/10/12.
35. Ward, pp. 136–137.
36. Albany *Knickerbocker Press*, 18/1/11.
37. Davis, p. 255; FDRL, RSSP, FDR to James Barkley, 4/4/11.
38. Freidel, p. 116; FDRL, RSSP, FDR to Murray, 3/4/11.
39. Ibid.
40. Ward, pp. 150–152.
41. Freidel, p. 116; FDRL, RSSP, FDR to H.W. Lunger, 30/1/28.
42. Freidel, p. 119; FDRL newspaper clippings.
43. Perkins, pp. 9–14.
44. Ibid.
45. Ibid., p. 14.
46. Davis, p. 266, Freidel, pp. 132–133; FDRL Speech File, People's Forum, Troy, NY, 3/3/12.
47. Freidel, pp. 139–140; PL, vol. II, pp.184–190.
48. Ernest K. Lindley, *Franklin D. Roosevelt: A Career in Progressive Democracy*, p. 102.
49. Arthur S. Link, *Wilson: The Road to the White House*, pp. 116–117.
50. Ward,. p. 183.
51. Eleanor Roosevelt, *TIMS*, pp. 187–188.
52. Ibid.
53. Freidel, p. 149.
54. Ward, p. 197; Davis, p. 152; Lela Stiles, *The Man Behind Roosevelt*, p. 37.
55. Ward, pp. 198–199; Freidel, p. 152; Davis, p. 301.
56. Ward, p. 217; Freidel, p. 155.
57. FDRL letter from E. Peabody; Ward, p. 202.
58. PL, vol. II, p. 199.
59. Ward, p. 202.
60. Ray Stannard Baker, *Woodrow Wilson: Life and Letters*, pp. 236–251.
61. Josephus Daniels, *The Wilson Era (TWE)*, vol. I, *Years of Peace*, p. 188; FDRL, Howe to FDR, 11/4/14.
62. Davis, pp. 334–339; Freidel, p. 232; *Chicago Examiner*, 27/4/14.
63. Freidel, p. 164; Ward, p. 209; FDRL, Henry B. Wilson to FDR, 7/7/13.
64. Freidel, pp. 164–166, 169–170.
65. Ibid; Ward, p. 214.

66. PL, vol. I, p. 480.

67. Mrs. Josephus Daniels, *Recollections of a Cabinet Minister's Wife*, pp. 3–5.

68. Ward, p. 217.

69. Daniels, *TWE*, vol. I, p. 165.

70. Ward, p. 224.

71. Ibid., p. 227; FDR 879th Press Conference, 11/2/43, PPA.

72. Ward, p. 228; James MacGregor Burns, *Leadership*, p. 32; Michael R. Beschloss, *Kennedy and Roosevelt*, p. 46.

73. Freidel, p. 273; *New York Times*, 30/3/15, p. 8.

74. Freidel, p. 179; Ward, p. 238; *New York Times*, 13/3/14, 11/4/13.

75. FDRL, personal letter to Governor Martin Glynn, 26/1/14.

76. FDRL, TWW to FDR, 1/4/14; Ward, p. 239.

77. FDRL, letter of President Wilson to FDR, 1/4/14; Ernest K. Lindley, *Franklin D. Roosevelt: A Career in Progressive Democracy*.

78. PL, vol. II, pp. 237–238.

79. Ibid.

80. Freidel, p. 238; PL, vol. II, p. 225.

81. PL, pp. 245–246.

82. Freidel, p. 185; *New York Times*, 8/9/14.

83. Eleanor Roosevelt, *TIMS*, p. 220; FDRL, PSF 151.

84. Ward, p. 297.

85. Ibid., p. 299.

86. Ibid., p. 201; Freidel, pp. 242–243; Davis, p. 392.

87. An example of this: PL, vol. II, pp. 261–265; *New York Times*, 17/12/14.

88. Ward, p. 306.

89. PL, vol. II, pp. 325–327.

90. Ward, p. 319.

91. Ibid., p. 324.

92. Davis, p. 429.

93. FDRL, RASNP, trip to Haiti and Santo Domingo, speech text; Freidel, pp. 276 et seq.; Ward, p. 327; Davis, p. 435 et seq.

94. Ward, p. 330; Freidel, p. 279.

95. Ward, p. 330; FDRL, RASNP, trip to Haiti and Santo Domingo.

96. Ward, p. 331.

97. PPA, toast to president of Haiti, 14/10/43.

98. Ibid.; informal remarks at dinner of Trustees of FDRL, 4/2/39.

99. Freidel, p. 292; Davis, p. 446.

100. Ward, p. 337.

101. Ibid., p. 340; Freidel, pp. 298–300; FDRL, diary of FDR, 9/3/17.

102. Ward, p. 340.

103. Ibid.; Josephus Daniels, *Cabinet Diaries (CD)*, 18/3/17.

104. Davis, p. 455.

105. Ibid., p. 456.

106. Ibid., p. 457.

107. Ibid., p. 459; Ward, p. 345; Freidel, p. 301.

108. Freidel, p. 301; Davis, p. 459; Ward, p. 346.

109. Freidel, p. 302.

CHAPTER 3

1. FDRL, ASNP, personal file, Camp, FDR, 25/7/17.

2. *New York Tribune*, 4/7/18.

3. Ibid.

4. Frank Freidel, *F.D.R.*, vol. I, *The Apprenticeship,*. p. 323.

5. Geoffrey Ward, *A First Class Temperament*, vol. II, p. 342.; FDRL, PPF 3946, FDR letter to Captain Beardall, 22/8/41.

6. Ward, pp. 348–349.

7. Ibid., p. 350.

8. Ibid; *Wall Street Journal*, 11/5/17.

9. PL II, p. 352; Freidel, vol. I, pp. 309–311; Kenneth S. Davis, *FDR*, vol. I, *The Beckoning of Destiny, 1882–1928*, p. 465; Ward, p. 355.

10. PL II, pp. 355–356.

11. Davis, p. 414; Ward, p. 354; Ernest K. Lindley, *Franklin D. Roosevelt: A Career in Progressive Democracy*, p. 160.

12. Davis, p. 475.

13. FDRL, PPF FDR; Freidel, vol. I, p. 317.

14. Lindley, p. 159.

15. PL II, p 351

16. Ward, p. 382.

17. Ibid.; Josephus Daniels, *Cabinet Diaries (CD)*, May 1918, pp. 302–305.

18. FDRL, ASNP, personal, FDR to John Mack, 18/6/18; FDR to President Wilson 8/7/18.

19. FDRL, Howe Papers, L.M. Howe to ER, 17/8/18.

20. Freidel, vol. I, p. 344; Josephus Daniels, *The Wilson Era (TWE)*, vol. II, *Years of War*, p. 263; Daniels, *CD*, 18/6/48, p. 379.

21. PL II, p. 379; FDRL, FDR diary, 11/7/18.

22. PL II, p 391

23. Carol Felsenthel, *Alice Roosevelt Longworth*, p. 255; Ward, p. 393.

24. PL II, p. 393.

25. Ward, p. 394.

26. Ibid., p. 396.

27. PL II, pp. 409–410.

28. Ibid., p. 411.

29. Ibid., pp. 427–428.

30. Ibid., pp. 393–394.

31. Ibid., pp. 431–432.

32. Freidel, vol. I, pp. 361–362; FDRL, ASNP, E. McCauley in FDR Europe diary.

33. FDR to Margaret Suckley, 15/10/41, Elliott Roosevelt, ed., PL, vol. IV, pp. 433–434.

34. Ibid., p. 434.

35. Admiral Nicholas Horthy, *Memoirs*, Internet edition, p. 107; J.F. Montgomery, *Hungary, the Unwilling Satellite*.

36. Daniels, *CD*, 5/9/18; Daniels, *TWE*, vol. I, p. 264.

37. Daniels, *CD*, 10/9/18.

38. FDRL, ASNP, FDR letter to Geddes; Ward, p. 40.

39. FDRL, ASNP, FDR to J. Daniels, 27/8/18; FDR to L. Davis, 11/10/18; Pauillac Pilot, 7/8/18; PL II, pp. 439–440.

40. Freidel, vol. I, p. 367.

41. Davis diary, 22/8 and 10/9/18; PPA 1935; pp. 249–252; Freidel, vol. I, pp. 366–367; Ward, p. 405; Davis, pp. 527–528.

42. Secretary of the Navy Annual Report, 1919, p. 12; Freidel, vol. I, p. 369; PL, pp. 366–368.

43. Freidel, vol. I, p. 369 (23/9/18).

44. Davis, p. 492.

45. PL II, pp. 349–350.

46. Jonathan Daniels, *Washington Quadrille*, pp. 116–117; Felsenthel, p. 137; Ward, p. 366.

47. Ward, p. 415.

48. Murray Kempton, *New York Review of Books*, 15/4/82, pp. 3–4; Ward, p. 415.

49. Freidel, vol. I, p. 337; Ward, p. 417; FDRL, RP 1920-8; FDR to H.H. Richard, 28/6/21.

50. PL II, pp. 444–448.

51. Ibid., p. 447.

52. Ward, p. 422.

53. PL II, pp. 435–455.

54. Frank Freidel, *F.D.R.*, vol. II, *The Ordeal*, pp. 9–10; FDRL, DNC Box 692, F.H. Allen to FDR, 16/8/30.

55. Freidel, vol. II, p. 7.

56. Ibid., p. 8.

57. Davis, pp. 554–560; Freidel, vol. II, p. 14.

58. Daniels, *TWE*, vol. II, p. 265.

59. Eleanor Roosevelt, *TIMS*, p. 289.

60. Joseph P. Tumulty, *Woodrow Wilson as I Knew Him*, Appendix, 6/1/19.

61. Ray S. Baker, *American Chronicle*, p. 470; Daniels, *TWE*, vol. II, p. 256; Davis, p. 500—(Davis took the canard seriously).

62. Ward, p. 453.

63. Freidel, vol. II, pp. 52–54; Davis, pp. 607–608; Ward, p. 45.

64. Joseph P. Lash, *Eleanor and Franklin*, p. 243; Arthur M. Schlesinger Jr., *The Age of Roosevelt*, vol. I, *The Crisis of the Old Order: 1919–1933*, p. 369.

65. Lash, p. 243; Joseph Alsop, *FDR: A Centenary Remembrance*, p. 67.

66. Ward, p. 452.

67. FDRL, RF-BPP, Newport Matters Box 30, FDR manuscript, 18/7/21.

68. Ibid., FDR press release, 18/7/21.

69. Ward, p. 487.

70. U.S. *Senate Report of the Committee of Naval Affairs*, 1921.

71. Ibid., p. 29.

72. Ward, p. 570.

73. FDRL, RF BPP, Box 30, FDR press release, 18/7/21.

74. Ibid.; Statement of Service, Thomas M. Osborne; Providence, RI, *Journal*, 22/1/20; Ward, p. 445.

75. Ward, pp. 467–468.

76. FDRL, AP Scrapbook, *New York Times*, 2/2/20.

77. Carroll Kilpatrick, ed., *Roosevelt and Daniels*, pp. 77–78.

78. Freidel, vol. II, p. 28; Davis, pp. 603–604; Daniels, *CD*, pp. 512–515.

79. Davis, p. 596; Schlesinger, p. 14; Sigmund Freud and William C. Bullitt, *Woodrow Wilson: A Psychological Study*, pp. 271–272.

80. FDRL, New York Bar Association, Box 2, 3/3/19, p. 26.

81. Davis, p. 582.

82. Alice Roosevelt Longworth, *Crowded Hours*, pp. 285–286.

83. Daniels, *TWE*, vol. II, p. 473.

84. Freidel, vol. II, pp. 57–58.

85. Ward, p. 476.

86. Ibid., p. 490.

87. Francis Russell, *The Shadow of Blooming Grove: Warren G. Harding and His Times*, p. 39.

88. Ward, p. 512.

89. Ronald Steel, *Walter Lippmann and the American Century*, p. 169.

90. PL II, pp. 493–494.

91. Freidel, vol. II, p. 75.

92. Freidel, vol. II, p. 74, Charles S. Graves to Henry Cabot Lodge, 4/7/20, and Lodge to Graves, 26/7/20.

93. Davis, p. 616.

94. PL II, pp. 496–497.

95. Ward, p. 515.

96. Ibid.; Davis, p. 616.

97. PL II, p. 495.

98. Ward, p. 519.

99. PL II, pp. 489–490.

100. Ibid.

101. Daniels, *CD*, 6/8/20; Freidel, vol. II, p. 76.

102. Russell, p. 409; Freidel, vol. II, p. 76; Ward, p. 521.

103. PL II, pp. 495–508.

104. Ibid.

105. Freidel, vol. II, p. 78; FDRL, F.W. Tanasig to FDR, 12/8/20.

106. FDRL, Sara Roosevelt diary, 9/8/20; *New York Times*, 9/10/20.

107. Ward, p. 520.

108. Harold Ickes; *The Secret Diary of Harold Ickes, 1933–1936*, p. 699.

109. Ibid.

110. Ibid.

111. Ward, p. 545; Freidel Papers; FDRL, oral history.

112. *New York Times*, 18/9/20.

113. Ward, p. 532.

114. *New York Times*, 9/8/20; FDRL, Speech File, Box 1, 18/8/20.

115. FDRL, Speech File, Box 2–21, 23/8/20.

116. *New York Times*, 18/9/20.

117. Ward, p. 536.

118. FDRL, Speech File, Box 2, Centralia, 21/8/20.

119. FDRL, McCarthy letter to FDR, 8/101/20; Freidel, vol. II, p. 86; Ward, p. 541.

120. Freidel, vol. II, p. 86.

121. Eleanor Roosevelt, *TIMS*, p. 316.

122. FDRL, ASNP, Box 30, Newport Matters, Supreme Court of New York: *Franklin D. Roosevelt v. John Rathon.*

123. Ward, p. 553.

124. Ibid., p. 555; Freidel, vol. II, p. 90; FDRL, Cox to FDR, 20/10/20; FDRL, FDR to Cox, 23/10/20.

125. FDRL, FDR to Coolidge, 3/11/20; Freidel, vol. II, p. 90.

126. Alfred Steinberg, *Mrs. R,* p. 121.

127. FDRL, ASNP, Box 7, FDR to M. Hale, 6/11/20.

128. Ibid., Box 11, FDR to Louis B. Wehle, 6/11/20.

129. Ward, p. 557

130. Ibid., p. 556.

131. PL II, pp. 392–393.

132. Ward, p. 559.

133. *New York Times,* 8/1/21.

CHAPTER 4

1. Eleanor Roosevelt, *This Is My Story (TIMS),* chap. 12.

2. FDRL, Eleanor Roosevelt Papers, Condolences, Box 2, ER to James R. Roosevelt, 14/8/21.

3. Ibid., RFP, Box 17, Sara Roosevelt to Frederic H. Delano, 2/9/21.

4. *New York Times,* 27/8/21.

5. Geoffrey Ward, *A First Class Temperament,* vol. II, p. 598; Kenneth S. Davis, *The Beckoning of Destiny, 1882–1928,* vol. I, p. 661.

6. Ward, p. 599.

7. Ernest K. Lindley, *Franklin D. Roosevelt: A Career in Progressive Democracy,* p. 203; Ward, p. 601; Frank Freidel, *F.D.R.,* vol. II, *The Ordeal,* p. 102; Davis, p. 662.

8. *New York Times,* 16/9/21.

9. John Gunther, *Roosevelt in Retrospect,* p. 226; Freidel, p. 103; Ward, p. 605; Davis, pp. 663–664.

10. Freidel, p. 103.

11. Gunther, p. 224; Ward, p. 609; Davis, p. 666.

12. Ward, p. 690.

13. James Roosevelt and Sydney Shalett, *Affectionately, F.D.R.: A Son's Story of a Lonely Man,* p. 246.

14. Ibid.; Ward, p. 611.

15. Davis, p. 677.

16. Roosevelt and Shalett, p. 158.

17. Ward, p. 617.

18. Eleanor Roosevelt, *TIMS,* p. 336.

19. FDRL, RP 1920–1928, President Wilson to FDR, 4/7/21.

20. Freidel, p. 123.

21. FDRL, condolence message, President Wilson to FDR, 16/9/21.
22. Ibid., President Wilson to ER, 9/11/21.
23. FDRL, RFBPP, FDR to L. Davis, 20/4/24; President Wilson to FDR, 5/1/22; RFBPP, Box 35.
24. Ward, p. 623; FDRL, RFBPP, Howe, F&D clients.
25. Ward, pp. 624–625.
26. Richard Thayer Goldberg, *The Making of Franklin D. Roosevelt*, p. 88.
27. Ward, p. 631; Michael Teague, *Mrs. L.*, p. 166.
28. FDRL, Marion Dickerman Oral History Project; Ward, p. 632.
29. Wilhelmine Wright, "Crutch Walking as an Art," ("CWA") *American Journal of Surgery*.
30. Ward, p. 630.
31. Ibid., pp. 634–636; Wright, "CWA."
32. Eleanor Roosevelt, *TIMS*, p. 350.
33. Roosevelt-Vanderbilt National Historic Sites Oral History Collection, G. Palmer–B. Haviland interview, 31/12/47.
34. Henry Moskowitz, *Alfred E Smith: An American Career*, p. 288.
35. Ward, p. 653.
36. FDRL, Small Collections, oral history; Frank Freidel–Louis Depew interview.
37. Turnley Walker, *Roosevelt and the Warm Springs Story*, pp. 6–9.
38. Ward, pp. 54–55.
39. FDRL, RFBPP, Box 4, FDR to McAdoo, 13/12/27.
40. FDRL, Speech File, Madison Square Garden, 31/10/36.
41. Freidel; p. 147; FDRL, RFB PP, FDR to Kimball, 20/7/23.
42. FDRL, RFBPP, F. Andree letter to FDR, 20/7/23; FDR to Andree 31/7/23.
43. Ibid., p. 138.
44. *New York Times*, 5/5/24.
45. *Chicago Tribune*, 17/7/34.
46. *New York Times*, 4/6/22, section VII, p. 2.
47. *New York Times*, 6/2/23; FDRL, RFBPP, FDR to Henry Ford, 23/1/24.
48. FDRL, RFBPP, FDR to EF Lawrence; FDR 6 mos. statement, 23/10/24; *New York Times*, 12/5/23.
49. FDRL, PPF 7553, FDR to A. Jenks, 20/5/4.
50. Freidel, p. 59; Freidel–ER interview, 3/9/52.
51. Freidel, p. 159.
52. FDRL, RFBP, Box 36, F. Tams to FDR, 20/12/22.
53. Ward, p. 662.
54. Ward, p. 663.
55. Freidel, p. 189; FDRL, FDR to C. Glass, 17/3/23.
56. FDRL, RFBPP, Box 376, Weong to II Log, 27/2/23.
57. Nathan Miller, *The Roosevelt Chronicles*, p. 137.
58. FDRL, Henry Morgenthau Jr. Papers, Presidential Diary, vol. 5, 27/1/42; Ward, p. 255; Jack Beatty, *The Rascal King: The Life and Times of James Michael Curley (1875–1958)*, p. 449; Michael R. Beschloss, *The Conquerors*, p. 51.
59. FDRL, ER Papers, Correspondence, Box 13, Folder 2, ER to Sara Roosevelt, 16/1/18.
60. FDRL, RFBPP, letter from S.E. Bertron to FDR, 27/8/24; Freidel, p. 187.

61. FDRL, RFBPP, Box 35, FDR to George Draper, 12/2/23.

62. Freidel, pp. 114–115; Ward, pp. 670–671; *Poughkeepsie Courier*, 19/6/21; FDRL, RFBPP, FDR to Henry Wallace, 30/7/42, PPF 446.

63. Davis, p. 686.

64. FDRL, RFBPP, FDR, "Shall We Trust Japan?" *Asia Magazine*,. vol. 23, 7/23.

65. FDRL, Campaign of 1924, Box 12, G. McWin to FDR, 30/6/24.

66. FDRL, RFBPP, Box 41, FDR review of C. Bowers's book, *New York World*, 19/11/25.

67. Ward, p. 681.

68. Ibid., pp. 672–673.

69. Ibid., p. 672.

70. Ibid., p. 678.

71. Ibid., pp. 676–677; F. Perkins, Columbia Oral History.

72. Ward, p. 709.

73. Bernard Asbell, *The FDR Memoirs*, p. 244; Ward, p. 709.

74. Conversation with William Safire, 8/7/02.

75. Asbell, p. 244.

76. PL II, p. 538.

77. Ibid., p. 545.

78. Freidel, p. 235; Marley F. Hay, 4/50, Columbia Oral History Project.

79. FDR letter to *Baltimore Sun*, 13/8/23.

80. FDRL, RFBPP, Box 41, Haiti memo, 1922.

81. Freidel, p. 237.

82. FDRL, RFBPP, Box 5, FDR to Al Smith, 21/5/23; Smith to FDR, 5/6/23.

83. *New York Times*, 9/6/24.

84. FDRL, RBFPP, Box 41, press release, 25/4/24.

85. Ward, p. 683.

86. FDRL, RFBPP, FDR to D.S. Hawkins, 22/3/24.

87. Davis, p. 738.

88. Freidel, p. 165.

89. FDRL, RFBPP, 1924. Campaign Papers, Box 10, FDR to Glenn Frank, 12/8/24.

90. M. Sullivan, *Our Times*, p. 333.

91. Davis, p. 753.

92. FDRL, 1924 Campaign Papers, Box 11, FDR to LaFollete, 3, 9/6/24.

93. Ibid., FDR to Marjorie MacCracken, 13/5/24.

94. Ward, p. 692.

95. FDRL, RBBPP, G.M. Palmer–Moses Smith interview, 15/1/48.

96. Freidel, p. 180; FDRL, RFBPP, I.B. Dunlap to FDR, 10/7/24; Davis, p. 757; Ward, p. 699.

97. FDRL, 1924 Campaign Papers, J.A. Farley to FDR, 2/5/24.

98. FDRL, 1924 Campaign Papers, G.H. Ruth to FDR, 13/6/24.

99. Freidel, p. 181; FDRL, 1924 Campaign Papers, H.T. Rainey to FDR, 13/6/24.

100. John Morton Blum, ed., *Public Philosopher: Selected Letters of Walter Lippmann*, p. 163, Lippmann to FDR, 27/6/24.

101. Ted Morgan, *FDR: A Biography*, p. 272.

102. Freidel, p. 169.

103. FDRL, 1924 Campaign Papers, FDR to Willard Saulsbury, 9/12/24.

104. Ibid.
105. Ward, p. 701.
106. Eleanor Roosevelt, *This I Remember*, pp. 31–32.
107. Davis, p. 782; FDRL, Mrs. C.L. Hamlin, *Memories of FDR*.
108. FDRL, 1924 Campaign Papers, FDR to Willard Saulsbury, 9/12/24.
109. Davis, p. 774.
110. Donald Day, *Franklin D. Roosevelt's Own Story*, p. 82.
111. Freidel, p. 193.
112. Ward, pp. 725–726; FDRL, RFBPP, D.S.Carmichael, *FDR Columnist*.
113. FDRL, RFBPP, Box 1, FDR to V.L. Black, 31/8/25.
114. Davis, p. 795; Freidel, p. 197.
115. PL II, p. 571.
116. Robert Skidelsky, *Oswald Mosley*, p. 150.
117. Ibid., pp. 148, 150.
118. PL II, p. 596.
119. Ward, p. 755.
120. Ibid., pp. 623–624, 755.
121. Ibid., p. 746; Davis, p. 808.
122. Theodore Lippmann, *The Squire of Warm Springs*, p. 241.
123. Conversation of Lady Soames with author, 12/7/02.
124. Ward, pp. 748–749.
125. Ibid., p. 752; Freidel, p. 216.
126. Ward, p. 753.
127. Richard O'Connor, *The First Hurrah*, p. 162; I.J. Huthmacher, *Senator Robert Wagner and The Rise of Urban Liberalism*, pp. 51–52; Davis, pp. 806–807.
128. Ward, p. 779–780.
129. Davis, p. 792; Robert Moses, *Public Works: A Dangerous Trade*, pp. 141–142; Roosevelt and Shalett, p. 167; FDRL, RFBPP, Box 5, V.L. Black to FDR, 22/4/25.

CHAPTER 5

1. Kenneth S. Davis, *The Beckoning of Destiny, 1882–1928*, vol. I, p. 819; Richard O'Connor, *The First Hurrah*, p. 197; PL III, FDR to C. Bowers, pp. 45–46.
2. *Chicago Tribune*, 28/7/28; *New York Times*, 28/6/28; PL II, p. 639; *New York World*, 29/7/28 (Durant).
3. Franklin D. Roosevelt, *Foreign Affairs*, July 1928, pp. 3–16; Davis, vol. I, p. 818.
4. *New York Times*, 8/11/28, 13/11/28; PL III, FDR to Senator B. Wheeler, pp. 129–130.
5. Frank Freidel, *F.D.R.*, vol. III, *The Triumph*, p. 9; *New York Times*, 5/12/28, 10/12/28.
6. Freidel, vol. III, p. 9; Samuel I. Rosenman, *Working with Roosevelt*, p. 28.
7. Frances Perkins, *The Roosevelt I Knew*, pp. 51–52; Freidel, vol. III, p. 17.
8. Emily Smith Warner, *The Happy Warrior*, pp. 183–184, 240; Kenneth S. Davis, *The New York Years, 1928–1933*, vol. II, p. 60.
9. Davis, vol. II, p. 64.
10. Freidel, vol. III, p. 3.
11. *New York Times, New York Herald Tribune, New York World*, 2/1/29.
12. *New York Times*, 3/1/29.

13. Ibid., 8/4/29.

14. *New York Times*, 29/3/29; FDR Public Papers—Governor, 1929, pp. 518–519.

15. FDRL, Governor Office File, letters to James C. Bonbright, 12/10/29, and to L. Davis, 5/12/29; Freidel, vol. III, p. 104.

16. Freidel, vol. III, p. 81.

17. Davis, vol. II, p. 94.

18. *New York Times*, 15/1/30; *Brooklyn Eagle*, 16/3/30.

19. FDRL, GPNY, Box 37, FDR letter to P.L.Herrick, 21/6/29; Freidel, vol. III, p. 73.

20. PPA, 1928–1932, xii; Freidel, vol. III, pp. 5–6.

21. *New York Times*, 30/12/28.

22. PL III, p. 119; FDR to W.I.Sirovich, 5/11/30.

23. *New York Times*, 4/8/29.

24. Freidel, vol. III, p. 80

25. Ibid., p. 86.

26. *New York Times*, 25/11/29.

27. FDRL, GP, Box 163, Sioux City, Iowa, *Tribune*; Freidel, vol. III, p. 96.

28. FDRL, GP, Box 77, FDR to B. Sullivan, 31/12/29.

29. Freidel, vol. III, p. 159.

30. Joseph P. Lash, *Eleanor and Franklin*, p. 336.

31. *New York Times*, 5/11/30; Freidel, vol. III, p. 167.

32. Davis, vol. II, p. 214.

33. Freidel, vol. III, p. 204.

34. PCA (Hungerford letter); Frank Freidel, *F.D.R.*, vol. II, *The Ordeal*, pp. 186–187; FDRL GP, FDR-1, D.L. Corbett, 22/1/25.

35. Freidel, vol. III, p. 183.

36. Ibid., pp. 188–189; John T. Flynn, "The Bank of the United States," *New Republic*, 28/1/31.

37. Davis, vol. II, p. 253.

38. Freidel, vo. III, p. 223.

39. Davis, vol. II, p. 250.

40. Freidel, vol. III, p. 236.

41. Davis, vol. II, p. 260; Freidel, vol. III, p. 253; FDRL, GP, FDR to Florence Stryker, 16/2/32.

CHAPTER 6

1. Rexford G. Tugwell, *The Democratic Roosevelt*, p. 213.

2. *New York Times*, 22/6/32; Gene Fowler, *Beau James*, pp. 314–315.

3. Frank Freidel, *F.D.R.*, vol. III, *The Triumph*, p. 298.

4. Ibid., p. 301; James A. Farley, *Behind the Ballots*, p. 123.

5. Freidel, vol. III, p. 293.

6. Farley, p. 142.

7. H.L. Mencken, *Making a President*, pp. 158–159, 166–167; Freidel, vol. III, pp. 303, 311.

8. Kenneth S. Davis, *FDR*, vol. II, *The New York Years, 1928–1933*, p. 332.

9. David Nasaw, *The Chief: The Life of William Randolph Hearst*, p. 456.

10. Ibid., p. 408

11. Freidel, vol. III, p. 316.

12. Eleanor Roosevelt, *This I Remember*, pp. 60–61; Freidel, vol. III, p. 324.

13. Farley, pp. 170–171; Freidel, vol. III, p. 331.

14. Herbert Mitgang, *Once Upon a Time in New York*, p. 202.

15. Ibid., pp. 221, 227.

16. Ibid., p. 229; Arthur M. Schlesinger Jr., *The Age of Roosevelt*, vol. III, *The Politics of Upheaval: 1935–1936*, p. 627.

17. Freidel, vol. III, p. 336; Samuel I. Rosenman, *Working with Roosevelt*, pp. 83–84.

18. FDRL, PPF, R.R. McCormick to FDR, 19/7/32 and 6/8/32; Freidel, vol. III, p. 341.

19. FDRL, PPF, W.R. Hearst to FDR, 8/7/32 and 6/9/32, FDR to W.R. Hearst, 5/9/32; Freidel, vol. III, p. 342.

20. Bascom N. Timmons, *Garner of Texas*, p. 168.

21. Davis, p. 362.

22. Freidel, vol. III, p. 343.

23. Ibid., p. 361.

24. Ibid., p. 363.

25. Ibid., p. 364.

26. Ibid., p. 358; Raymond Moley, *After Seven Years*, p. 53.

27. Freidel, vol. III, p. 368.

28. William E. Leuchtenberg, *Franklin D. Roosevelt and the New Deal, 1932–1940*, p. 13; Grace Tully, *F.D.R.: My Boss*, p. 60.

29. Michael Barone, *Our Country*, p. 59.

30. *New York Times*, 9/11/32; Freidel, vol. III, p. 371.

31. Leuchtenberg, p. 21n.

32. Ibid., p. 53.

33. Ibid., p. 28.

34. All economic comparative statistics are from the Institute for International Economics, Washington, D.C., courtesy of C. Fred Bergsten, director, and W. Arthur Lewis, *Economic Survey, 1919–1939*.

35. Stimson diary, 22/11/32; Frank Freidel, *F.D.R.*, vol. IV, *Launching the New Deal*, p. 35; Davis, p. 402.

36. Freidel, vol. IV, p. 52.

37. Ibid., p. 120.

38. Ibid.

39. Ibid.

40. Ibid., p. 106.

41. Ibid., pp. 103–104; Lindsay to Simon, 30/1/33, E.L. Woodward and R. Butler, *Documents on British Foreign Policy, 1919–1939*, 2nd series, vol. V, pp. 748–751.

42. Freidel, vol. IV, p. 110; FDRL, Longhand Box, 10/1/33; Claudel to Paul-Boncour, 11/1/33, *Documents Diplomatiques*, 1st series, vol. II, pp. 414–417.

43. Freidel, vol. IV, p. 105; *London News-Chronicle*, 10/11/32.

44. Freidel, vol. IV, p. 105; FDRL, Norman Davis to FDR, 15/10/32.

45. Adolf Hitler, *Last Political Testament*.

46. Freidel, vol. IV, p. 106.

47. Davis, p. 420.

48. Freidel, vol. IV, p. 142.

49. Ibid., pp. 143–144.

50. Ibid., p. 150.

51. Ibid., p. 153.

52. Ibid., p. 173; Davis, p. 431.

53. Freidel, vol. IV, p. 171.

54. Ibid., p. 173.

55. Frances Perkins, *The Roosevelt I Knew*, pp. 182–183.

56. Ibid., p. 183.

57. David Reynolds, *From Munich to Pearl Harbor*, p. 30.

58. Freidel, vol. IV, p. 177.

59. Leuchtenberg, p. 39; Agnes Meyer diary, 25/2/33.

60. Leuchtenberg, p. 40.

61. FDRL, PPF, 28/2/33.

62. Farley, p. 208; Freidel, vol. IV, p. 197.

CHAPTER 7

1. Frank Freidel, *F.D.R.*, vol. IV, *Launching the New Deal*, p. 196.

2. Ibid., p. 197; *Washington Post*, 4/3/33.

3. Freidel, p. 198.

4. Ibid., p. 203n.; Francis Bacon, *De Augmentis Scientiarum*, book VI, chap. III.

5. There is a persistent view, but no consensus among Roosevelt scholars, that he said this, but if so the circumstances are unclear. The likeliest possibility is that he uttered these or similar words in a jocular social moment on returning to private life and arranging his income in 1920, after ten years as a public official. It is, at most, a witticism, and not a philosophical keystone.

6. Robert Skidelsky, *Oswald Mosley*, p. 296.

7. Hollinger Collection, 7/7/33.

8. FDRL, PPF 434 BL (Breckinridge Long).

9. George Martin, *Madame Secretary: Frances Perkins*, p. 12.

10. Freidel, p. 208.

11. Ibid., p. 210.

12. Rexford G. Tugwell, *The Democratic Roosevelt*, pp. 270–271.

13. Freidel, p. 274; Arthur M. Schlesinger Jr., *The Age of Roosevelt*, vol. II, *The Coming of the New Deal: 1933–1935*, p. 14.

14. Gary Aichele, *Oliver Wendell Holmes: Soldier, Scholar, Judge*; Richard A. Posner, *The Essential Holmes*. Both authors point out that in context it was likelier that Holmes was speaking of Theodore Roosevelt, whom he had known much better than Franklin.

15. Letter of James A. Prozzi, *New Republic*, 5/7/93; Joseph P. Lash, *Dealers and Dreamers*, p. 102; Thomas G. Corcoran, *Memoirs*, p. 8.

16. FDRL, PPF 2280, O.W. Holmes to FDR, 16/3/33.

17. Letter to author from Arthur M. Schlesinger Jr., 25/5/02. Dr. Schlesinger wrote: "Scholars today tend to agree with Judge Posner that Holmes was talking about TR." (This is at least as unjust a comment about Theodore Roosevelt, who had a more

energetic but less subtle and devious a mind than Franklin, but that is not strictly relevant to this book.)

18. Lash, p. 277.
19. Bascom N. Timmons, *Jesse H. Jones*, pp. 198–200.
20. John Dos Passos, "The Radio Voice," *Common Sense*, February 1934.
21. Freidel, p. 254; Sir Ronald Lindsay to Sir John Simon, A 2336/17/45, Public Records Office (UK).
22. William E. Leuchtenberg, *Franklin D. Roosevelt and the New Deal 1932–1940*, pp. 46–47.
23. Ibid., p. 174: "Of all the forest planting, public and private, in the history of the nation, more than half was done by the CCC"; John Guthrie, "The CCC and American Conservation," *Scientific Monthly*, LVII (1943), pp. 401–402; Bernard Roth, "Remember the CCC," *Soil Conservation*, XVIII (1953), p. 205; Schlesinger, pp. 338–340.
24. Schlesinger, p. 201.
25. Freidel, p. 324.
26. Kenneth S. Davis, *FDR*, vol. III, *The New Deal Years, 1933–1937*, p. 150.
27. Ibid., p. 152.
28. Schlesinger, p. 437.
29. *Time*, 17/4/33, p. 17.
30. John Weitz, *Hitler's Banker Hjalmar Horace Greeley Schacht*, p. 149; FDRL, PPA, Morgenthau diary, 15/5/33; Freidel, p. 397.
31. Freidel, p. 390.
32. FDRL, PSF, Box 32, Diplomatic Correspondence—Germany.
33. Freidel, p. 403.
34. Ibid.
35. Morgenthau diary, 22/5/33; Freidel, p. 404.
36. David Reynolds, *From Munich to Pearl Harbor*, p. 29.
37. Schlesinger, p. 209.
38. Ibid., p. 211.
39. Cordell Hull, *Memoirs*, vol. I, pp. 250–255; Schlesinger, p. 210.
40. Edward J. Flynn, *You're the Boss*, p. 215.
41. Davis, pp. 192–193.
42. Leuchtenberg, p. 201n., cites Frances Pingeon, *French Opinion of Roosevelt and the New Deal*, M.A. essay, Columbia University, 1962.
43. Freidel, p. 474.
44. Ibid., p. 493.
45. Leuchtenberg, p. 82.
46. Ibid., p. 83; Fred Israel, "The Fulfillment of Bryan's Dream: Key Pittman and Silver Politics, 1918–1933," *Pacific Historical Review*, XXX (1961), p. 380.
47. Schlesinger, p. 251.
48. Hugh S. Johnson, *The Blue Eagle From Egg to Earth*, p. 208; Leuchtenberg, p. 65.
49. Schlesinger, p. 282.
50. Davis, p. 289.
51. Schlesinger, p. 248; FDRL, RP, FDR to Colonel E.M. House, 21/11/33.

52. James Chace, *Acheson: The Secretary of State Who Created the American World*, p. 66.
53. Ibid., pp. 65–68.
54. Ibid.
55. Ibid.
56. Schlesinger, p. 242, quotes from and about Acheson and "agrarian revolution." The same quotes are in most serious histories of the early Roosevelt administration.
57. Chace, p. 68.
58. Schlesinger, p. 242.
59. Lash, p. 148.
60. Leuchtenberg, p. 205; FDRL, PPF 743, G. Peek to FDR, and FDR to G. Peek, 12/11/35 and 22/11/35. Peek had negotiated a barter deal for the sale of surplus American cotton, which Roosevelt had approved, but which Hull persuaded him to revoke as incompatible with the administration's free trade policies.
61. Schlesinger, p. 258.
62. Ibid., p. 284.
63. See p. 1019, re response of Eugene O'Neill.
64. FDRL, proceedings of National Emergency Council, 23/1/34, cited in Leuchtenberg, p. 122.
65. Max Freedman, *Roosevelt and Frankfurter: Their Correspondence 1928–1945*, p. 382.

CHAPTER 8

1. Joseph P. Lash, *Dealers and Dreamers*, p. 179; Frank Freidel, *F.D.R.*, vol. II, *The Ordeal*, p. 130.
2. Kenneth S. Davis, *FDR*, vol. III, *The New Deal Years, 1933–1937*, p. 320.
3. Frank Freidel, *F.D.R.*, vol. IV, *Launching the New Deal*, pp. 111–112.
4. Michael R. Beschloss, *Kennedy and Roosevelt*, p. 88.
5. Rexford G. Tugwell, *The Democratic Roosevelt*, pp. 349–350.
6. Douglas MacArthur, *Reminiscences*, p. 101.
7. Freidel, vol. IV, p. 126; Stimson diary, 9/11/32.
8. PCA, 16/6/34.
9. Davis, p. 335.
10. Ibid., p. 334.
11. William E. Leuchtenberg, *Franklin D. Roosevelt and the New Deal, 1932–1940*, p. 112.
12. Ibid., p. 93.
13. Ibid., p. 86.
14. Ibid., p. 92; Raskob to Shouse, 7/7/32; Shouse mss.
15. Leuchtenberg, p. 92; *New York Times*, 25/8/34.
16. Leuchtenberg, p. 99.
17. Ibid., p. 97.
18. Ibid.
19. Arthur M. Schlesinger Jr., *The Age of Roosevelt*, vol. III, *The Politics of Upheaval: 1935–1936*, p. 49.
20. Ibid., p. 66.
21. Ibid., p. 67.

22. Leuchtenberg, p. 99; *Time*, 6/5/35.

23. Leuchtenberg, p. 105; *New York Herald Tribune*, 4/1/35.

24. Leuchtenberg, p. 101.

25. Schlesinger, vol. III, p. 20.

26. Ibid., p. 22.

27. Ibid., p. 23; Leuchtenberg, p. 101.

28. Schlesinger, vol. III, p. 72.

29. Ibid., p. 25

30. Davis, p. 409.

31. Schlesinger, vol. III, p. 120 (via Stephen Early).

32. Ibid., p. 119.

33. Ibid., p. 80.

34. Davis, pp. 647–648.

35. Schlesinger, vol. III, p. 181.

36. Ibid., p. 173.

37. Leuchtenberg, p. 91.

38. Michael R. Beschloss, *The Conquerors*, p. 208.

39. Ibid.

40. Hugh S. Johnson, *The Blue Eagle From Egg to Earth*, pp. 242, 371–375, 385–386; Arthur M. Schlesinger Jr., *The Age of Roosevelt*, vol. II, *The Coming of the New Deal: 1933–1935*, pp. 153, 157; Donald Richberg, *My Hero*, p. 174, and *The Rainbow*, p. 182; Harold L. Ickes, *The First Thousand Days*, p. 197; Perkins, *The Roosevelt I Knew*, pp. 206, 240 241.

41. Schlesinger, vol. II, p. 500.

42. Ibid.; Raymond Moley, *After Seven Years*, pp. 295–298, *New York Times*, 25/10/34.

43. FDRL, OF 846; David Nasaw, *The Chief: The Life of William Randolph Hearst*, p. 502; Schlesinger, vol. II, p. 507.

44. Leuchtenberg, p. 125.

45. Garner accused Roosevelt of being afraid of John L. Lewis and notoriously absented himself from Washington when Roosevelt was pressing legislative objectives he didn't share. Ted Morgan, *FDR: A Biography*, p. 485.

46. Cordell Hull, *Memoirs*, vol. I, pp. 21, 196; Leuchtenberg, p. 203.

47. Schlesinger, vol. II, p. 426.

48. Freidel, vol. IV, p. 400.

49. Leuchtenberg, p. 149.

50. Lash, p. 134.

51. Ibid., pp. 282, 353.

52. Ibid., p. 282.

53. Terry Teachout, *The Sceptic*, pp. 7–8.

54. Schlesinger, vol. II, p. 565.

55. Teachout, pp. 7–8.

56. Fred Hobson, *Mencken*, pp. 382–383.

57. Ibid.

58. Ibid.

59. Leuchtenberg, p. 197; Borah to James Nelson, 7/12/35, Borah mss., Box 391.

60. Schlesinger, vol. III, p. 244.

61. Ibid., p. 248.
62. Ibid., p. 27.
63. Ibid., pp. 245–246.
64. See Chapter 11.
65. Davis, p. 502.
66. Harry S Truman, *Years of Destiny*, pp. 145–146; Schlesinger, pp. 251–252.
67. Davis, p. 544.
68. Leuchtenberg, p. 133; Schlesinger, vol. III, pp. 308–309; Perkins, pp. 188–189, 282–285.
69. Schlesinger, vol. III, p. 141.
70. T. Harry Williams, *Huey Long*, pp. 812, 836, 837.
71. Leuchtenberg, p. 126.
72. Ibid., p. 133.
73. Ibid., p. 130.
74. Ibid., p. 158.
75. Davis, p. 473.
76. Davis, p. 517.
77. Lash, pp. 253–254.
78. Schlesinger, vol. III, pp. 387–388.
79. PCA, 6/3/35.
80. Ibid., 23/9/35.
81. Morgenthau diary, 20/5/35; John Morton Blum, *Roosevelt and Morgenthau*, p. 127.
82. Schlesinger, vol. II, p. 402.
83. Leuchtenberg, p. 152.
84. Schlesinger, vol. III, p. 305.
85. Nasaw, p. 487.
86. Ibid., p. 512; Davis, p. 543.
87. PPA, 1935, pp. 271–272.
88. FDRL, PPF 62.
89. Nasaw, p. 502.
90. Schlesinger, vol. III, p. 328.
91. Davis, p. 554.
92. FDRL, PSF, Box 32, Diplomatic Correspondence—Germany.
93. Ibid., 27/11/33, 9/5/35.
94. Ibid.
95. Ibid.
96. Leuchtenberg, pp. 210, 221–222; William Dodd and Martha Dodd, eds., *Ambassador Dodd's Diary*, p. 126.
97. Ibid.; Dodd; Leuchtenberg, p. 126.
98. FDRL, PSF, Box 50, Diplomatic Correspondence—Russia.
99. Leuchtenberg, p. 198; *Today*, 21/12/35.
100. Davis, p. 523.
101. Leuchtenberg, p. 166; *Emporia Daily Gazette*, 26/8/35.
102. Leuchtenberg, p. 163; Schlesinger, vol. III, p. 392.

CHAPTER 9

1. Kenneth S. Davis, *FDR*, vol. III, *The New Deal Years, 1933–1937*, p. 575.
2. FDRL, OF 1403, Gerald L.K. Smith to FDR; William E. Leuchtenberg, *Franklin D. Roosevelt and the New Deal, 1932–1940*, p. 180.
3. Ibid.
4. Ibid.
5. Ronald Steel, *Walter Lippman and the American Century*, p. 316.
6. Arthur M. Schlesinger Jr., *The Age of Roosevelt*, vol. III, *The Politics of Upheaval*, pp. 376–377.
7. Kenneth S. Davis, *FDR*, vol. III, *The New Deal Years, 1933–1937*, p. 583.
8. Ibid.
9. PCA, 15/5/36.
10. FDRL, PSF, Box 41, Diplomatic Correspondence—Breckinridge Long—Italy.
11. Ibid., 7/2/34.
12. Ibid., 28/2/34.
13. PCA, 8/3/36.
14. Leuchtenberg, pp. 221–222.
15. Hugh Thomas, *The Spanish Civil War*, p. 363; Manuel Azana, *Memoirs*, vol. IV, p. 630.
16. Lela Stiles, *The Man Behind Roosevelt*, p. 299.
17. Davis, vol. III, p. 603.
18. Stiles, p. 300.
19. Arthur M. Schlesinger Jr., *The Age of Roosevelt*, vol. III, *The Politics of Upheaval: 1935–1936*, p. 582.
20. Leuchtenberg, p. 194.
21. Arthur M. Schlesinger Jr., *The Age of Roosevelt*, vol. II, *The Coming of the New Deal: 1933–1935*, p. 402.
22. Schlesinger, vol. III, p. 579.
23. Joseph P. Lash, *Dealers and Dreamers*, p. 274.
24. Schlesinger, vol. III, p. 584.
25. *New York Times*, 13/3/37; Leuchtenberg, p. 181; Schlesinger, vol. III, p. 552.
26. *New York Times*, 22/5/36; Schlesinger, vol. III, p. 552; Leuchtenberg, p. 181.
27. FDRL, PPF 321, George Cardinal Mundelein; *Chicago Times*, 15/9/36.
28. FDRL, PPF 321, George Cardinal Mundelein.
29. Leuchtenberg, p. 182.
30. Ibid., p. 183.
31. FDRL, PSF, Box 41, Diplomatic Correspondence—Vatican.
32. Charles J. Tull, *Father Coughlin and the New Deal*, pp. 151–152.
33. Ibid., p. 151.
34. Schlesinger, vol. III, p. 610.
35. Lash, p. 280.
36. Michael Barone, *Our Country*, pp. 102–106; Harold F. Gosnell, *Champion Campaigner*, p. 166; Leuchtenberg, p. 187.
37. Ibid.; *Fortune*, XVIII (July 1938), p. 37.
38. Lash, p. 374; FDRL, PSF, 12/9/39.

39. Schlesinger, vol. III, p. 655.

40. Leuchtenberg, p. 183.

41. Schlesinger, vol. III, p. 273.

42. David Burnham, letter to *Washington Post*, 26/1/97; Christopher Ogden, *Legacy: A Biography of Moses and Walter Annenberg*, p. 209.

43. Schlesinger, vol. II, p. 570.

44. Robert A. Caro, *The Path to Power*, pp. 742–753.

45. Ogden, p. 213.

46. Ibid., pp. 222, 239.

47. Ibid., pp. 236–237.

48. Ibid., pp. 209–213.

49. Ibid., p. 244.

50. Leuchtenberg, p. 175.

51. PCA, 24/11/36.

52. Leuchtenberg, p. 209; Donald Dozer, *Are We Good Neighbors?*, p. 31.

53. PCA, 12/12/36.

54. Davis, vol. III, pp. 659–660.

55. Thomas, p. 576.

56. Lash, p. 5.

CHAPTER 10

1. Joseph Alsop and Turner Catledge, *The 168 Days*, p. 145.

2. Joseph P. Lash, *Dealers and Dreamers*, p. 5.

3. Ibid., p. 295.

4. Ibid., p. 296.

5. Richard Lowitt, *George W. Norris: The Triumph of a Progressive, 1933–1944*, pp. 185–190; Alsop and Catledge, pp. 95–96, 185–190.

6. Max Freedman, Roosevelt and Franfurter: Their Correspondence, 1928–1945, p. 382.

7. A.T. Mason, *Brandeis: A Free Man's Life*, p. 626; Kenneth S. Davis, *FDR*, vol. IV, *Into the Storm, 1937–1940*, p. 72.

8. Davis, p. 81.

9. Arthur M. Schlesinger Jr., *The Age of Roosevelt*, vol. III, *The Politics of Upheaval: 1935–1936*, p. 456.

10. Lash, p. 300.

11. William E. Leuchtenberg, *Franklin D. Roosevelt and the New Deal, 1932–1940*, pp. 242–243.

12. Davis, p. 91.

13. Ibid., p. 94.

14. Alben W. Barkley, *That Reminds Me*, p. 156.

15. Davis, p. 96.

16. Ibid., p. 106.

17. Lash, p. 298.

18. Davis, pp. 342, 651.

19. There is a possibility that the Spanish Republicans destroyed much of Guernica themselves, but this is of little importance to the fact of illegal German intervention

and of flagrant German disregard for the traditional rules of warfare in respect of civil populations.

20. David Reynolds, *From Munich to Pearl Harbor*, p. 38.

21. FDRL, PF, FDR Foreign Affairs, V5.

22. Ibid., V6.

23. Davis, p. 129.

24. Lash, p. 383.

25. Samuel I. Rosenman, Working with Roosevelt, p. 167.

26. Leuchtenberg, p. 245; *American Economic Review*, XXIX (March 1939), pp. 170–182.

27. Lash, p. 320.

28. Leuchtenberg, p. 256.

29. Lash, p. 325; Robert Jackson, *Secret Diary II*, pp. 287–288.

30. Leuchtenberg, p. 247; *New York Times*, 27/12/37, 30/12/37, 31/12/37.

31. Schlesinger, p. 498.

32. Leuchtenberg, p. 249; Morgenthau diaries, pp. 396–401, 434–435.

33. Davis, pp. 209–210.

34. Leuchtenberg, p. 250.

35. Ibid.; James MacGregor Burns, *Roosevelt: The Lion and the Fox*, p. 346; Letter of Bernard De Voto to Garrett Mattingly, 15/6/38, De Voto mss. Box 2; TRB; "Washington Notes," *New Republic*, XCIV (1938), pp. 358–359.

36. Davis, pp. 215–216.

37. Morgenthau diaries, p. 421.

38. Ibid., p. 22.

39. Hollinger Collection, p. 64.

40. Leuchtenberg, p. 254.

41. Schlesinger, p. 428.

42. Michael R. Beschloss, *Kennedy and Roosevelt*, p. 157.

43. Leuchtenberg, p. 284.

44. PL, p. 785.

45. *New York Times*, 17/6/38.

46. Harold Ickes, *Diaries*, 12/5/38; Davis, p. 253.

47. Anthony Eden, *Facing the Dictators*, pp. 625–628; Iain McLeod, *Chamberlain*, p. 16.

48. Eden, p. 633.

49. FDRL, PSF, Box 50, Diplomatic Correspondence — France.

50. David E. Lilienthal, *Journals*, p. 74; Davis, p. 182.

51. FDRL, PSF, Foreign Affairs — Great Britain, V9, J.P. Kennedy, 11/3/38.

52. FDRL, PSF, State, Welles, V9.

53. FDRL, PSF, Diplomatic Correspondence — Ireland, Cudahy to FDR, 6/4/38.

54. FDRL, PSF, Diplomatic Correspondence — Spain, 31/8/38.

55. Davis, p. 197.

56. Hugh Thomas, *The Spanish Civil War*, p. 825.

57. Ibid.

58. Robert Herzstein, *Roosevelt and Hitler: The Prelude to War*, p. 234.

CHAPTER 11

1. William E. Leuchtenberg, *Franklin D. Roosevelt and the New Deal, 1932–1940*, p. 266.
2. Kenneth S. Davis, *FDR*, vol. IV, *Into the Storm, 1937–1940*, p. 264.
3. Michael R. Beschloss, *Kennedy and Roosevelt*, p. 175.
4. Ibid., p. 167.
5. Beatrice Berle and Travis Jacobs, *Navigating the Rapids*, pp. 183–184.
6. PCA, photograph album of his visit.
7. Richard M. Ketchum, *The Borrowed Years, 1938–1941: America on the Way to War*, p. 59.
8. Ibid., p. 58.
9. Ibid., p. 54.
10. Ibid., pp. 61–62.
11. Ibid.
12. Davis, p. 329.
13. Bullitt was now coordinating the American diplomatic effort in Western Europe under direct orders from Roosevelt, and encouraging the possibility of American involvement in an anti-Nazi coalition; Kenneth P. Jones, ed., *U.S. Diplomats in Europe, 1919–1941*, pp. 169ff; *Documents Diplomatiques Francais*, vol. 2, 11, 12, Francois-Poncet to Bonnet. Kennedy was left completely in the dark.
14. Ketchum, p. 63.
15. Ibid., p. 65.
16. David Dilks, ed., *The Diaries of Sir Alexander Cadogan, O.M., 1938–1945*, p. 102. Cadogan had serious misgivings about the appeasement policy.
17. Davis, p. 335.
18. Beschloss, p. 172.
19. Ibid., p. 176.
20. Davis, p. 337.
21. Ketchum, p. 77. Description of Gamelin in footnote is from Alistair Horne, *To Lose a Battle: France, 1940*, p. 117, and was uttered by Air Chief Marshal Sir Arthur Barratt.
22. PPA, 1938, pp. 532–535.
23. PCA, 26/9/38.
24. Ketchum, p. 76.
25. Ibid.
26. Ibid., p. 77.
27. Davis, p. 340.
28. Harry Fitzgibbons, *William Bullitt, Ambassador Extraordinaire*, unpublished dissertation, Harvard College, 1958, p. 93.
29. Davis, p. 342.
30. Ketchum, p. 79.
31. Ibid.
32. Andrew Roberts, *The Holy Fox*, p. 299.
33. Beschloss, p. 182.
34. FDRL, PSF, Diplomatic Correspondence — France, WCB.
35. Telford Taylor, *Munich: The Price of Peace*, p. 42.

36. Ketchum, p. 81.
37. Beschloss, p. 177.
38. Davis, p. 344.
39. Ibid.
40. Taylor, p. 59.
41. William Phillips, *Ventures in Diplomacy*, p. 219.
42. Ibid., pp. 219–220.
43. PL II, p. 818; Leuchtenberg, p. 285.
44. David Reynolds, *From Munich to Pearl Harbor*, p. 39.
45. Davis, p. 345.
46. Ibid.
47. John Lukacs, *Churchill: Visionary, Statesman, Historian*, p. 65.
48. Reynolds, pp. 42–43.
49. Davis, p. 355.
50. Leuchtenberg, p. 281; *New York Times*, 2/11/38.
51. Hollinger Collection, p. 25.
52. PL IV, pp. 827–828.
53. *New York Times*, 13/7/38.
54. David Brinkley, *Washington Goes to War*, p. 36.
55. Reynolds, p. 51.
56. All polls are from Robert Herzstein, *Roosevelt and Hitler: The Prelude to War*, and most were taken by Gallup.
57. Ibid.
58. PPA, 1938, pp. 602–604.
59. Jeffrey S. Gurock, ed., *American Jewish History*, vol. V, pp. 144–156.
60. Herzstein, p. 234.
61. Hollinger Collection, p. 27.
62. Davis, pp. 372–373.
63. PPA, 1938, p. 615.
64. Anthony Eden (Earl of Avon), *The Eden Memoirs: The Reckoning*, pp. 41–42.
65. Reynolds, p. 46.
66. Donald Cameron Watt, *How War Came*, p. 96.
67. Ibid.
68. Davis, p. 402.
69. Herzstein, p. 317.
70. Davis, p. 408.
71. Ibid., p. 409.
72. Ibid.
73. Herzstein, p. 317.
74. Watt, pp. 124–125.
75. Davis, p. 403.
76. Herzstein, p. 254.

CHAPTER 12

1. Kenneth S. Davis, *FDR*, vol. IV, *Into the Storm, 1937–1940*, pp. 420–421; Harry S. Truman Library, Truman Papers, Personal Notes folder, Family Correspondence File.
2. Davis, p. 391.
3. Susan E. Tift and Alex S. Jones, *The Trust*, p. 171.
4. Albert Speer, *Inside the Third Reich*, p. 339.
5. Davis, p. 426.
6. Ibid., p. 424.
7. Ibid., p. 432.
8. William E. Leuchtenberg, *Franklin D. Roosevelt and the New Deal, 1932–1940*, p. 287; William K. Hutchinson, *News Articles on the Life and Works of Honorable William E. Borah*, U.S. Senate, 76th Congress, 3rd Session (1940), p. 39.
9. David Reynolds, *From Munich to Pearl Harbor*, p. 54.
10. Ibid.
11. Richard M. Ketchum, *The Borrowed Years, 1938–1941: America on the Way to War*, p. 396.
12. Robert Herzstein, *Roosevelt and Hitler: The Prelude to War*, p. 251.
13. Robert Dallek, *Franklin D. Roosevelt and American Foreign Policy, 1932–1945*, p. 186.
14. Davis, pp. 439–440.
15. Donald Cameron Watt, *How War Came*, pp. 258, 264.
16. Davis, p. 438.
17. Winston S. Churchill, *The Second World War*, vol. I, *The Gathering Storm*, pp. 389–390.
18. Lord William Strang, *Home and Abroad*, pp. 193–198, 314–316.
19. Sarah Bradford, *George VI, the Reluctant King, 1895–1952*, p. 393.
20. Davis, p. 453.
21. Herzstein, p. 225.
22. Watt, p. 269.
23. Herzstein, pp. 288–289.
24. Ibid., p. 295.
25. Ibid.
26. Reynolds, p. 56; Patrick J. Hearden, *Roosevelt Confronts Hitler: America's Entry into World War II*, p. 133; Cordell Hull, *Memoirs*, vol. I, p. 656; Edward M. Bennett, *Franklin D. Roosevelt and the Search for Security: American-Soviet Relations, 1933–1939*, pp. 159 et seq.; Herzstein, p. 28.
27. Davis, p. 461.
28. Ibid., p. 491.
29. Herzstein, p. 297.
30. Ibid., pp. 299, 306.
31. PPA, 1939, pp. 455–458.
32. Herzstein, p. 298.
33. Watt, p. 579.
34. Herzstein, p. 306.

35. Warren F. Kimball, *Churchill and Roosevelt: The Complete Correspondence*, vol. I, pp. 24–25.
36. Dallek, p. 211.
37. Frank Freidel, *Franklin D. Roosevelt: A Rendezvous with Destiny*, p. 323.
38. Leuchtenberg, p. 293.
39. William Phillips, *Ventures in Diplomacy*, pp. 222–223.
40. Hollinger Collection, p. 78.
41. Reynolds, p. 67.
42. Leuchtenberg, p. 295 et seq.
43. Kimball, pp. 33–34.
44. PPA, 1940, pp. 85–94.
45. Davis, p. 520.
46. Ibid., p. 313.
47. Herzstein, p. 313.
48. Ibid., p. 320.
49. Andrew Roberts, *The Holy Fox*, p. 198.
50. Ibid., p. 196.
51. FDRL., Newsreel #201-3105-4; Geoffrey Ward, *Before the Trumpet*, vol. I, p. 62.

CHAPTER 13

1. Doris Kearns Goodwin, *No Ordinary Time*, p. 13.
2. Ibid., p. 39.
3. Winston S.Churchill, *The Second World War*, vol. II, *Their Finest Hour*, p. 42.
4. Warren F. Kimball, *Churchill and Roosevelt: The Complete Correspondence*, vol. I, p. 38.
5. Ibid., p. 39.
6. Ibid., p. 40.
7. Ian Kershaw, *Hitler, 1936–1945: Nemesis*, pp. 516–517.
8. John Lukacs, *Five Days in London, May, 1940*, p. 217.
9. Kimball, p. 42.
10. David Reynolds, *From Munich to Pearl Harbor*, p. 79.
11. Ibid.
12. PPA, 1940, pp. 259–264.
13. Kimball, pp. 43–44.
14. Ibid., p. 44.
15. Ibid., pp. 45–46.
16. John Lukacs, *Churchill: Visionary, Statesman, Historian*, pp. 52–53.
17. Reynolds, p. 81.
18. Kimball, pp. 46–49.
19. Ibid., pp. 49–51.
20. Ibid., pp. 51–52.
21. Charles de Gaulle, *The Complete War Memoirs*, vol. I, *The Call to Honor*, p. 80.
22. Goodwin, p. 24.
23. Geoffrey Ward, *American Originals*, p. 24.
24. Kenneth S. Davis, *FDR*, vol. IV, *Into the Storm, 1937–1940*, p. 583.

25. Reynolds, p. 70.

26. Davis, p. 535.

27. Ibid., p. 586; *Max Freedman, ed., Roosevelt and Frankfurter: Their Correspondence, 1928–1945*, pp. 531–534.

28. Davis, p. 590.

29. Ibid.

30. de Gaulle, p. 57.

31. Alben W. Barkley, *That Reminds Me*, p. 186.

32. Davis, pp. 593–594.

33. Adam Cohen and Elizabeth Taylor, *American Pharaoh: Mayor Richard J. Daley, His Battle for Chicago and the Nation*, p. 451.

34. Hedley Donovan, *Roosevelt to Reagan*, pp. 20–21; Goodwin, p. 134.

35. Andrei Gromyko, *Memoirs*, p. 5.

36. Goodwin, p. 42.

37. Ibid.

38. Kimball, pp. 56–57.

39. Reynolds, p. 85.

40. Reynolds, p. 86.

41. Goodwin, pp. 147–148.

42. Davis, p. 611.

43. Ibid., p. 610.

44. Lukacs, *Churchill*, p. 64.

45. Richard M. Ketchum, *The Borrowed Years, 1938–1941: America on the Way to War*, p. 586.

46. Goodwin, p. 151.

47. Richard Overy, *The Battle of Britain: Myth and Reality*, pp. 126–128.

48. Reynolds, p. 96.

49. Ibid., p. 99.

50. Ibid., p. 100.

51. Goodwin, p. 163.

52. Ibid., pp. 185–186; Time, 11/11/40, pp. 17–18.

53. Samuel I. Rosenman, *Working with Roosevelt*, p. 249.

54. Matthew and Hannah Josephson, *Sidney Hillman: Statements of American Labor*, p. 488; Goodwin, p. 184.

55. PCA, 23/10/40.

56. Robert Herzstein, *Roosevelt and Hitler: The Prelude to War*, p. 358.

57. Steve Neal, *Dark Horse*, p. 167; Edward Willkie quoted in Barnes, *Willkie*, p. 258.

58. John Cooney, *The American Pope*, p. 122.

59. Michael R. Beschloss, *Kennedy and Roosevelt*, p. 220.

60. Robert E. Sherwood, *Roosevelt and Hopkins*, p. 191.

61. Neal, p. 167; Barnes, p. 25.

62. Ketchum, p. 525; Davis, p. 621; Amanda Smith, ed., *Hostages to Fortune: the Letters of Joseph P. Kennedy*, p. 489; Goodwin, p. 187.

63. Davis, p. 616.

64. Rosenman, p. 248.

65. Arthur M. Schlesinger Jr., *The Age of Roosevelt*, vol. III, *The Politics of Upheaval: 1935–1936*, pp. 624–625.

66. James MacGregor Burns, *Roosevelt: The Lion and the Fox*, p. 452; Sherwood, pp. 199–200.

67. James MacGregor Burns, *Roosevelt: The Soldier of Freedom*, pp. 3–4.

68. Joseph P. Lash, *Eleanor and Franklin*, p. 633.

69. Michael Barone, *Our Country*, pp. 143–144.

70. Frances Perkins, *The Roosevelt I Knew*, p. 113.

71. Barone, p. 144.

CHAPTER 14

1. David Reynolds, *From Munich to Pearl Harbor*, p. 104.

2. Michael R. Beschloss, *Kennedy and Roosevelt*, p. 226.

3. Ibid., p. 229.

4. Warren F. Kimball, *Churchill and Roosevelt: The Complete Correspondence*, vol. I, p. 81.

5. Ibid., pp. 102–109.

6. Reynolds, p. 105.

7. Kenneth S. Davis, *FDR*, vol. V, *The War President, 1940–1943*, p. 89.

8. Doris Kearns Goodwin, *No Ordinary Time*, p. 204.

9. William Lasser, *Benjamin V. Cohen*, pp. 214–215, 236.

10. Goodwin, p. 195.

11. Reynolds, p. 108.

12. Kimball, pp. 114–116.

13. PPA, 1940, pp. 711–712.

14. Freidel, p. 325.

15. See pp. 346–347.

16. Davis, p. 101.

17. Kimball, p. 131.

18. Andrew Roberts, *The Holy Fox*, p. 287.

19. Davis, p. 103.

20. Davis, p. 108.

21. Goodwin, pp. 211–212.

22. PPA, 1941, p. 11.

23. Winston S. Churchill, *The Second World War*, vol. III, *The Grand Alliance*, p. 23.

24. Davis, p. 123.

25. Davis, p. 124.

26. Goodwin, p. 212.

27. Davis, p. 127.

28. Ibid., pp. 125–126; Goodwin, p. 213.

29. Ibid.

30. Davis, p. 153.

31. Joseph P. Lash, *Roosevelt and Churchill*, p. 285.

32. Davis, p. 116.

33. Kimball, p. 143.

34. Reynolds, p. 114.

35. Winston S. Churchill, *The Unrelenting Struggle: War Speeches (TUS)*, pp. 78, 79.

36. Reynolds, p. 119.

37. Davis, p. 137.

38. Goebbels, *The Goebbels Diaries, 1939–1941*, p. 240.

39. Robert Herzstein, *Roosevelt and Hitler: The Prelude to War*, p. 327.

40. Reynolds, p.114.

41. Davis, p. 159.

42. Robert E. Sherwood, *Roosevelt and Hopkins*, p. 280; Davis, p. 163.

43. Conversation with author, 10/10/02.

44. Kimball, p. 145.

45. Ibid., p. 151.

46. Davis, p. 152.

47. Kimball, p. 180.

48. Ibid., p. 181.

49. Ibid., p. 182.

50. Andrei Gromyko, *Memoirs*, p. 40.

51. Kimball, p. 185.

52. Reynolds, p. 132.

53. FDRL, PSF 6, Britain King and Queen.

54. Reynolds, p. 134.

55. Davis, p. 170.

56. Reynolds, p. 115.

57. Ibid., p. 116.

58. Ibid., p. 130.

59. Davis, p. 204–205.

60. Churchill, *TUS*, pp. 176–181.

61. Reynolds, p. 109.

62. Ibid., p. 136.

63. Ibid.

64. William Leahy, *I Was There*, pp. 37–38.

65. Robert Skidelsky, *John Maynard Keynes*, vol. III, *Fighting for Britain*, p. 116.

66. Ibid., p. 363.

67. Davis, p. 237.

68. James Chace, *Acheson: The Secretary of State Who Created the American World*, p. 82.

69. Ibid., p. 81.

70. Chace, p. 74

71. Ibid., p. 81.

72. Ibid.

73. Mahan regarded the Philippines as "troublesome," a place the United States had been "pitchforked into," and that they were "less a property than a charge" and doubted they could be defended. Robert Seager, *Alfred Thayer Mahan: The Man and His Letters*, pp. 394–395.

74. Chace, p. 86.

CHAPTER 15

1. Kenneth S. Davis, *FDR*, vol. V, *The War President, 1940–1943*, p. 251.
2. Joseph P. Lash, Roosevelt and Churchill, 1939–1941, p. 391.
3. Davis, p. 251; Henry H. Arnold, *Global Mission*, p. 247. Frances Perkins makes no mention of this in her memoirs.
4. PCA.
5. Ibid.
6. Davis, p. 262.
7. James Chace, *Acheson*, pp. 84–87.
8. Davis, p. 265.
9. Winston S. Churchill, *The Second World War*, vol. III, *The Grand Alliance*, pp. 431–432.
10. Lash, pp. 447–448.
11. David Reynolds, *From Munich to Pearl Harbor*, p. 145.
12. Ibid., pp. 145–146.
13. PCA, letter to Margaret Suckley.
14. Official British film of Atlantic Conference, screened at Argentina on 50th anniversary of the meeting, August 1991.
15. Sir John Rupert Colville, *Fringes of Power: 10 Downing Street Diaries, 1939–1945*, p. 428.
16. Lash, pp. 400–403.
17. Davis, pp. 275–276; Porter McKeever, *Adlai Stevenson: His Life and Legacy*, pp. 78–79.
18. Reynolds, p. 149.
19. Warren F. Kimball, *Churchill and Roosevelt: The Complete Correspondence*, vol. I, p. 237.
20. PPA, 1941, pp. 384–392.
21. Davis, p. 288.
22. Ibid., p. 286–287.
23. Isaac Deutscher, *Stalin: A Political Biography*, p. 465; Alex De Jonge, *Stalin and the Shaping of the Soviet Union*, p. 406.
24. Reynolds, p. 152.
25. Ibid., p. 153.
26. PPA, 1941, pp. 406–413.
27. Reynolds, p. 156.
28. Hollinger Collection.
29. Reynolds, pp. 156–157.
30. Clement R. Attlee, *As It Happened*, p. 173.
31. Davis, p. 316.
32. Ibid., p. 317.
33. Kimball, pp. 275–276.
34. Reynolds, p. 165.
35. Ibid., p. 162.
36. Kimball, p. 277.

37. B. Mitchell Simpson, *Admiral Harold R. Stark: Architect of Victory, 1939–1945*, p. 107.

38. Reynolds, p. 162.

39. Ibid., pp. 164, 167.

40. Simpson, pp. 108–109; S. Sebag-Montefiore, *Stalin: The Court of the Red Tsar*, p. 356, quoting Russian sources including Zhukov.

41. Stimson diary, 27/11/41; Davis, p. 334.

42. William L. Langer and Everett S. Gleason, *Undeclared War: 1939–1940*, p. 899.

43. Ibid.

44. Davis, p. 334.

45. Ibid., p. 336.

46. Hollinger Collection.

47. Davis, p. 338.

CHAPTER 16

1. Ian Kershaw, *Hitler, 1936–1945: Nemesis*, p. 517.

2. Winston S. Churchill, *The Second World War*, vol. III, *The Grand Alliance*, pp. 608–609.

3. Life Magazine Books, *Call to Arms*, p. 91; Charles de Gaulle, *The Complete War Memoirs*, vol. I, *The Call to Honor*, pp. 213, 782.

4. Richard M. Ketchum, *The Borrowed Years, 1938–1941: America on the Way to War*, pp. 775–776.

5. James MacGregor Burns, *Roosevelt: Soldier of Freedom*, p. 165.

6. Gordon W. Prange, *At Dawn We Slept: The Untold Story of Pearl Harbor*, p. 39; Ketchum, pp. 553–555.

7. A.M. Sperber, *Murrow: His Life and Times*, pp. 206–208; Kenneth S. Davis, *FDR*, vol. V, *The War President, 1940–1943*, p. 342; Burns, p. 165.

8. Davis, p. 347.

9. Burns, p. 165.

10. Kershaw, p. 446; J.P.M. Showell, ed., *Fuehrer Conferences on Naval Affairs*, pp. 244–246.

11. Count Galeazzo Ciano, *Diaries*, 8/12/41.

12. Michael Bloch, *Ribbentrop*, p. 347.

13. William L. Shirer, *The Rise and Fall of the Third Reich*, pp. 897–900.

14. Warren F. Kimball, *Churchill and Roosevelt: The Complete Correspondence*, vol. I, pp. 294–309.

15. Charles Osgood, *Funny Letters from Famous People*, p. 38.

16. PPA, 1941, pp. 587–592.

17. Davis, p. 369.

18. Churchill, p. 670.

19. Ibid., p. 673.

20. David Brinkley, *Washington Goes to War*, p. 35.

21. Cordell Hull, *Memoirs*, vol. II, p. 847.

22. Davis, p. 378.

23. Churchill, p. 666; Hull, pp. 961–962, 1127–1138.

24. Churchill, p. 667.
25. Charles de Gaulle, *The Complete War Memoirs*, vol. II, *Unity*, p. 571.
26. de Gaulle, vol. I, p. 220.
27. Churchill, p. 686.
28. Davis, p. 384.
29. Churchill, p. 691.
30. Ibid., p. 687.
31. Ibid., p. 606.
32. Douglas MacArthur, *Reminiscences*, p. 117.
33. D. Clayton James, *The Years of MacArthur*, vol. II, pp. 3–19; David Reynolds, *From Munich to Pearl Harbor*, p. 165. Richard Connaughton, *MacArthur and Defeat in the Philippines*.
34. See chapter 14, p. 646.
35. Forrest C. Pogue, *George C. Marshall*, vol. II, *Ordeal and Hope*, pp. 246–248.
36. Ibid.
37. James, pp. 96–97; MacArthur, p. 139.
38. PCA, 15/11/21.
39. James, p. 131.
40. Ibid., p. 132.
41. MacArthur, pp. 99–100.
42. Barbara W. Tuchman, *Stilwell and the American Experience in China 1911–1945*, p. 300.
43. Ibid., p. 382.
44. Davis, p. 419.
45. FDRL, PSF, Box 83, Departmental File, George C. Marshall.
46. Kai Bird, *The Chairman: John J. McCloy and the Making of the American Establishment*, p. 152.
47. Ibid., p. 153.
48. Henry L. Stimson and McGeorge Bundy, *On Active Service in Peace and War*, p. 406.
49. Bird, p. 154.
50. Richard Gid Powers, *Secrecy and Power: The Life of J. Edgar Hoover*, p. 250.
51. Bird, p. 157.
52. PPA, 1942, p. 178.

CHAPTER 17

1. Kenneth S. Davis, *FDR*, vol. V, *The War President, 1940–1943*, p. 457.
2. James F. Byrnes, *All in One Lifetime*, p. 155.
3. Davis, p. 628.
4. PPA, 1942, p. 230.
5. Ibid., p. 228.
6. William D. Leahy, *I Was There*, p. 86.
7. Davis, p. 466.
8. Chapter 15, p. 649, et seq.
9. Warren F. Kimball, *Churchill and Roosevelt: The Complete Correspondence*, vol. I, p. 449.

10. William Lyon Mackenzie King Papers, National Library of Canada, FDR to WLMK, 27/4/42, copy furnished to author through the courtesy of journalist and historian Lawrence Martin.

11. Kimball, pp. 421–422.

12. Davis, p. 493; Winston S. Churchill, *The Second World War*, vol. IV, *The Hinge of Fate*, p. 324; Kimball, p. 458.

13. Davis, p. 495.

14. Ibid., p. 497.

15. Forrest C. Pogue, *George C. Marshall*, vol. II, *Ordeal and Hope*, p. 331.

16. Kimball, p. 489.

17. Davis, p. 501.

18. Ibid., p. 504.

19. Churchill, p. 377.

20. Ibid., p. 383.

21. Ibid.

22. Ibid., p. 387.

23. Kimball, p. 517.

24. Davis, p. 531.

25. Ibid., p. 534.

26. Soviet Union Foreign Ministry, *Stalin's Correspondence with Churchill, Attlee, Roosevelt, and Truman*, p. 56.

27. Churchill, pp. 464–465; Davis, p. 565.

28. Churchill, p. 476.

29. Ibid., p. 479; Kimball, pp. 560–562.

30. Ibid. (Kimball).

31. Churchill, p. 487.

32. Kimball, p. 563.

33. Churchill, p. 494.

34. Ibid., p. 493.

35. Ibid., p. 501.

36. H.A. De Weerd, *Great Soldiers of World War II*, p. 270.

37. Clement R. Attlee, *As It Happened*, p. 173.

38. A. Merriman Smith, *Thank You, Mr. President*, pp. 123–124.

39. Kimball, pp. 587, 589, 591–592.

CHAPTER 18

1. Steve Neal, *Dark Horse*, p. 258.

2. William Roger Louis, *Imperialism at Bay: The United States and the Decolonization of the British Empire, 1941–1945*, p. 199.

3. Charles de Gaulle, *The Complete War Memoirs*, vol. II, *Unity*, p. 335.

4. Forrest C. Pogue, *George C. Marshall*, vol. II, *Ordeal and Hope*, p. 402.

5. Geoffrey Ward, ed., *Closest Companion*, p. 183.

6. Richard Norton Smith, *The Colonel*, pp. 410, 433–439.

7. Anecdote told to author by James Hoge, eventual editor of the New York *Daily News*, and of *Foreign Affairs*.

8. *Middle East Quarterly*, March 2000, p. 94.

9. Robert Murphy, *Diplomat Among Warriors*, p. 70.

10. Hugh Trevor-Roper, ed., *Hitler's Table Talk, 1941–1944*, pp. 441–442.

11. Martin Blumenson, ed., *The Patton Papers*, vol. II, p. 123.

12. Murphy, pp. 120–121.

13. Kenneth S. Davis, *FDR*, vol. V, *The War President, 1940–1943*, p. 675.

14. Dwight D. Eisenhower, *Crusade in Europe*, p. 100.

15. Waverly Root, *The Secret History of the War*, vol. 2, pp. 464–465.

16. Murphy, p. 129.

17. Rick Atkinson, *An Army at Dawn: The War in Africa, 1942–1943*.

18. Davis, p. 689; Martin Blumenson, *Mark Clark*, p. 109.

19. Atkinson, p. 165.

20. Warren F. Kimball, *Churchill and Roosevelt: The Complete Correspondence*, vol. II, p. 4.

21. Ibid., p. 5.

22. Davis, p. 701.

23. Eisenhower, p. 131.

24. de Gaulle, p. 359.

25. Ibid., p. 381.

26. Churchill, pp. 645–647.

27. Peter Tompkins, *The Murder of Admiral Darlan*, p. 184.

28. Eisenhower, pp. 107, 112, 113.

29. de Gaulle, p. 378.

30. Tompkins, p. 199.

31. Churchill, p. 647.

32. Kimball, pp. 42–43.

33. Davis, p. 757.

34. Doris Kearns Goodwin, *No Ordinary Time*, p. 400.

35. PCA.

36. Ibid.

37. de Gaulle, pp. 387–388.

38. Forrest C. Pogue, *George C. Marshall*, vol. III, *Organizer of Victory*, p. 18.

39. Sir Alan Brooke, *Diaries*, p. 361.

40. John Grigg, *1943: The Victory That Never Was*, pp. 168–169.

41. Ibid., pp. 196, 218.

42. Carlo D'Este, *Patton: A Genius for War*, p. 449.

43. Brooke, pp. 360–361, 364.

44. Ibid., p. 362.

45. de Gaulle, p. 392; Goodwin, p. 406.

46. Atkinson, photo cut-line following p. 204.

47. Churchill, p. 611.

48. de Gaulle, p. 398.

49. Churchill, p. 621.

50. PCA.

51. Churchill, pp. 687–691.

52. Ibid., p. 687.

53. Pogue, pp. 32–34.

54. Grigg, p. 209; Chester Wilmot, *The Struggle for Europe*, p. 713.

55. Churchill, p. 694.

56. Ibid.

57. Ibid.; Goodwin, p. 408.

58. Goodwin, p. 408; Eric Larrabee, *Commander in Chief: Franklin Delano Roosevelt, His Lieutenants & Their War*, p. 39.

59. Lady Soames is aware of the history of the painting and is my source.

CHAPTER 19

1. Warren F. Kimball, *Churchill and Roosevelt: The Complete Correspondence*, vol. II, p. 150.

2. Doris Kearns Goodwin, *No Ordinary Time*, p. 410.

3. Kimball, pp. 52–53.

4. James MacGregor Burns, *Roosevelt: Soldier of Freedom*, p. 328.

5. William L. Shirer, *The Rise and Fall of the Third Reich*, p. 964; Kenneth S. Davis, *FDR*, vol. V, *The War President, 1940–1943*, p. 725.

6. Fred L. Israel, ed., *The War Diary of Breckinridge Long*, p. 104.

7. Ibid., pp. 146–148.

8. Ibid., pp. 173, 216.

9. Ibid., p. 216.

10. Ibid.

11. Ibid., p. 128.

12. Henry L. Feingold, *The Politics of Rescue*.

13. Davis, p. 729.

14. Michael R. Beschloss, *The Conquerors*, p. 66.

15. Ibid.

16. Dwight D. Eisenhower, *Crusade in Europe*, pp. 408–409.

17. Carlo D'Este, *Patton: A Genius for War*, p. 720; George S. Patton, *War As I Knew It*, p. 95.

18. Peter Hebblethwaite, *Pope John XXIII: Shepherd of the Modern World*, pp. 187–188.

19. Goebbels, *The Goebbels Diaries, 1942–1943*, p. 241.

20. Burns, pp. 342–343.

21. Ibid., pp. 361–362.

22. Goodwin, pp. 417–418.

23. Anthony Eden, *The Eden Memoirs: The Reckoning*, pp. 371–372.

24. Ibid., p. 373.

25. Ibid.; Burns, p. 365.

26. Eden, p. 373; Burns, p. 365.

27. Eden, p. 373.

28. Burns, p. 366.

29. Goodwin, p. 425.

30. Burns, p. 368.

31. Winston S. Churchill, *The Second World War*, vol. IV, *The Hinge of Fate*, p. 830.

32. Forrest C. Pogue, *George C. Marshall*, vol. III, *Organizer of Victory*, p. 199.

33. Churchill, p. 798.
34. Barbara W. Tuchman, *Stilwell and the American Experience in China 1911–1945*, p. 371.
35. Sir Alan Brooke, *Diaries*, pp. 404, 479.
36. Ibid., p. 59.
37. Tuchman, p. 371.
38. Ibid., p. 370.
39. Ibid., p. 371.
40. Brooke, p. 478.
41. Burns, p. 377.
42. Hollinger Collection, p. 15; Edwin P. Hoyt, *Yamamoto*, pp. 248–250.
43. Burns, p. 371.
44. Pogue, p. 212.
45. Kimball, p. 219.
46. Gary Kern, "How 'Uncle Joe' Bugged FDR," *Studies in Intelligence*, June 2003.
47. Kimball, p. 285.
48. Basil Liddell-Hart, *History of the Second World War*, p. 488; Michael Bloch, *Ribbentrop*, pp. 385–386; H.W. Koch, "The Spectre of a Separate Peace in the East: Russo-German Peace Feelers, 1942–44," *Journal of Contemporary History*, vol. 10, pp. 531–547; Alexander Dallin, *German Rule in Russia, 1941–1945: A Study of Occupation Policies*, p. 186.
49. Bloch, p. 387; Joachim von Ribbentrop, *The Ribbentrop Memoirs*, pp. 170–171.
50. Ibid.
51. Burns, pp. 373–374.
52. Brooke, pp. 417–418.
53. Kimball, pp. 300, 307.
54. Goodwin, pp. 450–451.
55. Henry L. Stimson and McGeorge Bundy, *On Active Service in Peace and War*, pp. 431–438.
56. Pogue, p. 261; Brooke, p. 441.
57. Pogue, pp. 257–259; Brooke, pp. 437, 441–442.
58. Pogue, pp. 247, 250.
59. Ibid., p. 250.
60. Kimball, pp. 487–488, 507.
61. Pogue, p. 249.
62. Brooke, pp. 445–446.
63. Ibid., p. 447.
64. Winston S. Churchill, *The Second World War*, vol. V, *Closing the Ring*, p. 102 (English edition).
65. Ibid., p. 104 (English edition).
66. Joseph P. Lash, *Love, Eleanor*, p. 508.

CHAPTER 20

1. James MacGregor Burns, *Roosevelt: Soldier of Freedom*, p. 399.
2. Keith Eubank, *Summit at Teheran*, p. 140.

3. Ibid., p. 144.

4. Sir Alan Brooke, *Diaries*, pp. 472–473.

5. Eubank, p. 150.

6. FDRL, PSF, Diplomatic Correspondence—Blg., Box 24, 23/12/38.

7. Michael R. Beschloss, *The Conquerors*, pp. 22–23.

8. Robert Skidelsky, *John Maynard Keynes*, p. 363.

9. Eubank, pp. 150–156.

10. Barbara W. Tuchman, *Stilwell and the American Experience in China 1911–1945*, p. 398.

11. Brooke, p. 479.

12. Tuchman, p. 403.

13. Forrest C. Pogue, *George C. Marshall*, vol. III, *Organizer of Victory*, pp. 306–307.

14. Winston S. Churchill, *The Second World War*, vol. V, *Closing the Ring*, p. 296.

15. Pogue, p. 307.

16. Brooke, p. 481.

17. Churchill, p. 301.

18. Anthony Eden, *The Eden Memoirs: The Reckoning*, p. 491.

19. FDRL, OF 200, *Trip of FDR to Cairo and Teheran, Nov. 12–Dec. 15, 1943*, 26/11/43.

20. Ibid., 27/11/43.

21. Ibid.

22. Churchill, pp. 302–303 (English edition).

23. Beschloss, p. 23.

24. Elliott Roosevelt, *As He Saw It*, pp. 174–176.

25. Eubank, p. 197.

26. Sergo Beria, *Beria: My Father*, p. 93.

27. Ibid.

28. Ibid.

29. A.H. Birse, *Memoirs of an Interpreter*, p. 155.

30. Eubank, p. 259.

31. Brooke, p. 484.

32. Sir Alexander Cadogan, *Diaries*, p. 582.

33. Churchill, p. 306; Pogue, pp. 310–311.

34. Churchill, p. 304.

35. Walter Laqueur, *Stalin*, p. 204; Hugh Trevor-Roper, ed., *Hitler's Table Talk 1941–1944*, p. 361.

36. Eubank, p. 286.

37. Beschloss, p. 25.

38. Eubank, p. 288.

39. Lord Moran, *Churchill, Taken from the Diaries of Lord Moran*, p. 146.

40. Eubank, p. 295.

41. William D. Leahy, *I Was There*, p. 245; Eubank, p. 304.

42. Pogue, p. 313.

43. Eubank, p. 311.

44. Ibid., p. 314.

45. Churchill, p. 330.

46. Ibid.

47. Charles E. Bohlen, Minutes, *FRUS Cairo and Teheran*, p. 555.

48. Moran, pp. 149–151.

49. Churchill, p. 331.

50. Ibid., p. 342.

51. Frances Perkins, *The Roosevelt I Knew*, pp. 83–85; Combined Chiefs of Staff, Minutes, *FRUS Cairo and Teheran*, pp. 555–564.

52. Ibid.

53. Churchill, pp. 348 et seq.; Eubank, p. 367.

54. Eubank, p. 381.

55. Arthur Bryant, ed., *Triumph in the West*, p. 72.

56. Pogue, p. 321.

57. Burns, p. 416.

58. D. Clayton James, *The Years of MacArthur*, vol. II, pp. 88–89.

59. Ibid., p. 88; MacArthur's letter to Fellers, 18/6/43.

60. Beschloss, pp. 29–30.

61. FDR diary, Cairo-Teheran.

62. Carlo D'Este, *Patton: A Genius for War*, p. 425.

63. FDR diary.

64. *U.S.S. Iowa Action Report*, 22/12/43; Eubank, p. 402.

65. Eubank, p. 409.

66. Ibid., p. 340.

67. Goebbels, *The Goebbels Diaries, 1942–1943*, pp. 542–544.

68. Doris Kearns Goodwin, *No Ordinary Time*, p. 479.

69. Warren F. Kimball, *Churchill and Roosevelt: The Complete Correspondence*, vol. II, p. 641; Bruenn-Clinical Notes.

70. Samuel I. Rosenman, *Working with Roosevelt*, p. 411.

71. Kimball, p. 637.

72. Ibid., p. 641.

CHAPTER 21

1. Peter Collier and David Horowitz, *The Roosevelts: An American Saga*, p. 349; FDRL, oral history, Martha Gellhorn.

2. ER to Lorena Hickock, 16/10/36, in Doris Faber, *The Life of Lorena Hickock, E.R.'s Friend*, p. 221.

3. Ted Morgan, *FDR: A Biography*, p. 676. The poem is entitled "The Lady of Eleanor."

4. Ibid., p. 674.

5. Henry Brandon, "A Talk with an 83-year-old Enfant Terrible," *New York Times Magazine*, 6/6/67.

6. Carol Felsenthal, *Alice Roosevelt Longworth*, pp. 194, 195. "The joke was on us" was reported to me separately in conversation with David Brinkley, Katherine Graham, and President Richard Nixon, and has been reprinted in several places. Given the stature of my informants and the fact that the comment was evidently correct, I believe it to be true.

7. Doris Kearns Goodwin, *No Ordinary Time*, pp. 434–435.

8. Collier and Horowitz, p. 394.

9. Ibid., pp. 395, 396; Belle Willard Roosevelt diary, Spring 1940.

10. Ibid., p. 360; Elliott Roosevelt, *A Rendezvous with Destiny*, p. 248.

11. Collier and Horowitz, p. 344.

12. James Roosevelt and Sydney Shalett, *Affectionately, FDR: A Son's Story of a Lonely Man*, p. 90.

13. Collier and Horowitz, p. 345.

14. Ibid., p. 366.

15. Roosevelt and Shalett, p. 89.

16. Elliott Roosevelt, *Rendezvous*, pp. 37ff.; Collier and Horowitz, p. 371.

17. Collier and Horowitz, p. 378.

18. Lillian Rogers Parks, *A Family in Turmoil*, pp. 149–150; Collier and Horowitz, p. 363.

19. Collier and Horowitz, p. 414.

20. Ibid., p. 426

21. H. Paul Jeffers, *Theodore Roosevelt Jr.: The Life of a War Hero*, p. 264.

22. Ibid., p. 424.

23. Collier and Horowitz, p. 429.

24. FDRL, PPA, 1944, pp. 34, 36.

25. James MacGregor Burns, *Leadership*, p. 390.

26. James MacGregor Burns, *Roosevelt: Soldier of Freedom (RSF)*, pp. 434–435.

27. Ibid., p. 437.

28. Ibid., pp. 463–472.

29. Warren F. Kimball, *Churchill and Roosevelt: The Complete Correspondence*, vol. II, pp. 701–702.

30. Ibid., pp. 718–720.

31. Ibid., p. 721.

32. Ibid., p. 722.

33. Stimson's notes of the meeting, in Burns (*RSF*), p. 459.

34. Kimball, vol. II, pp. 706–707.

35. Ibid., p. 742.

36. Ibid., p. 765.

37. Warren F. Kimball, *Churchill and Roosevelt: The Complete Correspondence*, vol. III, p. 61.

38. Ibid., p. 65.

39. Ibid., p. 73.

40. Ibid., p. 69.

41. Kimball, vol. II, pp. 725–726.

42. Kimball, vol. III, p. 31.

43. Ibid., p. 43.

44. Ibid., p. 80.

45. Ibid., p. 82.

46. Ibid., p. 11.

47. Ibid., pp. 54, 74, 87.

48. Ibid., p. 60.

49. Ibid., p. 118.

50. Ibid., p. 46.

51. FDRL, PSF, Box 41, Diplomatic Correspondence—Benito Mussolini.

52. Michael R. Beschloss, *The Conquerors*, p. 30.

53. Ibid., p. 32.

54. Ibid.

55. Ibid., p. 77.

56. Ibid., p.32. When Winant's counselor in the London embassy, George F. Kennan, visited Roosevelt on April 3, 1944, Roosevelt acknowledged that his design on the National Geographic map had been arbitrary and told Kennan to tell Winant he could subscribe to the Anglo-Soviet proposal. FDRL, OF correspondence between FDR and Edward Stettinius, February 18, 19, and 21, 1944 (Roosevelt declined to give Stettinius the text of what had been agreed at Teheran). George Kennan, *Memoirs, 1925–1950*, pp. 170–171.

57. William Lord Strang, *Home and Abroad*, pp. 213–214.

58. Bernard Asbell, *Mother & Daughter: The Letters of Eleanor and Anna Roosevelt*, p. 177.

59. Elliott Roosevelt, *As He Saw It*, p. 220.

60. Kimball, vol. III, p. 60.

61. Robert A. Slayton, *Empire Statesman*, p. 398.

62. Asbell, p. 176.

63. Burns, *RSF*, p. 455; Goodwin, p. 498.

64. *New York Times*, 8/5/44, p. 18.

65. Simon Berthon, *Allies at War*, p. 297.

66. Ibid., p. 296.

67. Ibid., p. 298.

68. Ibid.

69. Kimball, vol. III, p. 145.

70. Berthon, pp. 304–305.

71. Charles de Gaulle, *The Complete War Memoirs*, vol. III, *Salvation*, p. 554.

72. Ibid., p. 555.

73. FDRL, PSF, Box 31, Diplomatic Correspondence—Charles de Gaulle.

74. Kimball, vol. III, p. 163.

75. Berthon, p. 305.

76. FDRL, PSF, Box 31, Diplomatic Correspondence—Charles de Gaulle.

77. de Gaulle, p. 558.

78. Ibid.

79. Hastings Lord Ismay, *The Memoirs of General Lord Ismay*, p. 357.

80. Kimball, vol. III, p. 162.

81. FDRL, ER interview, Graff Papers; Goodwin, pp. 507–508.

82. Berthon, p. 309.

83. Ibid., pp. 310–311.

84. Burns, *RSF*, p. 475.

85. Kimball, vol. III, pp. 166–168.

86. *New York Times*, 7/6/44; Stephen Ambrose, *D-Day*, p. 495; Goodwin, p. 510.

87. Burns, *RSF*, p. 475.

CHAPTER 22

1. Jim Bishop, *FDR's Last Year*, p. 105.
2. Ibid., p. 89.
3. Eric Larrabee, *Commander in Chief: Franklin Delano Roosevelt, His Lieutenants & Their War*, p. 315.
4. Ibid., p. 351.
5. Bishop, p. 93.
6. James MacGregor Burns, *Roosevelt: Soldier of Freedom, (RSF)*, p. 511; James Mac-Gregor Burns, *Leadership (L)*, p. 282.
7. Steve Neal, *Dark Horse*, p. 316; Joseph Barnes, *Willkie*, pp. 371–372.
8. FDRL, OF 4040, Wendell L. Willkie.
9. Doris Kearns Goodwin, *No Ordinary Time*, p. 513.
10. Warren F. Kimball, *Churchill and Roosevelt: The Complete Correspondence*, vol. III, pp. 198–199.
11. Ibid., pp. 218–219.
12. Martin Gilbert, *Winston S. Churchill*, vol. VII, *Road to Victory*, p. 1283.
13. Kimball, p. 198.
14. Ibid., p. 226.
15. Ibid., pp. 263, 267.
16. Ibid., pp. 277–278.
17. Ibid., p. 308.
18. Ibid., pp. 287, 298.
19. V.J.. Esposito, ed., *West Point Atlas of American Wars*, vol. II, map 110.
20. FDRL, PSF, Box 31, Diplomatic Correspondence—Charles de Gaulle.
21. Raoul Aglion, *Roosevelt and De Gaulle*, p. 175.
22. Charles de Gaulle, *The Complete War Memoirs*, vol. III, *Salvation*, pp. 573–575.
23. J.W. Pickersgill and D.F. Foster, eds., *The Mackenzie King Record*, vol. II, p. 67.
24. Ibid., p. 69.
25. FDRL, PSF, Box 31, Diplomatic Correspondence—Charles de Gaulle, C 44-5.
26. William D. Leahy, *I Was There*, p. 43.
27. Ibid., p. 75.
28. Ibid., p. 142.
29. Ibid., p. 244.
30. Ibid., p. 411.
31. Ibid., pp. 339–340.
32. Goodwin, p. 542.
33. Ibid., p. 520.
34. Ted Morgan, *FDR: A Biography*, p. 726.
35. Ibid.
36. Bishop, pp. 115–116.
37. Morgan, p. 727.
38. John C. Culver and John Hyde, *American Dreamer: The Life and Times of Henry A. Wallace*, p. 348.
39. Alben W. Barkley, *That Reminds Me*, p. 169.
40. Goodwin, p. 540.

41. Bishop, p. 113.
42. Culver and Hyde, p. 348.
43. Ibid.
44. Ibid.
45. Goodwin, p. 527.
46. Harry S Truman, *Memoirs: Years of Trial and Hope, 1946–1952*, p. 191.
47. Frank Walker, *Quiet Confidant*, p. 154.
48. Morgan, p. 728.
49. Culver and Hyde, p. 350.
50. Allen Drury, *A Senate Journal*, p. 218.
51. Goodwin, p. 527.
52. Grace Tully, *F.D.R.: My Boss*, p. 2767.
53. Walker, p. 170.
54. Culver and Hyde, p. 355.
55. Ibid., p. 356.
56. Ibid., p. 359.
57. Barkley, p. 190.
58. Truman, p. 190.
59. Morgan, p. 729.
60. James Roosevelt and Sydney Shalett, *Affectionately, FDR: A Son's Story of a Lonely Man*, pp. 351–352; James Roosevelt, *My Parents: A Differing View*, p. 279.
61. Culver and Hyde, p. 363.
62. Joseph P. Lash, *A World of Love*, p. 132; FDRL, Esther Lape Papers, Box 5, ER to Esther Lape, 29/7/44.
63. Smith, Amanda P., ed., *Hostages to Fortune: The Letters of Joseph P. Kennedy*, p. 612.
64. Ibid., p. 608.
65. Morgan, p. 732.
66. Burns, *RSF*, p. 489.
67. Goodwin, p. 532.
68. Larrabee, pp. 346–347.
69. FDRL, PPF 4914.
70. Larrabee, p. 354.
71. Ibid., p. 393.
72. Ibid.
73. E.B. Potter, *Nimitz*, p. 319.
74. Samuel I. Rosenman, *Working with Roosevelt*, p. 458
75. Goodwin, p. 532.
76. Rosenman, p. 458. The only occasions in his life when Roosevelt seemed to be close to tears in the presence of others, after outgrowing infancy, were when then SEC chairman William O. Douglas told him Roosevelt's son James had tried to fix a case before the SEC on behalf of a person who had paid him to do so, because it was the Democrats' "turn to make money" (Peter Collier and David Horowitz, *The Roosevelts: An American Saga*, p. 366); after the box of his mother's mementos of his childhood and youth was delivered, following her death (p. 661); and on this occasion.
77. *New York Times*, 14/8/44, p. 14.

78. Geoffrey Ward, *A First Class Temperament*, vol. II, p. 776.
79. FDRL, PSF, Box 31, Diplomatic Correspondence—France (Charles de Gaulle).
80. Burns, *RSF*, p. 509.
81. Kimball, pp. 285, 294.
82. Ibid., p. 288.
83. Ibid., p. 295.
84. Ibid., p. 296.
85. Ibid., p. 311.
86. Ibid., p. 313.
87. Winston S. Churchill, *The Second World War*, vol. VI, *Triumph and Tragedy*, p. 127.
88. Ibid.
89. Ibid., p. 128.
90. Sir Alexander Cadogan, *Diaries*, p. 718.
91. Kimball, p. 316.
92. Morgenthau diary, 25/9/44.
93. Michael R. Beschloss, *The Conquerors*, p. 138.
94. Morgenthau diary, 24/8/44, 25/8/44.
95. Martin Gilbert, *Churchill: A Life*, p. 412; Beschloss, p. 123.
96. Beschloss, p. 148.
97. Ibid., pp. 126–127.
98. Ibid., p. 108.
99. Ibid.
100. Pickersgill, p. 88.
101. Churchill, p. 132.
102. Forrest C. Pogue, *George C. Marshall*, vol. III, *Organizer of Victory*, p. 433.
103. Ibid., p. 437.
104. Churchill, p. 130.
105. Ibid., p. 129.
106. Beschloss, p. 125.
107. Ibid., p. 124.
108. Kimball, p. 317.
109. Beschloss, pp. 148–149.
110. Smith, p. 609.
111. Beschloss, p. 130.
112. Sir Alan Brooke, *Diaries*, pp. 591–592.
113. Bishop, p. 143.
114. Beschloss, p. 134.
115. Churchill, p. 142.
116. Goodwin, p. 546.
117. Ibid., p. 547.

CHAPTER 23

1. David McCullough, *Truman*, pp. 324–327; Harry S Truman, *Memoirs: 1945, Year of Decisions*, p. 5.
2. J.W. Pickersgill and D.F. Foster, eds., *The Mackenzie King Record*, vol. II, pp. 65–66.

3. William D. Leahy, *I Was There*, p. 255.

4. Michael Barone, *Our Country*, p. 179.

5. Samuel I. Rosenman, *Working with Roosevelt*, p. 478.

6. *Time*, 2/10/44, p. 22.

7. Sir Alexander Cadogan, *Diaries*, p. 667.

8. Charles E. Bohlen, *Witness to History*, pp. 162–163.

9. Winston S. Churchill, *The Second World War*, vol. VI, *Triumph and Tragedy*, p. 198.

10. Warren F. Kimball, *Churchill and Roosevelt: The Complete Correspondence*, vol. III, pp. 348–351.

11. Ibid., p. 350.

12. Ibid., p. 351.

13. Churchill, p. 208.

14. Barbara W. Tuchman, *Stilwell and the American Experience in China 1911–1945*, p. 490.

15. Ibid., p. 492.

16. Ibid., p. 494.

17. Ibid., p. 499.

18. Ibid., p. 501.

19. Ibid., p. 516.

20. D. Clayton James, *The Years of MacArthur*, vol. II, p. 557.

21. Eric Larrabee, *Commander in Chief: Franklin Delano Roosevelt, His Lieutenants & Their War*, p. 404.

22. Ibid., p. 406.

23. Ibid., p. 408.

24. Ibid.

25. Ibid., p. 410.

26. Kimball, p. 376.

27. Barone, p. 178.

28. Ibid., p. 179.

29. Doris Kearns Goodwin, *No Ordinary Time*, p. 579.

30. FDRL, PPF 8921, O. Welles, 12/10/44. Amongst those who had been members of "Hollywood for Roosevelt" in 1940, almost all of whom remained supporters in 1944, were Lucille Ball, George Bancroft, Tallulah Bankhead, Robert Benchley, Joan Bennett, Irving Berlin, Charles Bickford, Humphrey Bogart, James Cagney, Andy Devine, Melvyn Douglas, Alice Faye, Henry Fonda, John Ford, John Garfield, Ira Gershwin, Betty Grable, Samuel Goldwyn, Katharine Hepburn, John Huston, Walter Huston, Nunnally Johnson, Garson Kanin, Jerome Kern, Dorothy Lamour, Pat O'Brien, George Raft, Claude Rains, Edward G. Robinson, Rosalind Russell, Myron Selznick, Jack Warner, Billy Wilder, and Jane Wyman.

Tallulah Bankhead, daughter of former House speaker William Bankhead, explained Roosevelt's appeal to the entertainment community in her memoirs: "Aside from their conviction that Roosevelt was our ablest man in such critical times, they admired him for his eloquence, for his gifts as a phrase-maker, for his theatrics, for his ability to touch their hearts as well as their minds" (*Tallulah*, p. 276). Spirited and witty, as well as an attractive woman, Ms. Bankhead once landed a theatrical part that required a natural redhead, from a skeptical producer, by performing an impromptu double cartwheel in front of him while wearing a loose skirt and unencumbered by underclothing.

Meetings with Roosevelt pop up in the memoirs of actors and actresses of the period as among the highlights of their lives, from Katharine Hepburn, who called him "the most powerful and fascinating of personalities. . . . What a character!" (*Me*, p. 174), to Myrna Loy, who described him as "My hero" in her autobiography.

31. Michael R. Beschloss, *The Conquerors*, p. 99.
32. FDRL, PPF 8921, O. Welles, 13/12/44.
33. FDRL, PPF 8853, J. Steinbeck, 24/8/44.
34. Mark Schorer, *Sinclair Lewis*, p. 727.
35. Millicent Bell, *Marquand*, pp. 367–368.
36. Louis Sheaffer, *O'Neill, Son and Artist*, vol. II, p. 462.
37. Joseph Blotner, *Faulkner*, p. 412.
38. James MacGregor Burns, *Roosevelt: Soldier of Freedom*, p. 529.
39. Harry S Truman, *Memoirs: Years of Trial and Hope, 1946–1952*, p. 193.
40. Goodwin, p. 554.
41. A. Merriman Smith, *Thank You, Mr. President*, p. 159.
42. FDRL, PPF 8880, Thomas E. Dewey, 13/11/44.
43. Burns, p. 533.
44. Kimball, p. 383.
45. Ibid., p. 385.
46. Burns, p. 532.
47. Churchill, p. 218.
48. Charles de Gaulle, *The Complete War Memoirs*, vol. III, *Salvation*, p. 723. Today, Clemenceau's statue faces de Gaulle's; one block to the south of them, along what is now Avenue Winston Churchill, is a statue of Winston Churchill; and the street immediately to the west is Avenue Franklin D. Roosevelt running from the Seine across the Champs Élysées. Thus does Paris commemorate the four statesmen to whom France chiefly owed its survival through the twentieth century.
49. Ibid.
50. Churchill, p. 219.
51. Bernard Asbell, *The FDR Memoirs*, p. 413.
52. Beschloss, p. 167.
53. Robert Ferrell, *The Dying President*, p. 114.
54. Kimball, p. 439.
55. de Gaulle, pp. 736–757.
56. Pickersgill and Foster, eds., p. 69.
57. Beschloss, p. 174.
58. Goodwin, pp. 566–568.
59. Joseph P. Lash, *A World of Love*, p. 161.
60. Goodwin, p. 570.
61. Ibid., p. 571.
62. V.J. Esposito, ed., *West Point Atlas of American Wars*, vol. II, map 160.
63. Frances Perkins, *The Roosevelt I Knew*, p. 148.

64. Beschloss, p. 101; FDRL, PSF, Box 41, Diplomatic Correspondence—Italy (J.P. Kennedy–S. Welles), 5/4/39; FDR's comments to George VI: Sarah Bradford, *The Reluctant King*, p. 297.

65. *Correspondence of President Roosevelt with Pope Pius XII*, pp. 61–64.

66. Robert Conquest, *Stalin*, p. 246.

67. Alden Hatch, *Edith Bolling Wilson, First Lady Extraordinary*, pp. 243, 271–272.

68. Goodwin, p. 573.

69. Frank Freidel, *Franklin D. Roosevelt: A Rendezvous with Destiny*, p. 578.

70. Ibid., p. 577.

71. Ibid., p. 578–579.

CHAPTER 24

1. James MacGregor Burns, *Roosevelt: Soldier of Freedom*, p. 603.

2. Doris Kearns Goodwin, *No Ordinary Time*, p. 575.

3. Anthony Eden, *The Eden Memoirs: The Reckoning*, p. 512.

4. Ibid.

5. Edward Stettinius, *Roosevelt and the Russians*, p. 75.

6. Ibid., p. 75.

7. Winston S. Churchill, *The Second World War*, vol. VI, *Triumph and Tragedy*, p. 300.

8. Sergo Beria, *Beria: My Father*, p. 104.

9. Rudy Abramson, *Spanning the Century: The Life of W. Averell Harriman, 1891–1986*, p. 370

10. Michael R. Beschloss, *The Conquerors*, p. 179.

11. Stettinius, p. 99.

12. Ibid., p. 304.

13. Ibid., p. 99.

14. Letter to author of Antony Beevor, author of *The Fall of Berlin* and *Stalingrad*, 20/1/03.

15. Frank Freidel, *Franklin D. Roosevelt: A Rendezvous with Destiny*, p. 580; Stimson diary, 31/12/44.

16. Martin Gilbert, *Winston S. Churchill*, vol. VII, *Road to Victory, 1941–1945*, p. 1174.

17. Stettinius, p. 111.

18. Ibid.

19. Ibid.

20. PCA, see pp. 372–373.

21. Charles E. Bohlen account; official U.S. Yalta transcript (YT), p. 543.

22. YT, p. 544.

23. YT, p. 547.

24. Antony Beevor, *The Fall of Berlin*, p. 81.

25. Ibid., pp. 81–82.

26. Stettinius, p. 129.

27. Ibid., p. 90.

28. Robert Dallek, *Franklin D. Roosevelt and American Foreign Policy, 1932–1945*, p. 518.

29. Goodwin, p. 579.

30. De Jonge, *Stalin and the Shaping of the Soviet Union*, p. 454.

31. Stettinius, p. 161.

32. Ibid.; Churchill, vol. VI, p. 316.

33. Dallek, p. 511.

34. YT, p. 721.

35. Dallek, p. 518.

36. YT, p. 766.

37. George McJimsey, *Harry Hopkins*, p. 369.

38. Beria, p. 101.

39. YT, p. 782.

40. Ian Grey, *Stalin: Man of History*, p. 411.

41. De Jonge, p. 435.

42. Sir Alexander Cadogan, *Diaries*, p. 706.

43. Stettinius, pp. 204–205.

44. De Jonge, pp. 452–453.

45. Beschloss, p. 238.

46. Sir John Colville, *Fringes of Power*, p. 564. Colville's version of this is of a "little British lion," but this became a theme of Churchill's as his status as the third power became more clear, and "donkey" was his preferred allegory.

47. Stettinius, p. 88.

48. Winston S. Churchill, *The Second World War*, vol. III, *The Grand Alliance*, p. 443.

49. Cadogan, p. 632.

50. Arthur Bryant, ed., *Triumph in the West*, p. 400.

51. Ibid., p. 411.

52. Anvil-Dragoon.

53. Bernard L. Montgomery, *History of War*, p. 518.

54. Ibid., p. 544.

55. Ibid.

56. Ibid., p. 529.

57. Goodwin, p. 576.

58. Eden, p. 512.

59. Stettinius, p. 72.

60. Cadogan, p. 702.

61. Stettinius, p. 72.

62. Abramson, p. 371.

63. James Byrnes, *All in One Lifetime*, p. 256.

64. Stettinius, p. 73.

65. Dallek, p. 519.

66. Goodwin, p. 585.

67. McJimsey, p. 363.

68. Ibid.

69. Goodwin, p. 576.

70. Freidel, p. 581.

71. Warren F. Kimball, *Forged in War*, p. 341.

72. Robert Ferrell, *The Dying President*, pp. 106–107.

73. FDRL, PSF, Box 24, Diplomatic Correspondence — William C. Bullitt.

74. Bohlen, p. 141.

75. Ibid., p. 209.

76. Andrei Gromyko, *Memoirs*, pp. 85, 98.

77. Ibid., p. 98.

78. J.W. Pickersgill and D.F. Foster, eds., *The Mackenzie King Record*, vol. II, pp. 69, 325.

79. Freidel, p. 578; Frances Perkins, *The Roosevelt I Knew*, p. 14.

80. Dallek, p. 521.

81. Beatrice Berle and Travis Jacobs, *Navigating the Rapids, 1918–1971*, p. 477.

82. Geoffrey Ward, ed., *Closest Companion*, p. 397.

83. McJimsey, p. 372.

84. Dallek, p. 533.

85. Ibid., p. 534.

86. Ibid.

87. Ibid.

88. Bohlen, p. 211.

89. Ibid.

90. Ted Morgan, *FDR: A Biography*, p. 735.

91. Burns, p. 578; Morgan, p. 756.

92. Ward, ed., p. 396.

93. Freidel, p. 581.

94. Churchill, vol. VI, p. 348.

95. Perkins, p. 142.

96. Bohlen, pp. 205–206.

97. Samuel I. Rosenman, *Working with Roosevelt*, p. 522.

98. Lord Moran, *Churchill, from the Diaries of Lord Moran*, p. 257.

99. Rosenman, p. 522.

100. Ibid.

101. Ibid., p. 528.

102. Joseph Alsop, *FDR: A Centenary Remembrance*, p. 230.

CHAPTER 25

1. Edward Stettinius, *Roosevelt and the Russians*, p. 311.

2. Robin Edmonds, *The Big Three: Churchill, Roosevelt, and Stalin in Peace and War*, p. 419.

3. Warren F. Kimball, *Churchill and Roosevelt: The Complete Correspondence*, vol. III, p. 549.

4. Ibid., p. 563.

5. Ibid., p. 564

6. Ibid., p. 571.

7. Frank Freidel, *Franklin D. Roosevelt: Rendezvous with Destiny*, p. 600; *Le Figaro*, 11/3/45, 12/3/45.

8. Robert Ferrell, *The Dying President*, p. 111; David Kennedy, *Freedom From Fear*, p. 808.

9. J.W. Pickersgill and D.F. Foster, eds., *The Mackenzie King Report*, vol. II, pp. 325–326, 329.

10. Doris Kearns Goodwin, *No Ordinary Time*, p. 596; Samuel I. Rosenman, *Working with Roosevelt*, p. 546.

11. Ferrell, p. 111.

12. Ibid.

13. Ibid., p. 112; Michael R. Beschloss, *The Conquerors*, p. 196; Jonathan Daniels, *White House Witness*, p. 266.

14. James MacGregor Burns, *Roosevelt: Soldier of Freedom (RSF)*, p. 595.

15. Ibid.

16. Freidel, p. 601.

17. Kimball, pp. 587–588.

18. FDRL, PPF 7177, Albert Einstein.

19. Antony Beevor, *Berlin*, pp. 194–195.

20. Beschloss, p. 204.

21. Dwight D. Eisenhower, *Crusade in Europe*, p. 399.

22. *Papers of General Dwight David Eisenhower*, vol. IV, p. 2394.

23. Forrest C. Pogue, *George C. Marshall*, vol. 3, *Organizer of Victory*, p. 534.

24. Eisenhower Papers, p. 2394.

25. Harry S Truman, *Memoirs: 1945, Year of Decisions*, p. 215.

26. Ibid., pp. 314–315.

27. Carlo D'Este, *Patton: A Genius for War*, p. 721.

28. Ferrell, p. 115.

29. Geoffrey Ward, ed., *Constant Companion*, p. 400; Ferrell, p. 111.

30. Ward, ed., pp. 402–403; Beschloss, p. 203.

31. FDRL, PSF, Diplomatic Correspondence, Box 32.

32. Kimball, p. 612.

33. Ibid., p. 617.

34. Beschloss, p. 188.

35. Kimball, p. 622.

36. Ward, ed., p. 414.

37. Ibid., p. 423.

38. Kimball, pp. 633–637; Truman, pp. 14–17.

39. Ward, ed., p. 411; Beschloss, p. 207.

40. Ronald Steel, *Walter Lippmann and the American Century*, p. 417; Walter Lippmann, *Today and Tomorrow*, 7/4/45.

41. Ward, ed., p. 413.

42. Ibid; Ferrell, p. 118.

43. Ward, ed., p. 414.

44. Beschloss, p. 211.

45. Ibid, p. 212.

46. Ibid., p. 179.

47. Ibid., p. 401; Ferrell, p. 114.

48. Ferrell, p. 117; Elizabeth Shoumatoff, *FDR Up Close*, pp. 78–79.
49. Ward, ed., p. 415.
50. Alex Shoumatoff, "Personal History," *The New Yorker*, 3/5/82.
51. Ward, ed., p. 418.
52. Ferrell, p. 119.
53. Ward, ed., pp. 418–419.
54. William D. Hassett, *Off the Record*, p. 335.
55. Noah D. Fabricant, "FDR, The Common Cold and American History," *Eye, Ear, Nose and Throat Monthly*, March 1958.
56. Samuel I. Rosenman, *Working with Roosevelt*, p. 411; CEH, VJM 2/57.
57. Fabricant.
58. Goodwin, p. 603.
59. Ferrell, p. 140.
60. Goodwin, pp. 603–604.
61. Ibid., p. 604.
62. D.B. Hardeman and Donald C. Bacon, *Rayburn: A Biography*, pp. 308–309; Truman, p. 341.
63. Goodwin, p. 611.
64. Ibid., p. 612.
65. Ibid., p. 631. At tea with James Roosevelt's former wife, Betsy Cushing Roosevelt Whitney, in 1947, Lucy expressed concern to know that she was the only extramarital lover FDR had ever had. Ted Morgan, *FDR: A Biography*, p. 207.
66. Martin Gilbert, *Churchill: A Life*, pp. 835–836.
67. Goodwin, p. 615.
68. *New York Times*, 7/6/47.
69. Goodwin, p. 606.
70. Ibid.
71. Ibid.
72. Ibid., p. 604; PCA.
73. James Chace, *Acheson*, p. 103.
74. Ibid., pp. 3, 596, 740.
75. Charles E. Bohlen, *Witness to History*, p. 210.
76. James MacGregor Burns, *Leadership*, p. 282; Goodwin, p. 608.
77. Ferrell, p. 143.
78. Nicholas Halasz, *Roosevelt Through Foreign Eyes*, p. 320.
79. Beevor, p. 204.
80. Burns, *Leadership*, p. 601; William L. Shirer, *The Rise and Fall of the Third Reich*, p. 1110.
81. Charles de Gaulle, *The Complete War Memoirs*, vol. III, *Salvation*, p. 900.
82. Goodwin, p. 621.
83. Edvard Radzinsky, *Stalin*, p. 493.
84. Lord Moran, *Churchill, Taken from the Diaries of Lord Moran*, p. 310.
85. Chace, p. 740.
86. John Gunther, Roosevelt in Retrospect, p. 18; Goodwin, p. 606.
87. Robert Herzstein, *Roosevelt and Hitler*, p. 413.

88. Isaiah Berlin, *Personal Impressions*, p. 26.

89. Theodore Lippmann Jr., *The Squire of Warm Springs: FDR in Georgia 1924–1945*, p. 241.

90. Eleanor Roosevelt, *This I Remember*, p. 117.

91. J.V. Stalin, *Leninism*.

92. John Keegan, *The Mask of Command*, section 4.

93. Goodwin, p. 630.

94. A.J.P. Taylor, *Oxford History of England: English History,1914–1945*, p. 577.

Bibliography

A comprehensive bibliography for the study of Franklin D. Roosevelt and his time would include a practically unlimited number of books and other sources. He makes at least a cameo appearance in an astonishing number of American and foreign biographical and historical works of the period and in a great many works of fiction as well. Documentary sources are also overwhelmingly extensive. The books listed here and the other sources cited among the footnotes were those that were more than cursorily consulted.

Foreign Relations of the United States (Washington, D.C.: U.S. Government Printing Office):
  The Conferences at Cairo and Tehran (1961), hereafter referred to as FRUS
    Tehran 1944 (1966).
  The Conference at Quebec (1972), hereafter referred to as FRUS Quebec 1945
    (1967–1968).
  The Conferences at Malta and Yalta (1955), hereafter referred to as FRUS
    Yalta.

Abramson, Rudy. *Spanning the Century: The Life of W. Averell Harriman, 1891–1986*. New York: Morrow, 1992.
Acheson, Dean. *Present at the Creation: My Years at the State Department*. New York: Norton, 1969.
Adamic, Louis. *Dinner at the White House*. New York: Harper & Brothers, 1946.
Adams, Henry H. *Harry Hopkins: A Biography*. New York: Putnam, 1977.
Aglion, Raoul. *Roosevelt and De Gaulle: Allies in Conflict, A Personal Memoir*. New York: Free Press, 1988.
Aichele, Gary. *Oliver Wendell Holmes: Soldier, Scholar, Judge*. Boston: Twayne, 1989.
Albion, Robert G. *Makers of Naval Policy*. Annapolis, Md.: Naval Institute Press, 1980.
Alinsky, Saul. *John L. Lewis: An Unauthorized Biography*. New York: Putnam, 1949.

Allen, Frederick Lewis. *Only Yesterday.* New York: Harper & Brothers, 1931.

Alsop, Joseph. *FDR: A Centenary Remembrance.* New York: Random House, 1982.

Alsop, Joseph, and Turner Catledge. *The 168 Days.* Garden City, N.Y.: Doubleday, Doran, 1938.

Ambrose, Stephen. *Citizen Soldiers: The U.S. Army from the Normandy Beaches to the Bulge to the Surrender of Germany: June 7, 1944–May 7, 1945.* New York: Simon & Schuster, 1997.

———. *D-Day: June 6, 1944: The Climactic Battle of World War II.* New York: Simon & Schuster, 1944.

———. *Eisenhower: Soldier, General of the Army, President-Elect, 1890–1952.* New York: Simon & Schuster, 1983.

———. *Eisenhower and Berlin, 1945: The Decision to Halt at the Elbe.* New York: Norton, 1967.

———. *The Supreme Commander: The War Years of General Dwight D. Eisenhower.* New York: Doubleday, 1970.

Anderson, Jervis. A. *Philip Randolph: A Biographical Portrait.* New York: Harcourt Brace Jovanovich, 1973.

Armstrong, Anne. *Unconditional Surrender: The Impact of the Casablanca Policy on World War II.* New Brunswick, N.J.: Rutgers University Press, 1961.

Arnold, Henry H. *Global Mission.* New York: Harper, 1949.

Asbell, Bernard. *The FDR Memoirs.* Garden City, N.Y.: Doubleday, 1973.

———. *When FDR Died.* New York: Holt, Rinehart & Winston, 1961.

———, ed. *Mother & Daughter: The Letters of Eleanor and Anna Roosevelt.* New York: Coward, McCann & Geoghegan, 1982.

Ashburn, Frank D. *Peabody of Groton.* New York: Coward McCann, 1944.

Atkinson, Rick. *An Army at Dawn: The War in Africa, 1942–1943.* New York: Henry Holt, 2002.

Attlee, Clement R. *As It Happened.* London: Heinemann, 1954.

Azana, Manuel, *Memoirs,* vol. IV.

Backer, John. *The Decision to Divide Germany: American Foreign Policy in Transition.* Durham, N.C.: Duke University Press, 1978.

Bacon, Francis. *De Augmentis Scientarum.*

Baker, Ray Stannard. *American Chronicle: The Autobiography of Ray Stannard Baker.* New York: Scribner, 1945.

———. *Woodrow Wilson: Life and Letters.* 8 vols. Garden City, N.Y.: Doubleday, 1927.

Baldwin, Hanson W. *The Crucial Years, 1939–1941.* New York: Harper & Row, 1976.

Bankhead, Tallulah. *Tallulah: My Autobiography.* New York: Harper & Brothers, 1952.

Barber, Noel. *The Week France Fell.* New York: Stein & Day, 1976.

Barkley, Alben W. *That Reminds Me.* New York: Doubleday, 1954.

Barnard, John. *Walter Reuther and the Rise of the Auto Workers*. Boston: Little, Brown, 1983.

Barnes, Joseph. *Willkie*. New York: Simon & Schuster, 1952.

Barone, Michael. *Our Country*. New York: Free Press, 1990.

Baruch, Bernard M. *Baruch: The Public Years*. New York: Holt, Rinehart & Winston, 1960.

Beach, Edward L. *The United States Navy: 200 Years*. New York: Henry Holt, 1985.

Beard, Charles A. *President Roosevelt and the Coming of the War, 1941*. New Haven, Conn.: Yale University Press, 1948.

Beasley, Maurine H. *Eleanor Roosevelt and the Media: A Public Quest for Self-Fulfillment*. Chicago: University of Illinois Press, 1987.

Beatty, Jack. *The Rascal King: The Life and Times of James Michael Curley (1875–1958)*. Boston: Perseus, 1992.

Beevor, Antony. *The Fall of Berlin, 1945*. New York: Viking, 2002.

Bell, Millicent. *Marquand: An American Life*. Boston: Little, Brown, 1979.

Bellow, Saul. *It All Adds Up: From the Dim Past to the Uncertain Future*. New York: Viking, 1994.

Bellush, Benjamin. *Franklin D. Roosevelt as Governor of New York*. New York: Columbia University Press, 1955.

Bellush, Bernard. *He Walked Alone: A Biography of John Gilbert Winant*. The Hague: Mouton, 1968.

Bennett, Edward M. *Franklin D. Roosevelt and the Search for Security: American-Soviet Relations, 1933–1939*. Wilmington, Del.: Scholarly Resources: 1997.

Berezhkov, Valentin. *At Stalin's Side: His Interpreter's Memoirs from the October Revolution to the Fall of the Dictator's Empire*. New York: Birch Lane, 1994.

Berg, Roland H. *The Challenge of Polio: The Crusade Against Infantile Paralysis*. New York: Dial Press, 1946.

Beria, Sergo. *Beria: My Father*. London: Duckworth, 2001.

Berle, Beatrice, and Travis Jacobs, eds. *Navigating the Rapids, 1918–1971: From the Papers of Adolf A. Berle*. New York: Harcourt Brace Jovanovich, 1973.

Berle, Beatrice Bishop. *A Life in Two Worlds*. New York: Walker and Company, 1983.

Berlin, Isaiah. *Personal Impressions*. Edited by Henry Hardy. New York: Viking, 1981.

Berthon, Simon. *Allies at War*. London: HarperCollins, 2001.

Beschloss, Michael R. *The Conquerors: Roosevelt, Truman, and the Destruction of Hitler's Germany 1944–1945*. New York: Simon & Schuster, 2002.

———. *Kennedy and Roosevelt: The Uneasy Alliance*. New York: Norton, 1980.

Biddle, Francis. *In Brief Authority*. Garden City, N.Y.: Doubleday, 1948.

Biddle, George. *An American Artist's Story*. Boston: Little, Brown, 1939.

Bird, Kai. *The Chairman: John J. McCloy and the Making of the American Establishment*. New York: Simon & Schuster, 1992.

Birkenhead, Earl of. *The Prof. in Two Worlds: The Official Life of Professor F.A. Lindemann, Viscount Cherwell.* London: Collins, 1961.

Birse, A.H. *Memoirs of an Interpreter.* New York: Coward McCann, 1967.

Bishop, Jim. *FDR's Last Year.* New York: Morrow, 1974.

Bloch, Michael. *Ribbentrop.* New York: Crown, 1993.

Blotner, Joseph. *Faulkner: A Biography.* London: Chatto and Windus, 1974.

Blum, John Morton. *From the Morgenthau Diaries.* 3 vols. Boston: Houghton Mifflin, 1959, 1965, 1967.

————. *Joe Tumulty and the Wilson Era.* Boston: Houghton Mifflin, 1951.

————. *Roosevelt and Morgenthau.* Boston: Houghton Mifflin, 1970.

————. *V Was for Victory.* New York: Harcourt, 1976.

————, ed. *Public Philosopher: Selected Letters of Walter Lippmann.*

Blumenson, Martin. *Mark Clark.* New York: Congdon & Weed, 1982.

————. *The Patton Papers.* Boston: Houghton Mifflin, 1972.

Boelcki, Willi A., ed. *Secret Conference of Dr. Joseph Goebbels: The Nazi Propaganda War, 1939–1943.* New York: Dutton, 1970.

Boettiger, John. *A Love in Shadow.* New York: Norton, 1978.

Bohlen, Charles E. *Witness to History: 1929–1969.* New York: Norton, 1973.

Bosworth, Allen R. *America's Concentration Camps.* New York: Norton, 1967.

Bradford, Sarah. *The Reluctant King: The Life and Reign of George VI, 1895–1952.* New York: St. Martin's, 1990.

Bradley, Omar, and Clay Blair. *A General's Life.* New York: Simon & Schuster, 1983.

Brinkley, David. *Washington Goes to War.* New York: Knopf, 1988.

Brinkley, Douglas, ed. *Dean Acheson and the Making of U.S. Foreign Policy.* New York: St. Martin's, 1993.

Brinkley, Douglas, and D.R. Facey-Crowther, eds. *Atlantic Charter.* New York: Macmillan, 1994.

Brinnin, John Malcolm. *The Sway of the Grand Saloon: A Social History of the North Atlantic.* New York: Delacorte Press, 1971.

Brooke, Sir Alan. *Diaries.*

Brough, James. *Princess Alice.* Boston: Little, Brown, 1975.

Browder, Robert Paul, and Thomas Smith. *Independent: A Biography of Lewis W. Douglas.* New York: Knopf, 1986.

Brownell, Will, and Richard N. Billings. *So Close to Greatness: A Biography of William C. Bullitt.* New York: Macmillan, 1987.

Bruenn, Howard J. "Clinical Notes on the Illness and Death of President Franklin D. Roosevelt." *Annals of Internal Medicine,* vol. 72 (April 1970).

Bryant, Arthur, ed. *The Turn of the Tide, 1939–1943,* vol. I, *A History of the War Years Based on the Diaries of Field Marshall Lord Alanbrooke.* Garden City, N.Y.: Doubleday, 1957.

————, ed., *Triumph in the West,* vol. II, *A History of the War Years Based on the Diaries of Field Marshall Lord Alanbrooke.* Garden City, N.Y.: Doubleday, 1959.

Buhite, Russell. *Decisions at Yalta: An Appraisal of Summit Diplomacy*. Wilmington, Del.: Scholarly Resources, 1986.

————, and David W. Levy, eds. *FDR's Fireside Chats*. Norman, Okla.: University of Oklahoma Press, 1992.

Bullitt, William C. *For the President, Personal and Secret: Correspondence Between Franklin D. Roosevelt and William C. Bullitt*. Edited by Orville H. Bullitt. Boston: Houghton Mifflin, 1972.

Bullock, Alan. *Hitler: A Study in Tyranny*. New York: Harper & Row, 1962.

————. *Hitler and Stalin: Parallel Lives*. New York: Knopf, 1992.

Bunker, John. *Liberty Ships: Ugly Ducklings of World War II*. Annapolis, Md.: Naval Institute Press, 1972.

Burner, David. *Herbert Hoover: A Public Life*. New York: Knopf, 1979.

Burns, James MacGregor. *Leadership*. New York: Harper & Row, 1978.

————. *Roosevelt: The Lion and the Fox*. Vol. 1, 1882–1940. New York: Harcourt, 1956.

————. *Roosevelt: Soldier of Freedom*. Vol. 2, 1940–1945. New York: Harcourt, 1970.

Busch, Noel F., *What Manner of Man*. New York: Harper & Brothers, 1944.

Butcher, Harry C. *My Three Years with Eisenhower: The Personal Diary of Captain Harry C. Butcher, USNR, Naval Aide to General Eisenhower, 1942 to 1945*. New York: Simon & Schuster, 1946.

Butler, Smedley D. (as told to Lowell Thomas). *Old Gimlet Eye: The Adventures of Smedley D. Butler*. New York: Farrar & Rinehart, 1933.

Byrnes, James. *All in One Lifetime*. New York: Harper, 1958.

————. *Speaking Frankly*. New York: Harper, 1947.

Cadogan, Sir Alexander. *The Diaries of Sir Alexander Cadogan, O.M., 1938–1945*. Edited by David Dilks. New York: Putnam, 1972.

Campbell, Thomas, and George Herring. *The Diaries of Edward R. Stettinius, Jr., 1943–1946*. New York: New Viewpoints, 1975.

Carmichael, Donald Scott. *FDR Columnist*. Chicago: Pellegrini & Cudahy, 1947.

Caro, Robert A. *The Path to Power: The Years of Lyndon Johnson*. New York: Knopf, 1982.

————. *The Power Broker: Robert Moses and the Fall of New York*. New York: Knopf, 1974.

Carter, Richard. *Breakthrough: The Saga of Jonas Salk*. New York: Trident Press, 1966.

Cebula, James E. *James M. Cox: Journalist and Politician*. New York: Garland, 1985.

Chace, James. *Acheson: The Secretary of State Who Created the American World*. New York: Simon & Schuster, 1998.

Chadakoff, Rochelle, ed. *Eleanor Roosevelt's My Day*. Vol. I, *Her Acclaimed Columns, 1936–1945*. New York: Pharos Books, 1989.

Chamberlain, Rudolph W. *There Is No Truce: A Life of Thomas Motto Osborne.* New York: Macmillan, 1935.

Chambers, Whittaker. *Witness.* Chicago: Regnery Gateway, 1984.

Chandler, Alfred, and Louis Galambos, eds. *The Papers of Dwight David Eisenhower.* Vols. 4, 5, and 9. Baltimore: Johns Hopkins University Press, 1967, 1970.

Charmley, John. *Churchill: The End of Glory.* New York: Harcourt, 1993.

Childs, Marquis. *I Write from Washington.* New York: Harper, 1942.

Chuev, Felix, and Albert Resis, eds. *Molotov Remembers.* Chicago: Ivan Dee, 1993.

Churchill, Winston S. *The Second World War.* 6 vols. Boston: Houghton Mifflin, 1948–1953.

——. *The Unrelenting Struggle: War Speeches.*

Ciano, Count Galeazzo. *Diaries.* Garden City, N.Y.: Doubleday, 1945.

Clark, James C. *Faded Glory: Presidents out of Power.* New York: Praeger, 1985.

Clemens, Diane Shaver. *Yalta.* New York: Oxford University Press, 1970.

Cohen, Adam, and Elizabeth Taylor. *American Pharaoh: Mayor Richard J. Daley, His Battle for Chicago and the Nation.* Boston: Little, Brown, 2000.

Cohen, Michael. *Churchill and the Jews.* London: Cass, 1985.

Cole, Wayne S. *America First: The Battle Against Intervention, 1940–1941.* Madison, Wisc.: University of Wisconsin Press, 1953.

Collier, Peter, and David Horowitz. *The Roosevelts: An American Saga.* New York: Simon & Schuster, 1994.

Colville, Sir John Rupert. *Fringes of Power: 10 Downing Street Diaries, 1939–1955.* New York: Norton, 1985.

Complete Press Conferences of Franklin D. Roosevelt. New York: Da Capo, 1972.

Conn, Stetson, and Byron Fairchild. *The Western Hemisphere: The Framework of Hemispheric Defense.* Washington, D.C.: Office of the Chief of Military History, 1960.

Connable, Alfred, and Edward Silberfarb. *Tigers of Tammany Hall: Nine Men Who Ran New York.* New York: Holt, Rinehart & Winston, 1967.

Conquest, Robert. *Stalin: Breaker of Nations.* New York: Viking, 1991.

Cook, Blanche Wiesen. *Eleanor Roosevelt.* Vol. I, 1884–1933. New York: Viking Penguin, 1992.

Coon, Horace. *Colossus on the Hudson.* New York: Dutton, 1947.

Cooney, John. *The American Pope: The Life and Times of Francis Cardinal Spellman.* New York: Times Books, 1984.

Cooper, John Milton, Jr. *The Warrior and the Priest: Woodrow Wilson and Theodore Roosevelt.* Cambridge, Mass.: Harvard University Press, 1983.

Cowles, Virginia. *The Astors.* New York: Knopf, 1979.

Cox, James M. *Journey Through My Years: An Autobiography.* New York: Simon & Schuster, 1946.

Craig, Gordon. *The Germans.* New York: Putnam, 1982.

———. *Germany: 1866–1945*. New York: Oxford University Press, 1978.

Cray, Ed. *General of the Army: George C. Marshall: Soldier and Statesman*. New York: Simon & Schuster, 1990.

Cronon, E. David, ed. *The Cabinet Diaries of Josephus Daniels, 1913–1921*. Lincoln, Neb.: University of Nebraska Press, 1963.

Culver, John C., and John Hyde. *American Dreamer: The Life and Times of Henry A. Wallace*. New York: Norton, 2000.

Dall, Curtis B. *FDR: My Exploited Father-in-Law*. Washington, D.C.: Liberty Lobby, 1970.

Dallek, Robert. *Franklin D. Roosevelt and American Foreign Policy, 1932–1945*. New York: Oxford University Press, 1979.

Dallin, Alexander. *German Rule in Russia, 1941–1945: A Study of Occupation Policies*.

Daniels, Jonathan. *The End of Innocence*. New York: Da Capo Press, 1954.

———. *Washington Quadrille: The Dance Beside the Documents*. Garden City, N.Y.: Doubleday, 1968.

———. *White House Witness 1942–1945*. Garden City, N.Y.: Doubleday, 1975.

Daniels, Josephus. *Editor in Politics*. Chapel Hill, N.C.: University of North Carolina Press, 1941.

———. *The Cabinet Diaries of Josephus Daniels, 1913–1921*. Lincoln, Neb.: University of Nebraska Press, 1963.

———. *Our Navy at War*. New York, 1922.

———. *Tar-Heels Editor*. Chapel Hill, N.C.: University of North Carolina Press, 1940.

———. *The Wilson Era: Years of Peace 1910–1917*. Chapel Hill, N.C.: University of North Carolina Press, 1944.

———. *The Wilson Era: Years of War and After 1917–1923*. Chapel Hill, N.C.: University of North Carolina Press, 1946.

Daniels, Mrs. Josephus (Adelaide Worth Bagley Daniels). *Recollections of a Cabinet Minister's Wife 1913–1921*. Raleigh, N.C.: Mitchell Printing Company, 1945.

Davis, Fred. *Passage through Crises: Polio Victims and Their Families*. Indianapolis: Bobbs-Merrill, 1963.

Davis, Kenneth. *FDR*. Vol. I, *The Beckoning of Destiny, 1882–1928*. New York: Putnam, 1972.

———. *FDR*. Vol. II, *The New York Years, 1928–1933*. New York: Random House, 1986.

———. *FDR*. Vol. III, *The New Deal Years, 1933–1937*. New York: Random House, 1986.

———. *FDR*. Vol. IV, *Into the Storm, 1937–1940*. New York: Random House, 1993.

———. *FDR*. Vol. V, *The War President, 1940–1943*. New York: Random House, 2000.

———. *Invincible Summer: An Intimate Portrait of the Roosevelts.* New York: Atheneum, 1974.

Dawidowicz, Lucy. *The War Against the Jews.* New York: Holt, 1975.

Day, Donald. *Franklin D. Roosevelt's Own Story.*

De Jonge, Alex. *Stalin and the Shaping of the Soviet Union.* New York: Morrow, 1986.

D'Este, Carlo. *Patton: A Genius for War.* New York: HarperCollins, 1996.

Deutsch, Harold. *The Conspiracy Against Hitler in the Twilight War.* Minneapolis: University of Minnesota Press, 1968.

Deutscher, Isaac. *Stalin: A Political Biography.*

De Weerd, H.A. *Great Soldiers of World War II.* New York: Norton, 1944.

Divine, Robert A. *Roosevelt and World War II.* Baltimore: Johns Hopkins University Press, 1969.

Dodd, William, and Martha Dodd. *Ambassador Dodd's Diary.* New York: Harcourt Brace and Company, 1941.

Donovan, Hedley. *Roosevelt to Reagan: A Reporter's Encounter with Nine Presidents.* New York: Harper & Row, 1985.

Dows, Olin. *Franklin Roosevelt at Hyde Park.* New York: American Artists Group, 1949.

Dozer, Donald. *Are We Good Neighbors: Three Decades of Inter-American Relations 1930–1960.*

Draper, George. *Acute Poliomyelitis.* Philadelphia: P. Blakiston's Son, 1917.

———. *Infantile Paralysis.* New York, 1927.

Drury, Allen. *A Senate Journal.* New York: McGraw-Hill, 1963.

Dulles, Allen. *The Secret Surrender.* New York: Harper & Row, 1966.

Dunn, Robert. *World Alive: A Personal Story.* New York: Crown, 1956.

Dunne, Gerald T. *Grenville Clark: Public Citizen.* New York: Farrar, Straus & Giroux, 1986.

Dutton, David. *Anthony Eden: A Life and Reputation.* London: Arnold, 1997.

Eden, Anthony. *The Eden Memoirs.* Vol. I, *Facing the Dictators.* London: Cassell, 1962.

———. *The Eden Memoirs.* Vol. II, *The Reckoning.* Boston: Houghton Mifflin, 1965.

Edmonds, Robin. *The Big Three: Churchill, Roosevelt, and Stalin in Peace and War.* New York: Norton, 1991.

Eisenhower, David. *Eisenhower at War, 1943–1945.* New York: Random House, 1986.

Eisenhower, Dwight D. *Crusade in Europe.* Garden City, N.Y.: Doubleday, 1948.

Erickson, John. *Road to Berlin: Continuing the History of Stalin's War with Germany.* Boulder, Colo.: Westview Press, 1983.

Esposito, V.J., ed. *West Point Atlas of American Wars.* New York: Praeger, 1960.

Eubank, Keith. *Summit at Tehran.* New York: Morrow, 1985.

Faber, Doris. *The Life of Lorena Hickok: E.R.'s Friend.* New York: Morrow, 1980.

Fairchild, Byron, and Jonathan Grossman. *The Army and Industrial Mobilization*. Washington, D.C.: Office of the Chief of Military History, 1959.

Farley, James A. *Behind the Ballots: The Personal History of a Politician*. New York: Harcourt Brace & World, 1938.

———. *Jim Farley's Story: The Roosevelt Years*. New York: Whittlesey House, 1948.

Farr, Finnis. *FDR*. New Rochelle, N.Y.: Arlington House, 1972.

Feingold, Henry L. *The Politics of Rescue: The Roosevelt Administration and the Holocaust 1938–1945*. New Brunswick, N.J.: Rutgers University Press, 1970.

Felsenthal, Carol. *Alice Roosevelt Longworth*. New York: Putnam, 1988.

Fenno, Richard. *The Yalta Conference*. Boston: Heath, 1955.

Ferdon, Nora. *Franklin Roosevelt: A Biological Interpretation of His Childhood and Youth*.

Ferrell, Robert H. *Choosing Truman: The Democratic Convention of 1944*. Columbia, Mo.: University of Missouri Press, 1994.

———. *The Dying President: Franklin D. Roosevelt, 1944–1945*. Columbia, Mo.: University of Missouri Press, 1998.

———. *Woodrow Wilson and World War I, 1917–1921*. New York: Harper & Row, 1985.

Fest, Joachim. *The Face of the Third Reich: Portraits of the Nazi Leadership*. New York: Pantheon, 1970.

———. *Hitler*. New York. Harcourt, 1974

Fish, Hamilton. *FDR: The Other Side of the Coin*. New York: Vantage Press, 1976.

Fleming, Thomas. *The New Dealers' War: Franklin D. Roosevelt and the War Within World War II*. New York: Basic Books, 2001.

Flynn, Edward J. *You're the Boss*. New York: Viking, 1947.

Flynn, John T. *Country Squire in the White House*. New York: Doubleday, Doran & Co., 1940.

———. *The Roosevelt Myth*. Garden City, N.Y.: Garden City Publishing Co., 1948.

Fowler, Gene. *Beau James*. New York: Viking, 1949.

Frankfurter, Felix. *From the Diaries of Felix Frankfurter*. Edited by Joseph P. Lash. New York: Norton, 1975.

Franklin D. Roosevelt Library. *The Press Conferences of Franklin D. Roosevelt*. 22 vols.

Freedman, Max, ed. *Roosevelt and Frankfurter: Their Correspondence, 1928–1945*. Boston: Little, Brown, 1967.

Freidel, Frank. *F.D.R.* Vol. I, *The Apprenticeship*. Boston: Little, Brown, 1952.

———. *F.D.R.* Vol. II, *The Ordeal*. Boston: Little, Brown, 1954.

———. *F.D.R.* Vol. III, *The Triumph*. Boston: Little, Brown, 1956.

———. *F.D.R.* Vol. IV, *Launching the New Deal*. Boston: Little, Brown, 1973.

———. *Franklin D. Roosevelt: A Rendezvous with Destiny*. Boston: Little, Brown, 1990.

Freud, Sigmund, and William C. Bullitt. *Woodrow Wilson: A Psychological Study.*

Gaddis, John Lewis. *The Long Peace: Inquiries into the History of the Cold War, 1941–1947.* New York: Columbia University Press, 1987.

———. *Strategies of Containment.* New York: Oxford University Press, 1982.

———. *The United States and the Origins of the Cold War, 1941–1947.* New York: Columbia University Press, 1972.

———. *We Now Know: Rethinking Cold War History.* New York: Oxford University Press, 1997.

Galbraith, John Kenneth. *A Life in Our Times.* Boston: Houghton Mifflin, 1981.

Gallagher, Hugh Gregory. *FDR's Splendid Deception.* New York: Dodd, Mead, 1985.

Gallup, George. *The Gallup Polls: Public Opinion, 1935–1971.* Vol. I, 1937–1948. New York: Random House, 1972.

Gaulle, Charles de. *The Complete War Memoirs.* New York: Simon & Schuster, 1964.

Geddes, Donald Potter, ed. *Franklin Delano Roosevelt: A Memorial.* New York, 1945.

Gellman, Irwin. *Secret Affairs: Franklin Roosevelt, Cordell Hull and Sumner Welles.* Baltimore: Johns Hopkins University Press, 1995.

Gerard, James W. *My First Eighty-Three Years in America.* Garden City, N.Y.: Doubleday, 1951.

Gilbert, Martin. *Auschwitz and the Allies.* New York: Holt, 1981.

———. *Churchill: A Life.* London: Heinemann, 1991.

———. *The Holocaust.* New York: Holt, 1985.

———. *The Second World War.* New York: Holt, 1991.

———. *Winston S. Churchill.* Vol. VI, *Finest Hour: 1939–1941.* Boston: Houghton Mifflin, 1983.

———. *Winston S. Churchill.* Vol. VII, *Road to Victory: 1941–1945.* Boston: Houghton Mifflin, 1986.

———. *Winston S. Churchill.* Vol. VIII, *Never Despair, 1945–1965.* Boston: Houghton Mifflin, 1988.

Gill, Anton. *An Honourable Defeat: A History of German Resistance to Hitler, 1933–1945.* New York: Holt, 1994.

Goebbels, Joseph. *The Goebbels Diaries, 1939–1941.* Edited by Fred Taylor. New York: Putnam, 1983.

———. *The Goebbels Diaries, 1942–1943.* Edited by Louis Lochner. Garden City, N.Y.: Doubleday, 1948.

Goldberg, Richard Thayer. *The Making of Franklin D. Roosevelt: Triumph Over Disability.* Cambridge: ABT Books, 1981.

Goldhagen, Daniel. *Hitler's Willing Executioners: Ordinary Germans and the Holocaust.* New York: Knopf, 1996.

Goodhart, Philip. *Fifty Good Ships That Saved the World: The Foundations of the Anglo-American Alliance*. Garden City, N.Y.: Doubleday, 1965.

Goodman, Jack, ed. *While You Were Gone: A Report of Wartime Life in the U.S.* New York: Simon & Schuster, 1946.

Goodwin, Doris Kearns. *No Ordinary Time: Franklin and Eleanor Roosevelt: The Home Front in World War II*. New York: Simon & Schuster, 1994.

Gosnell, Harold F. *Champion Campaigner: Franklin D. Roosevelt*. New York: Macmillan, 1952.

Gould, Jean. *A Good Fight: The Story of FDR's Conquest of Polio*. New York: Dodd, Mead, 1960.

——, and Lorena Hickok. *Walter Reuther: Labor's Rugged Individualist*. New York: Dodd, Mead, 1972.

Graebner, Norman A. *Roosevelt and the Search for a European Policy, 1937–1939*. Baton Rouge: Louisiana University Press, 1987.

Graff, Robert D., Robert Emmett Ginna, and Roger Butterfield. *FDR*. New York: Harper & Row, 1963.

Graham, Frank. *Al Smith: American*. New York: Putnam, 1945.

Graham, Otis L., Jr., and Meghan Robinson Wander, eds. *Franklin D. Roosevelt: His Life and Times: An Encyclopedic View*. Boston: Da Capo, 1985.

Grant, James. *Bernard Baruch: The Adventures of a Wall Street Legend*. New York: Simon & Schuster, 1983.

Greer, Thomas H. *What Roosevelt Thought: The Social and Political Ideas of Franklin D. Roosevelt*. East Lansing, Mich.: Michigan State University Press, 1958.

Grey, Ian. *Stalin: Man of History*. Garden City, N.Y.: Doubleday, 1979.

Grigg, John. *1943: The Victory That Never Was*. New York: Hill & Wang, 1980.

Gromyko, Andrei. *Memoirs*. New York: Doubleday, 1989.

Grose, Peter. *Gentleman Spy: The Life of Allen Dulles*. Boston: Houghton Mifflin, 1994.

Gunther, John. *Roosevelt in Retrospect*. New York: Harper, 1950.

Gurewitsch, A. David. *Eleanor Roosevelt: Her Day*. New York: Interchange Foundation, 1973.

Gurock, Jeffrey S., ed. *American Jewish History*, vol. V. New York: Routledge, 1997.

Hacker, Louis M., and Mark D. Hirsch. *Proskauer: His Life and Times*. Montgomery, Ala.: University of Alabama Press, 1978.

Hagedorn, Herman. *The Roosevelt Family of Sagamore Hill*. New York: Macmillan, 1954.

Halasz, Nicholas. *Roosevelt Through Foreign Eyes*. Princeton, N.J.: D. Van Nostrand, 1961.

Hallgren, Mauritz A. *The Gay Reformer: Profits Before Plenty Under Franklin D. Roosevelt*. New York: Knopf, 1935.

Hamby, Alonzo. *Man of the People: A Life of Harry S Truman*. New York: Oxford University Press, 1995.

Hamerow, Theodore. *On the Road to the Wolf's Lair: German Resistance to Hitler*. Cambridge, Mass.: Belknap, 1999.

Hamlin, Mrs. C.L. *Memories of FDR*.

Handlin, Oscar. *Al Smith and His America*. Boston: Little, Brown, 1958.

Harbaugh, William H. *Lawyer's Lawyer: The Life of John W. Davis*. New York: Oxford University Press, 1973.

Hardeman, D.B., and Donald C. Bacon. *Rayburn: A Biography*. Texas Monthly Press, 1987.

Hareven, Tamara. *Eleanor Roosevelt: An American Conscience*. Chicago: Quadrangle, 1968.

Harriman, W. Averell, and Elie Abel. *Special Envoy to Churchill and Stalin, 1941–1946*. New York: Random House, 1975.

Harrity, Richard, and Ralph G. Martin. *The Human Side of FDR*. New York: Duell, Sloan & Pearce, 1960.

Hart, Albert Bushnell, ed. *Theodore Roosevelt Cyclopedia*. New York: Roosevelt Memorial Association, 1941.

Hassett, William D. *Off the Record with F.D.R.: 1942–1945*. New Brunswick, N.J.: Rutgers University Press, 1958.

Hastings, Max. *Overlord: D-Day and the Battle for Normandy*. New York: Simon & Schuster, 1984.

Hatch, Alden. *Edith Bolling Wilson: First Lady Extraordinary*. New York: Dodd, Mead, 1961.

Haynes, John Earl, and Harvey Klehr. *Venona: Decoding Soviet Espionage in America*. New Haven, Conn.: Yale University Press, 1999.

Hearden, Patrick J. *Roosevelt Confronts Hitler: America's Entry into World War II*. DeKalb, Ill.: Northern Illinois University Press, 1987.

Hebblethwaite, Peter. *Pope John XXIII: Shepherd of the Modern World*. Garden City, N.Y.: Doubleday, 1985.

Hepburn, Katharine. *Me: Stories of My Life*. New York: Knopf, 1991.

Herken, Gregg. *The Winnipeg Weapon: The Atomic Bomb in the Cold War*. New York: Knopf, 1980.

Hershan, Stella K. *A Woman of Quality*. New York: Crown Publishers, 1970.

Herzstein, Robert. *Roosevelt and Hitler: The Prelude to War*. New York: Paragon House, 1989.

Hickok, Lorena. *The Road to the White House: FDR: The Pre-Presidential Years*. New York: Scholastic Book Services, 1962.

Hirsch, H.N. *The Enigma of Felix Frankfurter*. New York: Basic Books, 1981.

Hitch, Charles J. *America's Economic Strength*. New York: Oxford University Press, 1941.

Hitler, Adolf. *Last Political Testament*.

Hobson, Fred. *Mencken*. New York: Random House, 1994.

Hodgson, Godfrey. *The Colonel.* New York: Knopf, 1990.

Hoff-Wilson, Joan, and Marjorie Lightman, eds. *Without Precedent: The Life and Career of Eleanor Roosevelt.* Bloomington, Ind.: Indiana University Press, 1984.

Hofstadter, Richard. *The American Political Tradition and the Men Who Made It.* New York: Vintage Books, 1973.

Holt, Dr. L. Emmett. *The Care and Feeding of Children: A Catechism for the Use of Mothers and Children's Nurses.* New York: Appleton, 1912.

Hoopes, Townsend, and Douglas Brinkley. *FDR and the Creation of the UN.* New Haven, Conn.: Yale University Press, 1997.

Hoover, Herbert. *The Memoirs of Herbert Hoover.* 3 vols. New York: Macmillan, 1951–1952.

Hoover, I.H. ("Ike"). *Forty-Two Years in the White House.* Boston: Houghton Mifflin, 1934.

Hough, Richard. *The Greatest Crusade: Roosevelt, Churchill and the Naval Wars.* New York: Morrow, 1986.

Howe, George. *Northwest Africa: Seizing the Initiative in the West.* Washington, D.C.: Office of the Chief of Military History, 1957.

Hoyt, Edwin P. *Yamamoto: The Man Who Planned Pearl Harbor.* New York: Warner Books, 1991.

Hull, Cordell. *The Memoirs of Cordell Hull.* 2 vols. New York: Macmillan, 1948.

Hunter, Lieutenant Francis T. *Beatty, Jellicoe, Sims and Rodman.* Garden City, N.Y.: Doubleday, 1919.

Hurd, Charles. *When the New Deal Was Young and Gay: FDR and His Circle.* New York: Hawthorn Books, 1965.

Huthmacher, I.J. *Senator Robert Wagner and the Rise of Urban Liberalism.*

Ickes, Harold L. *The Autobiography of a Curmudgeon.* New York: Reynal & Hitchcock, 1943.

———. *The Secret Diaries of Harold L. Ickes.* Vol. I, *The First Thousand Days 1933–1936.* New York: Simon & Schuster, 1953.

———. *The Secret Diaries of Harold Ickes.* Vol. II, *The Inside Struggle, 1936–1939.* New York: Simon & Schuster, 1954.

———. *The Secret Diaries of Harold L. Ickes.* Vol. III, *The Lowering Clouds, 1939–1941.* New York: Simon & Schuster, 1954.

Irons, Peter. *Justice of War: The Story of the Japanese American Internment Cases.* New York: Oxford University Press, 1983.

Isaacson, Walter, and Evan Thomas. *The Wise Men: Six Friends and the World They Made.* New York: Simon & Schuster, 1986.

Ismay, Lord Hastings. *The Memoirs of General Lord Ismay.* New York: Viking, 1960.

Israel, Fred, ed. *The War Diary of Breckinridge Long.* Lincoln, Neb.: University of Nebraska Press, 1966.

James, D. Clayton. *The Years of MacArthur*, vol. II. Boston: Houghton Mifflin, 1975.

Jeffers, H. Paul. *Theodore Roosevelt Jr.: The Life of a War Hero*. New York: Ballantine, 2003.

Johnson, Gerald W. *Roosevelt: An American Study*. London: Hamish Hamilton, 1942.

Johnson, Hugh S. *The Blue Eagle from Egg to Earth*. Garden City, N.Y.: Doubleday, Doran, 1935.

Johnson, Walter. *William Allen White's America*. New York: Henry Holt, 1947.

Jones, Jess H., with Edward Angly. *Fifty Billion Dollars: My Thirteen Years with the RFC*. New York: Macmillan, 1951.

Jones, Kenneth P., ed. *U.S. Diplomats in Europe, 1919–1941*.

Jones, Robert H. *The Roads to Russia: United States Lend-Lease to the Soviet Union*. Norman, Okla.: University of Oklahoma Press, 1969.

Josephson, Matthew, and Hannah Josephson. *Al Smith: Hero of the Cities*. Boston: Houghton Mifflin, 1969.

———. *Sidney Hillman: Statements of American Labor*. Garden City, N.Y.: Doubleday, 1952

Kearney, James R. *Anna Eleanor Roosevelt: The Evolution of a Reformer*. Boston: Houghton Mifflin, 1968.

Keegan, John. *The Mask of Command*. New York: Viking, 1987.

Kempton, Murray. *Part of Our Time*. New York: Simon & Schuster, 1965.

Kennan, George. *Memoirs, 1925–1950*. Boston: Little, Brown, 1967.

Kennedy, David M. *Freedom from Fear: The American People in Depression and War, 1929–1945*. New York: Oxford University Press, 1999.

Kennedy, William. *O Albany!* New York: Viking, 1983.

Kershaw, Ian. *Hitler, 1889–1936: Hubris*. New York: Norton, 1999.

———. *Hitler, 1936–1945: Nemesis*. New York: Norton, 2000.

Ketchum, Richard M. *The Borrowed Years, 1938–1941: America on the Way to War*. New York: Random House, 1989.

Keyes, Frances Parkinson. *Capital Kaleidoscope: The Story of a Washington Hostess*. New York: Harper & Brothers, 1937.

Kilpatrick, Carroll. *Roosevelt and Daniels*. Chapel Hill, N.C.: University of North Carolina Press, 1952.

Kimball, Warren F. *Churchill and Roosevelt: The Complete Correspondence*. 3 vols. New York: HarperCollins, 1988.

———. *Forged in War: Roosevelt, Churchill and the Second World War*. New York: Morrow, 1997.

———. *The Juggler: Franklin Roosevelt as Wartime Statesman*. Princeton, N.J.: Princeton University Press, 1991.

Kinnaird, Clark, ed. *The Real FDR*. New York: Citadel, 1945.

Kissinger, Henry. *Diplomacy*. New York: Simon & Schuster, 1994.

Kleeman, Rita Halle. *Gracious Lady: The Life of Sara Delano Roosevelt.* New York: Appleton-Century, 1935.

Koch, H.W. "The Spectre of a Separate Peace in the East: Russo-German Peace Feelers, 1942–44." *Journal of Contemporary History,* vol. 10, pp. 531–547.

Koskoff, David. *Joseph P. Kennedy: A Life and Times.* Englewood Cliffs, N.J.: Prentice Hall, 1974.

Krock, Arthur. *Memoirs: Sixty Years on the Firing Line.* New York: Funk and Wagnalls, 1968.

Kubizek, August. *Young Hitler.*

Kuklick, Bruce. *American Policy and the Division of Germany: The Clash with Russia over Reparations.* Ithaca, N.Y.: Cornell University Press, 1972.

Lacey, Robert. *Ford: The Man and the Machine.* Boston: Little, Brown, 1986.

LaFeber, Walter. *America, Russia and the Cold War.* New York: John Wiley, 1976.

Laloy, Jean. *Yalta: Yesterday, Today, Tomorrow.* New York: Harper, 1988.

Lamb, Richard. *Churchill as War Leader.* New York: Carroll and Graf, 1991.

Lamont, Thomas W. *Across World Frontiers.* New York: Harcourt Brace, 1951.

Lane, Franklin K. *The Letters of Franklin K. Lane.* Boston: Houghton Mifflin, 1922.

Lane, Frederick C. *Ships for Victory: A History of Shipbuilding Under the U.S. Maritime Commission in World War II.* Baltimore: Johns Hopkins University Press, 1951.

Langer, William L., and Everett S. Gleason. *Undeclared War: 1939–1940.* New York: Harper & Row, 1952 1953.

Laqueur, Walter. *Russia and Germany: A Century of Conflict.* Boston: Little, Brown, 1965.

———. *Stalin: The Glasnost Revelations.* New York: Scribner, 1990.

———. *The Terrible Secret: An Investigation into the Suppression of Information About Hitler's "Final Solution."* London: Weidenfeld and Nicolson, 1980.

Larrabee, Eric. *Commander in Chief: Franklin Delano Roosevelt, His Lieutenants & Their War.* New York: Harper & Row, 1987.

Lash, Joseph P. *Dealers and Dreamers.* Garden City, N.Y.: Doubleday, 1988.

———. *Eleanor: The Years Alone.* New York: Norton, 1972.

———. *Eleanor and Franklin: The Story of Their Relationship.* New York: Norton, 1971.

———. *Eleanor Roosevelt: A Friend's Memoir.* Garden City, N.Y.: Doubleday, 1964.

———. *Life Was Meant to Be Lived: A Centenary Portrait of Eleanor Roosevelt.* New York: Norton, 1984.

———. *Love, Eleanor: Eleanor Roosevelt and Her Friends.* Garden City, N.Y.: Doubleday, 1982.

———. *Roosevelt and Churchill, 1939–1941: The Partnership That Saved the West.* New York: Norton, 1975.

———. *A World of Love: Eleanor Roosevelt and Her Friends, 1943–1962.* New York: Doubleday, 1984.

Lasser, William. *Benjamin V. Cohen: Architect of the New Deal.* New Haven, Conn.: Yale University Press, 2002.

Lawrence, David. *Diary of a Washington Correspondent.* New York: H.C. Kinsey, 1942.

Leahy, William. *I Was There.* New York: Whittlesey House, 1950.

Leffler, Melvyn. *A Preponderance of Power: National Security, the Truman Administration and the Cold War.* Stanford, Calif.: Stanford University Press, 1992.

Leighton, Isabel, and Gabrielle Forbush. *My Boy Franklin.* New York: Ray Long and Richard Smith, 1933.

LeTissier, Tony. *Battle of Berlin.* New York: St. Martin's, 1988.

Leuchtenberg, William E. *Franklin D. Roosevelt and the New Deal, 1932–1940.* Ithaca, N.Y.: Cornell University Press, 1983.

———. *In the Shadow of FDR: From Harry Truman to Ronald Reagan.* Ithaca, N.Y.: Cornell University Press, 2001 (3rd ed.).

Liddell-Hart, Basil. *History of the Second World War.* New York: Putnam, 1970.

Lilienthal, David E. *The Journals of David E. Lilienthal.* Vol. I, *The TVA Years.* New York: Harper & Row, 1964.

Lindley, Ernest K. *Franklin D. Roosevelt: A Career in Progressive Democracy.* New York: Blue Ribbon, 1931.

———. *Halfway with Roosevelt.* New York: Viking, 1936.

———. *The Roosevelt Revolution.* New York: Viking, 1933.

Link, Arthur S. *The Road to the White House.* Princeton, N.J.: Princeton University Press, 1947.

Lippman, Theodore, Jr. *The Squire of Warm Springs: FDR in Georgia, 1924–1945.* Chicago: Playboy Press, 1977.

Longworth, Alice Roosevelt. *Crowded Hours.* New York: Scribner, 1933.

Looker, Earle. *This Man Roosevelt.* New York: Brewer, Warren & Putnam, 1932.

Loucheim, Katie, ed. *The Making of the New Deal: The Insiders Speak.* Cambridge, Mass.: Harvard University Press, 1983.

Louis, William Roger. *Imperialism at Bay: The United States and the Decolonization of the British Empire, 1941–1945.* New York: Oxford University Press, 1978.

Lowitt, Richard. *George W. Norris: The Triumph of a Progressive, 1933–1944.* Champaign, Ill.: University of Illinois Press, 1978.

Ludwig, Emil. *Roosevelt: A Study in Fortune and Power.* New York: Viking, 1938.

Lukacs, John. *Churchill: Visionary, Statesman, Historian.* New Haven, Conn.: Yale University Press, 2002.

———. *Five Days in London.* New Haven, Conn.: Yale University Press, 1999.

———. *The Last European War: September 1939–December 1941.* New Haven, Conn.: Yale University Press, 2001.

———. *1945: Year Zero.* New York: Doubleday, 1978.

Lyon, Peter. *Eisenhower: Portrait of the Hero.* Boston: Little, Brown, 1974.

MacArthur, Douglas. *Reminiscences.*

MacCracken, Henry Noble. *Blithe Dutchess.* New York: Hastings House, 1958.

Mackenzie, Compton. *Mr. Roosevelt.* New York: Dutton, 1944.

MacLeish, Archibald. *The Eleanor Roosevelt Story.* Boston: Houghton Mifflin, 1965.

MacLeod, Iain. *Chamberlain.* London: Muller, 1961.

MacMillan, Harold. *War Diaries: Politics and War in the Mediterranean: January 1943–May 1945.* London: MacMillan, 1984.

MacNeil, Neil. *Forge of Democracy: The House of Representatives.* New York: David McKay, 1963.

Maisky, Ivan. *Memoirs of a Soviet Ambassador, 1939–1943.* London: Hutchinson, 1967.

Manchester, William. *American Caesar: Douglas MacArthur, 1880–1964.* Boston: Little, Brown, 1978.

Marcus, Sheldon. *Father Coughlin: The Tumultuous Life of the Priest of the Little Flower.* Boston: Little, Brown, 1973.

Marks, Frederick W., III. *Wind over Sand: The Diplomacy of Franklin Roosevelt.* Athens, Ga.: University of Georgia Press, 1988.

Marshall, George Catlett. *The Papers of George Catlett Marshall.* Vol. II, *We Can't Delay, July 1, 1939–December 6, 1941.* Edited by Larry Bland. Baltimore: Johns Hopkins University Press, 1981.

Marshall, Katherine Tupper. *Together: Annals of an Army Wife.* New York: Tupper & Love, 1946.

Martin, George. *Madame Secretary: Frances Perkins.* Boston: Houghton Mifflin, 1976.

———. *Truman.* New York: Simon & Schuster, 1992.

Marx, Rudolph. *The Health of the Presidents.* New York: Putnam, 1960.

Mason, A. T. *Brandeis: A Free Man's Life.* New York: Viking, 1946.

Mastny, Vojtech. *Russia's Road to the Cold War: Diplomacy, Warfare, and the Politics of Communism.* New York: Columbia University Press, 1979.

Mayle, Paul D. *Eureka Summit: Agreement in Principle and the Big Three at Tehran, 1943.* Newark, Del.: University of Delaware Press, 1987.

McAllister, James. *No Exit: America and the German Problem, 1945–1954.* Ithaca, N.Y.: Cornell University Press, 2002.

McCullough, David. *Mornings on Horseback.* New York: Simon & Schuster, 1982.

———. *The Path Between the Seas.* New York: Simon & Schuster, 1978.

———. *Truman.* New York: Simon & Schuster, 1991.

McElvoy, Anne. *The Saddled Cow.* London: Faber, 1992.

McEneny, John J. *Albany: Capital City on the Hudson.* Albany, N.Y.: Windsor, 1981.

McIntire, Ross. *White House Physician.* New York: Putnam, 1946.

McJimsey, George. *Harry Hopkins: Ally of the Poor and Defender of Democracy.* Cambridge, Mass.: Harvard University Press, 1987.

McKeever, Porter. *Adlai Stevenson: His Life and Legacy.* New York: Morrow, 1989.

McWilliams, Carey. *Prejudice: Japanese Americans, Symbol of Racial Intolerance.* Boston: Little, Brown, 1944.

Mencken, H.L. *A Choice of Days.* New York: Knopf, 1980.

———. *Making a President.* New York: Knopf, 1932.

Miller, Merle. *Plain Speaking: An Oral Biography of Harry S Truman.* New York: Putnam, 1973.

Miller, Nathan. *FDR: An Intimate History.* New York: Doubleday, 1983.

———. *The Roosevelt Chronicles.* Garden City, N.Y.: Doubleday, 1979.

Mitgang, Herbert. *Once Upon a Time in New York.* New York: Free Press, 2000.

Moffat, Jay Pierrepont. *The Moffat Papers.* Edited by Nancy H. Hooker. Cambridge, Mass.: Harvard University Press, 1956.

Moley, Raymond. *After Seven Years.* New York: Harper, 1939.

———. *The First New Deal.* New York: Harcourt Brace and World, 1966.

———. *27 Masters of Politics in a Personal Perspective.* New York: Greenwood, 1949.

Montgomery, Bernard L. *History of War.*

Montgomery, J.F. *Hungary, The Unwilling Satellite.*

Moran, Lord. *Churchill, Taken from the Diaries of Lord Moran: The Struggle for Survival, 1940–1965.* Boston: Houghton Mifflin, 1966.

Morgan, Ted. *FDR: A Biography.* New York: Simon & Schuster, 1985.

Morgenthau, Henry, Jr. *Germany Is Our Problem: A Plan for Germany.* New York: Harper, 1945.

Morgenthau, Henry, Sr. *All in a Life-Time.* New York: Doubleday, 1926.

Morgenthau, Henry, III. *Mostly Morgenthaus: A Family History.* Boston: Ticknor and Fields, 1991.

Morison, Elting. *Admiral Sims and the Modern American Navy.* Boston: Houghton Mifflin, 1942.

———. *Turmoil and Traditions: A Study of the Life and Times of Henry L. Stimson.* New York: Atheneum, 1964.

Morison, Samuel Eliot. *The History of United States Naval Operations in World War II.* 15 vols. Boston: Little, Brown, 1947–1962.

Morris, Edmund. *The Rise of Theodore Roosevelt.* New York: Ballantine, 1979.

Morrison, Joseph L. *Josephus Daniels: The Small-d Democrat.* Chapel Hill, N.C.: University of North Carolina Press, 1968.

———. *Josephus Daniels Says . . . An Editor's Political Odyssey: From Bryan to Wilson and FDR, 1894–1913.* Chapel Hill, N.C.: University of North Carolina Press, 1962.

Morse, Arthur D. *While Six Million Died: A Chronicle of American Apathy.* Woodstock, N.Y.: Overlook Press, 1983.

Mortimor, Edward. *The World That FDR Built: Vision and Reality.* New York: Scribner, 1988.

Morton, H.V. *Atlantic Meeting.* New York: Dodd, Mead, 1943.

Mosch, Theodore R. *The G.I. Bill: A Breakthrough in Educational and Social Policy in the United States.* New York: Exposition Press, 1975.

Moscow, Warren. *Politics in the Empire State.* New York: Knopf, 1984.

———. *Roosevelt and Wilkie.* Englewood Cliffs, N.J.: Prentice Hall, 1968.

Moses, Robert. *Public Works: A Dangerous Trade.* New York: McGraw-Hill, 1970.

Moskowitz, Henry. *Alfred E. Smith: An American Career.* New York: Thomas Seltzer, 1924.

Mosley, Nicholas. *Rules of the Game: Sir Oswald and Cynthia Mosley, 1896– 1933.* London: Secker & Warburg, 1982.

Mosley, Sir Oswald. *My Life.* New Rochelle, London: Nelson, 1968.

Murphy, Bruce Allen. *The Brandeis-Frankfurt Connection: The Secret Political Activities of Two Supreme Court Justices.* New York: Oxford University Press, 1982.

Murphy, Lawrence R. *Perverts by Official Order.* New York: Harrington Park, 1988.

Murphy, Robert. *Diplomat Among Warriors.* London: Collins, 1964.

Muskie, Stephen O. *Campobello: Roosevelt's "Beloved Island."* Camden, Maine: Down East Books, 1982.

Nadeau, Remi. *Stalin, Churchill and Roosevelt Divide Europe.* New York: Praeger, 1990.

Naimark, Norman. *The Russians in Germany: A History of the Soviet Zone of Occupation, 1945–1949.* Cambridge, Mass.: Belknap, 1995.

Nasaw, David. *The Chief: The Life of William Randolph Hearst.* Boston: Houghton Mifflin, 2000

Neal, Steve. *Dark Horse: A Biography of Wendell Willkie.* Garden City, N.Y.: Doubleday, 1984.

Nelson, Daniel J. *Wartime Origins of the Berlin Dilemma: A Study in Alliance Diplomacy.* Tuscaloosa, Ala.: University of Alabama Press, 1978.

Nesbitt, Henrietta. *White House Diary.* New York: Doubleday, 1948.

Neufeld, Michael, and Michael Berenbaum. *The Bombing of Auschwitz: Should the Allies Have Attempted It?* New York: St. Martin's, 2000.

Neustadt, Richard E. *Presidential Power and the Modern President: The Politics of Leadership from Roosevelt to Reagan.* New York: Free Press, 1990.

Newton, Verne, ed. *FDR and the Holocaust.* New York: Oxford University Press, 1996.

Nisbet, Robert. *Roosevelt and Stalin: The Failed Courtship.* Washington, D.C.: Regnery, 1988.

Notter, Harley. *Post-War Policy Preparation, 1939–1945.* Washington, D.C.: U.S. Government Printing Office, 1950.

O'Connor, Raymond. *Diplomacy for Victory: Franklin Roosevelt and Unconditional Surrender.* New York: Norton, 1971.

O'Connor, Richard. *The First Hurrah: A Biography of Alfred E. Smith*. New York: Putnam, 1970.

Ogden, Christopher. *Legacy: A Biography of Moses and Walter Annenberg*. Boston: Little, Brown, 1999.

Osgood, Charles. *Funny Letters from Famous People*. New York: Broadway Books, 2003.

Overy, Richard. *The Battle of Britain: Myth and Reality*. New York: Norton, 2000.

Parks, Lillian Rogers. *The Roosevelts: A Family in Turmoil*. Englewood Cliffs, N.J.: Prentice Hall, 1981.

Parrish, Michael. *Felix Frankfurter and His Times*. New York: Free Press, 1982.

Parrish, Thomas. *Berlin in the Balance: 1945–1949*. Reading, Mass.: Addison-Wesley, 1998.

———. *Roosevelt and Marshall: Partners in Politics and War*. New York: Morrow, 1989.

Partridge, Bellamy. *The Roosevelt Family in America*. New York: Hillman-Curl, 1936.

Paterson, Thomas. *On Every Front: The Making of the Cold War*. New York: Norton, 1979.

Patton, George S. *War As I Knew It*. Mariner Books, 1995 (reissue).

Paul, John. *A History of Poliomyelitis*. New York: Yale University Press, 1971.

Pearson, John. *The Private Lives of Winston Churchill*. New York: Simon & Schuster, 1991.

Penkower, Monty Noam. *The Jews Were Expendable: Free World Diplomacy and the Holocaust*. Detroit: Wayne State University Press, 1983.

Penrose, E.F. *Economic Planning for the Peace*. Princeton, N.J.: Princeton University Press, 1953.

Perkins, Dexter. *The New Age of Franklin Roosevelt 1932–1945*. Chicago: University of Chicago Press, 1957.

Perkins, Frances. *The Roosevelt I Knew*. New York: Viking, 1946.

Perlmutter, Amos. *FDR and Stalin: A Not So Grand Alliance, 1943–1945*. Columbia, Mo.: University of Missouri Press, 1993.

Persico, Joseph E. *Piercing the Reich: The Penetration of Nazi Germany by American Secret Agents During World War II*. New York: Viking, 1979.

———. *Roosevelt's Secret War: FDR and World War II Espionage*. New York: Random House, 2001.

Perrett, Geoffrey. *America in the Twenties: A History*. New York: Simon & Schuster, 1982.

———. *Days of Sadness, Years of Triumph: The American People, 1939–1945*. New York: Coward, McCann & Geoghegan, 1973.

Phillips, Harlan B., ed. *Felix Frankfurter Reminisces*. New York: Reynal and Company, 1960.

Phillips, William. *Ventures in Diplomacy*. Boston: Beacon Press, 1952.

Pickersgill, J.W., and D.F. Foster, eds. *The Mackenzie King Record.* Vol. II, 1944–1945. Toronto: University of Toronto Press, 1968.

Pogue, Forrest C. *The Education of a General, 1880–1939.* New York: Viking, 1963.

———. *George C. Marshall: Ordeal and Hope, 1939–1942.* Vol. II. New York: Viking, 1966.

———. *George C. Marshall: Organizer of Victory, 1943–1945.* Vol. III. New York: Viking, 1973.

Posner, Richard A. *The Essential Holmes.* Chicago: University of Chicago Press, 1992.

Potter, E.B. *Nimitz.* Annapolis, Md.: Naval Institute Press, 1976.

Powers, Richard Gid. *Secrecy and Power: The Life of J. Edgar Hoover.* New York: Free Press, 1987.

Prang, Gordon W. *At Dawn We Slept: The Untold Story of Pearl Harbor.* New York: McGraw-Hill, 1981.

Pringle, Henry F. *Alfred E. Smith: A Critical Study.* New York: Macy-Masius, 1927.

———. *Theodore Roosevelt: A Biography.* New York: Harcourt Brace, 1931.

Radzinsky, Edvard. *Stalin.* New York: Doubleday, 1996.

Read, Anthony, and David Fisher. *The Fall of Berlin.* New York: Norton, 1992.

Rees, David. *Harry Dexter White: A Study in Paradox.* New York: Coward, McCann & Geoghegan, 1973.

Reilly, Michael F. *Reilly of the White House.* New York: Simon & Schuster, 1947.

Reynolds, David. *From Munich to Pearl Harbor: Roosevelt's America and the Origins of the Second World War.* Chicago: Ivan R. Dee, 2001.

Rhodes, Richard. *The Making of the Atomic Bomb.* New York: Simon & Schuster, 1986.

Ribbentrop, Joachim von. *The Ribbentrop Memoirs.* London: Weidenfeld & Nicolson, 1954.

Richberg, Donald. *My Hero.* New York: Putnam, 1954.

———. *The Rainbow.* New York, Doubleday, Doran, 1936.

Roberts, Andrew. *The Holy Fox.* London: Orion, 1997.

Robertson, David. *Sly and Able: A Political Biography of James F. Byrnes.* New York: Norton, 1994.

Robinson, Corinne (Roosevelt). *My Brother Theodore Roosevelt.* New York: Scribner, 1922.

Robinson, Edgar E. *The Roosevelt Leadership 1933–1945.* Philadelphia: Lippincott, 1955.

Rollins, Alfred B., Jr. *Roosevelt and Howe.* New York: Knopf, 1962.

———, ed. *Franklin D. Roosevelt and the Age of Action.* New York: Dell, 1960.

Rommel, Erwin. *The Rommel Papers.* Edited by Liddell Hart and Basil Henry. New York: Harcourt Brace, 1953.

Roosevelt, Eleanor. *The Autobiography of Eleanor Roosevelt*. New York: Harcourt Brace, 1961.

——. *It Seems to Me*. New York: Norton, 1954.

——. *My Day*. New York, 1938.

——. *On My Own*. New York: Curtis, 1958.

——. *This I Remember*. New York: Harper, 1949.

——. *This Is My Story*. New York: Harper and Brothers, 1937.

——. *Tomorrow Is Now*. New York: Harper, 1963.

——. *You Learn by Living*. New York: Harper, 1960.

——, ed. *Hunting Big Game in the Eighties*. New York: Scribner, 1933.

——, and Helen Ferris. *Your Teens and Mine*. Garden City, N.Y.: Doubleday, 1961.

——, and Lorena Hickok. *Ladies of Courage*. New York: Putnam, 1954.

Roosevelt, Elliott. *As He Saw It*. New York: Duell, Sloan & Pearce, 1946.

——, ed. *FDR.: His Personal Letters*. 2 vols. New York: Duell, Sloan & Pearce, 1947, 1948.

——, and James Brough. *Mother R: Eleanor Roosevelt's Untold Story*. New York: Putnam, 1977.

——, and James Brough. *A Rendezvous with Destiny: The Roosevelts of the White House*. New York: Putnam, 1975.

——, and James Brough. *An Untold Story: The Roosevelts of Hyde Park*. New York: Putnam, 1973.

Roosevelt, Franklin D. *FDR: His Personal Letters*. Vol. I, *The Early Years*. Edited by Elliott Roosevelt. New York: Duell, Sloan & Pearce, 1947.

——. *How I Am Going to Conduct My Responsibilities*. Original owned by author, 1982.

——. *Public Papers and Addresses of Franklin D. Roosevelt*. Edited by Samuel I. Rosenman. 1937–1940, 4 vols. New York: Macmillan, 1941. 1941–1945, 4 vols. New York: Harper, 1950.

Roosevelt, James, with Bill Libby. *My Parents: A Differing View*. Chicago: Playboy Press, 1975.

——, and Sidney Shalett. *Affectionately, F.D.R.: A Son's Story of a Lonely Man*. New York: Harcourt Brace, 1959.

Roosevelt, Nicholas. *A Front Row Seat*. Oklahoma City: University of Oklahoma Press, 1953.

Roosevelt, Sara Delano (as told to Isabel Leighton and Gabriel Forbush). *My Boy Franklin*. New York: Crown, 1933.

Roosevelt, Theodore. *Theodore Roosevelt: An Autobiography*. New York: Scribner, 1924.

Roosevelt, Mrs. Theodore, Jr. *Day Before Yesterday*. Garden City, N.Y.: Doubleday, 1959.

Root, Waverly. *The Secret History of the War*. New York: Scribner, 1946.

Rosenman, Samuel I. *Working with Roosevelt*. New York: Harper, 1952.

————, ed. *The Public Papers and Addresses of Franklin D. Roosevelt.* 13 vols. New York: Random House, 1938–1950.

Rubinstein, William. *The Myth of Rescue.* New York: Routledge, 1997.

Ruddy, T. Michael. *The Cautious Diplomat: Charles E. Bohlen and the Soviet Union. 1929–1969.* Ohio: Kent State University Press, 1986.

Russell, Francis. *The President Makers: From Mark Hanna to Joseph P. Kennedy.* Boston: Little, Brown, 1976.

————. *The Shadow of Blooming Grove: Warren G. Harding in His Times.*

Sainsbury, Keith. *The Turning Point: Roosevelt, Stalin, Churchill, and Chiang Kai-Shek, 1943: The Moscow, Cairo and Teheran Conferences.* Oxford.: Oxford University Press, 1985.

Savell, Isabella. *The Executive Mansion in Albany: An Informal History, 1856–1960.* Brunswick, N.J., 1971.

Schlesinger, Arthur M., Jr. *The Age of Roosevelt.* 3 vols. Boston: Houghton Mifflin, 1957, 1959, 1960.

Schmidt, Hans. *Maverick Marine: General Smedley D. Butler and the Contradictions of American Military History.* Lexington, Ky.: University Press of Kentucky, 1987.

Schorer, Mark. *Sinclair Lewis: An American Life.* New York: McGraw-Hill, 1961.

Schriftgiesser, Karl. *The Amazing Roosevelt Family, 1613–1942.* New York. Wilfred Funk, 1942.

Schulz, Duane. *The Doolittle Raid.* New York: St. Martin's, 1988.

Schwarz, Jordan A. *Liberal: Adolf A. Berle and the Vision of an American Era.* New York: Free Press, 1987.

Seager, Robert. *Alfred Thayer Mahan: The Man and His Letters.* Annapolis, Md.: Naval Institute Press, 1977.

Seaton, Albert. *Stalin as Warlord.* London: Batsford, 1976.

Sebag-Montefiore, Simon. *Stalin: The Court of the Red Tsar.* London: Weidenfeld and Nicolson, 2003.

Sharp, T. *Wartime Alliance and the Zonal Division of Germany.* Oxford: Clarendon, 1975.

Sheaffer, Louis. *O'Neill, Son and Artist.* Boston: Little, Brown, 1973.

Sherry, Michael. *The Rise of American Air Power: The Creation of Armageddon.* New Haven, Conn.: Yale University Press, 1987.

Sherwood, Robert E. *Roosevelt and Hopkins.* New York: Harper & Brothers, 1948.

Shirer, William L. *The Rise and Fall of the Third Reich.* New York: Simon & Schuster, 1960.

Shoumatoff, Elizabeth. *FDR's Unfinished Portrait: A Memoir.* Pittsburgh: University of Pittsburgh Press, 1990.

————. *FDR Up Close.*

Simpson, B. Mitchell. *Admiral Harold R. Stark: Architect of Victory, 1939–1945.* University of South Carolina Press, 1989.

Sinclair, Andrew. *The Available Man: The Life Behind the Mask of Warren Gamaliel Harding*. New York: Macmillan, 1965.

Sitkoff, Harvard, ed. *Fifty Years Later: The New Deal Evaluated*. New York: Knopf, 1985.

Skidelsky, Robert. *John Maynard Keynes: Fighting for Freedom, 1938–1946*. New York: Viking, 2001.

———. *Oswald Mosley*. New York: Holt, Rinehart & Winston, 1975.

Slayton, Robert A. *Empire Statesman*. New York: Free Press, 2001.

Smith, A. Merriman. *Merriman Smith's Book of Presidents: A White House Memoir*. New York: Norton, 1972.

———. *Thank You, Mr. President*. New York: Harper & Brothers, 1946.

Smith, Amanda P., ed. *Hostages to Fortune: The Letters of Joseph P. Kennedy*. New York: Viking, 2001.

Smith, Arthur D. Howden. *Mr. House of Texas*. New York: Funk & Wagnalls, 1940.

Smith, Gaddis. *Dean Acheson*. New York: Cooper Square, 1972.

———. *Roosevelt, the Sea, and International Security*.

———. *Sharing Secrets with Stalin: How the Allies Traded Intelligence, 1941–1945*. Lawrence, Kan.: University Press of Kansas, 1996.

Smith, Gene. *When The Cheering Stopped*. New York: Time Life Books, 1964.

———. *The Shattered Dream*. New York: Morrow, 1970.

Smith, Richard Norton. *The Colonel: The Life and Legend of Robert R. McCormick*. Boston: Houghton Mifflin, 1997.

———. *An Uncommon Man: The Triumph of Herbert Hoover*. New York: Simon & Schuster, 1984.

Smyser, W.R. *From Yalta to Berlin: The Cold War Struggle over Germany*. New York: St. Martin's, 1999.

Soames, Mary, ed. *Winston and Clemmie: The Personal Letters of the Churchills*. Boston: Houghton Mifflin, 1999.

Speer, Albert, *Inside the Third Reich*. New York: Macmillan, 1970.

Sperber, A.M. *Murrow: His Life and Times*. New York: Freundlich Books, 1986.

Stalin, J.V., *Leninism*. New York: International, 1942.

Steeholm, Clara, and Hardy Steeholm. *The House at Hyde Park*. New York: Viking, 1950.

Steel, Ronald. *Walter Lippmann and the American Century*. Boston: Little, Brown, 1980.

Stein, Harold, ed. *American Civil-Military Decisions: A Book of Case Studies*. Birmingham, Ala.: University of Alabama Press, 1963.

Steinberg, Alfred. *Mrs. R: The Life of Eleanor Roosevelt*. New York: Putnam, 1958.

———. *Sam Rayburn: A Biography*. New York: Hawthorn Books, 1975.

Stettinius, Edward R. *The Diaries of Edward R. Stettinius Jr., 1943–1946*. Edited by Thomas M. Campbell and George C. Herring, New York: New Viewpoints, 1975.

———. *Lend-Lease: Weapon for Victory*. New York: Macmillan, 1944.

——. *Roosevelt and the Russians: The Yalta Conference.* Garden City, N.Y.: Doubleday, 1949.

Stewart, W.J., and Charyle C. Pollard. *Franklin D. Roosevelt, Collector.*

Stiles, Lela. *The Man Behind Roosevelt: The Story of Louis McHenry Howe.* Cleveland: World, 1954.

Stimson, Henry, and McGeorge Bundy. *On Active Service in Peace and War.* New York: Harper, 1947.

Strang, Lord William. *Home and Abroad.* London: Andre Deutsch, 1956.

Sutton, Anthony C. *Wall Street and FDR.* New Rochelle, N.Y.: Arlington House, 1975.

Tanehaus, Sam. *Whittaker Chambers: A Biography.* New York: Random House, 1997.

Tannenbaum, Frank. *Osborne of Sing Sing.* Chapel Hill, N.C.: The University of North Carolina Press, 1933.

Taubman, William. *Stalin's American Policy: From Entente to Détente to Cold War.* New York: Norton, 1982.

Taylor, A.J.P. *Course of German History.* London: Hamish Hamilton, 1945.

——. *Oxford History of England: English History, 1914–1945.* New York: Oxford University Press, 1978.

Taylor, Telford. *Munich: The Price of Peace.* New York: Doubleday, 1979.

Teachout, Terry. *The Skeptic: A Life of H.L. Mencken.* New York: HarperCollins, 2002.

Teague, Michael. *Mrs. L: Conversations with Alice Roosevelt Longworth.* Garden City, N.Y.: Doubleday, 1981.

Teichman, Howard. *Alice: The Life and Times of Alice Roosevelt Longworth.* Englewood Cliffs, N.J.: Prentice Hall, 1979.

Thomas, Hugh. *The Spanish Civil War.* New York: Harper & Row, 1961.

Tift, Susan E., and Alex S. Jones. *The Trust.* Boston: Little, Brown, 1999.

Timmons, Bascom N. *Garner of Texas.* New York: Harper & Brothers, 1948.

——. *Jesse H. Jones.* New York: Henry Holt, 1956.

Tittle, Walter. *Roosevelt as an Artist Saw Him.* New York: Robert M. McBride, 1948.

Toland, John. *Adolf Hitler.* New York: Doubleday, 1976.

Tompkins, Peter. *The Murder of Admiral Darlan.* New York: Simon & Schuster, 1965.

Trachtenberg, Marc. *A Constructed Peace: The Making of the European Settlement, 1945–1963.* Princeton, N.J.: Princeton University Press, 1999.

Trevor-Roper, Hugh. *Hitler's Table Talk, 1941–1944.* New York: Oxford University Press, 1988.

——. *The Last Days of Hitler.* New York: Macmillan, 1947.

Trohan, Walter. *Political Animals.* Garden City, N.Y.: Doubleday, 1975.

Truman, Harry S. *Memoirs: 1945, Year of Decisions.* New York: Doubleday, 1955.

——. *Memoirs: Years of Destiny.* New York: Doubleday, 1956.

———. *Memoirs: Years of Trial and Hope, 1946–1952.* New York: Doubleday, 1956.

Truman, Margaret. *Harry S Truman.* New York: Morrow, 1973.

Tuchman, Barbara W. *Stilwell and the American Experience in China 1911–1945.* New York: Macmillan, 1971.

Tugwell, Rexford G. *The Art of Politics as Practiced by Three Great Americans: Franklin Delano Roosevelt, Luis Munoz Marin and Fiorello H. LaGuardia.* Garden City, N.Y.: Doubleday, 1958.

———. *The Democratic Roosevelt.* New York: Doubleday, 1957.

———. *In Search of Roosevelt.* Cambridge, Mass.: Harvard University Press, 1972.

———. *Roosevelt's Revolution.* New York: Macmillan, 1977.

Tull, Charles J. *Father Coughlin and the New Deal.* Syracuse, N.Y.: Syracuse University Press, 1965.

Tully, Grace. *F.D.R.: My Boss.* New York: Scribner, 1949.

Tumulty, Joseph P. *Woodrow Wilson as I Knew Him.*

Ulam, Adam. *Expansion and Coexistence: Soviet Foreign Policy, 1917–1973.* New York: Praeger, 1974.

———. *Stalin: The Man and His Era.* New York: Viking, 1973.

"Unofficial Observer" (pseudonym for John Carter Vincent). *The New Dealers.* New York: Literary Guild, 1934.

U.S. Department of State. *Documents on Germany, 1944–1959.* Washington, D.C.: U.S. Government Printing Office, 1959.

———. *Documents on Germany, 1944–1970.* Washington, D.C: U.S. Government Printing Office, 1971.

———. *Documents on Germany, 1944–1985.* Washington, D.C.: U.S. Government Printing Office, 1985.

———. *Foreign Relations of the United States.* Washington, D.C. U.S. Government Printing Office.

U.S.S.R. Ministry of Foreign Affairs. *The Tehran, Yalta and Potsdam Conferences.* Moscow: Progress, 1969.

Venkataramani, M.S., ed. *The Sunny Side of FDR.* Columbus, Ohio: Ohio University Press, 1973.

Volkogonov, Dmitri. *Stalin: Triumph and Tragedy.* Rocklin, Calif.: Prima, 1992.

Walker, Frank. *Quiet Confidant: The Autobiography of Frank C. Walker.* Colorado: University Press of Colorado, 1997.

Walker, R. *Edward R. Stettinius.* New York: Cooper Square, 1956.

Walker, Turnley. *Roosevelt and the Warm Springs Story.* New York: A.A. Wyn, 1953.

Walter, Lord. *The Good Years: From 1900 to the First World War.* New York: Harper & Brothers, 1960.

Ward, Geoffrey. *American Originals.* New York: HarperCollins, 1991.

———. *Before the Trumpet: Young Franklin Roosevelt, 1882–1905.* New York: Harper & Row, 1985.

———. *A First-Class Temperament: The Emergence of Franklin Roosevelt.* New York: Harper & Row, 1989.

———, ed. *Closest Companion: The Unknown Story of the Intimate Friendship of Franklin Roosevelt and Margaret Suckley.* Boston: Houghton Mifflin, 1995.

Ware, Susan. *Partner and I: Molly Dewson, Feminism and New Deal Politics.* New Haven, Conn.: Yale Univesity Press, 1987.

Warner, Emily Smith, with Hawthorne Daniel. *The Happy Warrior.* Garden City, N.Y.: Doubleday, 1956.

Watkins, T. *Righteous Pilgrim: The Life and Times of Harold L. Ickes, 1874–1952.* New York: Henry Holt, 1990.

Watt, Donald Cameron. *How War Came.* New York: Pantheon, 1989.

Wehle, Louis B. *Hidden Threads of History: Wilson Through Roosevelt.* New York: Macmillan, 1953.

Weil, Martin. *A Pretty Good Club: The Founding Fathers of the U.S. Foreign Service.* New York: Norton, 1978.

Weinberg, Gerhard. *A World at Arms: A Global History of World War II.* New York: Cambridge University Press, 1994.

Weinstein, Allen. *Perjury: The Hiss-Chambers Case.* New York: Knopf, 1978.

Weiss, Nancy J. *Farewell to the Party of Lincoln: Black Politics in the Age of FDR.* Princeton, N.J.: Princeton University Press, 1983.

Weitz, John. *Hitler's Banker Hjalmar Horace Greeley Schacht.* London: Warner, 2001.

Welles, Benjamin. *Summer Welles: FDR's Global Strategist.* New York: St. Martin's, 1997.

Welles, Sumner. *The Time for Decision.* New York: Harper, 1944.

Werner, M.R. *Tammany Hall.* Garden City, N.Y.: Doubleday, Doran, 1928.

Werth, Alexander. *Russia at War, 1941–1945.* London: Pan, 1965.

West, J.B., with Mary Lynn Kotz. *Upstairs at the White House: My Life with the First Ladies.* New York: Coward, McCann & Geoghegan, 1973.

Whalen, Richard J. *The Founding Father.* New York: New American Library/World, 1964.

White, William Allen. *The Autobiography of William Allen White.* New York: Macmillan, 1946.

White, William S. *Majesty and Mischief: A Mixed Tribute to FDR.* New York: McGraw-Hill, 1961.

Wigal, Donald, ed. *The Wisdom of Eleanor Roosevelt.* New York: Citadel, 2003.

Wilkins, Roy. *Standing Fast: The Autobiography of Roy Wilkins.* New York: Viking, 1982.

Williams, T. Harry. *Huey Long.* New York: Knopf, 1969.

Wills, Garry. *Certain Trumpets: The Call of Leaders.* New York: Simon & Schuster, 1994.

Wilmot, Chester. *The Struggle for Europe.* London: Collins, 1952.

Wilson, Edith. *My Memoir.* Indianapolis: Bobbs-Merrill, 1939.

Wilson, Theodore. *The First Summit: Roosevelt and Churchill at Placentia Bay, 1941.* Boston: Houghton Mifflin, 1969.

Winfield, Betty Houchin. *FDR and the News Media.* Chicago: University of Illinois Press, 1990.

Wolfskill, George, and John A. Hudson. *All But the People: Franklin D. Roosevelt and His Critics, 1933–1939.* London: MacMillan, 1969.

Woodward, E.L., and R. Butler. *Documents on British Foreign Policy, 1919–1939.* 2nd series, vol. III.

Woolner, David, ed. *The Second Quebec Conference Revisited: Waging War, Formulating Peace: Canada, Great Britain and the United States in 1944–1945.* New York: St. Martin's, 1998.

Wyman, David. *The Abandoment of the Jews: America and the Holocaust, 1941–1945.* New York: Pantheon, 1984.

Yergin, Daniel. *Shattered Peace: The Origins of the Cold War and the National Security State.* Boston: Houghton Mifflin, 1977.

Young, James C. *Roosevelt Revealed.* New York: Farrar & Rinehart, 1936.

Youngs, J. William T. *Eleanor Roosevelt: A Personal and Public Life.* Boston: Little, Brown, 1985.

Zeller, Eberhard. *The Flame of Freedom: The German Struggle Against Hitler.* Boulder, Colo.: Westview Press, 1994.

———. *The U.S. in Germany, 1944–1945.* Princeton, N.J.: D. Van Nostrand, 1957.

Zevin, Ben D., ed. *Franklin D. Roosevelt: Nothing to Fear.* New York: Houghton Mifflin, 1946.

Ziegler, Robert H. *American Workers, American Unions 1920–1985.* Baltimore: Johns Hopkins University Press, 1985.

Zukowsky, John, and Robbe Pierce Stimson. *Hudson River Villas.* New York: Rizzoli, 1985.

Photo Credits

The photographs in this book are courtesy of the Franklin D. Roosevelt Library with the exception of the following:

With the Democratic candidates for president of 1924 and 1928 . . . Keystone Pictures/ZUMA Press

At the pool in Warm Springs in 1925 . . . St. Louis Post Dispatch

Roosevelt in general session court in New York . . . Bettmann/Corbis

Presidential nominee FDR establishes a precedent . . . Keystone Pictures/ZUMA Press

Humorist Will Rogers introduces FDR . . . Bettmann/Corbis

FDR campaigns for president in Seattle . . . Bettmann/Corbis

Election night, November 8, 1932 . . . AP/Wide World Photos

President Hoover joins the President-elect . . . Bettmann/Corbis

FDR expertly carved the turkey . . . Bettmann/Corbis

Relations with General Douglas MacArthur . . . Brown Brothers, Sterling PA

Joseph P. Kennedy, a bad appointment . . . Bettmann/Corbis

Roosevelt in his custom-designed Ford . . . Bettmann/Corbis

FDR in a characteristic pose . . . T. McAvoy/Time Life/Getty Images

Roosevelt delighted his followers . . . Bettmann/Corbis

After perspiring through a long hot evening . . . Bettmann/Corbis

Roosevelt's 1940 Republican opponent . . . AP/Wide World Photos

General George C. Marshall . . . Alfred Eisenstaedt/Time Life/Getty Images

Showing his imperturbability . . . T. McAvoy/Time Life/Getty Images

Joint press conference with Winston Churchill . . . Bettmann/Corbis

Roosevelt's Fireside Chat on "Progress of the War," . . . T. McAvoy/Time Life/Getty Images

The President and his chosen successor . . . Bettmann/Corbis

Another of his greatest rhetorical triumphs . . . Bettmann/Corbis

Three million New Yorkers stood in the rain . . . Bettmann/Corbis

One more time, as on many previous election nights . . . AP/Wide World Photos

The Big Three at Yalta . . . Courtesy of Robert Hopkins

Lucy Mercer Rutherfurd as she appeared . . . Courtesy of Guy Rutherfurd

Leaving Warm Springs, April 13, 1945 . . . Bettmann/Corbis

Index

PublicAffairs is a publishing house founded in 1997. It is a tribute to the standards, values, and flair of three persons who have served as mentors to countless reporters, writers, editors, and book people of all kinds, including me.

I.F. STONE, proprietor of *I. F. Stone's Weekly*, combined a commitment to the First Amendment with entrepreneurial zeal and reporting skill and became one of the great independent journalists in American history. At the age of eighty, Izzy published *The Trial of Socrates*, which was a national bestseller. He wrote the

BENJAMIN C. BRADLEE was for nearly thirty years the charismatic editorial leader of *The Washington Post*. It was Ben who gave the *Post* the range and courage to pursue such historic issues as Watergate. He supported his reporters with a tenacity that made them fearless and it is no accident that so many became authors of influential, best-selling books.

ROBERT L. BERNSTEIN, the chief executive of Random House for more than a quarter century, guided one of the nation's premier publishing houses. Bob was personally responsible for many books of political dissent and argument that challenged tyranny around the globe. He is also the founder and longtime chair of Human Rights Watch, one of the most respected human rights organizations in the world.

For fifty years, the banner of Public Affairs Press was carried by its owner Morris B. Schnapper, who published Gandhi, Nasser, Toynbee, Truman, and about 1,500 other authors. In 1983, Schnapper was described by *The Washington Post* as "a redoubtable gadfly." His legacy will endure in the books to come.

Peter Osnos, *Founder and Editor-at-Large*